DECISIONS
FOR HEALTH

Free Copy

DECISIONS
FOR HEALTH

FOURTH EDITION

Clint Bruess
University of Alabama–Birmingham

Glenn Richardson
University of Utah

Chapters 6 and 8 written by
Susan J. Laing
Department of Veterans Affairs
Medical Center
Birmingham, Alabama

Chapter 22 written by
Les Chatelain
University of Utah

Brown & Benchmark
PUBLISHERS

Madison Dubuque, IA Guilford, CT Chicago Toronto London
Caracas Mexico City Buenos Aires Madrid Bogota Sydney

Book Team

Editor *Ed Bartell*
Developmental Editor *Megan Rundel*
Production Editor *Debra DeBord*
Designer *Lu Ann Schrandt*
Art Editor *Mary Powers*
Photo Editor *Rose Deluhery*
Production Manager *Beth Kundert*
Visuals/Design Developmental Specialist *Janice M. Roerig-Blong*
Visuals/Design Freelance Specialist *Mary L. Christianson*
Marketing Manager *Pamela S. Cooper*

Brown & Benchmark
PUBLISHERS

A Division of Wm. C. Brown Communications, Inc.

Executive Vice President/General Manager *Thomas E. Doran*
Vice President/Editor in Chief *Edgar J. Laube*
Vice President/Production *Vickie Putman*
National Sales Manager *Bob McLaughlin*

Wm. C. Brown Communications, Inc.

President and Chief Executive Officer *G. Franklin Lewis*
Senior Vice President, Operations *James H. Higby*
Corporate Senior Vice President and President of Manufacturing *Roger Meyer*
Corporate Senior Vice President and Chief Financial Officer *Robert Chesterman*

The credits section for this book begins on page C.1 and is considered an extension of the copyright page.

Copyedited by Wendy Nelson

Cover image © Uniphoto Picture Agency

Copyright © 1985 by Wadsworth, Inc.

Copyright © 1989, 1992, 1995 by Wm. C. Brown Communications, Inc.
All rights reserved

A Times Mirror Company

Library of Congress Catalog Card Number: 94–71248

ISBN 0–697–15224–3

No part of this publication may be reproduced, stored in a retrieval system, or transmitted, in any form or by any means, electronic, mechanical, photocopying, recording, or otherwise, without the prior written permission of the publisher.

Printed in the United States of America by Wm. C. Brown Communications, Inc., 2460 Kerper Boulevard, Dubuque, IA 52001

10 9 8 7 6 5 4 3 2 1

To Susan J. Laing, with thanks for her creative writing, her constant support, and her role in a beautiful relationship.

To Kathleen, for strength, comfort, support, and happiness. To my children, Brannon, Tavan, Jordan, and Lauren, for ongoing special moments, mutual trust, and strong hope for the future.

BRIEF CONTENTS

CONTENTS

PART E

Relationships and
Sexuality 9.1

PART F

Alcohol, Tobacco, and Psychoactive Drugs   13.1

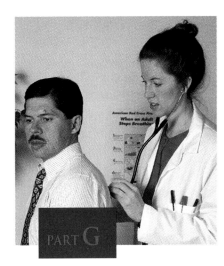

PART G

Illness and
Disease   16.1

Choices and the World Around You   19.1

PREFACE

It was once assumed that those possessing health knowledge would always behave in a manner conducive to their health. But this "fallacy of the empty vessel" (that people could be filled with knowledge to guarantee "proper" behavior) has given way to the understanding that healthy attitudes and sound decision-making skills are just as important as the knowledge itself. As educators, we don't feel it is our right to promote specific health behaviors; rather, we feel it is our responsibility to ensure that our students develop the skills to make informed health-related decisions throughout life.

The need for college students to become informed and intelligent health consumers is as great as ever. There is a flood of information about health-related issues, products, and services. Students of all ages must make daily health decisions. Therefore, one of the most important college courses is a personal health course that provides current information and teaches students how to sort out and use that information.

Between us, we have taught personal health courses at seven different colleges and universities, and we have found continual challenges in at least three areas. First, with so much ongoing research and the constant development and advocacy of new products and services, we are challenged to provide up-to-date information about a great variety of topics related to personal health. Second, with the many personal health students outside the typical college age range, we are further challenged to present material on health needs and issues that arise throughout life. Finally, with the vast amount of information available—much of it complex, confusing, often controversial, and even contradictory—we are challenged to present personal health material as clearly, concisely, and logically as possible.

We have responded to these challenges in a text that instructors and students can use to make the personal health course a more valuable learning experience. By providing up-to-date information, by involving the students in activities related to various health issues, and by providing a framework on which students can build sound decision-making skills, this text will enable students to become informed health consumers who are also skilled decision makers.

THE DECISION-MAKING PROCESS

Decisions for Health, Fourth Edition, is unique in many ways, but particularly in its thorough emphasis on decision making. The first chapter lays the groundwork for the development of decision-making skills, with its emphasis on total health, health behavior, and health decision making. The remaining chapters build on this theme while dealing with mental health and stress choices; choices related to aging and death; nutrition, physical activity, and weight control choices; sexual choices; choices related to use of chemicals; choices and disease; and choices and the world around you. These chapters help the student, the health consumer, integrate health-related information into an overall decision-making model. Health is primarily a product of lifestyles, and students will find that they can use this text to help improve their lifestyles and, hence, improve their health.

CONTINUING FEATURES

We have addressed the problems and challenges involved with teaching a personal health course, responded to comments from users of the first, second, and third editions and continued the integration of the following elements into *Decisions for Health:*

1. Chapter Outlines
2. Health Assessments
3. Issues
4. Commitment Activities
5. Key Questions, Summaries, and Additional Readings
6. Lifestyle Contracts
7. Glossary
8. Index

Chapter Outlines give the reader an "up-front" overview of what to expect in the chapter.

Health Assessments, found in each chapter, give the student an opportunity to assess present health status or feelings related to health topics contained within the respective chapter. These were developed especially for *Decisions for Health* and help the reader become personally involved in the content.

Issues are highlighted throughout *Decisions for Health* by presentations of opposing sides of many contemporary controversies. Consideration of these issues helps students become more involved while learning about health and health decisions.

Commitment Activities are found at the end of every chapter and are designed to prompt readers to act on health problems they have been considering within the chapter. It is well known that long-lasting health behavior changes are more likely to occur if learners are immediately and actively involved in appropriate positive health activities.

Key Questions, Summaries, and *Additional Readings* are expected by students and instructors, and we have provided them for each chapter: Key questions help the reader focus on where we are going; summaries help the reader recall where we have been; and additional readings provide motivated learners with sources of more information. Many new readings have been added for this edition.

Lifesyle Contracts, also developed especially for this book, are found at the end of each major part of the book. They are part of a systematic approach to making commitment to lifestyle change, and help you consider health decisions that might alter behaviors and improve your health.

The *Glossary* facilitates understanding of necessary health terminology. You should find our running glossary much more helpful than the standard glossary found only at the end of a typical text.

The *Index* provides ready access to every topic in the book.

We also retained our model for action based upon resiliency skills. As explained in chapter 1, the model rests upon protective skills and adjustment skills to promote healthy living. The theoretical base of this model is at the cutting edge of thinking in health education.

WHAT'S NEW IN THIS EDITION?

Users of the book and professional reviewers encouraged us to retain the helpful features found in previous editions. With some alterations, we have done that. For the sake of improvement, we have updated assessments, issues, and commitment activities where needed. We have added new issues where appropriate. We have made the lifestyle contracts more comprehensive so they reflect information contained within each major part of the book. The running glossary has been expanded to be more helpful.

While we have always emphasized a comprehensive view of health, in this edition we evolved into the use of a mind/body/soul concept of health that further broadens the view of health as a positive state of being. Implications of this expanded view are found in every chapter.

In addition, the following new elements have been integrated into *Decisions for Health:*

1. Healthy People 2000 Objectives
2. Health Updates
3. The World Around You boxes
4. Personal Skills and Experiences
5. Personal Insights

Healthy People 2000 Objectives, national health promotion and disease prevention objectives, have been integrated into each chapter where appropriate. They help the reader see how personal health decisions relate to overall national goals.

Health Updates provide additional facts and recent developments related to health. They also help to dispel many health myths.

The *World Around You* feature helps learners consider multicultural influences on health decisions. In addition, the bigger picture of community, national, and international health issues are confronted.

Personal Skills and Experiences boxes give examples of actions that can be taken to promote health or prevent health problems. As indicated throughout the text, learning facts about health is never enough. Healthy behaviors are a must in order to make a real difference.

Personal Insights have been added at the request of readers and have been applauded by reviewers. They provide actual examples of health decisions related to the content being considered.

Previously we included information on safety as an appendix. Because of increased emphasis on safety as well as injury prevention, a new chapter has been added that focuses on these important health issues.

A great deal of new and updated information has been blended into the fourth edition. This is true both for the information within the text and for the many learning aids throughout every chapter.

TO THE INSTRUCTOR

At the end of each major part of the book, we have provided a lifestyle contract for potential use by the student. The process of assessing health behavior, providing instruction, and then contracting for behavior changes is an appropriate formula for helping students make commitments to improve their health status. *Please pay particular attention to chapter 1, where the use of the lifestyle contracts is described in detail.*

Most researchers believe that students should effectively modify only one or two behaviors at one time. An attempt to modify numerous behaviors will likely result in frustration and failure in several areas.

The purpose of the contract experiences in this text is to allow students the opportunity to consider the behavioral changes that can occur with each topic area. After consideration of the assessments, and their own degrees of readiness and motivation, students may then select the areas that fit their needs and complete the lifestyle contracts that correspond with those areas. It is assumed that some of the contracts will be left blank and reserved for another time.

We hope that these contracts will provide a means to help students improve their health status using the best techniques available today. Good luck in working with your students in this regard.

SUPPLEMENTS

A number of aids are available to help both the instructor and the student experience the best learning situation possible while using *Decisions for Health*.

INSTRUCTOR'S MANUAL

The *Instructor's Manual* that accompanies *Decisions for Health* is designed to promote an optimal learning experience for students, while providing an invaluable and easy-to-use resource for instructors. The *Instructor's Manual* is divided into three sections. Section 1 contains learning objectives, a chapter overview, a chapter outline, discussion questions, teaching strategies, decisions stories, research issues, and audiovisual resources for all chapters. Section 2 is devoted to resources related to personal health. Section 3 contains twenty-nine transparency masters and a text-referenced listing of the transparency acetates in the *Personal Health Transparency Set*.

PERSONAL HEALTH TRANSPARENCY SET

This set of over fifty transparency acetates with many in full color is available to adopters of *Decisions for Health*.

MICROTEST

The test questions found in the *Test Item File* are also available on the computerized testing program, MicroTest III. This program allows instructors to effortlessly create tests, scoresheets, and answer keys, thereby saving hours of preparation time. MicroTest III is available in Macintosh, DOS, and Windows versions.

CALL-IN SERVICE

For those instructors who do not use the computerized program there is a convenient call-in/mail-in service. Using the *Test Item File* and the order form, an instructor can choose test questions and place a request order, and within two working days Brown & Benchmark will put in first-class mail a test master, a student answer sheet, and an answer key for fast and easy grading. Call your local Brown & Benchmark Sales Representative or call the Brown & Benchmark Help Line at 1–800–258–2370 for more information.

INSTRUCTOR'S RESOURCE KIT

To facilitate the use of all the ancillaries, a binder containing an unbound copy of the *Instructor's Manual, Test Item File*, the *Personal Health Transparency Set*, a guide to using the videotapes, and a description of the computerized software is available to qualified adopters of *Decisions for Health*.

INSTRUCTIONAL VIDEOTAPES

Adopters of *Decisions for Health* can select instructional videotapes from a varied series of programs appropriate to their own personal health course. These videos feature a variety of programs to stimulate class discussions and provide more in-depth coverage of selected topics. Call your Brown & Benchmark Sales Representative for more details.

SOFTWARE

Interactive programs for health and nutrition assessment are available to adopters of *Decisions for Health*. Call your Brown & Benchmark Sales Representative for more details.

UNIVERSITY OF CALIFORNIA, BERKELEY "WELLNESS NEWSLETTER"

This well-respected newsletter is provided to instructors who adopt *Decisions for Health*. The "Wellness Newsletter" will help instructors of personal health classes keep up-to-date on the latest health news throughout the year.

VIDEODISKS

Qualified adopters of *Decisions for Health* are eligible to receive our *Brown & Benchmark Personal Health Videodisk* or other exciting videodisks.

TESTWELL

This self-scoring wellness assessment was developed by the National Wellness Institute. It can be packaged with the text for a minimal charge.

"THE AIDS BOOKLET," THIRD EDITION

This sixty-four-page booklet is updated every six months and provides additional coverage of this devastating disease. It can be packaged free of charge with the textbook.

ADDITIONAL SUPPLEMENTS

Brown & Benchmark Publishers also publishes Annual Editions® and Taking Sides®. In addition to the *Annual Edition: Health 95/96*, both series offer selections in areas relevant to personal health, such as sexuality, drugs, and nutrition.

ACKNOWLEDGMENTS

A number of people have contributed to the development of this book, and we would like to thank the most obvious ones. The book profited greatly from the direct contributions of Susan J. Laing. In addition to her overall suggestions, her combined creativity and expertise resulted in excellent chapters on nutrition and weight control as well as an outstanding instructor's manual and a new student manual. Our editor, Ed Bartell, has been helpful with his suggestions and true to the spirit of publishing the best possible books. We appreciate what he does.

Finally, we would like to thank the many reviewers who provided helpful suggestions by reviewing all or part of this book. We hope they see their hours of work coming to fruition within the text. They are

- M. Betsy Bergen
  Kansas State University
- Kathie C. Garbe
  Youngstown State University
- Susan Graham-Kresge
  University of Southern Mississippi
- Willie Harris
  Valdosta State College
- Ray Johnson
  Central Michigan University
- Bobby E. Lang
  Florida A&M University
- Loretta Liptak
  Youngstown State University
- Ric Matthews
  San Diego Miramar College
- Sandra E. Mimms
  Alabama State University
- Millie Naquin
  Southeastern Louisiana University
- Barbara A. Thompson
  Florida A&M University
- E. Johnson Vaughn
  Norfolk State University
- Deitra Wengert
  Towson State University
- H. Patrick Woolley
  East Central College
- Marie Zannis
  Nicholls State University

DECISIONS
FOR HEALTH

PART A

Decision
Making and
Health

Health Behavior and Health Decisions

Health is a national preoccupation.

Each day you make decisions that affect your well-being now and in the future. How can you know which choices are best? A steady stream of health information flows from many sources, and many of these sources are unreliable. For example, weight-loss schemes and stress-reduction programs abound. How can you know which products or programs are best?

Today more college students are interested in developing a meaningful philosophy of life as a life goal, and fewer are committed to being very well off financially ("Attitudes of College Freshmen" 1993). This is but one example of interest in an overall high quality of life.

There is national interest in health. In fact, health promotion and disease prevention objectives have been developed by the government. The most recent edition of these objectives, *Promoting Health/Preventing Disease: Year 2000 Objectives for the Nation* (1990), contains major goals related to infant mortality, life expectancy, chronic disability, years of healthy life, and disparity in life expectancy. The government's goal of increasing years of healthy life to at least 65 years is a clear indicator of the interest in improved quality, as well as quantity, of life. The objectives include these:

1. Reduce overweight among people ages 20 through 74 to a prevalence of no more than 20 percent. (Recently the incidence was 25.7%.)

2. Increase to at least 80 percent the proportion of people age 21 and over who use food labels to make food selections. (Recently the proportion was 74%.)

3. Increase to at least 60 percent the proportion of people age 6 and older who participate in moderate physical activities 3 or more days per week for 20 or more minutes per occasion. (Recently the incidence was 50%.)

Although abundant information is available about health, and we are interested in health, surveys show that we actually know little about health. Furthermore, we have few guidelines for evaluating all the advice offered. This book provides basic information and the necessary decision-making techniques to make intelligent choices about health. It also makes reference to the specific objectives for the nation

Issue

What Does Health Mean? How Should It Be Measured?

People have generally accepted very limited definitions of health. As long as they feel okay, they think they are healthy. It is common for people to not know what it really feels like to be healthy.

- Pro: People have become so accustomed to being overweight, not having excellent physical stamina, living with constant stress, and using chemicals to try to feel better that they think of health in only a very limited way. If they do not have obvious disease symptoms, they say they are healthy. This is indeed a very limited definition.

- Con: More people are understanding what it means to be healthy. They don't settle for just making it through the day; they want to have extra stamina to do things they enjoy. They are willing to go out of their way to implement sound health decisions. They are not defining health in a limited way. They have a good feeling for the fact that health is a complex matter that involves all areas of our lives.

What does health mean to you? What do you have to do to be healthy by your definition? What has been the difference at the times in your life when you have been healthier than at other times? Do your family members and close friends look at health the same way you do? What are the similarities and differences? Why do you think these exist?

that relate to topics being discussed. In this first chapter we explore what health means, what influences your health behavior, and how to make wise health-related decisions.

TRADITIONAL VIEWS OF HEALTH

Historically, different cultures have viewed health in different ways. At times, health problems have been attributed to the gods or to unsanitary conditions. Even today, individuals in many cultures and subcultures continue to view health as merely the absence of illness or infirmity (lack of vitality). According to this view, you must be healthy if you aren't sick. For some, poor living conditions, poverty, and lack of medical care make unthinkable the concept that health might be more than the absence of disease.

Modern medicine in our culture emphasizes scientifically proven treatment with drugs and surgery and prevention of disease and health problems through vaccinations, cleanliness, and good health practices. Many people in our culture, however, are going beyond this view of health and striving toward an optimal state of living that is much more than freedom from disease.

These individuals view health as an overall positive condition consisting of several components—including mental, emotional, social, physical, occupational, and spiritual health. (In some definitions of health, the number of components and their definitions may vary; however, the general ideas are similar.)

Mental health is the capacity to cope with life situations, grow emotionally through them, and develop to your fullest potential. **Emotional health,** while related to mental health, is the ability to express emotions comfortably and appropriately. It might include choosing *not* to express emotions in certain situations.

Social health includes good relations with others, the presence of a supportive culture, and successful adaptation to the environment. **Physical health** is what many individuals think of first when they consider overall health. It includes efficient bodily functioning, resistance to disease, and the physical capacity to respond appropriately to varied events.

Occupational health includes feelings of comfort and accomplishment related to your daily tasks (Eberst 1985). For those who are employed outside the home, aspects of their job make up occupational health. For those who work at home or remain at home for other reasons, their occupational health would still be a function of daily tasks. For example, you might assess this component of health by answering questions like these: Do I feel a sense of accomplishment about my daily tasks? Am I basically happy with the way I spend most of my "occupational" time?

Spiritual health is also an important component of overall health (Bensley 1991). While spiritual health has not always been viewed as a component of health in our culture, there is increased recognition that it is significant in health-related decision making (Goodloe and Arreola 1992). Optimal spiritual health includes the ability to discover and express your purpose in life; to learn how to experience love, joy, peace, and fulfillment; and to help yourself and others achieve full potential (Chapman 1987). For some, spiritual health includes the belief in a Supreme Being, but for others this is not necessary. Spiritual health might include answers to the questions Who am I? Why am I here? and Where am I going? Complete the Health Assessment exercise to get a clearer picture of the health components in your life.

A continuum can be constructed for each dimension of health, with poor health and optimal health labeled for each dimension. For examples of optimal and poor health in various dimensions, see the continuums in figure 1.1.

Though it is easier to speak separately about them, the components of health actually form a whole. The word **health,** in fact, comes from an Old English root meaning "wholeness." There are numerous examples showing how a change in any one of the components affects the others. If your social environment subjects you to racial prejudice and discrimination, you might develop anxiety and a lowered sense of self-worth as a result. This in turn can lower your resistance to disease. If your level of social health is not what

Occupational health is an important component of our overall health.

you want it to be, your self-concept (a part of mental health) might be negatively influenced, and your eating and exercise patterns (part of physical health) might be negatively altered. If you are pleased with your progress in a fitness program, your good feelings can have a positive impact on your self-concept and even your relationships with others. Well-being in all dimensions is necessary for comprehensive health. The interaction of all dimensions of health is shown in figure 1.2.

mental health
The capacity to cope with life situations, grow emotionally through them, and develop to your fullest potential.

emotional health
The ability to express emotions comfortably and appropriately.

social health
Good relations with others, the presence of a supportive culture, and successful adaptation to the environment.

physical health
Efficient bodily functioning, resistance to disease, and the physical capacity to respond appropriately to varied events.

occupational health
Having feelings of comfort and accomplishment related to your daily tasks.

spiritual health
The ability to discover and express your purpose in life; to learn how to experience love, joy, peace, and fulfillment; and to help yourself and others achieve full potential.

health
Well-being in all dimensions of life.

Health Skills and Attitudes

1. Are you happy with your

social health status	_____ Yes	_____ No
physical health status	_____ Yes	_____ No
emotional health status	_____ Yes	_____ No
occupational health status	_____ Yes	_____ No
spiritual health status	_____ Yes	_____ No
mental health status	_____ Yes	_____ No

2. Are you motivated to enhance your health in reference to

social health status	_____ Yes	_____ No
physical health status	_____ Yes	_____ No
emotional health status	_____ Yes	_____ No
occupational health status	_____ Yes	_____ No
spiritual health status	_____ Yes	_____ No
mental health status	_____ Yes	_____ No

3. Are you actively doing something to improve your

social health status	_____ Yes	_____ No
physical health status	_____ Yes	_____ No
emotional health status	_____ Yes	_____ No
occupational health status	_____ Yes	_____ No
spiritual health status	_____ Yes	_____ No
mental health status	_____ Yes	_____ No

For the following items, mark what you would probably do in each case.

4. You are at a party and some of your friends offer you some type of drug that you really don't want to try, but they are very persistent. What would you do?
   a. Definitely go along with them
   b. Probably go along with them
   c. Probably not go along with them
   d. Definitely not go along with them

5. Some of your friends are pressuring you to go to a movie that you really don't want to see or feel it is wrong to see. What would you do?
   a. Definitely go along with them
   b. Probably go along with them
   c. Probably not go along with them
   d. Definitely not go along with them

6. Some other students found an exact copy of a test you are going to take tomorrow, and they want you to go and study the test with them, but you think it is wrong. What would you do?
   a. Definitely go along with them
   b. Probably go along with them
   c. Probably not go along with them
   d. Definitely not go along with them

7. I do those things that are consistent with what I believe.
   _____ Agree   _____ Disagree

8. I rarely do things that I think are morally wrong.
   _____ Agree   _____ Disagree

9. I behave in accordance with my value system.
   _____ Yes   _____ No

10. I seem to have plenty of energy to do what I have to do.
    _____ Yes   _____ No

11. I am rarely too tired to do something I want to do.
    _____ Yes   _____ No

12. I have a zest for living.
    _____ Yes   _____ No

Scoring

Questions 1–3 help you assess your motivation and pursuit of health. If you answered "no" to any of these questions, evaluate whether you should do something about that dimension of your health. One dimension can drag down other dimensions, and conversely, efforts to enhance a dimension of health can positively affect the other.

Questions 4–6 are an assessment of your peer resistance skills. Score your responses as follows:

For each "a" give yourself 1 point
For each "b" give yourself 2 points
For each "c" give yourself 3 points
For each "d" give yourself 4 points

A score of 10 or more points indicates good peer resistance skills. A score of 7 to 9 points indicates moderate peer resistance skills. A score of 6 or less points indicates poor peer resistance skills.

Questions 7–9 assess whether your behaviors are consistent with your value system. An answer of "no" to any of these questions might suggest conflict between what you believe is right and what you are doing, resulting in guilt. Congruence between these two important dimensions of health is important for happiness.

Questions 10–12 assess your energy level and quality of life. Positive responses indicate a zest for living and the energy to live life to the fullest. Negative responses indicate that you should do something to find that zest. The chapters in this book will give you some suggestions to find increased energy.

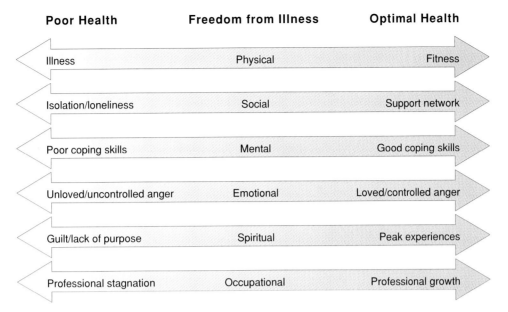

Figure 1.1

The dimensions of health.

Health is dynamic rather than static. It is constantly changing, and your choices can directly influence your level of health, regardless of your current physical health, social situation, and environmental and cultural surroundings. Your health and health maintenance are uniquely yours. You and another individual may differ considerably in blood pressure, weight, and the amount of sleep you get, although you might have similar diet and exercise habits. What health means, too, is likely to be different for you than for someone else. You might be content with a small circle of friends, for example, while another individual needs a variety of social interactions to feel socially healthy. What health means to you might be very different from what health means to someone in Africa, or in Canada, or even next door. A sample continuum for total health could be constructed, as was done for each component in figure 1.1.

A "MIND/BODY/SOUL" VIEW OF HEALTH

Recently, a "mind/body/soul" view of health evolved that has further broadened the view of health as a positive state of being. There is increasing scientific evidence that mind/body/soul interactions are at the root of both health and disease. For our purposes, *soul* refers to your purpose in life, your reasons for existence, and the essence of what motivates you.

Proponents of mind/body/soul health would not speak of health in terms of the components we have outlined. Instead, they would present the components as integrated into a broader view of mind, body, and soul. In fact, Dr. Robert Ader indicates that mind and body are an integrated unit and we study them (the components) separately just for convenience (Moyers 1993).

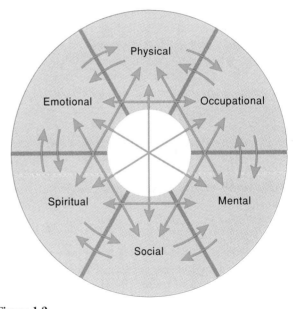

Figure 1.2

Interaction of all dimensions.

The mind/body/soul view of health expands the comprehensive view of health we've just described to show how the various components of health intimately interact. For example, if you fail a test, your emotional, social, and spiritual dimensions of health might be affected. You might not feel like going out, might feel depressed, or might not be motivated to exercise. The total reactions of your mind and body combine to influence how you feel. A bodily reaction (exercise) might really be difficult because of a mind experience (failure).

The ancient Greeks knew that the mind can affect the body's health. The Chinese have also known this for many

HEALTH UPDATE

Stress and Colds

Many people who become infected with a cold virus develop no cold symptoms. Researchers now believe that your history of psychological stress might explain this.

In one study, college students who stayed well, even when infected with a cold virus, reported about a third as many stressful events as those who got sick. Researchers concluded that psychological stress influences both the physiological response to cold viruses and the perception of cold symptoms ("Stress and Colds" 1993). Your perception of stressful events as well as what you do to control stress in your life can have an impact on your actual disease symptoms.

---

centuries. Dr. William Osler, the great nineteenth-century physician who was the father of modern medicine, said: "The care of tuberculosis depends more on what the patient has in his head than what he has in his chest" ("Can Your Mind Heal Your Body?" 1993).

There is still no comprehensive, unifying theory to explain just how the mind affects the body, but various types of research are beginning to show us much more about their relationship. It has long been known that the body undergoes numerous physical changes, such as increased heart rate and blood pressure, muscle tension, and hormonal changes, as a result of stress. It was not until 1974, however, that a discovery made by Robert Ader stimulated the current interest in mind/body/soul health (Moyers 1993).

Through experimentation, Ader found evidence that the nervous system and the immune system are intimately connected. He gave rats sweetened water together with an injection of a drug that suppresses the immune system. This caused the number of an important kind of cells in the rats' immune system to decrease. Later, Ader showed that giving the same rats only the sweetened water (without an injection) produced the same effect. Their bodies had "learned" to respond to a sweet taste by decreasing their immune function.

Similar experiments have been successfully repeated by others. Scientists are finding that there are many connections between the brain and the immune system. For example, nerve endings have been found in the tissues that produce and store immune-system cells, and immune-system cells have been shown to respond to chemical signals produced by the nervous system. These findings have generated a relatively new field known as psychoneuroimmunology, or PNI (*psycho-* for mind, *neuro-* for the nervous and hormonal systems, and *immunology* for the immune system). The basic idea behind PNI is that psychological reactions can suppress the immune system enough to increase the risk of physical illness ("Can Your Mind Heal Your Body?" 1993).

Many mind/body/soul relationships have been shown in recent years. For example, when individuals who have survived a stroke (a loss of blood supply to the brain) become depressed, their chances of long-term survival drop greatly. Social isolation (not having support from family and friends) after a serious medical event like a stroke also interferes with recovery ("Stroke Survival and Depression . . . and Isolation" 1993). On the other hand, emotional support helps people survive serious illness. People living in stable, well-developed social environments tend to have fewer problems with heart disease and recover better if they do have a heart attack ("Life Support" 1993). Group support can help improve and prevent many medical problems. People who feel isolated have three to five times more deaths from all causes than do people with good group support (Moyers 1993).

When we think of various influences on health, we often think of many of them as coming from the outside environment. But each influence is mediated by context—our perceptions and interpretations of the situation. For example, people who fast for a long time by personal choice tend to be less hungry than people who do so for external reasons (such as lack of money). Not only are they less hungry, but they also have fewer physiological changes—state of mind has shaped state of body. Harnessing the power of the mind (in an awareness of context that is called "mindfulness") can also have a positive effect on perception of pain, withdrawal symptoms when stopping smoking, or prevention of many health problems (Langer 1989). This is fundamental to a basic premise of this book—that *you can control your health!*

We don't always understand just how we control our health, but perhaps it will help to consider how you learned to ride a bike. Chances are, someone else held the bike as you pedaled, to keep you from falling until you learned to balance. Then, without your even knowing it, that person probably let go and you were riding on your own. You controlled the bike without even knowing you had learned how. In some respects, we control our health in the same way without knowing for sure what we do. But, just as on the bike, at some point we discover that we are in control. We learn how to recognize and use the control we possess over illness through mindfulness (Langer 1989).

Thus, there is increasing scientific evidence that mind/body/soul interactions are at the root of both health and disease. Psychological factors have a role in causing the onset and course of many chronic disorders. Psychological factors can also promote a positive state of health. In addition, psychological, emotional, psychosocial, and behavioral interventions are at least as effective as many purely medical treatments (Pelletier 1992).

Health behavior change is also influenced by multiple interactions. For example, a national survey indicated that Canadians understand they can take action, individually and

Factitious Disorders

An interesting, but negative, example of the intimate relationship between the mind and the body is a **factitious disorder.** This is a condition in which people literally make themselves sick in order to gain sympathy or enjoy some other form of emotional reward (Dortch 1994). They use physical symptoms as a socially sanctioned way to communicate their psychological distress.

At one end of the spectrum of factitious disorders are hypochondriacs. They genuinely believe they are sick, and they become so obsessed with their bodily functions that any slight irregularity causes them real alarm. At the other end of the spectrum are patients with Munchausen syndrome, a disorder named for a German baron. These people spend lots of time traveling from hospital to hospital and duping doctors into doing costly diagnostic procedures.

It is not known what causes factitious disorders. We would hope, however, that a better understanding of mind/body/soul relationships will go a long way toward preventing them.

---

collectively, to improve their health. Factors outside the formal medical-care system, such as the support of family and friends and reliance on personal, spiritual, or community resources, were felt to be extremely important in improving health behavior ("Most Canadians Report Good Health" 1993).

Throughout this text you will see examples of how mind/body/soul health relates to the topic at hand. Potential ways to optimize health are explained. The process begins by assessing your health status related to each topic, so Health Assessment exercises appear in each chapter. You will find a Lifestyle Contract at the end of each part of the book. Completing the contract will help you develop a plan for the health behavior changes you need to make to move toward optimal health.

Consistent with the increasing scientific evidence that mind/body/soul interactions are basic to both health and disease, each remaining chapter of this book contains boxes entitled "Personal Skills and Experiences." Many of these boxes emphasize interactions of the mind, body, and soul and focus on health decisions related to the content of the particular chapter.

At the end of each part, and in selected chapters, you will find boxes with more information about PNI (psychoneuroimmunology). They provide further examples of mind/body/soul interactions specifically related to various health topics.

HEALTH FOR WHAT?

Good health is essential to a good quality of life. To enjoy life more, to be more productive, and to live at a higher level are the primary reasons for pursuing good health.

HEALTH AND LIFESTYLE

Not long ago, the greatest strides in improving human health were made by individuals doing something for others, such as digging city sewer systems and developing vaccines for diseases. There is still much to be done, but in the industrialized world, at least, the greatest future improvements in health will result from actions each of us takes, not from what others do for us.

Many health problems are actually self-inflicted. Lung cancer and various circulatory ailments often result from an individual's choice to smoke cigarettes. Degeneration of the circulatory and respiratory systems is often traced to a lifetime of relative physical inactivity.

Lifestyle—your customary pattern of behavior—dramatically affects your health. Your decisions concerning personal care, drugs, sexual relations, and other health-related matters can help or hinder you throughout life.

CONTROL AND RESPONSIBILITY

Clearly, some factors that influence the length or quality of life, such as gender at birth and the health history of your ancestors, are completely out of your control. But, for other factors, such as where you live, the quality of your drinking water, and the kind of work you do, it *might* be within your control to change them, depending on your age, the amount of money you have, and other circumstances. Many health-related factors clearly *are* within your control—such as what you eat and whether you smoke, take sleeping pills nightly, exercise regularly, practice stress management, or drink heavily. It may also be possible to reduce your risk from factors that cannot be changed, such as heredity, if you understand how these factors affect well-being. For example, if early death due to stroke runs in your family, you can alter your lifestyle in an attempt to reduce your likelihood of having a stroke. This will certainly improve your physical health and reduce your risk for stroke.

Many experts believe that the next major health revolution in the United States will be a direct result of improved lifestyles. To develop a healthier lifestyle, you need (1) an awareness of your present patterns of behavior and their health consequences, (2) adequate health knowledge,

---

factitious disorder
A condition in which people literally make themselves sick to gain sympathy or enjoy some other emotional reward.

Your decisions probably influence your health more than anything else.

(3) the capacity to make intelligent decisions about health issues based on this knowledge and self-awareness, and (4) the ability, motivation, and desire to put your decisions into practice. One example of the direct effects of these four factors is the reduction of cardiovascular disease in the United States in the past 20 years. Many individuals have learned how their behavior patterns influence the development of this disease, have acquired sound knowledge about the disease, and have made more-intelligent decisions to reduce the likelihood of developing the disease.

CONSISTENT HEALTH BEHAVIOR

Most people are inconsistent in their health behavior. They might exercise regularly but go years without a physical examination. Others are critical of marijuana smokers but regularly overindulge in alcohol. Still others take pride in shopping wisely for health products but fail to use the same consumer skills when making other health decisions.

Do such inconsistencies mean that we really don't value our health? Sometimes. But to conclude that someone doesn't value health because her or his health behavior is inconsistent ignores the fact that good health is not always an individual's top priority. For example, a woman who runs into a burning building to save the life of a family member is more concerned with saving that person's life than with protecting her own health.

We often do things that affect our health positively or negatively, though the motivation might not be health related. For example, a man may follow good dental practices just to look more attractive or eat certain foods for their taste and appearance rather than for their nutritional value.

Sometimes motivation conflicts with desires for health and well-being. For example, a woman might want to have sexual intercourse but fear an unwanted pregnancy. Not all

activities need be health oriented, but understanding your motivations and the health-related consequences of your behavior can help you plan more effectively for your future well-being.

MOTIVATIONS FOR HEALTH BEHAVIOR

Actions are influenced by many factors. For example, you might delay seeking medical attention because you suspect that your symptoms are a sign of something serious. Fear about health can also prevent individuals from acquiring information they need to make sound decisions and from facing health problems in a rational and constructive way. As complicated as motivation for health behavior can be, four main motivations underlie most health behavior: social pressure, habits, attitudes and values, and knowledge.

SOCIAL PRESSURE

Actions we take in order to appear more masculine or feminine, to gain praise, to avoid embarrassment, or to appear more mature are all motivated by **social pressure**—that is, by the belief that we need to go along with or rebel against others' actions or expectations. Because we are social animals, our thoughts and actions are heavily influenced by the opinions and actions of others, particularly those of our peers (our social equals).

Our actions, then, are strongly influenced by our perceptions of the extent to which family, friends, and associates engage in a particular type of health behavior (i.e., the behavior's social acceptability). Peer and family influence can be an important tool in promoting health (Norman 1987). One good example of how social pressure has changed attitudes and behavior is the problem of drinking and driving. Alcohol-related fatalities used to be considered accidents; today there is a tendency to view them as being the result of a driver's criminal or immoral behavior in driving after drinking alcohol.

HEALTH HABITS

When an action is performed routinely and without thought, it becomes a **habit.** Health habits can be a result of social or parental pressure and might positively or negatively affect your health. Most children, for example, began to brush their teeth nightly because their parents insisted. Many began to smoke because they desired acceptance from an admired family member or friend who smoked.

---

social pressure
The belief that you must go along with or rebel against others' actions or expectations.

habit
An action that is performed routinely and without thought.

Observing others can influence health behavior.

The more often an act is repeated, the easier it becomes, and the more comfortable and self-assured you feel in doing it. As habits become increasingly ingrained, you may forget both your original reasons for doing them and their potential health effects.

ATTITUDES AND VALUES

Attitudes and **values** influence health behavior in many ways. Attitudes are feelings about facts and behaviors. Values are ideas we believe in and cherish. You might engage in some practices, such as running, reading, or eating sweets, purely for pleasure—you have a positive attitude toward them. These activities might have beneficial, harmful, or no real consequences for health. You might engage in or avoid other behaviors because of personal or religious values. Your values might dictate whether or not you choose to become a vegetarian or to smoke, drink, or have premarital sexual activity. It is clear that values we place on health do influence specific health behaviors (Abood and Conway 1992).

Health-related behavior can also reflect specific attitudes toward health. Have you ever been in excellent physical condition and run, swum, or done some other physical activity relatively easily for long periods of time? If so, you probably know that it feels great to be in good shape. Knowing what this feels like can influence your attitude toward a physically active lifestyle. Not knowing this sensation can have the opposite effect.

If we fail to recognize the influence of health behaviors on our present and future health, we are again viewing health in a very limited fashion—as simply the absence of disease. If, on the other hand, our attitudes and values cause us to prevent health problems and promote positive health by making wise health decisions today, we are consciously considering the consequences of our health behaviors.

KNOWLEDGE

Though we might not always act as reasonably as we could, we are not simply the victims of emotions, habits, and environmental influences. We take action or avoid action mainly because we are aware of the health benefits or risks. For instance, you might eat certain foods, refuse to ride with a drunk driver, and get periodic physical checkups because you know the health consequences of these behaviors.

Because individuals seem most at ease when what they know is consistent with their attitudes and values, they often seek information to support personal attitudes while ignoring information that does not. This tendency takes effort to overcome. We find many reasons to ignore information we receive. Instead, we tend to respond to knowledge only when it becomes important to us. For example, some individuals pay no attention to salt intake until they develop high blood pressure. This discrepancy between personal health behavior and general health knowledge is one of the biggest problems in the field of health education.

Motivations for health behavior can be complex. Individuals who want to change a behavior need to consider social pressures, habits, attitudes and values, and knowledge about the health behavior. For example, if you want to quit smoking, you must consider role models and possible sources of support; when, where, and why you acquired the habit of lighting a cigarette; personal values and reasons for quitting; and what is known about the benefits of being a nonsmoker.

In addition, you could be motivated because you will feel better about yourself if you don't smoke, you will feel good enough to enjoy things that have been difficult to do because of the smoking (such as jogging with friends who jog every morning), or you will be able to taste your food better. The chances of successfully changing a health behavior increase dramatically when you adopt an approach that considers your motivations.

CULTURAL INFLUENCES

We are learning more about how much our culture influences our health behavior. Cultural norms and the impact of subcultures are two examples of this.

CULTURAL NORMS

Though each of us may feel that the four motivating forces—social pressure, habits, attitudes and values, and knowledge—are uniquely our own, we usually share them

attitudes
Feelings about facts and behaviors.

values
Ideas we believe in and cherish.

Issue
Mandating Health

Is it ethical to require people to behave in a certain way if their health or the health of others will be improved by doing so? For example, consider these possible mandates:

1. People should be required to wear seat belts in automobiles.
2. Certain sexual behaviors should be prohibited.
3. There should be legislation against marijuana, alcohol, and tobacco.
4. Exercise periods should be required in school and at work.
5. Factories should be required to contain their pollutants.

- Pro: Society shoulders the burdens of paying and caring for people who don't take care of themselves; therefore, we have the right to require people to safeguard their health.

- Con: Society has no right to interfere with the private lives of its citizens. By the same standard, society is not obliged to bear the cost of caring for those who don't safeguard their health.

How far should we go in trying to control people's health behavior? Should there be rules and laws, or should we simply educate people and have healthy behavior be voluntary? What would you do to promote more-positive health behaviors? List specific steps you would take. Would they include mandates about healthy behavior, such as the five possibilities mentioned above?

TABLE 1.1	CULTURAL INFLUENCES AND THEIR HEALTH RESULTS	
Cultural Influence	**Health Result**
The need to eat food with friends or business acquaintances	Intake of unnecessary calories
The need to use a car to reach certain destinations	Lack of physical activity, which contributes to health problems
The pressure to achieve status and be "successful"	Stressful mental and physical condition
The acceptance of smoking in public places	Polluted air for all people in the area

Cultural and subcultural practices can influence health. For example, fried foods traditionally form part of the diet in certain subcultures. Because this diet results in a high intake of cholesterol, these groups have a higher incidence of ill health than other groups do. It is easy to overlook the influence of cultural practices on health. Consider, for example, the list of cultural influences and their health results shown in table 1.1.

Cultural expectations, or **norms,** play a large role in behavior. Some help us and others interfere with our potential to lead healthy, happy, and productive lives. Which of the norms listed below are present in groups to which you belong? What health consequences do you think each might have?

a. It is expected that people spend more time watching sports than participating in them.

b. It is acceptable for people to smoke without asking others present if it is all right to do so.

c. It is usual for people to eat more food than they want or need.

d. It is acceptable for people to have coffee and a roll instead of a nutritional breakfast in the morning.

e. It is expected that people drink alcohol, even when they don't really want it, simply to be part of the group.

f. It is usual for people to accept high tension levels in their lives, thinking that is the way life is.

g. It is acceptable for people not to wear seat belts when doing so is inconvenient.

with many others. The personal values that we believe so strongly to be distinctively our own are usually a product of what we have learned from others. If our teachers had been radically different, our values and beliefs would probably have been different as well. The collection of shared practices, rules, values, and beliefs of a large group of people constitutes their **culture.** People in the United States, for example, have been generally assumed to believe in majority political rule and religious tolerance, and to drive on the right side of the road—these are shared aspects of the culture.

SUBCULTURES

Smaller groups within society—such as Chinese Americans, Irish Americans, and college students—may have distinct practices that set them apart from other groups, even though they share society's major cultural values. Each of these groups is considered a **subculture.** Even within subcultures, enormous variability can exist. For example, in groups such as Hispanics, African Americans, and Asian Americans, languages, values, attitudes, and predominant socioeconomic classes vary greatly.

culture
The shared practices, rules, values, and beliefs of a large group of people.

subcultures
Smaller groups within a society that might have distinct practices that set them apart from other groups, even though they share the society's major cultural values.

norms
Cultural expectations.

Are there others you could add to the list?

Many factors influence health behavior. When you are trying to change a health behavior, you are most likely to be successful when you have appropriate information, access to needed health and social services, and a supportive social environment (Mann, Tarantola, and Netter 1992).

It all boils down to making decisions that improve your health and enhance your well-being. Your view of what health means, your reasons for valuing a healthy lifestyle, and your motivations in choosing health behaviors are all components of the health choices you make. Let's look more closely at a model for promoting optimal health and resiliency (the ability to prevent and/or bounce back from disruption) (Richardson et al. 1990).

A MODEL FOR ACTION

Throughout life there are obstacles and problems. Our health skills and the way we handle problems directly influence our quality of life. The mind, body, and soul strive for balance. Examples of balance can be found related to all health components. For example, when your biological functioning varies from normal, your body's mechanisms try to regain balance. When your psychological functioning is out of balance (e.g., when you have uncontrolled anger), you can initiate ways to return to a balanced state. The mechanism might be socially appropriate (vigorous exercise, relaxation techniques) or inappropriate (violence, property destruction), but over time you can usually revert to the balanced (unangered) state.

Spiritual balance can best be viewed as a blending of values and behavior. It exists when you choose a value or belief system that provides guidelines for living and then abide by that system. If blending does not occur between values and behavior, imbalance of the spiritual component of health results. This can cause feelings of guilt, for example, which subside when values and behaviors are again aligned.

LIFE-EVENT REACTIONS

Throughout life, challenges and stressors appear in many forms. These are **life events**—the many positive and negative influences that can cause disruption or changes. Life events can result in pressure to engage in addictive behaviors (such as excessive television watching, use of chemical substances, food misuse, or inappropriate sexual behavior.)

How well you handle life events determines how healthy you will be. Greater health skills will help you develop better health and handle problems in a more positive way. Understanding protective skills, negotiation, disruption, and disorganization are basic to health promotion.

Protective Skills

Certain **protective skills** (skills to protect yourself from problems) prepare you to deal with life's problems while promoting higher levels of health. For example, you can learn protective skills to enhance such biological factors as tolerance for pain, healing capabilities, fitness level, and state of fatigue. While the degree of protective skills varies from person to person, many can be enhanced by exercise, rest, meditation, proper nutrition, and avoidance of harmful substances.

Additional skills to help protect you are explained throughout this text. Examples are stress-management skills, decision-making skills, and value/behavior congruence. Not all skills are necessary at all times, but some must be functional to provide at least minimal protection.

Negotiation

We need to develop skills to negotiate life events. Which negotiating mechanism or stress-management technique is best depends on the nature of the life event and its effect. For example, you might find that ignoring an individual with a negative attitude might be the best tactic; however, another person might choose to use a different method, such as talking with the individual and finding a way to deal with the problem. You might negotiate problems easily, or you might have difficulty dealing with them, in which case you will probably experience disruption.

life events
Challenges and stressors, both positive and negative, that can cause disruption or changes in our lives.

protective skills
Skills you can use to protect yourself from problems.

CALVIN AND HOBBES copyright 1990 Watterson. Reprinted with permission of UNIVERSAL PRESS SYNDICATE. All rights reserved.

Disruption

Individuals who lose concentration, become angry, and fail to negotiate effectively have problems dealing with their daily lives. They are out of balance and cannot function effectively. The long-term effect of the **disruption** could be positive or negative. For example, after living through a disruption, the person might have learned better ways to deal with anger so that it doesn't cause disruption in the future. On the other hand, disruptions can have negative results, such as causing so much turmoil that people lose their perspective and stop trying to control their anger.

Flach (1989) suggests that experiencing disruption in life can be beneficial. Although being out of balance is unpleasant, disruption can be part of a process that enhances **resiliency** (the ability to prevent or bounce back from disruption). The person can become better skilled, better able to bounce back from problems, and stronger. For example, if you fear certain social situations, you might become more resilient by participating in such situations and finding ways to be successful in them. Disruption forces the resilient individual to look inward, adapt to life events, and possibly develop new skills.

Disruption can be an opportunity to grow and learn. Although the mechanism involved is different, muscle development is somewhat analogous. After strenuous exercise, muscles are fatigued and "torn down." Although the individual is initially weaker and exhausted, the body responds by making the muscles a little stronger than before the exercise experience. The enhancement of psychological or spiritual resiliency is not as predictable as muscle development, from a temporal perspective, but recovery and growth are inevitable for the resilient person.

Many individuals take on challenges because they know they will present growth opportunities. A disruption is not necessarily negative. It can be an exciting opportunity to accomplish something. Sometimes disorganization occurs, however, and this can also help people effectively face the challenge of growth.

Disorganization

Disorganization is a temporary state that occurs when one or more of the components of health become disrupted.

Perhaps a new challenge requires you to formulate a plan without the benefit of having previous related experiences. This can cause a state of disorganization. Or there might be a complete collapse of your view of the world, as might happen when someone close to you dies. This might require building a new support system, establishing a new social life, or making other major adjustments. The part of life that is most affected by the life event must become disorganized in order to create a place for the new.

Individuals do not usually stay in a state of disorganization for long. They must establish a new state of balance in order to function. When you need to do this, you might think about what you have experienced and how you might avoid the problem next time. Attempts to return to balance ideally result in positive adjustment.

DECISION-MAKING SKILLS

Adjustment is the process of returning to balance. It can involve creatively putting your life back together or recovering through systematic problem solving. The process of adjustment may take a few minutes or several years, depending upon the severity of the life event and the adjustment capacity of the individual.

A crucial part of adjustment and prevention is making sound health decisions. Each day you make decisions that affect your health. When a decision is made, it often affects other decisions. There might even be a series of needed decisions—each decision might influence the next one. Even our friends in the comics, like Calvin and Hobbes, are sometimes faced with this dilemma.

disruption
A life event that can cause an individual to become out of balance and unable to function effectively.

resiliency
The ability to prevent or bounce back from a disruption.

disorganization
A temporary state that arises when one or more of the components of health become disrupted.

Figure 1.3

A decision tree: deciding whether to use alcohol at a party.

A **decision tree** diagrams the possible choices and steps in decision making. Figure 1.3 illustrates the choices and steps that might be used when deciding whether to drink alcohol. Even this simple example shows that health decisions are often quite complex.

You can have greater control over personal health if you understand how decisions are made and what influences them. We'll now look at how to make decisions and then at what is needed to put these decisions into practice.

Taking an active role in health decisions is a four-stage process of thought and action: (1) **recognition** of a health-related problem, (2) **evaluation** of alternative courses of action, (3) **implementation** of the course decided on, and (4) **review** of the decision.

Recognition

Only when we recognize that there are ways to promote our health or reach a goal can we make a conscious decision. If you drink alcohol or smoke cigarettes, for example, you might decide you need to think about quitting when friends quit, when you read an article on the physical dangers of smoking or drinking, or when you feel negative physical effects. Or you might feel a need to begin an exercise program because you want to feel better, because of changes in your physical appearance, or because you want to be able to be active with young children. To make the best decision, you should define as precisely as possible the issue you want to resolve or the goal you want to reach. For example, does "drinking" include beer and caffeinated drinks? Does "smoking" mean marijuana as well as tobacco? What would be the purpose of the fitness program?

Evaluation

Once you have recognized the need to make a decision, it is time to gather relevant information, analyze the possible choices, and decide on the best alternative. For example, your decision could be to only drink wine with dinner guests or not to drink before a long commute. Your decision might be to stop smoking altogether or to set aside time each day for a fitness program.

---

decision tree
A diagram of the possible choices and steps involved in making a decision.

recognition
The first stage in making a health decision, in which we become aware that there are ways to promote our health or reach a goal, and that we must make a decision.

evaluation
The second stage in making a health decision, in which we gather relevant information, analyze the possible choices, and decide on the best alternative.

implementation
The third stage in making a health decision, in which we put into practice a decision we have reached through analysis and learning.

review
The fourth stage in making a health decision, in which, after putting a decision into practice, we engage in periodic review of our progress.

PERSONAL SKILLS AND EXPERIENCES

Health Behaviors to Improve Your Health

There are things you can do to improve your health as a result of the topics discussed in this chapter. The following is a partial list of some of the behaviors that could enhance your health.

1. Make decisions based on thorough knowledge and on considering your alternatives, without being influenced by your peers.

2. Resist the influence of others when it is inconsistent with your personal values.

3. Behave in accordance with your personal values.

4. Make an active effort to improve or maintain an optimal health status.

5. Actively strive to achieve health occupationally, spiritually, physically, socially, and emotionally.

6. Become motivated to change any behaviors that threaten your mind/body/soul health.

7. Take time to enhance the spiritual dimension of your health.

The resilient person has the ability to bounce back from life's disruptions.

Implementation

Once you reach a decision based on analysis and learning, it is time to put it into practice. In the case of alcohol consumption or cigarette addiction, your decision might be to quit outright or to cut down gradually. If fitness is the goal, changes in your daily habits may be needed. In these cases, only your personal behavior is being altered. In other health matters, however, you might conclude that the environment also must be changed, for you to have a healthier life. Suppose, for example, that you live near a chemical plant whose waste is polluting streams and seeping into the water supply. If you decide not to move, talking to neighbors and petitioning officials to halt the pollution are two possible courses of action.

Review

After you put your decision into practice, periodically review your progress. Are desired results being achieved, or should another alternative be tried? You might decide to quit alcohol or cigarettes completely instead of just cutting down. Or you might decide to try different exercises as part of your fitness program.

After making your decision, you might learn something new that raises questions about your choice. If so, start the decision-making process again. In fact, according to different

circumstances, many of your choices will require you to rethink your decision. Personal and group values will also strongly influence your decisions.

The major influences on decision making are the same ones that affect health behavior in general: social pressure, habits, attitudes and values, and knowledge. For example, a man might reluctantly decide to sniff cocaine at a party because his friends urge him to (that is, they exert social pressure) and he wants their acceptance. Or a woman might decide to eat junk food, for instance, simply because that's what she usually has for dinner (habit).

Attitudes about disobeying the law can influence whether an underage individual drinks. A woman who knows little about prenatal care (that is, she lacks knowledge) might make an uninformed and potentially disastrous decision to take certain drugs.

Research is lacking on why some individuals are more likely than others to behave in ways that promote their health. It does seem, however, that those with more-positive behaviors feel better about themselves, their bodies, their appearance, and their feelings of moral and personal worth (Bergmann and Greenberg 1991).

ADJUSTMENTS TO PROMOTE OPTIMAL HEALTH AND RESILIENCY

There are four basic ways to adjust to life events: resilient adjustment, balanced adjustment, faulty adjustment, and problematic adjustment.

Resilient Adjustment

Resilient adjustment is the optimal type of adaptation. The key is to benefit from all that a life event offers. While adjusting, we learn new skills, gain more self-understanding, and

---

resilient adjustment
The optimal type of adaptation to life events, benefiting from all that the event has to offer.

PERSONAL SKILLS AND EXPERIENCES

Decision Making Related to Mind/Body/Soul Health

Understanding decision-making steps is important, but they must also be understood in relation to mind/body/soul health. There is no sure way to tell a good decision from a bad one. We can't judge by the chosen behavior alone, because a practice that is good for one person or group might not be good for another. Should we have an affair outside marriage? We might answer this question very differently if we lived in the Muslim world, where the consequences of an affair are often much more severe than they are here. Similarly, we might judge an 80-year-old person's decision to continue smoking as reasonable, but the same decision by a pregnant woman as thoughtless.

The best preliminary way to judge the quality of your decision is to carefully assess the process you used in arriving at it and to see how the process and decision relate to your mind, body, soul, and their interdependence. Here are some examples.

Mind

When you are evaluating alternative courses of action and considering which one(s) to select, are you flexible? Can you listen fairly to various viewpoints? Do you realize that not everyone wants to behave just as you do? Are you open to the "facts"—even if they disagree with what you have believed?

Body

You must have knowledge about bodily functioning if you are going to make wise decisions. For example, knowing how physical activity affects the body is basic if you are planning an exercise program. Understanding basics about nutrition is essential if you are to eat wisely. Appreciating the intricacies of bodily functioning can help you prevent health problems. Did you examine all the relevant information, or just the information you wanted to hear?

Soul

How emotional are you when considering health decisions? Does your purpose in life promote or conflict with healthy decisions? Are there health practices, such as eating certain foods or using some forms of contraception, that go against your values? How do your values relate to "facts" about health? Can you be objective when making health decisions, or are your choices likely to be influenced by many outside factors?

Interdependence

As you follow the four-stage decision-making process (recognition, evaluation, implementation, and review), you will experience the interdependence of mind/body/soul factors. For example, what choices acceptable to you will be influenced by your values, your knowledge, and perhaps the influence of other people. Are you being realistic about your chances of success with your choice? Can you feel comfortable with the decision in the future? Does your chosen course of action fit with your values and goals in life, or are you simply responding to social pressure or habit? You will be most likely to successfully change your health behavior if you believe in what you are doing, you know that the facts reinforce your efforts, and others are supportive. Finally, are you willing to put the effort into making the decision work?

better comprehend personal, social, and environmental influences. Through the experience, resilient individuals put life back together in a way that results in more protective skills to adjust to future life events. For example, perhaps the next time you experience problems with personal relationships, you will know new ways to work them out.

Balanced Adjustment

Balanced adjustment means returning to the same level of functioning that existed prior to the life event. Those who return to the same level do not learn from their experience and will likely have similar problems until they learn from the life event. For example, an individual who has difficulty controlling body weight might lose weight in a weight-control program but not learn how to prevent the problem from occurring again. The same reasons for failure are likely to come up repeatedly.

Faulty Adjustment

Faulty adjustment results when the impact of the life event is so great that the individual has fewer protective skills than before the event. In the face of failure, there may be a loss of self-esteem, of a sense of adventure, or of high expectations. Generally the individual makes a minimal attempt at balanced adjustment but ultimately becomes resigned to a lower level of functioning. It is as if the person thinks it is not possible to do well and must settle for much less.

Many health topics discussed throughout this text relate to faulty adjustment. For example, some people experience problems with alcohol, tobacco, lifestyle diseases, obesity, or sexuality. If the problems are life threatening or cause dysfunctions, there may be problematic adjustment.

balanced adjustment
Returning to the same level of functioning one was at prior to a life event.

faulty adjustment
Emerging from a life event with fewer protective skills than one had before the event.

Problematic Adjustment

Problematic adjustment reflects the need for psychotherapy. Individuals demonstrate problematic adjustment to life events by abusing chemical substances, becoming violent, threatening or even attempting suicide, showing difficulty controlling behaviors, and becoming antisocial. For example, trying to escape reality with an excessive use of alcohol or other drugs and losing your temper for no reason are signs of problematic adjustment.

The model for promoting optimal health and resiliency is illustrated in figure 1.4. Individuals are represented in the circles as negotiating with life events, going through disruption and disorganization, and then adjusting in one of four ways. Wise health decisions, influenced by many factors, result in an increase in the ability to deal with life events.

STRENGTH INTERVENTION AND LIFESTYLE CONTRACTING

The focus of this book is on high levels of health rather than on health problems. Emphasizing strengths is a powerful way to help make health decisions that promote optimal health and, at the same time, make it easier to continue implementing these decisions (Richardson and Berry 1987).

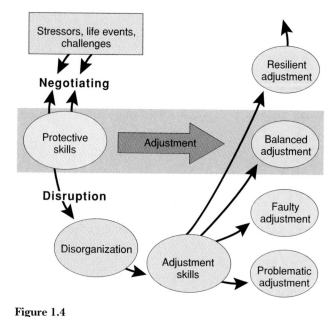

Figure 1.4

A model for promoting optimal health and resiliency.

This figure is reprinted with permission from *Health Education*, 1990, pp. 33–39. Health Education is a publication of the American Alliance for Health, Physical Education, Recreation and Dance, 1900 Association Drive, Reston, VA 22091.

problematic adjustment
Responding to a life event with behaviors—such as drug abuse, violence, or suicide attempts—that indicate a need for psychotherapy.

strength intervention
Influencing health behaviors by building on existing strengths.

lifestyle contracting
Making a personal plan for improving health behaviors.

Strength intervention means influencing health behavior by building on existing strengths. It is the basis for the remainder of this chapter, which focuses on **lifestyle contracting** (making a personal plan for improving health behaviors) as an important way to improve health. To use this method, you must first understand the four stages of strength intervention: assessing, nurturing, freeing, and optimizing (fig. 1.5).

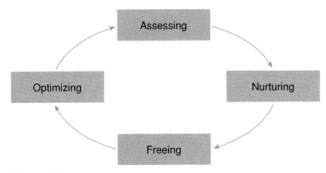

Figure 1.5
Stages of strength intervention.

Assessing means determining personal strengths, motivations, existing support systems, barriers to lifestyle change, and factors determining comfort and happiness. **Nurturing** means giving care and attention to the factors that produce strength in life. Remember the concept of total health and the interaction of all components of health (see fig. 1.1) and note that building strengths in one health area (such as physical health) can positively affect another health area (such as mental health). Focusing on strengths provides a boost in other dimensions of life.

Freeing means achieving freedom from disabling habits. At the negative end of the continuum for each component of health, a burden is implied. At the opposite end of the continuum there is freedom from such burdens.

Although subject to individual interpretation, the disability end of the spiritual dimension could be defined as guilt. One might believe a set of values is right, for example, but behave differently than those values dictate. Freedom can be conceptualized with any health risk factor. It might include liberation from the effects of such factors as distress, hate, excess weight, or tobacco.

Optimizing means striving to reach high-level health in one health component at a time. This means incorporating positive health behaviors. For example, you might focus on how to become happier in your workplace to improve your occupational health. Although you might focus only on optimizing one health component (such as occupational health) at a time, you will also affect the other health components, perhaps without even realizing it.

Assessing your personal strengths is a logical place for you to start when you are considering health behavior change. Complete the Health Assessment exercise on page 1.20 before continuing.

Lifestyle contracting is used in all parts of this book to help you consider health decisions that might alter your behaviors and improve your health. *Lifestyle contracting* is a systematic approach to making a commitment to lifestyle change. Strength intervention seems to be the most pleasant and effective approach to lifestyle contracting.

A lifestyle contract is shown in figure 1.6 on page 1.23. Refer to this figure as we discuss various parts of the contract. We will discuss all parts of the contract, but *not all parts may*

need to be used for every health behavior change. You will want to choose the areas in which your health needs the most improvement and do lifestyle contracts in those areas. Use the parts of the contract that are most pertinent to you and your desired behavior. For example, you might want to stop smoking, lose weight, and manage stress better. Another person might prefer to improve communication skills and nutritional practices.

Select a behavior you want to change. We'll use improving eating habits as an example, just to illustrate how lifestyle contracting might work, but you need to select a behavior that *you* want to change. You will build on your existing strengths (strength intervention) and use the results of your health assessments. Additional Health Assessment exercises are found in each chapter of this text to help assess your present attitudes and health behavior.

You have already done initial *assessing*, so the next factor to consider (part I.A.1 of the lifestyle contract in fig. 1.6) is whether the strength area needs *nurturing* (giving care and attention to factors that produce strength). For example, perhaps you eat nutritiously when you eat meals at home, but not so nutritiously when you eat out. Or perhaps eating with certain people influences your eating habits positively. Wherever you have strengths related to the health behavior you want to change, you can nurture the strengths to make them even stronger. When you know how the necessary strength, comfort, and support will be provided, go on to freeing.

Freeing (part I.A.2) means achieving freedom from habits that inhibit the behavior you want. Perhaps the junk food in the kitchen is so attractive that you can't stay away from it. Or maybe your friends often ask you to grab a quick bite at a fast-food restaurant. What might you do to free yourself from such habits that get in the way of your goal?

Then comes *optimizing* (part I.A.3), which means working to reach a higher level of health in one component at a time. For example, you are probably trying to improve your eating habits to improve your physical health. For now, being aware of that is all that is needed. There is no additional impact on your behavior choices from optimizing unless you also decide to do other things to improve your physical health. However, as you will read shortly, we generally recommend focusing on only one or two health behaviors at a time—though changing

assessing
Determining one's personal strengths, motivations, existing support systems, barriers to lifestyle change, and factors that determine one's comfort and happiness.

nurturing
Giving care and attention to the factors that produce strength in life.

freeing
Achieving freedom from disabling habits.

optimizing
Striving to reach high-level health in one health component at a time.

Personal Strengths Questionnaire

1. List the people now living who consistently make you the happiest and give you the most support, strength, or comfort.
   a. _____
   b. _____
   c. _____
   d. _____

2. List, in order, the specific activities (types of exercising, recreating, reading, visiting, and so on) that make you the happiest or make you feel good.
   a. _____
   b. _____
   c. _____
   d. _____

3. When you were younger, what activities gave you strength, comfort, happiness, or support? Reflect on one or several ages. Select those things from the list that you do not do now (e.g., listening to music with friends, going to movies, dancing, camping, going on trips by yourself).
   a. _____
   b. _____
   c. _____
   d. _____

4. Describe some elements of an ideal or fantasy day that you could have if you had no responsibilities or commitments but yet are within your moral and financial limitations.
   a. _____
   b. _____
   c. _____
   d. _____

Building on Success

5. Reflect for a moment on the past several years and write down any habits you broke, any habits you intentionally started, or behaviors that you modified and were able to continue to the present. Check any of the following items or write some that are not listed.
   _____ Stopped smoking
   _____ Lost weight
   _____ Began an exercise program
   _____ Improved a relationship with someone
   _____ Improved my diet
   _____ Stopped eating so many sweets
   _____ Started using time management or organized my day better
   _____ Stopped drinking (or excessive drinking)
   _____ Began to give more time to loved ones or friends
   _____ Became less moody
   _____ Others (list) _____

6. If you were able to answer #5, identify which of the following approaches you used to make those changes (mark as many as apply).

   Family support
   Friend(s) support
   Read some material on it and did it myself
   Just made up my mind to do it
   Got professional help
   Made it part of the enjoyable things I do
   My physician (health professional) told me to do it
   I felt the time had come to make the change
   Others (list) _____
   _____

7. Check the reason(s) you changed a habit in the past:
   _____ I just felt ready to change
   _____ I was motivated to change
   _____ There was an incentive for me to change
   _____ The idea of a change seemed fun
   _____ I was challenged by the idea of changing
   _____ I was encouraged by significant people in my life
   _____ I had a positive attitude about the change
   Others (list) _____
   _____

8. Check the reason you chose the habit you chose (please check all appropriate responses):
   _____ I knew I would feel better if I changed this habit
   _____ An important person in my life helped me select this behavior
   _____ It was something I always wanted to change
   _____ I kept hearing about it from the media or other sources
   Others (list) _____

Locus of Control (Perceived Control over Your Life)

9. My health status is determined mostly by how I live.
   _____ Agree _____ Not Sure _____ Disagree

10. How I feel is determined mostly by how my doctor and other health professionals care for me.
    _____ Agree _____ Not Sure _____ Disagree

11. Whether I get sick or not is a matter of good or bad luck.
    _____ Agree _____ Not Sure _____ Disagree

12. I am in control of my health.
    _____ Agree _____ Not Sure _____ Disagree

13. If I actively do things to improve my health, I will undoubtedly feel better.
    _____ Agree _____ Not Sure _____ Disagree

14. Whether I am sick or well has little to do with how I live.
    _____ Agree _____ Not Sure _____ Disagree

(Continued on page 1.21)

HEALTH ASSESSMENT

Scoring

Most of these assessments are to help you complete a lifestyle contract that is explained in this chapter. Questions 1–4 help you reflect on areas of personal strength. Questions 5–8 help you consider past successes in changing a health behavior. Using the same principles and methods you used to change past behavior will help you plan your current health challenge.

Questions 9–14 will help determine your perspective of control over your health, or health locus of control. Score as follows:

Questions 9, 12, and 13	Questions 10, 11, and 14
Agree = 3 points	Agree = 1 point
Not sure = 2 points	Not sure = 2 points
Disagree = 1 point	Disagree = 3 points

Total your points. The following is an interpretation of your score.

14–18 points = You perceive yourself as in control of your health status.

11–13 points = You perceive yourself as in moderate control of your health and some control by those around you or chance.

below 11 points = You perceive yourself as a product of your environment or your health is controlled by chance or other people.

The lifestyle analysis form is to help you plan your behavior change project. You will be able to look at this tool to determine where you can incorporate positive behaviors into your lifestyle.

Lifestyle Analysis

Directions: Take a "typical" day for you. A generally stressful day should be the typical day you reflect on. As best you can, note the activities you do during different times of the day. Indicate the periods when you eat, sleep, drive, work, recreate, watch television, take breaks during work, socialize, and so on until another activity is listed. For example, if you generally go to sleep at 11:00 P.M. and wake up at 6:30 A.M., you need only write sleep once at 11:00 P.M. and then write your next activity at 6:30 A.M.

12:00 A.M. (noon) _____
:15 _____
:30 _____
:45 _____
1:00 P.M. _____
:15 _____
:30 _____
:45 _____
2:00 P.M. _____
:15 _____
:30 _____
:45 _____

3:00 P.M. _____
:15 _____
:30 _____
:45 _____
4:00 P.M. _____
:15 _____
:30 _____
:45 _____
5:00 P.M. _____
:15 _____
:30 _____
:45 _____
6:00 P.M. _____
:15 _____
:30 _____
:45 _____
7:00 P.M. _____
:15 _____
:30 _____
:45 _____
8:00 P.M. _____
:15 _____
:30 _____
:45 _____
9:00 P.M. _____
:15 _____
:30 _____
:45 _____
10:00 P.M. _____
:15 _____
:30 _____
:45 _____
11:00 P.M. _____
:15 _____
:30 _____
:45 _____
12:00 P.M. (midnight) _____
:15 _____
:30 _____
:45 _____
1:00 A.M. _____
:15 _____
:30 _____
:45 _____
2:00 A.M. _____
:15 _____
:30 _____
:45 _____

(Continued on page 1.22)

3:00 A.M. _____	:30 _____
:15 _____	:45 _____
:30 _____	8:00 A.M. _____
:45 _____	:15 _____
4:00 A.M. _____	:30 _____
:15 _____	:45 _____
:30 _____	9:00 A.M. _____
:45 _____	:15 _____
5:00 A.M. _____	:30 _____
:15 _____	:45 _____
:30 _____	10:00 A.M. _____
:45 _____	:15 _____
6:00 A.M. _____	:30 _____
:15 _____	:45 _____
:30 _____	11:00 A.M. _____
:45 _____	:15 _____
7:00 A.M. _____	:30 _____
:15 _____	:45 _____

even one behavior can affect more than one health *component* without your even realizing it. For example, when you quit smoking to improve your physical health, you will experience other, nonphysical benefits—such as feeling better about yourself for each day you don't smoke, positive feedback in the form of social support and encouragement from friends and family, and an enhanced social life because nonsmokers appreciate your smoke-free presence.

The most vital decision-making assessment is the identification of individual **motivation** (part I.A.4). It is better to work on something you want to work on and build on the success for future behaviors. If you would like to improve your eating habits, but you really aren't motivated to, it might be better to wait until some other time and choose a health behavior that you are motivated to change.

Building on success (part I.A.5) helps bring about health behavior change. For example, perhaps you have previously been successful in changing other health behaviors. You could use what you learned to now alter your eating habits. Think about what you did in the past to help change your health behavior, and decide what aspects could help you now. In addition, successes with simpler problems can help build the confidence you need when you deal with more-difficult problems. (It might be helpful to again look at items 5–8 on the Personal Strengths Questionnaire, since those items deal with building on success.)

Barriers to change (part I.A.6) should also be considered. Finances, working hours, social support (or lack of it), and the like may dictate that a different behavior be selected or modified based on feasibility. For example, perhaps your school schedule combined with your work schedule makes this a terrible time to try to improve your eating behavior. It might make sense to wait awhile to help ensure success. It is important, however, not to use barriers as an excuse to avoid altering an important health behavior.

Most behavior change specialists recommend contracting for no more than one or two behaviors at a time (part I.B). Attempting several behaviors at once generally results in failure. It might be possible to contract for more than two

motivation
The feeling of being impelled or of desiring to do something that leads you to engage in an activity.

building on success
Using what you learned in previous successful attempts at changing your health behavior to change another health behavior.

barriers to change
Aspects of your life—such as finances, working hours, or lack of social support—that might require you to revise your plan for changing a health behavior.

◆ **Lifestyle Contracting Using Strength Intervention** ◆

I. Behavioral selection

   A. Factors to consider before making a behavioral selection

      1. Nurturing _____

      2. Freeing _____

      3. Optimizing _____

      4. Motivation/readiness _____

      5. Building on success _____

      6. Barriers to change _____

   B. Behaviors I will change (no more than two)

      _____

      _____

II. The plan

   A. General plan _____

   B. Substitution _____

   C. Linking behaviors _____

   D. Combining strength and weakness _____

   E. When _____

   F. Where _____

   G. Intensity _____

   H. Preparation _____

   I. With whom _____

III. Support groups

   A. Who _____

   B. Role _____

   C. Organized support _____

IV. Trigger responses _____

V. Starting date _____

VI. Date/sequence the contract will be reevaluated _____

VII. Evidence of reaching goal _____

VIII. Rewards when contract is completed _____

IX. Signature of client _____

X. Signature of facilitator _____

XI. Additional conditions/comments: _____

Figure 1.6

Lifestyle contracting using strength intervention.

behaviors if they are closely related, such as weight control, fitness, and eating habits; however, this should be done only with extreme caution.

While you are formulating your general plan (part II.A), it is important that you be detailed to avoid pitfalls that might not be apparent at first. Questions that need to be resolved include how, when, where, and with whom. For example, what will you do to improve eating habits? Will certain people assist you? What activities, such as trips to the grocery store, might need changing? Other parts of the lifestyle contract, such as building on strengths and substitution, relate to the general plan.

The most obvious way to change behavior is **substitution** (part II.B)—substituting positive behaviors for negative behaviors or for nonproductive time. You might eliminate one television show and replace it with time to cook a nutritious meal. Or you might choose restaurants where the choices are more nutritious, substitute exercise, or devote time to spiritual reading. There is also substitution in cases where an unhealthy activity is deleted from a lifestyle. For example, to

take away late-night snacking without replacement generally results in failure. One man petted his dog every time he had a craving for a late-night snack, another chewed sugarless gum, and another jumped on his minitrampoline.

Linking behaviors (part II.C) is done to help increase the likelihood of reaching your goal, and for time efficiency. The possibilities are limited only by your creativity. Examples include listening to a tape of class notes while shopping at the grocery store, or working on communication skills with spouse or partner while cooking a nutritious meal.

substitution
Substituting positive behaviors for negative behaviors or for nonproductive time.

linking behaviors
Performing two or more activities simultaneously to increase the likelihood that you will reach your goal.

PERSONAL SKILLS AND EXPERIENCES

Your Choices and Decisions

Perhaps one of the most exciting discoveries in the last two decades is the rediscovery and the medical confirmation of the power of the mind and its interaction with the body. Ancient philosophies and practices have always linked the mind and the body, but modern medicine has functioned on the idea that for every physical disease, there is a physical cause. For example, to prevent disease, one gets an immunization; to prevent heart attack, one should exercise and eat a low-fat diet; and if one has a bacterial infection, one should take penicillin.

In the early 1980s, physicians started to ask themselves why, although people are constantly exposed to microorganisms (viruses, bacteria, etc.), sometimes the organisms are activated and cause disease while other times the bacteria and viruses rest in respiratory passages without any harmful effect.

At the same time, some amazing documented cases of "miraculous" healings of serious diseases began to be reported. In one such case, a Mr. Wright was given about 2 weeks to live by his physicians. His body was bloated with tumors the size of oranges that had to be drained of 1 to 2 quarts of fluid each day. The medical staff was merely attempting to make him as comfortable as possible until his inevitable death. Mr. Wright heard about a new experimental cancer drug called Krebiozen and told his physician that he wanted to try it. It just so happened that the hospital where Mr. Wright was dying had been selected as an experimental site for the new drug. Because the physician wanted to experiment with patients who had a better chance of survival, he was reluctant to let Mr. Wright take the drug. Mr. Wright persisted and finally received permission to use the drug. After one injection of Krebiozen, the tumors reduced to half the size in 2 to 3 days, and, within 2 weeks, Mr. Wright went home apparently in total remission and free of tumors.

Some time later, which happened to be a day or two after the drug Krebiozen was reported in the media to be ineffective, Mr. Wright returned to the hospital with the tumors again. The physician, knowing that something more than the drug was at work, then put Mr. Wright in a control group for a "new" Krebiozen. This meant that Mr. Wright would not receive the drug, but rather would receive an injection of sterile water. The administration was given with great ceremony by the physician and with great anticipation by Mr. Wright, who perceived the administration to be a double dose of the "new" drug. After a few days the tumors again disappeared. A few months later, renewed reports citing the ineffectiveness of Krebiozen were made public and, shortly after, Mr. Wright died (Locke 1986).

Other case studies relate astonishing accounts of patients with multiple personalities with one personality having diabetes, tumors, or allergic reactions to certain substances.

When a new personality emerged, the conditions were no longer evidenced. Tumors disappeared in a few days, symptoms of diabetes disappeared, and allergies were no longer existent (Borysenko 1987).

Studies in medical literature demonstrate longer survival rates of patients with AIDS, cancer, or heart disease if they have positive personality traits. People with optimism, hope, faith, a cause or purpose, a fighting spirit, and a determination to overcome a disease do live longer and are happier.

Intuitively, we have known for years that if you are too busy to get sick, you are not as likely to get sick. When we are experiencing the most stress, are most depressed, when we are grieving, or most upset, we tend to get sick more often. Conversely, we also know that when things are going along smoothly, when we are excited about living, when we have a cause and purpose, and when we are working toward goals, we seem to have more energy and are healthier. Why is this?

The relatively new and exciting medical field that studies this phenomenon is called **PSYCHONEUROIMMUNOLOGY (PNI)** (Ader, Felten, and Cohen 1991). This is the study of the way that we think *(psycho)*, which then affects the central nervous system *(neuro)*, and then affects our immune system *(immunology)*. Much of the study of the field of PNI has been to understand how the immune system is triggered. Scientists have found that "no major sector of the immune system is without a hard-wire connection to the brain" (Locke and Colligan 1986).

The total picture of the interaction of the mind and body involves a two-directional network. How we think can affect our body, and how fit our body is can affect the way we think.

Studies show that when we have a fighting spirit, are optimistic, have a cause in life, and have great hope, our immune system can be fortified. There are actually more elements available in our immune system (i.e., macrophage, T-cells, and B cells) to fight the invasions of foreign microorganisms (Locke and Colligan 1986; Borysenko 1987).

A precaution about PNI is important to understand. How you think can in fact either weaken or fortify your immune system. This is **not** to suggest that you can think diseases away, but you can help the process. If you are sick, IT IS IMPORTANT TO FOLLOW A PHYSICIAN'S TREATMENT PLAN, but you can supplement the physician's plan by believing that treatment will work, that with proper treatment you will overcome the problem, and that you feel medicines and treatments working. If you are not sick, IT DOES NOT MEAN THAT YOU DO NOT NEED PERIODIC PHYSICIAN EXAMINATIONS. It means that positive thinking will help to keep you well.

Implications

Ask yourself the question, "How can this information help me?" At the end of each of the parts of this text will be a discussion of the implications of PNI for your lifestyle. The essence of all the recommendations will be to help you overcome negative mind and body states and promote positive states. There are four key elements in successful adoption of positive states.

(Continued on page 1.25)

PERSONAL SKILLS AND EXPERIENCES

1. Live through repeated and varied new experiences in the social, emotional, cognitive, physical, and spiritual domains of living.

2. When making decisions, take advantage of outcomes of those decisions (positive or negative) to learn and improve your decision-making skills.

3. Through experiences and decisions, focus on understanding yourself better so that you can refine your decision-making skills.

4. Become aware of or establish a cause in your life. A cause is more than a goal or something you do for yourself. A cause is generally made up of many goals that generally involve improving the condition or welfare of someone or something besides yourself (help your family, preserve the environment, help a kid or kids, help the elderly, or numerous other worthy causes).

Here are some things that might help you attain optimism, a fighting spirit, hope, or a cause:

1. When you experience a setback in life or are depressed or anxious, talk to yourself and get excited about this mental state. You can perceive it as a great opportunity to learn a new coping skill. Turn the negative state into a positive one.

2. Consider a variety of ways to establish a cause in your life. Think about your own environment and people you interact with, take a close look at your natural environment, visit some residents in a home for the elderly, visit some youth organizations, visit a homeless shelter, and see where you can potentially volunteer to help people or things.

3. Do something you haven't done before. After you think of something, learn how to do it or get a role model or someone else to show you how, and then do it. Successful experiences might include anything in life, such as trying to cook, iron, sew, or make something; trying out for a play or team; visiting a different religious ceremony; trying meditation, yoga, horseshoes, tennis, etc. Take a different type of class at your school, maybe a recreational class to learn to fish, scuba dive, or play chess.

References

Ader, R., D. L. Felten, and N. Cohen, (Ed.). *Psychoneuroimmunology (Second Edition)*. San Diego: Academic Press (1991).

Borysenko, J. *Minding the Body, Mending the Mind.* Reading, MA: Addison-Wesley Co. (1987).

Hall, N. R. S. and M. P. O'Grady. "Psychosocial Interventions and Immune Function" in R. Ader, D. L. Felten, and N. Cohen, (Ed.). (1991) *Psychoneuroimmunology (Second Edition)*. San Diego: Academic Press, p. 1075.

Locke, S. and D. Colligan. *The Healer Within: The New Medicine of Mind and Body.* New York: E. P. Dutton (1986).

An important psychological principle is evident when you *combine a strength and a weakness* (part II.D). If the two are somewhat matched, the strength usually wins out. The strength provides a supportive environment and promotes success. For example, one man who wanted to improve his eating habits determined that his primary strength dimension was social and his primary support person was his wife. He was most likely to be successful if initially he ate as many meals as possible with his wife, at home. He might then progress to improving his eating habits in any social situation while with his wife, and then move to eating better in other situations as well—even when his wife is not present.

The question of *when* (part II.E) is personal and is also influenced by outside factors. For example, improving eating habits means finding the right time of day to fit in food shopping, finding the time to prepare food, or altering meal times entirely. Controlling body weight has different "when" implications, and stopping smoking has still others. It is important to consider the timing of events that can affect your attempts to improve your health behaviors.

The issue of *where* (part II.F) may or may not be critical, but you should consider it. In regard to changing eating habits, it could mean where you eat or where you buy your food. In the case of exercise programs, you need to build in bad-weather alternatives to good-weather activities, such as cross-country skiing, snowshoeing, exercise bikes, or other acceptable alternatives. Another "where" consideration is convenience. At the beginning of a program, when you are highly motivated, you might be willing to drive to an appropriate restaurant or food market. When your motivation is not so high, however, convenience might be a greater factor.

Intensity (part II.G) is probably not applicable to a contract to improve eating habits, but it is applicable to some health behavior changes, such as an exercise program. Even though most parts of the contract will apply to all strength-improvement programs, there may be a few parts that do not.

Preparation (part II.H) usually becomes obvious once the plan is designed. It could involve getting equipment in which

---

intensity
The level of energy with which you pursue your new health behaviors.

preparation
Securing the aids—such as equipment, information, or social arrangements with other people—you need in order to be successful in changing your health behaviors.

a.

b.

Substituting one behavior for another might help promote health. For example, substituting the behavior in *(b)* for the behavior in *(a)* would be helpful.

to prepare new kinds of food, learning nutritional information, making arrangements to meet people at a certain time and place, or other acts that are needed in order to be successful.

With whom (part II.I) is another consideration that might not always be necessary, but it can be very helpful. Some goals can be accomplished alone; others might be enhanced by the presence and even the assistance of another person. In our example, it might be easier for you to improve your eating habits if you eat more often with certain people.

One or more **support groups** (part III of the lifestyle contract) can help increase your chances for success. In the Health Assessment exercise, you identified people from whom you derive comfort, support, happiness, and inner

Issue

Planning for Health Behavior Change

The best way to change health behavior is to carefully plan for change. This means you should work out a plan, such as a lifestyle contract, and follow it religiously.

- Pro: If we're going to bring about change, we can't leave things to chance. Considering behavioral theories, strength intervention, and the many parts of lifestyle contracting is a must. It's the only real way to succeed.

- Con: Strong people can change health behavior without taking the time to go through all those steps. It is simply a matter of deciding to do it and then doing it. No detailed plan is needed.

Is an explicit plan for health behavior change necessary for you? Do you think it is necessary for most other people? Why or why not?

strength. These individuals are ideal members of a support group to facilitate and sustain your efforts to improve your eating habits. The support group can fulfill several functions, such as giving you casual reminders to follow the contract, participating with you, providing praise, listening, and monitoring your progress.

People who fail in their contracts usually fail during the first 6 to 8 weeks of the program. They seem to fail because they lack motivation and want to give up, and consequently they drop out of the program. **Trigger responses** (part IV of the lifestyle contract) can help prevent this. Sample triggers might include putting pictures of nutritious food on the refrigerator, looking at a picture of yourself when you were leaner if you are trying to lose weight, or reading about nutrition in good sources. By being creative, you can think of trigger responses that will work best for you.

In some cases the **starting date** (part V) should be immediately, but sometimes it will take a little time to contact support people, purchase equipment, or learn appropriate information. Careful selection of the starting date is important, particularly when you need time to get ready.

It is a good idea to set a time, within 2 to 4 weeks of the start of your program, to *reevaluate your lifestyle contract* (part

support group
A group of people from whom you derive comfort, support, happiness, and inner strength, and who can help in your pursuit of improved health behaviors.

trigger responses
Positive responses to triggers (items that remind you of your health behavior goal) that help you succeed at reaching your goal.

starting date
The date you select to start working at changing your chosen health behavior.

PERSONAL SKILLS AND EXPERIENCES

New Year's Resolutions

It is common for New Year's resolutions to involve health behavior change. For most people, the toughest part is keeping the momentum going well into the new year. You must view taking control over your health behavior as something you will do for the rest of your life, not just for the next few weeks or months. To help make sure that your resolutions are successful, do the following:

1. Make sure your resolutions reflect *your* choices, not someone else's.

2. Enlist support from friends or family members.

3. Limit your exposure to people who tend to reinforce the habit you're trying to break.

4. Set realistic goals. Lofty goals are a setup for failure, and they increase stress.

5. Focus on one or two important changes at a time. Don't try to make too many changes at once.

6. Find a role model for inspiration, or set yourself up as a role model for your children or other people.

7. Analyze the forces behind your bad habit and target them in your plan for achieving your goal. If eating is your way of coping with stress, a stress-reduction plan might be more effective than a diet.

8. Think of your goal in a positive light. Instead of vowing to lose weight, for example, decide to adopt a healthier lifestyle.

9. Give yourself rewards as incentives. It's a good idea to choose rewards that reinforce the behavior you want to achieve—like new clothes, if you're involved in an exercise program.

10. Consider a stress-reduction program. Stress relief can open doors to many positive changes.

11. Vow to feel happier. Feeling happy will bolster your commitment to accomplishing other goals.

12. If you have a setback, don't throw in the towel.

From "Keeping New Year's Resolutions About Better Health Practices" in *Health Education Reports* 14(1), January 16, 1992, pages 6–7. Reprinted by permission.

VI). Most people overlook some considerations at the start, and you might need to modify your contract to accomplish your desired outcome. Modifications will probably be a matter of when, where, or intensity (starting out gradually to make the change).

How will you know when you reach your goal? *Specifying the criteria for the goal's having been met* (part VII) helps you determine when you will be happy with your achievement. Examples might be when you enjoy your meals more, when you find you are not as tempted to eat fast food, or when you feel benefit from eating better.

When you are in the process of identifying the behavior you want to change, consider what your standard for success will be. For example, will you need to eat better every meal of every day? most of the time? three days a week? If you slack off, at what point are you no longer successful?

Most psychologists suggest that you build in a **reward** (part VIII) when you have accomplished your goal. This is appropriate if you want to do so, but for some people the sense of accomplishment and control might be reward enough. One word of caution, however, is that your rewards should not be in conflict with your accomplishment of your goal. Buying a hot fudge sundae to celebrate better eating habits is an example of such a conflict.

This type of contracting is not legally binding, of course, but a signature represents commitment. Do not sign (part IX) until you are ready to make a commitment and are determined to comply with the contract. Getting the signature of a facilitator (someone to help you fulfill your contract) (part X) is another way to help you promote success. Careful planning, thinking through all of the steps described, and determination to change are all necessary ingredients for success.

Are you ready to make some positive changes in your health? Use the Health Assessment exercise you completed earlier to create your own lifestyle contract by filling in the blank contract in figure 1.6.

Now we're ready to explore many health topics that relate to the promotion of optimal health and resiliency. Our goal is to inspire you to strive for optimal health with the realization that disruption and disorganization will occur at times. In working toward your optimal state of living, you will find it invaluable to understand the close relationships between the mind, body, and soul; use positive adjustment skills; and make sound decisions about your health. You can also take specific actions, such as assessing your health status and using lifestyle planning, to help you strive toward optimal health and adjust resiliently to life events. Decisions for health are some of the most important decisions you will ever make.

SUMMARY

1. Despite the availability of abundant health information, most of us actually know little about our health.

2. Health has been defined in many ways. It is often viewed as a positive state of being that includes mental health, emotional health, social health, physical health, occupational health, and spiritual health. Recently, a mind/body/soul view of health evolved that has further broadened the view of health as a positive state of being.

---

reward

An enjoyable gift, consistent with your health behavior goal, that you give yourself when you have accomplished your goal.

3. Personal lifestyle dramatically affects health, but most individuals are inconsistent in their health behavior.

4. There are many motivations for health behavior. They include fear, social pressure, health habits, attitudes and values, knowledge, and cultural influences.

5. To change behavior, you must understand biological, psychological, and cultural factors, as well as the interplay among them.

6. Health and what is done about it are not simply an individual affair—they are connected to larger cultural issues. You can choose to alter many influences to arrive at a balance conducive to optimal health.

7. Protective skills, negotiation, disruption, disorganization, and adjustment skills are parts of a model for action to promote optimal health.

8. One health decision can have many ramifications for other health decisions. Making decisions about and acting on health issues involves recognition, evaluation, implementation, and review.

9. Social pressure, habits, attitudes and values, and knowledge can influence decision making. Cultural and subcultural norms and practices also impact decision making and health.

10. Strength intervention includes four stages: assessing, nurturing, freeing, and optimizing.

11. Lifestyle contracting can systematically help with health behavior change. In the preparation of a lifestyle contract, many factors must be considered, including building on success, barriers to change, substitution, linking behaviors, combining strengths with weaknesses, support groups, and triggers to action.

12. The best way to improve health lies in what we do or do not do—both to and for ourselves—not in what others do for us.

COMMITMENT ACTIVITIES

1. Circle the number on this continuum that you think best represents your current health status:

1   2   3   4   5   6   7   8   9   10

Poor health   ↔   Optimum health

Why did you rate yourself as you did? List the conditions or behaviors that you believe prevent you from reaching a higher level of health (for example, overeating, smoking, overwork).

1. _____
2. _____
3. _____
4. _____
5. _____
6. _____

7. _____
8. _____
9. _____
10. _____
11. _____

Which of these behaviors are you willing to change? As you go through this book, pay special attention to conditions or behaviors you are willing to change, then commit yourself to making needed changes. For those things you are not yet willing to change, commit yourself at least to learning more about them. From time to time, reassess yourself on this continuum. (Adapted from Marshall W. Kreuter, "An Interaction Model to Facilitate Health Awareness and Behavior Change" in *Journal of School Health,* November 1976, pages 543–545.)

2. The same continuum idea can be used to evaluate community health. Ask community members to assess the level of health in their neighborhood or town, then identify conditions that are roadblocks to better community health. What can be done to move your community's health closer to a 10?

3. List five of your health behaviors. Carefully examine them for inconsistencies and ask yourself why the inconsistencies exist. For each inconsistency, consider what you can do to increase positive health behavior (create consistency). How can you reduce barriers to action? Are you willing to do so?

4. For the next 5 days, jot down daily at least three decisions you make related to your health. Then evaluate the decisions based on the information in this chapter.

5. Develop a personal model of decision making for health, based on the material in this chapter and other sources. Follow the steps in your model as you make health decisions. Remember to evaluate your model occasionally and to revise it as necessary.

REFERENCES

Abood, D. A., and T. L. Conway. 1992. "Health Value and Self-Esteem As Predictors of Wellness Behavior." *Health Values* 16, no. 3 (May/June): 20–26.

"Attitudes of College Freshmen." 1993. *ERS Bulletin* 20, no. 7 (March): 1.

Bensley, R. J. 1991. "Defining Spiritual Health: A Review of the Literature." *Journal of Health Education* 22, no. 5 (September/October): 287–90.

Bergmann, B. L., and J. S. Greenberg. 1991. "A Study of the Psychosocial Profile of the Health Promoting Adult." *Journal of Health Education* 22, no. 6 (November/December): 354–62.

"Can Your Mind Heal Your Body?" 1993. *Consumer Reports* 58, no. 2: 107–15.

Chapman, L. S. 1987. "Developing a Useful Perspective on Spiritual Health: Well-Being, Spiritual Potential, and the Search for Meaning." *American Journal of Health Promotion* (Winter): 31–39.

Dortch, I. 1994. "Doctors As Detectives." *UAB Medical Center Magazine* 38, no. 2 (Spring): 2–5.

Eberst, R. 1985. "Defining Health: A Multidimensional Model." *Journal of School Health* 54, no. 3 (March): 99–104.

Goodloe, N. R., and P. M. Arreola. 1992. "Spiritual Health: Out of the Closet." *Journal of Health Education* 23, no. 4 (May/June): 221–26.

Langer, E. J. 1989. "The Mindset of Health." *Psychology Today,* April, 48–51.

"Life Support." 1993. *Consumer Reports on Health* 5, no. 3:25.

Mann, J., D. Tarantola, and T. Netter. 1992. *A Global Report: AIDS in the New World.* Cambridge: Harvard University Press.

"Most Canadians Report Good Health, Despite Increased Stress." 1993. News Release from Health and Welfare Canada describing results of Canada's Health Promotion Survey, 27 March.

Moyers, B. 1993. *Healing the Mind.* New York: Doubleday.

Norman, Ross. 1987. "Health Behavior: The Implications for Research." *Health Promotion* 25, no. 2:2–9.

Pelletier, K. R. 1992. "Mind-Body Health: Research, Clinical, and Policy Applications." *American Journal of Health Promotion* 6, no. 5 (May/June): 345–58.

Promoting Health/Preventing Disease: Year 2000 Objectives for the Nation. 1990 Washington, D.C.: Public Health Service, U.S. Department of Health and Human Services.

Richardson, G. E., and N. F. Berry. 1987. "Strength Intervention: An Approach to Lifestyle Modification." *Health Education* 18, no. 3 (March): 42–46.

Richardson, G. E., B. L. Neiger, S. Jensen, and K. L. Kempfer. 1990. "The Resiliency Model." *Health Education* 21, no. 6. (November/December): 33–39.

"Stress and Colds." 1993. *Consumer Reports on Health* 5, no. 6 (June): 59.

"Stroke Survival and Depression . . . and Isolation." 1993. *Consumer Reports on Health* 5, no. 5:51.

Wong, D., and W. C. S. Wilkinson. 1991. "The View from the Inside: Serving Asian Communities." *MIRA* 5, no. 1:5–7.

ADDITIONAL READINGS

Garrity, J. M. 1991. "Understanding and Supporting Healthy Behavioral Change." *SIECUS Report* 20, no. 1 (October/November): 8–10. Describes factors that are likely to influence health behavior change and outlines ways that people can support the health behavior change of others.

Goleman, D., and J. Gurin, eds. 1993. *Mind/Body Medicine.* New York: Consumer Reports Books. Contains many chapters that, as the editors put it, "sort out the truth about mind/body medicine from the many fictions that surround it." Examples are mind and immunity, hostility and the heart, infertility and the emotions, exercise for stress control, healthy attitudes, and working with your doctor.

Halpern, C. R. 1992. "The Political Economy of Mind-Body Health." *American Journal of Health Promotion* 6, no. 4 (March/April): 288–91+. Indicates that research shows that a new set of effective methods (such as meditation, yoga, supportive group therapy, and guided imagery) can assist healing; however, there are economic, political, social, and professional barriers to the use of these methods.

Healthy People 2000: Summary Report. 1992. Boston: Jones & Bartlett. Provides a summary of how the national health promotion and disease prevention objectives were developed, background information, and the actual objectives.

LIFESTYLE CONTRACT

There are several things you can do to improve your health as a result of the topics discussed in this chapter. The following is a partial list of some of the behaviors that could enhance your health status.

Health Behaviors

1. Select a personal strength area in your life and nurture it.
2. With major or minor decisions, take time to complete a decision tree or go through the steps of making a good decision.
3. Assess your risks of disease or death and determine which of those can be removed, and remove them.
4. Do activities that can, over time, modify your locus of control to a more internal perspective; for instance, try imagery strategies (picture yourself in control of many situations) or consciously change a behavior—both of these have been shown to be helpful in modifying people's perspective on control.

In this chapter you have learned to complete a contract using strength intervention. The assumption for the example here is that the person is not receiving the strength, comfort, and support he or she should be from some activities that used to be strength areas.

Sample Lifestyle Contract

I. Behavioral selection

  A. Factors to consider before making a behavioral selection

    1. Nurturing _This is what I will do_

    2. Freeing _____

    3. Optimizing _____

    4. Motivation/readiness _____

    5. Building on success _____

    6. Barriers to change _____

  B. Behaviors I will change (no more than two)

    Play my guitar and sing to help me relax and it makes me feel good

II. The plan

  A. General plan _I will do it when I talk to my two kids at bedtime_

  B. Substitution _Instead of just talking, I'm going to sing and play_

  C. Linking behaviors _Time with kids and playing my guitar_

  D. Combining strength and weakness _____

  E. When _8:30 p.m. – bedtime_

  F. Where _In the kids' room_

  G. Intensity _n/a_

  H. Preparation _Bring out my old songbook from several years ago and get my guitar from my folks_

  I. With whom _My two kids_

III. Support groups

  A. Who _My wife_ _My kids_

  B. Role _For the few times I've done it, the kids like it, so I'll have them badger me_

  C. Organized support _n/a_

IV. Trigger responses _I'll put a picture of a guitar over the kids' bed_

V. Starting date _This Wednesday_

VI. Date/sequence the contract will be reevaluated _One month_

VII. Evidence of reaching goal _Relaxed evening – guitar skills_

VIII. Rewards when contract is completed _I feel so good when I play–that short escape will be reward enough_

IX. Signature of client _____

X. Signature of facilitator _____

XI. Additional conditions/comments: _____

Mental Health and Stress Management

CHAPTER 2

Optimal Health of the Mind and Soul

KEY QUESTIONS

What is the mind and soul health revolution?

What is the health of the mind?

What is the health of the soul?

What is personal health? What is interdependent health?

What are some characteristics of the healthy mind and soul?

What are some of the dimensions of self-understanding?

How do I acquire healthy states of the mind and soul?

How do I practice personal skills of the mind and soul?

What are meditation and imagery?

What are some interdependent skills of the mind and soul?

CHAPTER OUTLINE

The Mind and Soul Health Revolution

The Healthy Mind

The Healthy Soul

Personal and Interdependent Enrichment of Mind and Soul

Personal Enrichment of the Mind and Soul

The Goal of Personal Enrichment of the Mind and Soul

Self-Understanding: Understanding the Nature of Your Mind and Soul

Personal Skills and Experiences to Enrich the Mind and Soul

Process for Acquiring Personal Health of the Mind and Soul

Interdependent Enrichment of the Mind and Soul

Communication Skills

Assertiveness

Trust

Promoting Causes (Altruistic Dreams)

Summary

Healthy People 2000 Objectives

- Establish mutual-help clearinghouses in at least twenty-five states (nine states in 1989).

- Increase to at least 50 percent the proportion of primary-care providers who routinely review with patients their cognitive, emotional, and behavioral functioning and the resources available to deal with any problems that are identified.

- Increase to at least 75 percent the proportion of providers of primary care for children who include assessment of cognitive, emotional, and parent-child functioning, with appropriate counseling, referral, and follow-up in their clinical practices.

Most of us can remember times when we have felt in love, afraid, angry, confused, excited, rejected, powerful, weak, confident, or sorry, at least briefly. Sometimes we feel as if we are on a mental and emotional roller coaster as we range from wondering if we are "going crazy" with so many problems to "floating on air" because we feel so good. The purpose of this chapter is to examine the characteristics and skills that promote the "ups" in life and promote mental and soulful health. This chapter will also provide guidelines on how to acquire optimal states, skills, and characteristics of the mind and soul through the resiliency model.

THE MIND AND SOUL HEALTH REVOLUTION

Our understanding of the natural ups and downs, as well as of the pathway to optimal mental and soulful health, is much clearer today that it was even 10 years ago. We find ourselves in the middle of a major health revolution characterized by a uniting of thought among modern medicine, modern psychology, ancient philosophical wisdom, sociology, and hundreds of "self-help" books that provide guidelines for obtaining optimal levels of health. The united approach is reflected in this chapter as we study the essence of health of the mind and soul, which leads to our happiness, sense of fulfillment, hope, contentment, and living in a state of appreciation.

The roots of the revolution stem principally from medicine and psychology; other disciplines are evolving in harmony with these. For example, modern medicine, most notably in the field of mind/body healing, or **psychoneuroimmunology (PNI),** suggests that a patient's having the will to live makes the difference between living or dying in many cases (Pellitier 1992; Borysenko 1987). The medical revolution was dramatized and explained in a PBS television program hosted by Bill Moyers and a partner book, *Healing and the Mind* (Moyers 1993). That series demonstrated that when they learned to find their sources of energy, were optimistic, had hope and faith, felt loved, had a fighting spirit, and had a purpose for living, many patients with life-threatening illnesses seemed to experience remarkable healings and had zestful lives.

Modern psychology is experiencing a reflective reevaluation of its roots (the root word *psyche* in psychology means "soul"). The book *Care of the Soul* by Thomas Moore (1992) is an example of the parallel evolutionary movement in psychology to refocus on the soul. The essence of modern psychology and ancient wisdom is that optimal states—optimism, hope, perceived love, happiness, hardiness, control, fulfillment, and cause and purpose in living—are healthy to the psyche, or the soul. Medical and behavioral scientists are exploring the ancient wisdom of the Aikido, Ayurveda, and Kneipp and philosophers such as Socrates, Plato, and Aristotle.

It becomes clear to us that optimal health of the mind and soul is the process and experience of acquiring these optimal states of feeling, thinking, and sensing that can result in being fulfilled, happy, zestful, and enjoying, or at least appreciating, the mental and emotional roller coaster we experience in life. We will first explore the nature of mental and soulful health. We know from the collective wisdom described above that the body, mind, and soul are, at their basic levels, interconnected and, theoretically, made of the same elements. We distinguish among them only for convenience and to help us understand and focus, because we have limited abilities to conceptualize all dimensions working together simultaneously.

THE HEALTHY MIND

Mental health involves our thinking processes, including learning, coping, solving problems, planning, decision making, creating, focusing, and performing mental functions.

psychoneuroimmunology (PNI)
The study of the way we think (*psycho-*, "mind"), the effects of our thinking on our nervous system (*neuro-*), and the effects of our nervous system on our immune system (*immunology*).

mental health
The capacity to cope with life situations, grow emotionally through them, develop to our full potential, and grow in awareness and consciousness.

Understanding, accepting, and maximizing who you are is critical to good mental health.

Many people refer to thinking as occurring on the left side of the brain (Williams and Stockmeyer 1987). The term *mental health* often carries a neutral or negative connotation; many associate it with such terms as *mental disorder* and *mental institution*. But just as health can be seen as more than simply the absence of disease or infirmity, so mental health can be viewed as positive rather than just avoiding mental infirmity, mental illness, distress, anxiety, neurosis, or psychosis. Optimal mental health requires the acquisition of skills and characteristics to effectively encounter and grow through setbacks, opportunities, challenges, adversity, stressors, and other life events. The experience of growing through adversity is *resiliency*.

THE HEALTHY SOUL

The soul has been defined as "the immaterial essence, animating principle, or actuating cause of an individual life" and "the moral and emotional nature of human beings" (*Merriam-Webster's Collegiate Dictionary*, 10th ed.). Our soul is our purpose in living, powerful emotions, the reasons for our existence, our spiritual orientation and nature, and the essence of what motivates us. It is living from the heart. The soul has been neglected in professional literature until recently (Moore 1992; Csikszentmihalyi 1990), largely because soul is difficult to measure. With some reflective insight, it is clear that within each of us there is a force or feeling, perceived either from external forces or from within ourselves, that motivates us to act in life. Identifying, nurturing, and adhering to the soul results in happiness, zest, vitality, power, and all of the other important elements of life. The essence of health of the soul is that it gives life meaning and fulfillment.

Issue

RECOGNIZING THE SOUL

We are in the middle of a health revolution, and health professionals are suggesting that we should believe strongly, have faith, be optimistic, and have fun if we can. The issue is whether we can buy into this soul concept in a professional setting. The concepts of soul, spirit, inner force, Chi, and following your heart are different for each person, and they are difficult to quantify. Members of the scientific world are divided among themselves about these.

- Pro: Everyone has felt inclinations to do something, been moved by a humanitarian scene, felt good inside, and felt some direction in his or her life. If everyone can feel it, then we ought to take advantage of it, not deny it, and use the power of the soul to our advantage.
- Con: It is just too vague. People feel the "spirit" and then they proselytize and try to convert others to their way of thinking. This feeling is private and shouldn't be dealt with except in a religious setting.

Do you ignore or deny the soul in you, or do you try to identify it, nurture it, and act on it? This book provides some guidance on acting on the soul if you choose to do so.

Because the soul is a major concept that is triggering the health revolution, we will examine the soul further. Moore (1992, p. xi) stated:

The great malady of the twentieth century, implicated in all of our troubles and affecting us individually and socially, is "loss of soul". When soul is neglected, it doesn't just go away; it appears symptomatically in obsessions, addictions, violence, and loss of meaning.

The soul has to do with our genuineness, depth, attachments, love, living with heart, and finding fulfilling work and rewarding relationships. Moore goes on to say that

We have come to know the soul only in its complaints: when it stirs, disturbed by neglect and abuse, and causes us to feel its pain. All of these symptoms such as emptiness, meaninglessness, vague depression, disillusionment, a yearning for personal fulfillment, a loss of morals and values, and a hunger for spirituality reflect a loss of soul. We yearn excessively for entertainment, power, intimacy, sexual fulfillment, and material things, and we think we can find these things if we discover the right relationship or job, the right church or therapy. But without soul, whatever we find will be unsatisfying, for what we truly long for is the soul in each of these areas.

Health of the soul is the essence of life, our motivational nature, and our purpose and meaning in living. As we look around at science, philosophy, and religion, there is always some reference to the soul, although the nature and name varies. Socrates talked about his "daimon" or inner guide around 400 B.C. Jung spoke of the "collective self." The Aikido call the inner energy source "Chi" (Moyers 1993). Campbell suggested that "we follow our bliss," and Castenada called it "choosing a path with heart" (Osbon 1991). Christian and non-Christian religions suggest that we have a "spirit" within us, or that there is a powerful external force (God) and that His/Her/Its Spirit is something we have access to for strength and guidance. Carl Rogers (1961) taught that deep within each of us there is a desire and force for good—a being that wants to succeed—and Rogers's therapeutic approach was to uncover and free that inner self. We will call the enrichment of the daimon, the spirit, Chi, the collective self, the inner guide, bliss, living by the heart, living with nature, or God's Spirit within us "soulful health" or "health of the soul."

PERSONAL AND INTERDEPENDENT ENRICHMENT OF MIND AND SOUL

There are two ongoing processes that enrich our minds and souls: personal enrichment and interdependent enrichment (fig. 2.1).

Personal Enrichment

In one sense, we experience personal health of the mind and soul. We see the world around us out of our own eyes and with our own perceptions of what the world is really like. We feel joy, pain, and happiness; we learn, make decisions, and solve problems in our own imaginations. In this sense the outside world exists only because we perceive that it exists. We acknowledge only those we care to acknowledge. The process is personal.

Interdependent Enrichment

At the same time as we are fortifying ourselves from within, we are also receiving influence and stimuli from the outside world. Interdependent enrichment is the experience of gaining strength, support, and comfort from other people and the world around us. We breathe air, see people, touch objects, shake hands, hug, push, listen, express, and live with others. Our personal experience is greatly influenced by and interdependent with the world around us. The process of experiencing the healthy mind and soul is greatly influenced by other people and our environments, including our experience of their personal worlds as dimensions of our environment.

PERSONAL ENRICHMENT OF THE MIND AND SOUL

We will discuss the goal of personal enrichment of the mind and soul, the nature of the mind and soul, skills for the mind and soul, and the process of enriching the mind and soul.

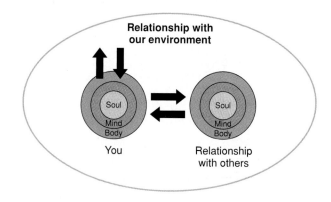

Figure 2.1

We have a relationship with our environment and with other people.

THE GOAL OF PERSONAL ENRICHMENT OF THE MIND AND SOUL

There are many terms used to describe the positive goal states of mind and soul. *Optimal health, wellness,* and *well-being* are a few of them. Maslow used the term *self-actualization* to describe the goal of personal enrichment.

Self-Actualization

The journey to experiencing optimal mental and soulful health first requires the fulfillment of basic needs. Abraham Maslow (1962) suggested that we have a hierarchy of needs and that positive states of mental and soulful health occur after the fulfillment and satisfaction of needs that are lower in the hierarchy, such as basic needs. The lower needs must be fulfilled before we can reach our human potential.

The needs hierarchy begins with basic physiological needs. The major concern of people who are starving or dying of thirst is foraging for food and water. Developing their self-esteem, furthering their education, working on their social skills, and developing their talents, except as these relate to foraging for food, are far removed from their thoughts. Again, the premise of the hierarchy is that basic needs must be fulfilled before higher needs can be fulfilled. Basic physiological needs (for food, air, water, and sleep) must be met before one can focus on safety needs (for shelter, emotional safety, and freedom from danger). After meeting our safety needs, we seek to love and be loved. When love needs are met, then needs for self-esteem (a sense of personal worth) can be met, which finally leads to self-actualization.

Self-actualization, which means fulfilling one's human potential as well as satisfying most of one's human basic

---

self-actualization

Fulfilling one's human potential along with fulfilling one's basic needs (physiological needs and needs for safety, love, and self-esteem).

Self-Actualization

Directions

Check off the characteristics that apply to you.

_____ I have an accurate perception of, and feel comfortable in, my surroundings (no fear of the unknown).

_____ I can accept people, despite their faults.

_____ I have long-term goals, and I work hard to attain them without letting the goals disrupt my life.

_____ I have a capacity to be spontaneous, natural, and simple.

_____ Occasionally I need solitude and privacy, which might appear to others as aloofness or absentmindedness.

_____ I have an independence of mind and am not greatly influenced by external forces, such as media, propaganda, or salespersons.

_____ I continually enjoy beauty.

_____ I have a variety of spiritual experiences, with feelings of ecstasy, power, or a close spiritual source of strength.

_____ I have a feeling of sympathy for all, no matter who they are or what they have done.

_____ I recognize my imperfections and have a capacity to experience guilt, anxiety, and sadness.

_____ I have a strong capacity for love and an intense closeness with a few friends.

_____ I have an ability to look at life in unique, refreshing ways.

_____ I have a philosophical sense of humor—seeing human life and situations that accompany it in a humorous light.

_____ I focus on and enjoy the process of obtaining a goal, rather than not being happy until I reach the goal.

_____ I have a democratic character structure (I place little emphasis on race, creed, color, or socioeconomic status), gained by learning from and listening to all people.

_____ I accept the cultural norms of others, but personally I can transcend these to reach higher norms.

_____ I accept the nature of life and the value of human nature, I withhold judgment about others, and I treat everything as part of life.

_____ I feel a cooperation between my head and my heart, rather than a war between basic instincts and conscience or between lust and righteousness.

Scoring and Interpretation

Few people can check all of the indicators honestly, so you might want to score your percentage of self-actualization. Simply total the number of blanks that you marked and divide by 18. The resulting percentage is your percentage of self-actualization. For example, you might be 60 percent self-actualized.

---

needs, represents the highest level of mental and soulful health, according to Maslow's hierarchy of needs. This hierarchy is shown in figure 2.2.

Maslow felt that few people are self-actualized because cultural, social, and motivational constraints inhibit people from achieving this high level of functioning. He studied the lives of Abraham Lincoln, George Washington Carver, Thomas Jefferson, Eleanor Roosevelt, and fifty-six others who were, in his estimation, self-actualized. Self-actualization is the product of a healthy mind and soul. Do the Health Assessment exercise to see if you have any of the traits Maslow correlates with self-actualization.

As you consider some of the descriptions of self-actualization, you might be wondering how you can improve your score or, more important, feel happier and have more inner peace. The process of personal enrichment that is described in the following pages will help guide you to a higher level of self-actualization.

SELF-UNDERSTANDING: UNDERSTANDING THE NATURE OF YOUR MIND AND SOUL

This chapter is about mental and soulful characteristics that will give you strength, comfort, support, power, and a sense

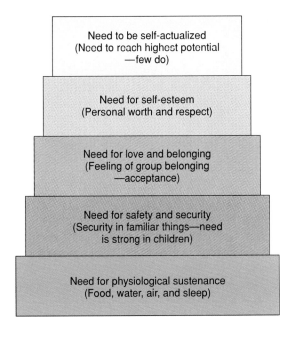

Figure 2.2

Maslow's hierarchy of needs.

Source: Data for diagram based on Hierarchy of Needs from *Motivation and Personality*, 3d edition, by Abraham H. Maslow, revised by Robert Frager et al. New York: Harper & Row, 1954, 1987.

Issue

Building Strengths Versus Dealing with Problems

There are two approaches to health enhancement. One is to identify our problems and try and do something about them. The government generally focuses on problems. When there is a drug problem, we get a drug czar; when we have a high incidence of AIDS, we provide money for research; when we have violence, we react again with plans and money. The second approach is to strengthen people as much as possible so that they stay as far away from problems as possible. The best drug prevention is to strengthen people and let them live for a dream, so that they don't have time for drugs anymore.

- **Pro:** It is much more enjoyable to work on strengths, and when you focus on them, problems seem to be less important. It is more fun, enjoyable, and rewarding to focus on positives, and it is easier to work on them than to focus on our problems.
- **Con:** Having some idealistic dream is not the real world. To be happy and productive, we need to get rid of our problems.

How will you direct your life? By worrying and attacking problems, or by merely having a dream and working toward it?

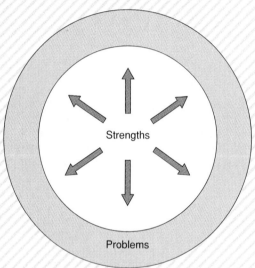 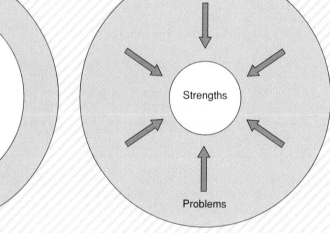

We can focus on our strengths and they will grow, or we can focus on our problems and they will grow.

of well-being. Space does not allow us to describe all the characteristics of the healthy mind and soul, but this section will identify some of the most important. It was Socrates, in about 400 B.C., who said, "Know thyself." An important process that continues throughout your lifetime is trying to understand who you really are. The following are some things to consider when you are trying to understand yourself.

Your Needs

Reflect again upon Maslow's hierarchy of needs. The optimal state of mental and soulful health is self-actualization, but if your more-basic needs are not being met, then, according to the theory, you need to work to meet those needs before you can become self-actualized. Many of us might be able to rise above those basic needs to be self-actualized in some situations. We have all heard of cases where a starving person gave what little food he had to someone else, or a person in a dangerous situation sacrificed her own life to save the lives of others. But more commonly we function optimally at higher

levels only when our basic needs have been fulfilled. Use the Health Assessment exercise to determine if you are in a position to fulfill your self-actualization needs.

If we are struggling with our basic needs, it is difficult to rise above them to feel good about ourselves. There are some people who do struggle daily for basic needs but still find an ability to provide service and care to others. But it might require much of our energy to fulfill our physical and safety needs. It might require additional effort to get a job or move our residence. This chapter will provide guidelines for fulfilling our needs for self-esteem and to be loved.

Your Development

Erik Erikson (1963) described the naturally occurring growth steps as developmental stages and indicated that for the healthy mind and soul we need to master different skills associated with different stages.

Fulfillment of Needs

Directions

Check off the statements that are true of you.

_____ I am confident that on most days I will be able to get adequate water, food, sleep, and air.

_____ I live in a place where I feel generally safe, secure, and stable.

_____ I love other people and feel loved by others. I belong to a family or group.

_____ I feel good about myself. I feel a sense of self-worth and self-respect.

Interpretation

If you were able to check all of the above, then the needs that must be fulfilled before you can experience self-actualization may have been met. If you left any of the items blank, you might want to consider dealing with those needs.

The baby enters the world and obtains its first major impression—whether its needs and wants will be satisfied or neglected. The relationship, primarily with the mother, largely determines whether the infant will have a trusting impression, which is accomplished by warm, close, loving, fulfilling relationships, or a sense of mistrust, which stems from neglect, being ignored, a lack of tender touching, and frequently having wants unfulfilled.

In the second and third years of life, the major tasks are toilet training and walking. If the child finds success and support in accomplishing these tasks, then a feeling of independence, control, pride, confidence, self-esteem, or autonomy is likely to result. On the other hand, if toilet training is mishandled and results in a traumatic ordeal, then the child may experience shame and doubt, accompanied by the lack of confidence to face and control the environment and him- or herself.

The child of age 4 to 5 learns that he or she can travel and explore on his or her own. Children have a strong attraction to the parent of the opposite sex that eventually leads to some disappointment, because they ultimately lose out to the same-sex parent. They develop a sense of what they want and develop initiative to obtain gratification. Parental rules become restrictive and, when broken, result in guilt. Serious guilt occurs when the child is made to feel guilty about self-initiated activity.

In the child of 6 to 12 years, sexual drives become relatively latent (dormant). During these years, the child seeks to be industrious and craves recognition but is also very sensitive to criticism. He or she tries to channel this industrious nature into socially accepted channels. Too much criticism will result in feelings of inferiority.

This age (12–17 years) is often described as the period of "identity crisis," in which the individual is no longer a child but not yet an adult. The stage is marked by tremendous physical growth, emotional development, social skill development, and value clarification. The adolescent who works through these crises feels comfortable with his or her unveiling identity, while unsuccessful completion of this stage promotes societal role confusion in the adolescent.

Between the ages of approximately 17 and 23 years, the individual faces the challenge of developing intimate relationships with members of his or her own sex and, usually more important, members of the opposite sex. Intimacy implies that mutual interaction promotes creativity, energy, responsibility, and happiness. Isolation, or failure to develop intimate relationships, results in pessimism, cynicism, and unhappiness.

Adults either find themselves actively engaged in raising children, developing professional careers, enhancing their moral or spiritual existence, and other generative activities that promote satisfaction, or they become engrossed in self-absorption and gratification of material needs, contributing little to others.

As older people reflect on their past, they may feel the sense of accomplishment and satisfaction that leads to ego integrity, or, if they regret having accomplished few of their goals, they may then despair because they know they cannot relive the past. People who experience ego integrity have a sense of personal dignity, believe in the value of human existence, and feel comfortable with their place in the community.

Each stage has alternative outcomes, such as "trust versus mistrust" and "autonomy versus shame and doubt." A person in the final period of the "identity crisis," or in the young adult stages where the alternative outcomes of the crisis are "intimacy" and "isolation," needs to develop communication skills and become more open so that intimate relationships can result. By "intimacy," Erikson neither means marriage nor implies sexual or physical closeness. Nonsexual friendships are as important as sexual relationships, and emotional, intellectual, social, and spiritual intimacy is as important as physical intimacy.

Erikson would have people learn from his theories that they need to develop friendships, communicate, share happy and sad times, give and receive, and understand how mutually shared experiences are more fulfilling than experiences one has in isolation.

Your Temperament

Each of us is unique, and we all think and act differently from everyone else. Understanding who you are, living within your basic nature, and then maximizing your strengths

Your Temperament

Directions

For each continuum, fill in the rectangle representing the place on the continuum that best characterizes you.

Interpretation

You can see your tendencies toward certain temperaments. You can maximize these as shown in table 2.1.

Internal Locus of Control
I see myself as master of my own destiny. By putting forth effort, I will achieve my desired outcomes. When I decide to engage in enriching experiences, I do so without significant help from others.

External Locus of Control
I see myself as a product of my circumstances and/or influence from parents, friends, or chance. I do what I do largely because my family or colleagues do it.

Affective
I make most choices based upon feelings and personal relationships, and I give emotional value to issues. I am attracted to the terms *humane, sympathy, devotion,* and *understanding.*

Objective
I make choices based on impersonal, objective, and logical judgments. I am attracted to the terms *principles, policy, laws, criteria,* and *firmness.*

Imaginative
I am creative and innovative. I think about the future, explore the world beyond realities, think of what could be rather than what is, and enjoy daydreaming and fantasizing.

Practical
I rely on and believe in facts, experience, what is, and reality-based thinking.

Introvert
I prefer solitude to recover and gain energy. I feel awkward or lonely in a crowd. I am quiet, reserved, and have trouble finding things to talk about with people I do not know well. I enjoy working alone.

Extravert
I like to be around people because I am energized by them. I am uninhibited, outgoing, easy to meet, friendly, assertive, and have many social contacts. I am comfortable talking before large groups, like to mingle, and am lonely when not with people for significant periods of time.

Pessimistic
I feel that no matter how hard I try, things will probably not turn out very well.

Optimistic
I approach life's challenges, opportunities, or problems believing that the best will result, whether it be the planned outcome or one that happens by chance.

Decisive
I like to come to decisions quickly and adhere to them. I take deadlines seriously. I like terms such as *decided, closure, planned, completed, settled,* and *deadlines.*

Open
I prefer to keep things open-ended and not rush into decisions. I like to remain flexible and feel that deadlines are just guides. I like the words *fluid, flexible, open-ended, tentative,* and *options.*

---

are key components of the healthy mind and soul. Part of your basic nature is acquired through experience, and some of who you are is inherent.

Temperament is the product of many factors, including experiences, disruptions, growth processes, and genetics. Temperament is the general characteristics of how you act, perceive, think, and feel. Your temperament determines how well you can cope with the stressors, life events, and adversities that occur on a regular basis. Understanding your temperament helps to understand how and why you do the things you do. Use the Health Assessment exercise to see what temperament traits apply to you. Table 2.1 lists some temperament characteristics and describes how you can live within your nature and maximize your strengths.

temperament
The mental mechanisms, traits, experiences, and complex intricacies of individuals that determine how they behave, feel, and think.

TABLE 2.1   LIVING WITHIN YOUR TEMPERAMENT

Many of us try to be what we are not and therefore find ourselves in frustrating, draining, and challenging situations. It is important to understand yourself and then maximize your strengths.

Consider who you are and then use the following examples as general guidelines to plan your life and to live within your personality and temperament.

If You Are	You Face the Potential Problem	Your Solutions Might Be
Introverted	Working in groups (draining and nonproductive)	Do your most challenging and creative work alone
Extroverted	Working alone (draining and nonproductive)	Do your most challenging and creative work with others
Imaginative	Being compelled to do practical and repetitive work (frustrating)	Make the job you do creative and futuristic, and imagine what could be
Practical	Being compelled to do futuristic and creative work (frustrating)	Choose a job that is based on facts and experience
Affective	Overrelying on feelings, relationships, and values (poor decisions)	Consider policy and rules and logical consequences before making decisions
Objective	Overrelying on facts, rules, and policy in making decisions (coldhearted)	Consider the exception to the rule and people's feelings, emotions, and circumstances
Decisive	Being too inflexible and potentially missing better options (missed opportunities)	Consider flexibility if deadline is reached and quality could be enhanced with time or other options
Open	Having trouble completing tasks because of being too flexible (poor work ethic and lack of accomplishment)	Take deadlines and goals more seriously and work toward completion
Risk taking	Venturing and losing too much (fewer resources)	Carefully consider outcomes
Conservative	Not getting ahead because of fear of venturing (stagnation—few resources)	Venture with fairly safe projects with a high likelihood of success
Traditionalist	Being compelled to do actions that compromise your traditional values (guilt)	Live by your values

Source: From G. E. Richardson, *Resiliency Training Manual*. Bountiful, Utah: Privately printed, n.d.

Your Psychological Hardiness

The characteristic of the mind and soul that has been suggested as the antidote or buffer for excessive stress is psychological hardiness (Kobasa, Maddi, and Kahn 1982), or a stress-resistant personality (Flannery 1987). Optimal mental and soulful health includes the hardy or stress-resistant personality. If you see school as a challenge, are committed to it, know that you are in control of what grades you receive, have good social support, and are experiencing a healthy lifestyle, then it might be that you are insulated to some degree from the negative effects of stress and have a better chance to experience positive states of mind and soul. Complete the Health Assessment exercise on hardiness to consider how psychologically hardy you are.

As we engage ourselves in our causes and pursue our dreams, we surface from those experiences with increased control, commitment, and challenge. The key to increasing hardiness is to challenge ourselves, learn new skills, and experience new activities. Self-esteem plays a role in this.

Your Self-Esteem

"**Self-esteem** refers to the evaluation a person makes and customarily maintains with regard to him- or herself. Self-esteem expresses an attitude of approval or disapproval and indicates the extent to which a person believes him- or herself capable, significant, successful, and worthy" (Coopersmith 1981).

We can face a significant number of negative experiences and still have good health of the mind and soul if we have positive self-esteem. It is interesting that we are not born with concerns about being good or bad, smart or stupid, pretty or ugly, lovable or unlovable, but we develop these ideas from significant people in our lives. We form self-images, which are pictures of ourselves that have been created from parents', teachers', and peers' input. Our self-image is the content of our perceptions and opinions about ourselves. The positive or negative attitudes and values by which we view ourselves, and the evaluations or judgments we make about our self-image, form our self-esteem. Use the Health Assessment exercise to better understand your general level of self-esteem.

self-esteem
Perceived sense of self-worth, self-confidence, and satisfaction with oneself.

Hardiness

Circle the number that indicates how much the description fits you.

1 = Very much like me
2 = Somewhat like me
3 = Not like me

1   2   3   When I have a task or job to do, I can see myself accomplishing it.

1   2   3   In life, I plan my activities, and generally events occur as I anticipated.

1   2   3   I generally see myself as having control over my life.

1   2   3   I become very involved in tasks I do at work, in the community, or at school.

1   2   3   I enjoy spending time improving the place where I live and the people I live with.

1   2   3   Most people would think that I am generally devoted and dedicated and not easily diverted by short-term pleasures.

1   2   3   I really enjoy regular challenges in work, home, or school.

1   2   3   I generally take on assignments, problems, and opportunities with vigor.

1   2   3   I enjoy doing things that challenge my abilities.

Scoring and Interpretation

Total the numbers you circled, and see where your total falls in the following scale of psychological hardiness.

24–27 = Very hardy
16–23 = Somewhat hardy
Below 16 = Not hardy

If you did not score as high on self-esteem as you would have liked, doing the following can enhance your self-esteem:

1. Try **positive verbalization** (Girdano, Everly, and Dusek 1993). For instance, write down some positive personality traits that you like about yourself and reflect on them. Continue to identify and reflect on additional positive traits. For persons with low self-esteem, it is healthy to spend reflective time dwelling on positive traits.

2. Accept compliments from others. Saying "Thank you" to a compliment, rather than shrugging it off, helps to enhance self-esteem.

3. In your daily planning, be sure to include activities that you do well or are likely to succeed at. For example, play a game you do well, do homework in your better subjects, or make a point of talking with someone who loves you. Enjoy the experience.

Empowerment

Empowerment is a perspective that results from successful experiences when people, organizations, or communities gain mastery over their affairs. We sense that we can make an impact on our environment by assuming control, making decisions, and influencing others. The intent of this book is to suggest you can be empowered, in a large part, to control your health status, feelings, and environment, and, in this case, how healthy you are in mind and soul.

There are many steps to empowering oneself, but perhaps the best is through successful experiences. You can follow the guidelines for enhancing the health of the mind and soul that will be presented later in this chapter. Part of that process is to set and attain goals to positively affect others and the world around you.

Your Value/Behavior Congruence

A strong mental and soulful condition that nurtures health is to align the way you act and behave with your values and beliefs. Belief and value systems reflect what we feel is right or wrong, ethical or unethical, and are an important part of the health of the mind and soul. Values, morals, and beliefs might be of people's own choosing, or they might have been imposed by family members, friends, religious leaders, or other sources and finally adopted by individuals. These values can be changing or very stable. Contemplating your values and behaving in accordance with them is a key to happiness. One of the most devastating experiences people can have is to believe that something is wrong, and yet to do it anyway—acting contrary to their values. Many young college students, for example, are experiencing the freedom from parental influence for the first time, and they begin to experiment with drugs, sexual behaviors, or even dishonesty that had been forbidden in the protective environment of home.

---

positive verbalization
The experience of saying, thinking, or writing down positive things about personality traits or skills that one likes about oneself and frequently reflecting on these traits and skills.

empowerment
A process or mechanism by which people, organizations, and communities gain mastery over their affairs.

Self-Esteem

Directions

For each item, write *a* in front of each statement that describes you and write *b* in front of each statement that does not describe you.

1. ____ People generally like me.
2. ____ I am comfortable talking in class.
3. ____ I like to do new things.
4. ____ I give in very easily.
5. ____ I'm a failure.
6. ____ I'm shy.
7. ____ I have trouble making up my mind.
8. ____ I am popular with people at school.
9. ____ My life is all mixed up.
10. ____ I often feel upset at my home, room, or apartment.
11. ____ I often wish I were like someone else.
12. ____ I often worry.
13. ____ I can be depended on.
14. ____ I often express my views.
15. ____ I think I am doing okay with my life.
16. ____ I feel good about what I have accomplished recently.

Scoring

Total the number of matches you have with the following key.

1. a	2. a	3. a	4. b
5. b	6. b	7. b	8. a
9. b	10. b	11. b	12. b
13. a	14. a	15. a	16. a

Interpretation

Interpret your total number of matches, as follows:

12–16	You have high self-esteem.
8–11	You have moderately high self-esteem.
4–7	You have moderately low self-esteem.
0–3	You have low self-esteem.

The result of the value/behavior incongruence can be mental debilitation and guilt. Guilt negatively affects self-esteem, the ability to study, social interactions, emotions, energy levels, and other dimensions of health.

To better understand **value/behavior congruence** in your life, complete the Health Assessment on page 2.14.

There are only two realistic strategies for coping with value/behavior incongruence—behave in accordance with your values, or alter your values so that they are aligned with your behaviors. Altering the value system is generally time-consuming and painful, whereas self-discipline and commitment can alter behaviors, in most cases, almost immediately. Sometimes an attempt to change one's value system can cause greater and lower self-esteem than an attempt to alter one's behavior.

Your Locus of Control

Perceived control over one's life, health, happiness, success, and future is an important concept in mental health. When our sense of control diminishes due to disability, illness, incarceration, or other causes, there may be a decrease in our coping abilities. The psychological perspective of control is termed **locus of control.** The two extremes of control are internal locus of control and external locus of control. An internal locus of control is the perspective that you are the master of your own fate, that you are in control of your own destiny, health, and happiness. An external locus of control is the perspective that you are the product of an environment, greatly influenced by models, friends, or environmental conditions. Persons with an external locus of control often view themselves as being subject to powerful others (bosses, friends, physicians, etc.) or being victims of chance or luck. Most experts suggest that an internal locus of control is necessary for becoming self-actualizing. Various exercises can help you gradually shift toward a more internal locus of control. Assess yourself for locus of control by doing the Health Assessment exercise on page 2.14.

If you score high on internal locus of control, then you perceive yourself as being in control, and your best approach to healthful living is to learn as much as you can and improve yourself on your own. If you score high on external control, then your best experiences for healthier living will be in the company of others. Support groups can be very important for you. If your locus of control is both internal and external, then a combination of support with internal motivation and control is optimal for you. For example, you might want to work on the behavior by yourself, but get congratulated by someone close to you.

Your Self-Efficacy and Faith

Self-efficacy is having the belief that you can accomplish a specific task or change a selected behavior. Although Albert

value/behavior congruence
Harmony between what someone believes to be right and how that individual acts. Value/behavior congruence results in inner peace; incongruence results in feelings of guilt.

locus of control
An individual's balance between internal and external control. With internal control, people perceive themselves as the masters of their own fate and outcomes as the results of their own actions. With external control, people perceive themselves as the products of their environment and their role models, their actions as directed by others, and the outcomes of their actions as due to chance or powerful others.

self-efficacy
The conviction that one can accomplish a desired outcome.

Value/Behavior Congruence

Directions

For the following statements, circle the letter for the response that is most true of you.

	Almost Always	Frequently	Sometimes	Rarely	Never
1. I feel guilty for some dishonesty in my school work.	A	B	C	D	E
2. I find myself going against my sexual moral standards.	A	B	C	D	E
3. I feel inner peace.	A	B	C	D	E
4. In part of my life, I have to do things that make me feel uncomfortable.	A	B	C	D	E
5. My moral standards are matched by what I do.	A	B	C	D	E

Scoring

For questions 1, 2, and 4, score as follows:

A=1, B=2, C=3, D=4, E=5

For questions 3 and 5,

A=5, B=4, C=3, D=2, E=1

Total your scores for the five questions.

Interpretation

20–25 = You have high value/behavior congruence.
12–19 = You have moderate value/behavior congruence.
5–11 = You have low value/behavior congruence.

Locus of Control

Directions

For the following statements, circle the letter for the response that is most true of you.

	Almost Always	Frequently	Sometimes	Rarely	Never
How I feel is largely up to me and in my control.	A	B	C	D	E
Good health is a matter of good luck.	A	B	C	D	E
The habits I have are largely because of the people around me.	A	B	C	D	E

Scoring

For question 1, score as follows:

A= 5, B=4, C=3, D=2, E=1

For questions 2 and 3,

A= 1, B=2, C=3, D=4, E=5

Total your scores for the three questions.

Interpretation

12–15 = Your locus of control is largely internal.
7–11 = Your locus of control is both internal and external.
3–6 = Your locus of control is largely external.

General Self-Efficacy

Directions

For the following statements, circle the letter for the response that is most true of you.

	Almost Always	Sometimes	Rarely
When I say I am going to do something, I do it.	3	2	1
When I have a project to do, I will make sure it gets done.	3	2	1
When I feel the need to modify the way I act, I can picture myself accomplishing the task.	3	2	1
When I take on a challenge, I am confident I can do it.	3	2	1
I complete tasks I set out to do.	3	2	1

Scoring

Total the numbers you have circled.

Interpretation

13–15 = You have high self-efficacy.
10–12 = You have moderate self-efficacy.
5–9 = You have low self-efficacy.

Bandura (1989) indicated that self-efficacy is a trait that applies to a specific task or function, we can also have a general sense of self-efficacy; in general, we can see ourselves accomplishing just about any reasonable task or changing just about any undesired behavior. Self-efficacy is a powerful characteristic of health of the mind and soul.

Faith adds a deeper dimension of soul to self-efficacy. Rather than believing that our strength to accomplish a task comes only from within, we can, in faith, add the dimension of being able to access an external spiritual source of strength to reinforce our own efforts. In other words, some people believe that with the help of their spiritual source of strength they can accomplish things they could not normally do if they relied solely on their own strength. But whether we believe that we can fortify the mind, body, and soul through our own efforts (self-efficacy) or that we can do that with the additional force of an external spiritual source of strength, the outcome of a positive state of mind and soul is the same. Use the Health Assessment exercise to estimate your own general level of self-efficacy.

To increase your level of self-efficacy, you need to take on challenges in life that you have a reasonably good chance for success at. Challenges will cause disruptions in your life, but with persistence you can experience a resilient adjustment. You will sense personal growth when you succeed at a challenge, and this will increase your self-efficacy and your belief that you will be able to succeed at future challenges.

Optimism

To have **optimism** is to believe that good outcomes will result from our actions. We take on challenges and respond positively to opportunities, face our problems head-on, if we have an optimistic outlook. The opposite of optimism is pessimism—thinking that the worst possible outcomes will result from our actions or the actions of others. Some pessimism adds a useful touch of realism to our endeavors, but optimism is a motivating force that generally improves our chances of success. Martin Seligman's book *Learned Optimism* (1991) suggests guidelines for people who get discouraged easily, get depressed more than they want to, or fail more than they think they should. He suggests examining the ABCs of pessimism:

1. *Adversity:* What is the challenge you face that causes you to become depressed, frustrated, or negative?
2. *Belief:* How do you think of yourself as a result of facing the adversity, and how does that belief operate in your everyday life?
3. *Consequence:* How do you act as a result of the adversity and your belief system?

For example, let's assume you have been on a diet-and-exercise program for a month. Suddenly, you let up for a day and overeat at a social gathering (adversity). You feel, "I am so weak and I'll never look good" (belief). Then you react by thinking, "I might as well go ahead and pig out, because I've already blown my diet-and-exercise program" (consequence).

After analyzing by the ABCs, Seligman suggests ways to deal with the pessimistic outlook: through distraction, disputation, and distancing.

---

optimism

The perception that experiences and events will turn out for the best.

It is normal to feel emotional swings from happiness to hurt and anger.

1. *Distraction:* Stop the existing thought process and think about something you like. In the case of the diet, you probably shouldn't think of pie and ice cream; perhaps think of a loving experience, something you like to do that is fun, or perhaps another distractor. As you are thinking, catch any negative thoughts that arise, say to yourself, "Stop," and then focus on positive thoughts.

2. *Disputation:* Analyze the adversity, the belief, and the consequences, and think of arguments for each of the steps. For example, refuting the adversity, you may think, "So I went off the diet one day. I can get back on tomorrow. I have a whole month and only one bad day, so I can bounce back tomorrow," or "I did well for a month—this was kind of a short vacation. I've been doing pretty well." Refuting the consequence, the plan might be, "Okay, I took one day off, and I'll be back at it tomorrow."

3. *Distancing:* Realize that your beliefs are just that—beliefs that may or may not be true. Try to look at beliefs as something that are not part of you, but that you can look at objectively and finally throw away. In the example of the belief "I am a weak person," you can look at that thought as a temporary state that is now gone and decide that you are going to continue with your diet-and-exercise program.

Your Emotions

People need to continually practice the many skills involved in developing relationships. These skills are based on emotions, feelings, and personality traits. The basic emotions are love, anger, and fear; all others are really combinations of these three or are secondary outcomes of these primary emotions. Jealousy, for example, is a combination of anger and love. Understanding one's emotions and those of significant others is crucial to successful social interaction.

The emotions affect our lives very powerfully. This is often demonstrated by actions and reactions, under the influence of intense anger, fear, or love, that are often out of character for a person. The sway of emotions often finds people regretting things they did when they were emotionally distressed. By understanding the emotions, we can better recognize in ourselves, and in the people we care about, one of the forces that affect actions. Though love may be the most important emotion for people to understand, an understanding of anger and fear is also essential.

The communication of all feelings is vital for optimal interpersonal relationships. According to Branden (1980), "Relationships are not destroyed by honest expressions of anger or any other emotion," but "relationships die every day as a consequence of anger that is not expressed. The repression of anger kills love, kills sex, kills passion" (140).

The degree of hurt that people feel is generally proportional to the amount of love they feel; the more people love, the more they can be hurt. The intensity of these emotions can be compared to a pendulum of a clock: As love increases, the pendulum swings farther in both directions (fig. 2.3).

To cope with hurt, many of us experience a secondary emotion—subconscious or conscious anger. In one sense, we can see that intense anger is a reflection of the degree of hurt; and if the anger is expressed appropriately (without causing physical harm or deep emotional hurt), it is easy to recognize the depth of love as well. It is important to note, though, that the expression of anger through abuse or inappropriate actions is not excused by the fact that the anger might represent depth of love as well. We need to learn to cope with anger appropriately. Some people shut off the

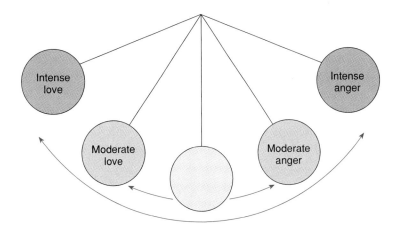

Figure 2.3
The emotional pendulum: love and anger.

swing of the pendulum altogether by denying all emotion. "When a couple is in a love quarrel, it is very common to see each of them shut down, disconnect from the depth of their feelings for each other, disconnect from the depth of their love, so as to protect themselves in case things don't work out. They become impersonal" (Branden 1980, 166).

How you feel is a function of your emotions. By controlling your emotions you can choose to be optimistic, hopeful, challenged, and excited, and to have a fighting spirit. You can also decide to feel self-pity, depression, and helplessness.

PERSONAL SKILLS AND EXPERIENCES TO ENRICH THE MIND AND SOUL

We have discussed the nature of the healthy mind and soul, and you had the opportunity to assess yourself to determine your nature. We will now treat some of these specific characteristics and skills and provide guidelines for learning these skills and for acquiring some of these traits. If you have not learned or experienced these skills before, then this process will serve as a positive disruption from which you will surface resiliently with new skills or characteristics.

Imagery
We all have the natural ability to daydream and fantasize when we think about what we could be doing or when we are contemplating our problems. Daydreaming or **imagery** is a powerful skill that we can use to perform a number of functions—for instance, to relax, meditate, problem-solve, make decisions, mentally rehearse physical skills, pray, and reinforce learning. Our minds and souls are in our imaginations. Others can't see the way we think or feel. There are many forms of imagery, including meditation. To be effective, imagery must be clear, powerful, and meaningful. It will help to position yourself comfortably in a chair, or flat on the floor with your legs and arms uncrossed. Take a few deep breaths, holding each for a moment and then releasing it smoothly and fully. Then mentally rehearse your actions—in giving a speech, communicating with a friend, having an interview, getting in touch with your spiritual source of strength, and so forth—or just go to a relaxing

Imagery exercises can help you achieve health of the mind and soul.

place in your mind. In your mind's eye you can see things, imagine how they would feel, look for color, see the movement, smell the smells, and imagine the touch. All of these elements help create powerful imagery.

Meditation
There are many forms of **meditation.** They vary in method, but all use some form of imagery. One emphasizes mindlessness; another emphasizes mindfulness. Some forms promote

imagery
What one sees, hears, smells, tastes, and feels through the mind's eye; meaningful fantasizing or daydreaming.

meditation
The skill of focusing (on a mantra, for instance) to reach a state of relaxation.

PERSONAL INSIGHT
A Case of Resiliency

From a health educator:

After I presented the concept of resiliency at an alcohol and drug conference, a beautiful Hispanic woman came up to meet me and told her story, which exemplifies the resiliency process model. She described herself as having been, at age 15, someone who had done it all. She described her comfort zone (regular routine) as hardly ever having been at home, spending most of her time with a gang, having tried every drug available to her, having robbed convenience stores, and having been expelled from school. Her disruption came when she realized that she was pregnant. One of the gang members said he'd marry her, and he did. After 6 months, just before the baby was born, he left her. When the baby was born, a change came over her and she decided to keep the baby. She determined at that time that she would make sure that her baby girl would not live the same life that she had led. This became her dream that would last a lifetime. She immediately changed, left the gang, and struggled for years. While living on welfare, she first earned her G.E.D. Then she graduated from college and ultimately became a clinical psychologist with a specialty in helping pregnant teenage adolescents. When I met her, she had remarried and had three additional children, and the daughter who had prompted her dream was in graduate school. Her cause had focused first on her own child and then broadened to encompass other young, unwed mothers. The mental health traits of having a dream, having the persistence and work ethic to make the dream happen, and using negative experiences as a child as a lifelong avenue to help others provide an example of the resiliency process.

particular sitting positions; others suggest that the body simply be comfortable. Opinions also vary on the steps needed to reach a state of deep relaxation and contemplation. Some recommend the repetition of a mantra (a special sound or image) to tune in the mind and tune out the mind's busy activity; others suggest that the practitioner listen carefully to the silence or the small sounds around, incorporating them into the meditation and into the body.

Most people find that one method or another suits them better than the others. This seems to depend upon personality and life experience rather than on the greater effectiveness of one method over another. Whatever the method, however, the intent and basic practice are the same. Meditation is a way to relax the body's musculature and quiet the mind's ceaseless activity by becoming a participant observer of one's own inner activity of consciousness and by practicing being aware of being aware. This awareness in and of itself seems to effect a spontaneous release of stress. Try the following meditative exercises focusing on breathing and a mantra.

For the breathing exercise, lie on your back in a comfortable position. Take some slow, deep breaths using your diaphragm (moving your stomach, not your chest). Close your eyes and imagine the air going into your lungs and filling them. Then imagine the air being exhaled and with it stress and tension leaving your body. Continue to picture this until you are quite comfortable. Then imagine that you are floating on an ocean in a raft. With each inhalation, imagine yourself rising with a gentle wave; with each exhalation, feel yourself going down with the wave. Continue to focus on the gentle up-and-down motion of the waves that corresponds with your breathing.

For the mantra exercise, start by selecting a mantra. This can be an image (flower, cross, heart, etc.) or a word (love, peace, relax). Focus on the image, or repeat the word in your mind over and over, for a period of 15 minutes or more.

Optimal Learning

By attending school, reading, listening to educational television, and challenging yourself, you are experiencing a powerful skill of the mind: learning. Each new piece of information that you learn reflects some disruption, but usually you quickly resiliently adjust by thinking how that new information fits with what you already know. The result is a broader picture or worldview. To maximize your learning is to take advantage of the time available to you for learning and to assure that you are ready, able to absorb the information, able to retain the information, and able to then apply and utilize it. The following guidelines will help to optimize your learning.

1. Create an environment that is conducive to learning. Eliminate irregular noises, interruptions, phones, and such. Surround yourself with things that are related to the subject you are learning. For example, a civil engineer might have pictures of bridges and buildings under construction, and a person who is learning a language might have pictures of the country where the language is spoken and its people.

2. Clear your mind of distractions. Make that nagging phone call, write that note, write down the tasks that need to be done after your learning time and assign ample blocks of time for them to be accomplished. If other distracting thoughts enter your mind during the process of learning, quickly write them down and deal with them another time.

3. Clear your body of distractions. Loosen your collar; stretch your back, shoulders, and neck; and assume a comfortable position. (And be sure to get ample rest at night so you won't be drowsy during your learning time.)

4. Do some mental readiness exercises. Reflect upon the importance or pleasure that the knowledge will give you. Mentally picture the edge it might give you, how it will help make you more functional or happier, or give you more hope. Try to give the information some value, such as the following.

   Personal meaning. You can best become ready to learn by finding personal meaning in your learning experience. You can accomplish this through discussions with others or personal reflection.

   Facts related to a conceptual understanding. Look for facts that deepen your understanding.

   How things work. Try to apply the information to see if and how it works.

   Self-discovery. Challenge yourself to teach yourself. Learn through trying different experiences and then judging the value of the knowledge to yourself.

5. Do a mental relaxation exercise (such as the imagery exercise described earlier).

6. Present the material to yourself according to your own learning style—in the mode you learn from most easily (reading, visuals, listening, etc.). If reading is your best mode, do the reading in the way you most enjoy (e.g., read a page, then think about it, highlight important points, take notes). If watching self-help videos is your best mode, listen to the videos in the way that is best for your learning style. As you are learning, periodically associate images with your learning. For example, if you need to remember several terms, such as *water, nutritious, jogging, stress, woman, weight lifting,* and *breathing,* create in your mind a mental picture of a *woman* in a pool of deep *water,* with her lungs *breathing,* while she is aqua-*jogging.* At the same time, she is *weight lifting* (holding barbells in her hands) in the water and someone is feeding her *nutritious* food. Imagine, too, that each time she exhales, the word *stress* floats out of her mouth. If you can imagine such a scene, then you will retain those words and instantly remember them. This skill can work for a number of learning tasks.

7. Mentally apply the knowledge. To retain and truly learn, apply each concept that you learn as you learn it. Ask yourself periodically, "How can I apply this?" or "So what?"

8. Reinforce the knowledge. Depending upon your learning style, you should try something that will ensure that you understand it. One of the best ways is to try to explain to someone else what you have learned; if no one is around, then pretend that someone else is there.

The experience will inevitably result either in a more thorough understanding or in more questions that can be answered by reviewing the given material. In group learning it is fun to reinforce the information by playing games with the information. Perhaps you can ask each other questions as if you were on a popular TV game show. If relevant, try to apply the information in some way. If you have learned about communication, try communicating. If you have learned about meditation, imagery, or self-hypnosis, try those skills.

Nurturing Strengths, Positive Addictions, and Flow
Nurturing your strengths, or having **positive addictions,** is a way of improving your mental and soulful health. Nurturing your strengths builds resources for coping and establishes havens in life where you can feel good and comforted. This principle is particularly important as it relates to health of the mind and soul. Glasser (1976) describes behavior strengths as positive addictions, those activities that people do to give themselves strength. Examples include meditation, exercise, hobbies, and imagery. He suggests that a positive addiction includes the following six elements:

1. The activity is something noncompetitive that people choose to do and can devote about an hour each day to.

2. It is possible to do it easily, and it doesn't take a great deal of mental effort to do it well.

3. It can be done alone or, rarely, with others, but it does not depend upon others to do it.

4. There should be an accompanying belief that it has some value (physical, mental, or spiritual).

5. There should be the belief that through persistence it will result in improvement, but this is completely subjective.

6. The activity must be one that a person can do without any self-criticism.

Developing positive addictions or nurturing your personal strength areas will reinforce and strengthen your coping potentials.

Csikszentmihalyi (1990) describes "flow" as the experience when our entire being is entranced in an optimal state; it is what "the sailor holding a tight course feels when the wind whips through her hair, when the boat lunges through the waves like a colt—sails, hull, wind, and sea humming a harmony that vibrates in the sailors veins" (p. 3). Flow is our body, mind, and soul being so caught up in an activity that we lose track of time and perhaps even of where we are.

---

positive addictions
Activities that an individual participates in regularly that make that person stronger.

Fighting Spirit and Hope

Psychoneuroimmunology suggests that patients with a fighting spirit and hope are the patients that will most likely get well. We can acquire a fighting spirit and hope by practicing some mental skills. Try the following.

Select a place where you can be alone and relaxed, close your eyes for a moment, and do some imagery. First prepare yourself by concentrating on your breathing, and breathe with your diaphragm (meaning that your abdomen expands and contracts, not your chest). Think of a challenge you face or a problem you have yet to solve. Think of what you are going to do to meet the challenge or solve the problem, and how you can benefit from it. While pondering, turn on some music (selected in advance) that is motivational to you. With the music in the background, picture yourself meeting the challenge. Feel yourself with that fighting spirit. Feel your emotions getting higher and higher and your readiness to do something peaking. When you feel unstoppable and ready in this peak emotional state, take a mental and emotional photograph. Remember how ready you feel and how ready you are. When you need to get back into this state, replay the music and repeat the experience.

Sense of Humor

One of the more enjoyable ways to enhance your mental and soulful health is to focus on your sense of humor. Laugh more when appropriate. Learn to see the humor in your situation. Learn to tell funny stories or jokes to your friends and reflect on funny things that have happened to you. Choose funny movies to watch. Try not to take life so seriously.

There are many other characteristics and skills you can develop to enhance your mental and soulful health. The essence of this is to provide yourself with new experiences, challenges, and opportunities—and enjoy the process of being disrupted and momentarily taken aback by having to learn something new. Then celebrate your resilient adjustment. You will find new personal skills. These same principles also apply to interdependent relationships.

PROCESS FOR ACQUIRING PERSONAL HEALTH OF THE MIND AND SOUL

The essence of developing healthy states, characteristics, and skills of the mind and soul is to resiliently adjust after new experiences or challenges. Before the challenge, we can learn, in nonupsetting ways, techniques for dealing with prospective problems. For example, we can learn personal problem solving, the steps in becoming more assertive, decision making, and how to promote self-esteem; techniques for these are described later in this chapter. It is one thing to learn about how to maximize potentials, and another to actually go through a new experience where the potentials are used.

We can plan to take on new challenges to utilize these skills, or we can wait until unexpected events occur and then use the skills. The three methods for acquiring mental and soulful health characteristics are to (1) learn the techniques

in a nondisruptive way, (2) challenge yourself to do something that you haven't done before but that you have a good chance of doing successfully, and (3) wait until some adversity happens to disrupt you and then view it as a challenge and learn the techniques suitable for overcoming that obstacle.

For an analogy that helps to conceptualize this experience, consider the fact that each of us has a worldview. As we look out at the world, we see other people, environments, and events around us. Each of these is a part of our worldview puzzle. Family, friends, school, community activities, religion, and so on, all make up this worldview and have their place in our intact worldview. When a new piece of the puzzle becomes apparent (a new challenge, an uncontrolled life event, new information, a new person), then the puzzle must be agitated or fall apart a bit to make room for the new piece. After some agitation, when the puzzle is put back together to make room for the additional piece, the worldview is bigger, growth occurs, and some coping skills have been acquired. The coping skills are those with which we put the pieces back together and fit the new piece into an appropriate place.

For example, for a student who moves away from home to begin college, the new pieces include adjustments to a new roommate, new living conditions, perhaps a new means of transportation, stronger academic demands, and perhaps a new social life. At first such students are awkward, less confident, and homesick, and they question their ability to perform well academically. Over time, however, through resilient adjustment, these students will develop better study habits, expand their social network, and have a new place of comfort (in addition to home) in the new living conditions. Students who do not adjust resiliently might drop out of school and go home. Students who adjust resiliently develop new coping skills, and the ones who drop out do not.

Planned disruptions, like going to college, are challenges to undertake if there is a good likelihood for success. Usually we probably shouldn't take on a challenge if there is a strong likelihood of failure. This is not to suggest that we should not try things that appear difficult if we are motivated to do so. Great people in society generally become great because they have overcome overwhelming odds. If we are able to make **resilient adjustments**—if we have resiliency skills (a work ethic, tenacity, a cause or purpose, and good problem-solving capabilities)—then few obstacles will stop us. But it is not helpful to reinforce a sense of failure by repeatedly taking on challenges that are too difficult. A more successful approach, generally, is to start with lesser challenges and build resiliency skills and self-confidence before taking on major challenges.

resilient adjustment
The process of coping with a disruptive, stressful, or challenging life event so that one has more protective and coping skills after the event than one had before it.

We can take planned steps to learn resilient adjustment. Events that result in some disruption, self-questioning, and confusion can be seen as opportunities for growth (Rutter 1987). This is not to suggest that we should actively look for problems; rather, we should seek new challenges and opportunities that we have not had before. When confronting a new challenge, we must do some **introspection** (reflecting on our personal resources and traits), perhaps acquire some new traits or skills, adapt some existing ones, and work to meet the challenge with the best possible arsenal of mental health coping traits and skills to perform optimally. The process of **planned disruption** and subsequent enhancement of mental health coping skills is described below.

Step I

Consider your dreams in life. Select the dream that is most important to you before proceeding to the next step. Select, for example, wanting to be a good student with good study skills.

Step II: Short- or Long-Term Goals

To accomplish the dream, it is necessary to plan a series of short-term and long-term goals that should be held constantly in mind. In our example, the dream of being a good student with good study skills, your long-term goal might be to be a good student, and your short-term goals might be to learn study skills that lead to the long-term goal.

Step III: Readiness/Lifestyle Planning

As your specific goals become clear, you can plan and prepare mentally and physically to accomplish those goals. You should develop a specific plan or lifestyle contract to know the how, when, where, with whom, and intensity of the plan. In your pursuit of being a good student, you might want to identify what good study skills are and where to get them.

Step IV: Self-Efficacy

Bandura (1977, 1989) believes that a critical component of behavior change or the acquisition of a goal is that we believe or perceive that we are capable of making the change. Self-efficacy is specific to certain kinds of situations, like attaining a selected goal. We must sincerely believe that we can accomplish the tasks necessary to accomplish the goal. In our example, self-efficacy would be your believing in your heart and mind that with these skills you will be a good student.

Step V: Action

When you are mentally ready, have a plan, and sincerely believe that you can accomplish the goal, then you implement the plan. This is the action portion and the last planned phase in the process of voluntarily subjecting yourself to disruption in order to experience growth. Engage in this plan with great perseverance and tenacity. Get the self-help books or take the workshops to develop the skills you want.

Step VI: Disruption/Disorganization

The disruption that is likely to occur when you try to accomplish a goal or realize a dream can be mild to severe.

Disruption and disorganization merely imply that you encounter a situation or challenge you have not experienced before. In our example, you might find it more difficult than you expected to develop these skills, and you may be taken aback by them.

Step VII: Renew Dream

It is always important, in the disruption stage, to remember and renew the dream that initially motivated your planned growth process. That is, know that you are disrupted but that when you get through this you will be a better student.

Step VIII: Introspection

Introspection is the personal experience of assessing available personal resources to deal with a disruption. It is an opportunity to reactivate little-used skills, modify them to fit a new situation, or identify new skills necessary to resolve the disruption and reach the goal.

In our example, you might need to discover some things about yourself, such as whether you are a visual learner, a verbal learner, or maybe an applied type of learner.

Step IX: Skill Acquisition

New, reactivated, or modified skills necessary to meet the mental disruption might include personal problem solving, assertiveness, value/behavior congruence, communication, or internalization of control. It might be that you need to learn effective communication skills to solve your problem.

Perhaps you need to change approaches, based upon your learning style, to acquire the skills you need. Since skill acquisition is the focus of our example, this step reinforces your overall efforts.

Step X: Renewed Action

With your new, modified, or reactivated skills or approaches, you can experience a resilient adjustment, and your initial action plan or your renewed action plan can be completed. The new skills you needed for resilient adjustment were likely not evident in your initial planning and became necessary during your process of growth. Your action plan proceeds with your new skills, and you should carry it out again with tenacity, sensitivity, and perseverance. In your pursuit of being a good student, you recommit with your new approaches to the study habits you want.

Step XI: Resilient Adjustment

Once you have reached your specific goal, as evidenced by responsive recognition by others, you emerge to a new and higher state of health of your mind and soul. With renewed

introspection
The experience, often triggered by a need to cope, of assessing one's personal resources, traits, and past experiences in order to deal with adversity.

planned disruption
Intentionally orchestrated life events and challenges that, after some adjustment, will help us to function comfortably at a higher level.

confidence, you set additional goals to accomplish your dream. You will find it internally rewarding to reflect upon your mental and soulful growth process and appreciate your newly acquired skills. You can feel your study skills working in your class work.

Planned, or controlled, opportunities for growth can be short-term and last just a few minutes, or they can be long, drawn-out experiences requiring several coping-skill enhancement opportunities to cope with the total experience.

In summary, the growth and development of the mind and soul is the constant process of acquiring new and refined coping skills in the face of adversity, opportunities, challenges, and new information. The healthy perspective to take is to view each challenge or life event as an opportunity to become stronger.

We have discussed in some detail the personal enrichment of the mind and soul. We now turn to interdependent enrichment of the mind and soul, which involves the relationships we have with others. We focused first on the personal process because we can be happy within our own personal worlds, but life is greatly enriched by also having positive relationships with others. Unfortunately, we also can experience unhappiness in relationships.

INTERDEPENDENT ENRICHMENT OF THE MIND AND SOUL

In life, we are born dependent upon parents or guardians to take care of and nurture us. We gradually learn to do things on our own and ultimately become independent. Perhaps the "rite of passage" into adulthood is when we leave our home and live in the world on our own. Then many of us also develop positive relationships and become interdependent. Interdependence is experienced when two or more independent people who are fulfilling their potentials of mind, body, and soul interact in such a way that the resultant combined level of happiness, productivity, and energy is greater than the simple addition of those characteristics of the independent people. When couples, friends, or coworkers work well together and give to the relationship, each feeding upon the other, the multiplying effect is extremely rewarding. Interdependence occurs among coworkers, couples, friends, families, church congregations, neighborhoods, cultures, communities, and nations. The key skills required to experience interdependence are communication skills, assertiveness, trust, and the promotion of causes.

COMMUNICATION SKILLS

Communication skills are essential to optimal interdependent relationships. When people talk, they generally focus on one of four levels of communication: (1) information giving, (2) directing or arguing, (3) exploring, and (4) self-disclosing. Table 2.2 summarizes the main features of each level.

To be happy in life, we need the very important skill of being able to effectively communicate emotions, feelings, thoughts, and ideas. Listening, understanding, and

Sharing your feelings openly is an important part of mental health.

empathizing with others when they share feelings, emotions, and thoughts are also critical for optimal interdependent relationships. After you understand the levels of communication, try the following with someone you know well.

Practice changing the level of communication. If you ever find yourself in a level 2 exchange (argument) with a friend, loved one, or business associate, take control by moving the exchange up to level 4. To better understand how to move from level 2 to level 4, think to yourself, "Why am I trying to blame, accuse, or deny?" "What are my true feelings on this?" Start with "I feel this way . . ." and express true feelings. Do not say "I feel that your problem is. . . ." Express your own state and let them worry about theirs. Remember that communicating on level 4 is very difficult for people because self-disclosure leaves you vulnerable; so it must be done with caution and trust. But it is the most effective and efficient form of communication. To resolve and enrich relationships, work toward level 4, express how you truly feel about the situation, and do not try to tell the other person how she

T ABLE 2.2	FOUR LEVELS OF COMMUNICATION

Level 1 Information giving: Sociable, friendly, conventional, and playful; emphasizes thinking and does not indulge disclosure

Level 2 Directing/Arguing: Directing, persuading, blaming, demanding, defending, praising, assuming, competing, evaluating, advising, and withholding; emphasizes feelings and little disclosure

Level 3 Exploring: Tentative, elaborating, exploring, speculating, searching, pondering, wondering, proposing, reflecting, and receiving; necessitates work and thinking and little disclosure

Level 4 Self-Disclosing: Aware, active congruent, accepting, responsible, disclosing, responsive, understanding, caring, and cooperative; necessitates work, disclosure, and feelings

Source: S. Miller, et al., *Connecting: Skills Workbook.* Littleton, Colo.: Interpersonal Communication Programs, 1989.

PERSONAL SKILLS AND EXPERIENCES

Activities to Enrich the Mind and Soul

Mind

All thinking is in the mind, as is all our imagery. To practice a relaxing imagery exercise, try the following.

> With your eyes closed, imagine that you are floating, perhaps on a cloud, and that you are rising upward. The temperature is perfect, and you have no fear as you float high in the sky looking at the views below. As you are traveling, you pass over a beautiful blue sea. You feel so good, so relaxed. You notice that you are floating down to a small island and feel yourself gradually coming to a stop on a sandy shore. It is beautiful. Gentle waves push onto the shore. Inland you see beautiful trees. Smell the smells of the fresh ocean breezes, and hear the sounds of the waves. Walk along the shore. You notice that you are barefoot and can feel the wet sand under your feet and the occasional waves lapping at your toes. Among the trees you notice a hammock tied between two trees. Walk over to the hammock and sit down, then lie down. Feel the security of the hammock around your shoulders as you swing back and forth. Feel that gentle swinging and rocking. You see the blue sky, hear the sounds around you, and are so comfortable and relaxed.

Imagine other scenarios that might be more relaxing or comfortable for you: a mountain scene or a hot bathtub in a hotel, for example.

Body

You can improve your thinking and feeling when you get the left side of your brain to be occupied with performing some repetitive, nonthinking, aerobic activity that frees the right side of your brain to create, ponder, think, problem-solve, or have soulful experiences. Try the following exercise to see if you do not think much more clearly when you are distracting your psychomotor center (the part of your brain that makes your body work).

If you are physically able, take an extended walk (or do some other comfortable form of movement) and ponder the following questions after a few minutes. Ponder the process of resilient adjustment. Reflect upon some personal experiences you have had in the past. Think of any experience that caused changes in your life—such as a new baby, getting married, moving, changing jobs, taking new classes, a family illness or death, a change in a child's behavior, a new boyfriend or girlfriend, or changing majors. As you exercise, picture and ponder the experience in light of the process of resilient adjustment. How did you recover from the change? Resiliently? If so, what did you learn? Did you recover to your comfort zone with loss (dysfunctionally)? What did you lose?

On another occasion, take your walk (or engage in some other form of restful exercise) and think again about your optimal health progress and some situations in your past that you may not have responded well to (after which you reintegrated to your comfort zone with loss, or dysfunctionally).

Now relive the events in your mind as you walk and think of ways you could reintegrate resiliently in that situation if you had the chance to do it over.

Having experienced walking and thinking about a subject, most people will agree that they think much more clearly, can work out problems, and do better planning while doing something physical. Mental and soulful experiences can be enriched when we are washing dishes, driving, cleaning, gardening, or doing other repetitive tasks. (In these cases, doing repetitive tasks doesn't result in boredom because we are taking advantage of them to be productive.)

Soul

To better get to know your soul, consider where you receive your strength of soul. That strength probably rests in one of the following perspectives:

1. A belief in a Supreme Being or Beings
2. A belief in the natural order of the environment, and gaining direction and insight by being in harmony with nature
3. A belief that all humans are endowed with an inner guide or force to provide direction and that it is our role to find and nurture that inner guide
4. A combination of two or more of the previous three perspectives

Having identified your source of strength of the soul, use your imagination to get in touch with that source. Read the following scenario and then close your eyes and experience it.

> In a relaxed state, picture in your mind that you are going to travel to the place where you feel most in harmony with your soul. To feel your inner soul, you may want to listen to some special music in a favorite real or imaginary place to feel your inner guide. You may want to travel in your mind's eye to a natural setting if you sense that your source of strength is from the environment. If you believe in a Supreme Being, then you may want to travel to your perception of what heaven might be like. Take the time to feel your soul or spirit in the environment you choose. Imagine the beauty, splendor, sense of love, and comfort of this place. The true self is in this place. If you are in the presence of a being or force, feel the love of the force. Visualize the being as clearly as you can. Feel the unconditional love, sense of purpose, meaning, and power of this state. Spend some time enjoying this scenario, communicating with this force or being. If you are with your true self, feel your self-love and purpose.

After you have completed the exercise, write something about the connection between your soul and the power in your life.

_____

_____

_____

_____

_____

or he feels. You do not communicate on this level most of the time, only when you need to. We do spend most of the time at level 1, information exchange.

The special value of communication is to openly communicate with those with whom you want to have a powerful relationship. Holding back, blaming, or other communication shortcomings only hinder the relationship. This is the rule for business, romantic, friendship, or familial relationships. Simply being aware of these levels will help your communication. As you talk with someone, be aware of what level you are communicating at.

If you can come to understand what types of communication are used in different circumstances, you will have accomplished the first step in maximizing communication.

ASSERTIVENESS

Interdependent actions can range from being totally passive to being overly aggressive; moderate, healthy action is termed "assertiveness." People who behave passively withdraw, rarely say anything, particularly with strangers, and are extremely shy. **Aggressive behavior** is pressing one's opinion to the point of violating the rights of others to express themselves freely. When being aggressive, a person might be hostile, not listen to others' opinions, and dominate conversations.

Assertiveness is feeling comfortable enough with yourself to speak to others and make statements that represent your own feelings and thoughts. Most people are not assertive, because they are concerned about hurting other people's feelings or are unsure of themselves. Finding the delicate balance between nonassertiveness and aggressiveness is difficult. Assertive people have the following qualities:

1. They are free to reveal themselves.
2. They can communicate with other people on all levels.
3. They have an active orientation to life (they go after what they want).
4. They act in a way they themselves respect.
5. They sense the freedom to say no.

Try the Health Assessment exercise to help determine how assertive you are.

We can become more assertive by training ourselves. Assertiveness training is the process of mentally preparing and practicing assertive behaviors until they become natural. The gradual process of turning a passive person into an assertive person is usually accomplished one step at a time. Here are some steps by which you can become more assertive:

1. Begin by greeting others.
2. When you can greet others, try giving compliments.
3. Then, in a group, try starting statements with "I," such as "I think . . ." or "I tried . . ."
4. Try asking "Why?" to get additional information.
5. Share some feelings spontaneously.
6. Try disagreeing when appropriate, if you really disagree.
7. Maintain eye contact (Girdano and Everly 1986).

TRUST

One of the best analogies for describing how to build trust in a relationship is the analogy of an emotional bank account (Covey 1989). We can imagine making deposits into the emotional bank account by being courteous, listening intently, doing favors, being honest, and following through with promises. Conversely, we can make withdrawals by being dishonest, being rude, being discourteous, lying, not following through on promises, and being selfish. The idea is that we need to continually make deposits into the emotional bank account to allow us the luxury of making an occasional withdrawal. In real-world terms, it seems that we need about ten deposits for every withdrawal that we make. Many people lose others' trust because they neglect making deposits with them.

PROMOTING CAUSES (ALTRUISTIC DREAMS)

The promotion of a cause is perhaps the most important interdependent aspect of the soul. A cause is a dream that involves service and altruistic effort for others. We feel good when we are engaged in a cause we believe to be good. The key elements of a cause are these: (1) Causes help others or something in addition to helping yourself; (2) causes consist of a series of goals; and (3) causes require that you give of your time, talents, or resources for their fulfillment. The following skills are ways of identifying or creating your cause in life.

1. Complete the cause checklist. The following checklist gives examples of causes in life. Go through this checklist and see how many, if any, you are working toward. If you are not involved with any of the causes here, this list might trigger some ideas and help you discover what your causes are. Your causes are things that are central to your life's motivation, and you are willing to sacrifice time and resources for them.
   ____ Your family
   ____ The environment
   ____ Children
   ____ The homeless
   ____ The elderly
   ____ Handicapped children/adults
   ____ Victims of certain afflictions
   ____ A church or religion

aggressive behavior
Expressing views and opinions in ways that diminish the views and feelings of others.

assertiveness
A mean between aggressiveness and passivity, in which people feel comfortable enough with themselves that they can freely express to others their own feelings and thoughts.

Assertiveness

Directions

Circle the number for the response that best describes you.

	Almost Always	Most of the Time	Some of the Time	Rarely	Never
1. I generally express my legitimate rights to others.	5	4	3	2	1
2. I generally express my wants and needs to others.	5	4	3	2	1
3. I generally express my feelings and ideas to others.	5	4	3	2	1
4. I allow others to express their feelings and ideas to me.	5	4	3	2	1
5. I allow others to express their wants and needs to me.	5	4	3	2	1
6. I do not hurt other people physically or emotionally when expressing my views, feelings, or ideas.	5	4	3	2	1
7. The outcome of a discussion where opinions differ is usually a compromise.	5	4	3	2	1
8. When differences occur, I try to assure a "win-win" outcome.	5	4	3	2	1
9. I use body language to make my point (eye contact, strong but not offensive voice, and erect posture).	5	4	3	2	1

Scoring/Interpretation

Total your scores for all nine items and interpret your total score as follows:

    35–45 = You are assertive.
    25–34 = You are moderately assertive.
Below 25 = You are unassertive.

____ A sociocultural movement

____ A political movement

____ Other special group

2. Turn your goals into causes. Another approach to identifying your causes is to analyze and turn your individual goals into causes. As you strive toward a personal goal, such as becoming more fit in order to reduce stress in your life, you enhance your perspective on that goal and can make it a cause that would benefit others. Your perspective might be that if you reduce stress, then you will be a more patient mother, father, or partner. Consider the following checklist of personal goals and consider how they could be transformed into causes (suggested transformations are in parentheses).

____ Being well liked (this can be accomplished by giving service to others)

____ Being happy (true happiness comes by giving service)

____ Being needed (provide someone else with their needs)

____ Financial success (giving you the means to help others who may be in need or to provide opportunities for people you care about)

____ Feeling important and worthwhile (this occurs when you make significant contributions of your time and talents to others)

____ Being loved and supported (this happens by giving love and support)

____ Control or power (so that you can help others—Robin Hood thinking)

____ Independence (so that you can contribute to a relationship and not have to rely on others too much)

____ Being socially skilled (so you can have a positive effect on others)

____ Trusting yourself (so you can trust others)

____ Being confident (to be able to help others)

____ Being spiritual (so that others can benefit from you)

____ Being physically fit (so you can play with children, accomplish service for others less fortunate than you)

____ Being intellectually competent (to be able to teach others)

3. Consider your job as a cause. It might be that to this point you have not evolved to have a cause, but you can shape personal goals into causes. For example, your employment can be viewed as something you have to do to provide support for yourself and others, or you can consider your contribution to society in whatever you do. Most types of employment offer some type of service or contribution to society. Focus on that contribution rather than on monetary rewards.

THE WORLD AROUND YOU
Guidelines to Good Relationships

Common in almost all cultures are the basics of good relationships. The following are some general guidelines to improving relationships with the people you care about. These are general enough that you can adapt these to your cultural heritage.

1. Enter a relationship with the idea of giving more than you expect to ever receive. Give what you most want to receive in that relationship.

2. Live in a state of appreciation for the relationship rather than seeking to find others (e.g., to climb higher in business or find a new challenge romantically). Ask yourself, are you living in a state of appreciation for what you have rather than looking for what you could possibly get? The quality of the relationship depends upon your mental state of appreciation and concern. Thoughts like How am I so lucky to work with you? be your friend? have you as my spouse? are healthy thoughts. Express those feelings, and experience them when you see the other person's face.

3. Relationships (with loved ones, colleagues, friends) often fail because we take them for granted or they become too routine or commonplace. Continue to court (do nice things to make a friend, maintain good collegial and romantic relationships), share activities that are enjoyable, and give to the relationship to keep it alive and spontaneous.

4. Think about how you can enhance the relationship. Remember that two people feeling the power of body, mind, and soul working together creates synergism, a multiplying effect. Interdependence occurs when we nurture our relationships.

5. Be sure that you are staying within the bounds of what you and your partner consider moral conduct and of your cultural guidelines. In business or with friends, be sure to mutually maintain ethical standards to avoid problems and ensure mutual trust.

6. In a disagreement, think of your true feelings. If you are angered call a "time-out" to think before you talk. Try to avoid saying something to your partner/friend/colleague that you might regret.

7. Try to find out what really makes your partner/friend/colleague feel loved and appreciated. (Is it receiving gifts? Being taken somewhere? Expressions of appreciation and concern?) Then do some of those things.

8. If you are feeling the negative outcomes of a relationship, particularly guilt, be sure that you attempt to purge them. If you have done something you feel guilty about, discontinue that behavior. Find a way to forgive yourself, including getting the counsel of a religious leader if you need it.

4. Look to the community for a cause. You may want to take some time to look for a cause. Being in a rut, living day to day, and just surviving generally means that you are missing out on much happiness in life. Try looking for a cause.

- Promote the arts in your community.
- Visit a rest home or a retirement center for the elderly.
- Visit a homeless shelter.
- Provide service to someone you know or who lives in your area.
- Visit a school and see where you can help.
- Take a look at your natural environment—is there something you could do?

5. Look to literature for causes. Many people have suggested that there are few heroes or heroines in contemporary society. Professional athletes are seen as having problems with drugs and as being obsessed with multimillion-dollar contracts, gossip magazines continually sully the reputations of movie stars, and so on. Of course there are many exceptions to the rule, and some teachers, business leaders, religious leaders, athletes, and other popular personalities are good role models.

In literature we can find heroes who do not change, for all members of the family. Children's classical literature is full of children and animals with personality who make their way in the world in spite of great adversity. Some were orphans or had some major disadvantage (e.g., Dumbo with the big ears, the ugly duckling). Adults can also find heroes and role models in literature. The reason these characters are heroes or heroines is that they had causes in their lives, and even though they faced much adversity, they persisted and finally accomplished their goals. Biographies of heroes throughout the ages will again provide role models. Good novels with heroes and heroines are still magnificent and motivational.

This chapter on the health of the mind and soul is an important foundation for the rest of the chapters in this book. Much of our happiness, excitement, energy, and healthy living starts with a healthy mind and soul. If we understand who we really are, have dreams of what we want to become, and learn skills of the mind and soul, we are on our way to personal life enrichment. When we have our dreams set and are working toward them, we can find friends and partners to share in our dreams in the pursuit of interdependent enrichment of the mind and soul.

PERSONAL SKILLS AND EXPERIENCES

PNI Action

Psychoneuroimmunology (PNI) is the study of the interaction of the mind, the central nervous system, and the body's immunological system. PNI studies show that people with a fighting spirit, a cause or dream, optimism, hope, faith, and self-efficacy actually build their immune systems and fortify themselves against diseases of the mind and body. The essence of mental health is to experience these states at least once a day. It is difficult, and probably not healthy, to expect to always be upbeat. We need disruptions occasionally to grow. The following PNI action involves body, mind, and soul and is a prescription for attaining optimal states at least once daily.

Step 1: Warm up and do some aerobic exercise for at least 30 minutes if you have been exercising regularly without any physical problems. If you cannot exercise aerobically, skip this step.

Step 2: After completing your aerobic exercise, do some slow stretching exercises. Be sure not to stretch to the point of pain or to shake or bounce during the stretch.

1. To stretch your groin and thigh muscles, do the foot pull. Sit on the floor, bend your legs so that the soles of your feet touch. Pull on your feet while pressing your knees down with your elbows.

2. To loosen your back and hamstring muscles, do the seated toe-touch. Sit on the floor with your legs stretched straight out in front of you. Point your toes, and slide your hands down your legs until you feel the stretch. Holding this position, slowly lean forward, and try to touch your toes.

3. The wall stretch will loosen your Achilles tendon and calf muscles. Stand about 3 feet from a wall with your feet slightly apart; put your hands flat on the wall. Keeping your heels on the ground, slowly lean forward.

4. To stretch your lower back muscles, try the knee-chest pull. While lying on your back, clasp one knee and slowly pull it to your chest. Hold for 10 to 30 seconds, then repeat with the other knee.

Step 3: After stretching, lie down on your back and experience the positives of physical readiness.

With your eyes closed, concentrate on your breathing. Breathe in through your nose and fill your lungs. Inhale so that your diaphragm is doing the work. Your stomach should be moving in and out with the inhalations and exhalations, and your chest should not show any movement. Visualize the air going in through your nose, down the trachea, and into your lungs. With each exhalation imagine the air going out, carrying with it stress and tension. Each exhalation brings a feeling of increased relaxation.

With your eyes still closed, feel the tingling of your body as it recovers from the exercise. Listen to your heart beat. Feel the blood arrive in your fingers. Feel the warmth and heaviness of your body in this relaxed state.

Get in touch with your soul. Feel love for people and those you care about. Sense your spiritual source of strength. Consider all the good things that you have in life and feel appreciation for what you have and have accomplished. Feel good about yourself and resolve to do better. If you are in a time of chaos, feel confident that you will emerge from the disruption with growth and experience. Feel optimism, hope, and the fighting spirit within you. Before you get out of this state, select the emotion that is part of you and that will help you with your day. Is it the warrior, the peacemaker, the guide, the confidant, or the scholar (Richardson, in press). Assume that state with all hope and confidence.

After the exercise, ready yourself for the next activity, but stay reflective of the positive state you experienced.

SUMMARY

1. We are in the midst of a medical and psychological revolution that combines ancient wisdom, modern science, and the integrated nature of the mind, body, and soul.

2. Mental health enriches our thinking processes, which include learning, coping, solving problems, planning, decision making, creating, focusing, and performing mental functions.

3. The soul is your purpose in living, powerful emotions, your reasons for existence, your spiritual orientation and nature, and the essence of what motivates you.

4. Optimal states of mind and soul include being able to access your sources of energy, being optimistic, having hope and faith, feeling loved, having a fighting spirit, and having a purpose for living.

5. Self-actualization, which means fulfilling human potential as well as satisfying most of the basic human needs, represents the highest level of mental and soulful health, according to Maslow.

6. There are two ongoing processes that enhance health: independent and interdependent growth and enhancement.

7. An important part of mental and soulful health is to better understand yourself in terms of your needs, stages of development, personality, self-esteem, hardiness, empowerment, value/behavior congruence, self-efficacy and faith, optimism, and emotions.

8. The process for gaining mental and soulful skills is through planned and unplanned disruptions, which means that you should challenge yourself and take advantage of your setbacks.

9.   Planned disruptions include the process of learning new skills such as imagery, meditation, and promoting a cause.

10.   Interdependent skills include communication, trust, assertiveness, and promoting causes.

COMMITMENT ACTIVITIES

1.   Plan a disruption by yourself, with your family, or in class. Take on a challenge with others, such as learning a new skill. When you try something new as a group or individually, think about the disruptive state, your confusion, and then how you felt when you accomplished your task. Discuss how it felt to resiliently reintegrate.

2.   Agree with a friend to tape a conversation you have together. After you tape it, sit down together and analyze how much of the conversation took place at level 1, how much at level 2, and so on.

3.   Take 15 minutes to sit on the campus grounds and watch people passing and greeting each other. How many people greet each other who do not seem to know each other? Take a chance today and say "Hi" to someone you do not know. Then think about what happened. How did you feel before you did it? How did you feel afterward?

4.   Write down individually, and then as a group, your perspective on your soul. Determine the circumstances that make you aware of the soul (e.g., music, feeling loved, fear, excitement, disappointment).

REFERENCES

Bandura, A. 1977. "Self-Efficacy: Toward a Unifying Theory of Behavior Change." *Psychological Review* 84: 191–215.

Bandura, A. 1989. "Human Agency in Social Cognitive Theory." *American Psychologist* 44, no. 9:1175, 1184.

Borysenko, J. 1987. *Minding the Body, Mending the Mind.* Reading, MA: Addison-Wesley.

Branden, N. 1980. *The Psychology of Romantic Love.* Los Angeles: Tarcher.

Budd, M. A. 1993. "Human Suffering: Road to Illness or Gateway to Learning." *Advances* 9, no. 3 (Summer): 28–35.

Coopersmith, S. 1981. *S.E.I.: Self-Esteem Inventories.* Palo Alto, CA: Consulting Psychologists Press.

Covey, S. R. 1989. *The Seven Habits of Highly Effective People.* New York: Simon & Schuster.

Csikszentmihalyi, M. 1990. *Flow: The Psychology of Optimal Experience.* New York: HarperPerennial.

Erikson, E. 1963. *Childhood and Society.* 2d ed. New York: Norton.

Flannery, R. B. 1987. "Toward Stress-Resistant Persons: A Stress Management Approach to Treatment of Anxiety." *American Journal of Preventive Medicine* 3, no. 1:25–30.

Girdano, D. A., and G. S. Everly. 1986. *Controlling Stress and Tension: A Holistic Approach.* Englewood Cliffs, NJ: Prentice Hall.

Girdano, D. A., G. S. Everly, and D. Dusek. 1993. *Controlling Stress and Tension: A Holistic Approach.* 4th ed. Englewood Cliffs, NJ: Prentice Hall.

Glasser, W. 1976. *Positive Addiction.* New York: Harper & Row.

Kobasa, S. C., S. R. Maddi, and S. Kahn. 1982. "Hardiness and Health: A Prospective Study." *Journal of Personality and Social Psychology* 42: 168–77.

Maslow, A. H. 1962. *Toward a Psychology of Being.* New York: Van Nostrand.

Merriam-Webster's Collegiate Dictionary. 1993. 10th ed. Springfield, MA: Merriam-Webster.

Moore, T. 1992. *Care of the Soul.* New York: HarperCollins.

Moyers, B. 1993. *Healing and the Mind.* New York: Bantam.

Osbon, D. K. 1991. *A Joseph Campbell Companion.* New York: HarperCollins.

Pellitier, K. R. 1992. *Mind As Healer, Mind As Slayer.* New York: Dell.

Richardson, G. E. in press. *The Resiliency Training Manual.* Dubuque, IA: Brown & Benchmark.

Rogers, C. R. 1961. *On Becoming a Person.* Boston: Houghton Mifflin.

Rutter, M. 1987. "Psychosocial Resilience and Protective Mechanisms." *American Journal of Orthopsychiatry* 57, no. 3:316–31.

Seligman, M. E. P. 1991. *Learned Optimism.* New York: Knopf.

Williams, R. H., and J. Stockmeyer. 1987. *Unleashing the Right Side of the Brain.* Lexington, MA: Stephen Greene Press.

ADDITIONAL READINGS

Covey, S. R. 1989. *The Seven Habits of Highly Effective People.* New York: Simon & Schuster. Covey describes optimal mental and soulful health as involving seven habits: proactivity, beginning with the end in mind, putting first things first, creating win-win situations, synergy, listening first in order to understand, and "sharpening the saw."

Csikszentmihalyi, M. 1990. *Flow: The Psychology of the Optimal Experience.* New York: HarperPerennial. Flow is the combined body, mind, and soul optimal state that we have all experienced at some point in our lives. In the flow state we are so wrapped up in a project or experience that we lose track of time and where we are, and forget about our worries. This book describes how to create flow experiences at home, at work, and other places for optimal mental and soulful health.

Glasser, W. 1976. *Positive Addiction.* New York: Harper & Row. This is a classic book by Glasser. He derives, from observations of many people, some ideas on how to find activities you can use to more effectively cope with pressures and lose yourself in positive activities.

Miller, S., D. Wackman, E. Nunnally, and P. Miller. 1989. *Connecting: Skills Workbook.* Littleton, CO: Interpersonal Communications Program. In this handbook on interpersonal communication, the focus is on awareness and the levels of communication, as described in this chapter.

Moore, T. 1992. *Care of the Soul.* New York: HarperCollins. Moore's book provides deep insights into human nature and the power of the soul.

Moyers, B. 1993. *Healing and the Mind.* New York: Bantam. Bill Moyers recaps his PBS television program of the same title in this exploration into modern science and ancient wisdom through interviews with experts in this new, evolving field of study.

Richardson, G. E. in press. *The Resiliency Training Manual.* Dubuque, IA: Brown & Benchmark. According to Richardson, the principle experiences of resilient living are self-discovery, paradigm orientation, dream making, supportive goal setting, experiences of the soul, transcending, and adapting. This book applies these principles to couples, families, communities, and corporations.

CHAPTER 3

Managing Stressors

Healthy People 2000 Objectives

- Reduce suicides to no more than 10.5 per 100,000 people (a 10% decrease).

- Reduce adverse effects of stress to fewer than 35 percent of people (an 18% decrease).

Some of us feel as though we are constantly swimming upstream as we face stressors in life.

Adversity, competitiveness, and the hectic nature of contemporary society can cause individuals a great deal of stress, and many people do not have the skills to avoid becoming overwhelmed. This chapter will describe the relationship between stress and health and will suggest strategies for managing the adversity and external pressures, as well as the personal thoughts, that create stress.

Stress can be positive—it can help people perform better, have higher energy levels, be more efficient, and reach peaks in personal experience. Stress can also be negative—it can result in personal difficulties, overload, frustration, and dysfunction. Negative stress can result in medical and psychological problems; positive stress can result in high-quality life experiences.

THE NATURE OF STRESS AND STRESSORS

Hans Selye, a pioneer in the study of stress, defined **stress** as the "non-specific response of the body to any demand made upon it" (Selye 1977). Any physiological response of the body to demands from external environmental cues (people, situations, elements), internal mental processes (worry, fear, happiness), or physiological processes (drugs, sugar, biorhythms) is stress. Such physiological arousal is generally called the **stress response.** The stress response is demonstrated in a temporary state by muscles becoming tense, brain waves moving rapidly, heart rate increasing, blood

pressure increasing, adrenalin and other hormones flowing through the system, and other responses that will be described later.

What triggers the stress response is a **stressor.** The stressor can be an emotional experience, an intellectual challenge, a social situation, a spiritual experience, environmental pollutants, or nutritional or physical stimulants.

Stress is basically a positive element in our lives and should be used in a positive way. It is important not to become stressed to the point of becoming counterproductive and ill. Selye used the term **eustress** to describe positive stress and the term **distress** to describe negative stress (figs. 3.1 and 3.2).

Eustress is productive, healthy stress, and distress is counterproductive, unhealthy stress. To conceptualize this, suppose there were no stress at all. By the definition of stress, this would mean that people would have no physiological arousal. Even when people are asleep or comatose they have some physiological activity, but even 24 hours of sleep per day would not be healthy. Stress increases with activity, such as waking up, exercising, eating, communicating with others, facing daily challenges, working hard, or playing; and activity improves people's health status and increases their productivity. If stress levels become extreme—with continual overstimulation, extreme competitiveness (to the point of hostility), a complete lack of recreational activities, or chronic sleep deprivation—then we experience the negative aspects of stress. Figure 3.3 shows the rise in productivity and health as a result of stress. At some point productivity and health peak, and if stress continues to increase, it is followed by decreased health and productivity until serious psychological and physiological health problems result. The excessive stress, in such forms as increased opportunities, responsibilities, and

stress
A nonspecific physiological response of the body to any demand made upon it.

stress response
The physiological arousal that occurs as a result of stressors.

stressor
A person, situation, or thought that triggers the stress response.

eustress
Positive stress.

distress
Negative stress.

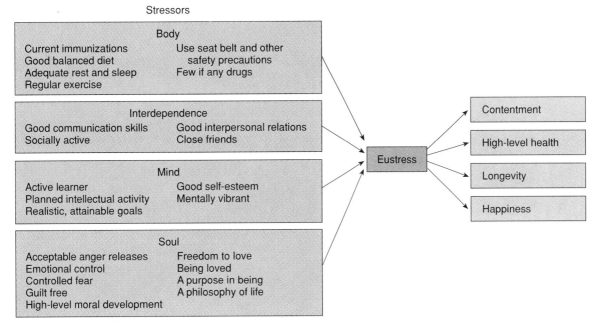

Figure 3.1

Eustressful lifestyle: stressors that may lead to contentment, high-level health, happiness, and longevity.

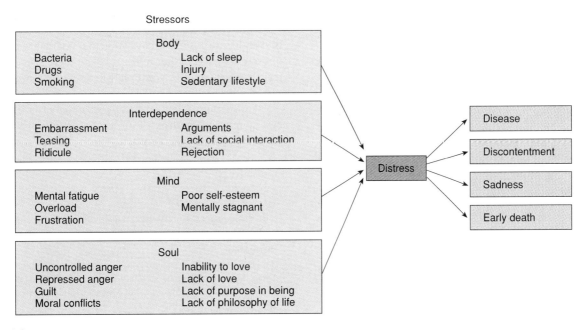

Figure 3.2

Distressful lifestyle: stressors that may lead to discontentment, disease, sadness, and early death.

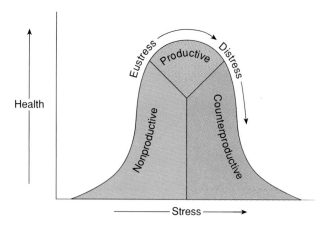

Figure 3.3
Relationship between health, productivity, and stress.

arguments, becomes counterproductive. One purpose of this chapter is to help you discover your ideal stress load so that you can perform at optimal levels.

STRESS AND PEAK PERFORMANCES

Olympic records are rarely made during practice. Most often they are made in the heat of competition, with crowds cheering—a stressful situation. An actor's best performance will be before a large audience full of expectations, not during rehearsals. Many people are most productive when they must meet a deadline, another stressor. Hanson (1986) has suggested that optimal stress loads result in longevity, peak performances, and the balance of getting enough stress but not overloading. If people find that they have excess time or nonproductive time, they should say yes more often to challenges. This certainly applies to lonely or bored people.

Hanson also suggested that stress can optimize personal potentials by motivating people to acquire beneficial skills and habits—such as laughter and good humor, proper diet, the formation of realistic goals, an understanding of stress, the practice of relaxation skills, sufficient sleep, good training for current or future jobs, living within one's financial means, and working hard to maintain a stable home life. Others have suggested that having good self-esteem, effective partner communication, social support, decision-making skills, a purpose in life, good self-management skills, time to play, assertiveness skills, control of one's perceptions, and self-awareness are also conducive to peak performance (Detert and Russell 1987).

GENERAL ADAPTATION SYNDROME (GAS)

The response of our bodies to stress moves through three stages, which Selye (1977) called the **general adaptation syndrome (GAS):** (1) the alarm stage, (2) the resistance stage, and (3) the exhaustion stage.

During the **alarm stage,** the body's defenses are called on to battle against a particular stressor. This is the **fight-or-flight response** triggered by a real or perceived threat. Hormonal stores are depleted as they are pumped into the blood, blood vessels constrict, heart rate increases, respiratory rate increases, pupils dilate, energy is utilized in tensing the muscles, and other aspects of the fight-or-flight response occur. If the stressor is so damaging that life cannot go on (e.g., fatal gunshot wounds or carbon monoxide poisoning), then the organism dies in the alarm stage, perhaps within a few moments or within a few days.

No organism can maintain itself in the state of alarm forever, so the body begins to adapt by entering the **resistance stage.** It generates more hormones and builds up energy stores to resist the stressor. In this stage the body attempts to restore the homeostasis, or the normal balance of its systems, it had before the alarm stage.

Over weeks, months, and even years, if the stressor is not removed, the body loses its ability to resist the stress, and it enters the **exhaustion stage.** In this final stage, reserves are eventually used up and lowered resistance makes the body susceptible to disease. The weakest and most susceptible organs or sites will be the likely targets of disease. Often the debilitating process in the body is irreversible and the organism dies. In other cases rehabilitative medicine can reverse the damaging process.

Remember that there are physical stressors, such as a broken leg, exposure to environmental pollutants, smoking, or even a particle of dust in the eye, and there are psychological stressors, such as continued worry, loneliness, depression, or chronic anxiety.

A worrying student is a simple example of how the general adaptation syndrome can work its destruction in our bodies. Suppose that a student enters college with bright

---

general adaptation syndrome (GAS)
The three stages through which our bodies respond to stress: alarm, resistance, and exhaustion.

alarm stage
The first stage of the general adaptation syndrome, characterized by an immediate increase in muscle tension, heart rate, blood pressure, brain activity, and other physical peaking responses.

fight-or-flight response
The alarm stage of the stress response; involuntary physiological response to sudden danger, characterized by quick action.

resistance stage
The second stage of the general adaptation syndrome, characterized by the body's attempting to return to homeostasis by building energy stores and hormones.

exhaustion stage
The third stage of the general adaptation syndrome, characterized by the fatiguing of organs and a depressed immune system, with resultant disorders of the organs.

hopes of becoming a physician but fares poorly on her first exam in chemistry and biology. Upon receiving the poor grade, the student enters the alarm stage, with self-doubt, worries about disappointing her parents, and fear of personal failure. Her body pours excessive digestive juices into her stomach to increase the metabolism of her food for energy. After a few days of this worry, her body responds to the imbalance by building up its energy stores and resisting the wear and tear of the digestive juices on the lining of the stomach. Her body rebuilds the worn lining. But after the student has worried constantly for months, her body's energy stores are depleted, and it can no longer repair the damage done by the digestive juices; the stomach wall develops an ulcer, which is characteristic of the exhaustion stage. Even one of ten physicians, who know about the effects of stress, suffers from stress-related problems (Scott 1989).

THE STRESS RESPONSE

Like other animals, humans have an involuntary or automatic response to sudden danger as well as a uniquely voluntary psychophysiological response to stress. This fight-or-flight response (the alarm stage of the GAS) includes the capacity for both sudden action and quick movement. This greatly intensified physical action is controlled by the nervous system and hormonal secretions (stimulating hormones) that produce a high state of arousal in the muscles. This high state of arousal also stimulates various organs, such as the heart, lungs, eyes, ears, and sweat glands.

PATHWAYS OF VOLUNTARY AND INVOLUNTARY STRESS RESPONSES

Figure 3.4 demonstrates the two pathways that trigger the voluntary and involuntary stress responses. The involuntary response, triggered by a sudden noise, touch, or other stimulus, travels through the hypothalamus (the centers of primitive and automatic response) in the brain, which stimulates the sympathetic nervous system (stimulating the

The physiological stress response is triggered by mental and social stressors.

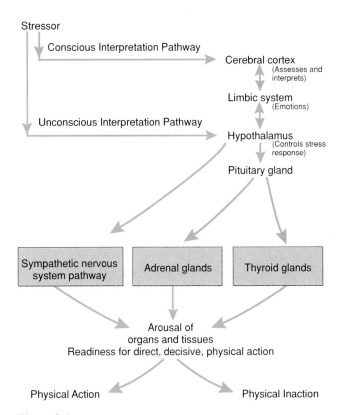

Figure 3.4
CNS pathway of the stress response.

larger brain system) and arouses the body for action. After the sudden involuntary response, the cerebral cortex evaluates the danger of the stimulus to determine whether the state of arousal is necessary.

The pathway for voluntary responses travels through the cerebral cortex (where we think, assess, and interpret), the limbic system (the center of emotions), and the pituitary gland, which stimulates the adrenal glands and the thyroid gland to secrete hormones to trigger the stress response, if the cerebral cortex determines that the state of arousal is appropriate.

INDICATORS OF THE STRESS RESPONSE

The specific responses of the body (physical action), whether triggered voluntarily (from thinking) or triggered involuntarily (as a primitive response), include the following:

1. A sharp increase in blood pressure (to increase the availability of oxygen)
2. An increase in the blood sugar (energy for muscles)
3. Quick conversion of glycogen (stored carbohydrates) and fats into energy (to sustain high energy utilization)
4. Increased respiration (to increase the availability of oxygen)
5. Increased muscle tension (readiness for quick applications of strength)
6. Pupil dilation (for visual acuity)

7. A release of thrombin (a blood-clotting hormone that resists wounds)

8. Suppression of digestion (to give the body full reaction capacity)

9. A release of cortisone (to resist allergy attacks and dust)

10. A release of thyroid hormone (to speed up the body's metabolism for energy)

11. A release of endorphins (the body's own painkillers)

12. A release of cholesterol in the blood (for endurance fuel)

The fight-or-flight response (fig. 3.5) once served a very useful purpose, for primitive people, but that cannot always be said for it today. The same primitive physical readiness response occurs in us when we take an examination, interview for a job, or get angry with someone. We cannot fight or flee, because these are usually socially unacceptable, even though our body is at a peak state of readiness to do something physical. There is no real need for the elevated energy, tension, and blood pressure.

Unfortunately, the body cannot differentiate among stressors. The hormones secreted into the blood as a physiological response create a cumulative effect of continued stress. For example, by the time you stub a toe, burn a finger on the stove, argue with your spouse or roommate, or get caught in a traffic jam, your physical readiness to fight or flee is high—and you will find yourself on the edge for the rest of the day until you release that energy.

STRESS AND DISEASE

Stress has been positively linked to a number of diseases and psychological conditions. In particular, **psychosomatic diseases**—diseases that are psychological in origin—are directly associated with stress. In the exhaustion stage of the general adaptation syndrome, the wear and tear of chronic stress on the body results in psychosomatic disease.

Psychosomatic diseases are of two types: (1) **psychogenic psychosomatic disorders** are structural and functional disorders, such as migraine headaches, ulcers, asthma, backaches, and skin reactions, that result from emotional stress (Girdano, Everly, and Dusek 1993); (2) **somatogenic psychosomatic disorders,** such as colds or coronary artery disease, result when the body's resistance is reduced by chronic emotional distress. Stress also acts as a catalyst for some organic diseases such as cancer or arthritis, if they are already present, accelerating their growth. This suggests that most diseases might have a psychosomatic component. Table 3.1 lists some of the diseases that have a stress component.

Psychological problems associated with distress include high levels of anxiety, irritability, fear, sleep problems, loss of appetite, overeating, inability to relax or enjoy normal activities, compulsive behaviors, ritualistic ways of coping, overdependence on alcohol or drugs, and overdependence on other people. In addition to the personal expense of destructive stress, the resultant psychological and physical

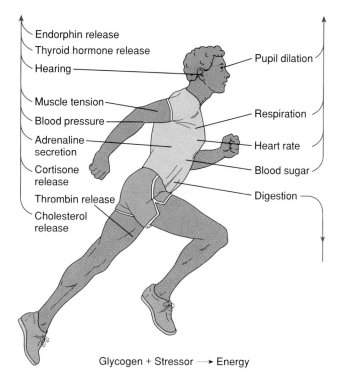

Glycogen + Stressor ⟶ Energy

Figure 3.5
The fight-or-flight response to stress.

problems cost businesses millions of dollars each year in health-care costs, lower productivity, and absenteeism (Sommerville 1989).

STRESSORS AND THE STRESS-MANAGEMENT MODEL

Figure 3.6 shows a simplified view of how the stress response occurs that gives some insight into how to manage stress. When embarrassing situations, school demands, personal interactions with others, or other external events occur, we consciously or subconsciously interpret the external stressors. We decide whether the external event is a positive stressor, a negative stressor, or an unimportant external event. This decision represents perceptual control dictating whether a message will be sent to the physiological system to respond to the stressor or ignore it. Maxie Maultsby (1986), the author of rational emotive therapy, has suggested that our perception of

psychosomatic diseases
Physical symptoms that have an emotional or mental origin.

psychogenic psychosomatic disorders
Structural or functional disorders, such as migraine headaches, ulcers, and asthma, that are worsened or caused by mental or emotional distress.

somatogenic psychosomatic disorders
Disorders that occur when the body's resistance (immune system) is weakened as a result of stress.

T ABLE 3.1	DISEASES AND CONDITIONS THAT HAVE STRESS AS A COMPONENT

Cardiovascular Diseases
Coronary artery disease
Hypertension (high blood pressure)
Angina (pain in the chest due to insufficient blood to the heart)

Muscle-Related Disorders
Tension headaches
Grinding and clenching of teeth
Shoulder and backaches

Allergic Diseases
Asthma
Hives
Hay fever
Allergic cold or swelling

Oral Conditions
Tooth decay
Ulcerated gums
Canker and cold sores
Tics (uncontrollable facial muscle contractions)
Habits such as thumb sucking, nail biting

Miscellaneous Diseases
Skin rash
Loss or graying of hair
Dandruff
Arthritis and rheumatoid arthritis
Overproduction of pituitary or thyroid hormones
Hypoglycemia (low blood sugar)
Infectious mononucleosis and other infectious diseases
Ulcers of the stomach or colon
Cancer
Depression
Diabetes
Gout
Warts
Premenstrual tension
Inflammation of vein walls

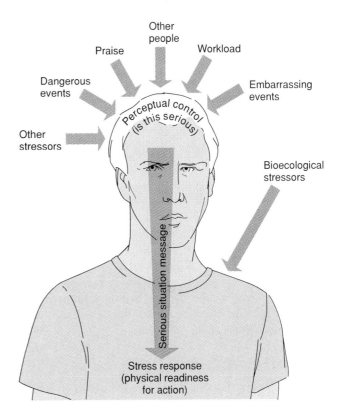

Figure 3.6
Stress-management model.

life events dictates how we feel. For example, you might view a midterm examination as a distressor if you perceive the exam as the teacher's way of finding weaknesses in order to lower grades. You might view the exam as a eustressor if you perceive it as an opportunity to show the teacher how much you know. Losing a job can be viewed as the end of the world or as an energy-producing opportunity to improve. You are not in control of all external events, but you are in control of how you respond to them mentally and emotionally. Once you understand that you can control how you interpret your stressors, you can also control important aspects of your stress response (Mansfield 1990).

However, some stressors such as bioecological stressors, do not allow for perceptual control. For example, when you are exposed to caffeine, drugs, noise, or pollution, your body has a direct physiological response, whether or not you interpret the external influence as a stressor. Through planning, you can avoid caffeine, noise, and so on, but once you have been exposed to them, you will experience the stress response.

The stress-management model presented in this chapter will explain the points of personal intervention for managing external stressors, perceptual stressors, and the stress response. By learning to control these, you can learn to reduce your physiological response to stressors.

One of the best ways to learn to control the stress response and to see the interaction of the mind and body is to try biofeedback. The technique of **biofeedback** uses instruments to measure bodily functions and translate them into immediate sensory feedback on specific physiological mechanisms, such as muscle tension. You can learn to control, to some degree, such involuntary functions as heart rate, blood pressure, brain-wave activity, body temperature, and muscle tension by responding to the biofeedback instruments and learning to consciously raise or lower the physiological measure.

biofeedback
Electronic feedback about bodily functions from machines that measure those functions. Used to observe physiological reactions to thought processes and for controlling the stress response.

For example, an electromyograph can measure muscle tension using surface electrodes. The subject is placed in a comfortable position, electrodes are placed on the skin, and resting muscle tension is measured in microvolts. The feedback can be auditory (e.g., soft beeps being given at a particular rate or pitch) or it can be a visual scale display. With auditory beep feedback, the rate of the beep slows down, or the pitch lowers, as the subject becomes more relaxed and the muscles less tense. Conversely, the beeps get faster, or the pitch goes higher, if the tension increases. Using biofeedback, you can learn to control biological stress indicators such as heart rate, muscle tension, and temperature in bodily extremities; by controlling these bodily functions, you can reduce your physiological arousal level when you are exposed to stressors.

For a simple example of biofeedback, take your own heart rate. First, rest and record a baseline heart rate. Then think fearful or exciting thoughts and retake your heart rate—most likely it will be higher. Then think for a while of being in a relaxing place, and take your heart rate—most likely it will be lower again.

EXTERNAL STRESSORS

You are constantly bombarded by external stressors, some of which you notice and some of which you ignore. It is important to be able to identify unnecessary external distressors, such as noise, potentially embarrassing situations, potential arguments, or elective classes that are far too difficult for you at the moment, and then avoid them. The key to controlling external stressors is to control or avoid particular stressors, and to learn to cope with those that can't be controlled or avoided. The following descriptions of some specific stressors may help you identify and manage some of your external stressors. Health Assessment exercises and a few suggestions for stress management are provided to help you determine whether these external stressors are causing distress in your life and what you can do about them.

Frustration

People experience **frustration** when they try to reach a desired goal and are prevented from accomplishing it. This can happen with major goals, as when trying to get into law school but scoring too low on the law boards, and with minor goals, as when trying to study quietly but being disturbed by noisy roommates. Frustration is frequently a cause of distress.

Overstimulation

When people find themselves incapable of meeting the demands placed on them in certain situations, they are overstimulated, or overloaded. Types of **overstimulation** include time pressures, excessive responsibility or accountability, lack of support, or excessive expectations from themselves or others. Do the Health Assessment exercise to see if you are overstimulated by external sources.

We can choose to be happy even when facing external stressors.

Adaptive Causes of Stress

Adaptive stress is the stress people experience when they try to maintain homeostasis or equilibrium in the face of change. Extreme life changes can also increase the incidence of distress and disease among humans (Holmes and Rahe 1967). Further, the effects of life changes are cumulative. Having to move several times in a year, for example, can wear down your resistance as much as the death of a loved one can. Change, of course, is a necessary element of growth and development, but when it is too intense it can become distressful.

The human body naturally fights to maintain its systems in a state of equilibrium, but change disrupts this balance. Trying to maintain the equilibrium is stressful. There are countless potential change stressors, and their effects vary from one individual to the next.

Do the Health Assessment exercise to see how much adaptive stress you have experienced recently.

Bioecological Stressors

In the world around us there are innumerable **bioecological stressors,** both environmental and nutritional, that bypass our

---

frustration
Being thwarted in one's pursuit of a desired goal.

overstimulation
A level of demands placed on an individual that exceeds that individual's capacity to respond.

adaptive stress
Stress due to the attempt to maintain equilibrium or homeostasis in the face of change.

bioecological stressors
Environmental or nutritional stressors, such as noise or a lack of nutrients.

perceptual control of stress and directly produce a stress response. Figure 3.7 provides examples of bioecological stressors.

Environmental Stressors Pollutants activate the body's immune, circulatory, and hormonal systems to ward off invading germs—this is a stress response. Those foreign elements, whether hidden in water pollution, air pollution, or food contamination, constitute real stressors. People should carefully consider environmental stressors when deciding on a place to live.

Loud noises also increase the stress level. Rock concerts or constant proximity to an airport not only promote deafness but also can raise blood pressure, heart rate, and hormone levels and produce other symptoms of the fight-or-flight response.

Nutritional Stressors Nutritional stressors abound on the grocery shelves, and they are prominently and prolifically advertised. Though much research remains to be done on the effects of refined sugar, some of its effects as a stressor are already quite evident. In addition to promoting tooth decay, which is stressful in itself, sugar may be linked to hyperactivity, heart disease, and vitamin depletion. Sugar, with no vitamin content of its own, saps vitamin stores in the body during the metabolic and digestive processes.

Sugar is also linked with hypoglycemic (low blood sugar) symptoms, which include afternoon drowsiness, lack of energy, and general "blahs." When high concentrations

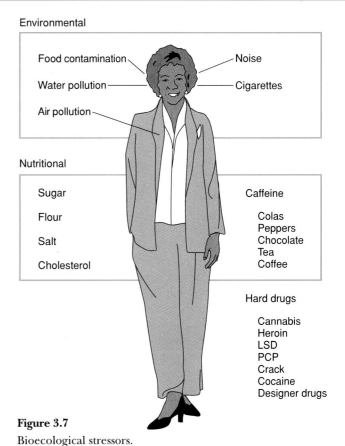

Figure 3.7

Bioecological stressors.

3.9

Are You Stressed Out by Overstimulation?

Directions

For each statement, circle the response that is most true of you.

	Always	Often	Sometimes	Rarely	Never
1. I have been given too much responsibility.	5	4	3	2	1
2. I get depressed when I think of everything I have to do.	5	4	3	2	1
3. People demand too much of me.	5	4	3	2	1
4. I often find myself without enough time to complete my work.	5	4	3	2	1
5. Sometimes I feel that my head is spinning or I get confused because so much is happening.	5	4	3	2	1

Scoring

Total the numbers you have circled.

Interpretation

5–11 = You have little stress from overstimulation.
12–16 = You have moderate levels of stress from overstimulation.
17–25 = You have high levels of stress from overstimulation.

Ideas for Management

1. Establish priorities among your list of tasks to be done, allow plenty of time to accomplish each task, and follow your list.

2. Learn to say no when appropriate, and avoid overloading yourself.

3. Delegate responsibility to others when possible, or ask for help in fulfilling your responsibilities.

4. Break a large task down into small parts rather than trying to do the whole thing at once.

5. Admit that you cannot do everything, and accept the fact that you are human.

6. Don't get caught up in the myths that lead to inefficiency (Semler 1989), namely, thinking that quantity of work is more important than quality, no one else can achieve the same results as you, and specific problems are urgent.

---

of refined sugar are consumed without vegetables, complex carbohydrates, or proteins, the body produces high levels of insulin. Insulin normally would be at work on slowly digested proteins, fats, and complex carbohydrates, but with only sugar in the bloodstream it moves the sugar into the cells for energy. The sugar is quickly burned up, leaving the insulin, but little sugar, in the bloodstream—and thus, hypoglycemia.

Though there is no conclusive evidence yet, it appears that refined white flour can induce stress symptoms similar to those produced by refined sugar. Other nutritional stressors are salt (which can be linked to high blood pressure), foods high in cholesterol, and drugs—such as caffeine—contained in foods. Many soft drinks (such as colas, Dr. Pepper, Mountain Dew) also contain significant amounts of caffeine, as do chocolate, tea, and coffee. Obviously, alcohol, tobacco, and other "recreational" drugs are stressors. As should also be obvious, poor skills in consumer decision-making can readily increase a person's stress level.

Working against **biorhythms** is also a way to increase stress. People are different in their biorhythms. Some people are morning people—that is, they are alert, mentally and physically sharp, and most productive in the morning. Other people take a while to get going in the morning but are alert and awake in the afternoon, evening, or night. People should plan to do their most difficult and challenging tasks when they are most alert.

Ideas for Management Here are some suggestions for managing bioecological stressors:

1. Reduce your consumption of alcohol, tobacco, caffeine, and other drugs.

2. Avoid exposure to loud noises, such as loud stereos, airplanes, and rock concerts.

3. Chart your biorhythms (natural ups and downs) each day for a month.

4. Plan your day around your biorhythms. Do your most challenging tasks in the morning if you are a morning person, or in the evening if you are an evening person.

---

biorhythms

The natural physical, emotional, and mental highs and lows in our lives, which potentially can be charted and assessed.

Adaptation

Directions

For each item, write in the number of times in the last 12 months that you have experienced that life event.

	Number of Times	Point Value
1. Death of parent, spouse, or close friend	_____	90
2. Divorce or difficult separation, jail term, accident or serious illness, getting married	_____	55
3. Fired from work, pregnancy, sex difficulties, or financial difficulties	_____	45
4. Change in living environment, problems in class with a professor, problems with boss, or outstanding personal achievement	_____	30
5. Final exams, change in sleeping habits, or taking a vacation	_____	20
6. Change in recreational activities, minor illness, family reunion, change in eating habits, or Christmas	_____	15

Scoring

For each category, multiply the number you have written down times the point value of the category; then total all points.

Interpretation

Your total score indicates the level of adaptive stress you have experienced in the last 12 months.

290+	=	High level of stress caused by adaptation
145–289	=	Moderate level of stress caused by adaptation
below 145	=	Low level of stress caused by adaptation

Ideas for Management

1. Set up daily routines and rituals so that they become second nature, to reduce the amount of change in your life.
2. Plan regular time for doing specific tasks.
3. Establish one regular and predictable mental-health day per week when you truly relax (don't take a hectic vacation).
4. Practice relaxation (imagery, meditation, autogenics).
5. Avoid change, when possible.

Loneliness and Boredom

Loneliness and boredom are the opposite of overstimulation. Lonely people lack the particular kinds of stimulation that come with close friendships, and this is a cause of significant personal stress. **Loneliness** preys heavily on many people. For example, even when college students are surrounded by others, they often still feel lonely. The need for intimate relationships is often frustrated by the newness of the college environment, which for many represents the first major separation from home and family. Of course, the feeling of being lonely in a crowd is not unique to college students.

Boredom is a restlessness and weariness that sets in in reaction to monotonous, unchallenging tasks. Many jobs in today's technological society are stressful, not because they are dangerous or difficult, but because they are routine and monotonous and exclude workers from the satisfaction of seeing the end products of their labor.

Do the Health Assessment exercise to see whether you are experiencing the stress of boredom or loneliness.

PERCEPTUAL STRESSORS

As you have already read, people's perception of external events can influence whether they will have a stress response. Such perceptual control is largely contingent upon personality or behavioral habits. Some personality types and characteristics are more likely than others to perceive events as stressful.

loneliness
A lack of the stimulations provided by close friendships.

boredom
A lack of eustressors; weariness and restlessness in reaction to monotonous, unchallenging tasks.

Loneliness and Boredom

Directions

For each statement, circle the number of the response that is most true of you.

	Always	Often	Sometimes	Rarely	Never
1. I am most relaxed when I am busy.	5	4	3	2	1
2. I throw away old clothes, toys, and other mementos.	1	2	3	4	5
3. I enjoy being alone.	1	2	3	4	5
4. I feel the need to belong to a social group.	5	4	3	2	1
5. I get homesick easily.	5	4	3	2	1

Scoring

Total the numbers you have circled.

Interpretation

5–11 = You are neither lonely nor bored.
12–16 = You are moderately stressed by loneliness or boredom.
17–25 = You are highly stressed by loneliness or boredom.

Ideas for Management

1. When you anticipate a lonely time, plan something to constructively and enjoyably fill those hours.
2. Develop hobbies and skills that will put you in touch with others with the same interests.
3. Do something new and different.

Issue

To Persist or Not to Persist

It is difficult for people to make decisions when they are frustrated. Frustration, which is the thwarting of a goal, is a nagging stressor that could be eliminated by simply abandoning the goal. The issue is whether people should avoid the stressor by giving up the goal, or continue to strive toward the goal and persist.

- Pro: Sticking to the pursuit of a goal is good when you consider the personal satisfaction of sticking to something and accomplishing it. There are also rewards that you receive when you have reached the goal. We should live by the saying "If at first you don't succeed, try, try, again."

- Con: The time, energy, and resulting stress that you suffer from trying to reach a goal that you might never reach is not really worth it. If you can find something else that is similar to the goal you have set, with comparable rewards, it is better to give up the original goal and attain a more manageable one.

Should you continue to strive toward the goal and persist, or avoid the stressor and give up?

Type A and Type B Behavior Patterns

The **Type A** and **Type B behavior patterns** were described by Friedman and Rosenman (1974), who suggested a correlation between the Type A behavior pattern and cardiovascular disease. More-recent literature (Fischman 1987) has noted conflicting reports about stress-prone Type A behavior and its relationship to cardiovascular disease. Many studies have shown a higher incidence of heart disease for people with Type A personalities and other studies have not.

The controversy also stems from studies indicating that Type A individuals survive longer after a heart attack than Type B's do. The Type A behavior-pattern traits that seem to carry the highest risk (four to five times greater risk of dying of a heart attack) are a mistrusting nature, harboring feelings of anger, and aggressive expressions of hostility (Raymond 1989). The most conservative conclusion is that a person who

Type A behavior pattern
A pattern of behavior characterized by competitiveness, impatience, polyphasic thinking (thinking of two or more things at once), a sense of time urgency, and open or inward hostility.

Type B behavior pattern
A pattern of behavior characterized by taking one thing at a time, effective concentration, flexibility, and equanimity in the face of uncompleted daily tasks.

Type A and Type B Behavior

Directions

For each statement, circle the number of the response that is most true of you.

	Always	Often	Sometimes	Rarely	Never
1. I get upset when I have to wait in lines.	5	4	3	2	1
2. I get frustrated and angry when I don't get as much done as I had hoped.	5	4	3	2	1
3. I get upset if something is taking too long.	5	4	3	2	1
4. I make almost every activity I do competitive with myself or others.	5	4	3	2	1
5. I say or do things that hurt people when I am under stress.	5	4	3	2	1

Scoring

Total the numbers you have circled.

Interpretation

5–11 = You tend toward the Type B personality.

12–16 = You have moderate tendencies toward the Type A personality.

17–25 = You have strong tendencies toward the Type A personality.

Ideas for Management

1. Use your time more efficiently and effectively, and don't try to accomplish too much, too fast.

2. Talk positively and calmly to yourself, reduce your ego involvement in your activities, and remember that your whole reputation does not rest on any one action.

3. If you are easily distracted, practice concentration as you would practice any other skill. Do thought stopping by yelling "Stop!" aloud. Remember that you can accomplish only one thing at a time. Keep a notepad handy and list things to be done that occur to you when you are in the middle of another task.

4. Use imagery for a short escape.

5. Become committed to and challenged by, and try to gain control of, the tasks that you are called upon to do (psychological hardiness).

Type A behavior leads to frustration, fatigue, and overcommitment.

Issue

Is Success Worth the Sacrifice?

Many people who have become successful in life have taken on major responsibilities, abandoned enjoyable activities, and worked very hard. They have become workaholics, but they seem to have a lot of money.

- Pro: If you take on every opportunity that comes your way, extra credit for classes, extra jobs for more money, and service projects because you care, you will be exposing yourself to opportunities that might pay off for you financially, politically, and in knowing the right person. It is great to be known as an "up-and-comer" or a "mover and shaker."

- Con: If you take on too many things, you will likely get more frustrated because you cannot do as much as you want to, you probably won't do as good a job on the project, and you may miss out on some important recreational or social activities that build memories of the "good college days."

Should you go after success and sacrifice pleasures, or not? Why?

Issue

The Rewards of Stress

An increasing number of families now have two wage earners, due to economic pressures and personal preference. Many people see this situation as stressful; others see it relieving stress.

- Pro: When both parents work, it puts undue stress on them to find time to bring up their children; it requires that both parents perform two jobs instead of one, and it would be better if one parent stayed at home. That would lessen the income but also lessen the stress, and therefore, it would be better for all family members.

- Con: It is less stressful to both work and share home responsibilities than to be bound to one role in the family unit. Having two wage earners in the family permits parents to take on half the responsibility for both raising the children and bringing in income.

Which work/home situation do you think is less stressful? Why?

---

demonstrates Type A tendencies is probably going to experience the negative short-term results from stress, such as frustration, fatigue, overcommitment, and abrasiveness.

The Type A behavior pattern is characterized by an intense sense of urgency (the need to get as much done in as short a time as possible), aggressiveness and frequent hostility, strong motivation and competitiveness but a short temper, an intense achievement motive but frequently a lack of properly defined goals, and a lack of concentration on work because of the intrusion of distracting thoughts. A person with Type A behavior characteristics is likely to be highly stressed.

The person with the Type B behavior pattern takes life as it comes and does not get extremely upset at losing or at not attaining a goal. Type B personalities usually set more-realistic goals than Type A's do.

Do the Health Assessment exercise to see whether you tend toward a Type A or a Type B personality.

Poor Self-Esteem

Positive **self-esteem** is important to health of the mind and soul. Poor self-esteem is a perceptual stressor that has been shown to lead to numerous stress-related diseases and poor success in living. The self-fulfilling prophecy of not trying hard because we think we'll fail—and therefore failing—works against people who have low self-esteem. When people struggle to raise their self-esteem, their opportunities ("luck") usually also improve.

Anxiety-Prone Personality

Some people see their problems as worse than they really are; such individuals are prone to anxiety. For them, every stressful event seems to be a life-or-death situation. Though a torn blouse or shirt should be "just one of those things," it becomes a major embarrassment for these people. They also have difficulty recovering from such events and continue to relive crises for days and weeks afterward; this repeated review of such experiences becomes itself a stressor.

People who have an **anxiety-prone personality** can sometimes detect overt symptoms, such as a pounding heart, gurgling stomach, trembling hands, awkward speech, and other types of muscle tension. Do the Health Assessment exercise to evaluate your proneness to anxiety.

GENERAL APPROACHES TO MANAGING STRESS

The two best general approaches you can take to managing stress are to (1) do and think things that fortify you and maximize your potentials and (2) practice skills that reduce

---

self-esteem
Feelings of self-worth, self-confidence, and satisfaction with oneself.

anxiety-prone personality
A tendency to see problems as being worse than they actually are.

Anxiety-Prone Personality

Directions

For each statement, circle the number for the response that is most true of you.

	Always	Often	Sometimes	Rarely	Never
1. When I get nervous, I often feel my stomach knotting, my mouth getting dry, and my heart pounding.	5	4	3	2	1
2. When I get nervous, I can feel my muscles tense, my hands and fingers shake, and my voice becomes unsteady.	5	4	3	2	1
3. After a crisis, I relive the experience over and over in my mind, even though it has been resolved.	5	4	3	2	1
4. I know that I must resolve a crisis or it will bother me for a long time.	5	4	3	2	1
5. When nervous, I imagine the worst possible outcomes of the original crisis.	5	4	3	2	1

Scoring

Total the numbers you have circled.

Interpretation

5–11	You are not very prone to anxiety.
12–16	You are moderately prone to anxiety.
17–25	You are very prone to anxiety.

Ideas for Management

1. Do thought stopping as described in the Health Assessment exercise for Type A behavior.
2. Use imagery to control your thoughts.

---

the impact of stressors and help you control your stress response. Meditation and imagery are examples of positive ways to deal with stressors and control your stress response. This section will describe additional positive approaches to managing stress.

As you have read, stressors can trigger the physiological stress response either directly or via the individual's interpretation of the seriousness of the stressor. Stress management involves three kinds of skills, and thus three points of intervention: intentionally avoiding certain external forces or events, controlling one's stress response to perceptual stressors, and reducing one's stress responses after they occur.

TIME MANAGEMENT (FOR EXTERNAL FORCES)

A strategy to manage external stressors, especially for people who are extremely busy, is **time management.** Many people suffer frustration and overload because they waste a lot of their time. Careful planning and managing time effectively will help to make the most of the time available each day. Day planners are popular because they provide the opportunity to plan a day and reflect on the important happenings of that day, and they serve as a record of success. Make or purchase a day planner that gives you a place to list tasks you need to do, shows time slots for each day, and has a place where you can write comments on the day's activities. You

might be familiar with other time-management planners (e.g., Franklin Institute, Covey Leadership, or *One-Minute Manager*) available at bookstores and might prefer to use one of those approaches. If you are not familiar with other approaches, try the following general guidelines.

1. List all the tasks you need to do and estimate the amount of time you need to accomplish each task. For a major task, such as a class paper, break the task down into manageable parts (literature review, introduction, subheadings, and so on).
2. Add 10 percent more time (Type A's should add 20%) to each task, for a buffer.
3. Rank-order the tasks according to importance or due date.
4. Identify all available time to do the tasks. Mark out slots that are not available (classes, meetings, work commitments, time for exercise).
5. Place the tasks in available time slots according to your priorities. This will result in a realistic estimation of what you can get done in that day.

---

time management
The systematic matching of prioritized tasks with available blocks of time.

PERSONAL INSIGHT

Managing Stress

Ali was an African American who was raised in a large eastern city. His mother was single and was the sole support for her family. They did not have many luxuries, but they had enough to live on. Ali attended high school but always imagined that when he finished high school he would try to find a job in his neighborhood. School came easy for Ali and he enjoyed learning. Taking examinations actually made Ali feel good because he knew the material and it always felt good to get good grades. With the other high school juniors, he took the ACT examination and filled out forms for scholarships, but he didn't think much about it. During his senior year he worked part-time at a garage as a mechanic and began to learn the skill. He suddenly started to receive letters at home offering him scholarships to prestigious universities. One of the letters offered a scholarship that included room, board, tuition, and books. Suddenly his dreams began to soar. He could see a way to put himself through school and take advantage of his academic talents.

Ali left home the next fall and attended a major college. One of the conditions of the scholarship was that Ali maintain a 3.4 grade point average on a 4.0 scale. For the first time in his life, he began to worry about grades. He studied very hard for his rigorous classes. When it came time to take his first examination in a chemistry class,

he was extremely worried. He studied until late the night before and in the morning was extremely nervous, even though he felt prepared.

When he sat down to take the examination, he could feel his heart banging in his chest. He wrote his name on the examination but could feel his fingers were slippery on the pencil because his hands were so moist. He looked at the first question, which was multiple choice. He understood the question and knew the answer. He did note that some of the answers were very similar. He felt that one answer was right but then began to think that maybe the professor was being tricky, and he began to second-guess himself. He chose the answer he felt was right, then he changed to another answer, then changed back again. He felt himself panic and he became so anxious that he could no longer think. He didn't even finish the exam. In his head he kept seeing the line on the scholarship contract about maintaining a 3.4 GPA. In the next class session when he received his examination back, he found that he had received a D grade. He had known all the right answers but in his panic and second-guessing had put down wrong answers. His heart sank, and he thought of going back to his job as a mechanic. He called his mother and she recommended finding help on campus.

Ali saw a counselor, who talked to him about test anxiety. As a result of the time with the counselor, Ali learned

to relax and to study effectively. For the next examination, Ali prepared for the exam by thinking about the meaning of the information he was studying. He imagined himself combining chemicals and visualizing their reactions. He thought about the material during his regular exercise sessions that he had started. On the morning of the examination, Ali went for a jog and again conceptualized the material on the exam. When he arrived at the exam, he had exhausted his muscles with the jog so there was not so much energy to get nervous with. While the examinations were being passed to the class, he did some diaphragmatic breathing and mentally escaped for a moment. He continued to be aware of his breathing as he looked at the questions. In his mind he thought about how he was going to show the professor that his first examination was not representative of his knowledge, and he was excited about getting back on the positive side. He had learned through his experience that with this professor it was best to go with his first impression rather than second-guess.

Ali received an A on the second examination. His routine of studying while exercising, exercising before an examination, deep breathing, and mental preparation helped him to graduate cum laude at the university. Ali is now a successful pediatrician who helps children in the neighborhood where he grew up.

---

6. Upon completion of a task, write to the side how long it took you, and other comments that will help you plan in the future.

7. Any tasks you did not accomplish on a given day should be added to the list for the next day, coupled with new tasks. Plan your next day in the same manner.

When you are doing time management, you will often find it helpful to do weekly planning. For the weekly plan, include time for fun, nurturing relationships, and developing skills. These are the activities that promote your longer-range dreams in life. Also leave some flexibility in your daily and weekly planning to allow for crisis planning.

EXERCISE FOR THE STRESS RESPONSE

Exercise is one of the best strategies for reducing the stress response. Aerobic exercise utilizes the potential for physical activity generated by stressors—utilizing the hormones in the blood, and the oxygen provided from increased heart rate and blood pressure, fatiguing the tensed muscles, and allowing the person to return to a tired but relaxed state. By dealing directly with the stress response in this way, you act in accordance with what your fight-or-flight response prepares you to do. Fighting generally is not appropriate, but walking, jogging, cycling, swimming, and so on give the body the physical action it needs.

CREATIVE PERSONAL PROBLEM SOLVING (PERCEPTUAL MANAGEMENT)

Creative personal problem solving has been defined as a "cognitive-affective-behavioral process through which an individual identifies and discovers an effective means of coping with problems encountered in everyday living" (D'Zurilla 1986, 11). Poor decisions generally result in problems, which people then have to deal with. For example, if you choose to drink alcohol excessively at a social event, then you might be faced with the problem of getting home safely or waking up with a hangover.

The creative approach to personal problem solving incorporates both systematic and creative styles. Here is one set of systematic steps that could be followed:

1. Define the problem clearly (collect as many facts as possible). A problem, in essence, is the difference between what is and what should or could be.
2. Generate a creative list of alternative solutions to the problem.
3. Think through the probable outcomes of each of the alternative solutions.
4. Choose the best alternative.
5. Make preparations (acquire skills, materials, etc.) to enact the best alternative.
6. Enact the best alternative.
7. Evaluate the outcome.
8. Make modifications based on what you've learned from the experience.

The second step is where the most creative portion of personal problem solving occurs. When you are thinking of solutions, write down the most logical solutions; then do some creative exercises, like the following, to enhance these options.

1. Think beyond moral, realistic, and financial limits for solutions; in other words, think wild and crazy. If the problem is that someone close to you got drunk and emotionally hurt or embarrassed you, then think of wild and crazy solutions such as these: (a) Take him or her to another planet or to a space-age laboratory where there is no ethyl alcohol and the person can be reprogrammed; (b) throw the person in jail; or (c) have a superhero (or the president) take the person to the Bat Cave (or the White House) and tell him or her how hurt you are, how he or she is messing up his or her life, and how you wished he or she wouldn't drink. From such wild ideas might emerge ideas that are more realistic and that are practical ethically and financially. (For instance, when the person is sober, you could visit a holding cell for drunks, get the person to make a pact to not have alcohol at home or to limit alcohol consumption, help reprogram the person's thinking through

	Hurt	Fear	Love	Anger	Wishing to quit
Sporting events			X		
Billboards					X
Telegraph					
Letters					
Videos	X				
Computer programs					

Figure 3.8
Creative personal problem solving with a forced matrix.

communication, or have someone who has seen the person drunk describe how he or she is hurting people.)

2. Using a forced matrix for solutions means to put things together that normally are not put together, to come up with solutions. For example, on one side of a matrix, place messages or feelings that the person who got drunk needs to hear (hurt, love, wishing he or she would quit, anger), and on the other side of the matrix place some different ways to communicate messages (announcements at sporting events, billboards, telegraph, letters, videos, computer programs) besides talking (see fig. 3.8). Point to the square where two ideas cross, and see if some new ideas emerge. Normally one wouldn't think of making a video to tell someone you are hurt, or asking the announcer at a baseball game to broadcast your expression of love over the loudspeakers, or even putting a message on a hotel marquis.

WHEN STRESSORS EXCEED OUR ABILITY TO COPE

In the general model of resilient adjustment to disruptions, adjustment follows one of four tracks. So far in this chapter the focus has been on resilient adjustment, or successful coping through the acquisition of mental health skills. Sometimes, though, adversity and pressures might exceed your ability to cope resiliently—you do not learn from the experience, and you go back to the same routine. You might lose something in the process and end up with fewer protective characteristics than you had before the disruption. You might have a reduced zest in pursuit of goals, lower self-esteem, or reduced self-confidence. You might even adjust dysfunctionally and require therapeutic help to recover.

creative personal problem solving
A cognitive-affective-behavioral process through which an individual identifies effective means of coping with problems encountered in everyday living.

The model of dysfunctional adjustment provides another way to look at **mental illness.** Often mental illness is considered bizarre behavior and is associated with mental institutions. Actually, few sufferers of mental illness behave oddly, since most are quite sedate—if not by choice, then by medication. The minority who do exhibit unacceptable behavior draw the attention of the media. There are widespread stories, popular in horror movies, of escapees from mental institutions who execute bizarre murders. Simply stated, mental illness results from an imbalance between the external pressures on an individual and his or her ability to cope with or handle the pressures. People who are mentally stressed might have trouble coping with the pressures they are experiencing, but gradually they work through them. Mentally ill people, in contrast, can't see blind spots in their recovery and need a therapist to help point them out.

Sometimes a genetic weakness, a learned inability to cope, excessive pressures, or an inability to see a path to recovery force people to seek professional help. There is no disgrace in seeking professional help. Seeing a mental health professional is no different from seeing a physician to deal with a physical problem. By seeking professional help, people can improve their coping abilities and maintain a mentally healthy life. If the imbalance is excessive, serious psychological problems can result.

The way that some people cope during the imbalance varies with the severity of the stressor compared with the coping ability of the individual. Some coping abilities are healthy and others are unhealthy. The following sections briefly describe some of the psychological coping strategies and illnesses that result when reality is not faced or when people choose to escape reality by taking their own lives.

EGO DEFENSE MECHANISMS

Psychologists have observed how people react when their self-esteem is threatened. Daydreaming in class can help reduce boredom, but continued daydreaming can result in failing the class. Unhealthy mechanisms are those that keep people from facing reality. Some of the common coping strategies called **ego defense mechanisms** are listed in table 3.2.

MENTAL DISORDERS

Most of us suffer emotional distress at some time in our lives. For example, we might place great importance on performance in a particular examination, and if we do not do well, we might be depressed for a disproportionately long time afterward. Or we might become so entranced romantically by a person who does not reciprocate our interest that, for a time, we lose interest in everything else in our life. These are minor forms of mental distress. The first is an example of mild depression; the second, an example of obsession coupled with depression.

When we suffer from these lesser forms of mental distress, we remain very much in contact with our everyday lives and we do not lose touch with reality. When we are depressed by unreturned love, we can usually maintain our daily lives and interact with other people, even though we might not do so happily. When, before a sport event, an athlete is anxious about a performance, she or he might dream about it, wake up sweating, lose interest in food, and become irritable, but the athlete does not stop moving and acting appropriately in her or his environment.

At any stage of the life cycle, there are many forms of poor mental health that can arise if a person overuses defense mechanisms while still maintaining contact with the outside world. These disorders once were generally classified as neuroses but are now usually sorted into more-specific categories, as in table 3.3. Adjustment disorders involve mental distress arising from an inability to cope with changes in the environment, such as an inability to study because of anxiety about an examination, or an inability to adjust to limitations on activity due to physical incapacitation.

Psychoses are more-serious mental disorders where people lose contact with the outside world. Despite widespread disagreement on the origin of these diseases, it is clear that some people might be genetically predisposed to them, and most of these diseases are also subject to environmental influence. These more-serious disorders include organic brain syndromes, which arise from physical disturbance in the brain from injury or other trauma, as well as schizophrenic and paranoid disorders. Less extreme but equally troubling to the sufferer are personality disorders, in which the person tends to distort rather than escape from reality.

Most people experience some moderate phobias, or fears, such as **acrophobia** (fear of high places), **astraphobia** (fear of thunder and lightning storms), **claustrophobia** (fear of enclosed places), **mysophobia** (fear of contamination or germs), or **monophobia** (fear of being alone). Most people also experience moderate somatoform disorders and depression at one time or another, but eventually work through them.

mental illness
The inability to cope with life situations.

ego defense mechanism
A defensive, often unconscious, way of dealing with perceived inadequacies or stressors.

acrophobia
Fear of high places.

astraphobia
Fear of thunder and lightning storms.

claustrophobia
Fear of enclosed places.

mysophobia
Fear of contamination or germs.

monophobia
Fear of being alone.

TABLE 3.2 SOME EGO DEFENSE MECHANISMS

Mechanism	Process	Example
Compensation	Covering up weakness by emphasizing desirable traits or making up for frustration in one area with gratification in another.	If we are not considered physically attractive, we may lose ourselves in intellectual pursuits.
Denial of reality	Protecting oneself from unpleasant reality by refusing to perceive or face it.	Sexually transmitted diseases often go untreated because we deny their reality.
Displacement	Discharging pent-up feelings and emotions, which are usually hostile, on objects less dangerous than the ones that initially aroused the emotions.	The manager who is reprimanded by the boss at work in turn reprimands a spouse because a meal is late or cold.
Fantasy	Overcoming frustration by imagining that achievements have actually occurred.	Using college attendance to allow us to tell stories of great athletic or social accomplishments back home until the stories seem true.
Identification	Trying to become like something or someone else in thought or behavior; feeling increased self-worth by identifying with someone or something held in high esteem.	Wearing a football jersey similar to those worn by professionals, with the number of a favorite player.
Projection	Placing responsibility for one's own good or bad behavior on others or attributing one's own desires to others.	"I failed that exam because Professor X is a lousy teacher."
Rationalization	Thinking up "good" reasons to justify irrational behavior; attempting to prove that one's behavior is rational and justifiable and thus worthy of social and self-approval.	When angered we may throw a dish against a wall and break it, later rationalizing that "I didn't like that dish anyway."
Regression	Retreating to an earlier developmental level that doesn't carry the responsibilities or difficulties of the current level; retreating to an age that one had enjoyed and where one had resolved the crisis associated with that stage.	Going to a park and playing on the playground equipment or developing strong emotional dependencies on a physical caretaker when distressed.
Repression	Consciously or subconsciously preventing painful or dangerous thoughts from entering the consciousness; often called "selective forgetting," although the thoughts are not really forgotten, for they "slip out" in dreams or conversations.	"Forgetting" the name of our old love until we suddenly call our new love by the old one's name.
Sublimation	Converting socially unacceptable instinctual drives or impulses into socially acceptable behaviors or personally acceptable channels.	Diverting our sexual drives into wrestling or carrying someone just in fun can seem more acceptable than premarital sex.

SUICIDE

A method of dysfunctional coping for some is **suicide,** the intentional killing of oneself. Suicide is the denial of a human being's most urgent need, self-preservation, and contradicts the high value placed on human life. In the United States, roughly five thousand young people between the ages of 14 and 25 will kill themselves this year (more than 13 people per day), which is almost triple the rate of suicide of 30 years ago (White, Murdock, and Richardson 1987). With problems in reporting, masking, and interpretation in suicide statistics, the actual suicide rate might be twice this figure. Add to this the number of attempts, which may be as high as one hundred per completed suicide, and a mental health problem of major proportions emerges.

Why Suicide?

The thought of suicide crosses nearly everyone's mind at some time during the life cycle. Everyone feels helpless or worthless at times, and most people don't get through life without the loss of a loved one or a major disappointment that leads them to despair. Most people, though, can cope with these feelings. Why do others decide not to go on?

Some people—such as an impulsive person in the heat of anger, frustration, or disappointment, a person who has perhaps been jilted by a partner, or a teenager angry at parents—might commit suicide impulsively without giving any rational thought to it. Depression can make a person feel that life has no meaning anymore, that special problems will never be resolved, and that the best thing to do is to end it all. A person in constant pain, especially with a terminal illness, might see suicide as an escape from suffering; older people are most susceptible in this area.

suicide
Intentionally killing oneself.

HEALTH UPDATE

Dr. Jack Kevorkian

Physician-assisted suicide is doctors' helping terminally ill patients to commit suicide. Jack Kevorkian is a Michigan physician who has helped several terminally ill patients commit suicide. In Michigan, physician-assisted suicide is a felony, but in 1992 California and Oregon almost passed proposals to make it legal (Cotton 1993). The drama is ongoing, as Dr. Kevorkian has been arrested and released a couple of times. He was found innocent of disobeying the Michigan law in a recent court case even though he admitted to helping in a suicide. When in jail he has fasted in protest against the law against physician-assisted suicide.

TABLE **3.3**	DIAGNOSTIC CATEGORIES FOR MENTAL DISORDERS

Disorders usually first evident in infancy, childhood, or adolescence (developmental, disruptive behavior, anxiety, eating, gender identity, tic, elimination, and other disorders)

Organic mental syndromes and disorders (disorders include dementias, psychoactive substance-induced, unknown physical disorders)

Psychoactive substance use disorders

Schizophrenia

Delusional disorder (paranoid disorders)

Psychotic disorders not elsewhere classified

Mood disorders (bipolar and depressive disorders)

Anxiety disorders (phobia and panic disorders)

Somatoform disorders (conversion disorders or hypochondriasis)

Dissociative disorders (multiple personality, hysterical neurosis, etc.)

Sexual disorders (paraphilia such as exhibitionism or voyeurism and sexual dysfunctions)

Sleep disorders (insomnia and other disorders)

Factitious disorders (intentionally produced physical or psychological symptoms)

Impulse control disorders not elsewhere classified (kleptomania, pathological gambling)

Adjustment disorder

Psychological factors affecting physical condition

Personality disorders

V codes for conditions not attributable to a mental disorder that are a focus of attention or treatment

Additional codes

From the American Psychiatric Association: *Diagnostic and Statistical Manual of Mental Disorders, Third Edition, Revised.* Washington, DC, American Psychiatric Association, 1987. Reprinted by permission.

Many people who attempt suicide are trying to communicate with those around them—asking a spouse to come back, asking parents for attention, and so on. Attempted suicides might deliver the message, but they seldom alter the situation.

Increased Risk for Suicide

The following circumstances might increase the risk of suicide.

1. Religion with no taboos against suicide. Religion is a particularly strong influence on suicide rates. The Catholic Church has strong sanctions against suicide, and predominantly Catholic nations have lower suicide rates than do mixed or predominantly Protestant nations. Protestant Sweden has a suicide rate twice that of the United States, and twelve times that of Catholic Ireland.

2. Urban-setting residences. Modern urban settings seem to abound with anomie (a restless alienation in which normative standards of conduct and belief are weak), which creates a higher risk of suicide for urban residents.

3. High unemployment. Suicide rates increase and fall with economic cycles.

4. Availability of method. Access to automobiles, firearms, and potentially lethal drugs also increases the risk.

5. Gender. Males are more likely to complete the suicide, females are more likely to make an attempt at suicide.

6. Race. Risk for successful suicide is in this order, from highest to lowest risk: white males, black and other nonwhite males, white females, black and other nonwhite females.

7. Family relationships. Single-parent households, poor intrafamily relationships, and having few siblings are factors associated with higher risk than other family characteristics.

8. Psychiatric profile. Depression, acting-out behaviors, inability to cope with stress, a tendency toward alienation, and isolation are high-risk factors (White, Murdock, and Richardson 1987).

Prevention of Suicide

Suicide prevention usually includes two different interventions: crisis intervention and counseling or psychotherapy. Crisis intervention is necessary before counseling can take place, and it includes relieving the person's isolation and reestablishing his or her social ties, relieving the person's anxiety and sleeplessness, removing any lethal weapons from the person's possession, and attempting to postpone the final suicide decision.

Anyone who threatens to commit suicide should be taken seriously.

Crisis Intervention   Anyone who threatens to commit suicide should be taken seriously. There are four recommended steps for helping someone who might be suicidal:

1. First, try to find out how deeply troubled the individual really is. Even though you might hesitate to bring the subject up, it is better to directly discuss the matter than to ignore it. If the person has not seriously intended suicide, discussing it is not likely to plant the idea. Further, potentially suicidal people are less likely to kill themselves if they can have a meaningful conversation with someone who cares about them.

2. Do not challenge the individual to act on a suicide threat she or he has made. Such a challenge might force the person to go through with the act.

3. Urge the person to postpone the decision. Help the individual to see that suicide is always an available option but one that, once chosen, cuts off all other options. Therefore, it should be delayed as long as possible.

4. Intervene early in the crisis situation. Suicidal thoughts usually arise when an individual feels that all other options have been exhausted. Frequently the person's perspective is limited by the immediate pressure of the situation, and an outsider is needed to help find other solutions and give the person the courage to try them.

There are many suicide prevention and crisis intervention centers throughout the United States, some sponsored by schools and church groups, others by the community. A suicide prevention center is a place that a person in crisis can call to get emergency advice, help, and referral. Volunteers are trained to calm the caller, assess the problem, and refer the caller to professional help. Some centers assign a team to travel to the person in crisis. The center usually has a 24-hour telephone service. Follow-up and referral services include emergency-room services, outpatient clinics, inpatient programs, and educational and consultation services for the entire community.

Counseling   Follow-up of suicidal people is best handled by trained psychotherapists. They can provide help with any psychological or social disturbances in the person's life. For example, they can help the person improve his or her self-image, find satisfactory social resources, learn alternative coping mechanisms, and explore developing a satisfying life plan.

Befriending a Person Who Might Be Contemplating Suicide
The Samaritans, an international, privately funded suicide prevention agency founded in 1953, have suggested the following guidelines for befriending a suicidal person (Langone 1986).

1. Befriending is played by ear. There are no formulas, just some safe guidelines.

2. You must be yourself. Anything else feels phony, sounds phony, and won't be natural to you or to the person who is talking to you.

3. Your job is to listen. You want to make a relationship with the other person so that they feel they can trust you enough to tell you what is really on their mind.

4. What you say or don't say is not as important as how you say it.

5. Deal with the person, not just the problem. Talk as an equal, not a counselor.

6. Give your full attention; listen for feelings as well as facts.

7. Don't feel you have to say something every time there is a pause. Silence gives you both time to think.

8. Show interest, and invite the person to continue without giving them the third degree. Simple questions like What happened? What's the matter? are not threatening.

9. Steer toward the pain, not away from it. The person wants to tell you; you have to provide the opening to let them.

10. Try to see and feel things from the other person's point of view. Be on their side.

11. Let the person find their own answers, even if you think you see an obvious solution.

12. Many times there are no answers and your role is simply to listen, to be with the person, and share the pain.

PSYCHOANALYSIS AND PSYCHOTHERAPY

When anxiety, depression, or abnormal behavior become serious, people can now seek help with little risk of being ridiculed for doing so. Such problems can be treated like diseases that are treated by a health-care provider, but in this case they are treated by a psychologist, psychiatrist, or counselor. There are many schools and kinds of **psychotherapy** available, from **psychoanalysis** (in which an individual might spend years with an analyst working through unresolved developmental stages, conflicts, and traumatic experiences that may have caused the present disorder) to family therapy (which operates on the principle that a family is a unit with hidden rules and expectations that can sometimes hurt rather than help its members if enforced without loving awareness).

SOURCES OF HELP

The following are some of the many sources of help for emotional problems.

1. Community religious leaders. For mild problems, trained religious leaders such as ministers, priests, and rabbis can give good and compassionate counsel, consistent with your values. They usually receive a counseling course in their training and an experiential internship.

2. Physicians. Your family physician hasn't the expertise of a psychologist or psychiatrist but does receive 12 weeks of training during medical school, normally has some experience with other emotionally troubled patients, and can refer you to a counselor.

3. Counselors. Universities and colleges usually have free or inexpensive student-counseling services. Often the counselors are doctoral students who study for 6 to 8 years to be counselors or psychologists. They are supervised by experienced university professors who are themselves experts. Severe cases can be referred to these professors.

4. Licensed clinical psychologists. Licensed clinical psychologists have a Ph.D. and at least 3,000 hours of clinical experience. Though they charge for their services, the help they give is often excellent.

5. Psychiatric social workers. These professionals usually have an M.A. or M.S. and extensive counseling experience. Many of them work at community health clinics.

6. Psychiatrists. Psychiatrists are physicians who have gone through medical school but have specialized in psychopathology. Psychiatrists are costly but usually the choice for people with severe mental problems requiring medication.

7. Licensed marriage, family, and child counselors (MFCCs). These professionals usually have an M.A. and extensive counseling experience. Many are in private practice.

8. Self-administered therapy. You can work on mild disorders yourself by reinforcing your healthy behaviors and replacing your unhealthy behaviors with healthier ones. Imagery can also be useful. For example, to avoid, control, or eliminate an undesirable behavior, associate it with a nasty or unpleasant image (e.g., imagine either being nauseous or burning your clothes every time you have a cigarette). For another example, by imagining yourself effectively coping with a feared situation, you can learn to no longer fear it (e.g., if you suffer extreme anxiety about exams, imagine yourself successfully completing the exam).

If you are wondering how to get in touch with someone in the community who can help you, look in the yellow pages under "Mental Health"; there is usually some type of community mental health center that can either help you or refer you to a qualified professional.

SUMMARY

1. Stress is a physiological response to stressors as manifested by increased heart rate, blood pressure, muscle tension, hormonal secretions, and brain-wave activity. Stress responses are either involuntary, taking a path through the hypothalamus and sympathetic nervous system, or voluntary, taking a path through the cerebral cortex, limbic system, hypothalamus, pituitary gland, and thyroid gland.

2. Eustress is positive stress that can result in peak performance and increased health; distress is negative stress and can result in disease.

3. The general adaptation syndrome is the body's response to distress that can lead to disease. The stages include alarm, resistance, and exhaustion.

4. The stress-management model identifies three points where stress-management and mental health skill development can occur: managing external stressors, developing mental/perceptual health skills, and managing the physiological stress response.

5. External stressors include failure to attain goals, overstimulation, adaptation, bioecological stressors, loneliness, and boredom.

6. Perceptual stressors include the Type A behavior pattern, poor self-esteem, and anxiety-prone personality.

7. General approaches to managing stress include time management, exercise, and creative personal problem solving.

---

psychotherapy
Any mental method of treating a disease, especially nervous disorders.

psychoanalysis
A type of psychotherapy in which patients reflect on their lives in order to find solutions to problems.

PERSONAL SKILLS AND EXPERIENCES

Dealing with Stress

Mind

Thinking rationally (logically) about things rather than tainting the issues with reactionary emotions is the specialty of Maxie Maultsby (1986), who is the author of rational self-counseling. Rational self-counseling helps put stressful thoughts, emotional feelings, or physical actions into perspective. Maultsby suggests that before making a decision to deal with stress, the questions below should be addressed.

1. Is my thought based on fact?
2. Will acting on my thought best help me protect my life and health?
3. Will acting on my thought best help me achieve my short- and long-term goals?
4. Will acting on my thought best help me avoid my most dreaded conflicts with other people?
5. Does my thought best help me feel the emotions I want to feel?

Body

Progressive relaxation is a technique, originally developed by Edmund Jacobson (1929), in which one relaxes by focusing on tensing and relaxing the muscle groups of the body. To experience progressive relaxation, concentrate on one area of your body at a time. Tense the muscles in one area for about 5 seconds and be sensitive to the resulting varied physical states, but end by relaxing the muscles and focusing on the relaxed state. Following is the list of commands that you can give yourself during this exercise.

- Tense your feet by curling your toes, and then relax.
- Tense your calf muscle by pointing your toes, and then relax.
- Tense the front of your lower leg by pulling the toes up, and then relax.
- Tense your upper leg muscles, and then relax.
- Tense your hand muscles by making a fist with both hands, and then relax.
- Tense your forearm muscles by bending your wrists toward your biceps, and then relax.
- Tense your outside forearm muscles by pulling your fists up, and then relax.
- Tense your biceps by bending your elbows, and then relax.
- Tense your abdominal muscles, and then relax.
- Tense your shoulder and neck muscles by pulling your shoulders up, and then relax.
- Tense your buttocks muscles, and then relax.
- Tense your facial muscles by clenching your jaw and making a scrunched-up face, and then relax.
- Now let all your muscles assume the relaxed state, making sure all muscle groups are free from tension.

Soul

You probably think of your soul as either a force greater than you are from which you could gain strengths; or a part of nature and your ecosystem; or an inner force or guide within you; or some combination of the previous three. When you encounter stressors, take the opportunity to put your life into perspective and get in touch with your soul. "Living with heart," "following your bliss," and "listening to your inner guide" are all important concepts of the soul and key in dealing with stressors.

Directions

1. Plan a time in a day when you can take at least half an hour and forget your daily responsibilities. You may want to go to a park, go out at night under the stars, or seclude yourself in some isolated place, even if it has to be a closet.
2. When alone, close your eyes and picture your soulful source of strength. Picture as clearly as you can the place you might be in, and feel the power of the force. You will likely have feelings of love, warmth, and energy when you are in that state. If you can imagine shape or color, do so.
3. Now communicate with your soul, or with yourself, about your life and where you are going with it. Are your causes or goals noble and aligned with your perception of good? Rehearse in your mind the dream or cause you want to pursue.
4. Commit or recommit yourself to living a life in harmony with your soulful source of strength.
5. Now reflect upon the stressor. How important is the stressor in light of the bigger picture of the soul that you have been contemplating? How can you manage or ignore the stressor in light of the strength of the soul?

8. Mental illness results from an imbalance between the stressors we face and our ability to cope with the stressors, creating blind spots and an inability to cope without the help of a therapist.

9. When stressors exceed our ability to cope, we can seek professional help without disgrace. There are many types of qualified health professionals who can help.

10. Suicide is often preventable if early warning symptoms are detected and befriending occurs.

COMMITMENT ACTIVITIES

1. A good activity to do in class or with a partner is to test your ability to reduce your heart rate by using breathing techniques, autogenic training, progressive relaxation, meditation, or imagery strategies. Sit at rest for some time, and then have a partner take your resting heart rate. Then practice one of the relaxation techniques. Have your partner keep his or her fingers on your pulse (at the wrist) the whole time you are doing the relaxation exercise. Periodically, the partner should take your resting heart rate. When you complete the exercise, see how your relaxation heart rate compares to your resting

PERSONAL SKILLS AND EXPERIENCES

An Exercise for Mind, Body, and Soul

Here is a routine for the body, mind, and soul that can help fortify you against illness and disease.

1. Write down a challenge of the mind or soul to ponder. This might be something as abstract as what your purpose or dream in life is, or what you are really like when you do not have roles to perform, or as specific as planning your day.
2. Do some form of repetitive aerobic exercise alone (walking, jogging, swimming, biking, etc.). While exercising, think about your challenge of the mind and soul and expect to get great answers.

3. After exercising, go through a series of flexibility exercises (yoga positions would be ideal). For example:
   —Stand with your feet shoulder-width apart, clasp your hands high over your head, and bend back as far as you can without falling over, and without pain, for about 10 seconds.
   —Sit on the floor with your legs straight out in front of you. Slowly bend forward and touch your toes and hold for about 10 seconds.
   —From the sitting position, roll onto your back and bring your feet high in the air as you support your back with your hands. Begin to do a backward somersault, but stop when your feet touch, and hold.
   —Lie on your stomach on the floor. Arch your head up and raise your legs and hold for 10 seconds.
4. Sit with your back straight (perhaps lean against a wall) with your legs crossed in front of you, close your eyes, and meditate for a few minutes.

heart rate taken at the beginning of the exercise. Repeat the exercise, exchanging roles with your partner. Practice various strategies until you can lower your heart rate at will.

2. All of us find ourselves under stress at times. This is true at all stages of the life cycle. Make a list of your stressors—people and situations that cause you stress, such as driving in traffic, exams, and so forth. Beside each item, write down the positive and/or negative ways you have managed this particular stressor. Later on, you will probably become aware of additional stressors that you didn't list and find new and positive ways of managing them.

3. Keep a personal stress diary during the next 3 days. Note which events cause you to feel stressed and whether you feel the stress is positive or negative. At the end of the 3 days, review your personal stress diary and honestly consider how you managed and coped with the stressful events you experienced. What might you have done to better cope with the stressor?

4. Take the opportunity to go through the process of adopting a new coping skill. Challenge yourself by trying something you have not done before. Go through the process of committing yourself, preparing, feeling the disruption, and gradually learning. For example, if you have never done meditation, progressive relaxation, self-hypnosis, or time management, try to practice one of them for a month. The process of disrupting your regular pattern of living in order to learn a new skill is an example of resilient adaptation.

REFERENCES

Cotton, P. 1993. "Rational Suicide: No Longer 'Crazy.' " *JAMA* 270: 797.

Detert, R. A., and R. Russell. 1987. "Identification and Description of Content Elements for Stress Management in Health Education." *Health Values* 11, no. 1:3–12.

D'Zurilla, T. J. 1986. *Problem Solving Therapy: A Social Competence Approach to Clinical Intervention.* New York: Springer.

Fischman, J. 1987. "Type A on Trial." *Psychology Today* 21, no. 2:42–64.

Friedman, M., and M. H. Rosenman. 1974. *Type A Behavior and Your Heart.* New York: Knopf.

Girdano, D. A., G. S. Everly, and D. A. Dusek. 1993. *Controlling Stress and Tension: A Holistic Approach.* 4th ed. Englewood Cliffs, NJ: Prentice Hall.

Hanson, P. G. 1986. *The Joy of Stress.* Kansas City: Andrews, McMeel & Parker.

Holmes, T. H., and R. H. Rahe. 1967. "The Social Readjustment Rating Scale." *Journal of Psychosomatic Research* 11: 213–18.

Jacobson, E. 1929. *Progressive Relaxation.* Chicago: University of Chicago Press.

Jola, I. K. 1970. "Helping: Does It Matter?" Paper presented at the meeting of the United Ostomy Association: Washington, DC.

Langone, J. 1986. *Dead End.* Boston: Little, Brown.

Mansfield, G. 1990. "You Can Manage Stress." *Safety and Health* 141, no. 2:60.

Maultsby, M. 1986. *Coping Better: Anytime, Anywhere.* New York: Prentice Hall.

Raymond, C. 1989. "Distrust, Rage May Be Toxic Core That Puts Type A Person at Risk." *JAMA* 261: 813.

Scott, C. D. 1989. "Coping with Stress." *JAMA* 262: 2466.

Selye, H. 1977. *Stress Without Distress.* New York: Signet.

Semler, R. 1989. "Senhor Semler's Planet." *Across the Board* 26: 10.

Sommerville, J. 1989. "Stress Treatment Costing Billions." *American Medical News* 32: 17.

White, G. L., R. T. Murdock, and G. E. Richardson. 1987. "Adolescent Suicide." *Physician Assistant* 11, no. 5:103–14.

ADDITIONAL READINGS

Borysenko, J. 1993. *Fire in the Soul.* New York: Warner. This book helps clarify what the soul is and how it can deal with problems in life.

Greenberg, J. S. 1993. *Comprehensive Stress Management.* 4th ed. Dubuque, IA: Brown & Benchmark. This is a comprehensive stress-management book that explains both concepts of stress management and stress-management strategies. It covers the scientific foundations, general applications, and specific applications of stress management.

Merrill, A. R. *Connections: Quadrant II Time Management.* Salt Lake City: Institute for Principled-Centered Leadership. Planning for the most important activities in life is more important than dealing with crises. This book helps you to diminish the number of crises in your life by bolstering your planning for truly enriching activities.

Miller, L. H., and A. D. Smith. 1993. *The Stress Solution.* New York: Picket. A good, comprehensive stress-management book that largely relies on cognitive approaches and presents some very practical strategies.

LIFESTYLE CONTRACT

By reading the chapters on mental health and stress management, you should have a good understanding of:

1. The power of good mental health
2. The skills to acquire good mental health
3. The process of acquiring good mental health skills
4. Stressors in your life
5. The points of intervention to manage stress
6. The value of stress and adversity in life when that adversity is used as a stepping stone for growth and improved health

You have also had an opportunity to assess your individual strengths and status as they pertain to mental health and stress. The application of these principles and skills in your life, if you are not already doing these things, is important. The outcome of reading this text is that you as a reader will learn new skills and adopt behaviors that will improve your health in any dimension. The prevention model that was presented in chapter 1 provides the framework whereby you can consider the relevance of the issues presented in this section and throughout the text. You can also reflect upon the health assessments contained in these first chapters that identified strengths and weaknesses that you may want to work on.

The following assessments and guidelines will take you through a systematic decision-making and lifestyle-contracting process that reflects the principles discussed in chapters 1–3. Each step is a necessary step in completing a successful health enhancement experience. The accomplishment of any of the steps is health enhancing in itself.

Preparations to Complete the Lifestyle Contract for Section II

I. Establish or confirm your purpose or cause in life. Reflect on the purposes or causes in life, either short-term or long-term, that you identified in chapter 2. Remember, there is a cause and effect for things that you do. If you are more assertive, then you may be better able to accomplish your goal of increased social health. If you do time management, then you may see an increase in your productivity and free time. As you reflect on your purposes, identify those that can be better realized if you had better mental health skills or were better able to control stress.

_____

_____

_____

II. Be psychologically hardy as it pertains to the accomplishment of the cause or purposes. Indicate the degree to which you sense control, are committed to, and challenged in pursuing the cause or purpose(s):

	Agree	Not Sure	Disagree
I know that if I work hard, I will achieve my goal or goals.	3	2	1
No matter what I do, the accomplishment of the goal depends on luck or if others will give me the break.	1	2	3
I am excited about and committed to accomplishing this goal.	3	2	1
I sense some ownership in this goal and that it is part of me.	3	2	1
This goal is a challenge for me.	3	2	1
This goal is not really that big of a deal.	1	2	3
Total			

Scoring

As it pertains to this goal or purpose I am:

Very hardy	17–18 points
Moderately hardy	14–16 points
Not very hardy	13 points and under

At this point, if you are not at least moderately hardy, then you should go back and consider your goals (causes) and reestablish some as suggested in chapter 2. Your lifestyle contract would be associated with the establishment of positive, realistic health goals in your life, which is an extremely healthy behavior.

III. Enhance your self-efficacy regarding the specific behavior that you want to modify for stress management and mental health and to help you to reach your goal. What kinds of mental health or stress-management traits or skills must you refine or acquire to take you a step closer to the attainment of your goal or dream? In the following assessment, in the first column identify the area that you feel would help you to work toward your goal or purpose in life with an X. In the second column, indicate the likelihood of your being able to perform or adopt the skill into your life. Indicate with:

V = Very likely   N = Not sure   U = Unlikely

_____	_____	Nurture a personal strength area
_____	_____	Improve decision-making skills
_____	_____	Shift toward a more internal locus of control
_____	_____	Increase my sense of empowerment
_____	_____	Increase my assertiveness
_____	_____	Improve my communication skills
_____	_____	Increase the number of my self-actualization traits
_____	_____	Reduce the excessive use of inappropriate self-defense mechanisms (substitute a better coping skill)
_____	_____	Increase my value/behavior congruence

(Continued on page 3.27)

LIFESTYLE CONTRACT

V = Very likely   N = Not sure   U = Unlikely

_____ _____ Be more open with my emotional self (or reduce openness)
_____ _____ Practice rational self-counseling
_____ _____ Practice imagery
_____ _____ Exercise at appropriate times to reduce stress
_____ _____ Learn and practice yoga
_____ _____ If frustrated, do goal analysis and substitution
_____ _____ Practice time management
_____ _____ Do thought stopping
_____ _____ Plan and do relaxation days or times
_____ _____ Reduce the consumption of nutritional stimulants (caffeine, nicotine, and others)
_____ _____ Practice progressive relaxation at appropriate times
_____ _____ Learn to say no when appropriate
_____ _____ Avoid exposure to loud noises and crowds
_____ _____ Do self-talk
_____ _____ Practice concentration skills
_____ _____ Do self-esteem-enhancing strategies
_____ _____ Ask for help if you feel out of control or helpless

The best behaviors to accomplish in your lifestyle contract are those with both an X and a V by them.

In the lifestyle contract that follows and is described in detail in chapter 1, the behaviors that will likely be selected will come from this list, since this contract is geared for the content in chapters 1–3. Lifestyle contracts will also follow the other parts of this book. You may choose a process goal, such as refocusing your life to work for a specific cause or purpose in your life, to increase your readiness for change, or do some exercises to increase your sense of empowerment.

The lifestyle contract that follows here will take some time to complete and should be done after some serious reflection on where you are going in your life and what you want to accomplish or be in life. Refer to chapter 1 for detailed guidance in this process.

Lifestyle Contracting Using Strength Intervention

I. Choosing the desired health behavior or skill.
  A. Check factors that you have considered before making the behavioral selection (your contract may be doing one of these).
    1. Is my purpose, cause, or goal better realized by the adoption of this behavior?
      _____ yes   _____ no

    2. Am I hardy enough to accomplish this goal?
      _____ yes   _____ no
    3. Do I feel that I can really acquire or accomplish this behavior?
      _____ yes   _____ no
    4. Do I first need to nurture a personal strength area?
      _____ yes   _____ no
    5. Do I need to free myself from the negative effects of a behavior (break a bad habit)?
      _____ yes   _____ no
    6. Do I want to optimize my potential by adopting a behavior?
      _____ yes   _____ no
    7. Have I considered the results of the assessments in the previous chapters?
      _____ yes   _____ no
  B. Behaviors I will change (no more than two)

    _____

    _____

II. Lifestyle Plan
  A. A description of the general plan of what I am going to do and how I will accomplish it (you may want to consider apperceptive experiences or successes in the past)

    _____

    _____

    _____

    _____

    _____

    _____

  B. Barriers to accomplishment of the plan (lack of time, facilities, motivation, or others)

    1. Identify _____

    _____

    _____

    2. Means to remove barriers (use problem-solving skills or creative approaches as described in chapter 3)

    _____

    _____

  C. Implementation of the plan (refer to the lifestyle analysis form in chapter 1)

Aging, Death, and Dying

CHAPTER 4

Healthy Aging

KEY QUESTIONS

What is aging?

What is the nature of the older population?

Is the percentage of the population that is elderly higher today than in the past?

What are some things that often occur, both mentally and physically, to older persons?

Why is it important for young adults to understand the process of aging?

What are some theories of aging?

What are some guidelines to healthful aging?

What are some resources for older people to get help for health-care costs and services?

How can you combat ageism?

How can you assure healthy aging?

CHAPTER OUTLINE

Healthy People 2000 Objectives

- Increase the years of healthy life to at least 65 years (baseline 62 years in 1980).

- Reduce hip fractures among people aged 65 and older so that hospitalizations for this condition are not more than 620 per 100,000 people (baseline 714 per 100,000 in 1988).

The following was a typical day for Larry Lewis of San Francisco: Larry woke up in the morning and jogged 5 to 7 miles through Golden Gate Park. He then walked to work, where he was on his feet most of the day working as a waiter, logging an additional 5 to 6 miles. In a senior olympics track meet, Larry ran the 100-yard dash in 17 seconds. This is not all that exceptional, until you consider that Larry was 103 years of age ("Run Dick, Run Jane" 1974). Bernice Nelson walks for an hour a day, bakes bread and cookies, drives her car, raises and cans vegetables, plays games and puts complicated jigsaw puzzles together with the neighborhood children, gives 30 or more service hours a week to her church, and does quilting marathons. Bernice is 80. Stephen Powelson, a 70-year-old man, has memorized twenty-two of the twenty-four books of Homer's *Iliad,* in Greek (Galvin 1988). Madge Rugg volunteers at a nursing home and helps, to use her words, the "little old ladies." Madge is in her eighties; some of her patients are in their seventies.

These people are role models of optimal health of the mind, body, and soul and in their relationships. These outstanding individuals demonstrate that if people have dreams and goals, and practice good mental and physical habits, **aging** can be positive. For many people it is a stressor to face the fact that we age—some have trouble accepting a few wrinkles or losing their skill in sports or their youthful figure. Some dimensions of aging cannot be changed, and it is healthy to accept those changes; but people also can maximize their potentials of mind, body, and soul with time and through repeated resilient adaptation to life experiences. Many will be able to age gracefully and productively like Larry Lewis, Bernice Nelson, Stephen Powelson, and Madge Rugg.

This chapter will focus on how to gain a healthy perspective on aging—something that is missing in many pockets of our society. Aging is a part of all life, and creative and healthful aging is the process of leading a healthy lifestyle and practicing wise consumer habits. The process of preparing for healthy and productive aging begins in youth. Healthy aging is as natural and important in your life now as it will be when you are older. Some of you who are reading this book are exemplifying a healthy aging process—you are older students back in school and taking courses for your own enrichment. Without the process of aging, people would miss out on much of the variety that comes with changing physical and psychological experiences in the world.

THE MULTIDIMENSIONAL PERSPECTIVE ON AGING

Sometimes aging is defined negatively, focusing only on the body and observing some obvious decline. Here is an example of a definition of aging that focuses on the body: "[Aging is a] post maturational process that correlates over time with increasing functional losses" (Phillips and Gaylord 1985). Simpler definitions say that aging is something like "the process of becoming physiologically and mentally older." In this book, aging is viewed as a multidimensional process during which, in many of the dimensions of health, one can become stronger or purer. Even in the dimensions of health in which people do not grow stronger in older years, such as the physical dimension, people can optimize their abilities within the limitations that arise from aging.

For an example of a dimension in which people can grow stronger with age, consider the health of the soul. In religious literature, both Western and Eastern, spiritual enhancement is viewed as a refining process. Over time, repeated experiences of the soul gradually enhance the spirituality of the individual. Those that live the longest have the greatest opportunity to refine their souls.

The mind can also be enhanced with age if it is not afflicted with disease. In most cultures, wisdom is viewed as a product of age and experience. The more decisions and outcomes a person experiences, the better prepared she or he is to make wise decisions in the future. Elders are often sought out for that wisdom. It is unfortunate that our society, on the whole, does not tap the valuable resources of the elderly.

Likewise, interdependence skills can be refined and maintained if they are continually used. Some of the most graceful, gracious, and mentally competent people in our society are well past retirement age. In Hispanic, African American, and other cultures that value extended family relationships, it is the grandparents that many children remember as exemplary role models and nurturers.

A thorough understanding of the multidimensional view of health leads to the conclusion that aging is desirable. It is through experience and time that people reach their full potential. Many of the rich human resources in our society are found in older people living in retirement homes. This chapter will focus on this precious human resource and how students can develop lifestyles now that will help them reach their potentials in their later years.

THE GROWING ELDERLY POPULATION

The number of people who are reaching retirement age and living longer is growing rapidly. Most of this group are also enjoying a higher quality of life now, with retirement communities and centers.

Older Americans, those 65 years and older, numbered 31.5 million people in 1990, or about one in every eight Americans. There are 18.7 million older women, compared to 12.8 million older men, with women still outliving men. In the year 1900 only 4 percent of the population in the United States were over 65, and only 0.2 percent were over 85. Now 12.8 percent are over 65 years of age, and 1.3 percent are over 85. By the year 2050, when many of you will be retired, 22.9 percent of the population will be over 65 (Logue 1993).

aging
The process of growing older.

Life expectancy was 59.3 years in 1930. It had risen to 69.6 years by 1954 and 74.7 years by 1985. For females the 1985 life expectancy was 78.2 years, and for males it was 71.2 years. Life expectancy for blacks was 69.5 years, and for whites it was 75.3 years (Siegel 1993).

The baby-boom generation is rapidly progressing toward retirement, and estimates are that 21.8 percent of the population, or 65.5 million Americans, will be over the age of 65 by the year 2030 (U.S. Bureau of the Census 1989). In light of the increasing numbers, it has been noted by many that the elderly are becoming a major social, political, and economic factor in our society. Today our older people are more educated, predominantly female, usually still in households, and mostly not in the workforce.

There are numerous reasons that Americans are living longer, including better medical care, better nutrition and fitness practices, and the vitality of retirement communities. This is a compliment to educational programs and medical science, and it is valuable information for younger people who want to have healthy elderly years. There are still many unanswered questions about the aging process that, when answered, will help others to grow old in a healthy manner. People who study the needs and impact of the elderly are called **gerontologists,** and their field is called **gerontology.** Gerontologists work with concern, care, and understanding to understand and effectively deal with the emotional, social, physical, mental, and spiritual needs of the elderly.

THE NATURE OF AGING

Gerontologists have discovered a good deal about the aging process. The following sections describe the physical aspects of aging, the mental aging process, some theories about why people age, and some interesting ongoing research to better understand the aging process. It is important to note that the characteristics described here do not necessarily apply to all older people. Many older people remain energetic and mentally alert until their death, and many others experience some of the negative effects of aging.

With increasing numbers of older people, millions of dollars each year are granted to study the aging process. The following are some of the areas that are being studied to see why people might lose some functions in these areas due to aging:

- Vision can decrease in color range, intensity, distance, width of field, and adaptability to darkness. This usually begins in our forties.
- Hearing loss begins at approximately age 20 and is progressive. As we grow older, we begin to lose our capacity to hear particular sound frequencies, especially the very high and very low frequencies.
- Other sensory areas are affected as well. The balance center (cochlea) becomes less sensitive, and people may lose their balance more often. Taste buds become less sensitive, and the number of buds declines. Touch sensations may also diminish.

- Psychomotor skills—the ability to move and coordinate muscle groups—can decline.
- Reaction time—the time it takes to receive a sensory stimulus and have muscle groups respond—increases.
- Speed and accuracy of movement decrease (Woollacott and Manchester 1993).
- Learning skills decrease slightly (Crook, Larrabee, and Youngjohn 1993).
- Memory skills decrease slightly (Fisher and McDowd 1993).
- Problem-solving abilities can decline.
- Creativity levels can diminish.
- Habit patterns can become more rigid; that is, we tend to persist in our habitual ways rather than adapt flexibly to new experiences and technology.
- Hunger drives are diminished; older people have smaller appetites than younger people.
- Sexual drives may decrease.
- Activity levels may decline.
- Nutritional needs change. Besides the adult RDAs, older people also need more calcium, vitamin B6, and vitamin B12 (because the aging body absorbs and utilizes these nutrients less efficiently) and must have adequate intakes of folacin, zinc, magnesium, and vitamin D (Andres and Hallfrisch 1989).

Many researchers feel that, for many of these functions, loss is a product of disuse. Some of the physical symptoms do not appear until retirement, when the person stops exercising, reading, or actively listening. Older people who continue to use the physical skills related to their former trade rarely lose their ability to perform similar skills.

DISEASES OF THE ELDERLY

Some physical diseases—most notably osteoporosis and Alzheimer's—are feared by the elderly. Do the Health Assessment exercise on page 4.6 to determine your risk for bone loss. The habits you acquire in youth can affect whether you get osteoporosis in old age.

Osteoporosis
Although whether a person will develop the disease is determined earlier in life, **osteoporosis** shows up mainly among the elderly, or, more specifically, postmenopausal women.

gerontologist
One who studies aging.

gerontology
The study of aging.

osteoporosis
A loss of bone material that can result in a loss of bone mass.

Risk for Bone Loss

Directions

Check off the categories that apply to you:

_____ 1. Postmenopausal woman and not taking estrogen.

_____ 2. Premenopausal woman.

_____ 3. Over 70 years of age.

_____ 4. Between 60 and 69 years of age.

_____ 5. Between 50 and 59 years of age.

_____ 6. Caucasian.

_____ 7. Slight bone frame.

_____ 8. Medium bone frame.

_____ 9. Intake of milk and dairy products is less than an equivalent of two glasses of milk per day (1 ounce cheese = one glass of milk).

_____ 10. Intake of milk and dairy products is an equivalent of two to four glasses of milk per day.

_____ 11. Lifestyle allows you to be exposed to 1 hour of sun per day, or you routinely drink a quart of vitamin D fortified milk per day.

_____ 12. Regular vigorous exercise four times per week or a physically demanding job (loading, walking stairs, and so on).

_____ 13. Your water supply is fluoridated or you take a supplement of 1 milligram per day.

_____ 14. You take glococortides for long-term treatment of asthma or rheumatoid arthritis, or you take anticonvulsive drugs for long-term treatment of seizure disorder.

Scoring

Total your points as follows for the items you checked:

Add 1 point for each: numbers 2, 5, 6, 8, 10
Add 2 points for each: numbers 1, 4, 7, 9
Add 3 points for each: number 3
Subtract 1 point for each: numbers 11, 12, 13

Interpretation

8 or more = You are at high risk for bone-loss disability
4–7 = You are at moderate risk for bone-loss disability
0–3 = You are at low risk for bone-loss disability

Osteoporosis is "a decrease in bone mass leading to an increased risk of fractures after minimal trauma" (Dempster and Lindsay 1993). Over 20 million people in the United States have osteoporosis, and it is the leading cause of hip fractures (Dempster and Lindsay 1993). About 700,000 fractures a year are attributed to osteoporosis. The primary risk factors associated with osteoporosis include consuming too little calcium, lack of exercise, lack of estrogen therapy for postmenopausal women, smoking, and drinking alcohol (Lindsay 1993). Other contributing factors include excessive protein consumption and lack of fluoride.

Asthenia/Cachexia

A syndrome called asthenia/cachexia manifests itself in the "wasting away" of a person, with obvious signs such as frequent falling, weight loss, decreased activity, and decreased food intake, and some less obvious signs such as poor wound-healing, recurrent infections, and ulcers (Verdery 1990). Sometimes the process can't be reversed, but in most cases, depending upon which of the many possible causes it is due to, reversal can occur. Some caregivers do not attempt to turn asthenia/cachexia around and merely let the person waste away.

Alzheimer's Disease and Other Dementias

The mental disease most dreaded by the elderly is **dementia,** and in particular **Alzheimer's disease.** Perhaps the most emotionally draining and demanding disease of the elderly, dementia is the loss of mental functions in an alert and awake individual, characterized by a group of symptoms including recent memory loss, loss of language functions, inability to think abstractly, inability to care for oneself, personality change, emotional instability, and loss of a sense of time or place. Dementia results from numerous causes. Three-quarters of all cases of dementia are caused by Alzheimer's disease (55% to 65% of cases) and strokes.

Alzheimer's disease is a chronic, degenerative, dementing illness, the cause of which is not yet known. No cure or intervention has been discovered yet to stop the progression of the disease. Research is being done that might identify genetic potentials for Alzheimer's (Toufexis 1993), and there is speculation that chemical imbalances might cause the disease (Baum 1993). Interventions such as music therapy have been shown to have some value (Lord and Garner 1993).

Specific symptoms in Alzheimer's patients include memory loss and intellectual impairment, wandering and agitation, depression, delusions, and family stress (Light and Lebowitz 1989).

---

dementia

A loss of mental functions, including memory loss, loss of language functions, inability to think abstractly, personality change, or inability to care for oneself.

Alzheimer's disease

A dementia marked by a distinctive, detectable loss or change of nerve cells.

More than seventy conditions can cause dementia. The following are some of the varieties of dementias, and their causes:

1. Dementias from degenerative diseases: Alzheimer's disease, Parkinson's disease, Huntington's disease, and others
2. Vascular dementia: cerebral embolisms, blood clotting, infarctions
3. Anoxic dementia: cardiac arrest, cardiac failure, carbon monoxide poisoning
4. Traumatic dementia: head injuries
5. Infectious dementia: AIDS, herpes, encephalitis, meningitis, brain abscess, neurosyphilis
6. Space-occupying lesions: brain tumors, hematomas, cancers, and other space-occupying lesions
7. Toxic dementias: alcohol, poisons
8. Others: epilepsy, posttraumatic stress disorders, heat stroke, multiple sclerosis, other autoimmune disorders, and others

Today, an estimated 2 million Americans suffer from severe dementia, which means that someone must care for them continually. An additional 1 to 5 million have mild or moderate dementia. There has been a dramatic increase in the number of cases of dementia: There are ten times as many people affected today as there were at the turn of the century. It is expected that there will be 60 percent more people affected in the year 2000 than there are today, and five times as many by the year 2040, when many college students reading this text will be at the susceptible ages (Toufexis 1993).

The progression of the disease varies with each case, but generally the disease is noticed by family, friends, or coworkers, and not the physician. Although sometimes the disease appears suddenly, most cases develop slowly and almost imperceptibly at first. A minor loss of memory, mental ability, or judgment that gets progressively worse is a common scenario.

The emotional and financial drain on families is enormous. On the average, an afflicted person lives with Alzheimer's disease for 8½ years before dying; some afflicted people have required 25 years of constant care before their death. The effects on family caregivers include diminished time for oneself, anger, and financial drain. In extended families and in cultures that tend toward extended families (particularly Hispanic and African American), where emotional ties extend to relatives (grandparents, uncles, aunts, cousins, etc.) outside the nuclear family, there tends to be a predominant belief that the caregiver could always be doing more and better.

To help those who must care for someone with dementia, national organizations, such as the Alzheimer's Disease and Related Disorders Association (ADRDA), have been formed to provide support. National attention has focused on the disease, which has been described in news magazines, films, talk shows, and several books. Dementia is becoming one of the most dreaded diseases of our elderly now and is projected to become an even more prevalent problem in the future.

MENTAL AGING

People who are well prepared for the mental aspects of aging and old age will be happier as they age than those who are not well prepared for it. Many people describe the negative effects of aging from a psychological perspective. When there is a greater understanding of why people age, some of the diseases may be eliminated.

In many cases, these results are apparent when visiting with older people. The negative aspect of mental aging is the focus on loss. The truth is that mental aging is largely in the control of the individual. Actively using the senses and emotions, having a positive outlook on life, and planning for old age will keep many people mentally vital. Only in the cases of disease will some of these functions be lost.

When physiological losses occur, some people experience a loss of control and autonomy. The inability to get somewhere, perform a task, or even remember something can result in frustration. The older we get, more family members and friends have died, and the loss of lifelong loved ones can be difficult to cope with. Another loss may occur when, because of medical problems, the elderly person needs constant monitoring. The elderly person may need to go to a nursing or retirement home, which results in a loss of privacy.

On the positive side, people who are prepared for old age will be able to cope because many of the losses will be avoided. Good financial planning will result in being able to keep a house and have a regular income. The aging process can be seen as a gain for the mentally healthy person—a gain of time and opportunity to see the world or develop new hobbies and interests. Many people start new businesses after retirement. Although there may be deaths of close friends and relatives, the socially active elderly person will have a strong support system to help him or her cope.

SEXUALITY AND THE ELDERLY

Until recently it was commonly believed that the loss of sexuality is characteristic of old age. But mental aging does not include the loss of the desire to be loved, to be nurtured, and to give love. One study of people 60 to 91 years of age reported that 83 percent were still sexually active (Botwinick 1984).

Males might show a gradual decline of sexual interest with age, but their sex drive does not cease unless they have decided to let it cease. It can take older males a longer period of time to have an erection and to ejaculate, but, barring organic problems, they are still quite capable of sexual intercourse at any age. Many times, men experience the "self-fulfilling prophecy" phenomenon; that is, they have erectile failure just because they have been given to believe,

Older individuals have needs to give and receive love and to be nurtured; sexual activity among the elderly is much more prevalent than society acknowledges.

by society, that sexual activity is for young people and that "dirty old men" should not be sexually active. Men who ignore such views can have long and enjoyable sexual lives.

Women's sexual activity generally does not decline until after age 60, and then it might decline only gradually. Many women become less sexually active merely because they do not have a sexual partner or their partners are no longer sexually active. Many women still masturbate. One survey showed that 88 percent of older women can still achieve orgasm (Botwinick 1984).

MENOPAUSE

Women's feelings about menopause have a bearing on their degree of sexual activity. **Menopause**—the end of menstruation—clearly signals to a woman that her reproductive years are over. This life change means different things to different women. Some feel a great sense of relief, and a sense of great freedom, that they no longer have to use birth control to avoid pregnancy. As a result, their sexual interest increases. Unfortunately, other women perceive menopause as a loss of their feminine identity and a loss of purpose; for these

women menopause can be followed by depression and major life disruption. Their interest in sexual activity might decrease, at least until psychological adaptation has occurred. After menopause, a woman's body produces less estrogen, and the shortage of estrogen can contribute to a decrease in bone density and osteoporosis. Many women take oral supplements of estrogen to reduce the impact of estrogen loss on bone density.

THEORIES ABOUT AGING

It is easy to observe the external bodily changes that occur with aging, but it is not so easy to pinpoint why these changes occur. Many theories have been proposed to explain the natural phenomenon of aging, but none has been proved to be the only correct one. Researchers are studying a variety of approaches to understand why we age. Animal studies include taking tissue and organs from old animals and transplanting them in young animals to see if this shortens the recipient's life span. Organs from young animals are also transplanted into old animals to see if this extends the life span of the older animals. Other approaches include studying brain size and longevity, environmental temperatures, metabolism rates, restricting caloric intake, cell reproduction, and genetic structure and changes.

A classic experiment performed by Hayflick (Finch and Schneider 1985) showed that in vitro human skin and lung cells could divide and replicate only a limited number of times before entering a phase in which cell chromosomes mutated and no longer faithfully replicated themselves. Cells would divide 35 to 63 times before reaching this stage. Cells from older people divided fewer times than the average. This study and many others have resulted in the following partial list of biological theories of aging.

1. Brain size theory. The idea that brain size determines longevity is based on studies comparing body and brain sizes of eighty-five animal species.
2. Biological clock(s) theory. This theory is that a biological or genetic clock or clocks predetermine how long we will live (Dice 1993).
3. Disposable soma theory. This theory suggests that aging results from the allocation of resources (e.g., intake of energy) among the various tasks to be performed by the body (e.g., growth, foraging, defense, repair). The optimal condition is to allocate as little energy as possible to somatic (body) repair and divert most energy to other functions. Over time, the need for repair becomes evident and, in the end, insurmountable, which is reflected as aging and death.
4. Pleiotropy theory. Pleiotropic genes are those that might have good effects in a young body but become harmful

menopause
The cessation of menstruation.

later in life due to a mutation or change. For example, a gene might play a positive role in the calcification of bone during early development but contribute to the calcification of arteries in later life.

5. Wear-and-tear theory. The body is much like a machine in that it can't be designed so that it won't break down. This theory supposes that, through constant use, cells, tissues, or whole organs just break down through several means, such as accumulated damage or genetic error.

6. Genetic theories. According to one of several genetic theories of aging, over time the body's cells lose the genetic information required to make the proteins necessary to rebuild the body.

7. Immunological theories. Scientists have also proposed theories linking aging to the immune system. Two of these theories suggest that the immune system is, in a sense, destroying the body from within. According to a third, the immune system might simply lose its vigor and no longer be able to fight off disease.

8. Error accumulation theory. The accumulation of harmful metabolic wastes implies that certain compounds are formed for which the cells have inadequate removal mechanisms (Dice 1993).

9. Cell-loss theory. The cell-loss theory supposes that the daily rate at which cells die varies for each individual and determines our longevity.

10. Nutritive theories. Animal experiments demonstrate that cutting down on food consumption by taking in only essential vitamins, minerals, and proteins prolongs life radically. As a result, some suggest that our nutritive habits contribute to how rapidly we age.

11. Environmental theories. Water pollution, radiation, the declining ozone layer, smog, and so forth may cause cells to be destroyed or cell walls to break down, thereby speeding the aging process.

12. Brain chemistry theory. According to the brain chemistry theory, aging is directly related to chemicals that transmit messages in the brain. With age, the number of transmitters decreases, which prevents the important centers in the brain from signaling other areas to produce the hormones necessary for bodily functions.

13. Cross-linking. Outward aging occurs as increasing numbers of proteins join connective-tissue fiber molecules in the skin, which forms wrinkles.

AGEISM

Understanding aging requires understanding not only the physical and mental aspects of aging but also its social aspects. The next sections discuss ageism and stereotyping, ageism and retirement, combating the stereotypes of old age, and combating ageism.

People can live happy, productive lives into their older years.

AGEISM AND STEREOTYPING

Ageism, discrimination based on age, is a powerful, socially reinforced prejudice in this society. Ageism is often a product of stereotyping—shared, conventional expectations about how people in a certain group behave, think, and relate. For instance, when an athlete on a sport scholarship walks into class, other students are likely to assume that person is "not too bright," "interested only in sports," and so forth. Stereotyping affects the way people vote, raise children, select doctors, teach in schools, and make other decisions.

The concepts of "young" and "old" as well as of "healthy" and "unhealthy" are defined in Western culture as polar opposites. If people value youth, they are not likely to also value old age. If people value activity and productivity, they probably do not also value physical restriction or a slower pace. A person who is seen as a competent, productive, healthy executive at the age of 69 might, one year later, at the age of 70, be seen as fickle, over-the-hill, out-of-date, senile, and unhealthy and be forced to retire.

Stereotyping is socially unhealthy for optimum human growth; among other things, it ignores individual variation. As a society, we must examine our views of growing older so that we can overcome cultural barriers and promote a healthier perspective on what it means to age in the United States.

AGEISM AND RETIREMENT

Competition for jobs, money, and other resources is fundamental to explaining the existence of ageism in a society

---

ageism
Discrimination based on age.

where productivity and independence are held up as prime measures of the value of human worth and dignity. The elderly no longer compete for jobs and money, and by retirement they are considered dependent and nonproductive. Where does this place the retiree on the Western continuum of human worth? Unfortunately, not at a level of high esteem. Contrast this with Eastern societies in which the elderly are venerated for their experience and wisdom.

COMBATING THE STEREOTYPES OF OLD AGE

One of the best-known organizations formed to combat the strong tendency to stereotype old age is the **Grey Panthers.** This group was formed by Maggie Kuhn in 1970 and now has more than ten thousand members across the nation. The National Institute on Aging was created in 1974 and is now involved in extensive research on the causes of physiological aging and on how to improve the quality of life in all stages of the aging process. As the percentage of older people in our communities continues to grow, the role of such organizations as the National Institute on Aging and the Grey Panthers will also grow.

Upon retirement—reflect on the many associations this word carries—people may experience several traumatic changes. Since the first childhood step, independence has been ingrained in people as an inherent and valued part of individual strength, and retirement signals financial dependence on the Social Security system and pension funds. Retirement can be a visible declaration to supportive children that it is now their turn to take care of their parents. This is not a welcomed concept in Western culture, which so highly values independence and self-sufficiency.

For many people, their job is a major source of their identity, and during the working years people accumulate a valuable store of knowledge that is found only in life, not in textbooks; yet the teaching role is often denied to retirees, those who are often best qualified to give advice on many matters. A good retirement plan should be directed toward building a future and should begin well before the transition into retirement begins. Part of retirement planning should ideally include (1) examining and evaluating one's present situation, (2) determining what satisfaction in retirement means personally, (3) developing short-range plans and a set of goals or objectives, (4) clarifying long-term objectives, and (5) evaluating progress.

It is not surprising that secondary impotence erectile failure due to psychological causes is also experienced by some older men at retirement age. The sense of uselessness and powerlessness they experience from having had to leave the work arena extends into the area of sexual activity. Women, too, suffer particular difficulties. Middle-aged women are often viewed as less desirable than men of the same age. For women, in the United States, a youthful appearance seems to be the most fundamental criterion of beauty, so as a woman's face and body mature, she tends to lose esteem in her own eyes and in those of others.

COMBATING AGEISM

What can be done to help eliminate ageism and make the lives of older people easier? First, we can improve the conditions and health of retired or nearly retired individuals who are having to make age- and work-related adjustments. We can more actively draw on the experience and wisdom of the elderly, and the elderly can actively seek creative outlets for their wisdom.

Second, we can clarify our values regarding independence, competition, and productivity and reexamine the premiums we put on youth and beauty. These values are deeply embedded in the structures of American society. The United States school system is based on competition; there is competition in men's and women's athletics, physical education classes, and recreation as well as in the grading system. Such extracurricular activities as choirs, bands, student body offices, and clubs also promote competition.

Self-actualization is a noncompetitive ideal that people can fully realize only if they have the time to work through Erikson's last life crisis: ego integrity versus despair. It is almost impossible to stand back from one's life and examine it with complete objectivity when one is working, but creative retirement offers the gift of unprogrammed time in which to fully realize this ultimate challenge of assessing, owning, and giving true meaning to one's life activities. As such, it is as important as any competitive undertaking or external productivity.

Third, we can see giving and receiving nurturing as both a masculine and a feminine characteristic and can equally value giving and receiving. Men who learn to nurture others may find it easier to receive nurturing whenever they need it, especially in their later years.

Spirituality and a sense of meaning and purpose in life are important values to be considered in the prevention of ageism. This seems to be particularly true for those who are approaching death and reaching out to deeper dimensions for comfort and strength. Spiritual experiences can be evoked through music, meditation, reading, religious activity, and the natural world, but often they arise through our contact with others who have experienced their own spirituality. Older people usually have come to terms with the last developmental crisis, and association with them helps prepare us for our own resolution of this crisis.

HELPING THE ELDERLY

When the elderly quit working and lose the ability to care for themselves in their older years, then the government and the family have some responsibility to help them. The following are current approaches to care.

Grey Panthers
A political organization designed to combat ageism and old-age stereotyping.

MEDICARE: GOVERNMENT AID TO THE ELDERLY

Even people who practice healthful living can have medical problems. With many elderly not able to afford medical care, the government has developed the **Medicare** program. Medicare is the largest health insurance program in the country for people of age 65 and older, disabled people under Social Security, and individuals with end-stage renal disease. Medicare, with its sister program Medicaid (health insurance for the poor), was instituted in 1965 by the U.S. Congress. The program has done much to reduce the financial burdens of the elderly and to allow them access to state-of-the-art health-care services. It has an annual federal budget of over $75 billion, and nearly 30 million elderly and disabled citizens benefit from it. Medicare is not free to the elderly—they must purchase the insurance much like other policies, except at more reasonable rates.

Historical increases in health-care expenditures, and a changing political and economic picture, have set the groundwork for major reforms in Medicare. In 1983, Congress enacted the prospective payment system (PPS), which is similar to the payment system for health maintenance organizations—with prepaid, fixed payments, rather than retrospective payments for services rendered. The Health Care Financing Administration, which oversees Medicare, is currently trying to contract with employer self-insurance plans, unions, and group health insurance companies so that in the future Medicare beneficiaries can elect to obtain Medicare coverage through their group insurance plans rather than through traditional Medicare, with the government paying the premiums. Attempts are also being made to price Medicare, which is currently based on average costs per patient, with new systems that would adjust the price of payment to the individual's health status.

With the number of elderly using Medicare increasing, these innovations in policy will affect young people, the future users of Medicare (Rovner 1991). People who take care of their health while they are young will probably be healthier in their senior years and will have financial benefits in terms of health-care premiums.

The current system in Medicare, with all of its benefits, is still inadequate, particularly in the area of preventive care. The costs of a physical exam that might detect a disease in its early stages would require a patient to pay an annual deductible amount plus a portion of the remaining costs. On a Social Security income of a few hundred dollars a month—where money must be spent on food and shelter—physical exams, eyeglasses, hearing aids, and other preventive measures are "luxuries" beyond many elderly people's budgets.

OPTIONS FOR CARE

What happens when people you love, such as parents or grandparents, become debilitated, perhaps as an indirect result of old age, and need care? Providing constant care is a difficult responsibility that requires an outlay of time, energy,

Issue
Social Security

Those of you who work will notice that a large portion of your check often goes to Social Security. Social Security is the way the government provides living expenses for the elderly. The idea is that when we are young, we put money into the Social Security system so that when we get older there will be some security there for us. A chief economic issue is that, with the increasing numbers of older people retiring, Social Security resources are very strained. The money you pay in now is not going into your security, but paying for someone's subsistence right now. The hope is that when you reach retirement age, the young will be giving you Social Security. The Social Security system is shaky, and some people have questioned it. Why should you have to pay Social Security now, when in fact the system might not even be in existence when the time comes for you to retire?

- Pro: People should pay it because it is our duty as a society to care for those who can't care for themselves. To stop now would be devastating to some people. If the government had to start paying, it would just have to increase taxes to cover Social Security anyway.

- Con: The Social Security system is not fair. People should be responsible for their own retirement program and plan for their retirement. If they don't, then that is their tough luck and they should rely on families or welfare for existence. Some people get Social Security that don't even need it. The current system has some real problems.

What is your stand on this issue? How can you plan now to avoid a potential economic problem when you retire?

and money. In this society there are three basic options for care of the debilitated elderly: home care by relatives, adult day care, and nursing homes.

Home Care by Relatives

Home care may require that a family member be home at all times. Whether home care is given by an elderly retired spouse or by one of the patient's children—who perhaps might have to quit his or her job to care for the parent—the financial resources of the caregiver can be seriously reduced by the demands of home care. All the same, many people choose the option of home care because they want to be sure that the ailing person's needs for love and care are met.

Medicare
A federally administered medical assistance plan for persons over the age of 65.

Residential settings:

In-home services may include home health care, personal care, chore services, and homemaker services to the client's house, apartment, or other residence. Some in-home health services are provided by home health-care agencies, most of which are certified by Medicare and must meet federal standards for staffing and range of services. Other services are provided by community agencies funded by federal, state, and local governments or nongovernmental organizations. Such agencies are generally not licensed or regulated.

Nursing homes are health-care facilities that provide 24-hour care, nursing, and personal services in an institutional setting. Most are certified to provide care under Medicare and Medicaid to eligible residents, and are regulated by states, subject to federal and state standards.

Board-and-care facilities are nonmedical residential care facilities that provide room and board and variable degrees of protective supervision and personal care. These range in size from foster care units with a few residents to large domiciliary facilities that house several hundred people. Many board-and-care facilities are licensed by state governments, but regulations are generally limited to physical structure and fire safety rather than patient care.

State mental hospitals are generally large state-funded institutions that provide acute and long-term psychiatric care primarily for mentally ill people, but also for some patients with dementia— especially those with behavioral symptoms that are difficult to manage.

Hospitals are facilities for medical care of those temporarily residing in them. The primary services available are diagnosis and treatment, but hospitals also often serve as foci for rehabilitation, case management, counseling, and family support. They may also be affiliated with nursing homes, day-care centers, home health agencies, or other settings and services.

Hospices are facilities for the care of terminally ill people. The emphasis in hospices is on alleviating symptoms and providing personal support, rather than cure and rehabilitation. Hospice services can be delivered in other settings, if the intent is to diminish suffering rather than prolong life.

Nonresidential settings:

Adult day-care centers are day treatment facilities, some of which provide intensive medical, physical, or occupational therapy. Others provide primarily social activities and personal services for several hours during the day. Adult day-care centers are licensed by some states, and must meet fire and safety codes of local jurisdictions, but are not subject to federal regulation unless they provide services reimbursed by Medicare or Medicaid.

Community mental health centers are psychiatric and psychological treatment facilities that provide a variety of mental health services for people with acute and chronic mental illnesses. Most services are provided on an outpatient basis. Most centers were originally developed in accordance with federal regulations tied to federal funding but are now regulated by states and funded by them, supplemented by federal funding through Mental Health Block Grants.

Outpatient facilities and clinics are medical settings for diagnosis and treatment of diseases. They may also become involved in delivering other services such as case management and counseling.

Senior centers are facilities intended for use by older Americans. They are often funded by a combination of private charity and local, state, and federal government contributions. Day care, recreational activities, family support, case management, and mental health services are available at some but not all senior centers.

Figure 4.1

Residential and nonresidential settings for the care of the elderly.

Source: From Office of Technology Assessment, 1986.

Geriatric or Adult Day Care

Many communities have day-care centers for older people; these are similar in function to those for children. People receive care during the day but are home alone or with families in the evening. This frees the family to work while ensuring that the elderly person's needs for love, responsibility, and companionship are satisfied.

Nursing Homes

Many people have determined that they can't provide adequate home care for older people and so have placed them in nursing homes. Nursing homes generally provide adequate complete physical care if needed, but they might not satisfy their clients' psychological and emotional needs.

For information about other settings for care for the elderly, see figure 4.1.

AGING: MYTHS VERSUS FACTS

Ageism is promoted largely by myths. It is hard to say exactly how some of these myths started, but most of them probably arose during times when disease was not as well controlled as it is now and older people were more subject to illness and infection. Following are some of the most prevalent myths about aging and the actual facts (Atchley 1980). How many of these myths have you believed?

- Myth 1: Aging causes death.
- Fact: Deaths are caused by accidents and disease, not by aging. The phrase *dying of old age* is accurate only in an indirect sense.

- Myth 2: Intellectual deterioration (senility) is inevitable.
- Fact: People who are intelligent during their middle years will probably be intelligent until they die.

- Myth 3: Old people lose interest in, and can't participate in, sex.
- Fact: Our needs for love, touching, closeness, and intimacy are basic in all developmental stages, including old age.

- Myth 4: Old people are ugly and unattractive.
- Fact: Many people who might have been considered unattractive as children or as adults actually become more attractive with age. A lively, happy person invariably radiates the beauty of personality. If all we perceive in older people is grayness and wrinkles, how will others see us when we are that age?

Volunteering in the community is one way older people remain socially active.

Issue
Aging in the East

Eastern countries' views of aging radically differ from Western views. In countries such as Japan, the older a family member grows, the more respect the family gives that member. In fact, in some places elderly parents set all the rules for the house, and all children living in the house, whether married with their own children or not, must abide by these rules, as must any spouses who have married into the family.

- Pro: The Eastern treatment of older people gives them respect for their life experience, assures them of care in their old age, and allows each family to care for its own members rather than expecting the family to care for strangers through the taxation process.

- Con: The Eastern treatment of older people is fine for the older people, but it prevents younger people, even those in middle age, from living their own lives to the fullest. Instead of fully developing their potential and giving their talents to the community at large, they are obliged to use all their energy and time on one or two people. They never acquire a sense of their own independence.

What is your opinion? Which system would you rather live under? At what age?

- Myth 5: Retirement causes people to get sick and die earlier than they would have had they not retired.
- Fact: Ill health is a major cause of retirement, but retirement does not cause ill health or mortality.

- Myth 6: Older people are neglected by their families. They tend to be geographically isolated from their children, and when they become disabled or ill, they are forced to enter nursing homes.
- Fact: A minority of families do become separated, but it is a misconception that all family ties are breaking down.

- Myth 7: Older patients have little in the way of recuperative powers.
- Fact: People generally vary in their ability to heal; some people in their eighties heal very well, while some in their thirties do not.

- Myth 8: Older people are old-fashioned and out of touch with the real world.
- Fact: Most company presidents, full professors, renowned writers, and leaders in most professions are near retirement age. Most of these leaders still consult for years after their retirement.

- Myth 9: All people tend to age at the same rate.
- Fact: In reality, people age at different functional rates of the mind, body, and soul; chronological age is not a factor.

- Myth 10: The aged are declining, disinterested, and disengaged.
- Fact: Elderly people are very interested in various areas, are tuned into others and world problems, and like to stay active.

- Myth 11: In their old age, people become inflexible and will not change even when presented with good reasons to.
- Fact: Some older people may seem unreasonable or inflexible because they have developed their particular personality traits and patterns over many years, but this relates only indirectly to chronological age.

- Myth 12: Old people are sweet, understanding, and tranquil.
- Fact: Elderly people have the same range of temperaments as any other age group.

Knowing the facts about aging makes it clear that with positive lifestyle habits we can live happy, productive lives even into our older years.

PERSONAL INSIGHT

Discovering the Wisdom of the Elderly

Many times we classify active, vital older people as good examples of healthy aging and those that are bedridden in nursing homes as poor examples of old age. Sometimes this perception is hard to change. The physical body might be in poor condition, but often the person's mental, social, spiritual, and intellectual capabilities are strong. Consider the following insight:

Tonight I had the opportunity to take twenty-five Cub Scouts to the Life Care Center to sing Christmas carols to the elderly. The boys wandered down the hallway and gave gifts they had made to each of the thirty-three residents. We were invited in many rooms and sang all five songs that we had practiced when they were wanted. I was particularly impressed with one woman who appeared to be in her nineties and was very sick. She was lying on her side and unable to even move under her own power. Her gray hair, bagging skin, and sunken eyes at first made her look so worn and tired, and ready to die. She had loose food in her mouth, which she had been apparently trying to swallow for some time since there was no food tray around. It appeared that most of her nourishment came through a tube in her arm. I was almost hesitant to enter, but when I asked if she would like to hear some carols, she whispered, "Yes." The boys came in hesitantly, but I encouraged them. They started to sing "Silent Night." They sounded particularly good this time as I think they were reverenced by this scene. After singing "Silent Night, Holy Night . . ." I noticed that she started to sing with us. She sang all five of our songs with us. The countenance of the boys changed from hesitancy to enthusiasm, recognizing the response. Her eyes sparkled and when the boys left, she beckoned me. The boys went on singing in other rooms. I stayed. I grabbed her hand, since she could not move it, and she said, "Thank you." In a short five or six minutes, I found a rich source of wisdom and experience. This woman had lived in Russia, crossed the iron curtain in the dead of night in fear of her life shortly after World War II. She stowed away in a ship to arrive in America and earned her citizenship. She loved America, had converted to a Christian church, and was so proud of her life. She told me so much and touched me so deeply. . . .

Source: From G. E. Richardson, excerpt from personal journal, December 16, 1987.

GUIDELINES FOR HEALTHY AGING

It is often assumed that if we live longer, we will enjoy more years of high-quality life. Russell (1989) projects that although people will be living longer in the future, 80 percent of that additional time will be spent sick or disabled. To have better odds of having a high quality of life in the older years, some guidelines should be followed (Roos and Havens 1991). One perspective of healthful aging is proposed by Dychtwald (1989), who suggests that retirement can result in either boredom or a "cycle life." The cycle life is to redo in retirement what occurred in the early part of the life cycle. In other words, people should return to school, change careers, and take part in sports and other skill-enhancement activities.

The conditions for healthy aging apply at any age. Do the Health Assessment exercise to see if you are developing the behaviors that will lead you to a happy, productive old age.

PRINCIPLES OF AGING APPLIED TO THE YOUNG

There are two main purposes to this chapter. The first is for students to improve their relationships with older people by talking with them and learning from them. The elderly have basic needs, just like younger people do, to be needed, to feel secure, to be loved, and to be productive. Younger people can help elderly people to meet those basic needs.

The second purpose is to help young people prepare for their elderly years. It is difficult for most young students to imagine ever being older, but, except for those who lose their lives early, everyone becomes old. Granted, the previous statement is obvious, but many young minds don't quite grasp it. Preparation for the late years begins as a young adult. For instance, the guidelines for successful physical aging apply to students in their youth. Eating right, exercising for a lifetime, controlling stress, avoiding drugs and tobacco, and other healthy behaviors are important.

Planning for retirement is also important. Job hunters should carefully examine retirement programs and benefits. When people retire, it is extremely important that they develop numerous avocational activities. It is obvious to an onlooker which people enjoy retirement and which people don't. Some of us will become "stir crazy" with nothing to do, yet some will create a whole new lifetime of avocational pursuits. With good health, strong relationships, hobbies, financial security, and a dream, people can make their older years a long-awaited, productive, and joyful capstone to life.

Healthy Aging

Directions

Check off all the statements that apply to you.

_____ 1. I accept my leisure and take time to enjoy relaxation.

_____ 2. I am active and exercise regularly. (You can start exercising and benefitting at almost any age if you are able [Fishman, 1993].)

_____ 3. I eat balanced meals and follow a good nutritional program.

_____ 4. I take an interest in life, enjoying nature, meeting others, and maintaining relationships.

_____ 5. I practice controlling my stress levels.

_____ 6. I am learning new skills to write better, play noncompetitive games, do crafts, garden, and so on.

_____ 7. I get adequate sleep but not too much.

_____ 8. I can communicate my feelings openly. (Men especially need to learn freedom of emotional expression; pent-up emotions are stressful.)

_____ 9. I give service for others and find service gratifying, healthy, and rewarding. (Altruism or service is healthy for the soul.)

_____ 10. I have chosen a safe living environment by avoiding pollution, crime areas, and other unsafe and unhealthy environments, if possible.

_____ 11. I add freshness to my life by acting and thinking creatively.

_____ 12. I am continually getting to know myself, and I accept and like who I am.

_____ 13. I have established a unifying philosophy of life, whether it be based on principle or on religion. (Establishing a sense of purpose that causes you to value life and motivates you to be productive is important to healthy aging.)

_____ 14. I have control and manage those areas of my life that are appropriate for me to manage and control (Wallhagen 1993).

_____ 15. I read and go to cultural events.

Interpretation

All of the above are guidelines to healthy aging and really a key to happiness throughout your life. The more you were able to check honestly, the happier you are; and if you continue with these practices, your older years will be more productive and happier as well.

PERSONAL SKILLS AND EXPERIENCES

Visualize Your Aging

Psychoneuroimmunology (PNI) is the study of the interaction of the mind, the central nervous system, and the body's immunological system. It has been shown that people with a dream, fighting spirit, optimism, faith, self-efficacy, and a sense of control can maximize their immune systems to ward off disease. Quality aging throughout your life is an opportunity to live the highest quality of life possible for you. The guidelines for healthy aging are described in this chapter. Try the following imagery exercise.

Imagine yourself graduating from college, selecting an occupation or life's work, and then training to become the best at whatever job you decide to do, be it a trade, a profession, or an unpaid job. Imagine selecting a dream partner—the romance, the emotions, and making a commitment by marriage or other arrangement. Visualize your professional and homemaking skills. Imagine that you become what you want to become in your mid years and have the lifestyle you want.

Imagine now you are approaching old age. Perhaps you decided to have children; visualize those children. Imagine the lifestyle that you would ideally like to have in retirement. Visualize where you would want to live and what activities you would like to do. Look at your mind, your body, and your soul. What kind of social engagement do you imagine?

Living the path that leads to that optimal lifestyle begins now.

PERSONAL SKILLS AND EXPERIENCES

Healthy Aging

Mind

General guidelines to healthy aging were described in the text. The following are some specific skills and experiences of the mind that will help you maximize the quality of your aging process, beginning now.

1. Health insurance: Make sure that you have the financial means to cover any unexpected medical expenses and to have regular physicals.
2. Planning for retirement: When 8 or 10 hours a day is suddenly given back to you when you retire, what will you fall back on? Plan and learn activities for the body, the mind, and the soul.
3. Financial needs: It is very difficult to live on Social Security alone, and you should plan for other income.
4. Estate planning: With time you will probably acquire property and other assets. If you want state law to dictate where your estate will go, then do nothing; but if you want your survivors to benefit without paying a lot to taxes, then estate planning is important.
5. Taking classes: Keep your mind functioning by taking classes.
6. Travel: Enrich your cultural and environmental experiences by traveling.
7. Reading: Stimulate your mind with enriching reading.
8. Watching the Public Broadcasting System and educational channels on television: There are many programs in the arts, sciences, politics, and health to keep you thinking (Solomon et al. 1992).

Body

The following are some specific skills and experiences to keep your body in the best condition possible throughout your life.

1. Play like a little child: Climbing trees, playing active games, doing somersaults, or playing on monkey bars sounds like "kids' stuff," but if adults would do these activities, they would be more flexible, stronger, and in better condition.
2. Learn to enjoy eating high-carbohydrate fruits and vegetables: You can develop a taste for good foods.
3. Select a good physician: Keeping with the same physician over the years will help the doctor notice small changes that may allow for prevention of serious problems.
4. Avocations: Avocations that require activity from your body are important—especially those that you can continue on through the retirement years (golf, tennis, bowling, Ping-Pong, swimming, gardening, and window shopping).
5. Use your body: Do active household chores like washing cars, vacuuming, fixing, cleaning, and making household items (Solomon et al. 1993).

6. Engage in aerobic exercises that you can do lifelong (walking, biking, rowing, dancing, etc.).

Soul

Perhaps the most important dimension of healthy aging is to live your life with heart. If you will establish principles to live by and then, throughout your life, live by those principles, you will experience an inner peace regardless of the condition of your mind and body. Living a life with good feelings and inner peace is difficult for some who are "trying to make a buck." When you live your life with your soul in charge, you are not as concerned about the wrinkles that show up, the body that is not as athletic as it was, or the sags that begin to show. The acquisition of faith, wisdom, and harmony become the indicators of happiness. Try the following imagery exercise.

Try to identify what you are really like at the core. It might help to imagine that the different faces you have had in life are going to be taken away from you. It will be like Halloween masks being taken off one at a time. Imagine the face of how you are supposed to behave as a student—then take it off. Take off the face of negative past experiences that may have soured you on some aspects of life. Get rid of the face you have as a family member. Do the same for all the other faces you might wear in other roles. When you get rid of all those faces, then you see who you really are. See yourself. Are you fun-loving, spontaneous, curious, loving, caring, teachable—much as you were as a child, perhaps, but now as an adult—childlike but not childish? Now imagine living your life as your true self throughout your life.

Interdependence

Some older people complain about being lonely. They find themselves in a retirement community or nursing facility, and visits from loved ones and friends are rare. Some people in our society have a tendency to "burn bridges" and to not nurture relationships. Part of aging healthfully is to continue to have strong social encounters. People who burn bridges find themselves lonely. Here are some guidelines for nurturing interdependent relationships to assure that you will continue relationships into your older years:

1. Socially engage yourself as much as you comfortably can.
2. Nurture family relationships with your parents, siblings, and children, and also with cousins, nephews, in-laws, and friends.
3. Continually "court" your friends and family. Do nice things for them. Make calls, drop them notes, help them when they need and want help.
4. Volunteer at any number of places where you can meet new people.
5. Be altruistic and provide service to neighbors and others. The old-time custom of taking some cookies over to a neighbor is still a good one (Solomon et al. 1993).

THE WORLD AROUND YOU

Combating Cultural Stereotypes

Transcendence has many meanings, but one important meaning is that we can rise above our racial biases and cultural stereotypes. It is fascinating that as children, when the dimensions of the soul are on the surface, we do transcend race and culture. Dimensions of the soul that are evident in childhood include the urges to have fun, to connect, to be loved, to love, to be a helper, to live, to create, and to be free. Little children play with each other, fulfilling these needs, no matter what their skin color or culture. They don't even need a common language.

But it doesn't take long in the school systems and in our society to impose biases. We develop tendencies to socialize with those who are more like us, and we might not really understand other people very well. We stereotype them, and friction sometimes occurs.

As the body begins to get older and we experience loss of optimal functioning, we again begin to find our soul. Soon we see people as people again rather than as a culture or race. We again need help from stronger people, we need to be loved and to connect.

We can see the elderly as a culture rather than as people. If, as the group between being children and being old, we can be like children and play with people regardless of skin color or culture, we will transcend. Rather than looking at old people as being "over the hill," we can look at them as a source of wisdom, experience, and tremendous insights. Culture is not important. The fact that the person is a human soul is. This nation is slowly transcending culture in many pockets of society—most notably at universities. We need to continue to promote that transcendence in the world around us.

TAKE ACTION

1. Make someone's retirement pleasant and rewarding by working on projects with him or her, visiting, traveling together, making things with the person, writing often, and so on.

2. Adopt a grandmother or grandfather at a local rest home, visit periodically, and share some activities (for instance, take him or her to a ball game or a musical).

3. Adopt recreational pursuits that you really enjoy and will be able to do for a lifetime.

SUMMARY

1. Aging is not just a physical experience, but an issue of the mind, body, soul, and relationships.

2. Most aspects of aging can be positive.

3. The percentage of older people in our society is growing rapidly.

4. There are some physical functions that seem to decline with age.

5. Osteoporosis is a dreaded disease characterized by a reduction in bone density.

6. Mental aging can result in either depression or a healthy outlook on life, depending on the makeup of the individual.

7. Both men and women experience healthy sexual relations well into their senior years.

8. Ageism is discrimination against people, especially against the elderly, because of their age. It should be combated by our society.

9. There are many myths about aging that can be refuted with factual information.

10. There are some guidelines for the elderly and young people to follow that will promote healthy aging.

11. Medicare is the largest insurance carrier in the country and takes care of most of the medical needs of the elderly.

COMMITMENT ACTIVITIES

1. If you have relatives who are older, make a better effort to be with them, learn from them, and give to them. If you do not have someone nearby, volunteer to spend an hour a week at a retirement village or rest home to help out and learn from the residents.

2. Examine the list of creative aging guidelines. Contract with yourself to modify your lifestyle to fit the healthy-aging lifestyle.

3. Locate two people in your community who have recently retired or are about to retire, perhaps a professor at school and a member of your family. Arrange a time to interview them, if they are willing, on their views of retirement. How does their attitude toward retirement reflect their attitude toward their life thus far?

REFERENCES

Andres, R., and J. Hallfrisch. 1989. "Nutritional Intake Recommendations Needed for the Older American." *American Journal of the American Dietetic Association* 89:1739–42.

Atchley, R. C. 1980. "Common Misconceptions About Aging." *Health Values: Achieving High Level Wellness* 5, no. 1:7–10.

Baum, R. 1993. "Chemical Imbalances in Alzheimer's Measured." *Chemical and Engineering News* 71, no. 19:6.

Botwinick, J. 1984. *Aging and Behavior.* New York: Springer.

Carr, B. R. 1993. "A Real-World Approach to Osteoporosis." *Patient Care* 27, no. 8:31–43.

Cox, C., and A. Monk. 1993. "Hispanic Culture and Family Care of Alzheimer's Patients." *Health and Social Work* 18, no. 2:92–101.

Crook, T. H., III, G. J. Larrabee, and J. R. Youngjohn. 1993. "Age and Incidental Recall for Simulated Everyday Memory Task." *Journals of Gerontology* 48, no. 1:45–48.

Dempster, D. W., and R. Lindsay. 1993. "Pathogenesis of Osteoporosis." *Lancet* 341, no. 8848:797–801.

Dice, J. F. 1993. "Cellular and Molecular Mechanisms of Aging." *Physiological Reviews* 73, no. 1:149–60.

Donow, H. S. 1992. "To Everything There Is a Season." *Gerontologists* 32, no. 6:733–79.

Dychtwald, K. 1989. *The Challenges and Opportunities of an Aging America.* Cited in S. Walton, "A Ride on the Age Wave." *Health,* July, 40, 88.

Finch, C. E., and E. L. Schneider, eds. 1985. *Handbook of the Biology of Aging.* New York: Van Nostrand Reinhold.

Fisher, L. M., and J. M. McDowd. 1993. "Item and Relational Processing in Young and Older Adults." *Journal of Gerontology* 48, no. 2:62–69.

Fishman, S. 1993. "Survival of the Fittest." *Health* 7, no. 3:58–65.

Fowles, D. G. 1989. *A Profile of Older Americans.* Washington, DC: American Association of Retired Persons.

Freundlich, N. 1993. "Quieting: Closing In on Alzheimer's." *Business Week,* 3 May, 112–13.

Galvin, R. M. 1988. "You're Not Losing Your Mind." *Across the Board* 25:50, 56.

Light, E., and B. D. Lebowitz. 1989. *Alzheimer's Disease Treatment and Family Stress: Directions for Research.* U.S. Department of Health and Human Services, Public Health Service, Rockville, Maryland.

Lindsay, R. 1993. "Prevention and Treatment of Osteoporosis." *Lancet* 341, no. 8848 (27 March): 797, 801, 806.

Logue, B. J. 1993. *Last Rights.* New York: Lexington Books.

Lord, T. R., and J. E. Garner. 1993. "Effects of Music on Alzheimer's Patients." *Perceptual and Motor Skills* 76, no. 2:451–56.

Phillips, H. T., and S. A. Gaylord. 1985. *Aging and Public Health.* New York: Springer.

Roos, N. P., and B. Havens. 1991. "Predictors of Successful Aging: A Twelve-Year Study of Manitoba Elderly." *American Journal of Public Health* 81, no. 6:63.

Rovner, J. 1991. "How Bad Is It? (Crisis in the Cost of Medical Care)." *Congressional Quarterly Weekly Report,* 16 February, 481.

Russell, C. 1989. "I Hate to Be a Party Pooper but . . ." *American Demographics* 11: 2.

Siegel, J. S. 1993. *A Generation of Change: A Profile of America's Older Population.* New York: Russell Sage Foundation.

Solomon, D. H., E. Salend, A. N. Rahman, M. B. Liston, and D. B. Reuben. 1992. *A Consumer Guide to Aging.* Baltimore: The Johns Hopkins University Press.

Toufexis, A. 1993. "Alzheimer's Clue." *Time,* 21 June, 59.

U.S. Bureau of the Census. 1989. *Current Population Reports: Population Profile of the United States, 1989.* no. 159. Washington, DC: Government Printing Office.

Verdery, R. B. 1990. " 'Wasting Away' of the Old: Can It and Should It Be Treated." *Geriatrics* 45, no. 6:26, 31.

Wallhagen, M. I. 1993. "Perceived Control and Adaptation in Elder Caregivers." *International Journal of Aging and Human Development* 36, no. 3:219–38.

Woollacott, M. H., and D. L. Manchester. 1993. "Anticipatory Postural Adjustments in Older Adults." *Journals of Gerontology* 48, no. 2:64–71.

ADDITIONAL READINGS

Richardson, M., and J. R. Richardson. 1990. *We've Got to Do Something About Mother.* Brookings, SD: OniPress. This reader-friendly book talks about eleven situations where people have struggled with care of older parents and what their solutions were.

Scrutton, S. 1992. *Ageing: Healthy and in Control.* New York: Chapman & Hall. This is an alternative approach to maintaining the health of older people. It includes such topics as medical ageism, allopathic medicine and old age, how to escape the psychology of medical ageism, maintaining social engagement, approaches to loss, death and dying, exercise, and nutrition.

Siegel, J. S. 1993. *A Generation of Change: A Profile of America's Older Population.* New York: Russell Sage Foundation. A comprehensive 600-page book that profiles the elderly in America. Chapters cover the gender, race, ethnic composition, geographic distribution, longevity, health, marital status, living arrangements, education, work, economic status, and other descriptors of the elderly.

Solomon, D. H., E. Salend, A. N. Rahman, M. B. Liston, and D. B. Reuben. 1992. *A Consumer's Guide to Aging.* Baltimore: The Johns Hopkins University Press. This 500+-page book is a practical lay approach to healthy aging written by three social workers and two physicians. It covers topics such as keeping fit, choosing health care, emotional balance, financial planning, moving, family roles, intimacy, retirement, and taking advantage of leisure time.

Death and Dying

Healthy People 2000 Objectives

- Increase years of healthy life to at
least 65 years (baseline 62 years
in 1980).

PERSONAL INSIGHT

Peace and Rewards in Death

My dad had diabetes since he was a teenager but in spite of it had lived a full life. He had raised his four children so that each was independent with their own children. Dad was 67 and had been feeling the long-term effects of diabetes. His vision was poor and he had to receive laser treatments regularly to try and save his sight, but he really couldn't drive anymore and go off to the mountains like he wanted. The circulation in his extremities was poor; in fact, he had dry gangrene in his toes. The doctors had told him that he would have to have his feet amputated someday. He also had a series of minor strokes, none seriously debilitating, but they were worrisome. He still tried desperately to be productive and although it might take him an hour to put in one screw with his poor vision, he was able to continue to make things, dreaming of the next time there would be a family reunion in the mountains.

Two weeks before he died, he and Mom came to visit me in my new house that I had been landscaping. He helped me load rocks and debris left from construction. He was happy when he could help. His life was a life of service to his wife, his children, his religion, and boy scouts. His major goal in life was to make sure Mom was left financially secure when he died and that his children were independent.

The night before he left on the plane, Dad and I sat under a big Texas sky and talked for hours. It was reminiscent of the many times we had talked under

the stars in the Sierras, Rockies, and deserts on boy scout and family camping trips. This time we talked about the impending amputation, his determination not to lose his legs, his life as he had lived it, and his not wanting to lose his dignity. "If it kills me, then let it be," he stated. It was at that time that Dad and I talked like we had never talked before. We had always hugged, kissed, and expressed love, but this time it was deeper, a sense of finality was in the air. We told each other how much we loved each other. I told him how he was my hero. I told him that much of what I had accomplished in sports, as a family man, and as a professional was just to try and make him proud of me. He always said he was proud of me and I lived for that. We talked about Mom's security, how he'd thought he'd lived an okay life. We shared our beliefs of life after death. We shared everything I would ever want to share. I am so grateful for that night. I still cherish that night.

There was a good possibility that I would see him in a few months when we would make our annual vacation out west to visit family. He was still working around the house and no one had said he might not live long, but somehow each of us knew that this would be the last time I would see my dad alive.

The next day, when I took Mom and Dad to the airport, we tried to talk lightly, planning our next outing, but each knew that we had had our last outing together. As he and Mom walked toward the gate, I snapped one last photograph, and he disappeared into the plane. Two weeks later, Mom

called and said that Dad had experienced a heart attack and may not make it through the night. We hurried to make a trip out to see him, but before we were able to leave, we received the news that Dad had died.

Dad had insisted that there not be a funeral, that he be buried immediately. We flew out immediately and buried him as he requested with only family members present. We then had a memorial service. A lot of people came to the memorial service, people we hadn't seen in years. It was a sad, yet joyous occasion. I felt so peaceful and grateful that I spoke at the memorial, giving me an opportunity to publicly acclaim the greatness of this humble man. I was so proud of the relationship we had and proud of the simple, but wonderful life this man had led. It seemed to me, and I expressed it, that his life was much like Camelot, a brief shining moment in history that will be remembered forever.

It was a time to rally around Mom. Each of the four children from all over the country and their spouses came, and we shared then, the love for each other that we hadn't shared in some time. It was a renewing, a new zest for living.

Although there was much sadness, and, oh, how I missed my Dad, there was a peace that I had not felt before, knowing that if death has to occur, what better way to part. I have thought of that moment many, many times since his death, and each time I was strengthened, comforted, and grateful.

Source: From G. E. Richardson, excerpt from personal journal, March through June, 1985.

Death is the climax of life as we know it. Most of us grieve at the loss of a loved one because we will no longer have the physical company of that person. As we ponder health of the mind and the soul, it is very difficult to think of a better way to feel the soul than in preparing for one's own death or seeing a loved one die. The heart aching does not feel good, but through this means you can be in touch with the health of your soul and get to know something about your heart. Consider the Personal Insight story of how positive a death can be.

THE AMERICAN PARADOX

Our American culture is caught in a paradox. On one hand, we are fascinated with death, as evidenced by the popularity of television shows and movies that include significant amounts of violence and death. On the other hand, we deny that we are mortal or that others close to us could die—until we are faced with a life-threatening situation. We are a death-denying society and therefore do not prepare when faced

Comfort Scale

How comfortable are you about talking about death? Complete this exercise and decide.

Directions

Circle the response that best reflects how you feel.

a = comfortable
b = somewhat comfortable
c = somewhat uncomfortable
d = uncomfortable

1. How comfortable do you feel talking about death and dying?   a b c d

2. How comfortable would you feel if called upon to visit and support someone you cared about who had been declared terminally ill? (Mark your degree of comfort for the person's being in each of the states listed below.)

   Denial (think they will beat the disease)   a b c d

   Anger (mad at you, physicians, and/or others)   a b c d

   Bargaining (pleading with God to change the situation and their pledge to do better)   a b c d

   Depression (sadness, may not even talk)   a b c d

   Acceptance (wants to get affairs in order and bid farewell to loved ones)   a b c d

3. How comfortable would you be in providing support for a friend or relative who had someone close to them die? Mark the degree of comfort for support in the cases listed below.

   Child losing parent   a b c d

   Parent losing child   a b c d

   Loss of someone who was in their later years (e.g., grandparent)   a b c d

4. If you were to die and someone else could use one of your organs, what degree of comfort would you feel in making your organs available for donation upon your death?   a b c d

5. If it was your misfortune to have something happen to you that would leave you in a coma and only kept alive through artificial life support, with little hope for survival, how comfortable would you be in signing (before the coma) a statement indicating that you would not like to be kept alive in that state?   a b c d

6. If someone you felt responsible for was kept alive only by life support, and you knew that they would not want to remain in this state, how comfortable would you be in ordering the withdrawal of the life-support equipment?   a b c d

Scoring

Total your score by assigning the following points to your responses:

a = 4
b = 3
c = 2
d = 1

Interpretation

This exercise measures your comfort in being able to deal with death and death-related experiences. The interpretation of your score is as follows:

18–24 = High degree of comfort.
12–17 = Moderate degree of comfort.
0–11   = Not comfortable in handling death-related experiences. The behaviors and concepts suggested in this chapter may help you in becoming more comfortable.

---

with our own death or the death of a loved one. Many of us have not talked with our parents or grandparents about where we want to be buried, what kind of funeral or memorial service arrangements we would prefer, whether we want to be buried or cremated, whether we want our organs donated, what death means to us, and our beliefs about life after death. We might not have a will because we deny that death could happen to us at a young age. With the combined fascination with death and denial of death in society, we are often ill prepared psychologically to cope with the death of a loved one.

This chapter is devoted to the understanding of death as a natural part of life. For the health of the mind and soul,

death can be the ultimate stressor and one of the greatest challenges to our mental coping abilities. Those of us who have already experienced the death of someone close to us recognize how all-consuming the impact of this stressor is and how it forces us to use our entire coping repertoire. But, as described above, death can also be the beautiful culmination of a life. This chapter provides guidelines and insights to better prepare you for your own eventual death and to help you prepare for the financial losses that might accompany, and coping skills you will need in order to accept, the death of a loved one.

THE CONCEPT OF DEATH

Death is the natural outcome of life, whether people live it healthily or unhealthily, but the thought of a loved one's dying, or of dying ourselves, is so unpleasant that we often repress it. When we do discuss death with others, we tend to avoid direct description in favor of such euphemisms as "passed away," "taken away," "gone to the great beyond," or even "kicked the bucket" or "knocked off."

When does death actually occur? At first the question seems simple. The historical common-law definition was that death occurs when the lungs and heart cease to function. By this definition, however, people who have had heart attacks and who have been revived by cardiopulmonary resuscitation would have died. Today's life-support machines can keep people "alive" if they cannot breathe on their own or their heart will not beat on its own. Machines will clean the blood if the body's organs can't do it and feed people if they cannot eat. Even when people are not emitting any brain waves, they can still "function" artificially. When, then, is a person actually dead?

There are several ways to define death, depending upon where you live and the circumstances of the death. For example, brain death is the cessation of the brain processes as indicated by a flat electroencephalogram (in other words, modern technology can find no indication of brain activity). Clinical death is the absence of heartbeat, breathing, and eye reflexes and the presence of algor mortis (the chill of death) and rigor mortis (rigidity of skeletal muscles). Clinical death involves the whole organism, while biological death refers to the death of particular organs. Cellular death occurs when irreversible damage to individual cells prevents them from dividing (Bardis 1981).

Harvard Medical School (Ad Hoc Committee 1968) has developed a clearer definition of death, based partly on our new ability to measure the brain's electrical activity. According to this definition, an individual is dead when the following four criteria are met:

1. Unreceptiveness and unresponsiveness: The patient is totally unresponsive to applied painful stimuli, such as poking with pins.
2. Unresponsiveness in breathing: For over an hour, the patient shows no spontaneous muscular contractions or breathing.
3. Lack of reflexes: The knee-jerk reflex is absent, or the pupils do not contract when light is pointed in the eye.
4. Flat electroencephalogram (EEG): For 20 minutes, the patient's brain does not generate an electrical impulse or brain wave.

According to this definition of death, a person kept functioning by life-support systems is considered "alive" until the machines are shut off.

Learning to cope with and be prepared for death is part of the healthy mind and soul. Those of us who repress thoughts and discussions of death are generally unprepared when death does occur, and we have difficulty recovering or helping someone else recover from such a traumatic experience. By understanding the issues and feelings that arise in dying and mourning, we can help ourselves cope with the eventuality of death. The stages of dying and then the stages of mourning will be examined in the following sections.

STAGES OF DYING

Many of us, when we eventually die, will not know that it is coming. We might die from traumatic fatal injuries or massive coronaries, and we will not have time to prepare to disengage with life, as far as we know. However, some of us will have some advance notice of death because of terminal illnesses. In these cases, we can come to terms with the inevitability of our situation in a very immediate sense. Elisabeth Kübler-Ross (1969) has worked for years with many terminally ill and dying patients and has observed that many pass through five psychological **stages of dying:** (1) denial, (2) anger, (3) bargaining, (4) depression, and (5) acceptance. Given enough time, most terminally ill patients can and will pass through these stages, although they won't all go through them in the same order. Some may skip a stage, revert to an earlier stage, or get stuck in one stage. We cope with death either through these stages or in our own unique way. Each of us will experience the dying process with the same individuality that distinguishes us as a unique person.

DENIAL

When the news comes that death will be soon, denial is the easiest way to cope ("It can't be true, not me"). Dying people might believe that a cure will be found for the disease or that they will be the exception to the rule.

ANGER

When people realize that they really are going to die, they are likely going to become angry and ask "Why me?" Such anger is often directed at the medical staff, the family, or God. Dying people might feel that they are unjustly being taken from the living and should not have to go through the ordeal of dying.

BARGAINING

Bargaining is a final attempt to avoid the inevitable. Dying persons may plead with God, promising to reform their lives in exchange for a miraculous recovery.

stages of dying
Five predictable, but not universally applicable, psychological stages a person passes through in the course of a terminal disease: denial, anger, bargaining, depression, and acceptance.

DEPRESSION

When bargaining fails and they realize that the last hope is dimming, dying people are likely to feel depression and self-pity. They feel the loss of friends and loved ones, good health, and the freedom of home. It is natural in this stage to grieve. Thus is the self-pity, or "poor me," stage.

ACCEPTANCE

Acceptance of inevitable fate is difficult, but it eventually arrives for most, with time. Dying persons are then likely to want to make sure that all their personal and professional matters are taken care of, including wills and funeral arrangements, and to bid farewell to special people in their lives.

APPLICATIONS FOR CAREGIVERS

Understanding these stages can help us talk to and aid loved ones who are dying. For example, if a loved one is in the denial stage, we can respond by listening and giving hope. The denial stage is when the power of the healing mind and soul can turn the direction of a terminal illness back onto the road of healing (Goleman and Gurin 1993; Moyers 1993). Support people can provide hope and faith and encourage a fighting spirit to try and make that healing turn for the better.

When the dying person gives up and no longer denies, she or he might then be angry. Understanding that an angry stage is common can help us to be tolerant and feel less hurt when the anger is directed toward us. When the individual is in the bargaining stage, we might encourage the development of the person's spiritual dimension and self-forgiveness. This is also a time for great hope, optimism, faith, and self-efficacy (belief in oneself) so that we can help facilitate a turn in condition with the healing mind and soul.

Again, when we sense that the dying person is giving up, we might see a depression stage. We should continue to express love and not allow the person to be left alone unless the person wants to be alone. When the individual has reached the acceptance stage and wants to be open about dying, we should help the person in that acceptance and assure that her or his life's affairs are in order. When dying persons have accepted their own death, it can be frustrating for them if loved ones show denial, depression, or anger. If the person has accepted the actuality of his or her own death, then we survivors must accept it as well.

HOSPICES

Many people die in hospitals, often alone—with medical staff, but away from their families. They die as one of several patients in an intensive care unit, a patient in a numbered room, a case on a clipboard.

Most of us, however, want to die at home with loved ones, or in homelike surroundings. This desire has given rise to the **hospice** concept. To make dying a fulfillment of life

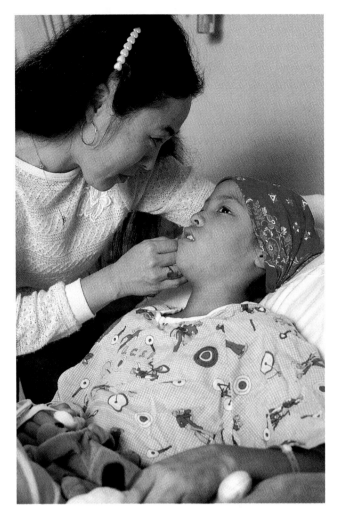

Loved ones can help provide hope and faith to a person who may be dying.

rather than a tragic end, the hospice provides either home care or a non-hospital-like atmosphere for the terminally ill. A hospice is a comfortable, homey place with a cheerful atmosphere. Volunteers visit and talk with dying patients, helping them to cope and offering them a sympathetic ear. Families visit freely without the restrictive hours or age limits common in hospitals. Within this temporary caring community, family and friends have the opportunity to encounter each other at the deepest levels and find mutual sustenance. Volunteers within the hospice program also make home visits for those who wish to die at home.

hospice
Care for the terminally ill in the home, or in a homelike setting, when attempts at a cure have been abandoned and the focus of care is on keeping the dying person comfortable and free from pain.

Hospices, although not available to all, aim to help individuals to die with dignity away from institutional settings.

Hospice is really a concept more than a place. There are hospice places, but most hospice patients are at home, cared for by family, hospice nurses, and volunteers. The focus of care is on providing loving support and pain management. Most hospice patients have painful, terminal diseases such as cancer and AIDS. In the almost two decades of hospice care in America, the movement has moved from being an alternative health-care approach to being an accepted part of American health care (Rhymes 1990). Medicare and other insurances now cover the cost of hospice care. To be reimbursed for hospice benefits, the patient must, among other things,

1. have a terminal illness with a life expectancy of 6 months or less,
2. have elected the hospice benefit, relinquishing other benefits except for the attending physician (i.e., no more curative treatments),
3. have no more than 80 percent of the payments be for home care (Rhymes 1990).

Access to hospice care has been limited to some degree by local unavailability, ignorance, and some restrictions of providers. The public and the health-care systems need to be continually educated in regard to hospices so that more terminally ill persons can receive care that allows them to die with dignity.

EUTHANASIA

Doctors face a dilemma. The Hippocratic oath dictates that the ultimate purpose in medicine is to preserve life, but doctors regularly encounter situations in which mercy dictates otherwise. One physician expressed it this way:

> How often have we encountered a patient in the last stages of a terminal disease? There are no mornings or evenings, no day or night, just the time between the narcotics that are necessary to relieve their unbearable pain. There are no thoughts of the future; just memories of the past and those are often clouded by the narcotics. ("Euthanasia" 1990)

Loved ones of the dying person also face the dilemma. When dying is prolonged and painful, as in some forms of cancer and AIDS, or when the recovery of a patient on life support seems impossible, the issue of euthanasia may arise

PERSONAL INSIGHT
Hospice in Action

My dad was a 78-year-old retired commercial artist who had his very own successful business for many years in Boise, Idaho. In his retirement years he golfed, barbecued for family, and loved watching sports from his easy chair in the family room. He began to feel ill and, after some extensive tests, found that he was in the advanced stages of cancer. The cancer had progressed to the point where treatment was not an option, so he and the family opted for the hospice program. The program was very thoroughly explained to Dad and

to the family, and the hospice personnel were readily available to answer any question that we had. Dad spent much of his time in his easy chair. Family visited him regularly, and the nurses from the hospice program made regular visits. The family was told what they could expect when the dying process began, and it was this information that helped us to recognize when he did begin to die. We called the hospice nurse, and she quickly came to his home to be with my mom, one of my sisters, and me. She not only monitored his physical signs but gently explained to us what was happening and what

we could expect to happen next. This was a great help to us at what was the most difficult time any of us had ever been through. When the moment of death was very near, our greatest concern was for Dad and that he know how very much we loved him. We felt the need to express our love to him and also to let him know that we would be all right and it was time for him to let go and pass from this life. He died with courage and dignity but most of all in an atmosphere of great love.

Source: Kathleen Richardson, March 28, 1990.

for them as well. Euthanasia (from the Greek words for "good death") means the promotion of an easier, swifter death for reasons of mercy. Because of the various circumstances involved, four types of euthanasia can be distinguished.

In voluntary **indirect euthanasia,** a patient on life-support machines or drugs asks the physician (or sometimes another trusted person) to withdraw the support if a change in his or her condition merits it. For example, a patient might ask ahead of time that support be removed if recovery becomes impossible, or a terminal cancer patient might refuse treatment except for pain, so as to die more quickly. This is indirect euthanasia because the physician does not actively promote death (as by administering a fatal drug), yet no special treatment is used to keep the patient alive; if death comes, it is natural. It is voluntary because the patient requests it.

Involuntary indirect euthanasia usually involves a comatose patient on life support. In this instance, relatives arrange to have the patient's life support removed. The term *involuntary* is applied because the patient did not personally choose to have life support removed.

In voluntary **direct euthanasia** (or voluntary mercy killing), the patient asks to have a fatal drug administered if his or her condition worsens. Involuntary direct euthanasia (involuntary mercy killing) occurs when the patient lapses into a coma and the relatives arrange for administration of the fatal drug. Both forms of direct euthanasia are illegal.

One of the dilemmas created by our advanced technology is our ability to keep people "alive" on life-support machines. For instance, if the brain does not have the capability to send messages to the heart and lungs to keep them working, a machine can do it. There are several questions you may want to ask.

1. Is it a disservice to let a person with almost no hope for recovery survive as a mental vegetable?
2. Would you want to be kept alive by a machine if you had little hope of recovering with your mental faculties intact?

3. Do you think others you care about would want to live or die in this situation?
4. Does "pulling the plug" constitute taking a life, or is the life already taken?
5. Have you talked with your loved ones and learned their feelings? Is it a good idea to raise the topic with them just in case?

One approach to resolving the problem of euthanasia has been enacted by the organization Choice In Dying, Inc. They have developed the **living will,** a simple statement individuals write to indicate that, if their condition requires life support, they wish to have no life-support systems and to let nature alone decide their fate. To get free information about writing a living will, you can contact Choice In Dying:

Choice In Dying, Inc.
200 Varick Street
10th Floor
New York, NY 10014-4810

Some hospitals now require or request living wills from patients when they are admitted, so that the physicians have

indirect euthanasia
Removing life-support systems from an individual so that she or he can die naturally.

direct euthanasia
Administering a lethal injection, or performing some other action to cause death, in order to free a dying patient from suffering.

living will
A document that states what medical interventions a person does or does not want to be taken if that person becomes incapacitated and cannot participate in decisions about his or her medical care.

HEALTH UPDATE

Status of the Living Will

In 1990, the U.S. Supreme Court endorsed the living will. Three years later, studies showed that living wills (advance medical directives) have had little impact on the way people are actually treated at the end of their lives.

Only 10 to 20 percent have completed a living will, and more disturbing is the fact that some doctors given the living will do not follow it. It is recommended that in your living will you get as specific as possible, let other people know your wishes, and appoint a person in the family as your agent to make sure it is done. It is helpful to consider as many conditions as possible and indicate what you want to be done. For example, do you want cardiopulmonary resuscitation, mechanical respiration, artificial feeding, major surgery, kidney dialysis, chemotherapy, or antibiotics? Be specific for situations such as coma with no chance of coming out, with a small chance of coming out, being a vegetable not knowing anyone or being able to speak, having a terminal illness, and other conditions (Consumer's Union 1993).

DEPARTMENT OF HEALTH & SOCIAL SERVICES
Division of Health
DOH 0060 (Rev. 12/91)

Effective Date
December 11, 1991
s. 154.03(1),(2)

PLEASE BE SURE YOU READ THE FORM CAREFULLY AND UNDERSTAND IT BEFORE YOU COMPLETE AND SIGN IT

DECLARATION TO PHYSICIANS

1. I, _____, being of sound mind, voluntarily state my desire that my dying may not be prolonged under the circumstances specified in this document. Under those circumstances, I direct that I be permitted to die naturally. If I am unable to give directions regarding the use of life-sustaining procedures or feeding tubes, I intend that my family and physician honor this document as the final expression of my legal right to refuse medical or surgical treatment and to accept the consequences from this refusal.

2. If I have a **TERMINAL CONDITION**, as determined by 2 physicians who have personally examined me, I do not want my dying to be artificially prolonged and I do not want life-sustaining procedures to be used. In addition, if I have such a terminal condition, the following are my directions regarding the use of feeding tubes (check only one):

   a. Use feeding tubes if I have a terminal condition ___

   b. Do not use feeding tubes if I have a terminal condition ___

   c. If I have not checked either box, feeding tubes will be used.

3. If I am in a **PERSISTENT VEGETATIVE STATE**, as determined by 2 physicians who have personally examined me, the following are my directions regarding the use of life-sustaining procedures and feeding tubes:

   a. Check only one:

   Use life-sustaining procedures if I am in a persistent vegetative state ___

   Do not use life-sustaining procedures if I am in a persistent vegetative state ___

   If I have not checked either box, life-sustaining procedures will be used.

   b. Check only one:

   Use feeding tubes if I am in a persistent vegetative state ___

   Do not use feeding tubes if I am in a persistent vegetative state ___

   If I have not checked either box, feeding tubes will be used.

4. By law, this document cannot be used to authorize: a) withholding or withdrawal of

any medication, procedure or feeding tube if to do so would cause me pain or reduce my comfort; and b) withholding or withdrawal of nutrition or hydration that is administered to me through means other than a feeding tube unless, in my physician's opinion, this administration is medically contraindicated.

5. If I have been diagnosed as pregnant and my physician knows of this diagnosis, this document has no effect during the course of my pregnancy.

Signed_____

Date_____

Address_____

I know the person signing this document personally and I believe him or her to be of sound mind. I am not related to the person signing this document by blood, marriage or adoption, and am not entitled to and do not have a claim on any portion of the person's estate and am not otherwise restricted by law from being a witness.

Witness_____

Witness_____

This document is executed as provided in chapter 154, Wisconsin Statutes

Note: This form can be duplicated

Division of Health, P.O. Box 309, Madison, WI 53701

Source: State of Wisconsin.

---

some directive. It is important to specify your wishes to your survivors, physicians, and hospital administrators in a written legal document that is in accordance with your state laws.

Cases that raise the issue of euthanasia show the complexity of the personal and ethical decisions we may face. On the one hand, we want to cling to the life of a patient, particularly to that of a loved one. Many medical and religious perspectives point to preserving life at all costs. On the other hand, keeping the person on life-support systems is expensive, and medical bills can quickly mount to astronomical figures, leaving survivors in severe financial difficulty.

LIFE-AFTER-DEATH EXPERIENCES

Our modern ability to snatch individuals from the jaws of death by technological means is partly responsible for the resurgence of claims of having experienced life after death. Earlier, life after death was considered a religious topic, beyond the realm of psychologists, medical doctors, and health educators. Raymond Moody's books *Life After Life* (1975) and *Reflections on Life After Life* (1977) and K. Osis and E. Haraldsson's book *At the Hour of Death* (1977) have given credence to the issue for other professionals. And controversial

Issue

Dr. Jack Kevorkian

Dr. Jack Kevorkian, of Michigan, has admitted to helping patients commit merciful suicide. At this writing there have been at least seventeen people, all facing painful and certain death, who have committed suicide in Dr. Kevorkian's presence, usually by inhaling carbon monoxide through a mask. Dr. Kevorkian's suicide machine is set up in the back of Dr. Kevorkian's van. Dr. Kevorkian has been tried by a Michigan court and found innocent of breaking the Michigan law, even though he admits to having assisted in another's death. The jury felt the law was unconstitutional.

This type of physician-assisted suicide clouds the distinction between active and passive euthanasia. New terms have been suggested: *physician-assisted suicide (PAS)* for a physician's providing a patient with a different means of death, such as a lethal drug the patient can take, and *physician-committed voluntary active euthanasia (PCVAE)* for a physician's administering a lethal drug to the patient with the patient's consent (Celocruz 1992). Here are some of the questions you need to resolve for yourself:

1. Is euthanasia, whether active or passive, a political or a religious issue (Dworkin 1993)?
2. Can the physician's motive be questioned in PAS? Can the physician's motive be questioned in PCVAE?
3. Should Dr. Kevorkian be punished as a criminal? For murder? Or for a lesser crime?
4. Should we really believe that there is a difference between active and passive euthanasia?

- Pro: Physician-assisted suicide is merciful, and if the suicide is chosen by the patient, then it is the most humane thing that we can do as a last gift to the patient.

- Con: It is hard to tell where this will all stop with physician-assisted suicide. We could become extreme and suddenly physicians will supply carbon monoxide and masks to people who are depressed. If we open the door, it will be hard to know where it will stop.

Discuss these questions with your classmates and see how varied the responses are.

discussions of life after death by Kübler-Ross (1974) have heightened this debate. We still see numerous books in the popular market with accounts of those who have "died" and then been brought back to life (Eadie 1992). Whether the life-after-death experience is a preview of after-death experiences or a psychological or physiological reaction to the void created at death will continue to be debated. What is important is not whether these reported experiences are true, but what they mean to people.

Near-death experiences that people have reported include seeing apparitions of people from the "postlife," being out of their bodies and able to look down upon themselves with great interest, seeing beings of light, experiencing a peaceful existence in a beautiful setting, having instantaneous panoramic playbacks of their lives, and traveling through dark tunnels. These experiences reportedly have occurred just as the person was dying or between the time when they had "died" (their heart had stopped) and the time when they were revived.

The following three factors are common to these reports:

1. The patient enjoys the death experience; it is peaceful, serene, and, in most cases, positive.
2. The patient "returns" with a new zest for living and a sense of the meaning of life, including a strong desire for knowledge and an increased emphasis on loving.
3. People who come back would not take their own lives to recapture the death experience because they have a renewed sense of purpose among the living; they no longer fear death.

If the life-after-death phenomenon is accepted, an additional stage might be added to Kübler-Ross's stages of dying. The additional stage could be called "mood elevation" (Richardson 1979), because the dying person would not only accept death but move into a positive state of happiness, love, and peacefulness. **Thanatologists** (scientists who study death and dying) report that fear of the unknown is a major problem in coping with death. If we accept the fact of death and the idea that death might be a pleasant passing into another existence, the coping might become easier and the fear reduced. For example, members of religious groups with strong beliefs in postmortal existence seem to have low anxiety levels about death and have an ability to adjust sooner following a death of a loved one than do people without such beliefs.

WILLS AND TRUSTS

Legal documents help ensure that our estates will go to the people we want them to go to. Some people make a will. In the will, all parties who are to share the estate are designated, or specific properties can be designated to go to specific persons. Wills can be prepared for as little as $150–$300—or more, depending on how complicated the will is. In many states, wills may have to go through probate, which generally involves a lawyer's proving before the courts that a document is genuine and valid. Court and legal fees are taken from the estate. Figure 5.1 is an example of a simple will.

If you put your estate into a trust before you die, all people whom you want to benefit from your estate share in the

---

thanatologist
A person who studies death and dying.

Death Preparation Scale

How prepared are you for death? Complete the following assessment and see how you rate.

Directions

Please check all the things that you have done, leave blank if you have not done these things.

_____ Completed an organ donor card.

_____ Made out a living will.

_____ Talked to clergy or spiritual mentor about life, death, and life after death.

_____ Made out a personal will.

_____ Talked with parents about how they would like their funerals to be, memorial versus funeral, cremation versus burial, type of casket, where they would like to be buried, viewing versus nonviewing, music selections, and so on.

_____ Talked with parents or grandparents, other family members, and friends about their beliefs about death and life after death.

_____ Completed a funeral arrangement form that you can get at a funeral home in your community so that, in the event of your death, others will know your wishes.

_____ Mentally rehearsed (in imagery) counseling or visiting with someone who has been declared terminally ill.

_____ Mentally rehearsed how you would comfort someone who had a family member or friend die (e.g., child losing parent, parent losing child, loss of grandparents, sudden and tragic versus expected losses).

_____ Talked with parents or grandparents about their will. Learned who the executor is, how the estate would be divided, how the surviving spouse would be cared for, if underaged children were involved, who would take custody, and so on.

Scoring

Total the number of checks you have made.

Interpretation

This exercise helps you determine how prepared you are to deal with the death of a loved one. All of the activities will make very difficult situations more manageable. Any of you who have experienced the death of a loved one will recognize how important these items are. Interpret your score as follows:

9–10 = Very well prepared
5–8 = Moderately prepared
0–4 = Poorly prepared

When you get to the end of the chapter, complete the Lifestyle Contract there to help you become better prepared to deal with death.

---

trust. Upon your death, the trust already belongs to the designated people, and so, rather than spending weeks in probate, the trust can be executed immediately and with minimal, if any, legal fees. A simple trust might take $700 to $900 to set up.

If you choose to neither make a will nor set up a trust, your estate will be subject to your state's laws for automatic wills. Upon your death, your estate would go through probate and your properties would be distributed according to your state's guidelines.

THE PURPOSE AND PRICE OF FUNERALS

When someone in our family dies, two experiences demand our time and attention: We must do something with the body of the deceased person, and we must cope with the loss. For the survivors of a death, recuperation can be a slow, painful ordeal, usually entailing funeral arrangements and a period of mourning. One of the most difficult tasks to accomplish when a loved one has died is making funeral arrangements. This is made somewhat easier if the dying person is able to be involved in planning the funeral. Survivors report that it helps them to cope and face the death when they have the opportunity to plan the funeral with the dying person (Vernon 1993).

BURIAL

When we do not have the opportunity to plan a funeral with the dying person before they die, and if we do not otherwise have directions from them about their wishes regarding a funeral, many of us will find it hard to make the necessary consumer decisions sensibly in the midst of our grief. We might discover later that we spent more than we could really afford to bury our dead. Americans are beginning to purchase less-expensive funerals. Many feel that normal funeral costs are far beyond their financial resources and that the emphasis

Will of Glenn Earl Doe

I, GLENN EARL DOE, a resident of Davis County, Utah, declare that this is my will.

FIRST: I revoke all wills and codicils that I have previously made.

SECOND: I am married to KATHLEEN READING DOE and all references in this will to "my wife" are to her. All references in this will to "my children" shall include my son BRANNON DOE, TAVAN DOE, JORDAN DOE, LAUREN DOE and any other children born to or adopted by me.

THIRD: I give all of my estate, both real and personal property, or my interest in any such property, not otherwise specifically disposed of by this Will or in any other manner, together with any insurance on the property, to my wife if she survives me for (30) days, and if she does not, to my children who survive me for that period in equal shares.

FOURTH: If my wife does not survive me and, at my death, any of my children are minors, (1.) I appoint my brother, VICTOR RAY DOE, as guardian of the person and estate of my minor child or children. If he shall for any reason fail to qualify or cease to act as such guardian, I appoint my sister, CAROLYN DOE SMITH, as such guardian in his place.

(2.) So long as my children who are under the age of (18) eighteen, the guardian shall apply their share of my estate for the benefit of my children. The guardian of my children's estate shall have the power in his or her discretion to determine what is necessary for their proper support care, maintenance, and education, after taking into consideration, to the extent the guardian shall deem advisable the estate, income, and resources of my children.

FIFTH: I nominate my wife, KATHLEEN READING DOE, of Bountiful, Utah, as executrix of this Will, to serve without bond. If she shall for any reason fail to qualify or cease to act as executrix, I nominate VICTOR RAY DOE, my brother, as executor, to serve without bond.

SIXTH: I have not entered into either a contract to make wills or a contract not to revoke wills.

I subscribe my name to this Will this_____day of _____1990, at Bountiful, Utah.

_____
GLENN EARL DOE

On the date above written, GLENN EARL DOE declared to us, the undersigned, that the foregoing instrument, consisting of three (3) pages including the page signed by us as witnesses, was his Will and requested us to act as witnesses to it. He thereupon signed this Will in our presence, all of us being present at the same time. We now, at his request, in his presence and in the presence of each other, subscribed our names as witnesses.

Residing at:
_____
_____

Residing at:
_____
_____

Residing at:
_____
_____

Figure 5.1
An example of a simple will.

on "paying last respects" is mainly a sales pitch by funeral directors and morticians. In many states, **embalming** (replacing the body's blood with preserving fluid) is required if burial does not occur within 24 hours of death. Embalming is one expense many of us can now avoid. Rather than purchasing an expensive casket, people today often use inexpensive wooden caskets or build their own. Rather that renting a funeral chapel, many have their loved ones buried and then hold the memorial service in the church or home. One reason for this is that if they spent a small fortune on a funeral, ultimately they would grieve over the financial burden as much as for the loved one.

CREMATION

Cremation is an alternative to burial. Increasingly more consumers (about 18% today) are choosing cremation because it costs less, it is more sanitary, it preserves land, and most people live far from family burial plots. In cremation, the body is usually placed in an inexpensive casket (although this is not necessary) and then burned in a special furnace called a "retort." The body and casket are reduced to ashes, which are either scattered, buried, or placed in an urn (a stone or metal container) and stored in a columbarium (a special place in a cemetery) or a mausoleum (a building designated specifically for cremated remains).

Some religions have sanctions against cremation, and some people feel that cremation isn't natural. Survivors may see cremation as destructive of the loved one, or may want a grave to visit. It is important to talk with loved ones who are likely to die before you are, so you can make arrangements in accordance with their desires.

CRYONIC SUSPENSION

In 1983 a group of physicians lowered the body temperature of a cancer patient 32 degrees from the usual 98.6 degrees for 40 minutes to induce a state of hypothermia, stopped the heartbeat, created a state of suspended animation, and were able to perform surgery (McShane 1983). In the process, they advanced one step closer to the dream that many scientists have had for many years, of freezing patients to create a state of total-body suspension in order to fight such diseases as cancer and heart disease. Not only is the scientific community

embalming
The process of removing blood from a dead person and replacing it with preserving fluid.

cremation
The process of burning a corpse in a furnace to reduce it to ashes.

interested in the procedure, but consumers are fascinated with the idea that, it they contract an incurable disease, they could be suspended and later, after a cure for the disease is found, revived and cured. It seems to be part of the quest for eternal life.

Cryonic suspension is a deep-freeze burial, which occurs in a cryotorium. The humans that are suspended are called "cryons." *Cryobiology* is investigation and experimentation on bodies that are well below normal body temperature. *Cryonics* comprises all disciplines and programs centered on human cold storage (Smith and Hall 1986).

Scientists have been successful in the freeze preservation of cells, blood serum, semen, and some large organs. Although cryonics has been successful in the transplanting of human organs, there has yet to be a success in the revival of an entire human body that has been suspended. Many people have contracted to be frozen upon death for fees of about $12,000 and an annual charge of $2,000 for maintenance. The obvious challenge to law and medicine relates to definitions of death, legal complexities and estate planning, and other medical and legal complications.

THE PRICE OF BEREAVEMENT

Funeral costs vary in different parts of the country. Table 5.1 shows a range of prices of typical funerals. Many of the costs could be avoided by burying or cremating immediately without ceremony. The total costs represented by these selected funeral homes would range from $1,980 to $30,105.

GRIEF

When we know a loved one is dying, we often go through stages of grief similar to those Kübler-Ross (1969) describes for the dying person. Survivors, too, may deny that death is coming and become angry, sometimes at the patient, especially if they depend on the dying person. They may spend much time in prayer, bargaining for the person to recover; they get depressed; ultimately, they usually accept their lonely state.

When someone close to us dies, we experience **bereavement** (Kutscher 1980), the objective fact of loss. Bereavement may bestow the label *orphan, widow, widower,* or *survivor.*

---

cryonic suspension
Deep-freezing human corpses in case, when a cure has been discovered for the condition from which the person died, the person can be revived and cured.

bereavement
The loss we experience when someone close to us dies.

grief
Intense emotional suffering that is a normal reaction to bereavement; its physical symptoms include a tight throat, shortness of breath, the need to sigh, and feelings of emptiness.

mourning
Social customs for bereavement, such as wearing black and having funerals.

TABLE 5.1   THE PRICE OF BEREAVEMENT

Burial Service Charges	
Services of the funeral director and staff	$295–$390
Use of facilities for viewing/visitations	$60–$100
Use of facilities for funeral ceremony	$175–$300
Use of facility to shelter remains	$80–$130
Automotive equipment (prices for 50-mile radius and $1 per mile per vehicle over 50 miles)	
Transfer remains to funeral home	$60–$100
Hearse	$75–$100
Limousines	$60–$80
Service vehicle (floral van)	$45–$60
Embalming	$110–$220
Other preparation of body: restoration, special care for autopsied remains, dressing ($50), hair care ($20), cosmetics ($50), etc.	$95–$225
Opening and closing a grave	$350–$600
Subtotal	**$1,405–$2,305**
Cremation	
Direct cremation without any attendant rites or ceremonies in an unfinished wood box	$590–$925
Direct cremation with container provided by the purchaser	$470–$625
Subtotal	**$1,060–$1,550**
Other Purchases	
Caskets (wooden box, cloth covered $190) to seamless (for longer preservation) metals such as bronze ($4,950) or copper ($10,500)	$190–$10,500
Casket containers ($75 wood to $1,600 metals or porcelain)	$75–$1,600
Grave markers: flat stone ($110), upright ($300) to statues ($13,000)	$110–$13,000
Cemetery plots	$150–$1,000
Urns	$50–$1,000
Burial clothing	$0–$200
Flowers, musicians, register books, acknowledgement cards, memorial programs, and so on	$0–$500
Subtotal	**$575–$27,800**

Grief is a normal reaction to bereavement; it is also a coping process of readjusting to life without the deceased. Physical symptoms that often accompany grief include a tightening of the throat, shortness of breath, a need for sighing, an empty feeling in the stomach, weakness, tension, or pain. Anger or indifference are among the possible emotional responses to bereavement.

Mourning is a social response to the state of bereavement. In our culture, people often wear black, have funerals, and follow other cultural patterns of expression.

When you know a loved one is dying, you may feel very much alone and begin to experience stages of grief similar to those of the dying person.

Children need to be included in the grieving experience.

NORMAL GRIEVING

C. M. Parkes defined the grief process in terms of a phasic progression of psychological and social experiences (Smith 1985). The first phase, according to Parkes, is a period of numbness. This is the first reaction of feeling stunned, paralyzed, and dulled by the news of a death. This stage serves an anesthetizing or protective function. The numbness stage lasts hours or days and is followed by the second stage, searching.

Searching occurs after we have recognized the reality of the loss and set in motion the psychological process of adjusting to the loss of the loved one. Anxiety, yearning, preoccupied thinking about the deceased, sobbing, crying, and subjection to delusions typify this stage. Many times these delusions are hypnagogic—that is, they happen when we are falling asleep. For example, widowed persons have reported hearing the spouse's voice in the other room—and they even get up, almost expecting to find them there—or hearing them drive up in a car and waiting for them to come up the stairs. The searching phase usually takes 5 to 14 days but can linger up to a year. The emotion from this stage is anger, which may be directed at the deceased, family members, or physicians but is more often repressed. The anger, which might seem unjustified to the grieving person, results in the other dominant emotion, guilt. During the searching process, we often discover missed opportunities in relationships, which also results in guilt. Anger and guilt require venting, which is where another person can help someone who is grieving.

The third stage is reactive depression, which is characterized by "sleep and eating disruptions, apathy and malaise, dysfunctions in higher mental activities, and disorganization in certain other behaviors" (Smith 1985). The death of a loved one throws our lives out of focus, changes goals, adds new responsibilities, and results in other major shifts in lifestyle.

In the final stage, readjustment, the bereaved person gradually assumes certain roles and functions that were previously performed by the deceased. We create a new life, and the depression is reduced or ceases. Researchers suggest that many of us will adjust after 1 year but others may take as long as 2 years to reach a fully functional lifestyle.

TALKING WITH CHILDREN ABOUT DEATH

When someone significant in their life dies, children can be immeasurably affected, largely because they were not given preparation for the death (Marks 1991). Here are some things to consider and some guidelines to follow when you need to talk with a child about death.

1. The ideal person to talk with a child about death is someone the child can trust, have confidence in, and feel is both open and sincere (Savicki 1985).

2. Before a significant death, prepare the child by talking about the ill person (Hansen and Frantz 1985). "Since Gramma became sick, what have you been feeling or thinking?"

3. Consider the age and development of the child. At age 3 to 4, there is a lack of clear understanding of death: Death is a temporary departure. At ages 5 to 9, children have a more realistic concept of death and accept its definitiveness, but it might be viewed as a unique entity of the deceased, like a spirit, a ghost, or living in heaven. After age 9, children have a clearer understanding of the irreversibility of death (Savicki 1985).

4. While each person has his or her own way of talking with a child, a helpful starting point is to review the meaning the deceased had for you and for the child, using phrases such as "Do you remember when . . . ?" "What do you remember most about . . . ?" and "If you could tell . . . one more thing, what would you say?" (Savicki 1985).

5. Talking about the future will stress the permanence of death and how the child will be affected: "Things will be different now, but we'll always remember the good times together . . ." or "We're really going to miss . . ." "What will you miss the most?" (Savicki 1985).

6. Be honest in answering the child's simple questions, such as "Why do people die?" or "Do you still eat and breathe when you die?" (Savicki 1985).

7. Protecting children from the funeral when they understand what is happening is generally not advised unless the child chooses not to attend. Leaving them out of a family event will increase their insecurity, and they will miss opportunities to grieve (Savicki 1985).

8. Preparation for the funeral is important. Tell the child that "Gramma will look different now" (if there is going to be an open casket) and "Grown-ups will be silent, sad, and weepy" (Hansen and Frantz 1985).

9. Remember that a child's grief, if it is not properly faced, can resurface unexpectedly (Hansen and Frantz 1985).

HELPING A GRIEVING ADULT

To help an older person, there are some basic things that you can do.

1. Listen, hold, touch, and understand anytime during the grieving process, which might be 1 to 2 years. Some people may never recover completely. Let the person share the grief with you. They may be angry with you one day and need to hold you the next, so be prepared.

2. Reassure them that their feelings of guilt, sadness, despair, and any other feelings that they might have are normal.

3. Try and put them in touch with other people who are grieving. Parents who have lost a child through a particular disease or suicide should share their experiences with others in similar circumstances.

EARLY DEATH

MISCARRIAGE

In a miscarriage, a developing fetus is suddenly delivered before its life can be sustained, and the pregnancy is terminated. Most miscarriages occur before 3 months of development. Depending upon your perspective of when life begins, you might see a miscarriage as a form of death. Some people have a very difficult time and must cope with the loss—especially if the pregnancy was wanted. According to Hutti (1992), reactions vary: Those who felt the reality of their pregnancy and ascribed a personality to the fetus experience the most grief. Those who acknowledged that the pregnancy was real but did not ascribe a personality to the child feel a sense of loss. Feelings of slight concern and acceptance are evident among those who did not have any sense of being pregnant.

STILLBIRTH AND PERINATAL DEATH

Pregnancy and birth are normally joyful experiences for parents and families. For some, it is very difficult to get pregnant. Once a couple gets pregnant, they begin to dream, fix up rooms, make purchases, select names, and tell many people. Unfortunately, in 1 to 2 percent of the cases (Smith 1985), a baby will be **stillborn** (dead at birth) or have a **perinatal death** (die within hours or days after delivery). Obviously many parents are not ready for the death and are devastated. Psychologically, parents grieve differently over newborns than they would over someone they have known well, since they have no memories of the child to cherish. Therapists recommend that the child be named, be seen by the parents (if not, take photographs for later viewing), and have formal funeral services, which provides a mechanism for grieving and identification with the child (Smith 1985).

SUDDEN INFANT DEATH SYNDROME (CRIB DEATH)

Sudden infant death syndrome (SIDS) is the sudden death of an infant or young child, with no apparent cause of death. Infants who die of SIDS are generally discovered by a parent or babysitter early in the morning or at a periodic check. The

stillbirth
The birth of a dead infant.

perinatal death
The death of an infant within hours or days after its birth.

sudden infant death syndrome (SIDS)
A syndrome that occurs among apparently healthy babies, generally between one and three months of age, involving sudden death without warning, usually while the infant is sleeping.

infant is instinctively taken into the arms of the parent or caregiver, who frantically attempts to resuscitate the baby. SIDS is rarely reported in infants younger than 1 month of age; peak incidents occur at 2 to 3 months of age, and 90 percent of SIDS deaths occur under 25 weeks of age. SIDS is the largest single cause of postnatal death, accounting for 2 to 3 deaths per 1,000 live births each year (Smith 1985). Although there are no apparent causes of SIDS, the most likely SIDS victims, based on several studies, are those born prematurely, during winter months, to young mothers, to smoking or drug-dependent mothers (particularly to those using methadone), and to mothers who have had little or no prenatal obstetrical care. One final factor that links the majority of SIDS victims is that they die while they are sleeping.

Numerous theories have arisen in an attempt to explain the mystery of SIDS. The theory that has the greatest support is the apnea theory, which refers to the interruption of breathing or respiratory function generally during rapid eye movement (active) sleep, creating a situation of greater vulnerability to asphyxiation.

SIDS is one of the most traumatic crises parents may face. The infant's death is so unexpected and the explanations about cause are so vague that parents are ill prepared, guilt ridden, and stunned by the loss. A SIDS death magnifies the normal grieving process, which may prolong the recovery process.

Some innovations are available for monitoring children during the night. Colin Paton, an 18-year-old young man, won an award for developing an easily assembled monitor that can be attached to a baby's stomach and senses when the baby stops breathing. After the baby goes for 15 seconds not breathing, the monitor sounds an alarm, which automatically stops when breathing resumes (Coghlan 1993).

DONATING ORGANS

Medical science has advanced to the point that there are few organs that cannot be used to help someone else live a much better-quality life. People are waiting months to receive new eyes, lungs, hearts, livers, and other organs. It has been shown that parents cope better with their child's death, and find solace, by donating the organs of their brain-dead child. They feel that if their child must die, then at least some other child in the world will live; the child's life, though short, is thus given meaning.

Perhaps one of the most precious gifts that we can give to another person would be to donate our organs at our death. Even though we die, we have the opportunity to provide our vital organs so that others can see, breathe, and continue to enjoy life itself. The way to do this is either to identify yourself

Issue
Donating Organs

A decision you can make now is to, in the event of your death, donate your organs to someone who may need them to live. Perhaps mentally your response to this is "yes, perhaps," and emotionally it is "no."

- Pro: Many people's lives are saved, improved, or extended when they receive an organ transplant. People can see better, live without kidney dialysis, have a more functional heart, breathe better, and regain other functions because someone donated their organs. There are thousands of people just waiting for a donor organ and suffering until they can receive it. We will be dead, so why should it matter?

- Con: It is a moral issue. We weren't born to ultimately be all cut up when we die. The thought of taking parts of me after I am dead and giving it to another person is more than I can handle. When I am buried, I want all of my body in the grave, I don't want my organs walking around in other people.

What do you feel about organ donation? If you feel willing to donate, which ones will you donate? If you do not feel willing to donate, why not? Do you know how to have your organs donated if you do die?

as an organ donor on your driver's license or to complete an **organ donor card.** An example of an organ donor card is shown in figure 5.2.

DEATH AS A POSITIVE FORCE IN LIFE

With all the negative emotions and readjustments that accompany death, there are some positive outcomes. When families are close and communicate feelings openly, death can be fulfilling. Death can draw the survivors closer together and help them to reevaluate the priorities in their lives, change behaviors, and grow from the experience.

organ donor card
A card indicating that, upon the bearer's death, specific organs are to be donated for organ transplants or research.

MINNESOTA DEPARTMENT OF PUBLIC SAFETY
Driver and Vehicle Services Division/108 Transportation Building/St. Paul, Minnesota 55155

In the hope that I may help others, I hereby make this anatomical gift, if medically acceptable, to take effect upon my death. I give any needed organs or parts for the purpose of transplantation.

(PLEASE PRINT) Donor's Name _____
First   Middle   Last

Date of Birth _____
Month   Day   Year

SIGNED BY THE DONOR IN THE PRESENCE OF THE WITNESSES SET FORTH BELOW
If donor is under 18 years of age BOTH parents, a legal guardian or parent or parents having legal custody must also sign in the presence of these witnesses.

Signature of Donor _____   Date _____

Address _____
Street   City   Zip   State

Signatures of both parents,
legal guardian or parent(s) _____   _____
having legal custody.

_____   _____
Witness   Witness

THIS IS A LEGAL DOCUMENT UNDER THE UNIFORM ANATOMICAL GIFT ACT OR SIMILAR LAWS. You are hereby notified that all personal data furnished on this document is part of a public record and transcripts may be issued to anyone.
PS-33204-03 Donor Card

GIFT OF LIFE ORGAN DONOR PROGRAM

Transplantation of some human organs is now a reality because of advances made in medical technology. One of the major problems is the shortage of transplantable organs. The Minnesota Department of Public Safety, Driver and Vehicle Services Division, through an act passed by the State Legislature, now give anyone the opportunity to indicate on the Driver License or Minnesota Identification Card that, upon death, needed body organs may be used for transplantation, if medically acceptable.

If you desire to register in the Organ Donor Program, complete the form on the reverse side and present it **with** your Driver License or Minnesota Identification Card application.

PLEASE NOTE:
1. **PRINT** your first, middle and last name.
2. **PRINT** your date of birth. (Month, day and year)
3. **In the presence of two witnesses, WRITE your name in the space provided for "signature of donor" and if under 18, BOTH parents, a legal guardian or parent(s) having legal custody WRITE their names in the spaces provided and have the two witnesses sign the document.**
4. **PRINT** your complete residence address.

The "DONOR" designation will then be indicated on your Driver License or Minnesota Identification Card. The designation may be removed by applying for a duplicate license or **new** Minnesota Identification Card.

If the donor cannot sign, the Donor Document may be signed for the donor at the donor's direction, in the donor's presence, and in the presence of two witnesses who must sign the document in the donor's presence. **If the donor is under 18 and cannot sign no "Donor" designation may be added to the Driver License or Minnesota Identification Card.**

If you do not wish to register in the Organ Donor Program, proceed with the Driver License or Minnesota Identification Card application as indicated thereon, disregarding this document.

Figure 5.2
Organ donor card.

TAKE ACTION

1. Become an organ donor.
2. Make out a living will.
3. Talk to someone in the clergy or another spiritual mentor about life, death, and life after death.
4. Talk with your parents or significant others about how they would like their funerals to be planned: memorial service versus funeral, cremation versus burial, viewing versus nonviewing, music selections, and so on.
5. Talk with your parents or significant others about their wills and find out who the executor is, what the surviving spouse's circumstances would be; who would take custody of underaged children if any are involved; and so on.
6. Mentally rehearse how to comfort someone who may be dying or who has lost a loved one who has died.
7. Purchase a family burial plot or mausoleum space, if one of these is your family's choice for treatment of the body after death.

PERSONAL SKILLS AND EXPERIENCES

PNI and Dying

Psychoneuroimmunology is the study of the interaction of the mind, the central nervous system, and the body's immunological system. PNI studies show that people with a fighting spirit, a cause of dream, optimism, hope, faith, and self-efficacy actually build their immune systems and fortify themselves against diseases of the mind and body. The deciding factor between dying of a disease and living has often been the state of mind and soul. But note that we should view PNI information with caution. The states of mind and soul are factors that can tip the scales one way or the other. Sometimes the disease is so strong that even the strongest will cannot resist its devastation.

To maximize your immune system daily, and especially in the time of disease, you need to have hope, optimism, and a fighting spirit. The natural state of denial in the case of terminal illness is an especially powerful state. To have hope and a fighting spirit in that stage might be the difference between living or dying. As we help others cope with their death, we may want to provide supportive hope in the early stages of denial and bargaining. PNI tells us that quicker healing, less-severe symptoms, and healthier living are acquired by attaining peak states of mental and soulful health. The key ways are these:

1. Have a cause, mission, purpose, or dream in life.
2. Challenge yourself with new, empowering, and varied life experiences.
3. Get to know your true nature.

8. Complete your own funeral arrangements in the event of your death and keep a record of this with your will so that others will not have to guess what you would like for funeral arrangements or feel obligated to buy an expensive service.

SUMMARY

1. At some time, everyone must deal with the death of a loved one and his or her own eventual death. There are ways to be better prepared for death.

2. People who die gradually often pass through five identifiable stages: denial, anger, bargaining, depression, and acceptance.

3. Understanding the psychological stages of dying can help people to cope better with their own death and provide support for others who are dying.

4. Hospices provide a more humane approach to death than is possible in hospitals.

5. Euthanasia is an issue that many people must face.

6. The life-after-death phenomenon is reported by many people who have approached death, and their experiences have positive implications for everyone.

7. Funerals can be very commercialized. Consumers must beware of unnecessary expenses and, before their death, learn the wishes of loved ones in regard to funerals.

8. Grieving is a difficult coping task that generally consists of numbness, searching, reactive depression, and readjustment.

9. Talking to a child or an adult who has just experienced the death of a loved one is difficult, but this support is very important. Special consideration is necessary in the case of SIDS or stillbirths.

10. Death can be a positive experience for the survivors, under the right circumstances.

COMMITMENT ACTIVITIES

1. In your state there are laws that regulate funerals, organ donation, euthanasia, and living wills, as well as a statute that defines when a person is legally dead. Find out what the laws are in your state regarding death-related procedures.

2. Is there a hospice near you? If so, arrange a time to visit and volunteer to help out for an afternoon so that you can get the feel of the place. If they have time, talk with staff members about their attitude toward death and dying. How does it compare with your own?

3. Spend some time in your college library reading about how different cultures deal with death and dying. Which of those you read about seem to address our human needs most effectively? Why?

4. There are many views of death, life after death, grieving customs, and methods of disposing of the body. Invite foreign students, religious leaders, or others to class; or have a class discussion in which class members describe their customs and talk about life after death (resurrection, reincarnation, and so on), how to grieve (tearing clothes, public grieving, purging ceremonies, etc.), and so on. Customs vary dramatically within our own country.

REFERENCES

Ad Hoc Committee of the Harvard Medical School to Examine the Definition of Brain Death. 1968. "A Definition of Invisible Coma." *Journal of the American Medical Association* 205: 337–40.

Bardis, P. D. 1981. *History of Thanatology.* Washington, DC: University Press of America.

CeloCruz, M. T. 1992. "Aid in Dying: Should We Decriminalize Physician-Assisted Suicide (PAS)?" *American Journal of Law and Medicine* 18, no. 4:369–94.

Coghlan, A. 1993. "Prize Winning Monitor Could Cut Cot Deaths." *New Scientist* 137, no. 1860:19.

Consumer's Union. 1993. "Last Rights: Why a 'Living Will' Is Not Enough." *Consumer Reports on Health* 5, no. 9.

PERSONAL SKILLS AND EXPERIENCES

Preparing for Death

Mind

This chapter has mentioned several activities that can help prepare you mentally for another's death. The following is a condensed list of things that you can do to make your own eventual death easier on your survivors.

1. Fill out an organ donor card.
2. Write out the music, speakers, and other wishes for your own funeral.
3. Write out your own obituary.
4. Purchase or identify a burial spot where you would like your remains to rest.
5. Write out whether you want to be cremated or buried.
6. Make a living will.
7. Make a will or establish a trust so that you know how your estate will be distributed.
8. Inform your lawyer and the executor of your will or estate of where you have filed your will or established your trust.
9. If you have dependent children, indicate how you want your children to be cared for in the case of your death and the death of your spouse.
10. Make sure your health insurance and life insurance are adequate to help your survivors.

To help you make some of these preparations, complete the following form.

Body

Something we all have in common is that we will someday die. Some of us will go in younger years, and others will be older. We might not have a lot of control over when we die. We do have some control over the quality of our life and the quality of our death. We may be able to choose to have a slow, painful death and disability for many years if we smoke, overeat, become sedentary, and lack purpose for living. Or we may be able to experience a higher quality of life through regular exercise and other healthful practices. Your quality of life, and subsequent quality of death, will be better if you

1. play throughout your life,
2. exercise throughout your life,
3. eat nutritiously throughout your life,
4. have active avocations, and
5. use your body daily as much as you can.

Soul

One of the reasons that we deny death the way we do is that we do not want to face negative emotions. We want to be happy, be in love, have positive spiritual experiences, be enriched with music, and feel other positive dimensions of the soul. But when we have to mourn or face loss, we deny and avoid it. Moore (1992) suggests that we should embrace all parts of the soul. The aches we experience when we contemplate death and loss are part of us as well, and we should get to know ourselves better. The experience and skill of the soul is to look at death as an opportunity to become genuine, to explore deep within your heart, to take advantage of the music that often accompanies funerals, and get in touch with your feelings. One way to express your soul and to cope is to tell stories about the times you had with the loved one—it will make you laugh and cry. Death is a chance to get to know the real you. Death removes the layers of roles and expectations we all suffer from in daily living and frees the soul to come to the surface.

If you have had a death in the family recently, reflect upon that event and note how the side of you that was on the surface during the death experience is different from the one that attends class. If you have not experienced a death of someone close to you, then imagine that it happened and get in touch with your soul.

Interdependence

A very difficult activity to do is to talk with loved ones about eventual death—theirs and yours. It is extremely helpful to you, and to others who will survive you, if you discuss the different aspects of death that have been covered in this chapter. You may want to talk about your own situation and their situation as it pertains to the following topics. This is a mind/body/soul experience of interdependence.

1. Share your feelings about an afterlife.
2. What do you each want at your funerals or memorial services, if you want those?
3. Do you each want to donate your organs?
4. What do you want in your obituaries?
5. Where do you each want to be buried, or where to you want your cremated remains to rest?
6. What are your religious feelings?
7. Write out whether you want to be cremated or buried.
8. Do you each have living wills, and what are your feelings about life support?
9. Discuss the advantages and disadvantages of wills versus trusts.
10. Discuss what you each would want to happen if you die? What about the children? What about remarrying? moving?
11. Discuss the adequacy of your life and health insurance. Is it adequate to cover funeral and medical expenses so that your death will not inflict a financial burden on survivors?

(Continued on page 5.19)

Service Instructions

Name_____

Conducting church preference_____

Services at: funeral home ☐ church ☐ graveside ☐
Pallbearers selected by: family ☐ funeral home ☐
Music selected by: staff ☐ family choice ☐

Specific selections:

1. _____

2. _____

Preferred speakers:

1. _____

2. _____

Prayers:

1. _____

2. _____

Preference of flowers:_____

Clothing:_____

Jewelry:_____

Glasses:_____

Donations to:_____

Obituary: yes ☐ no ☐   Out-of-town paper_____

Obituary picture: yes ☐ no ☐

Obituary

_____
_____
_____
_____

Cemetery Property Details

Do you have a deed to cemetery property? yes ☐ no ☐

Deed located in: home ☐ bank ☐ other ☐

Name of cemetery:_____

City:_____ State:_____

Property in name of:_____

Name of mausoleum or garden:_____

Section_____ Tier_____ Lot_____ Space(s)_____

I would prefer:_____

Interment_____ Entombment_____ Cremation_____

Vital Statistics and Historical Data

Name_____
    First   Middle/Maiden   Last

Address_____

_____
   City   County   State   Phone

Birthplace_____
               City   State

Date of birth_____ Social Security no._____

Employed by_____

Occupation (or retired from)_____

Single ☐ Married ☐ Widowed ☐ Divorced ☐

In city since_____

Spouse of_____ Maiden name_____

Father's Full Name_____

Mother's Maiden Name_____

Date of Marriage_____

Place of Marriage_____

Information Regarding Estate

My attorney is_____

My bank is_____

Additional bank or banks_____

Safe deposit box in_____ Box no._____
          Name of Bank

Location of key_____

Real estate owned_____

Location of deeds_____

(This information is confidential and very important in case of a common disaster.) I (have) (have not) made a will. If a will has been made, the Executor is:

_____
      Name   Address

A copy is kept:_____

Notify following insurance companies, unions, lodges, etc., paying death benefits:

1. _____

2. _____

Dworkin, R. 1993. "Life Is Sacred: That's the Easy Part." *New York Times Magazine,* 16 May, 36.

Eadie, B. J. 1992. *Embraced by the Light.* Placerville, CA: Goldleaf Press.

"Euthanasia." 1990. *American Medical News,* 27 July, 24.

Goleman, D., and J. Gurin, eds. 1993. *Mind Body Medicine.* New York: Consumers Union of the United States.

Hansen, J. C., and T. T. Frantz, eds. 1985. *Death and Grief in the Family.* Rockville, MD: Aspen.

Hutti, M. H. 1992. "Parents Perceptions of the Miscarriage Experience." *Death Studies* 16, no. 5:401–15.

Kamisar, Y. 1993. "Active Versus Passive Euthanasia." *Trial* 29, no. 3:32–37.

Kübler-Ross, E. 1969. *On Death and Dying.* New York: Macmillan.

Kübler-Ross, E. 1974. *Questions and Answers on Death and Dying.* New York: Macmillan.

Marks, J. 1991. "We Have a Problem." *Parents Magazine,* January, 47.

McShane, L. 1983. "Hopkins Saves a Life with New Technique." *Washington Post,* 12 October, C1.

Moody, R. A. 1975. *Life After Life.* New York: Bantam.

Moody, R. A. 1977. *Reflections on Life After Life.* New York: Bantam.

Moore, T. 1992. *Care of the Soul.* New York: Harper Collins.

Moyers, B. 1993. *Healing and the Mind.* New York: Doubleday.

Osis, K., and E. Haraldsson. 1977. *At the Hour of Death.* New York: Avon.

Rhymes, J. 1990. "Hospice Care in America." *Journal of the American Medical Association* 264: 369–72.

Richardson, G. E. 1979. "The Life After Death Phenomenon." *Journal of School Health* 49: 451–53.

Savicki, S. D. 1985. "Talking with Children About Death: Six Pragmatic Guides." In *Loss, Grief, and Bereavement,* edited by O. S. Margolis, et al. New York: Praeger.

Smith, G. P., and C. Hall. 1986. "Cryonic Suspension and the Law." *Omega* 17, no. 1:1–7.

Smith, W. J. 1985. *Death in the Human Life Cycle.* New York: Holt, Rinehart & Winston.

Szanton, A. 1992. "Changing Styles Bring Cremation Industry to Life." *American Demographics* 14, no. 12:25–26.

Vernon, J. 1993. "It's Your Funeral." *New Statesman and Society* 6, no. 248:22–23.

ADDITIONAL READINGS

Cecil, R. 1991. *The Masks of Death.* London: Book Guild. This is an intriguing book with many quotes and perspectives on the concept of providence, the evangelical way of death, violent death, sudden death, images of the afterlife, a view of the cults, and right-to-die issues.

Kübler-Ross, E. 1969. *On Death and Dying.* New York: Macmillan. This is a classic in the field of thanatology, describing in detail the psychological stages of dying.

Logue, B. J. 1993. *Last Rights.* New York: Lexington. Logue talks about the trends among the elderly and the growing force of frailty and then presents a case for "death control." The bias of this book is for leniency toward suicide and physician-assisted suicide.

Moller, D. W. 1990. *On Death with Dignity.* Amityville, NY: Baywood. Technology, individualism, stigmas of the dying, and social isolation are the key topics in this book. It has some interesting insights into our cultural biases.

Moody, R. A. 1975. *Life After Life.* New York: Bantam. A fascinating book with descriptions of "life after life" experiences by people who had been declared dead but then were revived.

Platt, L. A., and V. R. Persico. 1992. *Grief in Cross-Cultural Perspective.* New York: Garland. This book discusses the social meaning of death and perspectives on death of cultures other than mainstream white American culture. Views of death from Madagascar, Whalsay, Islam, Peru, the Yolngu of Australia, and Maya Indians of meso America, among others.

Rosen, E. J. 1990. *Family Facing Death.* Lexington, MA: Lexington Books. This book deals with coping with loss, understanding the family system, the role of caregivers, euthanasia, anticipatory grief, and helping.

LIFESTYLE CONTRACT

After reading and pondering the last 2 chapters on choices and the aging process and death and dying, you should have a good understanding of:

1. the nature of healthy aging.
2. what some of the things are that you can do to mentally and fiscally prepare for your own death or the eventual death of someone close to you.
3. the nature of the death and dying process.
4. what some things are you can do now for your own healthy aging experience.

Lifestyle Contracting Using Strength Intervention

I. Choosing the desired health behavior or skill.

A. Keeping in mind the purposes in life and goals you identified, consider one or two health behaviors related to aging and death and dying (from the lists in the chapters or your own creation) that will help you reach your goals. In order to assess your likelihood of success, ask yourself questions similar to those used in previous sections such as these:

1. Is my purpose, cause, or goal better realized by adoption of this behavior?

_____ yes _____ no.

2. Am I hardy enough to accomplish this goal? (This means I feel I can do it if I work hard, am committed to do it, am challenged by it, and see myself in control enough to make it happen.)

_____ yes _____ no.

3. Is this a behavior I really want to change and that I feel I can change?

_____ yes _____ no.

4. Do I first need to nurture a personal strength area?

_____ yes _____ no.
(If yes, be sure to include this as a part of the plan.)

5. Do I need to free myself from the negative effects of a behavior (break a bad habit)?

_____ yes _____ no.
(If yes, be sure to include this as a part of the plan.)

6. Have I considered the results of the assessments in the three previous chapters?

_____ yes _____ no.

("Yes" answers to the first three questions are a must in order to be successful. It might be wise to consider a different behavior if you can't honestly answer "yes" to these questions. Your answers to questions 4–6 ought to provide insights for your consideration in making your plan.)

B. Behaviors I will change (no more than two)

_____

_____

II. Lifestyle Plan

A. A description of the general plan of what I am going to do and how I will accomplish it. Consider successes you have had in the past since they may help you consider the best ways to carry out this plan.

_____

_____

_____

_____

_____

_____

B. Barriers to the accomplishment of the plan (lack of time, materials, support, etc.)

1. Identify the barriers: _____

_____

_____

2. Means to remove the barriers (use problem-solving skills or creative approaches).

_____

_____

_____

C. Implementation of the plan

1. Substitution (putting positive behaviors in place of negative ones) _____

_____

_____

2. Linking Behaviors _____

_____

_____

3. Combining a strength and a weakness _____

_____

_____

4. When _____

5. Where _____

6. Preparation _____

_____

(Continued on page 5.22)

LIFESTYLE CONTRACT

7. With whom _____

_____

_____

III. Support Groups
A. Who: _____

_____

B. Role: _____

_____

_____

C. Organized support: _____

_____

IV. Trigger responses: _____

_____

_____

V. Starting date: _____

VI. Date/Sequence the contract will be reevaluated: _____

_____

VII. Evidence(s) of reaching the goal: _____

_____

_____

VIII. Reward(s) when contract is completed: _____

_____

_____

IX. Signature of student _____

X. Signature of facilitator/instructor _____

XI. Additional conditions/comments _____

_____

PART D.

Nutrition, Physical Activity, and Weight Control

CHAPTER 6

Nutrition: Healthy Food Choices

KEY QUESTIONS

What factors affect food choices?
What is the nutritional status of Americans?
What are the components of good nutrition?
Why is it important to plan for good nutrition?
What can be done to eat inexpensively and nutritiously?
What are some nutritional concerns that should be considered by athletes, the elderly, and vegetarians?

CHAPTER OUTLINE

Food Choices of Americans
Nutrition Basics
Carbohydrates
Proteins
Fats
Vitamins
Minerals
Water
Eating Nutritiously
Food Choices
Eating Well on a Shoestring
Fast Foods and Frozen Foods
Dining Out
Nutrition and the Consumer
Nutrition Labeling
Food Additives
Special Nutritional Considerations
Vegetarians
Athletes
Individuals Under Stress
Nutritional Needs Throughout Life
Take Action
Summary

Healthy People 2000 Objectives

- Among people aged 2 and older, reduce dietary fat intake to an average of 30 percent of calories or less and average saturated fat intake to less than 10 percent of calories.

- Increase to at least 5,000 brand names the availability of processed food products that are reduced in fat and saturated fat.

- Increase to at least 90 percent the proportion of restaurants and institutional food service operations that offer identifiable low-fat, low-calorie food choices consistent with the Dietary Guidelines for Americans.

- Increase complex-carbohydrate and fiber-containing foods in the diets of adults to five or more daily servings of vegetables (including legumes, such as beans and peas) and fruits, and to six or more daily servings for grain products.

- Decrease salt and sodium intake so at least 65 percent of meal preparers prepare foods without adding salt, at least 80 percent of people avoid using salt at the table, and at least 40 percent of adults regularly purchase foods modified or lower in sodium.

- Increase to at least 85 percent the portion of people aged 18 and older who use food labels to make nutritious food selections.

- Achieve useful and informative nutrition labeling for virtually all processed foods and at least 40 percent of fresh meats, poultry, fish, fruits, vegetables, baked goods, and ready-to-eat carry-away foods.

- Increase to at least 45 percent the proportion of people aged 35 through 44 who have never lost a permanent tooth due to dental caries or periodontal diseases.

HEALTH UPDATE

Nutrition Trends

- American cheese consumption is on the rise, which is likely due to our consumption of pizza. Americans consumed 25 pounds of cheese per person in 1990.
- Consumption of poultry products has increased steadily since 1970.
- Americans consumed 64 pounds of poultry per person in 1990.
- Egg consumption has dropped from 276 eggs per person in 1970 to 187 eggs per person in 1990.
- Milk consumption has dropped from 214 pounds per person in 1970 to 88 pounds per person in 1990.
- Fruit consumption has risen from 18 pounds per person in 1970 to 90 pounds per person in 1990.
- Although coffee intake is down, caffeine levels have remained the same due to our consumption of chocolate and soft drinks.
- Sugar consumption has increased 15 pounds per person since 1970, mostly due to our consumption of soft drinks.
- Americans continue to consume more food per person than ever.

Source: From Candy Sagon, *L.A. Times/ Washington Post.*

"You are what you eat." This is one of those statements we have all heard since childhood. However, the results of good or bad nutritional choices are not immediate. If we overeat, or eat too much junk food, we might feel guilty, but we usually don't see dramatic physical changes the next day. This lack of immediate cause-and-effect results makes it hard for us to appreciate that good nutritional choices really do make a difference in our health over a number of years.

Although Americans are interested in **nutrition,** this interest often does not translate into eating a healthy diet. We have access to a wide array of healthy foods, but might not select the most nutritious items. Knowledge often is not enough to influence our behavior.

Our interest in nutrition has translated into an over-abundance of advertising, including much that promotes the nutritional advantage of products, whether or not those products actually have those advantages. Since much more money is spent on advertising the less nutritious foods than on advertising the more nutritious foods, we need to be informed consumers in order to differentiate fact from fiction.

Eating would be a very simple activity if we ate only when hungry and applied our knowledge of nutrition in making our food choices. However, it is much more complex than that. Young children learn to associate food with good times and bad times. These behaviors continue in adulthood. Individuals reach for food to feel better in times of disappointment and to celebrate in times of happiness. Food becomes a coping mechanism for some. We see the connection of mind, body, and soul in considering how we relate to food.

FOOD CHOICES OF AMERICANS

Although we have an almost endless number of food items to choose from, most of us eat fewer than a hundred foods. Parents have much to do with influencing children's eating habits.

Foods are so readily available to Americans, we should have the best diets in the world. Unfortunately, easy access to food does not result in good decisions. Many Americans have problems that relate to excessive eating rather than to dietary deficiencies.

During the 1970s the primary focus of food guides was on receiving adequate amounts of nutrients (Welsh, Davis, and Shaw 1992). However, as the connection between excess intake of foods and chronic diseases became evident, the focus changed. We now know that dietary factors are associated with six of the ten leading causes of death in the United States, including coronary heart disease, some types of cancer, stroke, non-insulin-dependent diabetes mellitus, chronic liver disease and cirrhosis, and atherosclerosis ("Institute Offers 'Clear-Cut' Diet Plan to Reduce Disease Risk" 1992, p. 2). The most recent dietary guidelines published by the U.S. Department of Agriculture and the U.S. Department of Health and Human Services (1990) point to preventing disease by avoiding excesses. The guidelines include these:

- Eat a variety of foods.
- Maintain healthy weight.
- Choose a diet low in fat, saturated fat, and cholesterol.
- Choose a diet with plenty of vegetables, fruits, and grain products.
- Use sugars only in moderation.
- Use salt and sodium only in moderation.
- If you drink alcoholic beverages, do so in moderation.

Greater significance is given to body weight and the intake of fats in the most recent guidelines. The guidelines also include more practical information on how to apply the guidelines in planning our diets (Welsh, Davis, and Shaw 1992). Our nutritional decisions involve options related to behavioral and motivational choices and the decision-making process.

Healthy People 2000 lists nutrition as one of its health promotion priorities and includes twenty-one nutrition objectives. The report acknowledges the correlation between poor nutritional practices and chronic diseases and the change in focus of Americans from nutritional deficiency to

nutrition
Eating a diet that is rich in the nutrients needed for good health.

Nutrition

This assessment provides you with an opportunity to assess your nutrition habits.

Directions

Check off each item that accurately depicts your behavior.

Nutrition Habits

_____ 1. I usually eat breakfast.

_____ 2. I don't skip meals.

_____ 3. I don't have small snacks such as potato chips, candy, cookies, and soft drinks between meals.

_____ 4. I eat a variety of foods, including fruits, vegetables, meats, breads, and dairy products.

_____ 5. I usually eat a light evening meal.

_____ 6. I rarely eat at fast-food restaurants. When I do, I select nutritious foods.

_____ 7. I eat breakfast each day.

_____ 8. I drink at least 10 cups of water each day.

_____ 9. I never add salt to food.

_____ 10. I consider nutritional value when selecting food.

Carbohydrates

_____ 11. I eat three or more servings of nonfried veggies each day.

_____ 12. I select 100 percent whole wheat bread.

_____ 13. I eat four or more servings of fresh fruit each day.

_____ 14. I rarely eat candy bars or pastry.

_____ 15. I either skip desserts or have fresh fruit for dessert.

_____ 16. I rarely eat sugar-coated cereals.

Protein

_____ 17. I eat fish or shellfish three or more times a week.

_____ 18. I eat beans, split peas, or lentils four or more times a week.

_____ 19. I eat unprocessed red meat (steak, roast beef, lamb, pork chops) no more than two times per week.

_____ 20. I don't eat processed meats (hot dogs, sausage, bologna).

_____ 21. I bake, boil, broil, or poach fish, poultry, or meat.

Fat

_____ 22. I trim visible fat from meat.

_____ 23. I drink 0.5 percent or skim milk.

_____ 24. I eat at most two egg yolks per week.

_____ 25. I never eat fried foods.

_____ 26. I rarely put butter or cream cheese on bread or toast.

Scoring

Give yourself 1 point for each item you checked, and total your score.

Interpretation

Your score on this assessment indicates the quality of your nutrition habits. Interpret your score as follows:

22–26	= Excellent
17–21	= Good
16 or below	= You might want to consider some ways to improve your diet

---

PERSONAL INSIGHT

Family Eating Habits

I grew up in the Midwest at a time when a typical breakfast consisted of eggs, bacon, white toast with jam, and whole milk. A typical dinner included meat, potatoes, white bread, canned veggies (except in summer, when they were fresh) and dessert. My father loved to eat and especially enjoyed marbled meats that had not been trimmed of extra fat. I can still remember seeing him add salt to foods before tasting them because he enjoyed the flavor that salt added to foods. When I was 8 years old, my father was diagnosed with a heart condition and was placed on a low-fat, low-sodium diet. This was a radical change for all of us. I can recall how awful foods tasted without the sodium and what a change this was.

As a child it is very difficult to see the impact of behavior on health because our actions do not have an immediate effect on our health. Something that might happen 20 or 40 years later seems like a lifetime away and really isn't important until a certain event brings it home to you. The event for me related to my father's health. He died when I was 10. I suspect that cigarette smoking was the main reason, but I know that diet had a part in it, too. The long-term effects of health behavior were made very real to me the day he died.

TABLE 6.1 RDAS FOR ADULT MEN AND WOMEN

	Age	Weight (lb)	Height (in)	Protein (g)	Fat-Soluble Vitamins				Water-Soluble Vitamins		
					Vitamin A (mcg RE)[a]	*Vitamin D (mcg)*	*Vitamin E (mg)[b]*	*Vitamin K (mcg)*	*Vitamin C (mg)*	*Thiamin (mg)*	*Ribo-flavin (mg)*
Males	15–18	145	69	59	1,000	10	10	65	60	1.5	1.8
	19–24	160	70	58	1,000	10	10	70	60	1.5	1.7
	25–50	174	70	63	1,000	5	10	80	60	1.5	1.7
	51+	170	68	63	1,000	5	10	80	60	1.2	1.4
Females	15–18	120	64	44	800	10	8	55	60	1.1	1.3
	19–24	128	65	46	800	10	8	60	60	1.1	1.3
	25–50	138	64	50	800	5	8	65	60	1.1	1.3
	51+	143	63	50	800	5	8	65	60	1.0	1.2

[a]mcg—microgram = 1/1,000,000th gram; RE—retinol equivalent = 1 mcg retinol or 6 mcg beta-carotene

[b]mg—milligram = 1/1,000th gram

Note: Recommended Dietary Allowances (RDAs) are established by the National Research Council of the National Academy of Sciences and published by the government. The RDA for any given nutrient represents the amount considered "adequate to meet the known nutrient needs of practically all healthy persons."

Reprinted with permission from *Recommended Dietary Allowances: 10th Edition*. Copyright 1989 by the National Academy of Sciences. Courtesy of the National Academy Press, Washington, D.C.

the emphasis on chronic disease prevention and health maintenance (*Healthy People 2000* 1992, 93–95). The recent progress in this area is reflective of the impact of national concerns regarding nutrition.

NUTRITION BASICS

All of us need food to stay healthy. We need to replenish our cells by ingesting food. Food passes through the digestive system and is transformed from today's meal into tomorrow's energy, renewal, and growth. If too much food, too little food, or too much food of low nutritional value is consumed, our health is negatively impacted.

Digestion begins in the mouth. Saliva produced at the sight, smell, or thought of food contains **enzymes** (compounds that speed the rate of a chemical reaction), which break down carbohydrates, and mucus that moistens food. Food moves through the esophagus into the **stomach,** where enzymes and stomach acids mix with the food. A meal usually leaves the stomach within 2 to 3 hours after consumption and passes into the **small intestine,** where it stays for 3 to 10 hours. The small intestine is narrow and about 10 feet long. Most of a meal (95 percent) is digested in the small intestine, where enzymes from the intestinal cells and the **pancreas** mix with the food during muscular contractions. Nutrients are absorbed from the small intestine into the bloodstream for use by the cells. The remaining solid waste moves from the small intestine to the **large intestine,** where it remains for 1 to 3 days before the waste products are eliminated from the body.

Nutrients, the nourishing elements in food, include carbohydrates, proteins, fats, vitamins, minerals, and water. The kinds and amounts of nutrients contained in foods

vary. No single food provides all of the nutrients in the amounts needed for growth and health. In fact, over forty nutrients are needed by the body. Consequently, a diet that

digestion

The processes by which the body breaks down food to extract the nutrients it needs for energy, renewal, and growth.

enzymes

Proteins that catalyze biochemical reactions, such as digestion, in the body.

stomach

A principal digestive organ, part of the alimentary canal, located in the abdomen above the small intestine, where enzymes and stomach acids mix with food to start breaking down the food in order to extract nutrients from it.

small intestine

A narrow, 10-foot-long portion of the alimentary canal, extending from the stomach to the large intestine, where almost all digestion takes place. Enzymes from the intestinal walls and the pancreas break down food into nutrients, which are absorbed from the small intestine into the bloodstream.

pancreas

A long gland behind the stomach that secretes digestive enzymes as well as hormones, such as insulin.

large intestine

The lower end of the alimentary canal, below the small intestine. Solid waste moves from the small intestine to the large intestine, where it remains for 1 to 3 days.

nutrients

The nourishing elements in foods, including carbohydrates, proteins, fats, vitamins, minerals, and water. The body needs over forty nutrients for proper functioning and good health.

TABLE 6.1 RDAS FOR ADULT MEN AND WOMEN—CONTINUED

Water-Soluble Vitamins				Minerals						
Niacin (mg)	Vitamin B_6 (mg)	Folate (mcg)	Vitamin B_{12} (mcg)	Calcium (mg)	Phosphorus (mg)	Magnesium (mg)	Iron (mg)	Zinc (mg)	Iodine (mcg)	Selenium (mcg)
20	2.0	200	2.0	1,200	1,200	400	12	15	150	50
19	2.0	200	2.0	1,200	1,200	350	10	15	150	70
19	2.0	200	2.0	800	800	350	10	15	150	70
15	2.0	200	2.0	800	800	350	10	15	150	70
15	1.5	180	2.0	1,200	1,200	300	15	12	150	50
15	1.6	180	2.0	1,200	1,200	280	15	12	150	55
15	1.6	180	2.0	800	800	280	15	12	150	55
13	1.6	180	2.0	800	800	280	10	12	150	55

includes a variety of foods from all of the food groups is needed to provide the necessary nutrients.

Food supplies energy to support the body's activities. This energy comes from the carbohydrates, proteins, and fats in food and is measured in calories. A calorie is a unit for measuring the heat or energy produced by food when it is burned by the body. A calorie raises 1 gram of water 1 degree Celsius. Food energy is usually expressed in terms of **kilocalories (kcal)** because a calorie is such a small unit of heat measurement. A kilocalorie is the amount of heat it takes to raise 1,000 grams of water 1 degree celsius. Calories are also a measure of the energy we expend in different activities. Water, minerals, and vitamins do not supply calories. However, they assist the body in using the calories supplied by carbohydrates, protein, and fat.

To have a healthy diet, we need to consume a variety of nutrients in varying amounts. **RDAs, or Recommended Dietary Allowances,** are the levels of nutrient intake necessary for the maintenance of good nutrition for most healthy persons, as determined by the Food and Nutrition Board of the National Research Council of the National Academy of Sciences (see table 6.1). The RDAs are intended to help us meet our nutritional needs through foods rather than with vitamin supplements. They are not daily recommendations, but are nutrient levels needed over time and should be the average intake for vitamins and minerals in a 3- to 7-day period (Guthrie 1990). You should not try to plan meals based on the RDAs. Supplements are recommended only in the few cases where deficiency is commonly observed, such as iron deficiency in women ("New Recommended Dietary Allowances" 1990).

RDAs are used by the U.S. Department of Agriculture to establish standards for food assistance programs, assess nutritional status, and evaluate food supply. These standards influence the way in which nutritional content of food is listed on labels.

Information about the nutrients may be helpful to you in improving your diet. The six major nutrient groups are carbohydrates, protein, fats, vitamins, minerals, and water.

CARBOHYDRATES

Carbohydrates supply to our bodies the energy that is needed for daily activities. Some people associate carbohydrates with excess calories, but complex carbohydrates, such as pasta, are a positive alternative for a protein dish high in fat. Carbohydrates are also metabolized faster and more efficiently than proteins.

Carbohydrates are composed of carbon, hydrogen, and oxygen. Their major function is to provide a continuous

kilocalorie (kcal)
The amount of heat needed to raise 1,000 grams of water 1 degree Celsius.

Recommended Dietary Allowance (RDA)
The recommended nutrient intake that meets the needs of almost all people of the given gender and age group.

carbohydrates
Nutrients that supply most of our energy for daily activities. Carbohydrates supply 4 calories per gram.

energy supply to the cells of the body. Carbohydrates supply four calories per gram and can be categorized as either simple or complex. Simple carbohydrates are composed of one or two simple-sugar units, while complex carbohydrates are composed of longer chains of sugar units.

Simple Carbohydrates

Sugars are **simple carbohydrates** that are found naturally in foods such as fruit, milk, and some vegetables, including beets and peas. Sugars refined from sugar cane and sugar beets are also added to foods such as candy, soft drinks, and ice cream.

Simple carbohydrates provide immediate energy, while complex carbohydrates provide longer-lasting energy. As carbohydrates enter the body, they are changed into glucose, the energy source for cells. Cells use this energy, along with proteins, vitamins, and minerals, to repair themselves, make new cells, and carry out their work. **Glucose** is found in molasses, corn syrup, honey, and fruits and is classified as a **monosaccharide** because it contains only one molecule of sugar. Fructose is a monosaccharide found in fruits.

Disaccharides are simple carbohydrates formed from two monosaccharides. They include sucrose (simple table sugar), which is a combination of fructose and glucose; lactose (found in milk products), which is a combination of glucose and galactose; and maltose, which is formed by the combination of two glucose molecules.

Sugar Intake   Americans consume more than 130 pounds of **sugars** and sweeteners per person each year (Liebman 1990a). Because sugar is highly refined, and therefore quickly digested, you might continue to eat when you otherwise wouldn't. Sugary snacks are filled with **empty calories** (calories that provide no vitamins, minerals, or protein). Your nutrition will be negatively affected when you substitute sugary items for foods with nutrients. The increased use of artificial sweeteners has not curtailed sugar consumption. In fact, sugar consumption has continued to grow.

It is difficult to find commercial foods that have been prepared without sugar. Sugar is included not only in the sweet foods, but also in sauces, some baby foods, almost all fruit drinks, salad dressings, canned and dehydrated soups, pot pies, frozen TV dinners, bacon and other cured meats, some canned and frozen vegetables, most canned and frozen fruits, yogurt, and breakfast cereals. The most frequently advertised product on Saturday morning television is breakfast cereal, and many of the presweetened cereals contain nearly as much sugar in one serving (1 cup) as half a can of pop ("TV Feeds Kids Steady Diet of Sugary-Food Ads" 1991).

There are over a hundred sweet substances identified as "sugar," including fructose, dextrose, lactose, and maltose, but the word *sugar* is commonly used to refer to sucrose. Some sugars aren't quite as bad for the teeth as sucrose; otherwise, there's virtually no difference among them. There is

Sugar is hidden in many foods.

no nutritional value in any of the sugars, other than calories ("Honey vs. Sugar" 1992).

The $7 billion cereal business is getting bigger as food manufacturers target children for an even larger share of the 33 percent of cereal business that children currently control. Although there have been sugar-coated breakfast cereals for years, manufacturers are now pulling out the stops with the newest wave of presweetened cereals that incorporate themes from the most current movies, toys, and crazes. One of the biggest concerns about such sugar consumption is that it is difficult for children to get a proper nutritional balance when so many of their calories come from sugar. Children's cereals are 44 percent sugar, while adult cereals are 10 percent sugar ("Kid's-Eye Cereals" 1990). See table 6.2.

simple carbohydrates
Sugars that are found naturally in fruit, milk, and some vegetables; assimilated quickly, providing immediate energy.

glucose
A simple, monosaccharide carbohydrate found in molasses, corn syrup, honey, and fruits.

monosaccharides
Simple carbohydrates with a molecular structure containing only one sugar molecule.

disaccharides
Simple carbohydrates, including sucrose, lactose, and maltose, formed from two monosaccharides.

sugar
Sweet, water-soluble, simple carbohydrates, including monosaccharides and disaccharides.

empty calories
Calories from foods, such as sugary snacks, that have no nutritive value (no vitamins, minerals, or protein).

TABLE 6.2   SUGAR CONTENT OF CHILDREN'S CEREALS

	Teaspoons of Sugar per Cup*		Teaspoons of Sugar per Cup*
½ can soda pop	5	Frosted Flakes	3.5
General Mills		Fruity Marshmallow Krispies	3.5
Apple Cinnamon Cheerios	3.5	Honey Smacks	5
Body Buddies-Natural Fruit	1.5	Just Right with Fiber Nuggets	2
Booberry	3.5	Nut & Honey Crunch O's	4.5
Cheerios	less than .5	Nutri-Grain Wheat	1
Cocoa Puffs	3.5	Product 19	1
Count Chocula	3.5	Raisin Bran	4.5
Frankenberry	3.5	Rice Krispies	1
Golden Grahams	3	Special K	1
Honey Nut Cheerios	3.5	**Nabisco**	
Kix	.5	Spoon-Size Shredded Wheat	0
Lucky Charms	3	**Post**	
Nature Valley 100% Natural Cereal (all flavors)	4.5	Alpha-Bits	3
		Cocoa Pebbles	3.5
Trix	3	Fruity Pebbles	3.5
Wheaties	1	Grape Nuts	3
Kellogg's		Honeycomb	2
All-Bran	0	Sugar Golden Crisp	4
Apple Jacks	3.5	**Ralston Purina**	
Bran Flakes	2	Bill & Ted's Excellent Cereal	3.5
Cinnamon Mini Buns	3.5	Cookie-Crisp Chocolate Crisp	3.5
Cocoa Krispies	3.5	Corn Chex	1
Corn Flakes	.5	The Jetsons	3.5
Corn Pops	3	Slimer! and the Real Ghostbusters	4
Double Dip Crunch	3	Teenage Mutant Ninja Turtles	3
Froot Loops	3.5		

*Serving sizes have been standardized to 1 cup. Four grams of sugar equal 1 level teaspoon. Values have been rounded to the nearest ½ teaspoon.

Reprinted with permission from the November 1991 issue, *Tufts University Diet & Nutrition Letter,* 53 Park Place, 8th floor, New York, NY 10007.

Although a number of diseases have been linked with sugar intake, tooth decay is the most obvious problem caused by excessive consumption of sugar. Dental caries (cavities) begin when oral bacteria lower the pH of the mouth from a normal 6.7 to 5.5 or lower. It is thought that bacteria (probably streptococci) convert carbohydrate to plaque, which deposits on the teeth. The bacteria between the plaque and the tooth enamel produce acids that dissolve tooth enamel. In this protected area, bacteria are not reached by saliva or by tooth brushing, so they continue to erode enamel. If the enamel is thin or weak, the process moves very quickly; bacteria eat through the dentin and can enter the pulp cavity. At this point it might be impossible to save the tooth by drilling and filling.

The frequency of eating sugar, the amount of sugar retained on the teeth, and the length of time the sugar remains in the mouth are more important than the total amount of sugar consumed ("Diet and Dental Caries" 1994).

The more often sugar is present in the mouth, the more opportunity the oral bacteria have to metabolize sugar, produce acid, and erode tooth enamel. A large amount of sugar consumed once a day is far less damaging to the teeth than a small amount consumed several times a day. Sticky snacks high in sugar are particularly harmful because the bacteria on the teeth continue to make acid and erode the enamel. It is better to snack on foods such as apples or carrots, because they clean the teeth.

There are several things you can do to maintain healthy teeth and gums: (1) Floss daily; (2) brush regularly with a soft nylon brush with rounded bristles, making a circular motion with the brush at a 45-degree angle with the gum line;

(3) avoid tooth whiteners (which erode enamel) and toothpastes or powders with sugar for flavoring; and (4) rinse your mouth with water several times a day.

Ways to Improve Your Diet   Sugar is the most common ingredient added to food, so it takes a conscious effort to reduce the sugar intake in your diet. Here are some suggestions that might help you decrease your intake of sugar:

1. Read labels for hidden sugars (look for ingredients ending in *-ose*) and select products with the fewest. Foods high in sugar will have it listed as one of the first ingredients. Choose items in which sugar does not appear or appears late in the ingredient list.

2. Decrease your intake of foods and beverages containing sugar. Be aware of soft drinks and presweetened products such as cereals.

3. Select fresh fruits or fruits packed in water or their own juices rather than syrup.

4. Prepare foods at home instead of buying commercially produced foods, which tend to be high in sugars. Gradually decrease the amounts of sugar you add to recipes.

5. Substitute spices, such as cinnamon, for sugar to bring out the flavor of foods.

6. Explore ways to decrease the amount of sugar you add to beverages and other foods.

7. Substitute fruit for sweetened desserts or snacks.

Complex Carbohydrates

Complex carbohydrates are composed of three or more simple sugars that are bonded together. They must be converted to simple carbohydrates before being used by the body. Complex carbohydrates include starch, fiber, and glycogen. **Starches** form the major part of American diets and are found in foods such as whole-grain bread, potatoes, rice, and vegetables (see table 6.3). Starches are an important part of the diet and provide great nutritional benefit. Another important form of carbohydrate is fiber.

Fiber   Fiber is found in the walls of plant cells and in the tough structural parts of plants, like the stringy part of celery or the bran of wheat and other cereals. It is not digested in the small intestine. Fiber can be soluble or insoluble. Insoluble fiber speeds the passage of food through the digestive tract and might help prevent the development of **carcinogens** (cancer-causing agents) in the colon. It might also help prevent constipation and hemorrhoids. Good sources of insoluble fiber include beans and whole grains (with the outer bran layers).

Soluble fibers are digested and slowly absorbed in the large intestine. They might help control diabetes and lower **cholesterol** (a waxy fatlike substance that circulates in the blood). Although several studies (Kirby et al. 1981; Van Horn et al. 1986) showed a drop in cholesterol levels associated

Fiber plays an important role in our diet and can be found in whole grains, fruits, and vegetables.

complex carbohydrates
Carbohydrates, including starch, fiber, and glycogen, composed of three or more simple sugars bonded together.

starch
A form of complex carbohydrate found in such foods as whole-grain bread, potatoes, rice, and vegetables. An important, highly nutritious part of the diet.

fiber
A form of complex carbohydrate found in plant cell walls. Insoluble fiber, found in beans and whole grains, aids digestion and might be protective against cancer. Soluble fiber, such as guar, psyllium, and pectin, might help control diabetes and lower cholesterol.

carcinogens
Cancer-causing substances.

cholesterol
A waxy fatlike substance that circulates in the blood; cholesterol buildup (plaque) on artery walls has been implicated in atherosclerosis. Found only in animal food sources.

TABLE 6.3 — THE HEALTHIEST VEGETABLES

Vegetable (½ cup cooked, unless noted)	Score	Vit. A.	Vit. C	Folate	Iron	Copper	Calcium	Fiber
Sweet potato, no skin (1)	582	✔	✔	•		✔		✔
Carrot, raw (1)	434	✔	✔					•
Carrots	408	✔				•		•
Spinach	241	✔	✔	✔	✔	•	✔	•
Collard greens, frozen	181	✔	✔	✔	•		✔	NA
Red pepper, raw (½)	166	✔	✔					
Kale	161	✔	✔			•	•	•
Dandelion greens	156	✔	✔	NA	•	NA	•	•
Spinach, raw (1 c)	152	✔	✔	✔	•		•	•
Broccoli	145	✔	✔	✔				
Brussels sprouts	128	✔	✔	✔	•			✔
Broccoli, frozen	127	✔	✔	✔			•	•
Potato, baked, w/skin (1)	114	NA	✔	•	✔	✔		✔
Mixed vegetables, frozen	111	✔	•					✔
Winter squash	110	✔	✔	•		•		•
Swiss chard	105	✔	✔	NA	✔	NA	•	•
Broccoli, raw	100	✔	✔	•				•
Snow peas	90		✔	NA	•			
Mustard greens	85	✔	✔	NA		NA	•	•
Kohlrabi	82		✔	NA		NA		
Romaine lettuce (1 c)	78	✔	✔	✔		NA		
Cauliflower	77		✔	•				•
Cauliflower, raw	77		✔	•				•
Asparagus	75	✔	✔	✔		•		•
Green peppers, raw (½)	67	•	✔					

✔ Contains at least 10 percent of the U.S. RDA

• Contains between 5 percent and 9 percent of the U.S. RDA

Note: The score for each vegetable was developed by adding up its percent of the U.S. RDA for six nutrients plus fiber. There is no U.S. RDA for fiber, so a value of twenty-five grams was assigned. If no number was available (NA) for a nutrient, it was assigned a value of zero. This could make the scores of some vegetables lower than they should be.

Copyright 1991, CSPI. Adapted from *Nutrition Action Healthletter*, (1875 Connecticut Ave., N.W., Suite 300, Washington, D.C. 20009-5728. $20.00 for 10 issues). Reprinted by permission.

---

with consumption of oat bran, the results from another study showed no difference in the effects of eating oat bran and eating low-fiber refined flour (Swain et al. 1990). However, the researchers in the latter study indicated that soluble fibers such as guar, psyllium, and pectin do lower cholesterol (Liebman 1990b). It was shown in a recent study that adding fiber to the diet does lower cholesterol levels. Participants in the research had moderately high cholesterol levels (220–300 mg/dL) and were divided into two groups. Fat consumption for each group was cut to 30 percent. One group consumed 25 grams of fiber per day, and the other group consumed 20 grams of fiber per day. At the end of 1 year the group with the higher fiber intake had cholesterol levels 13 percent lower, while the other group had a 9 percent drop in cholesterol levels ("High Fiber, Low Cholesterol" 1993). Figure 6.1 shows the amounts of fiber in some familiar foods.

This issue is likely to be debated for a long time. However, there are some practical aspects to consider. Because the daily consumption of fiber in the United States (10–15 grams) is two to three times lower than the levels recommended by the National Cancer Institute (20–30 grams), it is probably a good idea to increase the consumption of fiber if appropriate (see table 6.4). This increase needs to be made gradually to allow the body to adjust to the increased intake of fiber. Fluid intake also needs to be increased to prevent the constipation that can result from increased fiber intake. The known way to lower cholesterol is to eat less saturated fat and cholesterol (Liebman 1990b).

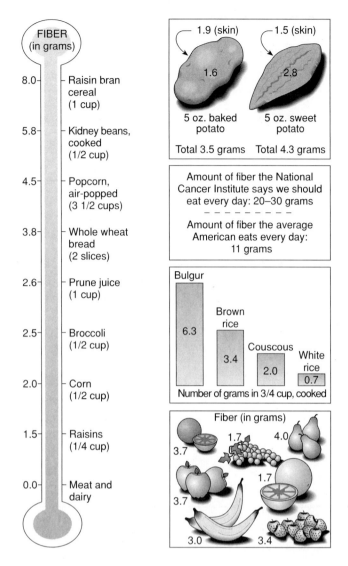

Figure 6.1

The fiber facts.

Copyright 1993, CSPI. Adapted from *Nutrition Action Healthletter* (1875 Connecticut Ave., N.W., Suite 300, Washington, D.C. 20009-5728. $20.00 for 10 issues). Reprinted by permission.

Glycogen, the third form of complex carbohydrate, is formed in the body from extra glucose. Extra glucose is converted into fatty acids and stored by the body in the liver and in muscle as a source of energy. The glycogen is converted into glucose when needed and is made available to the body for quick energy.

Ways to Improve Your Diet Our diets contain fewer complex carbohydrates than they should, and we need to make a conscious effort to increase our consumption of these foods. This effort is worthwhile because of the many nutrients provided by complex carbohydrates. Many health agencies encourage consumption of fruits and vegetables. Fruits and vegetables supply only 1 percent of the fat in the American diet, and they supply at least 90 percent of vitamin

C and beta-carotene—antioxidant nutrients that might prevent damage to body tissues and ward off debilitating diseases ("Nuts and Bolts of Fruits and Vegetables" 1993). Here are some suggestions that might help you increase your intake of these foods:

1. Investigate ways to increase your consumption of complex carbohydrates. Analyze your diet and determine where more complex carbohydrates can be added.
2. Use whole-grain flour when baking.
3. Substitute foods containing complex carbohydrates for foods containing simple carbohydrates.
4. Select fresh fruits and vegetables when possible.
5. Add whole-grain breads and rolls to your meals.
6. Prepare cold grain salads. Add vegetables to your cooked grain and toss with low-fat or nonfat dressing. ("Grains and Beans: The Key to a Low-Fat Diet" 1993)

PROTEINS

Proteins are the second most common nutrient in the body, next to water. They comprise about 16 percent of body weight and are made up of carbon, oxygen, hydrogen, and nitrogen. They supply 4 calories of energy per gram.

Proteins are part of nearly every cell and help build bone, muscle, skin, and blood. Proteins help protect us from disease, because they are the major ingredient in antibodies; they regulate body functions, because they assist in the formation of hormones; and they control chemical activities because of their role in forming enzymes. Oxygen, iron, and nutrients are transported to the cells of the body through proteins.

Although the primary function of protein is the building and repair of the body, calories from protein will be used to supply energy if the supplies are inadequate from carbohydrates and fats. Proteins are not an efficient or effective source of energy, because calories that might have been used to repair and maintain the body will be used to supply energy. This should be of special interest to those who fast to lose weight, because protein in muscles will be depleted if there are inadequate supplies of fats and carbohydrates for energy.

glycogen
Extra glucose that is stored in the body for future use.

proteins
Essential nutrients that are a part of nearly every cell in the body. Proteins primarily function to build and repair body tissues, but they also help protect us from disease, regulate body functions, control biochemical bodily processes, and provide extra energy. Protein supplies 4 calories per gram.

TABLE 6.4 FIBER CONTENT OF GRAINS AND BEANS

Grains (½ Cup, Cooked)	Percentage of Recommended Daily Intake[1]	Beans (1 Cup, Cooked)	Percentage of Recommended Daily Intake[1]
Whole wheat	30%	Pinto	78%
Rye	29	Red (Mexican)	72
Barley	27	Cranberry (Roman)	71
Triticale	20	Black-eyed peas (cowpeas)	66
Pearled barley	17	Navy	64
Rolled oats	16	Red kidney	60
Bulgur wheat	16	Lima, baby	58
Amaranth	9	Cannellini	52
Buckwheat groats	9	Great Northern	43
Corn grits	9	Chickpeas (garbanzos)	41
Quinoa	9	Lentils	40
Wild rice	8	Black (turtle)	40
Brown rice	7	Split peas	39
Millet	5	Fava (broad)	37
White rice	2	Pink	36

[1]While there is no U.S. RDA for fiber, the usual recommended daily intake is a total of 25 grams.

"Fiber Content of Grains and Beans" Copyright 1993 by Consumers Union of U.S., Inc., Yonkers, NY 10703-1057. Reprinted by permission from *Consumer Reports on Health*, October 1993.

Proteins are comprised of approximately twenty different **amino acids,** or chemical compounds. Nine of these amino acids cannot be made or synthesized in the body but must be obtained through food. These are called "essential amino acids." Foods containing all nine of these amino acids are known as "complete" proteins. Proteins from animal sources tend to be complete, while proteins from vegetable sources are not. Although many of the products derived from animals are good sources of protein (milk, meat, poultry, and fish products), they can be high in fats and cholesterol.

Protein is broken down and rebuilt in nearly every part of the body; as much as 3 to 5 percent of the protein in the body is replaced each day. Once enough protein has been eaten to supply bodily functions, the excess is broken down for energy or stored as fat. More protein is needed by females when they are pregnant or breast-feeding.

Protein Consumption

Although some individuals may be concerned about consuming enough protein, their intake is probably sufficient because there are large amounts of protein in many commonly consumed foods. In the United States children consume twice the U.S. RDA for protein, the average middle-aged man consumes 60 percent more than the U.S. RDA for protein, and the average middle-aged woman consumes 25 percent more than the U.S. RDA for protein (Roberts 1989).

There is growing evidence that excess protein can contribute to osteoporosis, heart disease, and certain cancers. Although some earlier research showed a connection between eating protein and kidney disease, more-recent studies have not produced direct evidence that eating protein causes kidney disease in healthy individuals (Schardt 1993).

Ways to Improve Your Diet

The major recommendation regarding protein is to eat the amount recommended by the U.S. RDA and to eat plant proteins rather than animal proteins. Here are some suggestions that might help you do this:

1. Feature complex-carbohydrate dishes as the main course for meals, and use meats and poultry as side dishes.
2. Limit the serving size when eating meat (2–3 oz of cooked meat, poultry, or fish).
3. Increase your consumption of plant proteins.

amino acids
Chemical compounds that are the constituents of proteins. The nine essential amino acids cannot be synthesized by the body and must be obtained in the diet; foods containing all nine of these are called "complete proteins."

HEALTH UPDATE

The Truth About Movie Popcorn

Popcorn is usually considered a healthy snack. However, it can turn into a snack that is high in calories and in fat, both saturated and trans, depending on how it is prepared. In a study of movie theater popcorn conducted by the Center for Science in the Public Interest, it was found that a large popcorn without "butter" had 80 grams of fat, including 50 grams of saturated fat. That is approximately the amount of saturated fat that is in six Big Macs. Adding "butter," which is actually partially hydrogenated soybean oils and includes saturated and trans fats, made the fat content jump to 130 grams. Saturated and trans fats raise cholesterol.

Source: From "Popcorn: Oil in a Day's Work" in *Nutrition Action Healthletter* 21(4):9 (May 1994).

FATS

Although fat has some negative characteristics, it is essential for the proper functioning of the body. **Fats** protect the vital organs against injury, provide insulation against the cold, and depress hunger pangs. They supply 9 calories per gram and are a concentrated source of energy when carbohydrate supplies are insufficient, such as during prolonged exercise. In addition, fats enhance the taste of food and transport the four fat-soluble vitamins (A, D, E, and K).

Triglycerides are the major source of dietary fat and comprise 95 percent of our fat intake. Fat is transported by the blood to the muscles, where it is used for energy (McGlynn 1993, 157). Excess fat is stored in **adipose cells** (fat cells), which can increase in size fifty times to store excess fat, and new adipose cells will be formed when the existing cells are full (Wardlaw and Insel 1990, 132). Fat is initially stored around organs and in muscles. By the time we can see the bulges in our bodies, the other storage areas are full.

Fatty Acids

Fat cells are composed of fatty acids and glycerol. The structure of the fatty acid determines whether or not the triglyceride is a dietary problem. Fatty acids are classified as **saturated, monounsaturated,** or **polyunsaturated,** depending on the number of hydrogen atoms that are bonded to the molecule. Saturated fatty acids contain the maximum number of hydrogen atoms (i.e., they are saturated with hydrogen), are usually from animal sources, and are solid at room temperature. Monounsaturated fatty acids have one double bond between their carbon atoms and are found in olive and canola oils. Polyunsaturated fatty acids contain two or more double bonds between the carbon atoms. Safflower, corn, and soybean oils contain polyunsaturated fatty acids. The unsaturated fatty acids are usually liquid at room temperature and are found in plant sources. Palm oil, palm kernel oil, and coconut oil are highly saturated fats even though they are from plant sources. Vegetable oils are often hydrogenated or partially hydrogenated (hydrogenation is the process of adding hydrogen to polyunsaturated or monounsaturated fats), which increases their saturation, and may become more saturated when they are used repeatedly at high temperatures (Roberts 1990). The fat that is produced from this process is **trans fat.** Trans fat is unsaturated fat that raises cholesterol possibly as much as saturated fat does. The process of partial hydrogenation makes oils firmer and less perishable. The hardened vegetable fat appears to be as destructive to the arteries as the saturated fat it replaced ("Can Vegetable Oils Harden Your Arteries?" 1993). The major sources of trans fat are fast foods, packaged baked goods, and margarine. Because of the new finding regarding trans fat, it is advisable to keep your combined intake of saturated fat and trans fat below the limit of 10 percent of your total calories (see table 6.5). It is felt that each gram of trans fat raises LDL cholesterol as much as a gram of saturated fat does (Wootan and Liebman 1993).

And speaking of that 10 percent limit of total calories from saturated fat—that refers to an upper limit of 10 percent. You would have greater health benefits if your consumption of saturated fats were 7 to 8 percent or lower

---

fat
An essential nutrient for proper functioning of the body, fats protect the vital organs, provide insulation, enhance the taste of food, and transport the fat-soluble vitamins. Fats supply 9 calories per gram.

triglycerides
The major form (95 percent) of our dietary fat.

adipose cells
Cells that store bodily fat. These can increase fifty times in size, and new adipose cells are created when existing cells are full. Fat cells.

saturated fat
Saturated fatty acids, which come mainly from animal sources and are solid at room temperature. They have been implicated in heart disease and should be kept to a minimum in the diet.

monounsaturated fat
Monounsaturated fatty acids, which are liquid at room temperature and found in plant sources, such as olive and canola oils. A healthy source of dietary fat when not heated.

polyunsaturated fats
Polyunsaturated fatty acids, which are liquid at room temperature and found in plant sources, such as safflower, corn, and soybean oils. A healthy source of dietary fat when not heated.

trans fat
Unsaturated fat that might raise cholesterol as much as saturated fats do.

TABLE 6.5   WHERE THE FATS ARE

	Serving Size	Trans Fat (g)	Saturated Fat (g)	Trans and Saturated Fat Combined	
				Combined Total (g)[1]	Percent of Daily Limit[1]
Fats and Oils					
Butter	1 tbsp	0.6	7.2	7.8	30%
Vegetable shortening	1 tbsp	3.4	3.6	7.0	27%
Margarine-butter blend, stick	1 tbsp	2.1	4.5	6.6	25%
Margarine, stick	1 tbsp	3.1	2.3	5.4	21%
Margarine, tub	1 tbsp	1.6	2.1	3.7	14%
Margarine, liquid	1 tbsp	1.2	1.8	3.0	11%
Spread, tub	1 tbsp	1.2	0.9	2.2	8%
Light spread, tub	1 tbsp	0.9	1.1	2.0	8%
Margarine, diet, tub	1 tbsp	0.9	1.1	2.0	8%
Corn oil, unhydrogenated	1 tbsp	0.0	1.7	1.7	7%
Extra light spread, tub	1 tbsp	0.4	1.1	1.5	6%
Prepared Foods					
Fried fish sandwich, 1	6.5 oz	8.2	5.7	13.9	53%
Fried fruit pie, 1	4.5 oz	5.9	7.7	13.6	52%
Doughnut, plain, 1	1.8 oz	5.0	4.3	9.3	36%
French fries	3 oz	4.4	2.8	7.2	27%
American cheese, imitation	1 oz	4.0	2.1	6.1	23%
Danish, small, 1	2 oz	3.7	2.0	5.7	22%
Cookies, assorted varieties	1 oz	3.2	2.2	5.4	21%
Cheese puffs	1 oz	3.4	1.9	5.3	20%
Potato chips	1 oz	3.0	1.7	4.7	18%
Corn chips	1 oz	2.8	1.7	4.5	17%
Tortilla chips	1 oz	2.5	1.4	3.9	15%
Crackers, round, fat-coated, 8	1 oz	2.5	1.3	3.8	15%
Waffle, frozen, 1	1.4 oz	2.1	1.1	3.2	12%

No one has yet compiled authoritative figures on the trans-fat content of foods. As examples, we've assembled numbers from some recent analyses that were based on relatively small samples of each type of food. While the actual fat content of some brands may differ from the figures shown here, the numbers should be representative. The table's key column is the last one: the percentage of the daily recommended limit for trans and saturated fat combined. (That limit is 26 grams, based on a daily intake of 2350 calories.) Note that some people may eat much larger servings than the ones listed here. Polish off five ounces of cheese puffs, for example, and you've exceeded the daily limit.

[1]Based on an average total daily intake of 2350 calories, and a daily limit of 10% of those calories from trans and saturated fat combined. That equals a maximum of 235 calories, or 26 grams of the two fats combined (since each gram of fat contains 9 calories).

"Can Vegetable Oils Harden Your Arteries? Where the Fats Are" Copyright 1993 by Consumers Union of U.S., Inc., Yonkers, NY 10307-1057. Reprinted by permission from *Consumer Reports on Health*, June 1993.

(Liebman and Hurley 1993) (see table 6.6). Researchers are hesitant to recommend the lower numbers because we might think those numbers are too drastic and too unobtainable.

Cholesterol

Although cholesterol consumption has negative implications, cholesterol is crucial in a number of bodily functions. It is a component of cell membranes, is used to protect the nerve fibers, and assists in the production of certain hormones, including the sex hormones. Eight hundred to 1,500 milligrams of cholesterol are produced by the body each day. The body regulates the amount of cholesterol by producing less when more cholesterol is obtained through dietary

sources. However, this process does not function properly in 25 to 33 percent of the population ("Fear of Eggs" 1989). Cholesterol found in the blood is harmful because it accumulates on arterial walls, causing them to narrow. This can lead to **atherosclerosis** (the formation of fat deposits on the walls of the arteries) and sometimes to a heart attack.

atherosclerosis

A disease state in which fat deposits (plaques) collect on artery walls, narrowing the arteries and sometimes leading to heart attack.

Low-fat meals can be delicious.

Cholesterol is not soluble in water, and it is transported through the bloodstream with a protein carrier and triglycerides. This combination is called a **lipoprotein** (fatty protein). There are three types of lipoproteins involved with transporting cholesterol in the body. **High-density lipoproteins (HDL)** are considered good cholesterol because they remove other cholesterol from the walls of the arteries and transport it to the liver, where it is processed and excreted (Stamford 1990). Both **low-density lipoproteins (LDL)** and **very-low-density lipoproteins (VLDL)** are considered bad types of cholesterol because they allow the cholesterol to circulate in the bloodstream.

LDL transports two-thirds of the cholesterol in the blood ("Forget Cholesterol?" 1990). It appears that the cholesterol in both LDL and VLDL is on its way to the cells for storage. This can be harmful because the cholesterol can build up in and clog the arteries, resulting in a heart attack. The distribution of lipoproteins might be as important as the cholesterol level in the blood. A high ratio of HDL would appear to put individuals at lower risk of coronary heart disease. The ratio of total cholesterol to HDL should be less than 4.5:1 (McGlynn 1993, 18). There is evidence in research studies that oxidized LDL clogs the arteries and might increase the likelihood of heart attacks (Liebman 1991). The antioxidant properties of vitamin C are being studied to see if vitamin C can inhibit the oxidation of low-density lipoprotein cholesterol ("Can Vitamin C Save Your Life?" 1994). Other substances being studied for their antioxidant properties include vitamin E and beta-carotene ("Battling the Bad Fat" 1992). In an 8-year study of 87,000 female nurses, the women who ate the most produce rich in antioxidants (beta-carotene, vitamins C and E) were less than half as likely to suffer an ischemic stroke (impaired blood flow due to arterial blockage) ("Eating Around a Stroke" 1993).

Many individuals are looking for foods that will raise their HDL. However, HDL levels in blood are raised by getting the

TABLE 6.6   FREE SAT FAT (LESS THAN ½ GRAM)

Grain Foods
Bagel or pita bread
Breakfast cereals, hot or cold (except regular granola)
Fig bars
French or Italian bread
All grains
Muffin, McDonald's apple bran
All pastas
Popcorn, air-popped
Pretzels or fat-free chips
Tortillas, corn or flour

Vegetables
All vegetables

Fruits
All Fruits (except avocado and coconut) and juices

Dairy Foods
Milk, skim
Yogurt or cheese, fat-free

Protein Foods
Beans, split peas, or lentils
Cod, flounder, haddock, halibut, perch, pollock, sole, snapper, tuna, or shellfish[a]
Egg white or egg substitute
Tuna, canned in water
Turkey breast

---

[a]Shrimp is high in cholesterol.

Copyright 1993, CSPI. Adapted from *Nutrition Action Healthletter* (1875 Connecticut Ave., N.W., Suite 300, Washington, D.C. 20009-5728. $20.00 for 10 issues). Reprinted by permission.

lipoprotein
A substance, composed of protein, triglyceride, and cholesterol, that transports cholesterol in the bloodstream; a fatty protein. There are three kinds: high-density, low-density, and very-low-density lipoproteins.

high-density lipoprotein (HDL)
Considered "good" cholesterol, HDL removes other kinds of cholesterol from artery walls and transports it to the liver, where it is processed and excreted.

low-density lipoprotein (LDL)
Considered an undesirable form of cholesterol, LDL has been implicated in the formation of arterial plaque (atherosclerosis).

very-low-density lipoprotein (VLDL)
Considered an undesirable form of cholesterol, VLDL has been implicated in the formation of arterial plaque (atherosclerosis).

body to increase its production of HDL. This can be done by eating a diet rich in fiber, maintaining proper body weight, and exercising vigorously.

There is an interesting debate among doctors as to whether it is risky for cholesterol to be too low (below 160 mg/dL). Individuals with low cholesterol are more likely to die from lung cancer, other respiratory diseases, cerebral hemorrhage, alcoholism, accidental death, and suicide. However, it is unlikely that middle-aged Americans will have cholesterol levels that low, and lower blood cholesterol levels are preventive against heart attacks (one-third of which are fatal). A low-fat diet is the best way to achieve low blood cholesterol ("Is It Risky to Lower Your Cholesterol?" 1993). Another benefit of low-fat eating appears to be a decreased chance for blood clots in the short term ("The Immediate Benefits of Low-Fat Eating" 1993). Figure 6.2 uses a familiar food—milk—to illustrate what you should look for in creating a nutritious, low-fat diet for yourself.

Ways to Improve Your Diet

The average American consumes approximately 37 percent of total calories from fat, including 16 percent from saturated fat ("Where's the Fat?" 1990). The American Heart Association and the National Cancer Institute recommend that fat constitute less than 30 percent of total calories, with the amounts equally distributed among saturated, monounsaturated, and polyunsaturated fats. Daily cholesterol consumption, which is currently 400 to 600 milligrams daily, should be reduced to less than 250 milligrams daily. The following are some things that you can do to reduce your total intake of fat and cholesterol:

1. Select lean poultry and remove the skin before cooking it.
2. Avoid fried foods and breaded foods.
3. Select lean cuts of red meat, such as flank, round, and rump.
4. Prepare foods by baking, broiling, boiling, or microwaving rather than frying. Use a receptacle under the food to catch the fat drippings when broiling, rather than letting the food sit in the fat.
5. Select skim or low-fat milk products. If you drink whole milk, decrease the amount of fat by mixing it with skim milk. In time, increase the amount of skim milk you add until the milk is only skim milk. Select low-fat cheeses.
6. Select monounsaturated or polyunsaturated fats and oils. Check the label to be sure of the type of fats and oils.
7. Remove all visible fat from meat before cooking it.
8. Check labels for fats and select products with less fat.
9. Include more fish in your diet.
10. Limit your intake of foods from fast-food restaurants, since a high percentage (40%–50%) of calories in fast foods come from fat (Roberts 1989).

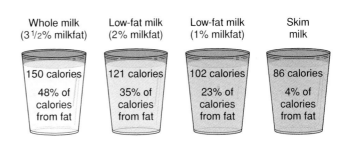

Figure 6.2

What's in an 8-ounce glass of milk? From the nutritional content labels on milk cartons, it appears that the differences between whole milk and skim milk are minimal. However, those numbers give the fat content as a percentage of the milk's *weight* rather than as the percentage of the milk's *calories* that come from fat. The percentages of calories from fat are illustrated here. The different kinds of milk all contain the same amount of protein (8 grams—one-sixth of an adult's need per day) and calcium (300 mg—one-third of an adult's need per day) in 8 ounces.

Source: Adapted from *Consumer Reports*, September 1991, page 627.

11. Cool cooked stew or soup and remove the fat before reheating and serving it (Hunter 1989).
12. Avoid products containing hydrogenated fats.
13. Reduce the fat in Chinese food by increasing the amount of rice and decreasing the size of the entree, ordering steamed veggies, and lifting the entree out of the sauce and onto the rice (Hurley and Schmidt 1993).

It has been found that a strong connection exists between the mind and the body related to low-fat eating. Findings in a study presented at the 1993 American Psychological Association meeting show that we can convince ourselves that foods high in fat are less appealing—we can fool ourselves into eating lots of high-fat foods without guilt. Eighty-two percent of 650 women who participated in a behavior-oriented program to reduce fat from 37 percent to 23 percent were still successful 5 years later. The participants in the control group chose high-fat foods over low-fat foods. They also were more forgetful about what they had eaten, the more they consumed (Elias 1993b).

VITAMINS

Vitamins are organic substances that are essential, in small amounts, for chemical reactions in the body. They do not provide energy, as some mistakenly believe, but combine with enzymes to enable the body to use other nutrients. Vitamins

---

vitamins

Organic substances essential, in very small amounts, for bodily chemical reactions. Vitamins combine with enzymes to enable the body to use other nutrients. Found in all foods except sugar, alcohol, and highly refined fats.

The Biosphere Diet

The eight individuals who spent 2 years living in Biosphere II consumed 12 percent of their calories from fat (compared to the U.S. average of 38%) and lost 15 percent of their body weight eating a diet full of grains, vegetables, and fruits. Their cholesterol level fell from 200 to 130, and their blood pressure dropped from 120/80 to 100/70.

The advantages of this type of diet for the general public include a healthier life and an extended lifespan. Studies in animals have shown that lifespans have been extended 50 percent on such diets (Elias 1993a).

Issue

Should the Government Regulate Vitamins?

The Food and Drug Administration has proposed a rule that would ban some vitamins and food supplements while classifying others as drugs available by prescription only. FDA officials indicate this is necessary to protect consumers from false claims, and to ensure that the products are not contaminated and contain the nutritional elements they are claimed to have. This would also prevent the selling of any brochure, book, or magazine article making an unapproved claim for a brand name product in the same location as the product (Long 1993).

- Pro: Health food stores should be able to sell any of these products. The choice should be theirs.
- Con: This regulation is necessary. There have already been too many deaths of individuals who bought contaminated products.

Do we need these regulations? Why or why not?

---

are found in all foods except sugar, alcohol, and highly refined fats and oils (McGlynn 1993). The body requires only 1 ounce of vitamins for every 150 pounds of food consumed (Wardlaw and Insel 1990, 306). Thirteen vitamins are absolutely necessary for good health.

Vitamins are categorized according to their solubility in either water or fat. The **fat-soluble vitamins** are vitamins A, D, E, and K, which are stored in and transported by the fat cells of the body. Because they can be stored in the body for long periods of time, it is not essential to consume foods containing them every day—and megadoses (amounts many times higher than the RDAs) of these vitamins can be toxic.

The **water-soluble vitamins** include the eight B vitamins and vitamin C. They are not stored in the body and need to be replenished every day. The supplies of these vitamins are continually being depleted or flushed out of the system through urine and perspiration. There are negative conditions associated with regular overconsumption. These include stomach inflammation, diarrhea, and kidney stones (Wardlaw and Insel 1990).

The vitamin content of foods is affected by processing procedures (e.g., vine-ripened items are more nutritious than those picked green), storage procedures (e.g., wilted vegetables are not as nutritious), and cooking procedures (e.g., extended cooking time usually results in a loss of vitamins).

There has been a great deal of controversy about vitamin supplements. Vitamins are involved in chemical reactions within the body and are needed in precise amounts. Amounts in excess of the RDAs are wasted. Most individuals who eat a balanced diet from a variety of foods do not need extra vitamins from pills. However, vitamin supplements might be recommended for heavy smokers, women on oral contraceptives, heavy drinkers, individuals with specific disorders, surgical

patients, and the elderly. There are no chemical differences between natural and synthetic vitamins. In a 10-year study of vitamin and mineral supplementation, no evidence of increased longevity was found (Kim et al. 1993).

MINERALS

Minerals are inorganic elements involved in a variety of metabolic functions. They are required in the body in varying amounts, whereas vitamins are required in very small amounts. Minerals are divided into two classifications: macrominerals and trace minerals. The macrominerals are

---

fat-soluble vitamins
The vitamins (A, D, E, and K) that are stored in and transported by fat cells. Because these are stored in the body, it is not necessary to consume them every day, and high supplemental doses can be toxic.

water-soluble vitamins
The vitamins, including the eight B vitamins and vitamin C, that are not stored in the body and need to be replenished every day. Regular overconsumption can produce physical ailments.

minerals
Inorganic elements necessary for essential metabolic functions. Macrominerals (e.g., calcium, magnesium, sodium, potassium, phosphorus, sulfur, chlorine) are required in relatively large amounts. Trace minerals (e.g., iodine, iron, cobalt, copper, manganese, zinc) are required in much smaller amounts.

required by the body in relatively large amounts and include calcium, magnesium, sodium, potassium, phosphorus, sulfur, and chlorine. The trace elements are required in much smaller amounts and include iodine, iron, cobalt, copper, manganese, and zinc.

Calcium

The mineral present in the largest amount in the body is **calcium.** The adult human body contains approximately 1,200 to 1,250 grams of calcium, with the vast majority of it in the bones and teeth (98 percent of it is located in the bones and 1 percent in the teeth).

Calcium is needed for growth and maintenance of strong bones and teeth. It is also needed to assist in blood clotting, to regulate the intercellular flow of fluids, to transmit nerve impulses, and to maintain the normal excitability of the heart muscle as well as other muscles. In addition, calcium might play a preventive role in several cancers, in **hypertension** (high blood pressure) ("Yet Another Reason to Drink Your Milk" 1992), and in preeclampsia (a mild form of hypertension in pregnant women) (Oestreicher 1990). Calcium is constantly moving in and out of the bones; as much as 20 percent of the calcium in the bones is replaced in the course of a year. Calcium is the major mineral most likely to be in short supply in the American diet, especially in females. Those who eat high-fiber diets need to include extra amounts of calcium, because fiber decreases by as much as 20 percent the body's ability to absorb calcium (Edell 1992). The average female consumes one-third to one-half the recommended intake of calcium, and the average male consumes three-fourths of the recommended intake ("Calcium: Vital for Women and Men" 1994).

Adequate supplies of calcium need to be maintained throughout life. It is especially important for college students to maintain their intake of calcium, because many consume soft drinks in place of milk. This can be a problem because of the decreased calcium intake and the excretion of calcium that results from consumption of fluids high in phosphorus, such as colas.

There was an indication in earlier research of a connection between calcium consumption and kidney stones. However, in recent research men who reported eating the most calcium had a much lower risk of kidney stones than men who ate the least calcium ("Calcium OK for Kidneys" 1993).

One of the results of calcium deficiency is **osteoporosis** (the loss of bone material, which can result in the loss of bone mass). Bones can become brittle, and more likely to break. Individuals with bulimia (an eating disorder characterized by binge eating often followed by vomiting) might be subject to the early onset of osteoporosis because their mineral consumption is often low. Postmenopausal women seem to be most likely to suffer from osteoporosis, though osteoporosis has also been diagnosed in men (Orwoll et al. 1990) and in premenopausal women as young as 35. There is a rapid loss of dense bone mass right after **menopause** (the cessation of menstruation), which makes postmenopausal women more susceptible to osteoporosis. Estrogen therapy increases calcium absorption, and postmenopausal women who do not receive supplements of estrogen have the lowest rates of calcium absorption (Wardlaw and Insel 1990).

Taking calcium throughout the growing years appears to be the most promising way to reduce the risk of osteoporosis in later years ("New Recommended Dietary Allowances" 1990) and for several years after menopause is completed. The decrease in estrogen at menopause results in a 15 percent lower bone mass. Since calcium is released from the bone at this time, dietary calcium will not make an impact until the process has stabilized (Oestreicher 1990). Current research supports the intake of calcium through the diet rather than calcium supplements, with low-fat or skim milk being one of the best sources of calcium (Clark 1990). Because weight-bearing activities are important in maintaining strong bones, activities such as jogging, walking, running, and dancing are recommended ("Weight-Bearing Exercises Help Prevent Bone Weakness" 1990). Individuals may want to monitor their intake of protein, since there is evidence that high-protein diets might contribute to osteoporosis ("New Recommended Dietary Allowances" 1990).

Risk factors for osteoporosis include female gender, advanced age, Caucasian or Asian heritage, a small frame, low

---

calcium

The most prevalent mineral in the human body, mostly contained in the bones and teeth. Necessary for the growth and maintenance of strong bones and teeth; also assists in blood clotting, regulation of intercellular fluid flow, nerve impulse transmission, and maintaining a regular heartbeat. Might help prevent several cancers and hypertension. Deficiency can result in osteoporosis in older women.

hypertension

Chronically high blood pressure, usually associated with arterial disease.

osteoporosis

A disease in which the bones lose bone material and become very porous and fracture easily. Especially prevalent in postmenopausal women. Preventive measures include regular lifelong calcium intake, weight-bearing exercise, and moderation of protein intake; after menopause, estrogen therapy is often used to increase the rate of calcium absorption.

menopause

The permanent cessation of menstruation; usually occurs between the ages of 45 and 55.

calcium intake throughout life, menopause before age 45, excess dietary protein, fiber, caffeine and/or alcohol, a sedentary lifestyle, and cigarette smoking ("Focus on Nutrition and Women's Health" 1993).

Sodium

Sodium and chloride are the components of table salt; sodium composes 40 percent of the salt molecule by weight. While sodium intake would be approximately 500 milligrams a day if no processed foods were eaten and no salt were added to food, the typical sodium intake of Americans is 3,000 to 7,000 milligrams per day (Wardlaw and Insel 1990, 384). Processed foods account for 77 percent of sodium intake (Mattes and Donnelly 1991).

Sodium is needed in the body to regulate the acid-base balance, to maintain the osmotic pressure of body fluids, and to preserve the normal irritability of muscle and the permeability of cells. Only 200 milligrams are needed per day, the equivalent of 0.1 teaspoon.

Although most individuals can adjust to different levels of sodium intake, approximately 50 million people have high blood pressure (140/90 or higher) (Liebman 1994). Fifteen to 20 million people are sodium sensitive (Williams 1990, 115). These individuals have a tendency to develop hypertension (a persistent elevation of blood pressure above normal levels). Since we have no way of knowing who is, or who will become, sodium sensitive, it is advised that the entire population reduce sodium intake ("Too Much Salt?" 1990). There is no known harm in moderate sodium restriction (*Healthy People 2000* 1992). It is doubtful that someone will consume too little sodium, because the body will prevent this by craving salty food (Edell 1991). Hypertension is rare in populations with low sodium consumption.

Ways to Improve Your Diet

We have acquired a taste for sodium and add it to foods out of habit. It is common to see someone salt food before tasting it. Reducing sodium consumption might take a special effort, because many of us are accustomed to the taste and because sodium is so prevalent in commercial products. Although vegetables are low in natural sodium, many foods of animal origin are high in natural sodium. These foods include meat, fish, poultry, milk, and eggs. Here are some suggestions that might help you reduce your sodium consumption:

1. Reduce or eliminate from your diet salty foods, such as cured or processed meats.
2. Reduce or eliminate salt added to foods.
3. Experiment with the flavor of other seasonings on foods rather than using salt.
4. Read labels and select low-sodium products. A food that is "sodium free" contains less than 5 milligrams of sodium per serving; a food that is "very low sodium" contains 35 milligrams or less of sodium; a food that is "low sodium" contains 140 milligrams or less of sodium; and a food that is "unsalted or no salt added" has only

Whereas fresh vegetables are low in sodium, frozen and canned vegetables often have large amounts of added sodium.

naturally occurring sodium, usually a minimal amount ("Does Salt Raise *Your* Blood Pressure?" 1994).

5. Select fresh produce over frozen or canned. A half cup of cooked fresh peas has 2 milligrams of sodium, while a half cup of cooked frozen peas has 70 milligrams, and a half cup of canned peas has 185 milligrams.
6. Limit your intake of processed foods.
7. Consider sodium intake when selecting foods at fast-food restaurants. Items such as triple cheeseburgers can contain from 1,354 to 1,953 milligrams of sodium (Roberts 1989).
8. Reduce your intake of salty snacks and replace them with fruits, vegetables, and unsalted snacks.

Iron and Potassium

Two other minerals that might be of special interest are **potassium** and **iron.** Potassium works with sodium to maintain

---

sodium

A component of table salt (sodium chloride). Necessary for many bodily functions. RDA is 200 milligrams per day. Overconsumption can result in hypertension as well as deplete the body's reserves of potassium.

potassium

A mineral that works with salt to maintain normal heartbeat and nourish the muscles. Found in vegetables, oranges, whole grains, and sunflower seeds. Deficiencies can cause heartbeat irregularities, insomnia, and nervous disorders.

iron

A mineral whose main function is to make hemoglobin. Found in animal organs (which are high in saturated fat), leafy green vegetables, whole grains, dried fruits, and legumes. Deficiency is common.

normal heartbeat and to nourish the muscles. Although sodium and potassium work together and must be in balance, sodium is associated with raising blood pressure, while potassium is associated with lowering it. Excessive ingestion of salt depletes the body's reserves of potassium, while the amount of sodium in the heart and muscles increases when the potassium amounts are low. Potassium deficiencies can cause heartbeat irregularities, insomnia, and nervous disorders. Sources of potassium include all vegetables, oranges, whole grains, and sunflower seeds.

Iron deficiency is one of the most common nutrient deficiencies. The main function of iron is to make **hemoglobin,** the part of the blood that transports oxygen from the lungs to the tissues. A daily intake of 18 milligrams of iron is recommended for women, and 10 milligrams is recommended for men. It is recommended that pregnant women increase their daily intake by an additional 15 milligrams ("New Recommended Dietary Allowances" 1990). Iron needs increase during menstruation, pregnancy, periods of rapid growth, or whenever there is a loss of blood.

Although animal organs are good sources of iron and are the sources that are most readily absorbed, they contain high amounts of saturated fats. Better nutritional choices are leafy green vegetables, whole grains, dried fruits, and legumes.

WATER

Water is the most important nutrient of all. One can survive for weeks without other foods, but only a few days without water, since the body cannot conserve or preserve water as well as the other nutrients. **Dehydration** (the removal of water from the tissues of the body) can result within hours and can be fatal.

Water transports the other nutrients to all cells, carries wastes away, and regulates body temperature. Approximately two-thirds of body weight is composed of water. Female bodies are approximately 50 to 55 percent water, while male bodies are approximately 55 to 60 percent water. An adult needs approximately 10 cups of water per day (Wardlaw and Insel 1990, 380).

The body uses protective measures to maintain water levels. After eating a meal high in sodium, you may be thirsty. This thirst response is the body's way of getting you to drink water to dilute the sodium and prevent reactions from the bodily organs. When there is too much water in the body, the brain signals the kidneys to remove more water in the urine.

Each day approximately 2.5 to 3.0 liters (approximately 10 to 12 glasses) of water are lost through urination, perspiration, and breathing. We take in water in three forms: in water and other liquids, in foods (foods such as melons and fruits contain 90 percent water), and as a product of cell oxidation. Water leaves the body through the kidneys, lungs, feces, and skin.

The normal means of acquiring water are sufficient under typical circumstances. However, you need to monitor your intake of fluids, especially when loss of water might exceed

Water is the best fluid-replacement drink for most activities.

intake, as in hot weather and during vigorous activity. Thirst cannot be relied upon as an indicator of water needs, because there is usually a delay between the need for water and the feeling of thirst. The thirst mechanism usually shuts off prior to rehydration, so you need to continue to drink water even if you are no longer thirsty.

EATING NUTRITIOUSLY

A variety of foods must be eaten in order to have a balanced diet. This takes some planning, particularly for college students who are responsible for making the majority of their food selection decisions and who might have limited time or money. It is not an impossible task to eat a healthful diet, though more than half of the adults in the United States are doing less than they could to eat a well-balanced diet ("Just What Is A Balanced Diet, Anyway?" 1992).

FOOD CHOICES

The four basic food groups have been replaced by the Food Guide Pyramid released by the U.S. Department of Agriculture in 1992 (figure 6.3) (Welsh, Davis, and Shaw 1992). Foods are divided into six groups, based on the similarity of nutrients. There is a wide variety of foods within these groups, and the portions recommended are relatively small (figure 6.4). Fats, oils, and sweets should be eaten sparingly because they tend to be high in calories and low in nutrients.

hemoglobin
The part of the blood that transports oxygen from the lungs to the tissues.

dehydration
The removal of water from body tissues. Common when water intake is low or temperatures are high, resulting in perspiration. Severe dehydration can be fatal within hours. An adult should drink 10 cups of water or other noncaffeinated, noncola liquid each day.

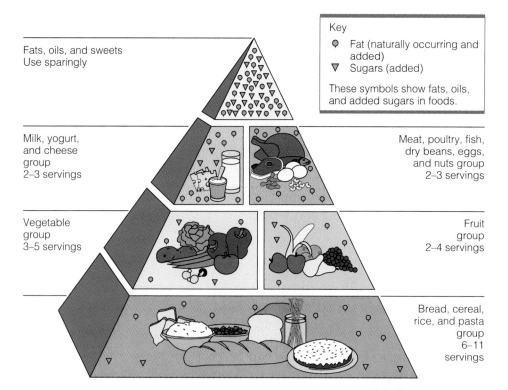

Fats, oils, and sweets
Use sparingly

Key
- Fat (naturally occurring and added)
- Sugars (added)

These symbols show fats, oils, and added sugars in foods.

Milk, yogurt, and cheese group
2–3 servings

Meat, poultry, fish, dry beans, eggs, and nuts group
2–3 servings

Vegetable group
3–5 servings

Fruit group
2–4 servings

Bread, cereal, rice, and pasta group
6–11 servings

Figure 6.3
Food Guide Pyramid: A guide to daily food choices.
Source: U.S. Department of Agriculture.

Food group	Typical size of one serving
Meat, poultry, fish, dry beans, eggs, and nuts [1] (2–3 servings)	2 to 3 oz. cooked meat, poultry, or fish (about the size of a deck of cards); 1 to 1 1/2 cups cooked beans; 2 to 3 eggs; 4 to 6 tbsp. peanut butter
Milk, yogurt, and cheese (2–3 servings)	1 cup milk or yogurt; 1 1/2 oz. natural cheese (that's a chunk measuring roughly 1" x 1" x 2 1/2"); 2 oz. processed cheese (about 2 slices)
Fruit (2–4 servings)	1 medium piece of whole fruit, such as apple or banana; 1/2 cup canned, cooked, or chopped raw fruit; 3/4 cup fruit juice
Vegetables (3–5 servings)	1 cup raw leafy vegetables; 1/2 cup other vegetables—cooked or chopped raw; 3/4 cup vegetable juice
Bread, cereal, rice, and pasta (6–11 servings)	1 slice bread; 1 oz. ready-to-eat cereal (this can range from 1/4 cup of Grape Nuts to about 1 cup of corn flakes to 2 1/2 cups of puffed wheat); 1/2 cup cooked cereal, rice, or pasta

[1] Total servings in this group should add up to the equivalent of 5 to 7 oz. of meat.

Figure 6.4
Serving sizes.

HEALTH UPDATE

Effects of Weather on Eating

An example of our connection to the world around us is seasonal affective disorder (SAD). One of the behaviors typical of SAD is our tendency during fall and winter to eat greater amounts of food that are higher in fat. Some theorize that this is a hibernation response to the shorter days and cooler temperatures, since there is no significant increase in activity level. When the temperatures cool and the hours of daylight increase, it is a good idea to be aware of your body's response and keep your food intake moderate.

It's a good idea to avoid these items, particularly when you are trying to lose weight. Foods in a specific group may have similar nutrients but can vary significantly in their overall nutritional values. We should select foods that are lower in sodium, fat (particularly saturated fat), and sugar, and higher in fiber and complex carbohydrates.

The food pyramid provides an extremely important guide for eating. Those who find they need to add or decrease items in their diets might want to do so gradually to ensure success.

The foods most likely to be underconsumed are fruits and vegetables. Only 23 percent of adult Americans meet the minimum goal for fruit and vegetable consumption, and most need to double their consumption of fruits and vegetables (Domel et al. 1993).

Researchers who tracked ten thousand people for fourteen years found that the fewer food groups in the diet, the higher the rate of death. Individuals who ate foods from the fewest food groups were 50 percent more likely to have died than those who consumed foods from all the food groups ("Food Groups" 1993).

THE WORLD AROUND YOU
Eating Nutritious Ethnic Foods

There is a wide variety of delicious ethnic foods. Many of these are also nutritious choices. Here are some suggestions for eating nutritiously when eating ethnic foods.

Caribbean

Caribbean foods feature the flavors of many countries that have influenced the development of these islands. Many of the basics are low in fat and high in nutrition.

- Good choices: Select grilled fish with cooked sweet potatoes and fresh fruit.
- Worst choices: Avoid dishes high in lard, butter, or cream.

Chinese

Chinese food often features veggies and rice. However, it can be high in fat and sodium due to the oils and soy sauce used in preparation.

- Good choices: Try a stir-fry of veggies and beef, pork, or chicken. Good side dishes include bok choy, snow peas, broccoli, and steamed rice.
- Worst choices: Avoid egg rolls and wontons, because they tend to be high in fat. Skip the deep-fried entrees.

Indian

Indian foods feature tasty dishes full of vegetable protein. Yogurt is often used as a topping or a marinade.

- Good choices: Lentils, chickpeas, beans, and rice are good choices.
- Worst choices: Avoid Indian curries made with coconut milk, ghee (clarified butter), and deep-fried foods.

Italian

Many Italian foods are quite nutritious. Pasta is fat free and a favorite of athletes.

- Good choices: Pasta with red clam sauce is a tasty treat, as is cioppino (tomato-based stew). Vegetarian minestrone soup is a good low-fat option.
- Worst choices: Avoid cannelloni, ravioli, lasagna, and tortellini, because they usually contain heavy cheeses and fatty meats. Be careful of rich cream sauces like alfredo and carbonara. Note that most Italian entrees are high in sodium (1,500 milligrams of sodium or more) (Hurley and Liebman 1994).

Japanese

Many Japanese dishes are healthy. However, you might wish to avoid soy or teriyaki sauce to reduce sodium.

- Good choices: Select steamed rice, steamed veggies, lean meats, and seafood. Sushi should be safe if the restaurant is clean and has a good reputation.
- Worst choices: Avoid the deep-fried (tempura) foods.

Mexican

Mexican dishes are healthy and low in fat until cheese and sour cream are added.

- Good choices: Select plain corn tortillas, refried beans, boiled black beans and rice, bean burritos or enchiladas, and soft tacos. Low-fat toppings include fresh salsa.
- Worst choices: Avoid the chimichangas and flautas because they are deep-fried. Other items high in fat include cheese enchiladas, cheese chili rellenos, and tortilla chips. Use guacamole sparingly.

Russian

Most Russian dishes center around cabbage, potatoes, and meat. They can be high in fat because of the meats and added lard.

- Good choices: Borscht is a stew of vegetables and is a good choice. Stuffed cabbage (without a sausage filling) is also a good choice.
- Worst choices: Avoid meat dishes and ones to which lard has been added.

Thai

Most Thai dishes focus on stir-fried veggies and rice. However, many of the dishes are made with coconut milk and cream, which are high in saturated fat and calories.

- Good choices: Stir-fries and steamed rice are your best choices.
- Worst choices: Avoid curries (high in fat) and deep-fried foods.

It is easy to eat only the foods we are familiar with. However, there are many nutritious food choices from other cultures.

Source: Adapted from Liz Applegate, "Ethnic Eats" in *Runner's World*, October 1993, pages 26–29.

Alcohol is not included in the new pyramid. Although it does contain calories, alcohol has no nutrients. One study showed that alcohol consumption makes the body burn fat more slowly and disrupts the body's normal disposal of fat (Suter, Schutz, and Jequier 1992).

Nutritious meals can be planned and prepared with minimal effort. Select ample supplies of fruits and vegetables, because they can be eaten raw and are especially good snacks. Some advance planning allows for more nutritious and more economical eating.

It is important to choose a variety of foods.

EATING WELL ON A SHOESTRING

As a college student, you might face some unusual challenges selecting nutritious foods and eating well. You might be away from home for the first time and in a situation where foods are served only at specific times, or be in living situations that require you fix your own foods. In either case, you have the challenge of eating well on a budget and doing so without a great investment of time.

When you are living in housing where meals are prepared and served at specific times, there are several things you can do to eat well and economically. Find out the serving times and obtain a copy of the menus for the week or month. Plan to eat at the serving times instead of missing meals and spending money on a fast-food meal or snacks. Review the menu before meals and determine what items to select. When reviewing the menus, consider the food groups and select the foods that are the most nutritious choices, despite the temptation to do otherwise. If there are few nutritious choices available, talk with the individuals in charge of the food service and make some positive recommendations to them. They are likely to be receptive to ideas

PERSONAL SKILLS AND EXPERIENCES

Eating Well for Less— What Can You Do?
Refer to the information in this section on eating well on a budget.

1. What can you do to eat better?
2. What can you do to eat more economically?
3. Where is the best place to shop?
4. What are your best tips for eating well and saving money?

like a salad bar if they know there is student interest. Meals are often included in the total cost of housing, so you have a right to be served healthy foods and get your money's worth for your investment.

Resist the temptation to go to a fast-food restaurant to save time if you are living in a location where meals are not provided. Plan a menu for a week that features low-cost foods. Skim milk and nonfat dry milk are good choices among dairy products; fresh produce in season is the best bet in the fruits and vegetables group; dried beans and peas are usually more economical than meat, poultry, and fish; and store-brand whole-grain and enriched grain products are the best choices in the breads and cereals category.

When shopping, buy in bulk and use coupons. Determine the cost savings in money and time in shopping at several stores. Although stores may be featuring different bargains, the time involved in going to several stores may not be worth the savings. If not, select the store where the prices are best, even though it might mean bagging your own groceries.

Think carefully before purchasing convenience foods that have been highly processed, such as hamburger helper products. These might not be good nutritional choices and usually cost more than similar items prepared at home. Chips and crackers might not be worth the cost, because they tend to be high in calories and low in nutritional value.

Buy foods that don't have handling costs included in the price. For example, it is less expensive to buy cheese and grate it yourself than to buy grated cheese, to buy whole chickens and cut them into pieces rather than to buy parts, and to buy the ingredients for trail mix or granola and make it yourself.

Plan for leftovers as part of the week's menu. Either include that food as part of another meal or combine it with something else for a new dish. Casseroles are a great example and allow for much creativity.

Give thought to storage so that foods don't spoil quickly. Refrigerate lemons in a plastic bag to make them last longer, and prevent mold on berries by washing them right before

Eating Nutritiously at Fast-Food Restaurants

It can be tougher to eat nutritiously at fast-food restaurants than at home, but there are ways to reduce the fat and calories. Here are some suggestions.

McDonald's

- Skip the tartar sauce on the filet of fish sandwich in order to eliminate one-third of the calories and two-thirds of the fat.
- Order the fat-free apple bran muffins instead of the Danish pastry.
- Skip the mayo when ordering the McDLT to save yourself 135 calories and 15 grams of fat.

Burger King

- Hold the mayo on the Whopper to skip 150 calories.

- Skip the mayo on the broiled chicken sandwich to eliminate 90 calories.
- Save 270 calories by choosing the Light Italian dressing rather than the regular dressings.

Taco Bell

- Skip the fried shell that holds the taco salad in order to remove half the fat and half the calories.
- Note that a bean burrito has half the fat of an order of nachos even though they have the same number of calories.

Pizza Hut

- Order the pizza without the cheese in order to skip 40 percent of the calories and 85 percent of the fat.
- Ask for extra veggies on your pizza.

Kentucky Fried Chicken

- Remove the skin from the fried chicken to cut calories in half and

to remove two-thirds of the fat. Note that the extra-crispy chicken has 45 percent more fat.

- Skip the fries, since they have more fat and calories than three orders of mashed potatoes and gravy.

Wendy's

- Avoid the potato salad, the cheddar chips, the pasta salad, and the cole slaw at the salad bar.
- Skip the chocolate chip cookies, as they contain more fat and the same number of calories as a single hamburger.

Baskin Robbins

- Choose a sugar cone rather than a waffle cone to reduce calories and fat.
- Order sorbet rather than ice cream.
- Vanilla and Very Berry Strawberry are low-calorie flavors of ice cream.

---

you eat them, rather than in advance. Store onions and garlic in a cool, dark place such as a basement. Submerge herbs, such as parsley, in water and refrigerate them to keep them fresh longer.

Cook large amounts or multiple servings and freeze the remainder for future meals. Securely wrap foods to prevent freezer burn, and mark each item with the date.

You might want to check with other students for ideas on saving money and eating well. They may suggest good places to shop and have some great tips for saving money.

FAST FOODS AND FROZEN FOODS

Fast foods have become a way of life for most Americans. Fast foods include the foods served by the chain restaurants that line our highways, while frozen foods include the trendy microwave meals sold in grocery stores.

Many fast foods are high in fat, sodium, simple carbohydrates, and calories. It is probably okay to eat these foods occasionally, but a steady diet of a burger, fries, and a coke is not recommended.

The food group most likely to be lacking in a fast-food meal is the fruits and vegetables group. However, fast-food restaurants have included salad bars and fruit bars to appeal

to the health-conscious consumer. If you choose the salad and fruit bar, resist the temptation to add high-calorie and high-fat dressings and toppings, if you want to eat nutritiously. Be sure to include several selections from the fruit and vegetable group at the next meal if you don't choose the salad or fruit bar (see table 6.7).

The most popular convenience foods are the frozen foods. Frozen meals have come a long way from the TV dinners introduced in the 1950s. Although they were quite a novelty at the time, they were far from delicious or nutritious. In recent years there has been a vast expansion of the frozen-foods market. *Consumer Reports* reviewed these foods and noted the following about light entrees: They contain 8 to 10 ounces of food, 200 to 300 calories, at most 50 milligrams of cholesterol, and 400 to 800 milligrams of sodium, and less than 30 percent of their calories come from fat. The regular entrees contained twice as much fat as the light entrees. The *Consumer Reports* writers found that light entrees were not a complete meal and that the taste could not compare to home cooking. Possible reasons for this included the use of inferior ingredients, second-rate recipes, and excessive processing ("Frozen Light Entrees" 1993). Even so, the light entrees are a vast improvement over the TV dinners of yesteryear.

TABLE 6.7   THE BEST, THE WORST, AND (SOME OF) THE REST

		Calories	Fat (tsp)[a]	Sodium (mg)[b]	Gloom[c]
	Breakfast Foods				
	McDonald's English Muffin w/butter	169	1	270	9
	McDonald's Hotcakes w/Butter & Syrup	413	2	640	20
	McDonald's Egg McMuffin	293	2¾	740	25
	McDonald's Biscuit w/Sausage & Egg	529	8	1,250	57
	Burger King Croissan'wich w/Sausage	538	9¼	1,042	61[d]
W	Hardee's Big Country Breakfast (Sausage)	1,005	16¼	1,950	97
	Burgers				
	McDonald's Hamburger	257	2¼	460	17
	McDonald's Quarter Pounder w/Cheese	517	6¾	1,150	45
	Wendy's Big Classic w/Cheese	640	9	1,310	56[d]
	McDonald's McD.L.T.	674	9½	1,170	56
W	Wendy's Triple Cheeseburger	1,040	15½	1,848	85[d]
	Jack-in-the-Box Ultimate Cheeseburger	942	15¾	1,176	88
	Chicken Sandwiches				
B	Carl's Jr. BBQ Chicken Sandwich	320	1¼	955	17
B	Hardee's Grilled Chicken Sandwich	330	2¾	1,240	25
	Jack-in-the-Box Grilled Chicken Fillet Sandwich	408	3¾	1,130	29
	Wendy's Chicken Breast Fillet Sandwich	430	4¼	705	27[d]
	Arby's Chicken Breast Sandwich	493	5¾	1,019	33
W	McDonald's McChicken Sandwich	490	6½	780	39
W	Arby's Roast Chicken Club Sandwich	610	8½	1,500	53
	Mexican Foods				
B	Jack-in-the-Box Chicken Faijita Pita	292	1¾	703	16
	Taco Bell Chicken Faijita	226	2¼	619	18[d]
B	Taco Bell Bean Burrito w/Green Sauce	351	2¼	763	17[d]
	Taco Bell Taco	183	2½	276	16[d]
	Taco Bell Steak Faijita	234	2½	485	18[d]
	Jack-in-the-Box Beef Faijita Pita	333	3¼	635	22
	Taco Bell Super Combo Taco	286	3½	462	23[d]
W	Taco Bell Taco Light	410	6½	594	39[d]
	Salads (No Dressings Added)				
B	McDonald's Chicken Salad Oriental	141	¾	230	7
B	Burger Kind Chicken Salad	140	1	440	9
	McDonald's Chef Salad	231	3	490	21
	Hardee's Chicken Fiesta Salad	286	3¼	533	26
	Jack-in-the-Box Mexican Chicken Salad	442	5¼	1,500	41
	Taco Bell Taco Salad w/out Shell	520	7	1,431	47[d]
	Wendy's Taco Salad	660	8½	1,110	45[d]
W	Taco Bell Taco Salad w/Shell	941	14	1,662	75[d]

[a]To convert teaspoons of fat to grams, multiply by 4.4.

[b]The recommended daily sodium intake for an adult is 2,400 mg.

[c]CSPI's "Gloom" rating ranks foods according to their fat, sodium, cholesterol, and vitamin and mineral content. The higher the number, the worse the food.

[d]"Gloom" rating was estimated without full information on fat content from manufacturer.

W = 1989 Worst, **B** = 1989 Best

Note: All information obtained from manufacturers.

Copyright 1989, CSPI. Adapted from *Fast Food Eating Guide,* published by CSPI, 1875 Connecticut Ave., NW, Washington, D.C. 20009–5728. Reprinted by permission.

HEALTH UPDATE

Kids' Snacks

Buying nutritious processed foods that are designed for kids is not easy to do. Experts convened by the Center for Science in the Public Interest determined that foods marketed for children closely resemble junk foods. The panel was unable to find a cookie, frozen dessert, granola bar, hot dog, or luncheon meat that met the group's standards. Many of the kids' foods have excessive amounts of fat, sodium, and sugar, which contribute to heart disease, cancer, and high blood pressure in later life. Refer to the following chart for the best of processed foods (Duston 1992).

- **Breakfast cereals:** Alpen (no salt or sugar added), Kellogg's Nutrigrain Wheat; old-fashioned or quick oats; Post Grape-Nuts, Weetabix, Wheatena.
- **Cheese:** Weight Watchers Low Sodium American.
- **Chips, pretzels, popcorn:** Arrowhead Mills Blue or Yellow Corn Curls (unsalted); Baja Bakery Rice & Bean Tortilla Bits Light; Guiltless Gourmet No Oil Tortilla Chips; Skinny's Corn Chips; Weight Watchers Microwave Popcorn; unsalted pretzels, all brands.
- **Cookies:** None.
- **Frozen dinners:** None.
- **Canned or shelf-stable entrees:** Fungle's Fun Foods, Health Valley Fast Menu, Hormel Health Selections Sweet and Sour Chicken.
- **Frozen entrees:** Health Choice spaghetti with meat sauce or macaroni and cheese: Tyson Looney Tunes Pasta.
- **Fast-food meals.** None.
- **French fries:** McCain Classic Cut, Golden Steak Fries or Crinkle Cuts; Ore-Ida Home Style Wedges, Dinner Fries, Golden Crinkles, Cottage Fries, Pixi Crinkles, or Lites Crinkle Cuts.
- **Frozen desserts:** None.
- **Frozen dessert bars:** FrozFruit Orange, Cantaloupe, Mango, Strawberry Lemon, Raspberry, Pineapple or Fruit and Yogurt.
- **Fruit beverages:** Orange, grapefruit, fortified apple or fortified grape juice.
- **Fruit snacks:** Nature's Choice Real Fruit Bars.
- **Granola bars:** None.
- **Hotdogs:** None.
- **Luncheon meats:** None.
- **Milk:** Skim or 1 percent low-fat.
- **Pizza:** Rice Crust Soy Cheese; Soypreme French Bread Garden Patch or Whole Wheat Cheese Style; Special Delivery Soya Kaas or Cheese; Tree Tavern Pizsoy.
- **Soup:** Campbell Low Sodium Split Pea, Low Sodium Chicken with Noodles, or Low Sodium Tomato; Hain Split Pea No Salt; Pritikin Split Pea, Lentil, Minestrone or Vegetable; Spice Hunter Quick and Natural.

Source: From Diane Duston, "Food Aimed at Kids Mostly Junk, Group Says." Associated press release in the *Birmingham News*, August 3, 1992, pages 1a, 6a.

DINING OUT

Some restaurants feature low-fat meals, but it is possible to eat nutritiously at any restaurant. Eat veggies and bread without butter before and during dinner. Skip chips with dip. Select items that are broiled, grilled, boiled, poached, steamed, or roasted rather than fried ("Low-Fat Dining Out" 1993). Avoid cheese- or cream-based dishes. Request salad dressing on the side and order a "light" dressing ("Just the Facts" 1993). If you prefer a topping on your baked potato, request plain yogurt or sour cream, as both have less fat than margarine or butter. Request the topping on the side of the potato and use it sparingly. Skip the other toppings for your salad and potato, such as cheese, bacon bits, and croutons. Don't hesitate to ask the server how items are prepared. Request a change if you prefer (baked rather than fried, sauce on the side rather than on the entree, visible fat trimmed from meat, the skin removed from poultry). Ask for veggies to be prepared without butter. Skip dessert or order fresh fruit or sorbet. Divide the entree in half and take home a "people" bag.

NUTRITION AND THE CONSUMER

Being a nutrition-conscious consumer involves more than just comparing prices. It also involves being able to interpret labels, evaluate nutritional claims in advertising, determine sound sources of nutritional information, and apply this information when making nutritional decisions, as well as being knowledgeable about food additives.

NUTRITION LABELING

It's important to use the nutrition labeling on a product in order to select the most nutritious foods. The FDA labeling program helps us identify the nutrient content of the foods we buy (figure 6.5). All labels with nutrition information must follow the same format, and any food that has an added nutrient or makes a nutritional claim must have a nutrition label.

Information on the label includes the following:

1. The serving size and number of servings in the container
2. The calories per serving and the number of calories from fat in each serving
3. The percentage of Daily Value (the percentage of the day's allotment of the nutrient that comes from this food) of total fat, saturated fat, cholesterol, sodium, total carbohydrates, sugars, dietary fiber, and protein in a serving

PERSONAL SKILLS AND EXPERIENCES

What's for Breakfast?

For years we have been told that breakfast is the most important meal of the day. The owners of fast-food restaurants heard that, also, and have been serving breakfast for years. However, the nutritional value of fast-food breakfasts might not be as high as it could be. The ideal breakfast should have 15 percent of its calories from protein, 30 percent or less of its calories from fat, and 55 percent or more of its calories from carbohydrates.

Review the breakfasts illustrated at the right and respond to the following questions:

1. What are the nutritional pluses and minuses of each breakfast?
2. What would make each breakfast more nutritious?
3. Which breakfast falls within the guidelines for an optimal breakfast?

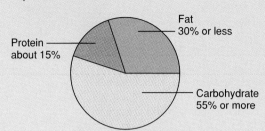

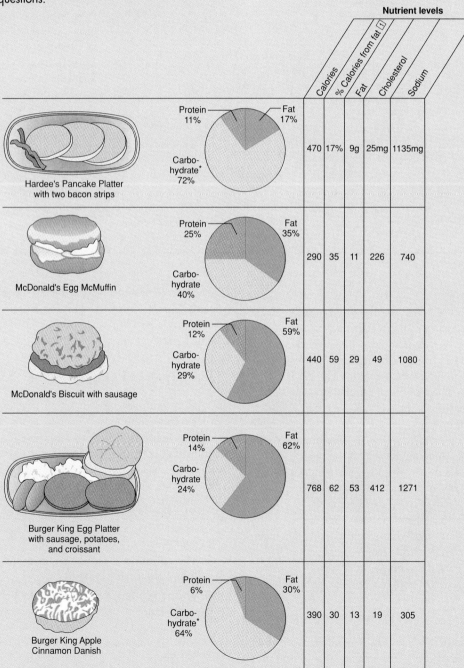

Nutrient levels

	Calories	% Calories from fat	Fat	Cholesterol	Sodium
Hardee's Pancake Platter with two bacon strips	470	17%	9g	25mg	1135mg
McDonald's Egg McMuffin	290	35	11	226	740
McDonald's Biscuit with sausage	440	59	29	49	1080
Burger King Egg Platter with sausage, potatoes, and croissant	768	62	53	412	1271
Burger King Apple Cinnamon Danish	390	30	13	19	305

*Includes an appreciable amount of sugar   Source: Adapted from *Consumer Reports on Health*, September 1991, pp. 625–629.

Nutrition facts

Serving size: ¹/₂ cup (114g)
Servings per container: 4

Amount per serving

Calories: 260	Calories from fat: 120

	% Daily Value*
Total fat 13g	**20%**
Saturated fat 5g	**25%**
Cholesterol 30mg	**10%**
Sodium 660g	**28%**
Total carbohydrate 31g	**11%**
Sugars 5g	
Dietary fiber 0g	**0%**
Protein 5g	

**Vitamin A 4% • Vitamin C 2% •
Calcium 15% • Iron 4%**

*Percentages (%) of. Daily Values are based on a 2,000 calorie diet. Your Daily Values may vary higher or lower depending on your calorie needs.

Nutrient		2,000 Calories	2,500 Calories
Total fat	Less than	65g	80g
Sat. fat	Less than	20g	25g
Cholesterol	Less than	300mg	300mg
Sodium	Less than	2,400mg	2,400mg
Total Carbohydrate		300g	375g
Fiber		25g	30g

1g fat = 9 calories
1g carbohydrates = 4 calories
1g protein = 4 calories

Figure 6.5
New nutrition labeling became effective in 1994, when labels such as this one replaced those in use since 1973.

4. A general guide to the amount of various nutrients (fat, saturated fat, cholesterol, sodium, total carbohydrates, and fiber) on a 2,000-calorie and a 2,500-calorie daily intake

5. The number of calories in 1 gram each of fat, carbohydrate, and protein

Most packaged foods will also list ingredients on the label. Each ingredient must be listed in the order of its concentration in a product, with the ingredient in largest concentration listed first.

Nutrition labeling can be used to serve better meals and save money. By reading and comparing labels, you can select the most nutritious foods and track calories. Individuals on special diets recommended by their physicians can use nutrition labels to help avoid restricted foods.

The new labels were required of all packaged foods in 1994 and reflect some of the health concerns of the American public, including the number of calories from fat and the amounts of dietary fiber, saturated fats, and cholesterol in a product. The new labels are required for all foods that are sources of nutrients, whereas the old labels were required only when a food was fortified or when a nutritional claim was made ("Nutritional Labels for the '90s" 1990). Even candy bars are required to have nutrition labels ("Unmasking Labels That Hide the Fat" 1992). The new labels do not apply to restaurant food; fresh fish, poultry, and meat; and fresh fruits and vegetables ("At Last, Food Labels That Make Sense" 1993).

The FDA has regulated standard serving sizes on labels and has developed standard definitions for nine terms used to describe products, including *high-fiber, light, low-sodium, cholesterol,* and *low-fat.* For example, products advertised as "light" or "lite" must have at least one-third fewer calories than the norm for that product. They must have at least 50 percent less fat if more than half the calories come from fat ("Unmasking Labels That Hide the Fat" 1992). "Low-fat" products must have at most 3 grams of fat per serving. These definitions should help us more accurately judge the nutritional value of different products. However, restaurants do not have to abide by these definitions.

Just because a product is advertised as being low in fat does not mean it is low in other ingredients you may wish to avoid. For instance, many of the light mayonnaises and salad dressings contain large amounts of sodium. Light mayonnaise can have as much as 170 percent more sodium than regular mayonnaise ("Hold the Mayo" 1992).

After the FDA began defining certain terms, some food manufacturers began labeling their food with other words that have not been defined. The latest term being used on labels is *healthy.* Many of the foods labeled "healthy" are anything but healthy. The FDA is considering defining implied claims like "healthy," much to the aggravation of the Grocery Manufacturers Association. You may wish to look at the number of products with *healthy* on their labels the next time you are in a grocery store (Hurley and Schmidt 1992).

Because there is so much misinformation in the field of nutrition, it is important for the consumer to be wary. Consider the following guidelines when you are trying to determine whether a source of information is credible:

1. Is one food or product promoted as the only one needed for good health?

2. Is the person promoting the product likely to experience personal gain?

3. Is there a variety of foods from the food groups recommended in the plan?

4. Would the person selling the plan or promoting the product be associated with reliable health information?

5. Is the person promoting the product a good role model?

FOOD ADDITIVES

Food additives include vitamins, food coloring, salt, and sugar. They are used for four purposes: (1) to maintain or

Issue

Chemical Residues in Food

Chemical residues from pesticides, vaccines, antibiotics, and other animal drugs are occasionally reported in meat and poultry. The primary reason for these residues to appear is failure to allow the animal's system to clear itself of a drug prior to slaughter. Diseased animals are not allowed to enter the human food supply, so animals may be treated with veterinary drugs prior to being slaughtered. The illegal residues usually are found in the kidneys, liver, or fat rather than in the muscle meat. The U.S. Department of Agriculture's Food Safety and Inspection Service is responsible for monitoring chemical residues in meat and poultry, while the Food and Drug Administration has set limits on the amounts of such residues in animal tissues intended for human consumption ("Illegal Residues in Meat and Poultry" 1992).

- Pro: The government has taken every precaution to ensure a safe food supply. Illegal residues are going to occasionally be found.

- Con: The government's standards are not strict enough. Tighter regulations should be enforced related to amount of time between administration of a veterinary drug and the slaughter of an animal that had been diseased.

Do you feel the government standards are strict enough? What do you think should be required?

improve nutritional value, (2) to maintain freshness, (3) to help in processing or preparation, and (4) to make foods more appealing.

One additive that might be added to bread in the near future is folic acid. This vitamin helps prevent open-spine defects and could easily be baked into bread. It is impossible to overdose on folic acid, so there is no risk associated with adding it (Butgereit 1993).

Additives are better controlled now than at any time in history. The FDA has the authority to regulate additives on the basis of safety, but it has no power over the number or need for additives in a product. The informed and selective consumer has the real power.

SPECIAL NUTRITIONAL CONSIDERATIONS

The nutritional information discussed in this chapter applies to the majority of healthy adults. There are several groups whose nutritional considerations merit special discussion. These groups include vegetarians, athletes, and individuals under stress.

VEGETARIANS

Most nutrients consumed by **vegetarians** are from plant sources. Vegetarian diets are becoming increasingly popular and are chosen for a number of reasons.

The types of vegetarian diets include vegan, lacto-vegetarian, and lacto-ovo-vegetarian. Vegans eat only plant foods. The vegan diet is the most difficult one to adhere to and to balance, from a nutritional perspective. Lacto-vegetarians eat plant foods and dairy products. Low-fat or skim milk products need to be used in the lacto-vegetarian diet to keep it low in fat. Lacto-ovo-vegetarians eat dairy products, eggs, and plant foods. This is the most common form of vegetarian diet in America.

All types of vegetarian diets can be nutritious if care is taken in food selection. Vegetarians typically have lower body weights, less constipation, lower blood pressure levels, less risk for heart disease and certain cancers, and more-favorable levels of blood cholesterol than the majority of the population. There are, however, some risks associated with a vegetarian diet. Vegetarian diets can be lacking in vitamins (including vitamin D, vitamin B-12, and riboflavin), minerals (including zinc, calcium, and iron), and amino acids. The greatest concerns regarding vegetarian diets relate to lack of vitamins D and B-12 and the difficulty of obtaining enough calories to meet energy needs.

Insufficient calories to meet energy needs is usually a problem for child vegetarians rather than adult vegetarians. Special efforts are needed to ensure that children consume adequate calories to meet the energy needs of their growing bodies.

Vegetarian women who become pregnant usually will not need to alter their diets if they are lacto- or lacto-ovo-vegetarians. Vegans need to be sure that they consume adequate amounts of protein, vitamin B-6, iron, calcium, and zinc, and they should take a vitamin B-12 supplement.

Once there was a concern that vegetables and grains lacked essential amino acids, but we now know that these foods contain amino acids in varying amounts rather than lack them entirely. High-quality protein can be obtained from plant sources if essential amino acids are present in a specific pattern so they can be used by the body as high-quality protein. Because vegetable foods contain varying amounts of the essential amino acids, vegetable protein foods must be combined so that one food provides what another is missing.

vegetarian

A person who eats a diet low in, or excluding, animal sources of food. Vegans eat only plants. Lacto-vegetarians eat plant foods and dairy products. Lacto-ovo-vegetarians eat dairy products, eggs, and plants. All these diets can be nutritious with careful food selection.

The foods can be eaten 3 to 4 hours apart and still complement each other. Vegetarians who consume a wide variety of foods are likely to obtain the needed amino acids. Here are some guidelines on how to pair up vegetable protein foods to achieve high-quality protein:

1. Pair legumes (dried peas, beans, lentils, peanuts) with grains (wheat, oats, rice, corn). Example: peanut butter on whole-wheat bread.
2. Pair legumes with seeds. Example: pea soup with sesame crackers.
3. Pair legumes with nuts. Example: mixed dry-roasted soybeans and walnuts.

ATHLETES

Most athletes are interested in all factors that will help them improve their performance, including nutrition. This is true of the professional athlete as well as the average American involved in fitness activities. Achieving top performance requires consuming a well-balanced diet. Top performances are not the result of eating particular foods.

There is a great deal of misinformation about nutrition and physical performance. One area of misinformation involves protein. Because muscles are made of protein, some people thought that a high-protein diet would build muscles. But muscles are built by exercising specific muscle groups, not by eating certain foods. Protein is needed for building tissue, but athletes do not need additional supplies, because most of us consume more protein than we need.

To get the energy they need, athletes need to consume adequate supplies of complex carbohydrates, the primary fuel needed by the muscles during exercise. Complex carbohydrates provide energy at a slow and gradual pace—unlike simple carbohydrates, which cause a rapid drop in blood sugar. Carbohydrate consumption for athletes involved in heavy training should be approximately 400 grams per day. It is best to consume a large portion of the carbohydrates within 2 hours after the end of training, because glycogen synthesis is the greatest then (Wardlaw and Insel 1990, 212).

Athletes have sought ways to store extra glycogen in the muscles and liver to delay exhaustion during endurance events. **Carbohydrate loading**—which involves depleting one's glycogen through exercise and diet followed by rest, and then "reloading" one's cells with glycogen by eating a high-carbohydrate diet—is no longer recommended. Most sport physiologists now recommend simply increasing the intake of complex carbohydrates 2 to 3 days prior to an endurance event ("Nutrition and Exercise: What Your Body Needs" 1993).

Athletes might need extra calories to meet the demands of training. The best advice for supplying these demands is to increase the portions of a well-balanced diet. It is not advisable to consume products high in fat or protein to add these extra calories.

Fluid replacement is extremely important for athletes, particularly those involved in endurance sports. Athletes involved in endurance activities can lose 6 to 8 pounds per hour, which is mostly water weight. A 3 percent weight loss can hamper performance; a 7 percent loss can disrupt the functioning of the heart and circulatory system (McGlynn 1993).

Water is still considered the best fluid-replacement drink; however, some of the most recent studies have shown that glucose solutions may be better than water for fluid replacement during prolonged exercise (activities that last longer than 90 minutes), provided that the concentration of glucose is less than 12 percent. The absorption rate is decreased at the 12 percent level, and the athlete may experience gastrointestinal distress (Powers and Howley 1990, 476, 484). It is recommended that athletes consume 2 cups of fluid 15 minutes before an event and 1 cup of fluid every 15 minutes for sport events that last longer than 30 minutes (Wardlaw and Insel 1990, 212). Salt tablets are never recommended as a means of replacing sodium lost during exercise, because they increase the likelihood of dehydration.

INDIVIDUALS UNDER STRESS

Diet is related to stress in several ways. Certain foods can produce a response similar to the stress response. Nutrients can be depleted during stressful times, and consumption of certain foods can worsen stress-related diseases.

Pseudostressors are substances in the diet that can produce effects similar to stress for certain individuals. These products can have a negative impact on health and may interfere with normal functioning by replicating sympathetic nervous system stimulation. The reaction may include an increase in the metabolic rate and a release of stress hormones that increase heart rate and metabolism (Greenberg 1990, 78). Dietary stressors include products containing caffeine, such as colas, coffee, tea, chocolate, and some over-the-counter drugs.

---

carbohydrate loading
A dietary practice some athletes use to prepare for competitive events. A severe reduction in caloric intake for several days prior to the event is followed by a very large intake of carbohydrates on the day prior to the event—the caloric reduction is meant to "empty" cells so that the large intake of carbohydrates can fill the cells with pure glycogen. No longer recommended.

pseudostressors
Dietary substances that can produce, in certain individuals, effects similar to those caused by stress.

PERSONAL SKILLS AND EXPERIENCES

Making Healthy Nutrition a Part of Your Life

Nutritional choices influence every aspect of life, because they influence how we feel. How we feel in turn influences the mind, the body, the soul, and the interdependence of all of these factors. For most of us, eating nutritiously requires some specific changes and a certain amount of commitment.

Directions: Complete the activities below to assess your health skills related to nutrition. If you successfully complete all of the activities, you have the prerequisites for making nutritious food choices a part of your lifestyle.

Mind

Decide whether eating nutritiously is important to you and what makes it important. Determine what you want to accomplish as a result of making nutritional changes.

Body

Evaluate your present eating habits. Consider how you feel as a result of your food choices. Determine your areas of strength and your weaknesses. Consider how the positive and negative aspects influence your health.

Soul

Determine whether the benefits associated with eating nutritiously are related to the values you hold. Consider immediate as well as long-term benefits.

1. Discuss the benefits of eating nutritiously with someone who is important in your life. Discuss ways in which nutrition impacts all areas of one's life.

2. Determine changes that will improve your nutrition. Evaluate what you need to do to successfully complete these changes.

3. You must have a certain level of commitment to successfully implement any long-term changes. Review the things you can do in other areas of your life to strengthen your commitment to, and your ability to make, these long-term dietary changes.

Although reactions vary among individuals, some people may find they are nervous and unable to sleep when they consume these products. Individuals who react this way should limit the intake of these products, particularly in the evening, and should check product labels for dietary stressors.

Stress can impact nutrition by depleting certain nutrients, particularly vitamin C and the B-complex vitamins. These vitamins are used to produce the hormone cortisol during periods of stress and are also used by the body to process products high in refined sugar. A diet deficient in these vitamins can result in depression, anxiety, nervous disorders, weakness, and sleep disturbances.

Consumption of large amounts of sugar over a short time can result in elevated levels of blood sugar followed by periods of hypoglycemia (low blood sugar). This source of dietary stress can result in trembling, anxiety, dizziness, fatigue, and lethargy, but this stress can easily be remedied by reducing the amount of simple carbohydrates one consumes.

Consumption of too much or too little or certain nutrients can worsen diseases related to stress. The likelihood of heart disease is increased by a diet high in saturated fats, which elevates the amount of cholesterol in the blood and its accumulation on artery walls.

If you are under prolonged stress, your immune system will be weakened and you might be more susceptible to the effects of stress. So nutrition is even more important during such times. People under stress tend to either significantly reduce their intake of food or eat snack food of low nutritional value. Instead, they should eat a well-balanced diet—and exercise regularly to work off the psychological products of stress that can accumulate in their blood and tissues. Good nutritional practices can enhance protective coping

skills. While nutritional choices may not appear to make an immediate impact on health, they have short-term as well as long-term effects. Good nutritional choices help ensure that individuals are in a strong physiological position to deal with the stressors they encounter.

NUTRITIONAL NEEDS THROUGHOUT LIFE

Although the same basic concepts of nutrition apply to individuals of different ages, specific needs change considerably at different stages. It is important to be aware of these different demands.

The most rapid period of growth is experienced by infants and children. Sound nutrition is required to meet these demands. Eating habits begun in these early years are especially important, and parents play a critical role in their formation. For example, a small child given soft drinks at meals might continue to want soft drinks rather than something more nutritious. On the other hand, regulating cholesterol intake in children has long been debated. There is currently no evidence that children with high cholesterol levels will also have high cholesterol levels as adults, so there is no consensus about the need for cholesterol screening in children (Payer 1993).

The teen years are the next most active stage of growth. Teens who experience a rapid growth spurt must consume adequate amounts of calcium, phosphorus, and vitamin D. Teens often eat many meals away from home, where there is no guarantee of nutritional quality.

Because pregnant women supply all of the nutrients to their developing fetus, their nutritional habits are especially important. The National Research Council's current Recommended Dietary Allowances include, for pregnant women, a 20 percent increase in protein consumption, a 50 percent increase in calcium consumption, a 16 percent increase in vitamin C consumption, and increased consumption of the B vitamins and vitamin D ("New Recommended Dietary Allowances" 1990). However, the guidelines from the Institute of Medicine state that pregnant women on balanced diets do not need extra vitamins (Institute of Medicine 1990). Expectant mothers should increase their iron consumption by 15 milligrams. It is recommended that lactating women consume 65 grams of protein; the same amount of calcium as pregnant women; higher amounts of vitamins A, B, and C than the levels recommended for the prepregnant female; and additional fluids to aid in milk production.

Major illnesses experienced by the elderly are related to malnutrition and obesity. Malnutrition in the elderly is often related to poor eating habits. Although 85 percent of elderly adults indicate that they are aware of the benefits of a healthy diet, 30 percent skip at least one meal a day ("Nutrition Screening Initiative" 1990). Many prefer not to cook for themselves and select snack foods that are low in nutrients. Multiple prescription drugs, taken by 45 percent of the elderly, can decrease appetite and absorption of nutrients ("Nutrition Screening Initiative" 1990). It is especially important for the elderly to eat well-balanced meals that are easily digested. Although (with the possible exception of calcium) the elderly do not need additional vitamins or minerals if they eat properly, they do need extra fiber to prevent constipation. The elderly might need to be especially careful about nutritional choices, as they might not need extra calories. Many of the elderly need to increase their consumption of dairy and grain products, while decreasing their intake of fats, sweets, and alcohol in order to maintain energy balance (Fanelli-Kuczmarski 1989).

TAKE ACTION

1. Develop an eating plan that will promote your overall health. (For example, eat breakfast every day, eat a well-balanced diet, and avoid sugar-coated cereals.)
2. Examine your diet for the past week, and determine ways it might be better. Develop a plan to improve the quality of your diet.
3. Consider what you might do to improve the quality of your nutrition when you eat away from home. Plan ways to implement these changes.
4. Devise a way to help a relative or close friend improve their personal nutrition. Include information they need to know and ways you will help them.
5. Think of a situation related to nutrition that has caused disorganization or disruption in your life (for example, a failed diet plan). Develop a plan to promote resilient reintegration in your life to prevent potential health problems in the future related to nutrition.

SUMMARY

1. The Year 2000 Objectives for the Nation acknowledges the correlation between poor nutritional practices and chronic diseases.
2. There are guidelines for improving the nutrition of Americans.
3. Useful elements of food are called "nutrients" and include carbohydrates, proteins, fats, vitamins, minerals, and water.
4. Needed levels of nutrients are indicated in the RDA.
5. Food supplies energy that is measured by kilocalories.
6. Americans need to eat more complex carbohydrates and fewer simple carbohydrates.
7. Protein intake is likely to be more than adequate in most individuals.
8. Fat supplies 9 calories per gram; proteins and carbohydrates supply 4 calories per gram.
9. HDL removes cholesterol from the walls of the arteries.
10. Vitamins do not provide energy but are needed for chemical reactions to occur in the body.
11. Inadequate supplies of calcium are associated with osteoporosis and other problems.
12. Fifteen to 20 million Americans are sodium sensitive.
13. Water is the most important nutrient of all.
14. The Food Guide Pyramid has replaced the basic four food groups. Foods are divided into groups based on the similarity of their nutrients.
15. Food additives allow us to store foods for long periods.
16. Ingredients on labels are listed in order of their concentration in the product.
17. Vegetarians need to be especially careful about getting needed amounts of vitamins, minerals, and amino acids.
18. The best fluid-replacement drink for most activities is water.
19. There are a number of things students can do to eat well on a budget.
20. An occasional fast-food meal is fine, provided that the needed nutrients are made up at the next meal.

COMMITMENT ACTIVITIES

1. Collect sample menus from local restaurants that advertise heart-healthy meals, lite dishes, diet plates, or dishes low in sodium. Analyze these to determine whether these are more nutritious than the other offerings.
2. Develop a list of changes to improve your nutrition. If you live in a dormitory, discuss these with the food supervisor to see which ones could be implemented.

3. Develop a list of guidelines and recommendations for selecting nutritious meals when eating out. Be sure the ideas are general enough to apply to restaurants serving a wide variety of foods.

4. Plan a trip to a local supermarket. Be a comparison shopper and use a product checklist that is developed by the class. Compare brands, sizes, nutritional content, and so on, and check the results with other members of the class.

REFERENCES

"At Last, Food Labels That Make Sense." 1993. *University of California at Berkeley Wellness Letter* 9, no. 6 (March): 3.

"Battling the Bad Fat." 1992. *Harvard Health Letter* 17, no. 3 (January): 6–7.

Butgereit, B. 1993. "Experts Favor Addition of Folic Acid to Bread." *Birmingham News,* 28 July, D1.

"Calcium OK for Kidneys." 1993. *Nutrition Action Healthletter* 20, no. 5 (June): 4.

"Calcium: Vital for Women and Men." 1994. *Consumer Reports on Health* 6, no. 2:13.

"Can Vegetable Oils Harden Your Arteries?" 1993. *Consumer Reports* 5, no. 6 (June): 57–59.

"Can Vitamin C Save Your Life?" 1994. *Consumer Reports on Health* 6, no. 1:25.

Clark, N. 1990. "Milk: Destroying the Myths." *Physician and Sportsmedicine* 18, no. 2:133.

"Diet and Dental Caries: An Overview." 1994. *Dairy Council Digest* 65, no. 1:1.

"Does Salt Raise *Your* Blood Pressure?" 1994. *Consumer Reports on Health* 6, no. 4:42.

Domel, S., T. Baranowski, H. Davis, W. Thompson, S. Leonard, P. Riley, J. Baranowski, B. Dudovitz, and M. Smyth. 1993. "Development and Evaluation of a School Intervention to Increase Fruit and Vegetable Consumption Among 4th and 5th Grade Students." *Journal of Nutrition Education* 5, no. 6 (November/December): 345–49.

Duston, D. 1992. "Food Aimed at Kids Mostly Junk, Group Says." *Birmingham News,* 3 August, 1a, 6a.

"Eating Around a Stroke." 1993. *Consumer Reports on Health* 5, no. 8:86.

Edell, D. 1991. "Your Built-In Salt Sensor." *Edell Health Letter* 2, no. 2 (February): 4.

Edell, D. 1992. "Calcium and Fiber at Odds." 1992. *Edell Health Letter* 11, no. 1 (December/January): 4.

Elias, M. 1993a. "Living Long, Lean on Biosphere Diet." *USA Today,* 19 November, D1.

Elias, M. 1993b. "Mind over Fatter: Leaner Diet Is All in Your Head." *USA Today,* 25 August, D1.

Fanelli-Kuczmarski, M. 1989. "Nutrition Education for Older Adults." *Nutrition News* 52, no. 3:9–12.

"Fear of Eggs." 1989. *Consumer Reports on Health* 54, no. 10: 650–52.

"Focus on Nutrition and Women's Health." 1993. *Dairy Council Digest* 64 no. 5 (July/August): 20.

"Food Groups: Variety . . ." 1993. *Consumer Reports on Health* 5, no. 9 (September): 99.

"Forget Cholesterol?" 1990. *Consumer Reports* 55, no. 3:152–56.

"Frozen Light Entrees." 1993. *Consumer Reports* 58, no. 1:27–31.

"Grains and Beans: The Key to a Low-Fat Diet." 1993. *Consumer Reports on Health* 5, no. 10 (October): 112.

Greenberg, J. 1990. *Comprehensive Stress Management,* 3d ed. Dubuque, Iowa: Wm. C. Brown.

Guthrie, H. 1990. "Recommended Dietary Allowances 1989." *Nutrition Today,* January/February, 43–45.

Healthy People 2000: National Health Promotion and Disease Prevention Objectives. 1992. Washington, D.C.: U.S. Department of Health and Human Services/Public Health Service.

"High Fiber, Low Cholesterol." 1993. *Consumer Reports on Health* 5, no. 4 (April): 30.

"Hold the Mayo?" 1992. *Consumer Reports on Health* 4, no. 4 (April): 30.

"Honey vs. Sugar." 1992. *Consumer Reports on Health* 4, no. 1 (January): 8.

Hunter, B. T. 1989. "Strategies to Reduce Dietary Fat." *Consumers' Research* 72, no. 4:29–31.

Hurley, J., and B. Liebman. 1994. "When in Rome . . ." *Nutrition Action Healthletter* 21, no. 1 (January/February): 5.

Hurley, J., and S. Schmidt. 1992. "Food Labels Get 'Healthy.'" *Nutrition Action Healthletter* 19, no. 6 (July/August): 8.

"Hurley, J., and S. Schmidt. 1993. "A Wok on the Wild Side." *Nutrition Action Healthletter* 20, no. 7 (September): 10–11.

"Illegal Residues in Meat and Poultry." 1992. *Consumers' Research* 75, no. 1 (January): 33–35.

"The Immediate Benefits of Low-fat Eating." 1993. *University of California at Berkeley Wellness Letter* 9, no. 7 (April): 1.

"Institute Offers 'Clear-Cut' Diet Plan to Reduce Disease Risk." 1992. *Health Education Reports,* 27 February.

Institute of Medicine. 1990. *Nutrition During Pregnancy.* Washington, D.C.: National Academy Press.

"Is It Risky to Lower Your Cholesterol?" 1993. *University of California at Berkeley Wellness Letter* 9, no. 6 (March): 1.

"Just the Facts." 1993. *Nutrition Action Healthletter* 20, no. 5 (June): 10.

"Just What Is a Balanced Diet, Anyway?" 1992. *Tufts University Diet and Nutrition Letter* 9, no. 11 (January): 3.

"Kid's-Eye Cereals." 1990. *Nutrition Action Healthletter* 17, no. 5 (June): 3.

Kim, I., D. F. Williamson, T. Byers, and J. P. Koplan. 1993. "Vitamin and Mineral Supplement Use and Mortality in a U.S. Cohort." *American Journal of Public Health* 83, no. 4 (April): 546–50.

Kirby, R. W., J. W. Anderson, B. Sieling, E. D. Rees, W. L. Chen, R. E. Miller, and R. M. Kay. 1981. "Oat Bran Intake Selectively Lowers Serum Low-Density Lipoprotein Cholesterol Concentrations of Hypercholesterolemic Men." *American Journal of Clinical Nutrition* 34 (May): 824–29.

Liebman, B. 1990a. "The Changing American Diet." *Nutrition Action Healthletter* 17, no. 4 (May): 8.

Liebman, B. 1990b. "Has the Oat-Bran Bubble Burst?" *Nutrition Action Healthletter* 17, no. 1 (January/February): 4.

Liebman, B. 1991. "The Clogging of an Artery." *Nutrition Action Healthletter* 18, no. 2 (March): 9.

Liebman, B. 1994. "The Salt Shake Out." *Nutrition Action Healthletter* 21, no. 2:5.

Liebman, B., and J. Hurley. 1993. "Putting the Squeeze on Saturates." *Nutrition Action Healthletter* 20, no. 4 (May): 5.

Long, Patricia. 1993. "The Vitamin Wars." *Health,* May/June, 45–54.

"Low-Fat Dining Out." 1993. *Consumer Reports on Health* 5, no. 5 (May): 53.

Mattes, R. D., and D. Donnelly. 1991. "Relative Contributions of Dietary Sodium Scores." *Journal of the American College of Nutrition* 10, no. 4:383–93.

McGlynn, G. 1993. *Dynamics of Fitness,* 3d ed. Dubuque, IA: Wm. C. Brown.

"New Recommended Dietary Allowances." 1990. *Consumers' Research* 73, no. 1:25–27.

"Nutrition and Exercise: What Your Body Needs." 1993. *University of California at Berkeley Wellness Letter* 9, no. 8 (May): 4.

"Nutritional Labels for the '90s." 1990. *Changing Times,* June, 100.

"Nutrition Screening Initiative" 1990. Press release by the American Academy of Family Physicians, the American Dietetic Association, and the National Council on Aging, 22 May.

"Nuts and Bolts of Fruits and Vegetables." 1993. *Tufts University Diet and Nutrition Letter* 11, no. 3:5.

Oestreicher, A. 1990. "Calcium Credited with Many Routes As Protective Factor." *Medical World News* 31, no. 4:22–23.

Orwoll, E. S., S. K. Oviatt, M. McClung, L. Deftos, and G. Sexton. 1990. "The Rate of Bone Mineral Loss in Normal Men and the Effects of Calcium and Cholecalciferol Supplementation." *Annals of Internal Medicine* 112, no. 1:29–34.

Payer, L. 1993. "Hyping High Cholesterol and Blood Pressure." *Consumers' Research* 76, no. 3 (March): 10–14.

Powers, S. K., and E. T. Howley. 1990. *Exercise Physiology: Theory and Application to Fitness and Performance.* Dubuque, Iowa: Wm. C. Brown.

Roberts, C. 1989. "Fast Food Fare and Nutrition." *Consumers' Research* 72, no. 12:30–33.

Schardt, David. 1993. "The Problem with Protein." *Nutrition Action Healthletter* 20, no. 5 (June): 5–7.

Schmidt, Stephen. 1991. "Stripped-Juice Tease." *Nutrition Action Healthletter* 18 (October): 9.

Stamford, B. 1990. "What Cholesterol Means to You." *Physician and Sportsmedicine* 18, no. 1:149–50.

Suter, P. M., Y. Schutz, and E. Jequier. 1992. "The Effect of Ethanol on Fat Storage in Healthy Subjects." *New England Journal of Medicine* 326, no. 15 (April): 983–87.

Swain, J. F., I. L. Rouse, C. B. Curley, and F. M. Sacks. 1990. "Comparison of the Effects of Oat Bran and Low-Fiber Wheat on Serum Lipoprotein Levels and Blood Pressure." *New England Journal of Medicine* 322, no. 3:147–52.

"Too Much Salt?" 1990. *Consumer Reports* 55, no. 1:48.

"TV Feeds Kids Steady Diet of Sugary-Food Ads." 1991. *Tufts University Diet and Nutrition Letter* 9, no. 9:7.

"Unmasking Labels That Hide the Fat." 1992. *Kiplinger's Personal Finance Magazine* 46, no. 2:92.

U.S. Department of Agriculture and U.S. Department of Health and Human Services. 1990. "Nutrition and Your Health: Dietary Guidelines for Americans." Home and Garden Bulletin 232. Washington, D.C.: Government Printing Office.

Van Horn, L. V., K. Liu, D. Parker, L. Emidy, Y. Liao, W. H. Pan, F. Giumetti, J. Hewitt, and J. Stamler. 1986. "Serum Lipid Response to Oat Product Intake with a Fat-Modified Diet." *Journal of the American Dietetic Association* 86, no. 6:759–84.

Wardlaw, G. M., and P. M. Insel. 1990. *Perspectives in Nutrition.* St. Louis: Times Mirror/Mosby.

"Weight-Bearing Exercises Help Prevent Bone Weakness." 1990. *Health Education Reports,* 7 June, 4–5.

Welsh, S., C. Davis, and A. Shaw. 1992. "Development of the Food Guide Pyramid." *Nutrition Today,* November/December, 12–23.

"Where's the Fat?" 1990. *Consumer Reports* 55, no. 3:158–59.

Williams, M. 1990. *Lifetime Fitness and Wellness: A Practical Approach* 2nd ed. Dubuque, Iowa: Wm. C. Brown.

Wootan, M., and B. Liebman. 1993. "The Great Trans Wreck." *Nutrition Action Newsletter* 20, no. 9 November: 10–11.

"Yet Another Reason to Drink Your Milk." *Tufts University Diet and Nutrition Letter* 9, no. 11 (January): 1.

ADDITIONAL READINGS

"FDA's Proposal for New 'Daily Values' for Nutrients." 1992. *FDA Backgrounder,* 12 February. The changes proposed for the revision of the nutrition label are discussed.

Liebman, B. "The Name Game." 1992. *Nutrition Action Healthletter* 19, no. 2 (March): 8. Shows some of the actual ingredients in products. The products shown contain far less of the ingredients advertised than one might expect.

Rose, A. 1992. "1990 Dietary Guidelines: Implications for Health Educators." *Journal of Health Education* 23, no. 5:293–95. The guidelines are compared with the 1985 version, and the significant changes are discussed.

CHAPTER 7

Physical Activity

KEY QUESTIONS

How is exercise beneficial to health?

What are the best ways to exercise?

Can you develop an exercise program on your own or is it necessary to see a physician?

How can you assess your present fitness levels?

Does it matter what kind of exercise you do?

How can an exercise program be designed to help you stay with it?

CHAPTER OUTLINE

Healthy People 2000 Objectives

- Increase to at least 30 percent the proportion of people aged 6 and older who engage regularly, preferably daily, in light to moderate physical activity for at least 30 minutes per day.

- Increase to at least 20 percent the proportion of people aged 18 and older, and to at least 75 percent the proportion of children and adolescents aged 6 through 17, who engage in vigorous physical activity that promotes the development and maintenance of cardiorespiratory fitness 3 or more days per week for 20 or more minutes per occasion.

- Reduce to no more than 15 percent the proportion of people aged 6 and older who engage in no leisure-time physical activity.

- Increase the proportion of worksites offering employer-sponsored physical activity and fitness programs as follows:

Worksite Size	2000 Target
50–99 employees	20%
100–249 employees	35%
250–749 employees	50%
750 and more employees	80%

- Increase community availability and accessibility of physical activity and fitness facilities as follows:

Facility	2000 Target
Hiking, biking, and fitness trail miles	1/10,000 people
Public swimming pools	1/25,000 people
Acres of park and recreation open space	4/1,000 people

Many college students participated in physical activities while growing up. Generally, the emphasis in school was on learning skills, and little attention was given to the relationship of health to physical activity.

In spite of the potential benefits of regular physical activity, relatively few Americans engage in it. In fact, only about 37 percent of high school students are vigorously active three or more times per week. Vigorous exercise is much less common among females (25%) than among males (50%) and among black students (29%) than among either white (39%) or Hispanic (35%) students. In addition, as females get older, fewer of them exercise. Almost 31 percent of ninth-grade females exercised vigorously three or more times per week, as compared to only 17 percent of twelfth-grade females ("Vigorous Activity Among High School Students" 1992). As for adults, almost 60 percent get little or no exercise ("First the Good News" 1992).

People in low-income groups exercise less than those who make more money. For example, about 65 percent of those who make $15,000 or less per year don't exercise often or at all; about 48 percent of those who make $50,000 or more per year do exercise ("USA Snapshots" 1993).

Less than 10 percent of the U.S. adult population exercises at the level recommended by the 1990 national health objectives: "Exercise which involves large muscle groups in dynamic movement for periods of twenty minutes or longer, three or more days per week, and which is performed at an intensity of 60 percent or greater of an individual's cardiorespiratory capacity." As children become older, move through adolescence, and enter early adulthood, fewer of them exercise with each year of increasing age (*Promoting Health/Preventing Disease* 1990).

Why should you be active? What is physical fitness, and what are its benefits? This chapter answers these questions, describes how to develop a personal exercise program, and discusses how physical activity is related to lifestyle.

PHYSICAL FITNESS AND ITS BENEFITS

You must be motivated in order to achieve and maintain physical fitness. The first step is understanding what physical fitness is and why it is important.

WHAT IS PHYSICAL FITNESS?

Physical fitness has many components. Traditionally they have included agility, balance, cardiorespiratory capacity, coordination, flexibility, muscular endurance, power, reaction time, speed, and strength. Currently, physical fitness is believed to consist of five components: muscle strength, muscle endurance, flexibility, body composition (degree of fatness), and cardiorespiratory endurance (American Academy of Pediatrics 1987). Although a high level of fitness in all of the traditional components is ideal, to get the health benefits of physical activity, only muscle strength, muscle endurance,

Obtaining the health benefits of physical activity does not demand a high level of skill.

flexibility, a favorable body composition, and cardiorespiratory endurance are needed. Most of the other components involve physical skills that are not basic to health.

Some individuals think of fitness as a state of being. We prefer to think of it as a way of life. It is best to develop an active lifestyle as children and continue the pattern throughout the life cycle, but it is never too late to start exercising. Even people in their fifties, sixties, seventies, and eighties can benefit from physical activity. In fact, regular physical activity, of the right type, retards much of the usual loss of physical capacity associated with aging (Kasch et al. 1990).

Physical activity must be continued throughout life, or fitness will be lost and health impaired. It is fairly simple to adjust people's exercise prescriptions as their needs change, but people must continue to be active.

HEALTH BENEFITS OF PHYSICAL ACTIVITY

Those who exercise regularly report that they feel better, have more energy, and often require less sleep. Regular exercisers often lose excess weight while improving their muscular strength and flexibility. Greater body satisfaction is associated with increases in exercise participation (Davis and Cowles 1991). In addition, regular exercise has been shown to reduce stress; enhance coping mechanisms; reduce anxiety, depression, and hostility; result in less hypochondria (thinking you are sick when you are not); increase general

physical fitness
A state of physical well-being currently believed to consist of muscle strength, muscle endurance, flexibility, body composition (degree of fatness), and cardiorespiratory endurance.

Testing Your Flexibility and Your Muscular Endurance

Flexibility Assessment

Place on the floor a box that is 12 to 15 inches high, any width, and at least 18 inches long. On top of the box place a ruler (a ruler taped to either the lowest row of bleachers or to a bench on its side would also work). Take off your shoes and sit with your knees straight and the bottom of your feet flat against the box. With a partner holding your knees straight (your partner can also help take the measurement), extend your arms forward with one hand placed on top of the other. Steadily reach as far forward as possible and maintain this position for 3 seconds. Do not bounce or jerk, and be sure to keep your legs straight.

The distance in front of or beyond the edge of the box that can be sustained for 3 seconds is measured and recorded. Determine in inches how far short you are of reaching the edge of the box (a negative score) or how many inches past the edge of the box you can reach (a positive score).

Scoring/Interpretation

	Women	Men
Normal Range (inches)	+4 to +10	–6 to +8
Average	+2	+1
Desired	+2 to +6	+1 to +5

Muscular Endurance Test

Lie down on a mat on your back with your hands interlocked behind your head, your knees bent at 90 degrees, and your feet held by a partner. Do sit-ups for 1 full minute, touching your elbows to your knees, and then returning to the starting position. Do as many sit-ups as you can. Your score is the number of sit-ups you are able to do during that period. (A word of caution—do not pull on your head or neck during the exercise, because this can cause harm to your spine).

Scoring/Interpretation

RATING SCALE FOR 1-MINUTE SIT-UP TEST

Rating	Age				
	20–29	*30–39*	*40–49*	*50–59*	*60–65*
Males					
Excellent	47	40	35	30	29
Good	41	35	30	25	24
Average	35	29	25	20	18
Fair	29	24	19	15	13
Poor	9	5	2	0	0
Females					
Excellent	42	37	30	21	20
Good	36	31	25	17	16
Average	30	26	20	12	11
Fair	24	20	15	8	6
Poor	3	1	0	0	0

From J. Gavin Reid/John M. Thomson, *Exercise Prescription for Fitness,* © 1985, p. 126. Adapted by permission of Prentice Hall, Inc., Englewood Cliffs, New Jersey.

---

well-being; and improve self-concept (Brill and Cooper 1993; Sacks 1993). Moreover, many who exercise regularly adopt a more healthy lifestyle—abandoning smoking, excessive drinking, and poor nutritional habits.

Some fear that repeated vigorous exercise, such as running, aerobics, and tennis, will harm their joints. A 5-year study by the Stanford Arthritis Center found that individuals running an average of 27 miles per week over 5 to 40 years were no more likely than sedentary nonrunners to develop early signs of arthritis in their hips or knees (*Health Education Reports* 1990, 5). Other studies also show that the most active people are no more likely than sedentary people to develop arthritis ("Exercise Isn't Arthritic" 1993). Exercise is beneficial for people with chronic disorders such as arthritis, diabetes, and hypertension ("Which Exercise Is Best for You?" 1994).

Sustained exercise improves the efficiency of the heart and increases the amount of oxygen the body can process in a given period of time. Evidence strongly suggests that when exercise is an integral part of daily activities it helps prevent coronary artery disease, helps maintain blood pressure within safe limits, controls body weight, and contributes to the control of diabetes ("Physical Exercise" 1990). Even modest exercise

(such as brisk walking for 30 to 45 minutes at 3 to 4 miles per hour, six to seven times a week) cuts the risk of cardiovascular disease (Phillips 1990).

There are also nutritional benefits from exercise. It helps control obesity, suppress the appetite, and conserve lean tissue instead of fat tissue, and it enables the physically active person to have a healthier quantity and quality of fats in the blood (Shephard 1989).

Additional benefits from exercise are continually added to an already long list. For example, many individuals with arthritis are now encouraged to increase their exercise levels. In addition to the usual health benefits, they can obtain improved joint mobility and pain control through physical activity (Samples 1990). Also, physical activity might reduce the risk of colon cancer (Cremmons 1990) and increase bone mass (Cooper 1989). Countless investigators have come to the same conclusion: Physical activity does benefit health.

Quality of life is probably far more important than quantity; however, strong evidence indicates that premature-death rates are significantly lower among the physically active. This is true with or without consideration of hypertension, cigarette smoking, extremes or gains in body weight, or early parental death (Paffenbarger et al. 1986). Exercise helps lengthen life as well as improve the quality of life. In fact, there is no single group that can benefit more from exercise than the elderly (Allison 1991).

Exercise compensates in several ways for the changes that accompany aging. It helps prevent the loss of muscle and can even help regain lost muscle. It helps preserve bone mass, prevent brittle bones, and even build bone. It boosts the resting metabolic rate and therefore aids in weight control, and it improves aerobic capacity just as it does in younger people ("Can Exercise Turn Back the Clock?" 1992). Exercise helps prevent hardening of the arteries as we get older (Vaitkevicius et al. 1993) and can even halt or reverse the buildup of fatty deposits in the coronary arteries ("Clearing Clogged Arteries" 1993).

People who continue to exercise have less anxiety and fewer depressive symptoms (King et al. 1993). They also have sharper minds, faster physical responses, increased resistance to some diseases, brighter moods, and even better sex lives (Fishman 1993).

To summarize, the health benefits of regular exercise include the following:

1. Improved physiological functioning
2. Improved appearance
3. Increased efficiency of the heart and lungs
4. Increased muscle strength and endurance
5. Reduced stress response
6. Protection from lower back problems
7. Possible delay in the aging process
8. Maintenance of proper body weight
9. Possible reduction of the risk of coronary heart disease
10. Naturally induced fatigue and relaxation (McGlynn 1993)

A physically fit person has greater ability to tolerate the challenges of daily life. It is important to note that the physical and psychological benefits of physical exercise combine to enhance resiliency. An excellent example of the mind/body relationship is also seen when physical activity is used to treat depression and enhance feelings of well-being and self-esteem ("Physical Exercise" 1990). It also increases resistance to stress, anxiety, and fatigue (Williams 1990, 48–49). Physically fit persons are better able to adapt through resilient adjustment when disruption and disorganization occur in their lives. Physical activity is an excellent example of a protective factor that enhances all of the components of health.

To understand what health benefits might be gained from physical activity, you need to know how exercise affects the human body. Specifically, understanding two general physiological principles will help you to have realistic expectations. The first one, the **principle of specificity,** means "You get what you train for." In other words, if you want to become stronger, it is imperative to train for strength and not for endurance. If you want to improve your ability to run long distances, it is important to lengthen the distances you regularly run. One physical capacity is not significantly improved by working on another. For example, doing many sit-ups daily won't improve your abdominal strength as effectively as will doing fewer sit-ups but with a weight held behind your head. Doing more sit-ups improves endurance, not strength. (A word of caution—when you use a weight during the exercise, do not pull on your head or neck, because this can cause harm to your spine.)

Related to the principle of specificity is the **overload principle.** Simply stated, the overload principle is that, in order to improve a physical capacity, a stress must be placed on the relevant part of the body. For example, if you desire increased strength, you must work with increasing amounts of weight. If increased endurance is your goal, you must perform the activity more times or for a longer period.

These principles help explain how you can improve three major systems of your body—the muscular, cardiovascular, and respiratory systems.

Unfortunately, there is a third principle, the **law of reversibility,** that must be considered. A significant reduction of working capacity begins to occur within days after training is stopped (the saying "Use it or lose it" definitely applies to physical fitness). A gradual decline of performance capacity results, as well as a decrease in size (**atrophy**) of muscle cells. Therefore, you must continue physical activity to maintain the benefits you achieve.

FITNESS OF MAJOR BODY SYSTEMS

Even though general physiological principles apply to all body systems, it is essential to understand some basics about specific systems. This is particularly true with regard to the muscular, cardiovascular, and respiratory systems.

---

principle of specificity
The principle that you must train specifically for the gains you wish to achieve (e.g., strength or endurance).

overload principle
The principle that improvement of a selected physical capacity requires that stress be placed on the relevant part of the body.

law of reversibility
The principle that a significant decrease in physical capacity will occur within days after training is stopped ("Use it or lose it").

atrophy
A decrease in size (as of muscle cells).

Anabolic Steroids and Performance

Anabolic steroids are growth-stimulating chemicals, some of which are found naturally in the body. They were developed synthetically to promote tissue growth in those who experienced atrophy because of prolonged bed rest. It did not take long for some individuals to wonder if anabolic steroids might be helpful in developing muscle mass and strength in athletes.

Steroids do not directly improve performance in aerobic activities, such as long-distance running, skiing, or swimming. They can help build lean body mass and improve strength in individuals involved in intense training activities, such as weight lifting, but the real possibility of harmful side effects greatly outweighs the questionable increase in performance. Anabolic steroids have been associated with liver dysfunction and liver cancer, an increase in the risk of coronary artery disease, a reduction of sperm production in males and a disruption in menstrual function in females, breast development in males and deepening of the voice and beard development in females, and adverse effects on psychological status (McGlynn 1993; Powers and Howley 1990).

FITNESS OF THE MUSCULAR SYSTEM

There are three types of muscles in the body: (1) involuntary muscles (in the blood vessels, stomach, intestines, and so on), (2) cardiac (heart) muscle, and (3) voluntary muscles (in the arms, legs, and so on). General physical activity helps to improve the functioning of all three types. In this discussion, we focus on the voluntary muscles.

From a physiological standpoint, a strength overload seems to lead to **hypertrophy,** which means that muscle fibers become larger and stronger. An endurance overload probably results in an improved blood supply to the working muscles. These are positive changes because they improve the health and functioning of the muscles.

The overload and specificity principles shed some light on the issue of isometric versus isotonic muscular activity, an issue that has been debated for many years. **Isometric activities** involve exerting muscular force against an immovable object (such as pulling on a chain attached to the floor) so that there is muscular contraction but no joint movement. **Isotonic activities** by contrast, involve exerting muscular force throughout the range of motion of a joint, as in lifting a heavy object. You can gain strength with either method, but it appears that isotonic activities are more practical for most people, and from a health standpoint it makes more sense to use a full range of joint motion. For example, isometric activities increase strength *only* at the specific joint angle at which training is done and can also cause potentially dangerous blood pressure fluctuations. Isotonic activities, on the other hand, develop strength throughout the entire range of motion and are applicable to everyday motions. To develop muscular endurance, isotonic activities are preferable because movement is needed to achieve the health benefits of physical activity.

A third type of muscle contraction is an **isokinetic contraction.** A muscular contraction is isokinetic when the speed of the contraction is kept constant against a variable resistance. Specialized equipment allows muscles to encounter maximum resistance throughout a complete range of motion.

While isometric, isotonic, and isokinetic methods can all produce significant gains in strength in relatively short periods of time, research seems to indicate that the isokinetic form of resistance training is superior to the other methods for strength gains (Brown 1986). Equipment needed for isokinetic contractions is quite expensive and probably only available at a well-equipped fitness center. Isokinetic contractions, however, do increase strength throughout the full range of motion and cause less injury and soreness than does either isometric or isotonic exercise (McGlynn 1993).

FITNESS OF THE CARDIOVASCULAR SYSTEM

The heart is a muscle, so it becomes stronger through use. As it becomes stronger, it doesn't need to work as hard to pump blood. This is why those in good physical condition tend to have low resting pulse rates. A resting pulse rate of 70 to 80 beats per minute is average, but it is not unusual to find physically fit people with resting rates around 40 to 50 beats per minute (figure 7.1). A low pulse rate allows the heart more rest and more time to fill with blood between beats so it can

hypertrophy
An increase in size and strength (as of muscle fibers).

isometric activities
Exercises that involve exerting muscular force against an immovable object to produce muscular contraction but no joint movement.

isotonic activities
Exercises that involve exerting muscular force throughout the range of motion of a joint.

isokinetic contraction
Exercises that involve a constant speed of muscular contraction against a variable resistance.

TABLE 7.1 CARDIOVASCULAR TRAINING EFFECTS

Cardiovascular Training Increases	Cardiovascular Training Produces	Cardiovascular Training Decreases
Tolerance to stress	Lower resting heart rate	Obesity-adiposity
Arterial oxygen content	Physical conditioning of muscles	Arterial blood pressure
Electron transport activity	Greater oxygen utilization	Heart rate
Efficiency of the heart	Greater stroke volume	Vulnerability to dysrhythmias
Blood vessel size	Lower heart rate for submaximal work	Stress response
Efficiency of blood circulation		Need of heart muscle for oxygen

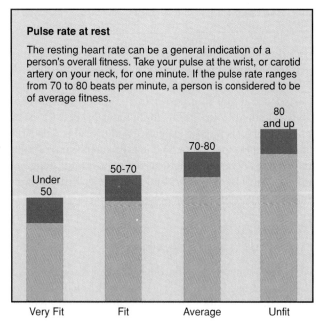

Pulse rate at rest

The resting heart rate can be a general indication of a person's overall fitness. Take your pulse at the wrist, or carotid artery on your neck, for one minute. If the pulse rate ranges from 70 to 80 beats per minute, a person is considered to be of average fitness.

Figure 7.1
Checking pulse rate.

better perform its task as a pump. As the heart muscle becomes stronger, it also becomes better able to withstand potential problems. If a heart attack (a condition where the heart muscle receives insufficient blood) should occur, a strong heart can deal with it much better.

Coronary is a general term referring to a heart attack that occurs because of a problem with the **coronary circulation.** Because the heart receives no benefit from the blood that flows through it, it needs to have its own circulation system (coronary circulation), which is strengthened by regular, total-body physical activity. In fact, endurance training over a number of years even affects the heart's anatomy. The coronary arteries develop a significantly greater capacity to dilate (become larger) (Haskell et al. 1993). The larger the arteries, the more efficient the supply of blood to heart tissue and the better the heart should be able to withstand problems. In addition, there is evidence that regular exercise can halt or even reverse the buildup of fatty deposits in the coronary arteries ("Clearing Clogged Arteries" 1993).

Increased circulatory efficiency, better coronary circulation, and more rest and strength for the heart all combine to enable the circulatory system to better resist cardiovascular disease and cope with problems that might develop. These valuable benefits can be obtained from a physically active lifestyle. Table 7.1 summarizes cardiovascular training effects.

FITNESS OF THE RESPIRATORY SYSTEM

Like the circulatory system, the respiratory system becomes more efficient as a result of physical activity. With regular activity, the breathing rate tends to decrease at rest, although this is difficult to observe because of the voluntary nature of breathing. As soon as you try to count your breaths per minute, you are conscious of the rate and alter the cadence.

As you regularly perform strenuous physical activity, your respiratory system develops more efficiency and an increased work capacity. A variety of related changes occur for this to happen, including the following:

1. *Greater possible maximal oxygen intake.* This means that the body's cells can take in a greater amount of oxygen. We already breathe in far more oxygen than we need, but our cells develop the capacity to use more of this oxygen.
2. *Decreased oxygen debt for the same work.* The muscular contractions involved in physical activity are made possible because of a chemical conversion process fueled by oxygen. After strenuous physical activity, we need oxygen in higher quantities for the chemical processes to "recharge." As fitness improves, the same work requires a smaller **oxygen debt.** Oxygen debt is the

coronary
The general term for heart attack.

coronary circulation
The heart's independent circulatory system, which is strengthened through regular total-body exercise.

oxygen debt
The amount of oxygen used during recovery from physical activity above the amount normally used during that same time at rest.

HEALTH UPDATE

Myths About Females and Physical Activity

1. *Myth:* If women exercise, they will develop large muscles, as men do.
   Fact: Men develop large muscles from some types of physical activity, but women generally do not. This is because women have much lower levels of the hormone testosterone.

2. *Myth:* Biological differences between males and females prevent females from developing high levels of fitness.
   Fact: There is little, if any, difference between males and females in this respect. Everyone can develop high fitness levels if they take appropriate steps.

3. *Myth:* Women cannot exercise for long periods of time.

Fact: Women have a higher percentage of body fat than do men (approximately 15% to 20%, versus 10% to 15% in men). This difference makes them particularly suited for endurance activities.

4. *Myth:* Women should not exercise during menstruation.
   Fact: Generally, there is no reason why activity patterns should be any different during menstruation. In fact, some women who experience discomfort during menstruation will find that physical activity helps relieve the discomfort. Regarding menstruation, however, it should be noted that severe, prolonged training, such as long-distance running, is associated with the cessation of menstruation and the absence of ovulation. Whether this happens because of exercise intensity or because of reduction of body fat is not known, but this situation is not harmful.

Incidentally, heavy exercise should not be relied on as a contraceptive method.

5. *Myth:* Physical activity is harmful to women's breasts.
   Fact: Activity itself is not harmful to women's breasts. Women would be wise, however, to use a good sport bra for proper support.

6. *Myth:* Pregnant women should not exercise.
   Fact: It might not be smart to begin training for the Boston Marathon when one is pregnant, but there is generally no reason why a pregnant woman cannot continue an established exercise program. Even those who have not been physically active can safely participate in an appropriately designed program (although it would be wise not to exceed the 70% level as shown in figure 7.2). In fact, maternal exercise does not decrease blood flow to the fetus as was once thought (Gauthier 1990).

amount of oxygen used during recovery from physical activity above the amount normally used during that same time at rest.

3. *Ability to withstand a higher oxygen debt.* Aside from requiring a smaller oxygen debt for the same work, the fit person can withstand a higher oxygen debt. The combination of these two factors enable the fit person to do more physical work with less discomfort than the relatively unfit person can do.

4. *Decreased oxygen requirement.* As the body becomes more efficient, it needs less fuel to do the same work. Because less oxygen is required for a given amount of physical work, oxygen debt for the same work is lower, the body can withstand a higher oxygen debt, and greater maximal oxygen intake is possible, the respiratory system of a fit person functions far more efficiently than that of an unfit person. This capacity is the keystone of health benefits derived from physical activity.

Physical activity is not a cure-all. The improvements in physical functioning, the psychological rewards, the tendency toward prevention of many diseases, and the use of physical activity for certain types of rehabilitation and treatment, however, combine to make exercise one of the more powerful health influences over which we have control. When you are establishing a lifestyle conducive to health, few activities will give you so much return for the investment as exercise.

DEVELOPING A PHYSICAL ACTIVITY PROGRAM

Most health-conscious people know the many benefits of exercise—that it reduces the risk of disease, increases stamina, builds strength, burns calories, and relieves stress. Many, however, do not know which exercise best fits their personal goals. An inappropriate exercise can ruin a developing exercise habit. It is important to identify the most effective workouts to fit your needs in order to obtain the most important goals of exercise ("Which Exercise Is Best for You?" 1994).

The decision whether to make exercise part of your lifestyle can be difficult, and it is likely to be influenced by a number of encouraging and discouraging factors. Even if we know the facts about physical activity, we often still do not lead physically active lives. We commonly say we don't have time. In reality, we make time for things we believe are important.

There are both encouraging and discouraging factors to influence our decision. These are some of the possibly encouraging factors: (1) Anyone can become physically fit, regardless of present condition. (2) The benefits can include better physiological functioning, loss of excess body fat, resistance to some diseases, more energy for daily living, and improved psychological outlook. (3) A variety of training programs are available to meet different tastes and requirements. (4) If realistic goals are set, regular progress can easily be seen.

Should You Exercise?

Directions

Mark any of the following that apply to you:

_____ Your physician said you have heart trouble, you have a heart murmur, or you have had a heart attack.

_____ You frequently have pains or pressure—in the left or midchest area, left neck, shoulder, or arm—during or right after you exercise.

_____ You often feel faint or have spells of severe dizziness.

_____ You experience extreme breathlessness after mild exertion.

_____ Your physician said your blood pressure is too high and is not under control. Or you don't know whether or not your blood pressure is normal.

_____ Your physician said you have bone or joint problems such as arthritis.

_____ You are over age 60 and are not accustomed to vigorous exercise.

_____ You have a family history of premature coronary artery disease.

_____ You have a medical condition not mentioned here that might need special attention in an exercise program (such as asthma or insulin-dependent diabetes).

Scoring/Interpretation

None of these factors will prevent you from exercising, but if you checked any of the above, you should first receive medical clearance from your physician to exercise.

THE WORLD AROUND YOU

Encouraging Couch Potatoes

In 1993 the President's Council on Physical Fitness conducted a national survey to better understand why so many Americans indulge in primarily sedentary lifestyles ("Couch Potatoes Know What They're Missing" 1993). Almost two-thirds of the respondents said they would like to exercise more but were unable to find the time. Yet their TV-watching patterns suggested they did have time, but instead chose to watch television.

Insufficient physical activity is a nationwide problem, but women, African Americans, and poor persons were disproportionately represented in the less-active group. Nearly two-thirds of the less-actives, however, said they would like to be more physically active, and nearly half said it would be easy to increase their activity level. (Yet they didn't.)

What would motivate relatively inactive persons to become more physically active? Improved health was the top motivation given, followed by greater strength and energy for daily life. Friends and family were identified as the most influential in encouraging less-actives to become more active. The single most effective encouragement was the companionship of a friend during physical activity. Spouses, boyfriends, and girlfriends were an especially strong influence.

This means you can be a very powerful influence in helping others begin and maintain physically active lifestyles. At the same time, it can be helpful for you to have someone close to you encourage your physical activity and perhaps even work out with you.

Source: From "Couch Potatoes Know What They're Missing, Need Encouragement" in *Health Education Reports* 15(22): 2–3 (November 18, 1993).

There are also discouraging factors, including these: (1) The body deteriorates with disuse, so activity must be engaged in regularly. (2) It is difficult to find the time to exercise and often inconvenient to have to change clothes and shower. (3) A time commitment is necessary in order to see significant changes. (4) Hard work is required, and even if a sensible program is used, there will be some muscle soreness and stiffness. (5) Injuries can occur, and adjustments to existing social activities might be necessary.

MEDICAL CHECKUPS AND STRESS TESTS

Once you make the commitment, the first step in developing your exercise program is to determine your present physical fitness level and how much strenuous activity your body can take. Some experts stress the need for a medical checkup, and perhaps an exercise stress test, before beginning an exercise program. Your responses to the Health Assessment exercise "Should You Exercise?" will help you decide whether

At least a simple self-test is essential prior to beginning a physical activity program.

TABLE 7.2	NORMS FOR THE 1.5-MILE RUN FOR COLLEGE-AGE STUDENTS 17 TO 25 YEARS OLD	
Percentile	**Males**	**Females**
99	7:21	8:42
90	8:53	11:23
80	9:13	12:00
70	9:27	12:25
60	9:42	12:46
50	10:00	13:14
40	10:16	13:44
30	10:34	14:17
20	10:54	14:38
10	11:30	15:23

From Larry Brown, *Lifetime Fitness*. Copyright © 1992 by Gorsuch Scarisbrick Publishers, Scottsdale, AZ. Reprinted by permission.

TABLE 7.3	ONE-MILE WALK CATEGORIES FOR 30- TO 69-YEAR-OLD HEALTHY ADULTS	
Category	**Males**	**Females**
Excellent	<10:12	<11:40
Good	10:13–11:42	11:41–13:08
High average	11:43–13:13	13:09–14:36
Low average	13:14–14:44	14:37–16:04
Fair	14:45–16:23	16:05–17:31
Poor	>16:24	>17:32

From: J. Rippe, J. Ross, R. McCarron, J. Porcari, G. Kline, A. Ward, M. Gurry and P. Freedson, "One Mile Walk Time Norms for Healthy Adults," *Medicine and Science in Sports and Exercise*, 18(2):521, 1986. Reprinted by permission.

or not to have a medical checkup. If you choose to have a checkup, your physician should examine your cardiovascular system and check your blood pressure, muscles, and joints.

As part of a medical checkup, or perhaps in place of it, you might decide to take an exercise stress test. If you do, choose the tester and the facility with care. Some authorities question the benefit or necessity of stress tests. Of course, people with obvious circulatory or other physical problems should seek medical advice before beginning an exercise program or taking a stress test. Others may opt for a self-test, such as those in tables 7.2 and 7.3. Although these tests are easy to administer and score, use caution. It is not wise to push yourself hard to score as well as you can—particularly if you have not been exercising regularly. The tests should be viewed as a rough indicator of present condition and nothing more.

Capacity for intense physical activity relates more to general health and present fitness level than to age. Strenuous physical activity can be performed safely and successfully by persons in their fifties, sixties, and beyond, if common sense is used.

For a long time there was an unwritten rule that females weren't supposed to be as active as males. But females need physical activity as much as males do, and they are not immune to the consequences of inactivity. Of course, some females are more successful at certain types of activity than some males are, but individual differences are more important than gender differences.

DESIGNING A CARDIOVASCULAR FITNESS PROGRAM

When you have determined your initial activity level, the next step is to design a program of activities. This includes scheduling exercise and deciding on intensity, duration, frequency, type of activity, and what accessories to use.

Issue

How Necessary Is a Medical Checkup Before Beginning an Exercise Program?

If you follow common sense and use sound self-tests, a medical checkup is not needed, particularly for college students who are in the 18–to–24 age group. Don't break your budget to get an expensive medical checkup that won't be of much use for your exercise plans.

- Pro: Emphasizing the need for a medical checkup sends a negative message. It makes individuals think that exercise is dangerous, and it isn't. It is necessary to do some personal assessments, such as those in this chapter, but nothing more in most cases. Besides, most doctors are not trained to assess fitness levels—they're trained to diagnose and treat injury and disease. The chance of finding an existing problem is so small that a medical checkup is not worth the time, effort, and expense.

- Con: Exercise is not usually dangerous, but it can be dangerous to some people. Perhaps you have hidden heart disease or another problem that you should know about *before* starting an exercise program. Regardless of your age, there can still be problems. A physician should check your cardiovascular system and your blood pressure, muscles, and joints. It will help you get started on a positive note by knowing that you are ready to become more physically active. There are so many reasons that people have difficulty starting and maintaining exercise programs that you want to be sure you are physically ready.

How important is a medical checkup before starting an exercise program? Should all people have one, or just people with certain problems? If you do well on the fitness self-tests in this chapter, does this mean that you don't need a medical checkup before exercising further? Why did you (or would you) decide to have, or not have, a medical checkup before starting an exercise program?

Schedule

A haphazard exercise program is likely to yield haphazard results. There is nothing magical about which days of the week, or what time of day, to exercise, but a regular schedule is necessary to obtain or maintain desired results. If a training session is missed, doubling the intensity of the next session will not make up for it.

Some people have feared morning exercise because they have heard that heart attacks are more likely in the morning. Research indicates, however, that there's no reason to wait until afternoon to exercise unless you prefer that time. Regular

exercise poses little risk of heart attack at any time of day ("Don't Fear Morning Exercise" 1993).

When you work out a schedule for your exercise program, remember to include time for warming up and cooling down. Warming up helps the body gradually adjust to activity. Specific warm-up activities will depend on the type of strenuous activity you plan to perform, but in general, mild total-body activity followed by stretching will help your body get ready to exercise. Cooling down, a gradual slowing of activity, is helpful for similar reasons. After a run, for example, you might cool down by slowing to a moderate jog, then a fast walk, and then a slow walk, and then finally do some stretching exercises.

Intensity

Perhaps the most important consideration in planning your personal exercise program is the **intensity** of activity you will use. The appropriate intensity is enough exercise to condition your muscles and cardiovascular system without pushing yourself too hard. Each individual's **target zone** is 60 to 80 percent of his or her individually measured **maximal aerobic power**—the point where, despite harder efforts, the heart and circulation cannot deliver more oxygen to the tissues without approaching exhaustion (Zohman 1983). Below the 60 percent level, there is little fitness benefit unless the individual has been bedridden for a while. (Lower levels are good for health, however, even if they don't produce fitness benefits.) Of course, people with lower fitness levels will have to start at a lower intensity and work up gradually.

There is a relationship between aerobic power and heart rate, as well as between age and maximal attainable heart rate. Figure 7.2 shows target zones for people of different ages. Usually, about 20 to 30 minutes in the *target zone* (not counting warm-up and cool-down time) provides a significant conditioning effect on the cardiovascular system.

You can determine whether you are in your target zone by counting your pulse. Place your hand over your heart or on the carotid artery (at the side of the neck); find the beat within a second, count for 10 seconds, and multiply by 6. Through trial and error, you can find the correct exercise intensity needed to put your pulse in the target zone. It is important to count your pulse immediately when you stop exercising, because the rate changes very quickly.

intensity
The repetitions and force used during exercise. The appropriate intensity is enough exercise to condition the muscles and cardiovascular system without overextending the body.

target zone
A level of exertion at 60 to 80 percent of the individual's maximal aerobic power.

maximal aerobic power
The level of exertion at which, despite harder efforts, the heart and circulation cannot deliver more oxygen to the tissues without approaching exhaustion.

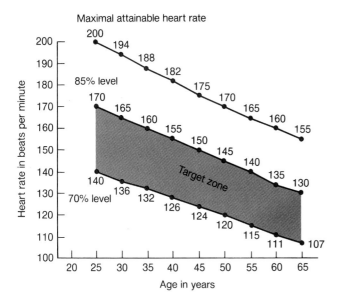

Maximal attainable heart rate

As we grow older, the heart rate that can be reached during all-out effort falls. These numerical values are "average" values for age, and one-third of the population may differ from these values. It is quite possible that a normal 50-year-old man may have a maximum heart rate of 195 or that a 30-year-old man might have a maximum of only 163. The same limitations apply to the 70 percent and 85 percent of maximum lines.

Figure 7.2

Target zones for physical activity.

From L. Zohman, M.D., *Beyond Diet: Exercise Your Way to Fitness & Heart Health,* CPC International, Englewood Cliffs, New Jersey.

Recognizing that some individuals can have trouble exercising at the intensity needed to reach their target zone, and also realizing that others might be willing to exercise only at lower intensities, some experts feel that too much emphasis is placed on developing and maintaining cardiovascular fitness. The opinion that low-level physical activity can help reduce the likelihood of heart disease is gaining support. In fact, beneficial effects on cholesterol and blood pressure occur from as low as 40 to 50 percent of maximal heart rate, and a target heart rate of 50 to 60 percent of maximum seems best for hypertensive people (Bankhead 1991). Also, participating successfully in low-level physical activity can encourage a person to gradually increase the intensity (Kasper 1990).

With any physical activity, it is important to progress slowly. It is unwise, and perhaps even dangerous, to attempt to increase exercise intensity or duration too fast.

Duration

Your long-range goals and present level of fitness will influence your exercise **duration.** Beginners might not be able to maintain the target rate for the recommended 20 to 30 minutes; it would be wise for them to increase their exercise time (at the target heart rate) gradually, until 20 to 30 minutes are possible. Longer periods of time will not provide greater health benefits. Longer work periods are necessary, however, for those interested in improving their performance in certain

activities. For example, if you want to improve your time in a 10-mile run, you must run progressively longer distances at progressively faster times in order to get better.

There is a trade-off between intensity and duration. For example, the higher the intensity of an activity, the more likely a person is to have injuries and soreness, and to drop out of the activity. From the standpoint of health, it makes sense to encourage medium-level intensity and longer-duration activity. To get health benefits, you must continue activity for the long term. Regardless of your exercise intensity, sticking with the program is the most vital recommendation (Terry 1993).

Frequency

Some individuals attempt to store the benefits of exercise by exercising strenuously only on weekends. Unfortunately, this doesn't work and can even be dangerous. **Frequency** is important. Benefits from exercise begin to be lost after even 2 or 3 days without activity. Three times is the *minimum* number of times per week to exercise, but daily activity is best. (Weight training, which should be done on alternate days, is an exception.)

It is unwise to exercise to the point of exhaustion. Simply following the suggestions given for intensity, duration, and frequency are sufficient.

When you design your personal fitness program, remember the guidelines of the American College of Sports Medicine (ACSM), a medical and scientific organization that provides information on sports medicine and exercise science ("ACSM Guidelines for Fitness Updated" 1990):

1. Train 3 to 5 days a week.
2. Work out at 60 percent to 90 percent of your maximum heart rate. (Note that the 90% level is only for people in top shape. Most of us should not exceed the 80% level.)
3. Exercise aerobically for 20 to 60 continuous minutes. (Note the key word *continuous.*)
4. The activity can be anything that uses large muscle groups and is rhythmical and aerobic in nature.

CHOOSING SUITABLE ACTIVITIES

About half of the population in this country currently exercise, and there are activities available to suit everyone. Among the most popular are aerobics, running or jogging, walking, water activities, cycling, rope skipping, and weight training. The potential benefits from different types of activity

---

duration

How long an exercise workout lasts.

frequency

Number of exercise workouts per week.

The health benefits of activity can be obtained in various ways.

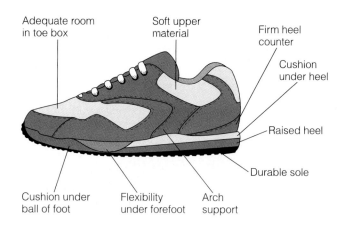

Figure 7.3

What to look for in a running shoe.

are similar, so individual preference is a major factor. You should choose an activity you like, so you will stick with it. You can combine different activities, and occasionally start and stop various ones, as long as you follow your overall program.

Aerobics

The term **aerobics** means any form of total body activity performed at a rate below that needed to produce oxygen debt. In other words, this means longer, moderately intense activity rather than shorter, high-intensity activity. In practice, the term has been used synonymously with *aerobic dance* for many years. This is changing, however, as many forms of aerobics have emerged—even to the point that aerobics has become a serious sport for some.

The amount of stress the body, mostly the joints and bones, receives from aerobics is referred to as the **impact.** Originally most aerobics classes emphasized high-impact activities. Then low-impact aerobics became popular, but they often did not provide sufficient activity for the cardiovascular system. More recently, middle-impact aerobics have become popular. The idea is to keep down the stress on the body but still have a strenuous workout.

There are countless variations on aerobics. These include step training or step aerobics (activity variations designed to move the body up and down off steps from 4 to 12 inches high), sports dance (aerobics using simulated sports moves), cross-training (combining aerobics with other forms of exercise, such as weight training), interval training (alternating low-intensity and high-intensity exercise in the same workout), and circuit training (aerobic floor exercise combined in a circuit with other types of exercise, such as stationary bikes, climbers, ski machines, and strength-training machines). Aqua-aerobics is also growing in popularity (Malanka 1990).

As with other forms of physical activity, it is important to progress slowly in aerobics. And be sure your aerobics instructors are properly trained.

Jogging or Running

As we define these terms, *running* is just faster than *jogging*. If you are physically ready to begin a running program, the most important consideration is to get proper shoes. They might seem expensive, but proper running shoes are a necessity. (See figure 7.3 for some basic requirements.) It is recommended that they have the following characteristics ("Shoes for Sports" 1986):

1. Well-cushioned heels, slightly raised to absorb impact, flared to provide stability, and rounded or beveled at the back to make forward movement easier.

2. A firm back portion of the shoe to stabilize the hindfoot and an Achilles pad to prevent irritation of the Achilles tendon as the foot moves up and down.

3. A flexible, cushioned midsole thicker than the sole of regular sneakers and with a surface that provides adequate traction.

4. Enough room in the toe box so toes do not touch the end, since they need enough room to move up and down.

5. A well-padded tongue to prevent irritation of the tendons along the top of the foot.

It isn't easy to tell how long running shoes should last. All of them lose a significant amount of resiliency after around 400 miles of running. Shoes should be replaced if they clearly feel less cushiony than they did when new. Visually, the only reliable sign of a worn-out shoe is a large

aerobics
Any form of total-body activity that raises the heart rate but does not produce oxygen debt (any longer-duration, moderately intense activity rather than shorter-duration, high-intensity activity).

impact
The amount of stress the body, especially the joints and bones, receives during activities like aerobics.

THE WORLD AROUND YOU
Running and Being

Over 15 years ago, Dr. George Sheehan wrote the book *Running and Being*. He spoke of his distance-running experiences in terms of mind, body, and soul. For example, the first part of his run was for his body, and the last part was for his soul. He says: "In the beginning the road is a miracle of solitude and escape. In the end it is a miracle of discovery and joy." (Although he doesn't refer to this directly, there are implications here for the mind, too).

Sheehan went on to talk about "a pace and silence that allow me to be myself." He said: "I become my body . . . I know that only in its fullness will I be all that I will be. I delight in my energy, my strength, my power as I pass by greening fields." "I feel myself come alive." "I am able to let my mind wander." "I am free to meditate, to measure the importance of things." "The energy of my body becomes an energy of the mind" "A tremendous energy pours through my body. I am whole and holy." "Man has no body distinct from the mind" (Sheehan 1978, 226–27).

This is a wonderful example of total health—illustrated by the intimate interrelatedness of all aspects of being. Other runners speak of a "runner's high," which is caused by chemical changes in the body during running. Distance running—for people who are trained for it—can be interdependence at its best.

Quotes taken from George Sheehan. *Running and Being*. New York: Simon & Schuster, 1978, pp. 226–227.

PERSONAL SKILLS AND EXPERIENCES

Running Safely
1. Don't wear jewelry.
2. Carry money for a phone call.
3. Run with a partner (a dog might be a particularly good partner).
4. Leave word of your running route with others.
5. Run in familiar areas.
6. Always stay alert.
7. Avoid unpopulated areas.
8. Don't wear headphones.
9. Ignore verbal harassment.
10. Run against traffic.
11. Wear reflective material if you must run in the dark.
12. Carry a whistle or other noisemaker.
13. Carry identification and medical information in the inside sole of a shoe and in a pocket.
14. Vary the running route and time if possible.

Source: From JoAnn Shroyer, "Becoming Streetwise: Guidelines for Female Runners" in *The Physician and Sportsmedicine*, 18 (2):121–125 (February 1990).

amount of uneven wear located anywhere on the sole ("Running Shoes" 1992). Besides good shoes, the only necessary ingredients are comfortable clothing and a desire to run.

Fitness is improved by increasing the distance run or by covering the same distance in less time. Most individuals find it more fun to vary or combine the two. Slow but steady progression is important in all forms of physical activity, and progress can be tracked with a chart and periodic measurement of your heart rate at rest and immediately following activity.

Walking

Walking has become increasingly popular as a form of total-body physical activity. If your goal is to burn off calories, walking can be effective. In fact, you will burn as many calories walking a mile as you will running a mile. The overload principle, however, reminds us that efficiency of the cardiovascular system is improved in direct proportion to the overload placed on it. In general, walking does not produce the same overload as running (although as the walking pace becomes faster and the running pace becomes slower, there is a point where the overloads are the same).

Walking does not stress the joints as much as running and aerobics do. It is probably easier for most people, as well. In addition, it can be done almost anywhere and requires no skills or major equipment.

Serious walkers might want to purchase walking shoes. Since walking isn't just slow running, a walker's shoe is different from a runner's shoe. A walker's shoe benefits from some cushioning, but too much can actually promote wobbling of the feet while walking. Walkers need more flexibility in the sole, and shoes that facilitate the heel-to-toe roll of a normal walking foot. Some walking shoes have a beveled heel or rocker profile—they're slightly rounded at the bottom like the runners on a rocking chair. Walking shoes must be comfortable, because walkers are often in their shoes longer than runners are. Details such as a padded collar and an Achilles notch are helpful ("These Shoes Are Made for Walking" 1990).

Issue

Is Walking Enough?

Walking can be enjoyable, and it burns calories, but does it involve sufficient overload to produce the desired benefits? Many argue that it does not tax the cardiovascular system enough to get health benefits.

- Pro: The cardiovascular system must be taxed at 60 to 80 percent of maximum in order to get optimal health benefits. Burning calories is helpful, and walking certainly has benefits, but higher-intensity activity is needed on a regular basis for health.

- Con: Walking burns calories just as well as more-intense activities. In addition, it does not have the risk of injury found in running and other activities involving greater stress to the body. Walking is all that is needed for health of the cardiovascular system.

Is walking enough exercise to get maximal health benefits? Use the information in this chapter to justify your answer. Be sure to answer these questions: What are your goals? How much activity do you need (type, amount, and intensity) to reach your goals? If you had different goals, would your answer change? Explain why or why not.

Water Activity

To provide real benefits, swimming, like running, must tax the cardiovascular system and raise the heart rate to appropriate levels; just paddling or floating is inadequate. Improvements in distance or time are as appropriate to strive for in swimming as they are in running. One advantage to swimming is that a cool-down period is less important, because the coldness of the water keeps the body temperature from rising.

Other physical activity in the water has become popular. Walking, running, and aerobics in water provide a safer and in many ways a more effective workout than the same exercises on land. Because water provides resistance to your movements, water workouts can burn calories faster and work your heart harder than similar land-based exercises—and also be easier on the joints. It would be a mistake, however, to substitute water workouts for all land exercises, because weight-bearing exercise is needed to help prevent bone loss ("Fitness Update" 1991).

Cycling

Cycling can be done outside with a rolling bicycle or inside with a stationary bicycle. Be sure that the bike is safe and that the seat and handlebars are at the correct height. When you sit on the saddle with the heel of your foot lightly resting on the pedal in the fully down position, your knee should be slightly bent; raise or lower the saddle to achieve this. Handlebars should be positioned so that your body is relaxed

and leaning slightly forward. Progressively increasing your distance covered and times traveled will have training effects that are similar to those in running and swimming.

Rope Skipping

Rope skipping is a great exercise that is inexpensive and allows mobility. In addition, both arms and legs are exercised, and you can use many jumping patterns. For best results, use a rope that just touches the floor or ground when you hold the ends at armpit level. Shorter or longer ropes make skipping more difficult.

Weight Training

Weight training involves building muscle strength and endurance and should not be confused with weight lifting, which is a competitive sport involving standardized lifts. In weight training, barbells and dumbbells provide resistance to the action of the muscles to be trained. To develop strength, use a relatively heavy load for few repetitions; to develop muscular endurance, increase the number of repetitions and lighten the load. (The 1-minute sit-up test in the Health Assessment exercise on page 7.3 is one example of a test for muscular endurance.) As your strength increases, apply progressively greater loads; as your muscular endurance increases, progressively increase the number of repetitions. From the standpoint of total health, it is unlikely that a weight-training program by itself will provide sufficient benefits to the circulatory system. It can be a fine addition, however, to another program designed to strengthen the circulatory system.

You might wonder whether free weights (barbells and dumbbells) or resistance machines are better for improving muscular strength or endurance. Individuals have their own preferences, but resistance machines have these advantages: There is less chance of injury, you can focus on a single muscle group, you will have consistent contraction throughout a full range of joint motion, and the machines are easy to use and fun. The disadvantages are they are expensive, less versatile (each maneuver takes place on only one plane), and bulky, and they can be uncomfortable or even unsafe if you are small. Free weights have these advantages: They are much cheaper, they provide unlimited variety to work virtually any muscle from any angle, they provide a whole-body workout because weights have to be lifted into position, they allow movement in three dimensions, and they can help improve balance. However, their disadvantages include possible injury if they are lifted incorrectly, the need for a training partner or "spotter" to guide your movements, and the need to develop some skill to balance the weight properly ("The Best Workout" 1993).

Before wearing weights around your ankles or wrists while exercising, consider the risks involved. Ankle weights can increase the risk of stress fractures of bones in the lower extremities and feet, and inflammation of the Achilles tendon—the tendon in the back of the ankle. Gravity triples the effect of an ankle weight on the foot and increases the tendency for feet to roll inward to handle the stress.

HEALTH UPDATE

Building Strong Abdominal Muscles

Strong abdominal muscles improve your appearance, help prevent low back pain, and may help prevent other health problems. Traditionally, the classic full sit-up—raising your head and shoulders off the floor all the way to your knees—was the standard way to strengthen abdominal muscles. Many experts now advise against full sit-ups, for two reasons: They can aggravate back pain, and abdominal muscles are used only during the initial lift. Once you've raised your shoulders a few inches off the floor, the hip flexors and other muscles take over the effort. The three exercises shown below are designed to avoid both of these problems. There is less lift, so the movement is concentrated where it does the most good and the least harm. Breathe slowly and steadily while doing these exercises, avoid jerky movements, and don't be surprised if you're sore for a day or two at first.

Pelvic tilt: Lie on your back with knees bent and hands relaxed by the side of your head. Tighten the muscles of your lower abdomen, tilting your pelvis and flattening your lower back onto the floor. (If you have trouble getting the hang of that, concentrate on curling your lower abdomen up toward your chest while pulling the stomach inward.) Hold, take a few breaths, and release.

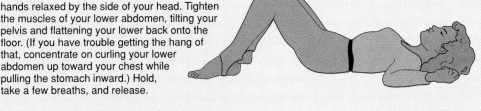

Partial sit-up: Lie on your back with knees bent. Cross your arms in front of your chest. Lift your head, shoulders, and upper back off the floor slowly. Hold for a count of three and slowly drop back down.
To increase the difficulty as you get stronger, place your hands loosely behind your neck, hold a light weight (one to five pounds) on your chest, or do the exercise on an incline board with your head at the low end.

Diagonal curl: Lie on your back with knees bent. Clasp your hands loosely behind your head. Lift your head, shoulders, and upper back off the floor slowly, pointing your right elbow toward your left knee. Hold for a count of three and slowly drop back down. Perform a full set of 8 to 12 repetitions. Then do the same thing, this time pointing your left elbow toward your right knee. To increase the difficulty, do the exercise on an incline board.

Wrist weights, when worn properly, are safer than ankle weights. Weights heavier than 0.5 to 2.0 pounds increase your risk of straining or tearing tendons that stabilize your shoulder joint, and they increase your chances of developing bursitis (inflammation of the lubricating sac that surrounds a joint).

Walking with a normal arm swing with handheld weights of 5 pounds or less is not enough to provide health benefits (Owens, Al-Ahmed, S. Moffatt 1989). So why use wrist or ankle weights at all, with so many apparent risks and little possible benefit? Simply exercising a little faster can increase your overload, and therefore your heart rate, without any of the risks of hand or ankle weights.

STEPS TO PROMOTE SUCCESS IN A PERSONAL FITNESS PROGRAM

Exercisers, particularly beginners, need abundant positive feedback, which increases their feelings of competence and intrinsic motivation (Rutherford, Corbin, and Chase 1992). This means that you and your exercise partners can help each other immensely by being supportive and by providing feedback about progress being made in the physical activity. For example, you can assist in providing performance information about running speed, fitness scores, or other results of physical performance. If you are not presently involved in an exercise program, the section for nonexercisers in the

Health Assessment "Initiation and Continuance of Exercise" will help determine the likelihood of your starting an exercise program.

For best results, a fitness program must be personal. Here are some steps to increase your chances of success:

1. *Make it personal.* Your program should be designed to fit your needs and goals rather than to compete with someone else.

2. *Proceed gradually.* You may want to progress quickly, but give your body a chance to adjust to the new activities.

3. *Set reasonable goals.* Don't expect too much too fast.

4. *Pick activities that you will continue.* Consider your interests and skills as well as available facilities.

5. *Consider medical and physical concerns* when selecting appropriate activities.

6. *Expect some soreness.* Some muscle soreness is natural and is nothing to worry about; if the soreness is extreme, you're probably ignoring step 2.

7. *Use total-body activity.* Emphasize activities for the circulatory and respiratory systems, where most of the health benefits are.

8. *Be regular.* The weekend athlete has highly questionable exercise habits that put an unnecessary strain on the body. Participate in vigorous activity at least three to four times per week, for at least 20 to 30 minutes each time. (Review information on target heart rate to help you determine what heart rate is "vigorous" for you.)

9. *Use several forms of exercise if possible.* You will be less likely to become bored if you vary your workouts (for instance, alternate swimming days and bicycling days).

10. *Determine and work out at your target heart rate* (figure 7.2). This is a good guide to correct activity intensity.

FACTORS INFLUENCING CHOICE OF PROGRAM

A number of factors influence the type of activity program you choose. For example, you need to consider your body condition and fitness level. An obese person might find swimming a more appropriate activity than tennis, at first. But regardless of body condition, everyone receives similar benefits from fitness activities.

Emotional temperament is also important. Some individuals are better suited to distance running, circuit training, or rope skipping than, say, weight training. Also consider motor ability and motor educability (some people learn physical skills easier and faster than others do). If you want to play tennis or another activity requiring a certain level of skill, take a realistic look at your present and potential skill levels. If you select activities that demand skills you do not possess, you are likely to get more frustrated than fit.

Availability is an obvious consideration. It is difficult to play racquetball if there are no courts in your community. If

PERSONAL SKILLS AND EXPERIENCES

Pros and Cons of Various Activities

Suppose a friend tells you that he or she wants to start an exercise program and asks you what kinds of activities are best. Prepare an outline of what you would say. Be sure to list various activities available, their advantages and disadvantages, and which activities are most likely to help your friend accomplish various kinds of personal goals.

Evaluate an exercise training facility carefully before joining.

you want team sports to be part of your program, you need people to participate and a way to organize the activities if appropriate team sports aren't already organized in your area.

TRAINING FACILITIES

Some individuals like to exercise at home, and others prefer to use training facilities. Advantages in using a training facility include socializing, having a regular place to change and shower, the availability of exercise equipment and trained instructors, the opportunity to participate in organized sports, and the promotion of self-discipline. Disadvantages include a possibly inconvenient location, the need to go to a set place (perhaps at a set time), the cost, and a feeling of obligation. If you are considering using a training facility, carefully check out the quality of the program, the instruction, and the equipment.

When evaluating an exercise training facility, you need to ask a number of questions. For example, are facilities available for aerobic exercise? This includes treadmills, exercise bicycles with a resistance control, a long swimming pool (at least 60 feet), and a running track or a large empty room that can be used for run/walk/jog sequences.

PERSONAL INSIGHT

Happiness and Physical Activity

For many years I've worked with people to try to help them improve their health and their level of fitness. One of the great things for me has been the chance to see so many people become so happy and even proud of themselves because of their involvement with exercise. This has happened countless times, but two instances stand out in my mind.

The first was when I was still in graduate school. I was teaching a basic fitness course for college students. The students spent most of their time participating in weight training and aerobic activity. I vividly remember two young men who worked together and became good friends. One was about 5 feet 6 inches tall and thin as a rail. The other was about 5 feet 10 inches tall and

relatively round. They soon became amazed that, although they did similar activities, the thin man gained weight and the rounder man lost weight. Both experienced happiness as they watched their physiques change in ways they desired. Even 25 years later I remember their strong positive feelings.

The second instance occurred only in recent years. I have always felt it was important to maintain a reasonable level of fitness and now, at age 52, I continue to run and be active. In the past 2 or 3 years I have observed people, particularly men, in their fifties and sixties who are "discovering" exercise. They have been relatively inactive for the past 20 to 30 years, and now, perhaps because of a desire to lose weight or a scare with a circulatory problem, have decided to start exercising again. Most have chosen to walk, jog, or use exer-

cise machines such as stair-stepping machines or stationary bikes. No matter what the form of activity, the results are the same. These people are literally bubbling over with happiness. They tell me they sleep better, feel better, feel less stress, and in many instances have returned to a body weight they had not seen for many years. They are so happy that they want to tell the world.

In both instances (with the college students and with the older men) I have enjoyed seeing their success and happiness with exercise programs. At the same time, however, I have to wonder why it took them so long to find this happiness. How can it be that more and more people learn about the benefits of leading an active life, but they still don't do it? Why don't more develop a lifestyle that will give them that happiness too?

Are members encouraged to attend three or more times weekly for fitness exercising? Some clubs permit members to attend as often as they wish yet subtly discourage regular attendance for fear of overloading the facility. Visit the facility on the days and at the times you wish to exercise, to make sure that they are not oversubscribed.

What kind of training do the instructors have? An instructor with a degree in exercise physiology or physical education probably knows the principles of aerobic conditioning exercise and can work with you on an effective program. It is also important for the instructors to be certified in first aid and CPR.

What kinds of exercise classes are offered? Classes that feature running, swimming, fitness dancing, and other aerobic activities usually indicate a good facility for developing and maintaining cardiovascular fitness. Classes in yoga, weight lifting, or calisthenics may promote muscle building or flexibility, but usually do not promote cardiovascular fitness.

Are other health programs available? If a facility offers diet consultation, smoking cessation, or other supplementary programs, it is health oriented and its exercise classes are probably geared to cardiovascular fitness.

Are adequate dressing and storage facilities available? Locking lockers should be provided so you can safely leave your valuables. The dressing room areas should be clean.

Is it preferable to join a club that is part of a chain? Only if the chain is oriented to cardiovascular fitness.

Is a good facility expensive? Not necessarily. If it meets the standards detailed above, a facility in the "Y" system is often adequate and inexpensive. Posh surroundings are not necessary, although they might add to your comfort.

YOUR PERSONALITY

When your fitness program matches your personality, you are more likely to stay with it, so psychological effect is one important consideration. At the same time, how you perform an activity might be just as important as the activity itself. For example, a runner who wants to relax and get physical benefits at the same time might choose to leave the stopwatch at home to avoid being too competitive.

Personality factors such as sociability, spontaneity, discipline, aggressiveness, competitiveness, mental focus, and risk taking can be used to determine the likelihood of an individual's staying with an activity. For example, compared to running, walking is more spontaneous, less aggressive, and takes less discipline. Racket sports are high in sociability, spontaneity, competitiveness, and focus, but low in discipline. Swimming is fairly high in discipline and low in sociability, spontaneity, and aggressiveness. If you're having trouble sticking to a fitness program, these ideas might help you to explain why and to reevaluate your psychological needs regarding a fitness program (Gavin 1989).

Initiation and Continuance of Exercise

Section I. Exercisers

This exercise is designed to determine the likelihood of your continuing to exercise throughout your life, which is a desirable attribute. Check all that apply to you. If you do not currently exercise, then skip to section II.

_____ 1. I exercise alone or enjoy exercising alone if no one else is around.

_____ 2. It is difficult for me to get motivated to exercise.

_____ 3. I exercise only because someone else encourages me to do it or I am in an organized sport.

_____ 4. Exercise is a high priority in my life.

_____ 5. I exercise all year around, not just in certain seasons.

_____ 6. I am unhappy or fidgety when I miss an exercise session.

_____ 7. My role model (hero) exercises.

_____ 8. I enjoy exercise.

_____ 9. I am "hooked" on exercise.

_____ 10. I plan to exercise all my life if possible.

Scoring

Give yourself points for each item you checked, as follows: Items 2 and 3 are each worth −2 points; the other items are each worth 2 points. Total your score.

Interpretation

Your score on this section indicates the likelihood that you will continue to exercise throughout your life. Interpret your score as follows:

10–16	=	High likelihood
4–9	=	Moderate likelihood
0–3	=	Low likelihood

If you scored low, then after reading this chapter you may be able to make some changes in your attitude and increase the likelihood of your continuing an exercise program throughout your life.

Section II: Nonexercisers

The purpose of this assessment is to determine the likelihood of your starting an exercise program. Mark all that apply to you.

_____ 1. I am really motivated to start an exercise program.

_____ 2. I used to exercise and liked it.

_____ 3. I've been wanting to start for a long time, but wasn't sure how to start.

_____ 4. I'm willing to try to start, but I doubt I will stick to it.

_____ 5. I am not sure exercise will help me much.

_____ 6. I don't like to exercise.

_____ 7. The benefits of exercise are not worth the time and effort.

_____ 8. I tried once and quit because I didn't like it.

Scoring

Give yourself points for each item you checked, as follows: Items 1–3 are each worth 2 points; items 4–8 are each worth −2 points. Total your score.

Interpretation

Your score on this section indicates the likelihood that you will start an exercise program. Interpret your score as follows:

2–6	=	High likelihood
0– −2	=	Moderate likelihood
−3– −10	=	Low likelihood

Hopefully, by reading this chapter, you can realize the benefits of exercise and become motivated to start. After reading the chapter, retest yourself on this if you scored low on likelihood of starting an exercise program.

MAINTAINING A FITNESS PROGRAM

The success of your fitness program depends on your keeping at it. If you begin an exercise program with unrealistic expectations, you might become frustrated and give up when those expectations aren't soon met. The Health Assessment exercise "Initiation and Continuance of Exercise" will help you determine the likelihood of continuing to exercise throughout your life.

Personal factors such as not being a smoker, being of normal weight, having a white-collar occupation, being self-motivated, knowing how to find the time, and having no medical contraindications increase the likelihood of maintaining a fitness program. Situational factors such as social support, convenience of a facility, and using low-intensity or moderately vigorous exercise (as compared to more strenuous programs) also help program continuation (Sallis 1986).

Social norms can play an important role in maintaining a fitness program. For example, healthy adults who think their physicians want them to exercise are motivated to do so. In contrast, adults (including those who want to exercise) who see their personal physicians as being opposed to exercise are less likely to be physically active (Godin and Shephard 1990).

WARM-UP AND STRETCHING

It has generally been assumed that warm-up activities are necessary before participating in physical activity. Because of this, some individuals warm up vigorously before participating in tennis, basketball, running, or other activities. This can do more harm than good.

Generally, it makes sense to warm up with activities that are the same as or similar to the workout activities. If you plan to run, jog slowly to warm up. If you are going to play racquetball, hit the ball easily for a few minutes or play a few easy practice points. This helps the body prepare itself.

Stretching is often misunderstood. People commonly stretch vigorously before activity because they think it will loosen them up; however, brisk toe-touches, for example, actually tighten muscles instead of stretching them. This is because when one set of muscles extends quickly, the opposite set naturally contracts. To avoid tightening muscles, it is important to stretch in a slow and steady manner. This allows for greater relaxation of the opposing muscle group, improves flexibility, and reduces the chance of injury to a muscle while stretching. The benefits of stretching before a physical activity are a matter of debate, but those who want to stretch should first do a mild form of total-body activity to raise their body temperature and then use only static stretching (no bouncing or bobbing).

Most individuals have been stretching incorrectly and for the wrong reasons. To improve flexibility, it probably makes more sense to stretch *after* physical activity than before. Stretching can also help the muscles recover from activity. Remember that a mild, total-body activity provides a better warm-up than stretching does.

IMPROVEMENT PATTERNS

Many of us are impatient and want quick results. Some benefits from exercise can appear after a couple of days, but significant improvement takes a couple of weeks. Also, we might retrogress before we get better. The initial overload stresses the body, and performance declines as internal forces are mobilized to repair stressed tissues. This decline lasts only a few days in most cases, but retrogression can occur again at any time during training—as the result of disease, poor nutrition, too little rest, or lack of motivation.

MUSCLE SORENESS

Some individuals become discouraged when starting a physical activity program because their muscles become stiff and sore at first. Experts are not sure about the exact reason for this. Some think soreness is due to microscopic tearing of the muscle fibers. Others feel that sore muscles result when waste products given off during chemical reactions in the body begin to collect in the muscle tissues and circulatory system. Mild activity, such as slow, rhythmic stretching exercises or even walking, stimulates the blood flow through sore areas and helps remove the waste products. Muscle soreness is common, but as the body gets more used to activity, the soreness usually diminishes greatly or even disappears.

GETTING THE DESIRED RESULTS

Misconceptions about the effects of certain activities can be discouraging. Some of us have used activity to try to lose fat from a certain part of the body (so-called **spot reduction**),

but this isn't really possible. When we lose weight, fat is lost from the entire body, even though the loss from some spots might be especially obvious.

If you perform activities for a certain part of the body, be sure the desired muscles are doing the work. For example, men commonly do arm curls in hopes of strengthening their triceps (muscles in the back of the upper arm), but that exercise is of little benefit to those muscles.

Don't confuse total-body activity with activity for certain parts of the body. For example, most bending, stretching, and other calisthenic exercises benefit certain body parts, but not the overall circulatory and respiratory systems. These activities are fine as long as you have appropriate expectations for them.

STALENESS

Sometimes we get bored with an activity program and feel "stale." It seems that no matter what we do, we feel tired and slow and don't get any better. For some people, it might be wise to consider more rest or even some time off from strenuous physical activity. For most individuals, however, **staleness** can probably be avoided by adding more variety to the physical activity program. This might mean using different types of activity, exercising in different places, or running various distances at different speeds. No one is sure what causes staleness, but most often it goes away by itself.

SOME CAUTIONS ABOUT EXERCISE

With all of the positive benefits of exercising, there are still some precautions:

1. Wearing a rubber or plastic suit can be dangerous. These suits cause elevated body temperature that can cause heat exhaustion. Also, weight lost from this practice is water weight, which is quickly regained when fluids are consumed again.

2. Gravity inversion devices (where you hang upside down to exercise) can be dangerous. Significant blood pressure increases have been found in individuals exercising upside down. Since blood pressure increases

---

stretching
Slow, gradual extension of muscle groups to warm them up before exercise in order to improve performance and diminish the chance of injury during physical activity.

spot reduction
Losing fat from localized areas of the body, which is not possible—fat is lost over the body as a whole, not in isolated areas.

staleness
Feeling tired and slow and as if you are not making progress in your exercise program.

anyway during exercise, further research is needed to determine the safety of gravity inversion devices.

3. Never end an exercise period with a wind sprint (an all-out burst of speed over a relatively short distance). Taper off slowly when ending exercise.

4. Exercises such as deep knee bends, the "duck walk," and holding the knees partially flexed for periods of time can cause knee joint injury.

5. Toe touching can cause lower back injury. This is particularly true if you have weak abdominal muscles. A good alternative is to sit on the floor with one leg extended and the other folded close to your body. Reach forward along the extended leg until you feel a gentle stretch in your hamstrings (muscles behind the thigh). Flex from the hips, keeping your back straight. Do this several times and repeat for the other leg ("Safe Alternatives to 10 Risky Exercises" 1993).

6. Doing sit-ups (which should be done with knees bent) by placing your hands behind your head can be dangerous, because a pulling action can injure the spine. A good alternative is to fold your arms on your chest.

MAINTENANCE

It might seem easier to maintain a desired fitness level than to get there, but maintaining optimal fitness requires regular activity. By being realistic about your personal qualities, selecting activities that make sense for you, and using the target zone principle, you can get satisfying results with a personal exercise program. Program maintenance is easier if you remember the following:

1. Pick rhythmic, repetitive activities that challenge your circulatory system at an appropriate intensity.

2. Do activities that are fashionable, provided that you like them. The "in" thing to do might be easier to continue.

3. Pick activities that you enjoy, that are suited to your needs, and that can be done year-round.

4. Make the activity more like play than like work. For example, sharing activity with friends or using music while exercising can be helpful.

5. Wear clothing appropriate for the exercise, considering temperature, humidity, proper footwear, and comfort.

6. Warm up and cool down.

7. Follow your program regularly, at least three times per week.

PERSONAL SKILLS AND EXPERIENCES

Cultural and Subcultural Differences in Physical Activity

There are subcultural differences in physical activity levels—and we don't know why. In some foreign countries, people walk a lot, use bicycles for transportation, and assume that activity is a basic part of their lives. Perhaps where you live it is common to drive two blocks to the grocery store to pick up a few small items—or to drive a block or two to visit a friend. A particularly entertaining pattern is seen among people who drive a few blocks to the gym to have a workout.

We don't have to go to foreign countries to see subcultural differences. For example, we know people who habitually walk to a destination only a few blocks away, or consistently use the stairs instead of elevators or escalators when going up or down only a few floors. If you habitually use stairs, it can be interesting if you are with a group and head for the stairs while others go in another direction to the elevator.

Personal habits can be a form of subculture. Some people choose to live in a subculture that values and practices a physically active lifestyle. Others are content with sedentary patterns. What can you do to influence your subculture?

Excuses for not being active might already be running through your mind. If you don't have motivation, no amount of information will lead you to physical fitness. But most excuses for inactivity are pretty flimsy:

- *"I don't have time."* Each of us wastes at least a few hours each week, and that's all the time you need. Make time for what you want to do.

- *"I don't have a place to exercise"* or *"I don't have anyone to exercise with."* Many forms of exercise require no special place, and although it might be nice to have someone else along, physiological benefits are not influenced by the presence of another person. In fact, many people report that their solitary exercise gives them time to think and be alone.

- *"I'm too old."* People of all ages need physical activity to keep their bodies functioning properly, and anyone can participate in a physical activity program.

- *"I'm too weak."* Using the target zone principle, it is simple to design a program for any individual need.

PERSONAL SKILLS AND EXPERIENCES

Fitness for Life

Being physically active is a way of life—influenced by, and influencing, mind, body, soul, and their interdependence. To get and keep benefits from total-body activity, you must make appropriate physical activity a part of your basic lifestyle. To do this, certain health skills are needed.

The following activities will help you determine if you have the needed health skills related to fitness. You will also see how they relate to the mind, body, and soul. If you can successfully complete all of them, you will have the prerequisites for a sound personal fitness program. Then, the rest is up to you.

Mind

Decide on goals and objectives for your personal fitness program. What do you want to accomplish and why?

Body

Determine your present fitness level. Do it in at least two different ways so you know where you should start in a personal training program.

Soul

Consider why a personal fitness program is important to you. How does it relate to what you value in life and what you want to accomplish in the short term as well as the long run?

Interdependence

1. Explain the health benefits of physical activity to a friend. Be sure to include information about the effects of physical activity on the muscular, cardiovascular, and respiratory systems as well as effects on mental health.

2. Outline a fitness program that meets your personal goals and objectives. Be sure to consider facilities needed, personality factors, and what can be done to assure that you follow and continue the program.

3. Finally, describe how you can help "guarantee" success and how you will know when you have been successful.

Just one more step is needed once you have the skills—do it!

- *"It's boring."* Vary the pace, the time of day, the type of activity, the clothes you wear, or anything else, if you need more variety.
- *"It's too cold/hot/humid/late/early/windy to exercise."* Honestly reevaluate your motivation and your exercise program if you often turn to this type of reasoning. If you value an active lifestyle, none of these excuses will prevent activity.

CREATING AN ACTIVE ENVIRONMENT

Many of us actually go out of our way to be sedentary. To counteract this tendency, the environment must be reorganized to provide activity. For many people, this means an adjustment in lifestyle.

ADJUSTING LIFESTYLE AND ENVIRONMENT

One way to adjust your lifestyle is to alter your daily routines to involve more exercise. For example, when you travel a relatively short distance, walk or bicycle. Replace your coffee breaks with exercise breaks, and use the stairs instead of elevators or escalators. With some creative thinking you can come up with other possibilities.

You can also encourage yourself to exercise by finding an apartment conducive to walking to school or by altering your home environment. Move the phone a few steps, and place objects on higher shelves to encourage stretching to get them. Other opportunities to stay active around the home include washing the car, raking leaves, and shoveling snow instead of paying others to do these tasks.

REWARDS

Rewards related to activity can also be helpful. For example, keeping an exercise chart will show your progress, thereby reinforcing your motivation to continue. Using exercise time to be active with other people can be a social reward. After you reach a personal goal, rewarding yourself with a new warm-up suit, a weekend vacation, or some other appropriate prize might be a motivator. You might make your access to physical activity easier by buying

While traveling, you many need to be especially creative and determined to maintain physical activity patterns.

exercise equipment—for instance, by buying a few weights, or installing a basketball basket so you won't have to make a trip to the gym.

EXERCISING WHILE TRAVELING

Exercising while traveling can present unique problems, but these can be overcome with a little creativity. When you are staying at a hotel, you can usually find safe places to jog; exercise rooms are becoming more common in hotels, and even hotel stairways can be used for a good workout. When you travel by car, you can take a short jog or walk at a rest stop.

Most of us are locked into daily routines, and it can be difficult to modify existing behaviors. After you assess your possibilities for modifying your routine, consider your personal needs, and make a realistic decision about which behaviors you can modify, then you must take action. Just thinking about exercising won't improve your physiological functioning.

SLEEP

We spend about one-third of our lives sleeping, yet researchers are still unable to explain why and how much we should sleep.

INSOMNIA

Many individuals at some time have **insomnia,** or difficulty sleeping, and some regularly experience sleep disturbance. Many tales have been told about how to promote sleep. Some common suggestions are to alter the amount of exercise, control sounds and lights, alter the time and amount of food consumption, avoid drinks containing caffeine, and avoid stressful situations just before going to bed.

Sometimes it might be helpful to try to reset the internal sleep clock. Most people have 24-hour rhythms that influence sleeping and waking patterns. A rhythm disturbance called "Saturday night insomnia" is caused by staying up late on weekend nights and sleeping later than usual on weekend mornings. This, and other rhythm disturbances, can often be helped by carefully maintaining a sleep routine. The key is to awaken at the same time, no matter what. The more serious your insomnia is, the more an established wake-up time is needed (Hauri and Linde 1990).

Some of these strategies work for some people but many are of little help to others. Individuals greatly vary in what helps them get to sleep.

SLEEP RESEARCH

The focus of investigations on sleep is on brain-wave patterns, shown on a **electroencephalogram (EEG).** These patterns differ when people are awake and asleep. Researchers have isolated four main stages of sleep (figure 7.4). During the relaxation period just before sleep, the rapid waves characteristic of most daytime brain activity are gradually replaced by longer and slower waves. Stage 1 of sleep is marked by even slower waves. During this stage, which lasts only a few seconds or minutes, we can be awakened quite easily.

Stage 2 of sleep produces faster brain waves and sleep is deeper; if you are awakened, however, you will not recall any dreams. Stage 3 shows dramatic physiological changes. Heartbeat slows, blood pressure and temperature fall, and the muscles become quite relaxed. Stage 4 is the deepest stage of sleep. In stage 4, it is hard to awaken you, you don't

---

insomnia
Difficulty sleeping.

electroencephalogram (EEG)
A machine that records and displays brain-wave patterns.

Figure 7.4

EEG waves for the stages of sleep.

move much, and your brain waves are mostly very slow. Sleep-walking and nightmares are most likely to occur during this stage. After stage 4, you go back through stages 3 and 2 and enter **rapid eye movement (REM) sleep,** a stage that includes dreaming about 85 percent of the time. Approximately 25 percent of a full night's sleep is spent in the REM stage. The cycle of moving back and forth through the stages of sleep generally occurs about three or four times each night.

DREAMS

Sleep affects how you feel, but feelings of happiness or un-happiness most strongly depend on dreams, although in ways that are not yet clear. "Bad" dreams (those perceived as nega-tive" outnumber "sweet" dreams (those perceived as positive) by four to one. Fear tops the list of emotional responses to dreams, followed by anxiety, guilt, anger, and sadness. Dreams are most commonly described as "confusing," "dis-turbing," "depressing," and "silly" (Fleming 1989).

There are countless theories concerning why individuals dream, including these: (1) Dreams happen because of unre-solved conflicts in the unconscious. (2) Dreams are simply a result of random activity. (3) Dreams are the brain's way of ridding itself of unwanted or overabundant associations stored during the day. And (4) dreams are powered by per-sonal conflicts (Kardong 1987).

Some individuals feel that in dreaming people can work out problems and feelings left unresolved during the day, but this is not known for sure. In laboratory settings, people de-prived of dreaming time show more severe symptoms of men-tal problems than those deprived of sleep at random intervals. Perhaps failure to dream interferes with the ability to restore the sense of competence to better go about your daily life.

Loss of even a single night's sleep can interfere with de-cision making, particularly when creativity is needed. For ex-ample, when twenty-four well-rested college students were challenged to come up with potential uses for a cardboard box or to imagine the consequences of some bizarre event, all of them had comparable scores on their ability to think of original ideas. After half of them had stayed awake all

night while the other half slept, however, the sleep-deprived students scored one-third to two-thirds lower in all areas (Lamberg 1989).

It seems that we need sleep and dreams. Although the exact reasons for this remain elusive, the relationship of sleep and dreams to health is beginning to be better understood.

TAKE ACTION

1. Begin an aerobic fitness program (jogging, swimming, aerobic dance, cycling, etc.) and stick with it for at least 3 months. Assess your results.
2. Set a goal to compete in or complete a 5K or 10K run and develop a plan to help you do it.
3. Pick a friend or relative who is sedentary and devise a way to help her or him become physically active using aerobic activities.
4. Think of a situation related to physical activity that has caused disorganization or disruption in your life (for example, an aborted physical activity program). Develop a plan to promote resilient reintegration in your life to prevent potential health problems in the future related to physical activity.

SUMMARY

1. Physical fitness has many components. Those most necessary for health are cardiorespiratory capacity, body composition, flexibility, muscular endurance, and muscular strength.

2. Health benefits of regular physical activity include improved physiological functioning, a more positive self-concept, reduced stress response, maintenance of proper body weight, possible reduction of the risk of coronary heart disease, possible delay in the aging process, and protection from lower back problems.

3. As a result of total-body physical activity, the cardiovascular system functions more efficiently. Flow of blood at the capillary level increases, heart muscle becomes stronger, resting pulse rate is lower, and coronary circulation is improved.

4. As a result of total-body physical activity, the respiratory system functions more efficiently. There is greater possible

---

rapid eye movement (REM) sleep
A stage of sleep that almost always includes dreaming.

maximal oxygen intake at the cellular level, a decreased oxygen debt for the same work, an ability to withstand a higher oxygen debt, and a decreased oxygen requirement.

5. Developing a physical activity program involves determining the present level of fitness, considering an exercise schedule, and deciding on intensity, duration, frequency, type of activity, and accessories.

6. Factors to consider when maintaining a fitness program include realistic expectations, warm-up and stretching, improvement patterns, muscle soreness, staleness, and maintenance.

7. An important part of an activity program is proper rest. Sleep and dreams are both needed, but the exact reasons for this remain elusive.

COMMITMENT ACTIVITIES

1. Cultural factors make it more or less likely that we will lead physically active lives. Unfortunately, for most of us, there seem to be more cultural factors interfering with physical activity than supporting it. Identify the cultural pitfalls that make it more difficult for you to lead a physically active life by making use of total-body activity. (For example, perhaps all your friends always use the elevator and drive very short distances while you might like to be more active. Or perhaps in your family people just don't exercise unless it is absolutely necessary—they might even think it is more healthful to continually rest and take naps. On a date, how would your date feel if you went for a walk instead of a drive?) Divide your list into two parts—factors you can't do much about and those over which you have control. Then, for a 2-week period, see if you can begin to eliminate the cultural pitfalls to physical activity over which you have control.

2. One factor that sometimes gets in the way of participation in physical fitness activities is the availability of facilities. This might mean simply a place to shower or a safe place to run. Assess the general availability of exercise facilities in your community. For example, can employees in local industries be active during their lunch hour if they so desire? Are local recreation facilities available during evenings and weekends? Are there attempts to provide facilities to meet a variety of needs? Are there safe places to walk, jog, swim, and ride a bike? If the answers to these questions are yes—great! If not, you have another challenge—what can be done about it?

3. Develop a 15-minute presentation on the benefits of regular exercise that you could make to a commercial organization. Your presentation should include probable benefits to the company as well as those to the individual employees. What kind of a beginning program would you recommend? Where might the managers and other employees go for help in developing a program?

REFERENCES

"ACSM Guidelines for Fitness Updated." 1990. *Running and FitNews* 8, no. 7 (July): 1.

Allison, M. "Improving the Odds." 1991. *Harvard Health Letter* 16, no. 4 (February): 4–6.

"American Academy of Pediatrics Statement on Physical Fitness and the Schools." 1987. American Academy of Pediatrics Committee on Sports Medicine and Committee on School Health.

Brill, P. A., and K. H. Cooper. 1993. "Physical Exercise and Mental Health." *Phi Kappa Phi Journal* 73, no. 1 (Winter): 44–45.

Brown, H. L. 1986. *Lifetime Fitness.* Scottsdale, Ariz.: Gorsuch Scarisbrick, 38.

"Can Exercise Turn Back the Clock?" 1992. *Consumer Reports on Health* 4, no. 3 (March): 21.

"Clearing Clogged Arteries." 1993. *Consumer Reports on Health* 5, no. 4 (April): 38–39.

Cooper, K. H. 1989. "The Basics of Bone." *Health* 21, no. 4 (April): 81.

"Couch Potatoes Know What They're Missing, Need Encouragement." 1993. *Health Education Reports* 15, no. 22 (18 November): 2–3.

Cremmons, A. N. 1990. "Activity May Reduce Risk of Colon Cancer." *Physician and Sportsmedicine* 18, no. 1 (January): 61.

Davis C., and M. Cowles. 1991. "Body Image and Exercise: A Study of Relationships and Comparisons Between Physically Active Men and Women." *Sex Roles* 25, nos. 1–2 (July): 33–44.

"Don't Fear Morning Exercise." 1993. *Consumer Reports on Health* 5, no. 7 (July): 71.

"Exercise Isn't Arthritic." 1993. *Consumer Reports on Health* 5, no. 11 (November): 119.

"First the Good News: Smoking Rates Down: But Americans Too Fat." 1992. *Health Education Reports* 14, no. 6 (26 March): 3–4.

Fishman, S. 1993. "Survival of the Fittest." *Health* 7, no. 3 (May/June): 59–64.

"Fitness Update." 1991. *Consumer Reports on Health* 3, no. 12 (December): 94.

Fleming, G. B. 1989. "The Stuff of Dreams." *Health* 21, no. 12 (December): 28–29.

Gauthier, M. M. 1990. "Maternal Exercise and Uterine Blood Flow." *Physician and Sportsmedicine* 18, no. 1 (January): 61.

Gavin, J. 1989. "Your Brand of Sweat." *Psychology Today*, March, 50–57.

Godin, G., and R. J. Shephard. 1990. "An Evaluation of the Potential Role of the Physician in Influencing Community Exercise Behavior." *American Journal of Health Promotion* 4, no. 4 (March/April): 255–59.

Haskell, W. L., C. Sims, J. Myll, F. G. Bortz, and E. L. Alderman. 1993. "Coronary Artery Size and Dilating Capacity in Ultradistance Runners." *Circulation* 87, no. 4 (April): 1076–82.

Hauri, P., and S. Linde. 1990. "Slumber Strategies." *Health* 22, no. 3 (March): 57, 88.

Health Education Reports 12, no. 8 (12 April): 5.

Kardong, D. 1987. "You Must Be Dreaming." *Runner's World*, June, 57–61.

Kasch, F. W., J. L. Boyer, S. P. Van Camp, L. S. Verity, and J. P. Wallace. 1990. "The Effect of Physical Activity and Inactivity on Aerobic Power in Older Men (a Longitudinal Study)." *Physician and Sportsmedicine* 18, no. 4 (April): 73–83.

Kasper, M. J. 1990. "Emphasis on Cardiovascular Fitness As a Barrier Toward Mobilizing the Sedentary Individual." *Health Education* 21, no. 4 (July/August): 41–45.

King, A. C. Taylor, C. Barr, and W. L. Haskell. 1993. "Effects of Differing Intensities and Formats of 12 Months of Exercise Training on Psychological Outcomes in Older Adults." *Health Psychology* 12, no. 4 (July): 292–300.

Lamberg, L. 1989. "Voyeurs in the Kingdom of Sleep." *Health* 21, no. 7 (July): 66–69.

Malanka, P. 1990. "Aerobics Rebound." *Health* 22, no. 3 (March): 59–65.

McGlynn, G. 1993. *Dynamics of Fitness.* Dubuque, Iowa: Wm. C. Brown.

Owens, S. G., A. Al-Ahmed, and R. J. Moffatt. 1989. "Physiological Effects of Walking and Running with Hand-Held Weights." *Journal of Sports Medicine and Physical Fitness* 29, no. 4 (December): 384–87.

Paffenbarger, R. S., R. T. Hyde, A. L. Wing, and C. C. Hseih. 1986. "Physical Activity, All-Cause Mortality, and Longevity of College Alumni." 1986. *New England Journal of Medicine* 314, no. 10 (6 March): 605–13.

Phillips, P. 1990. "Modest Exercise Program Proven to Cut Risk of CVD." *Medical World News* 31, no. 5 (12 March): 20.

"Physical Exercise: An Important Factor for Health." 1990. *Physician and Sportsmedicine* 18, no. 3 (March): 155–56.

Powers, S. K., and E. T. Howley. 1990. *Exercise Physiology.* Dubuque, Iowa: Wm. C. Brown, 88.

Promoting Health/Preventing Disease: Year 2000 Objectives for the Nation. 1990. Washington, D.C.: U.S. Department of Health and Human Services.

"Running Shoes." 1992. *Consumer Reports on Health* 4, no. 1 (January): 5.

Rutherford, W. J., C. B. Corbin, and L. A. Chase. 1992. "Factors Influencing Intrinsic Motivation Towards Physical Activity." *Health Values* 16, no. 5 (September/October): 19–24.

Sacks, M. H. 1993. "Exercise for Stress Control." In Mind Body Medicine, edited by Daniel Goleman and Joel Gurin. New York: Consumer Reports Books.

"Safe Alternatives to 10 Risky Exercises." 1993. *Consumer Reports on Health* 5, no. 9 (September): 100–101.

Sallis, J. F. 1986. "Exercise Adherence and Motivation." *Focal Points* no. 2:3.

Samples, P. 1990. "Exercise Encouraged for People with Arthritis." *Physician and Sportsmedicine* 18, no. 1 (January): 123–27.

Sheehan, G. 1978. *Running and Being.* New York: Simon & Schuster.

Shephard, R. J. 1989. "Nutritional Benefits of Exercise." *Journal of Sports Medicine and Physical Fitness* 29, no. 1 (March): 83–88.

"Shoes for Sports: Choose Carefully." 1986. *Better Health* 3, no. 4 (April): 1–2.

Terry, P. E. 1993. "Editor's Comment." *American Journal of Health Promotion* 7, no. 4 (March/April): 305–6.

"The Best Workout: Free Weights vs. Machines." 1993. *University of California Berkeley Wellness Letter* 9, no. 6 (March): 6.

"These Shoes Are Made for Walking." 1990. *Consumer Reports* 55, no. 2 (February): 88–93.

"USA Snapshots: Low-Income Groups Exercise Less." 1993. *USA Today,* 8 September, 1D.

Vaitkevicius, P. V., J. L. Fleg, J. H. Engle, F. C. O'Connor, J. G. Wright, L. E. Lakatta, F. C. P. Yin, and E. G. Lakatta. 1993. "Effects of Age and Aerobic Capacity on Arterial Stiffness in Healthy Adults." *Circulation* 88, no. 4 (October): 1456–62.

"Vigorous Activity Among High School Students." 1992. *Morbidity and Mortality Weekly Report* 41, no. 3 (24 January): 33–35.

"Which Exercise Is Best for You?" 1994. *Consumer Reports on Health* 6, no. 4 (April): 37–40.

Williams, M. H. 1990. *Lifetime Fitness and Wellness.* Dubuque, Iowa: Wm. C. Brown.

Zohman, L. R. 1983. *Exercise Your Way to Fitness and Heart Health.* CPC International.

ADDITIONAL READINGS

Bloch, G. B. 1990. "The Thinking Woman's Workout." *Health* 22, no. 1 (January): 56–58+. Describes a "hot" trend in health clubs called "interval circuit training" (ICT). The routine enhances many components of fitness.

Desharnais, R., J. Jobin, C. Cote, L. Levesque, and G. Godin. 1993. "Aerobic Exercise and the Placebo Effect: A Controlled Study." *Psychosomatic Medicine* 55, no. 2 (March/April): 149–54. Explains the results of a study designed to see if the placebo effect is involved in the exercise and psychological enhancement connection.

"How to Start an Exercise Habit You Can Stick With." 1993. *Consumer Reports on Health* 5, no. 7 (July): 69–71. Provides a guide to getting a workout that won't seem like work. Gives practical hints for starting a program and ways to track your progress.

Oman, R., and E. McAuley. 1993. "Intrinsic Motivation and Exercise Behavior." *Journal of Health Education* 24, no. 4 (July/August): 232–38. Gives the results of a study designed to determine the relationship between intrinsic motivation and exercise behavior. More-successful subjects attended more frequently, perceived themselves as being more competent, experienced more enjoyment, and put forth more effort.

CHAPTER 8

Achieving and Maintaining Healthy Weight

Healthy People 2000 Objectives

• Reduce overweight to a prevalence of no more than 20 percent among people aged 20 and older and no more than 15 percent among adolescents aged 12 through 19.

• Increase to at least 50 percent the proportion of overweight people aged 12 and older who have adopted sound dietary practices combined with regular physical activity to attain an appropriate body weight.

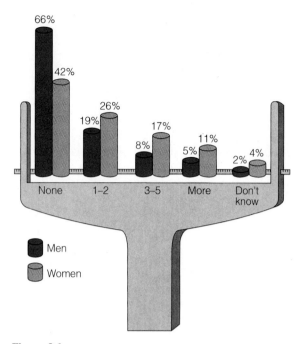

The authors of many weight control books prey upon the desire of the American public to be thin at any cost.

Figure 8.1

The number of times people tried to lose weight in 1991. Thirty-two percent of men and 54 percent of women tried to lose weight at least once during the year.

Source: Data from Bruskin/Goldring Research poll of 1,002 for Ultra Slimfast.

Many Americans strive for the "perfect" physique, as it is portrayed by the media, yet have a difficult time achieving that goal. The media have defined a norm for us that is unrealistic because very few can achieve this look, regardless of how much we diet and exercise.

Consequently, the diet business is a big one in the United States. At any given time 48 million adult Americans, including 60 percent of all adult women (DeAndrade 1993), are on a diet (see fig. 8.1), and we spend $35.8 billion annually on diet products (Thompson 1990). Ninety percent of Americans think they weigh too much (Hockey 1993) and are trying to lose an average of 30 pounds ("Losing Weight, Hot Foods, Life Expectancy" 1993). The majority of American girls have begun to diet by the time they are 13 (Stone 1993). Diet clinics are plentiful, and low-calorie foods are popular items. In fact, sales of low-calorie frozen foods have increased 15 percent each of the last several years (Hockey 1993). Fortunately, today's frozen light entrees are far more nutritious than their regular counterparts ("Frozen Light Entrees" 1993).

Despite the interest in diet products and services, very few individuals have long-term weight-control success (see figure 8.1). Only 3 to 5 percent of dieters keep off the weight they lose. Weight loss can be considered successful only when the weight is kept off for 3 to 5 years. In one survey, the average dieter regained half the weight lost in the first 6 months after ending the program and two-thirds of it in 2 years ("Washington Focus" 1993).

Americans know how to control their weight but continue to make food selections that are contradictory to weight loss. For example, many who are concerned about dietary fat or cholesterol still purchase ice cream, butter, and high-fat cheeses each week (Thompson 1990). It is important for us to internalize knowledge and modify our attitudes, if we want to change our behavior.

Authors of diet books and diet plans often take advantage of the American public's ignorance and misinformation by promising quick and easy plans that are very appealing. To effectively evaluate these plans, one must have sound knowledge of nutrition, exercise, and weight control.

One of the cultural aspects of body weight is that throughout history more emphasis has been placed on female thinness than on male thinness. The acceptable look for men has changed little over the years, while the preferred physique for women has changed every few years. The curvaceous look of Marilyn Monroe in the 1950s was followed by the skinny look of Twiggy in the 1960s. Today the athletic look of Cindy Crawford is popular, though there are some indications that the skin-and-bones look is coming back. The Barbie Doll, introduced by Mattel in 1959, depicts a physique far too slender to be healthy ("Barbie's Missing Accessory: Food" 1994).

Other cultures value a heavy physique for females because it is associated with wealth and power. Heavy women in the Yucatan are called "substantial" rather than fat. On the island of Mangaia, women are placed in "fattening" houses at puberty to ensure that they will be beautiful and can attract a spouse. Classical writings in India praise heavy women (Stone 1993).

Overweight is more prevalent in minority groups, particularly minority women, in the United States, and among the poor. In one study, 37 percent of women with incomes below the poverty level were overweight, compared with 25 percent of those above the poverty level (*Healthy People 2000* 1992).

WEIGHT CONTROL AND HEALTH

The percentage of overweight adults in the United States has steadily increased over the last several decades, making the problem of excess body fat a serious one in this country (Manson et al. 1990). Obesity affects 10 to 40 percent of schoolchildren; 80 percent of obese children become obese adults. Thirty-four million adult Americans (20% of U.S. adults) are considered obese (Manson et al. 1990).

Cosmetic reasons are often a primary motivation to lose weight. However, other factors to consider include the health risks associated with extra fat (see table 8.1). Extra body fat is associated with over twenty-six health conditions (Williams 1990), including heart disease, diabetes, hypertension, and cancer. There is definite evidence that loss of even half of one's excess weight prevents the development of type II diabetes ("Link Between Weight Loss and Diabetes II Prevention" 1992). Thin people also have a lower risk of dying. A study of male Harvard University alumni found the lowest mortality among those 20 percent below the U.S. average for men of comparable age and height ("Thin Is In" 1994).

Maintaining healthy body weight is an important factor in self-concept and emotional health, since most of us feel better physically and mentally when we attain a certain weight. In a study of freshmen female college students, a favorable body image was the only factor related to weight loss among those who lost weight (Hodge, Jackson, and Sullivan 1993). A study of 370 subjects found that overweight during adolescence has important social and economic consequences that are more important than those of many other chronic physical conditions. The researchers surmised that discrimination against overweight persons might explain these results. Women who had been overweight as adolescents had fewer years of school, were less likely to be married, had lower incomes, and had higher rates of poverty. Men who had been overweight were less likely to be married (Gortmaker et al. 1993). Positive weight-control practices enhance protective coping skills, while negative weight-control practices are very disruptive to both the mind and the body. However, knowledge about healthy weight does not always translate into maintenance of healthy weight.

There can be risks associated with dieting, however. Weight lost on a low-calorie diet might be muscle rather than fat. Loss of muscle can lower the metabolic rate, making it harder to keep weight off, since muscle tissue needs more calories to support it than fat does. Having a pattern of losing and regaining weight is especially dangerous. Participants in the Framingham Heart Study whose weight varied the most had a higher death rate than those whose weight varied the least ("Quit Watching the Scales?" 1993). Therefore, it is important to determine how great a risk your weight is and how much weight you need to lose to lower the risk. Those with diabetes and high blood pressure are especially likely to improve their health with weight loss ("Are You Eating Right?" 1992).

TABLE 8.1	RISKS OF BEING OVERWEIGHT (INCREASE IN RISK FOR DISEASE)		
	20% to 30% Overweight	40% or More Overweight	Deaths per Year
Cancer			
Male			
Colon/Rectum	26%	73%	29,100
Prostate	37%	29%	26,100
Female			
Breast	16%	53%	39,900
Cervix	51%	139%	6,800
Endometrium	85%	442%	2,900
Gallbladder	74%	258%	5,300
Ovary	0%	63%	11,600
Diabetes			
Male	156%	419%	14,859*
Female	234%	690%	21,928*
Heart Disease			
Male	32%	95%	289,461
Female	39%	107%	251,857
Stroke			
Male	17%	127%	61,697
Female	16%	52%	92,630

*This figure does not include the many diabetics who die of heart disease.

Sources: From *Journal of Chronic Diseases*, 32:563 1979; personal communication, John Lubera, American Cancer Society; Kathy Santini, National Center for Health Statistics, *Nutrition Action Healthletter*, January 1987, p. 7.

Issue

Achieving the Ideal

Americans value having a perfect body, which usually means being slim and well shaped.

- Pro: The emphasis on slimness is healthy. In view of all we know about the dangers of obesity, this cultural value makes us aware of what we eat and of the wellness we can experience if we exercise and eat correctly. We will feel better and live longer if we maintain a slim body.

- Con: The societal emphasis on slimness is based on fashion and may be the cause of much unhappiness to many individuals both over- and underweight.

What is your opinion of society's emphasis on slimness?

TABLE 8.2 ACCEPTABLE WEIGHTS FOR ADULTS

Height	Weight (lb)	
	19 to 34 Years	35 Years and Over
5'0"	97–128	108–138
5'1"	101–132	111–143
5'2"	104–137	115–148
5'3"	107–141	119–152
5'4"	111–146	122–157
5'5"	114–150	126–162
5'6"	118–155	130–167
5'7"	121–160	134–172
5'8"	125–164	138–178
5'9"	129–169	142–183
5'10"	132–174	146–188
5'11"	136–179	151–194
6'0"	140–184	155–199
6'1"	144–189	159–205
6'2"	148–195	164–210
6'3"	152–200	168–216
6'4"	156–205	173–222
6'5"	160–211	177–228
6'6"	164–216	182–234

Note: Values in this table are for height without shoes and weight without clothes.

Source: *Nutrition and Your Health: Dietary Guidelines for Americans*, 3d edition, p. 9. U.S. Department of Agriculture and U.S. Department of Health and Human Services, 1990.

OVERWEIGHT OR OVERFAT?

Determining your weight in pounds or kilograms is not necessarily the best indicator of whether or not you are overweight. It is more accurate to measure your percentage of body fat.

DETERMINING BODY WEIGHT

A traditional method of determining body weight involves the measurement of body mass by a scale. Based on this, **overweight** is defined as being 10 percent over desirable weight, and **obesity** is defined as being 20 percent over desirable weight. The reference most frequently used has been the Metropolitan Life height and weight table, in which the recommended weights are based on the mortality rates of individuals who purchase life insurance. Because this table has problems associated with it, it is being used less today. A far more accu-

overweight
Being 10 percent over desirable weight.

obesity
Being 20 percent over desirable weight.

body mass index (BMI)
Weight in kilograms divided by the square of height in meters.

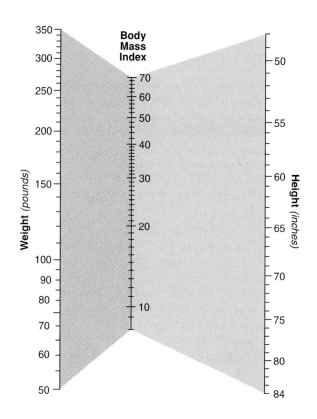

Your BMI is your weight in kilograms divided by the square of your height in meters. Because the BMI takes into account how tall you are, it's more useful than just weight in figuring out if you're too fat. Using this chart, make a mark next to your weight (without clothes) along the left-hand scale. Then make another mark next to your height (without shoes) along the right-hand scale. Draw a line connecting the marks. The point at which the line crossed the Body Mass Index scale down the middle of the chart is your BMI. The numbers on the chart have been converted to pounds and inches.

WHAT YOUR BMI MEANS

20 to 25: You're doing something right. People in this group live the longest.

26 to 30: You're overweight and have an increased risk of developing high levels of blood cholesterol, blood pressure, blood glucose, and blood insulin.

Above 30: Consider yourself obese. That makes you more susceptible to diabetes, coronary heart disease, cancer, and diseases of the digestive tract.

Below 20: You're fine . . . if you're in good physical shape and if you aren't suffering from a disease—like cancer—that's causing you to be underweight.

Figure 8.2

Body mass index.

Copyright 1993, CSPI. Adapted from *Nutrition Action Healthletter* (1875 Connecticut Ave., N.W., Suite 300, Washington, D.C. 20009-5728. $20.00 for 10 issues). Reprinted by permission.

rate chart is the one endorsed by the U.S. Department of Agriculture and the Department of Health and Human Services (see table 8.2), which provides for some weight gain as we age. There is no distinction between the weights of men and women, and there is a wide range of acceptable weights to allow for the differences in muscle and fat distribution.

Overweight and obesity can also be defined by using the **body mass index (BMI)** (see figure 8.2). In this method, weight in kilograms is divided by the square of height in meters. Males

Weight Control

Weight control is a complex experience compounded by many factors that will be described in this chapter. The purpose of this assessment tool is to examine the risk factors that lead to obesity. Often after high school, we reduce our energy expenditure, maintain our calorie consumption, and begin to gain weight gradually. This assessment helps you recognize the risks of becoming overweight in the next few years.

Biological Factors

1. By looking at your parents or grandparents when they were younger, would you say you had a genetic predisposition to obesity?
   a. yes
   b. no
   c. I don't know
2. How has your weight changed over the last 2 to 3 months?
   a. stayed the same
   b. lost some weight
   c. gained some weight
   d. up and down but basically the same
   e. I don't know
3. My metabolic rate is
   a. slow or low.
   b. fast or high.
   c. about average.
   d. I don't know.
4. Which of the following statements applies to you?
   a. I can eat a lot and not gain much weight.
   b. I eat less than those around me and still I gain weight.
   c. If I eat moderately, my weight stays about the same.

Behavioral Factors

5. Which of the following applies to you?
   a. I do not exercise regularly.
   b. I exercise some.
   c. I exercise regularly.
6. Which of the following best describe your eating habits? (Mark all that apply.)
   a. I deprive myself, then binge.
   b. I overeat regularly.
   c. I reward myself with food treats.
   d. I carefully monitor my diet and know how to count calories.
   e. I don't pay much attention to how I eat, just what comes naturally.

Psychological Factors

7. Indicate which of the following describes you. (Mark all that apply.)
   a. I have a lot of distress in my life.
   b. I am often bored.
   c. I am often lonely.
   d. I repress or can't feel emotions (such as anger, affection, fear, sadness, and so on).
   e. I tend to punish myself for my behaviors.
   f. I am often depressed.
   g. I am anxious or nervous.
   h. I am often frustrated.
   i. I feel resentment toward someone or something.
   j. I am often angry.
   k. I am defensive about my appearance or my actions.
   l. I am or was deprived of love.
   m. I am a passive person (nonassertive).
   n. I have a poor self-concept (poor self-esteem, self-worth, self-identity, self-image, self-confidence).
   o. I don't think I have a good-looking body.
   p. I don't think I am sexually attractive.

Environmental Factors

8. Which of the following applies to you?
   a. I had an unstable childhood.
   b. My family is not very supportive.
   c. My friends are not very supportive.
   d. I feel a lot of pressure to be thin and fit.

Scoring/Interpretation

Score each question as follows and then total your score.

Biological Factors

1a = 4	2c = 4	3c = 2
1b = 0	2d = 2	3d = 2
1c = 2	2e = 2	4a = 0
2a = 2	3a = 4	4b = 4
2b = 0	3b = 0	4c = 2

Behavioral Factors

5a = 4	6a = 4	6d = 0
5b = 2	6b = 4	6e = 2
5c = 0	6c = 4	

Psychological Factors
7a–p = 1 point for each response

Environmental Factors
8a–d = 3 points for each response

The areas assessed are all risk factors associated with obesity. The following interpretation assesses risk for each area (biological, behavioral, psychological, and environmental) and gives an overall risk assessment.

Biological
11 or more	=	high risk
6–10	=	moderate risk
0–5	=	low risk

Behavioral
12 or more	=	high risk
7–11	=	moderate risk
0–6	=	low risk

Psychological
11 or more	=	high risk
6–10	=	moderate risk
0–5	=	low risk

Environmental
8 or more	=	high risk
4–7	=	moderate risk
0–3	=	low risk

Overall Risk (total all scores)
40 or more	=	high risk
20–39	=	moderate risk
0–19	=	low risk

are considered overweight with a body mass index equal to or greater than 27.8; females are considered overweight with a body mass index equal to or greater than 27.3 (*Healthy People 2000* 1992). Individuals are considered obese at a body mass index of 30 (Wardlaw and Insel 1990). Low risk for mortality is associated with an index between 25 and 30, moderate risk for mortality is associated with an index between 30 and 40, and high risk for mortality is associated with a body mass index above 40. Twenty-five percent of American women 35 to 64 years old have a body mass index of 29 or higher (Vanitallie 1990).

The difficulty with using body mass as a determinant of weight is that there is no means of determining the proportion of pounds that are fat (adipose tissue) and the proportion that are lean tissue (muscle, cartilage, skin, bone, connective tissue, and nerves). Persons considered overweight according to the charts often do have a high amount of body fat. However, individuals with a high percentage of lean tissue (such as bodybuilders or football players) would also be classified by the charts as being overweight, even though most of the weight is from lean tissue. On the other hand, some people with a low percentage of lean tissue might not be classified as overweight because they fall within the normal range of the charts. A more accurate measurement assesses the percentage of body fat.

DETERMINING BODY COMPOSITION

Body composition is the percentage of fat versus the percentage of lean tissue, with body fat classified as essential fat or storage fat. Essential fat is necessary for staying alive and for maintaining normal body functioning. It is stored in the heart, lungs, muscle, bone, liver, spleen, kidneys, intestines, and central nervous system. Women usually have higher levels of essential fat (12 percent) than men (3 percent) to accommodate hormonal and reproductive functions.

Storage fat is the extra fat maintained by the body in the fat cells. Once the fat cells are formed, they never disappear; but they shrink in size when the amount of storage fat is lower (Wardlaw and Insel 1990). Because fat cells never disappear, fat babies often become fat adults. The location of this fat varies in each individual, although men tend to store extra fat in their midsection, and women tend to store fat in their buttocks, hips, and thighs prior to menopause. After menopause women tend to store fat in the abdomen. The waist-to-hip ratio is important, because there is a correlation between disease and fat stored in the midsection. It is thought that abdominal fat moves quickly to the liver, where the fat is changed to products that can raise blood cholesterol levels. In addition, abdominal fat cells are likely to be larger in size than regular fat cells. Large fat cells are linked with rises in blood sugar levels and blood pressure ("Quit

body composition
The percentage of fat versus lean tissue.

PERSONAL SKILLS AND EXPERIENCES

Compute Your Waist-to-Hip Ratio

1. Compute your waist-to-hip ratio by dividing the waist measurement by the hip measurement—for example, 30 ÷ 40 = .75.
2. A ratio above .80 for females and above .95 for males may put individuals at risk for heart disease, high blood pressure, and diabetes.

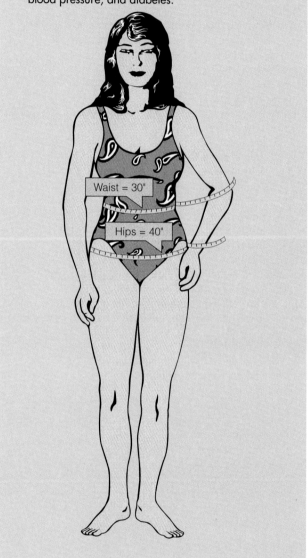

Watching the Scales?" 1993). However, weight in the midsection is easier to lose than weight around the hips and thighs (Schardt 1993). The waist-to-hip ratio can be computed by dividing the waist measurement by the hip measurement (see the Personal Skills and Experiences box). A ratio above .80 for females and above .95 for males may put individuals at risk for a number of diseases, including heart disease, high blood pressure, and diabetes (Thompson 1990).

Some storage fat is needed to protect the internal organs and insulate the body from cold, but it is not needed in excess amounts. Most experts recommend that body fat should not exceed 10 to 20 percent for males and 15 to 25 percent for females (Powers and Howley 1990). In one study researchers were commissioned to estimate average body fat based on data compiled by the National Institute of Health Information. It was found that average body fat for women is 31 percent, which is above the optimal range, and the average for men is 19 percent, which is within the optimal range ("How Fat Is America?" 1992). Problems associated with excess weight usually are associated with excess amounts of storage fat. The goal of weight-loss programs should be the reduction of storage fat, not the reduction of muscle or lean tissue.

One of the most precise ways of determining body fat is **hydrostatic weighing,** also known as underwater weighing. The results of hydrostatic weighing indicate overall density compared to water and are a comparison of body weight to body volume. The density figure determined by hydrostatic weighing is used in a specific calibration to determine the percentage of body fat (fig. 8.3). Underwater weighing is a precise method of determining body fat that requires a laboratory and expensive equipment, which are not readily available to most individuals. It is the criterion against which all other methods are compared.

The **skinfold technique** is the most common method for determining the percentage of body fat. Calipers are used to measure the amount of **subcutaneous fat** (fat beneath the skin). Approximately 50 percent of the body's fat is located beneath the skin, so the percentage of body fat can be estimated from these measurements. There are numerous sites that can be measured, including the abdomen, the back of the upper arm, the thigh, and the back. This technique is subject to error because of the difficulty in obtaining accurate measurements. However, measurements from three or four sites on different areas of the body provide a more precise percentage than do measurements from one or two sites. Dehydration can affect the results by 10 to 15 percent (McGlynn 1993).

There are several other techniques for evaluating body fat that are usually found in research settings. These include total-body electrical conductivity (TOBEC), bioelectrical impedance analysis (BIA), computer tomography, nuclear magnetic resonance, and infrared.

Although there is no single authoritative source for determining the gradations of fat based on body composition, references for these definitions are provided in table 8.3.

hydrostatic weighing
Underwater weighing, indicating overall body density compared to water density, and body weight compared to body volume.

skinfold technique
The use of calipers to measure the amount of subcutaneous fat to determine percent body fat.

subcutaneous fat
Fat beneath the skin.

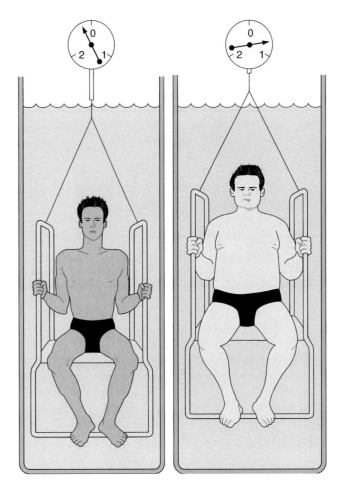

Figure 8.3
The underwater weighing method of estimating body density and proportion of fat to lean tissue. The scale weights of these two men are the same; under water, however, the leaner man on the left is shown to weigh *more* than the fatter man on the right, because lean tissue is heavier than water.

Calipers are used to measure subcutaneous fat.

TABLE 8.3	BODY FAT SCORE			
Male Percentage of Body Fat	Fitness Level	Female Percentage of Body Fat	Fitness Level
10	Very Lean	13	Very Lean
11–12		13–15	
12–14	Lean	17–18	Lean
14–15		18–22	
15–17	Acceptable	22–28	Acceptable
17–18	Fat	28–30	Fat
20+	Obese	30+	Obese

From George McGlynn, *Dynamics of Fitness.* Copyright © 1993 Wm. C. Brown Communications, Inc., Dubuque, Iowa. All Rights Reserved. Reprinted by permission.

FACTORS AFFECTING OBESITY

Several theories have been developed to explain the possible causes of obesity. These include explanations in terms of heredity, exercise, eating habits, fat-cell theory, and set point theory.

HEREDITY

There is increasing evidence of a genetic basis for body fatness. For years, heavy individuals have been told they weren't working hard enough to keep off the fat. This might not have been accurate, as they may have a genetic susceptibility to obesity and may have to work harder than individuals of normal weight to weigh less. Their distribution of body fat may closely resemble the distribution of fat in their biological parents (Nash 1987). For example, a female whose mother has large arms is also likely to have large arms. Researchers studying identical twins concluded that genetic influences on body mass index are substantial and that the childhood environment has little or no influence on this (Stunkard et al. 1990). Scientists studying the long-term effects of overfeeding in identical twins attributed the similarity of weight gain and fat distribution in the twins to genetic factors (Bouchard et al. 1990).

The genetic link to obesity is not a guarantee that individuals with a family history of obesity will always be heavy. They can attain lower fat levels and lower body weight.

EXERCISE

Exercise plays an important role in maintaining healthy weight, and it might be the most important key in this process. Exercise must be done on a regular basis, for the results to be permanent.

People who have a history of obesity in their family may want to watch their weight carefully.

Energy is supplied to the body through food in the form of calories. One pound of body fat contains approximately 3,500 calories. If more calories are consumed than are burned, fat is gained. Conversely, if fewer calories are consumed than are burned, weight is lost. Exercise is the only safe thing that can be done to increase the number of calories that are burned ("Diet vs. Exercise: What's Best?" 1992). Exercise raises the basal metabolic rate (the speed at which your body burns its fuel). Therefore, there is a double benefit from exercise—the burning of calories during exercise and the increase in the rate at which calories are burned after exercise (table 8.4).

In addition to exercise, individual activity levels are also important. You can increase your activity levels by changing many of your simple daily habits—for instance, walking stairs instead of taking the elevator, or parking at the far end of the parking lot instead of near the door. Avoid labor-saving devices, like self-propelled vacuum cleaners, because in saving you a little labor they decrease your caloric output.

TABLE 8.4 CALORIES BURNED PER HOUR BY SELECTED ACTIVITIES

Activity	Body Weight		
	100 lb	150 lb	200 lb
Mopping floors	144	216	288
Swimming (20 yd/min)	192	288	384
Tennis (beginner)	192	288	384
Weeding	228	342	456
Golf (carrying clubs)	270	405	540
Aerobic dancing (low impact)	276	414	552
Walking (4.5 mph)	288	432	576
Snow shoveling	312	468	624
Calisthenics	360	540	720
Jogging (5 mph)	360	540	720
Aerobic dancing (high impact)	372	558	744
Bicycling (13 mph)	426	639	852
Swimming (55 yd/min)	528	792	1056
Cross-country skiing (8 mph)	624	936	1248
Running (8 mph)	624	936	1248

Get in Shape, Stay in Shape "Calories Burned per Hour" copyright 1989 by Consumers Union of U.S., Inc., Yonkers, NY 10703–1057. Excerpted by permission from *CONSUMER REPORTS BOOKS*, 1989.

HEALTH UPDATE

When to Exercise?

One of the most important factors related to exercise is doing it on a regular basis. The best time to exercise is whenever you can. To lose weight, however, the best time to exercise is either before breakfast or before dinner. Exercising before breakfast is recommended because the levels of insulin in the blood are low, causing the body to burn fat rather than carbohydrates. You might want to have a small amount to eat before exercising so you don't become dizzy. Exercising before dinner can suppress the appetite and might relieve stress—which can be especially beneficial to weight control, since many individuals eat to relieve stress.

EATING HABITS

The foods we eat are an important factor in weight control. It has been shown in research that diet is even more important than previously thought. For years it has been thought that fat individuals craved the sugar in certain foods, but they might be craving the fat in food. A study in which participants rated the taste of milkshake-like drinks showed that obese individuals preferred drinks higher in fat and lower in sugar than those preferred by individuals of normal weight (Drewnoski et al. 1985). Other researchers have shown that overweight individuals like food that is flavorful and highly textured in addition to being high in fat (Simon 1989). Individuals who enjoy these qualities in food may find themselves dissatisfied when they severely reduce their calories. One solution is to learn to cook foods that are low in fat and calories, yet flavorful.

The fact that obese persons might crave fat is even more problematic considering that fat provides energy in a form the body most readily stores rather than burns. The energy in complex carbohydrates is almost never turned into body fat (Barnett 1986).

It is important to eat small, frequent meals in order to regulate the production of insulin. Insulin is responsible for fat storage and the production of body fat (Hockey 1993). If large meals are consumed, more insulin is produced to accommodate the extra calories and to store body fat. This becomes a vicious circle, because increased insulin levels result in decreased blood glucose levels, and when blood glucose levels fall we feel tired and hungry and have a desire to eat.

The psychological factors associated with eating can also be a problem. For many of us, food is a center of the social events in life and can be associated with celebrating good times as well as surviving bad times. Our desire for food can become very destructive if it becomes the focus of life and eating is used as a coping mechanism.

There is some evidence that personality type is a factor in food selection. Extroverts might have a more difficult time with weight management than introverts because they are stimulated by external stimuli.

Alcohol might play an important role in weight control. Researchers have found that alcohol makes the body burn fat more slowly and throws off the body's normal disposal of fat. The fat that is not burned is stored in the areas where individuals tend to put on weight. Participants in one study consumed 3 ounces of pure alcohol a day and burned about one-third less fat (Suter, Schutz, and Jequier 1992).

FAT-CELL THEORY

Adipose tissue is increased when existing fat cells fill with fat (**fat-cell hypertrophy**) and when the total number of fat cells increases (fat-cell hyperplasia). Proponents of the fat-cell theory hypothesize that obese individuals have more and larger adipose cells. There is disagreement over whether the number of fat cells becomes fixed early in life or whether the number can continue to increase throughout life. Once the

adipose tissue
Body tissue composed of fat cells.

fat-cell hypertrophy
The filling of fat cells with fat.

fat cells develop, they never decrease in number, but they can shrink in size if the stores of extra fat are decreased. Extra fat cells might influence the body to keep the cells full in an attempt to prevent the body from going into a state that it perceives as starvation (Nash 1987).

SET POINT THEORY

Set point theory is based on the concept that the body has an internal control mechanism that helps it maintain a certain level of body fat. This would explain why weight tends to return to a certain level after a loss or gain in pounds. The impact of dieting on metabolism supports this theory. Extreme restriction of calories depresses resting metabolism by as much as 45 percent (Katch and McArdle 1987). Since dieting alone may slow metabolism and inhibit efforts to lose weight, it is ineffective. The one thing that can lower the set point is regular aerobic exercise. The difference between thin individuals and many heavy individuals might be thin individuals' higher activity levels, not their lower caloric intake.

It appears that individuals who have the most difficult time attaining and maintaining normal weight are those who were obese as children (Nash 1987). It is important to prevent children from becoming obese. Rather than initiating rigid diets, it is better to serve healthy, low-fat meals, encourage physical activity, serve as a positive role model, and limit TV time ("Teen Obesity: A Heavy Burden Even in Adulthood" 1993). Adolescents spend an average of 20 hours a week watching television, and when doing so they go into a deeply relaxed state in which caloric expenditure is less than for ordinary sitting ("Concern for Couch Spuds" 1993). In addition, most adolescents do not have adequate knowledge to make healthy dietary changes (Perry-Hunnicutt and Newmann 1993).

SUCCESSFUL TECHNIQUES FOR ACHIEVING AND MAINTAINING HEALTHY WEIGHT

Exercise and diet are the primary factors in maintaining healthy weight. Achieving and maintaining healthy weight requires lifestyle changes and a lifelong commitment to these changes.

THE ROLE OF DIET

Some people who go on diets consider them to be temporary eating plans that must be tolerated for several days or weeks until a few pounds are shed. And, unfortunately, the reward some choose for themselves for having completed their diet is to go on an eating binge.

Our approach to diets must be changed, to have any hope of long-term success with weight loss. A "diet" must be permanent changes in eating habits. Don't waste time on dieting if you aren't committed to maintaining a healthy weight throughout your life. Individuals who are continually dieting and allowing their weight to yo-yo may be causing

some of the health problems previously blamed on obesity ("Fear of Fat" 1985). The negative health effects of losing and regaining weight are most obvious in individuals 30 to 44 years of age (Lissner et al. 1991).

If you repeatedly diet, you might actually cause your body to become fatter (Liebman 1987) and make it harder for you to lose weight (Stone 1993). When your body is continually denied food through dieting, its metabolism slows down as if it were reacting to a famine. Your body learns to gain weight back quickly and hold on to it when food supplies are next denied. There are also indications that regained weight contains a higher percentage of body fat ("Fear of Fat" 1985). There is no reason for you to diet unless you are going to permanently change your eating habits; otherwise you will just regain the weight.

Also consider your seasonal eating patterns. One research study found that humans, like animals, consume more calories in the fall than in other seasons. Those in the study consumed an average of 222 additional calories per day. We might have some physiological need to eat more in the fall even though we don't increase our activity level ("Falling Leaves, Rising Calories" 1992).

Food Selection

If you want to change your eating habits, you must pay close attention to the amounts and kinds of foods you eat. Good nutrition should be your first consideration when you contemplate reducing your weight. Here are some of the reasons:

1. It is more difficult to make nutritious food selections when you are consuming fewer calories.
2. By learning to select nutritious foods, you will be making an easy transition from weight loss to weight maintenance.
3. Poor nutrition during weight reduction can have serious, and even fatal, results.
4. Nutritional choices are especially important when nutritional needs are high, as during pregnancy.
5. Food choices can affect factors that influence weight control, such as diuresis, appetite, and satiety (Nicholas and Dwyer 1986).

A balanced diet should limit the intake of fat and simple carbohydrates. It should not exceed the recommended amount of protein (12 percent of total calories).

Calories consumed from products high in fat are more likely to be converted into fat than are calories consumed from carbohydrates or protein (Gurin 1989). Individuals who have a high-fat diet are more likely to be fat than are individuals who consume less fat. Become aware of food preparation

---

set point theory
The theory that the body has an internal control mechanism that helps it maintain a certain level of body fat.

PERSONAL INSIGHT

Weight Control

We all have friends who have struggled with maintaining healthy weight. The following is a description of the experiences of two of my friends.

I have known my friend Evad for years. When I first met him, he was heavy but not obese. Evad enjoys eating and especially likes lots of fatty foods high in calories. Therefore, it was not surprising to see that he was heavy. One day Evad announced he was going to lose weight before he went to his high school reunion. His friends were pleased to hear this and supported his efforts.

What I soon learned was that Evad was a yo-yo dieter. Over the years his weight has fluctuated by over 40 pounds. Evad's motivation for losing weight always coincides with some special event like his high school reunion. However, as soon as the event is over, Evad's weight goes up. Evad recently lost 28 pounds. As you might guess, there is another big event coming up in his life.

Another friend, AnnaMarie, has been heavy for years. Two years ago she decided to make some significant changes in her life. She began a weight-loss program using one of the expensive commercial programs. At the same time, she started a personal exercise program with a trainer. She lost lots of weight, bought all new clothes, and looked great. Now AnnaMarie has regained all of the weight she lost, and more, and cannot wear any of the new clothes she bought.

Although AnnaMarie and Evad want to be slender, they have not made permanent changes in their lives. The commitment to maintaining healthy weight has to be permanent, for weight loss to be permanent. Anyone can lose weight, but the challenge is in keeping off the weight.

A Dream Drug for Dieters

A new drug, Orlistat, has the potential of reducing fat intake by up to 270 calories a day. It does this by preventing some fat from entering the bloodstream. The action of two key enzymes in the digestive tract is partially blocked, preventing the breakdown and use of some dietary fat. Orlistat blocks approximately 30 percent of the fat ingested, regardless of how much is ingested.

The drug has been effective only when accompanied by significant changes in diet and exercise. Orlistat will most likely be limited to the morbidly obese when it does become available by prescription. Negative side effects include greasier stools and diarrhea (Elmer-Dewitt 1993).

Source: From Phillip Elmer-Dewitt, "Cake Eater's Dream?" in *Time* 142(4):54 (July 26, 1993).

methods and avoid fried foods, sauces, and creamed dishes. Condiments such as butter and sour cream can more than double the calories in a food item.

To consume adequate nutrients and to prevent your metabolism from slowing significantly, don't eat fewer than 1,000 to 1,200 calories per day. Caloric intake below that amount will likely prevent you from consuming enough food to get the nutrients you need.

Goals

One of the biggest frustrations of trying to lose weight is the amount of time it takes. It doesn't matter that the extra pounds and fat were added over several months or years.

When we are ready to lose weight, we want it off yesterday. Therefore, it is important to set realistic goals. Do not plan to lose more than ½ to 1 pound per week, because weight loss is more likely to be permanent if weight is lost slowly. Any diet that promises more weight loss in a week is not a good one. Keep in mind that the weight-loss process isn't always steady, and you might encounter several plateaus (periods when no weight loss occurs).

Changing Attitudes and Behaviors

If you are interested in permanent weight control, you might find it helpful to review your attitudes toward food and eating and determine the prompts that cause you to eat, since food is often eaten in response to factors other than hunger. Identifying those factors, and when and why they occur, will give you an opportunity to replace them with other behaviors as part of your behavior modification process.

One of the easiest permanent changes you must make in order to be certain of long-term success with weight control relates to the feeling of hunger. The strategy involves getting your brain to tell you that you feel full, so that you will eat less. After you have eaten something, the satiety center, located in the hypothalamus in your brain, will send you a signal that you are full. But there is a 20-minute delay from the time you eat to the time you get that signal. So, by drinking or eating something 20 to 30 minutes before mealtime, you can activate your satiety center and feel full by the time you are having your meal—and consequently you will eat less. There is no magical food that has to be eaten to cause this reaction—anything, including a glass of water or a piece of fruit, will do.

When you decrease the number of calories you consume, you must make better nutritional decisions. It is easier to get the nutrients you need when you consume several thousand calories per day, and harder when you consume

PERSONAL SKILLS AND EXPERIENCES

Suggestions for Modifying Your Behavior to Lose Weight

Food Purchasing
1. Plan meals in advance. Buy only what is on your list.
2. Don't shop when you are hungry.
3. Buy low-calorie snack foods.
4. Make nutritious food selections that include many complex carbohydrates.

Food Preparation
1. Don't sample foods while you are preparing them.
2. Prepare only the amount you need.
3. Put food on dinner plates in the kitchen rather than using serving plates on the table.
4. Use small plates.
5. Do not add high-fat items, such as sauces, to foods.

Eating
1. Drink a glass of water 30 minutes before eating.
2. Always eat in the same place.
3. Cut your food into small pieces.
4. Eat slowly.
5. Review the food selections at a party before eating anything.

Activity
1. Walk whenever possible. Be sure to wear comfortable shoes that provide support.
2. Look for ways to get more exercise in your daily activities. Take the stairs rather than the elevator, and park at the far end of the parking lot.
3. Schedule a time for activity each day. Start slowly and set realistic goals.
4. Substitute another behavior for eating at break times.

fewer. The Personal Skills and Experiences box on modifying your behavior to lose weight lists changes you might need to make when you are shopping, eating, and exercising, to achieve and maintain healthy weight.

Behavior modification is a requirement of any successful weight-loss program. It might seem simple to change your behavior so you eat less food, but the behavior modification process involved in weight control is far more difficult. This is most likely explained by the fact that our bodies have a biological resistance to losing weight, which also helps explain why individuals on very low-calorie diets who don't exercise regularly regain most of the weight they lose through dieting (Gurin 1989).

THE ROLE OF EXERCISE

Exercise plays a very important role in losing pounds and in keeping them off. Researchers who compared the effects of weight loss by diet only and by exercise only found that the group that was only exercising lost a higher percentage of calories from fat and had more success keeping off the weight than did the group that was only dieting (Liebman 1987).

Moderate exercise will suppress appetite, rather than increase it. You might want to exercise immediately before a meal to take advantage of that effect.

Another benefit of exercise is that it strengthens muscle tissue. Muscle tissue requires more calories than fat tissue does to maintain itself, so there is the added benefit that you will be burning additional calories as the percent of lean tissue increases. This is very important, because our resting metabolic rate accounts for approximately 70 percent of the calories we burn. We lose approximately one half pound of

Exercise burns calories and raises the metabolic rate.

muscle each year we age. It is important to maintain that lean muscle tissue through exercise as we get older. Although one type of tissue cannot change into another type of tissue (e.g., fat cannot change into muscle), fat cells can decrease in size as fat stores are decreased.

THE WINNING COMBINATION

The ultimate goal of any weight-loss program should be the loss of body fat, not just body weight. Those who combine diet and exercise lose more fat ("Exercise and Diet in Weight Loss" 1990) and are more likely to keep it off. In a comparison of average weight lost by groups, those who combined diet and exercise lost 13 pounds of fat tissue and gained 1 pound of lean tissue. Those who only dieted lost 9.3 pounds of fat tissue and lost 2.4 pounds of lean tissue (Rosato 1990). Keep in mind that it is desirable to increase lean tissue, because it burns more calories than fatty tissue. Exercise and sound eating habits will result in a steady weight loss that can be maintained on a permanent basis if you maintain your exercise and dietary changes.

You might fail to lose weight if you underestimate your calories consumed and overestimate your amount of exercise. In a study of ten obese individuals, the average subject underestimated food intake and overestimated physical activity by 50 percent ("Count Your Calories Carefully" 1993). These miscalculations can be due to denial about how difficult it is to lose weight rather than lack of knowledge ("But I Eat Like a Bird . . ." 1993). However, the tracking of exercise and diet in other studies of slim individuals has resulted in similar findings. Miscalculations can be a result of misjudging portions, underestimating calories in small amounts of high-fat, high-calorie foods (Alvarado 1993), and misjudging the calories in toppings and condiments (figure 8.4). Ads for fad diets claim large amounts of immediate weight loss, but much of this weight is from body fluids and lean tissue.

ASSESSING WEIGHT-CONTROL METHODS

There are lots of schemes for losing weight. The creators of these diets attempt to scientifically explain why their particular diet plan should work when others have not. When you consider that nearly 90 percent of Americans think they are overweight and 80 percent of fourth-grade girls are dieting, it is apparent that Americans need to be educated about sound methods for losing weight.

Recently, liquid diets have become more popular among those trying to lose weight. Sales of these products had slipped considerably after they were reviewed by the Federal Trade Commission in 1991. Some explanations for the return to popularity of liquid diets include celebrity endorsements and the increases in sales of all of these products when a new one is introduced. However, there is no scientific evidence to show that these products are any more successful now than they were before (Thomas 1993).

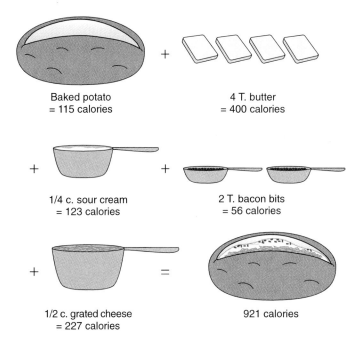

Baked potato = 115 calories

4 T. butter = 400 calories

1/4 c. sour cream = 123 calories

2 T. bacon bits = 56 calories

1/2 c. grated cheese = 227 calories

921 calories

Figure 8.4
The high-calorie baked potato.

It is impossible to evaluate all of the weight-control plans, because of the vast number available to the public. Some of these are very inexpensive; others are very costly. The cost of a 12-week outpatient weight-loss program can range from $108 to $2,120 (Speilman et al. 1992). Dieters on a variety of weight-loss programs did not rate any program better than the others. However, dieters who chose Weight Watchers were significantly more satisfied than those who chose another plan (Hellmich 1993). When contemplating a weight-control plan, consider the following:

1. Does it include a balanced diet with foods from all food groups?
2. Are the recommended foods easy to locate?
3. Are the recommended foods more expensive than regular foods?
4. Are the recommended foods ones the entire family can eat?
5. Are the recommended foods ones you would want to continue eating after the weight is lost?
6. Does the plan suggest some magical chemical combination that will burn off fat?
7. Does the plan suggest that calories don't count?
8. Is any mention made of evaluating body fat?
9. Is exercise a part of the plan?
10. Does the plan recommend exercise at least three times per week?
11. Does the plan suggest changing diet and exercise habits on a permanent basis?
12. Will anyone benefit financially through the sale of this plan?

If you answered yes to numbers 1, 2, 4, 5, 8, 9, 10, and 11, and no to numbers 3, 6, 7, and 12, you may have found a good weight-control plan. If not, you may wish to reconsider.

HIGH-RISK WEIGHT-LOSS PROCEDURES

Some people are so desperate to lose weight that they will try anything, including procedures that might injure their health. These procedures include insertion of a gastric balloon, gastroplasty (stomach stapling), intestinal bypass, jaw wiring, and liposuction. Except for liposuction, surgical procedures for weight loss are rarely done, though there is some indication of an increase in gastrointestinal surgery for severe obesity ("Obesity Surgery Regaining Favor" 1991). Unfortunately, these procedures don't teach good nutritional or exercise practices.

WHAT'S RIGHT FOR YOU?

Sometimes it's tough to know where and how to start a weight-control plan. The following suggestions provide some guidance.

- *Decide on a strategy.* First decide if you have a need and a desire to lose weight. Most individuals aren't at medical risk from extra poundage but are concerned about how they look. A high waist-to-hip ratio and medical problems related to excess weight are good reasons to lose weight. If you don't have a strong desire to lose weight, or if you look at a diet as just another temporary activity, it might be best for you to forget weight loss until you are seriously committed to making permanent changes.
- *Do some self-assessment.* Figure out what your favorite foods are and what activities you enjoy enough to do them on a regular basis. Do some reading. Go to the library and see what diet books are available. Look for one that takes a practical approach and includes exercise along with eating a variety of foods, limiting the intake of fat to at most 30 percent of total calories.
- *Review your diet history.* Do you occasionally gain just a few pounds and need only minor adjustments? Or is your weight out of control, giving you a need for a more formalized program? Choose a program that includes activity, teaches how to make wise food selections, and encourages behavior modification techniques. Some programs, such as TOPS (Take Off Pounds Sensibly), offer an inexpensive support group, while others are high-priced programs. A medically supervised program is recommended for individuals who have more than 50 pounds to lose, have a family history of obesity, and have health problems such as diabetes (Hamilton 1990).
- *Ensure your success.* Figure out what will help you be successful. Some of the things you can do include these:
  1. Set achievable goals. Aim to lose a realistic amount of weight, in a realistic amount of time. Plan to lose no more than one half to one pound each week, and be prepared for some plateaus along the way.

Issue

Regulation of Weight-Loss Facilities

Weight-loss facilities are under no regulatory commission. Some people feel there should be certain guidelines regarding the employees these facilities hire and the methods they endorse.

- Pro: Issues related to the health concerns of the population should be regulated. It is unthinkable that these businesses are under no guidelines.
- Con: This is a free country, and individuals in business should be able to do whatever they wish.

Based on the information from the text, which side would you support?

Issue

Liposuction

Your 14-year-old sister weighs 120 pounds and is 5 feet 4 inches tall. Although she appears small to you, she feels her thighs are too large. She has investigated liposuction and has started saving money for the procedure. She asks your advice the next time you are home.

- Pro: It is important for teenagers to have a good self-image. She should have the liposuction if it will improve her self-image.
- Con: There are too many problems associated with this procedure. Besides, she is too young, and the procedure is too expensive.

Based on the information in this chapter, what would you recommend? Why?

2. Plan a nutritious diet that includes moderate amounts of your favorite foods. Don't eliminate all of your favorite foods from your diet. Include foods that produce a feeling of fullness—for example, an orange is a better choice than orange juice because the fiber in the orange is filling and will reduce your appetite.

3. Eat a number of small meals rather than one large meal during the day. That way you will probably consume fewer calories and you will have less of a feeling of deprivation. Be sure to monitor your portion sizes carefully.

4. Keep busy and don't focus on dieting.

5. Include some type of exercise each day. Start slowly and set goals that are attainable.

6. Increase your normal level of activity. Walk briskly rather than slowly, and walk or bicycle rather than drive.

7. Reflect on your eating habits and behaviors, and don't eat unless you're hungry. Think of positive behaviors you can substitute for the old behaviors that previously influenced your eating.

8. Find others who will be supportive of your weight-loss plans.

9. Develop ways other than eating to deal with stress.

10. Think about your food decisions before social occasions. Since food is a focal point of most social gatherings, consider how to deal with that and what foods you will eat.

11. Accept some disappointments and setbacks. Reflect on why they happened and how they could have been avoided. Learn from them and go on. Dwell on your successes, not your failures.

12. Celebrate your successes—but learn to do this without food being the focal point.

SPECIAL CONCERNS FOR THOSE WHO ARE UNDERWEIGHT

Being underweight is a problem for close to 10 percent of the population (Williams 1990). Health problems associated with being underweight include, for females, the risk of delivering low-birth-weight babies, and, for females and males, surgical complications and longer recovery periods after illness. Females are considered underweight when their body fat is 12 percent or lower, and males are considered underweight when their body fat is 3 percent or lower. Underweight persons may be very concerned about their physical appearance and might feel that they look scrawny.

If you are underweight, try to determine the cause. It might be due to a medical condition, poor eating habits, nervous tension, or a genetic tendency. Once you have determined that the cause isn't medical, there are a number of things you can do:

1. Schedule regular mealtimes. You might prefer more-frequent meals of smaller portions rather than a few meals of large portions. You might be able to consume more calories in a day by doing this. Be sure to select healthy foods.

2. Increase your caloric intake by eating more complex carbohydrates. Unfortunately, people who are thin are often told to add high-calorie, high-fat foods such as milkshakes to their diet. This is bad advice; you should never add poor-quality food to your diet. The health risks associated with a high-fat diet affect the thin as well as the obese.

3. Plan regular exercise. Exercise will add contour and shape to your body by adding lean tissue. You are likely to look better and feel better when exercise is a regular part of your lifestyle.

EATING DISORDERS

Anorexia and bulimia are highly publicized **eating disorders.** Although these disorders are more frequently reported among white, upper-class females, they are increasingly being reported among minorities (Ballentine et al. 1991). Most patients with eating disorders are difficult to treat and can have chronic cases that require professional help (Yates 1990). Unfortunately there is no single approach that is effective (Gilbert 1986). Both disorders can be treated in the short run, but long-term success is not guaranteed with either (Mitchell 1990). Eating disorders are unusual in that they are the only psychiatric disorders that appear to be culturally determined by our society's preoccupation with thinness. Some speculate that the cultural obsession with thinness for women has promoted an acceptance of weight-loss programs that have created more problems than they have solved.

ANOREXIA NERVOSA

In **anorexia nervosa,** caloric intake is severely limited. Anorexia ("loss of appetite") nervosa ("of the nerves") involves the suppression of appetite rather than the loss of appetite. It has been described as self-induced starvation, or dieting gone out of control. Anorexics are focused on a goal of thinness and willingly starve themselves and overexercise to reach that goal (Bruch 1986). There was a time when individuals thought it was impossible to be too thin. We now know that being too thin can be harmful and even fatal.

Most anorexics are white females under 25 years of age who developed the condition in early adolescence or early adulthood and are from prosperous homes (Bruch 1986). Although the condition affects females 95 percent of the time, cases are reported among men, such as models, who are dependent on their thin physique for their employment. Male anorexia might be more prevalent than previously thought among college students. In an assessment of attitudes about weight and dieting among college students, 17 percent of males indicated that the most powerful fear in their lives was gaining weight or becoming fat (Collier et al. 1990). Less than 1 percent of the general population is anorexic (Williams 1992).

Weight loss in anorexics is usually achieved through fasting and extreme limitations on caloric consumption. Other methods include diuretics, laxatives, vomiting, strenuous exercise, and diet aids. Complications can result from all of these.

The body tries to maintain essential functions when calories are severely restricted. Less-vital functions will be slowed or stopped to preserve the functioning of the brain and heart. Anorexics might experience lowered body temperature, **amenorrhea** (absence of menstruation), and lowered blood pressure and respiration (fig. 8.5). Anorexia results in death in approximately 10 percent of all cases.

The anorexic may feel fat regardless of how much he or she weighs.

Although the exact cause of anorexia is unknown, it appears to involve a combination of psychological and environmental factors. The female anorexic might reject food in an attempt to avoid dealing with what she feels are society's demands that she become a superwoman. The weight loss can make the female anorexic look like a young girl, which some researchers feel is a conscious attempt to avoid dealing with issues related to intimacy and sexuality. Picky eating and digestive problems in early childhood may result in anorexia. Among college students, freshmen and seniors are more

eating disorders
Psychological disorders about food that appear to be culturally determined by our society's preoccupation with thinness.

anorexia nervosa
A condition in which the individual severely limits caloric intake due to appetite suppression; sometimes described as self-induced starvation. Can be fatal.

amenorrhea
Absence of menstruation.

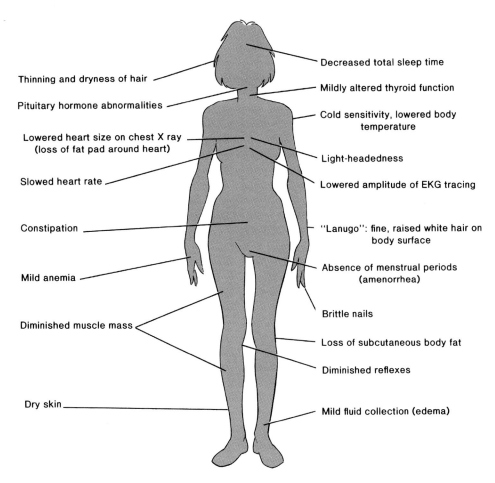

Decreased total sleep time

Mildly altered thyroid function

Cold sensitivity, lowered body temperature

Light-headedness

Lowered amplitude of EKG tracing

"Lanugo": fine, raised white hair on body surface

Absence of menstrual periods (amenorrhea)

Brittle nails

Loss of subcutaneous body fat

Diminished reflexes

Mild fluid collection (edema)

Thinning and dryness of hair

Pituitary hormone abnormalities

Lowered heart size on chest X ray (loss of fat pad around heart)

Slowed heart rate

Constipation

Mild anemia

Diminished muscle mass

Dry skin

Figure 8.5

Possible signs and symptoms accompanying weight loss in eating disorders.

Reprinted by permission. In *Eating Disorders Information Packet*, The National Anorexic Aid Society of Harding Hospital, Columbus, Ohio, 1990.

likely to report that their eating behaviors are affected by the stressful events and changes taking place in their lives. Society reinforces the perception that being slender is important. Anorexics might feel that their weight is the only factor they can control in a world where their expectations seem difficult to fulfill. A misconception of one's body size has long been considered a characteristic of anorexia; this can involve feelings about one's body that range from dissatisfaction to hatred (Cooper et al. 1987).

One of the most difficult things to understand about anorexia is the anorexic's self-perception. Regardless of how much weight has been lost, the anorexic still feels too heavy. Most anorexics continue dieting, and 79 percent still consider themselves overweight several years after hospital treatment (Yates 1990). Other characteristics of anorexia include an overly high activity level and the denial of hunger.

Many approaches are used in the treatment of anorexia, though the prognosis is not good. Drug therapy is used in 25 percent of cases, and behavior modification is used in 45 percent. A combination of approaches is also used. Most specialists recommend some period of hospitalization to ensure weight gain (Gilbert 1986) and family therapy. The prognosis for anorexics is worse than for bulimics (Mitchell 1990).

T ABLE 8.5   WARNING SIGNS

Anorexia Nervosa

Significant or extreme weight loss (at least 15%—with no known medical illness)

Reduces food intake

Develops ritualistic eating habits such as cutting up meat into extremely small bites and chewing every bite a large number of times

Denies hunger

Becomes more critical and less tolerant of others

Exercises excessively (hyperactive)

When eating, chooses low to no fat and low-calorie foods

Says he or she is too fat, even when this is not true

Has highly self-controlled behavior

Does not reveal feelings

Bulimia Nervosa

Makes excuses to go to the restroom after meals

Has mood swings

May buy large amounts of food and then it suddenly disappears

Unusual swelling around the jaw

Weight may be within normal range

Frequently eats large amounts of food, often high in calories (a binge) and does not seem to gain weight

May decide to purchase large quantities of food and eat it on the spur of the moment

Laxative or diuretic wrappers found frequently in the trash can

Unexplained disappearance of food in the home or residence hall setting

Binge Eating Disorder

Frequently eats a large amount of food that is larger than most people would eat during a similar amount of time

Eats rapidly

Eats to a point that is uncontrollably full

Often eats alone

Shows irritation and disgust with self after overeating

Does not use methods to purge

Additional Signs of Related Eating Disorders

Makes excuses to skip meals and does not eat with others

Develops a tendency to be perfect in almost everything

Conversation is mostly focused on foods or around body shape

Often hears other people's problems but does not share his or her own

Is highly self-critical

Worries about what others think

Thinks about weight and body shape most of the day

Begins to isolate more from friends and family

The odor of vomit is in the bathroom regularly

Repeatedly chews and spits out food—does not swallow large amounts of food

May purge and yet not binge eat

Note: The more warning signs a person has, the higher the probability that the person has or is developing an eating disorder.

From National Eating Disorders Organization at Harding Hospital. (1994). Eating Disorder Warning Signs. In *Eating Disorders Information Packet*, Worthington, Ohio: NEDO. (For more information write NEDO, 445 E. Granville Road, Worthington, Ohio 43085, (614) 436–1112.) Reprinted by permission.

BULIMIA

Bulimia ("insatiable appetite") is characterized by binge eating. It has been confused with anorexia nervosa because periodic bingeing is common to both disorders; however, a number of the characteristics are very different. Bulimics are usually older than anorexics and may have been anorexic earlier. Whereas anorexics are obsessed with thinness, bulimics have an obsessive fear of becoming fat.

The prevalence of bulimia in the general population is 2 to 3 percent (Williams 1992), with females comprising 95 percent of all bulimics. Bulimics tend to be close to normal weight and may appear to have normal eating habits. Bulimia usually begins in adolescence or early adulthood (Brey 1992). During their secretive eating binges, bulimics may consume 10,000 or more calories within a few hours. Afterward they try to purge the food through a variety of methods, including vomiting, laxatives, diuretics, and exercise. The anorexic may use these methods to lose weight; the bulimic uses them to avoid gaining weight. After the binge and purge are completed, the bulimic may feel depressed and discouraged about the behavior.

Bulimics tend to have a pattern of restrictive dieting followed by bingeing. Overcoming bulimia requires establishing a normal eating pattern that eliminates dieting. Although bulimics can hide their eating disorder from others, they are more likely than anorexics to seek treatment; however, they might expect immediate results and become frustrated with therapy (Yates 1990). Anorexics might request treatment only when others insist upon it. Warning signs can alert family and friends to the conditions (table 8.5).

---

bulimia

A condition in which the individual periodically binges and purges, out of an obsessive fear of becoming fat.

PERSONAL SKILLS AND EXPERIENCES

What to Do If You Think a Friend Has an Eating Disorder

You may want to know what to do if you suspect a friend has an eating disorder. It is important for your friend to receive professional help. Although there are no specific procedures to follow, you might consider some of these suggestions:

1. Observe the friend's behavior.
   a. Anorexia is usually easier to spot than bulimia because of the drastic physical changes associated with anorexic weight loss. The anorexic may try to conceal the weight loss by wearing bulky clothes. The anorexic also might refuse to eat food and might withdraw from friendships and engage in wild, obsessive exercise patterns.
   b. Bulimia can be more difficult to recognize because there might not be obvious personality or physical changes. Watch for purchases of enormous quantities of foods that disappear immediately. Another clue may be regular trips to the restroom immediately after meals.

2. Express your concern and encourage the person to seek professional help.
   a. Anorexics will usually deny that there is a problem and claim that they are in total control. They might think other individuals are jealous of their ability to master their weight. It is especially important to show support and concern, even though your friend might not seem to want it.
   b. Bulimics are more likely to be receptive to your comments, though they will usually deny that there is a problem. Your expression of concern and support is extremely important.

3. If the person refuses to seek help, find assistance. Although the anorexic is more likely to require hospitalization, both the anorexic and the bulimic may need this. Some helpful resources include your instructor for this class, the student health center, the counseling department and the student services center at your school, and the county health department. Remember, it is unlikely the person will get better on her or his own.

TAKE ACTION

1. Take action to relieve psychological problems (boredom, loneliness, depression, frustration, resentment, etc.) associated with overeating by seeking professional help and taking action.

2. Develop a plan to achieve and maintain your desired body weight in a healthy way, as described in the text.

3. Think of a situation related to weight control that has caused disorganization or disruption in your life (for example, a failed diet plan or an inability to control binge eating). Develop a plan to promote resilient reintegration in your life to prevent potential health problems in the future related to weight control.

SUMMARY

1. Despite the large number of individuals trying to lose weight, only 3 percent of them achieve permanent weight loss.

2. Achieving permanent weight loss requires making permanent lifestyle changes.

3. Extra body weight is a risk factor in heart disease, hypertension, diabetes, and cancer.

4. Body composition involves the percentages of lean tissue and fat tissue.

5. Body fat can be determined by a number of methods, including hydrostatic weighing and skinfold measurement.

6. Males are considered obese when their body fat exceeds 20 percent; females are considered obese when their body fat exceeds 25 to 30 percent.

7. Possible causes of obesity relate to heredity, exercise, eating habits, fat-cell theory, and set point theory.

8. Dieting can cause our bodies to become fatter, because the body retains fat to protect itself against perceived starvation.

9. Caloric intake should not go below 1,000 to 1,200 calories; a lower caloric intake will not provide all needed nutrients.

10. The best weight-control plans combine exercise and diet.

11. Weight-control plans that promise incredible results should be carefully scrutinized.

12. Individuals with eating disorders need professional help.

COMMITMENT ACTIVITIES

1. Vending machines can be found in most buildings on a university campus. See if those on your campus contain any nutritious foods. Work with your class to develop a plan to include nutritious, low-calorie foods in the vending machines.

2. Menus in student residence halls could be modified for those who want to control their weight. Work with the dietitian to create a "diet bulletin board" that lists the calories in each food for each meal. (This might include sample food selections for those on a daily intake of 1,200 calories.)

3. Medical science is continually improving care for individuals suffering from chronic diseases. Speak with faculty from your nutrition department to see what advances may have been made during the past year. Invite someone from the nutrition department of your school or from the local health department to speak to your class about specially prescribed diets.

4. Many communities have food programs that help individuals of various ages. Find out what is available in your community. Look into the WIC (Women, Infants, and Children) Program, the Child Nutrition Program, food stamps, Meals on Wheels, and the Elderly Feeding Program. Investigate the educational program that each provides.

REFERENCES

Alvarado, D. 1993. "Study Shows Dieters Eat Far More Than They Think." *Birmingham News,* 29 March, 1D.

"Are You Eating Right?" 1992. *Consumer Reports* 57, no. 19 (October): 644–51.

Ballentine, M., K. Stitt, J. Bonner, and L. Clark. 1991. "Self-Reported Eating Disorders of Black, Low-Income Adolescents: Behavior, Body Weight Perception, and Methods of Dieting." *Journal of School Health* 6, no. 9 (November): 392–96.

"Barbie's Missing Accessory: Food." 1994. *Tufts University Diet and Nutrition Letter* 11, no. 11 (January): 1.

Barnett, R. 1986. "Why Fat Makes You Fatter." *American Health,* May, 38–41.

Bouchard, C., A. Tremblay, J. Despres, A. Nadeau, P. J. Lupien, G. Theriault, J. Dussault, S. Moorjani, S. Pinault, and G. Fournier. 1990. "The Response to Long-Term Overfeeding in Identical Twins." *New England Journal of Medicine* 322, no. 21:1477–82.

Brey, R. 1992. "Eating Disorders and Eating-Disordered Behavior Among College Females." *Eta Sigma Gamman* 10, no. 1 (July): 64–72.

Bruch, H. 1986. "Anorexia Nervosa: The Therapeutic Task." In *Handbook of Eating Disorders,* edited by Kelly D. Brownell and John P. Foreyt. New York: Basic Books, p. 331.

"But I Eat Like a Bird . . ." 1993. *Tufts University Diet and Nutrition Letter* 1 1, no. 1 (March): 1.

Collier, S. N., S. F. Stallings, P. G. Wolman, and R. W. Cullen. 1990. "Assessment of Attitudes About Weight and Dieting Among College-Aged Individuals." *Journal of the American Dietetic Association* 90, no. 2:276–78.

"Concern for Couch Spuds." 1993. *Nutrition News* 55, no. 3 (Winter): 9.

Cooper, P. J., M. J. Taylor, Z. Cooper, and C. G. Fairburn. 1987. "The Development and Validation of the Body Shape Questionnaire." *International Journal of Eating Disorders* 6, no. 4:486.

"Count Your Calories Carefully." 1993. *Consumer Reports on Health* 5, no. 4 (April): 37.

DeAndrade, K. 1993. "A New Approach to Dieting and Weight." *Family Life Educator,* Fall, 4–10.

"Diet vs. Exercise: What's Best?" 1992. *Consumer Reports on Health* 4, no. 1 (January): 1–3.

Drewnoski, A., J. D. Sandeski, P. H. Iverius, and M. R. Greenwood. 1985. "Sweet Tooth Reconsidered: Taste Responsiveness in Human Obesity." *Physiology and Behavior* 35: 517.

Elmer-Dewitt, P. 1993. "Cake Eater's Dream?" *Time,* 26 July, 54.

"Exercise and Diet in Weight Loss." 1990. *Nutrition Today* 25, no. 1 (February): 4.

"Falling Leaves, Rising Calories." 1992. *Tufts University Diet and Nutrition Letter* 10, no. 8 (October): 1–2.

"Fear of Fat." 1985. *Consumer Reports* 50, no. 8 (August): 455–57.

"Frozen Light Entrees." 1993. *Consumer Reports* 58, no. 1 (January): 27–31.

Gilbert, S. 1986. *Pathology of Eating: Psychology and Treatment.* New York: Routledge & Kegan Paul, 129–32.

Gortmaker, S. L., A. Must, J. M. Perrin, A. M. Sobol, and W. H. Dietz. 1993. "Social and Economic Consequences of Overweight in Adolescence and Young Adulthood." *New England Journal of Medicine* 329, no. 14 (September): 1008–37.

Gurin, J. 1989. "Leaner, Not Lighter." *Psychology Today,* June, 33, 34.

Hamilton, K. 1990. "The Bulge Stops." *Health* 22, no. 5:54–55.

Healthy People 2000. 1992. U.S. Department of Health and Human Services, Public Health Service. Boston: Jones and Bartlett.

Hellmich, N. 1993. "Most Dieters Get Back Weight They've Lost." *USA Today,* 25 May, 8D.

Hockey, R. 1993. *Physical Fitness: The Pathway to Healthful Living,* 7th ed. St. Louis: Mosby Yearbook.

Hodge, C., L. Jackson, and L. Sullivan. 1993. "The Freshmen 15." *Psychology of Women Quarterly* 17: 119–26.

"How Fat Is America?" 1992. Press release from Diet Center, 8 January.

Katch, F. I., and W. D. McArdle. 1987. *Nutrition, Weight Control, and Exercise,* 3d ed. Philadelphia: Lea & Febiger.

Liebman, B. F. 1987. "Is Dieting a Losing Game?" *Nutrition Action Healthletter* 14, no. 2 (March): 10.

"Link Between Weight Loss and Diabetes II Prevention." 1992. *Health Education Reports,* 16 July, 6.

Lissner, L., P. Odell, R. D'Agostino, J. Stokes, B. Kreger, A. Belanger, and K. Brownell. 1991. "Variability of Body Weight and Health Outcomes in the Framingham Population." *New England Journal of Medicine* 324, no. 26:1839–44.

"Losing Weight, Hot Foods, Life Expectancy." 1993. *Nutrition Action Healthletter* 20, no. 6 (July/August): 10.

Manson, J. E., G. A. Colditz, M. J. Stampfer, W. C. Willett, B. Rosner, R. R. Monson, F. E. Speizer, and C. H. Hennekens. 1990. "A Prospective Study of Obesity and Risk of Coronary Heart Disease in Women." *New England Journal of Medicine* 322, no. 13:882–88.

McGlynn, G. 1993. *Dynamics of Fitness,* 3d ed. Dubuque, Iowa: Brown & Benchmark.

Mitchell, J. E. 1990. "The Treatment of Eating Disorders." *Psychomatics* 31, no. 1:1–3.

Nash, J. 1987. "Eating Behavior and Body Weight: Physiological Influences." *American Journal of Health Promotion* 1, no. 3 (Winter): 5–7.

Nicholas, P., and J. Dwyer. 1986. "Diets for Weight Reduction: Nutritional Considerations." In *Handbook of Eating Disorders,* edited by Kelly D. Brownell and John P. Foreyt. New York: Basic Books.

"Obesity Surgery Regaining Favor." 1991. *Medical World News* 32, no. 5:37.

Perry-Hunnicutt, C., and I. Newmann. 1993. "Adolescent Dieting Practices and Nutrition Knowledge." *Health Values* 17, no. 4 (July/August): 35–40.

Powers, S. K., and E. T. Howley, 1990. *Exercise Physiology: Theory and Application to Fitness and Performance.* Dubuque, Iowa: Wm. C. Brown.

"Quit Watching the Scales?" 1993. *Consumer Reports on Health* 5, no. 5 (May): 45–47.

Raciti, M., and S. Hendrick. 1992. "Relationships Between Eating Disorder Characteristics and Love and Sex Attitudes." *Sex Roles* 27, nos. 9–10:553–64.

Rosato, Frank D. 1990. *Fitness and Wellness: The Physical Connection.* St. Paul, Minn.: West.

Schardt, D. 1993. "Lifting Weight Myths." *Nutrition Action Newsletter* 20, no. 8 (October): 8–9.

Simon, C. 1989. "The Triumphant Dieter." *Psychology Today,* June, 48–52.

Sitton, S. C., and H. G. Miller. 1992. "The Effect of Pretreatment Eating Patterns on the Completion of a Very Low Calorie Diet." *International Journal of Eating Disorders* 10, no. 3:369–72.

Speilman, A., B. Kanders, M. Kienholz, and G. Blackburn. 1992. "The Cost of Losing: An Analysis of Commercial Weight-Loss Programs in a Metropolitan Area." *Journal of the American College of Nutrition* 11, no. 1:26–41.

Stone, J. 1993. "He's Just Big, She's Fat." *Health* 7, no. 3 (May/June): 67–70.

Stunkard, A. J., J. R. Harris, N. L. Pedersen, and G. E. McClearn. 1990. "The Body-Mass Index of Twins Who Have Been Reared Apart." *New England Journal of Medicine* 322, no. 21:1483–87.

Suter, P. M., Y. Schutz, and E. Jequier. 1992. "The Effect of Ethanol on Fat Storage in Healthy Subjects." *New England Journal of Medicine* 326, no. 15 (April): 983–87.

"Teen Obesity: A Heavy Burden Even in Adulthood." *Tufts University Diet and Nutrition Letter* 10, no. 11 (January): 1.

"Thin Is In." 1994. *Nutrition Action Healthletter* 21, no. 2 (March): 4.

Thomas, K. 1993. "Liquid Diets Inch Back onto Fat-fighters' Menus." *USA Today,* 9 September, D1.

Thompson, T. 1990. "Shape Up Diets." *Health* 22, no. 5:51–53.

Vanitallie, T. B. 1990. "The Perils of Obesity in Middle-Aged Women." *New England Journal of Medicine* 22, no. 13:929.

Wardlaw, G. M., and P. Insel. 1990. *Perspectives in Nutrition.* St. Louis: Times Mirror/Mosby.

"Washington Focus." 1993. *Health Education Reports* 15, no. 11 (June): 1.

Williams, M. 1990. *Lifetime Fitness and Wellness: A Practical Approach,* 2d ed. Dubuque, IA: Wm. C. Brown.

Williams, M. 1992. *Nutrition for Fitness and Sport,* 3d ed. Dubuque, IA: Brown & Benchmark.

Yates, A. 1990. "Current Perspectives on the Eating Disorders. II. Treatment, Outcome, and Research Directions," *Journal of the American Academy of Child and Adolescent Psychiatry* 29 (January): 1–8.

ADDITIONAL READINGS

Baer, J. T., and J. Taper. 1992. "Amenorrheic and Eumenorrheic Adolescent Runners: Dietary Intake and Exercise Training Status." *Journal of the American Dietetic Association* 92, no. 1 (January): 89–90. The authors report on an assessment of the dietary status of amenorrheic and eumenorrheic adolescent females. Because there are health risks associated with training vigorously and consuming a low-energy diet, the authors emphasize the need for appropriate energy intake to support performance as well as growth.

Kuczmarski, R. J. 1992. "Prevalence of Overweight and Weight Gain in the United States." *American Journal of Clinical Nutrition* 55, no. 2 (February): 495S–502S. The results from the Second National Nutrition Examination Survey (NHANES II) are discussed in this article. Data on overweight and weight gain in the United States are summarized by several demographic characteristics.

"Lose Weight with Big Meals." 1992. *Consumer Reports on Health* 4, no. 2 (February). Researchers at Columbia University found that women burned more calories when eating a large amount of food than when eating the same amount of food in small portions over several hours. They theorize that the digestive system needs to work much harder to digest the large amount of food and burns more calories in doing so.

By reading and working through the activities in the chapters on nutrition, physical activity, and weight control, you should have a good understanding of the following:

1. Basic nutrients and their importance to health
2. Practical health decisions that can promote good nutrition
3. Problems that can result from faulty health decisions about nutrition
4. Nutritional needs of special groups of people
5. The components of physical fitness and the health benefits of regular physical activity
6. The effects of total body physical activity
7. Practical ways to make health decisions about the development of a personal fitness program
8. Health problems associated with being overweight
9. Health decisions related to selection and use of a weight control plan
10. Eating disorders
11. The most effective and healthy ways to control body weight

There has also been an opportunity to assess your feelings about issues related to nutrition, physical activity, and weight control. Health-producing behaviors are enhanced by wise decisions about these three areas.

Since health decisions about nutrition, physical activity, and weight control are so basic to total health, it is appropriate to consider ways to strengthen your well-being related to these areas. The prevention model presented in chapter 2 provides the framework within which to consider the relevance of the issues presented in this section.

Lifestyle Contracting Using Strength Intervention

I. Choosing the desired health behavior or skill.

   A. Keeping in mind the purposes in life and goals you have identified, consider one or two health behaviors related to nutrition, physical activity, or weight control that will help you reach your goals. In order to assess the likelihood of success, ask yourself questions similar to those used in previous sections, such as:

      1. Is my purpose, cause, or goal better realized by adoption of this behavior?

         _____ yes _____ no

      2. Am I hardy enough to accomplish this goal? (This means I feel I can do it if I work hard, I am in control of what needs to be done, I am committed to do it, and the goal is a challenge for me.)

         _____ yes _____ no

      3. Is this a behavior I really want to change and that I feel I can change?

         _____ yes _____ no

      4. Do I first need to nurture a personal strength area?

         _____ yes _____ no
      (If yes, be sure to include this as a part of the plan.)

      5. Do I need to free myself from a bad habit in order to accomplish this goal?

         _____ yes _____ no
      (If yes, be sure to include this as part of the plan.)

      6. Have I considered the results of the assessments in the chapters on nutrition, physical activity, and weight control?

         _____ yes _____ no

These results may be helpful in developing a plan.

("Yes" answers to the first three questions are a must in order to be successful. It might be wise to consider a different behavior if you cannot honestly answer "yes" to these questions. Your answers to questions 4–6 ought to provide information for consideration in making your plan.)

   B. Behaviors I will change (no more than two)

      _____

      _____

II. Lifestyle plan

   A. A description of the general plan of what I am going to do and how I will accomplish it. (Consider apperceptive experiences—successes you have had in the past—since they may help you develop the best ways to carry out this plan.)

      _____

      _____

      _____

      _____

      _____

      _____

(Continued on page 8.23)

B. Barriers to the accomplishment of the plan (lack of time, feelings of others, frustration from previous failures, hesitation to take action, motivation, etc.)

   1. Identify the barriers: _____

   _____

   _____

   _____

   2. Means to remove the barriers (use problem-solving skills or creative approaches such as those described in the mental health chapter):

   _____

   _____

   _____

   _____

C. Implementation of the plan

   1. Substitution (putting positive behaviors in place of negative ones) _____

   _____

   2. Linking behaviors _____

   _____

   _____

   3. Combining a strength and a weakness _____

   _____

   _____

   4. When _____

   5. Where _____

   6. Preparation _____

   7. With whom _____

III. Support groups

   A. Who: _____

   _____

   B. Role: _____

   _____

   C. Organized support: _____

   _____

IV. Trigger responses: _____

   _____

   _____

V. Starting date: _____

VI. Date/Sequence the contract will be reevaluated: _____

   _____

VII. Evidence of reaching the goal: _____

   _____

VIII. Reward(s) when contract is completed: _____

   _____

   _____

IX. Signature of client: _____

X. Signature of facilitator: _____

XI. Additional conditions/comments: _____

   _____

   _____

   _____

   _____

   _____

Relationships and Sexuality

CHAPTER 9

Sexuality and Human Relationships

Healthy People 2000 Objectives

- Increase to at least 85 percent the proportion of people aged 10 through 18 who have discussed human sexuality, including values surrounding sexuality, with their parents and/or received information through another parentally endorsed source, such as youth, school, or religious programs. (Baseline: 66% of people aged 13 through 18 have discussed sexuality with their parents; reported in 1986.)

Sexuality and Human Relations

A number of internal and external forces in your life influence the decisions you make regarding sexual behavior. What you do may be in harmony with some of these forces and in conflict with others.

Directions

Give a value to the following forces in your life as they pertain to your sexual behavior (i.e., what makes you sexually active or what makes you refrain from sexual activity). If you are married, apply this tool to a specific sexual behavior such as your degree of fidelity to your spouse or your degree of sexual activity with your spouse.

a = a major force influencing my sexual behavior
b = a moderate force influencing my sexual behavior
c = an insignificant force influencing my sexual behavior

1. Religious influence — a b c
2. Family influence — a b c
3. How it feels when we kiss and hug — a b c
4. My own self-image (how I think I look to others) — a b c
5. My sense of right or wrong — a b c
6. Radio, television, or movies — a b c
7. How it feels to touch someone — a b c
8. How I learned to act — a b c
9. The way I feel inside — a b c
10. Literature (books, magazines) or music — a b c
11. Pleasure — a b c
12. My judgment — a b c
13. My sense of what I should and should not do — a b c
14. Friend's influence — a b c
15. Physical stimulation — a b c
16. Introversion or extraversion (how outgoing I am) — a b c
17. My morals or values — a b c
18. The expectations/relationship I have with boyfriend/girlfriend (for marrieds, consider friends other than spouse) — a b c
19. Fear of or anticipation of pregnancy — a b c
20. Desire to feel good about myself — a b c

Scoring

a = 3   b = 2   c = 1

Total values as follows from top to bottom of the four columns

Column A	Column B	Column C	Column D
1.____	2.____	3.____	4.____
5.____	6.____	7.____	8.____
9.____	10.____	11.____	12.____
13.____	14.____	15.____	16.____
17.____	18.____	19.____	20.____
Totals ____	____	____	____

Interpretation

Column A represents the degree to which your morals/values or beliefs influence your sexual behavior and decisions.
Column B represents the degree to which social forces influence your sexual behavior.
Column C represents the degree to which biological factors influence your sexual behavior and decisions.
Column D represents the degree to which psychological forces influence your sexual behavior and decisions.

The relative influences can be compared directly with each other to see which area is the strongest or if they are equal. You may interpret the results as follows:

11–15 major influence
6–10   moderate influence
1–5   insignificant influence

What do you really want to know when it comes to sexuality? It is often thought that we most often want to know about sexual functioning, sexual activities, or sexual morality. While all of these aspects are important and of interest, they are not the major areas of interest related to sexuality.

Dr. Ruth Westheimer, the well-known lecturer and radio and television talk show personality, has been receiving letters from male and female listeners and viewers since 1981. She notes that many of the letters are not specifically on sexual issues. Concerns about care and raising of children, family relationships, and companionship needs put 41 percent of the letters into the relationship category, with only 33 percent on sexual issues ("Educating America" 1987). Individuals are concerned about human relationships and how sexuality relates to these relationships. Consistent with this interest and need, it is appropriate to consider what sexuality involves. First, however, complete the Health Assessment on sexuality and human relations to see what forces most affect your decisions about sexuality.

Reading the chapters of this text that deal with aspects of human sexuality and participating in discussions about human sexuality are forms of sexuality education. You might wonder what will happen to your attitudes and behavior as a result of such sexuality education. There is no need for concern. Even after students take a semester-long human sexuality course, there is no change in their sexual behaviors. There are some changes in their sexual attitudes, as such students are generally more permissive about discussing sexuality and a variety of sexual topics (Weiss, Rabinowitz, and Ruckstuhl 1992).

SEXUALITY THROUGHOUT LIFE

When we hear the word *sexuality*, our thoughts often turn to people lying in bed participating in sexual acts, particularly sexual intercourse. This narrow view is as limited in vision as viewing health as merely absence of illness. Yet unless we have spent a great deal of time studying the topic of sexuality, the

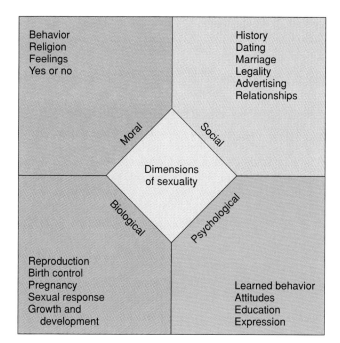

Figure 9.1

The four dimensions of human sexuality.

sound of the word will often excite our interest or make us feel slightly uncomfortable and shy—no matter how sexually experienced we are. But shyness and titillation are timid and immature responses to this powerful force in life. Sexuality is an essential part of each stage of the life cycle, and a thorough understanding of sexual natures and impulses, and of harmonious ways to express them, is vital to maintaining good health.

THE FOUR DIMENSIONS OF HUMAN SEXUALITY

Sexuality has four interacting dimensions: (1) social, (2) psychological, (3) moral, and (4) biological. Each of these dimensions influences and is influenced by the other three (figure 9.1).

The **social dimension of human sexuality** includes the cultural factors that influence your thoughts and actions, including historical influences, dating, interpersonal relationships, and all the sexually related beliefs and behaviors learned from the environment. In contemporary society, these cultural influences include advertising, radio, music and music videos, television, and literature, in addition to the traditional influences of family, school, and church.

The **psychological dimension of human sexuality** reflects attitudes and feelings toward ourselves and others. It is probably the clearest example of learned aspects of sexuality resulting from past experience. From birth, we get myriad signals about how to think and act. We might learn that some words are "wrong" or "dirty" and that certain body parts are "untouchable" or "unmentionable." We even learn to be careful about what conversation topics are proper with certain people.

The **moral dimension of human sexuality** is the basic question of right or wrong: "Should I or shouldn't I?" "Yes or no?" This dimension might be based on particular religious thinking or perhaps on some basic philosophy. Daily, we face dilemmas requiring moral decisions that affect and are affected by concepts of total human sexuality.

This dimension is a good example of how one dimension of sexuality can influence another. For example, it is known that sex guilt—that is, guilt about moral conduct in sexual situations—is related to sexual behavior. Since women might express greater sex guilt than men, and since those with stronger religious values seem to experience more sex guilt, consideration should be given to addressing religious values and the appropriateness of sexual activity as part of a relationship (Fox and Young 1989). Problems in one dimension of sexuality can lead to problems in another dimension. For example, guilt could lead to problems with a relationship.

The **biological dimension of human sexuality** is the one we usually think of first. It involves such considerations as physiological responses to sexual stimulation, reproduction, puberty, changes resulting from pregnancy, and growth and development in general.

The relationships among these dimensions of sexuality are many. For example, psychological stresses can influence a woman's menstrual cycle. Moral feelings might affect psychological reactions, and biological functioning could impact social relationships. It is a mistake to assume that any one dimension is more important than another; all four constantly work together—ideally, in harmony. The relationships among the social, psychological, moral, and biological dimensions constitute an individual's total sexuality. It is important to remember that sexuality relates more to what we are and not just to what we do. Although human sexuality is divided into dimensions for examination, it is in fact an indivisible whole.

sexuality
A four-dimensional (social, psychological, moral, biological) aspect of each person's personality that influences the person's total well-being.

social dimension of human sexuality
The sum of all the cultural factors that influence a person's thoughts and actions regarding sexuality.

psychological dimension of human sexuality
People's attitudes and feelings about themselves and others, regarding sexuality.

moral dimension of human sexuality
Basic questions of right and wrong regarding sexuality.

biological dimension of human sexuality
Aspects of sexuality involving physiological responses, reproduction, puberty, pregnancy, and growth and development.

SEXUALITY AND DECISIONS FOR WELL-BEING

Surveys indicate that at any given time in a college classroom, a great number of students are thinking about something related to human sexuality. Chances are, too, that many do more than just think about sexuality. Probably around three-fourths of the readers of this book are likely to have participated in sexual intercourse, and almost all are likely to have participated in some form of sexual behavior (Debuono et al. 1990; Flax 1992). In addition, there is a great deal of uncertainty about sexual knowledge among college students (Valois and Waring 1991). Myths, misinformation, and misconceptions about sexuality persist, in part because many of us are embarrassed to admit what we aren't sure of or just don't know. It is important, however, to separate fact from folklore so you can enjoy a healthy life ("Test Your Sexual I.Q." 1992).

Besides being the focus of much thought and behavior, sexuality influences interpersonal relationships, forms the basis of family life, and determines the reproduction of the species. Thus, sexuality is directly related to well-being in many ways. Being accurately informed about sexuality is, of course, crucial to future health and to making wise consumer decisions about it.

FAMILY FORMATION

Some argue that the institution of marriage is dying out, and the divorce rate has certainly climbed. The divorce rate does seem to have leveled off—about one in every two marriages ends in divorce. At the same time, married men and women are generally happier and less stressed than the unmarried (Coombs 1991).

Others argue that the quality of relationships cannot be measured with statistics. There may be more divorces, but this might mean that couples are ending low-quality relationships and entering into higher-quality ones. What *do* these observations mean? Central to any such discussion is how a mate is selected and what marital options exist.

MATE SELECTION

Many factors are important in choosing a mate. The single more important factor in mate selection is what is perceived as "love." At the same time, love seems most likely to occur between two individuals with certain similar and complementary backgrounds and traits.

In this society, the important **similarity factors** in mate selection seem to be social class, proximity of geographical location, intelligence, age, race, ethnic group, and religion. For example, we tend to choose mates of about the same education level, which is usually related to social class.

There are also **complementary factors.** For example, a person who needs to be dominant in personal relations

Perceptions of Ideal Body Shapes

Males and females tend to misjudge the body shape preferred by others. For example, using body silhouettes, females and males indicated the size of their own body figure, their ideal figure, and the figures most attractive to others. The female silhouette that women selected as most attractive was significantly thinner than the silhouette selected as most desirable by men. College men also misjudged the male silhouette preferred by women, exaggerating the extent to which women perceived large male physiques as ideal and desirable. Why do you think these misperceptions happened? How can we be realistic in our perceptions of body shapes?

Source: From Lawrence D. Cohn and Nancy E. Adler, "Female and Male Perceptions of Ideal Body Shapes" in *Psychology of Women Quarterly* 16: 69–79 (1992).

We are most likely to choose a mate who is similar to us in class, intelligence, race, and religion.

might select a relatively submissive mate, or someone who derives satisfaction from giving sympathy and emotional support might find a mate who derives satisfaction primarily from getting such sympathy and support.

similarity factors
Characteristics in which people are alike.

complementary factors
Characteristics by which people supplement each other.

Issue
Prenuptial Agreements

A **prenuptial agreement** is an arrangement made prior to marriage by those planning to be married. For example, the couple might agree not to have children, how to spend vacation time, how to share household tasks, or under what circumstances a move to another town would be considered. They might also agree on what will happen if the marriage should end. For example, they might agree on how to divide monetary assets, items owned individually before the marriage, or other items that might be acquired during the marriage.

- Pro: Prenuptial agreements are a good idea because too often problems arise concerning things that could have been worked out in advance. Also, preparing the agreement forces the couple to consider many aspects of their relationship and not just think everything will be rosy at all times.

- Con: Prenuptial agreements imply that there will be problems right from the start. Good relationships are built upon love and trust. If it is necessary to spell out details in advance, it is likely that there is not enough of either.

Do you think people should use prenuptial agreements? Why or why not? If you were going to use one, what would be the main points/topics to include? What should one person say to another about the reasons why it might be (or might not be) a good idea to have a prenuptial agreement?

THE WORLD AROUND YOU
Multicultural Differences in the Desire to Marry

According to South (1993), black men and women are significantly less desiring of marriage than are whites, and the racial difference among men is significantly larger than the racial difference among women. Compared to non-Hispanic whites of the same gender, Hispanic men are more likely, and Hispanic women less likely, to desire to marry. Racial and ethnic differences among women are attributable mainly to differences in educational attainment, while differences between black and white men result from differences in the anticipated benefits of marriage (South 1993). Also, black women have lower marriage rates because they place greater emphasis on having economic support in place prior to marriage and are more resistant to marrying someone who has fewer resources (Bulcroft and Bulcroft 1993).

Whether likenesses, differences, or some combination of the two are the primary reasons for mate selection, certain factors do seem to contribute to marital success. They have previously been identified (Saxton 1983) as these:

1. *Childhood background.* Characteristics such as parents who were happily married, a happy childhood, lack of conflict, and infrequency and mildness of punishment all are important to marital success.
2. *Age at marriage.* Earlier marriages seem to be less stable than later ones.
3. *Vocational preparedness.* We need sufficient training to undertake our own support and perhaps that of a family.
4. *Emotional maturity.* Relative independence and self-direction are important.
5. *Present interests and values.* Shared interests and values that seem to correlate most highly with marital happiness relate to sexual behavior, romantic love, children, and religion.

6. *Length of engagement.* A fairly long (6–14 months) engagement seems to be most effective.
7. *Adequate sexuality education.* Because sexual conflicts after marriage are major contributing factors to unhappiness, it seems clear that adequate sexuality education promotes marital happiness.

More recently, marital strengths identified by couples who had been married at least 30 years included intimacy balanced with autonomy, commitment, communication, religious orientation, and similar perceptions of the relationships (Robinson and Blanton 1993). Also, at least for wives, the perceived fairness of household labor is related to marital happiness (Ward 1993).

Although in past years, better-educated women have had lower marriage rates than those with less schooling, this seems to be reversing itself. In the coming years, more highly educated women will be more likely to marry. Going to college may delay marriage, but it seems to improve a woman's prospects for eventually getting married (Schmid 1987).

Until 1960, there were more males than females in the U.S. population. Since then, however, there has been a reversal in the gender ratio, with more women than men in almost all age groups. This has resulted in a shortage of marital

prenuptial agreement
Arrangements made prior to marriage, by those planning to marry, regarding assets, conditions of the marriage, situations that might arise, possible breakup, and other personal aspects of the relationship.

opportunities for women who might choose to get married, particularly women past age 25. Women over age 25 may need to consider younger men in greater numbers and not insist that the men they marry be of an equal or higher educational and economic status. Likewise, younger men may need to look more seriously at older women. This is particularly true as women gain higher educational and economic status ("Sex Ratio Imbalance Creates Fearful Women" 1986).

Gender differences can make a difference in expectations for yourself and for a future partner. For example, young women expect more success for their future husbands than young men do for their future wives. More women than men say their partners should be superior to themselves, and more men than women say their partners should be inferior to themselves. Some males may be threatened by bright, successful, capable women and therefore might not perceive them as eligible partners. Therefore, women may find that personal success reduces their opportunities for marriage. Men may feel compelled to choose high-status, high-paying careers; women may feel pressure to limit their educational and career goals (Ganong and Coleman 1992).

Obviously, we do not go through life with a checklist designed to rate potential mates, but you should know what characteristics seem important in the choice of a mate. In spite of some changes, the profile of the American wife remains rather traditional. The vast majority (93 percent) of married women live with their husband in their own household. Wives are usually a few years younger than their husbands. Four-fifths of all wives have at least a high school education and over one-seventh hold a college degree. Fifty-five percent of all married women are either employed or seeking work ("Profile of the American Wife" 1987).

Finally, there are reasons why some people do or don't get married. Reasons for getting married are many and varied, but certain factors emerge as particularly important ("Why Do Couples Get Married?" 1990):

1. *Mutuality.* Couples are more likely to marry if they are equally involved and are both in love.
2. *Interdependence.* Being equally involved is significant because interest in others causes breakups.
3. *Self-ratings.* Women who rate themselves higher on attractiveness, intelligence, and creativity are less likely to get married; however, men who rate themselves as desirable are more likely to get married.
4. *Individual readiness.* An individual's readiness depends on how much more schooling, career development, and development of other readiness factors the individual needs.
5. *Social networks.* This factor includes how well individuals know their partners, parental approval, and acceptance by friends.
6. *Similarity in parents' level of marital satisfaction.* As might be expected, people are more likely to get married if they feel that their parents were happily married.

There are also reasons why some women don't get married ("Why Some Women Don't Get Married" 1990). Some of these reasons could also apply to men; the list includes these:

1. Fear of loss of freedom
2. Fear of making the wrong choice of mate
3. Commitment to getting ahead in the business world and to not making sacrifices for a marriage
4. Not having found the right person to marry
5. Unwillingness to be emotionally or physically abused, flatter a man's ego unless the compliments are merited, act docile and submissive, or subjugate her needs to his
6. Needing someone to respect, enjoy, and communicate with on many levels and not just someone to pay the bills

FORMS OF FAMILY LIVING

The typical family today is quite different from the family of the past. People living 50 to 100 years ago may well have been part of an **extended family,** a family in which parents and children live with other relatives—a grandparent, for example, or an uncle or cousin—under the same roof. Now it is more likely that people grow up in and eventually form their own **nuclear family,** a family in which only parents and their children live together. Compared with many families of the past, people today are more likely to live some distance away both from where they grew up and from where relatives live.

The general shift from extended to nuclear families is just one of the changes that have altered modern family life. There appears to be less communication among family members than in the past, for example, due to television. The automobile has enabled family members to engage in activities away from each other and from home. The changing status of women in society, increased use of technology in the home, and economic constraints have also had significant impacts on family life.

In response to societal trends—and due to dissatisfaction with the traditional nuclear family—new forms of family structure have emerged. In many families, both husband and wife now work *and* share household and/or child-rearing responsibilities. Other families are **single-parent families** because of divorce, separation, death, or choice. These families are increasing in number and are becoming more workable than in

---

extended family
Parents, children, and other relatives living together under one roof.

nuclear family
Parents and children living together under one roof. Also called "conjugal family."

single-parent family
Family with only one parent.

An increasing number of children are living in single-parent families.

the past. The stigma of divorce has lessened due to its increasing prevalence, and women are more able to maintain families by themselves because of increased job opportunities.

Relatively high divorce and remarriage rates have drastically changed the profile of the American family in the past few decades. It is predicted that by the year 2000 the **stepfamily** (a family wherein one or both parents have children from a previous marriage) will be the predominant family structure in the United States and actually outnumber the nuclear family. Of all married-couple families with children under the age of 18, 40 percent are expected to become stepfamilies before the youngest child reaches age 18. Because this type of family structure is relatively new in large numbers, many questions about it remain unanswered. Some research indicates stepfamilies have more adaptability, but less cohesion, than nuclear families (Pill 1990).

Other forms of family-type relationships are much less common than those already mentioned, but it is still of interest to consider them. For example, in an increasing number of marriages, the partners have made a conscious decision not to have children. Other partners, both heterosexual and homosexual, are not marrying but **cohabiting** (living together without being married). Many of these couples have also chosen to remain childless.

Most cohabitation is very short-lived; two out of five such relationships are disrupted within a year. In addition, unions formed by cohabitation, including marriages preceded by cohabitation, are more likely to dissolve than are unions formed by marriage. Cohabitation rates are highest among women, whites, persons who did not complete high school, and those from welfare-receiving or single-parent families ("Rising Prevalence" 1990). Couples who cohabit before marriage report lower-quality marriages, lower commitment to the institution of marriage, more individualistic views of

marriage, and greater likelihood of divorce than do couples who do not cohabit (Thomson and Colella 1992; DeMaris and Rao 1992).

Other types of liaisons include **swinging,** which refers to a marital arrangement in which both partners include others sexually. Swinging seems to be more preferred by men than by women. Some couples find that sexual experimentation with others enhances their sexual activity with each other. Others believe that sexual activity should be enjoyed with a variety of people. Some people who swing like the opportunities for female and male homosexual behavior, group sexual activity, and a greater degree of openness between marital partners. Many others feel that swinging is immoral and destructive to relationships.

Another type of liaison within the basic marriage form is the **contractual marriage,** in which each partner agrees to review the marriage contract periodically. At the time of review, couples make agreements that provide direction for the next time period. These contractual arrangements are legally binding as long as they do not contradict existing laws. As a variation, prospective marital partners sometimes agree to certain conditions on which the relationship will be based; for example, the man might agree to do the housecleaning and cooking, while the woman might agree to work outside the home and help with the laundry and child-rearing chores.

A relatively new kind of liaison is the **commuter marriage,** in which spouses set up separate households and live apart for periods of from several days a week to months at a time. The main reason for doing so is pursuit of individual careers in different locations. Career development and satisfaction are the major benefits of this lifestyle, along with increased independence, greater self-sufficiency, and enhanced appreciation for spouse or family. Drawbacks include lack of emotional support and companionship. This is usually viewed by the couple as a temporary lifestyle that enables the meshing of career aspirations and family goals (Groves and Horm-Wingerd 1991).

stepfamily
A family in which one or both parents have children from a previous marriage.

cohabiting
Living together without being legally married.

swinging
A mutual agreement in which a married couple opens up their relationship to include sexual encounters with others.

contractual marriage
A marital relationship in which the partners agree to periodically review their marriage contract.

commuter marriage
A marriage in which spouses establish separate households and live apart for periods of time.

PERSONAL SKILLS AND EXPERIENCES

Improving Your Body Image

How we feel about our bodies and our appearance plays an important role in how we feel about ourselves in general. When we feel healthy, we are more likely to feel enthusiastic than when we feel sick or in poor shape. When we feel good about how we look, we're happier and likely to feel better about others. We're also often concerned with how other people react to our appearance. Many actions can help you improve your body image. Here are some examples:

1. Don't feel a need to apologize to others about every blemish you might see in your appearance. Chances are, others didn't notice them anyway. None of us is perfect.
2. Be careful about basing your body image on what you see and hear in advertisements. They are carefully produced to send certain messages to sell products. Few people look and act like what you see in the ads.
3. Attractive people are often judged by others to be more warm, interesting, friendly, considerate, and strong than those who are less attractive. With all of our defects, we can all do things to be more attractive. For example, the clothes you wear, the styles you use, and how you care for your physical appearance all have an impact. What can you do to be more attractive?
4. While you should be free to be yourself, the message you send about your appearance and the ones you receive from others might not always be the same. For example, a female might not wear a bra because she wants to be comfortable; a male might interpret that as her desire to look sexy. What messages are you sending by the appearance you present?
5. The way you move your body (body language) can also indicate how you feel about yourself. Watch what others do when they are nervous, happy, or sad. Use this information to control some of your body movements so they send the messages you want to send.

Body image is important. While you can't drastically change how you look, you have a lot to say about what clothes you wear, the physical condition of your body, your overall appearance, and how you move your body. What health actions will help you improve your body image?

FAMILY COMMUNICATION

Regardless of the form intimate relations take, communication is critical. Poor communication is usually associated with a lack of listening, an attempt to win, an inability to demonstrate understanding of another's viewpoint, and a rigidity that prevents consideration of alternative solutions.

UNSUCCESSFUL COMMUNICATION

An improvement in communication skills is likely to improve relationships. Consider the following discussion (Bruess and Greenberg 1994):

Barbara: Thanksgiving vacation is coming up, and I'd like you to come home with me and spend it with my family.

Paul: Now you ask! I've already told my folks to expect us for Thanksgiving dinner!

Barbara: You've got some nerve! You didn't even ask me if I wanted to go to your house for Thanksgiving.

Paul: Ask you? You've been hitting the books so much lately that I've hardly seen you long enough to say hello, much less to ask you to Thanksgiving dinner.

Barbara: Would you rather have me fail my courses? You're pretty selfish, aren't you?

Paul: I've had it! Either we're going to my house for Thanksgiving or you can say goodbye right now.

Barbara: In that case, goodbye!

In this example, both Paul and Barbara are out to win; that is, each is trying to control where the other spends the

Listening is an important part of successful communication.

Thanksgiving vacation. However, neither Paul nor Barbara can truly win in the situation described, because the only choices they've presented themselves with are (1) spend the vacation at Paul's house, (2) spend the vacation at Barbara's house, or (3) break up their relationship.

If they decide to spend the vacation at Barbara's, Paul will have to cancel his plans with his family and put up with the ensuing hassle. He's likely to feel that his wishes are not very important in the relationship, and he's likely to resent being at Barbara's for Thanksgiving. However, if they spend the vacation at Paul's house, Barbara will be resentful. She might feel that because she asked first, they should go to her house. Further, she may still resent Paul's assumption that he can make plans for them without bothering to consult her.

Thus, wherever they go, someone will be resentful, which will probably make Thanksgiving vacation uncomfortable and unenjoyable for all concerned. In other words, no matter who wins, both really lose. The third possibility, dissolving the relationship, is obviously a no-win solution.

SUCCESSFUL COMMUNICATION

How might Paul and Barbara better arrive at a decision about Thanksgiving vacation? Consider the following dialogue:

Barbara: Paul, Thanksgiving vacation is coming up, and I'd like you to come home with me and spend it with my family.

Paul: Now you ask! I've already told my folks to expect us for Thanksgiving dinner!

Barbara: You thought we'd go to your house for Thanksgiving vacation?

Paul: Yes, and my parents have already made preparations.

Barbara: Your parents would be upset if we canceled Thanksgiving dinner with them?

Paul: You bet! And I wouldn't want to be the one to tell them we're not coming.

Barbara: Your parents would really hassle you?

Paul: Yes.

Barbara: I suppose you'd feel embarrassed about changing plans that your parents thought were definite.

Paul: Yes, I guess I would.

Barbara: It sounds like you were really looking forward to our being together at your house and with your family this vacation.

Paul: Yes, I really was.

Barbara: I'm glad you included me in your Thanksgiving plans, but I really was looking forward to spending this vacation with you at *my* family's house. I haven't seen them for a while, and I know they'd really like you. Plus, I'm a little bothered that you didn't consult me before making your plans.

Paul: You have a point there. I'm sorry.

Barbara: Well, let's see if there's any alternative we haven't considered.

Paul: We could spend half the vacation at my house and half at yours.

Barbara: Or we could invite your family to my house.

Paul: How about staying here and not spending Thanksgiving with either of our families?

Barbara: If we spent half the vacation at each house, we'd waste a lot of time traveling.

Paul: It's not very realistic to expect my whole family to cancel their plans and go to your house.

Barbara: Well, if we stayed here, both families would be disappointed. That would be cutting off our noses to spite our faces.

Paul: Maybe we should spend Thanksgiving at one house and the next vacation at the other.

Barbara: That seems sensible. Since you've already made plans, let's spend Thanksgiving at your house.

Paul: Okay. Remember, though, the next vacation will be at your house.

LANGUAGE AND SEXUALITY

One factor that can contribute to communication problems is language—particularly language related to sexuality. Problems can arise when people do not have the same communication system and use different verbal comments, vocal styles, or nonverbal behavior. The basis for this is the lack of a precise sexual language.

At least four language systems have been developed for other purposes, but they are also used to communicate about sexuality. There are certain terms that parents often prefer to use with young children. This **child language** might be used to refer to body parts or bodily functions, or as terms of endearment. Because of this, children often grow up not knowing "proper" anatomical terms and feeling that such words are inappropriate to use.

As we grow up, we learn **street language** from peers and those who are a little older. These words seem to be power-laden and are the language of graffiti. This language can be used to impress others, but it is often socially unacceptable.

Euphemisms make it possible to avoid explicit terms while communicating with others. These include such expressions as *making love, sleeping together,* and *that time of the month.* **Medical-scientific language** is concrete and technical, and includes such words as *penis, vagina,* and *defecate.*

An awareness of various language systems can help promote better communication. You can develop a wide tolerance for language choice, try to talk in the language system of

---

child language
Terms parents often use with children to refer to body parts or body functions.

street language
The slang language of peers and age groups slightly older; used in graffiti.

euphemisms
Inoffensive expressions (such as *making love* and *sleeping together*) used to avoid use of more explicit terms.

medical-scientific language
Concrete, technical terminology.

THE WORLD AROUND YOU

Multicultural Influences on Communication About Sexuality

Most communication skills will be appropriate in any setting, but it is helpful to be aware of possible cultural influences on communication. For example, many Hispanics feel that discussions about sexuality are inappropriate, even among married people. For them, sexuality is a very private matter, especially for "respectable" women (Marin 1988). The black community tends to be more open about sexual messages. However, even though sexuality might be more openly discussed publicly and in black humor and music, within intimate relationships there is often a distinct imbalance of power between men and women that inhibits sexual communication (Mays and Cochran 1988). Finally, many Filipinos feel that it is inappropriate to discuss sexuality in mixed company. They would be more likely to communicate about sexuality in gender-specific and age-specific groups (Toleran 1991).

TABLE 9.1 FOUR LEVELS OF COMMUNICATION

Level	Characteristics
1. Information giving	Sociable, friendly, conventional, and playful; emphasizes thinking and does not indulge disclosure
2. Directing/Arguing	Directing, persuading, blaming, demanding, defending, praising, assuming, competing, evaluating, advising, and withholding; emphasizes feeling and little disclosure
3. Exploring	Tentative, elaborating, exploring, speculating, searching, pondering, wondering, proposing, reflecting, receiving; necessitates work and thinking and little disclosure
4. Self-disclosing	Aware, active congruent, accepting, responsible, disclosing, responsive, understanding, caring, and cooperative; necessitates work, disclosure, and feelings

Source: S. Miller et al., *Alive and Aware: Improving Communication in Relationships.* Copyright © 1975 Interpersonal Communication Programs, Minneapolis, MN.

the other person when possible, and change language choice when desirable. For effective communication, we must be sure we are speaking (and understanding) the same language.

RESOLVING INTERPERSONAL CONFLICT

Successful resolution of interpersonal conflict requires being prepared to work on level 4 in communication (see table 9.1). Level 4 communication requires that you take some risks, be open to others' input, reveal more of yourself, and be honest, among other things.

Active Listening

Reflective listening, or **active listening,** is paraphrasing the other person's words to be sure the meaning was received. It can also include describing feelings left unspoken. This shows an understanding of where the other person is coming from. For example, you might say, "Let me see if I understood what you said. Is it correct to say that you . . ." or "Is this a correct summary of your feelings?" (and then give the summary). Reflecting the words and thoughts of others shows them you care enough to understand their views. Once speakers appreciate this caring, they are more receptive to listening and to understanding your viewpoint. The net result is that each speaker not only better understands the other's point of view, but also is less insistent that his or her viewpoint is the only valid one.

Identifying Your Position

Besides reflecting the other's words and thoughts, it may also be necessary to identify your position—"where you are coming from." It is easier for others to understand your position

if you can explain your feelings. At the very least, stating your thoughts and feelings about a situation aids communication.

Exploring Alternative Solutions

The third step is to **brainstorm** alternative solutions. First list all possible solutions without evaluating them. This allows for creativity without judgment. Then evaluate these alternatives until a solution is reached. With this technique, it initially appears that no one wins, but in fact everyone wins.

PARENTING

You don't have to be a genius or a great scholar to be a good parent. A strong desire to do a good job, a sincere acceptance of children as human beings with needs, feelings, and rights of their own, and a warm and loving heart are important. Yet the decision to become a parent should not be taken lightly. In addition to the well-being of the parent and the child, there are also financial considerations. For example, the average cost of raising a child in midwestern urban areas from birth to age 18 is over $105,000 ("Cost of Raising a Child" 1991).

active listening
Paraphrasing a speaker's words to be sure that the message was understood.

brainstorming
Listing all solutions that come to mind, and evaluating them only after you're done listing.

THE WORLD AROUND YOU

Issues to Consider When Deciding Whether to Become a Parent

When a baby is born to you, you inherit a new set of joys, responsibilities, and decisions. Issues you must consider relate to your life, but they also relate to other people and to society. The following questions present some issues to consider in deciding whether to become a parent and how well you would cope with being a parent.

Does Having and Raising a Child Fit the Lifestyle I Want?

1. What do I want out of life for myself? What do I think is important?
2. Could I handle a child and a job at the same time? Would I have time and energy for both?
3. Would I be ready to give up the freedom to do what I want to do when I want to do it?
4. Would I be willing to cut back my social life and spend more time at home? Would I miss my free time and privacy?
5. Can I afford to support a child? Do I know how much money it takes to raise a child?
6. Do I want to raise a child in the neighborhood where I live now? Would I be willing and able to move?
7. How would a child interfere with my growth and development?
8. Would a child change my educational plans? Do I have the energy to go to school and raise a child at the same time?
9. Am I willing to give a great part of my life—*at least 18 years*—to being responsible for a child? And spend a large portion of my life being concerned about my child's well-being?

Raising a Child—What Is There to Know?

1. Do I like children? When I'm around children for a while, what do I think or feel about having one around all of the time?
2. Do I enjoy teaching others?
3. Is it easy for me to tell people what I want, or need, or what I expect of them?
4. Do I want to give a child the love she or he needs? Is loving easy for me?
5. Am I patient enough to deal with the noise and the confusion and the 24-hour-a-day responsibility? What kind of time and space do I need for myself?
6. What do I do when I get angry or upset? Would I take things out on a child if I lost my temper?
7. What does discipline mean to me? What do freedom, setting limits, and giving space mean? What is being too strict, or not strict enough? Would I want a perfect child?

8. How do I get along with my parents? What will I do to avoid the mistakes my parents made?
9. How would I take care of my child's health and safety? How do I take care of my own?
10. What if I have a child and find out I made a wrong decision?

What's in It for Me?

1. Do I like doing things with children? Do I enjoy activities that children can do?
2. Would I want a child to be "like me"?
3. Would I try to pass on to my child my ideas and values? What if my child's ideas and values turn out to be different from mine?
4. Would I want my child to achieve things that I wish I had but didn't?
5. Would I expect my child to keep me from being lonely in my old age? Do I do that for my parents? Do my parents do that for my grandparents?
6. Do I want a boy or a girl child? What if I don't get what I want?
7. Would having a child show others how mature I am?
8. Will I prove I am a man or a woman by having a child?
9. Do I expect my child to make my life happy?

Have My Partner and I Really Talked About Becoming Parents?

1. Does my partner want to have a child? Have we talked about our reasons?
2. Could we give a child a good home? Is our relationship a happy and strong one?
3. Are we both ready to give our time and energy to raising a child?
4. Could we share our life with a child without jealousy?
5. What would happen if we separated after having a child, or if one of us should die?
6. Do my partner and I understand each other's feelings about religion, work, family, raising children, and future goals? Do we feel pretty much the same way? Will children fit into these feelings, hopes, and plans?
7. Suppose one of us wants a child and the other doesn't? Who decides?
8. Which of the questions listed here do we need to thoroughly discuss before making a decision?

Although there is no exact way to score your results, honest answers to these questions will give a clear indication of your interest in being a parent. To clarify your feelings, discuss your results with a classmate or friend, and compare answers. Which responses are the *best* indicators of parental interest and readiness? Judging from your own answers, are *you* ready and willing to be a parent?

Source: National Alliance for Optional Parenthood.

PERSONAL INSIGHT
Sexuality Education by Parents

Having taught sexuality education courses at the college level for many years, I am comfortable talking about sexuality. I know that not everyone is as comfortable—particularly when talking about sexuality to his or her own children. Even many who talk freely about the subject with others will often have hesitation with their children.

Invariably, when someone with children learns that I have taught sexuality courses, one of the first questions is "At what age should I start to talk with my children about sexuality?"

Unfortunately, this question misses the whole point. Since sexuality has many dimensions, and since humans are sexual beings from birth, aspects of sexuality education are needed at all ages. It is not simply a matter of deciding to "do the educating" at a certain age. It is an ongoing process.

I am usually more polite than to say this, but what I feel like saying is this: "If you have to ask the question, you obviously have missed valuable years of formal and informal sexuality education already. The way you handle a baby, the emotions you show to family members, how you deal with

physical contact, how you handle nudity in the home, how you respond to the natural questions children have about sexuality—all of these and many other things are sexuality education. It doesn't start at a certain time. It goes on continuously."

But usually I don't say that, and instead I just provide a more subtle message about the importance of parents as sexuality educators. If you have children, you will be their primary sexuality educator—whether you choose to be or not. What you do and say will have a tremendous impact on them.

Unfortunately, some parents mistreat their children. Many have argued for a long time that the rights of children need special consideration. For example, over 20 years ago children's rights were highlighted in a special issue of a national counseling journal (Rotter and Crunk 1975). The articles in this special issue emphasized children's rights to health, a responsible family, a trained parent, development of confidence, receiving caring, becoming competent, being different from others, and a good education. Also in 1975, a "Bill of Rights for Children" was developed (Gordon and Wollin 1975). Among other rights, it indicated that every child has the right to be wanted, receive a variety of learning experiences, be protected against abuse and neglect, be provided with the best possible environment in which to develop, and receive good medical care.

SEXUALITY EDUCATION OF CHILDREN

All parents are sexuality educators of their children, whether they choose to be or not. The way parents verbally and physically treat infants contributes to early sexuality education. The love given to a tiny infant is part of the process of sexuality education, as is the way parents respond when their children explore their own bodies.

Many parent-child activities through the years have implications for sexuality education. Examples are toilet training, the use (or lack of use) of terminology for body parts and certain physical activities, showing affection to children or in front of children, the way parents regard the status and roles of men and women, how parents treat and value one another, and the way parents handle children's questions about topics related to sexuality.

Children deserve to be provided with sexuality education in an acceptable manner. It is up to parents to cover the real concerns of young people. For example, masturbation is one of their biggest concerns. They should learn that masturbation is, most of the time, a normal expression of sexuality at any age. It is also important for young people to learn that while behavior can be "abnormal," thoughts in and of themselves are not. All people experience a variety of thoughts and have sexual fantasies.

Boys need to understand about penis size, because size has no impact on function and size doesn't vary that much anyway. In addition, young people should realize that one or a few homosexual experiences don't make a person homosexual.

Young people are also curious about how to tell if they're really in love. Parents should never trivialize a child's love affair, but they can help children understand that there are different types of love (Gordon 1986).

Sexuality education has many benefits, including increased knowledge and improved self-concept. Among sexually inexperienced adolescents, it can even help postpone the first act of sexual intercourse ("Sex Education Can Delay Sexual Activity, Study Says" 1992).

In actual practice, sexuality education for children isn't much different from education in general. The basic principles of parenting, communication, and discipline apply in the same way no matter what the topic or situation. Sometimes the sensitive nature of sexuality makes it seem like the topic requires special handling, but sound parenting skills allow parents to provide their children with a good education about sexuality.

Issue

When and Why Should People Have Children?

Traditionally, individuals have been free to have children whenever they desired. This is still basically true, and many will argue that it is a fundamental right to have children.

- Pro: You should be able to have children whenever you desire and to have as many as you wish. It is not right for someone to tell others when, or under what circumstances, they can have children. This should remain one of the freedoms associated with living in the United States.

- Con: Before you have children, there should be strong evidence that you will be a good parent. You should know parenting skills, understand children, and be able to afford to raise children. There should also be limits on how many children one couple may have. While this is a free country, the rights of children and those outside of the family must also be protected.

Should you always be free to have children? Should other people be free to choose when they will have children and how many they will have? Should there be a legal procedure (perhaps with a board of "experts") used to determine when you can have children—and how many? What factors should be used to determine when you should have children, and who should decide?

IMPORTANT FAMILY FACTORS

There are a number of important factors parents can promote within a family that can make a difference in the health of that family (Manning 1992). For example, encouraging family communication, using family time well, and providing adequate affection are likely to result in children who feel wanted and loved. The degree of parental support is also important. It can make a big difference if parents support their children in an excessive manner (such as making excuses for them when they are wrong) or if they expect their children to be responsible for their actions.

Independence is also an important factor. At one extreme, some parents allow little individuality and respect for autonomy. At the other extreme, independence and individuality can be considered valuable. Abuse is also a factor. Dealing with stress by using psychological crutches such as drugs, alcohol, and physical abuse can have a significant influence on family health.

We remain sexual beings through all the days of our lives.

Finally, the degree of parental control can be important. Parents can behave so they are viewed as authoritarian and strict; or they can appear totally indifferent and ineffective in regard to discipline. Which combinations, and degrees, of these factors do you think are most important?

MYTHS AND FACTS ABOUT SEXUALITY AND AGING

As we have discussed, we are sexual beings at all ages. Children are often taught that older people are supposed to be **asexual,** that is, without sexuality. This can sometimes become a self-fulfilling prophecy—as individuals age, they feel they should be asexual themselves. But sexuality involves feelings, self-concepts, and relationships, as well as physical activity; so how could anyone be truly asexual? The myth that aging leads to asexuality persists, however.

What are the facts about aging and sexuality? Contrary to common belief, although physiological response may become a little slower and possibly less intense with age, the average person in good health maintains sexual interest, desire, and activity throughout the life cycle. We do know that as men get older they are more likely to have occasional problems with erectile functioning. In fact, more than half of all men aged 40 to 70 report this experience (Feldman et al.

asexual
Without sexuality.

1994). The major hindrance to sexual activity in older people, however, seems to be the attitude, not the body. Such factors as monotony, preoccupation with career, mental or physical fatigue, overindulgence in food or drink, physical or mental infirmities, and fear of unsatisfactory sexual performance can hinder sexual activity. Most of these factors, though, are strongly influenced by attitudes.

To deal with negative attitudes, it is wise to remember six rules on human sexuality and aging (Cross 1993):

1. *All older people are sexual.*
2. *Older people have a particular need for a good sexual relationship.* Because of other factors that might have caused difficult adjustments (such as retirement, loss of friends and loved ones, loneliness, reduced income, etc.), the warmth and security of a good sexual relationship can be very helpful.
3. *Sexual physiology changes.* Aging can result in slower physiological responses and change in appearance, but people with a healthy attitude can adapt to these changes.
4. *Social attitudes are often frustrating.* Society still tends to deny the sexuality of the aged, but younger people, and those who work with the aged, can be helpful in understanding the need for total relationships for people of all ages.
5. *Use it or lose it.* Sexual response is a physiological function that tends to deteriorate if not used. Regular sexual activity should be understood as healthy.
6. *Older folks do it better.* The elderly have the advantage of considerable experience, lots of time, and a mellowness that enables them to roll with the punches. There is no need for pressure to "perform" or to "prove oneself." These factors can lead to better (more enjoyable) sexual activity than at younger ages.

Attitudes toward **menopause,** which is the period of cessation of menstruation, are often negative; however, only a small number of women actually need medical help at this time. Most experience no loss of sexual satisfaction—provided that their attitudes don't get in the way.

Menopause occurs because of decreased production of estrogen by the ovaries. Some women experience "hot flashes" during menopause. This is usually reported as an intense feeling of heat or a sensation that the room suddenly became much warmer.

While most women do not experience severe symptoms during menopause, estrogen replacement therapy is available through a physician if such help is needed. Doctors may prescribe other drugs for relief of menopausal symptoms such as difficulty sleeping, headache, or depression. As the proportion of women nearing menopause increases, it is likely that we will learn even more about the mysteries surrounding this stage of life (Willis 1988).

Because of myths they have learned, many women fear menopause because they think it will mean a loss of sexual desire. Most women do not experience such a loss, however, and during and after menopause sexual activity is good for relationships and health. Women who have sexual intercourse regularly, once a week or more, seem to have fewer changes in sexual desire or in physical response (Barbach 1993).

You might hear about a so-called male menopause, but men do not have anything comparable to female menopause. Their hormone levels do not drop severely. Some people feel that boosting older men's testosterone levels will be helpful, but there is no proof that such treatment is helpful—and it can be harmful. For example, testosterone treatment can worsen existing cases of prostate enlargement and possibly of prostate cancer ("Do Men Go Through Menopause?" 1993).

There are many myths about **hysterectomies,** the surgical removal of the uterus, but generally the subjective level of the woman's sexual response before surgery will continue unchanged, with reassurance and adequate information. In many cases, a hysterectomy does not interfere with basic hormonal production, and it is the hormones that influence feelings and drives, not the presence or absence of a uterus. Many women, however, do experience a change in the orgasmic sensation: uterine contractions are no longer part of the clitoral-vaginal response.

Unfortunately, while combating all the myths about sexuality and aging, older people may search for some nutritional element to aid sexual performance. No food or chemical has ever been proven to improve sexual performance; any apparent effects are only psychological.

Numerous men at some time in their lives experience prostatic problems (problems related to the prostate gland) and might even need surgery; this does not usually bring their sexual activity to an end. Men who functioned well before surgery usually continue to do so afterward. There are exceptions, of course, but medical personnel and counselors can greatly help by encouraging positive attitudes as they discuss this matter with their patients or clients.

It is the mind, then, and not the body that tends to interfere with sexual activity at any age. An awareness of this will help you be better equipped to resolve sexuality-related problems both now and later in life. This is another wonderful example of a mind-body relationship.

menopause
The permanent cessation of menstruation.

hysterectomy
The surgical removal of the uterus.

PERSONAL SKILLS AND EXPERIENCES

Promoting Healthy Relationships

Many skills combine to help produce healthy relationships. Within families and other relationships, we must first be comfortable with our sexuality. Then, we have to understand our needs and desires as well as those of our partner or other person in a relationship. We must possess good communication skills. In addition, we need knowledge and understanding of the sexuality of others—regardless of the type of individual or the group from which they come.

While promoting healthy relationships is not as easy as baking a cake, we can copy the process. It is common to use a recipe for guidance when baking a cake. As an important action step, develop your own recipe for promoting healthy relationships. Organize your recipe into categories for mind, body, soul, and interdependence as appropriate by considering the following statements and questions. Compare your recipe with those written by others. How do the ingredients you used compare to those used by others? How does your emphasis on (or amount of) each ingredient compare to others?

Mind

I need to understand where my concept of sexuality came from.

Body

I need to consider how my perceptions of my body and attractiveness of others have an impact.

Soul

How do the things I value most in life relate to my feelings about others?

Interdependence

How do I react as a result of what others do—physically and intellectually?

SEXUALITY IN SPECIAL GROUPS

Older people are not the only group whose sexuality has been neglected or misunderstood. Myths abound regarding sexual activity among physically challenged people, mentally challenged people, and ill people.

PHYSICALLY CHALLENGED PEOPLE

For the purposes of this discussion, physically challenged individuals are those with any kind of physical difficulty, including changes in body contours due to accident or disease, or changes in body functioning that might relate to sexuality. While trying to see that these persons' basic needs are met, some have neglected the fact that the challenged are sexual beings. Concerns related to sexuality are often basic as well and need attention.

Depending on the type of physical challenge, various areas of concern need attention, including the feelings of loss of control over one's bodily functions, the inability to care for personal needs, the fear of being less of a person, and the feeling of being unacceptable. Almost always, the general issue of a challenged person's body image is fundamental. Education and counseling about body image are important and ideally should also involve the sexual partners of challenged persons.

For many years we have known aspects of sexual functioning that are important related to individuals who are paralyzed. For example (Woods 1975):

1. Some components of the human sexual response cycle, such as erection, are mediated by spinal cord reflexes. Therefore, it is unnecessary to have pathways from the brain to the sex organs. For example, stimuli resulting from pressure or tension in the pelvic organs or from touch excite impulses that can cause erection.

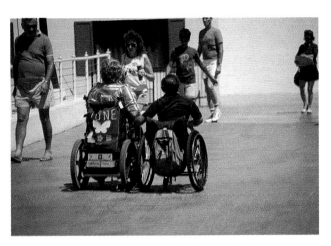

It's important to remember that disabled individuals are sexual beings too.

2. The level of the spinal cord lesion and the degree of interruption of nerve impulses influence the nature of sexual functioning in the patient with spinal cord injury. For example, the local reflexes important in female orgasm are thought to be integrated into the lumbar and sacral regions of the cord.

3. Gratification can be experienced from sexual responses other than those emanating from the sex organs during the human sexual response cycle. Many handicapped people highly develop other areas of stimulation.

4. Previous sexual practices might have to be modified as a result of spinal cord injury. For example, the positions in which one has sexual activity might have to be different. Sexual aids may be helpful.

We know that the successful adjustment of spinal-cord-injured males following injury involves many factors. Among them are a positive self-concept, having an understanding and supportive partner, and skillful sexuality education and counseling. Efforts need to be directed not only to patients, but to their partners and medical-care personnel as well (Alexander, Sipski, and Findley 1993).

Physically challenged people are an important part of society. In recent years much needed attention has been given to many of their needs, but there is still a failure to recognize and appreciate the sexuality of the physically challenged.

MENTALLY CHALLENGED PEOPLE

As with the physically challenged, until recently we have generally neglected the sexuality of mentally challenged individuals. Attention given to their sexual behavior was usually directed toward restricting that behavior, on the assumption that they were not interested in or could not handle sexuality. Fortunately, we now realize that mentally challenged people are sexual beings. They, too, need understanding and help in dealing with their sexuality. Often, there is a need to be explicit when working with mentally challenged people because they have lower reasoning levels. For example, educating the mentally challenged often requires showing them the actual positions for coitus with pictures and films so they fully understand.

Institutionalized mentally challenged individuals who are allowed to have sexual relationships can build feelings of affection and tenderness. As we increasingly recognize the rights of mentally challenged persons to participate in sexual activity, even institutionalized, severely challenged individuals can live happier, fuller lives.

ILL PEOPLE

Most of us have little experience with the very young, the aged, the physically disabled, or the mentally disabled. However, everyone knows someone who is ill, and everyone becomes ill on occasion. The ill are another group whose sexuality has mainly been ignored.

In the past, both patients and medical personnel avoided mentioning sexual topics, no doubt because both were too embarrassed to do so. Now, questions about sexual history are often asked in addition to regular questions about medical history. And doctors, patients, and partners are being encouraged to discuss, when relevant, how illness or other medical problems will affect sexual functioning.

Diabetes, neurological disorders, gynecological disorders, inflammation of the male's prostate gland, castration, rectal surgery, and heart attacks usually have a direct effect on sexual functioning. But persons with nonrelated physical problems often develop sexual problems because of psychological factors. Some, for example, feel guilty when they get sick and try to determine where the guilt lies. Because the

topic of sexuality is a leading producer of guilt, they might consciously or unconsciously avoid sexual activity. They might even allow illness to restrict their sexual life simply because they failed to ask medical personnel whether restriction was actually necessary (again note the interrelationships between physical and psychological aspects of total health).

To reduce sexual problems associated with illness, those who are ill need to feel that it is appropriate to discuss sexuality and need to be aware of guilt feelings. In addition, in all cases of illness, they should learn when they can safely return to normal sexual activity to avoid detrimental effects on their relationships as well as on their self-concept. Those who are ill also need to realize that sexual problems can be expressed through physical symptoms; a person who asks for an examination of the genital area because of a supposed concern about cancer may actually be seeking an "acceptable" way to talk about a sexual difficulty.

If we understand this relationship between illness and sexuality, we can help reduce the incidence of problems, both in and out of the hospital.

TAKE ACTION

1. Decide how you will educate your children (now or in the future) about sexuality.
2. Improve communication skills within your intimate relationships (friends, spouse, children, etc.).
3. Many people think negatively about some aspects of human sexuality. Develop a plan to reduce such negative thinking in your life so that sexuality can become a more positive aspect of your health decisions.
4. Recognize that people who have different sexual lifestyles have emotional needs, self-esteem needs, and acceptance needs just like anyone else.

SUMMARY

1. Sexuality has four interacting dimensions: social, psychological, moral, and biological.
2. Sexuality relates more to what we are than to what we do, and it is directly related to human health.
3. Some feel the quality of family life is deteriorating, while others feel we are entering into more high-quality relationships.
4. Both similarity factors and complementary factors influence mate selection.
5. Successful family communication involves feeling at ease with language about sexuality, using active listening, identifying one's position, and exploring alternative solutions.
6. Successful parenting demands considering the rights of children, personal feelings about children, and the sexual education of children.

7. Many myths exist about sexuality and aging.

8. Myths abound regarding the sexuality of people who are physically challenged, mentally challenged, or ill.

COMMITMENT ACTIVITIES

1. Traditional concepts of sexuality have been somewhat narrow-minded. As discussed in this chapter, a total concept of human sexuality involves many components. In the coming months, try to become more aware of your own prejudices in terms of human sexuality. In your thoughts and dealings with others, reduce the use of words and images that portray your behavior as superior or "normal" in comparison with that of others. Also, try to reduce comments that might reflect stereotypes about sexuality.

2. Although it is clear that we are sexual beings at all ages, the sexuality of older people has often been neglected. Visit a home for older people in your community. Talk with an administrator to see what provisions are made for sexuality at the home. Is privacy promoted? Are conjugal visits allowed? Are programs held on sexual topics?

3. Many factors play roles in determining whom we date and perhaps marry. Certainly love must be predominant, but numerous other factors also enter the picture. List the factors you consider most important in a person you would like to date and in a person you would like to marry. Is there any difference between your two lists? What will you do now and in the future to make your lists coincide with reality? In other words, how can you be sure you will end up with a person who meets your qualifications?

4. The sexuality of mentally and physically challenged people has often been ignored in training programs for people who work with these groups. Determine what is being done with the topic of sexuality in training programs for those who will work with the mentally or physically challenged in your area. Is it adequately covered for those who work in hospitals, clinics, or other facilities? If not, prepare suggestions for what might be done.

REFERENCES

Alexander, C. J., M. L. Sipski, and T. W. Findley. 1993. "Sexual Activities, Desire, and Satisfaction in Males Pre- and Post-Spinal Cord Injury." *Archives of Sexual Behavior* 22, no. 3 (March): 217–28.

Barbach, L. 1993. "The Pause: A Closer Look at Menopause and Female Sexuality." *SIECUS Report* 21, no. 3 (June/July): 1–5.

Bruess, C. E., and J. S. Greenberg. 1994. *Sexuality Education: Theory and Practice.* Dubuque, IA: Wm. C. Brown.

Bulcroft, R. A., and K. A. Bulcroft. 1993. "Race Differences in Attitudinal and Motivational Factors in the Decision to Marry." *Journal of Marriage and the Family* 55, no. 5 (May): 338–55.

Coombs, R. H. 1991. "Marital Status and Personal Well-Being." *Family Relations* 40 (January): 97–102.

"Cost of Raising a Child." 1991. *Youth Indicators 1991.* Washington, DC: U.S. Government Printing Office.

Cross, R. J. 1993. "What Doctors and Others Need to Know." *SIECUS REPORT* 21, no. 5 (June/July): 7–9.

DeBuono, B. A., S. H. Zinner, M. Daamen, and W. M. McCormack. 1990. "Sexual Behavior of College Women in 1975, 1986, and 1989." *New England Journal of Medicine* 322, no. 12 (22 March).

DeMaris, A., and K. V. Rao. 1992. "Premarital Cohabitation and Subsequent Marital Stability in the United States: A Reassessment." *Journal of Marriage and the Family* 54, no. 2 (February): 178–90.

"Do Men Go Through Menopause?" 1993. *Consumer Reports on Health* 5, no. 10 (October): 105–8.

"Educating America: What People Really Want to Know About Sex." 1987. *Sexuality Today* 10, no. 25 (25 May): 2–3.

Feldman, H. A., I. Goldstein, G. Dimitrios, D. G. Hatzichristou, R. J. Krane, and J. B. McKinlay. 1994. "Impotence and Its Medical and Psychosocial Correlates: Results of the Massachusetts Male Aging Study." *Journal of Urology* 151, no. 1 (January): 54–61.

Flax, E. 1992. "Most High-School Students Sexually Active, C.D.C. Finds." *Education Week* 11, no. 17 (15 January): 10.

Fox, E., and M. Young. 1989. "Religiosity, Sex Guilt, and Sexual Behavior Among College Students." *Health Values* 13, no. 2 (March/April): 32–37.

Ganong, L. H., and M. Coleman. 1992. "Gender Differences in Expectations of Self and Future Partner." *Journal of Family Issues* 13, no. 1 (March): 55–64.

Gordon, S. 1986. "What Kids Need to Know." *Psychology Today,* October, 22–26.

Gordon, S., and M. M. Wollin. 1975. *Parenting: A Guide for Young People.* New York: Oxford Book.

Groves, M. M., and D. M. Horm-Wingerd. 1991. "Commuter Marriages: Personal, Family, and Career Issues." *Sociology and Social Research* 75, no. 4 (July): 212–17.

Manning, T. M. 1992. "Definition of Family Factors That Make a Difference." Paper presented at national meeting of the Association for the Advancement of Health Education, April, Indianapolis.

Marin, B. B. 1988. "AIDS Prevention in Non–Puerto Rican Hispanics." Paper prepared for National Institute of Drug Abuse technical review, Rockville, MD.

Mays, V. M., and S. D. Cochran. 1988. "Issues in the Perception of AIDS Risk and Risk Reduction Activities by Black and Hispanic/Latina Women." *American Psychologist* 43, no. 11:949–57.

Pill, C. J. 1990. "Stepfamilies: Redefining the Family." *Family Relations* 39, no. 2 (April): 186–93.

"Profile of the American Wife." 1987. *Statistical Bulletin* 68, no. 2 (April–June): 18–21.

"Rising Prevalence of Cohabitation in United States May Have Partially Offset Decline in Marriage Rates." 1990. *Family Planning Perspectives* 22, no. 2 (March/April): 90–91.

Robinson, L. C., and P. W. Blanton. 1993. "Marital Strengths in Enduring Marriages." *Family Relations* 42, no. 1 (January): 38–45.

Rotter, J., and B. Crunk, eds. 1975. *Elementary School Guidance and Counseling* (Special Issue: Children's Rights). Washington, DC: American Personnel and Guidance Association.

Saxton, L. 1983. *The Individual, Marriage, and the Family.* 5th ed. Belmont, CA: Wadsworth.

Schmid, R. E. 1987. "College Degrees May Delay, Not Kill Chances of Marrying." *Birmingham News,* 19 January, 3B.

"Sex Education Can Delay Sexual Activity, Study Says." 1992. *Education Week* 11, no. 17 (15 January): 11.

"Sex Ratio Imbalance Creates Fearful Women." 1986. *Sexuality Today* 10, no. 19 (31 March): 1.

South, S. J. 1993. "Racial and Ethnic Differences in the Desire to Marry." *Journal of Marriage and the Family* 55, no. 5 (May): 357–70.

"Test Your Sexual I.Q." 1992. *Consumer Reports on Health* 4, no. 2 (February): 12.

Thomson, E., and U. Colella. 1992. "Cohabitation and Marital Stability: Quality or Commitment?" *Journal of Marriage and the Family* 54, no. 5 (May): 259–67.

Toleran, D. E. 1991. "Pakikisama: Reaching the Filipino Community with AIDS Prevention." *MIRA* 5, no. 1:8.

Valois, R. F., and K. A. Waring. 1991. "An Analysis of College Students' Anonymous Questions About Human Sexuality." *Journal of the American College Health Association* 39 (May): 263–68.

Ward, R. 1993. "Marital Happiness and Household Equity in Later Life." *Journal of Marriage and the Family* 55, no. 5 (May): 427–38.

Weiss, D. L., B. Rabinowitz, and M. F. Ruckstuhl. 1992. "Individual Changes in Sexual Attitudes and Behavior Within College-Level Human Sexuality Courses." *Journal of Sex Research* 29, no. 1 (February): 43–59.

"Why Do Couples Get Married?" 1990. *Behavior Today* 21, no. 39 (24 September): 4–5.

"Why Some Women Don't Get Married." 1990. *Behavior Today* 21, no. 39 (24 September): 5–6.

Willis, J. 1988. "Demystifying Menopause." *FDA Consumer* 22, no. 6 (July/August): 24–27.

Woods, N. F. 1975. *Human Sexuality in Health and Illness*. St. Louis: Mosby.

ADDITIONAL READINGS

Moss, Barry R., and Andrew I. Schwebel. 1993. "Defining Intimacy in Romantic Relationships." *Family Relations* 42, no. 1 (January): 31–36. Sharing of romantic intimacy is important, but there has been no definition of romantic intimacy. The authors propose a multidimensional definition of romantic intimacy and discuss concepts of love and intimacy.

Simon, Toby. 1993. "Sexuality on Campus—'90's Style." *Change* 25, no. 4 (September/October): 50–56. Discusses college students' concerns regarding sexuality. A university dean of student life summarizes discussions with a number of college students and provides sources of additional information.

Theisen, S. Carol, and Phyllis Kernoff Mansfield. 1993. "Menopause: Social Construction or Biological Destiny?" *Journal of Health Education* 24, no. 4 (July/August): 209–13. Explores biomedical and sociocultural models of menopause and discusses promotion of a healthy transition to menopause.

Tiedje, L. B., B. T. Tiedje, C. B. Worthman, G. Downey, C. Emmons, M. Biernat, and E. Lang. 1990. "Women with Multiple Roles: Role-Compatibility Perceptions, Satisfaction, and Mental Health." *Journal of Marriage and the Family* 52, no. 1 (February): 63–72. Examines alternative models of how women combine perceptions of role conflict and enhancement. Contains information about how women who combine the roles of mother, spouse, and professional perceive their multiple roles.

Sexual Response and Behavior

Healthy People 2000 Objectives

- Reduce physical abuse directed at women by male partners to no more than 27 incidents per 1,000 couples.

- Increase to at least thirty the number of states in which at least 50 percent of children identified as neglected or physically or sexually abused receive physical and mental evaluation with appropriate follow-up as a means of breaking the intergenerational cycle of abuse.

- Reduce rape and attempted rape of women aged 12 and older to no more than 108 incidents per 100,000 women.

- Reduce the proportion of adolescents who have engaged in sexual intercourse to no more than 15 percent by age 15 and no more than 40 percent by age 17. (Baseline: 27% of girls and 33% of boys by age 15; 50% of girls and 66% of boys by age 17; reported in 1988.)

Sexual Behavior Communication

Directions

Respond only regarding your sexual activity. If you do not participate in any sexual activity, skip this assessment. In regard to communication about sexuality with your partner, mark all of the following that apply to your relationship.

_____ 1. I tell my partner what feels good.

_____ 2. I tell my partner what hurts, if anything.

_____ 3. I avoid frequent sexual encounters because I do not like them.

_____ 4. I let myself just go with my feelings and behave the way I want to act during sexual encounters.

_____ 5. We have talked about and resolved how often to have sexual activity.

_____ 6. Sexual activity is a problem for us.

_____ 7. I have told my partner what I want during sexual activity.

_____ 8. My partner and I enjoy holding hands, kissing, and just talking as much as we do sexual activity.

_____ 9. It is important that each time we express love or date that it culminate in sexual intercourse to be a really meaningful experience.

Scoring

Give yourself the following points for the items you checked, and total your score.

1. = 2	4. = 2	7. = 2
2. = 2	5. = 2	8. = 2
3. = –2	6. = –2	9. = –2

Interpretation

This exercise indicates whether you have healthy communication in your sexual relationship. Interpret your score as follows:

6–10 = Your communication is healthy.

0–5 = Your communication is moderately healthy.

–1 – –6 = You need to improve your communication skills.

This chapter provides information you may have wondered about since your body first responded sexually. Even though basic biology is discussed here, keep in mind that responses are influenced by many other factors—there are many interrelationships among the dimensions of human sexuality. This is also an excellent example of mind/body/soul health. If you are currently in a sexual relationship, complete the Health Assessment on sexual behavior communication to see whether you have healthy communication in your relationship.

Tennov (1989, 45–50) describes **limerence** as the quality of sexual attraction based on chemistry and sexual desire. It is passionate love based on sexual attraction, a powerful feeling that can overcome basic reasoning. Relationships that are initially based on limerence can develop into deeper, long-lasting relationships, but it can be important to distinguish between love and limerence. "Crushes" experienced in the adolescent years are based upon limerence. Limerence is also used in the advertising media to sell products. Relationships that are based only upon limerence, and not upon communication and love, will probably be short-lived.

HUMAN SEXUAL RESPONSE

Do you recall the first time you had an erection or experienced vaginal lubrication? These are normal responses to sexual stimulation, but at the time you probably didn't realize that. Perhaps you had concerns about your response. The following sections explain what occurs when someone becomes sexually stimulated. Our goal is to help you understand the nature of sexual responses and appreciate that such natural responses vary among people.

THE MASTERS AND JOHNSON SEXUAL RESPONSE CYCLE

Around 30 years ago the research of William Masters and Virginia Johnson (1966) revolutionized our views of sexual behavior. Masters and Johnson gave us information about the phases of human sexual response, which is basically biological. That it is biological, of course, does not mean that it is "automatic" or "machinelike." Sexual responses are influenced by such factors as human relationships, mental stress, and individual beliefs. At the same time, this information about biological responses is basic to the understanding of our overall responses.

Masters and Johnson (1966) first studied more than eight hundred people in a laboratory situation, where the sexual responses of subjects could be monitored. They studied male and female responses during masturbation, intercourse, and mechanical stimulation, and discovered that the physiological response was essentially the same regardless of the type of stimulation used.

PHASES OF SEXUAL RESPONSE

Masters and Johnson discovered that human sexual response is an ordered sequence of events that can be divided into four phases: (1) excitement, (2) plateau, (3) orgasm,

---

limerence

The quality of sexual attraction based on chemistry and sexual desire.

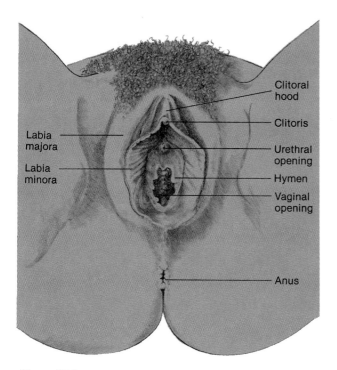

Figure 10.1

External genitalia of the human female.

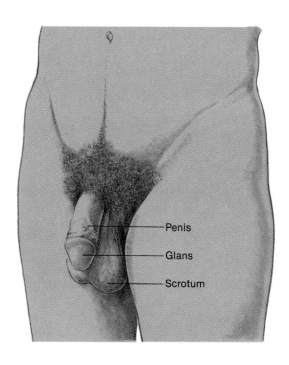

Figure 10.2

External genitalia of the human male.

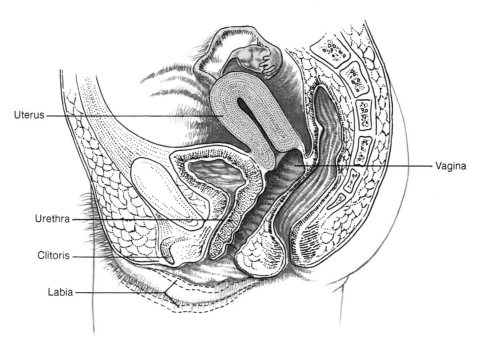

Figure 10.3

Some of the biological changes associated with female orgasm. The shape of the vagina changes so that the upper portion expands and the lower portion contracts to one-half of normal.

and (4) resolution. Contrary to earlier thinking, they also found far more similarities than differences between male and female responses. Figures 10.1 and 10.2 show relaxed ex-

ternal genitalia, and figures 10.3 and 10.4 illustrate changes associated with sexual response.

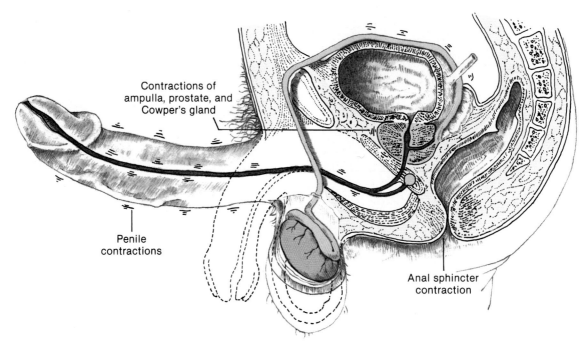

Contractions of
ampulla, prostate, and
Cowper's gland

Penile
contractions

Anal sphincter
contraction

Figure 10.4
Some of the biological changes associated with male orgasm.
The penis becomes engorged with blood and the testicles rise.

Excitement

In the **excitement phase** of human sexual response, in men, blood flows into the erectile tissue of the penis faster than it flows out, and the penis becomes erect. In women, the vagina quickly responds to stimulation by secreting lubrication (like sweating inside the vagina). Interestingly, male erections and female lubrication also occur during sleep approximately every 80 to 90 minutes.

In women, the clitoris, vaginal lips, nipples, and breasts tend to enlarge, while the vagina lengthens and the uterus elevates. In men, the testicles elevate. In both sexes, a skin flush may develop over the upper body and face. Additional changes might include increased muscle tension throughout the body, increased heart rate, and increased blood pressure. Men often experience tensing and thickening of scrotal skin.

Plateau

During the **plateau phase,** the changes that occurred in the excitement phase intensify. The penis and vagina become larger. The sex flush often becomes well developed and might spread over much of the body. The woman's *labia minora* often change color, ranging from bright red to a deep wine color. The man may experience a preejaculatory emission of two or three drops of fluid. If a pregnancy is not desired, extreme caution is needed because sperm have been found in this fluid.

Orgasm

Orgasm, usually the shortest stage of the sexual response, is quite similar in men and women. Both sexes experience

muscular contractions in the pelvic area that can last from a few seconds to about a minute. Muscular contractions and spasms may also occur in other parts of the body. Respiration, heart rate, and blood pressure all increase. The main difference between men and women is that men ejaculate and women do not, although some controversial research indicates that some women may experience a form of ejaculation as well if certain types of stimulation are used.

Some researchers say that female have a G (Grafenberg) spot—a patch of erectile tissue in the front wall of the vagina, directly behind the pubic bone—that acts something like a second clitoris. When this erogenous zone is stimulated by deep pressure, it is supposed to produce a vaginal orgasm distinctly different from a clitoral orgasm. Some researchers even report that sufficient stimulation of the G spot results in a form of female ejaculation. Other researchers feel this remains unproven.

excitement phase
The initial phase of human sexual response. Bodily changes include increased blood flow, vaginal lubrication, and penile erection.

plateau phase
The second phase of human sexual response, involving intensification of the responses begun in the excitement phase.

orgasm
The peak of pleasure in sexual excitement; the third phase of human sexual response.

Sexual Activity and Athletic Performance

No one really knows why, but for decades some people believed that sexual activity prior to an athletic event would hinder performance. Even today many coaches and athletic trainers feel strongly that athletes should avoid sexual activity prior to athletic participation.

It appears that participating in sexual intercourse just before competing won't affect athletic performance. Doctors gave sixteen professional athletes—ranging from cyclists to weight lifters—a thorough physical exam both before and 2 hours after having sexual intercourse. The results showed no difference in strength or endurance, with the exception of a stress test on a bicycle.

When the athletes did the bicycle test again 8 hours later, however, even that difference had vanished (Edell 1990).

While there is a lack of scientific information on the subject, most athletes today probably wouldn't hesitate to participate in sexual activity the night before an athletic contest. Depending upon the athlete's frame of mind, it couldn't hurt—and it might help (Thornton 1990).

A survey of 2,350 U.S. and Canadian women showed that many of the women believed that the G spot exists in the vaginal barrel. Those who reported orgasms from stimulation of the G spot were also more likely to report a spurt of fluid at the moment of orgasm (Darling, Davidson, and Conway-Welch 1990).

During orgasm, men usually experience expulsive contractions of the entire length of the *penile urethra* for several seconds. After several contractions, they are reduced in frequency; however, minor contractions continue for several more seconds. Contractions of secondary orgasms also facilitate the ejaculatory process.

In contrast to some earlier thinking that vaginal and clitoral orgasms were different, and in contrast to the information just mentioned about the G spot, Masters and Johnson claimed there is only one kind of female orgasm—a sexual one. This doesn't mean that women might not prefer different types of stimulation—just that the response is the same. Masters and Johnson also found that penis size makes *no difference* in either a man's sexual ability or a woman's sexual response.

In most males, the erection usually subsides after orgasm and cannot be attained again until some minutes, or even hours, have passed. The period during which a man is unable to have another erection is called the **refractory period.** Many women, however, are biologically capable of multiple orgasms within a relatively short period of time. There have been few investigations of this phenomenon, but in one study 42.7 percent of the female respondents had experienced multiple orgasms (Darling, Davidson, and Jennings 1991).

Resolution

During the **resolution phase,** in both sexes, the body tends to return to its preexcitement state. In addition, women often experience a widespread film of perspiration unrelated to the degree of physical activity. Men may experience similar perspiration, but it is usually confined to the soles of the feet and palms of the hands. This stage may last 10 to 15 minutes if orgasm has occurred, or a much longer time if it has not. Figures 10.5 and 10.6 show the male and female cycles of sexual response.

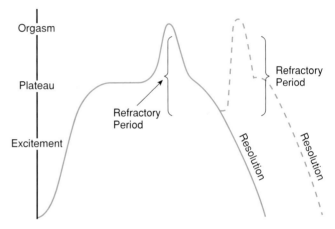

Figure 10.5

The typical male pattern of response. The dotted line indicates the possibility of a second orgasm and ejaculation after the refractory period.

William H. Masters and Virginia E. Johnson, *Human Sexual Response* (Boston: Little, Brown, 1966), p. 5.

OTHER THEORETICAL MODELS OF SEXUAL RESPONSE

Two other models of human sexual response should be mentioned. Watch for similarities and differences among the models.

Kaplan's Triphasic Model

Kaplan (1979) says human sexual response has a *desire* phase, an *excitement* phase, and a *resolution* phase. She feels it is possible to function well in one or two phases while

---

refractory period
The period following male ejaculation during which the male is unable to have another erection.

resolution phase
The fourth phase of human sexual response, when the body tends to return to its preexcitement state.

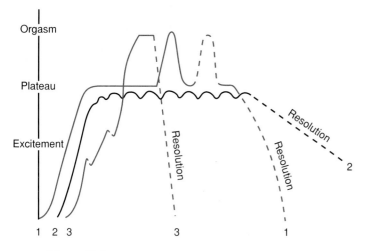

Figure 10.6

Three types of female response. Pattern 1 is multiple orgasm. Pattern 2 is arousal without orgasm. Pattern 3 involves a number of small declines in excitement and a very rapid resolution.

William H. Masters and Virginia E. Johnson, *Human Sexual Response* (Boston: Little, Brown, 1966), p. 5. Reprinted by permission of the authors.

having problems in the other. The unique component of **Kaplan's triphasic model** is the desire phase: a psychological, prephysical sexual response stage that is ignored by Masters and Johnson.

Zilbergeld and Ellison's Model

Zilbergeld and Ellison (1980) felt that the Masters and Johnson model focused exclusively on physiological aspects. **Zilbergeld and Ellison's model** consists of five components: (1) *interest or desire* (how frequently a person wants to participate), (2) *arousal* (how excited a person gets during sexual activity), (3) *physiological readiness* (e.g., erection or vaginal lubrication), (4) *orgasm*, and (5) *satisfaction* (a person's evaluation of how she or he feels).

Sexual satisfaction is a qualitative rather than a quantitative component. The quality of shared feelings is far more important than the number of orgasms experienced. It is also possible for a person to achieve sexual satisfaction without having the "peak" experience of orgasm every time.

SEXUAL DYSFUNCTION

Sexual dysfunction is a chronic inability to respond sexually in a satisfying way. While many prefer not to use these terms, female sexual dysfunction has traditionally been called *frigidity* and male sexual dysfunction has traditionally been called *impotence*. These labels do not apply when people are temporarily uninterested in sexual behavior or unable to respond sexually due to exhaustion, too much alcohol or other chemical substance, anger, and so on. The key word in the definition is *chronic*—that is, a consistent long-term inability to respond (Greenberg, Bruess, and Mullen 1993).

Sexual dysfunction can have many causes, but most experts agree that psychological causes are most common—another

example of strong mind/body/soul interrelationships. Men who are unemployed report more difficulties attaining an erection than do men who are employed. Wives of unemployed men also report greater erectile difficulties for their spouses than do wives of employed men. Marital satisfaction, however, can help reduce erectile difficulty (Morokoff and Gilliland 1993).

Some medications can cause sexual dysfunction. Men might have trouble achieving erection or might experience "dry" ejaculation in which semen travels back into the bladder. Women might have less vaginal lubrication or difficulty reaching orgasm. Both sexes may lose interest in sexual activity. It is important to communicate with your physician if these problems occur, since simple adjustments in dosages or drugs are often enough to reverse the sexual side effects ("Does Your Medication Impair Your Sex Life?" 1993). Sexual counseling has been helpful for many, but it has also caused consumer difficulties as a major area of health quackery.

Look again at the Health Assessment on sexual behavior communication at the beginning of this chapter. Now that you know more about human sexual response, review your responses to the statements and your score, if you are in a sexual relationship. What are the implications for your intimate relationships with others?

SEXUAL BEHAVIOR

While we emphasize total sexuality, we recognize that many individuals focus on specific sexual behaviors. Because of this, it is appropriate to briefly consider patterns of sexual behavior.

PATTERNS OF HETEROSEXUAL BEHAVIOR

Heterosexuals have sexual desire predominantly for members of the opposite sex. Most adults (aged 18 years and older) in the United States are sexually experienced and most are currently sexually active. Eighty-seven percent had only one sexual partner in the previous year. Eighteen percent of those sexually active engaged in unprotected intercourse with more than one partner during the past year (Leigh, Temple, and Trocki 1993).

Kaplan's triphasic model
A model of human sexual response, consisting of three phases: desire, excitement, and resolution.

Zilbergeld and Ellison's model
A five-component model of human sexual response.

sexual dysfunction
Chronic inability to respond sexually in a way that one finds satisfying.

heterosexuality
Having sexual desire predominantly for members of the opposite sex.

PERSONAL INSIGHT

Human Sexual Response As a Goal

It is helpful to know about human sexual response, but the information must be kept in appropriate perspective. Two people we know used the information to establish performance goals. Both were so interested in observing their own changes as they moved through the stages of human sexual response that it became difficult for them to enjoy their interactions with each other.

Once the female learned that multiple orgasms were biologically possible,

she set a personal goal of achieving at least three orgasms during one love-making session. She became so obsessed with trying to have multiple orgasms that sometimes she didn't even have one.

The male had set two goals. One was to help the female have multiple orgasms and the other was to see if he could ignore his refractory period and have multiple orgasms himself. As he tried harder and harder to reach the two goals, he found that he had difficulty maintaining his erection—or even getting one in the first place. Not only were the goals not reached, but soon

the couple's sexual relations in general were not very enjoyable.

This personal insight demonstrates the importance of the mind/body/soul relationship. It is helpful to learn about biological human sexual responses, but they are greatly influenced by emotional and spiritual factors. If you are not happy in a relationship, you will not respond effectively. If you aren't ready for sexual activity, you are likely to have the same thing happen. Or if you make sexual activity a contest or a goal, like our two friends did, problems can result. Human sexual response must be kept in perspective in relation to all parts of the person and the relationship.

Factors Influencing the Decision to Have Sexual Intercourse for the First Time

The transition to sexual intercourse is usually an important event. Factors influencing this transition can include these (Day 1992):

1. Females, regardless of age, are guided by religion, locus-of-control orientation, occupational desire, and self-esteem.

2. Males are typically more responsive than females to family and community influences.
3. Persons living in rural communities tend to have sexual intercourse earlier.
4. Females living with stepfathers tend to have sexual intercourse earlier than females living with biological fathers.
5. Persons with higher self-esteem and higher internal locus of control who have early sexual experiences are more likely to be high risk takers in general.
6. Males and females with deeper religious convictions tend to begin sexual intercourse later.

Note that the more risk factors present in adolescents' lives, the greater the likelihood that they will be sexually experienced. These risk factors include poor school performance, involvement in a committed relationship, a low level of parental education, frequent alcohol use, a history of sexual and/or physical abuse, a perception of limited economic opportunities, lack of school attachment, and permissive parental values about teenage sexual behavior (Small and Luster 1994).

Source: From Randal D. Day, "The Transition to First Intercourse Among Racially and Culturally Diverse Youth" in *Journal of Marriage and the Family* 54(11): 749–762 (November 1992).

Early Patterns of Sexual Behavior Before Marriage

Many history books give the impression that early Americans were sexually chaste before marriage. Careful reading, though, reveals that this was not the case. In the late 1700s in Massachusetts, one in three women in one church confessed "fornication" to her minister (Reiss 1973); the actual rate of participation was probably higher. Males on the western frontier relied heavily on prostitution for sexual gratification, and the women's liberation movement of the 1870s, designed mainly to ensure that women would have the right to vote, revealed numerous extramarital sexual affairs. Also, the first vulcanized rubber condom was displayed at the Philadelphia World's Fair in 1876. These apparently isolated events call into general question the supposed sexual innocence of our forebears.

Recent Changes in Sexual Behavior Before Marriage

The greatest increase in rates of premarital intercourse occurred in the first two or three decades of the 1900s (Bell 1966). The so-called sexual revolution began early in the 1900s, not in the 1960s and 1970s as many have thought. It appears that during most years of the twentieth century, well over half of all men had premarital sexual intercourse.

About 78 percent of high school males and females who had participated in sexual intercourse used some form of birth control during their most recent sex act. Fewer than half, however, used a condom (Flax 1992a, 10).

The average age to have sexual intercourse for the first time in the United States is 16 years for females and 15.5 years for males. Every 30 seconds a teenage girl becomes pregnant, and every 13 seconds a teenager contracts a sexually

Issue

Sexual Intercourse Before Marriage

Among a group of typical college freshmen, about half have participated in sexual intercourse and about half have not. Most of those who have participated have done so prior to marriage. Strong feelings exist about the pros and cons of sexual intercourse before marriage. Some of them are as follows:

- Pro: Premarital intercourse is okay as long as the individuals involved participate freely; no harm is done if they have freedom of choice, and the people involved can stop any time they so desire. Participating in premarital intercourse shows maturity, satisfies curiosity about sexual behavior, and can be a valuable learning experience in present or future relationships.

- Con: Premarital intercourse is acceptable only if there is a certain level of commitment between the people involved, perhaps a strong emotional commitment or even an engagement. Intimate relationships can be satisfying without intercourse. Also, some people feel that intercourse should occur only after marriage and is wrong before marriage under any circumstances.

Should people engage in sexual intercourse before marriage? What are the most important factors that should influence the decision? What do you think are the differences between those who choose to participate and those who don't?

THE WORLD AROUND YOU

The Image of "Recreational" Sexual Activity

Many college students feel that others expect them to participate in sexual activity but are not comfortable with that expectation. About 20 percent of women and 33 percent of men use alcohol more than normal to make it easier for them to participate in sexual activity. They often say they do so to lose their inhibitions.

In addition, from 20 to 40 percent of college women and 3 percent of college men say they have been physically or verbally coerced into sexual activity. More than 50 percent of college women have pretended to enjoy sexual activity, as have 10 percent of college men.

Source: From Wendy Luttrell and Peter Anderson, "Collegians Drink to Loosen Up Sexually." Paper presented at annual meeting of the Society for the Scientific Study of Sex, Chicago, November 1993.

transmitted disease. There are about 1 million teenage pregnancies a year, and 3 million teenagers—1 out of 6—will contract a sexually transmitted disease each year (Sroka 1991). Worldwide, sexual intercourse occurs more than 100 million times daily, resulting in nearly 1 million pregnancies and about 350,000 cases of sexually transmitted diseases ("Briefly Noted" 1992).

Approximately 50 percent of American adolescents do not use contraceptives the first time they engage in intercourse. Half of premarital pregnancies occur within the first 6 months after initiation of sexual intercourse ("How Healthy Are America's Adolescents?" 1990).

About 48 percent of females and 61 percent of males have had sexual intercourse by the time they reach college age. Studies of college students indicate that 75 to 80 percent of males and 60 to 70 percent of females have engaged in sexual intercourse (Reinisch et al. 1992). Exact numbers vary among studies. For example, in another study 33 percent of ninth-graders, 59 percent of tenth-graders, 69 percent of eleventh-graders, and 72 percent of twelfth-graders had participated in sexual intercourse (Jacobson, Aldana, and Beaty 1994).

Clearly there are many implications related to interpersonal relationships. For example, although the differences seem to be smaller than in the past, men still initiate sexual activity more frequently than women do. Women, however, no longer serve as the restrictors of sexual activity. They respond positively to initiations as frequently as men do (O'Sullivan and Byers 1992).

You may have wondered about the effect of sexual intercourse before marriage on the development of a relationship. This can be viewed in many ways. For example, when initial sexual intercourse is satisfying, the effect on the relationship is often positive for both females and males. Also, those who have high-quality relationships (involving love, commitment, and good communication) are more likely to report the effect of sexual intercourse as positive. The likelihood that intercourse will have a positive effect on the relationship is increased if the individuals develop competent decision-making and problem-solving skills in dating relationships (Cate et al. 1993).

As a final note on sexual intercourse before marriage, a cross-cultural comparison is interesting. College women from the relatively sexually restrictive U.S. culture report greater negative reactions to their first premarital intercourse than do their counterparts from the relatively sexually permissive Swedish culture. In addition, access to important information on responsible sexual decision making is severely limited in the more restrictive culture (Schwartz 1993).

Even in the United States, family structure and neighborhood characteristics can account for race differences in sexual activity. For example, attachment to family, educational aspirations, and perceived ability (or inability) to achieve educational goals are all important influences (Lauritsen 1994).

Sexual Behavior After the College Years

Behavioral statistics do not reflect the totality of sexuality, but they can still be interesting. Here are some for your consideration.

Sixty-seven percent of women aged 15 to 44 who have ever had sexual intercourse have had more than one partner, 41 percent have had four or more, 23 percent six or more, and 8 percent more than ten. Women in all age groups and racial or ethnic groups appear equally likely to have multiple partners while unmarried (Kost and Forrest 1992).

Ninety-five percent of men aged 20 to 39 have had vaginal intercourse, and 23 percent of them have had twenty or more partners. Twenty percent have engaged in anal intercourse, 75 percent have performed oral sexual activity, and 79 percent have received oral sexual activity. Only 2 percent of the men reported any same-gender sexual activity during the last 10 years, and only 1 percent reported being exclusively homosexual during that time (Billy et al. 1993).

Marital Sexual Activity

Two relatively recent social changes have had a great impact on marital sexual activity, particularly for women. The first is that more-reliable contraceptives have given women control of conception. The second change is the growing realization that women have as much right as men do to expect sexual satisfaction. How is sexual satisfaction achieved?

Sexual communication is vitally important to a harmonious marriage. The old assumptions that men naturally know how to perform sexually and that men know what women desire simply are not true. For instance, for many women, cuddling and closeness are more important than sexual intercourse. Some women may "exchange" intercourse for intimate body contact because such contact helps meet their needs for relaxation and security. These needs can be met only if the partners openly communicate.

What is known about the frequency of marital intercourse? Doddridge, Schumm, and Bergen (1987) report that the average frequency of marital intercourse for couples in their twenties and thirties is about 2 to 3 times per week. The rate drops off steadily throughout the life cycle. By the middle thirties and early forties, average coital rates are 1.5 to 2 times per week. Beyond age 50, these figures drop to once a week and less.

Call and Schwartz (1993) reported similar frequencies of marital sexual intercourse—about 12 times a month for couples in their twenties, and about 6 times a month for couples in their forties. They also reported that factors contributing to less sexual activity are an unhappy marriage, the presence of children under age 5, pregnancy of the wife, and older age. Each person, and each couple, however, is different.

Although you might be interested in how frequently other couples engage in sexual activity, using this information to bolster arguments is not effective. Informing your partner that most couples "your age" have intercourse 2.5 times a week does nothing to creatively resolve growing problems of sexual distance. Couples must work out acceptable

Communicating about sexual needs is a vital part of any sexual relationship.

levels, forms, and frequency of sexual activity for *themselves,* not for anyone else. What is relevant is that they communicate their sexual needs and expectations and reach a satisfactory agreement about their sexual activity together. After all, quality and meaningfulness are more important than frequency of sexual activity.

Difficulties with sexual language often cause communication problems. People have finally started to develop a public language about sexuality, but few have a private language for communicating about sexual behavior. Think, for example, of phrases designed to initiate or turn down sexual activity. An initiating statement might be "I think I'll take a shower," and a turn-down statement might be "I have to leave for work early tomorrow." Note which statements are straightforward and which ones sidestep or hint. Why do you think we have difficulty being direct about sexual relations?

Further evidence of the need for understanding and communication is the fact that wives tend to focus less on genital activies than do their husbands (Julien et al. 1992). This need not be a problem, but it does warrant discussion in an intimate relationship.

Extramarital Sexual Relations

In some circumstances, such as "swinging," both marriage partners openly acknowledge each other's extramarital sexual involvements. Extramarital sexual activity is usually secretive, though. It is often assumed that those who engage in extramarital sexual activity are having affairs and are emotionally involved in ongoing sexual relationships. Most extramarital sexual activity, however, is more casual; relatively few people have serious affairs.

How often does extramarital sexual activity occur? It is difficult to obtain accurate statistics on an activity that is generally not openly acknowledged. For men the frequency of extramarital activity appears to decrease with age; for women it appears to increase. A conservative estimate is that 50 to 75 percent of men participate in extramarital sexual activity at

HEALTH UPDATE

The Sexual Behavior of Men

In 1993 a nationally representative study of the sexual behavior of 3,321 U.S. men aged 20 to 39 showed that sexual acts vary according to social and demographic characteristics. Analysis of the data showed the following:

1. Ninety-five percent of the men had had vaginal intercourse.

2. Twenty-three percent had had twenty or more vaginal sexual partners.

3. Twenty percent of unmarried men had had four or more partners over a recent 18-month period.

4. Forty-one percent of never-married men and 32 percent of formerly married men did not have coitus during the 4 weeks preceding the interview.

5. Twenty percent of the men had engaged in anal intercourse. Of these, 51 percent had not done so in the previous 18 months, and 90 percent had not done so during the previous 4 weeks.

6. Seventy-five percent had performed oral sexual activity, and 79 percent had received oral sexual activity.

7. Two percent of sexually active men had had some same-gender sexual activity during the last 10 years, and 1 percent reported being exclusively homosexual during that period.

Source: From John O. G. Billy, Koray Tanfer, William R. Grady, and Daniel H. Klepinger, "The Sexual Behavior of Men in the United States" in *Family Planning Perspectives* 25(2): 52–60 (March/April 1993).

some point during their marriages. It is generally accepted that the incidence for women has increased significantly—perhaps doubled—since 1950, when sexuality researcher Alfred Kinsey noted his figure of 26 percent (Wyatt, Peters, and Guthrie 1988). It is interesting to note, however, that, in 1993, 93.6 percent of married people in a household probability survey of adults reported having only one sexual partner during the previous 5 years (Leigh, Temple, and Trocki 1993).

A number of social factors—such as religious beliefs, earlier patterns of sexual activity, and women's rights—tend to affect the incidence of extramarital sexual activity. Those who participate in premarital sexual intercourse, for example, are more likely to participate in extramarital sexual activity. The high divorce rate also may be related to higher rates of extramarital sexual activity. As conviction has grown that women should have more sexual rights than in the past, women have become more active seekers of sexual pleasure outside the marriage. Affluence is also a factor—the more money a person has, the greater the time and opportunity for extramarital sexual activity. Finally, the changing role of women in the labor force is also a factor—women today have a greater sense of autonomy than in the past, and working women have almost as much opportunity for extramarital sexual activity as working men do. Home demands, however, are still often stronger for the working woman than for the working man, which lessens the woman's opportunities.

How do individuals justify their extramarital sexual activity? Traditional justifications include sexual excitement, sexual curiosity, novelty or variety, sexual enjoyment, romantic love (getting love and affection and falling in love), emotional intimacy (intellectual sharing, companionship, understanding, respect, and enhancement of self-esteem), and extrinsic factors (such as career advancement and revenge). Women approve less of sexual justifications and more of love

justifications. Men seem to separate sexual behavior and love, and women believe that love and sexual behavior go together (Glass and Wright 1992).

Postmarital Sexual Behavior

The few studies on the sexual behavior of postmarital (widowed, separated, or divorced) people indicate that men continue to be as sexually active as they were during marriage, while women temporarily become less active after the marriage ends (depending on circumstances surrounding the ending) and then return to previous levels or reach even higher levels of sexual activity.

There are many more people today in a postmarital state than there were years ago. Higher divorce rates alone could account for this, but the ability of medical science to keep some people alive longer also contributes. Those who engage in postmarital sexual activity might discuss these relationships with their children, so children need to try to understand and communicate their reactions to their parents' relationships. Such communication contributes to the overall health of the family.

HOMOSEXUALITY AND BISEXUALITY

Homosexuality—sexual attraction and/or relations between members of the same sex—has received much attention in recent years. It is impossible to know at what age people know that they have homosexual interests. The topic is further

homosexuality
Having sexual desire predominantly for members of one's own sex.

Acceptance of Homosexuals

Mark those statements that apply to you.

_____ I am very comfortable talking to homosexual men and women.

_____ I have no negative feelings toward homosexuals.

Interpretation

If you marked both responses, you have an accepting attitude toward homosexuality. If you marked only one, then you have a moderately accepting attitude. If you did not mark either, you have a nonaccepting attitude and you should perhaps make an effort to get to know homosexuals and recognize their strengths.

Most homosexuals lead normal, well-balanced lives.

confused by the existence of numerous gradations in homosexual/heterosexual interest; in other words, a homosexual/heterosexual continuum exists, with exclusive homosexuality and exclusive heterosexuality at opposite ends. It is possible for someone to be at any point on that continuum. In the early 1990s, debates arose about the incidence of homosexuality. Traditionally it has been assumed that about 10 percent of the population are homosexual—including friends, classmates, teachers, and sport heroes. Many are questioning that percentage and feel it is actually much smaller.

Many heterosexuals don't think homosexuals have legitimate feelings and rights. Such thinking results from a fear called **homophobia,** which arises because *homophobes* accept one or more myths about homosexuality. Males with more traditional male-role attitudes, a religious fundamentalist orientation, and a parent who had completed fewer years of education are more likely to express homophobic views (Marsiglio 1993). Complete the Health Assessment on acceptance of homosexuals to help determine your feelings.

One myth is that homosexuals look different from others. Actually, it has traditionally been thought that about 10 percent of all homosexuals are what could be called "visible homosexuals," but more-recent studies estimate the proportion at 1 to 4 percent (Lopez and Chism 1993). In any case, homosexuals generally do not look any different from others.

Another myth is that homosexual males are effeminate and weak, while homosexual females are masculine and physically strong. In fact, sexual preference has nothing to do with one's body type or style of movement. Similarly, no relationship has been demonstrated between occupation and sexual preference. Male homosexuals are found in all walks of life—from football players and truck drivers to artists and corporate executives—as are female homosexuals.

There is also a myth that homosexuals lurk at street corners and seduce innocent children into lives of homosexuality. In reality, more heterosexuals than homosexuals take advantage of children. Either situation is intolerable, but it is unfair to blame only homosexuals for such behavior. A related myth is that homosexuals are unfit to be teachers. There is nothing about homosexuality that affects teaching ability.

Some believe the myth that all homosexuals are mentally disturbed. The American Psychiatric Association and American Psychological Association do not list homosexuality as an

homophobia
Fear of, hatred toward, or discrimination against homosexuals; a fear of homosexual feelings in oneself.

THE WORLD AROUND YOU
Homosexuals in Society

Sexual orientation has long been considered an interesting topic to discuss and study, but in recent years its interdependence with social, religious, and even political agendas has emerged. Traditionally, examples of personal-rights questions for homosexuals have centered on employment rights and the right to nondiscrimination because of sexual orientation. Recently we have seen interdependence of the sexual orientation questions in many areas:

- *The legal system.*   Attention has been given to issues such as the regulation of sexual behavior and the right to get married to a person of the same sex.
- *Politics.*   In President Clinton's 1992 presidential campaign and in his early years as president, questions related to rights and opportunities for people of

different sexual orientations influenced decisions and even ratings of candidates.

- *Medical insurance.*   Much attention has been given to the medical-care crisis in the United States. One issue has been whether people of the same sex who are living together can be covered under a "family plan."
- *Religion.*   The question of whether or not homosexuals should be allowed to be priests, ministers, or other church leaders has dominated many discussions among people from various religious groups.
- *Employment.*   Should homosexuals be allowed to serve in the military? Should they be law enforcement personnel or teachers? Many issues have been raised about employment opportunities for homosexuals.

This topic, which has always been controversial, is emerging today as having many social ramifications. This is an excellent example of how interdependence influences health decisions.

---

emotional disorder. Apart from the social persecution and difficulties they encounter, most homosexuals are happy with their lifestyles and partners, and lead well-balanced lives.

A related notion is that homosexuals develop their sexual preference because of problems in their family relationships. Obviously a poor family relationship can hinder anyone's development, but this theory of homosexual origins has not been substantiated. Many homosexuals do not regard their sexual preference as a "problem" at all, and researchers, so far, have been unable to explain what causes any sexual preference.

The question of whether homosexual orientation is biologically determined, socially learned, or a result of an interaction of the two has been a classic debate for over one hundred years. Most researchers have supported social or psychological factors as the primary causes of sexual orientation. Recently, however, increasing evidence indicates that biological factors might also be important. For example, the likelihood, among identical twins, that if one of the twins is homosexual the other will be also is high enough to suggest a strong biological basis for sexual orientation, even though the nature of the biological factors is yet to be understood (Whitman, Diamond, and Martin 1993). In addition, some researchers believe there is a gene that has significant influence on sexual orientation (Wheeler 1993).

Most heterosexuals have been taught that homosexuality is a second-class condition, and therefore they accept myths about homosexuals. As is readily seen, however, there is no solid foundation for any of these myths.

As a final point concerning awareness about homosexuality, it can be helpful for both homosexuals and heterosexuals to be aware that homosexuals in college classrooms may have specific concerns about their identity as lesbian or gay, their campus and classroom experiences, and their relationships with instructors and with their general learning (Lopez and Chism 1993). Understanding these concerns can help both homosexuals and heterosexuals be more healthy.

Bisexuality, or *ambisexuality,* is the enjoyment of sexual relations with members of both sexes. It is now widely believed that most individuals, left to their natural ways, are bisexual to some extent; so it seems to be the socialization process that produces predominantly heterosexual behavior. Some bisexuals are evenly divided between homosexual and heterosexual feelings, but most tend to lean one way or the other.

VARIATIONS IN SEXUAL PRACTICE

Many variations in sexual behavior are classified as abnormal, perverse, or problematic. We avoid these labels because most sexual behaviors can be seen as points on a continuum; it is difficult to judge when some specific variation becomes "abnormal" or "perverted." Exhibitionism is an example. Did you give some thought to the clothes you are wearing today? You probably chose them because you wanted to look nice; yet few would call you an exhibitionist for doing so.

Over the centuries, numerous variations in sexual practice have developed. Among the most common are masturbation, oral-genital contact, and sodomy.

---

bisexuality
Having sexual desire for members of both sexes.

Masturbation

Generally, **masturbation** is self-stimulation for sexual pleasure. Historically, many people considered it evil and detrimental to health. Even today, misconceptions about the supposed negative effects of masturbation persist.

Common myths are that masturbation leads to mental health problems, causes skin problems, or makes a male unable to have children. Other myths indicate that only males masturbate or that masturbation ceases after a person gets married. None of these is true.

It has been suggested, only half jokingly, that 99 percent of all males masturbate at some time in their lives and the other 1 percent lie! Probably 65 to 75 percent of females masturbate at some time. As one way to learn about bodies and feelings, masturbation can play an important role in healthy growth and development. In fact, children often masturbate unknowingly by exploring their bodies. In addition, masturbation provides a safe sexual outlet for many individuals.

Some individuals masturbate occasionally throughout their lives because they enjoy it. Others do not usually masturbate, but might at certain times in their lives, such as during separation from or illness of a partner. Still others find masturbation emotionally unsatisfying.

Some individuals wonder if it is possible to masturbate "too much." Actually, no harm is done to the body by masturbating frequently. Also, the body simply won't respond to sexual stimulation after a certain length of time. This is not harmful—it just indicates that the body has responded enough for a while.

Oral-Genital Contact

There are two basic types of **oral-genital contact**—fellatio and cunnilingus. **Fellatio** is defined as oral (mouth) contact with a male's genital area; **cunnilingus** is oral contact with a female's genital area. This is an excellent example of behavior that some think is disgusting and others think is erotic and desirable. Some individuals fear contact with such a "dirty" area of the body as the genitals; scientifically, however, this fear is unfounded. The genitals can be just as clean as any other area of the body; indeed, it has been suggested that if oral-genital contact is unclean, it is because of the many germs in the mouth!

Sodomy

The term **sodomy** refers specifically to anal intercourse, but has been used often to refer to almost any form of sexual behavior someone happens to think is not "normal." Some states have laws that define sodomy as any sexual activity between anyone other than a married couple; some states even outlaw certain sexual practices between a married couple, even though the couple participates in the activity in the privacy of their own home. In some states, the laws apply only to homosexuals, but in other states they apply to everyone. Such groups as the National Gay and Lesbian Task Force and the American Civil Liberties Union, however, have intensified their lobbying efforts to encourage states to repeal anti-sodomy laws.

Paraphilias

In addition to the practices just discussed, various sexual options are scientifically known as paraphilias. **Paraphilia** means love (*philia*) beyond the usual (*para-*). There are about thirty different paraphilias, and each one exists as a fantasy and as a practice.

There is a great difference between a sexual practice that is simply engaged in as a variation and does not adversely affect anyone else, and a practice that is engaged in compulsively and excludes consideration of others. For example, everyone has looked at other people's bodies in a locker room, but few people compulsively seek opportunities to watch others undress in the privacy of their own homes.

Voyeurism, or *scopophilia,* refers in a general sense to obtaining pleasure from watching others undress or engage in sexual behavior. Voyeurs, often shy, lonely, and lacking social skills, commonly fantasize about having sexual relations with those they watch and often masturbate while fantasizing. Voyeurs derive satisfaction from the fear of being caught, the anonymity of the person being watched, and the fact that the person does not know he or she is being watched. Generally, voyeurs are not violent and, in fact, are fearful of any contact with those they observe.

Exhibitionism is achievement of sexual gratification by exhibiting the body (particularly the genitals) to observers. The exhibitionist, commonly called a "flasher," receives gratification because of the victim's (observer's) response.

---

masturbation
Self-stimulation for sexual pleasure.

oral-genital contact
Use of one partner's mouth to sexually stimulate the other partner's genitals.

fellatio
Oral sexual stimulation of the male genitals.

cunnilingus
Oral sexual stimulation of the female genitals.

sodomy
Anal intercourse. The term is often applied disparagingly to any sexual practices believed not to be "normal."

paraphilia
Various forms of sexual desire or love (philia) beyond the usual (para-).

voyeurism (scopophilia)
Generally, obtaining pleasure from watching people undress or engage in sexual behavior.

exhibitionism
Achievement of sexual gratification by displaying one's genitals to observers.

Laws and opinions vary from state to state and individual to individual. Would you call this exhibitionism?

Exhibitionists might achieve orgasm by the very act of exposure, but more likely they masturbate, either while exhibiting or later.

Although it is often thought that exhibitionists are violent and aggressive, they are usually the opposite. It is rare for exhibitionists to do more than display the genitals. They do not want contact with the individuals to whom they exhibit themselves. While it may be difficult to do, generally the best response is to ignore an exhibitionist and continue usual activities. In this way, the exhibitionistic behavior is not reinforced.

Troilism refers to having sexual relations with another person while a third person watches. In one respect, it combines elements of exhibitionism and voyeurism.

Fetishism is sexual fixation on some object other than another human being. Almost anything can be the object of fixation—a knee, a shoe, silk, leather, and so on. As with other sexual behaviors, the fetish can exist on a continuum. In some cases, for example, a person might simply be attracted to a certain object; in other cases a person might not be able to sexually respond unless the object is present.

Frottage is the act of obtaining sexual pleasure by simply rubbing or pressing against another person. Frotteurs are likely to rub against people in crowds, on elevators, in buses, and on subways. It is even possible that the frotteur will achieve orgasm. Normally, no additional contact or other form of behavior follows.

Masochism is sexual gratification from experiencing pain; **sadism** is sexual gratification from inflicting pain on another person. For the masochist, the pain involved must be planned as part of an overall experience; accidentally hitting a finger with a hammer is not the kind of experience a masochist wants. Sadists, who make good partners for masochists, do not seem to be as common as masochists.

Sadism and masochism are good examples of sexual behaviors in which we need to differentiate between fantasy and behavior. For example, many more individuals report sexual fantasies involving masochism and sadism than actually participate in such behavior. It is possible to enjoy a sexual fantasy without wanting to participate in it in real life.

Nymphomania refers to an extremely high sex drive that dominates the lives of certain women. Most women who enjoy very frequent sexual activity, however, do not approach nymphomania. A similar sex drive in men is called **satyriasis.**

Bestiality, or *zoophilia,* is sexual contact with animals. Bestiality is most common among people who live on farms. It most likely occurs during adolescence, and most individuals make a transition to more common adult sexual relations with humans.

Transvestism is sometimes confused with *transsexualism* or with *homosexuality.* A *transvestite* prefers wearing clothes of the opposite sex and is likely to achieve sexual gratification from doing so. A transvestite, however, is not likely to be interested in a sex-change operation or in relating sexually to members of the same sex. In most instances, transvestites actually have "normal" heterosexual relationships in every way except for their tendency toward cross-dressing when alone or with an understanding partner. Historians have reported hundreds of stories of lifelong cross-dressers whose true behaviors were disclosed only after death (Heller 1992).

A **transsexual** believes he or she is "trapped" in a body of the wrong sex. This is not to be confused with homosexuality: Transsexuals want to relate sexually to persons of the opposite sex only if they can be in a body of the "proper" sex themselves; homosexuals want to relate sexually to persons of the same sex. Although it is an uncommon procedure,

troilism
Having sexual relations with another person while a third person watches.

fetishism
Sexual fixation on an object other than a human being.

frottage
Obtaining sexual pleasure by rubbing against another person.

masochism
Sexual gratification from experiencing pain.

sadism
Sexual gratification from inflicting pain on another person.

nymphomania
Extremely high sex drive in women.

satyriasis
Extremely high sex drive in men.

bestiality (zoophilia)
Sexual contact with animals.

transvestism
Sexual gratification from dressing like a member of the opposite sex.

transsexual
A person who feels "trapped" in a body of the wrong sex.

Issue

Should There Be Legislation Regulating Personal Sexual Behavior?

Historically, laws were passed to regulate such private sexual behavior among consenting adults as oral-genital contact and homosexual activity. Surprisingly, many of these laws are still on the books. They date back to early England and Puritan New England, they differ from state to state, and they are rarely enforced, but they are slow to be changed. In 1986, the U.S. Supreme Court ruled that states could pass laws to ban forms of sexual activity between consenting adults—even in private.

- Pro: These laws should be retained, because we have a societal and moral obligation to prohibit unacceptable behavior. People should not be allowed to participate in such activity, and if we repeal these laws, we are condoning perversion. If we don't have these laws, it implies that all sexual behaviors are acceptable.

- Con: Private sexual behavior among consenting adults is not a matter for the law. As long as there is legal consent of the participants, we have no reason to attempt to control personal sexual behavior. In fact, such laws are an inappropriate invasion of privacy. Not having laws regulating private behavior does not imply that all forms of sexual behavior are acceptable.

Should there be laws about private sexual behavior between consenting adults? If so, what kinds of sexual behavior should be regulated? What effect do laws about sexual behavior have on people's actual behavior?

surgery and chemical therapy can be combined to change a person's gender, but only after much psychological testing and investigation.

SEXUAL ABUSE

Most sexual behaviors are normally engaged in by personal choice. When any one of these behaviors involves some degree of forcing one individual's will on another, it can constitute **sexual abuse.** Some specific forms of sexual abuse—rape, obscene telephone calling, pedophilia, and incest—are unfortunately common in society. Accurate statistics are hard to obtain, but it appears that sexual abuse is increasing in the United States.

RAPE

Definitions of rape vary along several dimensions, including (a) the sexual behaviors specified, (b) the criteria for establishing

nonconsent, (c) the individuals specified, and (d) the perspective specified—that is, who decides whether sexual assault has occurred (Muehlenhard, Powch, and Phelps 1992). Complete the Health Assessment on rape prevention to evaluate the measures you are taking to avoid being raped.

The legal definition of **rape** differs from state to state, but a practical definition is "forcible sexual intercourse." When a female or male is forced to have sexual intercourse against her or his will, a rape is committed. Sometimes only the persons involved can tell when this is happening.

Some individuals feel there is no such thing as rape—that a woman, for instance, cannot be raped unless she cooperates. This is complete nonsense. A rapist can knock a woman unconscious, tie her up, physically injure her, use a knife or gun for coercion, or simply make strong threats. Just because most rapes do not involve physical injury beyond the sexual assault does not mean that those raped weren't forced; nor does it mean that those raped weren't injured psychologically.

Conservative estimates indicate that a woman is raped every 7 minutes and that a half million rapes occur each year in the United States. Twenty to 25 percent of American women have experienced attempted or completed rape (Tanzman 1992). In 1992 the National Victim Center reported that 683,000 adult women were raped in the United States in 1990. In addition, the center indicated that more than 12 million American women have been raped at least once in their life, 61 percent of those raped were younger than 18 at the time of the attack, and in 80 percent of cases the woman knew her rapist.

Women raped by men they know are less likely to make a report, because they question their role and responsibility in the attack, while women in a classic rape (i.e., attacked by a stranger) have the needed evidence to convince both themselves and others that they have been raped (Williams 1984). It also seems more likely that a rape will be reported if the offender did not have a right to be present where the assault occurred, if serious injury resulted from the assault, and if the individual raped was married (Lizotte 1985). In 90 to 95 percent of rapes, the rapist and the individual raped are of the same race, and most of the time they even live in the same neighborhood.

To better understand the motivations behind rape and to be able to assist rape victims more effectively, it is important to recognize that rape is a forcible violent act, not primarily a sexual one. Most rapists rape to be aggressive, to show their power, or to belittle the victim, not to obtain what we usually think of as sexual satisfaction. In fact, it is unlikely

sexual abuse
Forcing sexual behavior on another person against that person's will.

rape
Forcible sexual intercourse.

Prevention of Rape

Directions

Indicate which of the following you generally do.

_____ I make sure that my windows and doors are locked and my home is secure.

_____ I list my address in the phone book.

_____ I try to walk in lighted places.

_____ I occasionally hitchhike.

_____ I am careful not to let people know I will be alone.

_____ I do not let unknown people into my home without identification.

_____ I store my valuables in hidden and safe places.

_____ I am aware of surroundings and suspicious movements when alone.

_____ I try to travel with someone when possible.

_____ I have thought through what I would do if anyone ever tried to rape me.

Scoring

Give yourself the following points for each item you checked, and total your score.

1. = 2	5. = 2	8. = 2
2. = −2	6. = 2	9. = 2
3. = 2	7. = 2	10. = 2
4. = −6		

Interpretation

This exercise indicates the quality of the measures you are taking to prevent being raped. Interpret your score as follows:

8 or higher	=	Very good measures to prevent rape
0–7	=	Moderately good measures to prevent rape
−1–−8	=	Poor measures to prevent rape

PERSONAL SKILLS AND EXPERIENCES

How to Lessen Your Chances of Being Raped

It is impossible to act in a way that will guarantee you will never be raped; however, you can easily develop some protective habits that will lessen the chances.

At Home

1. When you are returning home, have your key ready and enter immediately.
2. Be sure that doors, door frames, window frames, locks, and hinges are secure.
3. Keep valuables out of sight—outside your house (perhaps stored at a bank), if possible.
4. Have good lighting in all interior and exterior areas.

On the Street

1. Be aware of your surroundings.
2. Be alert to suspicious or unusual movements.
3. Walk in well-lighted places, avoid deserted areas, and do not take shortcuts through dark areas.
4. Walk on the left side of the street, facing traffic, so you can see oncoming cars.
5. Never hitchhike.

Personal Precautions

1. Keep doors and windows locked.
2. In the telephone directory, list only your last name and initials.
3. Be cautious how you handle telephone calls; for example, never let a stranger know you're home alone.
4. Never let an unknown person enter your residence without proper identification unless *absolutely necessary*.
5. Have an emergency plan in mind, just in case.

that sexual satisfaction even occurs. Families of rapists often conform closely to the stereotypical American nuclear family, in which the husband is the breadwinner and the wife attends to children and the home. Rapists have been found to be more hostile toward women than men who do not rape, to have underlying anger motivations, to use dominance as a motive for sexual interaction, and to have underlying power motivations (Lisak 1991). Unfortunately, when many of us respond to the crime of rape, we tend to focus on its sexual rather than its violent aspects. Those who have been raped

and their loved ones need help through difficult times in the same way as those who experience other violent crimes.

There has long been debate about the best way to resist a rape attack. Some feel it is best to seem to "go along" with the attack until there is a safe way to escape. Others argue that it is better to resist immediately as strongly as possible. The effectiveness of women's resistance strategies for reducing the severity of sexual abuse and physical injury during sexual assaults was analyzed in a variety of assault circumstances (Ullman and Knight 1993). Particular resistance

Issue

Resisting Rape

If you find yourself in a potential rape situation, should you resist? If so, how much? It is difficult to know what is best to do in a potential rape situation. Many claim, however, that if you yell, kick, and scream, you will only aggravate the attacker and he or she will become much more violent—increasing your chances of being beaten or even killed. They are not saying you should willingly go along, but that you should "pretend" to go along until it is safe to flee. They say it is better to "only" have forced sexual intercourse than to be killed or maimed for life.

- Pro: As difficult as it may be to physically submit to unwanted sexual activity, it is better to do so than to put yourself in danger of severe injury or death. You and your family will have a much better life if you are in a condition to participate fully in it. Emotional scars can be healed more effectively than serious physical ones.
- Con: There is no way that it makes sense to "go along" with the attacker. It is best to kick, scream, run, and do everything else possible to get out of the situation. It would be impossible to live with the fact that you didn't do everything possible to prevent the attack.

What would you recommend? Should a person pretend to go along with a rapist until it is safe to escape, or is it better to physically resist as much as possible? What are the advantages and disadvantages of each approach? If you were actually being attacked, could you remember to do what you said you were going to do?

experienced attempted forced intercourse and 10 percent had experienced completed forced intercourse [Ward et al. 1991].)

2. Only 29 percent of men denied engaging in any form of sexually aggressive behavior, and 15 percent had intercourse against the woman's will (but none described it as rape).

3. Sixty-one percent of the men admitted they had fondled a woman against her will, 42 percent had forcibly removed a woman's clothing, and 37 percent had touched a woman's genitals against her will.

4. Thirty-five percent of men had ignored a woman's protest, 11 percent had used physical restraint, 6 percent had used threats, and 3 percent had used physical violence to coerce sexual contact.

5. Fifty percent of the men admitted to forced sexual activity.

Burkhart reported that most of the men were ordinary, not deranged perverts, and were doing what they thought they were supposed to do. Most of the offenders were very active in heterosexual relationships but simply saw women as objects of sexual pleasure. The women were likely to blame themselves and didn't view their treatment as strange or unusual.

There might be as many as five varieties of courtship rape. Each type arises at a different stage of a romantic relationship in terms of both the length of the relationship and previous sexual activity. For example, beginning date rape occurs during a couple's first few dates. Early date rape occurs after several dates, but before the couple has established sexual ground rules. Relational rape occurs after the couple's sexual ground rules have been established. The remaining two forms of date rape occur after a couple has or had an active sexual relationship, and they are distinguished by the presence or absence of battering (Shotland 1992).

More than 80 percent of the rapes on college campuses are committed by someone with whom the victim is acquainted; about 50 percent are committed on dates, and heavy drinking of alcohol and acquaintance rape often go together (Abbey 1991). Although women are fearful of walking alone on campus at night, the most common sexual assault is not the "stereotypical" rape attack, but instead one that occurs as part of the "normal" social environment on the campus (Ward et al. 1991).

One difficulty when trying to prevent date rape is a lack of understanding and communication between the sexes—particularly in interpreting sexual intentions. Programs are needed that focus on communication issues, gender differences, interpretation of nonverbal cues, support by friends,

strategies were effective in specific situations. Women who fought back forcefully were more likely to avoid rape than were women who did not fight back, regardless of whether a weapon was present. Forceful fighting resistance was related to increased physical injury when a weapon was present, but most physical injury was caused by nonlethal weapons. Women who screamed or fled when confronted with weapons experienced less severe sexual abuse. Increased physical injury was associated with pleading, crying, or reasoning indoors.

Date rape is much more common than most of us realize—probably the most common form of rape. Barry Burkhart, who has studied the topic since 1975, concluded the following ("Date Rape Is Occurring Too Often, AU Professor Says" 1987):

1. Twenty-five percent of women say they have had coerced intercourse, but only 15 percent of those incidents meet the legal definition of rape. (In another study, it was estimated that 20 percent of college women had

---

date rape
Raping a person one is on a date with or otherwise socially engaged with; acquaintance rape.

Date Rape

Directions

This exercise is for those who are single and dating. Mark all that apply to you.

_____ 1. When dating, most of the excitement is to see what degree of intimacy I will be able to reach with this person (i.e., how far we will go).

_____ 2. I test how far I will go (physical intimacy) with someone by progressive fondling (holding hands, putting arm around waist, rubbing back, chest, or breast and genitals) to see at what point the person will stop me.

_____ 3. When dating, I generally go with others or go somewhere public until I know someone.

_____ 4. I ask around about someone before I go out with her or him.

_____ 5. I make it very clear about what my values are about physical intimacy when dating before difficult situations arise.

_____ 6. I have tried to coerce or talk someone into having sexual activity with me.

Scoring

Give yourself the following points for the items you checked, and total your score.

1. = 3
2. = 3
3. = −2
4. = −3
5. = −3
6. = 5

Interpretation

3–11	=	You are potentially infringing on someone else's right to live within her or his value system and legal rights. You may be "date raping" or attempting date rape.
0–2	=	You have tendencies to infringe on someone else's right to live within her or his value system.
−1--3	=	You are practicing moderately healthy dating precautions to avoid date rape.
−4--8	=	You are practicing healthy dating precautions to avoid date rape.

and the influence of alcohol on date rape (Sawyer, Desmond, and Lucke 1993). Complete the Health Assessment on date rape, if you are single and dating, to see if you are taking healthy dating precautions.

Both males and females can help prevent date rape. Males need to be aware of social pressures, to communicate well with potential partners, to realize that being turned down is not a personal rejection, to accept an answer of no as meaning just that and not assume that previous permission for sexual contact applies to the present situation, and to realize that just because a woman might be dressed very attractively or even in a way that might seem "sexy," that doesn't mean that she wants sexual activity. Females also need to communicate clearly, to be assertive, to pay attention to what is happening, to be aware that nonverbal actions might send an unintended message, and to try not to put themselves in vulnerable situations ("Acquaintance Rape" 1986).

OTHER FORMS OF SEXUAL ABUSE

Erotic phone calling (or letter writing) is a form of erotic distancing. The person obtains sexual pleasure from a distance and not from direct contact with another person. Obscene telephone callers receive sexual gratification from making gross remarks over the telephone, usually suggesting that the receiver of the call meet them to have sexual relations (even

It is wise to learn techniques of self-defense.

erotic phone calling
Obtaining sexual pleasure from a distance; also done by letter writing, etc.

THE WORLD AROUND YOU
Societal Changes Related to Rape

Here are some changes that have occurred in recent years.

On College Campuses

1. Greater recognition of the need for more attention to the problem of rape
2. Better lighting and security on campuses
3. Courses in rape prevention and self-defense
4. Availability of escort services so women need not be alone on campus, particularly after dark

In Laws

1. Changes designed to facilitate conviction of rapists and sex offenders
2. Gradations of sexual offenses (for example, if rape cannot be proved, it might be possible to convict for sexual assault or another lesser charge)

3. Tendency to not allow a victim's background to be used in a trial unless it is determined to relate to the case

For Law-Enforcement Personnel

1. Training designed to help law-enforcement personnel become more sensitive to the problem of rape and sexual assault
2. Use of more female police officers
3. Better cooperation between law-enforcement personnel and medical and support personnel
4. Development of guidelines for handling of victims of sexual assault

Within the Community

1. Development of rape crisis centers to provide education, raise sensitivity to the problem, and aid victims of assault
2. Provision of shelters for victims of assault so they have a place to receive help
3. In general, a better understanding of the problem and more support

though the caller could never go through with this). The obscene letter writer is hoping for sexual gratification as well.

None of these offenders is likely to be violent or follow up on their calls or letters, but the suggestions might be violent and should be reported. The recommended response to obscene calls is to say nothing and hang up the phone.

Pedophilia is a form of sexual behavior in which an adult uses a child as the sexual object. Even though actual physical force might not be used, the child is unlikely to be able to effectively resist physically, emotionally, or psychologically.

Boys as well as girls are often sexual abuse victims. Experts believe that about 2.5 to 5 percent of the male population is sexually victimized in childhood or early adolescence, which translates to about 46,000 to 92,000 new cases of sexual abuse of boys each year. Most do not come to the attention of a professional.

Both men and women can be pedophiliacs, but males are most commonly the offenders. Unlike other men, child molesters associate sexual feelings with frustration and tension. The child molester's apparent fear of women, his emotional immaturity, and his preoccupation with sex apparently make him turn to children for sexual gratification (Johnston 1987). Pedophiles report being sexually abused as children significantly more often than other people do (Freund, Watson, and Dickey 1990). However, overall, pedophiles don't really differ in personality from the general population (Okami and Goldberg 1992).

Researchers cannot explain the relatively large numbers of sexually abused children who have no apparent adverse psychological symptoms (Finkelhor 1990). For those children who show symptoms, the initial effects of sexual abuse

include fear, anxiety, depression, and sexually inappropriate behavior. The most common long-term effects are depression, self-destructive behavior, anxiety, feelings of isolation, poor self-esteem, difficulty in trusting others, substance abuse, and sexual maladjustment (Finkelhor 1990; "Adult Survivors of Sex-Abuse in Crisis" 1990).

Incest is sexual abuse of children by, and other sexual behavior between, close relatives. The most commonly reported form is father-daughter, but brother-sister incest probably occurs more frequently. About 10 percent of all girls are subjected to some sexual encounter with a male relative; boys are less frequently involved in sexual activity within families. The United States has laws prohibiting incest, but it still occurs in all social classes, geographic areas, and ethnic and racial groups. Legal action is seldom taken.

Although the number of reported cases of incest in the United States is quite low, it probably occurs far more frequently than most of us realize. Because the experience occurs within the family, outsiders are not likely to be aware of it. Additionally, shame and guilt make it probable that family members will hide incest.

At least 25 percent of all women and 10 percent of all men in this country experienced some abuse as children, ranging from sexual fondling to intercourse. Boys who have

---

pedophilia
Adults using children as sexual objects.

incest
Sexual abuse of children by close relatives.

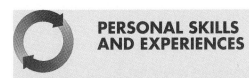

PERSONAL SKILLS AND EXPERIENCES

Helping Victims of Sexual Abuse

Though you might not be a trained counselor, if someone who has been sexually abused talks with you about what has happened, you can help by remembering the following points:

1. Listen in a supportive way, showing sympathy and concern. Ask questions and don't argue.
2. Encourage the person to express her or his feelings about the incident(s).
3. Help the person focus on actions that might be needed, such as seeking medical treatment or reporting to police.
4. The abused person must decide what to do; you cannot force him or her.
5. Help the person find professional follow-up services—professional counseling, crisis center guidance, legal assistance, or medical follow-up—and accompany the person if that is appropriate and if the person desires it.
6. Those who have been sexually abused can respond in almost any way. They can be hysterical, amazingly calm, or anything in between. Almost any (or no) reaction is "normal."
7. Let the person know you're available for help or support in the future.
8. Check back as often as necessary to see how the person is progressing toward full recovery.

been abused are far more likely to turn into offenders; girls are more likely to produce children who are abused. Abuse victims seem to be easy targets because they don't know how to take care of themselves. This may be due to poor self-image, lack of assertiveness, or the feeling they deserve to be punished (Kohn 1987).

Other relationships are coming to light related to sexual abuse. For example, nearly 66 percent of teenage girls who become pregnant were sexually abused as children. Compared with teenagers who became pregnant but who had not been abused, the victimized girls became sexually active at a younger age, were more likely to have used drugs and alcohol, and were less likely to use birth control (Flax 1992b).

Preventing child sexual abuse demands additional attention. Programs have been designed to educate children and adults to distinguish between appropriate and inappropriate touch, to say no to unwanted or uncomfortable touch, to tell a trusted adult if inappropriate touch occurs, and to identify their family and community support systems. In addition, college students have been encouraged to consider risks related to certain behaviors, the selection of a mate who will not abuse their children, and ways in which they will protect children from sexual abuse.

It is estimated that many childhood sexual abuse victims reach adulthood with no conscious memory of the abuse. Many events can trigger the recall of these memories. If you feel you may have been abused as a child, you would be wise to seek help from a professional who has experience treating adult survivors of childhood sexual abuse. If you know someone in this situation, encourage them to seek help.

Sexual harassment is probably one of the oldest forms of sexual abuse, but only recently has it received much attention. There are varying ways to define sexual harassment, but definitions usually include verbal abuse, sexist remarks, unwanted physical contact, leering or ogling, demand for sexual favors in return for some favorable treatment, a hostile environment, and actual physical assault (Fitzgerald and Ormerod 1991).

In 1991, the topic of sexual harassment received more attention from the media and the general public than ever before during the confirmation hearings of Judge Clarence Thomas as a U.S. Supreme Court justice. For days the media featured the sexual harassment charges leveled against Judge Thomas by Professor Anita Hill. The hearings prompted many people to discuss the topic and brought attention to the prevalence of sexual harassment. A number of issues were raised, such as, What constitutes harassment? Is it proper to make sexual harassment charges years after the alleged harassment? How does one decide who is telling the truth when sexual harassment charges are made?

Males and females can both be sexually harassed; however, females are more likely to be harassed. On college campuses, about 25 to 33 percent of female students and 40 to 50 percent of female faculty members have experienced sexual harassment (Shavlik 1992).

Sexual harassment frequently occurs at earlier ages than previously thought, and it often involves students harassing students. Among students in grades 8 through 11, 85 percent of females and 76 percent of males reported being sexually harassed in school. Peer harassment was more than four times as common as harassment by adults. One-third of the students said they had first experienced sexual harassment in grade 6 or earlier, and 60 percent had experienced harassment by grade 8 (Eaton 1993). In addition, 59 percent of students in grades 8 through 11 admit being the perpetrators of sexual harassment. Girls were nearly five times as likely as boys to be afraid at school and three times as likely as boys to feel less confident about themselves following sexual harassment (Bryant 1993).

sexual harassment
Any harassment of other people related to sexuality; includes verbal abuse, sexist remarks , unwanted physical contact, leering, ogling, catcalls, demands for sexual favors in return for favorable treatment, a hostile environment, and physical assault.

Issue

Are Pictures of Nudes a Form of Sexual Harassment?

For many years pinups—traditionally pictures of females with little of no clothes on, and recently also including such pictures of males—have been common in many workplaces. Little was done to limit the displaying of pinups. This changed in 1991 when a Florida federal court judge ruled that pictures of naked and scantily clad women qualify as sexual harassment under Title VII of the 1964 Civil Rights Act.

- Pro: The judge said that a "boys club" atmosphere is no less destructive to workplace equality than is a sign declaring "men only." He further indicated that females in a "sexually hostile" workplace are a captive audience to pornography and are usually reluctant to challenge superiors and colleagues over the issue. Therefore, since this is considered sexual harassment, the company involved must take down the photos and institute an antiharassment policy.

- Con: The Florida branch of the American Civil Liberties Union denounced the judge's ruling as a violation of free speech. Even at the trial, it was pointed out that such pictures would not offend the "average woman." Most pinups are found in so-called blue-collar workplaces and women represent only about 9 percent of such employees. In addition, no one is forced to look at the pictures—they have a choice. Therefore, displaying pinups should not be considered sexual harassment.

Should individuals be allowed to display pinups in the workplace? Is this an important issue or one that should be ignored? How would you feel if you worked in a place where pinups were displayed? Would your feelings be influenced by whether the pictures were of males or of females? Do you agree with the judge?

Each of us is responsible for what we do and how we handle what others do to us. Open and honest communication is needed to solve a sexual harassment conflict. A continuum of how sexual harassment responses are actually handled includes avoidance (ignoring and doing nothing), defusion (going along with it, stalling, or making a joke of it), negotiation (making a direct request to the harasser to stop), and confrontation (aggressively telling the harasser to stop or taking formal actions) (Gruber 1989).

Males and females may perceive sexual harassment differently. For example, females tend to interpret some behaviors as more harassing than do males, and subtle forms of harassment are often interpreted as more inappropriate by females than by males (Marks and Nelson 1993). Also, females and

males seem to interpret a male's actions differently when a female made prior commitments to a friendly relationship. Males' ratings of sexual harassment decrease when the female participates in increasingly informal, friendly interactions. Female ratings, however, remain relatively constant despite the female's friendly interactions (Williams and Cyr 1992).

Each person must examine his or her interactions with others with greater sensitivity to be sure the interactions are based on mutual respect—not stereotypes, faulty assumptions, or the erroneous opinions of others. We must form a new social contract based on mutual respect and regard for one another as human beings (Shavlik 1992).

COMMERCIAL SEXUAL BEHAVIOR

Some sexual activities exist mainly because of their relationship to money. Prostitution and pornography are the two most prominent examples, and they have become major social issues as well.

PROSTITUTION

Prostitution is a much studied, but not greatly understood, sexual variation. In a general sense, the term refers to any situation in which one person pays another for sexual gratification. The debate continues over whether prostitution should be made legal or not and what the effects of legalization would be.

Adolescent prostitution has become an increasing problem in the United States. There are between 600,000 and 900,000 female adolescent prostitutes, and at least 300,000 male adolescent prostitutes, under the age of 16. They commonly come from broken homes or have poor relationships with their parents. Prostitution is used as a means of economic survival (Nightingale 1985). There are reports of children setting up their own prostitution rings while still living at home, to earn spending money.

Therapy programs for prostitutes are usually not successful, for many reasons, particularly because many prostitutes do not feel they can receive help. Treatment programs have various components: self-help groups for women and families, a treatment group for adolescents, individual counseling, outreach, and advocacy.

PORNOGRAPHY

What is **pornography?** No answer to this question satisfies everyone. Some people feel that pornography, like beauty, is

prostitution
Any situation in which one person pays another person for sexual gratification.

pornography
Pictures or words intended to arouse sexual desire; often distinguished from erotica and artworks as being offensive, obscene, or harmful.

PERSONAL SKILLS AND EXPERIENCES

The Skill of Understanding

In the areas of sexual response and behavior, perhaps the most important skill is the skill of understanding. This means understanding how the body functions during sexual response and factors that influence this response. It means understanding variations of sexual behavior in a nonjudgmental way. It also includes understanding abusive sexual behavior, and other behaviors that might be classified as negative, to help prevent them and help others deal with them.

Personal characteristics related to the mind, body, and soul and their interaction contribute to the development of the skill of understanding. For example, knowledge, flexibility, and objectivity are a must. Honestly assess your present level of achievement in each of these areas.

Mind

Are you flexible when discussing sexual response and behavior? For example, are you willing to listen to various viewpoints?

Can you accept the fact that not everyone wants to behave just like you do? Do you take the attitude that "my mind is made up so don't confuse me with the facts," or do you consider new information and respect different opinions?

Body

Do you have adequate knowledge about human sexual response and various sexual behaviors? (One good way to test yourself is to pretend you are going to teach someone about these topics and see if you have enough knowledge to do so.)

Soul

Are you objective when discussing homosexuality, pornography, prostitution, incest, rape, and human sexual response? Can you be objective on some of these topics but not on others? (One indication is your degree of emotional response when discussing these topics. Of course, this response relates to what you value.)

If you want to successfully deal with the many topics in this chapter, you must have the skill of understanding. Assess yourself in the three areas listed above as well as their interdependence and, if needed, develop a plan to improve your abilities in each area.

---

in the eye of the beholder. Others feel that any pictures or words related to sexuality are disgusting. Defining pornography is particularly difficult because individuals can be led to interpret material as sexual or not by suggestions given to them before they view the material. When a story is preceded by introductory information that suggests sexual content, subjects tend to attribute sexual meaning to the story. Other subjects attribute a nonsexual meaning to the same story when it is preceded by introductory information that suggests the story does not have sexual content (Castille and Geer 1993). We must decide how we feel based on personal beliefs as well as on the "facts" about pornography.

Two classic sources from the 1970s still provide a foundation for understanding the effects of pornography. According to a report sponsored by the U.S. government (*Report of the Commission on Obscenity and Pornography* 1970) and a review of this report (Money and Athanasiou 1973), the following conclusions were drawn: Convicted sex offenders generally have been exposed to *less* pornographic and sexuality education materials during their lives than many "nonoffenders"; exposure to pornographic materials does not seem to alter a person's sexual behavior in the long run; and a person is only stimulated by portrayal of ideas or acts that turned him or her on in the first place—that is, pornographic materials do not seem to plant ideas in the mind that were not there all along. In addition, there is little, if any, difference in the responses of males and females to pornographic materials, and continued exposure to pornographic material tends to lead to boredom and indifference.

In contrast to the 1970 commission study, in July 1986 the Attorney General's Commission on Pornography (often called the Meese Commission after Attorney General Edwin

Meese) published its report, which linked hard-core pornography to sex crimes and made ninety-two recommendations for federal, state, and local governments to crack down on the $8 billion pornography industry in the United States. Many experts have questioned the findings of the Meese Commission. For example, the Society for the Scientific Study of Sex indicated that the commission's "evidence for a direct link between exposure to sexually explicit material, pornography, or violent pornography to consequences such as sexual violence, sexual coercion, or rape" is "incomplete and inadequate" ("SSSS Sees Meese Commission as Having Dire Effect on Future Sex Research" 1986). Many opposed to the commission's conclusions strongly indicate that it is not sex but violence that is an obscenity in our society (Donnerstein and Linz 1986).

In 1993 we saw an excellent example of this concern when the movie *Jurassic Park* was released. There was no sexual content, but many parents and psychologists wondered about the effects of the movie's violence on children.

There are many and varied opinions about pornography. Some religious groups claim that it propagates perverse sexual behavior and is immoral. Some women believe it promotes male power or leads to teenage psychological problems. On the other hand, producers of pornography argue that their products have positive effects. Many people purchase pornography for use in the privacy of their homes and cannot understand why a private matter should become a public problem (Leong 1991).

There seems to be no debate, however, when it comes to the topic of child pornography. Unanimous opposition to this form of pornography is apparent.

TAKE ACTION

1. Recognize that people who have different sexual lifestyles have emotional needs, self-esteem needs, and acceptance needs just like anyone else.

2. Sexually active students, as well as those who are not active at this time, can become process oriented (focusing on the enjoyment of the relationship and expressing feelings and love) rather than product oriented (focusing on sexual intercourse as the goal of a relationship). If appropriate, try to focus more on the quality of the relationship instead of on specific sexual behaviors.

3. Take precautions to reduce the risk of sexual abuse. This might relate to date rape, rape in other situations, or teaching children how to avoid sexual abuse.

SUMMARY

1. Limerence is the quality of sexual attraction based on chemistry and sexual desire.

2. Human sexual response is predictable and consists of certain phases.

3. A series of biological changes occurs in each phase of human sexual response.

4. There has been a great deal of premarital sexual behavior for decades and perhaps even centuries.

5. The quality of marital sexual activity is more important than the frequency of sexual activity.

6. Many myths exist about homosexuality, and some people have strong feelings about homosexual behavior.

7. Many varieties of sexual behavior exist. Variations in sexual practice include masturbation, oral-genital contact, and sodomy.

8. Psychosexual variations include voyeurism, exhibitionism, troilism, fetishism, transvestism, frottage, masochism, sadism, nymphomania, bestiality, and transsexualism.

9. Sexual abuse includes obscene phone calling, rape, pedophilia, incest, and sexual harassment.

10. Date rape is the most common form of rape.

11. Commercial sexual behavior includes prostitution and the use of pornography.

COMMITMENT ACTIVITIES

1. You already know more about human sexual response (having read this chapter) than most people do. Here's a chance to apply your knowledge in a practical way. Assume that a 14-year-old boy shares with you his concern about the way he feels when reading sexually oriented books, looking at sexually explicit pictures, or while on a date. He is wondering if there is something wrong with him because of the way his body seems to react. What should you tell him? Suppose a girl of a similar age and with similar concerns comes to you. What should you tell her?

2. Many feelings exist about variations in sexual behavior. We often find it hard to be objective about sexual behaviors we don't understand or agree with. Evaluate your own feelings about the many sexual behaviors discussed in this chapter. Are your feelings based on emotions or facts? From now on, try to better understand the feelings and behaviors of others and also be more sensitive to your own negative feelings about certain sexual behaviors.

3. Services exist in most communities for the sexually abused. It helps to know about them in the event that you or someone you care about needs them. Evaluate the services for survivors of sexual abuse in the community in which you live or attend college. Be sure to include services of law-enforcement agencies, hospitals, clinics, health departments, and voluntary groups. Which services would you recommend to someone who needs them?

4. Various community services are available for those with concerns or problems related to human sexual response, sexual orientation, or other aspects of sexual behavior discussed in this chapter. Make a list of such services available on your campus and in the community. Learn about each of the services. Which ones would you recommend to a friend who needs help?

5. Incest is a problem in most societies. Many experts think the best answer to this problem is prevention. Develop a plan for the prevention of incest. Be sure to include components that might be used in school and community educational programs.

6. Over the next weeks, spend some time each day clarifying where you believe you are on the continuum between exclusive heterosexuality and exclusive homosexuality. How comfortable do you feel about your position? What can you do about your comfort level?

REFERENCES

Abbey, A. 1991. "Acquaintance Rape and Alcohol Consumption on College Campuses: How Are They Linked?" *Journal of American College Health* 39 (January): 165–69.

"Acquaintance Rape: Is Dating Dangerous?" 1986. American College Health Association pamphlet. Available from ACHA, P.O. Box 28937, Baltimore, MD 21240.

"Adult Survivors of Sex-Abuse in Crisis." 1990. *Behavior Today* 21: 4.

Bell, R. 1966. *Premarital Sex in a Changing Society.* Englewood Cliffs, NJ: Prentice Hall.

Billy, J. O. G., K. Tanfer, W. R. Grady, and D. H. Klepinger. 1993. "The Sexual Behavior of Men in the United States." *Family Planning Perspectives* 25, no. 1 (January/February): 52–60.

"Briefly Noted." 1992. *Health Education Reports* 14, no. 14 (16 July): 7.

Bryant, A. L. 1993. "Hostile Hallways: The AAUW Survey on Sexual Harassment in America's Schools." *Journal of School Health* 63, no. 8 (October): 355–57.

Call, V., and P. Schwartz. 1993. "Age of Intimacy: Older Couples Slow Down a Bit." Paper presented at the annual meeting of the Society for the Scientific Study of Sex, November, Chicago.

Castille, C. O., and J. H. Geer. 1993. "Ambiguous Stimuli: Sex Is in the Eye of the Beholder." *Archives of Sexual Behavior* 22, no. 2:131–41.

Cate, R. M., E. Long, J. J. Angera, and K. K. Draper. 1993. "Sexual Intercourse and Relationship Development." *Family Relations* 42, no. 4 (April): 158–64.

Darling, C. A., J. K. Davidson, and C. Conway-Welch. 1990. "Female Ejaculation: Perceived Origins, the Grafenberg Spot/Area and Sexual Responsiveness." *Archives of Sexual Behavior* 19, no.1 (February): 29–47.

Darling, C. A., J. K. Davidson, and D. A. Jennings. 1991. "The Female Sexual Response Revisited: Understanding the Multiorgasmic Experience in Women." *Archives of Sexual Behavior* 20, no. 6 (December): 527–40.

"Date Rape Is Occurring Too Often, AU Professor Says." 1987. *Birmingham News*, 23 March, 3B.

Day, D. 1992. "The Transition to First Intercourse Among Racially and Culturally Diverse Youth." *Journal of Marriage and the Family* 54, no. 11 (November): 749–62.

Doddridge, R., N. Schumm, and M. Bergen. 1987. "Factors Related to Decline in Preferred Frequency of Sexual Intercourse Among Young Couples." *Psychological Reports* 60: 391–95.

"Does Your Medication Impair Your Sex Life?" *Consumer Reports on Health* 58, no. 8 (August): 87.

Donnerstein, E. I., and D. G. Linz. 1986. "The Question of Pornography." *Psychology Today* 20, no. 12: 56–59.

Eaton, S. 1993. "Sexual Harassment at an Early Age." *Harvard Education Letter* 9, no. 4 (July/August): 1–5.

Edell, D. 1990. "Sex Ruled Safe for Sports." *Edell Health Letter* 9, no. 4 (April): 3.

Finkelhor, D. 1990. "Early and Long-Term Effects of Child Sexual Abuse: An Update." *Professional Psychology: Research and Practice* 21: 325–30.

Fitzgerald, L. F., and A. J. Ormerod. 1991. "Perceptions of Sexual Harassment." *Psychology of Women Quarterly* 15: 281–94.

Flax, E. 1992a. "Most High School Students Sexually Active CDC Finds." *Education Week* 11, no. 17 (15 January): 10.

Flax, E. 1992b. "New Study Links Past Sex Abuse, Teenage Pregnancy." *Education Week* 11, no. 24 (4 March): 9.

Freund, K., R. Watson, and R. Dickey. 1990. "Does Sexual Abuse in Childhood Cause Pedophilia: An Exploratory Study." *Archives of Sexual Behavior* 19: 557–68.

Glass, S. P., and T. L. Wright. 1992. "Justifications for Extramarital Relationships: The Association Between Attitudes, Behaviors, and Gender." *Journal of Sex Research* 29, no. 3 (August): 361–87.

Greenberg, J., C. Bruess, and K. Mullen. 1993. *Sexuality: Insights and Issues.* Dubuque, IA: Wm. C. Brown.

Gruber, J. E. 1989. "How Women Handle Sexual Harassment." *Sociology and Social Research* 72, no.1 (October): 306.

Heller, S. 1992. "Scholar Finds Cross-Dressing Is a Central Part of Human Culture." *Chronicle of Higher Education* 38, no. 20 (22 January): A7–A8.

"How Healthy Are America's Adolescents?" 1990. *Target 2000.* American Medical Association.

Jacobson, B. H., S. G. Aldana, and T. Beaty. 1994. "Adolescent Sexual Behavior and Associated Variables." *Journal of Health Education* 25, no. 1 (January/February): 10–12.

Johnston, S. A. 1987. "The Mind of a Molester." *Psychology Today,* February, 60–64.

Julien, D., C. Bouchard, M. Gagnon, and A. Pomerleau. 1992. "Insiders' View of Marital Sex: A Dyadic Analysis." *Journal of Sex Research* 29, no. 3 (August): 343–60.

Kaplan, H. S. 1979. *Disorders of Sexual Desire.* New York: Simon & Schuster.

Kohn, A. 1987. "Shattered Innocence." *Psychology Today,* February, 54–64.

Kost, K., and J. Forrest. 1992. "American Women's Sexual Behavior and Exposure to Sexually Transmitted Diseases." *Family Planning Perspectives* 24, no. 3 (May/June): 244–52.

Lauritsen, J. L. 1994. "Explaining Race and Gender Differences in Adolescent Sexual Behavior." *Social Forces* 72, no. 3 (March): 859–84.

Leigh, B. C., M. T. Temple, and K. F. Trocki. 1993. "The Sexual Behavior of US Adults: Results from a National Survey." *American Journal of Public Health* 83, no. 10 (October): 1400–1408.

Leong, W. 1991. "The Pornography 'Problem': Disciplining Women and Young Girls." *Media, Culture, and Society* 13: 91–117.

Lisak, D. 1991. "Sexual Aggression, Masculinity, and Fathers." *Signs: Journal of Women in Culture and Society* 16, no. 2:238–63.

Lizotte, A. J. 1985. "The Uniqueness of Rape: Reporting Assaultive Violence to the Police." *Crime and Delinquency* 31, no. 2 (April): 169–90.

Lopez, G., and N. Chism. 1993. "Classroom Concerns of Gay and Lesbian Students." *College Teaching* 41, no. 3 (October): 97–103.

Marks, M. A., and E. S. Nelson. 1993. "Sexual Harassment on Campus: Effects of Professor Gender on Perception of Sexually Harassing Behaviors." *Sex Roles* 28, nos. 3/4:207–17.

Marsiglio, W. 1993. "Attitudes Toward Homosexual Activity and Gays As Friends: A National Survey of Heterosexual 15- to 19-Year-Old Males." *Journal of Sex Research* 30, no. 1 (February): 12–17.

Masters, W. H., and V. E. Johnson. 1966. *Human Sexual Response.* Boston: Little, Brown.

Money, J., and R. Athanasiou. 1973. "Pornography: Review and Bibliographic Notations." *American Journal of Obstetrics and Gynecology* 115 (January): 130–46.

Morokoff, P. J., and R. Gilliland. 1993. "Stress, Sexual Functioning, and Marital Satisfaction." *Journal of Sex Research* 30, no. 1 (February): 43–53.

Muehlenhard, C. L., I. G. Powch, and J. L. Phelps. 1992. "Definitions of Rape: Scientific and Political Implications." *Journal of Social Issues* 48, no. 1:23–44.

Nightingale, R. 1985. "Adolescent Prostitution." *Seminars in Adolescent Medicine* 1, no. 3 (September): 165–70.

Okami, P., and A. Goldberg. 1992. "Personality Correlates of Pedophilia: Are They Reliable Indicators?" *Journal of Sex Research* 29, no. 3 (August): 297–328.

O'Sullivan, L. F., and E. S. Byers. 1992. "College Students' Incorporation of Initiator and Restrictor Roles in Sexual Dating Interactions." *Journal of Sex Research* 29, no. 3 (August): 435–46.

Reinisch, J. M., S. A. Sanders, C. A. Hill, and M. Ziemba-Davis. 1992. "High-Risk Sexual Behavior Among Heterosexual Undergraduates at a Midwestern University." *Family Planning Perspectives* 24, no. 3 (May/June): 116–21.

Reiss, I. L. 1973. "Changing Trends, Attitudes, and Values on Premarital Sexual Behavior in the U.S." In *Human Sexuality and the Mentally Retarded,* edited by F. F. De La Cruz and G. D. La Veck. New York: Brunner/Mazel.

Report of the Commission on Obscenity and Pornography. 1970. Washington, DC: U.S. Government Printing Office.

Sawyer, R. G., S. M. Desmond, and G. M. Lucke. 1993. "Sexual Communication and the College Student: Implications for Date Rape." *Health Values* 17, no. 4 (July/August): 11–19.

Schwartz, I. M. 1993. "Affective Reactions of American and Swedish Women to Their First Premarital Coitus: A Cross-Cultural Comparison." *Journal of Sex Research* 30, no. 1 (February): 18–26.

Shavlik, D. 1992. "A Time for Change." *Higher Education and National Affairs* 41, no. 10 (18 May): 5.

Shotland, R. 1992. "A Theory of the Causes of Courtship Rape: Part 2." *Journal of Social Issues* 48, no. 1:127–43.

Small, S. A., and T. Luster. 1994. "Adolescent Sexual Activity: An Ecological, Risk-Factor Approach." *Journal of Marriage and the Family* 56, no. 1 (February): 181–92.

Sroka, S. R. 1991. "Common Sense on Condom Education." *Education Week* 10, no. 25 (13 March): 39–40.

"SSSS Sees Meese Commission as Having Dire Effect on Future Sex Research." 1986. *Sexuality Today* 9, no. 36 (23 June): 2–3.

Tanzman, E. S. 1992. "Unwanted Sexual Activity: The Prevalence in College Women." *Journal of American College Health* 406, no. 4 (January): 167–71.

Tennov, D. 1989. *Love and Limerence.* Chelsea, MI: Scarborough House.

Thornton, J. S. 1990. "Sexual Activity and Athletic Performance: Is There a Relationship?" *Physician and Sportsmedicine* 18, no. 2 (March): 148–54.

Ullman, S. E., and R. A. Knight. 1993. "The Efficacy of Women's Resistance Strategies in Rape Situations." *Psychology of Women Quarterly* 17: 24–38.

Ward, S. K., K. Chapman, E. Cohn, S. White, and K. Williams. 1991. "Acquaintance Rape and the College Social Scene." *Family Relations* 40 (January): 65–71.

Wheeler, D. L. 1993. "Study Suggests X Chromosome Is Linked to Homosexuality." *Chronicle of Higher Education,* 21 July, 6–7.

Whitman, F. L., M. Diamond, and J. Martin. 1993. "Homosexual Orientation in Twins: A Report on 61 Pairs and Three Triplet Sets." *Archives of Sexual Behavior* 22, no. 3:187–203.

Williams, K., and R. Cyr. 1992. "Escalating Commitment to a Relationship: The Sexual Harassment Trap." *Sex Roles* 27, nos. 1/2:47–72.

Williams, L. S. 1984. "The Classic Rape: When Do Victim's Report?" *Social Problems* 31, no. 4 (April): 459–67.

Wyatt, G., S. Peters, and O. Guthrie. 1988. "Kinsey Revisited, Part I: Comparisons of the Sexual Socialization and Sexual Behavior of White Women over 33 Years." *Archives of Sexual Behavior* 17: 201–39.

Zilbergeld, B., and C. R. Ellison. 1980. "Desire Discrepancies and Arousal Problems in Sex Therapy." In *Principles and Practice of Sex Therapy,* edited by S. R. Lieblum and L. A. Pervin. New York: Guilford.

ADDITIONAL READINGS

Craig, M. E. 1990. "Coercive Sexuality in Dating Relationships: A Situational Model." *Clinical Psychology Review* 10: 395–423. Provides a literature review related to coercive sexual behavior and presents a situational model to help explain coercive sexual behavior in dating situations.

Donnerstein, E. 1991. "Pornography: Research and Policy in a Free Society." *Contemporary Psychology* 36, no. 2:160–61. Provides an overview of research on pornography.

Herbert, T. B., R. C. Silver, and J. H. Ellard. 1991. "Coping with an Abusive Relationship: How and Why Do Women Stay?" *Journal of Marriage and the Family* 53, no. 2 (May): 311–25. Presents information about ways women cope with physical and emotional abuse while remaining with their abusive partners. This information helps develop an understanding of why they stay.

Hurley, Dan. 1993. "Getting to the Gist of Male Sexual Dysfunction." *Medical World News* 34, no. 3 (March): 50–59. Presents a roundtable discussion by four experts on male sexual dysfunction.

"Premarital Sexual Experience Among Adolescent Women." 1991. *Morbidity and Mortality Weekly Report* 39, nos. 51–52 (4 January): 929–32. Gives statistical data about the premarital sexual experience of 8,450 adolescent women and compares rates at different times.

Schmitz, Anthony. 1993. "A Shot in the Dark." *Health* 7, no. 1 (January): 22–24. Provides an overview of the controversial question: "Should sex offenders be forced to quell their urges with injections of a female hormone?" Pros and cons of the issue are discussed.

Strong, B., and C. DeVault. 1994. "The Influence of Popular Culture and the Media on Adolescent Sexuality." *Family Life Educator* 12, no. 4 (Summer): 4–10. Discusses influences on sexuality of television, videos, films, novels, and music. The need to teach young people about these influences is emphasized.

CHAPTER 11

Conception and Birth

KEY QUESTIONS

How do the male and female
   reproductive systems work?
How and when does conception occur?
What can be done for infertility?
What consumer decisions are involved
   in pregnancy?

CHAPTER OUTLINE

Healthy People 2000 Objectives

- Increase to at least 75 percent the proportion of mothers who breast-feed their babies in the early postpartum period and to at least 50 percent the proportion who continue breast-feeding until their babies are 5 to 6 months old.

- Reduce cigarette smoking to a prevalence of no more than 10 percent among pregnant women aged 20 and older.

- Increase smoking cessation during pregnancy so that at least 60 percent of women who are cigarette smokers at the time they become pregnant quit smoking early in pregnancy and remain abstinent for the remainder of their pregnancy.

- Reduce pregnancies among girls aged 17 and younger to no more than 50 per 1,000 adolescents.

- Reduce the prevalence of infertility (defined as the failure of couples to conceive after 12 months of intercourse without contraception) to no more than 6.5 percent.

- Increase to at least 40 percent the proportion of ever-sexually-active adolescents aged 17 and younger who have abstained from sexual activity for the previous 3 months.

- Reduce the infant mortality rate to no more than 7 per 1,000 live births.

- Reduce the fetal death rate (at 20 or more weeks of gestation) to no more than 5 per 1,000 live births plus fetal deaths.

- Reduce the incidence of fetal alcohol syndrome to no more than 0.12 per 1,000 live births.

- Reduce low birth weight to an incidence of no more than 5 percent of live births and very low birth weight to no more than 1 percent of live births.

- Reduce the cesarean delivery rate to no more than 15 per 100 deliveries.

- Reduce the primary (first-time) cesarean deliveries to 12 per 100 deliveries.

- Reduce the repeat cesarean deliveries to 65 per 100 deliveries.

- Increase abstinence from tobacco use by pregnant women to at least 90 percent and increase abstinence from alcohol, cocaine, and marijuana by pregnant women by at least 20 percent.

- Increase to at least 90 percent the proportion of women enrolled in prenatal care who are offered screening and counseling on prenatal detection of abnormalities.

One of the most crucial life-cycle phases is the childbearing years. Any decision about heterosexual intercourse almost always involves questions about having children. Among the most critical health decisions made are whether and when to have children, whether to use contraception and, if so, what type, and what should be done if a pregnancy occurs.

CONCEPTION: AN OVERVIEW

Conception is the fertilization of a female's egg by a male's sperm that results in pregnancy. Three conditions are necessary for conception to take place: (1) A mature egg must be in a position to be fertilized, (2) the sperm must reach the egg, and (3) there must be a suitable environment for the fertilized egg to grow.

THE MENSTRUAL CYCLE

Sometime during puberty, a girl reaches **menarche:** that is, she begins to menstruate. The reasons menstruation begins when it does are not exactly known. One hypothesis is related to the increase in body fat that occurs in puberty as a result of normal hormonal secretions. Interestingly, support for this hypothesis is found in women long-distance runners. Many women who habitually run long distances lose considerable body fat and cease menstruating. In fact, some experts estimate that as many as 50 percent of serious women runners will experience a cessation of menstruation (Reynolds 1987). At the same time, however, no one really knows why these runners cease to menstruate. There seems to be more to this than just a loss of body fat, since many thin female runners continue to menstruate and many heavier ones do not (Ullyot 1986).

In the female, maturation and arrival of an egg at a position in the body where it can be fertilized is just one stage in a larger cycle. **Menstruation** is the periodic discharge of blood from the **uterus** through the **vagina.** There are many myths about menstruation, including that a permanent wave will not take during menstruation, that sexual intercourse should not occur during menstruation, that women should not swim or exercise during menstruation, and that women cannot carry on usual work activity during the menstrual period. None of these myths is true. In fact, for many women, exercise can relieve possible menstrual cramps.

The **menstrual cycle** usually lasts approximately 28 days, although cycles vary in length from woman to woman and even for the same woman at different times. (Figure 11.1 illustrates the phases of this cycle.) No matter how many days the cycle lasts, the first day of menstrual flow (flow usually lasts about 5 days) is counted as the first day of the cycle. During the flow, hormonal (chemical) action that affects the upcoming cycle begins. The pituitary gland secretes **follicle-stimulating hormone (FSH),** which travels through the bloodstream and stimulates one of the **follicles** (small sacs in the ovary, each of which contains a developing egg cell) in a female's ovary to grow. As the stimulated follicle grows in size, the egg inside of it begins to mature. There are actually thousands of follicles in a female's **ovary** (all of which are present at birth), so clearly most eggs will never come to maturity (and a woman will never run out of eggs).

About the time the flow ends, the follicle stimulated by FSH begins to secrete the second **hormone** of the cycle, **estrogen.** As the estrogen level increases, it signals the lining of the uterus to thicken and become a hospitable place for a fertilized egg. The rising level of estrogen in the bloodstream also stimulates the pituitary gland to secrete a third hormone, **luteinizing hormone (LH),** into the bloodstream. The increased level of LH in the blood then causes the follicle to release the mature egg. This process of egg release is called **ovulation.**

Many individuals assume that ovulation occurs in the middle of the cycle. Most experts believe that ovulation actually occurs about 14 days before the onset of menstruation. So it is impossible to tell exactly when ovulation occurred

conception
Fertilization of an egg by a sperm resulting in pregnancy.

menarche
The onset of menstruation.

menstruation
Periodic discharge of blood from the uterus through the vagina.

uterus
The stretchable, pear-shaped organ in the female in which the fetus develops before birth; the womb.

vagina
The female organ that receives the penis during coitus and provides passage for the infant during birth.

menstrual cycle
The cycle of menstruation, usually lasting about 28 days, beginning with the first day of menstrual blood flow.

follicle-stimulating hormone (FSH)
A hormone secreted by the pituitary gland that stimulates the egg follicles.

follicle
Small saclike structures in the ovary that contain developing egg cells.

ovary
A gland in the female that contains eggs (ova) and certain hormones.

hormone
A chemical glandular secretion that regulates or stimulates bodily processes.

estrogen
A female hormone, possessed in different degrees by both women and men, that aids in various bodily processes, such as promoting a healthy uterine lining for egg implantation.

luteinizing hormone (LH)
A hormone secreted by the pituitary gland that, in the female, causes ovulation.

ovulation
The release of an egg from an ovary.

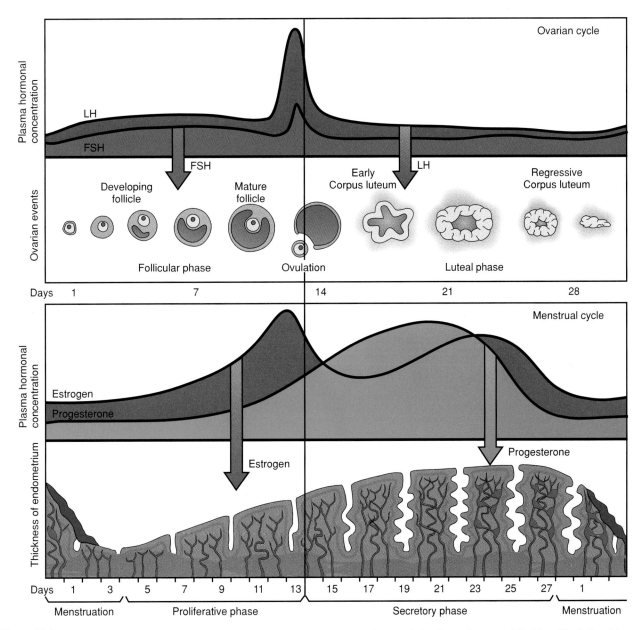

Figure 11.1

Major events in the female ovarian and menstrual cycles.

PERSONAL INSIGHT

How Times and Attitudes Have Changed

When I was a young boy, one of the big events at our house was going to the grocery store every Friday night. I could talk with the butcher and have samples of the meat and cheese that he was cutting. There might even be samples of some new products that our friends who ran the corner grocery store would share. It was truly an interesting and fun time.

I noticed that every so often there were cartons wrapped in plain brown paper among our groceries. I guess I wondered what they were, but I never asked. One day at home I was looking for a towel, and I noticed one of the cartons on the floor of our linen closet. I looked inside and discovered that the carton contained my mother's sanitary napkins. So the mystery of the plain brown wrapped cartons was solved.

Readers of this book will find this true story hard to believe, since "female products" are displayed openly on shelves today. We have come a long way in our openness toward some aspects of human sexuality, but still have a long way to go in others.

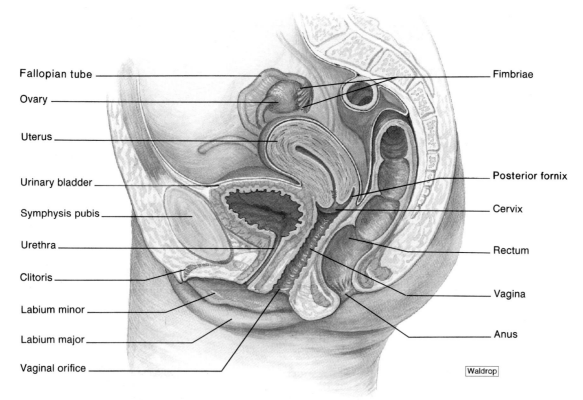

Figure 11.2

Cross section of the female reproductive system.

From John W. Hole, Jr., *Human Anatomy and Physiology*, 5th ed. Copyright © 1990 Wm. C. Brown Publishers, Dubuque, Iowa. All Rights Reserved. Reprinted by permission.

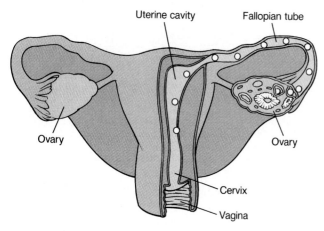

Figure 11.3

Female internal reproductive organs.

until 14 days after the event! This makes calculations of fertile times difficult. There is no problem if a woman has a 28-day cycle; she simply figures 14 days forward or backward from the onset of menstruation. But if a woman has a longer cycle, say 33 days, then ovulation is occurring not in the "middle" of her cycle, but closer to the end.

The average egg lives about 36 hours. A woman with a 33-day cycle would begin to ovulate on perhaps the nineteenth day of her cycle, and the egg would remain alive until sometime on the twentieth day. The maximum life of a male sperm, however, is about 72 hours; so the sixteenth

through the twentieth day of the cycle would be the prime fertilization time in this case. Remember, however, that cycles vary tremendously and the onset of menstruation varies for each woman within her cycle, so the time of potential fertilization is actually much longer than this. Even dietary changes can influence menstruation ("Diet Affects Menstrual Cycle" 1993).

After ovulation, the egg is sucked into the opening of the **oviduct,** or **fallopian tube** (figures 11.2 and 11.3). The follicle continues to produce estrogen, and the level of LH also increases. Because of the high level of LH, the tissue of the follicle changes color and begins to produce the fourth hormone of the cycle, **progesterone.** At this point the follicle is called the corpus luteum.

The combined secretions of estrogen and progesterone continue to cause the **endometrium,** or lining of the uterus, to thicken. In addition, the presence of hormones prevents the release of another egg, which prevents women from conceiving a second time within a few days of the first fertilization. If a woman becomes pregnant, these hormones will

oviduct (fallopian tube)
A pair of tubes in the female by which ova travel from the ovary to the uterus.

progesterone
A hormone that, in the female, works with estrogen to prepare the uterine lining for pregnancy.

endometrium
The lining of the uterus.

remain present at a relatively high level; if she does not, the levels of estrogen and progesterone will fall. This decrease in hormonal level brings about the menstrual flow (the total flow amounts to only around 4 tablespoons), and the entire process starts over. An unfertilized egg is simply removed from the body by the menstrual flow.

Most women experience mild premenstrual symptoms during the reproductive years. For a small number of women (fewer than 10 percent), the symptoms are temporarily disabling—disrupting social, family, and business relationships. The symptoms generally start 7 to 10 days before a woman's menstrual period. They might include fatigue, headache, depression, anxiety, clumsiness, binge eating, irritability, hostility, and lower abdominal bloating. Women with these severe symptoms have **premenstrual syndrome (PMS).** Although in some cases a woman's expectations can affect her reports of symptoms, premenstrual symptoms cannot be dismissed as simply a result of expectations (Klebanov and Jemmott 1992).

The female hormones estrogen and progesterone seem to play an important role in PMS, but the exact relationship is unclear. Some evidence indicates that women with full-blown PMS have lower than average blood levels of serotonin—a chemical found in the brain. Serotonin-raising drugs seem to reduce PMS problems ("Premenstrual Syndrome" 1993).

No single treatment is effective for all PMS sufferers, since the types and severity of symptoms vary a great deal. There is no known cure, but the most helpful strategies include these ("Premenstrual Syndrome" 1993):

1. Exercising regularly. Women who exercise are less likely than inactive women to have PMS.
2. Eating for relief. Eating complex carbohydrates, such as whole grains, breads, pasta, breakfast cereals, and potatoes can help by boosting serotonin levels.
3. Cutting down on salt. Women who tend to retain water toward the end of each cycle should try to consume less sodium.
4. Cutting back on caffeine. This may help women who become irritable or anxious before menstruation.
5. Cutting out alcohol. Since alcohol is a depressant, drinking it before menstruation can worsen depression.
6. Avoiding inappropriate remedies. Some physicians have recommended high doses of vitamin B-6 to reduce PMS symptoms, but there is little evidence that this does any good—and it can cause nerve disorders. Also, over-the-counter remedies such as PMS Multi-Symptom Formula Midol, Multi-Symptom Pamprin, and Premsyn PMS have little or no effect on PMS.

Much research is being done related to PMS. We still have lots to learn about it.

THE COURSE OF THE SPERM

Just as women are born with far more eggs than will ever come to maturity, men are provided with the capacity to

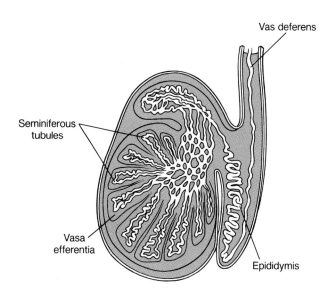

Figure 11.4
Cross section of testis.

produce millions of sperm each day, only an infinitesimal number of which will be used. **Sperm** are produced in the **seminiferous tubules** in the **testes.** These seminiferous tubules produce sperm through the combined hormonal action of follicle-stimulating hormone (FSH) and **testosterone.** Mature sperm are stored in the **epididymis** before traveling through the **vas deferens** in preparation for **ejaculation.** Figures 11.4 and 11.5 show the location of these organs.

---

premenstrual syndrome (PMS)
Physical and emotional symptoms that can occur before menstruation and that can sometimes be disabling.

sperm
Reproductive cells in the male.

seminiferous tubules
Coiled tubes in the testis in which the sperm are produced.

testes
Two oval glands in the scrotum that produce sperm and testosterone.

testosterone
The male hormone that promotes the development of the male sex drive characteristics and sex drive.

epididymis
A coiled tube between the seminiferous tubules and the vas deferens where the sperm mature.

vas deferens
A pair of tubes in the male, extending from the epididymis to the prostate, that serve as passageways for the sperm.

ejaculation
The expulsion of semen from the penis, usually accompanying orgasm.

Premenstrual Syndrome (PMS)

Directions

The first assessment here is for females and the second is for males, but both relate to premenstrual syndrome (PMS).

Female Assessment

Section A
On the following list, check off those things that you feel or experience just prior to your menstrual period.

____ I feel as though I am out of breath.

____ My nose bleeds for no reason.

____ My abdomen feels bloated.

____ My breasts are sore.

____ I get mouth sores or my mouth gets dry.

____ I develop cold sores.

____ My legs hurt or have cramps.

____ I feel dizzy or have fainting spells.

____ I feel like I am shaking inside.

____ I get sharp pains.

____ My skin itches and burns.

____ My joints hurt, swell, or feel stiff.

____ I get diarrhea or constipation.

____ I get bad headaches.

____ I get food cravings.

____ I get backaches.

____ Noise or light bothers me.

____ I get clumsy and drop or bump into things.

____ I feel fat or ugly.

____ I feel all alone in the world.

____ I cry for no reason.

____ Nothing can cheer me up.

____ I am really crabby.

____ I feel like committing suicide.

____ I get really angry.

____ I feel I am a failure.

____ I think I am going crazy.

____ I'm tired and have no energy.

____ I feel like people are out to get me.

____ I am extremely afraid.

____ I am out of control.

____ I can't get anything done.

____ I just can't laugh.

____ I just want to be alone.

____ No one listens to me.

____ I can't concentrate.

Section B
On the following list, mark those things that are general practices for you currently.

____ I rarely eat sweets or chocolate.

____ I do not drink coffee, tea, caffeinated beverages, or take No Doz.

____ I do not drink alcohol.

____ I usually get 7 to 8 hours of sleep at night.

____ I exercise 30 minutes or more, three to four times a week or more.

____ I get plenty of vitamins through natural sources or take vitamin supplements.

____ I avoid excessive stress.

____ I eat four to six small, well-balanced meals daily.

Interpretation
Section A is a symptom checklist for PMS. If you checked any of the symptoms because the symptoms make you less functional than normal and, in severe cases, very debilitated, then you may be suffering from PMS. The more symptoms you checked off, the more likely it is that PMS is a problem for you.

Section B is a list of things that you can do to lessen the impact of PMS. If there are any items you have not checked, you may want to adopt that habit to see if your premenstrual discomfort decreases.

Male Assessment

Read the list of symptoms in Section A and note whether anyone you know demonstrates any of those symptoms just prior to her period. Respond to the following assessment items in reference to that person.

Check all of the following items that apply to you.

____ I feel sorry for her when she experiences some of those symptoms.

____ I try to be more understanding during the time just before and during her period.

____ Because I know that hormones are affecting her, I can deal with her problem and not let it bother me.

____ I try to avoid fights and do not discuss important decisions or try to resolve arguments during this time in her cycle.

____ I know that she really doesn't mean some of the things she says while she is feeling bad, so I don't let it bother me.

Interpretation
If you did not think of anyone who experiences any of the PMS symptoms, then there are no results to be given. If you did think of someone, then it is important for you to consider the items you did not check. It is extremely important that you understand, have compassion, easily forgive, and help the person you know through hard times that males have difficulty understanding. If you did not check all items, then you are lacking in your ability to help and cope with PMS as a support person.

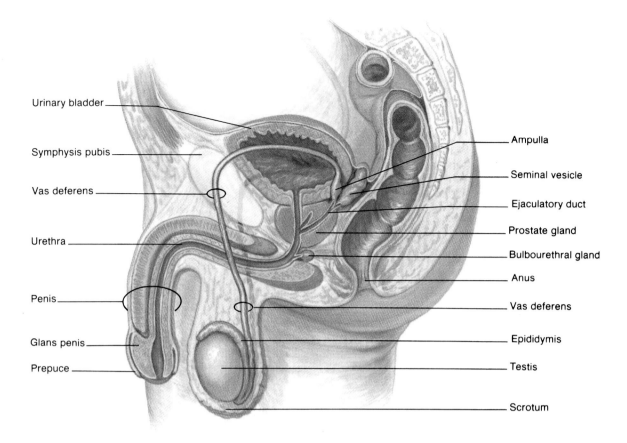

Figure 11.5

Cross section of the male reproductive system.

From John W. Hole, Jr., *Human Anatomy and Physiology*, 5th ed. Copyright © 1990 Wm. C. Brown Publishers, Dubuque, Iowa. All Rights Reserved. Reprinted by permission.

As the sperm pass through the vas deferens, they are joined by fluid secretions from the **seminal vesicles.** This fluid consists mainly of fructose, a simple sugar that provides nutrition for sperm. As the sperm and fluid continue their journey toward ejaculation, the **prostate gland** adds several chemical substances that help neutralize the acid in the vagina as well as possibly assist the sperm if they attempt to fertilize an egg.

The fluid mixture still needs one more secretion before it is completely prepared for ejaculation. The final fluid comes from the **bulbourethral glands,** also called **Cowper's glands.** This fluid lubricates and chemically neutralizes the **urethra** before sperm pass through. This is necessary because urination acidifies the urethra and the sperm need a neutralized passageway to survive the voyage.

Assuming the sperm are ejaculated into a vagina and no contraceptive measures are used, the sperm set out in search of an egg to fertilize. Most of the millions of sperm ejaculated do not survive the expedition. A few dozen probably reach the egg, if one is ready. Scientists believe that the first sperm to penetrate the egg might create a chemical change that shuts out all other surviving sperm. The head of this sperm proceeds to the center of the egg, where **chromosomes** (the parts of cells that contain hereditary factors) from the egg and the sperm become knitted together within a few hours. At this time, all inherited traits of the baby are determined, and the egg is now fertilized.

The union of a sperm and an egg produces a single cell called the **zygote.** The zygote begins to divide about 30 hours after fertilization. It splits into two cells, and then these two

seminal vesicles
A pair of glands in the male that provide a portion of the ejaculate that contributes to the activation of the sperm.

prostate gland
A male organ located below the bladder; it secretes fluid that is part of semen.

bulbourethral glands (Cowper's glands)
Tiny pea-shaped organs located below the prostate that secrete a fluid during sexual arousal.

urethra
The tube through which urine passes from the bladder out of the body.

chromosomes
The part of the cell that contains the hereditary factors (genes).

zygote
The single cell resulting from the union of an egg and a sperm, and the multicell organism that develops from cell division during the first week after fertilization.

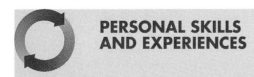

cells split into four cells, eight cells, and so on. The unborn child is called an **embryo** from approximately 1 to 8 weeks after fertilization and a **fetus** thereafter.

INFERTILITY

Just as many couples want to prevent conception, others wish to enhance their chances of conceiving. For those who want children, **infertility**—the inability to reproduce—can be distressing. There are varied estimates of the amount of infertility in the United States. Higgins (1990) indicates that infertility affects 15 to 20 percent of married couples in the United States and its incidence is increasing.

CAUSES OF INFERTILITY

The cause of infertility can be psychological. For example, anxiety related to intercourse can result in sexual dysfunction in males or in muscular spasms that obstruct the fallopian tubes in females. Also, the menstrual cycle in females and the sex drive in males can be influenced by stress. There is little evidence, however, that stress alone can cause lasting infertility. Women have conceived under extremely stressful conditions, such as during wartime (Seibel and McCarthy 1993).

There can be physical reasons for infertility. For example, it can be caused by physical barriers separating sperm from an **ovum** (the female's egg), the failure of successful implantation of the fertilized egg in the uterus, or problems in the normal development of the embryo.

If a male's ejaculate contains fewer than 20 million sperm cells (a condition called **oligospermia,** or low sperm count), the chances of conception are not good. In addition, if the sperm do not effectively neutralize acid in the urethra or vagina, conception may be impossible. Blocked fallopian

tubes, dysfunctional ovaries, an improperly functioning uterus, or inappropriate hormonal functioning, which can even be caused by drastic changes in body weight ("Infertility As a Function of Body Weight" 1992), in the woman can also lead to infertility.

Infertility can cause personal problems and problems in relationships. In addition, the loss of sexual pleasure can occur along with grief, anger, guilt, and depression (Higgins 1990).

TREATMENT OF INFERTILITY

Couples who are having difficulty conceiving would be wise to get a medical examination to determine the cause of the infertility. The male's medical examination focuses on sperm production and delivery. The female's medical examination is designed to assess regularity of ovulation, condition of the cervical mucus (for example, the mucus could contain antibodies against a male's sperm or could form a plug that blocks the passage of sperm), and the possible presence of infections or scar tissue. Evaluation of infertility problems should begin with the male. Because of new technology, many men who were previously unable to father a child can now do so (Burns 1994).

If the cause is medical and identifiable, procedures involving hormonal, chemical, nutritional, or surgical therapy are available to attempt to correct the situation. As an example of medical capabilities in this area, consider the 1978 birth of the first "test-tube baby." In this instance, the mother's fallopian tubes were blocked, preventing sperm from reaching and fertilizing an ovum; therefore an egg was surgically removed from the mother and fertilized by sperm from the father outside their bodies. The fertilized egg was then implanted in the mother's uterus for development and eventual birth.

Overheating of the testes will contribute to decreased sperm production. This might be the result of wearing tight underwear. Whether or not this is the case, the shift to boxer shorts is one of the least expensive and least difficult things to try. (It would not be wise, however, to rely on tight underwear as an effective contraceptive method.)

Some physicians might also caution against too-frequent sexual intercourse (more than once every 36 hours), on the

embryo
The unborn young from approximately 1 week after fertilization to about 8 weeks after fertilization.

fetus
The unborn young from about 8 weeks after fertilization until birth.

infertility
The inability to reproduce.

ovum
Egg.

oligospermia
Low sperm count.

Issue

Artificial Insemination

In recent years, many scientific developments have enhanced our ability to begin and sustain pregnancies in ways that your grandparents, and perhaps even your parents, would never have even dreamed about. We can remove eggs and sperm from people and combine them in a laboratory. We can take an egg from one female, fertilize it, and place it in the uterus of another female. We can even freeze fertilized eggs and use them later. Artificial insemination is a wonderful procedure that can enhance the lives of many people.

- Pro: Many couples unable to bring about a pregnancy have been able, using artificial insemination, to experience a pregnancy together and bring loved children into the world. They have wanted a child so badly that they have made personal and financial sacrifices to use God-given scientific information to enhance life.

- Con: Artificial insemination is immoral and interferes with God's plan for reproduction. Fertilization should occur only inside a female and not inside a test tube. A sperm and an egg from a couple who are not married to each other should not be combined. Pregnancies should result only from natural insemination.

Where do you stand on artificial insemination? How would you feel if you learned that your sister were going to have artificial insemination? How would you feel if your mother were going to be artificially inseminated to carry a baby for your married sister who was unable to successfully have a baby? Would you use artificial insemination in your relationship?

grounds that this reduces the number of healthy sperm. It is noteworthy that even experts cannot agree on what is best to do.

A procedure sometimes used by infertile couples is **artificial insemination.** In cases where the male's sperm count is not high enough or he cannot complete coitus, a donor can provide sperm that is introduced via a syringe into the woman's vagina. If a male's sperm count is consistently low, or if for some other reason he cannot fertilize an egg through sexual intercourse, another remedy is to collect samples of sperm over the course of several days and then instill the whole amount at the cervical opening. This is done in a physician's office as close to ovulation as possible.

---

artificial insemination
The introduction of sperm into a woman's vagina by means of a syringe.

If a donor is used, he is screened for health, intelligence, and physical resemblance to the father. A potential hazard of using donor sperm is the transmission of viral illness, including HIV infection. However, semen, like blood, can be screened for the presence of HIV antibodies.

In some cases drugs, commonly called "fertility drugs," can be used to stimulate ovulation. They can be helpful, but they also seem to cause more multiple births. For example, from the early 1970s until 1989, multiple births increased by 113 percent (from 29 to 62 per 100,000 live births) in white mothers and 25 percent (from 32 to 40 per 100,000 live births) in black mothers. These increases are thought to be a direct result of fertility drugs (Kiely 1992).

Psychological causes of infertility should be treated with professional psychosexual counseling. Great advances in such counseling have been made in recent years.

PREGNANCY

Parents now can and do take an active role in both their own health and that of their unborn child because of increased knowledge about factors influencing a healthy pregnancy and available options in delivery methods. Pregnancy-related decisions that years ago were not even considered are now quite necessary, as well as quite complex. More and more women are waiting until they are in their thirties—or even older—to have a baby. Since 1980, the overall fertility rate for women aged 30 to 34 increased 33 percent, and for

Teenage pregnancy is more common in the United States than in other Western countries.

For Married Couples Desiring Children

Directions

If as a couple you have tried to become pregnant and can't, check all of the following that apply.

_____ We have had complete physicals and know the cause of our infertility.

_____ We have considered adopting children.

_____ We have considered artificial insemination.

_____ We have considered foster children.

_____ We have received professional counseling on this matter.

Interpretation

Consider acting on any item you left blank.

Cloning: A New Scientific Debate

In October 1993 it was reported that human embryos had been cloned (meaning embryos were multiplied), presenting the possibility that identical children could be produced. This prompted a scientific debate that was probably the fiercest since the birth of the first test-tube baby about 15 years earlier.

Discussion included the possibility of producing identical babies in order to use them for spare parts for other babies, producing babies to order, and the potential desirability of prohibiting cloning. Supporters of cloning pointed out that it could help people have babies who otherwise could not, or it could allow a woman who knew she was about to become sterile (perhaps because of chemotherapy or exposure to radiation needed for medical treatment) to clone an embryo for future use. Of course there is also the ethical question of what should be done with a defective embryo. We will probably be hearing much more about this controversial scientific development.

Source: From Phillip Elmer-Dewitt, "Cloning: Where Do We Draw the Line?" in *Time* 142(19): 65–70 (November 8, 1993).

---

women aged 35 to 39 it increased 38 percent (Turner 1992). There is good news for them. There is no evidence that these older women have an increased risk of having a preterm delivery, a smaller infant or one with developmental problems, or an infant who dies during pregnancy. Because of medical advances, the few pregnancy-related problems that might occur in older women are readily manageable. Given sound counseling, appropriate prenatal care, and proper medical care throughout the pregnancy, the increasing number of older women having babies can look forward to excellent outcomes (Berkowitz et al. 1990; Resnik 1990).

While it is possible for teenagers to have healthy babies, there are a number of problems associated with teen pregnancy. Teenage pregnancy in the United States is far more common than in other Western countries—even though U.S. girls do not engage in sexual intercourse earlier or more frequently than girls in other countries do. If the present rates continue, 4 in 10 girls who are 14 years old will become pregnant before they are 20. Every 30 seconds a teenage girl becomes pregnant in the United States (Sroka 1991). The teenage pregnancy rate has recently stayed relatively constant—110 pregnancies per 1,000 girls (Portnes 1992). Approximately 1 million pregnancies are expected among 15- to 19-year-olds each year (Atwood and Donnelly 1993).

Teen mothers face reduced employment opportunities, unstable marriages (if they marry at all), low incomes, and increased health and developmental risks to their children.

Sustained poverty, frustration, and hopelessness are often the long-term outcomes. The national costs of health and social service programs for families started by teenagers amount to more than $19 billion a year (Wattleton 1989).

There are other tragic consequences associated with teenage pregnancy. Teenage mothers usually drop out of school and are unable to find jobs to support their children, unmarried teenage fathers rarely contribute financially to their children's support, and teenage marriages are at high risk for divorce. In addition, teenage mothers are more likely to have birth complications and are less likely to receive adequate prenatal care. Low birth weights and premature births, which can lead to problems such as childhood illnesses, neurological defects, and mental retardation, are common to teenage mothers ("March of Dimes Fact Sheet" 1991).

Although teenage girls in the United States do not engage in sexual intercourse earlier or more frequently than girls in other countries do, the main difference is probably the American attitudes toward sexuality. For example, the 1 million teenage pregnancies that occur in the United States each year seem to be related to a lack of openness about sexuality in society and restrictions on teenagers' access to contraception and teaching about sexuality in schools. Where there is more tolerance of teenage sexual activity, there seem to be *lower* pregnancy rates ("U.S. Far Exceeds Other Nations in Teen Pregnancy" 1987).

There are significant differences by race in the number of children born to women aged 15 to 34 that are either conceived before the woman's first marriage or born out of wedlock. These differences are a result of cultural background, economics, and use of abortion services.

Among whites, 33 percent of births are premaritally conceived, while among blacks the figure is 76 percent. In both races, fewer of these women than in previous years are getting married before the premaritally conceived child is born.

For Hispanics, the number of first children premaritally born or conceived is 49 percent. Among Asians and Pacific Islanders the rate is 29 percent. Rates of premarital conceptions also range widely by age group—from 92 percent of first births among women aged 15 to 17 to 9 percent among women in their early thirties (Turner 1992).

There also seems to be greater acceptance of out-of-wedlock births, and more women are approaching marriage and childbirth as two separate decisions (Cohen 1993). As a result, there is a sharp increase in the proportions of white, older, more educated, and more affluent women becoming mothers without marrying. Even though society seems to have changed its attitude toward unmarried mothers, this trend will probably increase the debate over the effects of single parenthood on children.

Sources: From R. Turner, "Birth to Women in Their Middle and Late 30s Have Risen Among Both Blacks and Whites Since 1980" in *Family Planning Perspectives* 24(2): 91–92 (March/April 1992); and from Deborah L. Cohen, "More Women Having Babies Without Marrying, Survey Finds" in *Education Week* 12(40): 22 (August 4, 1993).

DETERMINATION OF PREGNANCY

Pregnancy begins when an egg is fertilized by a sperm and is successfully implanted in the endometrium, or uterine wall, to be nourished. Pregnancy can be determined through several means. The most frequently used technique is to test the urine for the presence of **human chorionic gonadotropin (HCG),** a hormone produced by the placenta once implantation has occurred. Although pregnancy can be chemically determined as early as 10 days after conception, most pregnancy tests are conducted about 6 to 8 weeks after the last menstrual flow. When conducted and analyzed by a physician or laboratory technician, these tests are very reliable.

Pregnancy self-tests have become increasingly available. Such tests, which can be purchased at drugstores, measure the presence of HCG in urine. Manufacturers claim the tests are 90 percent accurate, but research indicates much lower accuracy rates (Hatcher et al. 1990). Accurate use of a test by an inexperienced person can be difficult. The most common error is a negative result that occurs because the test was used too early in pregnancy. An incorrect result is likely to mislead the woman and may cause delay in receiving a clinical evaluation and medical assistance.

Physicians have sophisticated equipment and tests that can detect pregnancy very early. One of these, sonography, which gives an image of uterine and other changes associated with pregnancy, will detect pregnancy within just a few weeks of conception ("Transvaginal Sonography Detects Early Pregnancy" 1992).

ENVIRONMENTAL AND GENETIC INFLUENCES: PRENATAL CARE

The first 3 months of pregnancy are the most important in the embryo's development. For this reason, if a woman suspects she is pregnant, she must act as though she is and seek **prenatal care.** Many factors can influence the health of the mother and the child. Even stress can produce major problems, such as premature delivery and low birth weight.

Today, more prevention-oriented activities, such as positive health practices for the woman and the developing baby, are encouraged. More and more the emphasis is placed on the quality of behavior and care and not just on the importance of a certain number of visits to the doctor. In fact, the American College of Obstetricians and Gynecologists recommends a reduction in the thirteen traditional visits to seven for healthy women who have previously had babies and nine for healthy women experiencing their first pregnancy (Young 1990).

Environmental Teratogens

Many factors in the mother's environment are suspected **teratogens** (substances that can cause birth defects or diseases in infants). There is a limit to what pregnant women can do to protect themselves from teratogens, but they can refuse chest or abdominal X rays during pregnancy, wear a lead apron during dental X rays, avoid raw meat, stay away from areas where pesticides are sprayed, avoid the use of aerosol containers, and have someone else clean the cat litter box (to avoid catching a defect-causing disease from the droppings).

pregnancy
The condition of having unborn young in the body.

human chorionic gonadotropin (HCG)
A hormone produced by the placenta once implantation has occurred.

prenatal care
Care prior to birth.

teratogens
Substances that can cause birth defects or diseases in infants.

Issue

Reducing Teen Pregnancies

It is clear that too many teenage girls are getting pregnant. U.S. teenagers have one of the highest pregnancy rates in the world—twice as high as in England and Wales, France, and Canada; three times as high as in Sweden; and seven times as high as in the Netherlands ("Teenage Sexual and Reproductive Behavior" 1991). The best way to reduce teen pregnancies is to be more open about them. There should be more open discussions and better access to accurate information. This includes information about contraception and free access to contraceptives. Only when it becomes more acceptable for teenagers to talk about sexuality and use reliable contraceptives, if they choose to have sexual intercourse, will we reduce the teen pregnancy problem.

- Pro: This is the only rational approach. No matter what is done, a significant number of teenagers will participate in sexual intercourse. Regardless of how one feels about this, the problem of pregnancy must be faced. Open discussions, decision-making activities, and access to reliable contraceptives for teenagers would go a long way in reducing teen pregnancies.

- Con: Having open discussions and access to contraceptives for teenagers implies that it is okay for them to participate in sexual activity, including intercourse. It would be better to emphasize why they should not participate in sexual activity and what problems are associated with sexual activity and teen pregnancy. If teenagers would better understand these problems, they would be more likely to abstain from sexual activity. Then there would not be so many teen pregnancies.

What do you think are the most effective ways to reduce teen pregnancies? If you could design a program to reduce teen pregnancies, what would it be?

Rh Incompatibility

Prepregnancy counseling is valuable for many reasons, one of which relates to Rh incompatibility. While the likelihood of this causing problems today has been greatly reduced, couples are still wise to reduce any possible risk. In **Rh incompatibility** the mother's blood is Rh negative (i.e., without an inherited protein substance) and the child's is Rh positive (i.e., with an inherited protein substance). Statistically, this combination is highly unlikely, but a woman with Rh-negative blood must be aware of the possibility. In response to the child's positive Rh factor, the mother's blood develops antibodies that could be harmful to a child's blood in future pregnancies. To remedy this situation, an injection (of Rhogam) that destroys the antibodies is given to an

Good prenatal care is important for both mother and child.

Rh-negative mother within 72 hours after delivery. This is done so that the next time she becomes pregnant the antibodies will not develop to a high enough level to do any damage.

Nutrition

Diet during pregnancy is extremely important. If a woman's diet is healthful, she has a much improved chance of remaining healthy during pregnancy and bearing a healthy child. Just because she is eating for two, however, does not mean she should eat twice as much. Only about 300 extra calories per day are needed.

In general, necessary vitamins are usually provided by a balanced diet that includes milk, bread, and fresh fruits and vegetables. It is particularly important that a pregnant woman get enough protein (for building new tissue), folic acid (for growth), iron (for the blood), and calcium (for growth of the fetal skeleton and tooth buds).

Rh incompatibility
A condition in which the mother's blood is Rh negative and her fetus's blood is Rh positive. This can create complications in future pregnancies because the mother's body develops antibodies in response to the child's positive Rh factor.

Promoting a Healthy Pregnancy

Directions

This assessment is for couples who might want to have children someday. Check all of the following that apply to you.

_____ The female partner smokes.

_____ The male partner smokes.

_____ The female drinks alcohol.

_____ The female takes drugs.

_____ The male takes drugs.

_____ The female fails to eat a well-balanced diet with plenty of iron and calcium.

Interpretation

This is an important list of behaviors that will increase the risk of birth defects or other problems. If you are performing any of the behaviors, then your risk of having problems is increased. If you have multiple factors, then the risk greatly increases with each item and with dosages or lack of good nutrition.

Ectopic Pregnancies

About 1.0 to 1.68 percent of pregnancies are **ectopic pregnancies**—implantation occurs outside the uterus. The embryo may attach itself to an ovary, one of the abdominal organs, or, most commonly, inside one of the fallopian tubes. Ectopic pregnancy should be suspected when a sexually active woman's period is a week late and she experiences abdominal pain. Other possible symptoms include absence of menstruation, vaginal bleeding, nausea, vomiting, and dizziness.

The incidence of ectopic pregnancy has quadrupled since 1970: to 1 in every 65 to 70 normal pregnancies. Risk factors for ectopic pregnancy include previous ectopic pregnancy, current intrauterine device use, fallopian tube surgery, previous pelvic inflammatory disease, and a prior history of infertility—particularly if there has been surgery to correct blocked fallopian tubes. All of these conditions can damage the lining of the fallopian tube so the egg and sperm can't be transported to the uterus. Ectopic pregnancies are now the leading cause of maternal death.

Source: From Richard E. Leach and Steven J. Ory, "Management of Ectopic Pregnancy" in *American Family Physician* 41(4): 1215–1218 (April 1990).

Poor maternal nutrition can lead to slower fetal growth, premature delivery, and low-birth-weight babies. Prematurity and low birth weight cause higher infant death rates, and malnourished babies with low birth weights may have brain damage and retardation. Pregnant women must remember that they are responsible for the health and nutritional needs of two individuals.

Tobacco, Alcohol, and Other Drugs

About twice as many premature and improperly developed babies are born to women who smoke as compared with women who do not smoke during pregnancy. There is also a higher risk of spontaneous abortion among women who smoke (Edwards 1992). Even when children of mothers who smoked reach 5 or 6 years old, they tend to score lower than their peers on intellectual and language tests ("Smart Moms Don't Smoke" 1993). The exact reason for this is unknown, but one theory holds that smoking during pregnancy prevents an adequate oxygen supply from reaching the fetus. In addition, women who smoke during pregnancy are almost three times as likely as women who do not smoke to have their pregnancy complicated by **placenta previa** (a condition in which the placenta partially or totally obstructs the cervical opening). Women who stop smoking before pregnancy are at no greater risk of placenta previa than are those who have never smoked (Rind 1992).

Moderate alcohol use can be harmful to the developing fetus, but heavier use of alcohol can cause great damage. **Fetal alcohol syndrome (FAS)** includes growth deficiencies before and after birth, damage to the brain and nervous system, and facial abnormalities. Mental retardation is also sometimes found in the children of alcoholic mothers.

In spite of these dangers, in one recent year in California alone there were over 67,000 newborns exposed to one

---

ectopic pregnancy
A pregnancy in which the fertilized egg implants outside the uterus.

placenta previa
Partial or total obstruction of the cervical opening by the placenta.

fetal alcohol syndrome (FAS)
Irreversible damage to the fetus caused by the mother's heavy use of alcohol during pregnancy.

or more drugs (including alcohol) in utero. In addition, more than 52,000 were exposed to tobacco. This amounts to more than 10 percent of all babies born in California that year (Klitsch 1994).

Almost every drug used by a pregnant woman will cross the placenta and enter the developing baby's circulation. Because it is not always clear which drugs will affect the embryo or fetus, even drugs that seem safe should be restricted. Drinking coffee slightly increases the risk of spontaneous abortion, premature birth, and possibly congenital defects (Edwards 1992). Aspirin should be avoided because it can cause fetal bleeding, and tranquilizers can cause fetal malformations.

Pregnant women addicted to drugs such as heroin, barbiturates, cocaine, crack, designer drugs, and amphetamines expose the fetus to many problems. Low birth weight and prematurity can occur, and the baby also becomes addicted, so the first days of life are a difficult time with withdrawal symptoms.

The effects of marijuana smoking on fetal development are unclear. The active chemical ingredients are known to cross the placental barrier, but there is insufficient research to predict the exact effects on the developing fetus. Some research, however, indicates that marijuana might be more damaging to a fetus than alcohol—especially if the mother's overall lifestyle is unhealthy. Women whose lifestyles combine smoking, drinking, marijuana use, and poor eating habits give birth to more infants with characteristics of fetal alcohol syndrome than do women who are just heavy drinkers. It is difficult to isolate any single detrimental factor, because people seldom use or abuse only one substance.

As you can see, many chemical substances can cause great harm during pregnancy, and even decisions about whether to take prescription drugs should be based on current research evidence. It is sensible to avoid any prescription drug unless it is prescribed by a physician aware of the pregnancy.

Physical Activity

Most healthy women can continue their regular physical activity patterns during pregnancy. Traditionally, women often were told to refrain from sports and sexual stimulation during the later stages of pregnancy and for 6 to 8 weeks following delivery. In most cases, however, there is no reason to refrain from general physical exercise or sexual stimulation at any time during a healthy pregnancy.

Many physicians recommend regular physical activity since maternal exercise doesn't affect fetal development. In addition, women who exercise during pregnancy have fewer complications during delivery and shorter labor. Their newborns are also less likely to show signs of fetal distress—strain on the heart during labor ("Exercising for Two" 1993). If extreme pain or spotting occurs, a physician should be consulted, but these symptoms are rare.

Many women do find sexual activity in the last weeks of pregnancy to be awkward, and some experience diminished sexual desire toward the end of pregnancy. Researchers, however, have concluded that sexual activity during pregnancy is safe (Bogren 1991; "Is It Okay to Have Sex?" 1993).

After birth, three factors determine how quickly a female can return to sexually stimulating activities: (1) when she feels like it, (2) when any surgical incision is fully healed, and (3) when all vaginal bleeding or spotting has ceased. Masters and Johnson (1966) found that these three criteria were usually met by the third week following delivery.

POTENTIAL COMPLICATIONS FOR THE FETUS

In spite of all precautions, complications may arise for the fetus during pregnancy. One means of detecting fetal abnormalities is by testing the amniotic fluid that surrounds the developing child. The process of extracting the fluid is called **amniocentesis (amniotic tap),** but it is not a routine procedure (figure 11.6). The fluid can be analyzed to detect various diseases, the sex of the child, and the exact age of the child. Amniocentesis is routinely recommended for women in their mid-thirties or older expecting a first or even third or fourth child. In the past, amniocentesis could not be done until the sixteenth week of pregnancy, but now it can be done as early as the eleventh week ("Amniocentesis Now Available in the First Trimester" 1992).

Another technique, **fetoscopy,** allows direct examination of the fetus. Using fetoscopy, physicians can actually see the fetus in the uterus and spot certain physical defects. They can even take blood and tissue from the fetus. The physician makes a small incision in the abdomen and inserts a pencil-lead-thin tube containing a scope with the ability to transmit light that enables physicians to see tiny areas of the fetus.

Another means of detecting fetal abnormalities is **chorionic villi sampling (CVS).** Pieces of the villi (thin tissue) protruding from the chorion (outer layer of the amniotic sac) are removed and analyzed for birth defects. One advantage of this technique over amniocentesis is that it can be done 8 to 9 weeks after conception. One disadvantage is the risk of spontaneous abortion following CVS has been higher than with amniocentesis. If you want to obtain CVS,

amniocentesis (amniotic tap)
Analysis of amniotic fluid taken from the intrauterine environment in order to detect fetal defects.

fetoscopy
Insertion of a viewing instrument into the womb to observe the fetus.

chorionic villi sampling (CVS)
The method of removing pieces of the villi (thin tissue) protruding from the chorion (outer layer of the amniotic sac) and analyzing it for fetal abnormalities.

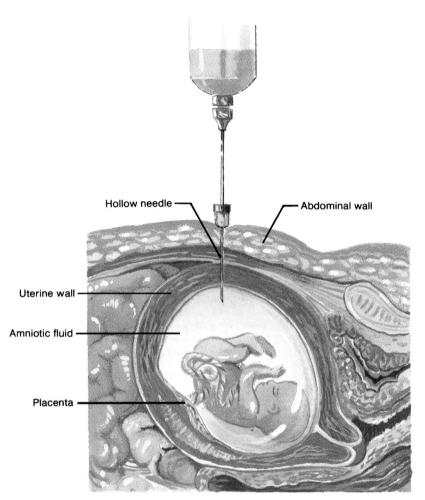

Hollow needle — | — Abdominal wall

Uterine wall —

Amniotic fluid —

Placenta —

Figure 11.6

Amniocentesis. Usually the fetus is first located by sonography—bouncing high-frequency sounds off it and recording the echoes. Then, about 10 ml of amniotic fluid, containing fetal cells, is withdrawn by a hypodermic needle inserted directly through the abdominal wall. The cells obtained by this method are grown in culture and then subjected to biochemical and chromosomal analysis.

From Stuart Ira Fox, *Human Physiology*, 3d ed. Copyright © 1990 Wm. C. Brown Publishers, Dubuque, Iowa. All Rights Reserved. Reprinted by permission.

it is crucial to go to a physician who is very experienced with the procedure. Those who are will keep the risk of spontaneous abortion extremely low ("How to Make CVS Safer for Yourself" 1993).

Ultrasound examinations are also useful during pregnancy. No radiation is used, so ultrasound is believed to be safer than X rays. The test can be used to estimate fetal age, exclude the possibility of an ectopic pregnancy, guide the needle during amniocentesis, evaluate atypical uterine growth, check for multiple fetuses, evaluate bleeding, check on fetuses at risk for birth defects, and evaluate complications during pregnancy to make sure the fetus is alive ("Ultrasound" 1985).

ultrasound
The use of sound waves for medical detection and treatment purposes.

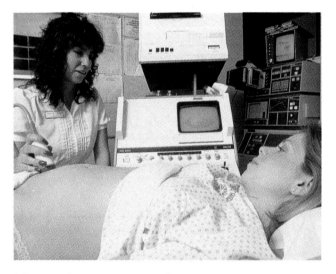

Ultrasound tests are common for pregnant women.

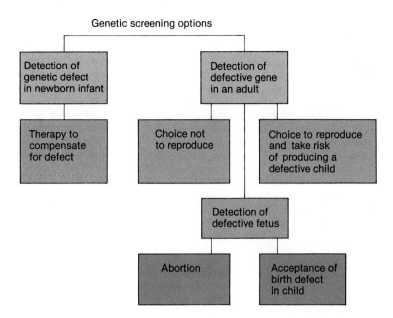

Genetic screening options

Figure 11.7
Flowchart describing genetic screening options.

Finally, to help identify certain birth defects early in pregnancy, screening programs based on a test for **alpha-fetoprotein (AFP)** in the mother's blood are becoming more common. The main object of testing pregnant women for AFP is early detection of neural tube defects. If the neural tube does not form properly, the result can be improper development of the brain and skull, or spina bifida ("split spine"). An abnormal result indicates that more-elaborate tests, such as amniocentesis or ultrasound, should be considered ("A New Prenatal Screening Program" 1987).

It is wise for potential parents to also pay attention to hereditary characteristics that can influence a baby's health. According to the March of Dimes Defects Foundation ("March of Dimes Fact Sheet" 1991), 20 percent of birth defects are inherited, 20 percent are environmentally caused, and 60 percent appear to result from an interaction between the two. Although it is not routinely pursued, **genetic counseling** can help prospective parents better understand their hereditary potential (figure 11.7).

Fortunately, most pregnancies result in the delivery of a healthy baby approximately 9 months after conception. As with health in general, making sound decisions before health problems occur greatly increases the likelihood of a healthy pregnancy.

FETAL DEVELOPMENT

Prenatal development is commonly regarded as having two stages. The **embryonic stage** lasts 2 months, and the **fetal stage** lasts from the beginning of the third month to birth. A 9-month pregnancy is usually viewed as consisting of three 3-month developmental periods called **trimesters.**

Most of the embryo's system and body parts form during the first trimester. The embryo is about 0.25 inches long at the end of the first month and 1.25 inches long at the end of the second month. The head is then almost half of the embryo's total bulk.

At the third month the fetus is 3 inches long. It can move, but the mother does not yet feel its movements. The greatest fetal growth occurs during the fourth month. The fetus is then 6 inches long and the head is about one-third of the body length. The fetus moves and can suck, and the mother can feel its movements.

During the fifth month the fetus is about 12 inches long, and it grows another 2 inches during the sixth month. By the seventh month, it is generally agreed, the baby can live outside the uterus. After the eighth month the fetus weighs a little over 5 pounds and is about 20 inches long. For the remainder of the pregnancy, the fetus will gain about 0.5 pounds a week.

POSSIBLE MATERNAL HEALTH PROBLEMS DURING PREGNANCY

Morning sickness (a condition of nausea and vomiting common in early pregnancy) is thought to be caused by hormonal changes, but the exact cause is unknown. For many women, small meals, avoiding strongly flavored foods, and eating toast and jelly in the morning before moving around seem to help. As the body adjusts to the pregnancy, morning sickness usually disappears.

Another potentially irritating, but not serious, condition is **chloasma,** or the "mask of pregnancy"—commonly, a yellow to brown patch of skin pigmentation on the faces of Caucasian women. It, too, is thought to be a result of hormonal action. The chloasma disappears after the pregnancy is over.

---

alpha-fetoprotein (AFP)
A test done during early stages of pregnancy to detect neural tube defects.

genetic counseling
Discussing one's hereditary characteristics with a trained counselor before deciding whether to have children.

embryonic stage
The first 2 months of pregnancy.

fetal stage
The stage of pregnancy from the beginning of the third month until birth.

trimesters
The three 3-month developmental periods of pregnancy.

morning sickness
A condition of nausea and vomiting common early in pregnancy.

chloasma
Commonly, a yellow to brown patch of pigmentation ("the mask of pregnancy") on the faces of pregnant Caucasian women; disappears when the pregnancy is over.

Stretch marks, also more common in Caucasian women, are visible white streaks in the skin of the breast and abdomen, which enlarge during pregnancy. They are thought to be caused by a weakening of tissue under the skin. In many instances, stretch marks do not disappear, although they may fade or lighten in time.

Hemorrhoids are swollen veins of the anal area. They can be caused by the increased flow of blood to the pelvic area during pregnancy. The result may be swelling, pain, and bleeding. The usual treatment is baths and topical creams.

Most women experience few, if any, problems during pregnancy, but there are potentially serious problems that should be understood. **Hypertension** (a high amount of pressure of the blood against the walls of the arteries—also called high blood pressure) induced by pregnancy can cause the **toxemias of pregnancy** (the hypertensive conditions of preeclampsia and eclampsia). In spite of the sound of the term, these conditions are not caused by poisons in the blood, as some people think. **Preeclampsia** is pregnancy-induced hypertension accompanied by swelling of the face, neck, and upper extremities. These body parts swell when tissues retain too much fluid. **Eclampsia** refers to the preeclampsia events, plus convulsions or coma, and it can be fatal. The causes of preeclampsia and eclampsia are unknown. Some swelling of the tissues is quite common during pregnancy and does not mean the presence of the toxemias of pregnancy.

BIRTH

It is important to understand the stages of labor. Then decisions related to the birth need consideration.

THE STAGES OF LABOR

In delivering a child (or children), a women goes through three stages of **labor,** as shown in figure 11.8. The first stage lasts an average of 10.5 hours for the first pregnancy and

hemorrhoids
Swollen veins in the anal area that can cause swelling, pain, and bleeding.

hypertension
High blood pressure.

toxemias of pregnancy
The hypertensive conditions of preeclampsia and eclampsia.

preeclampsia
Pregnancy-induced hypertension accompanied by swelling of the face, neck, and upper extremities.

eclampsia
Preeclampsia plus convulsions or coma; can be fatal.

labor
The process of childbirth.

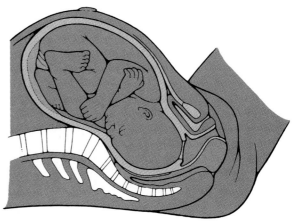

Stage 1

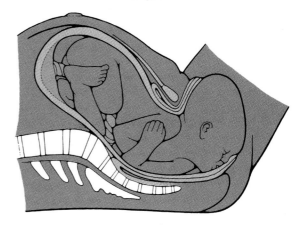

Stage 2

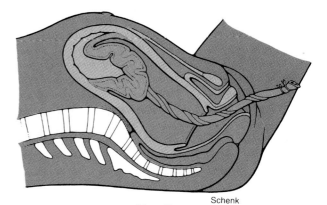

Schenk

Stage 3

Figure 11.8
The stages of childbirth, including discharge of the placenta (stage 3).

From Kent M. Van De Graaff and Stuart Ira Fox, *Concepts of Human Anatomy and Physiology,* 2d ed. Copyright © 1989 Wm. C. Brown Publishers, Dubuque, Iowa. All Rights Reserved. Reprinted by permission.

6.5 hours for later pregnancies, but it often lasts up to 20 hours. During this stage the neck of the cervix should dilate wide enough (4 inches) for the fetus to exit.

The second stage of labor is the time from full cervical dilation through birth of the child. It can last from a few

PERSONAL SKILLS AND EXPERIENCES

Promoting a Positive Relationship When Deciding Whether to Have a Child

Having a child is a major step in life. While pregnancies often occur with little, if any, advance thought, they can have a tremendous impact on human relationships. Even within a solid marital relationship, going through a pregnancy and adding another person to the relationship can be very trying. The decision to become pregnant should be based upon factors related to mind, body, soul, and interdependence. For example, reflect on the following.

Mind

Consider your feelings about your role within the relationship. Are you comfortable with your present role? with your partner's role? Are you willing to have the roles change as another person is brought into the relationship?

Body

Think about the physical changes that will occur during pregnancy to the person who is pregnant. Are you ready to deal with the changes in function and appearance? Will physical changes have an impact one way or the other on your relationship?

Soul

Think about your values. Will the presence of another person hinder or enhance what you think is important? Is it important for you to reproduce? Do you want a baby now? in the future?

Interdependence

Discuss with your partner the potential impacts of going through a pregnancy together. Discuss, also, the impact of having another person become part of your relationship. How will your lifestyles be influenced if you have a baby? Honestly assess the pros and cons for your relationship if you cause a pregnancy at this time. If you decide that it is a good time to cause a pregnancy, decide what you will do to promote a healthy relationship during the pregnancy and after the birth.

Many people cause a pregnancy without considering its impact on their relationship. You needn't follow that pattern. You can take actions to promote a good relationship whether or not you choose to cause a pregnancy. By carefully considering this important health decision, you will enhance your relationship no matter what you decide.

---

minutes to 2 hours in a normal delivery. An involuntary contraction and pushing of the abdominal muscles aids this process. To prevent tearing of the vaginal tissue, about 80 percent of women choose (with their physicians) to have an incision called an **episiotomy,** made in the vaginal opening right before delivery. There is both good and bad news about episiotomies. The good news is that they do reduce the number of minor vaginal tears during childbirth. The bad news is that the number of major tears increases ("Birthing Procedure Hurts Mother More Than It Helps" 1991). Some experts argue that nature should be allowed to take its course—which means not doing an episiotomy (Edell 1990b; Edell 1993).

The final stage of labor delivers the **placenta** (afterbirth). It usually takes up to half an hour.

Upon the baby's delivery, the **umbilical cord**—the cord linking the mother to the fetus and providing it with nourishment—is clamped and cut; the baby is checked for vital functions; and drops of silver nitrate are deposited in the baby's eyes to prevent blindness in case the mother has a gonorrheal infection.

Generally, the head of the fetus is the first body part to come out of the mother, but sometimes the fetus is positioned in the uterus with its buttocks set to come out first. A delivery in this situation (about 4 percent of all births) is termed a **breech birth** and calls for specific physician involvement to maneuver the fetus for birth. In other cases, the pressure on the head of the fetus can be so great as to decrease the fetus's oxygen supply; in these and other situations where the mother or baby would be endangered by vaginal delivery, the best procedure for birth might be a **cesarean section** (an incision in the woman's abdomen). Cesarean sections have become more common and now represent from 24 to 28 percent of deliveries in the United States. It used to be thought that once a woman had a cesarean she also had to have one for any future delivery. However, it has been found that from 40 to 80 percent of women could successfully avoid a repeat cesarean. This greatly reduces length of hospital stay, recovery time, and costs related to delivery ("C-Section Rates Remain High, But Postcesarean Vaginal Births Are Rising" 1990).

---

episiotomy
An incision made in the woman's vaginal tissue before she gives birth, to prevent its tearing during childbirth.

placenta
The organ connecting the fetus to the uterus via the umbilical cord.

umbilical cord
The cord that carries nourishment from the mother to the fetus.

breech birth
A birth in which the buttocks of the fetus are positioned to be delivered first.

cesarean section
The delivery of a baby through a surgical incision made in the mother's lower abdomen and uterine wall.

Decisions About the Birth

Directions

This assessment is for couples who are considering having children or who are in a pregnancy. If you ever plan to have children or are pregnant, check all that apply.

____ We have considered a Lamaze delivery.

____ We have considered a Leboyer delivery.

____ We have selected a physician or midwife with whom we are comfortable.

____ We have decided that the male will accompany the female during delivery.

____ We have chosen a hospital or home delivery that has the options we want (rooming-in, birthing rooms, and so on).

____ We have talked as a couple about the pros and cons of breast-feeding versus bottle-feeding.

____ We have looked into our family histories to discover any genetic diseases (e.g., diabetes) for which we might be carriers or know we have.

____ We have received genetic counseling (only if you have a history of a genetic disease).

Interpretation

If you have not talked about some of these items, perhaps you should do so.

While there might be good reasons for cesarean deliveries, the decision of whether or not to have one should be carefully considered. Some people feel there are too many cesareans done unnecessarily. For example, 30 percent of emergency cesarean sections performed at a British teaching hospital were judged later to have been unnecessary. There is also a high degree of disagreement among evaluators regarding the need for many of the other cesareans ("Evaluating the Cesarean Decision" 1990).

In one study, strongly encouraging physicians to use vaginal births and making cesarean delivery rates of individual physicians available to all other physicians in a hospital resulted in a dramatic decrease in the number of cesarean births performed. The total cesarean rates declined from 27.3 percent to 16.9 percent (Sokol et al. 1993).

DECISIONS ABOUT THE BIRTH

Because anesthetics to decrease the mother's pain during childbirth remain in the newborn long after birth, more and more women are choosing drugless births, or **natural childbirth.** One of the more popular methods of natural childbirth, the **Lamaze method,** is named after its developer, Fernand Lamaze. The Lamaze method is a program of formal class instruction designed to teach women how to relax through breathing exercises and how to bear down (using abdominal muscular contractions to help position the baby for birth) during the second stage of labor. Women are taught to consider labor as a time of work and concentration. They become active participants in the birth process, confident that they can help control their deliveries. Further, the father (or another person who serves as a partner) is taught how to coach the woman during childbirth—reminding her to relax, monitoring her breathing, telling her about her progress, and providing moral support.

WHERE TO DELIVER

Although hospital delivery is still the predominant choice, women are increasingly choosing home births. The advantages of home delivery include the familiar and comfortable setting, the potentially enlarged role of the father, faster recovery than from hospital births, and the opportunity to have the baby be an immediate part of the family and the family an immediate part of the birth. Since medical resources available at hospitals are unavailable in homes, however, home births are recommended only when the risk of complications appears low. The mother should be 20 to 30 years of age and should have no potential medical problems; she should also have been well nourished during the pregnancy, and have already had 1 to 3 full-term births without any complication. In any case, home birth should include the services of a qualified nurse-midwife or physician.

In some parts of the country there are **birthing centers.** A birthing center is usually connected with a hospital, although some are not. The center is designed to simulate the home environment, and the couple, along with their obstetrician and pediatrician, draw up a plan—based on their desires and potential medical needs—to guide the birthing center staff.

---

natural childbirth
Drug-free childbirth.

Lamaze method
A type of natural childbirth based on exercises in relaxation, breathing, and concentration on muscular contractions.

birthing center
A medical facility with a homelike atmosphere that is used for delivering babies.

THE WORLD AROUND YOU

Differences in Breast-Feeding Practices

It is interesting to note the different rates of breast-feeding among various groups. In the National Health Promotion and Disease Prevention Objectives (in Objective 2.11), it is pointed out that, in 1988, 54 percent of mothers used breast-feeding initially and 21 percent used it until their babies were 5 to 6 months old. Among certain population groups, however, the proportions were as follows:

	Initially	5 to 6 Months
Low-income mothers	32%	9%
African American mothers	25%	8%
Hispanic mothers	51%	16%
American Indian/ Alaska Native mothers	47%	28%

Initially, those using breast-feeding most are Hispanic mothers. At 5 to 6 months, however, those using breast-feeding most are the American Indian/Alaska Native mothers. How can you account for the differences seen in breast-feeding practices?

The homelike atmosphere of the birthing center facilitates relaxation with friends, family, and siblings. During labor, the mother may walk around and be near her loved ones. Usually no unexpected people, including hospital staff, are allowed inside unless an emergency occurs. If an emergency should arise, medical personnel and equipment are readily available.

Treatment of the Newborn

Another issue to consider is how to treat the newborn immediately after birth. There seemed to be little question about this matter until the ideas and practices of a French obstetrician, Frederick Leboyer, were publicized. Leboyer (1975) believes that entry into the world is a traumatic event for the infant and that everything possible should be done to make this transition gradual. He advises that newborns be delivered in dimly lit, quiet, warm rooms. Further, he argues that, rather than being held by their feet and spanked on their rears to induce breathing, babies should be placed on the mother's abdomen, where they can hear the heartbeat and begin breathing gradually. Finally, he advises that babies be placed in water at body temperature and bathed and rocked gently. Leboyer feels that babies born in this manner will be psychologically better off throughout the life cycle.

Rooming-in

Mothers who give birth in hospitals must also consider where the baby should be kept, in a nursery or in her room. Some feel that a mother who "rooms-in" with her first child tends to feel more competent and confident in her ability to mother than women whose babies are kept in hospital nurseries. Rooming-in, however, does not allow the mother as much rest and time to recover from childbirth.

Breast-feeding

Lactogenesis is the initiation of milk production after delivery; **lactation** is the breast-feeding (nursing) experience. If a woman decides to breast-feed, she must remember that what she eats or drinks will eventually reach the baby. (Doctors also recommend against taking birth-control pills while breast-feeding, because the hormones in the pills can end up in the breast milk [Edell 1990a].) A woman must also realize that sexual stimulation from breast-feeding is common and should cause no concern. Lastly, she should understand that she will probably have delayed onset of menstruation following delivery; however, this is not a reliable means of contraception. If another pregnancy is not desired, usual means of pregnancy prevention should be used after consulting with a physician.

Some argue for breast-feeding because a mother's milk gives the child the best nutrition available and provides antibodies that protect against disease. In addition, it can provide closeness between the mother and child, it saves money, and it does not require bottles and other equipment. Others argue that it is inconvenient, messy, and time-consuming and that adequate nutrition can be obtained from commercially available milk.

TO CIRCUMCISE OR NOT TO CIRCUMCISE

Circumcision, surgical removal of the foreskin of a male's penis, is the most commonly performed surgical procedure in the United States. (Although circumcision of the female has flourished in many parts of the world for centuries, we will confine this discussion to male circumcision because female circumcision is rarely seen in the United States.) Circumcision has been widely practiced throughout the world for religious, ritual, and hygienic reasons.

Particularly during the past 20 to 25 years, circumcision has been a controversial procedure in the United States. Some feel there is no absolute medical indication for routine circumcision of the newborn. They feel potential benefits should be balanced against the surgical risk, discomfort to the infant, and the use of medical and economic resources

lactogenesis
The initiation of a woman's milk production after she delivers a baby.

lactation
Breast-feeding.

circumcision
Surgical removal of the foreskin of the penis.

(Siwek 1990). Others feel that routine circumcision of new-born males has many potential advantages: The procedure helps prevent urinary tract infections, penile cancer, and sexually transmitted diseases (including AIDS). They feel that the risk of complications is low, it is more economical to perform the procedure early in life, and no evidence shows that penile hygiene alone is as beneficial as circumcision (Wiswell 1990).

Even a middle-of-the-road point of view exists on this issue. Some feel that although the risks of routine circumcision performed at birth are small, the benefits are uncertain. Therefore, it should be performed at the discretion of the parents and not as a part of routine medical care (Poland 1990). What do you think?

TAKE ACTION

1. Develop a plan for a woman who might want to be pregnant, so she can maximize her potential to have a healthy baby.

SUMMARY

1. For conception to occur, a mature egg must be in a position to be fertilized and sperm must reach the egg.

2. Many myths exist about menstruation. However, it is known that cycle lengths vary from woman to woman, and even for the same woman, that there are phases to the cycle that are controlled by hormones, and that it is difficult to calculate the most fertile time in the cycle.

3. There are many functions performed by the semen while it keeps the sperm alive and capable of fertilizing an egg.

4. Infertility can be caused by a number of factors, but today there are many ways to treat infertility.

5. In recent years, there have been more older females and younger females having babies in the United States.

6. Many factors can influence a healthy pregnancy.

7. Genetic counseling and the use of a variety of tests can be helpful to many couples interested in improving their chances of having a healthy baby.

8. A number of consumer decisions need to be made related to labor and delivery. These include the type of childbirth, the place for childbirth, immediate care of the baby after birth, and whether to circumcise a newborn male.

COMMITMENT ACTIVITIES

1. If you are a female (or if you are a male with a strong intimate relationship with a female), carefully follow your (or your partner's) menstrual cycle for 3 to 6 months. Through the use of careful record keeping, try to determine as closely as possible the time of ovulation during each cycle. What can you conclude after you have this information?

2. In many communities there are counseling centers and clinics designed to help couples who seem to be infertile. Locate some of these centers or clinics in your community and visit one to determine the types of services available, costs, and methods used to help infertile couples.

3. Visit your nearest chapter of the March of Dimes Birth Defects Foundation and gather information on birth defects. Compare the information you gather with the information in this chapter. Ask personnel with the March of Dimes about what can be done to help promote a healthy pregnancy and delivery.

4. Check with local hospitals to see what facilities are available for people wishing to have their babies away from the traditional delivery room. What are the hospital's policies about deliveries outside of the delivery room? Do they have any special facilities? Will the medical staff cooperate if a pregnant woman wishes to deliver her baby at home? Are there birthing centers away from the hospital? What would you decide about delivery if you (or your wife) were pregnant?

REFERENCES

"Amniocentesis Now Available in the First Trimester." 1992. *UAB Insight*, Winter, 12.

Atwood, J. D., and J. W. Donnelly. 1993. "Adolescent Pregnancy: Combating the Problem from a Multi-Systemic Health Perspective." *Journal of Health Education* 24, no. 4 (July/August): 219–27.

Berkowitz, G. S. et al. 1990. "Delayed Childbearing and the Outcome of Pregnancy." *New England Journal of Medicine* 322, no. 10 (8 March): 659–63.

"Birthing Procedure Hurts Mother More Than It Helps." 1991. *Edell Health Letter* 10, no. 10 (November): 7.

Bogren, L. Y. 1991. "Changes in Sexuality in Women and Men During Pregnancy." *Archives of Sexual Behavior* 20, no. 1 (February): 35–45.

Burns, J. 1994. "Male Infertility Updated." *UAB Insight* (Spring): 7.

Cohen, D. L. 1993. "More Women Having Babies Without Marrying, Survey Finds." *Education Week* 12, no. 40 (4 August): 22.

"C-Section Rates Remain High, but Postcesarean Vaginal Births Are Rising." 1990. *Family Planning Perspectives* 21, no. 1 (January/February): 36–37.

"Diet Affects Menstrual Cycle." 1993. *Edell Health Letter* 12, no. 1 (December/January): 6–7.

Edell, D. 1990a. "Q & A with Dr. Edell—Breast-Feeding." *Edell Health Letter* 9, no. 4 (April): 8.

Edell, D. 1990b. "Q & A with Dr. Edell—Episiotomies." *Edell Health Letter* 9, no. 4 (April): 8.

Edell, D. 1993. "Q & A with Dr. Edell—an Episiotomy." *Edell Health Letter* 12, no. 4 (April): 8.

Edwards, S. 1992. "Use of Coffee, Alcohol, Cigarettes Raises Risk of Poor Birth Outcomes." *Family Planning Perspectives* 24, no. 4 (July/August): 188–89.

Elmer-Dewitt, P. 1993. "Cloning: Where Do We Draw the Line?" *Time*, 8 November, 65–70.

"Evaluating the Cesarean Decision." 1990. *Family Planning Perspectives* 22, no. 6 (November/December): 245.

"Exercising for Two." 1993. *Consumer Reports on Health* 5, no. 8 (August): 88.

Hatcher, R. A., F. Stewart, J. Trussell, D. Kowal, F. Guest, G. K. Stewart, and W. Cates. 1990. *Contraceptive Technology*. New York: Irvington.

Higgins, B. S. 1990. "Couple Infertility: From the Perspective of the Close-Relationship Model." *Family Relations* 39, no. 1 (January): 81–86.

"How to Make CVS Safer for Yourself." 1993. *Edell Health Letter* 12, no. 4 (April): 5.

"Infertility As a Function of Body Weight." 1992. *UAB Insight*, Winter, 12.

"Is It Okay to Have Sex?" 1993. *Edell Health Letter* 12, no. 6 (June/July): 5.

Kiely, J. L., J. C. Kleinman, and M. Kiely. 1992. "Triplets and Higher Order Multiple Births." *American Journal of Diseases of Children* 146 (July): 862–68.

Klebanov, P. K., and J. B. Jemmott III. 1992. "Effects of Bodily Sensations on Self-Reports of Premenstrual Symptoms." *Psychology of Women Quarterly* 16: 289–310.

Klitsch, M. 1994. "Prenatal Exposure to Tobacco, Alcohol or Other Drugs found for More Than One in 10 California Newborns." *Family Planning Perspectives* 26, no. 2 (March–April): 95–96.

Leach, R. E., and S. J. Ory. 1990. "Management of Ectopic Pregnancy." *American Family Physician* 41, no. 4 (April): 1215–18.

Leboyer, F. 1975. *Birth Without Violence.* New York: Knopf.

"March of Dimes Fact Sheet." 1991. White Plains, NY: March of Dimes Birth Defects Foundation.

Masters, W. H., and V. E. Johnson. 1966. *Human Sexual Response.* Boston: Little, Brown.

"A New Prenatal Screening Program." 1987. *Harvard Medical School Health Letter* 12, no. 40 (February): 6–8.

Poland, R. L. 1990. "The Question of Routine Neonatal Circumcision." *New England Journal Of Medicine* 322, no. 18 (3 May): 1312–15.

Portnes, J. 1992. "Little Change in Teenage Programming Rate During '80's Found." *Education Week* 12, no. 2 (25 November): 8.

"Premenstrual Syndrome: Does Anything Help?" 1993. *Consumer Reports on Health* 5, no. 6 (June): 61–63.

"Pros and Cons of Norplant." 1992. *UAB Insight,* Spring, 13.

Resnik, R. 1990. "The 'Elderly Primigravida' in 1990." *New England Journal of Medicine* 322, no. 10 (8 March): 693–94.

Reynolds, G. 1987. "Running and Menstruation." *Runner's World,* March, 36–43.

Rind, P. 1992. "Smoking in Pregnancy Nearly Triples Women's Risk of Placenta Previa." *Family Planning Perspectives* 24, no. 1 (January/February): 47–48.

Seibel, M. M., and J. A. McCarthy. 1993. "Infertility, Pregnancy, and the Emotions." In *Mind Body Medicine,* edited by D. Goleman and J. Gurin. New York: Consumer Reports Books.

Siwek, J. 1990. "Circumcision: The Debate Continues." *American Family Physician* 41, no. 3 (March): 817–18.

"Smart Moms Don't Smoke." 1993. *Edell Health Letter* 12, no. 6 (June/July): 4.

Sokol, M. L., P. M. Garcia, A. M. Peaceman, and S. L. Dooley. 1993. "Reducing Cesarean Births at a Primarily Private University Hospital." *American Journal of Obstetrics and Gynecology* 168, no. 6, part 1: 1748–58.

Sroka, S. R. 1991. "Common Sense on Condom Education." *Education Week* 10, no. 25 (13 March): 39–40.

"Teenage Sexual and Reproductive Behavior." 1991. In *Facts in Brief.* New York: Alan Guttmacher Institute.

"Transvaginal Sonography Detects Early Pregnancy." 1992. *UAB Insight,* Spring, 12.

Turner, R. 1992. "Births to Women in Their Middle and Late 30s Have Risen Among Both Blacks and Whites Since 1980." *Family Planning Perspectives* 24, no. 2 (March/April): 91–92.

Ullyot, J. 1986. "Woman's Running: When Runners Don't Menstruate." *Runner's World,* July, 84–85.

"Ultrasound: Revelations About an Unborn Child." 1985. *Better Health,* April, 5–7.

"U.S. Far Exceeds Other Nations in Teen Pregnancy." 1987. *Health Link,* March, 45–49.

Wattleton, F. 1989. "Teen-Age Pregnancy: The Case for National Action." *Nation,* 24/31 July, 138–41.

Wiswell, T. E. 1990. "Routine Neonatal Circumcision: A Reappraisal." *American Family Physician* 41, no. 3 (March): 859–63.

Young, D. 1990. "How Can We 'Enrich' Prenatal Care?" *Birth* 17, no. 1 (March): 12–13.

ADDITIONAL READING

Bancroft, John, Lynn Williamson, Pamela Warner, Dilys Rennie, and Stephen K. Smith. 1993. "Perimenstrual Complaints in Women Complaining of PMS, Menorrhagia, and Dysmenorrhea: Toward A Dismantling of the Premenstrual Syndrome." *Psychosomatic Medicine* 55, no. 2 (March/April): 133–45. Compares four groups of women in terms of their reported menstrual symptoms. The authors present a theory describing factors that contribute to females' symptoms.

Neef, N. F., D. Scutchfield, J. Elder, and S. J. Bender. 1991. "Testicular Self-Examination by Young Men: An Analysis of Characteristics Associated with Practice." *Journal of American College Health* 39 (January): 187–90. The level of testicular self-examination awareness and practice of 404 male college students was determined. Results and characteristics associated with practice are discussed.

Turner, R. J., C. F. Grindstaff, and N. Phillips. 1990. "Social Support and the Outcome in Teenage Pregnancy." *Journal of Health and Social Behavior* 31 (March): 43–57. Presents information on the significance of social support for health and birth problems among adolescent mothers and their babies. The significance of support from family, friends, and partner are discussed.

CHAPTER 12

Preventing and Controlling Birth

Healthy People 2000 Objectives

- Reduce to no more than 30 percent the proportion of all pregnancies that are unintended.

- Increase to at least 90 percent the proportion of sexually active, unmarried people aged 19 and younger who use contraception, especially combined-method contraception that both effectively prevents pregnancy and provides barrier protection against disease.

- Increase the effectiveness with which family-planning methods are used, as measured by a decrease to no more than 5 percent in the proportion of couples experiencing pregnancy despite use of a contraceptive method.

- Increase to at least 50 percent the proportion of sexually active, unmarried people who used a condom at last sexual intercourse.

Contraceptive Behavior Assessment

Perhaps the most important aspect of this chapter is your sense of values and what you believe is right or wrong, particularly as it relates to sexual behavior, responsibility, human life, and when you feel life begins. The following assessment is designed to have you consider some very important questions that may help you to be in control, be responsible, and live in accordance with your sense of values.

1. Which of the following best describes you? (Mark all that apply.)
   a. Single, never married
   b. Married
   c. Divorced
   d. Widowed
   e. Separated
2. Which of the following best describes your feelings about sexual intercourse? (Select one response.)
   a. It's okay to have sexual intercourse with anyone you would like to have it with, if both partners think it's okay.
   b. It's only okay to have sexual intercourse with someone after you know them well and really love them.
   c. It's only okay to have sexual intercourse with someone after you have married them.
3. When do you think life begins? (Pick the closest time.)
   a. Before fertilization (egg and sperm separate)
   b. When the egg is fertilized
   c. When the egg implants in the uterus
   d. When the heart begins to beat
   e. Sometime between when the heart begins to beat and birth
   f. At birth
   g. After birth (when systems are stable)
4. Which of the following best describes your feelings? (Mark all that apply.)
   a. If I make a mistake, then I am responsible for the consequences.
   b. If I make a mistake, then I'll try not to do it again, but I'm really not responsible for the consequences.
   c. When I believe something is right, then I'll do it no matter what.

5. Which of the following best describes your behavior?
   a. I am sexually active. (When sexual opportunities come along, I will have intercourse with someone under the right conditions.)
   b. I have never had sexual intercourse, or I have in the past but I no longer have sexual intercourse.
6. Which of the following methods of birth control do you feel are wrong?
   a. Methods that are natural (abstinence, rhythm)
   b. Methods that act before fertilization (spermicides, condoms, birth-control pills, and so on)
   c. Operations that act before fertilization (tubal ligation or vasectomy)
   d. Methods that act after fertilization (IUD, morning-after pill)
   e. Methods that work after implantation and growth begins (abortion techniques)

Interpretation

This assessment deals with value/behavior congruence. When your values and behaviors are congruent (what you believe is what you do), then you will avoid negative emotions and guilt.

First compare your answers to numbers 3 and 6. If you believe life begins at fertilization, for example, any method of contraception that acts after fertilization or abortion should be avoided because your belief system would imply that you are taking a life. On the other hand, if you believe that life begins at birth, then any contraceptive or abortive method will be within your value system. Check for congruencies by making sure that the contraceptive or abortive methods you use (if you use them) are within your values limitations.

Consider numbers 1 and 2 together and then compare number 5. If you are single, for example, and checked number 2c and number 5a, then you have value/behavior incongruence.

Consider numbers 4 and 5 together. If you checked number 4a, which indicates responsibility, and number 5a, indicating sexual activity, and then you checked number 6b, c, and d, then maybe you should consider abstinence unless you are able to face consequences.

There are many potential areas you can check for incongruence. The point of this evaluation is to align your values and behaviors so that you are guilt free, do not make errors forcing you into responsibilities that you do not want, and are happy.

CONTRACEPTION

Contraceptive decisions are sometimes controversial. Understanding arguments for and against contraception, as well as options, is essential when making decisions about contraception.

ARGUMENTS FOR CONTRACEPTION

Many individuals use **contraceptives** to space pregnancies, limit family size, delay childbearing, or avoid pregnancy altogether.

Contraception allows us to decide whether and when we will have children. Because children conceived under such circumstances are planned for, we avoid bringing unwanted children into the world. For some women, a pregnancy

contraceptive
Any birth-control method or device.

THE WORLD AROUND YOU

Population Control

We hear about the overcrowding of some communities. We read about attempts to control the number of people who move to the United States from other countries. Sometimes we think about the "best" size for our family. All of these issues relate to the issue of population control. The topic often stirs up strong emotions in some people. Because of high living costs and shortages of space and other resources, many argue that our population should be controlled. They feel it has a large impact on the quality of our life.

- Pro: We have a social responsibility to control our population; if we don't, there will be increased overcrowding, housing shortages, general congestion, and possibly inadequate food supplies. Increased stress will also occur because of tension associated with crowds and decreased resources. Therefore, the government should institute population policies—such as tax regulations, educational programs, and distribution of birth-control devices and information—that will encourage people to have small rather than large families.

- Con: The population issue should be decided by each individual. Scientific discoveries in the future will ease tensions caused by population problems, and neither the government nor anyone else should tell people what to do about population. The major responsibility for the quality of life rests with individuals, not society.

Do you think there are reasons to control population size in the United States? Should we turn away people from other countries who want to move here? Should we provide tax incentives to help motivate people to have larger or smaller families? Should anything be done to control population? Why or why not?

might be medically dangerous, and contraception can protect their health. It can also help women avoid conceiving children with birth defects.

Contraception also provides a means for individuals to participate in sexual intercourse without much fear of pregnancy. Many women experience more freedom and self-actualization when they use contraception. This is particularly true for women who wish to pursue careers or other activities where unplanned pregnancies would be difficult. Lastly, contraception can also control population growth.

ARGUMENTS AGAINST CONTRACEPTION

Among the reasons commonly given for not using contraceptives are health risks and moral arguments. Some fear their bodies will be harmed by using birth-control pills or other methods, and others feel it is against the will of God to "artificially" interfere with a pregnancy. These individuals might consider abstinence or some other "natural" avoidance of pregnancy to be acceptable, but not any method that involves an artificial device or a chemical. Some individuals also find that certain contraceptive methods create a loss of spontaneity in sexual relationships. Finally, some minority-group social leaders have argued that government advocacy of contraceptive use for their group is meant to reduce their numbers and eventually exterminate them.

FORMS OF CONTRACEPTION

Deciding on the best contraceptive should involve consultation with a physician or appropriate persons who are trained to deal with contraceptive decisions and possess the latest information. Two of the current preferred methods (**oral contraceptives,** or the pill; and the diaphragm) require a physician's prescription. Sterilization requires a surgeon's help, and use of an **injectable** or implant requires visits to a physician. But all other methods considered here require at most a trip to the drugstore or another store that carries contraceptives.

Oral Contraceptives (the Pill)

The most effective method of contraception control today—short of abstinence or a surgical procedure—is the pill. Even though they're all generally referred to as "the pill," there are several varieties of oral contraceptives. The type of oral contraceptive used since the early 1960s contains both estrogen and progestin (synthetic progesterone) and is called the **combination pill.** A variation of the combination pill is called the **multiphasic pill.** This newer version varies the amount of estrogen and progesterone throughout the menstrual cycle to more closely match the amounts of these hormones naturally occurring in the female.

---

oral contraceptive
Birth-control pills; the pill.

injectable
Long-acting injectable contraceptive.

combination pill
A birth-control pill that contains both progesterone and estrogen and works by suspending ovulation.

multiphasic pill
A birth-control pill that varies the amount of estrogen and progesterone throughout the menstrual cycle to more closely match the naturally occurring amounts of these hormones in the female.

Many choices exist if the pill is the contraceptive method chosen.

The combination pill is almost 100 percent effective if taken properly. The user must take it regularly for 21 days or use supplementary contraception. The chemical reactions sparked by combination or multiphasic pills can be quite complicated. Simply described, the hormones trick the body into thinking it is pregnant; these hormones, estrogen and progesterone, work exactly as they do in the usual menstrual cycle. Recall that after ovulation, elevated levels of estrogen and progesterone prevent the release of another egg during the menstrual cycle. The pill elevates the levels of these hormones and suspends ovulation altogether. The menstrual cycle continues as usual for all practical purposes, but no egg is released and conception cannot occur.

The third type of oral contraceptive contains no estrogen and is called the progestin-only pill, or **minipill.** This pill is ingested daily throughout the menstrual cycle, but it often does not suspend ovulation. The progestin inhibits implantation and causes the cervical mucus to become thicker, making it more difficult for sperm to get through. Since the minipill contains only progesterone, it generally does not cause the side effects commonly associated with the combination pill. Researchers have concluded that it is a suitable and an equally effective alternative to the combination pill in all age groups ("Minipill May Have Broader Appeal" 1991).

Research shows that taking the pill presents fewer risks than going through a pregnancy. As with any medication, however, women who take the pill risk complications and side effects. A physician and client must decide if the benefits are worth the risk. The negative side effects of the pill are of two types: nuisance effects and medically serious effects. Fluid retention, weight gain, irritability, and change in sex drive fall into the nuisance category, while a tendency toward blood clots, hypertension, or gall bladder disease are medically more serious. In most cases, women's bodies adjust to the nuisance side effects after several menstrual cycles. If adjustment does not occur, however, a woman may decide that

this method is unacceptable. There is no reliable evidence that birth-control pills cause cancer—even after being used for 15 years or longer (*Better Health* 1987). It is generally recommended that women over 40, women who smoke, and women with liver function problems, hypertension, circulatory problems, sickle-cell disease, asthma, varicose veins, epilepsy, or migraine headaches should not take the pill. This does not mean that the pill causes any of these things—rather, it means that it is wise to be cautious if any of these conditions already exist. Better screening of potential pill users and lower hormone dosages have resulted in fewer reports of adverse side effects than 20 to 25 years ago.

Increasing evidence has shown that the pill has positive side effects. For example, it has been estimated that 50,000 hospitalizations are prevented each year by use of the pill. The pill has a direct positive effect on the following diseases: benign breast disease, ovarian and endometrial cancers, ovarian cysts, iron-deficiency anemia, **pelvic inflammatory disease (PID)** (PID leads to 1.2 million doctor visits and 276,000 hospitalizations annually [Althaus 1993a]), and ectopic pregnancy. In some cases, such as benign breast disease and PID, the protective effect increases the longer the pill is used (Hatcher et al. 1986; Edell 1990).

What happens when a female stops taking the pill? There is no strong evidence that the pill subsequently affects a woman's ability to become pregnant, increases her tendency to have multiple births, or in any other way alters her general health.

Other contraceptive techniques that also work by suspending ovulation are in various stages of experimentation and implementation. These include a capsule implant that is injected under the skin and releases hormones over a long period of time, an injection that works in essentially the same way, and a once-a-month (or other time interval) pill.

Injectables

Long-acting injectable contraceptives have been available for over a decade. On 10 December 1990, the U.S. Food and Drug Administration approved the marketing of Norplant, a contraceptive implant system. Six capsules 34 millimeters long inserted beneath the skin of a woman's upper arm release a steady, low dose of levonorgestrel (a synthetic progestin) for up to 5 years. The United States was the seventeenth country to approve the method for marketing. It is already thought to be the most effective reversible contraceptive method available, with a first-year use-failure rate of 0.2 pregnancies per 100 ("FDA OKs Hormonal Implant" 1990).

---

minipill
A birth-control pill that contains only progestin. The progestin inhibits implantation and causes the cervical mucus to become thicker, making it more difficult for sperm to get through.

pelvic inflammatory disease (PID)
Inflammation of the pelvic organs, such as the oviducts.

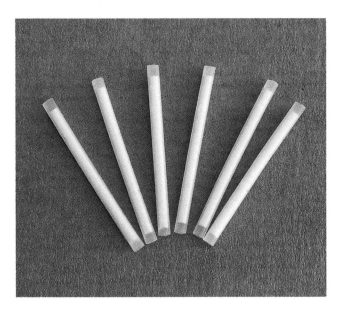

Norplant is becoming popular.

Some nuisance side effects (such as weight changes, headaches, and mood changes) have been reported among some Norplant users, but no serious side effects have been reported. Researchers have concluded that Norplant can be highly acceptable to most women seeking a convenient, effective, temporary method of contraception ("Hormonal Implants Prove to Be Highly Acceptable" 1990). The only downside to using Norplant seems to be abnormal menstrual flow. About 70 percent of users have flow that is unpredictable in amount, duration, and frequency ("The Pros and Cons of Norplant" 1992).

In 1992 the FDA approved Depo-Provera (a form of progesterone that can be injected), which is approved for use in over ninety countries. It is effective for about 3 months. To reduce accidental pregnancy, a woman should receive her first injection during the first week following the beginning of her menstrual cycle. The most common reason some women discontinue use of Depo-Provera is menstrual cessation. Women using injectables sometimes experience the same kinds of nuisance side effects (weight gain, dizziness, headaches, and depression) as do pill users, but these side effects can be more disturbing with injectables because a woman cannot stop the symptoms by immediately stopping use of the method (Klitsch 1993).

Injectables are about 99 percent effective, but some users report changes in menstrual patterns, some develop amenorrhea (absence of menstruation), and some report a delayed return to fertility after stopping use of the injectable. Injectables also have beneficial health effects. They often increase blood iron levels and protect against PID and ovarian and endometrial cancer ("Hormonal Contraception" 1987).

Emergency Contraceptive Pills

About 3.5 million unintended pregnancies occur each year in the United States, and about half of these are from contraceptive failure—usually as a result of human error. The term *morning-after pill* is commonly used, but the term *emergency contraceptive pill* is better because it avoids the incorrect implication that treatment must be delayed until the morning following unprotected sexual intercourse (Trussell et al. 1992). Postcoital hormonal treatment appears to prevent pregnancy by temporarily disrupting a woman's hormonal patterns. It disturbs the development of the uterine lining and disrupts the transport of the fertilized ovum through the fallopian tubes.

Simple postcoital hormonal treatments are available. The "Yuzpe" method involves taking four combined estrogen/progestin pills within 72 hours after unprotected intercourse (preferably as soon as possible) and taking two more 12 hours later. This method has replaced the older method involving high doses of an estrogen-like substance called **diethylstilbestrol (DES),** primarily because it has fewer side effects.

Another method consists of three tablets of danocrine (marketed in the United States as Danazol) taken within 72 hours of unprotected intercourse and repeated 12 hours later. This method has a lower incidence of nausea, vomiting, and breast tenderness than the "Yuzpe" method (Trussell et al. 1992).

An even newer method uses mifepristone (RU 486) as a postcoital contraceptive. When used within 72 hours of unprotected sexual intercourse, it has greater effectiveness and fewer side effects than the other two methods (Althaus 1993b). It blocks the effects of progesterone and brings on menstruation. You might read controversial articles about RU 486 because it can be used as late as 49 days after a woman's last menstrual flow. This means conception can have occurred, and RU 486 is then a method of nonsurgical abortion.

Diaphragm

The **diaphragm** also requires consultation with a physician. The diaphragm is a dome-shaped latex device that the woman places over the cervix to block the opening to the uterus, thereby preventing sperm from entering (figure 12.1). Used in combination with a spermicidal jelly or foam, the diaphragm was probably the most effective (about 85% to 90%) birth-control method before the advent of pills and injectables. It is important to use the diaphragm in combination with a spermicidal jelly, which lubricates the diaphragm for insertion and, more importantly, greatly increases its potential effectiveness. The diaphragm may be inserted just before intercourse, or

diethylstilbestrol (DES)
A synthetic estrogen used as a "morning-after" pill.

diaphragm
A round, latex, dome-shaped birth-control device for women that covers the entrance to the uterus (cervix); used with spermicidal jelly or foam.

PERSONAL SKILLS AND EXPERIENCES

How to Use Condoms Properly

- Latex condoms should be used because they offer greater protection against AIDS than natural membrane condoms.
- Condoms should be stored in a cool, dry place out of direct sunlight.
- Condoms in damaged packages or those that show obvious signs of age (brittle, sticky, or discolored) should not be used.
- Condoms should be handled with care to prevent puncture.
- Condoms should be put on before any genital contact. Hold the tip of the condom and unroll it onto the erect penis, leaving space at the tip to collect semen, yet being sure that no air is trapped in the tip of the condom.

- Adequate lubrication should be used, but only water-based lubricants should be used. Oil-based lubricants (such as petroleum jelly, cooking oils, shortening, and lotions) should not be used since they weaken the latex.
- If a condom breaks, it should be replaced immediately. If ejaculation occurs after condom breakage, spermicide should be used immediately. However, the protective value of postejaculation application of spermicide is not known.
- After ejaculation, care should be taken so that the condom does not slip off the penis before withdrawal; the base of the condom should be held while withdrawing. The penis should be withdrawn while still erect.
- Condoms should never be reused.

Source: From "U.S. Centers for Disease Control Give Recommendations for Proper Use of Condoms to Prevent STD Transmission" in *Health Education Reports* 10(7): 5 (March 1988).

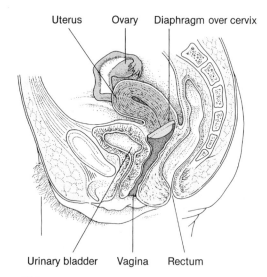

Uterus   Ovary   Diaphragm over cervix

Urinary bladder   Vagina   Rectum

Figure 12.1

Cross section of the female pelvis showing a diaphragm in position. Generally used in conjunction with a spermicidal jelly or cream, the diaphragm blocks sperm from entry into the uterus and thus prevents conception.

up to 6 hours beforehand. It is also important to leave the diaphragm in place for at least 6 to 8 hours after intercourse. If you have intercourse more than once during that 6 to 8 hours, an additional dose of spermicidal cream or jelly is recommended. Do not remove the diaphragm; use the plastic applicator to insert fresh jelly or cream in front of the diaphragm.

Use of the diaphragm introduces a factor not present with either pills or injectables: the user must insert the diaphragm before actual sexual intercourse, which some people find undesirable. There are no adverse side effects with the diaphragm, however, as there can be with pills and injectables. Women must consult their physicians to get a diaphragm that fits correctly and to learn proper insertion and

removal techniques. Never borrow another woman's diaphragm, because people are different sizes internally, just as they are externally. Also, after a pregnancy and after a body weight change of 6 pounds or more, a woman should be refitted for a new diaphragm.

Condom

Sometimes called **rubbers, condoms** cover the erect penis and prevent sperm from entering the vagina. Leading the list of nonprescriptive contraceptives, condoms can be quite effective (90% to 97%) if used properly (figure 12.2). Correct use involves following the U.S. Centers for Disease Control recommendations, which are listed in the Personal Skills and Experience box on proper condom use. There are no side effects or dangers associated with condom use. Some individuals object to condoms, claiming that condoms dull physical sensation and tend to interrupt sexual intercourse, but users should personally evaluate condoms for these characteristics.

Ever since the surgeon general's report on AIDS (Koop 1986), there has been a renewed interest in condoms. Although they are not a guaranteed barrier, condoms do seem to be helpful in reducing the likelihood of spreading sexually transmitted diseases—including HIV infection. (Animal-skin condoms, however, are not as effective for this purpose as latex condoms are.)

A few manufacturers have added the sperm-killing chemical nonoxynol-9 to some condoms, on the theory that it will inactivate any sperm that might spill from the condom. However, the effectiveness of the chemical for this purpose, or for additional disease protection, has not yet been proven. It is wise to combine use of a condom and a spermicidal

---

condom (rubber)
A latex sheath that covers the penis and catches ejaculated sperm; a birth-control device for men.

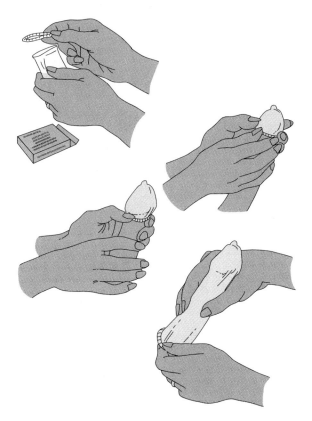

Figure 12.2

Most condoms, lubricated and plain, come packaged in foil and rolled, ready for use. The condom is placed over the head of the penis, with a space left at the tip to hold the semen when ejaculated. It is important to squeeze out the air as the condom is unrolled on the penis. Either partner can unroll the condom down over the glans and shaft of the penis to the base of the scrotum. The condom should be in place before any vaginal contact and removed immediately after ejaculation and withdrawal.

foam. Their combined effectiveness approaches that of oral contraceptives, and they also provide protection from sexually transmitted diseases.

Consumers' Union tested over forty varieties of condoms for defects and strength and surveyed over 3,300 of their readers to help accumulate additional facts about condoms. As a result of their research, the following summary statements can be made ("Can You Rely on Condoms?" 1989):

1. Women purchase 40 to 50 percent of condoms today, up from 10 percent a few years ago.

2. About one in four readers said that a condom had broken in the past year—about one in eight reported at least two incidents of breakage.

3. Overall about 1 condom in 140 broke. However, the type of sexual activity can make a difference. For example, the breakage for anal intercourse was 1 condom in 105 and for vaginal intercourse it was 1 in 165.

4. Intact latex condoms won't let the smallest microbes through. This means they can help prevent syphilis, gonorrhea, chlamydia, genital herpes, and HIV infection.

5. Failure rates have ranged from 5 to 15 percent, but strong motivation to use condoms properly could theoretically cut failure rates to 1 to 2 percent.

6. Condom quality has been improving. Much stricter FDA testing procedures are thought to account for this.

7. The amount of spermicide in condoms is no substitute for a vaginal spermicide that can be applied more liberally.

8. It makes sense to choose from among the condoms that did well in the Consumers' Union airburst test (the volume and pressure of air a condom can withstand before bursting). The results are available in *Consumer Reports* ("Can You Rely on Condoms?" 1989).

It is also important to pay attention to the expiration date on the condom package. In one study, about 3.5 percent of brand-new condoms broke during intercourse. Condoms less than 2 years old had a breakage rate below 10 percent, but about 19 percent of 7-year-old condoms broke during sexual intercourse ("Can You Count on Condoms?" 1993).

Due to increased interest in condoms, many recent studies have explored aspects of condom usage. Here are some examples: Properly used, condoms are unlikely to break or fall off. Only 1.5 percent broke or fell off during intercourse, and another 0.4 percent fell off during withdrawal. Most problems with condoms are a result of improper use (Althaus 1992). People who participate in other risky behaviors (such as use of illicit drugs, aggression, and cigarette-smoking) are less likely to use condoms. In addition, those who have more sexual partners are less likely to use condoms than are those with fewer sexual partners (Richter et al. 1993).

Adolescent women involved in relationships lasting less than 3 months are more than twice as likely to use condoms consistently than are young women in longer-term relationships (Edwards 1993). Men younger than 30 are more likely to use condoms than are men over 30, and condom use increases with years of education (Tanfer et al. 1993). Finally, many respondents report that using a condom "shows that you are a concerned and caring person." Consequences of using condoms are reported as making your partner think you have AIDS, being embarrassed when buying condoms, reduced sensation during intercourse, and being careful during intercourse so the condom is used properly. When purchasing condoms, most men look for those that are easy to put on, have the right amount of lubrication, and stay on (Grady et al. 1993). Think about these reports on condoms. Why do you think the results came out the way they did?

Did you know that there is also a female condom? Invented by a Danish physician in 1984, it is in limited use. A majority of men and women using it report it is easy to use

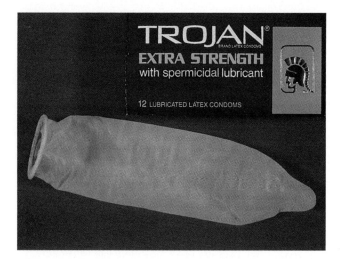

Male and female condoms.

and does not interfere with sexual response. Both men and women are more likely to report problems in achieving orgasm with the male condom than with the female condom ("Users Approve of Female Condom" 1991).

In 1993 the FDA approved the marketing of a female condom named Reality in the United States. It is not as effective as the male condom, and it costs around $2.50. It is a 7-inch-long polyurethane sheath with a ring on each end. The inner ring is inserted into the vagina, much like a diaphragm, while the other ring remains outside. The FDA required that the product label clearly indicate that male condoms are still more effective contraceptives and that female condoms have about a 26 percent failure rate. The manufacturer claims that, if used properly, the failure rate is only 5 percent. In 1994 it was reported that female condoms have only a 2.6 percent failure rate if used perfectly. Their effectiveness was equal to that of the diaphragm, greater than or equal to that of the cervical cap, and greater than that of the sponge (Trussell et al. 1994). It is thought that the polyurethane in the female condom may be more effective against viruses than the latex of male condoms, but not enough studies have been done to know for sure. At any rate, this relatively new product gives females an option if a male partner will not wear a condom.

Jellies, Creams, and Foams

A great variety of jellies, creams, and foams are available for women without a prescription in any drugstore. Figure 12.3 shows the application of a spermicidal foam. These products all work basically the same way—they are supposed to kill the sperm before it can complete its journey. By themselves, however, they are not nearly as effective as the methods already mentioned. For best results, they should be used in combination with a diaphragm or condom. The application method and the timing of use before intercourse will vary with the product, so it is important to read the instructions carefully. There are no known serious or adverse side effects,

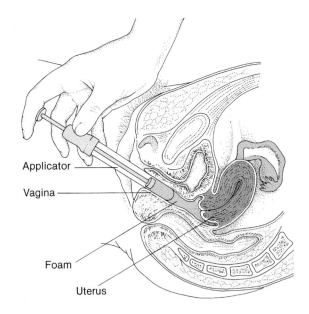

Figure 12.3

Application of spermicidal foam.

but some women and men report skin irritation from some products, just as might be expected from some deodorants or other products that contact the skin.

The effectiveness of a **spermicide** (a sperm-killing chemical) can be as low as 70 to 80 percent. To be effective, it must be inserted into the vagina as close to the time of intercourse as possible, but no more than an hour before. As it covers the cervix, the spermicide forms both a physical and a chemical barrier to sperm. To avoid interfering with the contraceptive action, a woman should not douche for at least 6 hours after intercourse.

spermicide
Sperm-killing chemical.

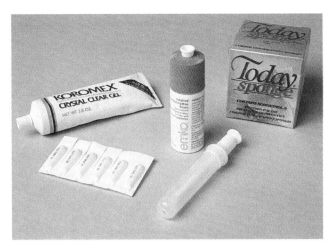

Many spermicides are available without a prescription.

Sponge

First marketed in 1983 under the brand name *Today,* the effectiveness of the spermicidal **sponge** is estimated to be 80 to 87 percent. It feels like a powder puff, is made of a special polyurethane material, and contains the spermicide nonoxynol-9. After being moistened with 2 tablespoons of water, the sponge is inserted into the vagina to cover the cervix, forming both a physical and a chemical barrier to sperm. It is believed to act in several ways: Its spermicide kills the sperm; the sponge itself absorbs the ejaculate; and it acts as a mechanical barrier to block the opening to the cervix. It should be left in place for at least 6 hours after intercourse but can be left in place and be effective for up to 24 hours. It should be discarded after use.

As with spermicides, a small percentage of users may experience irritations, and there are reports of difficulties in removing the sponge. There have been a few cases of toxic shock syndrome (TSS), a rare but potentially fatal illness among women using sponges. But the rate is very low—less than one TSS case per 3 million sponges used, and even this rate can be reduced if women carefully follow the directions on the leaflet accompanying the product.

As might be expected, women who continue to use the sponge view attributes of the sponge more positively than women who no longer use it. Those who continue to use it believe it is important for a contraceptive method to be obtainable without contact with a health professional, to not have to be washed or stored, and to be disposable (Beckman, Harvey, and Murray 1992).

Fertility Awareness (Rhythm Method)

A contraceptive method that requires little equipment and has been used for centuries is the **rhythm method,** also called natural family planning, the ovulation method, or **fertility awareness.** Effectiveness is highly variable, with estimates generally ranging from 53 to 86 percent. Avoiding pregnancy with this method requires having no intercourse during those times in the menstrual cycle when fertilization is likely to occur.

The most common variations are the basal body temperature method, the cervical mucus method, and the calendar method. They can be used together for increased effectiveness. The **basal body temperature (BBT) method** is based on the fact that the woman's temperature drops slightly, about 0.2 degrees Fahrenheit, just before ovulation. A day or so after the drop, a distinct rise (about 0.6 to 0.8°F) signals the beginning of ovulation. Unprotected intercourse must be avoided from the time the woman's temperature drops until her temperature has remained elevated for three consecutive days. Unfortunately, the woman's temperature can vary for other reasons, such as illness.

The **cervical mucus method** (also called **vaginal mucus method**) relies on the fact that cervical mucus changes from dry after menstruation to very slippery (almost like raw egg white) during ovulation to dry again after ovulation. A woman can check her cervical mucus several times a day by wiping herself with toilet paper before she urinates and observing any changes. At first, she many need help from a trained health professional to properly interpret her findings. Sometimes a woman may choose to combine the BBT and cervical mucus methods. When the two are used together it is termed the **symptothermal method.**

The **calendar method,** which is effective only when used with one or both of the methods just discussed, consists of keeping track of the number of days in the menstrual cycle in an attempt to pinpoint ovulation. If menstrual cycles are short, this method is highly unreliable. For best results, couples must be willing to carefully chart ovulation for a year's time and strictly adhere to a given regime. Table 12.1 shows how to calculate "safe" and "unsafe" days.

---

sponge
A relatively new contraceptive device that absorbs and kills sperm and serves as a barrier.

rhythm method (fertility awareness method)
A method of birth control based on abstinence from intercourse during the woman's fertile period.

basal body temperature (BBT) method
A method of birth control based on keeping track of the female's temperature changes during her menstrual cycle in an attempt to pinpoint ovulation.

cervical mucus method (vaginal mucus method)
Checking cervical mucus in an attempt to pinpoint ovulation.

symptothermal method
The combination of BBT and cervical mucus methods.

calendar method
Keeping track of the number of days in the menstrual cycle in an attempt to pinpoint ovulation.

Length of Shortest Cycle (Days)	First "Unsafe" Day After Start of Any Menstrual Period	Length of Longest Cycle (Days)	Last "Unsafe" Day After Start of Any Menstrual Period
20	2nd	20	9th
21	3rd	21	10th
22	4th	22	11th
23	5th	23	12th
24	6th	24	13th
25	7th	25	14th
26	8th	26	15th
27	9th	27	16th
28	10th	28	17th
29	11th	29	18th
30	12th	30	19th
31	13th	31	20th
32	14th	32	21st
33	15th	33	22nd
34	16th	34	23rd
35	17th	35	24th
36	18th	36	25th
37	19th	37	26th
38	20th	38	27th
39	21st	39	28th
40	22nd	40	29th

TABLE 12.1 THE RHYTHM METHOD OF CONTRACEPTION—HOW TO CALCULATE THE "SAFE" AND "UNSAFE" DAYS FOR COITUS

Issue

Contraceptive Use

Although older birth-control methods were not as sophisticated as those available today, probably from the beginning of time individuals argued about the pros and cons of controlling births. Strong positions have been taken on both sides of this issue.

- Pro: Births should be controlled with reliable methods. There should be no "accidents" or "unplanned pregnancies." In order to assure that a pregnancy occurs only when it is desired, the most reliable contraceptive method available should be used. It is crucial to review information on contraceptives, consider personal factors, and always use the most reliable contraceptive method.

- Con: Contraceptives might have benefits for some people, but in general they should not be used. Sexual intercourse, conception, and birth are natural processes. It is not right to interfere with them by using artificial means to control births. Reliable or not, contraceptives are contrary to natural laws and are not proper to use.

Are you able to take a stand on this issue? Do personal circumstances influence your point of view? Is it acceptable for people to use contraceptives whenever they wish to? Only at certain times and in certain situations? Explain your point of view to a friend and listen to his or her point of view.

Cervical Cap

The **cervical cap** is available on a limited basis and as an investigational device in some clinics around the country. It has long been popular in Europe. It is similar to, but smaller than, the diaphragm and is made of rubber, plastic, or metal. It is more difficult to insert than a diaphragm and fits snugly around the cervix.

Like the diaphragm, the cervical cap comes in different sizes, but it can probably be left in place for days or weeks. Generally, the cap must be removed during menstruation to allow for the menstrual flow to be removed from the body. There is, however, an experimental cap (the Goepp cap) that can remain in place up to a year. It has a one-way valve that allows menstrual products to flow into the vagina but doesn't allow sperm to enter the cervix. Although this method seems to hold some promise, its safety and effectiveness are still under investigation.

Intrauterine Device (IUD)

Of all methods of contraception, the **intrauterine device (IUD)** has been among the most controversial. IUDs are used by millions of women around the world (figure 12.4). In the

United States they were introduced in the early 1960s, and by 1982 they were used by over 2 million women (Hantula 1986). How the IUD prevents pregnancy is not known for sure, but there are several theories: (1) The presence of the IUD changes the chemical environment inside the uterus, preventing either fertilization or implantation. (2) The IUD causes the normal contractions of the uterine wall to be more violent than usual (although the woman doesn't feel them), which prevents implantation of a fertilized egg. (3) The IUD makes the egg travel more rapidly and, therefore, prevents the sperm from fertilizing it. (4) The IUD stops the sperm from getting through the uterus to the egg. (5) The IUD irritates the lining of the uterus and this prevents implantation.

cervical cap
A rubber, plastic, or metal contraceptive device that fits snugly over the cervix.

intrauterine device (IUD)
A small plastic or stainless steel contraceptive device that is placed inside a woman's uterus by a physician.

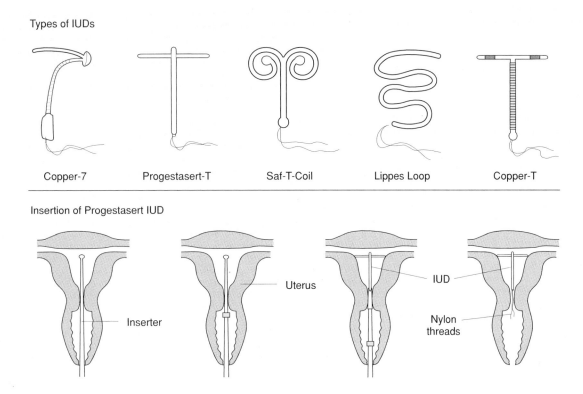

Figure 12.4
Intrauterine devices are made of flexible plastic, sometimes with copper or progesterone added. Before having an IUD inserted, a woman should discuss the pros and cons of available models with her health-care practitioner. After being straightened for insertion, the IUD's "memory plastic" resumes its original shape in the uterus. Some IUDs are designed to flex somewhat within the uterus to adjust to changes in the shape of the uterine cavity.

As early as 1974 one IUD, the Dalkon Shield, was taken off the market by its manufacturer, the A. H. Robins Company. In 1980 the company urged physicians to remove the devices from women still using them and in 1984 said it would pay all medical costs of such removal. By the end of 1985, Robins had paid out $520 million in more than nine thousand lawsuits related to serious side effects, and thousands of additional lawsuits were still pending (Hantula 1986).

The Saf-T-Coil was taken off the market by its manufacturer in 1982, and the Lippes Loop in 1985. The Copper-7, which had become by far the most popular IUD, and the Tatum-T were removed from the U.S. market in 1986 by their manufacturer, G. D. Searle and Company. It is interesting that this series of events was mainly a result of legal expenses and not medical complications.

In 1987 a copper IUD (the Copper-T 380, or TCu 380) was again put on the market, and expectations were that it would be widely used. In 1991 a slimline version of the TCu 380 became available. It might be helpful for women with small cervical canals, but there seem to be no other advantages of the newer model ("A Slimmer Copper T" 1991).

A 5-year evaluation of an IUD that releases low doses of levonorgestrel (the synthetic chemical in Norplant) showed the device to be as effective as the TCu 380—an advanced form of the Copper-T IUD. Each day it releases about one-third as much hormone as the Progestasert, which was the only hormonal IUD approved in the United States as of 1993. Effectiveness rates are about the same as for the TCu 380 (between 1.1 and 1.4 pregnancies per 100 users) ("The Low-Dose IUD" 1990).

Some experts feel that, because of all the negative publicity, some women are missing out on a good contraceptive option by not using an IUD. Ninety-eight percent of current IUD users are happy with the method; IUDs are far safer than most people assume, and the original negative statistics turn out to be misleading ("IUD Underused" 1992).

IUDs are changing rapidly, and it is difficult to keep up with the most recent information about them. As you read this, what is the current status of IUD use?

Ineffective Methods

Two other methods are sometimes classified as contraceptive but are ineffective and should not be considered reliable. These are **coitus interruptus,** withdrawal of the penis from

---

coitus interruptus
Withdrawal of the penis from the vagina before ejaculation.

PERSONAL SKILLS AND EXPERIENCES

Improving Contraceptive Effectiveness

Oral Contraceptive
Follow pill-taking instructions carefully and consistently. Use a backup method, such as foam or condoms, during the first month.

Intrauterine Device (IUD)
Have IUD inserted by experienced clinician. Frequently check IUD's position during the first few months. (User should feel thread in cervical opening but not the stem of the IUD). Use a backup method, such as foam or condoms, during the first 3 months and, if desired, at midcycle thereafter.

Diaphragm and Jelly
Use with every act of intercourse and leave in place for at least 6 hours after intercourse. Ask for thorough instruction with initial fitting and have fit checked annually by an experienced clinician. Inspect regularly for defects or holes. Avoid use of Vaseline or perfumed powders, as they can damage the latex. Always use ample amounts of spermicidal jelly or cream; add as necessary. Check position after insertion: front rim must be behind pubic bone, and dome must cover cervix.

Condom
Use with every act of intercourse. Put condom on penis before *any* penis-vagina contact, leave space in tip of condom for semen, and remove carefully to avoid spillage. Avoid damage to condom, handle carefully, and avoid heat and use of Vaseline. Buy a good brand and do not use condom that is more than 2 years old. Use foam along with condom.

Vaginal Spermicide
Use ample amounts with every act of intercourse. Follow instructions regarding time limits of effectiveness. When using foam, shake it *vigorously* before use. Use condoms along with spermicide.

Rhythm (Fertility Awareness)
Combine calendar, temperature, and mucus methods.

---

the vagina before ejaculation, and the **vaginal douche,** a stream of water or other liquid directed into the vagina for sanitary or medical reasons. The withdrawal method is common among young people because it is simple and requires no equipment. There is a real chance of pregnancy with this method, though, because sperm may seep out of the penis before actual ejaculation. These sperm are just as capable of fertilizing an egg as those ejaculated later. Sperm leaking from the penis, or deposited in a moist spot just *outside* the vagina, can swim into the vagina and up into the uterus. These facts, combined with the fact that the man is forced to withdraw when that's the last thing he feels like doing (and the woman probably isn't too happy about it either), make withdrawal a very ineffective method of contraception. The psychological frustrations of using this method also contribute to its undesirability.

The vaginal douche should not be considered an effective contraceptive. Sperm are good swimmers, and it is impossible for a female to douche quickly or thoroughly enough to wash out all of the sperm. Furthermore, the force of the douche might even push some sperm farther into the vagina and make pregnancy *more* likely. Figure 12.5 gives the effectiveness rates of the methods of contraception we have discussed.

STERILIZATION

Surgical **sterilization,** a procedure by which an individual is made incapable of reproducing, has rapidly gained popularity in the United States as a permanent way to prevent pregnancy. It is currently the most popular method used by couples over 30. After 15 years of marriage, two-thirds of all married couples have chosen sterilization (Randall 1992).

For either the man or the woman, sterilization simply involves blocking the anatomical roadway so that the sperm or egg can no longer make the trip to the meeting point. For men, this involves severing both of the vasa deferentia; for women, it requires severing the fallopian tubes. Some individuals believe that sterilization alters a person's physical abilities or sexual desires, but this is simply not true. For both men and women sterilization does *not* affect feelings, hormone production, or physical function.

In both the male operation (**vasectomy**) and the female operation (**tubal ligation**), there are a number of ways to sever and close off the tubes. Men and women can have these simple surgeries in about 15 to 20 minutes as outpatients in a hospital, clinic, or physician's office. The particular

---

vaginal douche
Directing a stream of water or other liquid into the vagina for sanitary or medical reasons.

sterilization
A surgical procedure that renders the individual incapable of reproduction.

vasectomy
A sterilization procedure for males in which the vasa deferentia are severed.

tubal ligation
A sterilization procedure for females in which the fallopian tubes are severed.

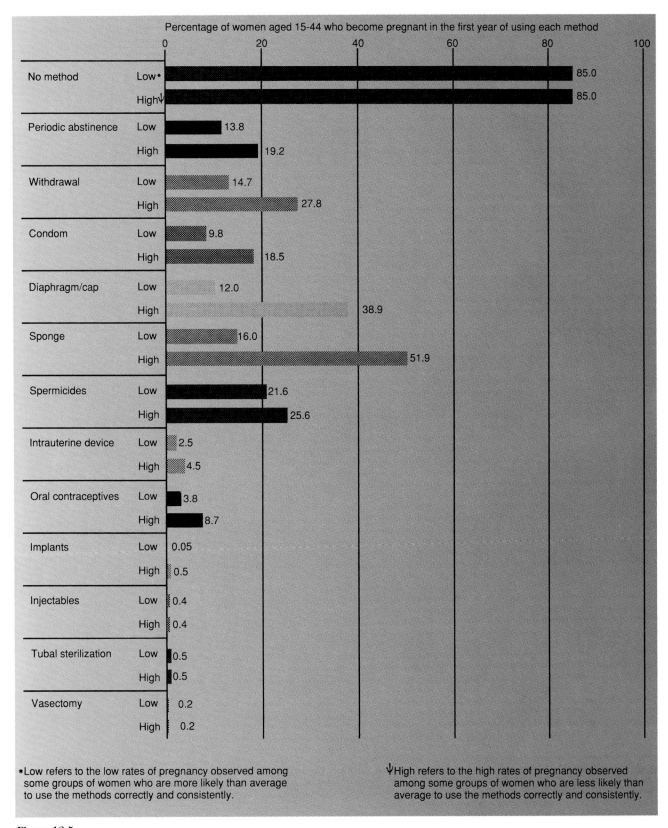

Percentage of women aged 15-44 who become pregnant in the first year of using each method

Method		Value
No method	Low*	85.0
	High↓	85.0
Periodic abstinence	Low	13.8
	High	19.2
Withdrawal	Low	14.7
	High	27.8
Condom	Low	9.8
	High	18.5
Diaphragm/cap	Low	12.0
	High	38.9
Sponge	Low	16.0
	High	51.9
Spermicides	Low	21.6
	High	25.6
Intrauterine device	Low	2.5
	High	4.5
Oral contraceptives	Low	3.8
	High	8.7
Implants	Low	0.05
	High	0.5
Injectables	Low	0.4
	High	0.4
Tubal sterilization	Low	0.5
	High	0.5
Vasectomy	Low	0.2
	High	0.2

*Low refers to the low rates of pregnancy observed among some groups of women who are more likely than average to use the methods correctly and consistently.

↓High refers to the high rates of pregnancy observed among some groups of women who are less likely than average to use the methods correctly and consistently.

Figure 12.5

Effectiveness of various birth-control methods. Note: Jones and Forrest (1992) have reported failure rates similar to those indicated. During the first year of use, they found 8 percent of pill users, 15 percent of condom users, 16 percent of diaphragm users, 25 percent of spermicide users, and 26 percent of those who practiced periodic abstinence became pregnant. Failure seemed to result more from improper and irregular use than from inherent limitations of the methods.

Source: Susan Harlap, Kathryn Kost, & Jacqueline D. Forrest, *Preventing Pregnancy, Protecting Health*, 1991, p. 35. © The Alan Guttmacher Institute.

PERSONAL INSIGHT

Feelings Associated with Sterilization

A man I know had a vasectomy several years ago. I had heard that some people were hesitant to be sterilized because of personal feelings or "hang-ups" about it, so I asked him some questions about his feelings, and the answers were very interesting. I asked him if it bothered him that he could no longer father a child. He said it didn't because he had no interest in having any more children. I asked him if he still felt like a man even though he could not reproduce. At first, he was surprised at the question. Then, he said that it never crossed his mind that the ability to reproduce would have an effect on feelings about being a man. After all, he said, all he had done was to sever the roadway for the sperm. He didn't change his functioning in any way. Why should a vasectomy change how he felt about being a man? His behavior was the same as before and nothing had changed. It seemed to me that he was comfortable with his decision because he had no "hang-ups" about needing to be able to reproduce to be a man.

In a similar vein, I talked with a woman who had a hysterectomy a month earlier. While the hysterectomy was not done for the purpose of sterilization, since her uterus was gone the woman could no longer reproduce. I asked her how she felt about the fact that some people might say she was an incomplete woman because she could not reproduce. She laughed and said that, since she discovered she had to have a hysterectomy, and during the time she was in the hospital and at home afterward, she never once thought about the fact that she could no longer reproduce. Like the man who had a vasectomy, this woman did not associate the ability to reproduce with her femininity. That seemed like sound reasoning to me. It is interesting the way some people develop certain feelings about what it means to be a male or female.

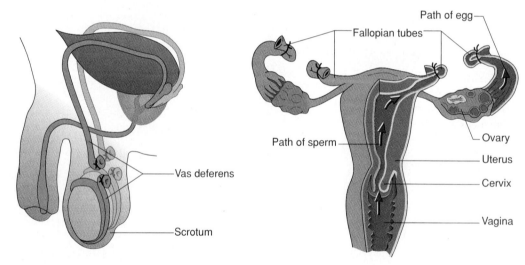

Figure 12.6

Vasectomy and tubal ligation compared. A vasectomy *(left)* is a comparatively simple surgical procedure. By comparison, tubal ligation *(right)* is somewhat more complex.

procedure and surroundings are a matter of choice between physician and patient. Figure 12.6 shows a vasectomy and a tubal ligation. After the procedure, a woman is immediately sterile. In a man's system, however, it takes some time to clear out all the sperm, and men are usually asked to bring an ejaculate sample to the doctor several weeks after a vasectomy to be sure they are "sperm-free."

It is generally accepted that sterilization has no long-term effects on women. Some individuals express concern about the effect of sterilization on the menstrual cycle, but sterilized women are unlikely to experience substantial changes in the duration of menstrual flow, cycle length, or midcycle bleeding ("Sterilization Is Unlikely to Alter Most Women's Menstrual Symptoms" 1990).

Some individuals suspect that vasectomies might make men more susceptible later to cardiovascular problems. Even men with vasectomies for longer than 10 years are no more prone to heart attacks, strokes, or other atherosclerotic problems than are nonvasectomized men their age.

A vasectomy is probably the safest and most effective means of contraception ("Vasectomy: Still a Good Choice?" 1993). Male sterilization is usually preferable to female sterilization for a variety of reasons. It is safer, just as effective, and less expensive, and there are fewer complications. In addition, regret is two-thirds again as high among women who have had tubal ligation as compared to men who have had a vasectomy ("Vasectomy Proves to Be Preferable to Female Sterilization" 1989). Why do you think more women would feel this way?

As is expected with any surgical procedure, complications occasionally accompany sterilization. Most sterilizations, however, are performed without complications or reported regrets; for those who know they want no more children, it is an ideal way to prevent pregnancy. Because reversal of the operation at a later time cannot be guaranteed, it should be considered a permanent procedure. Also, improved technology has increased the chances for successful reversal. For example, reversals done within 2 years are most successful (96%), with a 75 percent pregnancy rate. Done within 8 years, they have a better than 85 percent chance of producing sperm, with a pregnancy rate of more than 50 percent. Even when a vasectomy was done more than 15 years ago, a pregnancy rate of up to 30 percent is possible (Burns 1994). Research is under way, however, to find even better means of easily reversing the procedure; the installation of valves, the use of silicone plugs, and the perfection of surgical techniques hold promise for successful reversal in the future.

CONTRACEPTIVE DECISIONS

If there were a perfect contraceptive, it would be 100 percent effective, be very inexpensive or free, have no side effects, be reversible, be convenient and not messy, prevent sexually transmitted diseases, be accepted religiously and morally, and not interrupt sexual intercourse. None of the methods discussed, and none that are on the horizon, meet all these criteria. Individual feelings also determine whether or not a particular method is acceptable. Contraceptive decisions are influenced by considerations of safety, cost, reliability, convenience, religion, sociocultural factors, aesthetics, and whether a temporary or permanent method is desired.

The use of effective contraception by college men and women is primarily associated with the partner's support of contraception. Effective contraceptive use tends to begin only when the relationship reaches a stage at which intercourse becomes relatively predictable and when the partner is supportive of contraceptive use. Also, less-frequent intercourse is associated with condom use, and more-frequent intercourse is associated with use of the pill (Whitley 1990).

In one study of college students, oral contraceptives were the most favored contraceptive method, followed in order by abstinence, the condom, the diaphragm, the contraceptive sponge, female sterilization, the rhythm method, male sterilization, the vaginal suppository, the douche, the IUD, contraceptive foam, and withdrawal. Over a 5-year period, college students have become more favorable toward the condom and the diaphragm, but less favorable toward

THE WORLD AROUND YOU
Ethnicity and Contraceptive Practices

There are few studies of the similarities and differences in sexual behavior and contraceptive practices among the four major ethnic groups in the United States—blacks, whites, Latinos, and Asians. In general, ethnicity has little effect. This is particularly true if considerations are made for socioeconomic status.

While there are no major differences among ethnic groups in the United States, some interesting relationships were found in one major study.[a] For example, Latinos used birth control (any method) 11 percent less often than the other groups did. Asians used condoms about 10 percent more than whites, while blacks used them about 15 percent more than whites. Blacks also tended to use effective means of birth control more than the other ethnic groups did.

[a]Baldwin, J. D., S. Whiteley, and J. I. Baldwin. 1992. "The Effect of Ethnic Group on Sexual Activities Related to Contraception and STDs." *Journal of Sex Research* 29, no. 2 (May): 189–205.

rhythm, contraceptive foam, male sterilization, and IUDs. Less-effective methods seem to be receiving less use than in previous years (McDermott et al. 1993).

What do these facts mean in relation to your contraceptive decisions? What you do about your reproductive life may be one of the most important health decisions you make during your lifetime.

CONTRACEPTION AND THE FUTURE

There is a mixed picture regarding contraception and the future. On the one hand, researchers are trying to further improve various contraceptive methods and devices, and it is impossible to keep current with technological advances in contraception. On the other hand, some feel that since the United States is doing so little in contraceptive research, it has become the "global backwater in contraceptive research and development" (Randall 1992). This is because of legal liability issues, such as those discussed related to the IUD, and policies about governmental approval. Some feel that unless we immediately streamline the way our government approves new contraceptive products, we will be stuck for at least the next 10 to 15 years with the same contraceptive choices we have now. Already, in Western Europe and even in some less-developed countries, couples have a wider choice of contraceptive methods and greater access to the latest contraceptive technology than do couples in the United States (Randall 1992).

PERSONAL SKILLS AND EXPERIENCES

Conversing About Controlling Conception

You have heard people say that a birth of a baby was "an accident." Since you know about the male and female reproductive systems, how conception occurs, and how births can be controlled, you should have no "accidents." Having a baby and raising a child can be a wonderful experience, but it is also serious business. Babies should be created only by those who want them and are ready to be parents. To prevent "accidents," we need to communicate effectively in intimate situations and realize the consequences of our actions. Being comfortable with conversations about sexuality can help prevent "accidents." However, many people have difficulty talking with someone they care deeply about when it comes to sexuality.

Directions

To help prevent "accidents" and reduce stress, try the following as they pertain to body, mind, soul, and interdependence:

1. Mind: Consider your sexual feelings and how they relate to other parts of your life.

2. Body: Think about physical responses you have to sexual stimulation (this might be responses to pictures, movies, music, physical closeness, etc.). Consider what the effects of these responses might be on effective communication with another person.

3. Soul: Think about your values. What are your goals for this year, the next few years, and for the long term? What effects might your sexual behavior have on these goals?

4. Interdependence: If you have someone with whom you have an intimate relationship, discuss the possible impact of the three items above on your desires and behavior. For example, what do they have to do with sexual thoughts and behavior? What do they have to do with choices about controlling births? If you are not in an intimate relationship, find several classmates who do not mind sharing some of their thoughts (you and they might not be comfortable sharing all of your thoughts) on this subject.

Many "accidents" happen because people do not plan their behavior, consider their goals and values, or learn to communicate effectively in intimate situations. Taking these health actions can help prevent "accidents."

Those who practice fertility awareness, as well as those who have had difficulty conceiving, could be helped by a device that is available but not widely used. A small device, Bioself, consisting of an oral thermometer and a computer chip, gives repeated electronic beeps to remind the wearer that it is time to take her temperature. By using this device, the woman knows within 2 minutes if she is in a fertile phase of her cycle.

Researchers have developed a contraceptive device that immobilizes sperm by generating a weak current across the lining of the cervical canal. This is the gynecological equivalent of an electric fence. The device might be combined with a specially modified diaphragm or cervical cap, or attached to an intracervical implant and left in on a long-term basis ("Intracervical 'Electric Fence' Keeps Out Sperm" 1987).

Some researchers estimated that women will soon have new methods from which to choose—all modifications of the injectables already discussed. To varying degrees, all change or disrupt menstrual patterns. Biodegradable implants, placed under the skin, are expected to prevent pregnancy for 12 to 18 months. Injectable microcapsules prevent pregnancy for 1 to 6 months, and new monthly injectables are being developed as well. A vaginal ring can be placed by the woman in her vagina, where it gradually releases hormones and is effective for 3 months ("Hormonal Contraception" 1987). Finally, investigators are searching for new types of progestins. The hope is that they will inhibit ovulation as effectively as present forms of progestin, but have fewer or no side effects (Klitsch 1992).

A "missed-period pill" containing **mifepristone (RU 486)** seems to block hormonal action necessary for a pregnancy to begin. (Note that RU 486 was also discussed as a method of emergency contraception and as a potential nonsurgical abortion method.) This method, which might actually be considered a very early abortion, is thought to be very effective and has few side effects ("The Missed-Period Pill" 1987; Althaus 1993b).

Early French studies, which used mifepristone up to 3 weeks beyond the missed period, show an effectiveness rate of 96 percent. The administration of mifepristone seems to be a safe and effective method for the early termination of pregnancy (Segal 1990; Silvestre et al. 1990; Athaus 1993b). Because of the apparent safety and effectiveness of RU 486, in 1991 the American Association for the Advancement of Science encouraged the FDA to clear the way so RU 486 could be brought to the United States (Phillips 1991b). In 1993 the Clinton administration reconsidered policies of the previous two administrations that barred RU 486 from the Untied States. RU 486 then became available through a testing program. In 1994, RU 486 became available to Americans in Britain, as long as they stay for a follow-up exam a

---

mifepristone (RU 486)

A chemical that blocks the hormonal action needed to begin or sustain pregnancy.

week after administration of the drug. Chances are that, at the time you are reading this, the status of RU 486 has changed even further.

Developing a male birth-control pill seems to be more difficult than developing one for the female, but research continues in several directions. One of these is research on the compound Gossypol, which seems to inhibit enzyme activity necessary for sperm production. It decreases sperm production while not decreasing testosterone levels, but sperm production does not always return to normal when men stop taking it. It also seems to have potential negative effects on liver functions, gastrointestinal functions, and cardiac patterns and efficiency.

Other chemicals thought to have potential as a male contraceptive have been tried on animals. So far, none of these totally prevent sperm production. Those that are most effective also have unacceptable side effects, such as decreased six drive, decreased testosterone levels, and an inability to achieve an erection. Interestingly, weekly injections of testosterone seem to have promise as a safe and effective way to suppress sperm production ("A Male Contraceptive" 1991).

Contraceptive vaccines are also being explored. It makes sense that a vaccine in a female would prevent fertilization more effectively than a method that works after conception. Similarly, in the male there are attempts to develop a vaccine that will inhibit sperm production (Phillips 1991a).

Some experts still believe there will be fewer contraceptive methods at the end of the twentieth century than there were at the beginning. This is because of the prohibitive costs of liability insurance, the costs of developing new products, the amount of time before the FDA grants approval, and the costs involved in getting such approval ("Special Report on Contraception" 1986; Jenks 1990).

Since the introduction, over three decades ago, of the pill and the IUD, no fundamentally new contraceptive method has been introduced in the United States except Norplant. Many feel that new methods could become available if there were more support for their development (Mastroianni, Donaldson, and Kane 1990).

ABORTION

Abortion is premature expulsion from the uterus of a fertilized egg, an embryo, or a nonviable fetus. It can occur naturally (usually termed a **miscarriage** or **spontaneous abortion**) or be induced. Abortion differs from most contraceptive methods in that fertilization has already occurred before intentional or spontaneous action prevents the birth.

Abortion is one of the controversial issues of our day. In 1973 it became illegal for states to prohibit abortion in the early months of pregnancy, and many people considered abortion a female right. In 1989 the U.S. Supreme Court shifted the focus of the abortion controversy back to the states. This occurred because the Court showed a willingness to allow states a greater role in regulating abortion. This trend had not been seen since 1973 (Fulton 1990).

Abortion is one of the most controversial issues of our day.

Many legal questions are still being considered as a result of the 1989 Supreme Court decision. For example, when does the life of each human being begin? Do unborn children (if they can even be called "children") have rights? Can public funds be used for abortions? Whose permission is needed before an abortion can be performed? We will probably see the abortion controversy in the news for a long time to come. The United States, however, continues to have one of the higher abortion rates among developed countries ("Abortion in the United States" 1991). The number of abortions in the United States has leveled off at around 1.6 million per year. Women who have abortions are predominantly young (25% are under 20 years of age, and 33% are 20 to 24), unmarried (63%), and of poor to modest financial means. The national abortion rate is about 27.3 per 1,000 pregnancies ("Today's News" 1992).

MAJOR METHODS OF ABORTION

Whether you believe abortion is acceptable or not, you should understand a little about the process. Traditionally, the most common method of abortion has been **dilation and curettage (D&C),** a procedure that must be carried out within the first 12 weeks of pregnancy. This method involves dilation of the cervix (by inserting graduated sizes of instruments to stretch the opening) and scraping of the uterine cavity (curettage) to remove all developing tissues.

abortion
The premature expulsion of a fertilized egg, embryo, or fetus from the uterus.

miscarriage (spontaneous abortion)
A naturally occurring abortion.

dilation and curettage (D&C)
An abortion procedure that must be performed in the first 12 weeks of pregnancy; the procedure is also used to relieve excessive menstrual bleeding.

Issue

Should Abortions Be Legal?

Some of the pros and cons of abortion are listed below. Can you add any to the list?

- Pro:
  1. Government has no right to limit the freedom of a woman's choice.
  2. Human life doesn't begin until a fetus is capable of living outside the mother.
  3. Women should have the right to control their own bodies.
  4. Unwanted children should not be brought into the world.
  5. Women show few negative emotional reactions as a result of abortion; in fact, many show emotional benefit.

- Con:
  1. Government has no right to authorize destruction of a fetus or an embryo.
  2. Human life begins at the moment of conception.
  3. Humans do not have the right to take the lives of other innocent humans.
  4. Every human being—wanted or unwanted—receives its right to life directly from God.
  5. Women are psychologically damaged by abortion.

After adding your pros and cons to the list, how do you feel about abortion? Should abortions be legal? Can you make a statement that will apply in all situations, or do the circumstances matter?

A variation of this method is **suction curettage,** in which the contents of the uterus are sucked out as the uterine lining is scraped. Suction curettage is by far the preferred and most commonly performed abortion method today, due to its relative simplicity and lack of extreme pain.

Another method of abortion is **saline induction,** a procedure that cannot usually be performed until after 16 weeks of pregnancy. In this method, some **amniotic fluid** (fluid surrounding the fetus) is withdrawn through the abdominal wall and a saline (salt) solution is injected. The solution kills the **fetus** (the unborn child from the third month after conception on) and induces uterine contractions (labor) after 24 to 48 hours. The woman goes through labor to expel the dead fetus and the **placenta** (the organ that connects the fetus to the uterus through the umbilical cord). Sometimes a follow-up D&C is necessary to remove dead tissue.

The final major method of abortion is a **hysterotomy.** In this procedure, an incision is made through the lower abdomen and the wall of the uterus, and the fetus and related tissue are removed. This is used during the third trimester of pregnancy, is similar to what is done in a cesarean delivery at the end of a pregnancy, and involves several days of recovery in a hospital.

Some have feared that many women would have serious psychological consequences from abortions, but this does not seem to be the case. Although there may be sensations of regret, sadness, or guilt, evidence from the best scientific studies indicates that a legal abortion early in pregnancy is not hazardous to most women's mental health ("Lack of Evidence for Post-Abortion Syndrome Found" 1990).

Even among teenagers, those who chose to have an abortion were more likely to stay in school, were no more likely to have psychological problems, and were economically better off after 2 years than were those who decided to have a child. In addition, those choosing abortion were more likely to adopt a consistent contraceptive method and avoid a repeat pregnancy ("Study Finds No Negative Consequences for Teen Abortion" 1990).

FUTURE METHODS OF ABORTION

Extensive abortion research is being done with **prostaglandins,** fatty acid substances found naturally in the body. They can be injected into the uterus in a similar manner to the saline injection and induce labor much more quickly and simply. This method can be used between 12 and 16 weeks of pregnancy, a time when other methods so far cannot be used. Prostaglandin abortions are available in the United States on a limited basis and should probably still be considered to be in a research stage.

The missed-period pill (RU 486), already discussed as an emergency contraceptive measure and as a subject of

suction curettage
A type of abortion in which the uterine contents are sucked out through a narrow tube; the abortion method that is most widely used up through the twelfth week of pregnancy.

saline induction
A type of abortion in which a saline solution is injected into the amniotic sac; used during the second trimester of pregnancy.

amniotic fluid
The fluid surrounding the fetus in the uterus.

fetus
The unborn child from the third month after conception on.

placenta
The organ that connects the fetus to the uterus through the umbilical cord.

hysterotomy
A method of abortion in which an incision is made in the woman's abdominal wall and the fetus is removed.

prostaglandins
Fatty acid substances found naturally in the body. It might be possible to use these to induce labor during an abortion (still in research stage).

PERSONAL SKILLS AND EXPERIENCES

PNI and Sexual Choices

Psychoneuroimmunology (PNI), the study of the interaction between the mind, the central nervous system, and the body's immunological system, shows that people with a fighting spirit, optimism, hope, and faith can actually build their immune systems. The brain has the capability to self-medicate and to release a variety of mental and physical painkillers and motivating substances (neuropeptides) when the demand is there.

The topics that have been covered in this section have included several social, psychological, moral, and biological issues associated with sexuality and relationships. When considering the issues of love, family, intimacy, communication, sexual behavior (masturbation, homosexuality, and other variations), date rape, birth control, abortion, and other topics, the feelings and emotions as they pertain to PNI are quite clear. With negative experiences in sexuality and relationships, the outcome can be guilt, loneliness, rejection, sadness, pessimism, hopelessness, and depression. All of these emotions and feelings contribute to a weaker immune system, not to mention a poorer quality of living. On the positive side of sexuality and relationships, the resulting feelings can be warmth, love, caring, optimism, trust, happiness, security, and perceived emotional support. With these positive traits, we are looking at a fortified immune system and a good life quality.

Based on this generalization, it should be clear that there are two PNI intervention approaches. The first is to relieve oneself from the negative emotions, and the second is to maximize the emotions and feelings that come from the social, psychological, moral, and biological aspects of sexuality and relationships. The following is a series of questions you may want to consider to avoid the negative outcomes of a relationship and feel the positive outcomes. Remember that the positive fortifies.

If you are already in a relationship, consider these questions that (with positive response) can fortify positive outcomes of relationships.

1. Are you living in a mind state of appreciation for what you have rather than looking for what you could possibly get?
2. Are you in the relationships with the idea of giving to rather than seeing what you can get from it?
3. Are you avoiding a "take it for granted" mind state?
4. Are you staying within the bounds of what you and your partner consider moral conduct?
5. Have you talked about what each other considers moral conduct?
6. Do you avoid saying something you regret to your partner?
7. Are you aware of your emotional state when you are angry or are out of control?
8. Can you get over being angry soon?
9. Do you take pleasure in being close to someone and enjoying the moment as opposed to always looking to see how "far you can go?"
10. Are you spontaneous, playful, and fun in a relationship?
11. When you see your partner, do you link seeing them with positive emotional states?
12. Do you give what you most want in a relationship?
13. Do you try and find out those things that really make your partner feel loved? (Is it when I buy you something? Take you somewhere? Say I love you? Touch you a certain way? Play a certain way?)

If you are not in a relationship but want to be, consider some of the following questions.

1. Do you believe that you will find someone with whom you can have a good relationship?
2. Do you seek opportunities to meet people at places that will attract the types of partners that you would like to be with?
3. Are you being your natural yet best self when interacting with others as compared to putting on a phony front?
4. Are you looking for someone that has common interests, a compatible personality, and other commonalities or complimentary traits as opposed to superficial characteristics like physical attractiveness?
5. Are you friendly and assertive?

If you are feeling the negative outcomes of a relationship, particularly guilt, be sure that you attempt to purge that guilt. If you have done something that makes you feel guilty, then quit doing that behavior. Seek a means to forgive yourself. If relieving your guilt involves the counsel of or confession to a religious leader, then go through those steps to purge yourself.

Maximize your relationships by enjoying the process of dating, courting, and just being friends. People who worry about where the relationship is going, are not able to be themselves, or behave in a way to please others, generally see the stagnation of a relationship over time. When it is natural, honest, friendly, and fun, then relationships and the immune system can be fortified.

contraceptive research, might also be considered as a future abortion method—depending upon one's point of view. If it is readily available, an abortion decision could become a truly private matter. It would be as easy as visiting a physician, getting a few pills, returning home to swallow them as appropriate, and checking back with the physician a few days later to be sure everything went as planned. At any rate, since it is known that statistically an early abortion is safer than going through a pregnancy, it is likely that additional abortion research will continue.

TAKE ACTION

1. Be sensitive about comments made to couples who do not have children—especially if you know that they wish to have children.

2. If you choose to participate in sexual intercourse, but do not wish to cause a pregnancy, develop a plan for avoiding a pregnancy.

3. For many people, sexual activity is influenced by personal values. Develop a contract to promote consistency between your sexual activity and your values.

4. Think of a situation related to human sexuality that has caused disorganization or disruption in your life. Develop a plan to promote resilient reintegration in your life to prevent potential health problems related to sexuality in the future.

SUMMARY

1. There are a number of arguments for and against contraception. Decisions related to birth control have many health implications.

2. The most effective contraceptive method available is probably the pill. There are combination pills, multiphasic pills, minipills, and emergency pills.

3. Taking the pill is statistically safer than going through a pregnancy. In addition, the pill promotes a number of positive side effects.

4. Diaphragms and condoms can be effective barriers to sperm if care is used.

5. Spermicides used alone are less effective than previously mentioned methods, but they can help increase the effectiveness of other methods.

6. The sponge method seems to have promise as an effective contraceptive.

7. Fertility awareness is becoming more reliable as better ways to pinpoint ovulation are developed.

8. The cervical cap is considered experimental, and IUDs are available only on a limited basis in the United States.

9. Ineffective contraceptive methods include coitus interruptus and use of the vaginal douche.

10. Sterilization is very safe and effective, but should still be considered permanent.

11. Contraceptive research is still being done. Much of it involves ways that RU 486 might be used.

12. Abortion has been controversial through the years and remains so today. Medically, it is a safe procedure that can be done using various methods.

COMMITMENT ACTIVITIES

1. Population dynamics can be related to the quality of life. Too many or too few people in a given area might considerably influence the health of all. Survey your community to determine where overpopulation or underpopulation might contribute to potential health problems. Develop recommendations that could be used to help reduce these problems.

2. Many conception control services exist in most communities, but often individuals don't know about them. Assess the conception control services in the community where you live or attend college. Be sure to include services of planned parenthood, local or state health departments, the college, and private agencies. Also, be sure to include services designed to promote as well as prevent conception. Does your community seem to have services that are readily available and of high quality?

3. Think about your feelings concerning abortion. Is it always acceptable to you? Is it never acceptable? If it is acceptable, what circumstances make it so? After you have clarified your feelings, talk with people (particularly those who have strong feelings at both extremes on this issue) to be sure you understand why they feel as they do. Once you better understand where they are coming from, see if this new information has any effect on your feelings. Ask yourself the same questions again.

4. How do you feel about the need to control births and the use of contraceptives? What is appropriate in your own life? Once you have clarified your own feelings, outline a plan for communicating your feelings to a potential partner or your present one. How will you handle it if your partner feels differently about decisions related to birth control? Is there a way to reconcile any differences?

REFERENCES

"Abortion in the United States." 1991. In *Facts In Brief.* New York: Alan Guttmacher Institute.

Althaus, F. 1992. "Study Finds Low Condom Breakage Rate, Ties Most Slippage to Improper Use." *Family Planning Perspectives* 24, no. 4 (July/August): 191–92.

Althaus, F. 1993a. "PID Leads to 1.2 Million Doctor Visits and 276,000 Hospitalizations Annually." *Family Planning Perspectives* 25, no. 1 (January/February): 46–48.

Althaus, F. 1993b. "As Postcoital Contraceptive, Mifepristone Has Few Side Effects and High Efficacy." *Family Planning Perspectives* 25, no. 1 (January/February): 48–49.

Beckman, L. J., S. M. Harvey, and J. Murray. 1992. "Perceived Contraceptive Attributes of Current and Former Users of the Vaginal Sponge." *Journal of Sex Research* 29, no. 1 (February): 31–42.

Better Health 4, no. 2 (February 1987): 3.

Burns, J. 1994. "Male Infertility Updated." *UAB Insight* (Spring): 7.

"Can You Count on Condoms?" 1993. *Edell Health Letter* 12, no. 6 (June/July): 1–2.

"Can You Rely On Condoms?" 1989. *Consumer Reports* 54, no. 3 (March): 135–41.

Edell, D. 1990. "Good News About the Pill." *Edell Health Letter* 9, no. 4 (April): 4.

Edwards, S. 1993. "Young Women More Likely to Use Condoms with New Partners Who Prefer Method." *Family Planning Perspectives* 25, no. 1 (January/February): 45–46.

"FDA OKs Hormonal Implant." 1990. *Family Planning Perspectives* 22, no. 6 (November/December): 244.

Fulton, G. B. 1990. "Abortion . . . After Webster." In *Our Sexuality Update*. Redwood City, CA: Benjamin/Cummings (Winter): 7–8.

Grady, W. R., D. H. Klepinger, J. O. G. Billy, and K. Tanfer. 1993. "Condom Characteristics: The Perceptions and Preferences of Men in the United States." *Family Planning Perspectives* 25, no. 2 (March/April): 67–73.

Hantula, R. 1986. "IUDs." In *Spotlight on Health* (Macmillan Educational) 1:7.

Hatcher, R., F. Stewart, J. Trussell, D. Kowal, F. Guest, G. K. Stewart, and W. Cates. 1986. *Contraceptive Technology 1986–1987*. 13th ed. New York: Irvington.

"Hormonal Contraception: New Long-Acting Methods." 1987. *Population Reports*, Series K, 3 (March–April): K57–K87.

"Hormonal Implants Prove to Be Highly Acceptable." 1990. *Family Planning Perspectives* 22, no. 5 (September/October): 234–35.

"Intracervical 'Electric Fence' Keeps Out Sperm." 1987. *Sexuality Today*, 19 January, 3.

"IUD Underused." 1992. *Edell Health Letter* 11, no. 2 (February): 1–2.

Jenks, S. 1990. "Contraceptive Choices in U.S. Scarce, Experts Find." *Medical World News* 31, no. 5 (12 March): 37.

Jones, E. F., and J. D. Forrest. 1992. "Contraceptive Failure Rates Based on the 1988 NSFG." *Family Planning Perspectives* 24, no. 1 (January/February): 12–18.

Klitsch, M. 1992. "The New Pills: Awaiting the Next Generation of Oral Contraceptives." *Family Planning Perspectives* 24, no. 5 (September/October): 226–28.

Klitsch, M. 1993. "Injectable Hormones and Regulatory Controversy: An End to the Long-Running Story?" *Family Planning Perspectives* 25, no. 1 (January/February): 37–40.

Koop, C. E. 1986. *Surgeon General's Report on Acquired Immune Deficiency Syndrome*. Washington, DC: U.S. Public Health Service.

"Lack of Evidence for Post-Abortion Syndrome Found." 1990. *Behavior Today* 21, no. 17 (23 April): 6–7.

"The Low-Dose IUD." 1990. *Family Planning Perspectives* 22, no. 6 (November/December): 245.

"A Male Contraceptive." 1991. *Harvard Health Letter* 16, no. 3 (January): 7.

Mastroianni, L., Jr., P. J. Donaldson, and T. T. Kane. 1990. "Development of Contraceptives—Obstacles and Opportunities." *New England Journal of Medicine* 322, no. 7 (15 February): 482–84.

McDermott, R. J., P. D. Sarvela, R. S. Gold, D. R. Holcomb, J. K. D. Huetteman, J. A. Odulana. 1993. "Attributes Assigned to Contraception by College Students: 1985 and 1990." *Health Values* 17, no. 5 (October): 33–41.

"Minipill May Have Broader Appeal." 1991. *Family Planning Perspectives* 23, no. 1 (January/February): 5.

"The Missed-Period Pill." 1987. *Harvard Medical School Health Letter* 12, no. 5 (March): 1–2.

Phillips, P. 1991a. "Contraceptive Vaccines Inch Nearer to Clinical Trials." *Medical World News* 32, no. 3 (March): 17.

Phillips, P. 1991b. "Mainstream U.S. Scientists Back Controversial RU 486." *Medical World News* 32, no. 4 (April): 47.

"The Pros and Cons of Norplant." 1992. *UAB Insight*, Spring, 13.

Randall, T. 1992. "United States Loses Lead in Contraceptive Choices, R & D; Changes in Tort Liability, FDA Review Urged." *Journal of the American Medical Association* 268, no. 2 (8 July): 176–79.

Richter, D. L., R. F. Valois, R. E. McKeown, and M. L. Vincent. 1993. "Correlates of Condom Use and Number of Sexual Partners Among High School Adolescents." *Journal of School Health* 63, no. 2 (February): 91–96.

Segal, S. J. 1990. "Mifepristone (RU 486)." *New England Journal of Medicine* 322, no. 10 (6 March): 691–92.

Silvestre, L., C. Dubois, M. Renault, Y. Rezvani, E. Baulieu, and A. Ulmann. 1990. "Voluntary Interruption of Pregnancy with Mifepristone (RU 486) and a Prostaglandin Analogue." *New England Journal of Medicine* 322, no. 10 (8 March): 645–48.

"A Slimmer Copper T." 1991. *Family Planning Perspectives* 23, no. 1 (January/February): 5.

"Special Report on Contraception: Where Will We Be in the Year 2010?" 1986. *Sexuality Today* 9, no. 35 (16 June): 1, 2.

"Sterilization Is Unlikely to Alter Most Women's Menstrual Symptoms." 1990. *Family Planning Perspectives* 22, no. 1 (January/February): 44–45.

"Study Finds No Negative Consequences for Teen Abortion." 1990. *Behavior Today* 21, no. 8 (19 February): 6–8.

Tanfer, K., W. R. Grady, D. H. Klepinger, and J. O. G. Billy. 1993. "Condom Use Among U.S. Men, 1991." *Family Planning Perspectives* 25, no. 2 (March/April): 61–66.

"Today's News." 1992. United States Centers for Disease Control, Atlanta, Georgia, 30 June.

Trussell, J., F. Stewart, F. Guest, and R. A. Hatcher. 1992. "Emergency Contraceptive Pills: A Simple Proposal to Reduce Unintended Pregnancies." *Family Planning Perspectives* 24, no. 6 (November/December): 269–73.

Trussell, J., K. Sturgen, J. Strickler, and R. Dominik. 1994. "Comparative Contraceptive Efficacy of the Female Condom and Other Barrier Methods." *Family Planning Perspectives* 26, no. 2 (March/April): 66–71.

"Users Approve of Female Condom." 1991. *Family Planning Perspectives* 23, no. 1 (January/February): 5.

"Vasectomy Proves to Be Preferable to Female Sterilization." 1989. *Family Planning Perspectives* 21, no. 4 (July/August): 191.

"Vasectomy: Still a Good Choice?" 1993. *University of California at Berkeley Wellness Letter* 9, no. 8 (May): 1–2.

Whitley, B. E. 1990. "College Student Contraceptive Use: A Multivariate Analysis." *Journal of Sex Research* 27, no. 2 (May): 305–13.

ADDITIONAL READINGS

Campbell, Susan Miller, and Letitia Anne Peplau. 1992. "Women, Men and Condoms." *Psychology of Women Quarterly* 16, 273–88. Presents information concerning gender and ethnic differences in attitudes about condoms and about the impact of attitudes on condom use.

Coker, Ann L., Susan Harlap, and Judith A. Fortney. 1993. "Oral Contraceptives and Reproductive Cancers: Weighing the Risks and Benefits." *Family Planning Perspectives* 25, no. 1 (January/February): 17–20. Compares the lifetime incidence of cancer of the breast, cervix, ovary, and endometrium expected in pill users with the incidence expected in nonusers.

Klitsch, M. 1993. "Close to Half of Women Aged 13–44 Are at Risk of Unintended Pregnancy." *Family Planning Perspectives* 25, no. 1 (January/February): 44–45. Discusses the factors that make women at risk of becoming pregnant and compares some ethnic groups on their pregnancy rates.

Mays, Vickie M., Susan D. Cochran, Ellen Hamilton, Noel Miller, Laurie Leung, Sadina Rothspan, Jeffrey Kolson, Farrell Well, and Monica Torres. 1993. "Just Cover Up: Barriers to Heterosexual and Gay Young Adults' Use of Condoms." *Health Values* 17, no. 4 (July/August): 41–47. Explores the psychological and behavioral factors involved in the purchase and use of condoms. Discusses embarrassment, store display locations, packaging, and store personnel behavior.

LIFESTYLE CONTRACT

By reading and working through the activities in the chapters on human sexuality, you should have a good understanding of

1. human sexuality, its dimensions, its relationship to all people, and its connection to human well-being;
2. intimate relationships and communication;
3. parenting and sexual education;
4. human sexual response;
5. variations in sexual behavior;
6. human reproduction;
7. influences on a healthy pregnancy;
8. ways to control conception;
9. issues related to conception control.

There has also been an opportunity to assess your feelings about many sexual issues. It is clear that human sexuality is a topic that often causes strong reactions and feelings within many people. These can have a significant impact on health decisions. Since sexuality is an important part of health, it is appropriate to consider ways to strengthen your well-being related to sexuality and prevent potential problems.

Lifestyle Contracting Using Strength Intervention

I. Choosing the desired health behavior or skill.

A. Keeping in mind the purposes in life and goals you identified in the mental health chapter, consider one or two health behaviors related to human sexuality that will help you reach your goals. In order to assess the likelihood of success, ask yourself questions similar to those used in previous sections, such as these:

1. Is my purpose, cause, or goal better realized by adoption of this behavior?

_____ yes _____ no

2. Am I hardy enough to accomplish this goal? (This means I feel I can do it if I work hard, I am in control of what needs to be done, I am committed to do it, and the goal is a challenge for me)

_____ yes _____ no

3. Is this a behavior I really want to change and that I feel I can change?

_____ yes _____ no

4. Do I first need to nurture a personal strength area?

_____ yes _____ no
(If yes, be sure to include this as a part of the plan.)

5. Do I need to free myself from a bad habit in order to accomplish this goal?

_____ yes _____ no
(If yes, be sure to include this as a part of the plan.)

6. Have I considered the results of the assessments in the sexuality chapters?

_____ yes _____ no

These results may be helpful in developing a plan.

(Yes answers to the first three questions are a must in order to be successful. It might be wise to consider a different behavior if you cannot honestly answer yes to these questions. Your answers to questions 4–6 ought to provide information for consideration in your plan.)

B. Behaviors I will change (no more than two)

_____

_____

II. Lifestyle Plan

A. A description of the general plan of what I am going to do and how I will accomplish it. Consider successes you have had in the past, since they may help you consider the best ways to carry out this plan.

_____

_____

_____

_____

_____

_____

B. Barriers to the accomplishment of the plan (lack of time, feelings of others, my own hang-ups, motivation, etc.)

1. Identify barriers: _____

_____

_____

_____

2. Means to remove the barriers (use problem-solving skills or creative approaches such as those described in the mental health chapter):

_____

_____

_____

_____

C. Implementation of the plan.

1. Substitution (putting positive behaviors in place of negative ones) _____

_____

2. Linking behaviors _____

_____

(Continued on page 12.23)

12.22

LIFESTYLE CONTRACT

3. Combining a strength and a weakness _____
_____
_____

4. When _____

5. Where _____

6. Preparation _____
_____

7. With whom _____

III. Support Groups
   A. Who: _____
_____

   B. Role: _____
_____

   C. Organized support: _____
_____

IV. Trigger Responses: _____
_____
_____

V. Starting date: _____
_____

VI. Date/sequence the contract will be reevaluated: _____
_____

VII. Evidence of reaching the goal: _____
_____

VIII. Rewards when contract is completed: _____
_____

IX. Signature of client: _____
_____

X. Signature of facilitator: _____
_____

XI. Additional conditions/comments: _____
_____

Alcohol,
Tobacco, and
Psychoactive
Drugs

CHAPTER 13

Alcohol

Healthy People 2000 Objectives

- Reduce alcohol-related motor vehicle crash deaths to no more than 8.5 per 100,000 people (age adjusted) (a 12% decrease).

- Reduce alcohol use by schoolchildren aged 12 to 17 to less than 13 percent; marijuana use by youth aged 18 to 25 to less than 8 percent; and cocaine use by youth aged 18 to 25 to less than 3 percent (50% decreases).

In an ideal world, you would see people drinking alcohol responsibly or not drinking alcohol at all. People would drink one drink a day at dinner, socially, or to just relax after a busy day. Those who choose to drink would feel no pressure to try an alcoholic beverage, and alcohol would be considered just another drink. Even though there is alcohol abuse in the real world, you can create your own personal ideal world with regard to alcohol. You can drink responsibly or not at all. You can choose to ignore external pressures to drink. You can assess your family history of alcohol use and, if there is abuse of alcohol in your family, then you can choose not to drink. You can be in control of alcohol in your life.

Unfortunately, we do not live in an ideal world, and many people use alcohol as a crutch to escape their problems. Many people have a genetic predisposition to alcohol addiction. Accidents and crime are facilitated by alcohol. Alcohol abuse and dependence (i.e., alcoholism) are serious problems that affect about 10 to 15 percent of adult Americans, and about 3 out of every 100 deaths in the United States can be attributed to alcohol-related causes (U.S. Department of Health and Human Services 1990). Alcohol, because of its widespread use, causes more problems nationwide and internationally (Villalbi et al. 1991) than any other drug. According to the National Institutes of Drug Abuse, there are 10 to 18 million problem drinkers and alcoholics in the United States today. Unfortunately, only 1 out of 35 will effectively recover from alcoholism, and those who do will need to completely abstain from alcohol for the rest of their lives. The families of those alcoholics are often emotionally, socially, and spiritually devastated and, in some cases, physically abused. All of the problems associated with alcohol and alcohol abuse are estimated to cost our nation $117 billion per year in treatment and lost productivity (Parker and Harford 1992). It is unfortunate, too, in light of alcohol's being responsible for crime, a precursor to suicide, responsible for over half of all traffic accidents, a cause of disease, and a facilitator of death, that we Americans still offer the social gesture "Would you like a drink?"

The purpose of this chapter is not necessarily to suggest that we stop drinking (although that would be the safest action), but to suggest responsible habits, if you do choose to drink. Because any drinker has at least a one-in-ten chance of becoming an alcoholic, extreme caution and awareness should accompany any drinking habits. For nondrinkers, this chapter should encourage continued abstention based on the logic that if you never drink, you will never become an alcoholic. This chapter will also help nondrinkers to consider the relationship they may have with someone who drinks and help determine whether that person has a drinking problem and whether that problem is negatively affecting them.

THE ALCOHOL PROBLEM

Alcohol is something most of us have tried (estimates are that up to 92 percent of college freshmen have tried it), and it remains an accepted part of life on many campuses. Alcohol abuse is a major problem on most campuses ("Alcohol in Perspective" 1993). Some campuses (e.g., private institutions such as Baylor University and Brigham Young University) have banned alcohol from all college and university activities in an attempt to avoid the problems of alcohol. Others have alcohol programs, campus chapters of Students Against Driving Drunk (SADD), and other innovative educational and preventive programs to reduce the negative effects of alcohol. National campaigns and educational programs appear to have had some positive effect, but more must be done.

The most important aspect of using alcohol is for both drinkers and nondrinkers to understand the effects of alcohol, the potency of alcohol in different drinks, how many drinks can be consumed before irresponsibility ensues, and how to be a responsible host and drinker. It is appropriate to begin with understanding the nature of alcohol, the drug.

THE NATURE OF ALCOHOLIC BEVERAGES

The intoxicating ingredient in alcoholic beverages is **ethyl alcohol** (C_2H_5OH), which is a colorless liquid with a sharp, burning taste. There are other types of alcohols found in nature, but these are not used in drinks. **Isopropyl alcohol** is rubbing alcohol and is used to cleanse and disinfect. **Methyl alcohol** is wood alcohol and is extremely poisonous. Methyl alcohol is used in many industrial products, such as antifreeze.

Each of the major alcoholic beverages—beer and ale, wine, and liquor—contains a different percentage of ethyl alcohol and is made differently. Beer and ale are made by controlled fermentation of cereal grains plus malt. Hops might be added for a distinctive flavor. Wine is made by the fermentation of grapes and other fruit. Some wines, such as dessert wines (port and sherry), are fortified with the addition of more alcohol after the fermentation process is complete. Liquor is made by distilling an already fermented brew from grain, fruit, or molasses.

WHAT IS A DRINK?

In this chapter, reference will be made to a number of drinks. Although there is some variability in the amount of alcohol in each drink, as shown in table 13.1, a "drink" means 12 ounces of beer (4.1% alcohol), 4 ounces of regular wine (12.5% alcohol), 2 to 4 ounces of sherry or port (20% alcohol), or 1 ounce of liquor (50% alcohol).

ethyl alcohol
A colorless liquid (C_2H_5OH) that is the intoxicating ingredient in alcoholic beverages and is produced in the fermentation of grains and fruits.

isopropyl alcohol
Rubbing alcohol; also used to cleanse and disinfect.

methyl alcohol
Wood alcohol; an extremely poisonous liquid used in many industrial products.

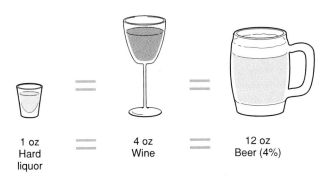

1 oz
Hard
liquor

4 oz
Wine

12 oz
Beer (4%)

These three drinks have the same alcohol content.

TABLE 13.1	PERCENTAGES OF ALCOHOL FOR SELECTED DRINKS	
Drink		**Alcohol (%)**
Beer		3–6*
Ale		6–8
Wine coolers		3.2–6
Hard cider		5–10
Champagne		12
Regular wines (red, white, rosé, sparkling)		10–16
Dessert wines		17–20
Whiskey		42–52
Brandy		40–50
Gin		27–45
Vodka		37
Cognac		45
Scotch		45

*Note: Depending on the state and brand.

From Dorothy Dusek and Daniel A. Girdano, *Drugs: A Factual Account*, 4th ed. Copyright © 1987 McGraw-Hill, Inc. Reprinted by permission of McGraw-Hill, Inc.

PROOF

The **proof** of a beverage is a measure of its alcohol content. Proof is given as roughly twice the value of the percentage of alcohol; for example, a beverage that is 50 percent alcohol would be given a value of 100 proof (O'Brien et al. 1992):

$$proof = 2 \times the\ percentage\ of\ alcohol$$

This designation is helpful in controlling drinking. It is not which drink is consumed—whether it is beer, gin, or wine—but the proof of the beverage that will help us know how much alcohol a person drinks. For example, beer ranges in proof from 6 proof (3% alcohol) to 12 proof (6% alcohol).

Interestingly, the term *proof* came from an early test of the quality of whiskey. The whiskey was mixed with gunpowder and then touched with a lit match. If the mixture did not light, then the alcohol content was low; if it flamed orange, then the alcohol content was too high; if it lit with a cool blue flame, then it was "proof" of a good whiskey (Dusek and Girdano 1987).

ALCOHOL ABSORPTION AND METABOLISM

When alcohol is swallowed, it passes down the esophagus and into the stomach; no digestion is required for it to have its effects. A small amount is absorbed directly into the bloodstream from the stomach, but the major portion passes into the small intestine, where it is absorbed directly into the bloodstream and carried rapidly to the brain.

The blood vessels carry alcohol to the various parts of the body. The liver is the organ most significantly involved in the metabolism, or breaking down, of alcohol. Approximately 90 percent of the alcohol is eliminated as a function of the liver, and 10 percent is eliminated by perspiration, exhalation, and urination. Enzyme action in the liver eventually converts alcohol into energy, carbon dioxide, and water. The process of metabolizing excessive amounts of alcohol over long periods of time has several debilitating effects on the liver that will be discussed later.

Alcohol is metabolized in our bodies at a fairly constant rate for most of us, but there is some variance from person to person. The average 150-pound person metabolizes approximately 0.5 ounce of absolute (100%) alcohol per hour. At that metabolic rate, taking one drink per hour will result in little, if any, alcohol in the blood; but if we drink faster than that, the alcohol begins to accumulate, resulting in a higher and higher blood alcohol concentration in the body.

BLOOD ALCOHOL CONCENTRATION

The safest approach to alcohol consumption is to avoid it; but if we choose to use this potentially devastating drug, we should learn about **blood alcohol concentration (BAC).** The amount of alcohol in the blood has clear psychophysiological effects, as shown in table 13.2.

To be a responsible drinker, you need to know how much you can drink and still be functional. It is important to err on the side of caution when planning to recreate or drive after consuming alcohol (Labianca 1992). The standard rule of one drink per hour might or might not be a good rule for any given person. You can easily calculate your own BAC for various numbers of drinks and different time frames to see what approximate concentration of alcohol would be in your system. BAC is a function of body weight, the number of drinks, and the time it takes to drink the number of drinks. The definition of one drink is one 12-ounce beer, 4 ounces of wine, or 1 ounce of 100-proof liquor.

proof
The measure of a beverage's alcoholic content, equal to roughly twice the percentage of alcohol in the beverage.

blood alcohol concentration (BAC)
The percentage of alcohol in the blood; usually measured in suspected drunken drivers.

TABLE 13.2 EFFECTS OF ALCOHOL

Number of Drinks	BAC	Effects[a]
1 drink	.02	More relaxed and loosened up
2.5 drinks	.05	High judgment impaired, loud, boisterous, disinhibited
5 drinks	.10	Judgment nil, muscle coordination depressed, staggers with walk, slurs speech
10 drinks	.20	Emotions erratic, memory impairment, couldn't put on a coat
16 drinks	.32	Stuporous and almost no sensory perception
20 drinks	.4–.5	Coma and may be near death

[a]Effects on a 160-pound person in a 1-hour period.

From J. Kinney and G. Leaton, *Loosening the Grip: A Handbook of Alcohol Information.* Copyright © 1991 Mosby Year-Book, St. Louis. Reprinted by permission.

To calculate your BAC, first convert your weight to kilograms by dividing your weight in pounds by 2.2. If you weigh 140 pounds, your weight in kilograms is 63.63 kg.

The formula* for BAC is this:

$$BAC = \frac{c}{BV} - (H \times .015)$$

Where c = number of drinks on one occasion × 14

BV = body weight × 8
H = the number of hours it takes you to drink the number of drinks you have on this one occasion

For example, for a person who weighs 140 pounds and has 3 drinks at a party between 8:00 and 10:00, the BAC at 10:00 would be:

140/2.2 (140 lb converted to kg) = 63.63

$$c = (3 \text{ drinks} \times 14) = 42$$
$$BV = (63.63 \text{ kg} \times 8) = 509$$
$$H = 10:00 - 8:00 = 2 \text{ hours}$$
$$BAC = (42/509) - (2 \times .015) = .052$$

Blood alcohol concentrations can be accurately obtained by testing blood samples, breath, urine, saliva, or even spinal fluid. If alcohol is found in these samples, the corresponding amount of blood alcohol can be calculated.

EFFECTS OF ALCOHOL ON THE BODY

Medically, alcohol is a depressant, a drug that slows the activity of the central nervous system, especially the brain and the spinal cord. In small doses, alcohol might psychologically seem to act as a stimulant, a drug that speeds up the bodily processes. As more alcohol is consumed, however, the activity of the central nervous system declines.

As we absorb the first drink, we are likely to feel better, gaining a sense of warmth and well-being. At the same time,

our ability to think clearly will begin to deteriorate. As we drink more and more, mental ability further deteriorates and physical coordination declines. Physical symptoms include staggering, slurred speech, and diminished sensitivity to glare and to certain colors and sounds. Alcohol can reduce our sense of fear, which accounts in part for the fights that break out among drinkers. Many unsafe sexual practices also occur under the influence of alcohol. Even though inhibitions are lowered by alcohol, sexual performance is actually often decreased.

Alcohol also affects specific bodily organs. Minor amounts of alcohol in the small intestine increase the flow of digestive juices, which may be mistaken for hunger pangs. Larger amounts of alcohol can irritate the throat, gullet, and lining of the intestine and stomach. Drinking alcohol also increases the urinary activity of the kidneys.

In the long term, alcohol can permanently affect several systems of the body. Chronic alcoholism can cause brain damage or brain disorders in a number of people. "Many studies have suggested that at least 50 percent of people who have been drinking heavily for years will develop some sort of brain disorder by the time they are forty" (Schlaadt and Shannon 1986). Brain atrophy can be as high as 50 to 100 percent in alcoholics.

The liver is the primary site of alcohol metabolism and is susceptible to alcohol abuse. Repeated use of alcohol causes the liver to swell and become tender. As alcohol abuse continues, liver function deteriorates into one of the three main types of disease: (1) fatty liver, (2) alcoholic hepatitis (which may be reversible with abstinence) (Woods, Hitchcock, and Meyer 1993), and (3) cirrhosis of the liver, which is not reversible.

Cirrhosis, the ninth leading cause of death in the United States (U.S. Department of Health and Human Services

*Source: Formula developed by Dr. Wayne Wiley, Director, Alcohol Abuse Prevention Project, Texas A & M University.

cirrhosis
A disease of the liver, manifested by scarring, that might be caused by excessive alcohol consumption.

Calculating Blood Alcohol Concentration

Whether you are a drinker or a nondrinker, calculate several BACs for different situations. See what your BAC would be for two drinks an hour, three drinks an hour, or four drinks in 2 hours. Determine the maximum number of drinks that you could have for different times to keep below a .04 BAC.

For a general picture of the relationship between body weight, number of drinks, and time, the blood alcohol concentration chart provides an overview.

Assess your ability to understand and calculate BAC by asking yourself the following question: Is it possible that you could be legally intoxicated while driving to school at 7 A.M. if you had alcoholic drinks the night before but had "slept it off"? Answer: Let's say you got home from studying and started drinking at 10 P.M. and finally went to bed at 1 A.M. During the time you were drinking, you and a friend drank three six-packs (you drank nine beers). After sleeping 5 hours and taking a shower, you drove to class at 7 A.M. If you weigh 140 pounds (use your own weight in the calculations), you would have a BAC of .11 (you would be legally drunk).

Weight												
100	1	2	3	4	5	6	7	8	9	10	11	12
120	1	2	3	4	5	6	7	8	9	10	11	12
140	1	2	3	4	5	6	7	8	9	10	11	12
160	1	2	3	4	5	6	7	8	9	10	11	12
180	1	2	3	4	5	6	7	8	9	10	11	12
200	1	2	3	4	5	6	7	8	9	10	11	12
220	1	2	3	4	5	6	7	8	9	10	11	12
240	1	2	3	4	5	6	7	8	9	10	11	12

Number of drinks in a two-hour period

BAC = 0.00 to 0.05 Be careful

BAC = 0.05 to 0.09 Driving impaired

BAC= 0.10 and over Do NOT drive

Blood alcohol concentration chart.
Source: From U.S. Department of Transportation.

1990), is characterized by diffuse scarring of the liver, which is a common complication of alcoholism. Those who have alcoholic cirrhosis and continue heavy drinking often die from **hepatic failure** (liver failure). Excessive alcohol consumption can also cause diseases of the heart and circulatory system. The most common of these is congestive heart failure, with symptoms including an enlarged heart, elevated diastolic blood pressure, and edema (retention of fluid in body tissues). Moderate drinking does not seem to affect the heart adversely, though it does cause the blood vessels to relax and dilate, and blood pressure falls slightly.

Alcohol consumption can also cause a pseudo Cushing's syndrome. Cushing's syndrome is characterized by an overproduction of hormones from the adrenal glands that results in physical disorders. An abnormally rounded face, obesity, hypertension, and carbohydrate metabolism problems are results of this disorder. It is believed that high amounts of alcohol consumption stimulate activity in the adrenal glands (Jeffcoate 1993).

In the gastrointestinal tract, regular alcohol use can cause inflammation of the esophagus and irritate peptic ulcers. Alcoholic beverages are also known to contain cancer-producing compounds. Tobacco users who also drink alcohol are at even higher risk of cancer. The mechanism of how tobacco with alcohol increases the risk is unclear; one theory suggests that alcohol is a solvent for cancer-producing compounds and enhances their penetration into susceptible areas.

Negative effects occur to many of the bodily organs, largely due to poor nutrition. Alcohol in the gut impairs the intestinal absorption of many nutrients, notably folate and vitamin B-12. Its empty calories also substitute for more-beneficial foods. In addition, alcohol, or one of the substances it changes into during metabolism, is a poison. Acetaldehyde, at high levels, is one of the chief substances that have been implicated in injury to the liver, heart, and other organs (Robbins and Kumar 1987).

WHY WE REACT DIFFERENTLY TO ALCOHOL

Some of us can drink alcoholic beverages all evening without any effects, while others are affected after a few sips of wine. Why do these variations occur? Five main factors appear to be involved: (1) time of consumption, (2) food consumption, (3) quantity, (4) body weight, and (5) gender (O'Brien et al. 1992). Keeping these factors in mind can help you decide how much to drink, what to drink, and how fast to drink.

Time of Consumption

A drink sipped slowly enough to last for an hour should cause no significant rise in blood alcohol concentration. The body will burn the alcohol at the same rate at which it is being absorbed into the bloodstream. If the drink is gulped, however, its effects will be felt immediately and will take about an hour to wear off.

---

hepatic failure
Failure of the liver to function properly.

Food Consumption

If you eat while you drink, or just before, the food in your stomach will slow the rate at which the alcohol is absorbed, and thus the alcohol will reach your brain at a slower rate. Foods that contain fat and protein are best (cheese, low-salt crackers, Swedish meatballs, cold cuts, and so on). Fruits are less effective at slowing down absorption.

Quantity

Beer and wine affect the central nervous system more slowly than liquor does. Beer and wine contain certain nutrients and other substances that slow the absorption of alcohol, resulting in a lower alcohol concentration in the blood. Carbonated substances added to alcoholic beverages speed the rate of absorption, because carbon dioxide relaxes the pyloric sphincter (the valve opening from the stomach to the small intestine) and allows alcohol to pass more readily into the small intestine. Sparkling burgundy and champagne have high carbon dioxide content and are absorbed faster than other beverages.

Body Weight

Someone who weighs 180 pounds has more blood and other bodily fluids than does a person who weighs 120 pounds. The same amount of alcohol will be more diluted in the bloodstream of the heavier person and thus will not show its effects as soon.

Gender

BAC is generally higher in women. Recent research indicates that women have less of the stomach enzyme gastric alcohol dehydrogenase, which neutralizes alcohol (O'Brien et al. 1992).

TOLERANCE

"Tolerance is a condition in which it takes increasingly larger amounts of alcohol to produce the same effects previously felt at lower levels of alcohol intake" (Dusek and Girdano 1987). An understanding of **tolerance** is critical to controlling alcohol. When you find that it takes two drinks instead of one to relax you, then you are developing tolerance. This means that your body is adapting to alcohol on the cellular level. Adaptation does not mean that you learn to function better—impairment is still evident at the same levels. This adaptation is the first step toward serious physiological addiction, even though some people might already be psychologically addicted.

Figure 13.1 represents how the effects of alcohol and tolerance work. Initially alcohol acts as a depressant. As with all drugs, after the depressing effect there is a stimulating effect that is part of the cause of a hangover. In figure 13.1, the black horizontal line in the top drawing represents normal bodily functioning. With one drink, there is a depressive action, which is followed, after the alcoholic effect wears off, by a stimulating effect. Over time, as the body develops tolerance, the body adapts to the alcohol,

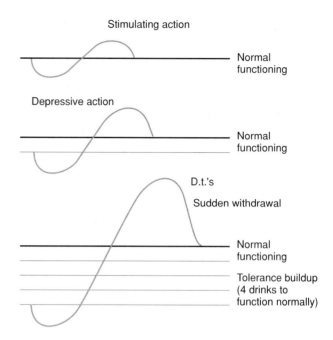

Figure 13.1
Alcohol and tolerance.

and the normal-functioning line drops some because the body begins to need alcohol to function optimally. With continued use, the normal-functioning lines drop more and more as tolerance increases. With problem drinking, when a person needs four or five drinks to get the same effect as one drink used to produce, then the person must have three or four drinks in his or her system to be able to feel okay.

A severe case is when someone who needs several drinks to function optimally is suddenly deprived of alcohol. The withdrawal effect of the drug is a rebound from the depressant effect of alcohol to a stimulating effect due to the lack of alcohol. For complete withdrawal, the person will experience the peak of the rebound stimulating effect. The stimulation is so severe that it is manifested by trembling and convulsions called the **delirium tremens (d.t.'s)**. The d.t.'s is a serious state of withdrawal that, without medical help, can result in death. Medical intervention generally includes mild injections of a depressant to reduce the peaking effects of withdrawal.

tolerance
The body's tendency to become less responsive to certain substances after repeated exposure. A person with low tolerance for alcohol has noticeable physiological responses from drinking a small amount of alcohol; a person with high tolerance for alcohol must drink much more alcohol to have those responses.

delirium tremens (d.t.'s)
Hallucinations and convulsive seizures that occur during withdrawal from alcohol.

Social drinking can lead to alcohol dependence.

ALCOHOL DEPENDENCE

Almost all social drinkers have experienced the immediate physical and psychological effects of overindulgence at one time or another, but they rarely drink to excess. Some people, however, develop a dependence on alcohol that leads to problem drinking and eventually to alcoholism. In alcohol dependency, a person experiences a craving or an uncontrollable desire for alcohol. At first the dependence is psychological, as the drinker builds up a certain level of alcohol tolerance; eventually, physical dependence can develop.

PSYCHOLOGICAL DEPENDENCE

Psychological dependence is the compulsive need for alcohol to relieve emotional discomfort. Alcohol-dependent people feel the need to escape from the tension and pressures confronting them in the real world, and they often find the social atmosphere of a bar more accepting of their behavior. Once involved in the bar scene, they need the sense of belonging given to them by the group.

PHYSIOLOGICAL DEPENDENCE

Physiological dependence does not occur as quickly as psychological dependence; generally, it takes from 3 to 15 years of heavy alcohol consumption, although young drinkers may develop a dependency after 1 or 2 years of heavy drinking. Someone physically dependent on alcohol experiences withdrawal symptoms when drinking is stopped or decreased.

DRINKING BEHAVIOR

WHO DRINKS?

Alcohol consumption is not confined to any particular age group or any other group in our society (figure 13.2), nor is alcoholism confined to any one group. Most alcoholics, however, tend to be married and/or living with families, so the impact of alcoholism on family life is high. The frequency of

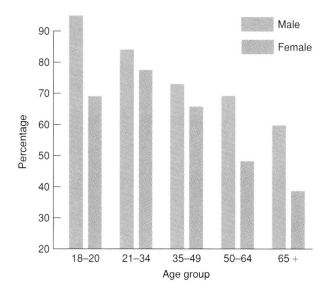

Figure 13.2
Percentage of male and female drinkers by age group. (Note: Results for the 18–20 age group must be viewed cautiously, since the number of respondents was small.)

alcohol consumption among American teenagers is about equal to that of adults, and alcohol is the leading psychoactive drug used by high school groups.

Until recently, most researchers have assumed that drinking, as both an activity and a problem, is associated more with men than with women. However, women's drinking has increased much more rapidly than men's over the last 50 years; although the percentage of women who drink is still lower than that of men, it comprises more than two-thirds of the female population.

As we grow older, we have less ability to metabolize alcohol, and many older adults respond to this by reducing their rate of alcohol consumption. A substantial percentage of the older population, however, suffers from alcohol addiction. Sadly, this abuse by older people often goes untreated because their behavior is quickly and conveniently explained away as symptomatic of old age (Braude and Char 1986).

WHY PEOPLE DRINK

We drink for many reasons. Some of us drink out of habit or family tradition, while others drink to celebrate religious, cultural, or social events, such as the champagne toast to a

psychological dependence
A state in which the user's craving for a particular drug might be so intense as to alter the user's behavior.

physiological dependence
Heavy consumption of a drug, such as alcohol, that results in the user's becoming dependent upon the drug and having withdrawal symptoms when the drug use is decreased or stopped.

bride and groom. For some, drinking is a way to show sophistication; drinking is thought to go hand in hand with elegance, as evidenced by the fine wine served with a good meal. The cocktail hour has become a great American pastime, with restaurants and bars promoting "happy hours" by serving reduced-rate drinks and appetizers for several hours in the early evening.

Some young people drink as a way of rebelling against their parents. Children of **teetotalers** (complete abstainers), for example, might drink excessively as a form of self-assertion against their parents, even while feeling guilty for doing so. Others of us drink to show that we're "one of the gang," to relax, to forget our problems, to relieve boredom, or simply because we enjoy doing so.

Still others of us drink because we wish to become intoxicated; we like the feeling that **intoxication** gives us. Intoxication is the direct result of alcohol's depressing the central nervous system. We tend to become talkative, sociable, and relaxed. For some, this is the way to loosen up in a social situation, regardless of possible alcohol dependence.

In the elementary school years, attitudes against drinking are high. Younger children do not think that people should drink often or to excess, and they think that drinking and driving are dangerous. After young people become drinkers, their attitudes and behaviors change to acceptance and tolerance of drinking, excessive drinking, and drinking and driving, and use of alcohol to cope with life crises (Carver, Kittleson, and Andrews 1991).

Psychologists have tried for years to understand the psychological reasons why people drink and become alcoholics. Although there are many theories, here are four basic theories, from which most others stem (Blane and Leonard 1987).

1. *Tension reduction theory.* People may drink to reduce stress and tension. If the drinking is successful in relieving the tension or problems, then the drinking is reinforced, and after some time the person will continue to drink to relieve tension.
2. *Personality theory.* There are certain personality types that are more prone than others to drinking. People with a certain personality type, whether through inheritance or learning, are more prone to drink. Personality characteristics associated with drinking include nonconformity, negative self-esteem, and certain negative cognitive styles (such as rationalization).
3. *Social learning theory.* This theory assumes that all drinking that progresses from incidental social use to alcoholism and abuse is governed by learning from others, cognition, and reinforcement from peers or effects of alcohol.
4. *Interactional theory.* This theory suggests that drinking is a function of the interaction between the person, his or her environment, and behavioral factors.

Other reasons for drinking include these:

1. To be accepted by friends, bosses, others with whom we associate
2. As a custom and part of the culture
3. As a way to forget about troubles
4. As a habit that we can't break
5. Made attractive by advertising and movies
6. Drinking by role models and heroes
7. Good taste
8. A way to show adulthood after years of not being able to legally drink
9. To reduce anxiety and stress
10. Experimentation and to relieve curiosity

Some of these reasons are less risky than others, in that some of them are less likely to lead to problem drinking. Which reasons do you think are "safer" reasons for drinking, and why?

RESPONSIBLE DRINKING

Responsible drinking of alcohol is a function of the drinker, the drinker's friends and family, social hosts, and servers of alcoholic beverages. Responsible drinking means making provisions to be taken home after drinking, understanding limits through the calculation of blood alcohol concentration, and recognizing when enough alcohol has been consumed. Responsible drinking is realizing that the toughest problem we may have is not whether to drink or not, but rather how we will live with the decision to be a drinker and the potential outcomes of drinking.

PERSONAL DECISIONS AND SOCIETY

Social life is very important to most students and can be a significant motivator. When social groups or individuals who are important to you offer you a drink, it may be difficult to say no thank you when you prefer not to drink or have had more to drink than you would like. Fraternity and sorority parties, and nightclubs, often socially revolve around drinking. When

teetotalers
People who never drink alcoholic beverages.

intoxication
The depressant effects of alcohol upon the central nervous system; drunkenness.

responsible drinking
Making provisions to be taken home if planning to drink, understanding limits through calculating blood alcohol concentration, and recognizing when enough alcohol has been consumed.

Am I Drinking Too Much?

Directions

Check every question to which your answer is yes.

_____ 1. Have I gotten drunk when I intended to stay sober?

_____ 2. When things get rough, do I need a drink or two to quiet my nerves?

_____ 3. Do other people say I'm drinking too much?

_____ 4. Have I gotten into trouble with the law, my family, or my business associates in connection with drinking?

_____ 5. Am I unable to stop drinking for a week or more?

_____ 6. Do I sometimes not remember what happened during a drinking episode?

_____ 7. Has a doctor ever said that my drinking was impairing my health?

_____ 8. Do I take a few drinks before going to a social gathering just in case there won't be much to drink?

_____ 9. Am I impatient while waiting for my drink to be served?

_____ 10. Have I tried to cut down, but failed?

_____ 11. Can I hold my liquor better than other people?

_____ 12. Has any member of my family been an alcoholic?

A positive response to any of these questions may necessitate abstinence from drinking or at least a restriction to no more than one drink per hour.

ordering a nonalcoholic drink at a club means having to hear the waiter yell, "Strawberry daiquiri, and make it a virgin!" it might seem difficult to avoid drinking.

In spite of the apparent social stigma, more people are finding the courage to say no when they have had enough to drink or when they don't want to drink at all. There are many ways to handle the situation, including being very open about being a nondrinker, covertly ordering a look-alike soft drink, or ordering a drink but never drinking it.

HELPING PEOPLE AND PROGRAMS

Because alcohol can impair judgment, it is important that roommates, family members, sorority sisters, fraternity brothers, and friends look out for each other for early signs of problems. Asking loved ones and friends when they are sober about potential problem drinking is awkward, but also important.

Many groups have been formed to educate us to avoid the problems associated with drinking alcohol. MADD (Mothers Against Drunk Driving) was started by a woman whose child was killed by a drunk driver; chapters of MADD exist all over the country to help prevent alcohol abuse and to treat and prosecute drunk drivers. Students Against Driving Drunk (SADD) and Removing Intoxicated Drivers (RID) have chapters around the country and on college campuses. These organizations try to reduce the number of drunk drivers on the road through providing education, rides, and awareness events.

RESPONSIBLE HOSTS AND GUESTS

Responsible hosting used to be an ethical issue of demonstrating concern and care for people attending socials as guests and watching to make sure that if they became intoxicated,

they would get home safely. Now it has become a legal issue as well. At this writing, most states have laws that cover prosecution of irresponsible social hosts, and only nine states have not yet considered the issue (Goldberg 1992). Consider the **host liability** in the following legal case.

> On January 11, 1980, Donald Gwinnell drove away from the home of Joseph and Catherine Zak after consuming reportedly 13 drinks of Scotch. Minutes later, while attempting to pass another car on a curve, he hit another car and injured Marie Kelly who suffered a broken ankle and lost six teeth. Gwinnell was legally intoxicated. Kelly sued Gwinnell and later included the Zak's in her suit. In 1984, the New Jersey Supreme Court ruled that "where the social host directly serves the guest and continues to do so even after the guest is visibly intoxicated, knowing that the guest will soon be driving home, the social host may be liable for the consequences of the resulting drunken driving." Several months later in one day of court, the Kelly case was settled with the Zaks paying $72,000 and Mr. Gwinnell paying $100,000. At least 12 states now include a provision in the law for action against social hosts for injury caused by their intoxicated guests. (Prugh 1986)

responsible hosting
Demonstrating concern and care for people attending social events you are hosting, making sure that if they become intoxicated, they will get home safely.

host liability
The legal responsibility of individuals who provide drinks to their guests. Courts have found hosts liable for individuals who have left the drinking occasion and later were responsible for traffic accidents.

PERSONAL SKILLS AND EXPERIENCES

Should You Drink?

Mind

With so much alcohol flowing in the United States, it is important to decide whether you will drink and how you will cope with those whose drinking habits differ from yours. This is a mental activity that you can practice before your next opportunity to drink or attend a function where there is drinking.

Decide whether you will abstain, drink occasionally, or drink frequently. Mentally work through how you plan to deal with the following situations if they arise.

1. Your date has been drinking when he or she comes to pick you up (or when you arrive to pick up your date, you can tell that he or she has been drinking).
2. Your date is drinking more at a party than he or she can handle.
3. You are the only nondrinker at a party where everyone urges you to have a drink.
4. Use the formulas in this chapter to determine how many drinks you can have and still drive safely (BAC less than .02).

Body

If you drink, consider how you feel physically the morning after drinking. Were you responsible enough not to have a hangover, or are you going to pay the price for irresponsibility? To maximize the potential of your body and to avoid losing coordination and control, do not drink more than one drink per hour. To avoid liver problems, headaches, and other problems, do not drink more than one drink per hour.

Soul

If you have an alcohol problem, the twelve steps of Alcoholics Anonymous is a soulful guide to gaining control:

1. We admitted we were powerless over alcohol—that our lives had become unmanageable.
2. We came to believe that a Power greater than ourselves could restore us to sanity.
3. We made a decision to turn our will and our lives over to the care of God as we understood Him.
4. We made a searching and fearless moral inventory of ourselves.
5. We admitted to God, to ourselves, and to another human being the exact nature of our wrongs.
6. We were entirely ready to have God remove all these defects of character.
7. We humbly asked Him to remove our shortcomings.
8. We made a list of all persons we had harmed and became willing to make amends to them all.
9. We made direct amends to such people whenever possible, except when to do so would injure them or others.
10. We continued to take personal inventory and when we were wrong promptly admitted it.
11. We sought through prayer and meditation to improve our conscious contact with God, as we understood Him, praying only for knowledge of His will for us and the power to carry that out.
12. Having had a spiritual awakening as the result of these steps, we tried to carry this message to alcoholics and to practice these principles in all our affairs.

Although the AA program is considered to be one of the most successful recovery programs, many people have questioned the first step, which suggests that people are powerless over alcohol. Some think that the first step should be stated that we believe we are capable of overcoming the effects of alcohol and only we are going to make the difference.

Source: *44 Questions and Answers About the AA Program of Recovery.* New York: Alcoholics Anonymous, 1952.

Whether it is an ethical issue or legal issue, it is important to carefully watch guests who are drinking.

Guidelines for Social Hosts

The following are some of the things you can do to be a responsible host (Source: From National Clearinghouse for Alcohol Information, Rockville, Md.).

• Do your best to establish and maintain a tension-free atmosphere. Guests should not have to drink in order to relax.

• Have food available before and during alcohol service, but avoid salty foods that promote thirst. High-protein foods, such as shellfish, meatballs, and chicken, are best at slowing the absorption of alcohol.

• Do not have an open bar. Deemphasize alcohol by putting the bar someplace out of the way. Serve your guests yourself or hire someone to do it. In either case, measure the alcohol carefully and use light doses.

• Have an attractive variety of nonalcoholic beverages on hand, and make them at least as easily and prominently accessible as the alcoholic drinks. If you are serving mixed drinks, be aware that noncarbonated mixers retard the absorption of alcohol into the bloodstream while carbonated mixers speed it up.

• If the event is a dinner-and-drinks affair, keep the drinking period short and have hors d'oeuvres available throughout.

- Don't push drinks. Respect your guests' right to refuse drinks. Make sure that nonalcoholic beverages are available during dinner as well as before.
- Never serve alcohol, or allow it to be served, to a guest who seems to be intoxicated.
- Stop serving alcohol at least an hour before the party is over.
- If, despite these precautions, a guest drinks to the point of impairment (not necessarily drunkenness) and you are not certain he or she will be driven home by a sober companion, then drive the guest home yourself, arrange for a taxi, or put him or her up in your home for the night. Never let a guest drive intoxicated.

Guidelines for Guests

The following are some of the things you can do to be a responsible guest (Source: From National Clearinghouse for Alcohol Information, Rockville, Md.).

- Support and cooperate with the efforts of your host or hostess to make the event safe and pleasant for all.
- Do not hesitate to exercise your right to refuse drinks or to avoid alcoholic beverages altogether.
- If you choose to drink, moderate your intake. If you arrive with a group, arrange for one member to take responsibility for doing the driving. That person should not drink alcohol on that occasion.
- Be aware that, while most people can metabolize about one standard drink every hour (a standard drink is one 12-ounce can of beer, 4 ounces of wine, or 1 ounce of spirits), metabolic rates vary.
- Women are more readily affected by alcohol than men are, because of lower average body weight, different tissue composition, and other factors.
- If a woman is pregnant or nursing, the safest decision for her and her baby is not to drink.
- Partygoers taking medication should be aware that many drugs—both prescription and over-the-counter—can interact with alcohol to produce unpleasant or even dangerous side effects. If in doubt, consult your physician or pharmacist.

Liability Lawsuits: Prevention Steps for Colleges and Universities

There are several things that university and college groups can do to reduce liability and damages associated with university functions where alcohol is served. The responsible hosting techniques described earlier in this chapter should be practiced in addition to, and with special emphasis on, the following (Source: From National Clearinghouse for Alcohol Information, Rockville, Md.):

- Ensure that nonalcoholic drinks are displayed with more or equal prominence as alcoholic drinks at an event.

- Make sure that plenty of food is available where alcohol is served, especially protein-rich items, such as cheese, crackers with protein toppings, and pizza, which slow the rate of alcohol absorption into the bloodstream.
- Develop alcohol-free events, such as dance marathons, dorm campouts, casino nights, and sports competitions, to take the place of traditionally alcohol-related activities.
- Eliminate "happy hours," discount prices, keg parties, and other practices that encourage the consumption of alcohol.
- Stop the service of alcohol an hour prior to the expected conclusion of any event.
- Establish an alcohol-problem awareness group on campus to educate students on responsible drinking.
- Restrict to appropriate levels the amount and kinds of alcohol served, according to the type of event, participants, and duration of the activity.
- Post notices stating the legal drinking age at the entrance and in beverage serving areas of campus functions where alcohol is served.
- Avoid open bars by requiring all campus alcohol service events to be attended by a responsible server at all times.
- Establish a designated-driver program, allowing the driver for a group to drink nonalcoholic beverages free of charge in order to lessen the risk of drunk-driving incidents.
- Take steps to ensure that the campus health services, the counseling center, and the disciplinary systems are sensitive to alcohol-related problems and are prepared to inform and intervene.
- Maintain adequate liquor-liability insurance.
- Provide due warning to the campus community on the health and safety hazards of alcohol abuse through educational and informational activities such as health fairs, panel discussions, demonstrations, film festivals, and a dedicated alcohol-problem awareness day or week.

RESPONSIBLE SERVING

There are many legal and ethical issues involved in a commercial establishment's serving alcoholic drinks. Successful lawsuits have been filed against bartenders and drinking establishments. Consequently, server intervention programs have surfaced around the country that train bartenders to spot potential drunk drivers, call them a cab, and quit serving them before legal drunkenness occurs.

Court rulings have been holding drinking establishments responsible for several types of behavior of their drinking customers. In a recent court case that involved the Las Vegas Sands Hotel and Casino, a federal judge ruled that the casino was responsible for the financial losses of a gambler. The casino employees allowed the customer to continue gambling although he was visibly drunk (Kaplan 1993).

Issue

The Lesser of Two Evils

Suppose that for some months now you have been working with a person responsible for important machinery that is potentially dangerous to others if not operated correctly. You have noticed that your coworker returns from lunch smelling of alcohol and frequently makes mistakes in operating the machinery. So far there have been no major accidents. Your coworker is a longtime and respected employee who supports a family with this job. If reported and the charge is proven, the coworker will lose the job and thus support for the family, and you may well lose the respect of other employees who go out drinking at lunch.

- **Pro:** The coworker should be reported. If reported, some help may be given, even though the person would no longer be able to hold that job. Once the person is out of the job, there will be no further risk to other employees from improperly operated machines.

- **Con:** It is the supervisor's responsibility, not yours, to ensure that the machines are being operated properly. The coworker has not yet made a bad mistake and has worked with the company for a long time. It is wrong to get someone fired and take away support from the family.

What would you do?

PROBLEM DRINKING

When alcohol begins to control a person's life, create accidents, cause arguments, and take the person away from activities he or she should be doing, that person may be considered a problem drinker. **Problem drinking** is repeated use of alcohol that causes physical, psychological, or social harm to the drinker or to others. The drinker is unable to cope or function "normally" without alcohol. The actual amount, frequency, or pattern of alcohol use is not particularly important; what is important is the person's consistent reliance on alcohol.

Complete the Health Assessment exercise on the risk of drinking problems to determine your risk for alcohol abuse. The Health Assessment includes a list of early indications of alcohol's becoming a problem. Those signs represent early symptoms of serious problems. Becoming seriously addicted is a subtle process, and people generally do not realize that they are sinking into alcoholic addiction.

PATHWAY TO PROBLEM DRINKING

The steps to alcoholism occur differently for every individual, but some common steps in the gradual decline might include the following (Strug, Priyadarsini, and Hyman 1986):

- *Step 1:* The occasional drink. A drink at a social gathering, at dinner as a cultural tradition, and an occasional drink for pleasure.
- *Step 2:* Initial use as a "crutch" or "escape." A drink for the purpose of calming nerves, to relax after a difficult day.
- *Step 3:* Frequent use of alcohol as a "crutch" or an "escape." Regular use of alcohol as a means to control stress.
- *Step 4:* Physical symptoms and overt symptoms. Routine psychological use of alcohol as a coping mechanism or escape, accompanied by occasional blackouts (not passing out, but not remembering events that occurred during drinking). Some preoccupation with alcohol, gulping first drinks, and drinking alone. Increasing tolerance.
- *Step 5:* Alcohol becomes central to lifestyle. Job, home life, appearance, possessions, and significant others become secondary to alcohol. Cannot stop at one drink. Interpersonal conflicts, resentment, and self-pity dominate.
- *Step 6:* Continuous drinking. Drinking starts in the morning and may continue. Daily routine of drinking everywhere one goes, danger of withdrawal and the d.t.'s if alcohol is not in the system at all times. Generally malnourished and has the "shakes."
- *Step 7:* Medical intervention or death.

ALCOHOLISM

Alcoholism is an old problem. Today, however, the problem has become one of America's top health problems: At least one in every ten adults—about 10 to 18 million Americans—are alcoholics! Alcoholism is a chronic condition associated with excessive consumption of alcohol (O'Brien et al. 1992). Alcoholics have so lost control over their drinking that they are consistently unable to refrain from drinking or to stop drinking before becoming intoxicated. Alcoholism differs from problem drinking in that the alcoholic not only suffers problems due to drinking but also suffers a loss of control.

Alcoholism is recognized by professional organizations as a disease. The disease process is a slippage or downward progression from social drinking to debilitating alcoholism. People who will need help in overcoming alcoholism include both those who have the powerful genetic predisposition to alcohol addiction as well as those that have become addicted by using alcohol as a coping mechanism. Professional intervention and Alcoholics Anonymous are the primary ways to curb the downward spiral to addictive ruin and begin the process of recovery.

problem drinking
Repetitive use of alcohol that causes physical, psychological, or social harm to the drinker or to others.

alcoholism
Loss of control in drinking; the inability to refrain from drinking; the inability to stop drinking before becoming intoxicated.

Risk of Drinking Problems

Directions

Circle all responses that apply to you.

1. If you still live with your parents or when you lived with your parents, it was (is) with
   a. both parents.
   b. mother only.
   c. mother and stepfather.
   d. father only.
   e. father and stepmother.
   f. neither.
2. Your parents are
   a. married.
   b. divorced.
   c. separated.
   d. widowed.
3. Mark any of the following situations that applies to you.
   a. I live at home with parent(s) who drink regularly.
   b. I socialize with friends or roommates who drink regularly.
   c. I live at or am a member of a sorority or fraternity that has alcoholic drinks at socials.
   d. I live with a spouse who drinks regularly.
4. When you have problems, whom among the following can you reach quickly and talk with freely?
   a. father/stepfather
   b. mother/stepmother
   c. friend
   d. girlfriend/boyfriend
   e. spouse
   f. no one really
5. Which of the following statements apply to you? (Mark all that apply.)
   a. I really enjoy the academic part of school.
   b. I am content with the grades I earn.
   c. I like school okay, but my grades are probably not as good as they could be.
   d. I don't like school.
   e. I am not getting grades I am happy with.
   f. I put a lot of pressure on myself to get good grades.
   g. My family puts a lot of pressure on me to get good grades.
   h. Someone else (i.e., coach, advisor, and so on) puts a lot of pressure on me to get good grades.
6. Mark all of the following that describe your family life (closeness and relationships) now and growing up.
   a. It was great growing up, but poor now.
   b. It was poor growing up, but good now.
   c. We did (do) lots of things as a family (vacations, outings, played games, and so on).
   d. We didn't (don't) do much as a family.

7. If you drink, indicate which of the following types of beverages you generally drink? (Leave blank if you do not drink.)
   a. beer
   b. wine
   c. wine coolers
   d. liquor (Scotch, gin, bourbon, vodka, and so on)
8. Which of the following best describes the drinking patterns of your best friends?
   a. They do not drink.
   b. They drink socially with no more than one or two drinks.
   c. They drink regularly, but not more than one or two drinks per time.
   d. They drink socially and occasionally get drunk.
   e. They drink regularly and get drunk often.
9. Which of the following best describes the drinking patterns of your immediate family (parents, siblings, grandparents)? Think of the family member(s) who drink(s) the most.
   a. They do not drink.
   b. They drink socially with no more than one or two drinks.
   c. They drink regularly but not more than one or two drinks per time.
   d. They drink socially and occasionally get drunk.
   e. They drink regularly and get drunk often.
10. Are any of your family members alcoholic or seriously abusing alcohol?
    a. father/stepfather
    b. mother/stepmother
    c. brother/sister
    d. one grandparent
    e. more than one grandparent
    f. no one in my family
11. Which of these statements best describes how you feel about yourself? (Mark all that apply.)
    a. I feel good about how I am.
    b. I wish I was the way I used to be.
    c. I don't like the way I am.
    d. I like my lifestyle and how I turned out.
    e. I want to be just like my mother (if female) or father (if male).
12. Which of the following best describes how you feel about religion? (Circle all that apply.)
    a. In my religion, it does not really matter whether you drink or not to be in good standing.
    b. My religion is not important to me.
    c. I am not religious.
    d. My personal religious beliefs are that drinking alcohol is okay.
    e. My personal religious beliefs are that drinking is wrong.

(Continued on page 13.16)

13. Which of the following applies to you? (Circle all that apply.)
    a. I am influenced by beer and wine cooler commercials on TV.
    b. I sometimes drink to escape my problems.
    c. I feel like I want to run away from my problems.
    d. I am sad a lot of the time.
    e. I am a happy person most of the time.
14. The following statements may describe your situation. (Circle all that apply.)
    a. People consider me rebellious.
    b. I do what I want to do no matter what other people think.
    c. I have a lot of problems that are difficult to deal with.
    d. I can handle just about every stress that is thrown at me.
    e. I am currently experiencing a lot of stress.
15. Which of the following best describes your drinking habits?
    a. I do not drink alcohol.
    b. I drink socially with no more than one or two drinks.
    c. I drink regularly, but not more than one or two drinks per time.
    d. I drink socially and occasionally get drunk.
    e. I drink regularly and get drunk often.

Scoring

Total the points you received based on the following key.

1. a = 0   b = 4   c = 1   d = 4   e = 1   f = 4
2. a = 0   b = 4   c = 4   d = 2
3. a = 5   b = 5   c = 5   d = 5
4. f = 5, for a–e if you were only able to mark 1 response give yourself 1, for two or more responses give yourself 0
5. a = 0   b = 0   c = 1   d = 2   e = 2   f = 2
   g = 2   h = 2

6. a = 4   b = 4   c = 0   d = 2
7. a = 1   b = 3   c = 2   d = 7
8. a = 0   b = 3   c = 3   d = 5   e = 7
9. a = 0   b = 3   c = 3   d = 5   e = 7
10. a = 7   b = 7   c = 6   d = 4   e = 6   f = 0
11. a = 0   b = 2   c = 3   d = 0   e = 0
12. a = 2   b = 2   c = 2   d = 2   e = 0
13. a = 3   b = 3   c = 3   d = 3   e = 0
14. a = 3   b = 0   c = 3   d = 0   e = 3
15. See interpretation that follows.

Interpretation

1. For moderate to high risk based on question 15.

   If you indicated response a, then you should refer to number 3 below to see what your risk is.

   If you selected response b or c, then you are already at a moderate risk. One out of ten social drinkers becomes an alcoholic.

   If you selected response d or e, you may already have a serious drinking problem.

2. You are low risk if you did all of the following:
   left question 3 blank
   selected two or more responses other than f on question 4
   selected 8a, 9a, 10f, 11a, 12e, and 15a.

3. From the total score for questions 1 through 14, interpret your risk of alcohol abuse as follows:

   Low risk   = See number 2 above or a score of less than 40.

   Moderate risk = 41–89.

   High risk   = See number 1 above or a score of 90 or higher.

Alcoholism creates problems for individuals, their families, and the community. Alcoholics lose their self-respect. Their health, happiness, and safety are affected, and this leads to ruined lives.

Three of every four alcoholics are reasonably well accepted members of their communities, not "skid row bums" as is often thought. Average alcoholics affect at least four others by their behavior. Loss of income and respect can lead to divorce, delinquency, crime, and even suicide.

Alcoholism can cause a huge drain on the community economy. Lost productivity, vehicular accidents, health and social service costs, and violent crimes stemming from alcoholism cost our nation billions of dollars each year.

CAUSES OF ALCOHOLISM

Alcoholism can potentially attack any of us without regard to social standing, occupation, intelligence, education, national

The conflict, marital problems, and family violence often caused by alcoholism can make growing up in an alcoholic home confusing and challenging.

origin, religion, or race. In fact, typical alcoholics include bright middle-management executives in their thirties who are married and living in middle-class neighborhoods. There are alcoholic middle-aged housewives who no longer have children at home and who have found little to occupy their lives other than drinking from a "hidden bottle." There are even 12- to 15-year-old alcoholics who go to school every Monday morning with a hangover. There are many theories about the causes of alcoholism, but no one has conclusively pinpointed a definitive cause.

Researchers are attempting to identify genetic predisposition to alcoholism. Many studies show that rats (Farrant and Cull-Candy 1993) and dogs (Kinney and Leaton 1991, 80) have predispositions to alcohol that these animals prefer alcohol to water. It appears that humans might also have predispositions and that some people can become alcoholics after their first drink.

STAGES OF ALCOHOLISM

Alcoholics have different drinking patterns, but all these patterns usually fall into similar stages (Blakeslee 1976):

  I. Early Stage
     Frequent drinking
     Increased tolerance
     Promises to quit but doesn't
     Changes in personality
 II. Middle Stage
     Conceals drinking
     Drinks alone, in the morning
     Work is affected
     Feels bad regardless of the amount consumed
III. Final Stage
     Loneliness and isolation
     Lives to drink
     Extreme personality changes
     Health is definitely affected

After a period of apparently normal drinking, the alcoholic begins a period of heavy social drinking during the early stages of alcoholism. The individual drinks more frequently, usually to relieve tensions, and develops an increased tolerance to the effects of alcohol. The person may experience blackouts and not remember the drinking episode. Other personality changes, including increased irritability and forgetfulness, are also likely to occur. The person promises to quit but promptly breaks the promise to cope with social stress. During this stage, which can last as long as 10 years, the person invents occasions for drinking if none exist.

The middle stages are characterized by a lack of control after taking the first drink. Drinking becomes a daily necessity, at any time of the day. The drinker is unable to abstain, even though the effects of drinking are pronounced. Definite physical, mental, and social changes occur in the alcohol-dependent individual, including severe guilt feelings, efforts to deny or conceal drinking, and general deterioration of normal social relationships within the person's family and professional life.

After a number of years of drinking, the alcoholic reaches the final stage—drinking to live and living to drink. The person's entire life revolves around obtaining and consuming alcohol. The alcoholic is usually isolated from family, friends, and coworkers; alcohol comes first. Health problems begin to appear: tremors, hallucinations, and malnutrition (because the alcoholic drinks rather than eats). Unless the alcoholic realizes there is a severe problem, she or he will likely lose everything, including family, job, and friends, and might eventually die from the health complications.

TREATMENT AND REHABILITATION

The only "cure" for alcoholism is complete **abstinence**—never drinking again. Several years ago, researchers thought that they could teach alcoholics to drink only socially. Studies showed that these behavior modification techniques worked for only 5 percent of alcoholics. In general, alcoholics are unable to stop drinking if they have even one sip of alcohol. To achieve abstinence, the alcoholic must admit there is a problem, sincerely desire to recover, and be willing to accept and stick with some form of treatment, whether self-imposed or institutional.

Most alcoholism treatment programs begin in a medical facility and include physical and psychological components. The first step in treatment is physical **withdrawal** from alcohol, a period in which the body adapts to functioning without alcohol. During withdrawal, hallucinations and convulsive seizures (d.t.'s) occur, and without drug assistance these can be very painful and dangerous. Sedation might be needed to help the person through this period. Vitamin injections may be given, because most alcoholics suffer from nutritional deficiencies. Tranquilizers might also be used to temporarily control anxiety, but they must be used with great care because of the danger of transferring dependence. Sometimes **Antabuse** therapy is used. Antabuse is a drug that prevents drinking because its intake with alcohol causes nausea, dizziness, and heart palpitations.

---

stages of alcoholism
Stages in the gradual decline from social drinking to alcoholism: The early stage involves increased drinking and tolerance; in the middle stage, one conceals one's drinking, drinks alone, doesn't function normally, and feels bad; in the final stage, one lives to drink and goes through extreme personality changes.

abstinence
Refraining from drinking any alcoholic beverage.

withdrawal
Symptoms that occur, due to physical dependence on alcohol, when an alcoholic person stops drinking. The symptoms range from a hangover to delirium tremens.

Antabuse
A drug that in combination with alcohol causes nausea, dizziness, and heart palpitations; used to deter persons from drinking.

The psychological component of the treatment program, psychotherapy, is provided to help the alcoholic face the problems that have caused and resulted from drinking. Group and individual therapy are available, depending on personal preference. The family of the alcoholic is often included in the therapy program to create a more supportive home environment for rehabilitation.

A number of excellent organizations assist in the **rehabilitation** of alcoholics. There are private counseling services, councils on alcoholism, and the Department of Veterans' Affairs, but perhaps the largest and most successful program is Alcoholics Anonymous (AA). Alcoholics Anonymous is a worldwide self-help organization with only one qualification for membership: The person must want to stop drinking. A person joins simply by attending a meeting, and members assist each other in maintaining sobriety. The AA program recognizes that the only cure is abstinence, which can be maintained through personal commitment, humility, a day-by-day plan for not drinking, and the "twelve steps" for personal recovery (see the Personal Skills and Experiences box "Should You Drink?" earlier in this chapter).

SOCIAL IMPACT OF ALCOHOL

The alcohol industry promotes drinking in spite of the negative consequences of drinking. The following is a list of some of those consequences ("Adverse Social Consequences of Alcohol Use and Alcoholism" 1986):

1. Traffic accidents. In one-third to one-half of all traffic fatalities, drivers had BAC of over .10. Drivers with BACs over .10 are three to fifteen times more likely to have a fatal crash than are drivers who have not been drinking.
2. Pedestrian accidents. Of the numerous pedestrians killed and injured by automobiles, 35 to 75 percent of the pedestrians had measurable BACs.
3. Airplane accidents. About 10 percent of fatal airplane crashes are caused by drunk pilots.
4. Occupational accidents. In 80 percent of job-related accidents, the employee had a measurable BAC.
5. Home and recreational accidents. In home accidents, one-third come from falls and another 20 percent come from burns and injuries from fire. In recreational activities, accidents come from drownings, falls, and other recreational activities. Studies have shown that 20 to 45 percent of these accidents involve persons with measurable BACs.
6. Homicide. Alcohol is involved in from 25 to 85 percent (there is wide range of variability in studies) of homicides.
7. Rape. The rapist will have been drinking alcohol prior to the rape in 50 to 81 percent of the cases.

The message is clear: If you drink, don't drive.

8. Marital problems. Forty percent of family court problems involve alcoholism in some way, and it is estimated that 33 to 40 percent of intact alcoholic couples have poor marital relationships.
9. Family violence. Although the abuse of children by their parents and the abuse of spouses by their marital partners are difficult to study, evidence suggests that alcohol is involved in 11 to 17 percent of child-abuse cases and from 29 to 71 percent of spouse-abuse cases.
10. Suicide. From 15 to 64 percent of suicide attempts, and up to 80 percent of completed suicides, have been associated with drinking alcohol at the time of the attempt.

DRINKING AND DRIVING

"If you drink, don't drive" is a familiar refrain today. Unfortunately, many persons disregard this message, and today alcohol is a leading factor in from 38 to 50 percent of all fatal automobile accidents (Kinney and Leaton 1991). Regardless of your own drinking behavior, it is important to understand the dangers presented by drinking drivers.

All fifty states have laws and penalties against driving under the influence of alcohol. Most states base "driving under the influence" on a person's blood alcohol concentration (BAC), as determined by a **breathalyzer** (breath tester) or

rehabilitation
The process of restoring a person's bodily or psychological functioning so that she or he can live a healthier life.

breathalyzer
A machine used to determine a person's blood alcohol content; usually used with drivers suspected of being drunk.

PERSONAL INSIGHT

A Tragic Lesson

Jodi was a 5-year-old girl who had just had a fun day at an amusement park. She and her two brothers and older sisters had been on rides all day and spent some of the time in the pool and water slides. They were exhausted. At about 5 P.M. they were to meet their mother, who was picking them up on her way home from work. The other children were standing by the curb in front of the amusement park while Jodi sat on the sidewalk.

John had been working on a service project sponsored by his fraternity. He had spent the day helping to build a batting cage at a local Little League baseball park. It was a warm day and John had several beers to quench his thirst. He lost track of the number of beers, but at the end of the project it was time to go home to his apartment. John got into his car and felt fine. He

was always cautious about driving after parties at night, but this was daytime. He thought that he probably hadn't had that many beers and that he must have sweated out most of the alcohol. John drove toward his apartment. He was thinking about his date that night and how much fun he would have. He caught himself going over the center line a couple times and thought that the alignment in his car must be off. He noticed that he went through a stop sign and was surprised that he hadn't seen it until he was into the intersection, but no other cars were there. He again found himself drifting into the opposing lane and swerved to miss an oncoming car, and then he heard a thud. He didn't pay much attention to it until he looked in the rearview mirror and saw some children screaming and circling something on the ground. He thought that maybe he could help. John pulled over to see if he could help. There was Jodi lying in a pool of

blood, and her brothers and sisters crying and panicked. One of Jodi's sisters yelled at John, "You've killed her—you've killed my sister!" How could he have, he thought; he was just driving along the road.

John stayed until the paramedics and the police arrived. The brothers and sisters told the police that John had swerved from the other side of the road and hit Jodi on the sidewalk. The tire tracks verified their statement. An examination of John's car revealed that the car was dented and blood splattered. At this writing, Jodi is still in a coma.

John's blood alcohol concentration was .11—he was legally drunk—and he was cited with a DUI. John's life is not the same now. He provides a lot of community service. He dropped out of college. He lives with guilt and remorse. He often visits Jodi and Jodi's parents. John doesn't drink anymore.

Issue

Drunk Driving: Losing Your License

Every state has the power to rescind the driver's license of a driver who has been convicted of driving while intoxicated. However, with the massive plea bargaining that occurs in some courts, very few drivers ever lose their licenses.

- Pro: Intoxicated drivers should lose their licenses because these drivers will drive drunk again, and the next time they might kill someone.
- Con: These drivers are not criminals in the same way that a robber or rapist is, and in most cases they need their cars to support a family, so their licenses shouldn't be rescinded.

Should problem drinkers (convicted more than once) and social drinkers (first-time offenders) be treated the same? Should mandatory treatment programs be required for either or both groups? If you could make the law, what would it be?

direct analysis of the blood. In many states a BAC of .08 or higher is classified as drunk driving; other states use a BAC of .10 as the criterion. Compulsive drinkers with consistently high BACs are involved in a disproportionate number of fatal crashes, even though they might be skillful drivers when sober.

The average person arrested for driving while intoxicated has a BAC of .20, which means that the person has probably had close to ten drinks and that his or her motor and sensory capacities are severely distorted. Such drivers are abusers of alcohol, not mainstream social drinkers. In the last several years, organizations such as MADD and RID have been attempting to make sure that drunk drivers, especially those who have been involved in fatal accidents, are taken to trial and for as long as possible, prevented from driving.

LEGISLATION OF ALCOHOL CONSUMPTION

Each state has its own statutes regulating the use, purchase, and sale of alcoholic beverages. However, many of these laws, particularly those prohibiting public intoxication and habitual drunkenness, have been found unconstitutional in recent

HEALTH UPDATE

Alcohol on Campus

Here are some facts about alcohol on college campuses.

1. As many college students will eventually die of alcohol-related causes as will receive master's and doctorate degrees.

2. Alcohol is the leading cause of death among young adults. Between 240,000 and 360,000 of the students in college in 1991 will eventually die as a result of drinking. This equals the entire undergraduate population of the nation's "Big 10" universities.

3. College students drink a total of more than 430 million gallons of alcoholic beverages annually—enough to fill an Olympic-size swimming pool on every college campus in the United States. This averages out to more than 34 gallons of alcoholic beverage per student per year.

4. Students attending college get drunk more often than do their counterparts who are not in college.

5. College students spend $4.2 billion annually on alcoholic beverages. This figure exceeds the amount spent on the nation's campus libraries, scholarships, and fellowships combined.

6. Nearly 7 percent of college freshmen drop out of college each year as a result of drinking, and drinking is a factor in 21 percent of all decisions to drop out of college.

7. Nine out of ten student deaths resulting from fraternity or sorority "hazing" are alcohol-related. (Eigen 1991)

Supreme Court decisions prohibiting the punishment of persons for public intoxication except as a misdemeanor. In various states, laws prohibit the following:

1. Public intoxication. Courts have interpreted a "public place" to include virtually every place but the home. Public intoxication has been decriminalized in approximately fifteen states.

2. Drinking in public. Some states prohibit this. Legal action could also occur under statutes that prohibit loitering and disorderly conduct.

3. Drunk and disorderly conduct. In some states, this is an offense.

4. Sale to minors. All states prohibit the sale of alcoholic beverages to "minors," but legal age varies from state to state.

FETAL ALCOHOL SYNDROME

A pregnant woman who drinks can cause her baby irreversible damage. Fetal exposure to alcohol is one of the leading known causes of mental retardation in the Western world, and treatment costs one-third of a billion dollars per year (U.S. Department of Health and Human Services 1990). Scientists still do not understand just how alcohol damages unborn children. They do know, however, that the ingestion of alcohol interferes with normal pregnancy, that the effects on the fetus are permanent, and that whether damage occurs depends on the basic metabolism of both the expectant mother and the fetus.

Fetal alcohol syndrome (FAS) is a pattern of physical, mental, and behavioral abnormalities often found among newborns whose mothers drank during pregnancy. Anatomical defects that may be signs of FAS include a small head circumference, a low nasal bridge, an underdeveloped groove in the center of the upper lip between the nose and lip edge,

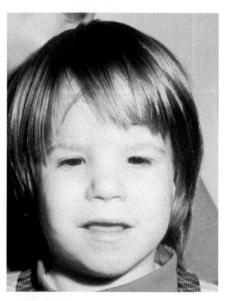

Fetal alcohol syndrome can result when pregnant women drink alcohol.

a thin reddish upper lip, a short nose, and a small midface. Potential effects of fetal alcohol syndrome are brain injury, mental retardation, and behavioral problems. A study that followed FAS-afflicted children 22 years after they were born found that childhood facial malformations were less prominent in adulthood but that cardiac and bone defects and misshapen hands persisted. These young adults were still mentally retarded and emotionally unstable (Dorozyaski

---

fetal alcohol syndrome (FAS)
Irreversible damage to the fetus caused by the mother's heavy use of alcohol during pregnancy.

1993). In addition, children born to alcoholic mothers are born dependent on alcohol; they go through withdrawal symptoms beginning during the first 24 hours after birth and lasting anywhere from 1 week to 6 months.

Not all women who drink alcohol during pregnancy will have babies with FAS. Genetic factors and other lifestyle variables might account for differences in outcome and might explain why some infants are spared the negative effects (U.S. Department of Health and Human Services 1990). Animal studies indicate that peak blood alcohol concentration levels, rather than drinking large amounts of alcohol over time, might be one critical variable. Researchers are working to identify women at greater risk of having babies with FAS. Risk factors such as length of drinking history, reported tolerance to alcohol, and history of alcohol-related illnesses are some of the factors being used to help identify those at highest risk (U.S. Department of Health and Human Services 1990).

To make a recommendation for safe levels of alcohol consumption for pregnant women in order to avoid FAS would be foolish. Genetic variability, bodily makeup, and psychological characteristics vary too much for such a recommendation. The only safe way to avoid FAS is to not drink during pregnancy.

There is an epidemic of addicted babies born to addicted mothers. The expense of dealing with FAS, helping the babies to recover form alcoholism, and the likelihood that the babies will be abandoned by the mothers are major problems in the United States today.

PROBLEMS FOR THOSE CLOSE TO ALCOHOLICS

You might be a nondrinker but come from an alcoholic family or have an alcoholic partner. There are potential problems that can surface in those types of relationships.

CODEPENDENCY

In their attempt to help a person who is experiencing drinking problems, caring support people sometimes are affected by the alcohol problem. **Codependency** is a condition in which people who are in a relationship with a problem drinker or an alcoholic are so entrapped by love and concern for the abuser that they lose their own identities in the process of trying to help. They essentially become addicted to the addict's behavior. Codependents are forced to hide their feelings, and the mental and emotional disruption is as destructive to the codependent as alcohol is to the abuser (Hogg and Frank 1992).

A child of an alcoholic mother learned to ignore her feelings and hide the secret of her mother's alcoholism and later married a man who abused alcohol and drugs. "He filled my needs as a codependent—I needed to be needed, and he needed me." Even after her husband got off drugs, she continued her codependent behavior until she went into therapy ("Codependency" 1989).

Figure 13.3
The process of becoming codependent.

The process of becoming codependent, according to Dr. Gary Jorgensen (1990), starts with the situation where someone becomes a victim of a problem drinker. People can become victims in alcoholic families or relationships if they are physically or emotionally abused, resulting in their losing their sense of self-worth. Victims form some core beliefs, such as "I must have done something to have caused my parents/partner to drink." A filtering process then occurs through conscious and unconscious thought, which is a product of family, genetics, temperament, and culture. After the filtering process, the codependent emerges thinking, "Anger is not okay." The codependent subsequently withdraws and is not directly angry with the person but might "act out" in other ways. Victims become anxious and form beliefs like "If I just show love, then he/she will be okay" and "I feel secure when I don't confront him/her. If I pray hard enough, God will deal with it." The final stage of codependency is when the codependent person becomes an enabler and thinks, "I will dance all around the behavior but never deal with it." Figure 13.3 shows this process.

Life is miserable for the person who has become trapped in a situation that, without confrontation and disruption, will not be solved. Help groups are available for codependents. If local groups can't be found, the national group Codependents Anonymous can be reached in Phoenix, Arizona, at (602) 944–0141.

codependency
A condition in which people who are in a relationship with a problem drinker or alcoholic are so entrapped by love and concern for the person that they lose their own identities in the process of trying to help.

Enabling and Codependency

Directions

If you have a close relationship with someone who, in your opinion, has an alcohol problem, then respond to the following statements. Circle the number of the response that most accurately describes your actions when you are with the person.

	Never	Sometimes	Frequently
1. I confront the person with his/her drinking problems.	2	1	0
2. I have to hide my real feelings around this person.	0	1	2
3. I know in advance of being with this person whether I will be loved or abused.	2	1	0
4. I feel like I am the cause of this person's drinking problem.	0	1	2
5. I cover for this person when he/she is drinking.	0	1	2

Scoring

Total the number of points circled.

Interpretation

0–1 points	You are probably not in a dysfunctional relationship with this person.
2–4 points	You are likely having some problems in this relationship as it pertains to his/her drinking. Read the section on enabling and codependency in this chapter, and you may need to seek some professional help.
5 or more	You are likely in a dysfunctional relationship with this person, either through enabling or as a codependent. You should seek counseling to help you in this relationship.

ENABLING

Enabling can be positive or negative. In the positive sense, support or skills can enable or help a person to succeed. In the negative sense, **enabling** means to help a person continue with abusive or dysfunctional behavior—such as abusing alcohol. "Enabling systems consist of that constellation of ideas, feelings, attitudes, and behaviors that unwittingly allow and/or encourage alcohol problems to continue or worsen by preventing the alcohol abuser from experiencing the consequences of his or her condition" (Anderson 1988). The enabler covers for the person by making excuses for his or her not attending parties, or not showing up at school or work. The enabler does not confront the person directly about the problem, thinking that in some way the problem will go away. However, disease prevention models show that growth occurs through the process of experiencing disruption or adversity, becoming disorganized, and, after that experience, acquiring more coping and protective skills than before the disruption. Enabling overprotects the addict from disruptions and confrontations; by shielding the addict from these challenges to growth, the enabler facilitates the addict's continuation of problem drinking.

The only way to help an alcoholic person you care about is to help them receive help. As a codependent or an enabler, you do not help the person. It is important to take a stand, confront the person, and not allow the behavior to continue. The result will be disruptive, and it is likely to be the only real way to help.

WHILE WAITING FOR THE RIGHT TIME TO HELP

Perhaps you have been close to someone who drinks too much. The following "dos" and "don'ts" might enable you to better handle such a situation (Department of Health, Education, and Welfare 1976).

Do

Remain calm, unemotional, and honest when talking to the drinker.

Let the drinker know you are learning about alcoholism.

Discuss the situation with someone you trust.

Maintain a healthy home environment.

Encourage new interests for the drinker.

Be patient: Live one day at a time.

Try to accept setbacks and relapses.

Refuse to drink with the drinker when he or she has been drinking.

---

enabling

A constellation of ideas, feelings, attitudes, and behaviors that unwittingly allow and/or encourage alcohol problems to continue or worsen by preventing the alcohol abuser from experiencing the consequences of his or her drinking behavior.

Don't

Punish, threaten, bribe, or preach.

Be a martyr.

Make excuses for the drinker.

Take over the drinker's responsibilities, leaving her or him with no sense of importance.

Hide bottles.

Argue with the drinker while he or she is drunk.

Drink along with the drinker.

Accept guilt for the other's behavior.

CHILDREN OF ALCOHOLICS

When children live with one or more alcoholics, they find themselves living in a chaotic household with rules that are never stable, hiding from parents who are episodically abusive and loving, riding with drunk drivers, and having no one to talk to about the horrid situation. These children are sometimes forced to run households in these dysfunctional families. One **child of an alcoholic (COA),** who was essentially robbed of his childhood, commented, "I grew up in a little Vietnam. I didn't know why I was there, and I didn't know who the enemy was" ("Alcohol and the Family" 1988). COAs learn to trust no one, and they don't learn how to experience joy.

When COAs grow up to become adult children of alcoholics (ACOAs), they tend to have the following characteristics (from J. G. Woititz, *Adult Children of Alcoholics,* quoted in "Alcohol and the Family" 1988). They

1. guess what normal behavior is
2. have difficulty following a project from beginning to end
3. lie when it would be just as easy to tell the truth
4. have difficulty having fun
5. overreact to changes over which they have no control
6. constantly seek approval and affirmation
7. feel that they are different from other people
8. are super-responsible or super-irresponsible
9. are extremely loyal even in the face of evidence that the loyalty is undeserved
10. tend to lock themselves into a course of action without giving consideration to consequences
11. judge themselves without mercy
12. have difficulty with intimate relationships
13. take themselves very seriously

The chances of an ACOA's becoming an alcoholic is 40 to 60 percent. Many ACOAs function extremely well and are

---

children of alcoholics (COAs)
People who grew up in dysfunctional families in which one or both parents were alcoholics.

PERSONAL SKILLS AND EXPERIENCES

PNI Action

Psychoneuroimmunology is the study of the interaction of the mind, the central nervous system, and the body's immunological system. It has been shown that people with a fighting spirit, optimism, hope, and faith can actually build their immune systems. Alcohol, on the other hand, has been shown to suppress many activities of the immune system. It makes AIDS patients more prone to infection, as it does with most people. It has been linked with poor nutritional practices (Roselle 1992). The PNI action is clear: Don't drink irresponsibly if you want to fortify your immune system and ward off disease. The highs and lows of alcohol result in a lack of hope, of optimism, of the fighting spirit, and of other positive mental health traits that help to fortify the immune system. Again: Either don't drink, or drink responsibly.

resilient in spite of their upbringing. Those who do survive are aware of their heritage and ensure that they do not develop a problem with alcohol, often by completely abstaining from alcohol. If you need help and can't locate a group locally, you can contact Adult Children of Alcoholics in Torrance, California, by calling (213) 534–1815.

If you drink responsibly, alcohol might never cause you any problems. But the precautions cited in this chapter are very important to consider when you take a drink.

TAKE ACTION

1. Reduce or stop your drinking. If you need to, seek professional help.

2. Drive with extreme caution, using defensive skills, when people might be abusing alcohol (e.g., after athletic events, on New Year's Eve). Don't drive if you've been drinking.

3. When hosting social events where alcohol is used, assure that all guests have a means of returning home safely. Deemphasize alcohol, or don't serve it at all; provide soft drinks and low-salt, high-protein foods.

4. Help someone else shake an addiction to alcohol, and do not enable their behavior. This might require confrontation and conflict.

5. Improve your refusal skills and increase your own self-confidence, self-esteem, and social problem-solving skills, and keep your purposes in life in focus. If your social group drinks alcohol, consider changing to groups that focus on something else, like productive service or natural ways of having fun. Spend more time with people who give you uplifts and enhance your strengths. Do some mental imagery to mentally rehearse saying no and to deepen your self-esteem and sense of well-being.

SUMMARY

1. There are 10 to 18 million alcoholics in the United States.

2. Drinking has slightly declined in the United States, due to the efforts of numerous organizations.

3. Ethyl alcohol is a depressant.

4. Alcohol is metabolized, mostly by the liver, at the rate of one drink per hour.

5. The number of drinks it takes to become an irresponsible drinker is determined by estimating blood alcohol concentration.

6. Negative physiological effects of excessive alcohol intake include brain disorders, cirrhosis, heart failure, and malnutrition.

7. Alcohol can cause both psychological and physiological dependence.

8. Tolerance is a condition in which it takes increasingly larger amounts of alcohol to produce the same effects previously felt at lower levels of alcohol intake.

9. Responsible drinking includes personal commitment and monitoring, helping others, responsible hosting, responsible serving, and being a responsible guest.

10. Problem drinking is repeated use of alcohol that causes physical, psychological, or social harm to the drinker or to others.

11. Alcoholism is a treatable disease, a condition in which people have so lost control over their drinking that they are consistently unable to refrain from drinking or to stop drinking before becoming intoxicated.

12. Enabling (in the negative sense) helps a person to continue or worsen an alcohol problem by preventing the alcohol abuser from experiencing the consequences of his or her behavior.

13. Codependency is a condition in which people are so entrapped by the love and concern they have for the abuser that they lose their own identities in the process of trying to help.

COMMITMENT ACTIVITIES

1. Alcohol use and social activities tend to go hand in hand. List your suggestions for dealing with irresponsible drinking at a university social function (if drinking is allowed at your university functions).

2. All fifty states and most communities have legislation that deals with the drinking driver. Find out what kinds of programs are available in your community for the driver convicted of a DWI (driving while intoxicated). Are there any such programs on your university campus? Work with the campus police department to develop such a program.

3. Discuss with your classmates ways to help your university community become more aware of the warning signs of potential problem drinking.

4. Visit an open meeting of Alcoholics Anonymous, Al-anon, or Ala-teen to hear a firsthand account of the problems associated with alcoholism.

5. Determine the kinds of treatment facilities available for alcoholics in your community. Invite one of the counselors to discuss treatment programs with your class.

REFERENCES

"Adverse Social Consequences of Alcohol Use and Alcoholism." 1984. In *Alcohol and Health.* Fifth Special Report to the U.S. Congress by the U.S. Department of Health and Human Services. Washington, DC.

"Alcohol and the Family." 1988. *Newsweek,* 18 January, 62–68.

"Alcohol in Perspective." *Berkeley Wellness Letter* 9, no. 5 (February): 4–7.

Anderson, G. L. 1988. *Enabling in the School Setting.* Minneapolis: Johnson Institute.

Blakeslee, A. L. 1976. *Alcoholism: A Sickness That Can Be Beaten.* New York Public Affairs Pamphlet No. 118A, 8–9.

Blane, H. T., and K. E. Leonard. 1987. *Psychological Theories of Drinking and Alcoholism.* New York: Guilford Press.

Braude, M. C., and H. M. Char. 1986. *Genetic and Biological Markers in Drug Abuse and Alcoholism.* National Institute on Drug Abuse Research Monograph, 66.

Carver, V. C., M. J. Kittleson, and V. J. Andrews. 1991. "Assessing Alcohol Consumption Attitudes of Adolescent Drinkers: Implications for Alcohol Education Programs." *Health Values* 15, no. 1:32–36.

"Codependency." 1989. *U.S. News and World Report,* 11 September.

Cohen, S. 1985. *The Substance Abuse Problems.* Vol 2. New York: Haworth Press.

Department of Health, Education, and Welfare. 1976. "Someone Close Drinks Too Much." DHEW pub. no. (ADM) 76/23. Washington, DC: Government Printing Office.

Dorozyaski, A. 1993. "Maternal Alcoholism: Grapes of Wrath." *Psychology Today,* January–February, 18.

Dusek, D. E., and D. A. Girdano. 1987. *Drugs: A Factual Account.* 4th ed. New York: Random House.

Eigen, L. E. 1991. "Alcohol Practices, Policies and Potentials of American Colleges and Universities: A White Paper." Washington, DC: U.S. Department of Health and Human Services, Office for Substance Abuse Prevention.

Farrant, M., and S. Cull-Candy. 1993. "GABA Receptors, Granule Cells and Genes." *Nature* 361, no. 6410 (28 January): 302–3.

Goldberg, J. M. 1992. "Social Host Liability for Serving Alcohol." *Trial* 28, no. 3 (March): 30–34.

Hogg, J. A., and M. L. Frank. 1992. "Toward an Interpersonal Model of Codependence and Contradependence." *Journal of Counseling and Development* 70, no. 3 (January–February): 371–76.

Jeffcoate, W. 1993. "Alcohol-induced Pseudo-Cushing's Syndrome." *The Lancet,* 341, no. 8846 (13 March): 676–77.

Jorgensen, G. Q. 1990. "Building Prevention Skills." Presentation made at the 39th School on Alcoholism and Other Drug Dependencies, University of Utah, Salt Lake City, June.

Kaplan, D. A. 1993. "Know When to Hold 'Em. Know When to Fold 'Em." *Newsweek,* 15 March.

Kinney, J., and G. Leaton. 1991. *Loosening the Grip: A Handbook of Alcohol Information.* St. Louis: Mosby Yearbook.

Labianca, D. A. 1992. "Estimation of Blood-Alcohol Concentration." *Journal of Chemical Education* 69, no. 8:628–33.

O'Brien, R., S. Cohen, G. Evans, and J. Fine. 1992. *The Encyclopedia of Drug Abuse.* 2d ed. New York: Facts on File.

Parker, D. A., and T. C. Harford. 1992. "The Epidemiology of Alcohol Consumption and Dependence Across Occupations in the U.S." *Alcohol World* 16, no. 2.

Prugh, T. 1986. "Social Host Liability: Kelly Versus Gwinnell." *Alcohol Health and Research World* (Summer): 32–35.

Robbins, S., and V. Kumar. 1987. *Basic Pathology.* Philadelphia: W. B. Saunders.

Roselle, G. A. 1992. "Alcohol and the Immune System." *Alcohol World* 16, no. 1:16–22.

Schlaadt, R. G., and T. T. Shannon. 1986. *Drugs of Choice: Current Perspectives on Drug Use.* Englewood Cliffs, NJ: Prentice Hall.

Strug, D. L., S. Priyadarsini, and M. M. Hyman. 1986. *Alcohol Interventions.* New York: Haworth Press.

U.S. Department of Health and Human Services. 1990. *Alcohol and Health.* Seventh Special Report to the U.S. Congress from the Secretary of Health and Human Services, NIAAA, Rockville, MD.

Villalbi, J. R., E. Comin, M. Mebot, and C. Murillo. 1991. "Prevalence and Determinants of Alcohol Consumption Among School Children in Barcelona, Spain." *Journal of School Health* 61, no. 3:123–26.

Woods, S. E., M. Hitchcock, and A. Meyer. 1993. "Alcoholic Hepatitis." *American Family Physician* 47, no. 5 (April): 1171–79.

ADDITIONAL READINGS

Blane, H. T., and K. E. Leonard. 1987. *Psychological Theories of Drinking and Alcoholism.* New York: Guilford Press. This book describes the many theories of alcohol abuse, with a chapter on each theory.

Edmeades, B. 1985. "Alcoholics Anonymous Celebrates Its 50th Year." *Saturday Evening Post,* July/August, 70–72, 102, 104. Gives the history and philosophy of Alcoholics Anonymous, still one of the best rehabilitation groups in the country.

Gibbons, B. 1992. "Alcohol: The Legal Drug." *National Geographic,* February, 3–35. This issue has a special section on alcohol and discusses its history and its social, physical, and emotional effects.

Johnston, J. 1991. *It's Killing Our Kids.* Dallas: Word. Jerry Johnston speaks to thousands of people each year, and this is a book that elaborates on his message. As a child of an alcoholic himself, he covers traditional topics such as codependency, the role of religion, and denial; he also tells his own story about dealing with his alcoholic mother.

Kinney, J., and G. Leaton. *Loosening the Grip: A Handbook of Alcohol Information.* St. Louis: Mosby Yearbook. A good general book about alcohol, dependence, effects on the body, medical complications, the cause of alcohol dependence, alcoholic behavior, and treatment for alcohol.

Miller, J. 1989. *Addictive Relationships: Reclaiming Your Boundaries.* Health Communications, Florida. A short book that describes the characteristics of destructive relationships and codependency and suggests approaches to confronting the problem. Suggestions on finding comfortable boundaries, degrees of involvement, and monitoring progress are provided.

CHAPTER 14

Tobacco

Healthy People 2000 Objectives

- Reduce the prevalence of cigarette smoking to no more than 15 percent of adults (a 48% decrease).

- Reduce the initiation of smoking to no more than 15 percent by age 20 (a 50% decrease).

An important decision in life is to try to keep our bodies as free from toxic substances as we possibly can. The cleaner the air, the better our bodies, minds, and souls will feel and function. We should be careful not to breathe too many gas and paint fumes or too many environmental pollutants. The air we breathe has direct access into our internal organs. Unfortunately, in today's industrial society, many of us are already forced to breathe air that contains toxins, and we have little control over this. It therefore becomes all the more important to do something about the aspects of air quality that we can control. A most devastating pollutant to our fresh air is tobacco smoke, whether it comes directly from a lighted cigarette, cigar, or pipe or from the exhalation of someone who is smoking. The optimal decision is to breathe the highest quality of air we can, to feel better, to feel invigorated, and to maintain the highest quality of health. The decision to smoke or to stay in places where there is a significant amount of tobacco smoke in the air is an important one that will be explored in this chapter.

If a new drug were to suddenly be proposed by a company for acceptance by the Food and Drug Administration, and it were shown that the drug contained some three thousand toxic chemicals, would double the risk of a fatal heart attack, would make the risk of death from chronic obstructive lung disease six times greater among users, would make the risk for dying from lung cancer ten times greater among users, and would contribute to over 300,000 deaths a year in the United States, there is little question that the drug would not be approved for consumer use. Yet those devastating effects are clearly established for tobacco smokers today. Given such common knowledge about tobacco's serious detrimental effects, it might be difficult to understand why tobacco is one of the drugs most widely used (exceeded only by caffeine and alcohol consumption) in the United States.

Because of politics and economics, we have made this deadly drug legal. You need to choose whether you will be a consumer of this legal, addictive, lethal drug. The purpose of this chapter is to make sure that your decisions about smoking and about being in smoke-filled places are based on a good understanding of the dangers of tobacco smoke.

THE NATURE OF THE TOBACCO PROBLEM

It is difficult for nonsmokers to understand why smokers start smoking. To be a smoker, we must actually learn how to smoke, because smoke inhalation by itself is not particularly pleasurable; to some of us, it is even nauseating. With practice, however, smokers learn to adjust the depth of inhalation and the frequency of puffs so that sidestream (inhaled) air and tobacco smoke are drawn into the lungs in a tolerable way. Through this "learning," a smoker's craving for nicotine (addiction) soon becomes the chemical motivation for smoking.

Nicotine can be a very deadly poison if taken in sufficient concentration; at normal smoking levels, it acts as a

Smoking, the leading cause of preventable death, causes great suffering for both smokers and their loved ones.

powerful reward, or "hook." Smokers seem to develop a level of daily nicotine consumption that they find satisfying. If they switch to a brand of cigarettes with less nicotine, they're likely to compensate by inhaling more deeply, smoking more cigarettes, or both.

Given the strong evidence for the detrimental effects of tobacco, along with the difficulty of learning how to smoke, you might think that smoking would not persist in our society, yet many Americans continue to smoke. The incidence of smoking peaked at 52 percent in 1965; it was 32 percent in 1987 and 28 percent in 1991 ("Who Dares? Smoking" 1993), and it is now just below 27 percent. Although fewer women than men smoke, the fastest growing segment of smokers is women under the age of 23. More than 80 percent of smokers start before the age of 21. Although percentages of smokers among black males (31%) and females (25%) compare closely to those for white males (28%) and females (24%), the percentages for other cultural groups are much higher. For instance, about 40 percent of Hispanic males smoke, although the percentage for Hispanic females is less (24%). Among youth, smoking prevalence among high school seniors declined from 28 percent in 1977 to 19 percent in 1987. Now, more adolescent females than males smoke (Kellie 1989).

Why Americans continue to smoke will be discussed in this chapter. Recently attention has focused on the powerfully addicting effect of nicotine, the active drug in tobacco, and how the use of tobacco is predicated on social, emotional, and spiritual forces as well. People who decide to use

For Smokers: Why Do You Smoke?

If you are a smoker, consider the following questions and answer honestly.

	Usually	Sometimes	Rarely	Never
1. Smoking (or using smokeless tobacco) helps to pick me up.	4	3	2	1
2. I like the feel of having something in my hand.	4	3	2	1
3. I only smoke (or use tobacco) when others smoke (or use it).	4	3	2	1
4. I associate smoking (or using tobacco) with pleasant or relaxing experiences.	4	3	2	1
5. When I run out of cigarettes (or smokeless tobacco), I feel an urgent need to get some more.	4	3	2	1
6. I smoke or use tobacco more when under stress.	4	3	2	1
7. Sometimes I reach for a cigarette or smokeless tobacco when I already have a cigarette lit or am already using tobacco.	4	3	2	1
8. I really like smoking (using tobacco products).	4	3	2	1
9. Smoking (using tobacco products) really keeps me going.	4	3	2	1
10. Unpacking, lighting, watching exhaled smoke (or the process of using smokeless tobacco) is part of the enjoyment of using tobacco.	4	3	2	1
11. If my friends and family didn't smoke or use tobacco products, I probably wouldn't smoke or use tobacco products.	4	3	2	1
12. I don't think I can go very long without smoking or using tobacco.	4	3	2	1
13. When angry or emotionally down, I generally smoke or use tobacco.	4	3	2	1
14. I often find myself smoking or using tobacco products and don't remember reaching for the tobacco or lighting the cigarette.	4	3	2	1

Scoring and Interpretation

Each of the following pairs of questions represents a reason for smoking or using tobacco. Total the scores for the two questions (range of 2 to 8). If you scored 7–8, then it is a strong reason why you smoke or use tobacco. If you score 5–6, then it may be a reason why you smoke. If you scored 4 or below on the two questions, it is probably not your reason for smoking or using tobacco.

Questions	Reason for Smoking/Using Tobacco
1, 9	Stimulation
2, 10	Need to handle things
3, 11	Need to fit in social
4, 8	Pleasure/enjoyment
5, 12	Addicted
6, 13	Coping
7, 14	Habit

tobacco will experience dramatic effects on their health status, and not only physically; their smoking will affect their social life, emotional nature, and occupational success.

In the United States, cigarettes were responsible for 418,690 premature deaths in 1990 by causing coronary heart disease, chronic obstructive pulmonary disease, cerebrovascular disease, other vascular and pulmonary diseases, lung cancer, other cancers, infant and neonatal deaths, lung cancers in nonsmokers, and deaths from fires caused by cigarettes (Slade 1989). Some 20 percent of all deaths in the United States were caused by smoking ("Cigarette Smoking" 1993). This translates into 1,200 deaths per day and 50 deaths per hour. C. Everett Koop, the former U.S. Surgeon General, stated:

There is no serious debate about the hazards of cigarette smoking. It is the chief avoidable cause of death in this country. It is a "disease" which each year is costing us billions of dollars in economic loss as well as much human suffering. (Koop 1986)

Tobacco's health toll is higher than that of all other addictive substances combined. About 57 million people in the United States are addicted to cigarettes, compared to about 18 million who are addicted to alcohol. Smoking costs the United States about $439 billion annually in medical expenses and lost workdays. Smoking a pack a day cuts a person's life expectancy by 6 years and adds about 18 percent to a person's medical bills.

For Smokers: How Heavily Do You Smoke?

This exercise will assess your current health status as it relates to your use of tobacco.

Directions

Keep a diary for 1 week. Record each cigarette smoked, or each time you chewed, dipped, or snuffed tobacco (number). Also indicate when you used it (time), where you were when you used it (place), what you were doing (activity), and what or who triggered the use of tobacco (prompt). A copy of the chart that follows can be wrapped around your cigarette pack or smokeless tobacco container with a rubber band to remind you to keep the record. A new chart can be attached to the pack or container each day.

Interpretation

For cigarettes: Calculate your average number of cigarettes per day for the week.

25 or more cigarettes per day	= You are a heavy smoker.
10–24 cigarettes per day	= You are a moderate smoker.
0–9 cigarettes per day	= You are a light smoker.

For smokeless tobacco: Calculate the number of chews or dips you have per day for the week.

10 or more per day	= You are a heavy user.
5–9 per day	= You are a moderate user.
0–4 per day	= You are a light user.

DAILY TOBACCO USE CHART

Number	Time	Place	Activity	Prompt

This information may not be new to you, but the chart you have completed will be helpful in quitting, as you will learn by reading this chapter.

Cigarettes have become a major international problem, fueled by American advertising. An estimated 1 billion people smoke 5 trillion cigarettes annually, resulting in 2.5 million deaths attributed to smoking. By the year 2000, the number of deaths is expected to rise to 4 million annually. While smoking rates are declining in industrialized countries at a rate of 1.5 percent per year, the rates are increasing at 2 percent per year in developing countries (Connolly 1989).

Tobacco is the most lethal commercial product sold in the United States and also the most heavily promoted. In spite of this, our government subsidizes tobacco growers more than $3 billion annually. A question we should all ponder is, What's wrong with this picture? Let's understand a little more about the physiology of smoking.

PHYSIOLOGICAL ASPECTS OF SMOKING

The negative physiological aspects of smoking are conclusive after 35 years of research and over 55,000 studies from eighty countries. Scientists now understand, for the most part, why smokers have three times the risk of sudden heart attack and 85 percent more lung cancer, and why women smokers who are pregnant have an increased risk of having premature babies, spontaneous abortions, stillbirths, and babies that live only a few hours or days (McGinnis 1987). The next sections present some of the details of the physiological effects of smoking.

The smoke from a lighted cigarette consists of a mixture of more than three thousand chemical substances that are dangerous to body tissues. These substances include tars, nicotine, and gases, such as carbon monoxide, hydrogen cyanide, and nitrogen oxide, that produce undesirable effects on health. The toxic effects of these gases and compounds with the nicotine is responsible for many cigarette-related deaths each year.

Tobacco products contain hundreds, if not thousands, of chemical additives used as flavors and fillers. No federal agency has any authority to require that these additives be disclosed or even removed if they are found to be harmful. Many of the additives used in tobacco products are suspected of being carcinogenic.

Tobacco **tar** is made up of hundreds of chemicals that together account for most of the known cancer-causing agents in cigarettes. Research has shown the tars to be carcinogenic (cancer-causing), and other chemicals in the tar to be cocarcinogens (substances that, although they do not directly cause cancer, can, in combination with other chemicals, stimulate the development of cancers).

Nicotine, an alkaloid poison, is the addictive element in tobacco. "Nicotine addiction is the most medically serious drug problem in the United States today with social, behavioral, physiologic, and pharmacologic aspects. . . . Nicotine regularly causes a true drug addiction in a high proportion of regular tobacco users" (Slade 1989). The addiction to nicotine is clear, as evidenced by the failure of nicotine-free tobacco-substitute products in the marketplace (Slade 1989).

The criteria for drug addiction used in the 1988 surgeon general's report are these:

1. There is a highly controlled or compulsive pattern of drug use.
2. Psychoactive or mood-altering effects are involved in the pattern of drug taking.
3. The drug functions as a reinforcer to strengthen behavior and lead to further drug ingestion.

Other criteria used in the report are tolerance, physical dependence, continued use despite harmful effects, pleasant (euphoric) effects, stereotypical patterns of drug use, relapses following drug abstinence, and recurrent drug cravings. All these criteria apply to nicotine addiction (Slade 1989). Nicotine's major effects on the body are cardiorespiratory stimulation and gastrointestinal hyperactivity, including irregular heart rhythms and effects on heart rate, blood pressure, cardiac output, oxygen consumption, and coronary blood flow. Nicotine, tars, and carbon monoxide are inhaled through cigarette smoking; in smokeless tobacco, nicotine is absorbed through the cheek and mouth membranes.

It is estimated that approximately 90 percent of the nicotine found in cigarettes will actually be inhaled and absorbed into the bloodstream. The body readily absorbs smoke, and some of the nicotine goes directly to the brain (Schlaadt and Shannon 1986).

Nicotine affects not only the respiratory and gastrointestinal systems, but also the brain, spinal cord, and peripheral nervous system. It can stimulate, and then depress, production of saliva, constrict the bronchi (the air passage tubes to the lungs), increase the amounts of free fatty acids in the bloodstream, and cause other effects as shown in figure 14.1.

Carbon monoxide (CO) is a deadly gas that is a by-product of burning tobacco. It is the same deadly gas that is in the automobile exhaust that pollutes the air. The reasons this gas is deadly rests in its powerful affinity to, or potential to bond with, hemoglobin. **Hemoglobin** is an iron-containing compound in red blood cells that carries oxygen to the cells of the body. There are four sites in hemoglobin where oxygen can attach to a red blood cell for the journey through the circulatory system to the cells. The fight between oxygen and

Carbon monoxide
(reduces oxygen carrying
capacity of the blood)

Tars
(carcinogens)

Nitrous oxide
(reduces the number of
white blood cells)

Additives
(suspected carcinogens)

Hydrogen cyanide
(increases nerve poison
and reduces cilia
function of lungs)

Nicotine affects the CNS
Heart rate ↑
Blood pressure ↑
Vasoconstriction ↑
Skin temperature ↓
Epinephrine release ↑
Adrenalin release ↑
Gastrointestinal tract activity ↑
Fatty acids in blood ↑
DNA synthesis of lymphocytes ↑
Physical dependence ↑
Psychological dependence ↑
Withdrawal symptoms ↑

Figure 14.1

Chemical elements and effects of tobacco smoke.

CO to attach to these sites is generally won by CO, because the CO chemical bond is two hundred times stronger than the oxygen chemical bond. The result is that the body's cells that rely on oxygen to function are deprived. Figure 14.2 demonstrates this process at the site of oxygen exchange.

Red blood cells returning from the circulatory trip to the tissues of the body have carbon dioxide (a by-product of metabolism) attached and are still carrying carbon monoxide (from the previous inhalation of smoke before the journey). At the oxygen exchange site in the lungs, the carbon dioxide and some of the carbon monoxide detach themselves from the red blood cell to be expired via the lungs. The detachments and expiration open some carrying sites on the red blood cells, and the fight between oxygen from the air and carbon monoxide from the smoke again wages.

tar
A dangerous and carcinogenic chemical constituent of tobacco smoke.

nicotine
An alkaloid poison; the addictive drug that is in tobacco.

carbon monoxide
A deadly gas that is a by-product of burning tobacco.

hemoglobin
An iron-containing compound in red blood cells that transports oxygen to the cells.

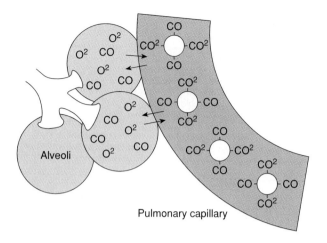

Figure 14.2

Exchange of oxygen and carbon monoxide.

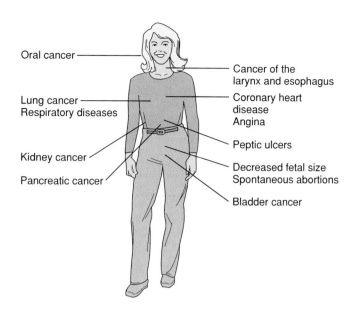

Figure 14.3

Diseases and disorders closely associated with tobacco use.

The result of this reduced supply of oxygen to the brain is impaired judgment, reducing the performance of a driver, a student on an exam, or an athlete in competition. Carbon monoxide can also lead to disturbances in rhythmic activity of the heart and promote atherosclerosis. When smoking is stopped, oxygen uptake improves soon after. Energy levels will return after a few months.

Carbon monoxide is particularly devastating to the unborn fetus of pregnant mothers. The CO is supplied to the fetus from the mother's blood, which travels through the umbilical cord and into the fetus's circulatory system. The result can be lower birth weight, premature delivery, and a greater risk of sudden infant death syndrome (crib death).

SMOKING AND DISEASE

Smoking tobacco negatively affects most of the systems of the body. Harmful toxins and cancer-producing agents can create problems in the heart, lungs, and many other vital organs.

DISEASES OF THE HEART AND BLOOD VESSELS

Coronary heart disease, a disease of the arteries that nourish the heart muscle, is the chief contributor to excess deaths in the cigarette-smoking population. Smokers have severe and extensive narrowing of the coronary arteries, which can lead to heart attack. Smoking is not only one of the three major risk factors for heart attack, but also a major risk factor for cardiovascular diseases affecting the peripheral blood vessels, vessels that constitute the circulatory system (Schlaadt and Shannon 1986).

Smoking also increases the possibility of recurrent heart attack and tends to lower the threshold for the onset of **angina,** the chest pain associated with heart disease. Women who smoke and use oral contraceptives increase their risk of heart attack, blood clots, and brain hemorrhaging (figure 14.3).

CANCER

The risk of developing lung cancer is ten times greater for cigarette smokers than for nonsmokers. The percentage of people with lung cancer has been increasing for several decades, and lung cancer is now the number one cause of cancer deaths.

Lung cancer risks for both sexes increase proportionately to the number of cigarettes smoked, the length of time people smoke, the age at which they started, and the amount they inhale (depth of inhalation). The tar and nicotine content of the cigarette smoked also affects lung cancer risk by irritating the lung tissue.

Other types of cancer caused by cigarette smoking include cancers of the larynx, esophagus, bladder, kidney, pancreas, and mouth. Using alcohol and cigarettes together tends to increase the incidence of laryngeal and esophageal cancer (American Cancer Society 1993).

RESPIRATORY DISEASE

Cigarette smoking slows down the action of the cilia in the lungs. The **cilia** are hairlike projections that help clean the lungs. When these cilia are immobilized, dust and dirt particles

---

angina

Chest pain associated with heart disease; can be brought on by smoking.

cilia

Hairlike processes, as in the bronchi, that move mucus, pus, and dust particles upward and out.

PERSONAL INSIGHT

A Victim of Tobacco Smoking

At the young age of 10 years old, Joyce went out with a group of her friends and found a pack of cigarettes that someone had apparently dropped. The girls got some matches and had their first smokes. Joyce didn't like it at first but continued to smoke. She smoked through junior high and through high school. She got married shortly after high school to a smoker, and they began their life together. Joyce had two children. At 35 years of age, Joyce had a persistent cough and sore throat. When she visited her doctor, she learned that she had cancer in her mouth and upper throat. She also

noticed that she had trouble breathing, and the tests revealed that cancer had gone to her lungs. Joyce went in for surgery, and one of her lungs was removed, along with much of her upper throat and mouth. The remaining lung was black from all the smoke over the years of smoking, but it still worked. In order for Joyce to breathe following her operation, a stoma (hole) was cut into her throat. She couldn't talk or eat normally. Cigarettes had taken half her lung, so walking was laborious, it had taken her voice, and she had to breathe through a hole in her throat. She knew that cigarettes had done this to her and she lamented it greatly. Upon visiting Joyce in the hospital, one of her dear friends who had tried to

help her quit smoking for years was shocked to see her continuing to smoke by placing the cigarette in the hole in her throat and making a seal around it. The addiction to nicotine was so powerful that she continued in spite of the fact that she knew she would die if she continued. She continued to smoke two packs a day through the stoma in her throat. Joyce died within 6 months after the operation. Joyce's husband, seeing what had happened to the woman he loved and feeling the responsibility of taking care of his children, realized that he was living the same suicidal pattern and, after a couple of attempts, finally quit smoking.

can cause lung inflammation and disease, even early in life; so children of parents who smoke are more likely to contract bronchitis and pneumonia during infancy and childhood.

Cigarette smokers also have more chronic coughs, phlegm production, wheezing, and other respiratory symptoms. Both men and women smokers tend to report more acute and chronic **bronchitis** (inflammation of the bronchi), **sinusitis** (inflammation of the sinus), and **emphysema.** Chronic smoking also leads to tissue changes in the respiratory tract. People with allergies, especially asthma, are more sensitive than other people to cigarette smoke.

DIGESTIVE DISEASE

Cigarette smoking is also associated with the incidence of stomach ulcer, or **peptic ulcer,** and increased risk of dying from this disease; smoking also tends to slow down the healing of peptic ulcers (Schlaadt and Shannon 1986).

GENDER AND CULTURAL VIEWS

We have been talking about the effects of smoking in general. There are some unique perspectives on smoking when we focus on African Americans and women.

AFRICAN AMERICANS AND SMOKING

Blacks might have a better perspective on smoking, as a group, than whites do. In a study by Royce (1993), it was reported that blacks, in comparison to whites,

1. had a stronger desire to quit smoking, and more serious attempts at quitting smoking in the past year,

2. had more favorable attitudes toward restrictions on access to tobacco,

3. were more likely to prohibit smoking in their cars, and

4. were more likely to see cigarette use as a problem in the community.

It was also reported in this study that blacks were more likely than whites to smoke within the first 10 minutes of awakening, which might mean that, for blacks, nicotine dependence is significant enough to make quitting very difficult even for lighter smokers.

WOMEN AND SMOKING

Women who smoke, like men who smoke, are at risk for cardiovascular disease, stroke, lung cancer, and chronic obstructive lung disease, but they have additional risks related to reproductive functions and osteoporosis. Approximately one in ten women will develop breast cancer. Smoking during pregnancy has an adverse effect on the well-being of the

bronchitis
Inflammation of the bronchial tubes in the lungs.

sinusitis
Inflammation of the sinuses.

emphysema
A chronic disease of the lungs that affects the air sacs, causes breathlessness, and can lead to death.

peptic ulcer
An ulcer in the stomach area.

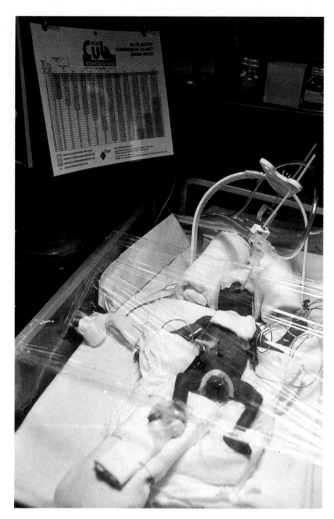

Smoking during pregnancy has adverse effects on the developing fetus and can lead to premature birth and complications during birth.

developing fetus. Smoking can reduce the size of the newborn; in fact, babies born to smoking mothers are on the average 200 grams (approximately 7 ounces) lighter than those born to nonsmoking mothers. Smoking mothers are also more likely to have a premature baby (who would also weigh much less than a full-term baby).

Smoking mothers have more complications than nonsmoking mothers during pregnancy; they have more spontaneous abortions, and the death of the unborn child is more likely. The mothers themselves also have more complications, including hemorrhaging and improperly developed placentas.

The more a woman smokes, the greater the risk to both herself and her child. Children of smoking mothers tend to have deficiencies after birth as well; physical growth, intellectual development, and emotional development may be affected for several years (Dusek and Girdano 1987).

Additionally, in 1986 the rate for lung cancer mortality reached that of breast cancer mortality in women. In 1988, lung cancer surpassed breast cancer as the leading cause of

cancer deaths in women, an outcome of increased smoking in women over the last few decades. The rate of lung cancer is twelve times higher for women who smoke than for nonsmoking women. Smoking also accounts for 41 percent of all coronary heart disease in women under age 65 (Kellie 1989).

OTHER FORMS OF TOBACCO USE

People consume tobacco in forms other than cigarettes. In this section we will discuss clove cigarettes, pipe and cigar smoking, and smokeless tobacco.

CLOVE CIGARETTES

Indonesian **clove cigarettes** were introduced in the United States about 1980, when surfers became acquainted with them in Australia. They became popular with "punk rockers" and "new wave" musicians. Their street name is *kreteks*, and they are sold under brand names like Jakarta, Kretek, Djarum, Pompa, and Garam. By 1985 kreteks were being sold in tobacco shops and specialty shops in every state. Kreteks contain about 60 percent tobacco and about 40 percent ground cloves. Some states have now enacted laws to ban all sales of the product. Scientific studies on the kretek are quite limited, but kreteks contain twice the tar and nicotine of most U.S. cigarettes because of the coarser and more potent tobacco. Reports of death, acute respiratory problems, and coughing up blood have surfaced from hospitals admitting kretek-using teenagers (Bailey and Lamarine 1986).

PIPE AND CIGAR SMOKING

Although the risk of lung cancer is less with pipe and cigar smokers, because the smoke usually is not inhaled into the lungs, there is still a significant risk of other problems. The increased health risks from pipe and cigar smoking include cancer of the lip, mouth, larynx, and esophagus. Because some of the tars are swallowed, there is also an increased risk of stomach cancer and urinary bladder cancer.

SMOKELESS TOBACCO

Smokeless tobacco is sold in three forms—snuff, loose leaf, and plug. Chewing tobacco may be packaged as loose-leaf tobacco, which is sold in a pouch. The user places the tobacco between the cheek and gum, and tobacco juice and saliva are expectorated. Chewing tobacco also can be found as plug tobacco, which is a solid brick form of tobacco. The user cuts

clove cigarettes
Sometimes called "kreteks," these contain about 60 percent tobacco, 40 percent ground cloves, and about twice the amount of tar and nicotine as most U.S. cigarettes.

smokeless tobacco
Tobacco that is used orally. It comes in snuff, looseleaf, and plug forms.

All the advertising in the world can't change the reality that the use of smokeless tobacco is a dirty and disgusting habit.

off a piece with a knife and chews it. **Snuff** is a finely ground tobacco sold in circular cans; it is usually placed between the cheek and gum ("dipping") or placed on the back of the hand and sniffed through the nose. Television and magazine advertisements have made smokeless tobacco falsely appear to be a healthy alternative to the smoking of tobacco. The advertisements also present a macho image of tobacco-chewing cowboys and athletes. Advertisements have made headway into social acceptance of smokeless tobacco in some settings where at one time it was considered to be a dirty, disgusting habit. The advertising success has resulted in a 52 percent increase in sales of smokeless tobacco since 1978. Most estimates are that 7 to 11 million Americans are using smokeless tobacco, though some estimates are as high as 22 million.

The reality is that chewing tobacco is a dirty habit, necessitating frequent expectorating (spitting) of the mixture of tobacco juice and saliva. It is also an unhealthy practice. Although smokeless tobacco does not produce the effects of carbon monoxide, tar, and other gases associated with cigarette smoking, it does have the following harmful effects (American Cancer Society 1993; Marty et al. 1986; McDermott and Marty 1986; Brubaker and Loftin 1987):

1. There is damage to the soft and hard oral (mouth) tissues.
2. There are excessive abrasions of tooth surfaces caused by abrasive grits in tobacco.
3. Smokeless tobacco contains nitrosonornicotine, a known cancer-producing agent.
4. There is an increase in heart rate and blood pressure.
5. Nicotine is absorbed into the body through the buccal mucosa (inner lining of the cheek) of snuff dippers and can produce cancers.

6. Dipping and chewing tobacco are also associated with the development of leukoplakia, which is a disease manifested by thick, white, irregular patches on the inner cheek, tongue, and other parts of the mouth in regular users. Leukoplakia often evolves into squamous cell carcinomas (malignant skin tumors).
7. Smokeless tobacco has been linked to suppressed immunological responses, which reduce the ability to ward off disease.
8. Use increases the number of dental caries.
9. Use is associated with gingival (gums) inflammation.
10. Infants born to mothers who used smokeless tobacco during pregnancy have decreased birth size.
11. Use is associated with cancers of the pharynx, esophagus, urinary bladder, and pancreas.
12. Use causes the teeth to darken and results in bad breath.

Regular use of smokeless tobacco can result in psychological addiction. Many people seek professional help in an attempt to quit using it. Addicted users of smokeless tobacco claim it helps them cope with problems, helps them perform better, and gives them a lift. Stopping use results in cravings and restlessness that many have described as being more difficult than the withdrawal symptoms associated with quitting cigarette smoking.

PSYCHOLOGICAL AND SOCIAL ASPECTS OF SMOKING

More and more smokers acknowledge the dangers and risks attributed to smoking and yet do not change their behavior. Even though almost all adolescents know the dangers today, approximately 19 percent of them smoke. Psychological influences seem to account for this early experimentation. Young people start because of rebellion, curiosity, peer pressure, and the belief that smoking makes one "grown up." The most common age for starting smoking is age 10 (fifth grade); for starting using smokeless tobacco, it is seventh grade. But the most intensive tobacco use prevention and education programs in the schools are in the tenth grade (Chen et al. 1991).

Family patterns influence teenagers' smoking behavior. Fewer smokers come from "intact" homes (where both a father and a mother are members of the household) than from homes where one or both parents are not present. Smoking practices of other family members, both parents

snuff
A type of tobacco that is inhaled through the nostrils, chewed, or placed against the gums.

For Nonsmokers: What Is Your Risk of Becoming a Smoker?

1. Circle all of the following that describe you.
   a. I used to smoke but quit over a year ago.
   b. I never smoked.
   c. I used to smoke but quit less than a year ago.
   d. My grades recently had a sudden decline.

   e. I recently went through a divorce or my parents recently went through a divorce.
   f. I have recently seen an increase in the amount of stress in my life.

Circle the appropriate response.

	Strongly Agree	Agree	Not Sure	Disagree	Strongly Disagree
2. The thought of smoking appeals to me.	5	4	3	2	1
3. My friends/family want me to start smoking.	5	4	3	2	1
4. The thought of dipping or chewing tobacco appeals to me.	5	4	3	2	1
5. My friends or family want me to start dipping or chewing tobacco.	5	4	3	2	1
6. I think smoking or using tobacco would help me cope better with my problems.	5	4	3	2	1
7. I want to start smoking but don't dare.	5	4	3	2	1
8. Smoke makes me nauseated.	1	2	3	4	5
9. Dipping or chewing tobacco is disgusting.	1	2	3	4	5
10. I like to chew or suck on things.	5	4	3	2	1
11. Smoking really doesn't hurt people.	5	4	3	2	1

Scoring

Total your points for questions 2 through 11.

Interpretation

Attitudes About Smoking
Interpret your total points for questions 2 through 11 as follows:

44 or higher	=	Your attitudes strongly incline you toward smoking.
23 to 43	=	Your attitudes do not incline you either toward or away from smoking.
22 or less	=	Your attitudes strongly incline you away from smoking.

Scoring high on this scale means that you should be careful to use healthy approaches to coping with life's stressors. Learn about stress management, nurture your personal strengths, and get support from family and friends.

Your Risk of Starting to Smoke
The following suggests your risk of starting to smoke (or of returning to being a smoker). If this scale indicates that you have a high or moderate risk, you should strongly resist smoking opportunities.

You have a high risk:	If on question 1 you selected *c* in combination with *d, e,* or *f* and you scored 40 or higher on the attitude scale.
You have a moderate risk:	If on question 1 you selected *a* in combination with *d, e,* or *f* and you scored 40 or higher on the attitude scale.
You have a low risk:	If on question 1 you selected *b* in combination with *d, e,* or *f* and you scored below 30 on the attitude scale.

Note: Over 90 percent of those who become regular smokers do so by the time they are 20 years of age. If you have never smoked, then you have likely learned to cope in other ways and are not likely to begin smoking. Please don't start and become one of the unfortunate 10 percent.

and older siblings, heavily influence teenagers. If both a parent and an older sibling smoke, that teenager is much more likely to smoke (Schlaadt and Shannon 1986).

Peer relationships and educational aspirations are also important. Adolescents who smoke generally have friends who smoke. Those who do not smoke seem to associate with nonsmokers, and those who plan to go to college have lower smoking rates than those who do not.

Until recently more boys than girls smoked, but now more girls than boys smoke. This may be due to how advertisers depict the changing sex roles in our society. For example, the slogan "You've come a long way, baby" is used in tobacco advertising to associate women's liberation with smoking.

Regardless of why people start, they tend to continue to smoke because they are accustomed to smoking in many situations and during many activities. The smoking habit becomes part of the daily routine. Watch the "chain reaction" that takes place when several smokers are sitting around a table and one person starts to smoke. Also, watch the way a smoker "lights up": Practically every movement is ritualistic. Learning these habits results in the constant desire for a cigarette during relaxing times, during boring times, during stressful times. It is particularly difficult for longtime smokers to quit, even though they understand the risks to their health.

If people are going to smoke during their lifetime, most will be smoking by the time they are 20 years old. Many start experimenting around the age of 12 for various reasons. They try to look older, they copy their parents, they are persuaded by their peers, the cigarettes feel good in their mouths (oral gratification reduces tension), or they develop an addiction very quickly.

Studies have shown that smokers more often have an external locus of control, that is, they are generally influenced by others around them (peers, advertisements, and heroes). Smokers tend to be more sensitive to stress and lack good coping skills. Smokers as a whole have lower self-esteem, are more insecure, have less self-confidence, and, as young smokers, tend to be alienated somewhat from society. This alienation is obvious from the fact that smoking by young people in schools is generally against the school rules, and it labels them as rule breakers (Dusek and Girdano 1987).

PASSIVE SMOKING

Passive smoking (sometimes called **involuntary smoking**) occurs when a nonsmoker breathes air that has been partially saturated by sidestream smoke. **Sidestream smoke** is the smoke that comes directly from the lit cigarette or from a smoker's exhalation that still contains the negative elements of tobacco smoke.

As many as 53,000 nonsmokers die each year from diseases caused by inhaling smoke released into the air by tobacco products (Heath and Glantz 1993). The 1986 surgeon general's report contained the following conclusions (Koop 1986):

1. Passive smoking is a cause of disease, including cancer, in healthy nonsmokers.
2. Children of parents who smoke, compared with the children of nonsmoking parents, have an increased frequency of respiratory symptoms and slightly smaller rates of increase in lung function as the lung matures.

The reason the surgeon general reached these conclusions is that one cigarette has been shown to release 70 milligrams of cancer-producing **particulate matter** (nongas) into the air and 25 milligrams of carbon monoxide. A smoke-filled room reaches 80 parts per million of smoke, which is considered hazardous to health by the Environmental Protection Agency (Dusek and Girdano 1987). McGinnis (1987) noted that sidestream smoke contains two and one-half times the amount of carbon monoxide that is in smoke inhaled directly from the cigarette by the smoker, and 70 percent more tar.

Additionally, it has been shown that for women who smoke during pregnancy, the growth of the fetus will be somewhat retarded. But it has also been shown that pregnant women who passively smoke will also have lower-birth-weight children (Zhang and Ratcliffe 1993).

Because sidestream smoke is dangerous and many people are very allergic to cigarette smoke, nonsmokers' demands have resulted in nonsmoking sections in public restaurants, smoke-free airlines, and nonsmoking rooms in hotels. The National Interagency Council on Smoking and Health has suggested a Nonsmokers Bill of Rights that includes the following rights that nonsmokers can claim to help protect everyone's health, comfort, and safety.

1. The right to breathe clean air. Nonsmokers have the right to breathe clean air, free from harmful and irritating tobacco smoke. This right supersedes the right to smoke when the two conflict.
2. The right to speak out. Nonsmokers have the right to express firmly, but politely, their discomfort and adverse

involuntary smoking (passive smoking)
Involuntarily inhaling smoke in the air from a person nearby who is smoking.

sidestream smoke
Smoke that comes directly from the source—such as a cigarette, cigar, or pipe or a smoker's exhalation—and still contains the negative elements of tobacco smoke.

particulate matter
Minute, harmful substances in cigarette smoke.

What Is Your Risk of Passive Smoking?

Directions

Circle any of the following

1. Circle any of the following situations where you associate indoors with people who smoke in your presence.
   a. Where I live
   b. At work
   c. At parties, social events, and clubs
   d. At school
   e. At my social or service organization meetings
   f. Other indoor activities
   g. No situations

For questions 2 through 4, consider the following reactions:

   a. I would allow them to smoke, even though I didn't want them to.
   b. I would allow them to smoke, because I wouldn't mind.
   c. I would ask them politely not to smoke, but not insist if they persisted.
   d. I would ask them politely not to smoke, and if they persisted, I would insist that they not smoke.
   e. I would demand that they not smoke.
   f. If a person persisted in smoking, I would leave or move.

Indicate which of the reactions you would have in the following situations:

2. A friend or family member asks if he or she can smoke in my house/room or car.
   a   b   c   d   e   f
3. A person I do not know very well asks if he or she can smoke in my room/house or car.
   a   b   c   d   e   f
4. In a nonsmoking section of a public place such as a restaurant or airplane, a person begins smoking.
   a   b   c   d   e   f

Scoring

Assign your answers the following points, then total your score.

Question 1:	*a, b,* or *d* =	3 points
	c, e, or *f* =	1 point
	g =	0 points
Questions 2, 3, and 4:	*d, e,* or *f* =	0 points
	c =	1 point
	a or *b* =	3 points

Interpretation

If your points total 10 or more, then you are likely being exposed to chronic sidestream smoke. If your points total is less than 3, then you are probably free of chronic excessive sidestream smoke.

---

reactions to tobacco smoke. They have the right to voice their objection when smokers light up without asking permission.

3. The right to act. Nonsmokers have the right to take action through legislative channels, social pressure, or any other legitimate means as individuals or groups to prevent or discourage smokers from polluting the atmosphere and to seek the restriction of smoking in public places.

FIGHTING THE TOBACCO WAR

A very difficult part of the "drug war" is fighting nicotine addiction. Many states rely on tobacco as a cash agricultural product, and many jobs are at stake in the growing, processing, manufacturing, and advertising of tobacco. This legal drug is creating more medical problems than any other drug in the drug war. This section will help the reader understand the power of the tobacco industry and cite some strategies in fighting the drug battle.

TOBACCO ADVERTISING

Tobacco advertising is a $2.8 billion business every year that focuses on specific populations, particularly youth, women, and cultural groups, in addition to the international market in developing countries. Since advertising on radio and

television was banned, advertising has become even more subtle. Cigarettes get better exposure in films than before. Philip Morris paid $350,000 to have Lark cigarettes prominently featured in *License to Kill*, a James Bond movie, and $42,000 for Lois Lane to smoke Marlboro cigarettes in *Superman II*. Cigarette advertisements still show up on television, with cigarette companies sponsoring sports events (e.g., the Virginia Slims tournaments) and cigarette ads on billboards at ball games, on cars in racing events, and so on.

The American Medical Association and other public health organizations have recommended a complete ban on cigarette advertisement. The tobacco industry argues that this type of ban would restrict free speech under the First Amendment. The U.S. Supreme Court ruled in 1975 that commercial advertisement is protected under the First Amendment. The ruling allowed state governments to regulate commercial speech and restrict the sale of hazardous products (Gostin and Brandt 1993). This is a real dilemma for our society.

The cigarette companies have employed a variety of tactics to promote sales of cigarettes in light of restrictive advertising laws. One ploy is to own several other companies with more acceptable products as a cover. It is difficult to boycott a tobacco company that also provides us with peanuts, beverages, candy, and cereals. For example, Philip Morris produces Marlboro, Merit, Benson & Hedges, Players, Virginia Slims, and Parliament, but also owns the Seven-Up Company,

Issue

Smoking in Public Places

Public opinion against smoking is on the increase, and smokers face several social and legal restrictions (Clark 1992). Many states and communities have issued rulings against smoking in public places.

- Pro: Anti-smoking groups feel that smokers pollute the environment with several toxic chemicals and that passive smoking presents significant risk to nonsmokers' health. They feel that smokers willing to quit should be provided with social and medical support. Those that are not willing to quit should be prohibited from endangering the lives of others (Leichtman and Merryman 1992). These nonsmoking groups feel that the rulings for public places are justified, as they are made for the good of all and passed by a majority. They protect all of us, including smokers, from the hazards of smoke-filled air. Nonsmokers in particular should not have their health penalized by the irresponsible actions of others.

- Con: Smoking groups feel that the ban on smoking will be unfair to the smokers, as research on effects of secondhand smoking is inconclusive (Leichtman and Merryman 1992). To regulate noncriminal behavior is to infringe on individual rights. To prosecute people for smoking in public is as ridiculous as it would be to prosecute a restaurant owner for having an open-air restaurant where people were forced to sit in the sun and therefore risked skin cancer. Regulating smoking behavior is like regulating sexual behavior—impossible and inappropriate.

What is the best solution to the problem of smoking in public places?

Issue

Advertising Smoking

Cigarette companies have spent billions of dollars linking cigarettes with the values and trends of the times. Young-looking models in the ads represent what every teenager wants to become. The subliminal, magical message of the ads is "If you smoke, you'll be popular, handsome/beautiful, and alive with pleasure." The companies even sponsor tennis tournaments, auto races, bowling championships, jazz festivals, and horse races. They are spending even more money on advertising and promoting cigarettes than they were before radio and television cigarette advertising was banned in 1971.

- Pro: Any company should have the right to advertise its product, provided it is not illegal to sell the product. It is not the government's right to interfere with this aspect of free enterprise. Individuals must decide for themselves whether to take any notice of the advertisements. We should not attempt to legislate good sense.

- Con: Each day more evidence is brought forward demonstrating that cigarette smoking is dangerous to our health. More and more people are attempting to give up smoking. There is no provable benefit observed from the habit of smoking. Tobacco companies should not be permitted to persuade people, particularly young people, to do something that is bad for their health just so the company can make a profit.

Should all types of cigarette advertising be banned?

General Foods (Post cereals), Kool-Aid, Jello products, Oscar Mayer Meats, Country Time, Good Seasons dressings, Minute Rice, Birds Eye, Tang, Log Cabin syrups, and others. R. J. Reynolds Tobacco Company, which produces Camel, Winston, Salem, Sterling, Bright, Doral, Winchester, and nine other brands of cigarettes, also owns Kentucky Fried Chicken, Canada Dry, Hawaiian Punch, Nabisco Brands, Life Savers, Planters Nuts, Blue Bonnet margarine, and many others. The other tobacco companies—Brown & Williamson Tobacco, Liggett Group, Lorillard, American Tobacco Company, U.S. Tobacco Company, and Culbro, Inc.—also own food companies, beverage companies, insurance companies, department stores, restaurants, and other businesses ("Tobacco Industry Conglomerates" 1986).

In 1991, Philip Morris spent some $60 million promoting a nationwide tour of the historic document the Bill of Rights. The implication is that smoking is a constitutionally protected right. People were left with a positive association between patriotism (which was heightened following the Persian Gulf war), rights of the people, and Philip Morris cigarettes. Local coalitions against smoking protested the tour.

Another ploy is to promote cigarettes with an image of "caring" about people. The cigarettes are presented as representing the "right of choice," yet the ads also claim to promote freedoms for nonsmokers and the hope that children will not smoke. People smoke and think, "What a nice company," while they are inhaling toxic chemicals and becoming addicted, and children are still watching older people smoke as role models of being "grown up."

One way to fight tobacco companies is to boycott the noncigarette products made by their other companies. Another strategy is to demand local legislation through boards of health to restrict access to tobacco products through limited licensing of vendors, eliminating vending machines, eliminating advertising by local stores, and keeping cigarettes behind the counters.

Tobacco liability suits might ultimately be successful. Several have been brought in recent years by individuals who

have developed major complications, such as lung cancer, from smoking. Litigation has a number of benefits for the overall effort to control the nicotine addiction epidemic. Liability suits typically claim that the plaintiff was addicted to tobacco and became addicted before the age of consent and before the legal age of sale. Although the plaintiff accepts some responsibility for smoking, the claim is that the responsibility should be shared with the tobacco company because of nicotine addiction, the inherently dangerous characteristics of the product, and the company's behavior (Slade 1989).

Cases alleging personal injuries from passive smoking are the new wave in smoking litigation. The Environmental Protection Agency has reported a link between passive smoking and lung cancer. The passage of the Americans with Disabilities Act of 1990 could mean that cigarette companies will become liable for illness and deaths attributed to passive smoking (Blum 1993). It will be interesting to see the evolution of this important legislation.

LEGAL RESTRICTIONS ON SMOKING

Nearly two-thirds of the American population report that they find it annoying to be near a person who is smoking. They believe that nonsmokers have the right to breathe air free of cigarette smoke. Governments at local, state, and national levels are attempting to intervene to help. Federal agencies regulate smoking on buses, trains, and airplanes, and some progress toward healthier air has been made in this respect. Smoking on intercontinental airline flights is now prohibited. The Interstate Commerce Commission permits smoking only in the rear 30 percent of seats on interstate buses. In trains, smoking is permitted only in designated cars. Enforcement of these regulations is not easy. If someone smokes in the nonsmoking section of the carrier, it is up to other passengers to ask the smoker to quit; if the smoker refuses to comply, the other passengers often must endure the smoke for the entire trip. The passengers may

then lodge a formal complaint, but this action does not eliminate the probability that the person will smoke illegally again in a similar situation.

Cigarette Labeling

Cigarette advertising and labeling are regulated by the Federal Trade Commission. The Federal Comprehensive Smoking Education Act is significant legislation that attempts to counteract the effects of cigarette advertising. The law requires that cigarette companies rotate the following four health warnings in conspicuous displays on cigarette packages and in their advertising (Koop 1986):

- Surgeon General's Warning: Smoking causes lung cancer, heart disease, emphysema, and may complicate pregnancy.
- Surgeon General's Warning: Quitting smoking now greatly reduces serious health risks.
- Surgeon General's Warning: Pregnant women who smoke risk fetal injury and premature birth.
- Surgeon General's Warning: Cigarette smoke contains carbon monoxide.

Organizations That Fight Smoking

Action on Smoking and Health (ASH) is a nonprofit organization in Washington, D.C., that was organized in the mid sixties to focus on the legal aspects of smoking. ASH was instrumental in removing cigarette advertisements from television, getting nonsmoking sections in commercial airlines, and working with states on clean air legislation. Current projects include action on the dangers of smoking, the dangers of smoke to nonsmokers, and economic losses from smoking (health and life insurance issues).

Legal Recommendations to Fight Smoking

Legal recommendations given by the health community to President Bush and Congress included these (Blakeman 1989):

1. Tobacco advertising and marketing must be severely restricted to eliminate their influence on our nation's children.
2. Excise taxes and user fees on tobacco products should be increased to raise revenues and discourage use by children.
3. The financial umbilical cord tying the federal government to the tobacco industry, the Tobacco Price Support Program, should be severed to reduce tobacco's undue political influence on the federal decision-making process.
4. The federal government must eliminate the cynical inconsistency between its domestic health policy and the way in which it exercises its international trade leverage

to open up tobacco marketing in other nations, thereby enabling American tobacco manufacturers to increase overall tobacco use in those countries.

In addition, policy-based smoking control programs focus on ten action alternatives that governments could adopt to control the smoking problem (Blakeman 1989):

1. Prohibition
2. Restriction of cigarette smoking
3. Reduction of hazardous substances in cigarette smoke
4. Restrictions on cigarette advertising
5. Public information education
6. Aid to people who want to quit
7. Taxation and other economic measures
8. International cooperation
9. Research
10. Economic sanctions

On the state level, 75 percent of all states have passed some legislation restricting smoking. You should be aware of the state and local laws that regulate the access and use of tobacco.

KICKING THE SMOKING HABIT

Obviously, the best way to fight the tobacco industry is to reduce the demand for tobacco products by not using them. Smoking cessation and smokeless tobacco cessation programs are somewhat effective (15 to 40 percent rates for permanently quitting).

The key to kicking the smoking habit is personal. People who highly value health usually have the easiest time quitting. Many adults quit primarily to set a good example for their children, because children of smoking parents tend to smoke. Others quit because they are disturbed by the unpleasant aspects of smoking—such as the smell of stale smoke in their clothing, bad breath, and stains on their fingers and teeth. Finally, some people like to master different situations, and perhaps awareness of this challenge to self-control would be sufficient incentive for them to begin kicking the habit. Table 14.1 on page 14.16 lists some activities that may help smokers kick the smoking habit.

NICOTINE-SUBSTITUTION APPROACHES TO SMOKING CESSATION

One of the better approaches to smoking cessation has been the use of federally approved prescriptions for **nicotine gum** (Nicorette). As with all prescriptions, nicotine gum should be used under the supervision of a physician. This approach to smoking cessation is to deal first with the behavioral aspects of smoking (the purchasing of cigarettes, the social aspects of

One approach to smoking cessation involves placing a nicotine patch on the skin.

smoking, etc.) but not to deal with the addiction to nicotine. Instead, nicotine is supplied in the nicotine gum (about 2 milligrams of nicotine per piece). Nicotine addicts chew about ten to twelve pieces per day, to a maximum of thirty pieces per day. After the behavioral aspects of smoking are overcome, then the smoker can suddenly or gradually reduce the consumption of nicotine gum. The advantage is that the smoker immediately stops the intake of carbon monoxide, tars, and other toxins and irritants. Smoking cessation rates vary dramatically depending upon the individual

---

nicotine gum
Sold under the name Nicorette, a gum that contains about 2 milligrams of nicotine and is designed to substitute for smoking cigarettes.

TABLE 14.1   ACTIVITIES TO HELP BREAK THE SMOKING HABIT

Type of Smoker	Reasons for Smoking	Activities to Substitute
Stimulation	You smoke to keep from slowing down.	Take a short walk instead of smoking.
	You smoke to stimulate yourself.	Try moderate exercise.
	You smoke to give yourself a "lift."	Take a mildly stimulating drink, such as tea or coffee.
Handling	Handling a cigarette adds to the enjoyment of smoking.	Play with a pencil, coin, paper clip, or any small object.
	Lighting a cigarette adds to the enjoyment.	Keep the hands busy by knitting, cooking, or engaging in another hobby.
	Watching the exhaled smoke adds to the enjoyment.	
Relaxation	Smoking is pleasant and relaxing.	Rewards help; use nonfattening food such as diet drinks, fruits, carrots, or celery.
	The best time for a cigarette is when you are comfortable and relaxed.	Start a new hobby or social activity.
		Change your behavior pattern or activity after meals.
Crutch	You smoke when you feel angry about something.	Consciously do something else when you feel tense.
	You smoke when you are upset.	Try deep breathing.
	You smoke when you want to take your mind off something.	Make up a phrase to say to yourself when you want to smoke. Practice it so it is almost automatic.
		Try sugarless gum or mints as a substitute.
		Splash cold water on your face.
		Practice conscious relaxation.
Habit	You smoke cigarettes automatically without even being aware of it.	Leave cigarettes in a different place; don't carry them.
	You sometimes light a cigarette with one already burning.	Wrap the package in paper and rubber band; make it difficult to get a cigarette.
	You sometimes find a cigarette in your mouth without realizing you put it there.	Designate nonsmoking areas of your home and workplace.
		Don't carry matches.

Source: From *Stop Smoking and How to Go About It*. Edinburgh, Scotland: Scottish Health Education Unit, 1979.

and the program, but from 17 to 65 percent smoking cessation rates have been reported. Many of those that quit smoking are still addicted to nicotine.

The same approach is used with the **nicotine skin or arm patch.** The smoker places a patch with nicotine on the arm, and about 20 to 24 milligrams (about 1 mg/hour) of nicotine is absorbed by the skin over a 24-hour period. The patch is changed each day. Side effects include mild to sometimes severe skin irritations (Higgins 1990). The Food and Drug Administration regulates nicotine when it is sold as a drug, as in Nicorette gum or in skin patches.

BEHAVIORAL APPROACHES TO SMOKING CESSATION

The twelve-step recovery approach (such as the one used by Alcoholics Anonymous), which has been successful with other kinds of chemical addiction, is also effective with nicotine addiction (Thanepohn 1990). The behavior component of smoking cessation is the most critical to being able to quit using tobacco. Group-therapy programs are usually sponsored by local voluntary health agencies. Volunteers including physicians, psychologists, and ex-smokers are trained to assist. Smokers who are attempting to quit are supported with **positive reinforcement** (which accentuates the positive aspects of quitting and rewards positive moves toward quitting) and group interaction, in which people share all of their experiences that might be helpful in the quitting process.

SMOKING CESSATION PROGRAMS

Several organizations have entered the field of group-therapy smoking-cessation programs in the last several years.

nicotine skin patches
Nicotine-containing patches placed on the arm that deliver about 1 milligram of nicotine per hour as a substitute for smoking.

positive reinforcement
A technique in which the positive aspects of a person's endeavor to break a habit—in this case, smoking—are rewarded.

The Likelihood of Your Being Able to Quit Using Tobacco Products

Directions

If you use tobacco, check all answers that apply to you, except where noted.

1. Which of the following statements best describes your feelings about quitting smoking or using smokeless tobacco?
   a. I do not want to quit smoking or using smokeless tobacco.
   b. Someday I would like to quit smoking or using smokeless tobacco, but not now.
   c. I would like to quit smoking or using smokeless tobacco now.
   d. I am very motivated to quit smoking or using smokeless tobacco now.

2. If you decided to quit smoking or using smokeless tobacco, who would be willing to support and help you quit? (Check all that apply.)
   a. All family members
   b. Some family members
   c. Roommates
   d. Good friends
   e. Other coworkers or students
   f. Spiritual or religious leader
   g. Other

3. People who are my heroes or someone I want to be like are
   a. smokers or users of smokeless tobacco.
   b. nonsmokers or do not use smokeless tobacco.
   c. I don't know.

4. My usual level of stress is
   a. very high.
   b. high.
   c. moderate.
   d. low.

5. Which of the following statements describes your feelings? (Check all that apply.)
   a. I don't think smoking/using tobacco has any negative effects on me.
   b. I tried to quit and failed, so I don't think I can quit again.
   c. I know why I smoke or use smokeless tobacco.
   d. I feel better about myself when I smoke or use tobacco.
   e. Because I can't stop using tobacco or smoking, I don't feel good about myself.
   f. I have been able to quit for short periods of time in the past.
   g. I feel more confident when smoking or using tobacco.

6. Which of the following statements best describes your feelings?
   a. I control whether I smoke (or use smokeless tobacco) or not.
   b. The only thing that prevents me from quitting is me.
   c. For me to quit, I just have to make up my mind.
   d. Whether I smoke (or use smokeless tobacco) or not depends a lot on other people.
   e. My smoking (or use of smokeless tobacco) is beyond my control.
   f. The way I was raised determined that I would be a smoker or a tobacco user.

Scoring

Score yourself on questions 1 through 6 as follows:

1. a = 1, b = 2, c = 3, d = 4
2. Give yourself 2 points for each answer you checked, for a maximum of 6 points.
3. a = 1, b = 3, c = 1
4. a = 1, b = 2, c = 3, d = 4
5. If a, then 1 point, if not selected give 3 points
   If b, then 1 point, if not selected give 3 points
   If c, then 3 points, if not selected give 1 point
   If d, then 1 point, if not selected give 3 points
   If e, then 1 point, if not selected give 3 points
   If f, then 3 points, if not selected give 1 point
   If g, then 1 point, if not selected give 3 points
6. If a = 3
   If b = 3
   If c = 3
   If d = 1
   If e = 1
   If f = 1

Total your points for questions 1 through 6. The following scoring system applies:

35–41	=	strong likelihood to be able to quit
27–34	=	good chance to quit, will need to work on attitude or support system
Below 27	=	chance, will need to make some attitudinal changes or improve relationships to be successful

PERSONAL SKILLS AND EXPERIENCES

Living Without Tobacco

Mind

Use creative personal problem-solving skills to resolve any problems that you may have with tobacco. If you are a non-smoker but are exposed to sidestream smoke, come up with some creative ways to solve the problem. For smokers, use your skills to figure out the best way for you to quit smoking or using smokeless tobacco and then implement your plan. Think through the important steps.

1. Define the problem clearly. Understand what tobacco is doing to your health and how other people perceive you. The problem, in essence, is the difference between what is and what should or could be.
2. Generate a creative list of alternative solutions to the problem. Think "wild and crazy" to brainstorm some innovative solutions to the tobacco problem.
3. Think through the probable outcomes of each of the alternative solutions.
4. Choose the alternative that is best within your moral and financial framework.
5. Make preparations (acquire skills, materials, etc.) to enact the best alternative.
6. Implement the solution.
7. Evaluate the outcome.

Body

If you are a smoker, look at your hands. Cup your hands over your mouth and breathe into your hand. How does your breath smell? How do your clothes smell? Ask others you trust how you smell. Imagine what your lungs might look like. It may be time to consider one of the smoking cessation pro-grams described in this chapter to quit smoking. Your body needs time to recover from the damage that may already have been inflicted. The sooner you quit, the sooner the recovery process can begin.

If you are a nonsmoker, think of how your body and clothes have smelled after being around tobacco smoke. Perhaps you can recall a mildly irritated throat or runny nose following exposure to smoke. Make a resolve to protect your body from smoke to avoid the immediate negatives, as well as the long-range dangers, of being in the presence of tobacco smoke.

Soul

Think for a moment of who you really are. When you get past experiences that have soured you about some parts of life and when you get past all the expectations others have of you (as a student, family member, employee, etc.), what are you really like? Are you fun-loving, loving, spontaneous, caring, and wanting to do good? As you picture that true self—the soul—how do cigarettes enter the picture? Do they really fit? How do you really feel about exposure to tobacco? Once you have established this, emotionally ready yourself to take action to avoid tobacco exposure to be in line with your true feelings.

Interdependence

In light of the reconfirmation that passive smoke can cause heart disease, cancer, and respiratory problems, interdependence on the part of the smoker and the nonsmoker is clear. Nonsmokers should practice assertiveness and communication skills to assure that they are not exposed to sidestream smoke unnecessarily. Be assertive to avoid passive smoking in buses, meeting rooms, restaurants, and other locations. Smokers, even with their freedom to smoke if they so desire, should no longer ask a nonsmoker if it is okay to smoke in their home, car, or other place. Instead, interdependent courtesy and caring for the welfare of others would dictate that you smoke only where others will not be affected.

PERSONAL SKILLS AND EXPERIENCES

Breathing Fresh Air

According to the PNI researchers, tobacco smoking inhibits the production of the protective substances of the immune system. Nicotine also promotes a roller-coaster effect—the drug first acts as a stimulant and then leads to a period of depression. As you consider how to maximize your strengths and to experience optimal living, you will see that being around tobacco smoke should be avoided. To have maximum ability to ward off disease, you should not include smoking in your daily activities. Smokers tend to get sick more often than nonsmokers. The PNI action is to seek and breathe deeply fresh clean air as often as possible. Focus on your breathing.

1. Breath with your diaphragm. Lie down and put your hand over your navel. As you breathe in, make your hand rise with your stomach. When you exhale, your hand should go down.
2. Concentrate on filling your lungs with fresh, clean air. Imagine that your lungs are filling with clean air and that you exhale any pollutants you've breathed in, in the past, with unclean air.
3. Seek fresh air as often as possible and enjoy the process of breathing.

SmokEnders

SmokEnders has chapters in more than thirty cities around the country. Participants attend nine weekly meetings, and reunions are organized after the final meeting for added reinforcement. SmokEnders also contacts participants periodically for a year after the completion of the program. The fee is high for this type of profit-making program.

Schick Laboratories

Schick Laboratories operates more than twenty smoking cessation centers around the country that conduct 1-hour individual therapy sessions for 5 consecutive days. The centers use behavior modification techniques and **aversion therapy** (negative reinforcement for smoking). After participants complete the initial program, they are reinforced for 8 weeks in weekly 1-hour group sessions. This type of program is quite expensive, but the fee includes 1 year of free service for anyone who has difficulty controlling the urge to smoke or who has resumed smoking.

The Seventh-Day Adventist "5-Day Plan"

The Seventh-Day Adventist 5-day plan is a successful withdrawal program that meets for 2 hours a day for 5 consecutive days. The clients are expected to quit smoking upon entering the program. At the end of 5 days, they will be over the physical withdrawal symptoms and receive much instruction to deal with the psychological aspects of withdrawal. The program substitutes exercise and nutrition for cigarettes. At the same time, the client is purged of other stimulants such as coffee, tea, colas, and alcohol. Clients are shown visuals of lungs with cancer and emphysema to reinforce the need to stop smoking. Clients are urged to seek help from their spiritual source of strength during withdrawal. For further information, contact any Seventh-Day Adventist Church or medical facility.

American Cancer Society's Stop Smoking Program

The American Cancer Society's Stop Smoking Program consists of eight 2-hour sessions, 2 days a week for a 4-week period. Specific guidelines for the program are contained in the *Stop Smoking Program Guide* published by the American Cancer Society, California division. Generally, the eight sessions consist of general emphases. Sessions 1 through 4 are for insight development. Sessions 5 through 8 are for resource development and for trying to go the first 48 hours without cigarettes. Sessions 9 and 10 follow the program and are used as support in the form of the I.Q. (I Quit) club.

Accurate success rates for these programs are unavailable because there have been few scientific follow-up surveys. People who run commercial smoking programs are often unaware of their failures, because people who don't stop smoking feel guilty and don't come back. Moreover, the high costs of many commercial programs are beyond the reach of many smokers.

Several companies suggest that filters they have developed, which reduce the tar and nicotine in cigarettes, can serve as a route to kicking the habit. Each cigarette progressively filters more and more nicotine out until very little gets through. Unfortunately, quitters using these filters seem unable to get past the last filter to become smoke-free.

Smoking Cessation Using Strength Intervention (Individualized Program)

The only strategy used in strength intervention is to quit cold turkey (i.e., for the client to select a day to quit smoking and not smoke after that day). If the individual wants to start with some of the other methods, such as switching to a lower-dose brand or gradually reducing the number of cigarettes smoked, those methods are used before the selected quitting day. In order for strength intervention to be effective, three screening factors must be considered. The first is the issue of readiness. If you do not feel that you really want to quit, then you must first resolve some readiness issues. Consider your score on the Health Assessment on your likelihood of being able to quit using tobacco. If you scored in the ready range, then you should proceed. If not, then you should engage in a readiness program. Your readiness program might include the following:

1. Read this chapter carefully, paying particular attention to those concepts that deal with diseases that result from smoking. You may also want to read additional material that is available from the American Cancer Society and the American Lung Association or the American Heart Association.

2. It is likely that someone you know or socialize with is a nonsmoker. Talk with that person about smoking, and seek her or his encouragement and support.

3. Do some imagery. The following scenarios can be used anytime, but they are particularly effective when you are smoking.

> **Scenario 1:** When you are smoking, close your eyes and imagine that you are able to see with Superman's X-ray vision. As you smoke, imagine that you see yourself in the mirror and, with X-ray vision, can see

---

aversion therapy
A type of treatment in which a specific behavior—in this case, smoking—is made undesirable through negative reinforcement.

the smoke you are inhaling go into your lungs. Picture the black tar making your lungs blacker and blacker. With each puff the healthy pink dims under the onslaught of the gray and black smoke. Picture your heart, straining as it beats faster than it wants to, under the influence of the smoke. Continue to watch your lungs deteriorate with each puff.

Scenario 2: Close your eyes and concentrate on how good you feel. Do not smoke at this time. Either sit or lie down, and relax, taking several deep breaths, enjoying this relaxed state. Now imagine that you begin to smoke, and feel a nauseating churning in your stomach. Concentrate on how you feel when you have a bad stomach flu and you are in pain. When you stop smoking, the ache goes away. When you imagine smoking, the nausea returns.

Scenario 3: Picture yourself as a nonsmoker. You no longer have a desire to smoke; you do not need to buy any more cigarettes. You are in control. Go through a typical day in your life, with people inviting you to smoke and you saying, "No thank you," and you feeling the power of controlling the cigarette, rather than it controlling you. Sense how good you feel, how fresh you smell, and how your teeth are brighter.

A second consideration before starting a smoking cessation program is the problem of barriers. If there are obstacles that make smoking cessation impossible or very difficult in your environment, then you must take some action to deal with those elements. For example, if you are under excessive pressure from school or a job, you will have a high level of stress. If significant others smoke or are not supportive of your quitting, that will also be a barrier for you. Some work must be done to remove those barriers. Do stress management, encourage family members or good friends to quit with you, or use other strategies necessary to quit smoking successfully.

The third prerequisite to quitting smoking is to nurture your strength areas and solicit support. Be sure that your activities and the people you are with are providing you with strength, comfort, support, and happiness. You will want to focus on those areas of strength and support as you overcome the smoking challenge.

If you are ready, have removed potential barriers, and have adequate resources for strength and support, then you can begin this program. The first step is to complete a lifestyle contract. (See the Lifestyle Contract at the end of this part of the book.)

Other methods of smoking cessation include hypnosis and acupuncture. **Hypnosis** has been used in various ways, but most often the individual is taught self-hypnosis as a way to stop smoking. Because **acupuncture** is a relatively recent development in this country, there have been few studies on its use as a smoking cessation technique. However, auricular (earlobe) acupuncture has been used for cessation purposes; participants who did quit using this method reported that cigarettes became distasteful. While the success reported for each of these methods alone is not particularly high, acupuncture in combination with psychotherapy or another therapy is showing noteworthy success rates (Blakeman 1989).

A decision that you can make in your life is to try to free yourself from the devastating effects of tobacco smoke. If you smoke now, quit. If you don't smoke now, don't start. If you don't smoke but are passively smoking, demand your rights to clean air. Just because there are many jobs and dollars hinging on the production of cigarettes does not mean that you need to smoke.

TAKE ACTION

1. Stop using tobacco. If you need to, get professional help.
2. Help someone else shake an addiction to tobacco, and don't enable their behavior.
3. Improve your refusal skills and increase your own self-confidence, self-esteem, and social problem-solving skills, and keep your purposes in life in focus. If your social group uses tobacco, consider changing to groups that don't. Do mental imagery to rehearse saying no to tobacco and to deepen your self-esteem and sense of well-being.
4. Learn healthy ways to deal with stress, such as getting vigorous exercise regularly, eating nutritiously, getting enough rest, and talking productively about your stressors with friends, family, or a counselor.
5. When seeking employment, look for a job that provides a smoke-free environment.

hypnosis
A physically induced altered state of consciousness in which the person can respond, within limits, to suggestions.

acupuncture
A medical technique that involves inserting needles into the skin and manipulating them to relieve pain and treat disease; also used to aid smoking cessation.

SUMMARY

1. Tobacco would not likely be accepted as a new drug if it were not already firmly established in the economic structure and personal lives of Americans.

2. Smoking tobacco is the chief avoidable cause of death in this country.

3. A cigarette contains three thousand chemical substances, including tars, nicotine, carbon monoxide, hydrogen cyanide, and nitrogen oxide.

4. Smoking increases the risks of heart disease, cancer, respiratory disease, digestive diseases, and complications in pregnancy.

5. Clove cigarettes, pipe smoking, and cigar smoking also result in significant health risks.

6. Smokeless tobacco increases the incidence of cancers of the mouth, throat, and stomach, and it is extremely difficult to quit using smokeless tobacco after becoming addicted.

7. People who smoke generally started, for numerous reasons, before reaching the age of 20.

8. People who do not smoke should avoid sidestream smoke because of the high amounts of gases and carcinogens in the smoke.

9. Health-care providers, voluntary agencies, and personal approaches to quitting are available to those who want to kick the smoking habit.

COMMITMENT ACTIVITIES

1. Call or write the local chapter of the American Cancer Society, American Lung Association, or American Heart Association to see if they provide smoking cessation clinics. See how you can help within these clinics or how you can spread the word of their availability.

2. The federal government no longer allows tobacco advertising or anti-smoking messages on television. Determine whether this regulation has created any problems for young people in our country. You might want to have a class debate about the pros and cons of cigarette advertising and anti-smoking messages on television.

3. Call the local health department and see if they have any morbidity and mortality statistics related to cigarette smoking in your community or state. Using population figures from current federal documents, compare your community figures to the national morbidity and mortality figures to find out whether smoking-related diseases and deaths are more prevalent in your locality.

4. Each cigarette package and cigarette advertisement must contain a warning about the health hazards of smoking. Using the examples given in this chapter and other information about smoking, rewrite the warning labels to be more-effective deterrents to smoking.

5. Using your university as a "community," develop a plan for a smoke-free environment within the university. You might want to write your own "clean air act." Determine what legislative actions could be taken to institute such an act, what role the mass media can play, and which student organizations should be mobilized to implement such a plan.

6. Plan to have a smoke-free day at the university, when all smokers agree to quit smoking for a day. Call the American Cancer Society and be a part of their "Great American Smoke-Out" or use their guidelines for your university's smoke-free day.

REFERENCES

American Cancer Society. 1993. *Cancer Facts and Figures: 1993*. New York: American Cancer Society.

Bailey, W. J., and R. J. Lamarine. 1986. "Clove Cigarettes: Problem or Symptom?" *Journal of School Health* 56, no. 1:2930.

Blakeman, E. M., ed. 1989. *Introduction: Final Report and Recommendations from the Health Community to the 101st Congress and the Bush Administration from the Tobacco Use in America Conference, Houston, Texas*. Washington, DC: American Medical Association.

Blum, A. 1993. "Secondhand Smoke Suits May Catch Fire; Some Lawyers See an Upsurge Following a New EPA Report." *National Law Journal* 15, no. 26 (March): 1.

Brubaker, R. G., and T. L. Loftin. 1987. "Smokeless Tobacco Use by Middle School Males: A Preliminary Test of the Reasoned Action Theory." *Journal of School Health* 57, no. 2:6471.

Chen, M. S., K. L. Schroeder, E. D. Glover, J. Bonaguro, and E. M. Capwell. 1991. "Tobacco Use Prevention in the National School Curricula: Implications of a Stratified Random Sample." *Health Values* 15, no. 2:39.

"Cigarette Smoking—Attributable Mortality and Years of Potential Life Lost—United States, 1990." 1993. *Journal of the American Medical Association* 270, no. 12 (22 September): 1408–11.

Clark, C. S. 1992. "Crackdown on Smoking." *CQ Researcher* 2, no. 45 (4 December): 1051–57.

Connolly, G. N. 1989. "The International Marketing of Tobacco." In *Final Report and Recommendations from the Health Community to the 101st Congress and the Bush Administration from the Tobacco Use in America Conference, Houston, Texas*, edited by E. M. Blakeman. Washington, DC: American Medical Association.

Dusek, D. E., and D. A. Girdano. 1987. *Drugs: A Factual Account*. 4th ed. New York: Random House.

Glasgow, R. E., J. F. Hollis, L. Pettigrew, L. Foster, M. J. Givi, and G. Morrisette. 1991. "Implementing a Year-Long Worksite-Based Incentive Program for Smoking Cessation." *American Journal of Health Promotion* 5, no. 3:192–99.

Gostin, L. O., and A. M. Brandt. 1993. "Criteria for Evaluating a Ban on the Advertisement of Cigarettes: Balancing Public Health Benefits with Constitutional Burdens." *Journal of the American Medical Association* 269, no. 7 (17 February): 904.

Heath, C. W., and S. A. Glantz. 1993. "Passive Smoke Provides Another Reason to Quit." *Patient Care* 27, no. 4 (28 February): 84–87.

Higgins, L. C. 1990. "Arm Patch May Help Kick the Butt." *Medical World News* 31, no. 11:29.

Kellie, S. E. 1989. "Tobacco Use: Women, Children, and Minorities." In *Final Report and Recommendations from the Health Community to the 101st Congress and the Bush Administration from the Tobacco Use in America Conference, Houston, Texas,* edited by E. M. Blakeman. Washington, DC: American Medical Association.

Koop, C. E. 1986. "The Quest for a Smoke-Free Young America by the Year 2000." *Journal of School Health* 56, no. 1:89.

Leichtman, A., and W. Merryman. 1992. "Are Smoking Bans Justified?" *CQ Researcher* 2, no. 45 (4 December): 1065–66.

Marty, P. J., et al. 1986. "Prevalence and Psychosocial Correlates of Dipping and Chewing Behavior in a Group of Rural High School Students." *Health Education* 17, no. 2.

McDermott, R. J., and P. J. Marty. 1986. "Dipping and Chewing Behavior Among University Students: Prevalence and Patterns of Use." *Journal of School Health* 56, no. 5:175–77.

McGinnis, J. M. 1987. Distinguished Scholar Lecture, University of Utah, Salt Lake City, 7 May.

Royce, J. M. 1993. "Smoking Cessation Factors Among African Americans and Whites." *American Journal of Public Health* 83, no. 2 (February): 220–27.

Schlaadt, R. G., and T. T. Shannon. 1986. *Drugs of Choice: Current Perspectives on Drug Use.* Englewood Cliffs, NJ: Prentice Hall.

Slade, J. 1989. "Nicotine Addiction." In *Final Report and Recommendations From the Health Community to the 101st Congress and the Bush Administration from the Tobacco Use in America Conference, Houston, Texas,* edited by E. M. Blakeman. Washington, DC: American Medical Association.

Thanepohn, S. G. 1990. "How to Kick the Butts." *U.S. Journal of Drug and Alcohol Dependence* 14, no. 1:1, 10.

"Tobacco Industry Conglomerates: Status Report on Diversification in the Tobacco Industry." 1986. *Smoking and Health Reporter* 3, no. 4:7.

"Who Dares? Smoking." 1993. *The Economist* 328, no. 7830 (25 September): A32–33.

Zhang, J., and J. M. Ratcliffe. 1993. "Paternal Smoking and Birthweight in Shanghai." *American Journal of Public Health* 83, no. 2 (February): 207–11.

ADDITIONAL READINGS

Blakeman, E. M., ed. 1989. *Introduction: Final Report and Recommendations from the Health Community to the 101st Congress and the Bush Administration from the Tobacco Use in America Conference, Houston, Texas.* Washington, DC: American Medical Association. This final report, available from the American Medical Association, Public Affairs Group, 1101 Vermont Avenue, N.W., Washington, DC 20005, is the most comprehensive and up-to-date report on the effect of nicotine addiction on society. The booklet includes discussions by the top people in the country on tobacco use by women, children, and minorities; nicotine addiction; federal regulation of tobacco products; cigarette excise tax; protecting nonsmokers; tobacco marketing and promotion; U.S. Agricultural policy on tobacco; the international marketing of tobacco; and grassroots lobbying.

Iverson, D. C. 1987. "Smoking Control Programs: Premises and Promises." *American Journal of Health Promotion* 1, no. 3. This is an excellent overview of smoking patterns, health implications of smoking, stages of smoking, and smoking cessation. Methods of controlling smoking in worksites, schools, and communities through physician, policy, and economic intervention are discussed.

Smoking and Health in the Americas: A 1992 Report of the Surgeon General, in Collaboration with the Pan American Health Organization: Executive Summary. 1992. Atlanta, GA: Department of Health and Human Services, Centers for Disease Control. Summary of findings on the epidemiology of smoking.

Surgeon General's Reports on Smoking and Health. Washington, DC: DHEW Publications: *Smoking and Women* (1980), *The Changing Cigarette* (1981), *Smoking and Cancer* (1982), *Smoking and Cardiovascular Disease* (1983). Information and research studies provided on specific topics each year.

Tollison, R. D., and R. E. Wagner. 1992. *The Economics of Smoking.* Boston: Kluwer Academic. This book covers the broad economic impact of smoking in a number of settings. It also includes discussions of tobacco warfare, public policy, taxation, markets, government action, advertising, self-interest versus public-interests legislation, and other topics.

Viscusi, W. K. 1992. *Smoking: Making the Risky Decision.* New York: Oxford University Press. This book is an overview of smoking that includes the economics of smoking, smoking behavior, risks for smoking, public opinion on smoking, and other risk-oriented topics.

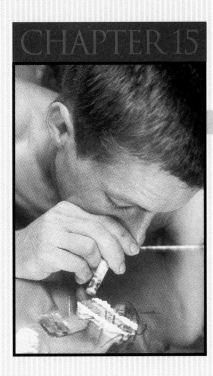

CHAPTER 15

Psychoactive Drugs

KEY QUESTIONS

What is the best decision for use and nonuse of drugs?

What is a psychoactive drug?

What are the skills and experiences of the mind, body, and soul that help deter drug use?

What are some reasons that people use drugs?

What is psychoactive substance dependence?

Why are designer drugs and freebased cocaine so dangerous?

Where are the classifications of drugs?

How does drug testing affect employees and athletes?

What does the term *drug abuse* mean?

For which classification of drugs is it the most dangerous to suddenly quit after using the substance for some time?

How can people avoid drug use or abuse?

CHAPTER OUTLINE

Evolving Patterns of and Perspectives on Drug Use

The War on Drugs

Motivations for Drug Use

Psychoactive Substance Dependence and Abuse

Genetic Vulnerability

The Addiction Cycle

Types of Psychoactive Drugs

Cannabis Products

Narcotics

Stimulants

Depressants

Hallucinogens

Drugs in Sports

Drug Testing

Drug Interactions

Drug Use and AIDS

Drugs and the Law

Take Action

Summary

Healthy People 2000 Objectives

- Increase by at least 1 year the average age at first use of cigarettes, alcohol, and marijuana by adolescents aged 12 through 17.

- Reduce drug-related deaths to no more than 3 per 100,000 people (baseline 3.8 per 100,000 in 1987).

- Reduce drug-abuse-related hospital emergency department visits by at least 20 percent.

There are many ways to have experiences that give us a natural high or flow experience (Csikszentmihalyi 1990). Rock climbing, jogging, listening to or playing music, reading a good book, romantic conversations—all can potentially provide us with peak experiences. We can escape many of our problems by not running from them but attacking them and solving them creatively. Our problems can become our strengths. Performance is enhanced best over time naturally through practice and work. The process for gaining optimal states of mind is through challenging oneself and growing from the experiences. People have more fun in life when they are in control and can enjoy their full sense of humor and comedy without being deadened by substances. We can make the decision to live a healthy lifestyle of fun, high performance, peak mental states, and happiness by following the guidance in this text.

Unfortunately, some people think that highs, escapes from problems, performing well, and having fun can be accomplished through artificial means. These people think that they can enhance performance by taking performance enhancers, study longer by taking caffeine, or escape their problems by taking drugs. This chapter is about the use of drugs in our society and, more importantly, your selective use of drugs.

EVOLVING PATTERNS OF AND PERSPECTIVES ON DRUG USE

Drug-use patterns in the United States have changed considerably during this century as a result of the changing needs, stresses, and lifestyles in our society, as well as the scientific understanding of drugs we have acquired through the years. During the nineteenth century, for example, medicines containing opiates (natural or synthetic derivatives of the opium poppy) were legally available and were taken without prescription for a variety of ailments. Many people, therefore, acquired a physical dependency on opium; that is, their body chemistry had been altered to rely on the drug, and withdrawal symptoms occurred when use of the drug ceased. This type of drug use was not covered by criminal law until 1914, when the Harrison Narcotic Act removed narcotics, opium, and opiumlike substances from the nonprescription drug list and classified their abuse as criminal behavior (Inciardi 1989).

During the 1960s the public began to view "drug users" less as criminal addicts and more as disruptive and rebellious youths. Drug use became widespread at the same time as campuses were in turmoil over civil rights and the Vietnam War. Many adults sympathized with student concerns and came to accept the use of drugs, especially marijuana, as a part of a larger social, economic, and political movement. By the time this movement subsided, Americans had attained a new level of awareness about drug use and abuse, an awareness that serves as the basis for our attitudes today (Dusek and Girdano 1993).

THE WAR ON DRUGS

In the mid 1980s the nation began its current aggressive war on drugs. Not since the 1960s has the country made such efforts to educate and to prevent drug use and abuse. *Time* magazine (15 September 1986) reported that angry residents in Harlem painted large red *X*s on crack dealers' doors and put stuffed animals in abandoned building windows as a symbolic gesture to reclaim them from drug users. In New Mexico two children turned in their parents to police for marijuana possession, and in California a girl turned in her cocaine-using parents. President Reagan made several national appearances with his wife in 1986 to stage the "war on drugs."

President Bush and his wife continued the war into the 1990s ("The War on Drugs [Continued]" 1991). Although some criticized Bush for not doing enough in treatment and prevention, his progress on the international front was going well. He worked with other countries, particularly in South America and Mexico, to crack down on the drug cartel and substitute other cash crops for the drug crops.

President Clinton's push is yet to be discovered in its entirety, but a major emphasis seems to be a get-tougher stand. He seeks funds for more law enforcement to help in the tough stand against gangs, crime, and drugs.

Drug testing in athletics, businesses, and government positions has created much controversy. In 1986, Congress allocated hundreds of millions of dollars to prevent and treat drug use and abuse. Almost every state in the union has a governor's council on drugs to deal with drug issues particular to each state.

Why is there a renewed war on drugs after 20 years? Some of the reasons are that the drugs available today are much more potent, dangerous, addicting, and available than ever before. The marijuana smoked today is twenty times more potent than the marijuana smoked in 1964. Cocaine, once labeled the "rich man's" drug, is not only cheaper, but it is easily transformed (freebased) into **crack,** a substance that is forty times as addicting as cocaine and is sold on the streets for a relatively cheap price.

Methamphetamine (speed), which is bad enough in its original state, has been refined into an intensified crystalline rock form (which first arrived here from Korea and Japan) that intensifies the addictiveness and debilitative nature of the drug.

Designer drugs, which can be mass-produced in a single laboratory, are made from readily available chemicals and are one thousand times as potent as heroin. Some botched batches have left a trail of users with Parkinson's-disease-like symptoms and other forms of brain damage.

With all the benefits of today's technology, opportunists have gained skills to develop drugs that can ruin people's lives. People have the knowledge to synthesize powerful narcotics for hundreds of dollars and make profits in the millions. Some of these drugs can turn healthy people into "basket cases" in a matter of a few days or weeks.

This chapter is designed to create an awareness of the new drug epidemic that has hit the United States. It is hoped that students will make wise decisions regarding the use of illicit, prescription, and over-the-counter drugs.

MOTIVATIONS FOR DRUG USE

Most people from 16 to 25 years old try drugs only once or twice as an experiment, because they are curious or because their friends are using drugs. Some people try drugs primarily for pleasure, recreation, or to help them through unpleasant situations. If you are not currently using drugs, do the Health Assessment exercise to evaluate your risk of becoming a drug abuser. The following list of reasons for using drugs has been suggested by experts (Schlaadt and Shannon 1986; Towers 1987):

1. To feel less afraid and more courageous
2. To find out more about oneself
3. To have a religious experience or come closer to God
4. To satisfy a strong craving or compulsion
5. To relieve boredom
6. To find altered states and increase the intensity of moods
7. To relieve tension or nervousness
8. To shut things out of one's mind
9. To recreate and have fun
10. To escape from boredom
11. To experience a different kind of awareness
12. To make it easier to be more social, begin conversations, and promote camaraderie
13. To find stimulating and sensational experiences
14. To feel less depressed or sad
15. To demonstrate rebellion against parents and social norms
16. Because of peer pressure
17. To escape life stressors and pain
18. To feel capable and wanted (to overcome a lack of self-worth)
19. To perform better in school, athletics, or work
20. To follow family modeling or deal with family inconsistencies

PSYCHOACTIVE SUBSTANCE DEPENDENCE AND ABUSE

According to the American Psychiatric Association, problem use of drugs is termed either *psychoactive substance dependence* or *abuse.* Dependence has both physiological and psychological components.

Physiological dependence is characterized by tolerance and withdrawal symptoms. Tolerance is a condition in which it takes increasingly larger amounts of a drug to produce the same effects previously felt at lower dosages. Withdrawal is the physical disturbance or cluster of symptoms that occurs when the drug is taken away or becomes unavailable. Withdrawal symptoms are an indication that the body has adapted to the presence of the drug, that the drug is required for the individual to function normally, and that the development of

crack
A freebased version of cocaine that is extremely potent, quick acting, addicting, and dangerous.

methamphetamine
A stimulant drug of abuse; also called "speed."

physiological dependence
A condition in which a person has a biochemical need to continue using a particular drug in order to prevent withdrawal symptoms.

Your Risk for Drug Abuse

This questionnaire is designed for those who are not currently using drugs. If you currently use drugs, then this does not apply to you. By "drugs" this questionnaire means prescription or illegal drugs that can be abused (e.g., cocaine, marijuana, speed, downers, heroin, Valium).

Directions

Please use the *a, b,* and *c* codes to respond to the following list of characteristics or situations.

a = This definitely applies to me or applied to me.
b = This somewhat applies or applied to me.
c = This does not apply and never did apply to me.

1. My parents (guardians) and I have a good relationship.   a   b   c
2. My parents (guardians) and I share our feelings openly and comfortably.   a   b   c
3. I place a lot of importance on achievement.   a   b   c
4. I am very sensitive to criticism by my friends.   a   b   c
5. It is not important for me to do things that are socially acceptable.   a   b   c
6. I am very religious.   a   b   c
7. I get very good grades.   a   b   c
8. Some of my friends use drugs.   a   b   c
9. I feel depressed quite frequently.   a   b   c
10. I grew up with only one parent in my home.   a   b   c
11. The people I live with now use drugs.   a   b   c
12. I have a rebellious nature.   a   b   c
13. I skip class frequently.   a   b   c
14. I have a low opinion of myself.   a   b   c
15. My parents (guardians) use(d) drugs.   a   b   c
16. I have experimented with drugs.   a   b   c
17. My home is chaotic and disorganized.   a   b   c
18. I often feel guilty.   a   b   c
19. I have feelings of insecurity.   a   b   c
20. I have often wanted to try a drug just to see what it was like.   a   b   c

Scoring

For questions 1, 2, 3, 6, and 7, score as follows:

a = 3 points
b = 2 points
c = 1 point

For all other questions, score as follows:

a = 1 point
b = 2 points
c = 3 points

Total your score for all twenty items.

Interpretation

This is a risk assessment tool, which means that numerous studies have shown that some people have a higher risk than others of becoming drug abusers. These risk factors do not mean that someone will become a drug abuser, but it does mean that people with a particular background have become drug abusers more frequently than those who do not have these characteristics. Your total points can be interpreted as follows:

20–33   High risk
34–46   Moderate risk
47–60   Low risk

physical dependence has occurred (Jensen 1987). "**Psychological dependence** is a condition in which the drug produces a feeling of satisfaction and a psychological drive that requires periodic or continuous drug use to produce pleasure or avoid discomfort" (Jensen 1987). The American Psychiatric Association (1987) suggests that any three of the following criteria are indicators of **psychoactive substance dependence.**

1. The substance is often taken in larger amounts or over a longer period than the person intended.
2. A persistent desire, or one or more unsuccessful efforts, to cut down or control substance use.

psychological dependence
A condition in which the user's craving for a particular drug is so intense that it alters the user's behavior.

psychoactive substance dependence
A maladaptive pattern of psychoactive substance use indicated by the presence of at least two of the following: (1) The substance is taken in larger amounts, for a longer time, than the user intended; (2) a persistent desire for the substance, with unsuccessful efforts to cut down or control substance use; (3) a great deal of time spent in activities necessary to get, take, or recover from the substance; (4) frequent intoxication (drugged state) or withdrawal symptoms when the user is expected to fulfill a major role at work, school, or home; (5) important social, occupational, or recreational activities abandoned or reduced because of the substance use; (6) continued substance use despite knowing that one has a persistent or recurrent social, psychological, or physical problem that is caused or exacerbated by the use of the substance; (7) marked tolerance; (8) the substance is often taken to relieve or avoid withdrawal symptoms; (9) symptoms of disturbance have persisted for at least one month or have occurred repeatedly over a longer period of time.

HEALTH ASSESSMENT

Checklist for Detection of Drug Use

This tool is designed to aid you in helping others who might be starting to use drugs. As a roommate, sibling, or friend, it may be your opportunity to help someone who is just starting out with drugs. Picture someone in your life who you care about and want to keep off drugs, and apply this questionnaire to them.

Directions

Mark a check by any of the symptoms that might apply to the person you have chosen for this assessment.

____ 1. Recent trend toward self-centeredness

____ 2. Motivation to achieve life goals has weakened

____ 3. Dress becomes noticeably more bizarre

____ 4. Whites of the eyes are often bloodshot

____ 5. Seems to be more sensitive to light

____ 6. Friends seem to change to a less desirable group

____ 7. Vague about social activities

____ 8. Capacity to think is impaired and has a poor short-term memory

____ 9. Emotions seem to be flattened

____ 10. Tends to react to frustration with increased irritability or anger

____ 11. Bottles of eye drops are found

____ 12. Has frequent infections, runny nose, chronic cough

____ 13. Uses gum or mints to cover breath

____ 14. Change in sleeping patterns (i.e., can't sleep until late and sleeps a lot during the day)

____ 15. Goes directly to own room and shuts door without interaction

____ 16. Loses appetite

____ 17. Blames others for problems

____ 18. Speech may be slurred or has difficulty speaking

____ 19. Does not answer when spoken to

____ 20. Frequently lies and maintains lie when truth is discovered

____ 21. Missing money or items from the home/room/apartment

____ 22. Frequent use of incense in their room

____ 23. Seems to be more secretive

____ 24. Needle marks or bruises on body

____ 25. Less attention to cleanliness

____ 26. Increased physical problems such as nausea, stomach problems, fatigue, sweats, trembling

____ 27. Evidences of drug use such as rolling papers, seeds, razor blades, mirrors, miniature spoons, miniature tubes, miniature bottles, or other drug paraphernalia

Scoring

Score one point for each item checked, except for items 24 and 27.

Interpretation

If item 24 or 27 is checked, then there is a strong likelihood that the person is at least experimenting with drugs.

For other items, note that something is going on that is prompting a behavior change. If you care about this person, investigation through effective communication and paying attention to other potential cues may help you to help this person before dependence or addiction takes place. These symptoms may not represent drug use, but could represent relationship, academic, or other types of problems.

Illicit drugs have infiltrated all segments of society.

3. A great deal of time is spent in activities necessary to get the substance (e.g., theft), taking the substance (e.g., chain-smoking), or recovering from its effects.

4. Frequent intoxication or withdrawal symptoms when expected to fulfill major role obligations at work, school, or home (e.g., does not go to work because hung over, goes to school or work "high," intoxicated while taking care of his or her children), or when substance use is physically hazardous (e.g., drives when intoxicated).

5. Important social, occupational, or recreational activities are given up or reduced because of substance use.

6. Continued substance use despite knowledge of having a persistent or recurrent social, psychological, or physical problem that is caused or exacerbated by the use of the substance (e.g., keeps using heroin despite family arguments about it, cocaine-induced depression, or having an ulcer made worse by drinking).

Steps to Drug Abuse

This tool is designed to assess where you are in the steps that can lead to potential drug abuse. All of you are at least on step 1, but consider other steps.

Directions

Mark all that apply.

_____ 1. I do not take drugs and have no idea how to get them.

_____ 2. I do not take drugs, but could get them if I wanted them.

_____ 3. I do not take drugs, but would like to try sometime.

_____ 4. I have tried some drugs (e.g., marijuana), but no longer use them.

_____ 5. I use some soft drugs occasionally and socially.

_____ 6. I use some soft drugs regularly.

_____ 7. I have experimented with harder drugs (cocaine, crack, heroin, speed, barbiturates), but no longer use them.

_____ 8. I use a variety of drugs socially, but regularly.

_____ 9. I take drugs regularly even when alone.

_____ 10. I need to take hard drugs regularly.

Interpretation

Look at the highest number you have marked. If there are any marks above number 2, you are at risk of abusing drugs. If you have checked number 5 or above, then you have a one-in-eight chance of becoming seriously addicted. If you have checked number 7 or above, then you have a one-in-three chance of becoming seriously addicted. If you have checked number 8 or above, you may already be seriously addicted. If you marked number 9 or 10, then you need help immediately to recover from your drug abuse problem.

---

7. Marked tolerance: A need for markedly increased amounts of the substance (i.e., at least a 50 percent increase) in order to achieve intoxication or the desired effect, or markedly diminished effect with continued use of the same amount.

There are two additional criteria, but these might not apply to cannabis, hallucinogens, or phencyclidine (PCP):

8. The substance often is taken to relieve or avoid withdrawal symptoms.

9. Some symptoms of the disturbance have persisted for at least 1 month, or have occurred repeatedly over a longer period of time.

Psychoactive substance abuse may be indicated by a college student who "binges on cocaine every few weekends. These periods are followed by a day or two of missing school because of crashing. There are no other symptoms" (American Psychiatric Association 1987). Other examples are when a student repeatedly drives under the influence of a drug or keeps using a drug even when the drug is irritating an ulcer and medical advice is to quit using the drug.

GENETIC VULNERABILITY

One frightening fact to consider is that people generally begin to use drugs through the influence of someone else who has had some drug experience. An assumption is that the new user's reaction to a drug will be the same as that of the person who influenced him or her to try the drug. There is substantial evidence that genetic vulnerability to drugs is a significant factor in becoming addicted (Pickens and Svikis 1988). Even if a

more experienced user reports minimal effect from a dose, a new user might become addicted immediately. Although everyone can become addicted through repeated use, some people are more vulnerable than others and can instantly become drug addicts after one or two experimental doses. The only safe course of action, particularly for those who are genetically vulnerable, is to never try drugs.

THE ADDICTION CYCLE

Stress reduction is a significant factor in drug use. Life is so pressing for some people that they choose to escape from life's problems temporarily, or get an extra boost to help them cope, through drug use. A common progression to drug abuse follows a series of events and feelings. First, it is likely that the person experiences negative events (a romantic breakup, the death of a close person, academic problems, financial worries, etc.). The resultant feelings are likely hurt, inadequacy, feeling "put down," rejection, abandonment, or fear. The feelings soon turn to anger and depression. The person might then act out these feelings by using drugs (or a variety of other addictions, like gambling, eating, sex, or shopping). After acting out, the person feels self-defeat, guilt, resentment, and shame, and acts out some more. Thus the cycle between negative feelings and acting out continues, which is an addiction cycle, as diagrammed in figure 15.1.

TYPES OF PSYCHOACTIVE DRUGS

Many different psychoactive drugs are used, each with a different physiological and psychological effect. In the remainder of this chapter, the use and effects of the major types of

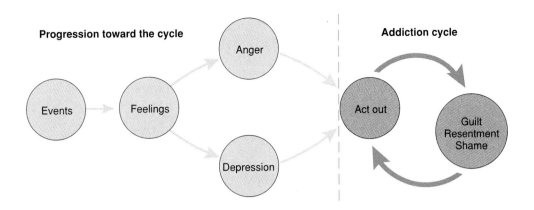

Progression toward the cycle

Events → Feelings → Anger

Feelings → Depression

Addiction cycle

Act out ⇄ Guilt Resentment Shame

Figure 15.1
Progression toward the addiction cycle.

psychoactive drugs (except for alcohol and tobacco) will be presented. Because of their frequency of use, cannabis products will be discussed first, followed by the two categories that have been the major reason for the renewed war on drugs, the narcotics and stimulants. Within these two classifications, the new "ice," designer drugs, and crack have emerged. The other classifications of drugs, each with their own potential dangers, are the hallucinogens and depressants.

CANNABIS PRODUCTS

Aside from alcohol and tobacco, **marijuana** is the drug most used for nonmedical purposes in the United States. More than 22 million Americans use marijuana regularly. Marijuana and its sister drug, **hashish,** come from the Indian hemp plant *Cannabis sativa,* which grows wild throughout most of the tropical and temperate regions of the world. Marijuana is the dried leaves and flowering tops of the plant; hashish is the processed resin. The solid form is dried resin, compressed into balls, cakes, or cookie-like sheets. The liquid form, hashish oil, is produced by a process of repeated extraction of the plant materials. Since marijuana is much more commonly used in the United States than hashish is, most of the discussion will center on the composition, use, and personal and social effects of marijuana.

Composition

Chemists have identified over 350 chemicals in marijuana and hashish, more than 50 of which are **cannabinoids,** chemicals found only in cannabis products. Many of their effects are only partially understood, but we do know that the major psychoactive drug found in marijuana is **delta-9-tetrahydrocannabinol (THC).** The THC content of marijuana (and thus its effect on users) can vary greatly, from less than 1 percent to as much as 5 percent, depending on where the plants were grown and what part of the plant is used. The marijuana smoked today can be twenty to a hundred times more potent than the marijuana commonly smoked in 1965 (Dusek and Girdano 1993). Today's high-tech **hydroponics** produces marijuana that is drastically more potent and more expensive than what

was smoked in the late sixties. Rather than an average of 1 to 4 percent THC, today's **sinsemilla** produces 17 percent and higher THC concentrations. Instead of a buzz, the results are hallucinations, heavier withdrawal symptoms, more depression, mood swings, and anxiety (Meacham 1990).

Marijuana and hashish work by entering the bloodstream and acting on the brain and nervous system. They can be either smoked or eaten but are about three times more potent when smoked. A single drop of hashish oil on a cigarette has the same effect as one marijuana joint; the effects are felt within minutes, reach their peak in 10 to 30 minutes, and may linger for 2 to 4 hours. Effects depend partly on the amount of THC but can also vary according to the expectations and past experience of the user.

There are numerous acute effects of marijuana use on the body. Low doses can induce mood changes involving euphoria, a feeling of restlessness, a sense of well-being, relaxation, laughter, hunger, or sleepiness. Larger doses can cause confusion and disorientation to the environment, which users call "getting stoned." There can be changes in

marijuana
A drug of abuse derived from *Cannabis sativa.*

hashish
The resin of the cannabis plant; a drug of abuse.

Cannabis sativa
The Indian hemp plant that produces marijuana and hashish.

cannabinoids
Chemicals found in marijuana.

delta-9-tetrahydrocannabinol (THC)
The major psychoactive drug found in marijuana.

hydroponics
The technology for growing plants (including marijuana) in nutrient solutions, with or without dirt as a medium or support.

sinsemilla
Marijuana grown with high-tech hydroponics that produces much higher THC levels than in marijuana grown in natural mediums.

sensory perception, including more vivid senses of sight, smell, touch, and taste. Marijuana effects are based largely on the expectations of the user and the setting.

Stronger doses of marijuana also produce other physiological reactions. There is a 30 to 60 percent increase in heart rate, depending on the dosage, which is not very significant in a healthy person but is potentially dangerous in a person with heart problems. Bronchodilation, an increase in the diameter of the air passages of the lungs, occurs. If inhaled deeply, the smoke may irritate these air passages.

Stronger doses can also produce changes in mental performance. Memory is impaired and time sense is altered, so performance on various tasks is impaired. High doses can also result in image distortions, a loss of sense of personal identity, fantasies, relaxed inhibitions, and **hallucinations** (visual or imaginary perceptions). There is definite impairment of driving skills, even after ordinary social use of the drug.

Heavy and prolonged use may also impair lung function. When tobacco and marijuana are inhaled together, there is a synergistic effect more intense than the sum of the effects of inhaling them separately. It appears that marijuana might be more pathogenic than tobacco, due to its greater irritant effect, the greater degree of upper-airway involvement, and the deeper smoking technique. Lung cancer has not yet been seen as a consequence of marijuana use, but this might be because the latent period for lung cancer extends over decades.

Extensive government research has also suggested that daily use of substantial amounts of marijuana can adversely impair aspects of reproduction. It can (1) decrease the levels of sex hormones in males and females; (2) reduce sperm count and the sperm's ability to move, and increase the incidence of abnormal sperm; (3) cause sexual dysfunction and impotence; (4) disrupt gonadal function; and (5) impair ovulation, cause defective menstrual cycles, and increase testosterone levels in females. It is not known if this last possibility can lead to problems with fertility or lactation or to cancer of the reproductive organs, but any drug that affects normal menstrual cycles might adversely affect fertility and reproductive health in later life. Researchers are also exploring the possible effects of marijuana use on chromosomes (Meacham 1990).

Since 1975, marijuana users have also had to worry about marijuana contaminated with **paraquat.** The U.S. and Mexican governments have tried to stop marijuana growing in Mexico by spraying the fields there with this defoliant (plant killer). If the sprayed crop is harvested immediately, however, it can still be sold; thus, much Mexican marijuana is contaminated by high levels of paraquat. Smoking paraquat-contaminated marijuana can cause irreversible lung damage.

Abuse Potential

Psychological dependence on marijuana depends on the frequency of use, ranging from little or no dependence in intermittent users to compulsive behavior in very heavy users. Individuals apparently do not become physically dependent

Issue

Still a Debate for Marijuana Decriminalization

The argument for the decriminalization of marijuana rests with the popularity of the drug, failures to control the use of the drug, inconclusive evidence of the long-range negative effects of marijuana use, the criminalization of users, and the exploitation of criminal elements.

- Pro: Two states have gone against the norm to attempt to decriminalize marijuana. Oregon's law reduces the possession of 1 ounce of marijuana to a citation (a misdemeanor and a fine of no more than $100) (Schlaadt and Shannon 1986). Laws are still strong for possession of more than an ounce. There does not appear to be an increase in use of marijuana as a result of the law. Alaska has legalized the growing of five marijuana plants for private use (Egan 1991).

- Con: Even though long-range studies cannot be conducted because marijuana use is illegal, it is obvious from the existing data that there are more carcinogens in marijuana than in cigarette tobacco. THC is a strong drug, and unless we want to have society of apathetic dropouts, we need to continue to fight the use of marijuana.

The legalization of marijuana continues to be a major issue. What should be done about it?

when marijuana is taken in relatively small amounts, but there is a possibility of dependence among very heavy users. **Withdrawal** symptoms from very high doses begin 6 to 8 hours after the last dose and include restlessness, irritability, tremors, nausea, vomiting, diarrhea, and sleep disturbances (Meacham 1990).

Cultural Aspects of Marijuana Use

As in the '60s and '70s, marijuana is again becoming the focus of young adult culture. Although marijuana use is gradually declining in the population as a whole, the youth culture is again "singing the praises of marijuana" (Farley 1993).

hallucinations
Visions or imaginary perceptions.

paraquat
A defoliant (plant killer); very poisonous.

withdrawal
Symptoms that occur, due to physical dependence on a drug, when the user stops using the drug.

Psychoactive Drugs 15.9

Rock and rap stars are including more references to marijuana in their lyrics, and trendy clothing also glorifies the use of the drug. The young culture seems to view marijuana as a symbol of simplicity and health consciousness (Zeman 1993).

Marijuana and the Law
The Marijuana Tax Act of 1937 regulated marijuana use until it was repealed by the more lenient Comprehensive Drug Abuse Prevention and Control Act of 1970. Possession of a small amount is usually considered a misdemeanor punishable by a fine. Often the misdemeanor does not become part of the person's permanent record.

Laws vary from state to state, but most still provide stiff penalties for possession or sale of a large quantity of marijuana and possession of hashish. Such acts may be considered felonies punishable by jail terms.

People still grow marijuana in the forests, on government land, or in their own homes. The U.S. Forest Service has set up hot lines in an effort to stop the illegal cultivation of marijuana in national forests (Howe 1992). Whether for personal use or for sale, the plant is still grown. A typical plant produces up to 1.5 pounds of marijuana, enough to generate $6,000 on the market. Homegrown sinsemilla, the high-potency marijuana, is available through mail-order seed catalogues; it was Oregon's highest-cash-value crop (Meacham 1990) and may be the nation's. Tucson and West Los Angeles have had days when the highest pollen count causing problems for allergy sufferers was from the flowering marijuana plant, likely due to indoor plant cultivation (Wise 1989).

NARCOTICS

Narcotics, the major problem of the '60s, appear to be making a major comeback in the wake of cocaine. Drug users are now mixing heroin and cocaine to produce a drug that results in a mix of emotional highs and lows, and death in some cases.

The term **narcotics** refers to opium and opium derivatives, such as **morphine, heroin,** and **codeine,** and to synthetic opiates, such as hydromorphone (**Dilaudid**) and **methadone.** Narcotics are indispensable in the practice of medicine because of their ability to relieve pain; however, this same ability accounts for a large portion of their abuse.

Under medical supervision, narcotics are used not only to relieve pain, but also to suppress coughs and relieve diarrhea. They are administered orally or injected into a muscle. As drugs of abuse, however, they are sniffed, smoked, or injected under the skin (**skin popping**). Most abusers inject narcotics into a vein, which is called **mainlining** (Carrol 1989).

The initial effects of narcotic use may be extremely unpleasant, ranging from drowsiness, apathy, and constipation to nausea, vomiting, and depression of the respiratory system. These effects, however, are usually followed by a state of euphoria.

Repeated use of a narcotic tends to increase tolerance, forcing the user to obtain larger and larger doses to get the same effects and to prevent withdrawal symptoms from occurring. Withdrawal symptoms are directly related to the amount of narcotic used daily. If the narcotic is withheld, symptoms will appear before the next scheduled dose, and withdrawal peaks at about 36 to 72 hours afterward. Initial withdrawal symptoms include watery eyes, runny nose, yawning, and perspiration. These are followed by restlessness, irritability, loss of appetite, insomnia, tremors, and severe sneezing. After 48 hours the user is weak and nauseous and might also experience stomach cramps and diarrhea. Pain and muscle spasms occur. The person often becomes suicidal. Without treatment, the symptoms will probably disappear in 7 to 10 days, but the psychological need will persist for several weeks.

Narcotics of Natural Origin
The opium poppy is the main source of nonsynthetic narcotics. The milky fluid of the dried plant is extracted and transported in liquid, solid, or powder form. There were no legal restrictions on the use of opium until the early 1900s, but today there are state, federal, and international laws governing the production and distribution of narcotic substances such as **opiates,** and there is little abuse of opium in the United States.

Twenty-five alkaloids can be extracted from opium and used to produce other narcotics. One group of alkaloids, the phenanthrene alkaloids (such as morphine and codeine), are used as **analgesics** (medicines that relieve pain) and

narcotics
Drugs of abuse that contain opium and opium derivatives.

morphine
A narcotic drug used to relieve pain; it can also be abused.

heroin
A synthetic narcotic drug of abuse.

codeine
A narcotic drug used to relieve moderate pain.

Dilaudid
A synthetic drug of abuse.

methadone
A synthetic narcotic drug of abuse; used as a treatment for heroin addiction.

skin popping
Injecting a drug directly under the skin.

mainlining
Intravenous drug injection.

opiates
Natural or synthetic derivatives of the drug opium, which is derived from the poppy plant.

analgesics
Medicines that relieve pain; painkillers.

cough suppressants. Another group, the isoquinoline alkaloids, have no significant influence on the central nervous system, so they are not drugs of choice on the illicit market. A small amount of opium is also used to make antidiarrheal preparations such as paregoric.

Morphine, the principal constituent of opium, is one of the most effective drugs known for relieving pain. It is used medically, usually for postoperative pain or pain associated with terminal illness. Abusers inject the drug intravenously; tolerance and dependence develop rapidly. Most codeine is produced from morphine. Compared with morphine, codeine produces less sedation and analgesia; thus, it is used for the relief of moderate pain and in combination with other products such as aspirin. It is by far the most widely used naturally occurring narcotic in medical treatment.

Heroin was medically used to reduce pain from 1898 until 1914, when it was shown to be highly habit-forming. Since then, it has become strictly a street drug. Pure heroin is a white powder with a bitter taste; it is rarely sold in unadulterated form on the street.

In the 1960s and early 1970s, a **bag** (a single dose of heroin) was about 4 to 7 percent heroin. Today it is about 40 percent pure. With the increased purity, the addiction rates are much higher. Also, the price of heroin has dropped from about $600 a gram to about $300 a gram (Brady 1993). With the high demand in the United States market, heroin produced in Afghanistan, Iran, Burma, Laos, Thailand, Mexico, and other places is pouring into the country ("The Return of a Deadly Drug Called Horse" 1989).

Unpurified heroin is usually some shade of brown in color, depending upon the impurities left from the manufacturing process and/or the presence of additives. A fix of heroin is usually injected directly into a vein. Because dependency becomes extreme, the user can rapidly go from using 20 or 30 milligrams a day to using 400 milligrams or more.

Heroin can enslave users so completely that they spend every waking hour determining how to get the next fix. Withdrawal symptoms begin 8 to 12 hours after each fix, so the user is continually on a physical and emotional roller coaster. It is difficult for users to hold a regular job, not only because of the constant need for the drug, but also because of the large income needed to support the habit. Many heroin users turn to crime to pay for the habit they have acquired.

Synthetic Narcotics

Synthetic narcotics have been developed that have helped drug addicts become productive members of society, but at the same time the technology has created a new threat in the form of "new heroin." Synthetic narcotics such as hydromorphone and methadone have been derived by modifying the chemicals found in opium. Hydromorphone (Dilaudid) abuse does not necessarily follow the same pattern as heroin, but the end result is the same dependency. Hospitals and pharmacies have administered it as a painkiller for more than 15 years, and heroin addicts now are turning to it when they are unable to get heroin. It is marketed in both tablet and injectable form. Its effects last for a shorter period, and it is more sedative than morphine, but its potency is much greater; thus, it is a highly abusable drug.

Methadone has the same general properties as morphine. It is a highly effective analgesic agent but more recently has been used for the treatment of narcotic dependence. Though methadone itself creates a dependency, the withdrawal symptoms appear more slowly and are less intense than those of heroin. Methadone maintenance programs are still prevalent in the United States today; heroin addicts can take methadone to avoid the withdrawal effects of heroin and be productive citizens in society (Stitzer, Iguchi, and Felch 1992).

Designer Drugs

A new threat is sweeping America. In 1979, a dealer unveiled a drug that looked like heroin; it was cut with milk sugar, and he called it "Asian White," the street name for the finest Southeast Asian heroin, and he charged a comparable price. He shortly lost two of his customers. One was found comatose in a motel room and the other died in a bathroom, and both had the obvious heroin paraphernalia—needle, syringe, and white powder. Forensic scientists examined the bodies, and they found no trace of heroin. Since that time, numerous chemicals have surfaced, each with slight variations, that have become known as **designer drugs.**

These drugs originally were legal because they were not considered controlled substances. When researchers found out that the chief ingredient of the drugs was **fentanyl,** this became a controlled substance and illegal. The drug-producing chemists then created a new drug that was similar to fentanyl but with a slight molecular variation that resulted in a legal or uncontrolled substance. The frustrating thing was that there were hundreds of variations of fentanyl, and the designer drugs, now called "China White" or "new heroin" (in the case of narcotics), use any number of the variations and in many cases are legal.

The base drug, fentanyl, is 100 times as strong as morphine and 20 to 40 times as strong as heroin. The analogs sufentanyl and lofentanyl are, respectively, 2,000 and 6,000 times as strong as morphine. Under controlled situations, these are effective anesthetics; in the illicit markets they result in a very fast "rush" and an extraordinary high. Their addictive power is overwhelming; it may take a couple of years

---

bag
A single dosage unit of heroin.

designer drugs
Many of these drugs use as their chief ingredient fentanyl, or a derivative, which produces a drug that is a hundred times as strong as morphine and twenty to forty times as strong as heroin. Designer drugs can imitate narcotics, cocaine, or hallucinogens.

fentanyl
A psychoactive substance that is the basis for some designer drugs.

to get addicted to alcohol, or a couple of months to become addicted to cocaine (not crack)—but it can take only one dose for fentanyl. Because of their potency, these drugs have varied and bizarre effects. They have been called the drug version of Chernobyl, a problem that was never imagined 20 years ago. It has been reported that students are smoking cocaine cut with the fentanyl, which has been called "juice."

Every abusable drug can be synthesized in a laboratory. In California, 20 percent of the heroin abusers are now using fentanyl instead of the more expensive heroin, and in some counties as many as 90 percent of the heroin abusers use fentanyl. These problems occur not only on the coast but throughout the United States. For example, a county in Pennsylvania recently reported sixteen overdose drug deaths due to fentanyl ("An Outbreak of Designer Drug–Related Deaths in Pennsylvania" 1991).

Some of these criminal chemists have botched batches and sold the drugs anyway. MPTP is a contaminant that was discovered in new heroin. After its distribution, MPTP left users suffering from the devastating symptoms of Parkinson's disease, in many cases after one dose. The brain uses MPTP to produce the toxin that causes Parkinson's disease (Shafer 1985).

MDMA (3,4-Methylenedioxymethamphetamine), which was outlawed in 1985 and is better known as "ecstasy," is a type of synthetic cocaine. **Ecstasy** is a drug hybrid, a cross between a hallucinogen, mescaline, and a stimulant, amphetamine ("New Data Intensify the Agony over Ecstasy" 1988). Labeled the LSD of the '80s and '90s, MDMA appears to stimulate the emotions and cognitive functions. It was taken recently in the United Kingdom by some young people at a "rave" party to obtain a warm, loving feeling, and fifteen people died from the resulting convulsions (Randall 1992). Before it was outlawed, it was used by psychiatrists to speed psychotherapy. As with most drugs, there seemed to be some positive effects in therapy, but in the streets it was abused and resulted in deaths and dependency. Some of the fatalities died of explosive high fever, convulsions, coagulation of the blood vessels, rhabdomyolysis (disintegration of skeletal muscle), and acute kidney failure (Henry, Jeffreys, and Dawling 1992).

Treatment of Narcotics Abuse

Treatment programs for narcotic abuse usually involve three stages: (1) crisis intervention, (2) detoxification, and (3) aftercare. Crisis intervention is the care undertaken to relieve whatever problem brought the user to the treatment center. If the user decides to continue in the treatment program, **detoxification** (the process of eliminating the drug from the user's system) must be started. This usually entails controlling the withdrawal symptoms so that the user will experience as few ill effects as possible. The initial concern is to determine polydrug use, the identity of the drugs used, and the degree of dependency on each drug. For example, barbiturate/alcohol withdrawal is more serious than continual use

and is treated first with mild barbiturates to gradually withdraw the individual. Methadone would likely be used for opiate users.

After the process of detoxification, the long, hard job of rehabilitation begins. There are several aftercare approaches currently available to those who choose to kick their habit. There are two basic, and opposing, philosophies of rehabilitative treatment for heroin abuse. In general, the maintenance programs (such as the British system and methadone maintenance) do not try to break the user's drug dependence. Rather, their goal is to make users' criminal or antisocial acts unnecessary by providing them with a monitored legal supply of narcotics. By contrast, the goal of abstinence programs is to help users become functioning members of society again by breaking the drug habit for good.

STIMULANTS

Drugs known as stimulants, or "uppers," speed up the central nervous system. There are probably as many legal stimulants on the market as there are illicit drugs in this category. The major legal stimulants that are widely used and abused are caffeine and nicotine. The two most dangerous and popular illicit drugs are cocaine and its freebased derivative, crack, and methamphetamine (speed, or **crank,** and its more potent crystalline form, "ice"). It seems that technology continues to discover new forms of synthetic stimulants, each more powerful than the previous one. For example, recently the illegal drug "cat" (methcathinone), which is similar to speed, was invented, and several dozen illegal "cat" labs have been raided since 1991 (Glastris 1993).

Physiological Reactions to Major Stimulants

Stimulants mimic the action of the sympathetic nervous system; that is, at proper dose levels, they increase system activity to respond to the need for improved mental and physical performance when fatigue impairs them. The physiological reactions to stimulants include increased heart rate and strength of contraction, elevated blood pressure, increased muscle tension, stimulation of adrenal glands to produce adrenaline, constriction of blood vessels, dilation of the bronchi in the lungs, relaxation of intestinal muscle, and increased blood sugar. These reactions combine to produce alertness, wakefulness, and attentiveness; thus, the drugs seem to make their

---

ecstasy
Also called "MDMA," this hybrid cross between amphetamines and the hallucinogen mescaline acts much like cocaine.

detoxification
The process of eliminating a drug from the user's body.

crank
Another nickname for the stimulant methamphetamine, or "speed."

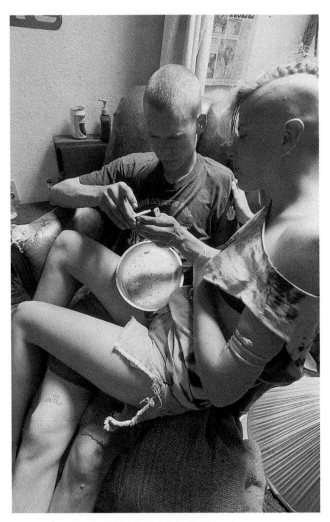

Crack is much more powerful and addictive than cocaine, with addiction sometimes occurring after a few uses.

users feel stronger, more decisive, and more self-confident. They can also act as appetite suppressants.

The drugs are quickly absorbed from the alimentary tract (digestive system) or from sites of injection. The effects are greatly intensified if stimulants are injected intravenously rather than taken orally or inhaled. Injection produces a sudden sensation known as a "rush," often described as orgasmic in nature, which probably results from the intense stimulation of the sympathetic nervous system. A period of euphoria occurs, which is usually followed by a period of depression (Carrol 1989). In order to remain "high," abusers must increase the dose level, which often leads to physiological dependence.

Caffeine

Most Americans take a legal stimulant, caffeine, each morning. It is fairly easy to ingest over 500 milligrams of caffeine in one day, which can be harmful. Table 15.1 shows the amount of caffeine in commonly used substances. Caffeine is a stimulant: It speeds the heart rate, temporarily elevates the blood pressure, interferes with sleep, and increases the fatty acid levels in the blood.

Caffeinism is acute or chronic overuse of caffeine and caffeine poisoning. The symptoms of caffeinism include anxiety, mood changes, sleep disturbances, and other psychophysical complaints. Caffeine intoxication is characterized by the described traits and consumption in excess of 250 milligrams of caffeine per day.

Caffeine withdrawal results in headache, irritability, lethargy, depression, muscle pain, mood changes, fatigue, sleep disturbance, and mild physiological arousal (Silverman et al. 1992). Even drinking two and a half cups of coffee per day can result in the withdrawal symptoms ("Withdrawal Seen for Coffee Drinkers" 1992).

Cocaine and Crack

Cocaine use has rocketed over the last decade; 22 million Americans having tried cocaine, and 15.2 percent of graduating high school seniors have tried it. One out of every 18 young people has used crack, and 6 million Americans use cocaine regularly (Clouet, Asghar, and Brown 1988). Just a few years ago cocaine was not considered addictive, but now it is recognized as a powerfully addicting drug. Even after treatment and months of abstinence, many people cannot resist its lure. The national cocaine hot line receives 1,200 calls per day, most of which are from users of crack or concerned family and friends of crack users. Other callers are users of powder cocaine.

In its pure form before being cut, cocaine is a white crystalline powder that looks much like sugar. Cocaine is also found in rock form and flake form (like shavings from a bar of soap). It is either snorted, liquified and then injected, or freebased and smoked.

Cocaine, the most powerful stimulant of natural origin, is extracted from the leaves of the coca plant, which has been cultivated in South America since prehistoric times. In South America, up to 90 percent of the adult male population living at high altitudes chew the leaves of the plant for refreshment and relief from fatigue.

The following statements are descriptive of the nature and effects of cocaine (Holtzman 1986):

1. General psychological stimulant that mimics the stress response by increasing heart rate, respiratory rate, body temperature, blood pressure, constriction of the blood vessels, and dilation of the pupils.

caffeinism
Acute or chronic overuse of caffeine, and resultant caffeine poisoning; symptoms include anxiety, mood changes, sleep disturbances, and other psychophysical complaints.

TABLE 15.1   CAFFEINE IN SELECTED SUBSTANCES (IN MILLIGRAMS)

Coffee (5 oz.)		Diet Pepsi	36
Brewed, drip method	60–180	RC Cola	36
Brewed, percolator	40–170	Cherry RC	36
Instant	30–120	Canada Dry Jamaica Cola	30
Decaffeinated, brewed	2–5	Canada Dry Diet Cola	1.5
Decaffeinated, instant	1–5	**Prescription Drugs**	
Tea (5 oz.)		Cafergot (for migraine headache)	100
Brewed, major U.S. brands	20–90	Darvon compound (for pain relief)	32.4
Brewed, imported brands	25–110	**Nonprescription Drugs**	
Iced (12 oz.)	67–76	No-Doz (alertness tablets)	100
Instant	25–50	Vivarin (alertness tablets)	200
Soft Drinks (12 oz.)		Aqua-Ban (diuretic)	100
Sugar Free Mr. Pibb	58	Aqua-Ban Plus	200
Mountain Dew	54	Anacin	32
Mello Yello	52	Excedrin	65
Tab	46	Midol	32.4
Coca-Cola (classic or new)	46	Vanquish	33
Diet Coke	46	Duradyne	15
Shasta Cola	44	Coryban-D capsules	30
Shasta Cherry Cola	44	Triaminicin tablets	30
Shasta Diet Cola	44	**Other**	
Mr. Pibb	40.8	Cocoa (5 oz.)	2–20
Dr. Pepper	40.8	Chocolate milk (8 oz.)	2–7
Diet Dr. Pepper	40.8	Milk chocolate (1 oz.)	1–15
Pepsi-Cola	38.4	Semi-sweet chocolate (1 oz.)	5–35
Big Red	38	Chocolate flavored syrup (1 oz.)	4

Denise Grady/© 1986 *Discover* Magazine. Reprinted with permission.

2. Reduces hunger and fatigue. The more fatigued the user, the more powerful the effect.

3. Temporarily increases reaction time and muscular strength, but then there is a letdown.

4. Acts as a local anesthetic.

5. If snorted, it reaches the brain in 3 to 5 minutes; if injected, it reaches the brain in 15 seconds; and if smoked, it reaches the brain in 5 to 7 seconds.

6. Psychological effects include anxiety, hallucinations, impotence, and insomnia.

7. Large doses may cause multisensory (visual, tactile, and auditory) hallucinations, paranoid delusions, quick changes in perception, impaired judgment, aggression, panic reactions, agitated depression, and a perception of power, which may make a person potentially antisocial and dangerous.

8. Death from overdose is due to respiratory failure on a lethal dose of about 1.2 grams at one time.

Freebasing cocaine has become very popular because the intensity of the cocaine high is dramatically more powerful and intense. It is comparable to methamphetamine in intensity. Up until 1985, freebasing was a dangerous process. Cocaine purchased on the street in its **adulterated** form was refined using water and ether or ammonia. The procedure removes most of the sugars and other substances, and leaves an intensive form of cocaine. The use of ether is extremely dangerous and has resulted in fires and explosions. In about 1985, freebasing began to be accomplished with common baking soda. Suddenly crack or rock emerged as a cheap (about $5 to $10 a hit), powerful drug, and it has swept America. It is generally sold as slivers or pellets (like soap shavings) in a vial, folding papers, or aluminum foil. According to

adulterated
Made impure by the addition of another substance.

experts, crack is many times more powerful and more addicting than cocaine, and addiction occurs sometimes after a few uses. It is so intense that it can cause instant death, particularly for a small percentage of the U.S. population who can't metabolize its enzymes ("An Invitation to Sudden Death" 1991). Crack triggers high blood pressure, brain damage, heart attacks, and strokes (Brooks 1993). Cocaine and crack have been responsible for many instant deaths in normally healthy people, and many of these deaths have received a great deal of attention, as in the case of athletes and Hollywood figures. Crack joins the designer drugs, methamphetamine (crank), and "ice" (refined methamphetamine, described later) as the most potent, quick-addicting, and dangerous street drugs of our times.

Cocaine powder is usually sniffed, or "snorted," through the nasal passages, but freebasing, vaporizing the cocaine, and inhaling the smoke has recently become popular among some heavy users. Within minutes the drug enters the bloodstream and is carried to the brain, where it serves as a central nervous system stimulant. The effects of cocaine, which last from 1 to 2 hours, have been described as extremely pleasurable; users say the drug makes them feel happier, more energetic, more seductive, more exciting.

Cocaine overuse can damage the mucous membranes of the nose. The drug acts as a **vasoconstrictor**—it narrows blood vessels and reduces the oxygen supply. The lining of the nose eventually deteriorates, and the septum (the cartilage that separates the nostrils) crumbles. Some chronic users have so abused this drug that they have "sniffed" holes in their noses that required surgical repair.

With chronic use of cocaine, new symptoms can develop from the constant stimulation and lack of rest. As tolerance increases, larger doses are required at shorter intervals until the user's life is largely committed to the habit. Tactile hallucinations can seem so real that some chronic users injure themselves attempting to remove imaginary insects from under their skin. Excessive doses can cause seizures and death from respiratory failure (Carrol 1989).

A major problem is the increasing number of cocaine babies that are being born to cocaine-abusing mothers. Cocaine babies begin life in the agonizing state of withdrawal and may go throughout life with severe physical problems in motor development, emotional problems, and learning disabilities (Carrol, 1989). Babies exposed to cocaine during fetal development may have low birth weights, be shorter, have smaller heads, and be born prematurely (Bateman et al. 1993).

Amphetamines

Amphetamine abusers usually follow one of two patterns. Some compulsively take low-dose oral amphetamines daily to maintain a fast pace, reinforce an outgoing personality, keep their mood elevated, and postpone the inevitable depression that follows discontinued use. They alternate stimulants and depressants, taking "uppers" in the morning and "downers," such as barbiturates or alcohol, at night.

The other pattern of amphetamine abuse involves the intravenous use of high-dose methamphetamine (speed or crank). In this pattern, the abuser goes on "runs"—episodes lasting from several hours to a few days, during which he or she remains "up" with continued injections. Within minutes after the initial injection, the user experiences an intense tingling sensation (a "buzz"), which is followed by more intense tingling sensations, muscle contractions, and a feeling of extreme pleasure. During a run, the user typically does not eat and thus loses weight and may experience other symptoms of malnutrition. The longer the run persists, the more problems occur, including a mood change from pleasant optimism and euphoria to hyperactive aggression. After the initial high, the user is left with an aftermath of potentially severe mental disorders and destruction of brain cells. Even though tolerance develops, overdoses of amphetamines are uncommon and rarely fatal (Dusek and Girdano 1993).

Ice

One of the latest high-tech forms of methamphetamine to arrive in the United States is a crystalline rock form called **ice.** The drug originated in Japan and Korea and gradually spread to Hawaii, where it has become a major problem (Cho 1990). On the mainland it arrived first at the West Coast, and it has reached most major cities on the mainland (Lerner 1989). Women seem particularly attracted to it; some consider it a weight-reduction drug. The sense of euphoria from ice lasts for up to 14 hours.

Ice can cause vitamin and mineral deficiencies, rapid loss of weight, and lowered resistance to disease. Prolonged use can cause lung, liver, and kidney damage. Side effects are somewhat puzzling but include anorexia, brittle bones, and wounds that won't heal (Culhane 1990).

In Hawaii, case studies indicate addiction after a single use. Users will take the drug for up to 4 days and then crash (sleep), just like with speed or crank.

Illicit amphetamine use closely parallels that of cocaine in the range of its short-term and long-term effects. Despite the risks, undercover laboratories continue to produce vast amounts of amphetamines, especially methamphetamine, for distribution on the illicit drug market.

Unfortunately, some amphetamines—such as phenmetrazine hydrochloride (Preludin), dexedrine, and methamphetamine—are often prescribed as diet pills. Many

---

vasoconstrictor
A drug that narrows the blood vessels and reduces the oxygen supply.

amphetamines
Stimulant drugs used to combat fatigue and suppress appetite; as drugs of abuse, commonly called "uppers."

ice
A crystalline rock form of methamphetamine (speed) that is more powerful and more addicting than the original methamphetamine.

states have already passed legislation that virtually bans the use of amphetamines for the treatment of obesity. Similar legislation is pending in several other states.

The Food and Drug Administration continues to approve the use of amphetamines in the treatment of narcolepsy and hyperactivity in children. Dextroamphetamine and methylphenidate (Ritalin) are the most effective drugs for the acute management of hyperactivity; about two-thirds of all hyperactive children treated with these drugs have shown improvement. The drugs seem to reduce aggressive and impulsive behavior in children, as well as improving goal orientation and attention span. Unlike the activating effects observed in adults, these drugs do not produce euphoria or overstimulation in hyperkinetic children, nor do they slow the children down or suppress their initiative. The medical reason for this is not well understood, but the calming effect does improve academic performance (Gerald 1981).

The treatment of cocaine and other stimulant abuse involves (1) the user's absolute abstention from all drugs, (2) teaching consequences of drug stimulation and alternative forms of stimulation, and (3) involving family members in the treatment when possible. Research is focusing on developing enzymes that could block the effect of cocaine and reduce the craving for the drug (Morell 1993).

DEPRESSANTS

Depressants are drugs designed to slow the functioning of the central nervous system. There are two classifications of depressants: sedative hypnotics and antianxiety drugs. Sedative hypnotics can calm the individual and thereby relieve anxiety and tension by inducing a state resembling natural sleep. The sedative hypnotics include **barbiturates,** such as phenobarbital and secobarbital, and **nonbarbiturates,** such as methaqualone (Quaalude) and glutethimide (Doriden), and alcohol. Antianxiety drugs calm the individual and relieve anxiety and tension but do so without inducing a hypnotic state.

If you suspect or know that you have become dependent on a particular drug or drugs, whether legally or illegally obtained, think about your choices concerning future use of this drug. You may wish to include the physical, psychological, social, and professional consequences of continuing or discontinuing use. As you consider your choices, locate a drug counselor who can assist you in making your decision.

Physicians often prescribe depressants to reduce tension and anxiety and counteract insomnia. Taken in excessive amounts, however, depressants produce a state of intoxication similar to drunkenness. These effects can vary not only from person to person but also from time to time in the same individual; invariably, however, excessive use of depressants results at least in impaired judgment, slurred speech, and loss of motor coordination. Users rapidly develop tolerance to the intoxicating effects, which can lead to overdosing.

Depressants vary in their potential for overdose, but users who have severe depressant poisoning can fall into a coma,

have a weak and rapid pulse, or have slow and shallow respiration. Users can even die from an overdose, generally from respiratory failure, if they do not receive medical attention.

Chloral Hydrate

Chloral hydrate, first synthesized in the 1860s, is the oldest of the hypnotic drugs. Its popularity declined with the advent of barbiturates, but it is still considered an effective sedative and hypnotic that is unlikely to induce tolerance (although it may be habit-forming). It disturbs rapid eye movement (REM) sleep less and depresses respiration less than the barbiturates do, but it does show some drug interactions. Chloral hydrate, when used with alcohol, was known as a "Mickey Finn," or "knockout drops." These drugs in combination reacted synergistically—that is, caused each other to be more powerful than when consumed alone. Chloral hydrate has been responsible for deaths when it has been used as a sedative for children with cardiopulmonary disease and complications resulted (Cohen 1993). Chloral hydrate is not considered a street drug.

Barbiturates

Some 2,500 derivatives of barbituric acid have been synthesized, but only about 15 remain in medical use. Doctors prescribe barbiturates in small therapeutic doses to calm nervous conditions and in large doses to induce sleep. These drugs are classified as ultrashort-, short-, intermediate-, and long-acting.

Because the ultrashort-acting drugs produce anesthesia within seconds and because their duration is also short, drug abusers do not seek them out; instead, they seek out the short- and intermediate-acting barbiturates with durations of up to 6 hours. Long-acting barbiturates are not marketable as illicit drugs because of the length of time needed for onset. One of the most dangerous aspects of all barbiturate use is the high risk of both physiological and psychological dependence.

Glutethimide (Doriden) and Methaqualone (Quaalude)

When it was introduced in 1954, glutethimide (Doriden) was thought to be a safe barbiturate substitute, but experience

depressants
Drugs used to decrease nervous or muscular activity; as drugs of abuse, commonly called "downers."

barbiturates
Sedative-hypnotic depressant drugs; as drugs of abuse, commonly called "downers."

nonbarbiturates
Depressant drugs such as methaqualone (Quaalude) and glutethimide. These drugs produce a calming effect and relieve anxiety and tension without inducing a hypnotic state.

chloral hydrate
The oldest synthetic sleep-inducing drug.

has shown that it has no particular advantage, and several disadvantages, compared to the barbiturates. Its sedative effects are similar to those of the intermediate-acting barbiturates, but because this drug's effects are of long duration (6 hours), it is difficult to reverse overdoses, and overdoses of this drug often result in death (Carrol 1989). Glutethimide overdoses have a mortality rate four times higher than barbiturate overdoses (Gerald 1981).

Methaqualone (Quaalude), also a synthetic sedative, has been widely abused because people mistakenly thought it was nonaddictive. Users often take Quaaludes to heighten a feeling of excitement. They say that they feel more in control than with other drugs and don't have to worry about hangovers, alcohol on their breath, or "bad trips," but the drug can impair reflexes and judgment. Large doses cause coma, sometimes accompanied by convulsions. Users rapidly develop dependence, and some say that it is easier to become dependent on this drug than on narcotics. The amount of methaqualone needed to overdose does not increase with a user's tolerance, so heavy users can overdose before the drug has even made them feel high. This drug also has a synergistic effect in combination with alcohol.

Tranquilizers

Tranquilizers are divided into two groups: major and minor. The major tranquilizers, such as Thorazine and Reserpine, are prescription drugs most often used in mental hospitals for the treatment of psychoses. They are not street drugs of abuse. The minor tranquilizers are used to relieve anxiety, tension, and muscle spasms, to produce sedation, and to prevent convulsions.

Meprobamate, synthesized in 1950, introduced the era of minor tranquilizers. It is also sold as Miltown, Equanil, Kesso-Bamate, and SK-Bamate. In onset and duration of action, meprobamate is similar to the intermediate-acting barbiturates, but it does not produce sleep and is less toxic. Excessive use, however, can result in psychological and physical dependence. Minor tranquilizers of the **benzodiazepine** family, including **Valium** and **Librium,** are the most widely prescribed medicines in the country. The FDA cites evidence that Valium is overprescribed and abused, and that it can cause psychological and physical dependence. Over 90 percent of the physicians in this country prescribe Valium for anxiety, muscle spasms, ulcers, and other anxiety-related psychosomatic disorders. Women users outnumber men 2.5 to 1. Valium is also a popular street drug. Although the benzodiazepines are less likely to cause dependence than the barbiturates, they have adverse effects on thought processes, coordination, and memory (Gillin 1991). The newer benzodiazepines, introduced in the mid 1970s, still have problems but are less likely to cause these side effects because they are metabolized much faster (Gillin 1991). One such new drug, triazolam, is the most commonly prescribed "sleeping pill" in the United States.

Librium (chlordiazepoxide) is also habit forming and overprescribed. It is common for users to experience clumsiness,

Drugs affect people from all walks of life.

drowsiness, and dizziness. Valium and Librium as tranquilizers cause drowsiness, respiratory depression, and a decrease in memory and motor functions. Valium and Librium, like almost any drugs, are dangerous to women who are pregnant, particularly during the first trimester. Side effects include skin rashes, lethargy, menstrual irregularities, conjunctivitis, overexcitement, constipation, stammering, slurred speech,

tranquilizers
Depressant drugs used medically to relieve tension and anxiety; as drugs of abuse, commonly known as "downers."

benzodiazepines
A general classification of tranquilizers that includes the most widely prescribed, Valium and Librium.

Valium
A widely prescribed tranquilizer that causes drowsiness and respiratory depression.

Librium
A widely prescribed minor tranquilizer used to treat anxiety.

hypertension, and thirst. Valium in combination with alcohol has a **synergistic** (multiplying) **effect** and can result in coma or death.

Valium dependence can occur with a dosage as low as 30 milligrams a day over time. Withdrawal from Valium can be as dangerous as barbiturate withdrawal, which is characterized by violent shaking and possible seizures.

Treatment for Withdrawal from Depressants
The treatment for withdrawal from depressants requires intensive care that should be given in a medical setting. Signs and symptoms of withdrawal first appear within 8 hours after the user discontinues the drug, and they become severe during the next 8 hours. They become even more severe after 24 hours and, if untreated, will likely develop into grand mal (major) convulsions at between 30 and 48 hours. After the first 48 hours, there may be recurrences of insomnia culminating in delirium, hallucinations, and marked tremors. This stage lasts about 5 days, ending in a long sleep. Treatment, or detoxification, consists of administering short-acting barbiturates to relieve the first symptoms and then tapering off with either the same drug or decreasing doses of a long-acting drug. Along with this treatment for the physical withdrawal from the drug, users need psychological help to prevent a relapse into drug use. Death is a real danger in uncontrolled, untreated withdrawal (Dusek and Girdano 1993).

HALLUCINOGENS

The hallucinogenic drugs discussed in this section—LSD, peyote and mescaline, psilocybin and psilocyn, and PCP—have much more powerful effects than marijuana and hashish do. They bring about greater excitation of the central nervous system, characterized by alterations of mood. These moods are usually **euphoric,** characterized by a feeling of extreme well-being, but can also be so severely depressive that suicide is possible.

When people use hallucinogens, their pupils dilate, their body temperature rises, and their blood pressure elevates. Senses of direction, distance, and time are distorted. These drugs produce **delusions** (false beliefs) and visual hallucinations, such as the intensification of color, the apparent motion of a fixed object, or the confusion of one object with another. The most common danger is impaired judgment, which can lead to accidents and rash decisions. Long after hallucinogens are eliminated from the body, users can experience spontaneous **flashbacks**—recurrences of the hallucinatory effects.

Lysergic Acid Diethylamide (LSD)
Lysergic acid diethylamide (LSD) is produced from lysergic acid, a substance derived from the ergot fungus, or "rust," that grows on rye and other grains (O'Brien et al. 1992). The LSD user gets the drug in a tablet or other consumable form. Because LSD is so powerful and the usual dosage (100 or 200

micrograms) is too small a quantity to weigh out, the drug is always found on tangible objects, such as sugar cubes, postage stamps, gelatin squares, or blotter paper (O'Brien et al. 1992).

Just how LSD acts to produce hallucinations is unknown. Successful treatment of a bad LSD trip can often be accomplished by friends who talk the user down in familiar surroundings. Minor tranquilizers have also proved useful.

LSD remains high on the list of drugs to be controlled. Because of the belief that the original laws were not stringent enough, legislators have passed even stiffer laws, and today the maximum federal penalty for first-time unlawful possession is a $5,000 fine and 1 year in jail. There has been some resurgence of LSD use, particularly among teenagers.

Peyote and Mescaline
Mescaline is the primary active ingredient of the fleshy parts, or buttons, of the **peyote** cactus. It can also be synthetically produced. It is legal in the United States to use peyote as a part of the religious rites of the Native American Church; outside this church community, the drug is used illegally.

Peyote or mescaline intoxication first brings on a feeling of contentment and hypersensitivity, which is followed by a period of nervous calm during which visual hallucinations often occur. A 350- to 500-milligram dose of mescaline produces delusions and hallucinations lasting 5 to 12 hours. As used in religious ritual, four to twelve peyote buttons are ingested, followed by a period of meditation during which visual aberrations, nausea, or vomiting may occur.

Peyote buttons can be found on the illegal drug market, but the extracted mescaline is rare; only about two in every hundred street samples offered as mescaline actually turn out to be the drug. Like LSD, no physical dependence seems to occur, but it is possible that some psychological dependence may develop. Tolerance to the drug develops very quickly.

---

synergistic effect
The result when the effects of two drugs used in combination are greater than the sum of their individual effects when used separately; a multiplying of effects.

euphoric
Characterized by a feeling of extreme well-being.

delusions
False beliefs that can occur in users of hallucinogens.

flashbacks
The recurrence of effects experienced on drugs, such as the intensification of colors, the apparent motion of a fixed object, or the mistaking of one object for another.

lysergic acid diethylamide (LSD)
A hallucinogenic drug of abuse.

mescaline
A hallucinogenic drug of abuse, derived from the peyote cactus.

peyote
A form of cactus; mescaline is derived from its buttons.

PERSONAL INSIGHT
A Story of PCP

Beth was raised in a small town in Kentucky. She belonged to a conservative Christian church and was very devout. After high school, she attended a university, where she did very well. By the spring semester, she had met several friends and enjoyed a healthy social life.

One evening, she was invited to a party with her group of friends and some people she did not know. She had never smoked or drunk alcohol in her life. At the party, some of the people she did not know very well persuaded her to try a marijuana joint. She took a few puffs. The people she did not know very well had laced the marijuana with PCP. In just a few moments, she began to feel very strange. She felt that she couldn't get her feet to touch the ground. As she reached for the floor, she became aware that she was on fire. The fire was so real in her hallucination that she began to beat her pants to put out the fire but it would not go out so she shed all of her clothes. With people laughing at her, she ran down the street naked. When exhausted, she fell down on a lawn and vomited on herself. The police came, but she thought they were going to attack her, so she screamed and kicked as they wrestled her into the police car. When the effects of the PCP finally wore off and Beth realized what had happened, she was so humiliated that she dropped out of the university.

One smoke, but a major life change for Beth.

Psilocybin and Psilocyn

Psilocybe mushrooms have also been used for centuries in traditional Mexican Indian religious services to produce visions and hallucinations. When these mushrooms are eaten, they affect moods in the same way that mescaline and LSD do. Their active ingredients, **psilocybin** and **psilocyn,** are chemically related to LSD. The hallucinatory experience is roughly comparable to that produced by LSD, except that the trip lasts about half as long. Dangers involved stem not from physical harm but from the potential for inducing psychotic states that remain long after the expected end of the experience. Tolerance to these mushrooms develops quickly, and a period of 5 days must elapse without use before the user can experience a "high" again from it. Psilocybin and psilocyn head the list of the most misrepresented drugs on the street; most mushrooms sold on the street are the grocery store variety spiked with LSD.

Phencyclidine (Angel Dust)

Phencyclidine (PCP) is sold under at least fifty names, including **angel dust,** *animal tranquilizer, crystal, supergrass,* and *killer weed.* In its pure form, PCP is a crystalline powder that readily dissolves in water; however, most illicit PCP contains contaminants that cause the color to range from tan to brown and the consistency to range from a powder to a gummy mass. It is most often applied to a leafy material, such as parsley, mint, oregano, tobacco, or marijuana, and smoked. The bizarre and volatile effects of this drug include numbness, slurred speech, loss of coordination, rapid or involuntary eye movements, and image distortions like those seen in a funhouse mirror. Severe mood disorders (sometimes violent or psychotic) can also occur. Because of the catatonic (trancelike) state often produced, evidenced by the inability to speak or walk, PCP effects are often indistinguishable from the effects of schizophrenia.

At one time, PCP was tested as a human anesthetic but was abandoned because of its bizarre aftereffects. Until 1979, it was used as a tranquilizer on large animals. PCP has perhaps the highest potential for bad experiences of any hallucinogen. Even emergency room professionals are not quite sure what to do for a "PCP freakout." Persons who are badly affected by this drug should be kept in a dark, quiet room because of their tendency to become hyperactive on high doses, and medical attention is definitely needed. Another problem is that PCP is often used to adulterate other drugs. Some drug samples alleged to be cocaine, for example, are partly or wholly PCP. The opposite problem can also occur—a user can believe that the drug is PCP when it is something else. This can cause a particular problem for a doctor trying to treat a drug overdose.

In the spring of 1978, PCP was added to the Comprehensive Drug Abuse Prevention and Control Act of 1970, which created much harsher penalties for possessing the drug. There are no legal manufacturers of PCP in the United States today.

DRUGS IN SPORTS

On 13 January 1986, the National Collegiate Athletic Association (NCAA) approved mandatory drug testing, and since that time there has been increased public awareness regarding drugs and athletes. Professional sports have also adopted drug testing. This has been facilitated by national media coverage of the cocaine-related deaths of several athletes as well as anabolic-steroid-related exclusion of some athletes from postseason bowl games. Mandatory drug testing has been the

psilocybin, psilocyn
Hallucinogenic drugs of abuse extracted from the psilocybin mushroom.

phencyclidine (PCP)
A hallucinogenic drug of abuse; also called "angel dust."

angel dust
The street name for phencyclidine, a hallucinogenic crystalline powder that produces bizarre and volatile effects.

Football player Lyle Alzado attributed his illness, which eventually led to his death, to the use of steroids.

to nitrogen-depleted prisoners of war. Steroids soon became available to weight lifers and other athletes. In the 1970s and early 1980s, there was widespread abuse among NCAA and professional sports until drug testing was instituted. Proponents of steroids claimed an increase in muscle strength, mass, and endurance, decreased recovery time between workouts, and improved physique. Critics claim that these beneficial effects are due primarily to expectancy and other factors associated with training (Lukas 1993). Physicians have dramatically reduced the number of steroids they prescribe, but the black-market supply of steroids has increased. About 1 million Americans still take anabolic steroids illegally (DuRant et al. 1993). Table 15.2 lists the potential effects of steroids (White et al. 1987).

Another hormone that some athletes are using in a dangerous attempt to get the "edge" in sports is **human growth hormone (HGH).** HGH is a natural hormone (a polypeptide with 191 amino acids) that is released from the pituitary gland and promotes general body growth. Until recently HGH could be obtained only in an expensive retrieval process from cadavers. Now HGH can be manufactured synthetically and has become available through physicians by prescription but also illegally "on the street" (White et al. 1989).

first strategy that has worked to curtail the widespread use of drugs in athletics. Athletes realize that they can lose their eligibility to compete in athletics if they have a positive test. New ways to get "the edge" in sports are through more natural means, such as self-hypnosis, meditation, and imagery, rather than steroids and cocaine.

Anabolic steroids are derived from the male hormone testosterone, which comes in pill form or injectable solution. In World War II, anabolic steroids were used effectively to increase aggressiveness in German soldiers and restore vitality

anabolic steroids
Substances derived from the male hormone testosterone; used to increase muscle bulk, but with serious side effects.

human growth hormone (HGH)
A growth-promoting hormone that occurs naturally in the body. It is sometimes abused and can result in giantism and other problems.

TABLE 15.2   EFFECTS OF STEROID USE

1. Helps the body utilize protein (protein synthesis).
2. Causes retention of water and salt.
3. Causes increased aggression.
4. Causes masculinization of females.
5. Decreases natural testosterone production in males.
6. Causes testicular atrophy.
7. Causes acne.
8. Causes gynecomastia (enlargement of breasts in males).
9. Increases red blood cell production (for anemics).
10. Accelerates growth in children (for growth retarded children).
11. Causes male pattern baldness.
12. Decreases sperm production.
13. Increases body hair in females.
14. Causes menstrual irregularities in women.
15. Causes deepening in voice in females.
16. Increases total serum cholesterol and lowers HDL.
17. Causes liver dysfunction.
18. Causes chemical imbalance in body.
19. Bone growth will stop (epiphyseal plates). Excess testosterone fools body into thinking puberty is passed. Young people who have not reached their full growth will have early secondary sex characteristics and stunted growth.
20. In abrupt cessation of use, depression results.
21. Euphoria is associated with aggressive effects of steroids.
22. Causes false psychological high.

Reprinted with permission from the *Journal of Health Education*, August/September 1987, pp. 32–34. *Journal of Health Education* is a publication of the American Alliance for Health, Physical Education, Recreation and Dance, 1900 Association Drive, Reston, Virginia 22091.

HGH is used therapeutically in children who can't produce their own HGH and would have been victims of disabling dwarfism. Athletes who indiscriminately use growth hormone may have problems with the medical condition acromegaly. Acromegaly is associated with heart problems, arthritis, impotence, and bony enlargement of the forehead, jaw, hands, and feet (White et al. 1989). Except for medical applications, use should be avoided by athletes as well as anyone else who thinks that HGH use would benefit them physically.

DRUG TESTING

In recent years the testing for drugs in athletes, federal workers, transportation service personnel, and a variety of other workers has become an important issue. Beginning with Utah in 1987, many states have implemented or are considering implementing mandatory drug testing of employees.

Drug tests are conducted by giving an employee about a 1-hour notice to provide a urine specimen (which is witnessed by an observer) to be analyzed for any abused drugs.

Issue

Employee Drug Testing

"It was impossible to get high anymore, or to stop," stated a 31-year-old former narcotics addict who at the time was in the last stages of his disease. As an addict he had needed eight to ten shots a day, and when he woke up he was either overdosing or detoxing. "My world was hopeless, and I was helpless. I had no more relationships, and I had accepted the fact that I was doomed to die alone, in fear."

This sounds like the confession of a street "junkie," but this confession ends with this: "By that point, I was either on the street scoring, or in the hospital working as an emergency room physician." He was spending the $1,500 per week he was earning in the emergency room for either heroin or designer drugs after he was suspected, rightly, of diverting drugs from the hospital pharmacy. Unfortunately, this physician's story is not uncommon among respected professionals. It is frightening to know that this physician worked for 4 years practicing medicine in his condition. To try to deal with this problem, some professions and businesses have made drug testing mandatory.

- Pro: It is imperative that drug testing be done. What kind of harm could this physician have done? What harm could a policeman, pilot, bus driver, or nuclear power plant operator do under the influence of drugs? Testing must be done.
- Con: Drug testing is an invasion of privacy. If people want to kill themselves with drugs, it is their option to do so. False positive tests can result in lost jobs.

Should employees be tested for drugs? What are you going to do when asked to take a drug test?

Employees and athletes who use drugs often go to great lengths to not get caught with drugs in their urine and devise schemes to beat the test. Reports of storing pouches of urine from nonusing friends to beat the test are common. Two specimens of urine are sent to the lab, one for an initial screening and a second to test for confirmation of a positive test. Two forms of analysis include the **immunoassay** and **gas chromatography/mass spectrometry (GC/MS)** tests. Immunoassays work by allowing selected antibodies to come in

immunoassay
A somewhat unreliable drug-testing technique that uses antibodies that bond to the drugs being tested for.

gas chromatography/mass spectrometry (GC/MS) tests
An accurate drug-testing technique that breaks down each drug and spreads each substance on a printout for easy identification.

TABLE 15.3 NCAA BANNED SUBSTANCES

Substance	Intensity	Positive Test with GC/MS After Use
Marijuana (THC)	Chronic user (daily)	Up to 1 month
Marijuana (THC)	Two times/week	1–3 days
Cocaine/Crack	Single dose	48 hours
Methamphetamine	Single dose	23 hours
Methamphetamine	Chronic user	48 hours
Opiates	Light to heavy	1–3 days
PCP	Light to heavy	7 days
LSD	Light to heavy	2 days
Quaaludes	Light to heavy	1 week
Barbiturates	Depending if short or long acting	30–76 hours
Valium/Librium	Chronic	Weeks to months

contact with drugs in the specimen. Antibodies are proteins that have sites where specific drugs will bind. An analysis of what drugs have bonded to the antibodies will provide a positive test. Some errors have occurred and, in unfortunate instances, employees have lost their jobs because of occasional false positive tests. GC/MS is a gas chromatograph that breaks down all substances in a specimen and spreads each test on a printout. This test is 99.9 percent accurate and has not had any reported errors. The only errors with GC/MS are human handling errors.

Students not yet employed must realize that drug testing might be a condition of future employment. Prospective employees who test positive usually will not be hired. Drug testing is being challenged in courts, with people refusing to be tested on the grounds of "invasion of privacy." In some cases, the court has ruled in favor of the person refusing to take a test.

Costs for drug tests in 1994 ranged from $25 to $35 for drugs of abuse and about $100 for drugs of abuse and anabolic steroids. Table 15.3 is a sample list of drugs banned by the NCAA that can be detected through drug testing and how long they can be detected after use. There are over three thousand brand-name drugs that contain a substance banned by the NCAA (1986).

DRUG INTERACTIONS

When two or more drugs are used at the same time, they might adversely interact. Drug interactions are of several types; perhaps the most serious is when the drugs act to multiply each other's effects. Such multiplication of effects is termed "synergism" (O'Brien et al. 1992). For example, barbiturates and alcohol each depress the central nervous system when taken alone, but when they are taken together, they increase each other's depressant effects and result in a "superdepressant." Alcohol potentiates the effects

of tranquilizers, antihistamines, and sedatives. Other kinds of potential problems occur when one drug inhibits the metabolism of another, displaces another from its plasma-binding site (thus allowing a greater amount to reach its receptor site, such as the brain), or alters elimination so that the drug is not passed from the body as quickly as it would be if taken alone.

A second type of interaction occurs when one drug acts as a therapeutic antagonist to another, thereby reducing or nullifying its effect. For example, caffeine nullifies the effect of sedatives, barbiturates reduce the effectiveness of major tranquilizers, alcohol reduces the effect of minor tranquilizers, and nicotine decreases the effectiveness of certain analgesics.

Cross-tolerance is the condition when tolerance to one drug will carry over to another in the same group (O'Brien et al. 1992). For example, a person who abuses alcohol and has built up a tolerance to its effects would have the same tolerance for barbiturates. It is difficult to anesthetize an alcoholic because of cross-tolerance. Cross-tolerance also occurs among a number of the hallucinogens.

Cross-addiction and cross-dependence follow the same principle, meaning that dependence on or addiction to drugs of the same group are mutual or interchangeable (O'Brien et al. 1992).

The possibilities of dangerous interactions are almost endless. Certainly, the safest action is to assume that the potential for a dangerous reaction exists whenever two drugs are taken at or near the same time.

cross-tolerance
The condition in which tolerance to one drug carries over to another drug in the same group.

PERSONAL SKILLS AND EXPERIENCES

Alternatives to Drugs

Mind

If you use drugs, think about the situations when you use drugs. Do you drink caffeinated soft drinks or coffee to keep alert while studying? Do you take aspirin for a headache? Do you take a sleeping pill to sleep at night? Instead of using an artificial drug to help stimulate your thinking, kill pain, or relax yourself, try some of the natural approaches to acquiring desired mind states.

1. To stimulate your thinking, try any of the following:
   - Play some music with an upbeat tempo—something that excites you.
   - Look at a picture or symbol that represents what you are going to do with your degree after you get through school.
   - Walk around for a while imagining your energy level continually rising.
   - Imagine people you care about around you and encouraging you to learn.
2. To kill pain, try to distract yourself from the pain by doing any of these activities:
   - Meditation
   - Imagery where you imagine the pain as an object that you can control—something that you can throw away
   - Imagery in which the painful area is numbed
   - Imagery in which your own painkillers (endorphins) are attacking and eliminating the pain
3. To go to sleep at night, do some of these relaxation exercises:
   - Meditation
   - Autogenics
   - Relaxation imagery

Body

Some people take drugs for thrills and excitement. Give your entire being a thrill by doing some activity that takes your breath away—stimulates your heart—and when done makes your feel good all over. High-adventure activities that you do not normally do will create an exciting feeling. Bungee jumping, river rafting, or a thrill ride at an amusement park are examples. At a less thrilling level, but still able to stimulate your own endorphin production, go rollerblading, jogging, swimming, biking, or even for a brisk walk. You can even feel a "rush" by simply jumping into a cold shower (if you have a healthy heart) to invigorate yourself all over. Even the pleasure of getting a good night's sleep, eating a healthy meal, or holding hands with someone can have an energizing effect.

Soul

One of the reasons why people take drugs is to have mystical, visionary, euphoric experiences. This artificial quest to find the inner soul is short-term and often laden with addiction and side effects. The developers of LSD and MDMA all thought that the drugs would enrich their souls. Among Native Americans, peyote is legal in religious services to enrich the spiritual domain of life.

The following are some activities that can be natural means for enriching the soul.

1. Read emotional or spiritual literature.
2. Listen to music that reminds you of growing up.
3. Listen to music that touches your soul.
4. Watch movies that touch the soul.
5. Meditate or do quieting, peaceful imagery.
6. Get in touch with nature by sitting in a natural scene and sensing your surroundings.
7. Lie down on a blanket at night in the out-of-doors and ponder nature and the order of the universe and cosmos.
8. Talk with your religious leader or attend religious services.

PERSONAL SKILLS AND EXPERIENCES

PNI Actions

Psychoneuroimmunology (PNI) is the study of the interaction of the mind, the central nervous system, and the body's immunological system. It has been shown that people with a fighting spirit, optimism, hope, and faith can maximize their ability to ward off disease. The use of some drugs reduces your immune levels. Marijuana has had the most research demonstrating resultant susceptibility to disease from lowered immune responses (Friedman, Klein, and Specter 1991). Most drugs artificially influence our mood states to produce anything from extreme highs, hallucinogenic experiences, and painkilling to extreme lows. When the body, mind, and soul are manipulated artificially, the body's responses to natural stressors are less effective.

How do you maximize your immune system? It should be obvious that you should use only drugs that are prescribed by a physician or nonprescription drugs used sparingly and appropriately. You then have the opportunity to acquire optimal mood states through natural means. The essence of maximizing your immune system consists in these practices:

1. Have a dream, cause, or mission in life.
2. Have positive, repeated, challenging, new, and rewarding life experiences that can result in good self-esteem, self-efficacy, faith, hope, and optimism.
3. Understand and love yourself.
4. Provide unconditional service to others.
5. Try to be more optimistic and hopeful.

DRUG USE AND AIDS

A detailed discussion of the HIV virus and AIDS must be deferred to a discussion of communicable diseases, but it should be noted that AIDS is a disease that has no cure. People who get AIDS will shorten their life significantly. One of the common ways of spreading AIDS is through the sharing of needles among drug users. Many professionals are looking to methadone maintenance programs as one way to curb AIDS, because even though the addict continues to receive a drug, at least the methadone maintenance programs provide sterile conditions and serve as an option for intravenous drug use. Some larger cities have even made sterile syringes available for drug abusers to avoid the sharing of needles.

DRUGS AND THE LAW

Laws are made in an effort to safeguard the members of our society; and the drug laws now in force are a combination of federal, state, and local laws that have accumulated since the passage of the Harrison Act of 1914. The most current federal law for the control of illicit drugs is the Comprehensive Drug Abuse Prevention and Control Act of 1970, Title II. More familiarly known as the Controlled Substances Act, this law was designed to control the distribution of all depressant and stimulant drugs as well as others with abuse potential.

Under the act, persons cannot lawfully manufacture, distribute or dispense, or possess with intent to distribute any of the drugs mentioned. The penalties vary, depending upon

the type of drug. The act also covers illegal possession (possession without a doctor's prescription) of the controlled drugs and assesses penalties for violation, with possible 1-year probation for a first-time offender caught in simple possession. Extra-stiff penalties may be administered for adults who break the law by distributing a controlled substance to a person under the age of 21.

Federal laws are enforceable throughout the United States, but individual states have their own laws, as do cities and counties. Though it is important to be aware of these penalties, it is more important that people know the statutes of the state in which they live, because the laws vary from state to state.

Decriminalization of drug use has resurfaced as a "hot" political topic in Washington, D.C. Some legislators and health professionals are in favor of removing the laws on drug use. The billions of dollars spent in trying to stop the importation of drugs and keeping citizens from growing or manufacturing their own are not being effective. The legal, political, agricultural, health, advertising, emotional, and psychological implications of such a debate are mind-boggling. A very important implication of this whole drug issue is your own personal behavior and choices. It is hoped that knowing the negative consequences of participating in any dimension of over-the-counter, prescription, or illicit drug use will help you to make healthy choices.

TAKE ACTION

1. If you use illicit drugs, stop using them. Seek professional help to do this.

2. Drive with extreme caution, using defensive skills, when people might especially be abusing drugs (e.g., after athletic events, on New Year's Eve). Never drive when you have been using illicit drugs.

3. Help someone else shake an addiction to drugs, and do not enable their behavior. This might require confrontation and conflict.

4. Improve your refusal skills and increase your own self-confidence, self-esteem, and social problem-solving skills, and keep your purposes in life in focus. If your social group uses drugs, change to groups that don't (find groups that focus on productive service, natural ways to have fun, acquiring skills and knowledge, personal growth, and so on). Spend more time around people who give you uplifts, enhance your strengths and self-esteem, and exemplify how you want to be.

5. Do mental imagery to rehearse saying no and to deepen your self-esteem and your natural, drug-free sense of well-being.

6. When seeking employment, find a job that provides a drug-free environment.

7. Be careful not to begin to rely on over-the-counter or prescription medications unless encouraged by a physician to do so.

8. Read more about chemical substances, and keep current on and aware of the changing drug scene.

9. Enhance your spiritual health.

SUMMARY

1. State-of-the-art chemical technology has produced some devastating new drugs, such as designer drugs and crack, that are quickly addicting and debilitating and can cause death.

2. People use drugs for a variety of reasons, including recreation, experimentation, coping, sensation seeking, and escape.

3. Psychoactive substance dependence involves both psychological and physiological factors.

4. Cannabis products are more potent today than they were 20 years ago, and they are some of the most widely used illicit drugs.

5. Natural and synthetic narcotics are still commonly abused; the fentanyl designer drugs are beginning to dominate the narcotic abuse scene.

6. Stimulants include the amphetamines, nicotine, caffeine, and cocaine (also freebased cocaine), which are some of the most addicting drugs in America.

7. Depressants are extremely dangerous, particularly when they are mixed with alcohol, because they have a synergistic effect with alcohol.

8. Hallucinogens include LSD, PCP, mescaline, psilocybin, and other drugs that create illusions and hallucinations.

9. Polydrug use can result in drug effects that are synergistic or antagonistic or show cross-tolerance.

10. Drug laws in our society are designed to prevent the manufacture, distribution, and possession of controlled substances.

COMMITMENT ACTIVITIES

1. If you know of someone who might be having trouble with cocaine or crack, you can call the Cocaine Hot Line by dialing, toll free, 1–800–COCAINE. They will identify your local Cocaine Anonymous chapter and provide other information for you.

2. Determine what your community has done to counteract the problem of drug abuse. You may want to visit a halfway house and talk to people there who are recovering from drug abuse. Ask them for help in developing a prevention program for young people in your community.

3. Interview a member of the police department whose responsibility lies in drug enforcement. Discuss the types of persons who take drugs and other problems specific to drug abusers, including drugs of choice in your community, legal aspects, and rehabilitation facilities.

REFERENCES

American Psychiatric Association. 1987. *Diagnostic and Statistical Manual of Mental Disorders.* 3d ed., rev. Washington, DC: American Psychological Association.

Bateman, D. A., S. K. C. Ng, C. A. Hansen, and M. C. Heagarty. 1993. "The Effects of Intrauterine Cocaine Exposure in Newborns." *American Journal of Public Health* 83, no. 2 (February): 190–94.

Brady, D. 1993. "Cheap and Deadly: Heroin Usage Is Up Because of a Price Drop." *Maclean's* 106, no. 14 (15 April): 54–55.

Brooks, A. M. 1993. "Crack—a Lethal Drug." *Current Health* 2, vol. 19 (April): 16–18.

Burchfield, D. J., V. W. Lucas, R. M. Abrams, L. Miller, and L. DeVane. 1991. "Disposition and Pharmacodynamics of Methamphetamine in Pregnant Sheep." *Journal of the American Medical Association* 265, no. 15 (17 April): 1968–73.

Carrol, C. R. 1989. *Drugs in Modern Society.* 2d ed. Dubuque, IA: Wm. C. Brown.

Cho, A. K. 1990. "Ice: A New Dosage Form of an Old Drug." *Science* 249 (10 August): 631.

Clouet, D., K. Asghar, and R. Brown. 1988. "Mechanisms of Cocaine Abuse and Toxicity." NIDA Research Monograph no. 88, U.S. Department of Health and Human Services, Public Health Service.

Cohen, M. R. 1993. "Chloral Hydrate Overdoses Implicated in Deaths." *Nursing,* 23, no. 5 (May): 25.

Csikszentmihalyi, M. 1990. *Flow: The Psychology of Optimal Experience.* New York: Harper Perennial.

Culhane, C. 1990. " 'Ice' Spreads to West Coast Area." *U.S. Journal of Drug and Alcohol Dependence* 14, no. 1:16.

DuRant, R. H., V. I. Rickert, C. N. Ashworth, and G. Slaven. 1993. "Use of Multiple Drugs Among Adolescents Who Use Anabolic Steroids." *New England Journal of Medicine* 328, no. 13 (1 April): 922–27.

Dusek, D. E., and D. A. Girdano. 1993. *Drugs: A Factual Account.* 5th ed. New York: McGraw-Hill.

Egan, T. 1991. "Life, Liberty, and Maybe Marijuana: Choosing Sides in Alaska." *New York Times,* 5 February 1991, B1, A16.

Farley, C. J. 1993. "Hello Again, Mary Jane." *Time,* 19 April, 59.

Friedman, H., T. Klein, and S. Specter. 1991. "Immunosuppression by Marijuana and Components." In *Psychoneuroimmunology,* 2d ed., edited by R. Alder, D. L. Felton, and N. Cohen, 931–53. San Diego: Academic Press.

Gallager, W. 1986. "The Looming Menace of Designer Drugs." *Discover,* August, 24–35.

Gerald, M. 1981. *Pharmacology: An Introduction to Drugs.* Englewood Cliffs, NJ: Prentice Hall.

Gillin, J. C. 1991. "The Long and the Short of Sleeping Pills." *New England Journal of Medicine* 324, no. 24 (13 June): 1735–37.

Glastris, P. 1993. "A New Drug in Town." *U.S. News and World Report,* 26 April, 20–21.

Henry, J. A., K. J. Jeffreys, and S. Dawling. 1992. "Toxicity and Deaths from 3, 4, Methylenedioxymethamphetamine." *The Lancet* 340, no 8816 (15 August): 384–87.

Holtzman, D. 1986. "Crack Shatters the Cocaine Myth." *Insight* 23 (June).

Howe, S. 1992. "Looking for Grass in the Forests." *Backpacker,* February, 9.

Inciardi, J. A. 1989. "Debating the Legalization of Drugs." *American Behavioral Scientist* 32, no. 3:232–33.

"An Invitation to Sudden Death." 1991. *USA Today,* February, 5.

Jensen, M. A. 1987. "Understanding Addictive Behaviors: Implications for Health Promotion Programming." *American Journal of Health Promotion* 1, no. 3:48–57.

Lerner, M. A. 1989. "The Fire of 'Ice.' " *Newsweek,* 17 November, 37.

Lukas, S. E. 1993. "Current Perspectives on Anabolic-Androgenic Steroid Use." *Trends in Pharmacological Sciences* 14, no. 2 (February): 61–69.

Meacham, A. 1990. "Potent Pot Causes More Health Problems." *U.S. Journal of Drug and Alcohol Dependence* 14, no. 1:13.

Morell V. 1993. "Enzyme May Blunt Cocaine's Action." *Science* 259, no. 5103 (26 March): 1828.

National Collegiate Athletic Association. 1986. *NCAA Banned Drugs Reference List.*

"New Data Intensify the Agony over Ecstasy." 1988. *Science* 239 (February): 864–66.

O'Brien, R., S. Cohen, G. Evans, and J. Fine. 1992. *The Encyclopedia of Drug Abuse.* 2d ed. New York: Facts On File.

"An Outbreak of Designer Drug-Related Deaths in Pennsylvania." *Journal of the American Medical Association* 265, no. 8 (28 February): 10–12.

Pickens, R. W., and D. S. Svikis. 1988. "Genetic Vulnerability to Drug Abuse." In *Biological Vulnerability to Drug Abuse,* edited by R. W. Pickens and D. S. Svikis. NIDA Research Monograph 89, U.S. Department of Health and Human Services, Pubic Health Service.

Randall, T. 1992. "Ecstasy-Fueled 'Rave' Parties Become Dances of Death for English." *Journal of the American Medical Association* 268, no. 12 (23 September): 1505–6.

"The Return of a Deadly Drug Called Horse." 1989. *U.S. News and World Report,* 14 August, 31–32.

Schlaadt, R. G., and T. T. Shannon. 1986. *Drugs of Choice: Current Perspectives on Drug Use.* Englewood Cliffs, NJ: Prentice Hall.

Shafer, J. 1985. "Designer Drugs." *Science,* March, 60–67.

Silverman, K., S. M. Evans, E. C. Strain, and R. R. Griffiths. 1992. "Withdrawal Syndrome After the Double Blind Cessation of Caffeine Consumption." *New England Journal of Medicine* 327, no. 16 (15 October): 1109–14.

Stitzer, M. L., M. Y. Iguchi, and L. J. Felch. 1992. "Contingent Take-Home Incentive: Effects on Drug Use of Methadone Maintenance Patients." *Journal of Consulting and Clinical Psychology* 60, no. 6 (December): 927–34.

Towers, R. L. 1987. *Student Drug and Alcohol Abuse.* Washington, DC: National Education Association.

"The War on Drugs (Continued)." 1991. *U.S. News and World Report,* 30 December, 21.

White, G. W. et al. 1989. "Preventing Growth Hormone Abuse: An Emerging Concern." *Health Education* 22, no. 4:4–8.

White, G. W. et al. 1987. "Preventing Steroid Abuse in Youth: The Health Educator's Role." *Health Education* 18, no 4:32–34.

Wise, T. 1989. "Weed It and Reap: Domestic Marijuana Production Soars with Drug War." *Dollars and Sense,* March, 12–15.

"Withdrawal Seen for Coffee Drinkers." 1992. *Facts on File* 52, no. 2710 (29 October): 823–24.

Zeman, N. 1993. "Turning Over a New Old Leaf." *Newsweek,* 8 February, 60.

ADDITIONAL READINGS

Carrol, C. R. 1989. *Drugs in Modern Society.* 2d ed. Dubuque, IA: Wm. C. Brown. This is an up-to-date, comprehensive textbook discussing in depth the causes, effects, descriptions, and problems associated with drug use and abuse.

Coombs, R. H., and L. J. West. 1991. *Drug Testing: Issues and Options.* New York: Oxford University Press. For a complete understanding of drug testing, this book is very good. It provides a history of drug testing, the politics, an explanation of which drugs are tested, techniques, applications to a variety of groups, and the ethical issues associated with testing.

Gallager, W. 1986. "The Looming Menace of Designer Drugs." *Discover,* August, 24–35. This article gives an excellent overview of designer drugs, how they surfaced, and their destructive effects.

Jensen, M. A. 1987. "Understanding Addictive Behaviors: Implications for Health Promotion Programming." *American Journal of Health Promotion* 1, no. 3:48–57. This excellent article provides an explanation of the psychology and physiology of addiction.

O'Brien, R., S. Cohen, G. Evans, and J. Fine. 1992. *The Encyclopedia of Drug Abuse.* 2d ed. New York: Facts On File. An excellent one-volume encyclopedia of general and specific information on drugs. Drugs, drug terms, cultural perspectives, and so forth are listed and explained alphabetically. It is written mostly in lay terminology.

LIFESTYLE CONTRACT

After reading and pondering the chapters on chemical substances and choices, you should have a good understanding of

1. the nature and devastating effects of alcohol, tobacco, and other types of substance use in human beings.
2. how dependence on these substances can disrupt one's life.
3. how substance use and abuse affect loved ones by potentially making them codependent and enablers.
4. the genetic variance between people, which leaves them either programmed to addiction with use or resistant to addiction of any substance.
5. substance abuse as "acting out" negative feelings, such as hurt, fear, and rejection.

Lifestyle Contracting Using Strength Intervention

I. Choosing the desired health behavior or skill.

A. Keeping in mind the purposes in life and goals you identified for health of the mind and soul, consider one or two health behaviors related to substance abuse that will help you reach your goals. In order to assess your likelihood of success, ask yourself questions similar to those used in previous sections, such as these:

1. Is my purpose, cause, or goal better realized by adoption of this behavior?

_____ yes _____ no.

2. Am I hardy enough to accomplish this goal? (This means I feel I can do it if I work hard, am committed to do it, am challenged by it, and see myself in control enough to make it happen.)

_____ yes _____ no.

3. Is this a behavior I really want to change and that I feel I can change?

_____ yes _____ no.

4. Do I first need to nurture a personal strength area?

_____ yes _____ no.
(If yes, be sure to include this as a part of the plan.)

5. Do I need to free myself from the negative effects of a behavior (break a bad habit)?

_____ yes _____ no.
(If yes, be sure to include this as a part of the plan.)

6. Have I considered the results of the assessments in the three previous chapters?

_____ yes _____ no.

("Yes" answers to the first three questions are a must in order to be successful. It might be wise to consider a different behavior if you can't honestly answer "yes" to these questions. Your answers to questions 4–6 ought to provide insights for your consideration in making your plan.)

B. Behaviors I will change (no more than two)

_____

_____

II. Lifestyle Plan

A. A description of the general plan of what I am going to do and how I will accomplish it. (Consider apperceptive experiences—successes you may have had in the past—since they may help you consider the best ways to carry out this plan.)

_____

_____

_____

_____

_____

_____

_____

_____

B. Barriers to the accomplishment of the plan (lack of help, overcoming the addiction, etc.)

1. Identify the barriers: _____

_____

_____

2. Means to remove the barriers (use problem-solving skills or creative approaches such as those described in the mental health chapter):

_____

_____

_____

C. Implementation of the plan

1. Substitution (putting positive behaviors in place of negative ones): _____

_____

_____

2. Confluence (combining a mental and a physical activity for time efficiency if possible)

_____

_____

(Continued on page 15.27)

LIFESTYLE CONTRACT

3. Systematic enhancement (using a strength to help a weakness): _____

4. When: _____

5. Where: _____

6. Preparation: _____
_____

7. With whom: _____
_____
_____

III. Support Groups
   A. Who: _____
_____
_____

   B. Role: _____
_____
_____

   C. Organized support: _____
_____

IV. Trigger responses: _____
_____
_____

V. Starting date: _____

VI. Date/Sequence the contract will be reevaluated: _____
_____

VII. Evidence(s) of reaching the goal: _____
_____
_____
_____

VIII. Reward(s) when contract is completed: _____
_____
_____

IX. Signature of student: _____

X. Signature of facilitator/instructor: _____

XI. Additional conditions/comments: _____
_____
_____

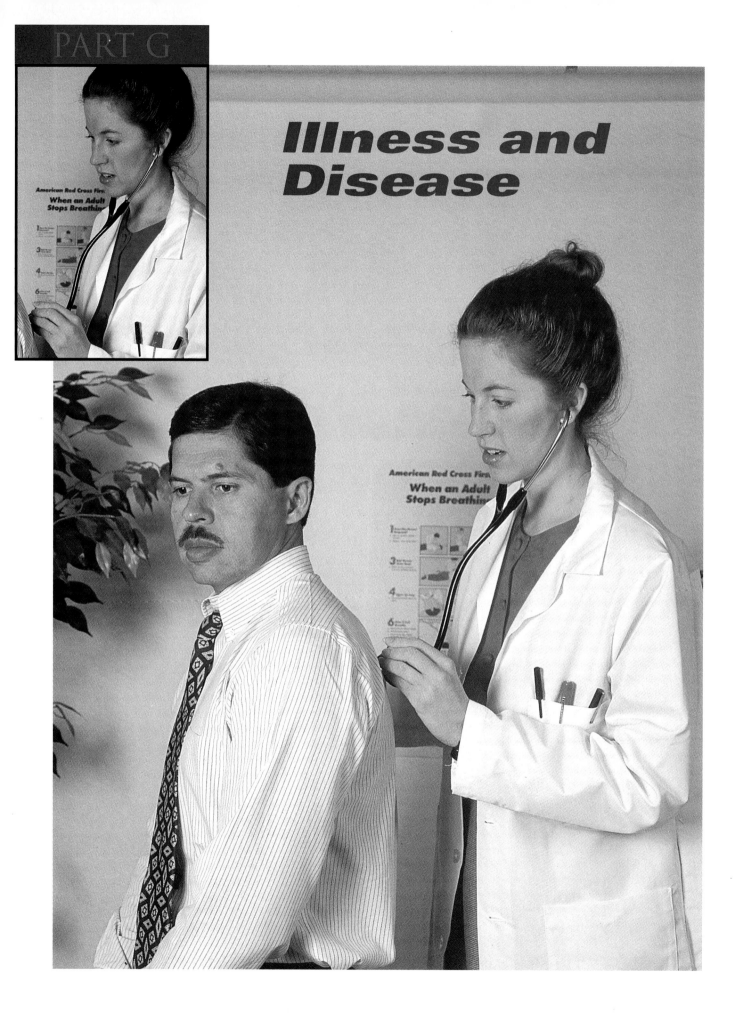

PART G

Illness and Disease

Communicable Diseases

Healthy People 2000 Objectives

- Confine HIV infection to no more than 800 per 100,000 people.
- Reduce gonorrhea infections to no more than 225 per 100,000 people (a 25% decrease).
- Reduce syphilis infections to no more than 10 per 100,000 (a 45% decease).

- Eliminate measles.
- Reduce epidemic-related pneumonia and influenza deaths to no more than 7.3 per 100,000 people aged 65 and older (a 20% decrease).
- Increase childhood immunization levels to at least 90 percent of 2-year-olds (a 20% increase).

Why do childhood diseases such as rubella and polio still exist when immunizations could prevent them?

Some of us wish that our society could be disease-free. The fact is that diseases can be eradicated, which means that they would no longer exist in a natural setting. Smallpox is an example of a disease that was eradicated. The International Task Force for Disease Eradication (ITFDE) was established in 1988 to help eradicate all possible diseases on a global scale to make the world disease-free ("Update" 1992). The organization has determined:

1. Mumps and rubella might be eradicable.
2. Neonatal tetanus is preventable but not eradicable.
3. Pertussis is not eradicable but can be controlled.
4. Yellow fever is not eradicable.
5. Diphtheria might be eradicable in the future.
6. Hepatitis B is not eradicable but transmission could be eliminated.

It seems that the goal of having a disease-free state won't be achieved until sometime in the distant future. In fact, just when we think we have some control over communicable disease, new problems emerge.

In America, there has emerged a renewed concern over communicable diseases that was not as evident just a few years ago. With the eradication of smallpox from the earth, many people believed that communicable diseases were no longer serious threats to life. Some people would still die from complications of influenza and pneumonia, but for most of us, if we contracted something communicable, like a sexually transmitted disease (STD), we would get an injection of penicillin and recover. This state of denial or apathy has been manifested by the fact that some parents do not even immunize their children against preventable diseases such as polio. However, today there is fear of contracting a new incurable plague—acquired immunodeficiency syndrome (AIDS). There is also fear of getting other incurable STDs.

This chapter will present the principles of communicable diseases, the most common of these diseases, and, more importantly, what can be done to avoid or control these diseases.

PRINCIPLES OF COMMUNICABLE DISEASES

Throughout the life cycle, we are subject to **communicable diseases—contagious diseases** that can be passed from one person or animal to another. Some of these diseases—including chicken pox, mumps, diphtheria, polio, German measles (rubella), measles (rubeola), and pertussis (whooping cough)—usually occur during childhood. With modern **vaccines,** most of these diseases are now fully preventable.

Unfortunately, there are other communicable diseases for which no adequate preventive vaccine has been developed. These include tuberculosis, typhoid fever, leprosy, syphilis, gonorrhea, encephalitis, typhus, ringworm, AIDS, and the common cold.

You should know which communicable disease you have had. Some of these diseases can be contracted only once, while others can be contracted many times. By providing a brief history of the communicable diseases you have had, you can help your physician understand your susceptibility to particular diseases.

Even early in this century, communicable diseases were by far the major cause of death in the United States. With the progressive improvements in sanitation and nutrition, the introduction of numerous vaccines, and the discovery

---

communicable disease
A disease that can be passed from one person to another.

contagious disease
A communicable disease.

vaccine
A preparation of dead or live attenuated (weakened) viruses or bacteria used to prevent infectious disease by inducing active immunity.

of penicillin and other antibiotics, there has been a marked decrease in the frequency of fatal communicable diseases in the U.S. population.

Today in our country, the leading reported communicable diseases (diseases that physicians must report to public health officials), such as AIDS, chlamydia, gonorrhea, and herpes, are sexually transmitted. Even though the common cold is not a reportable disease, we know that the cold and other upper respiratory ailments are also common, accounting for the majority of lost hours in both industry and school. With the exception of the influenza vaccine, scientists have been unsuccessful so far in developing a vaccine that prevents any of today's leading communicable diseases.

How does a communicable disease spread? A fight is constantly occurring in the body between invading microbes (one-celled microorganisms that cause disease) and bodily defenses. Whether a communicable disease is contracted depends on three factors: (1) The ability of the infecting microbes to invade the body and produce disease; (2) the number and virulence (ability to overcome bodily defenses) of microbes entering the body; and (3) the resistance put forth by the body's defenses, both natural and acquired.

The development of a communicable disease follows a regular pattern. First, the microbes enter the body through a natural opening in the body, such as a break in the skin or mucous membrane, or through the nose, lung, or intestine. The microbes attach themselves to cell surfaces and multiply to form a primary **lesion,** or abnormal change in the organ. At that time, the microbes begin to spread locally. Eventually, they spread through the body via the bloodstream and form "secondary" lesions in other tissues. The body's immune response is the body's ability to provide resistance to fight off the invasion.

AGENTS OF INFECTION

Communicable diseases are transmitted from human to human or from animal to human through several kinds of agents of infection: bacteria, viruses, rickettsias, parasites, and fungi.

BACTERIA

Bacteria are tiny cells similar to, but more primitive than, the cells that make up higher organisms. Like all living things, bacteria require food as a source of energy and a favorable environment in which to grow. Each species of bacteria has its own nutritional needs and a set of preferences concerning body temperature, oxygen level, and acid-alkaline balance. When bacteria invade the body, one of three things may happen: (1) The bacteria might die; (2) they might survive without causing death; or (3) they might survive and produce disease.

The diagnosis of an illness believed to be of bacterial origin is made by taking an appropriate specimen—for example, sputum, feces, urine, or a throat swab—and sending

it to a laboratory. The specimen is allowed to grow in a controlled atmosphere until colonies of bacteria are formed. These colonies have different characteristics, depending on the microbe (type of bacteria) that is the causative agent. When the particular microbe is distinguished, treatment can be started.

For an active bacterial infection, antibiotics are usually the physician's treatment of choice. Since antibiotics have come into widespread use, many strains of originally sensitive species have become resistant to particular antibiotics; the best known is probably a penicillin-resistant strain of gonorrhea.

If bacterial infection does occur, the body's immune defenses come into play. **Antibodies** are produced by specialized cells to combat the threatening microbes. These antibodies are then released into the bloodstream, where they provide immunity or resistance to a particular infection. People can also obtain immunity artificially. Vaccines containing weakened or killed microbes are used to induce the formation of antibodies without causing illness.

VIRUSES

Another type of disease-producing agent is the **virus.** Viruses are extremely small infective agents, so tiny that a special type of microscope is needed to make them visible at all. They are believed to be the simplest form of life, and they depend on living animal or vegetable cells to exist and multiply. Viruses are present in our bodies at all times, but various inner defense and immunity mechanisms usually keep them in check.

Some of the most common viral diseases include the cold, polio, hepatitis, influenza, measles, German measles, chicken pox, mumps, shingles, mononucleosis, and encephalitis. Even ordinary warts and "cold sores" are caused by viruses. Many types of upper respiratory infections and stomach upsets are also viral in nature. Scientists have identified about three hundred viruses that cause infections, half of which cause respiratory tract infections (Robbins and Kumar 1987).

lesion
An abnormal change in an organ due to injury or disease.

bacteria
Microscopic organisms that cause disease.

antibodies
Substances manufactured by the body to destroy invading organisms.

virus
The smallest intracellular infectious parasite that is capable of reproducing only in living cells. Viruses cause numerous diseases, including measles, mumps, AIDS, hepatitis, herpes, and rabies. Viruses are very difficult to control.

Most viral diseases, in contrast to those caused by bacteria, confer a permanent immunity on those who recover from them.

For many of the communicable diseases, after people have contracted them they are immune to having the disease again. This is called **active immunity** and occurs with diseases such as measles and chicken pox. There are important exceptions, however, such as the common cold, where repeated attacks can occur.

As with any infection, viral diseases are spread from one person to another in various ways, most often by inhaling germs from another's coughing or sneezing, or by using contaminated objects. Commonsense precautions, including avoiding unnecessary exposure to an infected person, are very important in reducing one's chances of catching a viral disease.

Antibiotics are extremely successful in treating bacterial infections, but they are useless for treating most viral diseases. Generally, for a patient who has caught a virus, a physician can only treat the symptoms until the body's natural defenses can overcome the invading virus.

OTHER AGENTS OF INFECTION

Rickettsias are minute bacteria-like organisms that seem to be on the borderline between bacteria and viruses. Like viruses, they require the presence of living cells and cannot be grown in the laboratory. These organisms grow in the intestinal tract of insects called **vectors**—usually bloodsucking insects, such as lice, rat fleas, mites, and ticks—which transmit the organisms from one host to another. Rickettsial diseases include typhus and Rocky Mountain spotted fever (Robbins and Kumar 1987).

An **animal parasite** living in the body of another animal might or might not produce disease in this host organism. In either case, it can spread to another host (such as a person) where it might remain until it dies. Animal parasites belong to two groups, protozoa and worms. **Protozoa** are one-celled animals and cause such diseases as amoebic dysentery, malaria, African sleeping sickness, and trichomoniasis—which are most prevalent in human beings in tropical areas and areas with poor sanitation. Worms live in the intestine and can become very long (up to 60 feet) or be very small. Although there are many types of worms, two common ones are tapeworms and hookworms. The tapeworm comes from infected beef or pork and is passed on to humans when the meat is poorly cooked. Hookworms, on the other hand, burrow directly into humans through bare feet walking on soil.

Fungi are parasitic organisms of simple structure that live in soil, rotting vegetation, and bird excreta. Examples of fungal diseases include candidiasis, ringworm and athlete's foot (which are contagious), histoplasmosis, and coccidioidomycosis.

IMMUNE RESPONSE

Our bodies fight the invasion of microbes in a variety of ways. One line of defense is the activation of white blood cells, also called "phagocytes," that recognize, attack, and destroy microbes or antigens (other foreign substances) when they enter the body.

Humoral immunity is the body's production of antibodies to fight a particular type of antigen. Antibodies are types of proteins that function to deactivate, rather than destroy, the antigen. They are manufactured to fit against the antigen to form an antigen-antibody complex, which becomes harmless. Once our body has triggered the production of an antibody, it remains in the bloodstream to ward off future invasions of the same antigen. Childhood diseases such as rubella produce antibodies, so we rarely get rubella more than once. **Immunization** is the process of triggering the formation of antibodies by injecting small doses of the disease in mild forms to create the antibody to ward off a serious attack. The immune response can also be fortified with antibiotics such as penicillin to help fight bacteria (but not viruses).

Interferon is a protein that has been shown to be effective against a variety of viral diseases. When a virus attacks a cell, interferon is produced, and although it does not protect

---

active immunity
Immunity to a disease, derived from having had either the disease or an injection of the infectious organism.

rickettsias
Just barely visible with a light microscope, these minute bacteria-like organisms must be in contact with living tissue and cannot be grown in a laboratory. They grow in the intestinal tracts of insects called "vectors," are considered borderline between bacteria and viruses, and might cause such diseases as typhus and Rocky Mountain spotted fever.

vectors
Organisms that transmit disease from one host (person or animal) to another.

animal parasite
Any animal (worms, lice, protozoa, etc.) that feeds on other organisms.

protozoa
One-celled animal parasites.

fungi
Parasitic organisms of simple structure that live in soil, rotting vegetation, and bird excreta.

immunization
The administration of a vaccine that prevents a person from getting a particular disease.

interferon
A chemical in our bodies that gives us natural immunity to specific diseases.

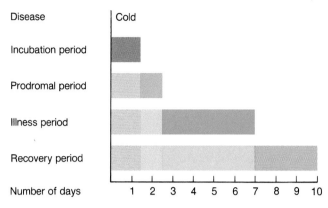

Figure 16.1

A typical course of the common cold.

the invaded cell, it does seem to inhibit the reproduction of the virus. The viral infection is thereby localized, and surrounding cells are protected. Interferon has great promise in treating heretofore incurable viral diseases.

Other mechanisms to defend against disease include the skin, tears (which can wash away bacteria), respiratory tract cilia (small hairs that move foreign particles out of the respiratory tract), and mucous membranes lining the air passages (which can catch foreign particles before they enter sensitive areas).

There are several stages in any communicable disease. If a microbe enters a **susceptible host**—one who is unable to resist infection—the disease will occur. The course that the disease normally follows can be divided into four stages: (1) incubation, (2) prodromal stage, (3) illness, and (4) recovery. (Figure 16.1 illustrates a typical course of the common cold.)

The **incubation stage** is the interval between the time from the entry of the microbe into the body until the first signs or symptoms appear. During this stage, the microbes multiply until disease symptoms are produced. This stage may be as short as a few hours, as with the common cold, or as long as several months or years, as with tuberculosis, but usually lasts from a few days to a few weeks. Diseases are highly contagious at the end of the incubation stage, just before symptoms appear.

The **prodromal stage** is the time during which nonspecific symptoms appear. This stage is characterized by fever, headache, and other aches and pains, such as watery eyes and the scratchy throat that precede other cold symptoms. Many diseases are extremely contagious during this stage, which may last from a few hours to several days.

The **illness stage** occurs next. The symptoms characterizing the specific disease begin to occur, such as the sneezing and runny nose that accompany the common cold or the skin rash characteristic of chicken pox.

The **recovery stage** begins when the body's defenses start to overcome the microbes and symptoms begin to

disappear. (In the cold, sneezing has often subsided and other symptoms are not as pronounced.) Microbes are still present, so recovery cannot be rushed. If we resume full activity too soon, a relapse can occur.

IMMUNIZATION

Medical research has produced a number of vaccines to prevent viral diseases, and people should be immunized against these diseases. There is always some risk associated with immunizations, such as the rare possibility of children's getting meningitis after taking their measles, mumps, and rubella (MMR) vaccine. But the risks are generally negligible compared to not being immunized for disease (Miller et al. 1993). Immunizations are available for many diseases (see table 16.1).

Adults should be immunized later in life for hepatitis B, measles, flu, pneumococcal infections, and rubella because childhood vaccinations do not provide the necessary protection (Eickhoff, Strikas, and Williams 1992). Adults most at risk are the elderly and those with underlying diseases.

SPECIFIC COMMUNICABLE DISEASES

Specific communicable diseases most common in adult population include the common cold, influenza, infectious mononucleosis, hepatitis, AIDS, gonorrhea, chlamydia, and other sexually transmitted diseases.

THE COLD

The most common of all communicable diseases is the **cold.** The cold itself is not a serious disease, but complications (such as pneumonia, in rare cases) can result from improper care of a cold.

---

susceptible host
An organism that is vulnerable to harboring and nourishing a parasite.

incubation stage
The disease stage between the time of infection and the appearance of symptoms.

prodromal stage
The disease stage during which nonspecific symptoms appear.

illness stage
The disease stage in which specific symptoms begin to appear.

recovery stage
The disease stage in which the body's defenses begin to overcome the microbes or the symptoms begin to disappear.

cold
The most common communicable disease. It is caused by viruses for which no vaccine has been developed.

TABLE 16.1   AN IMMUNIZATION CHECKLIST

Disease	Immunization Available?	When Given	Number of Doses	Booster
Chicken pox	No			
Cholera	Yes	When traveling to remote areas of some countries	2; 2–4 weeks apart	Every 6 months for maximal protection
Diphtheria	Yes[a]	2 months	3; 4–6 weeks apart	At 18 months; before entering school; repeat as needed
Influenza	Yes	To elderly, chronically ill, and others at high risk before flu season	1 per strain (type of influenza)	Yearly, as needed
Gonorrhea	No (experimental stage)			
Herpes genitalis	No (experimental stage)			
Measles (in combination with mumps, rubella)	Yes[a]	12 months	1	Possibly if high risk
Mumps (in combination with measles, rubella)	Yes[a]	12 months	1	Possibly if high risk
Pertussis (whooping cough)	Yes[a]	2 months	3; 4–6 weeks apart	At 18 months; before entering school
Plague	Yes	When traveling to certain countries, such as Vietnam	3; 4–12 weeks apart	Every 6–12 months, as needed
Polio	Yes[a]	2 months	2–3; 4–6 weeks apart	At 18 months; before entering school
Rabies	Yes	To exposed persons (animal bite)	14–21 daily injections	No
Rubella (in combination with measles, mumps)	Yes[a]	12 months	1 to 2 is now recommended	Possibly if high risk
Smallpox	No longer needed			
Tetanus	Yes[a]	2 months	3; 4–6 weeks apart	At 18 months; before entering school; as needed for wound management
Typhoid	Yes	For persons exposed to known carrier	2; 4 weeks apart	Every 3 years
Typhus	Yes	For persons traveling to certain remote areas of world	2; four or more weeks apart	Every 6–12 months
Yellow fever	Yes	For persons traveling to specific areas of world	1; at certain designated centers	

[a]Required for entry to school

From E. W. Hook et al., *Current Concepts of Infectious Diseases.* Copyright © 1977 John Wiley & Sons, Inc., New York, N.Y. Reprinted by permission of John Wiley & Sons, Inc.

At least fifty different viruses cause symptoms of the common cold, which appear 1 to 3 days after the virus enters the body. The first clue is usually a scratchy throat. Within a few hours, a stuffy nose develops and sneezing begins. High fever is not a normal symptom of a cold. When a high fever accompanies a cold, either a secondary infection or another disease is present.

Within 48 hours, the cold is usually full-blown, bringing teary eyes, runny nose, husky voice, obstructed breathing, and dulled senses of taste and smell. A moderate headache might be present. Once a cold has fully developed, it usually continues at its peak from 7 to 14 days. Too often, complications can occur that may lead to other, more serious chronic diseases.

No effective immunization has been developed to prevent the common cold, but there are some commonsense precautions, including getting enough rest, washing one's hands frequently, eating well-balanced meals, and avoiding unnecessary contact with people who have colds.

Immunization Checklist

Directions

For all of the immunizations listed below, indicate which applies to you according to the following scale.

a. Yes, I have had the immunization and I know the year.
b. Yes, I have had the immunization, but I don't know when.
c. I don't know if I have had the immunization or not.
d. I have not had the immunization.

1. Cholera	a	b	c	d
2. Diphtheria	a	b	c	d
3. Pertussis (whooping cough)	a	b	c	d
4. Tetanus	a	b	c	d
5. Influenza (flu)	a	b	c	d
6. Measles (rubella)	a	b	c	d
7. Mumps	a	b	c	d
8. Plague	a	b	c	d
9. Polio	a	b	c	d
10. Rabies	a	b	c	d
11. Typhoid	a	b	c	d
12. Yellow Fever	a	b	c	d
13. Typhus	a	b	c	d

Scoring/Interpretation

You should have circled *a* or *b* for the following, to be safe:

Diphtheria
Pertussis
Tetanus
Mumps
Measles
Polio

You should have had most of these as a child. If you know you have had them, you might not need to get immunization for them, because they generally have a lifelong effect. For measles, you will want to read the immunization schedule in table 16.1. If you selected *c* for any of the listed diseases, then you should contact your parents or medical records to find out. If you selected *d,* then you should contact your physician or local health department and see about getting immunized.

You should have checked *a* for tetanus, influenza, and rabies for the following conditions:

Tetanus: If you have a wound, particularly if it was a puncture wound caused by metal.
Rabies: If you have been bitten by an animal and cannot produce the animal for tests or verification.
Influenza: If you have respiratory problems, are 50 or older, or have another condition that is hazardous in connection with influenza. The immunization must be specific to each viral strain.

You should have marked *a* for the following conditions only if you plan to travel or have traveled out of the United States.

Cholera
Typhus
Yellow Fever
Plague
Typhoid

You should be immunized within 6 months of travel for each of these diseases. Immunizations specific to the country you will visit may vary this need. Check your local health department for specifics, if you plan to travel out of the country.

If you have marked *c* or *d* and plan to travel, then you should see the health department to be immunized.

The best treatment for the cold is quite simple (Hansen 1987): (1) Rest in bed during the early stages, as dictated by the severity of the symptoms; (2) drink lots of fluids or breathe humidified air (it will stimulate the fluid production in the respiratory passages, easing the pain of sore throat and reducing coughing); and (3) use an appropriate cold remedy. It is important to remember that any drug can cause an allergic reaction, so follow a physician's advice if there is any question about an over-the-counter drug.

Although there is no cure for the common cold, millions of dollars are spent on cold remedies that are geared toward treating the symptoms rather than curing the cold. There are some eight hundred over-the-counter cold medications (Smith and Feldman 1993). The following is a breakdown of their various functions (Hansen 1987):

1. Nasal decongestants help to open nasal passages by constricting the dilated nasal blood vessels.

Cold remedies don't remedy; they only mask the symptoms.

Symptoms Checklist

Directions

For the following list of symptoms, indicate those that you have experienced recently.

____ Chills
____ Weakness
____ Fever
____ Headache
____ Muscular aches and pains
____ Sore throat
____ Dry cough
____ Nausea
____ Vomiting
____ Physical discomfort
____ Lack of appetite
____ Lack of energy
____ Swollen lymph glands in the neck
____ Sore and tender lymph glands in the neck
____ Diarrhea
____ Tenderness in the liver area
____ Jaundice (yellowing of the skin or eye tissue)
____ Skin rash over much of the surface of the body
____ Swelling of the floor of the mouth
____ Coughing
____ Runny nose
____ Shortness of breath
____ Purple blotches on the skin
____ Sudden unattempted weight loss
____ Pain at the angle of the jaw
____ Skin eruptions
____ Yellowish or whitish discharge from the penis or vagina
____ Mild to intense burning when urinating

____ Cold sores or fever blisters on the genitals
____ Painless sores or chancres on genitalia or oral cavity
____ Unpleasant smelling discharge from penis or vagina
____ Itching or inflammation of the genitals
____ White curdlike discharge from the vagina
____ Warts on the genitals

Scoring/Interpretation

A problem with providing a symptoms checklist of this nature is that people often overreact and suddenly begin, by suggestion, to feel the symptoms described above. But, at the same time, it is important to have any symptoms checked to assure that any serious conditions that you may have are treated, especially if you lead a risky lifestyle (e.g., multiple sexual partners).

You will recognize that symptoms can be indicative of a number of problems, some serious and others that will pass with no harmful effects. To be safe, if you are manifesting any of the symptoms, and particularly if they do not pass in a couple of days, you should see a physician who can give you a definite diagnosis. The following are typical symptoms, some of which may or may not apply to you. The only sure diagnosis is via thorough medical tests, but the purpose of this assessment is to increase your awareness and encourage you to see a physician if any of these symptoms appear or persist.

The following are symptoms that are common with the following types of diseases.

Influenza

chills	sore throat
weakness	dry cough
fever	nausea
headaches	vomiting
muscular aches and pains	

(Continued on page 16.11)

2. **Analgesics** such as aspirin and acetaminophen are appropriate painkillers to relieve musculoskeletal pains.

3. Expectorants help to stimulate the formation of secretions in the respiratory passages and result in an increased flow and decreased viscosity of the sputum.

4. Antitussives are used to suppress dry coughing.

5. Local anesthetics such as throat lozenges are effective local painkillers that help relieve sore throats.

It is important to remember that many cold remedies have as many as ten active compounds, taking the shotgun approach to treating symptoms. The FDA has cited the dangers of the multiple ingredients in cold pills. It is better to recognize a particular symptom and purchase a medication to treat it specifically, as described in the list above, than to "shotgun." Unfortunately, some people waste a lot of money on questionable over-the-counter drugs.

It is important to follow the guidelines for the treatment of common colds. Secondary infections, such as pneumonia, can result if the body does not have the chance to build resistance to the virus. Excessive stress and lack of sleep can reduce the body's ability to ward off the virus.

INFLUENZA

Influenza, or "flu," is another **infectious** disease caused by a virus. One person contracts it directly from another by inhaling droplets that are spread by coughing and sneezing. It can also be indirectly communicated through the use of shared drinking glasses, towels, and other items.

analgesic
A medicine that relieves pain.

influenza
An infectious respiratory disease caused by a virus.

infectious
Contagious; communicable.

Infectious Mononucleosis

moderate fever
physical discomfort
lack of appetite and
    energy

lymph glands in neck become
    enlarged and tender
sore throat
white blood count elevates

Hepatitis

feel miserable
vomiting
diarrhea
fever

tenderness in the liver area
jaundiced (yellowish skin or
    eyes)

Chicken pox

skin eruptions

Rubella

rash
fever

swelling of the lymph glands

Mumps

swelling of the floor
    of the mouth
fever

pain near the angle of the jaw

Rubeola

rash that covers most
    of the body
coughing

runny nose
fever

AIDS

cough
fever
shortness of breath

symptoms of pneumonia
purplish blotches and bumps
    on skin

Gonorrhea

yellowish or whitish discharge from penis or vagina
mild to intense burning sensation when urinating

Nongonococcal Urethritis

same as gonorrhea

Herpes

cold sores on genitals
    or mouth
fever blisters on genitals

fever
headaches
lymph nodes enlarge

Syphilis

painless sore or chancre on penis or oral area (first stage)
rash over much of body (second stage)
ulcer on any part of the body (third stage)

Trichomoniasis

discharge from genitals with unpleasant odor
itching and inflammation of genitals

Monilia

white curdlike discharge from the vagina
intense itching

Genital Warts

warts on genitals

Influenza often affects many individuals in a community at the same time, producing an **epidemic.** Such epidemics generally last about a month and may occur in different sections of the country at the same time. Deaths from influenza occur mainly among older people or those with a chronic disease.

Symptoms of all types of flu are similar, but the severity of the illness varies. An attack begins suddenly. There may be a general feeling of weakness, chills, fever, headache, muscular aches and pains, sore throat, dry cough, nausea, and vomiting. These symptoms need not all be present. As a rule, the acute stage of the illness lasts only a few days, but weakness can persist for some time, especially among older or chronically ill people. With the onset of suspected influenza symptoms, people should go to bed as soon as possible, keep warm, and eat sensibly. If symptoms persist longer than a few days, or if fever remains more than slightly elevated, a physician should be consulted.

No known medicine will cure influenza. Antibiotics have no effect, although they are used to combat certain complications that may follow. If the complications are bacterial problems, then the use of antibiotics may be prescribed by a physician. Getting well without developing any dangerous complications depends on giving the body's immune system every known advantage while it fights off the infection. To treat influenza, do these things:

1. Go to bed when symptoms begin.
2. Keep warm and out of drafts.
3. Eat simple and agreeable foods.

epidemic
An outbreak of disease within a specified geographical area.

4. Drink plenty of water or other caffeine-free, nonalcoholic fluids.

5. Call the doctor if fever occurs.

6. Take any prescribed medication.

7. Get enough rest.

Vaccines that combine protection against the common strains of viruses, including the Asian strain, are available for high-risk groups. A single dose of vaccine is about 60 percent effective if given during the late autumn months, before the beginning of the usual influenza season. Influenza vaccine is recommended for anyone over 6 months of age who is at increased risk (due to age or medical condition) for complications of influenza. Health-care workers and others in close contact with high-risk persons, in addition to anyone that wishes to reduce the chance of becoming infected with the influenza, can be immunized (Centers for Disease Control 1990a). A serious disease that sometimes follows influenza or other viral infections is Reye's syndrome. During recovery from the disease, there is a sudden turn for the worse, with vomiting, delirium, convulsions, and even coma. Death can occur in 24 to 48 hours. Most milder forms are reversible. In severe cases, the infection results in a fatty change in the liver and encephalopathy (brain disease). This occurs in younger people from age 6 months to 17 years old (Robbins and Kumar 1987).

INFECTIOUS MONONUCLEOSIS

Infectious **mononucleosis** is a viral disease of the lymphatic system—the connecting link between the blood and the cells—and is extremely common among high school and college-age students. It is called the "kissing disease" because the virus seems to be transmitted in saliva, although not necessarily through kissing.

Symptoms of the illness begin about 1 or 2 weeks after exposure. At the onset, there is usually a moderate fever, a general feeling of discomfort, and a lack of appetite and energy. Lymph glands in the neck become enlarged and sometimes tender, and a sore throat is common and often quite severe. The spleen becomes enlarged about one-third of the time. Because outward symptoms are often misleading, diagnosis is made by a very specific blood test. When the disease is present, the total white blood cell count is elevated and the percentage of mononuclear cells, or *lymphocytes,* is higher than normal.

Few of us exposed to active cases of "mono" become infected. Nevertheless, we should avoid exposure to known cases. Some physicians treat patients with the medication acyclovir, but it appears to be ineffective (Healy 1993). There is no medication to cure mononucleosis. Bed rest is indicated when symptoms are severe. With rest, complete recovery with no aftereffects takes place after a period of up to several weeks (Robbins and Kumar 1987).

HEPATITIS

Hepatitis is another disease that has been a public health problem through the ages. Its name literally means "liver inflammation," which is one of the symptoms of the disease. There are several types of hepatitis. The most common are hepatitis A (formerly called "infectious hepatitis") caused by the hepatitis A virus (HAV), and hepatitis B (formerly called "serum hepatitis"), caused by the hepatitis B virus (HBV). A third category, known as non-A and non-B hepatitis, is caused by a hepatitis C virus (HCV), which includes hepatitis that is transmitted parentally and another kind that is transmitted through fecal contamination. About 28,500 cases of hepatitis A, 23,200 cases of hepatitis B, 2,500 cases of non-A and non-B hepatitis, and another 2,400 unspecified cases are reported annually, and these are probably only a fraction of the actual cases (Centers for Disease Control 1990b).

Type A, infectious hepatitis, is transmitted by direct contact with an infected person or with contaminated food or water. This type usually occurs in areas where many people live, such as a university residence hall or a military barracks. Type A can also occur when drinking water is polluted by backed-up sewers during a flood.

Type B, serum hepatitis, was previously thought to be transmitted primarily by blood transfusions or by hypodermic needles shared by illicit drug users. New evidence indicates that the virus can also be passed along by sharing a razor, manicure scissors, or anything else sharp enough to make a cut. Some people have been infected by nonsterile ear-piercing instruments. Type B can probably also be spread by close social contacts, including kissing, using someone else's toothbrush, or having sexual intercourse with an infected person or carrier.

Within the past several years, incidence patterns for both types of hepatitis have changed. In the past, rural areas seemed to have more cases, but today there are more cases in the cities. Although children once were the most affected group, today young adults are. This group typically contracts the type B virus.

Characteristically, people who have hepatitis feel miserable. Symptoms include vomiting, diarrhea, fever, tenderness in the liver area, and **jaundice**—a yellowing of the skin or eye tissue.

mononucleosis
A viral infection of the lymphatic system. Medication is not helpful; recovery is attained through rest.

hepatitis
A disease of the liver, of two types—infectious (hepatitis A) and serum (hepatitis B).

jaundice
A yellowing of the skin or eye tissue.

If hepatitis is suspected and illness lasts for more than 2 or 3 days, a physician should be consulted. Generally a blood sample is sent to the laboratory to test for hepatitis. If the tests are positive, the individual is usually put to bed, either at home or in a hospital, depending on the severity of the symptoms. Bed rest and inactivity may be prescribed for weeks or even months. During the acute stage, the person should be isolated, and throwaway dishes and utensils should be used to avoid contaminating others. The spread of hepatitis can be slowed by improved personal hygiene and sanitation, by the practicing of safe sex, and if intravenous drug users will avoid sharing needles.

LYME DISEASE

In 1976 an epidemic of what was first described as inflammatory arthritis clustered in the northeastern United States near the town of Lyme, Connecticut. The disease has now been reported from several locales within and outside the United States and appears to be spreading. After some experience with the disease, it became apparent that this condition affects more than just the joints, and the disease was renamed **Lyme disease** in 1979.

Lyme disease is caused by a newly identified spirochete called *Borrelia burgdorferi* that is transmitted by a specific tick (*Ixodes dammini*). The course of the disease follows in a series of three stages if left untreated. Lyme disease is difficult to diagnose because early symptoms are much like those of other diseases and blood tests used to detect Lyme disease produce unclear results (Stroh 1992). The progress of the disease is that first there are skin conditions that surface, beginning days to weeks after a tick bite and with a rash showing large, ring-shaped sores that may enlarge to several inches in diameter before fading. Next, in 10 to 15 percent of the cases, heart and neurological problems emerge. The heart problems include pericarditis (inflammation of the membrane that surrounds the heart) and atrioventricular blocks (disruption of the transmission of nerve impulses within the heart). Neurological problems include meningitis (inflammation of the membrane that covers the brain and spinal cord), encephalitis (inflammation of the brain), and cranial neuritis (inflammation of the nerves of the skull). The third stage is an arthritic condition, generally in the knees, and is manifest in about 50 percent of the cases.

Prevention of Lyme disease includes using a tick repellant, avoiding uncut grasses and weeds, and inspecting the skin for bites and ticks (Hamburger 1992). Lyme disease is treatable by antibiotics, including penicillin; if administered early, these are effective in preventing the secondary and tertiary symptoms of the disease. In light of the recent spreading of Lyme disease, anyone who receives a tick bite, particularly if a rash develops, should see a physician for possible treatment with antibiotics to prevent secondary and tertiary problems.

The development of a vaccine for Lyme disease might not be too far off. A sample vaccine in mice not only kept the mice from getting Lyme disease but also inoculated the ticks that sucked the blood of the immunized mice (Oliwenstein 1993).

TUBERCULOSIS

In previous editions of this text, we excluded a discussion of tuberculosis because it was so rare. Recently there has been an increased incidence of the disease, particularly in the third world countries. About 1.7 billion people carry the disease, and it is projected that about 3 million will die from it in 1993. Much of the fear is that the new strains of the disease are resistant to drugs that traditionally treat the disease (Boutotte 1993). Tuberculosis is a disease caused by the bacteria *Mycobacterium tuberculosis*. It usually involves the lungs but can affect any organ of the body. Tuberculosis flourishes where there is poverty, crowding, and chronic debilitating sickness. Tuberculosis accompanies AIDS in many cases. The disease is characterized by an inflammation and destruction of the lung tissue. The disease can be detected by a tuberculin test.

CHILDHOOD DISEASES

Three common childhood diseases are chicken pox, mumps, and rubella (German measles). Generally, one attack of each of these diseases confers lifelong immunity to the person, although there have been exceptions. Increasing the number of people, particularly children, who have been immunized for these diseases can dramatically decrease the number of cases in a community (Schlenker et al. 1992). A chicken pox vaccine is still being researched at this writing and hopefully will be available soon.

Chicken pox is caused by the virus *Varicella zoster*. Symptoms usually appear 13 to 17 days after exposure to someone with chicken pox. An infected person is contagious the day before the skin eruptions are present. The disease runs its course with the manifestation of a rash, skin eruptions, and fever. The symptoms disappear after 3 or 4 days, and this can be shortened to 1 or 2 days with a treatment of acyclovir ("Controversy About Chicken Pox" 1992). Itching can be severe and can be treated with antihistamines or by taking

Lyme disease
An infectious disease, caused by a spirochete transmitted by a tick, that develops in three stages—(1) rash, (2) heart problems, and (3) arthritis.

chicken pox
A disease caused by a virus and resulting in a rash, skin eruptions, and fever; itching may be severe but can be treated with antihistamines and taking warm baths with baking soda.

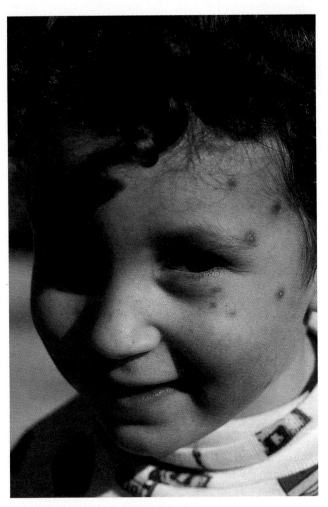

This child with chicken pox was contagious the day before this rash appeared.

warm baths with baking soda. Neurological complications such as temporary paralysis can occur in children who are recovering from chicken pox ("Cerebrovascular Complications of Primary Herpes Varicella-Zoster Infection" 1992).

Rubella, or German measles, is caused by the rubella virus, but its symptoms are generally mild and may go undetected until the rash appears. Additional symptoms of the disease include fever and swelling of the lymph glands. Sometimes called the "3-day measles," the disease actually lasts from 1 to 4 days. Symptoms appear 2 to 3 weeks after exposure. Rubella can be a devastating disease when pregnant women are infected, because of the high risk of deformity in the unborn fetus. The incidence of measles should be on the decline with the availability of immunizations, but there are still periodic outbreaks around the country (Centers for Disease Control 1991a). If you live in an area where measles outbreaks are common, or, most importantly, if there is a chance that you will become pregnant in the next 3 to 4 months, you should get a second vaccination if you have no contraindications or problems with taking the vaccine.

Mumps symptoms and signs are infection of the salivary glands, swelling of the parotid gland (in the floor of the mouth), fever, and pain near the angle of the jaw. Like other childhood diseases, the disease is spread through droplets from the respiratory passages by sneezing and coughing. Although uncomfortable, in children it is usually harmless and passes within a few days. The incubation period is 10 to 35 days. The mumps virus can be localized in the testes or ovaries, causing sterility in young people, particularly in young men. It can also localize in the brain, causing brain damage (although this is vary rare).

Rubeola, also called "red measles," is very contagious and can be manifested 10 to 12 days after exposure. This form of measles is more severe and may include fever, coughing, and runny nose followed by a rash that often covers the body in a couple of days. Rubeola lasts longer than rubella, in that it can take a week to 10 days to begin to recover. Rubeola is a serious disease that can lead to infections in the brain.

SEXUALLY TRANSMITTED DISEASES

Sexually transmitted diseases (STDs) are diseases that usually are spread by sexual contact. Eighty-six percent of the over 12 million cases occur per year in 15- to 29-year-olds. These diseases are spreading more rapidly than all other communicable diseases combined. According to the Centers for Disease Control and the U.S. Public Health Service, the problem of STDs has reached epidemic proportions, despite the fact that modern medicine has effective ways of diagnosing and treating the majority of these diseases.

Sexually transmitted diseases are highly contagious. A single sexual contact with an infected person can transmit the disease. Individuals who are sexually active face an increased risk of infection because sexual partners can unknowingly have one or more of the STDs and infect others.

These diseases affect individuals of all races, ages, and socioeconomic levels. This section will discuss AIDS, gonorrhea, nonspecific urethritis, herpes genitalis, syphilis, chlamydia, and other sexually transmitted diseases.

HIV INFECTION AND AIDS

Just a few short years after the eradication of smallpox from the world, a new communicable disease has emerged that is putting fear into the hearts of people around the world. Although **AIDS (acquired immunodeficiency syndrome)** has existed for some time, it was first identified in the United States in 1981 when five patients in Los Angeles were diagnosed

sexually transmitted diseases (STDs)
Diseases spread by sexual contact, including gonorrhea, syphilis, and herpes genitalis.

acquired immunodeficiency syndrome (AIDS)
A breakdown in the body's natural defenses that is spread through the exchange of bodily fluids (in sexual intercourse, needle sharing, etc.) and is often fatal. There is no known cure.

Behavioral Risk Factors for STD

Directions

Mark all that apply to you.

____ 1. I use syringes (for diabetes or drug use).

____ 2. I have had intercourse with more than one partner.

____ 3. I have never had intercourse with anyone.

____ 4. I am a practicing male homosexual.

____ 5. If I have sexual intercourse with someone, I use or ask my partner to use a condom.

____ 6. I participate in oral sexual practices (mouth to genitalia).

____ 7. I am married or have a permanent relationship with someone.

____ 8. My sexual partner has never had sexual intercourse with anyone but me.

Scoring

For each of the above statements that you checked, give yourself the following points:

1. = 3
2. = 4
3. = -5
4. = 4

If you checked 2 and 4, add 7 more points

5. = -1
6. = 4

If you checked 6 and 2, add 5 more points

7. = -5
8. = -7

Interpretation

Total the values for all questions to help determine how your lifestyle puts you at risk for contracting serious communicable diseases. Interpret as follows:

12 or higher	=	High-risk behavior
-3 to 11	=	Moderate-risk behavior
-4 or lower	=	Low-risk behavior

with the disease. Some researchers believe that **human immunodeficiency virus (HIV) infection** was born in experimental research on polio vaccines in the Belgian Congo in 1957, when some of the vaccines were contaminated and then infected green monkey tissues (Brownlee 1992). It should be noted that about 62.5 percent of the HIV infection cases are in Africa (Weeks 1992). Since 1981, the disease has spread very rapidly in spite of major efforts by the government, health professionals, and other organizations to warn people about the hazards. Some fifteen major pharmaceutical companies from the United States and Europe will share information and supplies related to human trials to fight AIDS ("AIDS Trial Collaboration Set" 1993). Annual international conferences are prompting tremendous cooperation in fighting this fatal disease.

There has been a dramatic increase in deaths due to AIDS. Health researchers are desperately trying to find a treatment for AIDS or a vaccine to prevent it. To compound the problem, several cases of AIDS appeared during the summer of 1992 in people who tested negative for AIDS. The thought that people with AIDS can be unaware that they are affected or ill is frightening.

Since the disease was first identified, the number of reported AIDS cases has spiraled—to a projected 270,000 cases

by the end of 1991; an additional 315,000 cases were reported by the end of 1993 in the United States alone, of which 195,000 have already died. It is estimated that, as of the end of 1993, 2 million people will have been infected with the virus in the United States, of which an additional 300,000 will likely come down with HIV infection and 20 to 30 percent will develop AIDS in the first 5 years after being infected. In the world, the numbers are much higher—an estimated 14 million people worldwide have HIV infection and about 2 million have AIDS (Cowley 1992). An estimated 2.5 million have already died from AIDS ("AIDS Pandemic Spreads" 1993). The World Health Organization predicts that by the year 2000 there will be 12 to 18 million cases of AIDS in the world ("AIDS: Spreading Fast . . ." 1992).

Just one decade after the disease was identified, the lifetime cost for treating HIV infection and AIDS for one person is about $80,000 (Lord 1989), with annual U.S. costs reaching $11 billion. Insurance companies are threatened by the

---

human immunodeficiency virus (HIV) infection
An infection that is present in persons who test positive for the AIDS virus, but symptoms are less severe than those of AIDS.

Many people demonstrate for better care of AIDS victims.

social, political, and economic costs of AIDS and are concerned about increasing their premiums even higher to deal with the high costs (Getz and Bentkover 1992).

Historically, HIV (human immunodeficiency virus), AIDS (acquired immunodeficiency syndrome), and ARC (AIDS-related complex) were thought to be distinct diseases. It is now believed that HIV disease (HIV positive) is a condition that ranges from no symptoms to the serious conditions of AIDS. The use of the term *ARC* is no longer current. The terms *HIV infection* and *HIV disease* refer to this continuum of disease, and the term *AIDS* suggests the end stages of the disease.

AIDS Virus

AIDS is caused by the human immunodeficiency virus (HIV), which has been variously named by scientists as the AIDS virus, HTLV-III (human T-lymphotropic virus type III), and LAV (lymphadenopathy-associated virus). The AIDS virus attacks white blood cells (T-lymphocytes) in human blood. The attack on the white blood cells results in damage to the immune system and destroys the body's ability to ward off other microbes. When the AIDS virus enters the bloodstream, antibodies are produced by the body, but they are ineffective in slowing the progression of the disease. Scientists do not know why these antibodies have no effect. The production of the antibodies makes detection easy. A simple blood test taken 8 to 12 weeks after infection detects the antibodies that have been produced to fight the AIDS virus. Routine practice is to take tests to positively confirm the HIV infection. A positive test means that one has the virus—it does not mean that one has AIDS.

An individual infected by the AIDS virus can develop either AIDS or HIV infection, or have no ill effects in spite of the production of antibodies. The incubation period for HIV infection is variable, generally ranging from 2 to 5 years, but shorter and longer time periods have been seen. A person who has developed AIDS will usually live 2 to 5 years before dying. Some AIDS patients have lived up to 9 and 10 years,

but once a person is diagnosed as having AIDS, the fatality rate approaches 100 percent (Moss 1992).

The range of symptoms for AIDS is varied, largely because of the breakdown of the immune system, allowing almost any opportunistic virus, bacteria, fungi, or other microbes to invade without the hindrance of an immune response from the body. Some of the symptoms and signs of AIDS are a persistent cough, fever, shortness of breath, symptoms of pneumonia, or symptoms of Kaposi's sarcoma. Kaposi's sarcoma, only rarely found in women with AIDS, is a once-obscure tumor that gained attention as an important complication of AIDS in males. It is a cancer that generally creates skin lesions on the legs, characterized by purplish blotches and bumps. The type of pneumonia that AIDS patients contract is *Pneumoncystis carinii pneumonia*, named after the opportunistic protozoa whose invasion rarely affects healthy individuals but is seen in 50 percent of AIDS patients.

If patients do not get AIDS, they may develop the less serious disease referred to as *HIV infection*. HIV infection is a condition in which the patient has tested positive for the virus but has symptoms that are generally less severe than AIDS symptoms. Symptoms of HIV infection can include loss of appetite, weight loss, fever, night sweats, skin rashes, diarrhea, tiredness, lack of resistance to infection, and swollen lymph nodes.

Some people are exposed to the virus and even form antibodies but show no ill effects even after many years; in fact they might never get AIDS or HIV infection. (See figure 16.2 for AIDS outcomes.) But because they have been infected by the virus, they can transmit the disease to others.

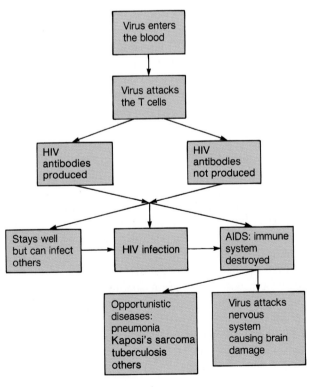

Figure 16.2

Outcomes of the AIDS virus in the blood.

Methods of Transmission of AIDS and High-Risk Groups

The AIDS virus has been found in many body fluids, including blood, semen, and possibly vaginal secretions (Moss 1992). Some reports suggest that the AIDS virus has also been found in tears and saliva, although transmission is not known to have occurred through this means. To date, the six methods of AIDS transmission that have been documented are these:

1. Homosexual or bisexual males making sexual contact with men who have the AIDS virus

2. Intravenous drug administration by contaminated needles

3. Administration of contaminated blood and blood products (although the risk of contaminated blood products has been greatly reduced since the implementation of required screening in 1985)

4. Blood-to-blood or body-fluid-to-body-fluid contact with an HIV-infected person

5. Transmission through heterosexual sexual activity

6. Passage of the virus from infected mothers to their newborns through the placenta

The percentages of AIDS deaths from infections via these sources are as follows, for the United States (Centers for Disease Control 1991b):

1. Homosexual and bisexual males comprise by far the largest group, accounting for 59.1 percent of the reported cases.

2. Intravenous drug users with no previous history of homosexuality are about 28 percent of the total number of deaths.

3. Hemophiliacs receive large amounts of plasma concentrates (blood transfusions) and make up about 1 percent of the AIDS deaths.

4. Other recipients of multiple blood transfusions constitute 3 percent of deaths.

5. Infants born to parents that are homosexual, bisexual, or intravenous drug users make up 1.2 percent of deaths.

6. Heterosexual sexual contact results in 4 percent of deaths.

7. No identified risk results in 3.3 percent of deaths.

In May 1991, the media reported the transmission of the AIDS virus through organ transplants from a person who had been murdered. Apparently the organ donor had been infected just prior to his death. The tests that were performed had not revealed the AIDS virus, so the organs were donated. Some of the organs were sterilized prior to transplants, but because of their size, or for other reasons, several of the organs were not. Consequently, three of the patients who received the transplants had died by the time of this writing, and eight more had tested positive for the AIDS virus.

Issue
People with Aids

When people become infected with the AIDS virus, a number of decisions and conditions follow. Suddenly they fear dying and wonder when full-blown AIDS will become apparent. They also must decide whether to tell other people that they have AIDS, since that would likely result in being labeled and having to endure social stigma. The wave of hysteria over AIDS includes discrimination, ostracism, homophobia, prejudice, and, in some cases, violence. An active interpersonal sex life is clearly out of the question for any ethical person. Many government agencies and businesses are requiring mandatory AIDS testing for their employees, so job security becomes a factor. Is this the best way to deal with the social and emotional aspects of the AIDS epidemic?

- Pro: People who get AIDS are contagious and are a potential threat to the community, to the workplace, in sports, or any other place. Quarantining is justified just as we sometimes do with other communicable diseases. We just do not know enough about this disease to know how to handle it. Until we know more, the stigmas, mandatory testing, and ostracism are important.

- Con: Most medical people assure us that as long as there is not blood-to-blood contact through needles, sex, or touching open wounds, then we cannot get AIDS. That is what we know. AIDS victims are going through emotional turmoil that those of us who do not have AIDS can only imagine. Why take away their income by not hiring them—they are going to need all the money they can make to deal with the medical costs of the disease. Why take creative, productive people out of the workforce? Rather than ostracism, this is a time for love, concern, caring, and support. We no longer have "leper colonies"—we found those to be inhumane.

What is your feeling about people with AIDS?

There has been concern among health workers who have been exposed to HIV-infected patients' blood, stools, and other body fluids. Although precautions against HIV infection are now mandatory and routine in hospital settings, one study showed that 3 out of 750 such workers tested positive for the AIDS virus and that those 3 had accidentally stuck themselves with contaminated needles. More recently, some 4,500 health-care workers in the United States have been reported to have the acquired immunodeficiency syndrome (Mishu et al. 1990).

Another study observed surgical services at a reputable hospital for 6 months, and in 30 percent of the operations at least one blood contact (a splash to the eyelash or on the skin) was observed (Panlilio et al. 1991). The chances for continual spread among health-care workers is high. The vast majority of these infections have occurred as a result of lifestyle rather than hospital accidents.

The questions then arise: Do patients of health-care workers need to be concerned about being exposed to the AIDS virus if their physician, nurse, dentist, or other health-care practitioner has HIV infection? Should the health professional be allowed to practice? One study reported on a surgeon with AIDS who had operated on 1,896 patients. Of the surviving patients, none had AIDS; of the 264 that had died, none had died of AIDS except for one—an intravenous drug user who likely contracted the AIDS virus from a contaminated needle. One news report in 1990 reported that the first person to contract the AIDS virus from a health-care provider was someone who contracted the disease from her dentist, who had AIDS. It might have been that during the course of injecting a painkiller, contact was made between a cut in the physician's hand and a sore in the patient's mouth, but the actual mode of transmission has not been determined.

Another report (Holmes, Karon, and Kreiss 1990) tracks the increased cases of AIDS attributed to heterosexual activity. From 1983 to 1988, the percentages of women who contracted AIDS from heterosexual activity went from 0.9 percent of reported cases to 4.0 percent. In men, during the same period, the rate rose from 0.1 percent to 1.4 percent. As the disease continues to infiltrate various segments of our society, the rate will likely continue to increase.

Anyone who has sex with a prostitute or has multiple sexual partners (male or female) is at higher risk of contracting AIDS. Anal intercourse, which is common among male homosexuals and some heterosexuals, is especially risky.

Prevention, Guidelines, and Myths

Couples who have monogamous relationships and are faithful to each other, and have been for the last 5 years or longer, have low risks of getting AIDS. If both partners have never had sex with anyone else and do not fall into the other categories we have listed, there is virtually no risk. It is important to know your partner well before engaging in sexual activities.

The surgeon general's report on AIDS (U.S. Department of Health and Human Services 1987) has described some personal measures that may help you protect yourself against AIDS:

1. If you have been involved in any high-risk sexual activities (e.g., multiple sex partners, unprotected sexual contact, or anal intercourse) or have injected intravenous drugs into your body, you should have a blood test to see if you have been infected with the AIDS virus.

2. If you have tested positive, or if you decide to engage in high-risk activities and choose not to have a test, you should tell your partner. If you jointly decide to have sex, you must protect your partner by always using a condom (rubber) during (from start to finish) sexual intercourse (vaginal or rectal), and avoid unprotected oral contact with sex organs.

3. A condom (rubber) should always be used during (from start to finish) sexual intercourse (vaginal or rectal). This is especially important if your partner has tested positive for infection with the AIDS virus, or if you suspect that your partner may have been exposed by previous heterosexual or homosexual behaviors, or if you suspect that your partner might have used intravenous drugs with shared needles and syringes.

4. If you or your partner is at high risk for having HIV infection, avoid mouth contact with the penis, vagina, or rectum.

5. Avoid all sexual activities that could cause cuts or tears in the lining of the rectum, in the vagina, or on the penis.

6. Single teenagers have been warned that pregnancy and contracting sexually transmitted diseases can be the result of only one act of sexual intercourse. They have been taught to say no to sex. They have been taught to say no to drugs. By saying no to sex and drugs, they can avoid AIDS, which can kill them.

7. Do not have sex with prostitutes. Infected male and female prostitutes are frequently also intravenous drug abusers; therefore, they may infect clients through sexual intercourse and other intravenous drug abusers by sharing their intravenous drug equipment. Female prostitutes also can infect their unborn babies.

The implication from the report is this—the only unprotected sex that should occur is in monogamous relationships (only one permanent partner) and when both partners are sure that they are antibody negative.

Research and the Future of AIDS

There are researchers all over the world who are frantically trying to learn to control AIDS. A few drugs are currently used to attempt to control AIDS, but only one of them that is approved for prescription use has shown some promise in slowing down the AIDS destruction: Early use of the drug AZT can delay the onset of AIDS but does not extend the life span of HIV-infected patients (Cowley 1993). AZT does not cure AIDS, has devastating side effects including myopathy (diseases of the muscle tissue), and destroys good cells in the body. Nothing is currently available that will cure AIDS.

Research continues to look for a vaccine, but some researchers suggest that the search for a vaccine is futile because HIV mutates so fast and can evade attempts to destroy it (Goldsmith 1993). The best approaches at present appear

PERSONAL INSIGHT

Ryan White

There are many stories of AIDS patients like Magic Johnson and Arthur Ashe, but the story that touched the hearts of many Americans was the courageous fight with AIDS by Ryan White. In April 1990 at the age of 18, Ryan White died of respiratory failure after living with fully developed AIDS for 5 years. Ryan's public story began in 1985 when he contracted the AIDS virus from contaminated blood transfusions. Ryan was a hemophiliac—he had bleeders' disease.

In August 1985, after it became known in Kokomo, Indiana, his town, that he had AIDS, Ryan was barred from entering Western Middle School because the school officials feared he would infect other students. The Centers for Disease Control issued guidelines that students with HIV infection be allowed in school and that their privacy should be protected. Consequently, in November 1985 an Indiana hearing officer ruled that Ryan could return to school in Kokomo.

The up-and-down battle to stay in school took a negative turn when an Indiana circuit court judge barred 14-year-old Ryan from attending class after his first day of school following a 15-month absence. This was a roller-coaster fight to be treated normally, and 4 months later Ryan returned to his seventh-grade class after a judge overruled the previous injunction to keep Ryan out of school. As a result of Ryan's entry into school, parents of twenty-seven students removed their children from the school for fear that their children could contract AIDS from Ryan.

In July 1986, parents of Kokomo dropped their legal fight to keep Ryan out of the classroom, and county officials agreed to let Ryan attend school if he used a separate bathroom and disposable utensils. Ryan did not have an easy life in Kokomo, being branded as the kid with AIDS.

In May 1987, Ryan's family decided to move 25 miles away from Kokomo to Cicero, Indiana. Some sensitive school officials from Cicero changed the quality of life for Ryan and his family with some excellent insights to prepare for Ryan's arrival. Parents and students were educated about AIDS. The community became sensitive to the personal trauma, helplessness, and challenge of AIDS patients and their families. When Ryan arrived at the Cicero schools, he was welcomed with open arms. Many students tried to make his life as normal as possible, and Ryan made many new friends. Even though he just wanted a normal life and to go to Indiana University, Ryan had already received national attention in his fight to stay in school in Kokomo. He touched the lives of many people, and many celebrities befriended Ryan. Ryan helped to change the image of the AIDS patients and helped people realize how widespread the disease is.

Ryan died in the presence of family and friends after attempting to live the life of a normal teenager. Ryan's name will be remembered for many reasons, including for the fact that when the federal government voted to provide medical and emergency support for ambulatory AIDS patients, the legislators, who also were touched by Ryan's life, titled it "The Ryan White Comprehensive AIDS Resources Emergency Act of 1990 (CARE)" (Kerr 1990).

No Good News

This update is a nonupdate on the fight against AIDS. We see signs from insurance companies as they talk about the ethics of denying insurance to AIDS victims, the increased load on primary physicians, and an appeal from medicine and science to open our avenues to find a cure. We need to look beyond what we have been doing, even the unorthodox approaches, because the ones being used now aren't working. When an AIDS patient shouted at President Clinton recently in a hospital for not doing anything about AIDS, President Clinton was unnerved and grateful that the young man still had "fight" left in him. The answer is somewhere within us. At the same time we see the denial of the problem. For instance, Shaquile O'Neil, a famous basketball player, publicly suggested that he doesn't really worry about getting AIDS and sees no need for him to take precautions.

to be multimodal therapy (a combination of several approaches to therapy) coupled with innovations in gene research (Goldsmith 1993). At the 1993 Berlin International Conference on AIDS, it was reported that there is a group of prostitutes in Africa who had been exposed repeatedly to HIV infection but have not been infected themselves (Altman 1993). Other research is looking at attempts to put the immune system back into balance and even destroying some of the good parts of the immune system (T-lymphocytes) to rebalance the immune system (Rennie 1993).

If all of this sounds discouraging, it is. The title of an article in *Nature* magazine—"A Disappointing Decade of AIDS" (Maddox 1993)—tells it all. Even though AIDS has become the most studied infectious disease of all time (Kelleher 1993), there is still no realistic hope of finding a cure in the near future. The hope for a vaccine has been dashed. An enormous amount of money has been given to research, and we still do not know what to do.

The only avenue that works now is prevention. If you have not been infected, your lifestyle is critically important to continue to avoid this disease. That is, you should have a monogamous sexual relationship, not use intravenous drugs, and avoid fluid-to-fluid contact with other people. There are some people, though, who make a point of spreading the disease. Some infected people intentionally try to have sex with noninfected people. It was reported in San Antonio, Texas, that some girls risk infection with AIDS as part of their gang sex rite ("Girls Report Risking Infection" 1993). Changes and new information about this dreaded deadly disease are evidenced each day. It is important for students to keep informed about the advances that are being made in the fight against AIDS.

If you have questions regarding any aspects of HIV infection and AIDS, you can call the AIDS Information line toll free, 24 hours a day, 7 days a week: 1-800-342-AIDS. For a worldwide perspective, call the World Health Organization at 1-202-861-4346.

GONORRHEA

Gonorrhea has been a major health problem in this country for many years. It has surpassed syphilis in frequency in the last decade and is still frequent on college campuses. Caused by the bacterium *Neisseria gonorrhoea*, it attacks mucous membranes of the penis, eyes, vagina, rectum, or throat, and can be spread by vaginal, oral, or rectal contact with other people of either sex.

Penile gonorrhea occurs within 3 to 7 days after contact. The disease causes a thick, whitish-yellow discharge or "drip" of pus from the penis, which is accompanied by a mild to intense burning sensation during urination. Sometimes a drip without burning, or burning without the drip, will occur, but either should be reported for medical treatment. Unfortunately, some men with penile gonorrhea have no apparent symptoms. If untreated, the disease can cause painful inflammation of the prostate gland, or scar tissue can build up inside the penis, leading to difficulty in urination or to sterility. Penile gonorrhea can also cause intense irritation and swelling of the testicles.

Women with vaginal gonorrhea usually have no symptoms, or the symptoms may be so slight as to go unnoticed. Occasionally a vaginal discharge and a burning sensation during urination may occur. Gonorrhea in women can become extremely serious, leading to **pelvic inflammatory disease (PID),** the leading cause of infertility in women. PID is an infection of the urethra (the channel for the passage of the urine from the bladder to the outside) that is evidenced by swelling and reddening. PID symptoms include difficulty or pain when urinating, bleeding between menstrual periods, and excessive vaginal discharges.

Men and women with rectal gonorrhea also might have no symptoms. When symptoms are present, however, they include a rectal mucus discharge, intense rectal irritation, a feeling of incomplete bowel movements, and burning pain during either intercourse or a bowel movement.

Symptoms of oral gonorrhea in both men and women usually go unnoticed. If symptoms are noted, they include a mild to severe sore throat, fever, and chills.

Gonorrhea is diagnosed with a smear test or a culture. For people with symptoms, gonorrhea is diagnosed with a smear test. A microscopic analysis is performed, using pus discharged from the penis or a scraping from the lining of the cervix. A culture is used to detect gonorrhea when no symptoms are present. In this test, scrapings are taken from the mucous membrane lining the suspected area and placed on a nutrient substance. The small, round bacterial colonies will grow in 24 hours, and a positive diagnosis can be made in about 48 hours.

Penicillin is the drug of choice in the treatment of gonorrhea. For people who are allergic to penicillin or have a penicillin-resistant strain of the disease (rare in the United States), tetracycline or spectinomycin is used. Men and women with known recent exposure to gonorrhea should receive the same treatment as individuals who have actually contracted the disease, and all diagnostic tests should be repeated after treatment to be certain the person is cured. Because no immunity develops, the same individual can contract gonorrhea over and over again; a one-time treatment does not prevent reinfection.

Gonorrhea is quickly and completely cured, without lasting damage to the body—if the disease is diagnosed and treated soon after infection. Inadequate treatment can cause symptoms to disappear, but further damage to vital organs may still occur, and the disease may be spread to others. Treatment with leftover antibiotics is ineffective because the amount or strength of the antibiotic is improper; in fact, this type of treatment could contribute to the development of resistant strains of the bacteria.

A pregnant woman who has gonorrhea can infect her baby at childbirth. The attending physician or midwife at birth can put silver nitrate into the eyes of a newborn infant to protect the child from gonorrhea.

CHLAMYDIA AND NONGONOCOCCAL URETHRITIS

Chlamydia is a disease that symptomatically is similar to gonorrhea. It results in the infections of several pelvic areas and if not treated can result in scarring of the fallopian tubes, ectopic pregnancies, and sterility. Other than the symptoms of

---

gonorrhea
One of the sexually transmitted diseases; the most frequently reported communicable disease.

pelvic inflammatory disease (PID)
Inflammation of the female genital tract; a complication in sexually transmitted diseases.

chlamydia
A disease that is symptomatically similar to gonorrhea. It results in the infections of several pelvic areas and sometimes in scarring and damage to some of the reproductive organs.

burning during urination, the infection does not seem to have any long-range effects in males, but an infected male can infect his partner.

Chlamydia trachomatis is a bacteria that acts much like a virus in the sense that it functions inside other cells. The difference is that it has its own RNA and DNA, unlike viruses (Robbins and Kumar 1987). Its action and resulting symptoms are much like the gonococcus bacteria, except that the symptoms are somewhat milder.

Chlamydia is part of a group of STDs that are called **nongonococcal urethritis (NGU)** or nonspecific urethritis (NSU) because they cause the inflammation of the urethra, but not by the gonococcus bacteria. Ureplasma urealyticum also causes NGU. *Chlamydia trachomatis,* in addition to causing NGU, is responsible for lymphogranuloma venereum (ulcer on the genitalia and enlargement of the lymph nodes of the groin); hyperendemic blinding trachoma (infection of the conjunctiva and cornea of the eye, which results in blindness); inclusion conjunctivitis (adult and newborn inflammation of the eye); cervicitis (inflammation of the cervix); salpingitis (inflammation of the uterine tube); proctitis (inflammation of the rectum); epididymitis (inflammation of the epididymis); and pneumonia in newborns.

NGU is the most prevalent STD in the United States today, accounting for some 4 million cases per year. The identification of NGU requires a smear and tissue culture. NGU caused by chlamydia is very important. The treatment for NGU and chlamydia is tetracycline, erythromycin, or doxycycline.

HERPES GENITALIS

Herpes, or **herpes genitalis,** is caused by the **herpes simplex virus type 2,** a virus closely related to the one that causes cold sores, fever blisters, and shingles (a nerve disorder). Exactly how that virus is transmitted is unknown, but it is thought to be spread by direct contact with an infected carrier.

Blisters appear on the genitalia 2 to 12 days after infection. Persons infected for the first time may also experience fever, headache, and enlarged lymph nodes. These symptoms may last 1 to 3 weeks.

At least 500,000 people are diagnosed with genital herpes each year ("Herpes" 1992). Recurrences of herpes are probable, as the virus is retained within the body in a dormant state and can break out again later. An expectant mother can pass the virus on to her fetus from a new infection or an old case that flares up and becomes active. Routine practice to avoid potential exposure is to deliver the baby as a cesarean birth if the mother has an active case of herpes.

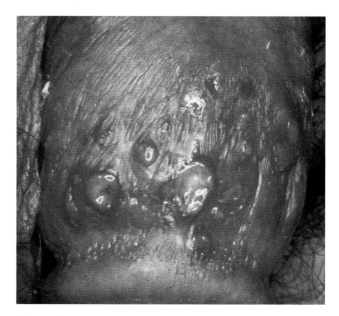

Herpes Corona.

There is still no effective cure for genital herpes. Locally applied compresses and antibiotic creams (such as acyclovir) are often prescribed to lessen pain from blisters and ulcerations, which run their course and disappear only to reappear at a later date. It is clear that herpes is highly contagious when blisters or lesions are present. It is suspected that herpes is contagious during the prodromal period (early stage) before blisters or lesions appear. Those with an active case of herpes should refrain from sexual contact until the virus becomes inactive, that is, until all scabbing has gone from the blisters. To protect against mild or hidden cases of herpes, condoms should always be used.

nongonococcal urethritis (NGU)
Several diseases, including chlamydia, are included among the nongonococcus urethritis diseases because they cause the inflammation of the urethra but not by gonococcus bacteria.

herpes genitalis
An incurable sexually transmitted disease characterized by cold-sore-like blisters caused by the herpes simplex virus type 2.

herpes simplex virus type 2
This virus causes herpes and is related to the virus that causes cold sores, fever blisters, and shingles. Blisters appear on the genitalia, and symptoms can last from one to three weeks. Recurrence is probable, and the disease in incurable.

SYPHILIS

Although unchecked **syphilis** can have serious consequences, the availability of penicillin and an organized control effort have the ability to almost eliminate the disease in the general population. There are still certain high-risk groups, however, including male homosexuals, migrant workers, and the poor. Syphilis was a major health problem in the early part of the twentieth century, but by the 1950s it was relatively uncommon. There has been a rise in syphilis cases since 1985, largely in association with cocaine use (Hook and Marra 1992).

Syphilis is caused by the bacterium *Treponema pallidum,* classified as a spirochete because of its corkscrew appearance. The spirochete is an extremely delicate organism that can't live for more than a few moments outside the human body; however, it can pass from person to person through direct physical contact.

The spirochetes burrow into the soft mucous linings of the sex organs, rectum, and throat. Once the organisms pass through the mucous membranes, they are carried throughout the body by the bloodstream. The course of untreated syphilis follows a series of stages that produce characteristic symptoms.

The average incubation period for syphilis is 21 days, but it can be as short as 10 days or as long as 90. During this time, the disease is present in the body but there are no symptoms and the disease cannot be detected. After the incubation period, the first outward symptom of syphilis, a red swelling, appears on the body at the point where the spirochetes first gained entrance. This sore, called a **chancre,** becomes eroded to form a small, painless ulcer with firm, hardened edges. Its surfaces produce a discharge seething with spirochetes. These spirochetes are also transported throughout the body by the lymph system and bloodstream. One to 5 weeks after its appearance, the chancre will disappear, even without treatment.

If an infected person does not get treatment in the initial stages of syphilis, the disease progresses into the still-contagious second stage of syphilis, the signs and symptoms of which appear 6 to 24 weeks after infection. The most prominent symptom is a skin rash that covers all or part of the body, especially the palms of the hands and soles of the feet. Other symptoms include the loss of large patches of hair, lesions or white blotches in the mouth, headache, chronic sore throat, joint pains, and swelling of the lymph glands. The signs may linger for only a few days or for as long as months at a time and then disappear. Relapses may occur, and new eruptions may appear over a period of a year.

If the infected person still remains untreated, the disease can progress to the latent stage, during which there are usually no outward signs or symptoms. This stage begins about 2 years after contact. During the latent stage, the microbes multiply relentlessly and begin to destroy the body's tissue, bones, and organs. The person is no longer contagious at this stage.

From the latent stage, the disease progresses to the late stage. This process usually takes 10 to 20 years. By this time, the destruction of tissue, bones, and organs is irrevocable. All body tissue is vulnerable, but the nervous system is most often affected. Frequent results include blindness, paralysis, deafness, insanity, and heart disease.

During pregnancy, syphilis is dangerous not only to the mother but also to the unborn baby. After the eighteenth week of prenancy, syphilis germs can cross the placenta from an infected mother to her fetus. The fetus might be stillborn, or might appear uninfected, only to develop symptoms several days or weeks—or up to 10 years—later. Early prenatal care, including a blood test for syphilis, is thus very important for pregnant women.

Penicillin remains the best and most effective treatment for syphilis. For those allergic to penicillin, tetracycline and erythromycin are the most effective substitutes.

MONILIA OR CANDIDIASIS

The yeast infection *Candida albicans* is the most frequent cause of disease, of all of the fungi. **Candidiasis,** also called **monilia,** is very common on college campuses, mostly among women. *Candida albicans* is present on the skin, mouth, vagina, large intestine, and rectum of many healthy people. At times a woman's body is upset through stressful circumstances or by taking antibiotics or birth control pills, and it is upset routinely during the menstrual cycle. Under these conditions organisms can flourish in large numbers, causing a yeast infection. The yeast infection is manifested by small sores on the labia. In infants, patchy sores in the mouth and diaper areas are symptoms. In men and women, infections can occur on the skin or mouth in addition to the genital

---

syphilis
A sexually transmitted disease caused by a bacterium *(Treponema pallidum),* with an incubation period of 12 to 20 days.

chancre
The first outward symptom of syphilis; a small, painless sore.

candidiasis (monilia)
A common vaginal yeast infection caused by flourishing *Candida albicans* due to an upset in a woman's internal balance.

areas. The infection often results in a white, curdlike discharge from the vagina, accompanied by intense vaginal and vulval itching. The infection can be spread through direct sexual contact or incidental contact from shared towels, toilet seats, and so on.

The test for monilia is done by taking a swab from the infected area, looking at it under a microscope, and making a laboratory culture. A vaginal cream or suppository will be prescribed for approximately 7 to 10 days after diagnosis. The condition can become quite persistent and difficult to control unless prescribed treatment is followed. Douching with clear water is recommended to relieve the itching. Both partners can help in the prevention of vaginal infections, but once an infection does occur, medical assistance should be secured (Robbins and Kumar 1987).

TRICHOMONIASIS

Trichomoniasis is a common infection caused by the protozoa *Trichomonas*. It is usually transmitted through sexual contact; however, *Trichomonas* can survive for several hours at room temperature on moist objects such as toilet seats, towels, and washcloths. Most infected males are carriers without symptoms who pass the organism on to women.

In women the infection is characterized by a profuse, frothy white or yellow discharge with an unpleasant odor, which is accompanied by itching and inflammation. The disease is diagnosed by an examination of the discharge and treated with the drug Flagyl. Both partners must receive treatment, or the organism will be passed back and forth (Robbins and Kumar 1987).

CONDYLOMAS (GENITAL WARTS)

Condylomas once were fairly rare, but the condition is now beginning to be diagnosed more frequently on college campuses, with an estimated 1 million cases per year. Both men and women can develop condylomas in the anal or genital regions. Evidence suggests that these warts are caused by a virus (human papillomavirus, or HPV infection) similar to the one that causes warts on other areas of the body. There are over sixty-six types of human papillomavirus that are associated with genital warts (Dover and Arndt 1992). The virus is transmitted by sexual activity and appears 1 to 3 months after infection. Genital warts are generally small, skin- or pink-colored growths. One or more may appear together or form clusters, and sometimes these can be very large, covering several centimeters.

Prescribed treatment with podophyllin, a brown liquid that is spread on the wart, can remove it. It is extremely difficult to rid the body totally of the warts, because one part of one wart will cause the continual spreading of warts. Early treatment is vital, as condylomas can spread and become more difficult to treat. Treated with podophyllin, about 15 to 50 percent of the cases will return. It appears that when treated with lasers and interferon, almost all cases are cured (Bauman 1992). Sexual intercourse should be avoided during the course of infection.

PEDICULOSIS PUBIS (CRABS)

Crabs, or pubic lice, are pinhead-size insect parasites that live in the hairy parts of the body, usually around the genitals; infestation by crabs is called **pediculosis pubis.** Some people have no symptoms, while others experience intolerable itching from these parasites. Crabs can be passed by physical contact during sexual intercourse or by contact with infected bedding, clothing, or towels.

Treatment includes a medicated lotion prescribed by a physician. Instructions with the lotion must be followed completely to eliminate both the crabs and their eggs. Sex partners and roommates must be treated at the same time to avoid repeat infections. Bedding, towels, clothing, and other washables are also treated.

PREVENTION AND CONTROL OF SEXUALLY TRANSMITTED DISEASES

Prevention and control of STDs should be a primary concern in communities throughout the United States, but the intimate nature of sexual concerns presents many problems. Guilt feelings, for example, make it difficult for people to talk about STDs and to seek proper medical care.

Though some people scoff at condoms, saying that they interfere with sexual activity, condoms can prevent the spread of some STDs. To be effective, a condom must be worn on the penis prior to and during any sexual activity. If

condyloma
A sexually transmitted anal or genital wart caused by human papillomavirus, treated with Podophyllin.

crabs
Insect parasites that can be passed from one person to another during close bodily contact; another name for pubic lice.

pediculosis pubis
A sexually transmitted disease caused by crabs or pubic lice, pinhead-sized insect parasites that live in the hairy parts of the body, usually around the genitalia. Some people have no symptoms, while others experience intolerable itching from these parasites.

PERSONAL SKILLS AND EXPERIENCES

Avoiding Communicable Diseases

Mind

Our main problem with communicable diseases is that we do not think about our actions and circumstances. Many of us get mumps, measles, influenza, and other diseases because we do not think about getting immunized. Some of us contract a sexually transmitted disease because we think that our partner isn't infected. It's almost as though we are thinking with our genitals and raging hormones instead of our minds. Some of us provide first aid to victims at a traffic accident with our bare hands because we do not think to have latex gloves in our car and so we risk having fluid-to-fluid contact. Some of us contract malaria or yellow fever because we travel abroad and we don't think to get additional immunizations.

Body

Communicable disease is always reflected in some functional problems in the body. We have sneezes and sniffles with a cold or a deterioration of the immune systems with AIDS. For many communicable diseases, the state of our body will determine whether we come down with the disease or not. Think about when you get a cold. Is it when you are tired and not getting enough sleep? Is it when you quit exercising or you are eating poorly? To protect your body from communicable disease, avoid exposure to the disease and also do the following:

1. Get adequate rest.
2. Exercise regularly.
3. Assure that you have been immunized appropriately.
4. Eat a nutritional diet.

Soul

Your soul is both the highs and the lows of your emotions and your sense of purpose in life. To increase your chances of avoiding communicable disease, you need to have an optimistic nature, have faith and self-efficacy, feel good about yourself, and experience inner peace. Here are the ways to accomplish all of these:

1. Nurture your soul through enriching music.
2. Think and write down your dream in life and work toward that dream.
3. Practice a religion, a theology, or a philosophy in life.
4. Do many acts of service and altruism for others—volunteer.
5. Optimal states of the soul (joy, happiness, hope, and faith) come through positive, challenging, empowering life experiences—challenge yourself.
6. Feel inner peace by assuring that the way you act or behave is in harmony with your personal sense of morals (what is right and wrong).
7. Find opportunities to laugh a lot. Play harmless practical jokes, see humorous performances, and joke with friends and family.

THE WORLD AROUND YOU

Practical Actions

The label *communicable disease* expresses powerful implications about the world around us. If we catch a disease, it is likely that it will be from another person. In our relationships it is extremely important for us to communicate openly and honestly about our state of disease. Consider the following specifics:

1. Most of us know when we are about to come down with a cold or other communicable disease. We may have early symptoms of sneezing, a scratchy throat, or fatigue. We might find ourselves on a date or with someone we care about during those times and begin to think romantic thoughts. Communication at that point, rather than exposing our partner, is to indicate that we feel ourselves coming down with a cold and that we are concerned about exposing our partner with the virus.

2. If we have a communicable disease, or suspect that we do, then open communication is extremely important. Interdependence should be nurturing others, not infecting others. We only have to think of the relationship in a few weeks if we infect others—trust will be destroyed because we knowingly infected someone else with our disease.

The key to rich relationships as it pertains to disease is open communication, responsibility, and assertiveness in protecting ourselves.

Issue

Abstinence and Safer Sex: A Voice from the Past

The fifties and sixties provided the groundwork for the sexual revolution, rebellion against the age-old morals of yesterday. The irresponsible phrase "If it feels good, do it" rang through the college campuses in the early seventies. At the same time, STD frequency began to increase. Today, we find ourselves in a real dilemma. The majority of college students are still sexually active, some with multiple partners. This means that anyone you come in contact with, unless he or she has abstained from sexual activity and also intravenous drug use for his or her whole life, is a potential carrier of a treatable or untreatable communicable disease. Is it time to go back to the old-fashioned morals?

- Pro: Abstaining from sex is the only sure way to avoid sexually transmitted diseases. There are several things that you can do to relieve sexual frustration without coming in direct contact with potential infected areas. Within your own moral limitations you can experience the degree of intimacy, touching, and even experience the pleasures of sex without having intercourse. Through effective communication with your partner about sexual limitations based on each other's morals, couples can set limits and monitor each other to stay within the limits and be guilt-free. Open communication with your partner about what feels good within those limitations can make you feel satisfied, feel emotionally close to your partner, and provide the foundation for a good relationship. It is just too dangerous to behave any differently.

- Con: Abstaining from sexual intercourse is frustrating. In building a lasting relationship, one should know the person socially, emotionally, and physically, which includes sexual compatibility. What would happen if you got married and found out that you were sexually incompatible?

What is your choice going to be, pertaining to safe sex?

used properly, the condom can provide complete protection against gonorrhea and NGU, and good protection against syphilis, herpes, and genital warts. The most protective condoms are made of latex; viruses may be able to penetrate natural lambskins and other nonsynthetic condom materials. The female condoms that are now being produced might provide even greater protection because of the strength of the strong polyethylene material they are made from and their more complete coverage of the genitals. Urinating and washing the genitalia and adjacent areas with soap and water immediately following intercourse affords a little protection against STDs. Spermicides (foams) may also be useful in prevention.

Sexually transmitted diseases can be controlled if persons who are exposed to them are alerted to the possibility of infection and advised about proper medical care. In most communities, there are STD epidemiologists who are experts in determining the source and spread of these diseases. An epidemiologist works with each patient to alert all sexual contacts about their exposure. In all states, minors may consent to their own confidential treatment, and in most instances confidentiality is maintained. The essential elements for controlling STDs include public education, screening high-risk groups, treating all infected persons, and identifying and treating sexual contacts.

Ten steps to prevention are highlighted below. Some of these provide very little protection (as we have already specified), others provide more. After reflecting on the following list, consider the Issues box entitled "Abstinence and Safer Sex: A Voice from the Past."

1. Be highly selective with sexual partners.
2. Wash with soap and water after coitus.
3. Have open communication with partners.
4. If a disease is contracted, avoid exposing partner.
5. Use latex condoms.
6. Urinating and douching after coitus might help.
7. Abstain from intercourse.
8. Talk openly with your partner about the potential for STDs (i.e., discuss openly your sexual histories).
9. Avoid unprotected oral-genital contact.
10. Watch carefully for symptoms of any disease, and seek medical help if you have any suspicions.

PERSONAL SKILLS AND EXPERIENCES

PNI Action

One of the best examples of how your mental state can help you stay disease-free could be to consider experiences you have had in your own life. Think of a time when you have had some deadlines, perhaps a paper due in a class or preparing for finals. In your mind, you might have been thinking, "If I can just make it through finals week, then I am going to relax." In your mind and soul, you were going to work very hard to do well, and you could hardly wait for the break. You just did not have time to get sick. Your entire body, mind, and soul were geared to finals week. Perhaps you can remember a time like this—as you turned in your final paper or completed your last examination, you breathed a sigh of relief. At that moment or shortly thereafter, you suddenly felt a sore throat or the sniffles of a cold coming on. You could hardly believe it. The second that you let down and had time to get sick, you got your cold.

We know that viruses and bacteria are harbored in an inactive state in the respiratory passages of our body and that they can remain inactive as long as we have the mind state not to get sick. They can become activated and infect us when we let down.

The key to maximizing our immune system against disease is to continually pursue an ongoing cause or purpose in life, be optimistic, have a sense of control, and have a fighting spirit. To experience these optimal states, consider all the skills and experiences of the mind, body, soul, and interdependence, and you will have done what you can do to maximize your immune system.

It isn't very likely that the world will ever be completely free from diseases, but you can create a personal world around you that immensely reduces your chances of contracting a communicable disease. You need to think, be immunized, live life with soul, protect your body, and carefully select your social and physical environments, and then you will have given yourself a somewhat protected world to live in.

TAKE ACTION

1. Avoid mucous contact, via drinking glasses, toothbrushes, sexual intimacy, sharing needles, and so on, with anyone infected with a communicable disease.

2. Before becoming sexually intimate with another person, get to know her or him very well—to the point where you can openly discuss your past sexual histories with each other.

3. Have regular physicals, to determine the health of your organs, the presence of any communicable diseases, or the presence of any chronic diseases, for early detection and treatment.

4. If you have a communicable disease, don't infect others. Stay at home, cover your mouth when you sneeze or cough, and keep your distance from others.

5. Make sure you have received all appropriate immunizations.

6. Practice preventive measures against contracting STDs.

SUMMARY

1. The development of any communicable disease follows a four-stage pattern: the incubation, prodromal stage, illness, and recovery.

2. Communicable diseases can occur whenever microbes enter the body and disrupt any of the vital processes.

3. Diseases are caused by bacteria, viruses, rickettsias, animal parasites, and fungi.

4. The common cold and influenza are two respiratory infections for which there are no cures, yet remedies are marketed.

5. Hepatitis and infectious mononucleosis, which can be passed along by such things as sharing razors and kissing, are prevalent in the college-age population.

6. Sexually transmitted diseases are spreading rapidly, and some of the most common strains, such as herpes genitalis and AIDS, are incurable.

7. AIDS is an incurable disease that almost always results in death and is infecting both homosexual and heterosexual populations.

8. Chlamydia, nongonococcal urethritis, gonorrhea, monilia, and other STDs are irritating diseases, extremely common among sexually active students on college campuses, that need medical treatment.

9. Preventive activities include abstinence, use of condoms, washing and douching, open communication with partners, seeking medical help for any symptoms, and safer sexual practices.

COMMITMENT ACTIVITIES

1. List the ways you could provide STD information to other students at your school. What kinds of materials would you use? Where would you look for current information relevant to your community? Check with the student health service or the residence hall council to see if a series of STD programs could be given at your university. How could you assist in setting up these programs?

2. List the "cold remedies" you have in your medicine cabinet. Decide why you use each medication. Is it for sneezing, coughing, headache, allergy, or something else? From now on, read the labels on all over-the-counter medications that you

buy for respiratory infections. Become as knowledgeable as you can about the ingredients contained in each medication. Consult your physician or the student health service if you have a doubt about any of these medications.

3. There are many misconceptions about STDs. Prepare a list of facts and a list of misconceptions about STDs; then ask some students at your university to judge the accuracy of each list. Report your findings to the class.

REFERENCES

"AIDS Pandemic Spreads." 1993. *The Futurist* 27, no. 3 (May–June): 56.

"AIDS: Spreading Fast . . ." 1992. *U.N. Chronicle* 29, no. 1 (March): 88.

"AIDS Trial Collaboration Set." 1993. *Facts on File* 53, no. 2737: 352–53.

Altman, L. K. 1993. "Immunity Study Offered at Berlin AIDS Meeting." 1993. *New York Times,* 9 June, A4, A7.

Bauman, N. 1992. "Interferon and Lasers May Cure Severe Condylomas." *Medical World News,* 33, no. 3 (March): 36–37.

Boutotte, J. 1993. "Guarding Your Airway Against T.B." *Nursing* 23, no. 20 (October): 66.

Brownlee, S. 1992. "Origins of the Plague: Scientists Are Searching for the Beginning of the AIDS Epidemic." *U.S. News and World Report,* 30 March, 50–52.

Centers for Disease Control. 1990a. "Prevention and Control of Influenza." *Morbidity and Mortality Weekly Report* 39, no. RR-7 (May).

Centers for Disease Control. 1990b. "Protection Against Viral Hepatitis." *Morbidity and Mortality Weekly Report* 39, no. S-2 (February).

Centers for Disease Control. 1991a. "Increases in Rubella and Congenital Rubella." *Journal of the American Medical Association* 265, no. 9:1076–77.

Centers for Disease Control. 1991b. "Mortality Attributable to HIV Infection/AIDS—United States, 1981–1990." *Morbidity and Mortality Weekly Report* 40, no. 3 (January).

"Cerebrovascular Complications of Primary Herpes Varicella-Zoster Infection." 1992. *The Lancet* 339, no. 8807 (13 June): 1449–50.

"Controversy About Chicken Pox." 1992. *The Lancet* 340, no. 8820 (12 September): 639–40.

Cowley, G. 1992. "For Users of AZT, Sobering News." *Newsweek,* 24 February, 63.

Dover, J. S., and K. A. Arndt. 1992. "Dermatology." *Journal of the American Medical Association* 268, no. 3:342–44.

Eickhoff, T. C., R. A. Strikas, and W. W. Williams. 1992. "Update on Adult Immunization." *Patient Care* 26, no. 15 (30 September): 113–21.

Getz, K. A., and J. D. Bentkover. 1992. "The Impact of AIDS on the Insurance Industry." *Journal of the American Society of CLU & ChFC* 46, no. 2 (March): 54–65.

"Girls Report Risking Infection with AIDS in a Gang Sex Rite." 1993. *New York Times,* 27 April, A9, C6.

Goldsmith, M. F. 1993. "For AIDS Treatment, Vaccines, Now Think Genes." *Journal of the American Medical Association* 269, no. 17 (5 May): 2189–90.

Hamburger, M. I. 1992. "Demystifying Lyme Disease." *Newsweek,* 11 May, A12.

Hansen, G. R. 1987. *Common Medicines.* 2d ed. Salt Lake City: G. Hansen.

Healy, B. P. 1993. "Oral Administration of Acyclovir Appears Ineffective in Treating Acute Infections of Mononucleosis." *Journal of the American Medical Association* 266, no. 21:2955.

"Herpes: The Fastest Spreading STD." 1992. *Berkeley Wellness Letter* 8, no. 12:6.

Holmes, K. K., J. M. Karon, and J. Kreiss. 1990. "The Increasing Frequency of Heterosexually Acquired AIDS in the United States, 1983–1988." *American Journal of Public Health* 80: 7.

Hook, E. W. III, and C. M. Marra. 1992. "Acquired Syphilis in Adults." *New England Journal of Medicine* 326, no. 16 (16 April): 1060–69.

Kelleher, C. 1993. "Beyond HIV: Assembling the AIDS Puzzle." *Omni* 15, no. 8:56–61.

Kerr, D. L. 1990. "Ryan White's Death: A Time to Reflect on Schools' Progress in Dealing with AIDS." *Journal of School Health* 60, no. 5 (May): 237–38.

Lord, J. 1989. *Infection, Your Immune System and AIDS.* 1990 ed. Enterprise for Education in Association with the Massachusetts Medical Society.

Maddox, J. 1993. "A Disappointing Decade of AIDS." *Nature,* 362 (4 March): 13.

Miller, E. et al. 1993. "Risk of Aseptic Meningitis After Measles, Mumps, and Rubella Vaccine in UK Children." *The Lancet* 341, no. 8851 (17 April): 979–82.

Mishu, B., W. Schaffner, J. M. Horan, L. H. Wood, and R. H. McNab. 1990. "A Surgeon with AIDS." *Journal of the American Medical Association* 264, no. 12:467–70.

Moss, A. 1992. *HIV and AIDS.* Oxford: Oxford University Press.

Oliwenstein, L. 1993. "Biting Back at Lyme." *Discover,* January, 53.

Panlilio, A. L. et al. 1991. "Blood Contacts During Surgical Procedures." *Journal of the American Medical Association* 265, no. 12:1533–37.

Rennie, J. 1993. "Balanced Immunity: Would Killing Some T-Cells Slow the Progress of AIDS?" *Scientific American,* May, 22–23.

Robbins, S. L., and V. Kumar. 1987. *Basic Pathology.* 4th ed. Philadelphia: Saunders.

Schlenker, T. L., C. Bain, A. L. Baughman, and S. C. Hadler. 1992. "Measles Herd Immunity: The Association of Attack Rates with Immunization Rates in Preschool Children." *Journal of the American Medical Association* 267, no. 6 (12 February): 823–27.

Smith, M. B. H., and W. Feldman. 1993. "Over-the-Counter Cold Medications: A Critical Review of Clinical Trials Between 1950–1991." *Journal of the American Medical Association* 269, no. 17 (5 May): 2258–63.

Stroh, M. 1992. "Picking Out Lyme's from Lemons (Misdiagnosing Lyme Disease)." *Science News* 141, no. 20:325.

"Update: International Task Force for Disease Eradication, 1990 and 1991." 1992. *Morbidity and Mortality Weekly Report* 41, no. 3 (24 January): 40–42.

U.S. Department of Health and Human Services. 1987. *Surgeon General's Report on Acquired Immune Deficiency Syndrome* Washington, DC: Government Printing Office.

Weeks, D. C. 1992. "The AIDS Pandemic in Africa." *Current History* 91, no. 565 (May): 208.

ADDITIONAL READINGS

Benson, H., and E. M. Stuart. 1992. *The Wellness Book: A Comprehensive Guide to Maintaining Health and Treating Stress-Related Illnesses.* New York: Birch Lane Press. This contemporary book on preventing stress-related illness incorporates the principles of psychoneuroimmunology and mind/body/soul approaches to prevention. Excellent reading.

Lord, J. 1989. *Infection, Your Immune System and AIDS.* 1990 ed. Enterprise for Education in Association with the Massachusetts Medical Society. An excellent 52-page booklet simply describing the immune system and how AIDS affects it. Some beautiful color photography and illustrations. Provides the reader with a broad understanding of the nature and history of the disease, prevention, and social and world impact.

U.S. Department of Health and Human Services. 1985. *1985 STD Treatment Guidelines.* Washington, DC: Government Printing Office. This government guide provides an overview of the treatments for and nature of several sexually transmitted diseases.

U.S. Department of Health and Human Services. 1987. *Surgeon General's Report on Acquired Immune Deficiency Syndrome.* Washington, DC: Government Printing Office. This is a frank and bold declaration of the nature of AIDS, high-risk populations, and how to prevent contracting AIDS.

CHAPTER 17

Cardiovascular Diseases

KEY QUESTIONS

How are chronic diseases prevented?

What is cardiovascular disease?

What is stroke?

What are some lifestyle decisions we can make that will reduce our chances of developing cardiovascular disease?

What are the different types of cardiovascular disease?

What are some examples of risk factors associated with cardiovascular disease?

How has medical technology been advanced to treat heart disease?

CHAPTER OUTLINE

Healthy People 2000 Objectives

- Reduce coronary heart disease deaths to no more than 100 per 100,000 people (a 26% decrease).

- Reduce stroke deaths to no more than 20 per 100,000 (a 34% decrease).

- Increase control of high blood pressure to at least 50 percent of people with high blood pressure HBP (a 108% increase).

- Reduce blood cholesterol to an average of no more than 200 mg/dL (a 6% decrease).

a.

c.

You can significantly and positively affect your future health and quality of life by developing the following prevention strategies: *(a)* exercise, *(b)* eat a diet low in cholesterol and saturated fat and high in fiber, *(c)* watch your weight, *(d)* make wise decisions about exposure to tobacco products.

b.

d.

When some health promotion consultants interviewed the chief medical director of a distinguished hospital, one of their questions was, "What do you think about wellness programs?" The physician, with deep thought, said, "Wellness may be all well and good, but if you give me a patient whose mother died of a heart attack at 50 and whose father also died of a heart attack at age 50, I'll show you a patient who is going to die at 50 with a heart attack."

This physician was trying to remind the health promotion consultants of the powerful genetic influence in heart disease. He then followed up with a statement that clarified his position: "But I will say this about leading a healthy lifestyle—that patient who exercises, eats right, maintains optimal weight, and is excited about living will have a marvelous 50 years."

We really don't know whether we can extend our lives or not, based upon our lifestyle, if the genetic cards are stacked against us. Jim Fix, for example, was an avid jogger who wrote books on running. Jim died of a heart attack running in his forties, but many speculate that he might have lived longer than he should have, based upon his genetic nature, and he was extremely active when he died.

Whether lifestyle or advances in medical and genetic research can change how long we live is a question that can be debated, but we do know that we can shorten life with our lifestyles. Preventing premature heart disease is what this chapter is about. Collectively we are looking at thousands of lost years that we can recapture with healthy living (see fig. 17.1). In this chapter we will look at maximizing the potential of our hearts for high-quality living as long as we live.

DISEASE PREVENTION

Since the beginning of the twentieth century, the overall death rate in the United States has been reduced from 17 per 1,000 persons per year to less than 9 per 1,000. Much of the credit for this reduction must go to the efforts we have made in prevention, based on knowledge gained from medical research. The once-great killers—typhoid fever, smallpox, and the plague—have been eradicated due to improvements in sanitation, housing, nutrition, and immunization.

Today the primary killer in the United States is chronic disease. Currently, 75 percent of all deaths in this country are

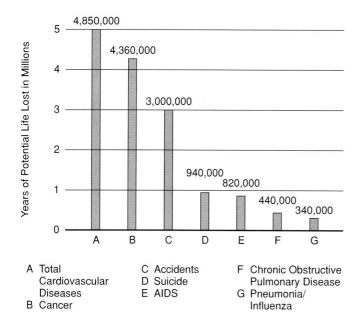

Figure 17.1

Estimated years of potential life lost before age 75, by cause of death (1989 U.S. estimates).

Source: From Centers for Disease Control and the American Heart Association.

due to **chronic diseases** that occur over a long period of time and are usually disabling, such as cardiovascular diseases and cancer. For a look at how chronic diseases and other causes of death cross cultures and genders, consider figure 17.2. For many of us, prevention of these diseases requires changes in lifestyle. Making these lifestyle changes depends on our understanding the basics of chronic disease and the impact of health habits we acquired during childhood and young adulthood, as well as on our sincere effort to change.

Most of us think that chronic disease, such as heart disease, is something that cannot happen to us. We are particularly vulnerable to this myth before we are 30 years old. But just as our daily decisions about nutrition and exercise will affect our future life expectancies, so we must deal daily with the issue of heart disease if we are to lessen our risks and enhance the quality of our lives. The food you have eaten today and the amount of exercise you have done today directly influence the health of your heart.

PREVENTION STAGES

Preventing the premature onset of heart disease, or any other disease, is a function of different levels of intervention. Prevention of disease means inhibiting the development of disease and interrupting or slowing the progression of disease after it has started.

Prevention can be divided into three stages: primary prevention, secondary prevention, and tertiary prevention. If any of your immediate relatives have suffered from any chronic disease, you might be predisposed to that disease. You can decide to take preventive measures now, before any disease symptoms occur. This is called **primary prevention.**

In some instances, a disease is already present but is being treated at an early stage. This is **secondary prevention**—prevention that attempts to keep the disease from worsening (such as bypass surgery or removal of a localized tumor). Unfortunately, no matter what lifestyle changes you make, you still might develop a major chronic disease at some stage in your life. Consequently, it is important to know the signs and symptoms of cardiovascular disease, cancer, stroke, diabetes, and other diseases, because it can help you seek early diagnosis and treatment.

Many of us have probably had (or known someone who has had) a disease and undergone rehabilitation to lessen or eliminate the sometimes serious effects. This process is known as **tertiary prevention.**

RISK REDUCTION: A PRIMARY PREVENTION STRATEGY

We can significantly influence our future health and increase our quality of life by developing prevention strategies, including controlling certain risk factors that increase the probability of chronic disease, disability, or premature death. There are a number of identified risk factors associated with potential cardiovascular diseases (heart attack, stroke, high blood pressure), cancers, digestive diseases, mental disorders, injury and poisoning, nervous system diseases, and sense organ diseases. Note that these are risk factors and not causes. Risk factors that are common to many diseases, in no particular order, include these:

1. Smoking
2. Hypercholesterolemia (high levels of cholesterol)
3. Lack of exercise
4. Poor nutrition (high-fat, high-salt, high-simple-sugar diet)
5. Obesity
6. Stress
7. Alcohol
8. Illicit drug use
9. High blood pressure
10. Exposure to carcinogens (excessive sun, pollutants, asbestos, etc.)

chronic disease
A drawn-out disease that cannot be cured.

primary prevention
Prevention of a disease before symptoms occur.

secondary prevention
Treatment of a disease at an early stage in an attempt to keep it from worsening.

tertiary prevention
Rehabilitation; the lessening or eliminating of the serious effects of a disease.

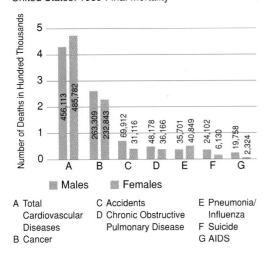

Leading Causes of Death, Males and Females
United States: 1989 Final Mortality

A Total Cardiovascular Diseases
B Cancer
C Accidents
D Chronic Obstructive Pulmonary Disease
E Pneumonia/Influenza
F Suicide
G AIDS

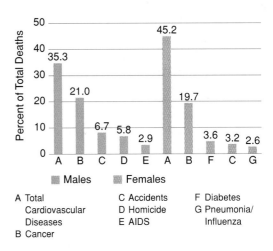

Leading Causes of Death for Black Males, Females
United States: 1988 Final Mortality

A Total Cardiovascular Diseases
B Cancer
C Accidents
D Homicide
E AIDS
F Diabetes
G Pneumonia/Influenza

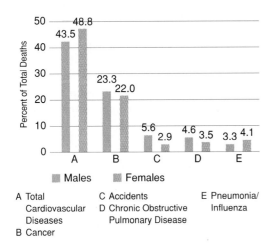

Leading Causes of Death for White Males, Females
United States: 1988 Final Mortality

A Total Cardiovascular Diseases
B Cancer
C Accidents
D Chronic Obstructive Pulmonary Disease
E Pneumonia/Influenza

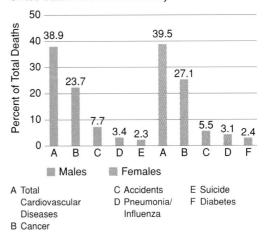

Leading Causes of Death for Asian or Pacific Islander Males, Females
United States: 1988 Final Mortality

A Total Cardiovascular Diseases
B Cancer
C Accidents
D Pneumonia/Influenza
E Suicide
F Diabetes

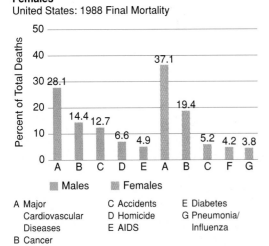

Leading Causes of Death for Hispanic Males, Females
United States: 1988 Final Mortality

A Major Cardiovascular Diseases
B Cancer
C Accidents
D Homicide
E AIDS
F Diabetes
G Pneumonia/Influenza

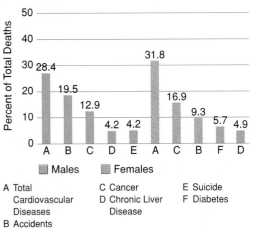

Leading Causes of Death for American Indian Males, Females
United States: 1988 Final Mortality

A Total Cardiovascular Diseases
B Accidents
C Cancer
D Chronic Liver Disease
E Suicide
F Diabetes

Figure 17.2

Leading causes of death for Americans.

Sources: From National Center for Health Statistics and the American Heart Association.

Risk of Cardiovascular Disease

Directions

Circle the number adjacent to the responses that are most accurate about you.

1. Gender

    3 Male

    0 Female

2. Family history of heart disease

    0 I am not aware of any of my parents or grandparents having died of a heart attack before age 60.

    1 One grandparent died of a heart attack before age 60.

    2 Two grandparents or one parent died of a heart attack before age 60.

    4 Three or more grandparents or one parent died of a heart attack before age 60.

    8 Both parents or all four grandparents died of a heart attack before age 60.

    10 One parent or two grandparents died of a heart attack before age 45.

3. Family history of high blood pressure, diabetes, or cholesterol ("family" in this question refers to brothers, sisters, mother, father, or grandparents).

    0 No one in my family has high blood pressure, diabetes, or high blood cholesterol.

    1 Only one member of my family has high blood pressure, diabetes, or high blood cholesterol.

    4 Two or three members of my family have high blood pressure, diabetes, or high blood cholesterol.

    6 Four or more members of my family have high blood pressure, diabetes, or high blood cholesterol.

4. Serum Cholesterol

    If you have had your cholesterol levels analyzed through blood analysis, what was your total cholesterol amount? If you have not had it checked, add 2 to your score since you do not know whether you are at risk.

    0 190mg/dL or below

    2 191–219mg/dL

    4 220–239mg/dL

    6 240–289mg/dL

    12 290–319mg/dL

    16 320mg/dL or higher

5. HDL (High-Density Lipoprotein) Cholesterol

    0 Over 50mg/dL or ratio of HDL to total cholesterol is one-fourth or better

    3 40–50mg/dL

    6 30–39mg/dL

    10 23–29mg/dL

    16 Below 23mg/dL

6. Smoking

    0 Never smoked

    1 Quit over 5 years ago

    2 Quit 2 to 4 years ago

    3 Quit about 1 year ago

    6 Quit during the past year

    If you still smoke, what is the number of cigarettes you now smoke:

    9 One-half to one pack a day

    12 One to two packs a day

    15 More than two packs a day

7. Blood Pressure

    0 120/75 or below

    2 120/75 to 140/85

    6 140/85 to 150/90

    8 150/90 to 175/100

    10 170/100 to 190/110

    12 190/110 or above

8. Exercise

    0 Aerobic exercise 4 to 5 times a week

    2 Aerobic exercise 2 to 3 times a week

    4 Aerobic exercise on weekends

    6 Occasional exercise

    8 Rarely exercise, if at all

9. Weight

    0 Always at or near ideal weight

    2 Presently 10 percent overweight

    4 Presently 20 percent overweight

    6 30 percent overweight

    8 Have been 20 percent or more overweight for most of my life

10. Are you a diabetic?

    0 No

    5 Non-insulin-dependent diabetic

    10 Insulin-dependent diabetic

11. Alcohol Consumption

    0 Zero to one drink per day (1 oz hard liquor, 4 oz wine, 12 oz beer = 1 drink)

    2 Two to three drinks per day

    4 Four drinks per day

12. Stress

    Do a formal stress assessment, or estimate your level of stress.

    0 Low stress

    3 Moderate stress

    6 High stress

Scoring

Total your points for the twelve questions.

Interpretation

Your total score indicates your risk for heart disease.

0–25	Low risk
26–50	Moderate risk
51–80	High risk
Over 80	Very high risk

Increasing evidence suggests that much of the incidence of chronic disease is generally due to the typical American lifestyle. Americans tend to eat foods high in saturated fat, sugar, and salt, while consuming lesser amounts of whole grains, breads, vegetables, and fruits. Many Americans drink large quantities of alcohol and smoke cigarettes. When these behavior patterns are added to our sedentary way of life, the result is an awesome incidence of chronic disease. If we are to make any change in the years to come, we must begin to value primary prevention, rather than the treatment and rehabilitation we focused on in the past.

CARDIOVASCULAR DISEASES

Cardiovascular diseases, which are diseases of the heart and blood vessels, have been the major cause of death in the United States for more than 40 years and account for over half of all deaths. The major types are hypertensive disease (characterized by continued elevation of blood pressure above the normal), coronary artery disease (a narrowing of the blood vessels that nourish the heart), and stroke (caused by a blockage of the blood supply to some part of the brain).

According to the projections for 1993 in *1993 Heart and Stroke Facts Statistics* by the American Heart Association (1992), estimates show that more than 70 million people in the United States today have some form of cardiovascular disease. The following are some other statistics of interest in the report:

1. In 1990, 930,000 Americans died of cardiovascular disease.
2. More than 2 of every 5 Americans die of cardiovascular disease.
3. About 70 million people suffer some form of cardiovascular disease, among the 250 million Americans. That is more than 1 out of every 4.

Heart disease earns its reputation as America's number one killer because the facts just cited mean that there are more deaths from cardiovascular disease than from all other causes combined. Many thousands of these deaths occur not among older people but among those in the prime of their lives. The cost of treating patients with cardiovascular disease will be approximately $117.4 billion in 1993 (Gunby 1993).

These statistics suggest that the cardiovascular diseases are presently beyond human control. Actually, however, of all the chronic diseases, these seem to have the most potential for primary prevention because of the knowledge we have gained about the risk factors. Studies show, for instance, that people who have heart attacks often have histories of high blood pressure, have high levels of blood cholesterol, smoke cigarettes, do not get sufficient exercise, are excessively overweight, have diabetes, and/or have a family history of heart attack in middle age. Each of these risk factors increases the chance of heart attack; in combination, they multiply the risk tremendously.

UNDERSTANDING MAJOR RISK FACTORS

You can prevent yourself from getting heart disease by understanding your risk factors, detecting any symptoms early, and modifying your lifestyle to reduce your risks. There has been a reduction of heart disease over the last few years because we are watching our diets, exercising, quitting smoking, and monitoring our blood pressure and cholesterol levels. The following sections discuss risk factors in more detail.

FAMILY HISTORY

It appears that the tendency toward heart disease is hereditary. If you have close relatives who died from heart disease between the ages of 40 and 60, that increases your risk for heart attack. Family history is a risk factor that cannot be controlled, so it is extremely important for high-risk people to carefully monitor the health of their heart by getting regular medical examinations and to reduce additional risks as described in the next sections.

CIGARETTE SMOKING

Cigarette smokers have higher levels of carbon monoxide in their blood than do nonsmokers. Carbon monoxide not only displaces oxygen in the blood but also tends to damage the arterial walls. Smoking makes the heart beat faster, raises the blood pressure, and narrows the blood vessels of the skin, especially in the fingers and toes. Given these facts, it is not surprising that numerous studies indicate that cigarette smokers are highly prone to heart disease. It is estimated that about 430,000 adults over the age of 35 died from smoking cigarettes and that about 201,000 of these deaths were from cardiovascular disease. It is also estimated that about 37,000 other deaths from cardiovascular disease involved exposure to environmental tobacco smoke (American Heart Association 1992).

HIGH BLOOD PRESSURE

Blood pressure is the force that flowing blood exerts against the arterial walls. Blood pressure varies from moment to moment, rising when we are excited and falling when we rest. In some individuals, however, blood pressure is always higher than normal. This condition is known as high blood pressure, or hypertension.

High blood pressure has been associated with an increased incidence of heart attack and stroke. When high

cardiovascular disease
Disease of the heart and blood vessels.

blood pressure
The force exerted by flowing blood against the artery walls.

blood pressure is not treated adequately, it can damage the heart, kidneys, and other organs of the body. Hypertension is a cardiovascular disease in itself, but because we feel no symptoms—no pain or discomfort—it is considered by some as a risk factor. Hypertension can go undetected for years because of the lack of alarming symptoms in the early stages. With regular medical checkups, we can uncover a case of high blood pressure while it is still in an early stage. Hypertension will be further described as a heart disease.

HIGH BLOOD CHOLESTEROL

High blood cholesterol can cause buildup on the arterial walls, narrowing the passageway through which the blood flows and leading to subsequent heart attack and stroke. The body generates its own cholesterol in addition to cholesterol that is ingested in foods. The amount of cholesterol manufactured by the body seems to be hereditary. A physician can measure the amount of cholesterol in the blood, and it is also common to see cholesterol screening programs at health departments or shopping malls. A diet that is low in cholesterol and saturated fat and high in fiber, particularly oat bran (Humble 1991), can help lower a blood cholesterol level that is too high. In difficult cases, hypercholesterolemia (high blood cholesterol disease) can be treated with medications.

It is difficult to make any absolute judgments about how high is too high a level of cholesterol. Robbins and Kumar (1987) state, "There is no single level of plasma cholesterol that identifies those at risk, the higher the level, the greater the risk." Studies have shown, though, that risk rises significantly once a plateau of 200 mg/dL is reached. Over 104 million American adults (58%) have blood cholesterol values of 200 mg/dL or higher, and about 49 million (27.7%) have levels of 240 or above (American Heart Association 1992).

DIABETES

Diabetes appears most frequently during middle age, usually in those of us who are overweight and live sedentary lifestyles. Diabetes can sharply increase the risk of heart attack, making control of the other risk factors even more important. (Diabetes is discussed at length later in this chapter.)

OTHER CONTRIBUTING FACTORS

Other factors contributing to heart disease include obesity, lack of exercise, and stress. Obesity usually results from eating too much and/or exercising too little. It places a heavy burden on the heart, but it is associated with coronary heart disease primarily because of its influence on blood pressure, blood cholesterol, and diabetes. About 47 million American adults are 20 percent or more over their desirable weight (American Heart Association 1992). A lack of exercise has been shown to be a risk factor for heart attack, and lack of exercise combined with overeating can lead to excessive weight—which is clearly a contributing factor.

Coronary heart disease is 1.9 times more likely to develop in those of us who are physically inactive as compared to those that are active and exercise. In spite of the well-publicized benefits of physical activity, only slightly more than one in five of us report physical activity lasting at least 30 minutes, five or more times per week. More than one in four Americans age 18 or older report no leisure-time physical activity (American Heart Association 1992). Some evidence suggests that stressful living habits also contribute to a higher incidence of heart attack.

To better understand how to prevent cardiovascular disease and how to cope with any such disease that occurs, it is useful to know something about the major cardiovascular diseases.

HEART DISEASES

In addition to hypertension, other specific heart diseases include arteriosclerosis and heart attack.

ARTERIOSCLEROSIS

Arteriosclerosis is the general term for three patterns of vascular disease, all of which cause thickening and a loss of elasticity of arteries. The most prominent pattern is atherosclerosis; less prominent are calcific sclerosis (calcium deposits on the arteries) and arteriolosclerosis (diseases of the small arteries and arterioles). The focus of this section is on atherosclerosis.

Atherosclerosis, or hardening of the arteries, is a degenerative disease that contributes to the development of high blood pressure, heart attack, and stroke. Atherosclerosis is a leading contributor to many heart attack and stroke deaths. During the disease process, the arteriole linings become thickened and roughened by deposits of fat, cholesterol, fibrin (a clotting material), cellular debris, and calcium.

The buildup on the inner walls eventually becomes hard and thick, and the arteries lose their ability to expand and contract. When this occurs, the blood has difficulty moving through the narrowed channels. It is then easier for a clot to form that might in turn block the channel and deprive the heart, brain, or another bodily organ of blood.

The deposits may grow for many years before the vessel becomes clogged enough to cause trouble (figure 17.3). When this does occur, however, that part of the body served by the clogged vessel is deprived of its blood supply. If

---

arteriosclerosis
A group of diseases characterized by the shrinking of, and loss of elasticity in, artery walls.

atherosclerosis
Hardening of the arteries; a degenerative cardiovascular disease that occurs when fat deposits build up in arteries.

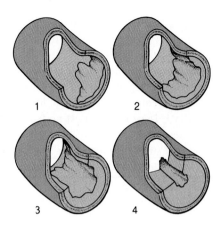

Figure 17.3
Progressive atherosclerotic buildup on artery walls.

blockage occurs in a coronary artery, the result may be a heart attack. If it occurs in a vessel leading to the brain, the result may be a stroke.

The atherosclerosis disease process is beginning to be clarified but is far from being totally understood. Part of the mystery that is being studied is the ratio of good cholesterol, or **high-density lipoprotein (HDL),** to bad cholesterol—**low-density lipoprotein (LDL)** or **very-low-density lipoprotein (VLDL).** High levels of HDL have been associated with lower risk of atherosclerosis. The exact function is not known, but it appears that HDL prevents plaque buildup and atherosclerosis. HDL is thought to carry the fats to the tissues of the liver where it is excreted in the bile. High levels of LDL are associated with increased risk of atherosclerosis because LDL seems to promote plaque buildup in the arteries. VLDL is associated with the triglycerides, which are also a form of fat, and also seems to contribute to atherosclerosis and coronary artery disease. Consequently, most physicians agree that the higher the HDL level and the lower the LDL level, the less risk there is of coronary artery disease. A ratio of 4 to 1 is considered a good ratio for total cholesterol to HDL (e.g., a total cholesterol of 200 and an HDL of 50). The higher the ratio the better—for example, a total cholesterol of 150 and an HDL of 50 would be a 3-to-1 ratio, which would be even better than 4 to 1.

HYPERTENSION

In the United States, more than 57 million people have some elevation of blood pressure (American Heart Association 1992). Even more alarming, 25 percent of those with hypertension are unaware of it, 25 percent are aware but are doing nothing to control it, and 25 percent are not receiving adequate treatment. Thus, only 25 percent of persons with high blood pressure are getting adequate treatment (American Heart Association 1986b).

Understanding Blood Pressure

With each beat of your heart, your blood pressure rises and falls within a limited range. Blood pressure is directly related to the amount of blood pumped through the heart, multiplied by the resistance of the vessels through which it is being pumped. If either the amount of blood or the resistance increases, as with atherosclerotic buildup, blood pressure rises. If your blood pressure remains elevated, you have high blood pressure.

High blood pressure adds to the workload of the heart and arteries, and the narrowed blood vessels might not be able to deliver enough oxygen to the body's organs. When the heart is forced to work harder for a long period of time, it tends to enlarge and can't keep up with the demands that are made on it. The arteries also show the wear and tear of high blood pressure by becoming hardened, less elastic, and scarred. When this happens, the blood is not delivered to the body's organs as it should be.

Causes of High Blood Pressure

In 90 percent of all cases of high blood pressure, the cause is unknown or idiopathic (Robbins and Kumar 1987). This type of high blood pressure is called **essential hypertension.** In the other 10 percent, the high blood pressure is known as secondary hypertension; with the correction of the primary health problem, generally renal disease, blood pressure usually returns to normal. The use of oral contraceptives is a common cause of hypertension. Oral contraceptives can raise blood pressure by increasing the blood volume, although the elevation is usually only slight. Overweight women who take birth control pills are particularly susceptible to high blood pressure.

Determining Blood Pressure

The only sure way to know if you have high blood pressure is to have your blood pressure taken with a **sphygmomanometer,** which consists of an inflatable rubber cuff that is placed around the arm and then inflated with air. The arm is squeezed with the cuff until the flow of blood momentarily stops. Then the air is released, and the blood begins to flow again. With a stethoscope, a trained person can detect both

---

high-density lipoprotein (HDL)
Considered "good" cholesterol, HDL removes other kinds of cholesterol from artery walls and transports it to the liver, where it is processed and excreted.

low-density lipoprotein (LDL)
Considered an undesirable form of cholesterol, LDL has been implicated in the formation of arterial plaque (atherosclerosis).

very-low-density lipoprotein (VLDL)
Considered an undesirable form of cholesterol, VLDL has been implicated in the formation of arterial plaque (atherosclerosis).

essential hypertension
High blood pressure, the cause of which is unknown.

sphygmomanometer
An instrument used to measure blood pressure.

systolic pressure and diastolic pressure. **Systolic pressure** is the first number that is recorded and is the highest pressure that occurs when the heart beats. It is noted on a readout from the sphygmomanometer (pressure recorded in millimeters of mercury) when the first beat is heard through the stethoscope when pressure begins to be released from the constricting cuff. It marks the beginning of blood flowing again during the heart contraction. **Diastolic pressure** is the pressure of the blood flow between heartbeats, or when the heart is relaxed. It is recorded secondly when the last beat is heard. Both numbers are then recorded as the blood pressure measurement (120/80, for example, called "120 over 80").

What is a normal blood pressure? Researchers have collected data on blood pressure, evaluated it statistically, and determined that 120 over 80 is the typically "normal" blood pressure for an adult. Lower and higher values are within the normal range. Blood pressure can be considered high if the systolic pressure is considered normal but the diastolic pressure is high (i.e., 130/105), when the systolic pressure is high and the diastolic pressure is normal (i.e., 180/80), or if both values are high (i.e., 160/100). The upper limits of normal are about 140/90 (fig. 17.4). Life expectancy and blood pressure are shown in table 17.1.

Treatment of High Blood Pressure

Many antihypertensive medications are available for the treatment of high blood pressure, including **diuretics** (which eliminate excess fluid and salt) and **vasodilators** (which widen narrow blood vessels). Antihypertensives include hydrochlorothiazide, stenolol, captopril, clonidine, diltiazem, prazesin, and prazosin (Materson 1993). In most cases, these drugs lower blood pressure, but often other actions must also be taken. If you are overweight and have high blood pressure, you can lower your blood pressure some by losing weight.

A controversial prevention strategy is the regular consumption of small amounts of alcohol. The effects in reducing blood pressure are clear, but the studies do not consider the dangerous effects on the liver or on drinking behavior (Russell et al. 1991). Reducing the amount of salt in the diet may also help.

HEART ATTACK

Heart attacks result from coronary artery disease or atherosclerosis of the coronary arteries. If a blood clot forms in one or more of these narrowed arteries and blocks the flow of blood to that part of the heart (fig. 17.5), a heart attack, or **myocardial infarction,** can occur. That part of the heart begins to die. Luckily, the heart has its own method of repair. If the damage is not too severe and the person does not die, other blood vessels begin to supply that area of the heart served by the blocked artery. One purpose of exercise is to enlarge the arteries and facilitate the development of collateral circulation. With **collateral circulation,** smaller blood vessels allow blood to flow to the part of the heart muscle served by a blocked main vessel, sometimes even before a

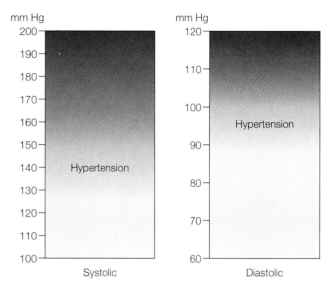

Figure 17.4

The American Heart Association identifies hypertension as a systolic pressure of 140 mm Hg or higher and/or a diastolic pressure of 90 mm Hg or higher. For a given individual, hypertension can start at ±10 mm Hg of these measures.

T ABLE 17.1	BLOOD PRESSURE AND LIFE EXPECTANCY OF A 35-YEAR-OLD MAN	
Blood Pressure		**Life Expectancy**
120/80		41.5 years
140/95[a]		37.5 years
150/100[a]		25 years
[a] Elevated pressure		

systolic pressure
The highest point of blood pressure, measured when the heart contracts.

diastolic pressure
The lowest point of blood pressure, measured when the heart relaxes.

diuretic
A type of medication that causes the body to eliminate water through urination.

vasodilators
Drugs or nerves that cause a widening of the opening of blood vessels.

heart attack
The death of part or all of the heart muscle due to cardiovascular disease; also known as myocardial infarction.

myocardial infarction
Heart attack.

collateral circulation
Circulation of the blood through smaller vessels when a major vessel has become blocked.

PERSONAL INSIGHT

Stress-Related Hypertension

I had just received an offer to become a department chairman of an academic department. To accept this job, I had to leave the state and move 2,000 miles. Selling the house in 1985 was not easy and I ended up leaving it in the hands of a realtor. To make a long story short, we had to rent a condo and still had a house payment on top of the rent. We didn't know where we wanted to live in this new place. The new job, changing from researcher and teacher to administrator, was a real adjustment. We finally sold our house, but because land was more expensive, decided to build ourselves. My wife acted as the general contractor and I acted as several subcontractors, doing rock work, insulation, siding, roofing, tile work, and numerous other jobs. We were getting close to the deadline to be out of our condo and we had no place to move, so I started putting in eighteen- to twenty-two-hour days trying to finish the house. I wasn't eating well,

grabbing a bite when I could. During the midst of all this, I was monitoring my blood pressure and it kept getting up higher and higher until it was 140 over 105. I checked in with a physician and he put me on blood pressure medication. After six months on medication and after completing our home, I decided that I would get off the medication through lifestyle change.

It was not easy. I started running again and figured I was about fifteen pounds overweight. An analysis of my diet showed a lot of fat and salt. The low-salt and low-fat diet was hard. Low-salt soups were horrible. No salt on eggs that I could only have once a week got to be a drag. No salt on baked potatoes and no sour cream made me dislike potatoes, but I started adding yogurt and did okay. I hardly ever had beef and ate lots of vegetables.

I had always had trouble running distances. After fifteen minutes, I was walking. I kept at it and finally got to thirty minutes a day about four or five times a week. My blood pressure would be lowest right after I ran. I quit

snacking late at night to try and lose weight as well. My blood pressure after four months was still high when I would quit my medication for more than four or five days.

In desperation, I entered a study at the university, where they were experimenting with medications. The first three weeks were to establish a baseline. During the first week, I qualified for the study (diastolic of over 100 qualified). Just when they were to put me on one of the medications, they said, "Sorry, you don't qualify; your diastolic is only 95." I was ecstatic. I kept off the medication and, after three more weeks, I was under 90. I went to my physician and told him I wanted to stay off, and he gave me his blessing as long as I monitored it carefully. After several more weeks of hard work and stress-control strategies, my blood pressure returned to 120 over 84, or normal. It remains that low as long as I continue to practice good health strategies—to date, eight months off medication.

Source: From G. E. Richardson, personal journal.

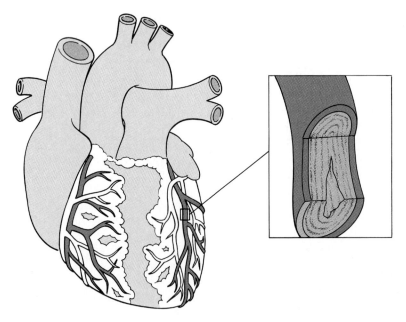

Coronary arteries (showing blocked artery)

Figure 17.5
Blocked coronary arteries cause heart attack.

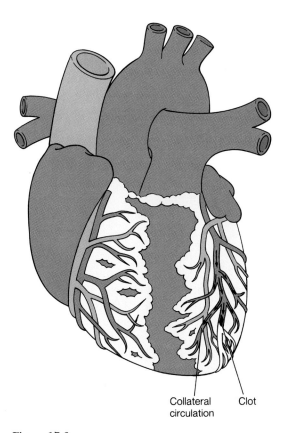

Figure 17.6
Collateral circulation.

heart attack occurs. An examination of runners' hearts showed that some of the runners had suffered heart attacks during their lifetimes and never knew it because of the collateral circulation created by exercise (fig. 17.6).

Another result of coronary artery disease can be chest pain, or **angina,** which warns of narrowed or blocked arteries before a heart attack occurs. Angina usually occurs at times of emotional excitement or unusual physical exertion.

Symptoms of Heart Attack
Unfortunately, many people who have heart attacks actually deny they are having a problem. So it is important to know the warning signals of a heart attack.

Heart attack is the nation's number one killer. When an attack occurs, there is no time for delay, as many victims can survive only if they get immediate medical care. Certain signs indicate that a heart attack might be occurring: (1) an uncomfortable pressure, fullness, squeezing, or pain in the center of the chest, lasting 2 minutes or more; (2) pain that spreads to the shoulders, neck, jaw, or arms; and (3) severe pain, dizziness, fainting, sweating, nausea, or shortness of breath. Not all of these signals are always present, and they sometimes subside and then return. If some or all of these signals do occur, get help immediately.

What to Do
You should know exactly what to do when a heart attack occurs. Many communities have emergency rescue services that can be called. Many cities have a 911 number to call paramedics who can administer **cardiopulmonary resuscitation (CPR).**

Sometimes the heart attack is so severe that the victim's heartbeat and breathing stop. If you are trained to administer CPR, you might save a life. If you are not, quickly find someone in the neighborhood or dorm who can help after you have called for emergency personnel. The 4 or 5 minutes it may take emergency personnel to arrive are critical. Many people have been trained in CPR, so you might be lucky and find someone who can start resuscitation. If you are not trained to administer CPR, you can check for breathing and a pulse at the carotid artery.

It is a good idea for all of us to be trained in cardiopulmonary resuscitation. Numerous lives have been saved regularly by brothers and sisters, roommates, and parents who were trained in CPR.

ADVANCES IN TREATMENT OF HEART DISEASE

Modern interventions to treat cardiovascular disease are amazing. If you ever find that you have heart disease, you could get a new donor heart, or your physicians could go inside your heart to see what is wrong, clean out the arteries, or implant a device to insure the rhythm of your heartbeat. The following sections briefly describe some of the current treatments for cardiovascular disease.

DIAGNOSIS

The actual diagnosis of heart attack is made by a physician and is based on the results of several tests taken at a hospital, either in the emergency room or in the coronary care unit (CCU). These units offer specialized treatment and around-the-clock care. The physician uses an **electrocardiogram (EKG),** a test that graphs the electrical impulses within the heart, along with blood tests, to identify levels of cardiac enzymes and to

angina
Chest pain associated with heart disease; can be brought on by smoking.

cardiopulmonary resuscitation (CPR)
An emergency measure to artificially maintain breathing and heartbeat.

electrocardiogram (EKG)
A test that measures electrical impulses in the heart, to determine whether the heart is malfunctioning.

determine whether a heart attack has occurred and whether there are any abnormalities caused by heart damage (American Heart Association 1986a).

ENDOVASCULAR SURGERY

There are several types of surgeries that allow the physician to go inside the coronary arteries and see and treat the problems directly. The goal of endovascular surgery is to dilate the coronary arteries that have been narrowed by atherosclerotic plaque and thus improve the blood supply to the heart and reduce the risk of heart attack. Endovascular surgeries include angiography, balloon angioplasty, laser angioplasty, and stent placement (Ahn and Eton 1993).

Angiography

A special technique called **angiography** shows the cardiologist where and how great the obstruction is. In essence, angiography involves sending a tiny camera into the coronary artery to identify obstructions.

Balloon Angioplasty

Another technique to facilitate the unrestricted flow of blood through the arteries is **angioplasty.** This process is much like cleaning a sewage line with a "snake." A small balloon-like instrument on the end of a wire is forced through the artery and flattens the clogs or buildup against the arterial wall to allow for a better flow of blood.

Laser Angioplasty

Laser angioplasty accomplishes the same function as balloon angioplasty, with equal success. Both continuous-wave lasers, delivered with contact probes, and pulsed lasers are able to remove plaque that blocks arteries (Lammer et al. 1992).

Stent Placement

After an angioplasty is performed, sometimes the arteries will abruptly occlude (close) after surgery. It is also likely that the arteries will narrow again a few months after angioplasty. One device that has been developed to help keep the arteries open and keep tissue from closing the artery is the placement of a stent, or mechanical support, inside the artery. Initial reports indicate improved functions in some patients, but, like in other forms of endovascular surgery, function declines over time (Serruys et al. 1991).

DRUG THERAPY

New classes of heart drugs are leading the revolution in treating heart disease. Beta-blocking drugs, first made available in the late 1960s, are effective in preventing second heart attacks and sudden cardiac arrests in patients who have had previous attacks. Calcium-blocking drugs prevent the coronary arteries from contracting and having spasms that block the flow of oxygen to the heart muscle. Physicians can now treat heart attack victims by injecting a specific enzyme into

the heart that prevents further damage to the heart muscle. Other drugs, including antiarrhythmia agents, are now being tested.

In **thrombolic therapy,** drugs are used to dissolve blood clots. Clot-dissolving drugs are used to treat both heart attack and stroke (Skolnick 1993).

CORONARY BYPASS SURGERY

In some cases, heart damage requires **bypass surgery.** A vein is removed from the patient's leg and grafted to the coronary artery above and below the obstruction, diverting coronary blood flow around the blockage. Many times, more than one bypass is needed.

HEART TRANSPLANTATION

The first heart transplant was performed in 1967, but within a few years almost all early advocates of transplants had abandoned the operation because of a mortality rate of up to 80 percent within a year following surgery. To prevent the body from rejecting the "new" heart, patients were often given huge doses of powerful **immunosuppressive drugs.** These drugs made patients more susceptible to other diseases, and the vast majority of transplant patients died from infection.

Transplant surgery has now been revived, however, because of the new drug cyclosporine, a fungal compound that blocks the production of white blood cells that cause rejection but not of those that fight infection. So the heart transplant now seems to have become a more successful operation. The transplants are now covered by Medicare.

So much progress has been made that now every year many Americans receive new hearts, and 70 percent of heart transplant recipients survive for more than 1 year. Combined heart/lung transplants have a 70 percent survival rate.

---

angiography
A diagnostic procedure through which the chambers and blood vessels of the heart are examined.

angioplasty
The process of clearing arteries using a balloon-type instrument on the end of a wire, much like cleaning a pipe with a plumber's snake.

thrombolic therapy
The use of drugs to dissolve blood clots.

bypass surgery
A surgical technique in which cardiologists take blood vessels from another part of the body and use them to replace obstructed coronary arteries. In single, double, triple, and quadruple bypasses, surgeons replace one, two, three, or four arteries, respectively.

immunosuppressive drugs
Drugs that suppress the immune system to prevent the body from rejecting a transplant organ.

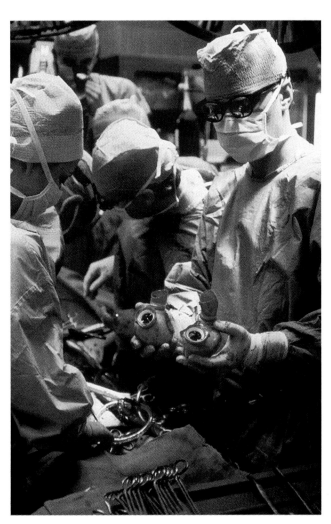

The Jarvik artificial heart.

Issue

Which Risk Is Higher?

A secondary prevention strategy against heart attack is bypass surgery. In this operation, an artery that is almost totally blocked, but still allowing blood to pass through, is replaced with a vein from another part of the patient's body. The replacement artery does not have plaque buildup and restores normal flow to the heart. In one open-heart surgery, a patient might have a triple (or quadruple) bypass, which means that three (or four) arteries are replaced. The patient avoids the heart attack and resulting necrosis by this operation. Over time, the plaque buildup may return, and the operation may need to be repeated.

Is this the best way to give a heart patient a full and active lifestyle?

- Pro: The mortality rate from the bypass operation has become very low, so the possibility of death is quite remote. The guarantee is clear coronary arteries after the operation, which might not happen just with lifestyle changes. It means instant relief from angina and improved life expectancy.

- Con: A program of drugs, diet, and moderate exercise can be just as effective as bypass surgery, and the mortality rate is about the same. Such a program is much less expensive than surgery, and the lifestyle change is beneficial. There is no break in work or school in most cases.

What do you think?

THE ARTIFICIAL HEART

In December 1982, medical history was made in Salt Lake City with the implantation of an artificial heart into the chest of a 61-year-old retired dentist who was suffering from congestive heart failure. The plastic heart, the **Jarvik-7,** was attached to the patient's atria, the ventricles having been surgically removed. The artificial heart, slightly larger than the average heart, was connected by tubes to a compressor that kept it pumping.

Life was not easy for this first recipient of an artificial heart. He was permanently tethered to 375 pounds of equipment, including two compressors, a backup compressor, a 3-hour supply of pressurized air to operate the heart in case of power failure, a drier to dehumidify the air, and mechanisms that controlled air pressure and heart rate. All this equipment rested on a cart that had to be kept 6 feet from the patient. The patient lived for over 3 months with this artificial heart, and the information acquired from this treatment was extremely helpful for future advances.

Since 1982, many patients have received transplants with Jarvik-7 or Jarvik 7-70 (a smaller version of the Jarvik-7) artificial hearts. The Jarvik 7-70 was developed because the

spherical shape of the Jarvik-7 ventricles did not fit easily into the chest. The Jarvik 7-70 fit better but had a 30 percent reduction in stroke volume (the amount of blood pumped with each heartbeat). A later version of the artificial heart is the Utah 100. Like the Jarvik 7-70, the Utah 100 is pneumatically powered and has a more oval shape to better fit into the chest cavity, but it has the same stroke volume as the original Jarvik-7 (Olson and De Paulis 1987).

The function of artificial hearts at this point is to allow the patient to live until a donor heart is found for transplantation. The average time that people have artificial hearts is 10 to 30 days. The longest time a person was on an artificial heart was 200 days.

Jarvik-7 artificial heart
An artificial heart that temporarily replaces a real heart until a donor can be found. The revised versions of the original Jarvik include the Jarvik-7, the Jarvik 7-70, and the Utah 100 Artificial Heart.

Recycled Donated Hearts

The heart of a 20-year-old man who shot and killed himself was transplanted into a 47-year-old man. The 47-year-old man had suffered many episodes of heart failure and at the time of the transplant, in December 1991, was bedridden. Although the transplanted heart was fully functional for 13 days, the recipient never fully recovered and was brain dead. Upon his death, the heart was again taken out and transplanted into a 58-year-old man who had had four heart attacks. The 58-year-old man was healthy and active a full year after his heart transplant (Pasic et al. 1993).

The artificial heart, though serving a good purpose, has not been perfected to the point of being problem-free. Artificial hearts are prone to thrombosis, stroke, bleeding, clotting around artificial biomaterial, and destruction of red blood cells (Grieger 1986). In late 1989 and 1990, the Food and Drug Administration (FDA) began putting several medical devices under scrutiny (Jones 1990). In January 1990, the FDA withdrew approval for use of the Jarvik-7 artificial heart (Merz 1990), largely for sloppiness in manufacturing and complications with some patients using the Jarvik-7. Researchers at the University of Utah Artificial Heart Laboratory and Humana Medical Center in Louisville, Kentucky, continue to refine the hearts by giving them softer pumping action to prevent the destruction of red blood cells, improving the anticoagulant drug balances, and better monitoring for early detection of stroke and other problems (Grieger 1986). It is projected that, by the year 2000, fully implantable and portable artificial hearts will be available. Penn State University researchers are near perfecting replacement hearts and lungs (Goldsmith 1993).

STROKE

Stroke is a sudden loss of brain function, usually as the result of some interference (either permanent or temporary) with the brain's blood supply. The extent of damage determines whether the stroke is minor and transient with no lasting effects, one that leaves the victim with some degree of disability, or one so major that the victim dies.

Stroke is a devastating and disabling human disorder. It has afflicted almost 2 million persons in the United States today and kills more than 145,000 annually (American Heart Association 1992).

The brain and its nerve cells depend on the oxygen and food brought to them by the bloodstream. When this supply is cut off for a period of time, the nerve cells die. Once these

cells have died, they cease to fulfill their tasks, such as making a body part move, reporting on sensations, or operating one of the senses.

CAUSES OF STROKE

There are four causes of stroke (fig. 17.7). One of the more common causes is a **cerebral thrombosis,** which occurs when a clot **thrombus** forms inside one of the arteries supplying blood to the brain and blocks it. These clots occur in arteries damaged by atherosclerosis.

Another form of stroke—**cerebral embolism**—can be caused by a wandering clot **(embolus)** that is carried in the bloodstream until it becomes wedged in one of the arteries leading to the brain.

When a defective artery in the brain bursts, another form of stroke—**cerebral hemorrhage**—occurs. Blood supply to the cells is cut off, and the cells can't function. In addition, accumulated blood from the burst artery can create pressure on the surrounding brain tissue. This pressure can interfere with brain function, causing mild or severe symptoms of stroke.

Arterial hemorrhage in the brain can be caused by a burst aneurysm. **Aneurysms** are blood-filled pouches that balloon out from weak spots in the artery wall; they are often associated with high blood pressure. Aneurysms do not always cause trouble, but when one bursts in the brain, the result is a stroke (American Heart Association 1992).

A stroke can occur at any time or place, during activity or rest. Typically those who have a cerebral hemorrhage suffer a sudden, severe headache and fall unconscious. When a cerebral embolism is the cause, the stroke comes on even

stroke
A cardiovascular disease in which the blood supply is cut off to a portion of the brain, causing paralysis, aphasia, and/or death.

cerebral thrombosis
The formation of a blood clot that blocks one of the arteries that supply blood to the brain.

thrombus
A blood clot, usually one located at the point where it was formed, in a blood vessel or a chamber of the heart.

cerebral embolism
A clot that is carried to the brain, where it blocks a small artery.

embolus
A wandering blood clot.

cerebral hemorrhage
Bleeding from a diseased artery that damages surrounding brain tissue.

aneurysm
A ballooning out of a vein, an artery, or the heart, due to a weakening of the wall by disease, traumatic injury, or an abnormality present at birth.

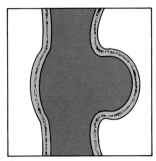

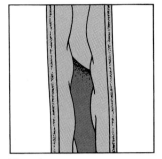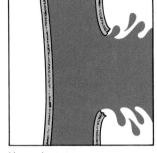

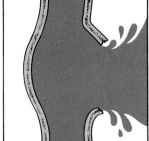

Figure 17.7
Causes of stroke.

WARNING SIGNALS

The warning signals of an impending stroke are (1) a sudden, temporary weakness or numbness of the face, arm, and leg on one side of the body; (2) a temporary loss of speech, or trouble in speaking or understanding speech; (3) a temporary dimness or loss of vision, particularly in one eye; and (4) unexpected dizziness, unsteadiness, or sudden falls (American Heart Association 1992).

Typically, the most visible sign of stroke is paralysis on one side of the body. Paralysis of the right side results from damage to the left hemisphere of the brain, which will also cause problems with speech and language (**aphasia**). These persons will also be slow and cautious when approaching an unfamiliar problem. Paralysis on the left side indicates damage to the right hemisphere of the brain (fig. 17.8). These persons have difficulty with spatial perception and tend to be quick and impulsive, often attempting unsafe activities.

After a stroke, some of the damaged nerve cells may recover, or their function might be taken over by other nerve cells in the brain. In this way, the part of the body affected by the stroke may eventually improve or even return to normal. Some persons recover quickly; others, however, suffer such serious damage that even a partial recovery takes a long time.

TREATMENT AND REHABILITATION

Treatment may include surgery and/or drugs. If a blockage has occurred in the carotid arteries of the neck, surgery called **carotid endarterectomy** is used to remove the atherosclerotic plaque buildup. If a blood vessel has been blocked by a clot, anticlotting drugs may be used either to prevent new clots from forming or to dissolve an existing clot (Skolnick 1993).

Most stroke patients can be rehabilitated with a program designed to teach new skills to replace those lost and to maintain and improve the patient's physical condition—another example of tertiary prevention.

OTHER TYPES OF HEART DISEASE

Of the other types of heart disease, the most common are rheumatic heart disease, congenital heart disease, and congestive heart failure.

more suddenly and without warning. A cerebral thrombosis is similar to a cerebral hemorrhage but usually occurs after inactivity.

RISK FACTORS

The risk factors of stroke are slightly different from those discussed for heart disease. Two of them, sex and race, can't be changed. The risk of stroke is greater in men than in women; however, women who take oral contraceptives increase their risk of stroke, and women who smoke heavily further increase their risk.

There are certain modifiable risk factors for stroke, however. Controlling high blood pressure or diabetes will reduce the risk, as will wise management of heart disease. An increase in the red blood cell count may be a risk factor of stroke, but this too can be modified through medical management.

---

aphasia
Loss of the ability to speak, usually caused by stroke.

carotid endarterectomy
Surgery used to remove plaque buildup in the carotid arteries of the neck.

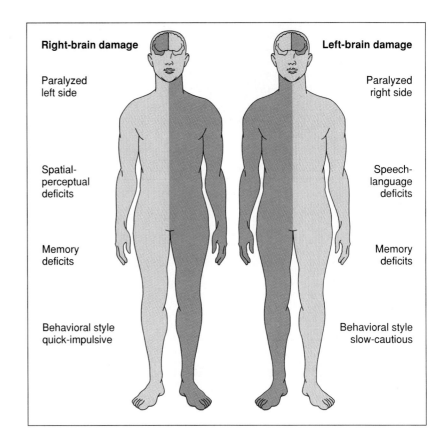

Right-brain damage

Paralyzed
left side

Spatial-
perceptual
deficits

Memory
deficits

Behavioral style
quick-impulsive

Left-brain damage

Paralyzed
right side

Speech-
language
deficits

Memory
deficits

Behavioral style
slow-cautious

Figure 17.8

Damage on one side of the brain affects the
opposite side of the body.

Source: Adapted from "How Stroke Affects Behavior."
American Heart Association (#50-1033), 1992 .

RHEUMATIC HEART DISEASE

An untreated streptococcal infection can develop into
rheumatic fever, which in turn can damage many of the
body's tissues, especially in the heart, joints, brain, and skin.
Rheumatic fever can cause permanent heart damage, known
as **rheumatic heart disease.** Anyone can develop rheumatic
fever, but it is found most often in children aged 5 to 15.

CONGENITAL HEART DISEASE

Congenital heart defects are abnormalities in the structure
of the heart that are present at birth. Most such defects either obstruct the flow of blood or reroute the blood. Unusual heart defects also occur, upsetting the electrical impulses responsible for the heartbeat. In most cases, the cause
of these defects is unknown, although German measles—if
contracted by the mother during the first 3 months of pregnancy—is one cause that has been identified.

CONGESTIVE HEART FAILURE

Congestive heart failure occurs as a result of damage to the
heart muscle caused by rheumatic fever, congenital heart defects, heart attack, atherosclerosis, or high blood pressure.

The heart muscle lacks the strength to properly circulate the
blood, so the blood flow is inadequate to meet all of the
body's needs.

TAKE ACTION

1. Don't smoke or drink coffee.
2. Attain and maintain an ideal weight (body fat
   composition).
3. If your cholesterol level is high, reduce it through
   exercise, diet, or prescription medication.
4. Learn to effectively manage your stress levels.
5. Monitor, and reduce if necessary, your blood pressure.
6. Eat low-fat foods and a balanced diet with lots of
   vegetables and fiber.

rheumatic heart disease
An inflammatory disease centered in the valves of the heart.

congestive heart failure
A condition in which the heart cannot pump the required
amount of blood, causing fluid to collect in the abdomen, legs,
and/or lungs.

PERSONAL SKILLS AND EXPERIENCES

Preventing Cardiovascular Disease

Mind

Chronic stress has been associated with heart disease. The hostile Type A behavior pattern as well as daily hassles are risk factors for heart disease. At the same time, the antidote for stress-related heart disease is hardiness: a sense of being committed, challenged, and in some sense in control in our lives. The following skills and experiences of the mind can help fortify your cardiovascular system.

1. Positive states of hardiness, self-efficacy, and self-esteem can be enhanced by challenging yourself and growing through repeated, empowering, positive, new life experiences.
2. Practice stress-management strategies, particularly positive imagery and creative personal problem solving.
3. Practice mental health skills such as understanding your mind, body, and soul; meditation; nurturing your strengths; and laughing.

Body

To improve the quality of your life and perhaps live as long as you possibly can, you can practice several skills and experiences of the body that will keep your heart functioning optimally:

1. At the first indication of elevated blood pressure or other symptom of heart disease, take one aspirin a day ("Aspirin for Stable Chronic Angina" 1993).
2. Do aerobic exercise four or five times a week.
3. Eat diets that are low in fat. Eat mostly complex carbohydrates, fruits, and vegetables.
4. Maintain your optimal weight.
5. Avoid smoking and passive smoking.
6. Have regular medical examinations.
7. Learn to take your own blood pressure.
8. If your moral standards allow you to drink and you do not have a history of alcoholic problems in your family, then one drink a day may be helpful in keeping your blood pressure down.

Soul

Positive states of the soul will also help you avoid chronic diseases and assure you a higher quality of life. To love others, feel loved, and have a means of releasing pent-up negative emotions such as anger in positive ways (e.g., walking it off) are ways of fortifying your defenses against chronic disease. Having a spiritual orientation and faith in positive forces greater than your own will help.

If each day you make sure that you spend some time getting in touch with your soul, you will be healthier. Perhaps when you are driving to school you can listen to some music that will touch your soul or to a motivational speaker. You may want to read some spiritual literature to touch your soul. Make a commitment to reflect upon who you are and where you are going with your life.

THE WORLD AROUND YOU

Preventing Heart Disease Through Good Relationships

Across cultures, heart-warming experiences with others promote a healthy heart. Anger and hostility with others are detrimental to the heart. Skills and experiences for keeping your heart healthy, then, include learning and practicing the skills of communication and loving others. Establish trust with others by doing favors, being honest, and doing what you say you are going to do. Doing acts of service and expressing unconditional love to others (giving without any expectation of receiving or having them owe you anything) not only make you feel good emotionally, but also help fortify your body. People who are married or are in a close intimate relationship with someone live longer than those who are not.

PERSONAL SKILLS AND EXPERIENCES

PNI Action

It might be hard to believe, but one way of guarding yourself against diseases is to provide service to others. Case studies in psychoneuroimmunology (PNI) have shown that watching humanitarian acts, watching humorous movies, and being engaged in a cause all strengthen the immune system. We know that a fighting spirit, optimism, hope, and periodically having a good laugh all fortify the body against heart disease. Reflect upon the skills of the soul and adopt them into your lifestyle. The combined effects of the skills of body, mind, soul, and interdependence will help to maximize your immune system.

SUMMARY

1. Prevention can be divided into three stages: primary prevention (taking steps to avoid the disease before symptoms occur), secondary prevention (treatment at an early stage of the disease), and tertiary prevention (rehabilitation).

2. Risk factors associated with heart disease include smoking cigarettes, obesity, hypertension, a diet high in fats and cholesterol, a high blood cholesterol level, and a lack of exercise.

3. Heart attack is the nation's number one killer.

4. The latest advances in cardiovascular medicine include heart transplantation, Jarvik 7-70 artificial hearts, cardiovascular risk identification and reduction, and angioplasty.

5. Stroke is a devastating disease characterized by a sudden loss of brain function that can lead to paralysis, loss of speech, and even death.

6. Other types of heart disease include rheumatic heart disease, congenital heart disease, and congestive heart failure.

COMMITMENT ACTIVITIES

1. Learn to take your blood pressure. It is likely that someone else in your class knows how. Ask the instructor to provide some sphygmomanometers and stethoscopes so that you can learn. After you know how to take your blood pressure, you will benefit from purchasing a blood pressure kit so that you can monitor your blood pressure throughout your life.

2. As you prepare to do your lifestyle contract for this part of the book, become aware of the resources available in your community to help you. You and your class might want to go to the American Heart Association to help you understand how to modify the cholesterol or salt in your diet, lose weight, quit smoking, or control your blood pressure. The AHA has several pamphlets that can help you reduce your risk of heart disease.

3. There are often clubs or meetings of people who have had bypass operations or who are rehabilitating from heart attacks. Either attend one of the meetings or invite someone who has had one of the operations to talk to your class.

4. Many people who suffer heart attacks are saved by those who are trained to do cardiopulmonary resuscitation (CPR). Your local chapter of the American Heart Association or the American Red Cross offers CPR classes. Take the opportunity to become trained in CPR. It is likely that your college or university has classes in first aid and CPR. You never know when you will need this skill.

REFERENCES

Ahn, S. S., and D. Eton. 1993. "Endovascular Surgery for Peripheral Arterial Occlusive Disease." *American Family Physician* 47, no. 2 (1 February): 423–30.

American Heart Association. 1986a. *After a Heart Attack.* Dallas, TX: American Heart Association.

American Heart Association. 1986b. *How You Can Help Your Doctor Treat Your High Blood Pressure.* Dallas, TX: American Heart Association.

American Heart Association. 1992. *1993 Heart and Stroke Facts Statistics.* Dallas, TX: American Heart Association.

"Aspirin for Stable Chronic Angina." 1993. *Patient Care* 27, no. 5 (15 March): 82–83.

Goldsmith, M. F. 1993. "After Two Decades, Penn State Researchers May Be Near Perfecting Replacement Heart and Lungs." *Journal of the American Medical Association* 269, no. 8 (24 February): 966–69.

Grieger, Lisa. 1986. "MDs Hit FDA Restrictions on Artificial Heart Cases." *American Medical New,* 21 February.

Gunby, P. 1993. "Two New Reports Help Put Nation's No. 1 Killer Disease Challenges into Perspective for 1993." *Journal of the American Medical Association* 269, no. 4 (27 January): 449–50.

Humble, C. G. 1991. "Oats and Cholesterol: The Prospects for Prevention of Heart Disease." *American Journal of Public Health* 81, no. 2 (February) 159–60.

Jones, L. 1990. "House Panel Puts FDA Regulation of Medical Devices Under Scrutiny." *American Medical News,* 9 March, 2–3.

Lammer, J., et al. 1992. "Pulsed Excimer Laser Versus Continuous-Wave Nd." *The Lancet* 340, no. 8829 (14 November): 1183–88.

Lange, R. A., and L. D. Hillis. 1993. "Immediate Angioplasty for Acute Myocardial Infarction." *New England Journal of Medicine* 328, no. 10 (11 March): 726–28.

Levin, S. 1991. "Aquatic Therapy." *Physician and Sportsmedicine* 19, no. 10 (October): 119–24.

Levy, R. I., and J. Moskowitz. 1982. "Cardiovascular Research: Decades of Progress, a Decade of Promise." *Science* 217: 121–29.

Materson, B. J. 1993. "Single Drug Therapy for Hypertension in Men: A Comparison of Six Antihypertensive Agents with Placebo." *New England Journal of Medicine* 328, no. 13 (1 April): 914–21.

Merz, B. 1990. "FDA Cites Deficiencies, Withdraws Approval for Jarvik-7 Artificial Heart." *American Medical News* 33 (26 January): 1–2.

Olson, D. 1987. "ISAO International Registry: Bridge-To-Transplant Experience with the Jarvik-7 and the Jarvik-7-70 Total Artificial Heart." *Artificial Organs* 11, no. 1:63–68.

Olson, D., and R. De Paulis. 1987. "Does the Artificial Heart Work?" Experimental and Clinical Proceedings of Advances in Cardiology, 1 May, Bordighera, Italy.

Pasic, M., et al. 1993. "Brief Report: Reuse of a Transplanted Heart." *New England Journal of Medicine* 328, no. 5 (4 February): 319–20.

Reid, K., and L. Vikhanski. 1992. "The Sun's Ominous Side: Skin Cancer." *Medical World News* 33, no. 2 (February): 18–25.

Robbins, S. L., and V. Kumar. 1987. *Basic Pathology.* Philadelphia: Saunders.

Russell, M., M. L. Cooper, M. R. Frone, and J. W. Welte. 1991. "Alcohol Drinking Patterns and Blood Pressure." *American Journal of Public Health* 81, no. 4 (April): 452.

Serruys, P., et al. 1991. "Angiographic Follow-up After Placement of a Self-Expanding Coronary-Artery Stent." *New England Journal of Medicine* 324, no. 1 (3 January): 13–17.

Skolnick, A. A. 1993. "Rapid Clot-Dissolving Drugs Promising for Stroke." *Journal of the American Medical Association* 269, no. 2 (13 January): 195–97.

ADDITIONAL READINGS

American Heart Association. *1993 Heart Facts.* Dallas, TX: American Heart Association. This is an annual edition that explains the nature of heart diseases, stroke, and other cardiovascular incidence, and the mortality, symptoms, risks, and treatments for each disease.

Benson, H., and E. M. Stuart. 1992. *The Wellness Book: The Comprehensive Guide to Maintaining Health and Treating Stress*

Related Diseases. New York: Birch Lane Press. This is one of the best chronic disease prevention guides on the market, written primarily by the physician who authored *The Relaxation Response.* Covers mind/body disease prevention, the relaxation response, exercise, nutrition, stress management, and other specialties.

Goleman, D., and J. Gurin, eds. *Mind Body Medicine.* New York: Consumer's Report Book. This outstanding book covers many of the elements of optimal living and how your mind can optimize your body. The chapters "Mind and Immunity" and "Hostility and the Heart" are particularly appropriate.

CHAPTER 18

Cancer and Other Chronic Diseases

KEY QUESTIONS

What is cancer?
What are the warning signs of cancer?
What are the major sites of cancer?
How successful is treatment for
   different forms of cancer?
What are the warning signs of diabetes?
What are the warning signs of kidney
   disease?
What consumer decisions can we make
   to help prevent cancer and other
   chronic diseases?

CHAPTER OUTLINE

Cancer
Causes of Cancer
Prevention
Nutrition and Cancer
Early Detection
Types of Cancers
Cancer Treatment
Cancer Research
Diabetes Mellitus
Understanding Diabetes
Type I and Type II Diabetes
Causes of Diabetes
First Aid Treatment for Diabetics
Prevention and Guidelines for
   Diabetics
Diabetes Research
Hypoglycemia
Kidney Disease
Warning Signs of Kidney Disease
Diagnosis and Treatment of Acute
   Kidney Disease
Chronic Kidney Disease and Kidney
   Failure
**Chronic Diseases of the Respiratory
   System**
Chronic Bronchitis
Emphysema
Asthma
Warning Signs of Respiratory Disease
Prevention
Genetic Disease
Detection and Diagnosis
Prevention
Neuromuscular-Skeletal Diseases
Arthritis
Diagnosis and Treatment of Arthritis
Prevention
Take Action
Summary

Healthy People 2000 Objectives

- Reduce disability from chronic conditions to no more than 8 percent of the population (a 15% decrease).

- Reduce diabetes-related deaths to no more than 34 per 100,000 people (an 11% decrease).

We are entering one of the most exciting times of modern medicine, analogous to earlier years' eradication and control of some communicable diseases and the development of penicillin to treat bacterial diseases. The dramatic increase in knowledge about chronic diseases, such as cancer, diabetes, and multiple sclerosis, is based upon genetics. With almost every chronic disease, researchers are finding the locations of genes that may cure us, prevent the disease, or at least warn us of the disease. It is difficult to tell where this revolution is taking us, but it is likely that we will be asking ourselves some ethical questions about how far we can go in controlling who we are and what our weaknesses are, and in altering the creation of human beings while the fetus is still in the womb.

The good news is that we are on the verge of some very exciting discoveries as we enter the twenty-first century. In this chapter we will explore some of these chronic diseases, how they affect us, their prevalence, and also where we are in research in treating these problems. We will study cancer, diabetes, respiratory diseases, neuromuscular-skeletal diseases, kidney disease, and genetic diseases.

People who feel somewhat reluctant to read this chapter on chronic disease probably share a common fear—fear of what they can't control, particularly in the physical realm, in their lives, and in the lives of those close to them. Yet this fear can actually prevent people from taking control of their lives by taking the necessary steps to achieve and maintain optimal health.

Early detection of these diseases is important in combating their progress. Moreover, understanding their causes can help people better decide how to prevent them in the first place. By stopping smoking, for example, people can significantly lessen their risk of lung cancer; also, by sensibly protecting themselves from the sun at every age, they can lessen their risk of contracting skin cancer.

If you become knowledgeable about these diseases and their causes, effects, and treatments, you will find that your fear of the unknown is reduced. Until people understand the progression of breast cancer, for example, they can't do much more than sympathize with someone who has the disease. By understanding the limitations and changes that accompany chronic diseases, however, people can begin to help the affected person live a fuller life.

CANCER

The term **cancer** refers to a large group of diseases characterized by the uncontrolled growth and spread of abnormal or malignant cells. Cancer strikes at any age, but more frequently at advanced ages. Even so, cancer kills more children between the ages of 3 and 14 than any other disease. In fact, after cardiovascular disease, cancer is the leading cause of death in the United States; about 24 percent of all deaths in this country are caused by cancer. About 30 percent of people now living will eventually get cancer. More than 8 million Americans alive today have a history of cancer; 5 million of them were diagnosed with cancer 5 or more years ago. This year, however, another 1.17 million will be diagnosed as having cancer. About one of every five deaths in the United States is from cancer, which means that about 1,400 people per day die of cancer in the United States. Many might have been saved with earlier diagnosis and prompt treatment (American Cancer Society 1993).

There are more than a hundred basic, recognized forms of cancer, but the one characteristic they share is their malignant nature. Normally the body's cells reproduce themselves in an orderly manner. Worn-out tissues are replaced, injuries are repaired, and bodily growth proceeds normally. Occasionally, however, something happens, and certain cells undergo an abnormal change and begin the process of uncontrolled growth. These cells can grow into **tumors,** masses of tissues that are either benign or malignant. **Malignant tumors** are cancerous; **benign tumors** are not.

Benign tumors should also be watched carefully because they can change and become cancerous. Malignant tumors invade the surrounding normal tissue, kill it, and eventually spread to tissue in other parts of the body, where the invasive process is repeated.

At the beginning, cancer cells usually remain at their original site, and the cancer is said to be localized **cancer in situ.** If untreated, some cells may invade neighboring organs or tissue by direct extension, in what is called "regional involvement." If still untreated, the cancerous cells become detached and are carried through the lymph or blood systems to other parts of the body. This is called **metastasis.** When cancer metastasizes, it usually results in death.

CAUSES OF CANCER

The basic causes of most cancers are still unknown. Extensive research, however, has uncovered some predisposing factors that are connected to abnormal growth in certain cells and thus might cause cancer. Some of these factors are hereditary; others are environmental.

Our heredity plays a major role in the transformation of normal cells to malignant ones. In some unfortunate families,

cancer
A group of diseases characterized by the uncontrolled growth and spread of abnormal cells.

tumor
An abnormal mass of tissue.

malignant tumor
A cancerous growth.

benign tumor
An uncontrolled growth of cells that is not malignant but can disturb the function of an organ.

cancer in situ
Localized cancer that has not spread.

metastasis
The movement of detached cancer cells to other parts of the body through the bloodstream.

certain cancers occur with a frequency up to four times that of the general population. This is one reason why genetic research and intervention can make a major change in patients with cancer.

Certain environmental factors, such as radiation, seem to cause genetic changes, or mutations, by directly damaging the **DNA**—one of the essential substances that make up our genes. With new genetic research, we might be able to make corrections to these mutations. A wide variety of chemicals, and perhaps even viruses, can also cause these changes.

Cancer-causing substances (**carcinogens**) regularly create problems in whole populations. Asbestos fibers can produce cancer, for example, so people who work in asbestos factories are at high risk for cancers. There is also a relationship between industrial solvents and bladder cancer. And, as we well know, there is a powerful connection between smoking and lung cancer.

Viruses have been isolated that cause cancer in animals. For instance, a virus obtained from mice with breast cancer can cause the same malignancy in a second animal. So far, a specific cancer-causing virus has not been isolated in human beings, but researchers continue to explore this possibility. It seems only a matter of time until we find a virus that can be definitely linked to some forms of cancer (Robbins and Kumar 1987).

PREVENTION

Some cancers can be prevented. Your understanding of the controllable risk factors and early warning signs can help you make and act on decisions that could well save your life. For example, if we all stopped smoking, we would prevent most lung cancers. We would also prevent certain occupational or environmental cancers if we eliminated contact with the particular carcinogenic agents that cause them.

Smoking has been implicated not only in lung cancer but also in cancers of the mouth, pharynx, larynx, esophagus, pancreas, and bladder. Your decision about whether to smoke is important. The elimination of cigarette smoking can certainly decrease the incidence of cancer.

NUTRITION AND CANCER

There is significant research being conducted to show the relationship between cancer and diet (Fackelman 1993). Although several dietary carcinogens have been identified through laboratory studies with rats, no direct cause-and-effect relationships have been determined. There is strong evidence from statistics that the following dietary guidelines might reduce your risk of cancer.

1. Maintain an ideal weight. Obese persons (40 percent or more overweight) increase their risk of colon, breast, prostate, gallbladder, ovary, and uterine cancer.
2. Reduce the total amount of fat you consume. A diet high in fat may be a factor in breast, colon, and prostate cancers.
3. Eat more high-fiber foods such as whole-grain cereals, fruits, and vegetables. This might reduce your risk of cancer of the colon and bladder.
4. Eat foods high in vitamins A and C daily. Sweet potatoes, oranges, spinach, peaches, apricots, carrots, grapefruit, strawberries, peppers, and other yellow and dark-green vegetables supply these vitamins and may help reduce the risk of cancer in the larynx, esophagus, and lung. Do not use excessive vitamin A supplements, because of the potential for toxic buildup.
5. Eat cruciferous vegetables. These include cauliflower, brussels sprouts, broccoli, and cabbage.
6. Eat few or no salt-cured, smoked, and nitrate-cured foods, such as hams, pork, or bacon. There is more incidence of cancer of the esophagus and stomach in those who eat large amounts of these foods.
7. If you drink alcohol, drink only moderate amounts and especially do not drink in conjunction with the use of tobacco. Use of alcohol in conjunction with tobacco in any form increases cancer in the upper digestive areas and liver.
8. When possible, cook your food by roasting or stewing rather than frying or grilling ("Dietary Carcinogens Linked to Breast Cancer" 1993).

EARLY DETECTION

Most cancers, however, are not preventable, so early detection is a necessity. The American Cancer Society recommends safeguards for the prevention and early detection of cancer (table 18.1). As with many chronic diseases, cancer has specific warning signals that can alert us to possible problems. Perhaps the seven warning signs of cancer are easiest to remember:

C   Change in bowel or bladder habits
A   A sore that does not heal
U   Unusual bleeding or discharge
T   Thickening or lump in breast or elsewhere
I   Indigestion or difficulty in swallowing
O   Obvious change in wart or mole
N   Nagging cough or hoarseness

Everyone 20 to 40 years old should get a cancer-related physical examination at least once every 3 years; everyone over 40 should get one annually. Special tests and procedures are listed in table 18.1. These checkups should include

DNA
A nucleic acid found in all living cells that carries the organism's genetic information.

carcinogens
Substances that stimulate the development of cancer.

Cancer Risk

Directions

Indicate how many of your family members have had any of the following types of cancer. If only one member that you know of had the cancer, put a 1 in the blank; if two members, put a 2 in the blank; and over two members, place a 3 in the blank. ("Family members" in this questionnaire refers to parents, grandparents, siblings, aunts, or uncles.)

_____ 1. Colon and rectal cancer

_____ 2. Breast cancer

_____ 3. Prostate cancer

_____ 4. Skin cancer

_____ 5. Endometrial or uterine cancer

Scoring and Interpretation

Several cancers have been identified as running in families. If there is one member of the family who has had a particular cancer, then you are at a significant risk. If there are two or more family members who have had the same type of cancer then you would be at high risk. The cancers of the colon/rectum, breast, prostate, skin, uterus, and endometrium have shown significant intrafamilial risks. It is important to have regular cancer checkups if you have a family history of cancer.

TABLE 18.1 GUIDELINES FOR THE DETECTION OF CANCER FOR THOSE WITHOUT SYMPTOMS

Under Age 40

Checkup Every 1–3 Years	Checkup Every 3 Years	Monthly Self-Exam
Breasts	Thyroid	Breasts
Pelvic exam and Pap test	Testicles	Testicles
	Ovaries	
	Skin	
	Mouth	
	Lymph nodes	

Age 40 and Older

Annual Checkup	Checkup Every 1–3 Years	Checkup Every 3–5 Years	Monthly Self-Exam
Thyroid	Pelvic exam and Pap test	Colon and rectum: sigmoidoscopy for those over 50	Breasts
Testicles			Testicles
Ovaries			
Skin			
Mouth			
Lymph nodes			
Breasts (mamogram every 1–2 years for those 40–49, every year for those 50 and older)			
Colon and rectum: stool slide test for those over 50			
Prostate: digital rectal exam and antigen blood test			

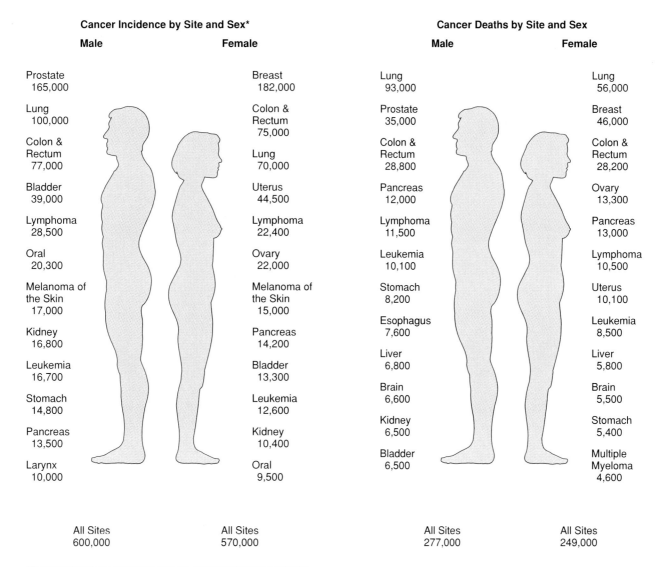

Cancer Incidence by Site and Sex*

Male	Female
Prostate 165,000	Breast 182,000
Lung 100,000	Colon & Rectum 75,000
Colon & Rectum 77,000	Lung 70,000
Bladder 39,000	Uterus 44,500
Lymphoma 28,500	Lymphoma 22,400
Oral 20,300	Ovary 22,000
Melanoma of the Skin 17,000	Melanoma of the Skin 15,000
Kidney 16,800	Pancreas 14,200
Leukemia 16,700	Bladder 13,300
Stomach 14,800	Leukemia 12,600
Pancreas 13,500	Kidney 10,400
Larynx 10,000	Oral 9,500
All Sites 600,000	All Sites 570,000

Cancer Deaths by Site and Sex

Male	Female
Lung 93,000	Lung 56,000
Prostate 35,000	Breast 46,000
Colon & Rectum 28,800	Colon & Rectum 28,200
Pancreas 12,000	Ovary 13,300
Lymphoma 11,500	Pancreas 13,000
Leukemia 10,100	Lymphoma 10,500
Stomach 8,200	Uterus 10,100
Esophagus 7,600	Leukemia 8,500
Liver 6,800	Liver 5,800
Brain 6,600	Brain 5,500
Kidney 6,500	Stomach 5,400
Bladder 6,500	Multiple Myeloma 4,600
All Sites 277,000	All Sites 249,000

*Excluding basal and squamous cell skin cancer and carcinoma in situ.

Figure 18.1

Leading sites of cancer incidence and deaths (1993 estimates).

Source: Data from *Cancer Facts & Figures—1993*, American Cancer Society.

examinations for cancers of the thyroid, lymph nodes, oral region, and skin as well as for nonmalignant diseases. Women might have pelvic examinations, and men might be examined for cancer of the testicles.

If cancer is suspected, a sample of a suspected tumor is usually obtained through a **biopsy**, a simple surgical procedure in which a small section of the tumor is removed and examined under a microscope. The presence of cancer is determined on the basis of the quantity and type of cells and their relative proportions to normal cells. Malignant cells are irregular in shape and size and show growth patterns that are irregular, invading the surrounding tissue and spreading to local and distant tissues. As the tumor grows and spreads, various symptoms may appear. If the tumor grows in soft tissue,

a lump may become evident; if it blocks the opening of a vessel, such as the bowel or the bronchi of the lung, some pain may be evident. Abnormal weight loss can also indicate cancer, because malignant cells tend to compete more successfully for nutrients than do normal cells. Naturally, the earlier the detection, the more likely a cure.

TYPES OF CANCERS

Because prevention, detection, and treatment are site specific in many cancer cases, each of the major cancer sites will be examined separately. Figure 18.1 shows the American Cancer Society's 1993 estimates of cancer incidence

biopsy
A surgical procedure in which a small section of a tumor is removed and microscopically examined for possible cancer.

Cancer Risk Checklist

A. Check off all of the following statements that apply to you.

_____ 1. I work in conditions where I am exposed to industrial chemicals, such as nickel, chromate, asbestos, and vinyl chloride.

_____ 2. I smoke one-half pack of cigarettes or less a day.

_____ 3. I smoke one to two packs of cigarettes a day.

_____ 4. I smoke two or more packs a day.

_____ 5. I have been smoking for over 15 years.

_____ 6. I work around people who smoke cigarettes in smoke-filled settings.

_____ 7. I use smokeless tobacco regularly.

_____ 8. I work in conditions where I am exposed to industrial chemicals and I smoke two or more packs a day.

_____ 9. I work with cadmium regularly.

_____ 10. I work with rubber, dye, or leather regularly.

_____ 11. I am fair skinned and often suntan or frequent tanning salons.

_____ 12. I work around coal tar, pitch, creosote, arsenic compounds, or radium.

_____ 13. I had some severe sunburns as a child.

_____ 14. I burn easily and do not tan very much.

_____ 15. I burn slightly, but get darker with each exposure to the sun.

_____ 16. During the right weather, I try to suntan and expose myself frequently (more than 30 minutes per time and two or more times per week).

_____ 17. I do not use sunblock or sunscreen (number 12 or higher).

_____ 18. I am generally about 20 percent or more overweight.

_____ 19. I eat processed meats (bologna, hams, bacon, and so on) more than three times a week.

_____ 20. I generally include fatty foods in my diet (mayonnaise, fried foods, beef, pork, and so on).

_____ 21. I drink three or more alcoholic drinks (one drink = 1 beer, 4 oz wine, or 1 oz liquor) when I drink.

_____ 22. I don't eat enough fiber or am not aware of what foods have a lot of fiber.

_____ 23. Generally, when I have a bowel movement, the feces sinks to the bottom of the commode (a floating stool is an indication of eating plenty of fiber).

_____ 24. I don't eat at least four servings of green and yellow vegetables or fruits daily.

_____ 25. I drink coffee daily.

B. Which of the following descriptions apply to you? (females only)

_____ 1. I am taking estrogen supplements.

_____ 2. I have an annual pap test or pap smear taken.

_____ 3. I give myself a monthly breast self-examination.

_____ 4. I have never had children, nor do I plan on having children.

_____ 5. I had my first child when I was over 30 years of age.

_____ 6. I had intercourse for the first time at an early age (mid teens).

_____ 7. I have multiple sex partners.

_____ 8. I have a history of infertility or failure to ovulate.

C. Which of the following symptoms do you have? (males and females)

_____ 1. Persistent cough.

_____ 2. Sputum streaked with blood.

_____ 3. Chest pain.

_____ 4. Recurring attacks of pneumonia or bronchitis.

_____ 5. Bleeding from the rectum.

_____ 6. Blood in the stool.

_____ 7. Change in bowel habits.

_____ 8. Breast changes that persist such as a lump, thickening, swelling, dimpling, distortion, retraction, or skin irritation.

_____ 9. Nipple scaliness, discharge, pain, or tenderness.

_____ 10. Intermenstrual or postmenopausal bleeding or unusual discharge.

_____ 11. Enlarged abdomen.

_____ 12. Digestive disturbances (discomfort, gas, distention), in women over 40, that are prolonged and unexplained.

_____ 13. Sore that bleeds and doesn't heal.

_____ 14. A lump in the mouth.

_____ 15. A reddish or whitish patch that persists in the mouth.

_____ 16. Difficulty in chewing, swallowing, or moving tongue or jaws.

_____ 17. Weak or interrupted flow of urine.

_____ 18. Frequent inability to urinate, especially at night.

_____ 19. Blood in the urine.

_____ 20. Urine flow that is not easily stopped.

_____ 21. Painful or burning urination.

_____ 22. Continuing pain in lower back, pelvis, or upper thighs.

_____ 23. Any unusual skin condition.

_____ 24. Change in the size, shape, or color of a mole or dark pigmented spot.

_____ 25. Scaliness of the skin.

_____ 26. Oozing, bleeding, or the appearance of a bump or nodule.

_____ 27. The spread of pigment beyond a border.

_____ 28. A change in skin itchiness, sensation, tenderness, or pain.

_____ 29. Paleness.

_____ 30. Fatigue.

_____ 31. Undesired weight loss.

_____ 32. Repeated infections.

_____ 33. Easy bruising.

_____ 34. Frequent nosebleeds or other hemorrhages.

D. Which of the following examinations have you had?

_____ 1. Digital rectal examination.

_____ 2. Stool blood test.

_____ 3. Proctosigmoidoscopy examination.

_____ 4. Breast cancer detection test.

_____ 5. Skin cancer examination.

(Continued on page 18.7)

Scoring and Interpretation

Sections A, B, and C: It is difficult to score a cancer risk test in terms of a generalized cancer risk, but this assessment does break down the various types of cancers into risks and symptoms. In the case of risk factors, it should be noted that if you check several risk factors for a particular type of cancer, then it is important for you to reduce those risk factors where appropriate. If you have any of the symptoms described, then you should see a physician to assure that the symptom is not cancer. Many of these symptoms could be symptomatic of different problems, many minor, but they also could be serious.

The following is a list of cancers with their risk factors and symptoms. If you have checked any of the above, then recognize your risk. If you have any symptoms, then see a physician.

Lung Cancer

Risks

- Cigarette smoking (the more you smoke, the higher your risk: Over two packs a day is a significantly higher risk)
- History of smoking (the longer you have smoked, the higher your risk)
- Exposure to industrial substances
- Involuntary (passive) smoking
- Exposure to radiation
- Combination of smoking and working around industrial substances (very high risk)

Warning Symptoms

- Persistent cough
- Sputum streaked with blood
- Chest pain
- Recurring attacks of pneumonia or bronchitis

Colon and Rectum Cancer

Risks

- Personal or family history of colon and rectal cancer
- Personal or family history of polyps in the colon or rectum
- Inflammatory bowel disease
- Diet high in fat
- Diet that is low in fiber

Warning Symptoms

- Bleeding from the rectum
- Blood in the stool
- Change in bowel habits

Breast Cancer

Risks

- Over age 50
- Personal or family history of breast cancer
- Never had children
- First child after age 30

Warning Symptoms

- Breast changes that persist such as a lump, thickening, swelling, dimpling, skin irritation, distortion, retraction
- Scaliness of the nipple, nipple discharge, pain or tenderness

Uterine/Cervical Cancer

Risks

- Early age at first intercourse
- Multiple sex partners
- Endometrial cancer, history of infertility
- Failure of ovulation
- Prolonged estrogen therapy
- Obesity

Warning Symptoms

- Intermenstrual or postmenopausal bleeding or unusual discharge

Ovarian Cancer

Risks

- Increases with age, peaking at 65–85
- Women who do not have children
- Late age of first live birth
- Late age of first pregnancy
- Low number of pregnancies
- Low number of years of ovulation
- Already have had breast, colorectal, and endometrial cancer
- You are a nun, Jewish, or never married

Warning Symptoms

- No obvious signs or symptoms until late in its development
- Enlarged abdomen caused by the collection of fluids
- Vague digestive disturbances in women over 40 (stomach discomfort, gas, distention) that persist and cannot be explained

Oral Cancer

Risks

- Cigarette, cigar, and pipe smoking
- Use of smokeless tobacco
- Excess use of alcohol

Warning Symptoms

- Sore that bleeds easily and doesn't heal
- A lump or thickening in the mouth
- A reddish or whitish patch that persists
- Difficulty in chewing, swallowing, or moving tongue or jaws

(Continued on page 18.8)

Prostate Cancer

Risks
- Age (over 65)
- Black Americans
- Some familial association
- High-fat diet
- Working with cadmium
- Diet and lifestyle

Warning Symptoms
- Signs and symptoms similar to infection or prostate enlargement
- Weak or interrupted flow of urine
- Inability to urinate frequently, especially at night, blood in the urine
- Urine flow that is not easily stopped
- Painful or burning urination
- Continuing pain in lower back, pelvis, or upper thighs

Bladder Cancer

Risks
- Smoking (the greatest risk factor)
- Male (four times greater risk for men than for women)
- Live in urban area
- Work with dye, rubber, leather
- Coffee drinking
- Artificial sweeteners

Warning Symptoms
- Blood in the urine
- Increased urination

Skin Cancer

Risks
- Excessive exposure to sun
- Fair complexion
- Occupational exposure to coal tar, pitch creosote, arsenic compounds, or radium
- White (blacks rarely have skin cancer)
- Severe sunburn in childhood may have effect later in life

Warning Symptoms
- Any unusual skin condition
- Change in the size, color, or shape of a mole or darkly pigmented growth or spot
- Scaliness
- Oozing, bleeding, or the appearance of a bump or nodule
- The spread of pigment beyond the border
- A change in sensation, itchiness, tenderness or pain

Pancreatic Cancer

Risks
- After age 30 (most are aged 70 to 90)
- Smoking
- Male
- Blacks (50 percent more common)
- Incidence of chronic pancreatitis, diabetes, and cirrhosis
- High-fat diet
- Coffee (possibly)

Warning Symptoms
- No early symptoms

Leukemia

Risks
- Down syndrome and other hereditary abnormalities
- Excessive exposure to radiation
- Little is really known, and hits all ages and sexes

Warning Symptoms
- Fatigue
- Paleness
- Weight loss
- Repeated infections
- Easy bruising
- Nosebleeds or other hemorrhages

Section D: Cancer can often be cured if it is detected early enough. If you have not had any of these examinations, you are taking the risk of late diagnosis of cancer, which could be a fatal risk. The practice of annual exams for cancer is especially important when you get into your thirties and older.

and death by site and sex. As the figure shows, lung cancer has the highest overall incidence and death rates in the population today, closely followed by cancer of the colon and rectum. Notice how patterns vary between males and females. Each site will now be treated separately.

Cancer of the Lung

Lung cancer kills more people than any other type of cancer. There are two types of lung cancer: small-cell lung cancer and non-small-cell lung cancer. Small-cell lung cancer is more likely to spread to other parts of the body (Ihde 1992).

The high-risk male smoker is aged 60 to 69 and has been smoking one or more packs of cigarettes per day for the past 40 years. The high-risk female smoker is aged 55 to 64 and has been smoking one or more packs of cigarettes per day for the past 30 to 35 years. Many of these people began smoking in college but were seemingly not affected for years; unfortunately, lung cancer often gives no warning of its presence until it is well advanced.

Due to the sudden recent increase in the incidence of smoking in women, lung cancer now kills more women than any other type of cancer, whereas just a few years ago breast

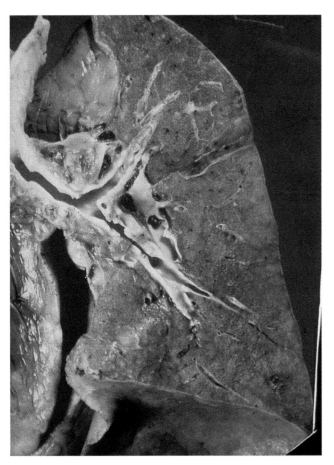

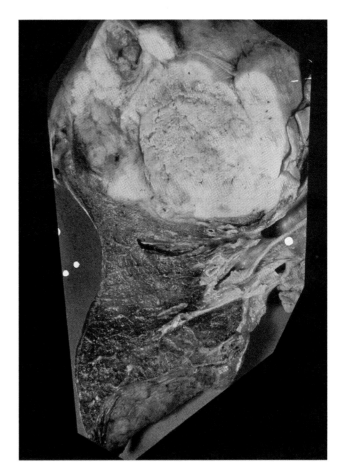

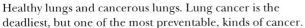

Healthy lungs and cancerous lungs. Lung cancer is the deadliest, but one of the most preventable, kinds of cancer.

cancer was the number one killer. Lung cancer has become the number one killer of women because of lifestyle, and yet lung cancer is one of the most preventable cancers if people avoid exposure to environmental carcinogens and tobacco smoke. Exposure to radon gas is also a risk factor (Bown 1992).

The earliest symptom of lung cancer is likely to be an ordinary cough that most persons will blame on "smoker's cough." As the disease progresses, the cough gets worse and blood-streaked sputum is expelled. Chest pain may follow. Attacks of bronchitis may also signal the early presence of lung cancer.

Surgery is the treatment of choice for lung cancer. However, because in one-third of all patients the tumor spreads from small-cell lung cancer, radiation and chemotherapy are frequently used as well. The outlook, or prognosis, for lung cancer patients is not good. Only 13 percent of them are alive and well 5 years after diagnosis and treatment. The real hope for the future lies in early detection (American Cancer Society 1993).

Cancer of the Colon and Rectum

More than 155,000 new cases of colorectal cancer are diagnosed each year, of which 60,900 result in death (American

Cancer Society 1993). Recent evidence indicates a relationship between this type of cancer and two other digestive diseases, chronic **ulcerative colitis** (ulceration and inflammation of the mucous lining of the large intestine) and **congenital polyposis,** a hereditary disease in which a number of polyps (a type of tumor) grow in the colon and rectum. Increasing evidence suggests that diet (e.g., a lack of fiber) might also play a key role in the development of this type of cancer. Scientists have identified a gene that is responsible for about 15 percent of the cases of colon and rectal cancer (Podolsky 1993).

The closer the colorectal cancer is to the rectum, the more pronounced will be the symptoms of an obstruction: rectal bleeding, constipation or diarrhea (or both), increased intestinal gas, and abdominal discomfort.

ulcerative colitis
Inflammation of the mucous lining of the large intestine.

congenital polyposis
A congenital disease in which a number of polyps grow in the colon and rectum.

Colorectal cancer can be detected at an early stage with readily available tests. About two-thirds of all victims can be saved if the disease is diagnosed early and treated promptly.

Surgery is the most effective method of treating colorectal cancer, but radiation and chemotherapy are sometimes used in combination with surgery. In many cases of colorectal cancer, a **colostomy** must be performed. This operation involves removal of the rectum and part of the colon. When the two ends of the bowel cannot be reconnected, an opening called a **stoma** is made in the abdominal wall, through which bodily wastes can be evacuated. With proper rehabilitation, the person can lead a normal, fully active life (American Cancer Society 1993).

People should decide whether to be tested regularly for colorectal cancer. Colorectal cancer can be detected at an early stage through the following diagnostic procedures: (1) a digital rectal examination, in which a gloved finger is inserted into the rectum to examine the anal area; (2) a fecal swab, in which fecal matter is taken and tested for **occult blood** (blood in such minute quantities that it can be seen only under a microscope); or (3) a proctosigmoidoscopy, in which a lighted tube is passed into the rectum and lower colon, allowing the physician to visually inspect about 12 inches of the colon wall. Fifty to 60 percent of all colorectal cancers can be detected by this last procedure. Physicians recommend an annual test for colorectal cancer, especially after age 50.

Breast Cancer

Although lung cancer is the number one killer of women out of all cancers, the breast is the leading site of cancer incidence in women and breast cancer still kills 44,000 women per year (American Cancer Society 1993). About 150,900 new cases are diagnosed each year, and 11 percent of women develop breast cancer at some time during their lives. Chances of developing breast cancer are less in the young (1 in 19,608) and very frequent in older women (1 in 8) (Rubin 1993).

Breast cancer is found most often among women aged 35 or older. The high-risk population includes women whose close relatives have a history of breast cancer, women who have never had children or have had a first child after the age of 30, and women who have a lump in the breast or nipple discharge.

When a curable breast cancer is found, the surgery may vary from a lumpectomy (removal of the lump and some adjacent breast tissue) to a simple mastectomy (removal of the entire breast) to a modified radical mastectomy (removal of the breast and lymph nodes in the armpits) to a radical mastectomy (removal of the breast, underlying muscles, and lymph nodes in the armpits). Radiation and/or chemotherapy may sometimes be used in combination with surgery.

When breast cancer is discovered before it spreads beyond the breast, current therapy is highly effective, with a 5-year survival rate of 90 percent (American Cancer Society 1993).

Most breast cancer is discovered by the woman herself or her partner. Women should examine their breasts each month, about a week after menstruation when the breasts are not tender or swollen (fig. 18.2). Partners should also become sensitive to any changes in the breast for early detection. After menopause, the breasts should be checked on a regular schedule (e.g., on the first day of each month). Women should have their first mammogram, which is more accurate than a breast self-exam, at age 35 to 40.

A **mammogram** is an X ray of the breast. It is more effective than a breast self-exam because it can detect extremely small breast cancers before they grow large enough to be detected by touch. The smaller the cancer is at the time of discovery, the better the chances are for cure. Researchers are attempting to isolate a gene that by mutating makes a woman more susceptible to breast cancer (Biesecker 1993).

Uterine Cancer

The term *uterine cancer* refers to cancer of the cervix (the neck of the uterus) and cancer of the endometrium (the lining of the uterus). Even though the two types of cancer strike the same organ, they are completely different in their risk factors, their detection mechanisms, and the populations they strike.

Cervical cancer is the most preventable of all internal cancers, and its incidence has steadily decreased over the years. It is most common today among low socioeconomic groups. The high-risk group includes those who have had frequent sexual intercourse before the age of 20 and those who have had multiple sex partners. The highest incidence is among women aged 40 to 49. With the advent of the Pap test, most of these cancers are diagnosed at the precancerous state and the cancer is removed, but any unusual bleeding should be taken as a warning signal.

Endometrial cancer afflicts mostly mature women, and diagnosis usually is made between the ages of 50 and 64. Risk factors include a history of infertility, failure of ovulation, estrogen therapy, late menopause, and a combination of diabetes, high blood pressure, and obesity. Signs of endometrial cancer include bleeding between menstrual periods, excessive bleeding during periods, and bleeding after menopause. Although the Pap test is highly effective in detecting early

colostomy
Surgical removal of the rectum and part of the colon.

stoma
An artificially created opening, such as an opening in the abdominal walls through which bodily wastes are excreted.

occult blood
Blood in such minute quantities that it can be seen only by microscopic examination.

mammogram
An X ray of the breast; more effective than a self-administered breast exam because it can detect extremely small breast cancers before they grow large enough to be detected by touch.

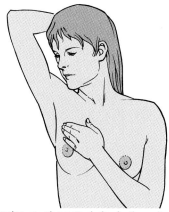

Examine your breasts during bath or shower; hands glide easier over wet skin. Fingers flat, move gently over every part of each breast. Use right hand to examine left breast, left hand for right breast. Check for any lump, hard knot, or thickening.

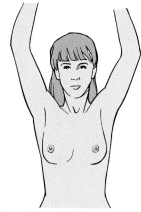

Inspect your breasts with arms at your sides. Next, raise your arms high overhead. Look for any changes in contour of each breast, a swelling, dimpling of skin, or changes in the nipple.

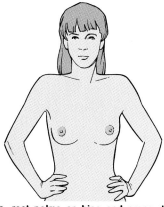

Then, rest palms on hips and press down firmly to flex your chest muscles. Left and right breast will not exactly match—few women's breasts do.
Regular inspection shows what is normal for you and will give you confidence in your examination.

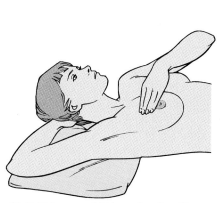

To examine your right breast, put a pillow or folded towel under your right shoulder. Place right hand behind your head—this distributes breast tissue more evenly on the chest. With left hand, fingers flat, press gently in small circular motions around an imaginary clock face.

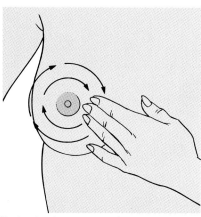

Begin at outermost top of your right breast for 12 o'clock, then move to 1 o'clock, and so on around the circle back to 12. A ridge of firm tissue in the lower curve of each breast is normal. Then move in an inch toward the nipple, keep circling to examine every part of your breast, including nipple. This requires at least three more circles.

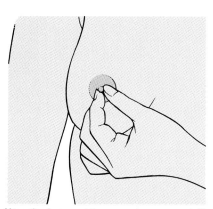

Now slowly repeat the procedure on your left breast with a pillow under your left shoulder and left hand behind head. Notice how your breast structure feels.
Finally, squeeze the nipple of each breast gently between thumb and index finger. Any discharge, clear or bloody, should be reported to your doctor immediately.

Figure 18.2

How to examine your breasts.

Source: Information is based on data available from the American Cancer Society.

cervical cancer, it is only 50 percent effective in detecting endometrial cancer. Women at high risk should have an endometrial tissue sample examined at menopause. The use of estrogen for postmenopausal women corresponded with the rise of uterine cancer in the '70s, but the incidence of cancer has since declined with the use of progesterone-related hormones used cyclically with estrogen for these women (Perskey et al. 1990).

Most physicians perform a dilation and curettage (D&C) on a woman suspected of having endometrial cancer, and tissue samples are then studied for abnormal changes. The overall cure rate for this type of cancer is about 75 percent.

Uterine cancer is usually treated by surgery, radiation, or a combination of the two. In precancerous stages, cervical cancer may be treated by **cryotherapy,** the destruction of cells by extreme cold, or by **electrocoagulation,** the destruction of tissue by intense heat. Precancerous endometrial changes may be treated with the hormone progesterone (American Cancer Society 1993).

cryotherapy
The destruction of cells through extreme cold.

electrocoagulation
Destruction of tissue by the use of intense heat.

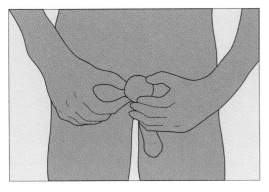 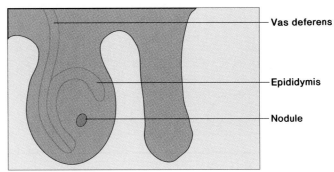

Figure 18.3

Performing a three-minute testicular self-examination. The time to examine the testicles is when the scrotum is loose, relaxed, and warm (e.g., during a shower or bath). Roll each testicle gently between the thumb and fingers of both hands, and, if you find any hard lumps or nodules or any changes from the previous examination in surface contours, then check with your physician soon. Do this exam monthly.

Women must decide whether to have a regular **Pap test,** a highly accurate test used to detect cervical cancer at an early stage and to show cell changes that could develop into cancer. The Pap test is a microscopic examination of cells scraped from the cervix, a simple procedure that can be a part of a regular pelvic examination. The American Cancer Society recommends that women have Pap tests annually for 2 years; if these tests are negative, they should then have a Pap test every 3 years.

Prostate Cancer

Cancer of the prostate is one of the more common cancers, but most of these cancers are small and without symptoms. Prostate cancer occurs most commonly in men beyond the age of 50. Typically, men with prostate cancer have a urinary obstruction that leads to pain on urination and to urinary infections. A rectal examination can often detect prostate cancer that has given no symptoms and is in an early enough stage that it can be completely cured. Blood tests to measure prostate-specific antigens may be more effective than a digital rectal examination for early diagnosis (Catalona et al. 1993). If the cancer is confined to the prostate, the entire gland and some surrounding tissues are removed. Impotence almost always results from this operation.

There are no preventative measures specifically designed for prostate cancer, although men who have had vasectomies appear to have a higher incidence of prostate cancer (Fackelman 1993). When a rectal examination is done for colorectal cancer on a man over the age of 45, the physician will also examine for prostate cancer.

Pancreatic Cancer

About 27,700 new cases of cancer of the pancreas are identified each year. Rates for this cancer are 30 percent higher in men than in women, and 40 percent higher in blacks than in whites. Pancreatic cancer is a silent disease that occurs without symptoms until the later stages of the disease, and then its principal symptom is nonspecific abdominal pain (Dimagno, Rich, and Steele 1992). Some progress is being made in getting earlier detection by using ultrasound (Doppman 1992). There is very little known about the disease except that is occurs with age and most cases occur in persons of about 65 to 79 years of age. Smoking is a definite risk factor, but chronic inflammation of the pancreas, diabetes, and a diet high in fat may be risk factors; treatment with radiation, surgery, or drugs is usually too late, and only 3 percent of patients live longer than 5 years after diagnosis (America Cancer Society 1993).

Testicular Cancer

Cancer of the testis occurs mostly in the 15- to 35-year-old age group, and this group is experiencing an increased frequency. The incidence of testicular cancer is about 2 out of every 100,000 males, with blacks having an extremely low incidence and Jewish males having twice the incidence of non-Jewish males. Although there is not a known cause, there does seem to be a genetic link. Testicular cancer is manifested by an enlargement of the testes. With early detection, 80 to 95 percent of the cases, depending on type of testicular cancer, will survive. If the cancer is allowed to spread, then survivability drops dramatically (Robbins and Kumar 1987).

After a man has had a physician's exam and been found not to have testicular cancer, he should regularly perform a testicular self-exam. The best time to perform this monthly self-examination is right after a warm bath or shower, when the scrotal skin is relaxed and loose. Examine each testicle by gently rolling it between the thumb and fingers of both hands (fig. 18.3). Any lump or swelling that you find, or any change since your last examination, should be promptly reported to your doctor.

Pap test
The microscopic examination of cells removed from an organ (usually the cervix of the uterus) for signs of cancer.

Sun blocks may provide some protection to help reduce the risk of skin cancer.

Skin Cancer

An estimated 700,000 cases of skin cancer occur each year in this country, most of which are highly curable **basal-cell** and **squamous-cell cancers** (named for types of skin tissue). The most serious skin cancer is malignant **melanoma,** which is distinguished by a dark brown or black pigmentation. Melanoma is on the rise, with rates increasing about 4 percent per year (American Cancer Society 1993). Thirty-two thousand Americans are diagnosed with melanoma each year, largely due to fun-in-the-sun lifestyles and the damaged ozone layer (Saltus 1992).

People are at increased risk of skin cancer if they are fair-skinned, particularly redheads and blonds, and burn easily. People who had severe sunburns as children are at higher risk. Sunbathing and using tanning salons and sun lamps are all high-risk behaviors. Sunbathing is becoming a higher-risk activity as the ozone layer in the atmosphere, which shields the earth from significant amounts of ultraviolet light, is slowly diminishing because of pollution. People are also at risk if they work around coal tar, pitch, creosote, arsenic compounds, or radium. It is not advised to frequent tanning salons or use sun lamps, particularly for fair-skinned persons ("Diagnosis and Treatment of Early Melanoma" 1992). African Americans rarely get skin cancer. The use of sunscreen or sunblock is the currently recommended strategy for prevention. There has been some debate among researchers regarding the use of sunscreens. Some are suggesting that elements in sunblock might inhibit sunburn but still allow penetration of the cancer-producing sun rays. By not burning, people tend to stay out longer and thus have higher risks of cancer (Gorman 1993). The safest solution is to cover as much of your body as possible for as long as possible (e.g., sit in the shade after swimming). Unless you are well pigmented, you should tan slowly and avoid burns.

Early detection is most critical. Watch your moles, freckles, warts, and other forms of skin markers for any change.

The earlier the identification, the greater the chances of living ("Malignant Melanoma" 1992). Study carefully the pictures of mole changes in figure 18.4.

There are four methods of treatment for skin cancer: surgery, radiation, electrodesiccation (tissue destruction by heat), and cryosurgery. For malignant melanomas, deep surgical excision is necessary, and removal of nearby lymph nodes is often required (American Cancer Society 1993). Researchers are close to developing new methods of treatment, including a melanoma vaccine (Field 1993), and they have identified the chromosomal site that causes a person to be susceptible to melanoma (Cannon-Albright 1992).

Oral Cancer

Cancer can affect any part of the oral cavity, including the lip, tongue, mouth, and throat. The incidence is about twice as high in males as females, especially in those over the age of 40. About 29,800 cases of oral cancer are reported annually. Heavy cigarette, cigar, or pipe smoking, drinking, the use of chewing tobacco, and chronic sun exposure place a person at higher risk. Modern methods of treatment are surgery and radiation therapy, with chemotherapy as a possible adjunct treatment (American Cancer Society 1993).

By having regular dental and physical checkups, you give your dentist and physician the opportunity to see abnormal tissue changes and to detect oral cancer at an early, curable stage.

Leukemia

Although it is often thought to be a childhood disease, **leukemia** strikes people of both sexes at all ages. Acute lymphocytic leukemia is the childhood form, whereas adults can have either acute or chronic leukemia.

In children and adults with acute leukemia, the first signs include enlarged lymph nodes, spleen, and liver. The person becomes fatigued and pale and suffers a weight loss, repeated infections, easy bruising, nosebleeds, and other hemorrhages. As the condition advances, these symptoms become more severe. The disease often progresses rapidly. Chronic leukemia progresses much more slowly; the symptoms are similar to those of acute leukemia, but they might not appear for years.

---

basal-cell cancer
A type of skin cancer.

squamous-cell cancer
A type of skin cancer.

melanoma
A form of skin cancer, usually malignant and involving dark pigmentation.

leukemia
Cancer of the blood-forming tissues.

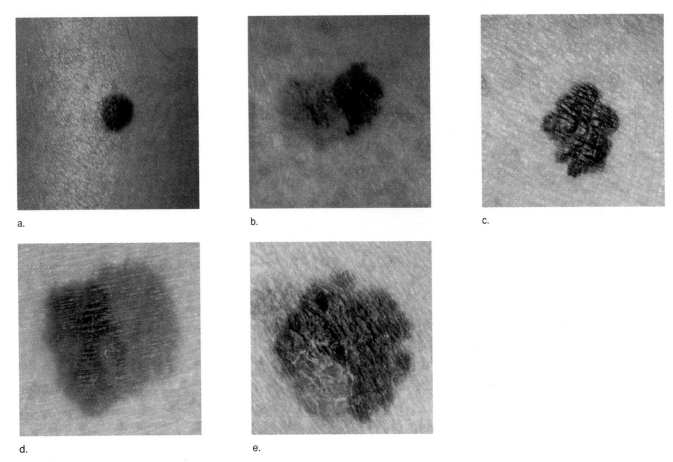

a.

b.

c.

d.

e.

Figure 18.4

The difference between a melanoma and an ordinary mole. A normal mole is an evenly colored brown, tan, or black spot in the skin. It is either flat or raised. Its shape is round or oval and it has sharply defined borders *(a)*. Here's the simple ABCD rule to help you remember the important signs of melanoma: *(b)* **Asymmetry.** One half does not match the other half. *(c)* **Border irregularity.** The edges are ragged, notched, or blurred. *(d)* **Color.** The pigmentation is not uniform. Shades of tan, brown, and black are present. Red, white, and blue may add to the mottled appearance. *(e)* **Diameter greater than six millimeters.** Any sudden or continuing increase in size should be of special concern.

The causes of most leukemia cases are unknown. There is some evidence of inherited susceptibility, as children with **Down syndrome** and other hereditary abnormalities have a higher incidence of leukemia than others. The genetic link, as with other cancers, also provides some hope. The gene that regulates interferon has been found to be faulty in many adults with leukemia. Leukemia has also been linked to excessive exposure to radiation and to certain chemicals, including benzene.

Early detection is often difficult, but when a physician does suspect the disease, diagnosis is made through blood tests and a bone marrow biopsy. Chemotherapy is by far the most effective method of treating leukemia patients, with transfusions of blood components and antibiotics used as supportive treatments, but the 5-year survival rate is only 38% (American Cancer Society 1993). Bone marrow transplants from unrelated donors can prolong the survival of some patients (Keernan et al. 1993).

Unfortunately, at this time there are no known preventive measures for leukemia.

CANCER TREATMENT

The goal of cancer treatment is complete cure; if that is not possible—and often it is not—treatment is aimed at controlling the disease and giving the patient as long and as full a life as possible. Surgery, radiation, and chemotherapy, alone or in combination, are the major means of treating cancer (American Cancer Society 1993).

Cancer is most often treated surgically. The surgeon removes not only the malignant tumor or organ but also a wide margin of normal tissue and often nearby lymph nodes. If all cancer cells can be eliminated at their site of origin, and if none have escaped into the bloodstream or lymph system,

Down syndrome
Congenital mental retardation and physical deformities caused by the presence of an extra chromosome in chromosome pair 21.

PERSONAL INSIGHT

The Devastation of Melanoma

Gregg was a high school athlete who became a coach, married, and had five children. He became an FBI agent. He was tall, strong, and a good father. Gregg had a mole on his back that he didn't watch carefully. When he and his wife finally noticed that it looked strange, the melanoma had already progressed to the second stage of the disease—infection of the lymph nodes. Gregg had some fifty operations on his lymph nodes to remove cancerous lumps. Unfortunately, this did not stop the disease, which progressed to the third stage, moving into the bloodstream and attacking the vital organs. Gregg went through chemotherapy. He lost his hair, vomited regularly, and could not hold food down, and it almost killed him. He survived the chemotherapy and hoped that the disease was arrested. The disease did go into remission for a short time, but finally, after 3 years of agony for Gregg and his family, he died. He had good insurance and had been able to relocate his family near extended family members, but he left a widow and five children, ages 5 through 17, to recover from the 3 years of misery.

Gregg's wife, Joy, now looks at the positive aspects of the experience. During those 3 years, they became closer than they ever were, and her religious convictions have become stronger. Her children still feel like they have been cheated.

Could this devastation have been avoided? Maybe. Survivability increases, the earlier cancer is detected. Joy now checks each child regularly for any danger signals of cancer.

---

surgery can effect a cure. Surgery is currently being used to treat cancers of the lung, breast, colon and rectum, uterus, prostate, bladder, head and neck, kidney, ovary, and thyroid.

Radiation is the second most common method of treating cancer. Today, about half of all cancer patients receive radiation therapy, either alone or in combination with some other therapy. X-ray machines of the past have been replaced with supervoltage equipment, such as the linear accelerator, that allows deeper penetration. The beams don't kill malignant cells outright but instead destroy their reproductive mechanism, so that once they die, no new cancer cells develop. Radiation is often the primary treatment for a number of cancers, including cervical cancer, head and neck cancer, Hodgkin's disease, brain cancer, and cancers of the larynx, pharynx, esophagus, oral cavity, bone, prostate, testes, and skin. Radiation treatment can cause unpleasant side effects, however, including diarrhea, difficulty in swallowing, itching, and a diminished sense of taste.

Chemotherapy—the use of drugs and hormones—is the preferred treatment when cancers have spread beyond the reach of surgery or radiation. Thus far, it has proved most effective among rarer forms of cancer, including melanomas, acute leukemia, and testicular cancer. At present, some fifty different drugs are being used, either alone or in combination. These drugs work because they interfere with the reproductive ability of the cancer cells. Unfortunately, chemotherapy can also cause serious side effects, including nausea, vomiting, diarrhea, anemia, lowered resistance to infection, and loss of hair.

In cancer treatment, the real hope for the future lies in earlier detection. Of course, the long-range hope in research is to be able to prevent the disease.

CANCER RESEARCH

Millions of dollars have been given to researchers to find a cure for cancer. Although there has been some success in

Issues

The Cure Versus the Complaint

One of the more difficult issues for a cancer patient to face is the side effects of cancer therapy. For example, radiation and chemotherapy often lower the white blood cell count so much that the patient is subject to serious infection from the mildest sources. These side effects can be more immediately disturbing to the patient than the disease itself.

- Pro: Cancer patients must be educated to be open to all forms of treatment, no matter how difficult or dangerous the side effects, because it is the only way that we know of that may put the cancer into remission.

- Con: Cancer patients should be encouraged to weigh the advantages and disadvantages of different treatments. They may wish to lead a shorter life free from disabling side effects than a longer life full of difficulties.

What would you do if you found yourself needing chemotherapy?

controlling cancer, there have been no cures. These are some of the latest approaches to identifying a cure (Source: From American Cancer Society, Inc.):

1. Interferon research. Interferon is a natural body protein that has been shown to work against viruses and also to fight cancer. Research is showing that interferon

---

chemotherapy
The use of specific drugs to treat a disease.

Gene Therapy

Not only is gene therapy beginning to show great signs of progress in curing some cancers, it is also helpful with chemotherapy. *Scientific American* reports (Gibbs 1993) that physicians hope to help patients tolerate more chemotherapy by genetically altering their bone marrow cells, allowing medications that are usually harmless to kill tumor cells.

therapy is working with some types of leukemia and lymphomas but is less successful for lung and colon cancer. The current thrust is to combine interferon with some of the other types of treatments to improve their effectiveness. This research will become less expensive because interferon can now be produced in a laboratory rather than having to be gathered from human blood.

2. Genetic engineering. Research to correct impaired immune systems and even modify heredity by transplanting foreign genes is the hope of genetic researchers.

3. Monoclonal antibodies. Tailor-made, highly specific antibodies are being developed that will be highly sensitive to cancer cells, yielding a technique for earlier detection of cancer, when treatment is most effective.

4. Mechanisms of carcinogenesis. Researchers are trying to understand how cancer begins. They are attempting to answer questions like these: Are there normal genes that serve as master switches for early tissue development, inducing normal cells to become cancerous later in life? If so, what turns them on? Can they be programmed to stay off?

5. Chemoprevention. Researchers are attempting to identify foods, beverages, and behaviors that will protect people against cancer. Agents such as vitamin A, vitamin C, vitamin E, the chemical element selenium, and other naturally occurring substances in brussels sprouts, cabbage, and certain other foodstuffs are possibly protective.

6. New drugs that inhibit cancer migration by blocking normal pathways of movement are being studied (Skolnick 1993).

DIABETES MELLITUS

Diabetes mellitus, with an annual U.S. death toll of about 35,000, is the seventh leading cause of death in the Untied States (Robbins and Kumar 1987). It is difficult to know exactly how many people have diabetes in the United States, because there are varying degrees of the disease, and many

people who have diabetes do not know that they do. But the number is estimated to be about 15 million (Randal 1992), or 1 to 2 percent of the population. There has been a dramatic increase in the number of people being diagnosed with diabetes, which was estimated at approximately 600,000 for a recent year and as increasing by 6 percent annually. A major reason is the new survivability of people with diabetes. At the turn of the century, before insulin was prescribed, people with diabetes died at an early age, not having the opportunity to marry and have children. With the discovery of insulin, people with diabetes can live long, productive lives and raise children. All of the children of diabetics will be carriers of the diabetes genes, although not all will be diabetic. Genetic researchers may have found the diabetic gene that provides hope for diabetics in the future (Bishop 1991).

UNDERSTANDING DIABETES

Diabetes mellitus is a chronic disorder affecting the natural metabolism of carbohydrates, fats, and proteins (Robbins and Kumar 1987). The cause of the ineffective use of carbohydrates in particular is defective or deficient insulin production. **Insulin** is a hormone produced by the pancreas that has several functions, including protein synthesis, glycogen (the form in which carbohydrates are stored in the body) formation in the liver and muscles, and glucose (simple sugar formed from carbohydrates) conversion to triglycerides (fats). The most critical function as it relates to diabetes is that it facilitates the movement of glucose across cell membranes so that the cells can use the glucose for energy. Insulin is normally released into the bloodstream when blood glucose levels are high, which means the insulin functions to reduce the level of blood sugar by transporting it into the cells or storing it for later use. In diabetes, the lack of insulin results in the buildup of dangerously high levels of sugar in the blood.

The inability to use the sugar in the blood is accompanied by the breakdown of glycogen (the storage form of carbohydrates) to additional blood sugar, which is normally inhibited by insulin. The high sugar level results in an overload of the kidneys, which are trying to reabsorb the glucose, and the result is excretion of sugar in the urine. Since the sugar can't be used for energy, fatty acids stored in fat deposits become the major energy sources. In the liver, fatty acids are oxidized into ketone bodies, which are used by the muscle, heart, kidney, and brain. In Type I diabetes, in particular, the formation of ketone bodies may exceed the rate of their utilization and result in **ketosis** (excessive ketone bodies, to

---

insulin
A hormone produced by the pancreas.

ketosis
In unmanaged diabetes, an excess of buildup of ketone bodies in the blood, which can cause coma or death.

T ABLE **18.2**	THE WARNING SIGNS OF DIABETES

The following symptoms are typical. However, some people with non-insulin-dependent diabetes have symptoms so mild they go unnoticed.

Insulin-Dependent Diabetes	**Non-Insulin-Dependent Diabetes**
(Usually occur suddenly)	(Usually occur less suddenly)
• Frequent urination	• Any of the insulin-dependent symptoms
• Excessive thirst	• Recurring or hard-to-heal skin, gum, or bladder infections
• Extreme hunger	• Drowsiness
• Dramatic weight loss	• Blurred vision
• Irritability	• Tingling or numbness in hands or feet
• Weakness and fatigue	• Itching
• Nausea and vomiting	

Reprinted with permission from the American Diabetes Association. Copyright © 1984 by the American Diabetes Association.

the point of toxicity, which can lead to coma and death). Because tissues seem to be starving for glucose, protein supplies from the diet and tissues are diverted from their primary function, that of building up body tissues, to breaking down proteins to be used as an energy source for the cells.

TYPE I AND TYPE II DIABETES

Type I diabetes, or insulin-dependent diabetes mellitus (IDDM), was formerly called "juvenile onset diabetes" and accounts for 10 to 15 percent of all cases of diabetes. Type I diabetes is the more severe form of diabetes, characterized by an absolute lack of insulin. The insulin levels in the blood are low due to a reduction in the **beta cells** mass in the pancreas. People with Type I diabetes require supplemental insulin for survival. The loss of beta cells is thought to be caused by an interaction of environmental influences (e.g., viruses, stress), genetic vulnerability, and autoimmunity (Robbins and Kumar 1987).

Type II diabetes, also called "non-insulin-dependent diabetes mellitus" (NIDDM), accounts for 85 to 90 percent of all diabetic cases. This form of diabetes is not as severe and generally occurs later in life (generally after 40). Insulin is produced by the beta cells but is insufficient to deal with the glucose load. Often, strict diets, weight loss, and exercise will manage type II diabetes. Warning signs of diabetes are shown in table 18.2.

CAUSES OF DIABETES

The exact cause of diabetes is open to debate. There appears to be both genetic and environmental risk factors.

Genetic Vulnerability

Diabetes mellitus, in part, is a family or genetic disorder, but the direct method of inheriting the trait is not known. Until recently, it was assumed that there was a single pattern

of genetic predisposition for both type I and type II diabetes, but studies with identical twins reveal that there is a difference. Among identical twins, for type I diabetes there is a 50 percent chance that both twins will be affected, but for type II diabetes there is a 90 percent chance that both will be affected. This means that there are environmental influences, particularly for type I diabetes.

Environmental Influences and Autoimmunity

A number of factors may contribute to the surfacing of diabetes among people who are genetically predisposed. Viral infections such as mumps, measles, and mononucleosis have been implicated for many years as directly or indirectly attacking the beta cells to reduce their mass and ability to produce insulin.

A most important factor among type II diabetics is obesity. Approximately 80 percent of type II diabetics are obese. Sometimes when type II diabetics attain an optimal weight, the symptoms of diabetes go away. Pregnancy, as a stress on the body, may result in temporary diabetes and many women revert to normal after delivering the baby. Other major stressors,

---

type I diabetes
Also called "insulin-dependent diabetes mellitus," formerly called "juvenile-onset diabetes"; the more severe form of diabetes, characterized by an absolute lack of insulin.

beta cells
The cells in the islets of Langerhans of the pancreas that produce insulin.

type II diabetes
Also called "non-insulin-dependent diabetes mellitus"; accounts for 85 to 90 percent of all diabetes cases. Not as severe as type I, and usually appears later in life (generally after 40). Insulin is produced by the beta cells but is not sufficient to deal with the glucose load.

including trauma, infections, and hyperthermia, can unmask diabetes in those harboring the hereditary trait. It is well known that insulin requirements increase under stress.

The classic symptoms of the disease include the three "polys": polyuria (passage of excessive amounts of urine), polyphagia (excessive eating), and polydipsia (excessive thirst). The three polys are accompanied by weight loss, fuzzy vision, and fatigue.

Outcomes of Diabetes

The detrimental outcomes of diabetes depend on two factors: the severity of the disease and the duration of the disease. Most problems result from the vascular system, as indicated by the fact that 80 percent of diabetics die from vascular disorders. Diabetics with the disease for 15 or more years will probably display one or more of the following conditions in mild or severe forms.

1. Myocardial infarction caused by atherosclerosis of the coronary arteries is the most common cause of death in diabetics.

2. Hypertension is more prevalent and severe in diabetics.

3. Kidneys are prime targets for diabetes. Renal failure is second only to myocardial infarction as a cause of death. Atherosclerosis of the kidneys and inflammation of the kidneys also occur.

4. Visual impairment, and sometimes total blindness, is a fear of diabetics that results from the thickening of capillaries of the retina of the eye.

5. Neuropathy is a disease of the peripheral nervous system, generally of the lower extremities, resulting in motor and sensory dysfunction (e.g., sexual impotence, bladder and bowel dysfunctions).

6. Stroke, which, again, results from the vascular problems.

7. Gangrene of the extremities from the lack of adequate blood supply to the hands and feet.

FIRST AID TREATMENT FOR DIABETICS

If you happen upon a person in distress who may have diabetes, there are some things that you can do to help.

1. If the person is conscious, ask the person if she or he is diabetic and if you can help.

2. If the person is not conscious, check to see if there is some form of identification. For instance, check to see if he or she is wearing a diabetes bracelet. Call for medical help.

3. If the person is having an **insulin reaction** or insulin shock, she or he has not eaten enough food, has exercised too hard, or has received too high a dose of insulin. If conscious, the person might experience emotional changes, headache, numbness, poor coordination, slurred speech, a staggering gait, a cold sweat, and rapid heartbeat. Many diabetics having a reaction have been falsely cited for driving while

intoxicated. Give the diabetic some candy or fruit juice, sugared (not diet) pop, or other sugar drink. Oftentimes the person has Lifesavers or honey packets in their possession. If the person is unconscious, call for medical help and do not give him or her anything that would have to be swallowed. A sugar cube under the tongue is okay if carefully observed, and it might help (Thygerson 1986).

4. **Diabetic coma** can result from overindulgence in food, too little insulin, injury, or decreased activity. High blood sugar and ketosis give the breath a peculiar, sweetish odor. The person may be thirsty, have abdominal pain, be nauseated, or vomit. You can provide fluids and get medical help.

5. If you can't distinguish between diabetic coma and a diabetic reaction, try giving the person a small amount of sugar, recognizing that the sugar will help the reaction but, in a small amount, will not have a measurable effect on the diabetic coma (Thygerson 1986).

PREVENTION AND GUIDELINES FOR DIABETICS

Diabetics who constantly monitor their blood sugar levels, have frequent insulin injections, and eat a nutritious diet have fewer complications than those who do not (Rubin 1993). Available monitoring equipment includes insulin pumps that are carried around constantly by the diabetic, automatically pump in needed insulin when blood sugar is high, and warn the diabetic to eat when blood sugar is low.

Naturally you would like to increase your chances of not getting this disease, but you need to understand that with autoimmune disorders such as diabetes, specific strategies for prevention are difficult to recommend. It is helpful to maintain ideal weight and eat nutritious food. Scientists at Berkeley and Stanford University offer direct evidence that physical activity can help prevent non-insulin-dependent diabetes ("Running Away from Diabetes" 1992).

Studies with mice have provided some future suggestions for prevention. Some Boston researchers identified two types of immune cells with opposing effects that determine whether diabetes-prone mice will develop the disease. By injecting the mice with a toxin that destroys the cell type that destroys the body's insulin factories, they have tipped the balance in favor

---

insulin reaction

A condition that occurs when the blood sugar level becomes too low; calls for immediate ingestion of certain carbohydrates. Insulin shock.

diabetic coma

A comatose state resulting from ketosis, the conversion of sugar buildup in a diabetic person's bloodstream into ketone bodies.

Some diabetics administer their own insulin injections.

of the insulin-protecting cell type, halting diabetes onset. In the future, people with a predisposition to diabetes might receive an injection to prevent the onset of diabetes (Cowen 1990).

DIABETES RESEARCH

Researchers have been developing an insulin-secreting artificial pancreas as a therapy for diabetes (Ross 1993). They are looking specifically at implants to the islets of Langerhans, which is the insulin-producing part of the pancreas. Researchers are also looking at the transplantation of live pancreatic cells as a way to regenerate insulin production. As with similar research on other chronic diseases, gene research is showing some progress, in that it has found that the gene that is involved with the metabolism of sugars may mutate and cause diabetes (Froguel 1993).

HYPOGLYCEMIA

Hypoglycemia is low blood sugar, which is just the opposite of hyperglycemia, or the high blood sugar evident in diabetes. Hypoglycemia reflects a malfunction of the body's mechanisms that regulate glucose balance. It can result from a variety of causes and is accurately diagnosed by a glucose-tolerance test. Symptoms include anxiety, hunger, heart palpitations, sweating, headache, weakness, and fatigue. Those who suffer from hypoglycemia are subject to emotional mood swings, depression, and trouble with thinking and recalling.

People suffering from this disorder are usually helped with a strict diet regimen. Frequent small meals that are high in protein and include starches rather than simple sugars often bring about marked improvement of symptoms.

KIDNEY DISEASE

Most of us have two kidneys located in the small of the back along both sides of the spine. They perform the vital processes of removing fluids and waste compounds from the blood and regulating the internal body chemistry by selective excretion or retention of various compounds. More than 18 gallons of blood pass through the human kidneys each hour, carrying nutrients to the body's tissues and waste products from the tissues, as well as transporting compounds necessary for internal chemical balance.

Each kidney has more than a million microscopic filters called **glomeruli.** If these filters cease functioning, the body retains increasing amounts of water, salt, and other substances. The body tissues then begin to swell, and waste products accumulate, causing a condition called **uremia.** If uremia grows progressively worse, death can result (Robbins and Kumar 1987).

WARNING SIGNS OF KIDNEY DISEASE

Several of the kidney diseases can be diagnosed at an early stage if we clearly understand the warning signs and promptly seek medical help. The warning signs of kidney disease are (1) swelling of body parts, especially the ankles; (2) lower back pain, just below the rib cage; (3) puffiness, especially around the eyes and particularly in children; (4) increased frequency or changes in the pattern of urination;

hypoglycemia
Low blood sugar.

glomeruli
A small cluster of capillaries located at the beginning of each uriniferous tubule in the kidney. Its function is to filter and remove wastes from the blood.

uremia
The accumulation of waste products in the body tissues.

(5) pain or unusual sensation associated with urination, and bloody or tea-colored urine; and (6) high blood pressure, affecting the efficiency of the body's waste-elimination process (Robbins and Kumar 1987).

DIAGNOSIS AND TREATMENT OF ACUTE KIDNEY DISEASE

The symptoms listed above may indicate an acute kidney disease, but only a physician can know for sure. Laboratory tests will confirm the problem if there is one.

Treatment of acute kidney disease and some less-serious chronic kidney disease includes diet, drugs, and sometimes surgery. The diet is modified to lower the intake of salt, water, and protein because the kidneys cannot do their job. **Diuretics** are used to help avoid fluid buildup in the body, and the antibiotics are given to control any infection that might be present. In cases where problems are caused by birth defects, any obstructions are surgically removed.

CHRONIC KIDNEY DISEASE AND KIDNEY FAILURE

In patients with chronic kidney disease, kidney function deteriorates gradually. When the kidneys fail, the victim has two courses of action: kidney transplantation or hemodialysis. A **kidney transplant** can be performed successfully in the patient who has lost most or all kidney function. A major reason that more kidney transplants are not done is that the kidney tissue of the donor and recipient must be matched. Many medical centers have waiting lists, and potential recipients must go on hemodialysis until a donated organ with a compatible tissue type becomes available. A donor and recipient who are closely related usually have the best chance for compatible tissue types and successful transplantation. The principal barrier to successful transplantation is the body's own immune system. If the defensive immune response of the body is not suppressed, it can destroy the foreign tissue within a short time. The recent development of more effective and less toxic special drugs to suppress the destructive immune response has increased the chances of successful transplantation.

Hemodialysis is the only hope of survival for a large number of persons who suffer from kidney failure. Hemodialysis is performed by an artificial kidney machine, a machine that takes over the blood-purifying function of the damaged kidneys. The machine is connected through a tube to the patient's arm or leg; the blood flows through the machine to be cleansed and is then returned through another tube to the patient's blood vessel. Dialysis treatments are administered several times per week for a period of approximately 9 hours (Burton and Martin 1978).

CHRONIC DISEASES OF THE RESPIRATORY SYSTEM

Chronic diseases of the respiratory system range from allergies to serious problems like emphysema. Allergies are very common and occur when the immune system cannot tell the difference between harmful and harmless substances—we react to nonharmful substances (Katzenstein 1993). Those of us with allergies experience reactions seasonally (depending upon the substance we are reacting to), with itchy eyes, scratchy throats, runny noses, and sneezing. The treatments for allergies include antihistamines, decongestants, steroid nasal sprays, and cromolyn sodium to reduce the symptoms. A physician can also provide you with an "allergy shot."

More serious chronic respiratory disease is usually caused by inhaling a harmful substance, such as bacteria, industrial pollutants, or organic matter to which we may be allergic. Major diseases include chronic bronchitis, emphysema, and asthma.

CHRONIC BRONCHITIS

Chronic bronchitis results from chronic inflammation in the bronchi of the lungs, which causes mucus to form, with resultant coughing. In many instances, this disease is due to cigarette smoking. It often precedes or occurs concurrently with emphysema (Purtilo 1978).

EMPHYSEMA

Emphysema is a form of lung disease that takes a number of years to develop. It is characterized by overinflation of the lungs and the destruction of the alveoli (air sacs), which are

---

diuretics
Medications that cause the body to eliminate water through urination.

kidney transplant
The implantation of a donor kidney when the patient's original kidneys have failed. Survival rates are vastly and steadily improving. Donor and recipient kidney tissues must match.

hemodialysis
The use of an artificial kidney machine to purify blood when the person's kidneys have failed.

chronic bronchitis
Persistent inflammation of the mucous membrane of the bronchi, evidenced by continual coughing and discharges.

emphysema
A chronic disease of the lungs that affects the air sacs and causes breathlessness and can lead to death.

PERSONAL SKILLS AND EXPERIENCES

Preventing Chronic Disease

Mind

When problems and negative situations arise in your life, you will either effectively handle the problem or you will struggle with it over time. Your abilities in self-counseling and creative personal problem solving, time management, and other skills of the mind will determine whether you resolve, learn, and grow from the problem or negative situation or whether you end up frustrated, upset, and depressed. Enhance your creative personal problem-solving abilities, your ability to manage time effectively, and your ability to ask yourself good questions and then come up with solutions. The positive mind state that results will give you control over your problems, and you will be able to fortify your immune system to prevent chronic disease.

Body

There are several precautions, pertaining to protecting and nourishing your body, that you can take to reduce the risk of cancer. Consider the following list of practices and put them into action in your own life (Source: From American Cancer Society, Inc.).

1. Reduce exposure to sunlight and tanning salons, especially if you are fair-skinned.
2. Wear a strong sunblock (number 15) when in the sun.
3. When possible, avoid breathing polluted air. If necessary, wear a face mask or air filter to avoid chronic or occupational exposure.
4. Do not smoke any form of drug.
5. Avoid refined sugars, refined flours, and other forms of junk food.
6. Eat a low-fat diet.
7. Avoid carcinogenic (cancer-causing) chemicals found in some processed foods (e.g., sodium nitrite in bologna, hams, and bacon) and in other sources (e.g., vinyl chloride, insecticides).
8. Avoid X rays, when possible.
9. Avoid obesity.
10. Keep alcohol consumption moderate if you drink.
11. Include cruciferous vegetables (broccoli, brussels sprouts, cauliflower, and cabbage) in your diet.
12. Do not smoke cigarettes.
13. Eat plenty of fiber.
14. Practice monthly breast self-examination (women).
15. Have a Pap test regularly (women).
16. Have an annual test for colorectal cancer, especially after the age of 50.
17. Practice regular testicular examination (men).
18. Have a regular physical examination from a physician.
19. Note the warning signs of cancer.

Soul

Positive states of the soul will also help you avoid chronic diseases and assure you a higher quality of life. To love others, to feel loved, and to have a means of releasing pent-up negative emotions such as anger in positive ways (e.g., by walking it off) are ways of fortifying your defenses against chronic disease. Having a spiritual orientation and faith in positive forces greater than your own will help. From psychoneuroimmunology (PNI) we know that a fighting spirit, optimism, hope, and an occasional good laugh fortify the body against chronic disease.

where gases are exchanged between the lungs and the bloodstream. Few people under the age of 50 have emphysema, but the average age of victims is getting lower, probably because many people are starting to smoke at an early age. Overstretched air sacs and an inability to breathe normally are characteristic of the disease. At first, the shortness of breath is hardly noticeable, but the condition gradually worsens until the victim has to limit physical activity. A person with advanced emphysema is often unable to walk up a flight of stairs without stopping (Robbins and Kumar 1987).

ASTHMA

Asthma occurs because of a hypersensitivity (allergy) to a particular substance or substances. When the allergic person inhales this substance, the lungs' airways narrow, and mucous plugs tend to form and obstruct the airways; exhaling is impaired, and wheezing occurs.

WARNING SIGNS OF RESPIRATORY DISEASE

Numerous signs and symptoms can indicate respiratory problems. Shortness of breath is a warning signal if it occurs during

asthma
A disease or allergic response characterized by bronchial spasms and difficulty in breathing.

THE WORLD AROUND YOU
Chronic Disease and Others

All people and cultures dread chronic disease. Cultures may differ in their prevalences of specific kinds of chronic diseases, but the bond that brings us all together is the fear we feel. One of the best things that we can do is to not stereotype or avoid people with cancer, diabetes, kidney disease, genetic diseases, or any other disease. Many of us have a tendency to be afraid of people when they are ill. Compassionate service and friendship for these people will not only help them better deal with the disease, but it will help fortify you against disease.

For you to guard against disease from the world around you, you can provide service to others in that world. Case studies in PNI have shown that even watching humanitarian acts (such as Mother Theresa doing service to people in India) fortifies the immune system. In your own life, doing acts of service and expressing unconditional love to others (giving without any expectation of receiving back or having them owe you anything) not only make you feel good emotionally, but also help to fortify your body.

Issue
Betting the Odds

Some couples who are planning to marry find out that one or both of them carries hereditary genes that may produce defects in any children they have together.

- Pro: The couple should go ahead and marry but should not have children. It would be unfair to the child(ren).
- Con: If the couple decides to marry, they should agree on whether to take the risk of having a child with a birth defect. It would be unfair to the parents to deny themselves that right as a couple.

What would you do? Would genetic counseling help in this situation?

everyday activities that have not caused breathing difficulty in the past. Coughing can also be a significant symptom, especially if it lasts for any period of time. Sputum production (particularly in the early morning) and coughed-up blood are signs of a serious problem that should receive medical attention. Chest pain can have a number of causes, including chronic lung disorders or infection, and should be reported to a physician.

PREVENTION

You can decide to protect your lungs and other organs of the respiratory system in various ways. First and foremost, do not smoke. Second, work to keep our atmosphere clean, because environmental pollutants can damage the respiratory system. If you work in an atmosphere with pollutants, wear a protective mask. Avoid becoming overweight, because the heavier you are, the harder your lungs must work.

GENETIC DISEASE

Genetic diseases are disorders of the hereditary material—the genes and chromosomes. Its victims are either born with the disorder or born with a susceptibility to develop the disorder later in life. Some genetic diseases are inherited in a complex manner involving multiple genes, whereas others involve multiple genes plus certain environmental factors. About 20 percent of all birth defects are genetically induced, 20 percent are environmentally influenced, and the rest result from the interaction of heredity and environment.

Genetic diseases create the nation's most serious child-health problem. The defects that occur are characterized by abnormalities of body structures and/or functions.

DETECTION AND DIAGNOSIS

Physicians can now detect many birth defects and genetic abnormalities before birth. Detection techniques include **amniocentesis** (analysis of the amniotic fluid taken from the intrauterine environment), **ultrasound** (the use of sound waves), and **fetoscopy** (insertion of a viewing instrument into the womb to observe the fetus). Physicians can plan treatment before the baby is born, if necessary; can determine fetal maturity to eliminate birth hazards; or can suggest abortion in cases of severe problems.

Relatively few genetic defects can be completely corrected, but many can be treated to slow, stop, or partly reverse harmful effects. Available types of treatment include corrective surgery; chemical regulation by drugs, hormones, vitamins, and dietary supplements; transplantation, including bone marrow transplants for immunodeficiency disorders; and rehabilitative training to help compensate for mental, physical, and sensory handicaps (*Birth Defects* 1981).

amniocentesis
Analysis of amniotic fluid taken from the uterus; a test used to determine whether fatal defects are present in the fetus.

ultrasound
The use of sound waves for medical detection and treatment purposes.

fetoscopy
The insertion of a viewing instrument into the womb to observe the fetus.

PREVENTION

For couples who suspect that their future children may be at risk of inheriting a disorder, genetic counseling is a necessity. One or both parents may know of a particular defect in the family history, or they may belong to an ethnic group at relatively high risk for a specific disease. If there is some risk of a defect, a genetic counselor can define the odds and explain the potential for treatment or care if the couple chooses to have children. This decision is one that only the parents can make, but they should have access to all the latest information before they make their choice.

NEUROMUSCULAR-SKELETAL DISEASES

Finally, a brief examination of diseases affecting the nervous, muscular, and skeletal systems is appropriate. Some of these diseases, such as arthritis, can result from the aging process of a particular system; others, such as muscular dystrophy and multiple sclerosis, have unknown causes.

ARTHRITIS

Arthritis is humanity's oldest known chronic disease. There are several types, all of which attack the body's joints, and the effects vary from slight pain to severe crippling and total disability. The word *arthritis* means inflammation of a joint. The three most common types are rheumatoid arthritis, osteoarthritis, and gout.

Rheumatoid arthritis is the most difficult rheumatic disease to control and can do the most damage to the joints. The condition usually begins between the ages of 20 and 50, with twice as many women as men being afflicted. It generally affects many joints but most commonly the small joints of the hands. Joint inflammation causes pain and swelling and, if uncontrolled, can cause destruction of the bones, deformity, and eventual disability. Its course is unpredictable. It flares up suddenly (perhaps as the result of emotional distress) and just as suddenly returns to remission. Usually, the first signs are fatigue, muscle stiffness (especially in the morning), and joint pain. Painful swelling begins, with nodules ranging from pea-size to walnut-size appearing under the skin. Joint motion is gradually lost and deformities develop.

Osteoarthritis seems to result from a combination of wear and tear on the joints and other unknown factors. It is much more common and less damaging than rheumatoid arthritis. Older people are its most frequent victims. The disease is characterized by degeneration of the joint cartilage. The cartilage develops small cracks and wears unevenly. Disability most often results from disease in the weight-bearing joints of the knees, hips, and spine. Common symptoms are pain and stiffness, especially in the fingers and in joints that bear the body's weight.

Gout is the easiest form of arthritis to detect and treat, and is the best understood. It usually occurs in men and commonly affects the joints of the feet, particularly the big

toe. Gout results from the deposit of too much uric acid (a body chemical) in the tissues. Uric acid crystals form in the joints, causing inflammation and severe pain. Attacks of gout may follow minor injury, excessive eating or drinking, overexercise, or surgery. Sudden attacks often occur for no apparent reason and may last for days or weeks.

DIAGNOSIS AND TREATMENT OF ARTHRITIS

An accurate diagnosis of rheumatoid arthritis can be made only by a physician after a careful physical examination. The treatment regime might include rest, physical therapy (including heat and corrective exercises), one of many drugs that control pain and inflammation, and, in some cases, surgery. The same general methods of diagnosis, treatment, and care are used for osteoarthritis. Surgical correction of deformed weight-bearing joints, especially the hips, has been effective in helping many osteoarthritic patients to walk again without pain.

Researchers are looking at combating arthritis by growing new cartilage in a laboratory to replace and repair cartilages damaged by osteoarthritis (Skerett 1993).

Gout responds more satisfactorily to treatment and is more effectively controlled than the other types of arthritis. The goal of treatment is to reduce the level of uric acid in the blood through drug therapy (Arthritis Foundation 1986). Exercise is recommended for arthritis sufferers, preferable in water.

PREVENTION

Although it is not yet possible to cure rheumatoid arthritis, it is possible for patients to cope successfully. The prime objective of treatment is to prevent joint destruction. The possibility of remission makes it crucial that all efforts be made to prevent joint destruction during the active stage. Rheumatoid arthritis is usually chronic and can last a lifetime, so physicians try to avoid the use of toxic drugs as much as possible. This requires that patients undergo treatment with lesser drugs at the earliest sign of recurrence. If rheumatoid

---

arthritis
A chronic disease characterized by inflammation of the joints.

rheumatoid arthritis
The most crippling form of arthritis, characterized by inflammation of the joints, stiffness, swelling, and pain.

osteoarthritis
A type of arthritis characterized by degeneration of the joint cartilage.

gout
A form of arthritis that commonly affects the joints of the feet, especially the big toe.

PERSONAL SKILLS AND EXPERIENCES

PNI Action

Psychoneuroimmunology (PNI) is the study of the interaction of the mind, the central nervous system, and the body's immunological system. It has been shown that people with a fighting spirit, optimism, hope, and faith can actually build their immune systems. The brain has the capability to self-medicate and to release a variety of mental and physical painkillers and motivating substances (neuropeptides) when the demand is there.

It is important to note here a major caution. How you think can in fact either weaken or fortify your immune system. This is not to suggest that you can think diseases away, but you can help the process. If you are sick, *it is important to follow a physician's treatment plan,* but you can supplement the plan by believing that treatment will work, that with proper treatment you will overcome the problem, and that mentally you will feel medicines and treatments working. If you are not sick, *it does not mean that you do not need periodic physician examinations* just because you are thinking yourself well. It means that positive thinking will help to keep you well.

Consider the following suggestions to help fortify you against disease and to help you when you become sick.

1. Believe in the treatment prescribed by your physician or, for minor illnesses, believe in your personal therapy (bed rest, positive thinking, etc.). For an illness, you might receive a prescription from your physician. You should start with positive thoughts. When you take the prescription, feel it working, imagine the pain going away, believe that it will work, and feel yourself becoming stronger, overcoming the illness.

2. Formulate a cause in your life. Work vigorously toward some goal, whether it be your studies, athletics, service, or another cause that demands that you function optimally. This is not meant to be frustrating or overloading, but something that is exciting for you. Make yourself comfortably too busy to get sick. Many case studies have been reported that, while working vigorously on a project, performance, or other cause, people may have been tired but not sick. At the moment when the performance was through, they would take a deep breath and relax, and then shortly they would feel a cold, sore throat, or other minor illness.

3. When you do behaviors to make you feel healthier (exercise, eat high-fiber foods, meditate, etc.), do some imagery and picture the power of the positive behavior. Imagine the fiber cleaning the digestive system, the exercise clearing arteries and expelling all the stress, and meditation calming and allowing your body to rebuild.

4. Challenge yourself. Do something you haven't tried and work at it until you do it well. Try a new activity, such as skiing, rollerblading, playing an instrument, or speed reading.

5. If you get sick, you may want to try repeated imagery. As you lie in bed with the illness, picture your immune system attacking the foreign antigens, imagine the battle, and see yourself winning. Repeat the scenarios over and over until you feel better.

---

arthritis is diagnosed early, and if prompt, individualized treatment is begun, severe crippling can usually be prevented or minimized.

Since osteoarthritis results from wear and tear on the joints, any protective care we can give our joints may deter the onset of this disease. This includes attention to overweight, poor posture, injury, or strain from our occupation or recreation.

Drugs can reduce excessive uric acid in the blood to prevent further attacks of gout. Though medical treatment is the most important area in the management of this disease, lifestyle also affects gout to some extent. Persons susceptible to gout should avoid or limit alcoholic beverages, maintain normal weight, get sufficient exercise, and avoid using drugs that are not absolutely necessary, because many drugs elevate the uric acid level (Arthritis Foundation 1986).

TAKE ACTION

1. Avoid hazardous chemicals and carcinogens (sun, asbestos, air pollution, etc.).

2. Don't smoke or drink coffee.

3. Attain and maintain an ideal weight (body fat composition).

4. Learn to effectively manage your stress levels.

5. Eat low-fat foods and a balanced diet with lots of vegetables and fiber.

SUMMARY

1. Cancer is characterized by the uncontrolled growth and spread of abnormal, or malignant, cells.

2. The cause of cancer is unknown, but risk factors are being identified in such forms as diet, exposure to industrial chemicals, smoking, and ultraviolet light.

3. The major sites of cancer include the skin, colon, lungs, rectum, breast, uterus, and mouth.

4. Treatment and research in cancer include chemotherapy, radiation treatment, and experimental studies using interferon, genetic engineering, and other approaches.

5. Diabetes mellitus is a disorder in which the body does not produce enough insulin, preventing the sugar in the blood from reaching the cells to provide energy.

6. There are two types of diabetes: type I, or insulin-dependent diabetes, and type II, or non-insulin-dependent diabetes.

7. Diabetes has warning signs and treatments. In addition, first aid for diabetics is important for people to know.

8. A number of different diseases can attack the kidneys, potentially leading to chronic kidney disease and kidney failure.

9. Chronic respiratory disease may be environmentally induced by cigarette smoking and industrial pollutants.

10. Genetic diseases cause more health problems for young children than any other type of disease. Many genetic diseases can be detected before birth.

11. Various diseases affect the neuromuscular-skeletal system. The most common ones affect the joints of the body; these include osteoarthritis, rheumatoid arthritis, and gout.

COMMITMENT ACTIVITIES

1. Take the time to look carefully at your body. Look at moles, warts, freckles, and any other lumps. Feel your armpits and groin for any unusual lumps. Look into a mirror to note any unusual changes. Be sure to monitor your skin carefully. Also, do a breast self-examination, if you are female, and a testicular self-examination, if you are male. If you spot anything unusual, please see a physician.

2. Genetic counseling should be available to all persons in the community. Determine where genetic counseling is available in your community. If such counseling is not available at your university health center, perhaps you could help develop a program. If it is available, what kinds of promotional activities can help students become aware of this service?

3. Find out if any industries in your area produce carcinogens. Which carcinogens are being produced? What has the industry done to lower risk or inform employees of the risk involved? Is there a risk to the community?

4. If you have not had a physical examination in the last year, decide to have one before the end of this semester. Develop a list of questions to ask your doctor about your own personal risk with respect to the diseases covered in this chapter.

REFERENCES

American Cancer Society. 1993. *Cancer Facts and Figures—1993.* New York: American Cancer Society.

Arthritis Foundation. 1986. *Basic Facts: Answers to Your Questions.* Atlanta: Arthritis Medical Information Series.

Biesecker, B. B., et al. 1993. "Genetic Counseling for Families with Inherited Susceptibility to Breast and Ovarian Cancer." *Journal of the American Medical Association* 269, no. 15 (21 April): 1970–74.

Birth Defects: Tragedy and Hope. 1981. White Plains, NY: March of Dimes.

Bishop, J. E. 1991. "Gene That Causes a Diabetes Type May Be Found." *Wall Street Journal,* 15 February, 84(w), B2.

Bown, W. 1992. "Cavers Risk Cancer from Underground Radon." *New Scientist* 135, no. 1838 (12 September): 4.

Burton, B., and A. A. Martin. 1978. "What You Should Know About Kidney Dialysis." *Pharmacy Times,* January.

Cannon-Albright, L. A., et al. 1992. "Assignment of a Locus for Familial Melanoma, MLM, to Chromosome 9p13-p22." *Science* 258, no. 5085 (13 November): 1148–52.

Catalona, W. J., et al. 1993. "Detection of Organ-Confined Prostate Cancer Is Increased Through Prostate-Specific Antigen-Based Screening." *Journal of the American Medical Association* 270, no. 8 (25 August): 949–55.

Cowen, R. 1990. "Mouse Study Suggests Diabetes Prevention." *Science News* 137 (31 March): 198.

Cowley, G. 1993. "Sharper Focus on the Breast: Early Detection of Tumors Is the Key to Fighting Cancer." *Newsweek,* 10 May, 64.

"Diagnosis and Treatment of Early Melanoma." *Journal of the American Medical Association* 268, no. 10 (9 September): 1314–19.

"Dietary Carcinogens Linked to Breast Cancer." 1993. *Medical World News* 34, no. 5 (May): 13–14.

Dimagno, E. P., T. A. Rich, and G. D. Steele. 1992. "Pancreatic Cancer: What You Need to Know." *Patient Care* 26, no. 6 (30 March): 151–65.

Doppman, J. L. 1992. "Pancreatic Endocrine Tumors—the Search Goes On." *New England Journal of Medicine* 326, no. 26 (25 June): 1770–72.

Fackelman, K. A. 1993. "Cancer Protection from Fruits and Veggies." *Science News* 143, no. 23 (5 June): 358.

Field, R. 1993. "Melanoma Vaccines Begin to Make Their Mark." *Medical World News* 34, no. 4 (April): 14–15.

Froguel, P. 1993. "Familial Hyperglycemia Due to Mutations in Glucokinase: Definition of a Subtype of Diabetes Mellitus." *New England Journal of Medicine* 328, no. 10 (11 March): 697–702.

Gibbs, W. W. 1993. "Sentries and Saboteurs: Mutating Patients' Genomes to Suit Their Medicine." *Scientific American,* October, 16–20.

Gorman, C. 1993. "Does Sunscreen Save Your Skin?" *Time,* 24 May, 69.

Ihde, D. C. 1992. "Chemotherapy of Lung Cancer." *New England Journal of Medicine* 327, no. 20 (12 November): 1434–41.

Katzenstein, L. 1993. "Allergies Nothing to Sneeze At." *American Health* 12, no. 4 (May): 44–49.

Keernan, N. A., et al. 1993. "Analysis of 462 Transplantations from Unrelated Donors Facilitated by the National Marrow Donor Program." *New England Journal of Medicine* 328, no. 9 (4 March): 593–602.

"Malignant Melanoma." 1992. *The Lancet* 340, no. 8825 (17 October): 948–51.

Persky, V., et al. 1990. "Recent Time Trends in Uterine Cancer." *American Journal of Public Health* 80, no. 8 (August): 935–39.

Pizzo, P. A. 1993. "Management of Fever in Patients with Cancer and Treatment-Induced Neutropenia." *New England Journal of Medicine* 328, no. 18 (6 May): 1323–42.

Podolsky, D. 1993. "An Advance on the Cancer Front." *U.S. News and World Report,* 17 May, 14.

Purtilo, D. T. 1978. *A Survey of Human Diseases.* Reading, MA: Addison-Wesley.

Randal, J. 1992. "Insulin Key to Diabetes but Not Full Cure." *FDA Consumer* 26, no. 4 (May): 15–20.

Robbins, S. L., and V. Kumar. 1987. *Basic Pathology.* Philadelphia: Saunders.

Ross, P. E. 1993. "Living Cure: Insulin-Secreting Implants Approach Human Testing." *Scientific American,* June, 1820.

Rubin, R. 1993a. "The Breast Cancer Scare: Women in Their 30's and Even 20's Are Increasingly Fearful." *U.S. News and World Report,* 15 March, 68–72.

Rubin, R. 1993b. "A Tighter Rein on Diabetes." *U.S. News and World Report,* 28 June, 68.

"Running Away from Diabetes." 1992. *Berkeley Wellness Newsletter* 8, no. 4 (January): 6.

Saltus, R. 1992. "Genetic Damage and Skin Cancer." *Technology Review* 95, no. 2 (February–March): 11–12.

Skerett, P. J. 1993. "Growing New Cartilage to Fight Arthritis." *Technology Review* 96, no. 3 (April): 10–11.

Skolnick, A. A. 1993. "Novel Therapies Dominate American Cancer Society's 35th Annual Science Writers Seminar." *Journal of the American Medical Association* 269, no. 17 (5 May): 2182–85.

Thygerson, A. L. 1986. *The First Aid Book.* Englewood Cliffs, NJ: Prentice Hall.

ADDITIONAL READINGS

American Cancer Society Readings are many and very good, including these:

Facts on Bladder Cancer
Facts on Bone Cancer
Facts on Breast Cancer
Facts on Cancer of the Brain
Facts on Cancer of the Larynx
Facts on Childhood Cancer
Facts on Colorectal Cancer
Facts on Hodgkin's Disease
Facts on Leukemia
Facts on Lung Cancer
Facts on Lymphomas and Multiple Myeloma
Facts on Oral Cancer
Facts on Prostate Cancer
Facts on Skin Cancer
Facts on Stomach and Esophageal Cancers
Facts on Testicular Cancer
Facts on Thyroid Cancer
Facts on Uterine Cancer

Each of these booklets contains information about the incidence, types, prevention, treatment, and prognosis of each of the types of cancer.

The American Cancer Society has good books on coping, for those who have cancer, including these:

Advanced Cancer: Living Each Day
After Breast Cancer: A Guide to Follow-up Care
Breast Biopsy: What You Should Know
Breast Cancer: Understanding Treatment Options
Breast Reconstruction: A Matter of Choice
Mastectomy: A Treatment for Breast Cancer
Parents Handbook on Leukemia

The Arthritis Foundation also has numerous excellent pamphlets, in its Arthritis Medical Information Series, providing an overview of nature of the disease, the diagnosis, treatment, and the prognosis of arthritic diseases. Some available titles, among many:

Basic Facts: Answers to Your Questions
Bursitis, Tendinitis, and Related Conditions
Coping with Pain
Exercise and Your Arthritis
Gout

After reading and pondering the chapters on diseases, you should have a good understanding of:

1. the nature and devastating consequences of communicable, cardiovascular, and other chronic diseases and cancer.

2. how to prevent some of the diseases through lifestyle change.

3. the importance of taking action by becoming immunized, avoiding stress, and avoiding the consumption of food or beverages that facilitate disease.

Lifestyle Contracting Using Strength Intervention

I. Choosing the desired health behavior or skill.

A. Keeping in mind the purposes in life and goals you have identified, consider one or two health behaviors related to disease prevention (from the lists in the chapters or of your own creation) that will help you reach your goals. In order to assess your likelihood of success, ask yourself questions similar to those used in previous sections, such as these:

1. Is my purpose, cause, or goal better realized by adoption of this behavior?

_____ yes _____ no.

2. Am I hardy enough to accomplish this goal? (This means I feel I can do it if I work hard, am committed to do it, am challenged by it, and see myself in control enough to make it happen.)

_____ yes _____ no.

3. Is this a behavior I really want to change and that I feel I can change?

_____ yes _____ no.

4. Do I first need to nurture a personal strength area?

_____ yes _____ no.
(If yes, be sure to include this as a part of the plan.)

5. Do I need to free myself from the negative effects of a behavior (break a bad habit)?

_____ yes _____ no.
(If yes, be sure to include this as a part of the plan.)

6. Have I considered the results of the assessments in the 3 previous chapters?

_____ yes _____ no.

("Yes" answers to the first 3 questions are a must in order to be successful. It might be wise to consider a different behavior if you can't honestly answer "yes" to these questions. Your answers to questions 4–6 ought to provide insights for your consideration in making your plan.)

B. Behaviors I will change (no more than 2)

_____

_____

II. Lifestyle Plan

A. A description of the general plan of what I am going to do and how I will accomplish it. (Consider apperceptive experiences—successes you may have had in the past—since they may help you consider the best ways to carry out this plan.)

_____

_____

_____

_____

_____

_____

B. Barriers to the accomplishment of the plan (lack of time, materials, support, etc.)

1. Identify the barriers: _____

_____

_____

2. Means to remove the barriers (use problem-solving skills or creative approaches):

_____

_____

_____

C. Implementation of the plan

1. Substitution (putting positive behaviors in place of negative ones): _____

_____

_____

2. Confluence (combining a mental and a physical activity for time efficiency if possible):

_____

_____

3. Systematic enhancement (using a strength to help a weakness): _____

_____

_____

(Continued on page 18.28)

LIFESTYLE CONTRACT

4. When: _____

5. Where: _____

6. Preparation: _____
_____

7. With whom: _____
_____
_____

III. Support Groups
  A. Who: _____
_____
_____

  B. Role: _____
_____
_____

  C. Organized support: _____
_____

IV. Trigger responses: _____
_____
_____

V. Starting date: _____

VI. Date/Sequence the contract will be reevaluated: _____
_____

VII. Evidence(s) of reaching the goal: _____
_____
_____

VIII. Reward(s) when contract is completed: _____
_____
_____

IX. Signature of student: _____

X. Signature of facilitator/instructor: _____

XI. Additional conditions/comments: _____
_____
_____

Choices and the World Around You

CHAPTER 19

Environmental Health

Healthy People 2000 Objectives

- Eliminate blood lead levels above 15µg/dL in children under age 5.

- Increase protection from air pollutants so that at least 85 percent of people live in counties that meet EPA standards.

- Increase protection from radon so that at least 40 percent of people live in homes tested by homeowners and found to be or made safe (a 700% increase).

In the movie *Dances with Wolves,* a soldier (played by Kevin Costner) ventures into the West to staff an abandoned post during the closing years of the Civil War. He lives alone and finally makes friends with the Native Americans who live nearby. The soldier writes in a journal his impressions and experiences in the natural environment. Many of us who viewed the movie almost wished that we could have an experience of living on the land and reflecting on the beauty of nature. Consequently, national forests and parks are the targets of many of our vacations. We flock to be in preserved forests and deserts. We love to camp in recreational vehicles and tents to get back to nature.

THE WORLD AND THE ENVIRONMENTAL CRISIS

Most of us appreciate natural settings and are fearful that industrialization and growing populations will destroy some of the natural areas we love. The issue of preserving our natural environment and avoiding the toxins of industrialization is a problem that has been recognized by almost all people around the world. In an effort to protect the planet we have regular world conferences on pollution.

For example, in June 1992, in Rio de Janeiro, representatives from around the world came together to work on what could have been a major worldwide agreement to try to preserve the environment. Over a hundred world leaders and 30,000 participants gathered to consider these questions ("Earth Summit" 1992a):

- What kind of planet will our children inherit?
- Will they have room to roam, air to breathe, and food to eat?
- Will they ever see an eagle flying free or enjoy the solitude of a pristine mountain lake?

These questions arise in this era because we hear information like this ("Earth Summit" 1992a):

- The world has lost 500 million acres (an area one-third of the size of the United States) of trees since 1972.
- Over 10,000 endangered species of animals have become extinct.
- Brazilians are burning the rain forest for farmland, which will promote global warming.
- The oceans are littered with plastics, tar balls, and other refuse, and they are rapidly losing fish.
- The garbage dumps, oil spills, sewage discharges, drift nets, and factory ships are only visible problems with the sea; 70 to 80 percent of maritime pollution comes from the sediment and contamination that flows into the seas from land-based sources, topsoil, fertilizers, pesticides, and industrial waste.

One purpose of the Earth Summit in Rio was to sign the Biodiversity Treaty, which would call upon industrial nations to give the developing world financial incentives to protect their natural ecosystems, endangered plant and animal species, and rain forests. It seemed to be a difference of perspective of the Northern Hemisphere versus the Southern Hemisphere of the world, because the North looks at the forests as a treasure in dealing with the greenhouse effect to absorb carbon dioxide and keep global warming in check. The United States with all its industrialization is still not as bad as what Russian citizens have to live amid—the aftermath of nuclear accidents, nuclear testing, and massive air and water pollution (Perera 1993). Northwestern Russia has been labeled "the most polluted area in the world" ("Nuclear Winter" 1993). Mexico City has the undesirable distinction of being the city with the worst air pollution in the world (Gardels and Snell 1993). The Northern, industrialized areas fear the loss of the world's natural areas and want them to be preserved. Meanwhile, the developing nations of the Southern Hemisphere see the same forests as resources for potential farmland, exportation of exotic woods, free sources of fuel, and lumber. When all these countries met together, they brought with them a variety of opinions, but the United States was the only country not willing to sign the Biodiversity Treaty. The decision that we have to make as a world community is between (1) economic growth, which necessitates producing steel, cutting trees for lumber, and other forms of industrialization, and (2) protecting the world from environmental pollution, acid rain, the destruction of the protective ozone layer, the elimination of thousands of endangered species of plants and animals, and the warming of the planet. As Margaret Thatcher, then prime minister of England, put it in her famous "Green Speech" to the Royal Society, "With all these enormous changes in population, agriculture, use of fossil fuels concentrated into such a short period of time, we have unwittingly begun a massive experiment with the system of the planet itself" (Woodell 1989).

THE ENVIRONMENTAL HEALTH PROBLEM

An individual exists in an environment that is either conducive to health or detrimental to health. The conditions where people live can be either environmental stressors or positive factors, both of which affect our mental health, stress level, and physical well-being (fig. 19.1). Air pollution, noise, water pollution, chemicals, trash, land abuse, and other environmental conditions can negatively affect our outlook on life and our mental health, and they can ultimately destroy us.

POPULATION GROWTH

Figure 19.2 demonstrates the normal population growth curve and how, after a certain population saturation is reached, the species ultimately destroys itself. Figure 19.3 shows the projected world population growth, which is a matter of concern to some of us. It appears that the world has reached its peak in growth. On a positive note, humans are not mice confined in a cage. The world is very large, with

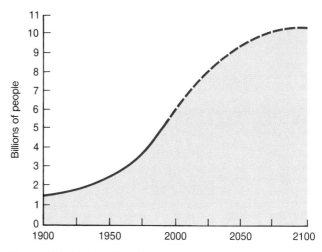

Source: United Nations Population Division

Figure 19.3

World population growth, 1900–2100.

Source: Data from *World Population Prospects, 1992.* United Nations Publication, table A.1.

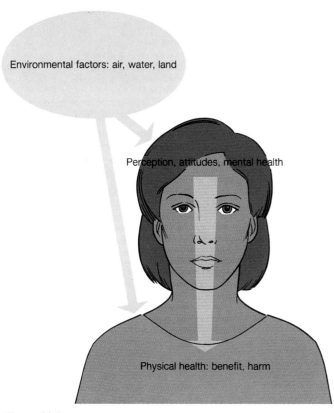

Figure 19.1

The effect of environmental factors on perception, mental health, and physical health.

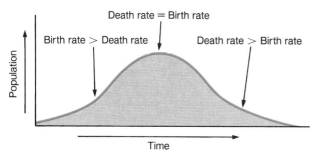

Figure 19.2

The normal population growth curve.

The worldwide population explosion is a medical, economic, political, and moral issue.

huge areas of land that have not been developed. Humans have the ability to adapt, destroy waste products, and develop chemicals that can sterilize and disinfect. How far human resourcefulness will take us is a concern of many environmental health specialists. Limiting family size, increasing efficient food production, and removing waste are worldwide concerns. They are of particular concern in densely populated areas. In some places of the world, overpopulation results in multiple families living together in single-family dwellings. Life expectancy is shortened because of improper waste removal, poor sanitary conditions, and the rapid spread of disease. The population explosion is not only a medical, economic, and political issue, but a moral issue.

The more people there are, the more air pollution there is from autos; the more waste to be removed; the more homes to be built, which uses up wood from the forests; the more development and expansion into the ever-decreasing natural landscape; the more factories to be built; and so on. With more people, the higher our chances are of breathing bad air, getting contaminated water, and being exposed to toxic substances. This picture sounds dismal, but it is difficult to find a positive outcome of natural resource waste. The positive side of the picture is that there are measures that we can take to avoid toxic substances and demand good control from federal, state, and local governments. In more-developed countries, for example, the population growth is much less than that in less-developed countries (fig. 19.4).

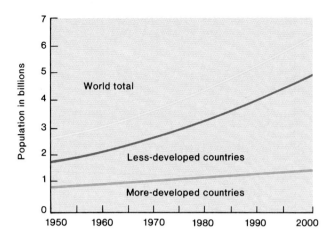

Figure 19.4

World population growth, 1950–2000.

Source: Data from *World Population Prospects, 1992.* United Nations Publication, table A.1.

For an understanding of how the air, water, and land are being threatened by contamination, a basic understanding of the concept of toxicity is necessary.

TOXICITY

Almost any chemical can be toxic (poisonous) if people are exposed to excessive amounts of it. **Toxicity** depends on the exposure level and the dose at which various negative effects occur. Because we are constantly exposed to chemicals, it is important to know as much about them as possible to avoid overexposure.

We will not suffer from toxicity without exposure to a chemical. **Exposure** is the pathway or means by which we come into contact with the chemical. Understanding how exposure occurs is an important step in preventing toxicity. **Risk assessment,** as it applies to the study of environmental health, is the scientific estimation of the likelihood of health problems' occurring as a result of exposure to chemicals. The estimation of risk is based on studies that show amounts of exposure and consequential health problems that have resulted over time. Risk assessment is the key in determining safe working conditions, products that will be sold on the open market, building materials, and other government-controlled materials.

toxicity

How poisonous a chemical is, depending on exposure, dose, and negative effects.

exposure

Along with dose, one of the two factors that determine toxicity. Exposure can occur through direct contact or inhalation.

risk assessment

In the study of environmental health, the scientific estimation of the likelihood of health problems' occurring as a result of exposure to chemicals.

Issue

Population Growth

Some countries (such as India and China) are now imposing mandatory birth-control measures to help control their population. Couples are allowed to have only one or two children. Many health professionals feel that the United States should also put a limit on family size. Although the likelihood of that happening is slim, from a constitutional perspective, do you favor it for other countries where this can happen? Do you favor it for people on welfare in this country?

- Pro: If we advocate population control, then we can avoid the prospect that rising numbers will promote poverty and famine. It is amazing to see countries where they can hardly feed their people, still having large families. It certainly makes sense to limit family size. If they don't limit the size, then they will probably starve to death. This should be particularly true for low-income people. Even in this country, if people on welfare are going to be subsidized by the government, then perhaps they should be limited while they are on welfare, in light of the economic deficit facing the United States.

- Con: This is a moral and spiritual issue first and an economic and political issue second. Restricting family size is a major infringement of human rights and is inhumane. This policy is not in reference to dogs or cats, but loving couples who want offspring to carry on traditions and family names and to create family units. Just because someone is on welfare does not mean they should also lose their dignity, their need for family, or their need to be loved. Furthermore, if we look at high-population countries, such as Japan, that are densely populated, we see some of the wealthiest countries in the world. Whereas China, which is not as densely populated, is poorer. The true key to economic well-being is a free capitalistic system that allows us to produce more than we consume ("The More the Merrier" 1993). Technology and free enterprise evolve as the need arises.

How would you react to governmentally imposed restrictions on family size? What do you think that we ought to do about population growth, as a world community?

Whether a chemical is toxic is also dependent upon potency. Potency is the ability of the chemical to cause cancer or other problems. For chemicals in the body, potency is expressed in terms of milligrams of chemical per unit of body weight (kilograms) per day. For example, benzene has a potency of, or an ability to cause cancer at an exposure of, 0.052 mg/kg/day. Potency may also be determined by a cumulative

Toxins in Your Environment

Directions

Do a home inspection to determine any forms of toxicity that you might be exposed to. The intent is not to make you overly anxious but to help you consider potential sources of problems where you live. The checklist (adapted from Williams 1993) indicates the potential problem that could result from excessive exposure to a substance.

_____ Carbon monoxide from faulty furnaces, stoves, heaters, and car exhausts (headaches, drowsiness, and irregular heartbeat)

_____ Methylene chloride and other solvents in paint, glues, and thinners (nerve disorders)

_____ Radon 222 from "radioactive" soils, rocks, and some water supplies (lung cancer)

_____ Styrene in carpets and plastic products (kidney and liver damage)

_____ Benzopyrene from tobacco smoke and wood stoves (lung cancer)

_____ Formaldehyde from furniture filling, paneling, particle board in furniture, and foam insulation (irritation of the eyes, throat, skin, and lungs, and nausea and dizziness)

_____ Tetrachloroethylene residue from dry-cleaned clothes (nerve disorders)

_____ Paradicholorobenzene from air fresheners and mothball crystals (cancer)

_____ Chloroform from chlorine-treated water in hot showers (cancer)

_____ 1,1,1-trichloroethane in aerosol sprays (dizziness and irregular breathing)

_____ Nitrogen oxides from unvented gas stoves, kerosene heaters, and wood stoves (lung irritation, cold-like symptoms, and headaches)

_____ Asbestos from pipe insulation, fireproofing, and ceiling and floor tiles (lung disease and cancer)

_____ Tobacco smoke from cigarettes (lung cancer, respiratory disease, and heart disease)

_____ Pesticides from fruit and vegetables (heart problems and nerve disorders)

Interpretation

If you have checked anything, then you need to determine the potential risk and remove the risk if possible.

---

analysis. For example, exposure to 93 milligrams of benzene over a person's lifetime causes an increased risk of cancer to 1 in 1,000 people. Sometimes the potency of exposure is based on the surrounding water or air that we drink or breathe. The units then become parts of the chemical to total parts in the air or water. For example, cancer risks increase when the amount of benzene that will be inhaled with the air is 5,500 parts per million, or when the amount ingested with water is 550 parts per million.

ROUTES OF EXPOSURE TO CHEMICALS

Chemicals are moved from one place to another in a variety of ways, and we can be exposed to the same chemical from a variety of sources. The chief mediums for chemicals include air (gases or vapor), water (liquid substances in the ground, on the ground surface, or in the rainwater), soil or sediments (chemicals mixed with dirt), and the food we eat (animals or plants).

Movement of chemicals between mediums depends on the chemical properties of the substance, but the chemicals can be changed or moved through metabolism (e.g., bacterial change or eating), chemical transformation (as in exposure to ultraviolet light), exposure to heat (e.g., liquids into gas forms), and in conjunction with other chemicals (e.g., nontoxic sodium nitrite into carcinogenic nitrocimines). Chemicals can then be moved into our bodies by inhalation, absorption, or ingestion.

WATER POLLUTION

Water pollution can occur through bacterial, chemical, and thermal contamination.

BACTERIAL CONTAMINATION

By now, you should be fully aware that you cannot take safe drinking water for granted. Most municipal water-treatment facilities are equipped only for bacterial decontamination, which is accomplished by chlorination of the water. Thus, water leaving municipal water-treatment facilities is tested only for (1) absence of **coliform bacteria** and (2) presence of a **chlorine residual.** The chlorine residual is the amount of chlorine added minus the amount used up in the decontamination process. A chlorine residual in a water sample indicates that the bacteria have been killed and that some chlorine remains in the water to kill bacteria that enter after the water leaves the plant. Too many dangerous bacteria in drinking water can spread waterborne diseases.

---

coliform bacteria

A group of bacteria whose presence in drinking water is suggestive of fecal contamination.

chlorine residual

Chlorine that is left in a water system to destroy any remaining bacteria.

Often water pollution occurs because of laziness
or carelessness.

CHEMICAL CONTAMINATION

Routine daily tests for the myriad possible chemical or radiological contaminants in a water supply are impractical, so these tests are conducted only in special instances. Consequently, chemical and radioactive waste dischargers have a heavy responsibility to institute at least minimal pollution controls. If you know of any industries that discharge wastes into local lakes, rivers, or streams, find out about their pollution-control policies.

Threats to human health posed by chemical contamination of water supplies are much more serious than those posed by biological contamination, because chemicals can persist in the environment for a much longer time. Much of the biological contamination of water supplies can be treated at municipal water facilities; the effects of chemical contamination can be virtually irreversible. For instance, widespread use of high-nitrate fertilizers and concentrated feedlots (cattle-feeding areas) has contaminated many underground water sources with nitrates to levels that exceed drinking water standards. Once an underground water supply is contaminated in this way, purification is practically impossible. If young children ingest water high in nitrates, methemoglobinemia (a fatal blood disease) can result. In addition to acute disease episodes, the effects of chemical contaminants can be chronic. Low levels of chemical contaminants in water might not be noticed until they are ingested and concentrated in the body over a long period of time.

THERMAL AND RADIOACTIVE POLLUTION

Thermal and radioactive pollution of water are other ways we pay for industrialization. In **thermal pollution,** excessive heat is added to the natural water supply, causing detrimental changes in the aquatic balance. This excess heat is usually derived from power plants situated near rivers, lakes, or streams that use the inexpensive nearby water source to cool their equipment. Raising the water temperature even a few degrees, however, can change the ways fish and plants obtain their food. For example, if the water temperature is too high, the fish may have to migrate; fish in a lake with no feeder streams are not able to escape the overheated water. Heated water also contains less dissolved oxygen because heat drives it out of the water. Plants need the oxygen for respiration. Without enough oxygen, water plants die, and the fish that depend on them for food must migrate or die.

Radioactive pollution of water can be even more insidious than thermal pollution. Discharges into natural waters by nuclear plants are the most common source of radioactive wastes. This influx of radiation can make the water unusable for humans or for water life.

THE REGULATION OF WATER POLLUTION

The 1972 amendment to the **Federal Water Pollution Control Act** of 1948 is considered "landmark" legislation because, for the first time, national goals for water quality were announced. These national goals were to improve water quality so that all navigable waters (interstate and intrastate) would be clean enough for swimming, recreation, and fish and wildlife by July 1983.

The Clean Water Act of 1977 and subsequent legislation provided tangible federal support to implement the provisions of the 1972 amendment to the Federal Water Pollution Control Act. The program that perhaps effected the most dramatic improvement to water quality was the funding of efforts to upgrade municipal sewage-treatment facilities. As a result, fish have returned to waters they had abandoned, and the recreational appeal of Lake Erie, for example, which was a dying lake, has been revived.

Because of the number of oil spills in the oceans and waters, the 1990 Oil Pollution Act was enacted to require petroleum tanker operators to have safety procedures in place that will contain and clean up any oil spills. The Department of Justice has shown that it is serious about the law and recently fined Texaco and U.S. Oil and Refining some $14.7 million to pay for spills in Fidalgo Bay and in Tacoma ("First Penalties Levied Under U.S. Oil Pollution Act" 1993).

thermal pollution
Damage to an aquatic ecosystem through an increase in heat in the water.

radioactive pollution
Damage to an aquatic ecosystem through the addition of radioactive matter into a natural body of water.

Federal Water Pollution Control Act
A law enacted in 1948 that announced the first national goals for water quality.

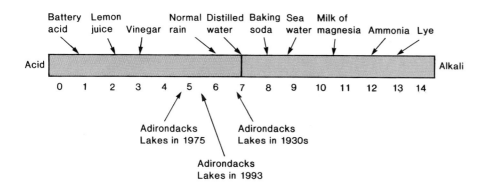

Figure 19.5

A pH scale showing acid rain in relation to other substances.

Reprinted by permission of Waveland Press, Inc., from Anne Nadakavukaren, *Man & Environment: A Health Perspective*, Second Ed., Copyright © 1986, 1984. Third Edition published 1990 by Waveland Press, Inc., Prospect Heights, Illinois.

Besides governmental efforts, there has been progress by the chemical industry in water pollution control. One particular example of industrial initiative is Dow Chemical's use of bacteria to turn specific chemical wastes into harmless end products.

However, governmental efforts and industrial initiatives are not enough by themselves to improve our water quality. We must all participate. To start, we can learn more about the water pollution problems in our communities and express our concerns to elected officials. One letter at the federal level is believed to have as much influence on policy as twenty-five votes. Further, we can make our lifestyle compatible with improved water quality by using water frugally and not littering on our natural waters. Whether and how we extend a heritage of cleaner water is up to us.

ACID RAIN

Acid precipitation in the form of snow, rain, hail, and fog is a recent concern that wasn't even recognized when the Clean Air Act was passed. **Acid rain** has a pH less than 5.6. The pH scale ranges from 0.0 to 14.0, with 0.0 representing the strongest acids and 14.0 representing the strongest alkali. The pH of distilled water is 7.0. Rain is usually slightly acidic at 5.6 because of its tendency to react with atmospheric carbon dioxide (fig. 19.5).

The extent of the acid rain problem was originally observed as a local problem, occurring near industrial centers. Now the phenomenon occurs hundreds of miles from the original sources, causing the pH of previously unpolluted lakes to change from normal to acidic, killing fish and other forms of wildlife. For example, the sparkling Adirondacks lakes in New York, once known for their excellent trout fishing, are now devoid of fish. Minnesota's Boundary Waters Canoe Area is on the brink of suffering the same fate. Reports of mysterious disappearances of fish come from everywhere from Ontario and Quebec (140 Ontario lakes are now devoid of fish) to the waterways of Scandinavia (10,000 lakes no longer have fish). The Black Forest of Germany and Roan Mountain of North Carolina have also been affected by acid rain. The Rockies and Sierra Nevada mountains are under threat, too. Such lakes are acid dead, having been poisoned by sulfuric and nitric acid falling from the sky (Nadakavukaren 1986).

Acid rain control programs are in full swing in many of these areas, particularly in the Adirondacks lakes, and it is now projected that by the year 2010 the lakes might again be able to support brook or lake trout (Rubin et al. 1992). The key to the program is getting the pH balance back to normal.

AIR POLLUTION

The **Clean Air Act (CAA)** is the most important federal law protecting the air that we breathe. It establishes ambient (outside) air standards for seven pollutants and emission standards for those seven and other chemicals. The CAA does not have jurisdiction over workplace exposure. The seven noncarcinogenic pollutants have been labeled **criteria air pollutants** because they are **threshold** chemicals and safe levels can be established. The pollutants include carbon monoxide, lead, nitrogen dioxide, hydrocarbons, ozone, particulates, and sulfur dioxide (see table 19.1).

acid rain
Rain that has a pH of less than 5.6.

Clean Air Act (CAA)
A law that establishes emission standards and air standards for six pollutants.

criteria air pollutants
A group of substances identified under the Clean Air Act for which outside air standards are set. The substances include carbon monoxide, lead, nitrogen dioxide, hydrocarbons, ozone, particulates, and sulfur dioxide.

threshold
The safe level of exposure for a particular chemical—as opposed to nonthreshold chemicals, which are dangerous at even very low doses.

TABLE 19.1   SELECTED POLLUTANTS AND THEIR EFFECTS

Pollutant	Form	Effects
Total suspended particulates (TSP)	Solid or liquid	1. acts synergistically with SO_2 as respiratory irritant 2. grime deposits 3. obscures visibility 4. corrodes metals
Sulfur dioxide (SO_2)	Gas	1. respiratory irritant 2. corrodes metal and stone 3. damages textiles 4. toxic to plants 5. precursor of acid rain
Carbon monoxide (CO)	Gas	1. aggravates cardiovascular disease 2. impairs perception and mental processes 3. fatal at high concentrations
Nitrogen dioxide (NO_2)	Gas	1. respiratory irritant 2. toxic to plants 3. reduces visibility 4. precursor of ozone 5. precursor of acid rain
Ozone (O_3)	Gas	1. respiratory irritant 2. toxic to plants 3. corrodes rubber, paint
Hydrocarbons (HC)	Gas	1. precursor to O_3 2. some types are carcinogens
Lead (Pb)	Metal aerosol	1. damage to nervous system, blood, kidneys

Reprinted by permission of Waveland Press, Inc., from Anne Nadakavukaren, *Man & Environment: A Health Perspective,* Second Ed., Copyright © 1986, 1984. Third Edition published 1990 by Waveland Press, Inc., Prospect Heights, Illinois.

Sources of pollutants covered under the CAA include emissions from automobiles, which carry significant amounts of all the criteria pollutants except ozone and sulfur dioxide.

The **Environmental Protection Agency (EPA)** has identified **hazardous air pollutants** that are generally considered to be carcinogenic, including these:

- asbestos
- benzene
- beryllium
- mercury
- radionuclides
- vinyl chloride

The CAA requires the EPA to set emission standards with an ample margin of safety to protect the public health. The EPA does not have authority to regulate the release of chemicals other than criteria and hazardous air pollutants. Indoor air quality (radon accumulation, carbon monoxide, and formaldehyde, for example) is generally not controlled.

One of the most insidious and potent environmental hazards is **radon** (Nero 1993). Radon is a naturally occurring gas that results from the radioactive decay of radium, found in many types of rocks and soils. Radon enters buildings through cracks in their foundations (Williams 1993). Radon is also found in drinking water, although few deaths are attributed to waterborne radon (Stone 1993). About 6 percent of U.S. homes have high levels of radon. Radon has been linked to lung cancer and is responsible for almost 10 percent of lung cancer deaths (Castleman 1993). Home test kits are available to measure radon levels in homes.

KINDS OF AIR POLLUTION

Air pollution can have both natural and artificial origins. Because of the natural sources of pollution, the air in our

Environmental Protection Agency (EPA)
A federal agency responsible for the protection of air and water, and other environmental concerns.

hazardous air pollutants
Substances in the air that are generally considered carcinogenic. The EPA has identified six such substances: asbestos, benzene, beryllium, mercury, radionuclides, and vinyl chloride.

radon
A naturally occurring gas that results from the radioactive decay of naturally occurring radium.

Avoid as much air pollution as you can, particularly on smog alert days.

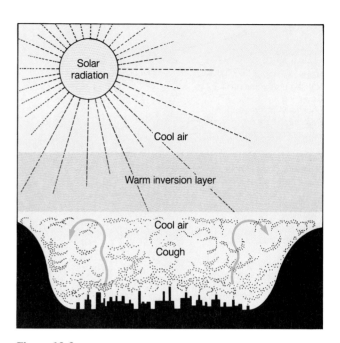

Figure 19.6
Thermal inversion, triggered by a high-pressure area, traps pollutants in a layer of cool air that cannot rise to carry the pollutants away.

atmosphere has probably never been pure. Naturally generated air pollution—such as volcanic ash, windblown dust, and pollen—is almost unavoidable during certain times. Artificially generated air pollution, such as factory smoke and auto exhaust, began on a large scale about the time of the Industrial Revolution and quickly added both insult and injury to human health and the environment.

Visible air pollution, such as smoke and soot from factories, became recognized and even accepted as the price of industrialization in Europe in the 1700s. It took only about 25 years before artificially generated pollution exceeded nature's capability to purify the air in heavily industrialized areas. When weather conditions accentuate the effects of artificially generated air pollution, the number of human illnesses and deaths rises. In the 1800s, air pollution ordinances were passed that seemed to be effective in reducing smoke.

Perhaps the real reason for the improvement in the visible air quality during the 1950s was the shift from coal to petroleum as our primary energy source. But this change in energy sources did not solve the air quality problem. By the middle of the twentieth century, "invisible" air pollution emerged as the leading culprit of unhealthy air, and air quality actually deteriorated even further.

This deterioration resulted from the proliferation of the motor vehicle and the availability of relatively inexpensive fuel. Americans became addicted to the personal convenience that motor vehicles offered. Work and leisure revolved around the car. At one point, the rate of vehicle registrations even surpassed the birth rate!

THE NATURE OF AIR POLLUTION

When a concoction called **photochemical smog**—the product of sunlight acting on auto and industrial exhausts—became our major air pollutant, nature's job of cleaning the air became even more demanding. Not surprisingly, transportation is still the single greatest contributor to air pollution in this nation. Chemically, the major gaseous air pollutants are carbon monoxide, nitrogen oxides, and the sulfur oxides, while the major solid components of air pollutants are **hydrocarbons** and particulates. Figure 19.6 shows how smog gathers in a populated area.

Here again lies the root of the industrialization versus preserve the forest debate. To clean the air, we need forests to produce oxygen, but we also need to lumber the forest for industrialization.

HEALTH CONSEQUENCES OF AIR POLLUTION

One danger of these air pollutants is their invisibility. Without formal testing, people never know where the chemicals are being emitted or how much is present. Air pollutants can affect the human body in many ways, some of which are shown in figure 19.7.

photochemical smog
The primary air pollutant; the product of sunlight acting on automobile and industrial exhausts.

hydrocarbons
Organic compounds of hydrogen and carbon that have a high energy content and are often used as fuel.

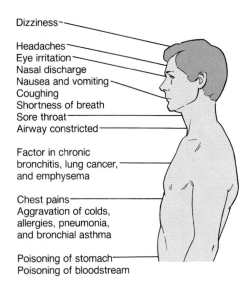

Dizziness

Headaches
Eye irritation
Nasal discharge
Nausea and vomiting
Coughing
Shortness of breath
Sore throat
Airway constricted

Factor in chronic
bronchitis, lung cancer,
and emphysema

Chest pains
Aggravation of colds,
allergies, pneumonia,
and bronchial asthma

Poisoning of stomach
Poisoning of bloodstream

Figure 19.7
Some possible effects of air pollution on the human body.

THE GREENHOUSE EFFECT AND GLOBAL WARMING

The **greenhouse effect** (fig. 19.8) is the "effect that the accumulation of carbon dioxide and other gases in the earth's atmosphere has on the balance between the energy the earth receives from solar radiation and the energy it loses by radiation from its surface back to space" (Leaf 1989). The Industrial Revolution focused on fossil fuel (coal and oil), whose by-product is, among other gases, carbon dioxide. The carbon dioxide and other greenhouse gases, like methane, nitrous oxide, and chlorofluorocarbons, are largely transparent to the sun's rays, including ultraviolet light, that warm the earth's surface. Usually the sun's warming rays bounce off of the earth's surface and go back out into space; but greenhouse gases act like water vapor—they absorb the longer infrared waves reflected by the earth and trap the warmth in the earth's atmosphere.

This balance of gases is critical. If there were no gases, there would be another ice age, because no warmth would be retained in the atmosphere; but as we produce more gases than necessary to maintain the earth's warmth, a slow warming occurs. Experts differ in opinion on global warming. Some suggest that we are witnessing a slow warming rate of about 0.3 degrees Celsius every decade. This amount may seem trivial, but a warming of between 2 to 5 degrees Celsius is about the difference between current conditions and the last ice age. Others have monitored some temperatures since

1950 (but not in all locations) and failed to detect the warming trend—in fact the temperatures have dropped. If global warming is occurring, it might do the following:

1. Turn fertile and arable areas into deserts and move prime agricultural areas north (e.g., from the United States into Canada) and to higher elevations

2. Melt the polar ice caps and, depending on the amount of melt, raise sea level by 3 to 20 feet, displacing millions of people living near coasts

3. Increase precipitation (heat increases evaporation, but it would likely be unevenly dispersed); produce quick runoffs and increased flooding where winter normally holds water in snow

4. Turn agricultural lands into deserts, causing widespread famine and population displacement

Much research is being done to understand the effects of global warming. Core drillings in Greenland ice show the frequent changes of the world's climate over the past 40,000 years (Lehman 1993). We will learn more and more about this serious problem.

THE THINNING OF THE STRATOSPHERIC OZONE LAYER

Another environmental disturbance that humans are causing is the depletion of the ozone layer in the stratosphere. The **ozone layer** is a kind of shield protecting us from the sun's ultraviolet radiations. Ultraviolet light is divided into three arbitrary subregions, based upon their place on an electromagnetic spectrum. Ultraviolet C includes wavelengths of 200 to 290 nanometers and is the most damaging to life; the ozone layer shields us from exposure to this. Ultraviolet B (wavelengths of 290 to 320 nanometers) is not as damaging to life as ultraviolet C, but it is many times more damaging than ultraviolet A. The pathological consequences of ultraviolet B

greenhouse effect
The effect that the accumulation of carbon dioxide and other gases in the earth's atmosphere has on the balance between the energy the earth receives from solar radiation and the energy it loses by radiation from its surface back into space.

ozone layer
Part of the stratosphere that acts as a shield protecting against the sun's ultraviolet light.

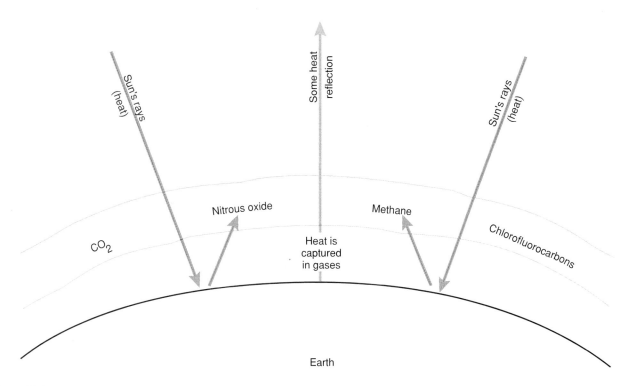

Figure 19.8
The greenhouse effect.

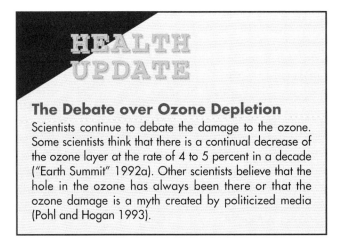

The Debate over Ozone Depletion

Scientists continue to debate the damage to the ozone. Some scientists think that there is a continual decrease of the ozone layer at the rate of 4 to 5 percent in a decade ("Earth Summit" 1992a). Other scientists believe that the hole in the ozone has always been there or that the ozone damage is a myth created by politicized media (Pohl and Hogan 1993).

and C are chiefly attributable to their disruption of DNA and proteins in the body (Leaf 1989). The ozone layer blocks these rays from reaching the earth's surface.

It has been only in the last decade or so that scientists have understood what we are doing to the ozone. Chlorofluorocarbons (used in aerosols), refrigerants, nitrous oxide (from internal combustion engines), and other industrial products rise to the stratosphere, become reactive with the ozone, and destroy the ozone. Ozone is formed naturally by the action of sunlight on the rare molecules of oxygen in the stratosphere. It does regenerate but very slowly. The half-life of recovery of ozone is 3 to 5 years.

In the spring of 1985, a hole in the ozone layer was discovered and thereafter grew to the size of a continent. In March 1988, the thinning of the ozone layer was noted over the North Pole.

HEALTH EFFECTS OF GLOBAL WARMING AND OZONE LAYER DEPLETION

The health effects of global warming via the greenhouse effect and the holes in the ozone were forecast by Leaf (1989) as the following:

1. There will be an increased production of respiratory irritants that will add to the current levels of air pollution and lead to increases in lung diseases such as bronchitis, asthma, and chronic obstructive pulmonary disease.

2. More ultraviolet C radiation will penetrate to the earth's surface and raise the incidence of skin cancers and cataracts.

3. Excessive ultraviolet light will also compromise the immune system, and, in combination with the increasing unsanitary conditions caused by other sources of pollution, this will lead to an increase in infectious diseases.

4. As the ocean levels rise from glacial melting, waterborne infections will also multiply.

5. Decreased food supplies will be the most serious repercussion of global and climatic environmental changes.

REDUCING AIR POLLUTION

Reducing air pollution from any one source is not a simple task. Vehicle emissions alone involve several pollutants, and different pollutants require different reduction methods, each of which has inherent technological problems. However, the greatest hindrance to real progress in reducing air pollution is that we currently value economics and energy above the environment. Until we rearrange our priorities, no fundamental progress will result. As members of this society who care and are concerned about the environment, we must each contribute to making all members of our society more environmentally conscious.

We need to not only reduce the amount of pollution but also plant as many trees and plants as possible. Forests absorb huge amounts of carbon dioxide, more than we originally thought (Hilchey 1993). The preservation of forests is essential to reducing air pollution.

Attempts to clean up the air were spurred by the environmental movement, which had its most profound impact in the early 1970s. The U.S. Environmental Protection Agency was established during these years, and many environmentally related laws were passed. Among these laws were the Clean Air Amendments that specified automobile emission standards for cars produced after 1975 and 1976.

Though major strides in automobile air pollution control were made, none of the clean-air goals were entirely attained. Why? Part of the answer can be traced to our lifestyle values. For example, the Arab oil embargo of 1973–1974 forced a greater change in lifestyle than perhaps any other event in the 1970s. Gone were the days when gasoline cost only 25¢ to 35¢ per gallon. Now a gallon of gasoline costs over $1 and availability is sometimes uncertain.

When a decision had to be made on whether to add the costs of environmental quality to the rising cost of gasoline, politics and economics won out. Auto manufacturers were permitted to delay implementation of costly pollution-control efforts in favor of energy efficiency. Economics and energy, rather than environmental quality, dictated decisions. Hence, our lifestyle values seemed to have shifted.

If we were to reverse this trend, we must act to preserve environmental quality, making it as important as economic and energy considerations. There are reasons why goals related to the big three Es—economics, energy, and environment—should not be pursued simultaneously.

LAND POLLUTION

Ironically, recent efforts to abate water and air pollution have made land pollution an even greater problem than it has been in the past. This is because there are only three repositories for the wastes of society: the land, the water, and the atmosphere. The environment is an interconnected system, and restrictions imposed on any one of these three repositories inevitably lead to an overflow on the other two. For example, restrictions on water disposal of sludge (organic wastes from the treatment of water) have resulted in more land disposal of sludge. The ban on open burning of garbage and debris to reduce air pollution has likewise meant that the burden of disposal has been transferred to the land. Furthermore, the trend is to look more and more to land as the ultimate repository for hazardous chemical and radioactive wastes. The earth has literally become a pit for all undesirable substances.

The sheer increase in the bulk and weight of solid waste has further aggravated the disposal problem. In 1960 each person in the country generated approximately 2.7 pounds of solid waste per day; now that amount had risen to approximately 4 pounds per day. This trend represents about a 1 percent increase in solid wastes per person per year. At the other extreme, each citizen in Calcutta discards about 1 pound of solid waste per day. Over 90 percent of the world's waste is dumped into landfills, at a rate of approximately 340 million metric tons per year (Williams 1993).

Consider all the packaging and wrappings for food, the boxes and bags for clothes, and the plastic we dispose of daily without thinking. It adds up. While the amount of solid waste has grown steadily, the means for its disposal have been limited. Traditionally, solid waste has been incinerated, buried in **sanitary landfills,** or converted by resource recovery **(recycling).**

Each method has inherent benefits and risks. No one method of solid waste disposal is best for all kinds of waste. For example, resource recovery is usually the most environmentally responsible method; however, potential health hazards require incineration rather than recycling of hospital

sanitary landfill
An area where solid waste is buried.

recycling
The reuse of specific materials, such as the aluminum in cans.

Issue

Two Environmental Concerns

In light of the recent Earth Summit in Rio de Janeiro, it has become clear that there are two major concerns in society pertaining to the environment. The economic concerns for industrialized nations as well as for developing countries are to provide jobs and better living conditions and to help the poor, hungry, and homeless; using natural resources will provide jobs, produce lumber for homes, clear land for farming, make land available for housing and cities, and other benefits. The environmental concerns have been emphasized throughout this chapter; using natural resources produces pollution, limits the earth's ability to clean itself up, and kills fish, game, and other wildlife.

- Pro: Why should people who are starving and living in awful conditions today be that concerned about the future? They need to get food, fuel, and shelter today to be able to survive. Technological advances will occur that will help us make artificial trees that will use CO_2, clean the water, and replace the ozone layer, and we'll be able to propel all of our pollutants into outer space.

- Con: How important is it to be able to produce steel, plastics, and other industrialized products when you can't even breathe clean air, drink pure water, or enjoy a natural setting that is not trashed? This whole world needs to work together and help each other out of this mess or we'll all end up poisoning ourselves. The United States should have signed the biodiversity treaty, and then many others, until we have solutions to our diminishing natural environment.

Discuss this with your class.

Issue

Government Regulation of Pollution

Many people feel that the government has been too lenient in the legislative laws and guidelines regarding pollution. Technology exists to dramatically reduce the amount of air pollutants produced by automobiles and factories, but the stricter guidelines have not been imposed. These people feel that allowing factories to dump moderate amounts of pollutants into lakes and oceans is being too lenient. People want the governments—federal, state, and local—to crack down.

- Pro: It is easier to prevent problems than to clean up pollutants. There is a limited amount of water and land, and if we as a society mess it up, then we will have to live or die with it. Future generations depend on our cracking down now.

- Con: If the government were to crack down harder, it would cost billions of dollars to install the high-tech pollution devices in cars and industry. The costs of automobiles, which are already high because of the additional pollution devices, will skyrocket; and each product that is manufactured in a factory that installs pollution controls will also skyrocket in price. The consumer loses if these devices are installed, because the factory must continue to make money or it will go out of business.

How are you going to vote when "tough" environmental legislation is proposed?

---

wastes. In selecting the best disposal method, people must consider energy and economics; however, as with air quality enhancement, lifestyle values should guide attitudes and actions. The time for solid waste to be "out of sight, out of mind" has passed. The country is in sight of land pollution, and people must exercise their insight to minimize its hazardous effects on health and environment.

The Resource Conservation and Recovery Act (RCRA) and the Comprehensive Environmental Response, Compensation, and Liability Act (CERCLA, or Superfund) are the two current federal laws governing regulation of present and future land disposal practices and cleanup. The Toxic Substances Control Act (TSCA) is the federal law that regulates the production and use of new chemicals and previously unregulated chemicals. Before a new chemical can be produced for industrial or commercial use, the EPA must review the available toxicological database. The EPA has the power to regulate any chemical judged to pose an unreasonable risk of injury to human health or to the environment. Types of control include labeling, banning, disposal methods, exposure precautions, and required consumer information.

NOISE POLLUTION

With technology, increasing population, more air travel, and industrialization comes more noise. With construction equipment, amplifiers, jet engines, street traffic, trains, school bells, vacuum cleaners, televisions, compact disc players, and other noisemakers, we are abusing our ears. This abuse often results in hearing dysfunctions. Hearing loss results from destruction of the delicate hair cells in the inner ear. These hair cells convert fluid vibrations in the inner ear into nerve impulses that are carried to the brain, resulting in the sensations of sound. Damage to the hair cells can cause partial hearing loss, such as a softening of sounds or a loss of certain frequencies (generally the higher frequencies) or complete hearing loss. Hearing loss is generally associated with prolonged exposure to noise of over 70 to 85 decibels (Nadakavukaren 1986).

Noise-induced hearing loss is progressive and is usually not accompanied by such overt symptoms as pain or bleeding. Noise has been implicated in both temporary (acute) and cumulative (chronic) effects on human health. Sudden noises can produce immediate blood vessel dilation, increases in blood pressure, heart-rate changes, and hormonal secretions. Continuous noise can exact a toll on mental health and increase our susceptibility to infection and gastric disorders. Steady levels of loud noise have led to a higher incidence of cardiovascular and balance problems among exposed workers than among nonexposed workers (Evans 1982). In addition to these problems, nerve damage from loud noises can produce hearing impairment that can't be restored by hearing aids or surgical procedures.

How irritating and damaging sound is depends on frequency (pitch) and amplitude. Pitch measures the speed of the vibrations in **hertz (Hz).** People can hear from 10 to 20,000 Hz. Amplitude is a measure of the force behind the vibration or loudness. Amplitude is measured in **decibels (dB),** which range from 0 (where normal ears can begin to hear) to 194 (the theoretical maximum loudness of pure tones). Decibels are logarithmic, which means that 20 dB is one hundred times as loud as 0, 30 dB is 1,000 times as loud as 0 dB, and so on. Comparative sounds and measured decibels are shown in table 19.2.

Excessive noise not only results in hearing loss but is a safety hazard as well, being responsible for many accidents. A worker in an auto glass factory caught his hand in a piece of equipment and screamed for help, but no one could hear him to come to his aid because of excessive factory noise, and he lost his hand. Two people who were waiting to see Senator Robert Kennedy's funeral train pass through the city were struck by a locomotive because they hadn't heard the warning whistle, which had been drowned out by the noise of the news media helicopters and secret service. While jogging or walking on streets, many of us listen to music with headphones and never hear oncoming cars. Many people have been struck by vehicles while doing this.

The federal government has tried to reduce excessive noise with the passage of the Noise Control Act, which regulates new commercial products that are considered to be major noise sources. Regulations mandating mufflers on cars have greatly reduced city noise.

You can control how much noise you are exposed to and how much hearing damage you will suffer. If you are forced to work around or be around loud noises, you can wear ear protectors. You can choose to be in front of the speakers at a concert or a dance or to be farther away from them.

TABLE 19.2 SOUND LEVELS AND HUMAN RESPONSE

Common Sounds	Noise Level (dB)	Effect
Air-raid siren	140	Painfully loud
Jet takeoff	130	
Discotheque	120	Maximum vocal effort
Pile driver	110	
Garbage truck	100	
City traffic	90	Very annoying, hearing damage
Alarm clock	80	Annoying
Freeway traffic	70	Phone use difficult
Air conditioning	60	Intrusive
Light auto traffic	50	Quiet
Living room	40	
Library	30	Very quiet
Broadcasting studio	20	
	10	Just audible
	0	Hearing begins

Source: U.S. Environmental Protection Agency.

ENVIRONMENTAL THREATS FROM NUCLEAR POWER PLANTS

The benefits of nuclear energy are unquestioned. In a day of diminishing oil reserves when there is a need to have oil shipped from countries experiencing political unrest, having nuclear power is a good supplement. The dangerous part of nuclear power plants is the potential for massive destruction if accidents occur. The worst nuclear power disaster thus far occurred in the Soviet Union.

THE CHERNOBYL DISASTER

In April 1986, in Chernobyl, U.S.S.R., a 1,000-megawatt nuclear power plant suddenly broke down and resulted in the world's worst nuclear accident. From the resulting fire billowed smoke, gas, and radioactive particles into the air, causing radioactive fallout all over Europe and even in parts of the United States. It will be years before the total loss of life

---

hertz (Hz)
A measure of how irritating and damaging sound is. Hertz is the pitch of sound as indicated by the speed of the vibrations.

decibel (dB)
A numerical expression of the relative loudness of sound.

from this disaster is known, because not all resulting cancers have occurred yet. The process leading to the disaster had six steps:

1. The cooling system for the reactor failed.
2. The uranium fuel melted.
3. The graphite overheated and flammable gases resulted.
4. The mix exploded.
5. Radiation billowed out.
6. Emergency response measures faltered.

One part of the aftermath of the Chernobyl accident is the psychological scars on the inhabitants. Levels of anxiety about having radiation sickness and cancers, stress, and a strong desire to move away or have the government relocate them were prevalent among those who lived in the contaminated areas around Chernobyl (Ginzburg 1993).

THE THREAT OF NUCLEAR EXPLOSION

Radiation fallout can kill immediately or linger in the body for decades. The rem is the unit of measure for radiation. The following represents the dosage and health consequences:

Exposure	Effect
5,000 rem	Kills almost immediately
1,000 rem	Kills within days
400 rem over several days	Kills half of its victims within a month
150 rem over a week	Survivable

Radiation from fallout affects people differently, but it often causes immediate loss of appetite, nausea, and diarrhea. Often these initial symptoms disappear after a week, inducing a false sense of recovery. Then high fever sets in, and victims lose weight and become lethargic as their gastrointestinal tracts lose the ability to absorb nutrients. Damage to blood-forming tissue produces a drastic lowering of the white blood cell count, leaving the victim prey to infection.

It is important to be aware of these threats and be active politically, demanding that these energy-producing plants be carefully monitored and maintained.

EXAMPLES OF ENVIRONMENTAL LESSONS

In 1989, a widely publicized event was the oil spill along the Alaskan coast in Prince William Sound when the *Valdez*, an Exxon oil tanker, struck a reef and spilled 11 million gallons of oil. The captain was found to be intoxicated, and the result was a $2.5 billion cleanup operation and a devastating impact on the environment and wildlife. Some three hundred lawsuits were filed against Exxon and individuals, and

settlements have exceeded $1 billion. The disaster continues to be a source of controversy, with Exxon researchers claiming that there have not been any long-range effects on the environment ("Exxon Valdez Controversy Revived" 1993) and Alaskan authorities claiming there was a heavy impact from the spill and asking for more compensation (Pain 1993).

Saddam Hussein committed acts of ecoterrorism during the Gulf war. While the world community fights to limit waste, recycle, conserve, and protect, it is amazing how one man can cause so much destruction in such a short time. At the end of the war, when troops from Iraq were withdrawing from Kuwait, the orders from Hussein were to destroy the oil wells of Kuwait before they left. The consequences were devastating:

1. About 1,000 oil wells were destroyed.
2. Approximately 600 were set ablaze like orange fireballs all over the desert. It took until the fall of 1991 for these fires to be extinguished, after they had burned up enormous amounts of crude oil.
3. Oil was dumped into the Gulf waters, leaving a major oil slick that threatened the extinction of several species of sea life.
4. The smoke from the oil fires caused black clouds to cover areas of Kuwait. It appeared as night at noon. Soot from the fires fell like snowflakes, and oil droplets fell like greasy black rain. Temperatures were 20 degrees Fahrenheit hotter under the black clouds (Elmer-DeWitt 1991).

These selfish, thoughtless acts will take years for the area to recover from.

Underground petroleum pipelines have also been shown to have spills, even with careful inspections. For example, 358,000 gallons of diesel oil spilled from an underground pipe near Washington, D.C., in March 1993. The spill contaminated Sugarland Run Creek and part of the Potomac River ("Spill Prompts Policy Review" 1993). The Federal Department of Transportation will have to impose more stringent regulations on underground pipelines.

Contaminated sites that have been discovered where the land has been ruined include the "valley of the drums" near Louisville, Kentucky, where 17,000 drums (of which 6,000 were full of chemicals) were discovered. Apparently the owner of the land had been paid by industrial firms to haul their wastes to an approved site. Instead, he pocketed the money and dumped the chemicals on his own land, in some cases dumping the chemicals on the soil so he could reuse the drums. In Iberville Parish, Louisiana, a 19-year-old man was killed when a load of the chemical he dumped into a waste pit reacted with other chemicals there, forming a cloud of hydrogen sulfide gas that enveloped him and paralyzed

PERSONAL INSIGHT

The Love Canal

In 1963, Frank and his wife Suzanne bought a new, modest home for a great price in a small residential suburb of Niagara Falls, New York. They loved their little home, and the newlyweds were anxious to begin a family. There was a school near their new home and life was good.

Frank and Suzanne began to smell some horrible odors, as did others in their neighborhood, but that was not unusual for an industrial city. Frank and Suzanne had two children, and there were now four of them living in their home. In the mid 1970s during some heavy rains, Frank and Suzanne began to see chemicals oozing through their basement walls. Outside, they saw puddles of chemical wastes that never evaporated. Vegetation became scorched, and lawns died. There were holes that opened up in fields revealing large, corroded, leaking chemical drums. With neighbors, Frank and Suzanne complained to city officials and were not initially responded to; instead they received assurances that

everything was okay. Finally, in 1978, the EPA began to test the area around Frank and Suzanne's home and found twelve known carcinogens in the basements of the houses and in the soil. It was then that Frank and Suzanne heard the whole story.

The Love Canal was a dream of William Love, who dug the 7-mile navigable canal from above Niagara Falls to below the falls. His dream was to build a model industrial city using hydroelectric power. Mr. Love's dream faded when he went bankrupt in 1927, but the canal was used for fishing and recreation and was annexed by the city. In 1947, Hooker Chemical Company bought the land and received permission to dump chemical wastes into the canal. Over the years 21,000 tons of chemical wastes, acids, alkalis, solvents, and chlorinated hydrocarbons were disposed of at this sight. By 1953, the canal was so full of waste that it filled in and began to grow over with grass and weeds. Not many homes were near the area at the time, but Hooker then sold the site to the city for a token dollar.

Frank and Suzanne's home was built over the Love Canal. The EPA found benzene, dioxin, and numerous other chemicals. Finally, the area was condemned and President Carter proclaimed the area a national emergency. The state purchased Frank and Suzanne's home as well as those of their neighbors and they moved to another part of town. Frank and Suzanne and about five hundred other families were moved. Frank, Suzanne, and their two children seem to be okay at this writing, but studies of some of the other families are finding indications of elevated rates of miscarriage, birth defects, and chromosomal damage. The city did a lot to try to make the land safe for homes, and Frank and Suzanne noticed in the paper in 1990 that their old house on Love Canal was back on sale. The warning in the paper was that "the homes are safe, but not guaranteed." Many lawsuits, including Frank and Suzanne's, are still pending against Hooker Chemical, which ultimately became a subsidiary of Occidental Petroleum.

---

his lungs. The pit was operating without a permit. In Montague, Michigan, the Hooker Chemical Company built a factory that produced a highly toxic pesticide C-56. The factory had allowed the C-56 to be vented into the air near the tourist town of White Lake and had also let the C-56 ooze through the floor and onto the work areas below. Two billion gallons of ground water had been contaminated, and a million gallons of carcinogenic water flowed into White Lake daily (Nadakavukaren 1986).

More than a dozen serious accidents have plagued the U.S. effort to tame nuclear power. Among the worst ("The Chernobyl Syndrome" 1986):

1. 24 July 1959: A blocked cooling system caused twelve of forty-three fuel elements to melt in an experimental power reactor at Santa Susana, California, near Los Angeles. Radioactivity was contained.

2. 3 January 1961: Control rods were removed in error from the core of a military experimental reactor near Idaho Falls, Idaho. This caused a steam explosion that killed three technicians, one of whom was impaled by a control rod. These were the only deaths so far in the U.S. reactor operations. Radiation levels were very high in the plant, but the damage was contained.

3. 5 October 1966: Failure of a sodium cooling system caused a partial core meltdown at the Enrico Fermi demonstration breeder reactor 30 miles from Detroit. Radiation was contained.

4. 5 June 1970: A false signal from a meter at Commonwealth Edison's Dresden II plant in Morris, Illinois, was blamed for a 2-hour loss of control. A buildup of radioactive iodine at one hundred times the permissible level was contained.

5. 19 November 1971: The waste storage space at the Northern States Power Company's reactor in Monticello, Minnesota, filled to capacity and spilled over. More than 50,000 gallons of radioactive waste water flowed into the Mississippi River, and some was taken into the St. Paul water system.

6. 22 March 1975: A technician using a candle to check for air leaks set fire to electrical insulation at the Brown's Ferry reactor in Decatur, Alabama; cables controlling safety equipment burned out, and the cooling water fell to dangerous levels before a makeshift system was devised. No radioactive material was released.

7. 28 March 1979: In the worst U.S. commercial nuclear accident so far, a series of equipment failures and

THE WORLD AROUND YOU

Earth Day

In the spirit of Earth Day, it is extremely important to make a decision and encourage local, state, and national governments to deal effectively with the environmental dilemmas we face. Should we try to do something to help prevent continual pollution, the destruction of the ozone, and the greenhouse effect? Granted, on an international level, we need to continue to provide active political support for the international attempts at dealing with these problems, but it is here in the United States that we can make a significant impact. The United States, by its unwillingness to sign the Biodiversity Treaty, has set itself up as negative influence on the world cooperative efforts to preserve the earth's natural resources. The United States has only 5 percent of the world population but uses 25 percent of the world's energy and emits 22 percent of the carbon dioxide produced. The U.S. secretary of the interior gave permission to loggers to cut down 1,700 acres of ancient forest in the Pacific Northwest that is home to the threatened spotted owl, an endangered species. This will add to the thousands of animal species that have already become extinct.

human mistakes led to a loss of coolant and partial core meltdown at the Three Mile Island reactor in Middletown, Pennsylvania. The Nuclear Regulatory Commission later concluded that the plant came within an hour of catastrophic meltdown. Some radiation escaped into the air, but health risks were found to be minimal.

8. 7 August 1979: Highly enriched uranium was released from a secret nuclear-fuel plant near Erwin, Tennessee, and about a thousand people were contaminated with up to five times as much radiation as they would normally receive in a year.

9. 11 February 1981: Eight workers were contaminated when 110,000 gallons of radioactive coolant leaked into the containment building of the Tennessee Valley Authority's Sequoyah plant in Tennessee.

10. 25 January 1982: A steam-generator pipe broke at Rochester Gas & Electric Company's Ginna plant near Rochester, New York. Radioactive water spilled into the containment vessel, and some radioactive steam escaped into the air.

11. 9 June 1985: At least sixteen equipment failures and human error started a sequence similar to the Three Mile Island failure at Toledo Edison's Davis-Besse plant in Oak Harbor, Ohio. But auxiliary cooling pumps averted damage to the core.

12. 4 January 1986: A cylinder of uranium hexafluoride, a chemical used in nuclear-fuel production, was

improperly heated at a Kerr-McGee plant at Gore, Oklahoma. One worker died and a hundred were hospitalized; small levels of radiation were detected in the area.

RECYCLING

At the personal level you can help by recycling. New industries are springing up all over America to help recycle materials for continued use, thereby reducing the demand on landfills. Try to purchase products that have been recycled; this encourages reuse and encourages the formation and profitability of recycling companies. Recycle a variety of products that you use on a regular basis. Check your local community for locations to deposit recyclable materials. The following list identifies recyclable materials and how to prepare them for return.

1. Metals. Scrap metal dealers might accept some large appliances. Call first. Higher prices might be paid if metals are separate and clean.
2. Aluminum. Siding, cans, gutters, and other materials can be recycled at centers in most communities. Place them in a reusable trash barrel.
3. Tin cans. Rinse cans out. Remove ends and labels.
4. Plastics. Plastic beverage containers such as 2-liter pop bottles (#1 PET) or plastic milk and water containers (#2 HDPE) are currently accepted at some local supermarkets if washed and flattened. One company is now using recycled plastic bottles to make clothes.
5. Glass containers. Separate according to color (clear, brown, green) and rinse. Labels are okay to leave on.
6. Newspapers. Bundle newspapers with string for convenience and drop them off at scouting recycling bins, some stores, or recycling centers.
7. Cardboard. Must be unwaxed and corrugated, like a pizza box.
8. Paperboard. Unwaxed boxes such as those for crackers, cereal, and powdered laundry detergent. Just remove the inner linings before recycling.
9. Magazines. Take the magazines to doctor's offices, hospitals, nursing homes, day-care centers, barber shops, beauty shops, laundromats, tire stores, and other places that have waiting rooms where people may enjoy them (check with the organization first).

PROGRESS

We are making some progress. All representatives at the Earth Summit in Rio agreed that polluters should pay for the cost of pollution, that poverty should be eradicated, and that appropriate demographic policies should be adopted (e.g., birth control). Additionally, in 1982, after 10 years of hard negotiation, the Convention on the Law of the Sea was signed by 119 countries (only 35 have ratified it at this point), to give each country a 200-mile zone from their coast

TABLE 19.3 FEDERAL AGENCIES THAT HELP REGULATE POLLUTANTS

Area	Agency
Transportation	Department of Transportation
	U.S. Environmental Protection Agency
	U.S. Coast Guard
Waste disposal	U.S. Environmental Protection Agency
Air quality	U.S. Environmental Protection Agency
Water quality	U.S. Environmental Protection Agency
Spills	U.S. Environmental Protection Agency
Nuclear wastes	Nuclear Regulatory Agency
Drinking water	U.S. Environmental Protection Agency
Food	Food and Drug Administration
Other consumer products	Consumer Product Safety Commission
Fish and wildlife	Department of the Interior Fish and Wildlife Service
Occupational safety	Occupational Safety and Health Administration
Chemicals	U.S. Environmental Protection Agency
Pesticides	U.S. Environmental Protection Agency

Reprinted by permission of Waveland Press, Inc., from Anne Nadakavukaren, *Man & Environment: A Health Perspective*, Second Ed., Copyright © 1986, 1984. Third Edition published 1990 by Waveland Press, Inc., Prospect Heights, Illinois.

PERSONAL SKILLS AND EXPERIENCES

PNI Action

The essence of these PNI action boxes is to help you fortify yourself against disease. You can do this through positive mind and soul states. Exposure to positive environments can elevate moods and promote the maximization of the immune system. Studies cite how the environment aids in the healing process or, conversely, can trigger stress (Evans 1982). Hospital patients who recover in hospital rooms with windows seem to heal faster than those without a window. Conversely, the incidence of disease increases when temperature inversions occur and it is gloomy outside. Temperature inversions and being confined indoors promote depression, which in turn diminishes the effectiveness of the immune system.

To maximize your ability to avoid disease and to feel better, take as many opportunities as you can to be in clean, natural environments. Some people who experience temperature inversions in valleys by mountains will take the opportunity to drive up the mountain and get above the inversion layer to experience increased warmth, fresh air, and sunshine. People in cities will take opportunities to go to the local park and read or do work in order to invigorate their immune system.

for exclusive economic purposes but also with the responsibility to improve and maintain it. The Montreal Protocol on substances that deplete the ozone layer was established in 1987 and has been signed by 35 countries. It froze the production of chlorofluorocarbons at 1986 levels and mandates a 20 percent reduction by 1993 and a further decrease by 1998. Other conferences and meetings, such as the International Council of Scientific Unions and the World Meteorological Organization, are all trying to deal with the issue of ozone layer destruction. The U.S. government has several agencies to help regulate pollutants (see table 19.3).

Some attempts have been made to limit factory emissions by selling "pollution credits." Unfortunately, some companies are selling their "credits" (their rights to pollute) to other companies, so distribution problems are arising.

Recently Los Angeles, known as a city with a major air pollution problem, met the federal clean air standard for nitrogen oxide for the first time since monitoring began in 1976 ("The Los Angeles Area . . ." 1993).

Perhaps the most important evidence of progress is the growing awareness of environmental health among the citizens of the world. If we all do our own personal part to clean the environment, and the world leaders continue to talk, we may be able to work ourselves out of this problem. Hopefully we will be able to breathe fresh air, picnic next to clean natural waters, and live on unpolluted soil for many years to come.

PERSONAL SKILLS AND EXPERIENCES

Preserving and Benefiting from the Environment

Mind

There are several positive experiences that you can have to enrich your mind, pertaining to environmental health.

1. Set aside some time to consider how you can reduce your exposure to pollution through daily habits. How will you recycle products, dispose of oil or other chemicals, conserve energy in your home, or reduce the amount of trash you dispose of?

2. Write a letter to a representative or senator at the local, state, or national level on environmental issues around your home. It is surprising how few unsolicited letters some lawmakers receive. In conversation, one state senator said that if she received four or five unsolicited letters on an issue, it was of major importance.

3. Be mindful when exposed to positive elements of nature. For example, focus on the pleasure of clean water around you. Sense the refreshment of taking a shower or a bath, or swimming in a pool or a natural body of water. When in a park or other natural surroundings, be mindful of the energizing experience.

Body

In this chapter we have discussed the potential environmental hazards you might face on a regular basis. To protect your body and reduce your exposure to some of these toxic elements in our environment, there are several things that you can do:

1. Wear earplugs when anticipating being exposed to loud noises (rock concerts, construction equipment, etc.).

2. Wear a filter mask on high-air-pollution days.

3. Assure yourself that you are drinking water that is clean.

4. Choose a place to live that is environmentally healthy.

5. Keep your own living conditions free from environmental hazards by cleaning, avoiding aerosols, and disposing of household chemicals properly.

6. Assure that your home is low in radon gas concentration.

7. At your workplace, identify any potential environmental hazard, wear appropriate protective clothing to avoid exposure, and do something about getting the hazard cleaned up.

Soul

Intuitively, many of us sense some benefit from being in natural environments. Although there has been limited modern scientific evidence demonstrating an energy transfer, there is something intuitive about what happens when we embrace natural surroundings. Those of us who try this and become advocates through firsthand experience realize that it takes us to a higher level of consciousness and energy. These insights as they pertain to interdependence in the environment will become truths for you as you participate in and experience them. If, when you are done, you feel the benefit, then it is a truth and benefit for you, and you will want to continue having such experiences. We can realize harmony between ourselves and our environment. We feel connected rather than isolated and estranged from others. We feel ourselves as part of a divine, dynamic interrelated universe.

Some of the following activities might sound strange, but try them and see how you feel.

1. Meditate in stillness. In a natural setting, immerse yourself in the landscape, relax your body, do some relaxation techniques, observe the natural flow of your breath, and do not try to control it. During the pauses between inhalation and exhalation, focus on what you are feeling in the present.

2. Gaze at stars. Select music that makes you feel in harmony with nature, take a portable audiocassette player, lie down on a blanket away from street lights on a clear night and gaze at the stars. Then turn on the music softly and marvel at the magnificent universe.

3. Gaze at a campfire or fireplace. If you have a chance to sit around a campfire or a fireplace in your home, just gaze into the naturalness of the fire. Feel the warmth, watch the mesmerizing flames dancing, listen to the crackling. It is warm, assuring, and cleansing, and it provides a natural type of meditation.

4. Become part of nature. Go to a place in a natural setting and sit motionless for 20 minutes and wait for nature to return to its natural state. When you arrive, you generally disrupt or scare animals, so just sit motionless for a time, then observe natural happenings around you. Try to blend in. Listen for the silences between the sounds.

Personal Contributions to Maintaining the Environment

Circle the number in front of each item that you have done or are doing.

1. When camping or when I do not have access to culinary water, I purify water (or would purify water) using tablets according to instructions or boil it before drinking.
2. On high-pollution days, I wear a mask in extended exposure to the smog.
3. During temperature inversions, I try to reduce the buildup of air pollution by not burning in fireplaces and reducing my automobile travel as much as possible.
4. I have visited my water or sewage treatment facilities and water sources.
5. I try to avoid known carcinogens such as vinyl chloride, asbestos, benzene, mercury, X rays, and so on.
6. I make sure my car is tuned and has functional emission-control equipment.
7. I avoid noise pollutants (I sit away from speakers at concerts, select an apartment away from busy streets or airports, and so on).
8. I have written my representative in state or federal government about environmental issues.
9. I avoid using aerosol sprays.
10. I recycle plastics.
11. I recycle metals.
12. I recycle aluminum.
13. I reuse materials such as grocery shopping bags, cardboard boxes, etc.
14. I recycle tin cans.
15. I recycle glass containers.
16. I recycle newspapers.
17. I recycle cardboard.
18. I purchase recycled products.
19. I use products that have minimal packaging and avoid plastics.
20. I use as few paper products as possible.
21. I dispose of hazardous materials (old car batteries, used oil, or used antifreeze) at gas stations or other appropriate sites.
22. If I have children or when I have children, I will use a diaper service as opposed to disposable diapers.

Scoring and Interpretation

Count how many items you have circled. Ideally, you can be doing all these things, but if you are trying to do at least some, you can score yourself as follows:

17–22	Good contributions to maintaining the environment
12–16	Moderate contributions to maintaining the environment
Below 12	Need to consider the recommendations made in this chapter to help the environment

SUMMARY

1. In this day of rapid world population growth and high technology, the concern over food supplies, waste disposal, and nuclear accidents is evident.

2. Water from both ground and surface sources is being contaminated from the air (acid rain) and through waste dumping.

3. Legislative efforts have been enacted to prevent some dumping, but more must be done.

4. Much has been done in the fight for pure water, but more must be accomplished.

5. The air we breathe is contaminated by numerous chemicals, and it is wise for us on particularly smoggy days to stay indoors or breathe through a mask.

6. Concern over indoor air is also more evident today, given our "airtight" energy-efficient homes.

7. Noise pollution is a subtle form of pollution with no really painful symptoms, but it gradually results in hearing loss. Noise is also responsible for numerous accidents.

8. Land pollution came to the forefront of American awareness during the Love Canal incident in the 1970s and subsequent incidents with dumping infractions.

9. Perhaps the most devastating demonstration of the potential for problems is uncontrolled nuclear energy, such as the world saw during the Chernobyl incident.

10. With all these potential dangers, it is important for citizens to be aware and active in politics to control the threats to our environment.

11. A pollution-free environment is critical to physical health as well as to positive attitudes and outlooks.

COMMITMENT ACTIVITIES

1. The Environmental Protection Agency carefully monitors the water supplies of cities. Some sources are completely safe, others are marginal, and some water supplies contain chemicals or elements that are above recommended standards. Cities are given imperatives to clean up the water supply by certain dates. As a class, find out about the water source in your community and compare its safety to that of other communities' water supplies.

2. A good class project is to assess the environmental condition of your campus or community. Team up and examine the water treatment plant, discover the method for waste disposal (track your waste from your apartment or dorm to where it is deposited), determine the acid rain threat, and assess the degree of air pollution—report back to class.

3. When you go to your home or apartment, do a safety check. Look for anything that could cause an accident and check to see if you are prepared in case of an accident. For example, is there loose carpet that could cause someone to trip, particularly around stairs? Do you have a fire extinguisher and smoke alarm? Do you know how to call for emergency vehicles (is the 911 system available in your area?), and do you have other numbers posted? Do you have any exposed electrical wires, overloaded circuits, or dangerous appliances? Have you recently had your natural gas line checked for leaks? Are there any potential fire hazards, such as turpentine or gas that is not in sealed metal containers?

4. Locate the nuclear plant nearest to where you live. If it is close, visit it and ask questions regarding its safety and maintenance.

5. Learn to purify water several ways: using boiling, water purification tablets, or chlorine. Outdoor stores or sporting goods outlets often carry literature and tablets.

6. Learn about sewage treatment. How is sewage treated in your community? What is done with it after it is treated? Learn how people who are not on sewer lines deal with waste. Learn about septic tanks and drainage (leach) lines, and the kinds needed for particular kinds of soil (percolation tests). You can learn about this from your local health department.

REFERENCES

"Air Pollution Information Activities at State and Local Agencies—United States, 1992." 1993. *Journal of the American Medical Association* 269, no. 5 (3 February): 572–73.

Castleman, M. 1993. "Seeping Problems." *Sierra*, July–August, 44–45.

Dao, J. 1993. "A New, Unregulated Market: Selling the Right to Pollute." *New York Times*, 6 February, 1.

"Earth Summit." 1992a. *Time*, 1 June, 42–65.

"Earth Summit." 1992b. *Time*, 15 June, 35.

Elmer-DeWitt, P. 1991. "A Man-Made Hell on Earth: The Ecological Devastation of Kuwait Is Worse Than Imagined, but It Is Not the Planet-Wide Catastrophe That Some Predicted." *Time*, 18 March, 36.

Evans, G. W. 1982. *Environmental Stress*. Cambridge: Cambridge University Press.

"Exxon Valdez Controversy Revived." 1993. *Oil and Gas Journal* 91, no. 17 (16 April): 26–27.

"First Penalties Levied Under U.S. Oil Pollution Act." 1993. *Oil and Gas Journal* 91, no. 8 (22 February): 44.

Gardels, N., and M. B. Snell. 1993. "Mexico City Is an Omen: A Warning for Us About the Cost of Modern Progress." *Unte Reader*, January–February, 94.

Ginzburg, H. M. 1993. "The Psychological Consequences of the Chernobyl Accident: Findings from the International Atomic Energy Study." *Public Health Reports* 108, no. 2 (March–April): 182–84.

Grisham, J. W., ed. 1986. *Health Aspects of the Disposal of Waste Chemicals*. New York: Pergamon.

Hilchey, T. 1993. "A Forest Absorbs More Carbon Dioxide Than Was Predicted." *New York Times*, 8 June, 89, C4.

Hileman, B. 1993. "Plan to Prevent Climate Change Pleases Industry." *Chemical and Engineering News* 71, no. 11 (15 March): 6.

Leaf, A. 1989. "Potential Health Effects of Global Climatic and Environmental Changes." *New England Journal of Medicine* 321, no. 23:1577–83.

Lehman, S. 1993. "Flickers Within Cycles." *Nature* 361, no. 6411 (4 February): 405.

Nadakavukaren, A. 1986. *Man and Environment: A Health Perspective*. Prospect Heights, IL: Waveland Press.

Nero, A. V., Jr. 1992. "A National Strategy for Indoor Radon." *Issues in Science and Technology* 9, no. 1 (Fall): 33–41.

"Nuclear Winter: Pollution in Russia." 1993. *Economist* 326, no. 7798 (13 February): 84–85.

Oechel, W. C., S. J. Hastings, G. Vourlitis, M. Jenkins, G. Riechers, and N. Grulke. 1993. "Recent Change of Arctic Tundra Ecosystems from a Net Carbon Dioxide Sink to a Source." *Nature* 361, no. 6412 (11 February): 520–23.

Pain, S. 1993. "Exxon Gags Sound Researchers." *New Scientist* 137, no. 1860 (13 February): 6.

Pearce, F. 1993. "North Sea Crude." *Audubon*, May–June, 24–26.

Perera, J. 1993. "Dirty Habits Plague Russia's Health." *New Scientist* 137, no. 1854 (2 January): 9.

Pohl, F., and J. P. Hogan. 1993. "Ozone Politics: They Call This Science." *Omni*, June, 34–39.

Prather, M. J., and R. T. Watson. 1990. "Stratospheric Ozone Depletion and Future Levels of Atmospheric Chlorine and Bromine." *Nature* 344: 720–26.

Raloff, J. 1993. "Cotton, Fleece, and Beads." *Science News* 143, no. 21 (22 May): 332–33.

Rubin, E. S., M. J. Small, C. N. Bloyd, and M. Henrion. 1992. "Integrated Assessment of Acid-Deposition Effects on Lake Acidification." *Journal of Environmental Engineering* 118, no. 1 (January–February): 120–34.

"Spill Prompts Policy Review." 1993. *ENR* 230, no. 15 (12 April): 10.

Stone, R. 1993. "EPA Analysis of Radon in Water Is Hard to Swallow." *Science* 261, no. 5128 (17 September): 1514–16.

"The Chernobyl Syndrome." 1986. *Newsweek*, 12 May, 22–46.

"The Los Angeles Area in 1992 Met the Federal Clean Air Standard for Nitrogen Oxides for the First Time Since Monitoring Began in 1976." 1993. *Oil and Gas Journal* 91, no. 7 (15 February): 2.

"The More the Merrier: Reject the Dismal Prophets of Population Control." 1993. *Eastern Economic Review* 156, no. 19 (13 May): 5.

Walsh, J E. 1993. "The Elusive Arctic Warming." *Nature* 361, no. 6410 (28 January): 300–301.

Williams, M., ed. 1993. *Planet Management*. New York: Oxford University Press.

Woodell, S. R. J. 1989. "Forecasting Our Environmental Future (and That Was the Future)." *Futures* 21: 547–59.

ADDITIONAL READINGS

Caldicott, H. 1992. *If You Love This Planet*. New York: W. W. Norton. Caldicott lays out a plan to heal the earth and addresses the problems of the ozone, toxicity, species extinction, removal of trees, and overpopulation.

Fields, R., P. Taylor, R. Weyler, and R. Ingrasci. 1984. *Chop Wood, Carry Water*. Los Angeles: Tarcher. A book that will help you to become more sensitive to the environment through poetry and readings.

Freudenberg, N. 1984. *Not in Our Backyards: Community Action for Health and the Environment*. New York: Monthly Review Press. A good book on how to be active in controlling environmental pollutants from a political and community standpoint. The focus is on waste removal.

Kaplan, M. 1988. *Earth Song*. Crystal Heart Press. A book on how to become more sensitive to the natural environment.

Rothkrug, P., and R. L. Olson. 1991. *Mending the Earth.* Berkeley, CA: North Atlantic Books. Rothkrug and Olson lay out a plan to deal with the global environmental problems. The plan includes political action, environmental resources, technology, and numerous other dimensions.

Williams, M., ed. 1993. *Planet Management.* New York: Oxford University Press. An amazingly beautiful book with an overview of environmental health that includes beautiful color pictures and illustrations. The book looks like an encyclopedia and deals with specific environmental challenges throughout the world.

Health Products and the Consumer

Healthy People 2000 Objectives

• Increase to at least 75 percent the proportion of pharmacies and other dispensers of prescription medications that use linked systems to provide alerts to potential adverse drug reactions among medications dispensed by different sources to individual patients.

• Increase to at least 75 percent the proportion of primary-care providers who routinely review with their patients aged 65 and older all prescribed and over-the-counter medicines taken by their patients each time a new medication is prescribed.

Personal Consumer Skills

Directions

Circle the numbers in front of all of the following things that you do.

1. I make buying choices largely because of the advertisements I've seen or heard.
2. I read and understand labels on packaged foods before I purchase them for the first time.
3. I use laxatives regularly.
4. I use mouthwashes regularly.
5. I would purchase a name brand aspirin before I would buy a generic or cheap brand.
6. I follow directions carefully when taking medications like aspirin or cold remedies.
7. If a physician gives me a prescription, I always ask about possible side effects of the drug.
8. If a prescription works for me and someone else has the same problem I had, I would share my medications to help him or her get better.
9. I ask friends and family to see if anyone has a prescription medication to treat a problem that I have.
10. I take prescription medication only until I feel better.
11. If I purchased a health product that did not do what it was supposed to do, I would contact the Food and Drug Administration (FDA), the Federal Trade Commission (FTC), or the National Advertising Division (NAD).
12. I take antacids regularly.
13. I almost always take cold remedies when I get a cold.
14. I take sleeping aids.
15. I really don't keep track of how much medicine I use.

Scoring

Use the following key to total your scores. Give yourself the indicated value if you marked an item. Give yourself a zero if you didn't mark an item.

1. = −3
2. = 3
3. = −3
4. = −3
5. = −3
6. = 3
7. = 3
8. = −3
9. = −3
10. = −3
11. = 3
12. = −3
13. = −3
14. = −3
15. = −3

Interpretation

0 to 12	= You are practicing good consumer skills.
−1 to −16	= You will need to read this chapter carefully to improve your consumer skills.
−17 to −33	= You are practicing a number of poor consumer skills.

We are all consumers. Understanding total health and the factors motivating our health behavior, and learning to base our health decisions on sound questions and procedures, are basic to every facet of health. For example, all topics in this text involve consumer decision making. These decisions might relate to health information, health products, or health services.

Because total health relates to continual growth and improvement, there are several steps to creating a personal plan for better health: (1) assessing health-producing and health-destroying behaviors, (2) adopting health-producing behaviors in a systematic way so the behaviors are reinforced, (3) recognizing and accepting good feelings associated with high-level wellness, and (4) cognitively understanding why certain behaviors are related to health and positive feelings (Corry 1983).

All these steps can be accomplished by intelligent health consumers, and the idea is the same whether considering decisions about drugs, exercise programs, stress management, or other health matters. In the past, we may have felt like

Every day we are faced with decisions as consumers of health-care products.

health consumers only when buying a product or service related to medical care, but today consumer decisions are made when starting an exercise program, learning breast self-examination, stopping smoking, selecting medical insurance, and so on.

An example of the four-step process described above can be seen by considering physical fitness. A personal assessment of health-producing and health-destroying behaviors (step 1) might show a great deal of breathlessness when participating in moderate physical activity, a tendency to be completely exhausted at the end of the day, and an undesirable body shape. Adopting health-producing behaviors in a systematic way (step 2) might mean walking up steps instead of using the elevator, initiating a daily exercise program, and controlling food intake a little better. Recognizing and accepting the good feelings that result from the increase in health-producing behaviors (step 3) might be seen in greater personal confidence, increased energy throughout the day, and an improved self-image resulting from a change in body contours. Understanding why certain behaviors are related to health and positive feelings (step 4) is fundamental to the first three steps. This also makes it likely that there will be attempts to increase the incidence of other health-producing behaviors as well.

The entire contents of this text indicates the many topics that require intelligent consumer health decisions. Think for a moment about how consumers make decisions about such a variety of health topics. As decisions are made, certain information about health products, advertising, consumerism, health care, and quackery is basic. In this chapter some of this information is provided, in the hope that it will be applied to health decisions about the many other topics in the text. For consumers of life, it can be no other way.

THE VULNERABLE CONSUMER

Caveat emptor means "Let the buyer beware." Even in this age of warranties and money-back guarantees, most of us have bought a product that didn't work or didn't perform as promised and have found that there was little we could do about it. Like it or not, *caveat emptor* still applies today. This is commonly recognized when entering a used car lot, but it is equally important when making decisions about health products. Government regulations do not protect us from being cheated in the marketplace or ensure that health advertisements in magazines, on television, and on radio are accurate.

ADVERTISING

Because of advertising, we often buy health products we don't need or that don't perform according to our expectations. Advertisers exploit our psychological needs and emotions. An example of where advertising has helped convince us of the need for a product is facial cleansers. Women spend more than half a billion dollars a year on facial cleansers because advertising claims indicate that brand X leaves the skin "retexturized and younger looking," brand Y

"nourishes dry skin to give it more youthful elasticity," and brand Z provides a "refreshing first step to younger-looking skin." As with many cosmetic products, numerous claims are made, but the truth is that, like soap and water, they just take off the makeup ("Facial Cleansers" 1989).

Another example is tanning pills. These pills use a food-coloring agent that, if taken in extremely high doses, actually colors the skin. Not only are the major ingredients illegal for this use, but tanning pills can cause numerous health problems, such as allergic reactions, nausea, diarrhea, and itching and welts on the skin. In addition, they offer no protection from the sun ("Beware of Tanning Pills" 1991).

In a given day, around 23 percent of television time is advertisements. About 31 percent of these commercials contain health messages (Wallack and Dorfman 1992). Most of these messages are not designed to provide accurate and useful health information, but are supposed to make us feel good about a certain product.

Think of all the ads you have seen during the past week on television, in magazines, and in newspapers that concerned health-related products.

To understand our vulnerability to ineffective health products, we can't look at advertising pitches alone. After all, no one forces us to buy that new type of deodorant or that supposedly medicinal soap. To understand why we buy products that don't do any significant good, we must also look at why we are so susceptible to advertising in the first place.

CONSUMER INSECURITIES

We can be cheated when we are not well informed, are anxious about health, or are desperate for an affordable solution to a health problem. Many individuals are convinced that using sleeping pills or "pep" pills is safe without medical supervision. Others believe that copper bracelets cure arthritis, that extra vitamins supply energy, or that garlic cures anything. Some women have been convinced, by advertising and through myths handed down from one generation to the next, that douching is necessary. Interestingly, douching is more common among women who live in poverty. Also, women with less than a high school education are more likely to report douching than those with 16 or more years of schooling (56% versus 16%). Not only is douching unnecessary, but it has been associated with pelvic inflammatory disease (PID) and ectopic pregnancy (Aral, Mosher, and Cates 1992).

We are also vulnerable because we all have some anxiety that something serious could happen to our health or even that we will be disliked if we don't use that special mouthwash. Who hasn't felt some pain or other symptom and wondered if some dreadful disease had finally taken

---

caveat emptor
"Let the buyer beware."

hold? We might hesitate to seek competent medical attention for fear of knowing the truth, and head for the drugstore shelf instead.

The high cost of medical services further complicates the issue of consumer vulnerability. Regardless of whether we pay directly for health services or pay higher insurance premiums to get quality service, the cost is going up. As costs rise, it becomes increasingly tempting to try health products that appear to be less expensive and provide a quick fix. It's certainly cheaper to use a particular skin cream than it is to visit a physician who specializes in skin problems. It costs less to use diet pills than it does to seek medical care for weight control.

In this chapter, there is an emphasis on becoming more aware of vulnerabilities and learning to make more informed and skillful decisions about health products. First we will look at how to evaluate advertising claims about products, then at what to consider in purchasing and using medications, and, finally, at what our options are if we have been bilked or misled in purchasing health-related products. In the next chapter we look at how to make intelligent decisions about health-related services. All these consumer skills are basic to health decisions.

EVALUATING ADVERTISEMENTS

Think of various health-related advertisements from newspapers and magazines (you can even note the wording of an advertisement from television); then analyze each ad for informational content. In other words, how much are you actually told about the product or service in the ad? Which ad gives the least information? Which gives you most? Are they equally appealing?

In light of the many advertising techniques used to separate us from our money, we may feel hopelessly trapped. With so many professionals working to sell something for profit, how can we make wise consumer decisions about health products? First, we must learn how to systematically evaluate the advertising claims being made for a product. This might initially seem to be quite a lengthy process, but the eventual rewards are worth it.

We need to consider the psychological approach being used in ads. For example, is the approach related to emotions, needs, or wants? We must analyze the contents of the ad. What claims are made? Which statements are true? Is there any information left out? What are the positive and negative effects of the product? Is there a guarantee and, if so, what kind? What is the credibility of the people and the organization associated with the product? What questions do we need to ask to analyze the claims presented in the ad? Finally, is there anything about the medium used or the way the ad is presented that will influence our reaction to the ad?

Fortunately, there is help for consumers when it comes to evaluating advertisements and controlling them to some extent. The **Federal Trade Commission (FTC),** an agency

Issue

Advertising for Children

Young children have difficulty distinguishing between programs and commercials. They also have little or no understanding of commercials' persuasive intent. They are therefore very vulnerable to commercial claims and appeals (Kunkel and Roberts 1991).

Therefore, many individuals feel there should be strict controls on advertisements that reach children or on advertisements used in magazines and books and on television when children are the likely audience.

- Pro: Children are not yet mature consumers. They can't be expected to differentiate between accurate and inaccurate information about the latest breakfast cereal or chocolate-flavored syrup and to deal with misleading techniques. It is unethical to submit them to continual bombardment with commercial messages.

- Con: Children are capable of differentiating between accurate and inaccurate information. Ads geared to their level give children opportunities to develop decision-making skills they will need throughout life. It is the responsibility of parents to help their children learn about advertising and not up to the producer or government to control.

What do you think about ads for children? Does freedom of speech enter into this issue? Is it the responsibility of parents and teachers to be sure that children are wise health consumers (and good decision makers) or is that expectation too much? Does the age of the children make any difference?

of the federal government, has the power to halt what it deems deceptive or unfair advertising. A classic example of this occurred when mouthwash manufacturers claimed that their products not only helped combat bad breath but also prevented sore throats and colds, or at least eased their symptoms. The FTC decided that these claims were misleading and that the manufacturers could no longer make them.

Nearly forty other government agencies have some say in how certain types of advertising are presented. For example, the Civil Aeronautics Board looks at airline ads and the Food and Drug Administration reviews ads for pharmaceuticals. The effect of federal action is seen in statements like "Your mileage may vary" or in warnings by the surgeon general about the dangers of cigarette smoking.

FTC
Federal Trade Commission.

There is also some self-regulation. In 1971 several advertising associations and the Council of Better Business Bureaus created a **National Advertising Division (NAD)** to promote standards and handle complaints. The program is voluntary, but the NAD can turn over its findings to a regulatory agency for action.

The media also help, but how carefully ads are screened before they appear on radio and TV, and in newspapers and magazines, varies a great deal. The process often involves specialists in areas such as pharmaceuticals or children's food who look at thousands of ads each year. Children's ads receive special attention.

Some of the best scrutiny comes when the NAD responds to complaints about competitors' misrepresenting the facts, especially when two products are compared. The NAD also initiates its own investigations. Some people feel that advertising in general is now probably fairer, more accurate, and more honest than it has ever been. Many corporations, thanks to the consumer movement, have been forced to be far more public-minded than they were years ago.

Because there is no guarantee that advertisements and other sources of health information will be totally accurate, it is important for consumers to be able to identify differences between accurate and inaccurate information. The checklist in figure 20.1 can be very helpful for this purpose. The first part of the checklist is used to evaluate the qualifications of individual authors, the second part is to be used when an organization, agency, or other institution is the information source, and the third part focuses on the information itself (McKenzie 1987).

DECISIONS ABOUT COMMON DRUGS

Common drugs provide an excellent example of how we must make daily health decisions. Americans live in a drug-oriented society. Early in life we learn that if we don't feel well, we can take a pill to help, and that if we are hurt, we can use medicine to relieve the pain. Later, we learn we can even take pills if we feel too tired or not tired enough. Eventually, we might believe that pills or other medicines can take care of almost every problem. Individuals sometimes use drugs simply because they like their effects. Here the focus is on drugs used mainly as health products.

Drugs used primarily as health products are either **over-the-counter (OTC) drugs** or prescription drugs. Over-the-counter drugs, or proprietary drugs, can be purchased without a doctor's signature. Prescription drugs, by contrast, require a written order from a medical doctor in order to be purchased and can be sold only by a licensed pharmacist.

We need drugs of either type only when we have real health problems. Most of the time, making good health-related decisions and choosing a suitable lifestyle can greatly reduce the likelihood of needing any drugs at all—even in old age. Contrary to what the ads might say, a healthy lifestyle and a little time do cure many ills.

OTC DRUGS

Self-medication with over-the-counter (OTC) drugs is widespread. Most of these drugs are relatively ineffective, they are frequently used unnecessarily, and they may have adverse side effects. Some of the OTC drugs most frequently used and abused are laxatives, mouthwashes, and cold remedies.

Laxatives help eliminate feces and relieve constipation. Often, however, constipation can be relieved by changing dietary patterns, and regular physical exercise can promote regularity as well. Regularity does not necessarily mean a daily bowel movement must occur; thus, laxatives are usually not needed. Moreover, their continued use can be habit forming.

Cold remedies of the past included applying kerosene plasters to the chest or wrapping a dirty sock stuffed with salted pork and onion around the neck. Today's remedies smell better, but they come no closer to curing colds or shortening their duration than the old remedies did. The potency of over-the-counter cold products rivals anything requiring a prescription. All of these remedies, no matter how effective, only relieve symptoms. The infection must run its course ("Cold Remedies: Which Ones Work Best?" 1989).

So-called shotgun cold remedies (those supposedly designed to attack all cold symptoms) do not work well. In fact, research indicates that they often have undesirable side effects (such as drowsiness and impaired mental performance) and are no more effective than placebos are ("Which Cold Remedy Is Right for You?" 1994). When colds are treated, they are cured in about 7 days; if left untreated, they last about a week.

Television commercials give the impression that a wide variety of OTC drugs to relieve pain exist, but there are really only three choices: aspirin, acetaminophen, and ibuprofen. Aspirin, discovered in 1899, is quite common. It is available in several forms—tablets, capsules, buffered (Ascriptin, Bufferin), coated to reduce possible stomach irritation (Easprin, Ecotrin), and time-release. Acetaminophen (marketed as Tylenol, Anacin III, Valadol, Datril) was not widely used until it became a nonprescription drug in 1955. Acetaminophen and aspirin are equally effective for relief of minor pains, but unlike aspirin and ibuprofen, acetaminophen does not suppress inflammation. It does not irritate the stomach, as aspirin can do, but it can upset the stomach. Ibuprofen, available under brand names like Advil, Nuprin, Motrin IB, and Medipren, is one of the newest nonprescription pain medicines on the market. In practice,

NAD
National Advertising Division of the Better Business Bureau.

OTC
"Over-the-counter"—generally refers to drugs.

Question	Response		
	Yes	No	Not sure/Don't know
Part I. The author A. Background information on the author is provided.			
B. The author's educational background is in the discipline in which the author is writing. (Note: Be cautious of impressive titles easily confused with qualified professionals.)			
C. The author is a recognized expert in the discipline in which the author is writing.			
D. The author is a recognized member of a professional health organization in the area in which he/she is writing.			
Part II. The source A. The source is a recognized organization in the health field.			
B. The source is interested in sharing information, not in making a profit.			
Part III. The information A. The author uses misleading comparisons to encourage consumers to draw conclusions, such as "contains twice as much" and "up to eight-hour relief."			
B. The information is based on "personal observations" and not sound scientific data.			
C. The author uses testimonials of "cured" or "satisfied" consumers.			
D. The author uses statements including the words "new," "quick," "secret," or "amazing" as they relate to health.			
E. The information contains all-inclusive statements such as "this approach always works."			
F. The information is an advertisement used to make a profit.			
G. The information is inconsistent with other information on the same topic.			
H. The author uses few or no references to substantiate the point.			
I. The author uses sensationalism to emphasize points, such as "a product like this has never before been available to the public."			
J. The information defies common sense and seems unbelievable.			
"Yes" answers are desired in Parts I and II. "No" answers are desired in Part III.			

Figure 20.1

A checklist for evaluating health information.

aspirin and acetaminophen relieve pain as effectively as, and usually cost less than, ibuprofen ("OTC Pain Medications of Only Three Types Available" 1987; "Which Pain Reliever Is Right for You?" 1993).

DANGERS OF SELF-MEDICATION

There is a big difference between self-care and self-medication. Using OTC drugs is a form of self-medication. According to an old proverb, people who are their own doctors have fools for patients. Even with the current emphasis on optimal health, which includes self-care, this statement retains some truth, particularly when it comes to taking drugs.

What are the potential dangers of self-medication? One is that if we use drugs based on our own advice, we might use them longer than necessary. Also, chemical substances may repress symptoms and delay us from seeking medical treatment until a problem is serious or even uncontrollable. Further, because similar symptoms result from different problems, the wrong condition might be treated. No one likes to have disease symptoms, but they serve a purpose by showing that a health problem exists.

Self-medication can also result in taking drugs in doses that cause bodily damage. If we use more than one medicine at a time, we may alter the effects of each and end up with unintended side effects. In short, when putting chemicals into our bodies, we are betting we will benefit. Self-medication may diminish our chances of winning the bet.

PRECAUTIONS

No medication is completely harmless, and any chemical substance has the potential for problems. Consistent with other health-related decisions, we must decide if any potential risk, no matter how small, is worth the probable benefits from taking a substance.

The first precaution is to use only relatively harmless substances for self-medication (even though no substance is totally harmless). Aspirin, sodium bicarbonate (for simple indigestion), calamine lotion (for mild skin irritations and bites), milk of magnesia (as a laxative), and alcohol (as an antiseptic and for rubbing) can be used for minor problems. Intelligent use is not likely to cause harm.

A second precaution is to pay close attention to OTC drug labels. The labels must list the name of the product, the symptoms the product relieves, the contents, the quantity, the name and address of the manufacturer or packer, directions for use, warnings (such as limits on the length of use, possible side effects, total dosage in a day), and possible drug interactions. In addition, note the expiration date on the label; after that date, the product is not safe to use.

A third precaution is to check with the pharmacist about the OTC medication chosen. The letters **NF** or **USP** appear on some OTC drug labels; official standards for strength, purity, and identity are found in two reference books, the *National Formulary (NF)* and the *United States Pharmacopeia (USP)*, written by pharmaceutical experts. When a drug label contains either set of letters, the drug has been manufactured according to official standards. If your OTC drug labels do not contain all the information cited here, take the medications back to the place of purchase and find out why.

A fourth precaution is to follow label directions exactly; instructions for the use of a drug are given for good reasons. If you exceed the quantity or rate of dosage, you may harm yourself. Any negative reactions to medicine should be reported immediately to a physician or nurse practitioner.

PRESCRIPTION DRUGS

Prescription drugs are usually more powerful than OTC drugs. Prescriptions are required by law because only a trained and appropriate physician can correctly diagnose a specific problem and know the proper medicine and dosage. Those who promote drugs, however, know that while the physician writes the prescription, the patient often guides the pen. Nearly one-third of prescriptions for new products are now written at the request of the patient. This is why drug companies spend so much money promoting new drugs directly to potential consumers ("Miracle Drugs or Media Drugs?" 1992).

If you go to a physician and get a prescription, mention all medications you are using (both OTC and other prescription drugs) and any negative reactions you have had to any drug. Drug interaction can be harmful.

The general points made about OTC drugs also apply to prescription drugs. The labels on prescription drugs, however, do not give some of the basic information found on OTC drug labels. What the drug does, the possible side effects, and appropriate precautions are not usually on the label because it is assumed that this information is provided by the physician. The label is likely to have information on how much to take and how often. Check with your physician and/or druggist about the method of taking a drug and its possible side effects.

Drugs have three different names. One name is based on chemical structure, there is a shorter generic name used by pharmacists and physicians, and there is a brand name used by the manufacturer. For example, a variant of penicillin, which fights bacterial infection, is 6-amino-penicillanic acid, or ampicillin. Some brands are Amcill, Omnipen, and Polycillin. Several companies also make "generic" versions of the drug, which contain the same active ingredients as drugs sold under a brand name. In recent years, consumer interest in **generic drugs** has increased because they are often significantly cheaper than brand-name drugs.

There is a real payoff for shopping for the best price on prescription drugs. Prices for the same drug can vary by 100 percent or more in the same community. A brand-name drug in one pharmacy can cost twenty-two times more than the generic version in another ("Prescription for Savings" 1990).

Generic drugs are supposed to be of the same quality as drugs sold under specific brand names. If generics were always prescribed for the roughly 75 percent of major drugs available in that form, patients and insurers would cut their costs about $1 billion a year. Yet the FTC estimates that no more than $236 million per year is saved. The consumer can help by reminding the physician that generics can save money. This is particularly important because in a recent 10-year period prescription drug prices increased 88 percent—almost three times the general inflation rate and almost twice as fast as prices increased in the rest of the medical industry (Warden 1992).

NF
National Formulary.

USP
United States Pharmacopeia.

generic drugs
Similar compounds that are not necessarily produced under the same brand name.

Emphasis on the money-saving power of generic drugs raises questions about their quality. The **FDA** analyzed samples of the thirty most widely prescribed generics, however, and concluded that generics as a class are not inferior to brand-name drugs ("Update on Generics" 1990).

GUIDELINES FOR BEST RESULTS

Once you have detected a potential medical problem, consulted with a physician, and obtained a prescription drug to help deal with the problem, follow these guidelines to get the best possible results from the medication:

1. Follow the physician's instructions for taking the medicine. The dosage and length of time you take the drug are dictated by your individual situation. Don't stop taking the drug just because you feel better; there is probably a good reason why you are supposed to take it for a certain time period.

2. Ask the physician about possible side effects from the medication. If you have unexpected symptoms or side effects, report the problem to your physician at once.

3. Don't start taking new drugs without your physician's knowledge. Harmful drug interactions may occur.

4. Carefully follow label instructions about storing the medicine. Some drugs need to be refrigerated; others need to be kept dry.

5. Don't take a prescription meant for someone else and don't allow someone else to use one meant for you. The same drug can affect different individuals quite differently. Furthermore, you or the other person may have seriously misdiagnosed the problem.

6. Never mix different tablets or differently dated tablets in one bottle. You or someone—even a child—may take the wrong one and treatment would be difficult to diagnose.

7. When prescription drugs are no longer needed, dispose of them. This removes the temptation to let someone else try them or to use them yourself when they are no longer safe.

8. Find out what should be done if you inadvertently miss a dose.

Attention has been given to so-called "off-label" use of drugs in recent years. Once a drug is approved for one purpose, physicians can prescribe it for other purposes as well. Since the FDA approval process is expensive and takes a relatively long time, sometimes manufacturers will not go through the process just to get FDA approval for a drug that is already on the market. It is often suggested that consumers read the *Physician's Desk Reference (PDR)* to be properly informed about prescribed drugs. In the case of "off-label" prescriptions, however, it will be necessary to consult the *Complete Drug Reference (CDR)* instead. In addition to the FDA-approved uses that are listed in the *PDR*, the *CDR* lists accepted off-label uses—as judged by a panel of experts (Lipman 1993). This is an example of where proper communication with your physician is a must.

Drugs can serve a useful purpose in society. We must respect their value and power, however, and avoid the temptation to take them casually or without good medical cause.

DECISIONS ABOUT HOME HEALTH TESTING

One relatively new health decision relates to the use of do-it-yourself medical testing. Individuals test their eyesight, stool, urine, blood, and blood pressure in search of health clues related to vision problems, gastrointestinal diseases, infection, ovulation, pregnancy, diabetes, hypertension, and other conditions.

In 1993 the FDA approved the home test kit Choles Trac, which should allow you to test your own cholesterol level as accurately as professional testing by a medical laboratory. The home test, however, won't tell you all you need to know about your risk of coronary heart disease and how to lower it. For that, you'll still need to see a physician for a lipid profile, which measures other blood characteristics as well ("A Take Home Test for Cholesterol" 1993).

FDA
Food and Drug Administration.

THE WORLD AROUND YOU

Precautions When Taking Medicine

Taking medicine is an interdependent act in several ways. It is important for you to take them properly because of the interdependence of your treatment with the action of the medicine. Because of the interdependence of drugs with each other, it is crucial to avoid dangerous chemical interactions caused by taking more than one drug at a time without medical supervision. Finally, there is a type of social interdependence related to taking drugs. One person has success with a certain medicine and recommends it to another. This may be fine as long as the other person checks with a physician first to be sure the drug is appropriate; otherwise there is a real danger if one person uses a drug prescribed for another person. In summary, the following precautions relate to interdependence and use of medicines:

1. Many OTC medicines contain the same ingredients. By comparing labels and prices, we can save money, avoid an overdose, and avoid buying two medicines that do the same thing.

2. Many OTC medicines relieve symptoms without curing an illness. If symptoms persist, seek medical assistance.

3. All medicines influence bodily functions. Know what to expect in advance.

4. Medications often lose or gain strength with time. Pay attention to the expiration dates given on labels.

5. A medicine that is safe or appropriate for one person might cause adverse reactions for another. It is dangerous to take a prescription drug intended for another person.

6. It is dangerous to take more or less of a drug than is prescribed.

7. Drug combinations can cause problems. Seek medical help to avoid complications associated with interactions of different chemical substances in the body at the same time.

8. Make sure all tablets have childproof containers.

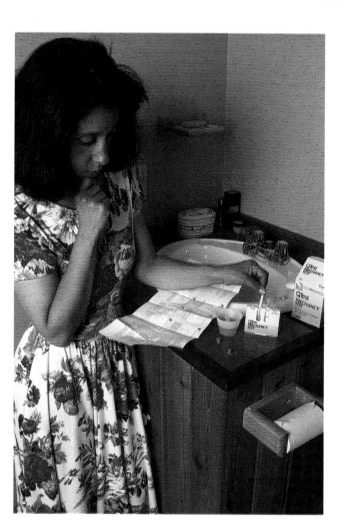

Although home pregnancy tests have become easier to administer, their accuracy rates vary. They are not foolproof tests.

Another home cholesterol test, Accumeter Cholesterol Self-Test, also became available in 1993. It is claimed that the test is as accurate as the tests that physicians use, but some physicians still have their doubts. Many are also concerned that a cholesterol test is only one part of a person's total health picture, and a "normal" result could make some people think they're fine when they need additional medical attention ("Qualms About Home Cholesterol Tests" 1993).

In general, there are three categories of self-testing products: (1) tests that help diagnose a specific condition or disease in those with symptoms, such as pregnancy test kits (used after a missed period); (2) screening tests that identify indications of disease in people without symptoms (e.g., testing stools for hidden blood); and (3) monitoring devices that provide an ongoing check for an existing condition and are used on the advice of a physician (e.g., blood glucose test kits for diabetics).

BENEFITS OF HOME TESTS

To consumers, this trend of self-reliance in health care can mean lower medical costs, a closer watch on chronic conditions, and earlier detection of health problems. A positive pregnancy test may prompt a woman to seek medical care early in her pregnancy; a woman being treated for infertility problems can pinpoint her time of ovulation; and regular blood pressure readings can provide helpful information to both patient and doctor. Thanks to convenient portable tests, individuals with some chronic health problems can maintain testing regimens away from home. An example is glucose monitoring, which has long helped diabetics keep their disease under control so they can live healthier and more normal lives.

Issue

Home Health Testing

Home health testing is a relatively recent development and can be controversial. With the increasing concern about the cost of visits to physicians and clinics, many people welcome the increasing availability of home tests for their convenience and money-saving characteristics. Others, however, are concerned that home tests will keep away from physicians and clinics people who really need professional help. Also, they are fearful that home health testing products will not be totally accurate or might even be faulty, prompting people to not seek treatment when they should, or to fear that problems exist when they don't.

It is still argued, however, that home health testing is a tremendous help to consumers. Proponents say that tests done at home save time and money and help people to be healthier than ever.

• Pro: The availability of an increasing number of home health tests helps consumers pay closer attention to their health. Tests provide information crucial to improving levels of health and decision making.

• Con: Home health tests may be of some use, but consumers need to exercise much caution in using them. Tests are not 100 percent accurate. They are also just one indicator and not close to a measure of overall health. Health decision making involves much more than just information obtained from home health tests.

Should home health tests be used? If so, under what circumstances? Would you use them at all? If so, what would determine whether or not you would use a home test?

PROBLEMS WITH HOME TESTS

The biggest problem with home tests is the risk of misinterpreting or overrelying on test results. A single abnormal reading is often taken as a "diagnosis" of a problem, or a return to a normal reading is taken as a "cure." Another problem is that once results of a home test are known, a person might not seek medical care. For example, a pregnant woman might not see her physician for appropriate prenatal care, whereas in the past she would have at least seen the physician to have a pregnancy test performed.

Making medical decisions without professional medical advice can be dangerous. Using the results of one test as a diagnosis is risky. A usual diagnosis by a physician involves an evaluation of the patient's medical history, a physical examination, other tests, and sometimes consultation with other medical experts.

No home test is 100 percent accurate, even under the best conditions, and results can differ from brand to brand. With a pregnancy test, for example, if enough of a certain hormone is present in a urine specimen, a signal should occur to indicate a possible pregnancy. But kits from different companies may indicate this signal at different hormonal levels, and not all women produce the hormone at the same rate. The accuracy of different brands of tests can vary a great deal.

HINTS FOR USING HOME TESTING KITS

Despite some problems with home tests, including questions about their accuracy, the future looks bright for manufacturers of home testing kits. On the horizon are plans for tests for syphilis, herpes, strep throat, and perhaps even acquired immunodeficiency syndrome (AIDS). These tests are likely to be around for quite some time, so it is wise to be aware of the FDA suggestions for their use (see the accompanying Personal Skills and Experiences box).

CONSUMER PROTECTION

Considering the many health products used and the many companies that produce them, it might seem a matter of luck that there aren't more problems. But there is much more than luck involved. Protection for the consumer does exist, even though it is not likely it will ever be perfect.

One informal type of consumer protection has been the close scrutiny of research findings. Typically, researchers have published their findings in medical journals. Supporters of this practice contend that this helps ensure credibility by allowing peers to critique the research. Critics say the process, which takes many months or even more than a year, can cause serious delays in the application of new treatments and can even cost patients their lives. They argue that major research studies receive intense independent scrutiny while they are under way, and thus the journal peer-review system may not be as necessary as before. Not sharing medical news until publication, they feel, can actually put patients in greater danger than allowing information and treatments to be released quickly. You will probably hear more about this issue. In the meantime, when do you think research information about health should be released?

OUR RIGHTS AS CONSUMERS

The consumer's *right to safety* has been partly protected by such agencies as the Consumer Product Safety Commission and the Environmental Protection Agency. Various national, state, and local agencies have the authority to investigate potentially unsafe products, procedures, or services, to recommend or effect corrections, and to order elimination of hazardous products. In addition, specific laws and regulations require the safety and effectiveness of prescription drugs,

PERSONAL SKILLS AND EXPERIENCES

Home Testing Safety Tips

The Food and Drug Administration offers the following precautions to promote home testing safety and effectiveness.

• For test kits that contain chemicals, note the expiration date. Because some chemicals may lose potency and affect results, do not buy or use a test kit if it is outdated.

• Consider whether the product needs protection from heat or cold. If so, don't leave it in the car trunk or by a sunny window on the trip home. At home, follow storage directions.

• Study the package insert. Read it through to get a general idea of what the test is about. Then go back and really study the instructions and pictures until you fully understand each step.

• If something isn't clear, don't guess. Consult a pharmacist or other health professional, or check the insert for a toll-free "800" number to call.

• Learn what the test is intended to do and what its limitations are. Remember, tests are not 100 percent accurate.

• If color is a part of the test and you're colorblind, get someone who isn't to interpret the results.

• Note special precautions, such as avoiding physical activity or certain foods and drugs before testing.

• Follow instructions exactly, including the specimen collection process, if that is a part of the test. Sequence is important. Don't skip a step.

• When collecting a urine specimen—unless you use a container from a kit—wash the container thoroughly and rinse out all soap traces, preferably with distilled water.

• When a step is timed, be precise. Use a stopwatch, or, at least, a watch with a second hand.

• Note what you should do if the results are positive, negative, or unclear.

• Keep accurate records of the results.

• As with medications, keep test kits that contain chemicals out of the reach of children. Throw away used test materials as directed.

---

medical devices, and OTC medicines; the safety of buildings and mobile homes; the remedy by automakers of safety defects found in cars; and other protections.

The *right to be informed* is basic, because we cannot make intelligent consumer decisions without enough information to protect ourselves from deception. There is a mandated and voluntary trend toward plain language in medical insurance policies and other contractual forms. In grocery stores, nutrition values and content statements now appear on food packages, as do unit prices on shelves. Consumer organizations have become more prominent in gathering and distributing practical information of value to consumers.

The *right to choose* has been supported by efforts to break up monopolies and encourage marketplace competition. Manufacturers can no longer set retail prices, as some once did under fair-trade laws. Bans that once kept prescription drug prices from being advertised are now illegal. The outlawing of mandatory fee schedules in general has given the consumer greater choice of medical services.

The *right to be heard* has been more evident than ever in recent years, both in government and in business circles. **Class action suits,** in which one consumer can pursue a remedy on behalf of all who have had the same problem, are commonly heard in the courts. Consumer affairs offices are often found in departments of the federal, state, and local governments, and within businesses. In some situations, not only are guidelines set up to protect the consumer in the first place, but simple processes for the resolution of problems and disagreement are provided as well.

How can you exercise your rights as a consumer? First, you must know where to go for assistance and how to seek redress for problems.

CONSUMER PROTECTION AGENCIES

No one has the time or expertise to check the contents, safety, and advertising of all health products. Fortunately, many government agencies at the federal, state, and local levels, as well as numerous private agencies, possess some of the resources needed to protect consumers from fraudulent claims and dangerous products. The most prominent agencies involved in consumer protection are discussed in the following sections.

Food and Drug Administration (FDA)

The FDA's major responsibility is to enforce laws designed to ensure that foods are wholesome, drugs and medical devices are safe and effective, cosmetics are harmless, and the labeling of such products is truthful. The FDA also has authority to require that manufacturers of medical devices prove the safety and effectiveness of their products before they put them on the market.

The development and approval of a new drug product comprise a long and involved process. Here is a simplified view of the steps the FDA takes.

1. A new drug is developed through research and is then subjected to screening tests and testing on animals. If it has the desired effects, more animal tests are done to

---

class action suit
A suit in which one person takes legal action on behalf of all who have had the same problem.

Issue

Government Regulation

Not everyone agrees on the amount of government regulation that there should be for health products and services. Simply put, the arguments supporting regulation center on the need for control of products and services to improve health. Arguments opposed to regulation often center on the need for individuals to make their own decisions and the fact that we cannot afford to financially support such extensive government services.

For example, some individuals argue that regulation of health-related products and services and associated industries is a legitimate and vital function of government.

- **Pro:** It is necessary for the government to regulate sanitation and selling and advertising practices and to even prohibit certain products. Individual choice is important, but individuals cannot always be expected to know, on their own, what is best. We need protection by the government, which has been established for that very purpose.

- **Con:** We should be free to make our own choices. Putting fluorides in water, prohibiting use of certain chemicals, preventing consumers from getting new drugs more quickly, and legislating what needs to be done to control pollution are examples of inappropriate governmental influence. It is important for consumers to be educated, but individual choice should not be limited by government interference.

How much government regulation do you think there should be? Do you feel that the government has gone too far with regulations on matters related to health? If you were the person making the final decisions, what kinds of regulations would you have related to health products and services?

see what dosage levels are poisonous, what the safe dosage level for humans might be, and whether there is a reason for human testing.

2. If tests indicate the drug can safely be tested on humans, the sponsor applies to the FDA for permission to conduct tests on humans. The sponsor must submit results of the animal studies and show that no human test subject will be exposed to an unreasonable risk.

3. Human testing is divided into three phases. Phase I determines what chemical action a drug has, how it is absorbed by the body, how it should be given, and what the safe dosage range is. Phase II involves testing on a limited number of patients for treatment or prevention of a specific disease. Phase III is the most extensive

testing stage. Studies are done to assess the drug's safety, effectiveness, and most desirable dosage in treating a specific disease in a large number of people.

4. If all stages are successful, the sponsor applies to the FDA for approval to market the new drug. The FDA reviews all available information to determine if the benefits of the drug when used properly outweigh the risks.

5. Once the FDA gives approval, the company is required to keep records relating to production methods for the drug and its safety and effectiveness. Any negative information must be reported to the FDA.

To ensure product safety, the FDA can take a number of possible actions. It can prevent the sale of a product, require that it be redesigned, demand that it be relabeled or packaged in a safer way, and take action against false or misleading labeling. The FDA can order the recall or removal of products from the marketplace or go to court to seize illegal products. It can also obtain injunctions against violators or prosecute manufacturers, packers, or shippers.

Federal Trade Commission (FTC)

The FTC was established in 1914 to protect consumers by keeping competition in the marketplace free and fair. The FTC is a consumer protection agency. In the area of health products, it is concerned with preventing misbranding, mislabeling, and fraudulent advertising.

The FTC's enforcement power is limited to issuing *cease and desist* orders, requiring that those responsible for deception stop their deceptive practices. Such orders can be appealed to the courts, however, and it may take months for a deceptive practice to be stopped.

The FTC and other public or private agencies cannot be aware of and deal with *all* deceptive health practices. In recent years, however, the FTC has dealt with such problems as advertisements for vitamin preparations that promise users increased sexual responsiveness, health books containing claims of unproven or questionable methods for curing cancer or heart disease, and advertisements for drugs promising cures for arthritis or other noncurable conditions. From a practical standpoint, the FTC is most likely to focus on deceptive practices in life-threatening situations.

U.S. Postal Service

The Postal Inspection Service of the U.S. Postal Service is responsible for preventing the mails from being used to defraud the public. It investigates mail-order fraud and protects consumers from harassment and from certain types of junk mail.

The Postal Service can refuse to deliver mail from a promoter, thus forcing the shutdown of a mail-order operation. The Postal Service can also take legal action, though it is more likely that such action results from a consumer complaint.

HEALTH UPDATE

The FDA's Restriction of Information

Some people feel that the FDA causes potential harm to consumers with policies that retard the spread of valuable information about approved drugs. For example, direct advertising of prescription drugs is allowed, but, if the ad contains information about the drug and the condition for which it is intended, the ad must also contain a "brief summary." This "brief summary" is actually a lengthy (one- or two-page) statement in small print listing side effects and contraindications associated with the drug. Many feel this information is worthless to consumers because it is overly technical and, if they want the drug, they will have to visit a physician anyway. The effect of the requirement, however, is that there are fewer and less-informative ads for prescription drugs because either the "brief summary" makes them so long that they are prohibitively expensive or the manufacturer gives little information to avoid the requirement for a "brief summary." The results are these:

1. A consumer might not be aware that a treatment exists for some condition, and so will not consult a physician.
2. A consumer might suffer some symptoms without realizing that they are symptoms of a disease.
3. A consumer might have been previously diagnosed with some then-untreatable disease for which a new treatment has since become available.
4. A remedy with reduced side effects might become available and the consumer would not know about it.

Therefore, some individuals argue that the FDA focuses mainly on the costs of deception and needs to focus more on costs to consumers of being denied access to valuable information (Rubin 1992).

State and Local Government Agencies

Many states and municipalities have agencies with responsibilities similar to those of national agencies. Almost every city and state has a department of consumer affairs that provides general consumer information and referrals. State and local health departments often have divisions regulating food and drugs, health facilities, medical-care licensing and services, veterinary health, product safety, occupational safety, and radiation control. These agencies might be more responsive than federal ones in dealing with a specific problem because they tend to be less bureaucratic.

Better Business Bureau

The Better Business Bureau is supported entirely by private businesses. Local bureaus assist with misunderstandings between customers and business firms, and they investigate questionable business activity and instances of apparently false advertising. While these bureaus can provide information on a specific company or charity, consumers must draw their own conclusions. Bureaus will not endorse a company, product, or person, or offer legal advice.

Chamber of Commerce

The Chamber of Commerce is a voluntary organization interested in publicizing, developing, and promoting commercial opportunities in communities. It acts as a communication vehicle between businesses and consumers and often has a business-consumer relations code. The Chamber strives to protect the health and safety of consumers by monitoring the design and manufacture of products as well as trying to eliminate fraud and deception.

Consumers' Union

Consumers' Union is the most important of a number of independent testing organizations designed to inform Americans about the quality of products we buy. Information from the Union is printed in its magazine, *Consumer Reports.* Consumers' Union does not accept paid advertisements or endorse products.

CONSUMER COMPLAINTS

When dissatisfied with a product or service, we should first honestly ask ourselves whether we used the product as labeled, carefully followed instructions, and had realistic expectations. If, after answering these questions, further action is needed, there are several relatively informal and appropriate steps to take.

INFORMAL ACTIONS

First, gather all relevant facts about the product or service, including names, dates, and circumstances. Any written evidence, such as a receipt, is helpful. In general, keep receipts, unused products, and records of transactions until the complaint is handled in a satisfactory manner. Then, if possible, go to the place where the product or service was received. If put off by a salesperson or clerk, ask to see the manager. If the manager does not provide satisfaction, talk to those of higher and higher authority until a solution is found.

If it is not possible to return to the place of purchase, make a phone call or write a letter. Be clear about the complaint and related facts. When connected with the proper person, ask the person's name and position and write it

PERSONAL SKILLS AND EXPERIENCES

Consumer Decisions Related to Mind, Body, and Soul

When making consumer decisions, it is helpful to consider influences related to the mind, body, and soul. Certainly one dimension influences another, but questions such as those listed below need to be considered. Perhaps you can think of additional questions that also need consideration.

Mind

1. When selecting this product or service, how influenced was I by advertising?
2. What is my motive for buying this product? (For example, am I trying to get rid of a headache? Am I trying to avoid headaches in the future?)
3. What can I do to avoid the need for this product or service in the future?

Body

1. Have I tried natural means of solving my problem before using medications? (For example, do I have a proper diet, follow a healthy exercise program, or use sound stress-control techniques?)
2. Do I "listen to my body" so I learn when things seem to be functioning well and when they don't?

Soul

1. Are my consumer habits in harmony with my basic values and what I think is important in life? (For example, do I do what I say, and do I act consistently with what I think is important?)
2. Are my consumer choices consistent with my cause and purpose in living? (For example, do I buy products that harm the environment, or do I use substances instead of positive health behavior to prevent problems?)

Finally, summarize what you need to do to improve your health skills and to bring them in line (make them consistent) with your values. Combine areas where you can to improve similar skills at the same time. Prioritize what you need to do and explain how you will do it. Pick your top priorities and begin improving your consumer skills.

There are many ways to register a consumer complaint.

down for future reference. Ask to speak with that person's superior if necessary, but listen to what the person on the other end of the line says. If wrong about the complaint, admit it. Ideally, you will be satisfied with the corrective action suggested; if not, more formal action can be pursued.

FORMAL ACTIONS

If direct contact with the company or appropriate individuals does not lead to satisfactory results, some of the following ideas may help:

1. Photocopy your original letter and send copies to city, county, or state voluntary consumer groups or governmental consumer agencies; your state's attorney general; the local Better Business Bureau; the appropriate business or professional association; national consumer groups; and the state and national office of Consumer Affairs.

2. If the company does business in interstate commerce, contact the appropriate federal government agency.

3. If the problem has to do with unfair or deceptive advertising or business practice, contact the FTC, and if the deceptive advertisement appears in the local media, contact the broadcaster or newspaper and request that they stop running the ad.

4. Advise the company in question that you are taking these steps and send them copies of all letters sent. Many companies fear the adverse publicity of letters and will provide satisfaction concerning the complaint.

5. If all these effects prove ineffective, your local voluntary or governmental consumer agency may assist you by writing letters and visiting the company. Government agencies often send out investigators and will take remedial action if it is justified.

6. As a last resort, you can sue the business in small claims court (the ceiling on recovery, depending on the state, is usually $500–$1,500). No lawyer is needed, and the filing costs are small. Contact the Small Claims Study Group, c/o John H. Weiss, Room 1, Quincy House, Cambridge, Massachusetts 02138, for advice on using these courts.

PERSONAL INSIGHT

Handling Consumer Problems

I know a person who is very successful in having consumer problems resolved. Over a period of several years, I've watched how she does it. While the tactics are not always exactly the same, problems are generally handled similarly. Perhaps the things she does will be helpful to you. Here they are:

1. She stays calm when talking with a representative of the organization about the problem. You know how you feel if someone starts yelling at you. It usually makes you want to fight—it doesn't make you feel like helping the person.

2. Even though she is calm, she makes her points firmly. She is aggressive, but not pushy. She indicates what was expected, what the problems are, and what she feels should be done about them.

3. She clearly explains her case. This may involve telling about the product or service and why it is not satisfactory.

4. One of the reasons she is able to state her case so clearly is that she prepares in advance. She thinks about what she wants to say and may even rehearse the words. She makes notes and uses them when she is talking with the appropriate person.

5. If the person she is talking with is unwilling or unable to take care of the problem, she asks to speak to that person's supervisor. While being courteous, she indicates that she will call or write the supervisor to try to remedy the situation. This is not a threat, just a statement that this is what she will do.

6. She gets the name of the person she is talking to and makes note of the name, date, and approximate time of day. This has often been useful in later conversations with that person or a supervisor.

7. She decides her priorities in advance. There is no point in complaining about ten things at the same time unless absolutely necessary. She may have more concerns, but is more successful dealing with two or three things at most. It is easy to get sidetracked with so many issues that the main ones never get addressed.

8. She keeps appropriate records. These often include receipts, charge slips, warrantees, and other related items. These are useful for many reasons, but they are essential when trying to have a problem rectified.

9. She listens carefully to what the other person is saying. Not only is this polite, but if she learns what the other person's main points are, she can use these to help deal with her problem. For example, she might realize that the person might be able to do certain things, but not others—or compromise in certain ways.

10. She is willing to compromise if needed, but not on the major issues. If someone is trying to be helpful, however, she is willing to listen to reason and settle for a reasonable solution.

11. She asks the person when she can expect some action. For example, she might ask how long it will take for a certain thing to happen. Or she might ask by which day something will be done, or when she will receive a replacement, or when the person will be back in touch, or when she should contact the company again.

12. She is consistent and persistent. She is consistent in that she says the same things and emphasizes the same points in repeated communications. She is persistent in that she continues to push for action in reasonable ways. This might mean follow-up phone calls, letters, or action with supervisors.

13. If possible, she does not pay for something until she is sure it is satisfactory. While this is not always possible, this is easy to do with many services. It is particularly easy to do if payment was made with a credit card. It is usually easy to inform the credit card company not to pay a certain bill if there are problems. Obviously, people are much more likely to want to help her if they have not yet been paid.

14. When the issue is satisfactorily resolved, she usually thanks those involved—often in writing with a copy to the person's supervisor. Not only is this courteous, but someday she may have reason to deal with the same people again. If not, perhaps someone else may benefit because she was courteous.

I hope these tips help you when dealing with consumer problems. They sure work well for her.

PROBLEMS WITH ADVERTISEMENTS

If you see or hear an ad you think is misleading or offensive, or if you have questions about an ad, you don't have to wait for one of the government or private watchdogs to act. You can complain. Chances are you will not be alone and others have similar concerns. Sometimes even a single letter can prompt action by the FTC. The National Advertising Division of the Council of Better Business Bureaus (NAD) routinely acts on consumer complaints.

Directing a letter to the proper agency is important. As you might guess, national agencies are more interested in national advertising and a local consumer agency or attorney general's office would be more interested in local advertising. Complaints about radio or TV ads can be directed to the station manager, and those from a newspaper or magazine can be sent to the publisher. Following are some additional addresses that might be helpful.

Division of Advertising Practices
Federal Trade Commission
Washington, DC 20580

National Advertising Division
Council of Better Business Bureaus
845 Third Avenue
New York, NY 10022
(Complaints about national ads aimed at children can be addressed to the Children's Advertising Review Unit at the same address)

Mail Order Action Line
Direct Marketing Association
Six E. 43rd Street
New York, NY 10017
(For complaints about mail-order ads)

CONSUMER RESPONSIBILITY

The ultimate responsibility for consumer protection is in your hands. Today help is available from legal sources, as well as from public and private agencies designed to help protect you. But it is a mistake to sit back and assume that everything is being taken care of for us. The size of the population, combined with the thousands of products and services available to consumers, makes it impossible for regulatory agencies and consumer interest groups to protect us fully.

How can you help promote consumer protection? First, keep informed on consumer issues by gathering and using information on health in general, using consumer protection organizations and legislation, and using the decision-making process. If consumer problems develop, take action on them. The solution to your problem might assist other consumers as well. Everyone has a responsibility to help rectify difficulties with health products or services. In the final analysis, we are our own consumer protection agency.

TAKE ACTION

1. Assess your motivation and reasons for purchasing health products.
2. Examine the outcomes and scientific basis of any self-medications or self-treatment that you use.
3. Become a wiser consumer of health products. For example, keep informed about consumer issues, read labels carefully, check out products before purchasing them, and buy generic drugs when possible.
4. Use your rights as a consumer to take action if you experience a problem with a medical product.

SUMMARY

1. A personal plan for better health involves assessing health-producing and health-destroying behaviors, adopting health-producing behaviors in a systematic way, recognizing and accepting the good feelings associated with high-level wellness, and understanding why certain behaviors are related to health and positive feelings.

2. In part because of advertising, people often buy health products they don't need or want.

3. In order to make wise consumer decisions, people must learn to systematically evaluate advertising claims being made for a product.

4. Many OTC drugs are ineffective and are used unnecessarily. There are potential dangers from self-medication.

5. Certain guidelines should be followed for best results when using prescription drugs.

6. One relatively new health decision relates to the use of do-it-yourself medical testing.

7. Consumers have the right to safety, the right to be informed, the right to choose, and the right to be heard.

8. Many government and private agencies exist to protect consumers.

9. Consumer complaints can be handled formally or informally. In either instance, certain steps should be followed.

10. The ultimate responsibility for consumer protection is in the hands of the consumer.

COMMITMENT ACTIVITIES

1. Collect at least six advertisements for health products. Evaluate the ads, using the guidelines presented in figure 20.1. Does the activity have any effect on your feelings about any of the advertisements?
2. Using the checklist for evaluating health information presented in figure 20.1, analyze health information you hear and see in the next several days. What can you conclude about the health information, based upon this analysis?
3. Examine a number of labels for OTC and prescription drugs. Are they consistent with the information presented in this chapter? Can you generalize about the labels?
4. Find out which consumer protection agencies exist in your home or college community. Visit representatives from three of the agencies and briefly interview them. Use questions such as the following and add your own:
   a. How does your agency help protect consumers?
   b. What are the most common consumer problems you see?
   c. How can individuals best work with your agency?
   d. How can consumers help prevent the problems you encounter?

5. Many of us are hesitant to take action when we notice a problem with an advertisement of something we bought. Perhaps we don't want to bother, would feel embarrassed, or don't know what to do. With any consumer problem you have had recently, or with one you have now, take action! You might visit the place of business to discuss your problem with a clerk, the store manager, or another official. Or you might write a letter to an appropriate person. At any rate, take action and don't give up until your problem is handled to your satisfaction. Use the suggestions in this chapter to guide your action.

REFERENCES

Aral, S. O., W. D. Mosher, and W. Cates. 1992. "Vaginal Douching Among Women of Reproductive Age in the United States." *American Journal of Public Health* 82, no. 2 (February): 210–14.

"Beware of Tanning Pills." 1991. *Consumers' Research* 74, no. 1 (January): 29–30.

"Cold Remedies: Which Ones Work Best?" 1989. *Consumer Reports* 54, no. 1 (January): 8–11.

Corry, J. M. 1983. *Consumer Health.* Belmont, CA: Wadsworth.

"Facial Cleansers." 1989. *Consumer Reports* 54, no. 6 (June): 408–10.

Kunkel, D., and D. Roberts. 1991. "Young Minds and Marketplace Values: Issues in Children's Television Advertising." *Journal of Social Issues* 47, no. 1:57–72.

Lipman, M. M. 1993. "Unapproved Prescriptions: Doctor Knows Best?" *Consumer Reports on Health* 5, no. 8 (August): 90–91.

McKenzie, J. F. 1987. "A Checklist for Evaluating Health Information." *Journal of School Health* 57, no. 1 (January): 31–32.

"Miracle Drugs or Media Drugs?" 1992. *Consumer Reports* 57, no. 3 (March): 142–46.

"OTC Pain Medications of Only Three Types Available." 1987. *UAB Report* (30 January): 5.

"Prescription for Savings: Shop Around." 1990. *Changing Times* 44, no. 2 (February): 102.

"Qualms About Home Cholesterol Tests." 1993. *Edell Health Letter* 12, no. 6 (June/July): 1.

Rock, A. 1993. "Cut Your Spiraling Drug Costs 70%." *Money,* June, 131–34.

Rubin, P. H. 1992. "The FEA's Prescription for Consumer Ignorance." *Consumers' Research* 75, no. 6 (June): 17–19.

"A Take Home Test for Cholesterol." 1993. *Consumer Reports on Health* 5, no. 5 (May): 54.

"Update on Generics." 1990. *Changing Times* 44, no. 2 (February): 102.

Wallack, L., and L. Dorfman. 1992. "Health Messages on Television Commercials." *American Journal of Health Promotion* 6, no. 3 (January/February): 190–96.

"Which Cold Remedy Is Right for You?" 1994. *Consumer Reports on Health* 6, no. 1 (February): 16–19.

"Which Pain Reliever Is Right for You?" 1993. *Consumer Reports on Health* 5, no. 11 (November): 122–24.

ADDITIONAL READINGS

Cornacchia, H. J., and S. Barrett. 1993. *Consumer Health: A Guide to Intelligent Decisions.* St. Louis: Mosby. Chapter 1 on dynamics of the health marketplace, chapter 5 on advertising, and chapter 27 on consumer laws, agencies, and strategies provide needed information related to basic consumer products and decisions.

Kazman, S. 1991. "The FDA's Deadly Approval Process." *Consumers' Research* 74, no. 4 (April): 31–34. Outlines the FDA approval process for new drugs and gives examples of deaths that might have been caused by "too much safety."

Warden, C. 1992. "The Prescription for High Drug Prices." *Consumers' Research* 75, no. 12 (December): 10–14. Gives an overview of trends in prescription drug prices and explains possible reasons for the relatively high increases.

CHAPTER 21

Using Health-Care Services

Healthy People 2000 Objectives

- Increase to at least 50 percent the proportion of primary-care providers who routinely assess and counsel their patients regarding the frequency, duration, type, and intensity of each patient's physical activity practices.

- Increase to at least 75 percent the proportion of primary-care providers who provide nutrition assessment and counseling and/or referral to qualified nutritionists or dieticians.

- Increase to at least 75 percent the proportion of primary-care providers who screen for alcohol and other drug use problems and provide counseling and referral as needed. Similar objectives are found for emotional and behavioral functioning, safety precautions, and occupational health exposures.

- Increase to at least 90 percent the proportion of hospitals, health maintenance organizations, and large group practices that provide patient education programs, and to at least 90 percent the proportion of community hospitals that offer community health promotion programs addressing the priority health-care needs of their communities.

- Increase to at least 70 percent the number of people aged 35 and older using the oral health-care system during each year.

- Increase to at least 50 percent the proportion of people who have received, as a minimum within the appropriate interval, all of the screening and immunization services and at least one of the counseling services appropriate for their age and gender as recommended by the U.S. Prevention Services Task Force.

- Increase to at least 95 percent the proportion of people who have a specific source of ongoing primary care for coordination of their preventive and episodic health care.

- Improve financing and delivery of clinical preventive services so that virtually no American has a financial barrier to receiving, at a minimum, the screening, counseling, and immunization services recommended by the U.S. Preventive Services Task Force.

Selecting Medical Care

Directions

Circle the letter in front of all responses that apply.

1. In selecting a physician, I would:
   a. ask my friends.
   b. pick someone who was geographically close.
   c. check to see with which hospital the physician is affiliated and call the administration for a recommendation.
   d. check to see how available he or she would be in an emergency and if out of town, how patients would get treatment.
   e. ask how much he or she charges for a visit.
   f. call the local or state medical society, and ask for recommendations in my area.
2. Under which of the following situations would you seek medical help? (Mark all that apply.)
   a. stomachache
   b. a persistent cough or sore throat
   c. a headache
   d. severe bleeding or deep cut
   e. persistent chest pain
   f. swallowing some mild poison
3. From which of the following health professionals would you feel comfortable and confident receiving treatment for a serious disease? (Mark all that apply.)
   a. allopathic physician (prescribes drugs or chemotherapy to treat diseases)
   b. osteopathic physician (heats, manipulates, or massages the musculoskeletal, nervous, and circulatory systems in addition to methods such as chemotherapy)
   c. chiropractor (aligns back to relieve impinged nerves)

   d. acupuncturist (inserts and manipulates needles to treat disease)
   e. naturopath (treats disease with natural herbs)
   f. faith healer (cures the disease through divine help)

Scoring/Interpretation

1. If you circled letters *a*, *b*, *d*, and *e*, which are good things to consider, then it appears you are assuming that the physician is well-respected among his or her peers. It is important to consider if friends are satisfied, and if the physician is reasonably priced, is closely located, and readily available for convenience and comfort.

   To determine competency, you should have selected *c* and *f* to check how hospitals and the professional society view the physician in terms of respect and competence. Find out information like the number of malpractice lawsuits against him or her and so on.
2. All of the reasons could be indicators of serious illness, but *a* and *c* would need to persist over some time before most doctors would recommend that you visit them. In most cases, these pass in a short amount of time. When in doubt, call and ask whether you should see the doctor or not.

   Letters *d* and *f* would necessitate immediate help by either traveling to an emergency room (if someone can drive you) or calling paramedics.

   Letters *b* and *e* are conditions that should be checked by a physician by appointment.
3. Only *a* and *b* are licensed to practice medicine. *C*, *d*, and *f* can supplement medicine, but cannot treat a serious disease. *E* is extremely questionable from a medical perspective and in treating a serious disease would be considered quackery.

Practically everyone at some time needs to see a medical specialist or use a medical facility, or is called upon to help someone with a serious medical problem. Providing some form of medical care and medical-care insurance for each person has become a virtual necessity. In this chapter, the major aspects of using medical-care services are examined: first, when to see a medical specialist and how to help the medical specialist help the patient; second, how to choose a medical specialist or medical facility, how to plan to pay for the medical care, and what to expect from current U.S. medical care; and, finally, what to avoid in the way of quack medical practices.

MAKING DECISIONS ABOUT MEDICAL CARE

In certain situations, such as a serious car accident or the sudden development of a severe pain, immediate medical care is needed. In other situations, such as when you have had a sore throat or have been coughing for a few days, it is

harder to determine whether or not to seek medical care. Potential decisions involve many questions, such as these: When should self-care be used? When should medical care be sought? What can be done to help the medical specialist help the patient? How should you go about finding a suitable medical specialist or medical facility?

WHEN TO SEEK MEDICAL CARE

Some individuals rely too much on self-care, figuring that a symptom will go away if left alone or if treated with over-the-counter medicine; many are not aware of the dangers of self-medication.

At the other extreme, some individuals rush to a physician the moment they feel a muscle twitch or get a headache. How can we know when to seek professional advice or care? Medical care should be sought in the following situations:

1. When a life-threatening situation exists. For example, any of the following conditions can lead to immediate death: severe bleeding, stopped breathing, ingestion of

THE WORLD AROUND YOU

Multicultural Differences in Preventive Care

While many of you probably regularly visit medical personnel because you believe it is one good way to help prevent health problems, not all people feel that way. For example, preventive medical care is not a common practice for some Hispanics. They believe that one goes to a physician only when one is really "sick." A common myth is that if you go to the physician when you are not sick, the physician will find something wrong and then you will certainly become sick (Sanchez 1987).

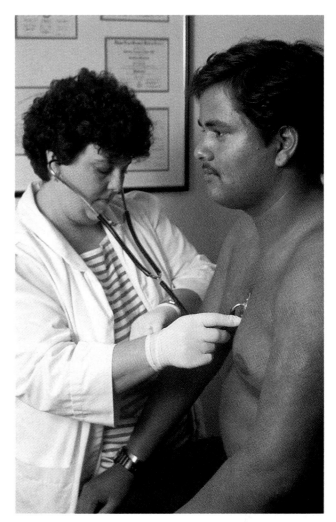

For regular care, it is important that we make informed decisions about our use of health professionals' services.

a poison, shock, or chest pains (which may precede a heart attack). In these situations, go to a hospital emergency room or call an ambulance.

2. When any bodily symptom (e.g., pain, swelling, fever) lasts for an unusually long time. For example, a sore throat usually lasts only 2 to 7 days.

3. When there is uncertainty. Call a physician's office and explain the problem.

You are the expert on your own body. You are the most sensitive to your bodily changes and are consequently the best early warning system regarding any changes in your well-being. If you experience unexplained symptoms, consult a physician as soon as possible.

DECIDING ON KINDS OF MEDICAL HELP

When a medical emergency occurs, there isn't time to choose a hospital or personal physician; sometimes there is no choice about who to see or where to go. But for regular care, it is important to make informed decisions about a personal physician and dentist.

Both **allopathic physicians** (those with doctor of medicine—M.D.—degrees) and **osteopathic physicians** (those with doctor of osteopathy—D.O.—degrees) are licensed to practice medicine and have had the required medical education. How, then, do you choose between them? They had to pass the same examinations for state licensure, and in most cases they would treat a patient similarly.

The major difference between an M.D. and D.O. lies in their philosophical approach to medicine. Allopathic physicians generally emphasize drugs and other forms of chemotherapy as the preferred means to treat disease. Osteopathic physicians emphasize the roles of the musculoskeletal, nervous, and circulatory systems in the management of bodily ailments. Consequently, some D.O.'s would apply manipulative therapy, such as massaging or heat treatment, in addition to chemotherapy. Another factor to consider is accessibility. This might be the distance of the physician's office

from your home or workplace, the practitioner's hours, the practitioner's weekend or vacation substitute, and financial costs. When you narrow the field to one practitioner, a visit allows you to consider such personal qualities as personality, patience, and the willingness to answer questions clearly. If you feel uncomfortable with the physician's opinion or personal qualities, seek out another physician.

The physician-patient relationship provides an excellent example of mind/body/soul health. There seems to be a powerful therapeutic value in a good physician-patient relationship. Individuals often report that they want to seek help from "their doctor" who knows them and in whom they have confidence. An interested physician who imparts confidence,

allopathic physician
A physician who has received a medical doctor degree (M.D.).

osteopathic physician
A physician who has been trained in a college of osteopathic medicine.

who is friendly and reassuring, who performs a thorough examination, and who is not overtly anxious about the patient is more likely to elicit a positive therapeutic response. In various situations, when physicians counsel and support active involvement of their patients, the patients are more likely to do what the physician recommends and they are also more likely to feel better sooner (Smith and Thompson 1993).

A **nurse practitioner** can extend a physician's services. Usually this individual is a registered nurse (RN) who has had additional education and experience, and who can assess patients' health histories, conduct physical examinations, and order and interpret diagnostic tests. The nurse practitioner works under the guidance of a licensed physician, but some states allow nurse practitioners to engage in private practice. Depending on their area of study, nurse practitioners can be called "family nurse practitioners," "pediatric nurse practitioners," "geriatric nurse practitioners," or "surgical nurse practitioners."

A **physician assistant (PA)** can also extend physicians' services. Under the supervision of a physician, the PA can do many things usually done by a physician. For example, they can perform physical exams, treat some ailments, prescribe some medications, and talk with patients about health problems. Most PAs work in physicians' offices, but some work in hospitals or other medical-care settings.

A **certified nurse-midwife (CNM)** is a licensed nurse with a graduate degree and national certification. A CNM may operate an independent practice for maternity and gynecological care. In thirty-two states and the District of Columbia a CNM can write prescriptions for drugs appropriate to their practice, such as prenatal vitamins, oral contraceptives, and treatments for basic gynecological problems. A CNM is trained to refer a patient to a physician when necessary. There can be significant cost savings when babies are delivered at birthing centers staffed by midwives. In a recent year, average fees for a midwife birth at a birthing center were $2,629, compared to $4,919 for a physician birth at a typical hospital (Clark 1993).

HOW TO HELP THE MEDICAL SPECIALIST HELP THE PATIENT

Medical care involves a partnership between patient and practitioner, not a one-way contract. Patients must articulate their problems, clearly state their needs and expectations, and fully cooperate in getting well. Remember, the physician-patient relationship is confidential, and only medical professionals with a "need to know" are authorized access to medical records.

Many people try to be "good" patients—they listen respectfully, they follow the physician's recommendations without complaint, and they try not to take too much of the physician's time with questions. Studies show, however, that "good" patients often feel sicker and die sooner than assertive patients. This is because "good" patients do not learn about their condition, think independently, or take action to

improve their health ("Take Charge of Your Health" 1993). Note the Personal Skills and Experiences box for suggestions on how to become a more assertive patient.

After the problem is described, the practitioner examines and tests the patient, and may order certain lab tests or X rays to help diagnose the problem before prescribing treatment. Throughout the visit, the patient needs to understand exactly what is going on. Ask for clarification on any treatment or medications, such as whether a medication can cause drowsiness or other side effects, what the dosage is, and when to take the medication. The cost of recommended tests, treatments, or prescriptions should also be learned, along with possible alternative and less costly options.

The practitioner may need to refer the patient to a specialist. In addition to family medicine or general practice, there are five major clinical specialties: (1) **internal medicine** includes such subspecialties as the study of heart problems, endocrine diseases and metabolism, and the digestive system; (2) **obstetrics and gynecology** is concerned with childbearing and diseases of women; (3) **pediatrics** is concerned with infants, children, and adolescents; (4) **psychiatry** deals with mental problems; and (5) **surgery.** A physician's training can be verified by calling the county medical society or checking the *Directory of Medical Specialists,* available in many public libraries. Other suggestions are found in the Personal Skills and Experiences box entitled "Shopping for a Physician."

---

nurse practitioner
A registered nurse with advanced training in a particular medical specialty.

physician assistant (PA)
A trained assistant who, under the supervision of a physician, does many basic tasks of a physician.

certified nurse-midwife (CNM)
A licensed nurse with a graduate degree and national certification who may operate an independent practice for maternity and gynecological care.

internal medicine
A medical specialty in which the physician deals with the functions of the internal systems of the body.

obstetrics and gynecology
Obstetrics is the medical specialty of caring for women during pregnancy, childbirth, and after birth. Gynecology is the medical specialty dealing with the health of the female reproductive organs.

pediatrics
The medical specialty dealing with the treatment of children.

psychiatry
The medical specialty dealing with the diagnosis, treatment, and prevention of mental illness.

surgery
The medical specialty dealing with operative procedures for correction of disease or deformity.

PERSONAL SKILLS AND EXPERIENCES

Becoming an Assertive Patient

1. Before the visit, jot down questions and concerns you want to discuss with the physician. Also, write down your symptoms so you will remember to tell the physician about them.
2. Consider bringing a friend or relative who can help ease your anxiety, make sure you cover everything, and recall what the physician said.
3. During the visit, mention immediately that you have some questions. Politely insist on time to describe your symptoms and ask questions.
4. Think carefully about tests. Is the test worth doing and worth the cost? Ask about the risk, discomfort, and cost of the test, and weigh them against potential benefits.

5. Think carefully about treatments. What are the odds that they will work? What are the possible side effects? What options are available?
6. Tell the physician if you are not happy with a recommended treatment—perhaps it can be adjusted.
7. Don't leave the physician's office with unresolved questions. Ask the physician for a summary of the visit to be sure you understand everything. Take notes on the main points.
8. If you are not satisfied with what you heard, get a second opinion and follow the same assertive steps.

Source: From "Take Charge of Your Health" in *Consumer Reports on Health* 5(11):117–119 (November 1993).

PERSONAL SKILLS AND EXPERIENCES

Being a Powerful Patient

The only way to make rational judgments about your medical care—especially decisions about surgery and therapeutic choices—is to become an expert so you can make up your own mind. When recommendations are made by your physician, there is more help out there than you might think to assist you in decision making. Here are some suggestions to get you started:

1. The National Health Information Center ([800] 336-4797) can refer you to appropriate organizations. It can also give you a list of over a hundred hot lines you can call.
2. There are national and local organizations for many diseases and disabilities. Examples are the American Lung Association, the American Cancer Society, and the American Heart Association. They are user-friendly and will send information and provide suggestions about where to seek help.
3. For less well known illnesses, call the National Organization for Rare Disorders at (203) 746-6518.

4. Support groups can be very helpful. The American Self-Help Clearinghouse publishes the *Self-Help Sourcebook* and will provide telephone numbers for clearinghouses in many states; call them at (201) 625-7101.
5. More than any other tool, the computer has reduced the gap between what physicians know and patients know. There are hundreds of databases available. Call Grateful Med ([800] 638-8480) for software that allows you to conduct your own search for in-depth articles on any medical subject. Information about other databases can be obtained by calling the Directory of Online Health-Care Databases at (503) 471-1627 or the Health Reference Center at (800) 227-8431.
6. If you are already into computer technology, you can get a list of health-oriented computer bulletin boards by calling (with a modem) (302) 994-3772.
7. Finally, there are data brokers who help meet the needs of both physicians and patients. Examples are Planetree Health Resource Center at (415) 923-3680, the Medical Information Service at (800) 999-1999, and the Medical Data Exchange at (503) 471-1627.

Source: Adapted from Steve Fishman, "The Powerful Patient" in *Health* 7(2), March/April 1993, pages 74–76.

A patient may be referred by a physician or go directly to one of these specialists or to another health professional, such as a **clinical psychologist** or a **licensed clinical social worker.** Licensed clinical psychologists hold a Ph.D. degree from an accredited school and specialize in emotional and psychological adjustment, as well as in temporary or chronic emotional difficulties and disturbances. The psychiatrist, who

clinical psychologist
A person with a Ph.D. degree who specializes in emotional and psychological adjustment.

licensed clinical social worker
A person with academic training in social work who specializes in emotional or psychological adjustment.

PERSONAL INSIGHT

Researching Your Own Illness

Jerry was 24 years old and prided himself on being in great physical shape. He even took a karate class several times a week, could put his fist through 3 inches of wood, and felt invincible.

One day, as he undressed for bed, he noticed a hard lump, about the size of a dime, on his left testicle. The next day he was given an examination, an ultrasound procedure, and a blood test. In his blood, the levels of hormone-like chemicals (signs of cancer) were elevated. His physician recommended surgery to remove the testicle.

So, the cancerous testicle was removed and a silicone prosthesis was put in its place. Jerry thought his problems were over, but 10 days later his physician informed him that they were not through yet. He said there was a chance that the cancer had spread to the lymph system. The standard follow-up procedure was a lymph node dissection—surgery lasting as long as 12 hours, during which the abdomen would be sliced open so physicians could remove the lymph nodes and examine them for cancer. The physician said the procedure had been around for a long time and that many physicians recommended it.

Jerry asked about side effects. In addition to the surgery itself, and the weeks of recovery, there was a chance that the operation could sever the nerve that permits ejaculation. Jerry was stunned because he was looking forward to the possibility of being a father some day.

The physician said that the decision was up to Jerry. The usually-in-control karate expert experienced many emotions. He had never had to make that kind of decision before. The physician was recommending a serious operation that might possibly save his life, but what about quality of life after survival? If he had the operation, he could end up unable to ejaculate. If he didn't have the operation, there was a chance that cancer cells would remain hidden in his body—then he could die before he had a chance to become a father.

Jerry felt victimized and out of control. He realized later that he felt that way because of lack of knowledge.

He decided to learn more about his condition. He called the National Cancer Institute in Bethesda, Maryland, and requested the names of the country's biggest cancer treatment centers. He called the closest one, asked for the urology department, and eventually got a physician on the line. After Jerry explained his situation, the physician offered to send him a special report on testicular cancer.

Then Jerry headed for the library, where he thumbed through back issues of the journal *Urology*. He found that Indiana University Medical School was doing major work and he called them. They referred him to more studies to read. He figured it was his life and worth some time for study.

After reading for a few days, Jerry learned that lymph node surgery had high cure rates—particularly when combined with chemotherapy. He also read that physicians in Denmark, which has the highest testicular cancer rate in the world, achieved high cure rates by using chemotherapy alone and avoiding surgery.

Jerry then discussed what he learned with his physician. He asked his physician the following questions: Is there any way to avoid the surgery? How do doctors know it is the surgery, and not the chemotherapy, that kills the cancer? What about chemotherapy alone? What about holding off on either surgery or chemotherapy?

Finally, Jerry and his physician agreed on a wait-and-see approach—no lymph node surgery—because the tumor that was removed had been so contained, and because the cancer had been caught at such an early stage. They also decided to postpone the chemotherapy for the time being. Jerry wanted to avoid the side effects.

Jerry knew that the risk he took in saying no to the surgery was a 20 to 30 percent chance that the cancer would recur, but he would be monitored with sensitive monthly blood tests and quarterly CT scans (high-definition X rays of the lymph system), which would pick up any cancer early. And if the cancer did recur, Jerry knew the same treatments would still be available, with an overall cure rate still above 90 percent. He had learned enough to know the risks, and he was content with his decision.

Some physicians may be put off by give-and-take sessions, but Jerry's experience was very positive. He found that his physician liked having a patient who took such an active interest.

Three years later, as this text went to press, Jerry's cancer had not returned, nor had his fertility been hampered. He was greatly relieved, since he was planning to get married in a few months. He said: "You really owe it to yourself to do what I did."

is also a physician, is likely to see patients who require medication as well as psychotherapy. The psychologist is more likely to see patients who do not require constant prescription medication for their specific emotional problems. Licensed clinical social workers specialize in the same areas as clinical psychologists.

Other health professionals include **optometrists** and **ophthalmologists.** An optometrist specializes in measuring visual acuity and prescribing corrective lenses. An ophthalmologist is an M.D. who specializes in the treatment of eye disorders and diseases. Clinical psychologists, optometrists,

and other health professionals function independently and outside a physician's realm of supervision, though they might choose to work with a physician to help a patient.

optometrist
A nonmedical trained person who specializes in measuring visual acuity and in vision correction.

ophthalmologist
A medical doctor who treats and performs surgery for eye disorders.

PERSONAL SKILLS AND EXPERIENCES

Shopping for a Physician

Locating a Physician

1. Call the local county or state medical society and ask for names of physicians in the area.
2. Find out what hospitals the physicians on your list are affiliated with.
3. Find out whether the physician can be reached easily in an emergency.
4. Inquire about the physician's fees.
5. Make a get-acquainted visit—an appointment before you get sick.

Getting to Know the Physician

1. Does the physician listen to the things you have to say?
2. Is he/she willing to share his/her overall view of medical care?
3. Will he/she help you stay healthy as well as treat you when you're sick?
4. Does his/her philosophy concerning use of drugs, reliance on tests, and so forth, agree with yours?
5. What is his/her background and education?
6. What specialists is he/she likely to send you to for surgery or other unusual problems?

Source: From Associated Press release in the *Birmingham News,* May 5, 1987, pp. 6g–7g.

Other health professionals include medical (lab) and X-ray technologists, as well as respiratory, physical, and occupational therapists.

SELECTING A HOSPITAL

One way to select a hospital is to follow a physician's recommendation. This should be a geographically accessible hospital where the physician has **patient-admission privileges.** If the physician does not have admission privileges, check further into both the physician and the hospital. In a small community, there may be only one hospital. If there is a choice of hospitals, what do you look for? The following three questions should be asked:

1. *Is the hospital accredited?* Hospitals are accredited by the Joint Commission on the Accreditation of Hospitals (JCAH). Accreditation represents voluntary compliance with hospital standards established by the JCAH.
2. *Is it a "teaching" hospital?* "Teaching" hospitals have formal programs for the training of medical personnel. Thus, a hospital affiliated with a medical school and giving medical residency training theoretically provides better medical care than a hospital that does not. But this is not always so. You should look at other criteria as well.
3. *Who "owns" the hospital?* There are three general categories of hospital ownership: voluntary (nonprofit, community), private (proprietary, "for-profit"), and public (government). Among these types, privately owned hospitals tend to be the least desirable. They usually offer a smaller range of medical services and fewer backup services, such as blood banks and therapeutic X rays, because many private hospitals have a limited focus. There are many exceptions to this generalization, however; in fact, many private hospitals offer *better* facilities than voluntary or government hospitals do. Once again, all factors should be considered.

Should we accept the convenience and possibly the lower prices offered by this urgent-care center?

NEW OPTIONS FOR MEDICAL CARE

In the past, treatment in either a physician's office or a hospital were our only real choices. As medical care has become more of a business, however, other delivery systems are available as consumer products.

Ambulatory-care centers are growing very rapidly. The National Association for Ambulatory Care indicates that in 1982 there were 600 urgent-care centers (for minor injuries and family care) in the United States, by 1985 there were 2,500, and by 1990 over 5,000. The number of "surgicenters" (for outpatient surgery) has also increased rapidly.

patient-admission privileges
The rights of a physician to admit patients to certain hospitals.

ambulatory-care center
A center that provides treatment for minor medical problems without an appointment.

THE WORLD AROUND YOU
Is This Treatment Necessary?

Medical procedures have a widespread influence. When they are needed, they can be lifesaving and improve the quality of life. But when they are performed unnecessarily, they can disrupt the lives of the patient and his or her family and friends. In addition, unneeded medical procedures will add to the total cost of medical care and increase insurance costs and the overall costs of medical-care delivery for everyone.

With the increased attention given to medical-care costs and quality, academic researchers, policy analysts, and insurance companies have paid more attention to medical procedures that might be unnecessary. The treatments listed below have attracted particular attention because of their cost and frequency. If your physician suggests one of these procedures, you'd be wise to think twice and seek a second opinion. This does not mean the procedure is bad or shouldn't be used, but it is a good time to question your physician about possible alternatives to the suggested treatment. Consumers need to ask the question: Is this treatment necessary?

Cesarean section. About one in four U.S. births is completed surgically. This rate may be about twice the ideal. Hospitals that have purposely tried to eliminate unnecessary caesareans have cut their rate about in half with no apparent increase in risk to mothers or babies.

Hysterectomy. After cesarean section, this is the second most common major surgery in the United States. As many as 27 percent may be unnecessary. Rates of hysterectomy vary greatly throughout the country, an indication that physician preference plays a big role in the decision to perform the operation.

Back surgery. It is thought that at least 14 percent of common back surgery is not needed. Usually back pain can be eliminated by bed rest, improving body mechanics, appropriate exercises, physical therapy, or some combination thereof.

Magnetic resonance imaging (MRI). This is a powerful new imaging technique that produces detailed pictures of internal organs without exposing the patient to radiation. Because it is virtually risk-free, it is especially likely to be overused as a defensive measure. An MRI procedure, however, costs about $1,000, so unnecessary ones greatly add to the cost of medical care.

Prostate surgery. Surgery for noncancerous enlargement of the prostate is often unneeded. Putting off the surgery may be a wise choice, and it is not particularly dangerous. When fully informed in advance of the risks, 80 percent of men in one HMO chose to postpone the operation.

Clot-busting drugs. These drugs, when given within 4 to 6 hours of a heart attack, can break up a blood clot blocking the coronary artery and greatly reduce damage to the heart muscle. All currently available clot-busting drugs are about equally effective, but one (streptokinase) has the lowest incidence of serious side effects and costs only about $200 per dose, as compared to about $2,000 per dose for its most common competitor.

Source: From "Health Care Dollars" in *Consumer Reports* 57 (7): 435–448 (July 1992).

HEALTH UPDATE

Using No-Appointment Medical Centers

Nationwide, emergency-care centers have sprung up. Their mission is to treat minor injuries or short-term illnesses of patients who have no physician or whose doctor is unavailable. They have a licensed medical doctor present at all times, promise to deliver prompt treatment to walk-in patients, and claim to cost less than a hospital emergency room. They are typically open evenings, weekends, and holidays in addition to normal daytime hours. There are several things you can do to decide in advance whether to use a certain center. They are

1. Ask your family physician what he or she knows about the center, its doctors, and staff.
2. Check on the center's reputation—how long has it been in operation and how is it regarded in your community?
3. Visit the center, meet the physician, and tour the facilities. Talk to patients, note professional credentials, request literature, and learn how the center functions.
4. Find out how the center maintains its records. Will the center communicate directly with your physician?
5. Ask how the center works with local hospitals and emergency ambulance services, and ask if there is life-support equipment available.
6. Find out whether an emergency center physician can bypass a hospital emergency department and admit a patient directly into the hospital if needed.
7. Ask how the center handles follow-up care.

Your decision about whether to use an emergency center or a hospital will ultimately depend on your judgment of the seriousness of the problem, the cost, convenience, and your trust in the facility. We will probably see more of this new consumer orientation to health care in the future.

Urgent-care centers provide treatment without an appointment. Minor problems, such as sprained ankles, sore throats, and cuts needing stitches, are handled. Urgent-care centers do not have the same sophisticated medical equipment or medical specialists found in a full-service hospital. The centers are usually open 12 to 16 hours per day. Critics have called them "Docs-in-a-box" or even "Medical McDonald's."

Surgicenters are capable of providing minor, low-risk, outpatient surgery. For operations such as a biopsy or removal of tonsils, the patient usually goes home within a few hours after surgery. Costs are less at a surgicenter because they can operate at fixed hours, with scheduled appointments, and don't require the expensive equipment of a hospital. Surgicenter patients must be referred by a physician or a hospital.

In the summer of 1991 there was another new development—medical information by telephone. In one case, members of a Massachusetts community health plan are able to use a home computer to get nonemergency medical information. In another case, which is much more controversial, people in New York and New Jersey can call a 900 number and ask questions of a licensed physician (Zoler 1991). Some feel medical information by telephone is a sign of a deteriorating relationship between physicians and patients. Others think it is a good way to get medical information. What do you think?

ALTERNATIVE MEDICAL SYSTEMS

Some individuals argue that the Western system of medicine is not the only acceptable way to deal with medical problems. They point out that other systems have been used from time to time with interesting results. At least one-third of people with common ailments such as back pain, depression, and anxiety turn to some form of unconventional medicine for help (McKeown 1993). In fact, some alternative therapies, such as acupuncture and chiropractic, are gaining respect from the medical establishment and from insurance companies ("Alternative Medicine Is Catching On" 1993).

The dangers of improper medical care are real and common; however, the danger of our labeling something as "improper" simply because we do not understand it is equally great. While we must always be careful not to place our mental or physical health in the hands of a fraud, we must be equally careful to remain open and curious about new procedures. For example, D.O.'s (osteopaths) were once thought of as quacks because their work was misunderstood. In the same way, chiropractors are often labeled as quacks, when in fact they might perform important services in certain circumstances.

Chinese medicine, including the use of herbs and acupuncture, was long thought to be superstitious hocus-pocus until some open-minded American physicians traveled to

An example of a Chinese herbal cure for AIDS.

China and began investigating Eastern treatment methods from a Western perspective. We are now discovering that Chinese medicine has much to offer the West and vice versa. Similarly, medicine from India is receiving increasing interest and respect from the West, and Western-trained doctors are studying age-old Indian techniques.

Many individuals turn to a nonmedical practitioner because it is easier and cheaper. In 1990, Americans made 388 million trips to primary-care physicians and 425 million visits to providers of unconventional medicine. This probably has as much to do with economics as it does with changing belief systems. There is even a newly formed National Institutes of Health Office for the Study of Unconventional Medical Practices (McKeown 1993).

What is most important is to choose practitioners and methods consistent with our needs, and these individuals should have good training, demonstrate their competence, and be respected in their fields of expertise.

CHIROPRACTIC

Chiropractic is based on the theory that diseases are caused by misalignments, or subluxations, of the spine. Chiropractors

---

urgent-care center
A center that provides treatment without an appointment for minor medical problems such as sprained ankles, sore throats, and cuts needing stitches.

surgicenter
A center capable of providing minor, low-risk, outpatient surgery.

chiropractic
A system of manipulative treatment, based on the teaching that all diseases are caused by impingement on spinal nerves and can be corrected by spinal adjustments.

locate subluxations by spinal analysis and X ray, then manipulate and adjust the spinal column. The goal is to properly realign the vertebral column to remedy disease or other problems.

Chiropractors in the United States are basically of two types—straights and mixers. Straights use spinal manipulation and massage only, but mixers use these techniques as well as heat, light, and diet therapy. Chiropractors are not legally authorized to perform surgery, prescribe drugs, or practice obstetrics, and they are not permitted to practice in any hospital accredited by the Joint Commission on the Accreditation of Hospitals. Chiropractors often claim they can treat acne, goiter, heart disease, obesity, prostate trouble, angina, and ulcers, among other conditions. In one recent year, 19 million people visited chiropractors (McKeown 1993).

No scientific proof supports the theory of chiropractic practice. Orthodox medicine has always violently opposed chiropractors. The attitude of some physicians is changing, and instances can be found where physicians and chiropractors work together; however, chiropractors are not generally accepted by most medical and health groups.

After reading the above information about chiropractic, the assistant to the executive vice president for professional affairs of the American Chiropractic Association took the liberty to write what he called a "more factual, balanced article regarding chiropractic" (American Chiropractic Association, personal correspondence, 2 March 1990). Consistent with our decision-making theme and with emphasis on the need to consider varying points of view, here is his information.

> Chiropractic is based on the premise that the relationship between structure and function in the human body is a significant health factor and that the relationships between the spinal column and the nervous system contribute to the disease process. The doctor of chiropractic conducts systematic physical, neurological, and orthopedic examinations using the methods, techniques, and instruments standard with all health professions. Chiropractors also include postural and spinal analysis unique to their profession. Diagnostic X-ray and standard and special laboratory procedures and tests are used to arrive at a differential diagnosis. The Chiropractor corrects, reduces, mobilizes or immobilizes articular abnormalities, particularly of the spine and pelvis, to normalize structural and functional relationships and relieve attendant neurologic, muscular, and vascular disturbances. These methods do not include prescription drugs or major surgery, thus avoiding the dangers therein. Patient care is conducted with due regard for environmental, nutritional and psychotherapeutic factors as well as first aid, hygiene, sanitation, rehabilitation, and physiological therapeutic procedures designed to assist in the restoration and maintenance of neurological integrity and homeostatic balance.
>
> There are approximately fifty thousand licensed chiropractors in the United States. Each state has a licensing board which governs the scope of practice. Every state and the District of Columbia license chiropractors upon completion of a minimum of two years prechiropractic education in the basic sciences and four years of chiropractic college. Some states require more education. Additional time is spent in internships, residency or other specialty programs. Chiropractors have hospital privileges in many hospitals throughout the United States although not yet in every state. (Description furnished by the American Chiropractic Association in 1991).

When deciding whether chiropractic medicine can help you, Dr. Dean Edell's (1990) observations might be helpful: Chiropractors, it's safe to say, are a mixed bunch. Some are good ones who are content to deal with muscular and skeletal problems that frustrate ordinary physicians. "Then there are ones I call embarrassments, the ones who want to be primary care physicians. This brand of chiropractor honestly believes that all diseases are caused by a pinched nerve or a misaligned spinal column."

Edell feels the consumer is caught in the middle of a dilemma, because some physicians would gladly refer a patient with neck or back pain to a good chiropractor—after first ruling out more serious problems. On the other hand, most doctors simply don't trust practitioners who haven't earned a medical degree.

For those who feel it might sometimes be appropriate to consult a chiropractor, Edell offers the following advice:

1. Try a chiropractor for neck or back pain after first visiting an internist to rule out cancer and other more serious ailments.

2. Be aware that chiropractors work best for people suffering moderate, chronic pain. Spinal manipulation can actually worsen many serious disorders, including herniated discs or arthritis.

3. Make sure to find a good one. Many doctors still publicly refuse to refer patients to chiropractors, but you'll probably find that quite a few doctors "secretly" know of a few you can trust. These are the chiropractors you'll want to patronize.

ACUPUNCTURE

Acupuncture existed as long as 4,500 years ago in ancient Chinese civilizations. In the early 1970s, when acupuncture became known in the United States, Western doctors seriously questioned the theory behind it.

Acupuncture is a medical technique that involves inserting and manipulating needles in the body to relieve pain and treat disease. The needles are much finer than syringe needles and seldom cause bleeding. By inserting needles at points often far from the area to be treated, the Chinese

---

acupuncture
A medical technique that involves inserting and manipulating needles in the body to relieve pain and treat disease.

Issue

Should You Use the Services of a Chiropractor?

The chiropractor's training often seems to be inadequate. Even if some chiropractors can be helpful, legitimate medical (M.D.) specialists are available to take care of problems related to the back and spine. In addition, properly trained physical therapists who work with physicians can do everything that a good chiropractor might do. There is no logical reason to use a chiropractor.

- Pro: While it might be possible that some chiropractors are well trained and treat only the problems they are trained to handle, many chiropractors lack sufficient training to deal with such important matters. Since properly trained medical specialists are available who can be assisted by professional physical therapists, there is no reason to use a chiropractor. In other words, why should you place important care in the hands of someone who is not trained as well as the appropriate medical doctor?

- Con: Some people report good results from using chiropractic services. Since chiropractors specialize in problems of the back and spine, it makes sense to use a chiropractor if that type of problem exists. It is even likely that the services will be cheaper and more easily obtained than the services of a medical doctor. Besides, if chiropractors weren't legitimate, they wouldn't be allowed to practice.

Would you use chiropractic services? Would you recommend that a family member or a good friend use chiropractic services? If your answer is yes to either of these questions, for what problems would you recommend a chiropractor? How would you select one? How would you refute the "pro" argument listed above? If your answer to both questions is no, how would you refute the "con" argument listed above? Find another student who answered differently than you did. Compare your responses.

claim to stop pain and restore health by rebalancing the life force. Needles are inserted and twirled at any of over 367 points where there may be blockages. The objective is to balance forces necessary for health.

Traditionally, the Chinese used acupuncture for back pain, arthritis, cancer, headache, nerve deafness, ulcers, blindness, and mental disorders. Today, the Chinese have generally modified their claims and indicate it is not appropriate for all diseases and cannot be used for structural damage or infection. How it stops pain is a mystery; however, it

does seem to be helpful in some cases of deafness, narcotics withdrawal, and chronic pain. In addition, it can provide effective anesthesia in some situations.

An estimated five thousand physicians in the United States use acupuncture in their practices to treat nausea, pain, and even depression. It is also being used to treat drug and alcohol addiction, and the cost of conventional treatment is about twenty times more than outpatient acupuncture sessions (McKeown 1993).

The study of acupuncture is in its infancy. Some evidence indicates it may be useful in controlling pain, controlling nausea and vomiting, and treating alcoholism and drug addiction. Even the evidence for these benefits, however, is limited and far from conclusive. Controlled research on acupuncture's other uses is almost nonexistent. There is also no comprehensive medical explanation for acupuncture's apparent effects. Nevertheless, acupuncture remains a well-established method of treatment in Asian cultures, where it has a long tradition. It is wise to consult your physician and try appropriate medical treatments before you consider acupuncture. Like other forms of alternative medicine, acupuncture should be used only as an adjunct to regular medical treatment, never as a substitute for it ("Acupuncture" 1994).

HERBAL MEDICINE

Herbal medicine has been practiced for centuries. It is the use of natural plant substances to treat illnesses, based on folk medicine and modern research. Ancient Egyptians established pharmacies based on myrrh, peppermint, olive oil, licorice, and other herbs in addition to plants, roots, and seeds.

Very little is actually known about the effectiveness of herbal medicines or what conditions they might be effective for. Herbal medicine has increased in popularity in recent years, perhaps because of soothing effects and a claim to be "natural." One danger is that some herbs are known poisons and it is almost impossible to control dosages. In addition, there is a danger of self-diagnosis and failure to use more-appropriate medical techniques.

HOMEOPATHY

Homeopathy, started in 1810, is medication based on the premise that diluted minidoses of various substances will

herbal medicine
The use of naturally occurring plants, roots, and seeds to fight disease.

homeopathy
Medical treatment based on the premise that administration of minute doses of various substances will energize the immune system to fight disease.

TABLE 21.1   FIVE TYPES OF FAITH-HEALING GROUPS

Group Name	Who Belongs	What They Practice
Christian	Most are middle-aged, middle-class; men outnumber women.	Most base healing on Jesus' healing ministry and the place of healing in early churches.
Metaphysical	Tend to be diverse groups—some made up of mostly older people with others within a range of ages. More commonly women than men.	These groups came from Christian Science, Unity, and Religious Science. They maintain church buildings and control religious teachings. Many of their beliefs are similar to psychic and occult groups.
Technique practitioners	Mostly middle-class including all ages—even children.	Techniques are usually applied one-on-one. Many are used including acupuncture, reflexology, naturopathy, rolfing, and other nonorthodox medicine.
Eastern meditation and human potential groups	Upper-middle-class and very well educated. Most are between 25 and 40, and women predominate.	They draw from Eastern forms of meditation and popular psychotherapy methods. Examples are sensitivity training, Transcendental Meditation, Jain yoga, and meditation.
Psychic and occult groups	Some within a broad age spectrum, but middle-aged are most common. Some groups have many men, but women are more common.	They emphasize gaining power and control over life. Groups are quite diverse and include Eckankar, Great White Brotherhood, Spiritual Frontiers Fellowship, and many unaffiliated psychic healing circles.

Source: From Meredith B. McGuire, "Healing Rituals in the Suburbs" in *Psychology Today,* 23 (½): 57–64 (January/February 1989).

energize the immune system into fighting disease. In larger doses, these substances would cause the same symptoms that the practitioner wishes to cure.

Some homeopaths give evidence of how basic homeopathic principles have been adapted by mainstream medicine. For example, digitalis is used to treat heart disorders, but it can create heart problems as well. Ritalin, a drug given to hyperactive children, is a stimulant, and radiation, used to shrink tumors, is a known cause of cancer.

Homeopaths believe that the body and mind are inseparable. Therefore, treatment is determined by the individual's body type, temperament, disposition, and behavioral tendencies (McKeown 1993).

Homeopathic remedies themselves are probably harmless even though they have not been tested for safety. Homeopathy does pose one real risk: that of seeing a practitioner who will ignore or misdiagnose early symptoms of a serious disease that needs medical treatment. Also, there is still no logical, scientific case to be made for homeopathy's benefits. The theoretical basis of homeopathy is highly implausible, and what experimental evidence exists is preliminary at best ("Homeopathy: Much Ado About Nothing?" 1994).

FAITH HEALING

Faith healing is based upon the belief that the mind, which controls the body, can cure disease through divine help. A basic premise is that the patient must have faith in healers because they are God's instruments. Techniques used include prayer, laying on of hands, witchcraft, and trance. Some who believe in the healing power of faith say that sickness does not exist except as a mental condition. Others turn to faith healing only when medical science has failed to cure them.

Many people now follow a wide range of beliefs and practices not sanctioned by mainstream medicine. More than 130 different groups of healers of five broad healing types (see table 21.1) have been identified. Most individuals who use faith healing also use conventional health care. In general, those who use any of the five broad healing types view health, illness, and healing from a perspective much broader than medicine's main focus on biological functioning (McGuire 1989).

The mainstream medical profession recognizes the power of faith to influence both psychological and physiological function (again, note the mind/body/soul relationship). There are also times when diseases reverse or cure themselves without medical intervention. This is referred to as **spontaneous remission.** If a sick person has been going to a healer, it might appear that the healer is responsible for the cure.

Faith healing has existed throughout history. In recent years, though, as individuals have realized that science cannot cure everything and that there is a strong connection between emotional and bodily disorders, there is an increased

faith healing
Techniques based upon the belief that the mind controls the body and can cure disease through divine help.

spontaneous remission
The reversal or cure of disease without medical intervention.

HEALTH UPDATE

The Office of Alternative Medicine

In 1993 the Office of Alternative Medicine, created by Congress in 1991 within the National Institutes of Health, awarded its first grants ("Exercise, Meditation, Yoga Get Alternative Medicine Money" 1993). Thirty grants were approved from more than eight hundred applications designed to test the validity of unconventional medical techniques—taking into account cultural and religious belief systems and the human dimension of medicine. The titles of the grant awarded included these:

- "Can Visualization Exercises and Progressive Muscle Relaxation Boost the Immune System?"
- "Can Acupuncture Help in the Treatment of Severe Depression in Women?"
- "Can Hypnosis Reduce Suffering from Chronic Low Back Pain?"
- "Can Hypnosis Accelerate Bone Healing in People with Fractured Ankles?"

It is interesting that an official arm of the U.S. government now grants money for these studies. It will be interesting to learn about the results.

Source: From "Exercise, Meditation, Yoga Get Alternative Medicine Money" in *Health Education Reports* 15(22):5 (November 18, 1993).

---

interest in faith healing. There is no proof of the efficacy of faith healing, however, because confirmed medical conditions are difficult to obtain.

PAYING FOR MEDICAL CARE

The average cost of a hospital room continues to increase, but room charges are only part of the cost of a hospital stay. As an example, in 1993 a typical 3-day hospital stay for an intestinal infection cost $4,307 ($918 for the room, $1,096 for pharmacy charges, $1,621 for radiology services, and $672 for laboratory services [Maschal 1993]).

Medical costs in the United States increase by over 15 percent per year. The average hospital stay costs around $4,000. Next to house payments and transportation costs, the largest outlay of money may well be for medical expenses.

Another way to look at the rapid increase in medical-care costs is to realize they are rising three times as fast as the general inflation rate. Ideas to control this drastic increase include reducing the amount of legal action related to medical care, not purchasing duplicative technology, limiting hospital stays, instituting price controls, establishing stronger requirements to be sure in-hospital procedures are necessary, moving more people to home health care, and limiting access to medical procedures beyond a certain point (White 1993).

METHODS OF PAYMENT

By planning ahead, we can make wise decisions about how to pay for medical expenses—decisions that meet our needs and are within our budgets. Remember, good health today does not protect you from a sudden catastrophe tomorrow.

College students are often underinsured or not insured at all. Find out whether or not your university or workplace provides a student insurance plan. Family medical insurance policies or an employer's medical plan might not cover all your medical needs. Extra insurance or extra savings may be needed. Medical expenses are too high to be taken for granted!

With the rising cost of health care, many people support the development of a national health-care system. The debate over this continues.

Paying for medical care directly is no longer feasible, given the high cost of medical services, but anticipated medical-care expenses can be financed in various ways. How best to do this so that all Americans are covered remains controversial. Whether you use a traditional health insurance plan, or a health maintenance organization (HMO), there is emphasis on "managed care." Managed care means practices such as restricting patients to a single primary-care physician who must approve all referrals to specialists, penalizing physicians who order too many tests or procedures, preapproving elective hospitalizations, and paying only the preapproved costs for medical procedures ("Health Care Dollars" 1992). Managed care, many argue, prevents physicians from setting fees as they wish. Unheard of in the United States until around 1983, managed care now occupies an ever-increasing share of the United States medical-care market. Many physicians fear it will do nothing but lower their incomes and increase the time spent justifying the care they prescribe and filling out paperwork. By 1993, however, at least half of all United States physicians were involved in at least one type of managed-care arrangement (Butterbaugh 1993).

Health insurance plans have traditionally been much more common than **health maintenance organizations (HMOs),** but this is rapidly changing. You may find various definitions of an HMO, but generally it is a group of doctors and hospitals that provides medical care. Commonly, a gatekeeper must approve all services before they are performed. Virtually all medical services are covered, including preventive care.

What are the differences in charges between health insurance plans and HMOs? Often, very little. Both charge very similar monthly fees; thus, some employers offer either option to their employees. There is also little difference in objectives—both provide subscribers with ways to pay for many medical-care expenses—but they achieve these objectives differently. For example, under a health insurance plan, you are reimbursed for medical expenses after you use the service. Under an HMO you pay fixed membership fees (instead of health insurance premiums) in advance. You pay a small charge for seeing a physician, but all other medical-care services are paid for. HMOs make higher profits if they can avoid incurring major medical expenses (for which they must bear the cost), so they actively work toward keeping people well through timely curative services and appropriate preventive care. In fact, one of the advantages of managed-care settings is that they provide many opportunities for disease prevention and health promotion. For example, the managed-care organization can identify particular health risks and problems of the enrolled population and develop strategies to address these risks. Programs might involve outreach to patients, chart reminders, and group health education ("Health Promotion Seen as Major Function of Managed Care" 1993).

Another difference between medical insurance plans and HMOs is the choice of physicians. Under a health insurance plan, you choose your physician, but under HMOs you must choose or be assigned to physicians who are part of that HMO. Furthermore, whenever you are within the geographic service area of the HMO, you must use the HMO for services to be covered. If you are outside the HMO's service area, however, the HMO arranges for payment to another physician.

In practice the line between health insurance plans and HMOs is becoming less and less distinct, and there are as many varieties of HMOs as there are insurance plans. To make the distinction even more ambiguous, major health insurance companies such as Blue Cross and Blue Shield have already established, or are in the process of establishing, HMOs.

HMO enrollments have been rising each year, but patient dissatisfaction seems to have increased with HMO efforts to hold down costs. Some individuals favor conventional pay-as-you-go doctoring because of shorter waiting time for appointments, easier access to specialists and hospitals, and more-stable relationships between patients and their physicians ("Second Thoughts on HMOs" 1987).

There are different types of plans within managed care, and you might find that the terminology used for these varies. In the **preferred provider organization (PPO),** a network of doctors and hospitals has agreed to give the sponsoring organization discounts from their usual charges. PPOs generally don't exercise tight management over medical care. They may require physicians to get the plan's approval before sending patients to a hospital, but they don't usually require members to choose a primary-care physician. If you join a PPO, you can go to any physician in the network whenever you want to. Therefore, there generally isn't a gatekeeper.

The **point-of-service plan (POS)** (also called an "Opt-Out HMO") combines some features of HMOs and PPOs. You can get care in or out of the network, but there is an in-network gatekeeper who must approve all services. You may find, however, that a lower portion of the costs are paid if you "opt out" and use medical services from outside the network.

For further information about health insurance options, write to the Health Insurance Institute, 277 Park Avenue, New York, NY 10017. For further information about HMO options, write to the Group Health Associations of America, 1717 Massachusetts Avenue, N.W., Washington, DC 20036.

WHAT IS RECEIVED FOR PAYMENT?

What can you expect from the money you put into the medical-care system now and in the future? Unfortunately, because the cost of medical care continues to rise, less and less can be expected. The upward spiral of medical-care delivery costs has not been matched with equivalent improvements in general health or medical-care delivery. In a few instances, slight declines in ill health have been detected. This problem became even more obvious in 1993, when Hillary Rodham Clinton was given a visible role in the medical-care cost problem.

The rising costs of medical care and the relative stagnation or even decline of delivery suggest that fundamental changes need to be made in the medical-care delivery system. Various forms of national health insurance have been proposed and debated in Congress, but to date no form of national health insurance has been approved. The ideal plan would include "womb-to-tomb" universal coverage of all Americans, but how such a project might be financed remains unresolved. Supporters of national health insurance

---

health maintenance organization (HMO)
A prepayment plan for medical care.

preferred provider organization (PPO)
A group of physicians and facilities that contract with an employer to give subscribers specific services at a price (often discounted) agreed upon in advance.

point-of-service plan (POS)
A medical-care plan combining some features of HMOs and PPOs.

PERSONAL SKILLS AND EXPERIENCES

Asking Questions About Managed Care

Your employer might allow you to choose from among various managed-care plans. Besides looking at such obvious points as costs and coverage, you will be wise to also find answers to these questions:

1. How dedicated is the plan to offering and promoting preventive service? The best plans promote preventive services, such as immunization, cholesterol screening, and educational programs.

2. Is the plan attuned to customer concerns? For example, does it periodically conduct a patient survey and disclose the results?

3. How much physician turnover does the plan experience each year? If a plan's turnover rate is much higher than 5 to 10 percent, there may be problems with physician morale and motivation.

4. Is the network accredited? This is not a must, but it is a plus. The accreditation agencies with the strictest requirements are the National Committee for Quality Assurance (for HMOs) and the American Accreditation Program (for PPOs).

5. When must I notify the plan before going to the hospital or when an emergency occurs, and how do I do it? If you ignore the rules, you could jeopardize your benefits.

6. Will I be penalized for going outside the network?

7. What happens if I see a specialist who is not in the plan?

8. Are all services offered by a physician in a network covered?

9. Who pays if my regular physician is unavailable and another physician is covering?

10. Are the physicians in the plan board-certified? This means they have passed certain tests for competency in their medical field. Also, have they been with the plan long? Are there complaints against them?

11. What is the physician's obligation to me if he/she leaves the plan while I'm in the hospital? The plan may require your physician to continue your treatment until you're discharged.

12. How does the plan handle mental health coverage? What are the benefits and who determines the care I will receive? What recourse do I have if I'm unhappy with my care?

Sources: Adapted from "Are HMOs the Answer?" in *Consumer Reports* (57)8:519–531 (August 1992); and from Lani Luciano, "How to Size Up a Doctor Network" in *Money* 22(7):110–116 (July 1993).

feel it is needed because of the rapidly rising costs of medical care, the maldistribution of medical services, and many other factors. Opponents feel nationalization and further institutionalization of an already depersonalized system would harm the consumer. Chances are, as you read this, debates about national health insurance continue.

Patients can influence the quality of care by exercising patient rights. The American Hospital Association has suggested the Patient's Bill of Rights that appears in the Health Update box. If you are dissatisfied with a medical-care facility, service, or provider, you can stand up for what you deserve. To proceed with a complaint, here are some tips:

1. Specify, verbally or in writing, the who, what, when, and where aspects of your complaint.

2. Find out to whom you should direct your complaint. This is usually someone in a supervisory position, such as a physician, chief nurse, or hospital administrator.

3. If you are unsatisfied, take your complaint to the next-higher level of supervision, as high as necessary. The ultimate local authority is usually the local medical society (for physicians) or the hospital board of trustees (for nurses and administrative matters).

4. If all else fails and your complaint has to do with a hospital, determine whether the hospital is accredited by the Joint Commission on the Accreditation of Hospitals (JCAH). If it is, you can write to the JCAH.

5. Remember to be clear and confident, and document all your complaints. No medical-care facility can afford too many patient complaints. Only by being informed and assertive can you make your personal health decisions influential at the community level.

As a final note on paying for medical care, there is a trend towards insurers' limiting the amount of time in a hospital or the type of care that can be reimbursed. For example, new mothers are increasingly being told that their insurer will pay for only 1 or 2 nights in the hospital after delivery of their children. Just a few years ago, 3 days was the standard for normal delivery, and it used to be even longer. In general, patients are being moved out of hospitals "quicker and sicker" because of increased rationing of treatment. At issue is not only control of medical-care costs, but also who should make important medical-care decisions for individuals—the individuals, their families, physicians, or third parties (insurers) interested in managing costs (Spencer 1993).

AVOIDING QUACKS

In television movies, the traveling "pitchman" of old is still seen proclaiming from the back of a covered wagon the wonders of his potions and pills. Covered wagons have long since been replaced by slick ad campaigns, but the same basic attempt is still seen to get money by providing useless

A Patient's Bill of Rights

Introduction

Effective health care requires collaboration between patients and physicians and other health care professionals. Open and honest communication, respect for personal and professional values, and sensitivity to differences are integral to optimal patient care. As the setting for the provision of health services, hospitals must provide a foundation for understanding and respecting the rights and responsibilities of patients, their families, physicians, and other caregivers. Hospitals must ensure a health care ethic that respects the role of patients in decision making about treatment choices and other aspects of their care. Hospitals must be sensitive to cultural, racial, linguistic, religious, age, gender, and other differences as well as the needs of persons with disabilities.

The American Hospital Association presents *A Patient's Bill of Rights* with the expectation that it will contribute to more effective patient care and be supported by the hospital on behalf of the institution, its medical staff, employees, and patients. The American Hospital Association encourages health care institutions to tailor this bill of rights to their patient community by translating and/or simplifying the language of this bill of rights as may be necessary to ensure that patients and their families understand their rights and responsibilities.

Bill of Rights*

1. The patient has the right to considerate and respectful care.
2. The patient has the right to and is encouraged to obtain from physicians and other direct caregivers relevant, current, and understandable information

concerning diagnosis, treatment, and prognosis.

Except in emergencies when the patient lacks decision-making capacity and the need for treatment is urgent, the patient is entitled to the opportunity to discuss and request information related to the specific procedures and/or treatments, the risks involved, the possible length of recuperation, and the medically reasonable alternatives and their accompanying risks and benefits.

Patients have the right to know the identity of physicians, nurses, and others involved in their care, as well as when those involved are students, residents, or other trainees. The patient also has the right to know the immediate and long-term financial implications of treatment choices, insofar as they are known.

3. The patient has the right to make decisions about the plan of care prior to and during the course of treatment and to refuse a recommended treatment or plan of care to the extent permitted by law and hospital policy and to be informed of the medical consequences of this action. In case of such refusal, the patient is entitled to other appropriate care and services that the hospital provides or transfer to another hospital. The hospital should notify patients of any policy that might affect patient choice within the institution.

4. The patient has the right to have an advanced directive (such as a living will, health care proxy, or durable power of attorney for health care) concerning treatment or designating a surrogate decision maker with the expectation that the hospital will honor the intent of that directive to the extent permitted by law and hospital policy.

Health care institutions must advise patients of their rights under state law and hospital policy to make informed medical choices, ask if the patient has an

advance directive, and include that information in patient records. The patient has the right to timely information about hospital policy that may limit its ability to implement fully a legally valid advance directive.

5. The patient has the right to every consideration of privacy. Case discussion, consultation, examination, and treatment should be conducted so as to protect each patient's privacy.

6. The patient has the right to expect that all communications and records pertaining to his/her care will be treated as confidential by the hospital, except in cases such as suspected abuse and public health hazards when reporting is permitted or required by law. The patient has the right to expect that the hospital will emphasize the confidentiality of this information when it releases it to any other parties entitled to review information in these records.

7. The patient has the right to review the records pertaining to his/her medical care and to have the information explained or interpreted as necessary, except when restricted by law.

8. The patient has the right to expect that, within its capacity and policies, a hospital will make reasonable response to the request of a patient for appropriate and medically indicated care and services. The hospital must provide evaluation, service, and/or referral as indicated by the urgency of the case. When medically appropriate and legally permissible, or when a patient has so requested, a patient may be transferred to another facility. The institution to which the patient is to be transferred must first have accepted the patient for transfer. The patient must also have the benefit of complete information and explanation concerning the need for, risks, benefits, and alternatives to such a transfer.

(Continued on page 21.17)

9. The patient has the right to ask and be informed of the existence of business relationships among the hospital, educational institutions, other health care providers, or payers that may influence the patient's treatment and care.

10. The patient has the right to consent to or decline to participate in proposed research studies or human experimentation affecting care and treatment or requiring direct patient involvement, and to have those studies fully explained prior to consent. A patient who declines to participate in research or experimentation is entitled to the most effective care that the hospital can otherwise provide.

11. The patient has the right to expect reasonable continuity of care when appropriate and to be informed by physicians and other caregivers of available and realistic patient care options when hospital care is no longer appropriate.

12. The patient has the right to be informed of hospital policies and practices that relate to patient care, treatment, and responsibilities. The patient has the right to be informed of available resources for resolving disputes, grievances, and conflicts, such as ethics committees, patient representatives, or other mechanisms available in the institution. The patient has the right to be informed of the hospital's charges for services and available payment methods.

The collaborative nature of health care requires that patients, or their families/surrogates, participate in their care. The effectiveness of care and patient satisfaction with the course of treatment depend, in part, on the patient fulfilling certain responsibilities. Patients are responsible for providing information about past illnesses, hospitalizations, medications, and other matters related to health status. To participate effectively in decision making, patients must be encouraged to take responsibility for requesting additional information or clarification about their health status or treatment when they do not fully understand information and instructions. Patients are also responsible for ensuring that the health care institution has a copy of their written advance directive if they have one. Patients are responsible for informing their physicians and other caregivers if they anticipate problems in following prescribed treatment.

Patients should also be aware of the hospital's obligation to be reasonably efficient and equitable in providing care to other patients and the community. The hospital's rules and regulations are designed to help the hospital meet this obligation. Patients and their families are responsible for making reasonable accommodations to the needs of the hospital, other patients, medical staff, and hospital employees. Patients are responsible for providing necessary information for insurance claims and for working with the hospital to make payment arrangements, when necessary.

A person's health depends on much more than health care services. Patients are responsible for recognizing the impact of their life-style on their personal health.

Conclusion

Hospitals have many functions to perform, including the enhancement of health status, health promotion, and the prevention and treatment of injury and disease; the immediate and ongoing care and rehabilitation of patients; the education of health professionals, patients, and the community; and research. All these activities must be conducted with an overriding concern for the values and dignity of patients.

---

or unneeded health products and services. **Quackery** uses discredited or unproven methods or devices to diagnose and/or treat a variety of diseases and other disorders. Today's pitchman is known as a **quack**—a practitioner or other individual who uses these methods or devices to deceive the public.

Many health problems and practices lend themselves to quackery. For example, in one recent year federal agencies cracked down on these frauds ("Gyps and Frauds" 1994):

1. Previously owned pacemakers. An enterprising man sold used or outdated heart pacemakers. Some had been dropped on the floor during surgery or removed from patients because they were faulty. The man sterilized them, packed them in relabeled boxes, and sold them as new.

2. A pinheaded strategy for eyestrain. Sets of darkened glasses with tiny openings that makers claimed would exercise and relax the eye muscles, improve vision, and "allow you to see things you've never seen before" were advertised to the public.

quackery
Methods and/or devices used to deceive the public about health/medical care.

quack
A person who uses discredited or unproven methods or devices to diagnose and/or treat diseases or disorders.

Issue

Medisave Accounts

When we enter the medical marketplace, 95 percent of the money we spend in hospitals is someone else's money at the time we spend it, 80 percent of all physicians' payments are made with other people's money, and so are 75 percent of all medical payments. While indirectly we pay for increased medical costs, at the time we use medical services it is usually an HMO or an insurance company that pays the major share of the bills. Some argue that this causes two problems: (1) Since we pay only a fraction of the real cost of medical care, we have an incentive to overconsume. We use medical services we don't need. (2) We have given control of our medical services to third-party payers (insurance plans and HMOs) by default. They pay most of the bills, so they make decisions about our medical care. One solution to this problem is a Medisave Account, or medical savings account. We would make tax-free deposits to Medisave accounts each year. Funds in the accounts would grow tax-free, and withdrawals would be permitted only for legitimate medical expenses. Any money not spent each year would continue to grow. Funds not spent during the working years could be spent on postretirement medical care or rolled over into a pension fund. From the fund, we would pay for "catastrophic" medical insurance that kicks in only after a relatively high amount, such as $4,000 to 5,000, has been spent out-of-pocket. The out-of-pocket costs, however, would also be paid out of the Medisave Account.

- Pro: Medisave accounts would give us more control of medical services used and help improve the physician-patient relationship. Such accounts would also save money because there would be an incentive for us to use only the medical services that we really need. The cost of medical insurance would be reduced, as would administrative costs of medical care and the cost of the actual medical care.

- Con: Consumers would not get needed medical care because they would be more interested in accumulating money in their accounts. In addition, they would have responsibility for making decisions related to medical care that they are not qualified to make. Decisions about medical care should be left to physicians, since they are the experts in the field.

Do you think Medisave accounts are a good idea? Would you establish one if they were available? How do you think most people would handle them? Would they increase or decrease the quality of medical care?

Sources: Adapted from John C. Goodman and Gerald L. Musgrave, "How to Solve the Health Care Crisis" in *Consumers' Research* 85(3):10–14 (March 1992); and from Peter L. Spencer, "More Patients Being Denied Health Care" in *Consumers' Research* 76(1): 25–26 (January 1993).

3. All-you-can-eat diet pills. The ads for these pills claimed you could pop a few pills and lose 6 to 10 pounds a week while eating large quantities of any kind of food you wanted.

The most obvious danger of quackery is the loss of money, but there are also other serious consequences. First, using quack treatments can delay receiving legitimate medical services, which can mean the difference between needing a simple, relatively inexpensive treatment and needing a complex, expensive treatment or even being beyond the point of successful treatment altogether. Second, patronizing a quack may lead directly to additional harm or even death, because some quack treatments and devices cause very serious problems. Third, it can promote dangerous self-medication.

THE LURE OF QUACKERY

Quacks find a receptive audience because we want to be vibrant, attractive, and interesting. We are often anxious about our health and want to find quick, inexpensive solutions to health problems. We might visit a reputable physician and be unhappy with the results. Physicians can't guarantee results or speedy recoveries, but quacks do, and we can easily take the bait. Or, in the case of terminal illness, we might turn to a quack as the last resort. We want to have hope, and quacks offer a promise.

The claims of quacks often appear plausible partly because of our relative ignorance of health matters, our inability to filter through the flood of information about new developments in medical care, and our frequent tendency to take what is seen in print as truth. Quack claims also appear believable because they play on modern fascination with technology. Humans have walked on the moon, life has been nurtured in test tubes, and polio has been virtually wiped out—if science and technology have brought these developments, why not a quick cure for cancer or instant relief from arthritis?

Another interesting aspect of quackery is the **placebo effect.** Scientists running controlled studies in laboratory settings discovered that subjects given, for example, a simple sugar pill were almost as likely to show subjective signs of improvement—and in some cases even objective improvement—as the subjects given an actual test drug for their problems. Apparently, expectations of receiving help have a great deal to do with the actual effect of a drug, activity, or service. It is easy to see how quackery can take advantage of this placebo effect by raising expectations of the miraculous curative powers of some drug or procedure. In fact, it is the

placebo effect
Subjects' showing improvement (e.g., after taking sugar pills) just because they expect to improve.

PERSONAL SKILLS AND EXPERIENCES

A Mind/Body/Soul Approach to Health Promotion

Over 20 years ago, a well-known writer, Norman Cousins, inadvertently taught us a lot about mind/body/soul health. After being diagnosed with a serious, debilitating (and life-threatening) disease, he became determined to fight it. One physician told him there was nothing that could be done, but another agreed to work with him. Following are some of the things he did.

Mind

1. He studied research reports and other information about his disease.
2. He checked out of the hospital and into a hotel. This allowed him more peace and quiet and no unnecessary interruptions.
3. He rented a movie projector and many comedy films. He viewed the films regularly and spent lots of time laughing at them.
4. He maintained a positive outlook.

Body

1. He learned many facts about how his body functioned and the specific effects of the disease upon his body.

2. He was very careful to get appropriate rest and sleep.
3. He used only the medications that he and his doctor agreed were absolutely necessary to help control his disease.

Soul

1. He maintained faith that what he was doing was well grounded medically and that it would work.
2. He maintained strong relationships with his physician and his family and friends.
3. He continued to believe in himself.

Interdependence

1. He balanced his daily activities—even though he was initially confined to bed.
2. As he gradually got better, he continued emphasizing mind/body/soul activities.
3. He emphasized the importance of the relationships among the activities he was doing. For example, laughter, medications, human interactions, rest, and gradually increased activity were all important and mutually beneficial.

Though it took months to do so, Norman Cousins returned to normal activity. His friends, and many physicians, were amazed. He did enjoy visiting with the physician who had told him there was nothing that could be done. Mr. Cousins's experiences were reported in a well-known book entitled *Anatomy of an Illness.*

We can be susceptible to quackery because of our strong desire to look and feel better.

expectation of improvement that does the curing, not the drug or procedure itself. Again, we have an interesting example of mind/body/soul relationships.

The self-limiting nature of many diseases also contributes to the success of quackery. Many diseases (for example, the common cold) go away even if nothing is done. Other diseases are cyclic. For example, the cancer victim might think he or she is "cured" during a time when the disease is not as evident. It is easy to see how someone who has visited a quack or used a quack remedy might think it was successful if symptoms seem to disappear.

MAJOR AREAS OF QUACKERY

Major target areas for quack promotions include arthritis, fitness, weight loss, and cancer. Nutrition and cosmetic quackery are also common (and phony supplements are a waste of money and can cause or mask real health problems ["Phony Food Supplements" 1993]). Even bogus AIDS treatments are increasing.

Arthritis quackery is common because over 40 million Americans suffer from arthritis, and the nature of the disease (pain comes and goes, and there is no cure) makes it fertile ground for fraud. Arthritis sufferers may actually believe they have been cured by a quack remedy during a time when the disease is in remission.

More than $2 billion is spent annually on quack arthritis cures such as snake venom, lemon juice, milk from vaccinated cows, and steroids. Some treatments can be extremely dangerous. It is important to remember that pain relief and inflammation treatments are not the same. Serious arthritic conditions should be treated by a doctor.

Fitness is a prime area for quacks because people want the benefits of exercise without actually exercising. Recent

HEALTH UPDATE

The Top Ten Health Frauds

Americans spend an estimated $27 billion a year on quack products and treatments. Over 38 million Americans have used a fraudulent health product within the past year. Here is the FDA's list of the top ten health frauds (but keep in mind that health fraud is not limited to these ten):

1. Fraudulent arthritis products.
2. Deceptive cancer clinics.
3. Bogus AIDS cures.
4. Instant weight-loss schemes.
5. Fraudulent sexual aids.
6. Quack baldness remedies and other appearance modifiers (such as cream to remove wrinkles or a device to "develop" the bust).
7. False nutritional schemes.
8. Chelation therapy. (This is an injection or tablet that is supposed to clean out the arteries. The FDA and the American Heart Association agree that there is no scientific evidence that chelation therapy works.)
9. Unproven use of muscle stimulators. (Claims are made that stimulators can remove wrinkles, perform face-lifts, reduce breast size, and remove cellulite. Claims are even made that they can reduce one's beer belly with no effort. They can't do any of these things.)
10. *Candidiasis* hypersensitivity. (Candida is a fungus found naturally on the body. It can multiply and infect the skin or mucous membranes. Promoters recommend antifungal drugs and vitamin and mineral supplements. These don't work, and the idea that some people are hypersensitive to candida has not even been proven.)

Source: From "The Top Ten Health Frauds" *Consumers' Research* 73(2): 34–36 (February 1990).

years have brought all sorts of "body toning" devices, such as electrical muscle stimulators and machines that vibrate body parts. Such devices are worthless for body toning and can even be dangerous, but they are advertised and sold as substitutes for exercising.

Weight-loss schemes might be the most popular form of quackery. Millions of people seek a painless and effortless way to win the battle of the bulge. Because proper diet and exercise take constant discipline and work, quack claims are especially appealing. The fact is, you can't lose weight unless the amount of food you eat is reduced and the amount of exercise you do is increased. There are no medicines or devices that make this process effortless.

Cancer quack cures are probably the cruelest and most expensive. Seriously ill individuals may spend thousands of dollars on ineffective quack treatments. Among the most popular quack cancer remedies are immune-enhancing therapies (to improve the immune system), metabolic treatments, and special diets. None of these are effective (Cassileth 1991).

There is no one device or remedy capable of diagnosing or treating all types of cancer. Cancer cannot be detected or treated solely through the use of machines. Before you are treated at a cancer clinic or use a product that is supposed to cure cancer, you would be wise to consult with a respectable physician and the American Cancer Society.

RECOGNIZING QUACKERY

Considering the many health decisions made in the world of advancing technology, how can we tell which health products and services are legitimate? Few rules apply in every situation, but here are some warning signs that quackery may be present:

1. A cure for the disease is guaranteed.
2. A special or "secret" formula or machine is discussed.
3. A quick and easy treatment and speedy cure are promised.
4. Health services are advertised, using case histories and testimonials from patients.
5. We are warned of the danger of orthodox drugs and treatments.
6. Claims are made of persecution by the medical community.
7. There is refusal to accept proven methods of medical research.
8. Claims are made of treatment methods that are better than surgery, X rays, and medically prescribed drugs.
9. Ingredients are not identified.
10. Support from experts is claimed, but they are not named or fully identified.

THE WORLD AROUND YOU
Cosmetic Surgery

In a recent year, more than 1 million cosmetic procedures were performed on Americans. Once these procedures were exclusively for the rich, but today an increasing number of middle-class Americans are getting skin-tightening and fat-removing cosmetic procedures. Traditionally, it was mostly women who had cosmetic surgery, but today nearly one out of every three cosmetic operations is performed on a man.

Why do so many people have cosmetic surgery? The only reason is to look better and/or younger, since no medical benefit is involved. This means we have surgery to feel better about ourselves and to look better for others.

Here are some interesting results from a recent Gallup poll of 1,015 adults:

1. Do you think cosmetic surgery is an acceptable way for an older adult to maintain his or her looks? (55% said yes and 43% said no.) Adults over age 50 were slightly less likely to approve than were younger adults. Also, those who earn $50,000 or more per year were more likely to approve than those who earn less than $30,000 per year (69% to 51%).

2. Do you think cosmetic surgery is an acceptable way for a young adult to improve his or her looks? (45% said yes and 52% said no.) Interestingly, 47 percent of those 30 or older approved, compared to 37 percent of those under 30.

3. Which do you find easier to accept: the idea of a woman having cosmetic surgery, or the idea of a man having it? (58% said a woman, 1% said a man, and 25% said either/both.) Again, younger adults were more conservative (16% said cosmetic surgery is equally acceptable for men or women, but 28% of those 30 or older okay both).

4. Which, if any, of the following do you find to be an acceptable procedure for a member of your immediate family?

nose job = 54%   liposuction = 31%
hair transplant = 54%   breast implant = 20%
face-lift = 48%   buttock implant = 14%

5. Do you think that cosmetic surgery will eventually become as routine as, say, dyeing one's hair? (57% said yes and 40% said no.)

Source: From Jeff Schein, "Cosmetic Surgery: A Nip and a Tuck" in *Consumers' Research* 75(9): 30–34 (September 1992); and from Ann Japenga, "Face Lift City" in *Health* 7(2): 47–55 (March/April 1993).

11. Claims are made for effectiveness for a variety of conditions (the broader a claim, the less believable it is).

12. The product is declared as all "natural." This probably means the product is some combination of vitamins and minerals and no different from a typical multivitamin pill.

13. Vague illusions are made to "published research," sometimes with an offer to supply references by letter.

14. The product is offered only through the mail or door-to-door.

Some mail services, such as those that sell eyeglasses or dental plates, might not actually be fraudulent but are of dubious value because interpretation, adjustment, or quality control by a health professional is crucial. For example, a mail-order urinalysis has been promoted by some firms for many years. A urinalysis is an important part of a medical examination but is of questionable value when conducted through the mail. Its results can also be misleading without a more thorough exam conducted and interpreted by a licensed physician.

If you suspect quackery in any health-related product or service, consult a physician, pharmacist, or other health professional. In addition, one of the consumer protection agencies or consumer organizations mentioned earlier might be contacted.

If you want to take legal action against a quack, you can get help from the National Council Against Health Fraud. This organization can refer you to an experienced lawyer, provide a registry of expert witnesses, give information on defense witnesses, and furnish a list of unproven, fraudulent, and potentially dangerous treatments. Contact the National Council Against Health Fraud, Inc., P.O. Box 1276, Loma Linda, CA 92354; phone (909) 824–4690 (Carlyon 1993).

Even though the ultimate responsibility for wise health decisions falls on the shoulders of consumers, we are not alone in the process. Help is available if we seek it and know how to use it.

TAKE ACTION

1. Assess your motivation and reasons for purchasing health services.

2. Become a wiser consumer of health services. For example, keep informed about the varieties of health services available and check out services before using them.

3. Use your rights as a consumer to take action if you experience a problem with a medical service.

4. Analyze your personal health insurance options and implement an insurance plan to cover you and your family in the best way possible.

PERSONAL SKILLS AND EXPERIENCES

PNI and Consumer Choices

Psychoneuroimmunology (PNI) is the study of the interaction of the mind, the central nervous system, and the body's immunological system. It has been shown that people with a fighting spirit, optimism, a sense of control, hope, and faith can actually build their immune systems. The brain has the capability to self-medicate and to release a variety of mental and physical painkillers and motivating substances (neuropeptides) when the demand is there.

The decision about health-care providers and consumer health is extremely important as it relates to PNI. You have learned that modern medicine has become extremely sophisticated and specialized. Medicines and technology continue to become more and more sophisticated. Often, the power of touch, hope, and optimism is neglected, and the members of the medical profession rely almost totally on technology for healing. Those physicians who provide hope, optimism, touch, a sense of control, and other human caring traits facilitate the healing experience.

Generally speaking, quackery thrives largely because of the belief that a certain fraudulent cure will work. Consumers believe something will work, and it does, through their own self-efficacy or faith. The methods by themselves do not work, but in combination with a patient who believes, the patient's hopes, fighting spirit, control, and optimism are raised. This may fortify the immune system so the patient feels better. Faith healings among religions also promote the positive states that may result in feeling better. This process has been demonstrated repeatedly when modern medicine has been administered to someone of another culture.

Someone who is offering some form of quackery generally offers something more than a traditional doctor's office visit. They give substantial time, touching, and take time to understand feelings. We can learn from that element of caregiving and take advantage of alternative forms of healing that can supplement doctors' orders. It is with some hesitation that this recommendation is made in light of how we have treated quackery in the past. It has been viewed as totally negative and worthless. The fact is, it may provide hope in some cases. The caution is twofold:

Never use a quackery method instead of a physician's recommendation, but perhaps the method can be used in harmony with the prescription. This is particularly true if you have strong faith in the method.

Secondly, do not spend much money on a questionable product in spite of claims. Unless you have money to throw away, you can create your own techniques to bolster your immune system.

With those cautions in mind, you may want to try some methods that are truly beneficial to reduce stress and provide a basis for hope, optimism, control, and a fighting spirit.

1. Take the opportunity to learn water therapy (Angelé 1980). Many of us know how good it feels to sit in a Jacuzzi and feel the benefits of water massage. The most famous form of therapy is the German Kneipp water application method and its therapeutic benefit. It is the 400-year-old science of warm and cold water applications to various parts of the body that result in a reduction of the stress response, a relaxing and calming effect, an enriched circulation, and stimulation of the skin. In essence, the process is to apply cold water (46°–50° F) on the skin, beginning with the arms (from fingers to shoulders), the legs (from the toes to upper leg), the face, and finally the body. Lay down, relax, and feel the wonderful sensation of the tingling skin following the experience. There are 160 different Kneipp applications. Many involve special equipment and are beyond the scope of this text but would be a viable compliment to traditional medical care.

2. Mentally feel the healing effects of acupressure massage. Massages in combination with acupressure can improve circulation, reduce muscle tension and pain, relieve pain, and help deeply relax the mind and body. Massage will take your mind off problems, let you focus on the positive touching experience, and produce a subtle calm over the whole body. The Chinese thoroughly studied the body, isolating and recording the points where knots and bands of excessive muscle tension frequently occur.

3. Enhance your spiritual dimension of living (if comfortable with this concept) as it pertains to faith, belief in a higher power, and practice accessing that power through the means dictated by your own belief system. Rituals or symbols (prayer or charms) to aid in the healing or preventive sense can help compliment medicine.

4. There are numerous other techniques that can make you feel good if you try them and believe that they will work especially if used in harmony with medical guidance. Examples include deep-muscle therapy, meditation, and self-hypnosis (Feltman 1989).

Issue

Quackery and Government Control

Many argue that the best way to deal with quackery is to have more government control. They feel that the best scientific evidence should be used to control quack products and services. They would give more power to agencies such as the FDA and the FTC and charge the government with developing stricter laws and regulations dealing with health products and services.

- Pro: We can't expect people to have the technical expertise to evaluate health information and services. Because technology changes so fast and people are so busy with other things, only experts can really know what is best. We should be able to assume that government agencies have taken sufficient steps to be sure that available health products and services are safe and beneficial. If we can't have that assurance, the products and services shouldn't be on the market.

- Con: Informed consumers are the ultimate protection against quackery. Most issues surrounding quackery are subtle, and agencies and legislation cannot deal with them. It makes sense to have the emphasis on education and decision making. This will result in better consumer information, sound decision-making abilities, and much less quackery.

How can quackery best be controlled? Is it best to spend more money on laws and other controls or to spend the money on consumer education? If you were in charge of reducing the amount of quackery in the United States, how would you do it?

5. Be alert for quackery and take action to help prevent it. Analyze ads, articles, and medical claims from other sources in a manner appropriate for a wise health consumer.

6. Develop a plan for others to help them become wiser health consumers.

SUMMARY

1. Decisions about medical care include when to use self-care, when to seek medical care, how to help the medical specialist help us, and how to find a suitable medical specialist or hospital.

2. Medical care should be used in a life-threatening situation, when bodily symptoms have lasted for an unusually long time, and when there is uncertainty.

3. To choose medical care, the consumer must know what kind of medical help is available, how to check credentials, and how to evaluate personal responses.

4. New options for medical care include urgent-care centers and surgicenters.

5. Alternative medical systems include chiropractic, acupuncture, herbal medicine, homeopathy, and faith healing.

6. Options for paying for medical care include individual insurance programs and various types of HMOs.

7. There are many rights to remember when being a patient.

8. Quacks find a receptive audience in the American population for a variety of reasons.

9. Major areas of quackery include arthritis, fitness, weight loss, and cancer.

10. There are a number of ways to recognize quackery.

COMMITMENT ACTIVITIES

1. Review several medical self-help books available in your college library or local bookstore. Do they seem to advocate sound procedures? Can you detect any quack practices in them? How do the books compare to the information in this text?

2. As noted in this chapter, the American Hospital Association has a "Patient's Bill of Rights." Determine which hospitals in your community post "A Patient's Bill of Rights" and have a written policy on handling patient complaints about the hospital's quality of care. If any hospital does not post the bill of rights or have a written policy for handling patient complaints, discuss the issue with a hospital administrator.

3. Collect information on several health insurance plans and an HMO, if one is in your area. What are the benefits and drawbacks of each? How would you choose among them?

4. Share your most recent experience as a patient in either a hospital or an office/clinic with other class members. Bring out your perceptions of the positive and negative aspects of your encounter with the medical-care system.

5. Pay attention to advertisements in some popular magazines. Using this chapter's guidelines for recognizing quackery, identify instances where quackery seems to be present. Write to the editors of magazines in which suspected quack practices or products are advertised. Point out the apparent quackery to them and inquire about their policies for accepting advertising. Request a written explanation.

REFERENCES

"Acupuncture." 1994. *Consumer Reports* 59, no. 1 (January): 54–59.

"Alternative Medicine Is Catching On." 1993. *Kiplinger's Personal Finance Magazine* 47, no. 1 (January): 98–99.

Angelé, K. H. *Your Daily Health Care with Kneipp.* Bad Worishofen, Germany: Kneipp-Verlag GMBH (1980).

Butterbaugh, L. 1993. "Exploiting Managed Care's Success." *Medical World News* 34, no. 2 (April): 22.

Carlyon, W. 1993. "The National Council Against Health Fraud, Inc." *HEXTRA* 18, no. 5 (November–December): 5.

Cassileth, B. R. 1991. "Questionable and Unproven Cancer Therapies." *Consumers' Research* 74, no. 9 (September): 20–23.

Clark, J. B. 1993. "New Choices in Who Cares for You." *Kiplinger's Personal Finance Magazine* 47, no. 11 (November): 124.

Edell, D. 1990. "How to Find a Good Chiropractor." *Edell Health Letter* 9, no. 4 (April): 2.

"Exercise, Meditation, Yoga Get Alternative Medicine Money." 1993. *Health Education Reports* 15, no. 22 (November): 5.

Feltman, J. (Editor) *Hands-On Healing.* Emmaus, Penn.: Rodale Press (1989).

"Gyps and Frauds: Update." 1994. *Kiplinger's Personal Finance Magazine* 48, no. 5 (May): 136–37.

"Health Care Dollars." 1992. *Consumer Reports* 57, no. 7 (July): 435–48.

"Health Promotion Seen as Major Function of Managed Care." 1993. *Health Education Reports* 15, no. 13 (1 July): 4.

"Homeopathy: Much Ado About Nothing?" 1994. *Consumer Reports* 59, no. 3 (March): 201–6.

Maschal, R. 1993. "The High Cost of a Hospital Stay." *Birmingham News,* 12 July, E1–2.

McGuire, M. B. 1989. "Healing Rituals in the Suburbs." *Psychology Today,* January/February, 57–64.

McKeown, L. A. 1993. "The Health Profession on an Alternative Mission." *Medical World News* 34, no. 4 (April): 48–60.

"Phony Food Supplements." 1993. *Edell Health Letter* 12, no. 1 (January): 1.

Sanchez, A. 1987. "Salud Popular: An Ethnographic Study of the Lay Health Beliefs and Health Seeking Behaviors of Hispanic Elderly. Ph.D. diss., University of Washington.

"Second Thoughts on HMOs." 1987. *Changing Times* 41, no. 5 (May): 33–38.

Smith, T. C., and T. L. Thompson. 1993. "The Inherent, Powerful Therapeutic Value of a Good Physician-Patient Relationship." *Psychosomatics* 34, no. 2 (March–April): 166–69.

Spencer, P. L. 1993. "More Patients Being Denied Health Care." *Consumers' Research* 76, no. 1 (January): 25–26.

"Take Charge of Your Health." 1993. *Consumer Reports on Health* 5, no. 11 (November): 117–19.

"The Top Ten Health Frauds." 1990. *Consumers' Research* 73, no. 2 (February): 34–36.

White, S. W. 1993. "Health Care and Genetics." *Phi Kappa Phi Journal* 73, no. 2 (Spring): 2–3.

Zoler, M. L. 1991. "Do Call-In Consults Enhance or Counterfeit Medicine?" *Medical World News* 32, no. 8 (August): 25.

ADDITIONAL READINGS

"Alternative Medicine: The Facts." 1994. *Consumer Reports* 59, no. 1 (January): 51–53. Gives an overview of current methods of alternative medicine, discusses pros and cons, and provides reasons some people take alternative medicine seriously.

Foulke, J. E. 1992. "Cosmetic Ingredients: Understanding Puffery. *Consumers' Research* 75, no. 6 (June): 25–27. Provides information about claims, names, and biological ingredients of cosmetics. Discusses the process of industry self-regulation in the cosmetic industry.

"Health Care Policy in America." 1993. *National Forum: The Phi Kappa Phi Journal* 73, no. 3 (Summer). This entire issue, devoted to the topic of health-care reform, includes articles on the case for a single-payer system, health-care reform and the goals of medicine, rationing health care, what the consumer wants, defensive medicine, community-care networks, the challenge of HIV infection, and other significant health-care reform topics.

Kazman, S. 1991. "The FDA's Deadly Approval Process." *Consumers' Research* 74, no. 4 (April): 31–34. Outlines the FDA approval process for new drugs and gives examples of deaths that might have been caused by "too much safety."

"What You Should Know About Medigap Policies." 1993. *Consumers' Research* 76, no. 1 (January): 27–30. Explains the need for Medicare supplemental insurance and outlines available options. Describes what is covered by various plans.

CHAPTER 22

Personal Safety

KEY QUESTIONS

What is personal safety?
Can you be completely safe from all risks?
What areas of your life pose a risk to you, related to personal safety?
How do you reduce your individual risk and increase your personal safety?
Who is responsible for your safety?
If acceptable risk is an individual decision, how do you set acceptable risk for yourself, related to personal safety?
How do awareness and preplanning reduce risk?
What agencies and organizations provide information and assistance in reducing personal safety risks?

CHAPTER OUTLINE

Medical Emergencies
Auto Safety
Home and Apartment Safety
Dorm Safety
Campus Safety
Disaster Preparedness
Safety and the Elderly
Violence
Recreational Safety
Hiking and Backpacking
Hunting and Fishing
Bicycling
Jogging and Walking
Swimming
Travel Safety
Travel by Aircraft
Travel by Automobile
Motel and Hotel Safety
Worksite Safety
Planning for Emergencies
Dealing with Emergencies
Take Action
Summary

Healthy People 2000 Objectives

- Reduce deaths caused by alcohol-related motor vehicle crashes to no more than 8.5 per 100,000 people.
- Reduce homicides to no more than 7.2 per 100,000 people.
- Reduce weapon-related violent deaths to no more than 12.6 per 100,000 from major causes.
- Reduce assault injuries among people aged 12 and older to no more than 10 per 1,000 people.
- Reduce rape and attempted rape of women aged 12 and older to no more than 108 per 100,000 women.
- Reduce by 20 percent the proportion of people that possess weapons that are inappropriately and therefore dangerously available.
- Increase to at least 85 percent the proportion of workplaces with 50 or more employees that offer health promotion activities for their employees.
- Reduce deaths caused by unintentional injuries to no more than 29.3 per 100,000 people.
- Reduce nonfatal unintentional injuries so that hospitalizations for

this condition are no more than 754 per 100,000 people.
- Reduce deaths caused by motor vehicle crashes to no more than 1.9 per 100 million vehicle miles traveled and 16.8 per 100,000 people.
- Reduce deaths from fall and fall-related injuries to no more than 2.3 per 100,000 people.
- Reduce drowning deaths to no more than 1.3 per 100,000 people.
- Reduce residential fires to no more than 1.2 per 100,000 people.
- Increase the use of occupant protection systems, such as safety belts, airbags, and child safety seats to at least 85 percent of motor vehicle occupants.
- Increase the presence of functional smoke detectors to at least one on each habitable floor of all inhabited residential dwellings.
- Reduce deaths from work-related injuries to no more than 4 per 100,000 full-time workers.
- Reduce work-related injuries resulting in medical treatment, lost time from work, or restricted work activity to no more than 6 cases per 100 full-time workers.

How Safe Are You?

The following assessment will help you determine your safety awareness and help you make good choices that will affect your daily life.

Directions

Answer yes or no to each of the following questions.

1. Have you taken a CPR (cardiopulmonary resuscitation) class within the last year?
2. Have you taken a first aid class within the last 3 years?
3. Do you keep emergency telephone numbers and instructions on or near your telephone at home and at work?
4. Have you checked the safety features in your car within the last 2 weeks to be sure that they are working properly?
5. Do you always wear a seat belt when traveling in a car?
6. Do you keep an emergency kit in your car, including tools, jumper cables, flashlight, warm clothes, first aid kit, and so on?
7. Do you completely clear snow and ice from all windows and lights before driving in winter conditions?
8. Does your home/apartment/dorm have smoke detectors, fire extinguishers, deadbolt locks, and a peephole to see who is at your door?
9. Are all primary and secondary exit routes from your home/apartment/dorm clear of obstructions and well lit?
10. Do you store, use, and dispose of chemicals in a safe and legal manner?
11. Do you live on the ground level of a building?
12. Do you live above the fifth floor of a building?
13. Do you know where the utility shutoffs are for your home/apartment/dorm, and do you know how to use them if you need to?
14. Do you have a "72-hour kit" in case of a disaster?
15. Do you choose day care for your children based only on a convenient location?
16. Have you taken appropriate steps to make your home/apartment safe for elderly visitors or occupants?

17. Did you look at safety factors such as location, lighting, windows, and exits when choosing your home/apartment/dorm?
18. Do you hike, bike, walk, or jog alone?
19. When choosing a route to bike, walk, or jog, do you drive along the route first to look for hazards?
20. When you go fishing, hunting, hiking, biking, walking, or jogging, do you tell someone where you are going and when you will return?
21. When traveling by air, do you keep medications, personal needs, money, and identification in your carry-on luggage?
22. When vacationing by car, do you plan your routes and stops ahead of time, and does someone know where you are and how to contact you every day?
23. When you begin a project such as painting, going on vacation, or going jogging, do you take time to think of and plan for safety considerations?

Scoring and Interpretation

The answer indicating safe behavior in response to questions 11, 12, 15, and 18 is no. On all other questions the answer indicating safe behavior is yes. Total your number of answers indicating safe behavior and interpret as follows:

20–23 = Your personal safety awareness is good to excellent.

17–19 = Your personal safety awareness is moderate, and you should review the sections that discuss the areas in which you practice unsafe behaviors.

16 or less = You need to increase your personal safety awareness. This chapter is for you. Remember, these are choices and decisions that affect your life every day.

Source: Courtesy of Les Chatelain, Director of Emergency Programs and Deputy Director of the Health Behavior Laboratory, University of Utah.

Statistics show that most people who die between the ages of 1 and 45 are killed in accidents—not only automobile accidents, but also falls, drownings, electrocutions, occupational accidents, and many other kinds of accidents that occur thousands of times a day (see National Safety Council 1993). There will be more than 10 million accidental disabling injuries this year in the United States, accounting for a total financial loss of over $100 billion. This does not even take into account the accidents that we recover from within a few weeks or the ones in which no one is hurt but property is damaged or cases of assault and other violence. How can you keep from becoming one of these statistics? You cannot completely, but there are many things you can do to reduce your

risk of having an accident and many more things you can do to lessen the damage and speed your recovery. That is what personal safety is all about.

MEDICAL EMERGENCIES

Medical emergencies are common in every community. You have probably been a bystander or personally involved in at least one medical emergency in the last year. It is a well documented fact that in 90 percent of all cases where CPR is performed by a nonprofessional care provider, the CPR is performed on a friend or family member of the provider. This means that you will probably be called upon to give

EMERGENCY TELEPHONE NUMBERS

Police_____   Ambulance_____

Fire Department _____   Poison Control Center_____

Your Address_____

Your Telephone Number_____

Nearest Major Intersection _____

Primary Physician_____   Dentist_____

Pediatrician_____   Ob/Gyn_____

Preferred Hospital _____

Others to contact in an emergency (day care, babysitting, food, friends, family)

_____

_____

Figure 22.1

Photocopy this page, complete the information, and post it near your telephone. In many areas, police, fire, and ambulance can be contacted by dialing 911.

first aid to someone you know. There is nothing more frustrating and guilt inducing than having to watch a friend or family member suffer or even die because you did not know what to do to help.

First, know how to get help. Have emergency telephone numbers posted on or near all telephones (fig. 22.1). The 911 system is in operation in most communities, but not all; know the emergency number for your area. You might not need the 911 services. It might be the Poison Control Center or your family physician that you need, and 911 cannot connect you with them. *All* emergency numbers should be posted. Other important information to post by your telephone

includes work telephone numbers; your address, including number coordinates for both your house and street; and telephone numbers of friends and family members. These people may be of assistance with such things as tending younger family members, transportation, or food preparation. You will be surprised at how difficult it is during an emergency to remember simple things like telephone numbers or where the kids are.

Second, be prepared to give the needed information to the dispatcher, who will ask for your name, the telephone number you are calling from, the exact location of the emergency, what happened, how many victims there are, what the victims' conditions are, and what help is being given. This means you will need to briefly assess the emergency prior to making the call. Lack of information can delay the response of needed personnel.

Third, provide basic emergency care. What care you can provide is very limited unless you are trained. You can obtain first aid and training in **cardiopulmonary resuscitation (CPR)** from many sources, including the American Red Cross, the American Heart Association, hospitals, community adult education programs, colleges and universities, church groups, and civic groups. It is recommended that you receive CPR training yearly and first aid training at least every 3 years. There are some things that can be done with little or no training. Immediately assess the emergency. Is it safe for you, the victims, and others to be in the area? Ask the victim what happened. If the victim can talk to you, she or he probably has adequate airway, breathing, and pulse. These should be assessed throughout your treatment. If the person does not respond to you, and someone else is present, send them immediately to call for medical assistance while you determine if the victim is breathing and has a pulse. If there is no breathing or pulse, treat these according to your training. Look for any bleeding. Most bleeding can be slowed down or stopped by applying pressure to the wound with your hand. Some type of clean barrier (such as a towel or clothing) should be placed between your hand and the wound to prevent infection of the victim or yourself. *Important:* Do not move the person unless you absolutely must, either to treat the victim or because the scene is definitely unsafe (it is usually best to keep the victim of an automobile accident in the car and in the position you find him or her in). Talk to the person and keep them calm. Be very reassuring. If the victim is too hot, try to cool them down. If the victim is too cold, try to warm them up. Always work within your training. Do all you can for the victims but do not attempt things you are not trained to do or cannot remember how to perform (see Emergency Cardiac Care Committees 1992; American Academy of Orthopaedic Surgeons 1992).

Lastly, while we all hope that we will never be involved in a medical emergency, we still need to be prepared. Have a first aid kit available. You may want to have one at home, in your car, and at work. Obtain health insurance if at all possible. With the cost of medical treatment these days, an accident can become a financial burden that you will never recover from. Some relatively inexpensive sources for health insurance are your school and/or work. Even if your work does not provide health insurance for free, it is often available at reduced costs through your employer. Select the appropriate care. A private physician, a specialist, a multispecialty clinic, a free-standing emergicenter, and a hospital emergency department may all be appropriate at different times. The key is not to overtreat or undertreat your emergency.

Not all medical emergencies come from outside influences. One common medical emergency comes from drug interactions. These can be from prescription or over-the-counter medications. In these days of medical specialization, many people see several different care providers, depending on the problem. You might have an orthopedic surgeon for your skiing injury, an ob/gyn for gynecological care, student

health services for colds and flu, a dentist for dental care, and an emergicenter for accidents. Any of these care providers could prescribe a medication that will interact with a medication prescribed by someone else. It is important that you inform care providers of all medications you are taking. Another precaution that you can take is to always use the same pharmacy when having prescriptions filled and ask the pharmacist if there could be any problems with over-the-counter medications that you select. Most pharmacies review all new prescriptions to determine if they will interact with any of your current prescriptions, but they can check only the prescriptions that were filled at that pharmacy. Always tell your pharmacist about medications that you are taking that were not purchased at that pharmacy or that are over-the-counter medications.

AUTO SAFETY

Our automobiles tend to be one of the most frequently overlooked areas in safety. Sure, we wash and wax the car, and if we are going on a long trip, we might have it "checked out," but when was the last time you checked the air pressure in your spare tire? Most automobile accidents and breakdowns occur within 5 miles of home. Almost all companies with large fleets of vehicles require the drivers to do a daily or weekly safety check, and yet most of us are comfortable with doing safety checks twice a year for "big trips." We typically do not go as many miles per day as a fleet vehicle, but we should still check our vehicles every 2 to 4 weeks. This inspection should include checking levels of fluids such as oil, coolant, transmission, and window washer fluids; lights, including front and rear, brakes, hazard flashers, turn signals, and interior lights; fan belts; brakes; tires; battery; and exhaust system.

No matter how good a condition the car is in, the most important factor is the driver. Take a moment before you climb into the driver's seat to assess your condition. We frequently think of drugs and alcohol and the impact they have on our ability to drive, but prescription medications and over-the-counter medications can have just as much effect. Our mental state can have a tremendous effect on our driving also. If you are tired, mad, stressed, depressed, or simply late for an appointment, your mind and thoughts are often not on driving. Studies have shown that we make an average of 400 decisions per mile of city driving, and 38 of those will be major decisions. If your mind is on an upcoming test or the person in the car with you or any of the many other places your mind can go while you drive, one of those 400 decisions could turn out badly.

cardiopulmonary resuscitation (CPR)
An emergency measure to artificially maintain breathing and heartbeat.

It is important to clear *all* windows, windshield wipers, lights, and air exchange ports prior to driving after a snowfall.

Even if you do regular maintenance and safety checks, you may still experience a breakdown or accident (see the section in this chapter called "Travel by Automobile"). In these cases you should have an emergency kit in your vehicle. This kit should contain first aid supplies, flares or other warning devices, flashlight, blanket, tools, jumper cables, tow cable, fire extinguisher, warm clothing, and coins to make a phone call. Some extra fluids such as oil and coolant can be helpful, but carrying extra fuel is discouraged.

None of the equipment mentioned is of any use if you do not know how to use it. One of the best examples of this was the person who arrived at an accident and decided to put flares out to warn oncoming traffic. After checking to see that there had not been any gasoline spilled, he proceeded to go through two books of matches trying to light the flares. It is important that you know how to use your jack as well as how to change the tire; one without the other is useless. A variety of places offer training in basic maintenance and repair of your vehicle and use of emergency equipment. These include automobile clubs, automobile dealerships, community adult education programs, and church and civic groups. If all else fails, ask a friend, but do it *before* you get stranded.

One out of every two people will be involved in a disabling or fatal car accident in his or her lifetime. On the average, people have one accident every 4 years. Auto accidents are the leading cause of death in the traditional college-age population. Auto accidents are the leading cause of occupational deaths. This is also one area where we, as individuals, can have the most impact on our safety. Maintaining our vehicles properly, wearing seat belts, not driving under the influence of drugs, alcohol, or mental distractions, following traffic laws and regulations, and taking periodic driver safety classes can drastically reduce the pain, death, and disability caused by auto accidents. Many agencies, including the National Safety Council, local and state health departments, and automobile clubs, such as the American Automobile Association (AAA), have classes and information on automobile and driving safety.

Issue

Are Safe Cars Worth the Cost?

Every year thousands of Americans lose their lives in automobile accidents. Automobile accidents are the leading cause of death in Americans ages 1 to 45. Over the past decade many federal and state laws and regulations have been enacted to force automobile manufacturers to build safer cars. Such things as airbags, mandatory passenger restraints, unitized body construction, and antilock brakes have been mandated.

- Pro: These laws and regulations have saved thousands of lives over the past decade and will continue to save lives in the future. A little inconvenience, such as having to wear your seat belt, is well worth the benefits.

- Con: These safety additions force the American consumer to spend significantly more money for their cars. This is another situation where government is interfering in our personal lives. These additions should be available for those who want them but not be forced on everyone. It should be the individuals who are being placed at risk that make the decision for themselves, not government.

While this is viewed as a public health issue, it is the individual who is put at risk. Should we have the right to determine our own needs, or is the "good of all" more important than the rights of an individual?

HOME AND APARTMENT SAFETY

There are many safety concerns to consider when choosing where to live. Look at the area you have chosen. If it is a high-crime area, it might not be your first choice; however, finances often dictate where we live. If this is the case, recognize that fact, and do all you can to make your selection as safe as possible. Walk around the outside of the building. Are there bushes or trees that would provide dark hiding places or access points for burglars or attackers? Are there adequate lights, and do they work? Pay particular attention to walkways, parking areas, and entrances. If snow is a problem in your area, ask how snow removal is taken care of and how soon after the snowfall removal occurs. Is access controlled at the entrance to the building, or can anyone enter? How is that access maintained? If you are looking at a multiple-story building, do not choose to live on the first floor or above the fifth floor. Burglaries and assaults occur most frequently on the first floor because access is much easier. Living above the fifth floor is a problem because it takes longer to evacuate from that height in case of a fire or disaster. Another problem with living above the fifth floor is that conventional rescue and fire-fighting methods are of limited use above that height and many towns do not have the specialized equipment needed.

PERSONAL SKILLS AND EXPERIENCES

Home Safety Walk-Through Checklist

Outside

Walkways

_____ In good condition (no large cracks, holes, or raised portions).

_____ Shrubs lining walkways kept trimmed small enough to prevent someone from hiding in or behind them.

_____ Any stairs in good condition.

_____ Snow and ice kept cleared.

_____ Adequate lighting, particularly in entryways, parking areas, and frequent-use areas.

Entrances

_____ Good lighting.

_____ Rain gutters in place and kept clean.

_____ Stairs and landings kept clear from clutter, ice, or water.

_____ Entrance doors are solid and close tightly.

_____ Peepholes in _all_ entrance doors.

_____ Deadbolt locks and security chains on all entrance doors.

Windows

_____ No broken glass.

_____ Close tightly.

_____ Locks working properly.

_____ Adequate window coverings for privacy.

_____ Insect screens in place and in good condition.

_____ Shrubs kept trimmed to prevent intruders from being able to hide.

Parking

_____ Adequate on-site parking.

_____ Adequate lighting.

_____ Direct and clear access to entrance.

_____ Surface in good condition.

_____ Adequate snow removal and drainage.

Grass and Play Areas

_____ Grass kept mowed and trimmed.

_____ No broken glass or other sharp objects.

_____ Fences in good condition.

_____ Hazards such as pools, ditches, and streams fenced off.

_____ Supervision of young children always provided.

Storage Areas and Utilities

_____ Wires (electricity, telephone, cable, etc.) properly suspended and at proper height.

_____ Utility meters (gas, electric, etc.) kept clear of obstructions.

_____ Chemicals stored away to prevent access by children or pets.

(Continued on page 22.7)

Look to see that exits are not used for storage or blocked in other ways that could obstruct your path during a fire or disaster.

Washrooms and storage areas are frequently locations of assaults and rapes. Look at the location of these areas in your facility. Is help readily available, are they adequately lighted, are they frequently used? Many times you will not get completely accurate information about this from the landlord or the person trying to rent or sell you the property. Don't be afraid to ask other tenants. Also look at the property at different times of the day and different days of the week to insure that you are seeing all of the potential hazards. These same things apply to your current home or apartment. Survey the outside of your house to see that all of these concerns are cared for.

After assessing the outside of your house or apartment, turn to the inside. Is there at least one smoke detector on each level of the house? Are the stairways well lit and in good repair? Are exterior doors solid (as opposed to hollow), and

do they have deadbolt locks and peepholes to see who is at the door? Are all windows equipped with functioning locks? Do all throw rugs have nonslide backs? Do showers and baths have nonslip surfaces or mats? Is access available to shut off utilities if needed, and do you know how to shut them off? Are emergency exits (fire escapes, chain ladders, push-out windows) in good repair? Is the hot water heater set at a low enough temperature to prevent accidental scalding? Are outlets ground-fault protected in the kitchen, bathroom, garage, and other areas where water is likely? Is there air conditioning so that doors and windows will not have to be left open during hot weather?

These are all physical characteristics about your house or apartment, but the most hazardous thing you will face at home is _you_. All of the things you look at inside and outside of your home must be used and maintained in order to protect you. If you do not check them periodically and repair or report them as needed, you might as well not have them. Your actions affect your safety around the home in many

PERSONAL SKILLS AND EXPERIENCES

_____ Chemicals and garbage disposed of safely and properly.

_____ Tools and sharp objects (including lawn mowers) stored away to prevent access by children.

Inside

Fire

_____ Flammable liquids stored outside whenever possible and never in a room with open flames such as pilot lights or fireplace.

_____ Smoke detectors in hallways of each level and batteries changed twice a year.

_____ Exit routes kept clear.

_____ Occupants know at least two exit routes from bedrooms and living rooms.

_____ No one allowed to smoke in bed.

_____ Adequate ashtrays available.

_____ Portable heating sources (electric, kerosene) used properly.

_____ Bedroom doors kept closed at night.

_____ Matches and lighters stored properly.

Electrical

_____ Outlets not overloaded.

_____ Extension cords not used in place of permanent wiring or placed in traffic areas.

_____ Electric appliances kept in good condition, including the cords.

_____ Unused wall plugs covered to prevent children from inserting objects.

_____ No exposed wiring in living areas.

_____ Occupants know location of the electrical panel, access is kept clear, and all switches are labeled.

_____ All repair and remodeling performed by a qualified electrician.

Miscellaneous

_____ Knives and sharp objects stored properly.

_____ Guns and ammunition stored separately and where children cannot gain access to them.

_____ Rugs backed with nonslip backing.

_____ Hot water heater set at no higher than 115 to 120 degrees Fahrenheit.

_____ Bathtubs and showers have nonslip surfaces.

_____ Doors and windows kept locked even when someone is home.

_____ Walking surfaces and stairs kept clear, clean, dry, and in good condition.

_____ Railings installed and in good condition in all stairways.

_____ Good lighting in all halls and stairways and adequate lighting in all other locations.

This is by no means a complete checklist of hazards and is intended only as a beginning point. Special populations such as the elderly, young, or handicapped will have particular needs that might not be addressed here. (See Doniger 1990.)

---

other ways. You should store guns separate from ammunition, and they should be where access is limited, preferably locked. Have first aid supplies available and emergency telephone numbers posted on or near the telephone (see the "Medical Emergencies" section of this chapter). Household chemicals should be stored where small children cannot gain access to them. All chemicals should be used in accordance with the label instructions and should be disposed of properly. If you or others smoke in your home, have plenty of ashtrays in convenient locations. _Never_ allow people to smoke in bed. Never use extension cords in place of permanent wiring. Do not overload electrical circuits; if you are "always blowing a fuse," there is a problem that should be evaluated by an electrician. Keep doors to bedrooms closed at night to slow the spread of smoke and fire (most deaths associated with fires occur from smoke inhalation).

Most major insurance companies that provide homeowner's and/or renter's insurance have information and home safety programs available. You usually do not need to have a policy with the company to get information or participate in their educational programs. Other resources for home safety include your local police department and fire department. Many police departments have a service where an officer will come to your home and, based on a brief inspection, give you some ideas on how to reduce your risk of burglary and assault. Most fire departments have either educational programs or programs where firefighters will come and inspect your home for fire hazards. For help with a self-evaluation, use the Home Safety Walk-Through Checklist found in the Personal Skills and Experiences box.

DORM SAFETY

Most of the information in the home and apartment safety section is applicable to living in dorms. There are some additional problems frequently seen in dorms, though. Keep your door shut and locked when you are not in the room and at night. Do not use extension cords or "splitters" to provide additional electrical outlets. Do not cook in your dorm room unless the room is designed to allow cooking and specific authorization has been given. Do not have excessive combustibles such as posters and pictures on the walls. Always evacuate the building when a fire alarm sounds, no matter how many false alarms there have been. Provide a medical history, including any special medical problems and any prescription medications you are taking, to the hall director in case you are involved in an accident. Know the quickest exit routes from your room, the bathrooms, the lounge, and other areas where you are likely to be spending a lot of time. Have someone whom you can tell where you are going and when you will be back, so it will be noticed if you are missing, and keep track of each other. Report any people or activities that are not "normal" in your dorm to the RA or campus police.

For more information on safety measures specific to dorm living, contact your dorm director, campus police, or residence halls student association.

CAMPUS SAFETY

We frequently feel very comfortable and safe on campus because of the amount of time we spend there. Because of this feeling of safety and a concentration of people (all operating on a fixed schedule), many campuses have become a target for crime. Most of the issues discussed in this chapter apply to the time you spend on campus.

Just because someone is in your class does not mean that they are incapable of theft or assault. Particularly after dark and at nonpeak hours, travel across campus in pairs or groups. Many campuses offer escort services through their security or police departments; use these services instead of taking unnecessary risks. Travel through buildings, where there is more light and there are people, rather than go around them while walking across campus. Be aware of where emergency phones are located. If you have to park a long distance away and expect to be on campus after dark, take time to move your car to a safer location when parking becomes available. Be particularly aware of weather that can cause slippery sidewalks, roads, and hallways. Take more time; it is better to be late than to fall and injure yourself. Carry a small flashlight in your book bag; you will be surprised how often you use it if it is available. Let friends or family know your schedule so they will recognize if you are late or missing. Report all suspicious people or situations, hazardous conditions, or utility/mechanical problems to the authorities. You are protecting others as well as yourself by reporting these situations.

Plan and prepare for emergencies that may arise while you are at school. Know what services are provided to students, and use them. You can find out about services available on your campus through the public safety department, student services department, student counseling services (academic and emotional), student health services, student associations and clubs, and student government.

When walking across campus at night, always travel in groups.

DISASTER PREPAREDNESS

Disasters come in many forms, including floods, fires, tornadoes, hurricanes, hazardous chemical spills, winter storms, and earthquakes. The one sure thing about disasters is that every location has the potential for at least one type of disaster. While there is little we can do to prevent them, we can do many things to lessen their effect and to allow us to return to normal as soon as possible.

One important thing to do is to recognize what hazards exist in your area. Most natural disasters have locations that are more seriously affected. For instance, floods affect river beds and low-lying areas. Earthquakes have fault lines and liquefaction areas. Avalanches and snowstorms affect foothills and mountains. Some areas are more prone than others to hurricanes and tornadoes. Take this information into consideration when choosing where to live. Building styles are affected differently also. For example, a single-story wooden structure will experience less damage than a multistory unreinforced brick building during an earthquake. This type of information can be gained about all natural disasters that you are likely to be exposed to. This information can be obtained from your local or state government, emergency preparedness agency, local engineering firms, board of realtors, or university engineering, architecture, or environmental studies department.

An important thing to know during and immediately after a disaster is how and where to turn off damaged utilities such as gas, water, and electricity. Being trained in first aid is very important. Knowing where to go and how to protect yourself during the disaster is essential.

Probably the most important thing is to prepare for disasters. Not all disasters can be predicted, and often we will not get any warning before they occur. It is important, though, to use any warning we get. Know how and where the

After a disaster, services are *very* limited for the first 72 hours. Having a 72-hour disaster kit on hand can make the difference between survival and reasonable comfort.

warning will come from. Will it be on TV or radio, or will it be sirens and/or individual contacts (not phone calls)? Use what time you have to secure belongings, but never risk your life to save an object. If told by authorities to evacuate the area, do not question that decision—just leave the area. Have a 72-hour kit available. A 72-hour kit contains supplies necessary to live on your own for at least 3 days. Experience tells us that utilities and services are disrupted immediately after a disaster but will be resumed in most areas affected within 72 hours. You should have adequate supplies of food, medications, fuel for heat and cooking, water, and personal needs. A more in-depth description of a 72-hour kit is available from the American Red Cross or your local emergency preparedness agency.

Local fire departments, state and local emergency planning agencies, and the Federal Emergency Management Administration (**FEMA**) are good resources for more information on disaster preparedness. Your campus should have a disaster plan, and campus administrators often are thankful for volunteer assistance in planning, preparedness, and recovery stages of disasters.

SAFETY AND THE ELDERLY

The elderly are a group frequently overlooked regarding safety. Because they are older, there are many physiological changes that not only increase their risk of accidents, but

Issue

Who Is Responsible for Natural Disasters?

Billions of dollars are spent by federal, state, and local governments to prepare for natural and man-made disasters and to help individuals and businesses recover from these disasters. Many individuals and businesses have insurance, or insurance is available to them to deal with these disasters. In many cases people choose to locate their homes and businesses on flood plains, in tornado corridors, on fault lines, or in hurricane-prone areas.

• Pro: We have a responsibility to our fellow human beings to eliminate pain and suffering whenever possible. If a disaster occurs that the victims could not prevent and did not cause, we should be sympathetic and help them rebuild their lives. If we do not assist them in becoming self-sufficient again, we will end up paying more in welfare and other social services to support them. How can we expect people not to live in towns that have been in a high-risk area for over a hundred years? We cannot just move these towns.

• Con: The large amounts of money spent on these occasional instances that affect a small percentage of the population could better be used to improve health care or education and have an effect on many more people. In most cases these people chose to live or establish their business in a high-risk area. We do not repay the business person whose business was robbed after the neighborhood has experienced urban blight—and he or she might not have chosen to locate in the blighted area, it might have come to them. There are adequate insurance policies available, and people who choose to live in high-risk areas should be required to be insured.

Is it society's responsibility to rebuild these lives at the cost of billions of dollars? Could this money be better used in other ways? Should we pay for victims' *choices*?

also cause them to be more seriously affected by incidents and to recover more slowly. Visibility of objects is a concern with the elderly. Small steps and irregular surfaces are frequently not noticed. These should be removed when possible or very visibly marked. Night vision is often impaired in the

FEMA
Federal Emergency Management Administration.

elderly, increasing the need for well-lighted walks, halls, and stairs. Elderly people often do not move or react as quickly. A task as simple as crossing the street can become a problem when traffic lights do not allow adequate time. As we age, we become shorter and tend to stoop, making it difficult to reach many items. Frequently used items should be stored on lower shelves, and secure step stools should be provided for access to higher items. The elderly are frequent targets for crime. Simply accompanying them on errands can prevent many of these attacks. Installation of handrails, nonslip backing on rugs, and nonslip surfaces in bathtubs and showers can prevent many falls. As we age, we are unable to adapt to changes in temperature as quickly, so special attention needs to be given to the elderly during the spring, fall, and particularly hot or cold spells. One of the most difficult decisions most of us will face is when to stop driving. It is very difficult to give up the freedom that our car affords us, but at some point the risks outweigh the freedom.

If the time comes that you participate in the selection of a retirement facility or nursing home, use the following resources to assist in choosing the facility. Choose a state-licensed facility, then contact the state licensing bureau and the Better Business Bureau to see if there have been any complaints filed against the facility. Ask your physician or care provider for recommendations. Spend several hours in the facility watching patient interaction and care. Talk to the residents/patients about their experience. Ask for references of families with residents in the facility. Lastly, go by your "gut feelings." If it is not right for you, it will probably not be the best choice.

For more information on safety issues for the elderly, contact the American Association of Retired Persons (AARP) or your local or state department of aging services.

VIOLENCE

Assault, robbery, and rape have been a problem for as long as humans have existed. There are no solutions, but there are many things we can do to reduce the risk of these problems. At least a portion of each section in this chapter is related to preventing assaults. The information in this section can be applied to many situations.

Whenever possible, travel in groups, particularly at night or in unfamiliar areas. Always be aware of your surroundings and what possible hazards exist. Whenever handling money, such as at stores or in a bank, always put the money securely away before leaving the check stand or teller window. Carry purses with straps that go around your arm or carry wallets in inside pockets or pockets that button. Do not carry excessive amounts of cash. Use cashier's checks or traveler's checks when a transfer of larger amounts of money is necessary.

Park in well-lit areas. Always have your keys ready before you reach your door. Pause briefly before you reach your car and look under the car and in the front and back seat. Always lock your car and house/apartment even if it will "just be a minute."

Issue

What Constitutes the Right to Bear Arms?

Homicide, suicide, and assault continue to be major health and social issues faced by all Americans. We have recently seen passage of the "Brady Bill" and a continued effort for gun control particularly focused on assault rifles and handguns.

- Pro: There is no need for assault rifles and handguns in today's society. All legitimate uses for guns can be achieved without handguns or assault rifles. While depression is usually a long-term problem, the act of suicide is often an impulsive act. If guns cannot be purchased without a waiting period, many lives lost to suicide by gunshot may be saved. If handguns and assault rifles are not available, many criminals will resort to less deadly forms of intimidation and threat.

- Con: There have been restrictions on the sale and purchase of guns and ammunition for as long as there have been guns; none of these have been shown to reduce crime or deaths. There are so many handguns and assault rifles on the streets now that it would take decades to get them all off the streets. If we restrict the sale and possession of any type of gun but *all* other countries do not, the guns will just be brought into this country illegally and still be used.

Is gun control the answer to violence in America? If gun control will not solve the problem, will it at least help? Do we have a right to have any gun we choose?

Carry valuable items in sacks or other coverings so others do not know what you have. Lock valuable items in the trunk of your car where they cannot be seen. Keep valuables in safes or safe deposit boxes. Have expensive jewelry and clothes appraised and keep written and picture documentation of them for identification, recovery, and insurance purposes.

Choose routes to travel based on safety, not on time or shortest distance. If you think you are being followed, go directly to a busy location such as a store and call the police. If someone runs into your car or stops quickly, trying to make you run into their car, drive directly to a busy location and call the police. Always walk "with a purpose"; looking flustered or confused makes you a better target.

If confronted by an individual or a group, answer their questions directly but do not volunteer any information. Act confident and self-assured but not confrontational or threatening. Observe them closely for later identification. Look for things like height and weight, tattoos, or license plate numbers. It is usually best to give them what they want. No monetary object is worth losing your life for.

Report all known or suspected cases of spouse abuse, child abuse, elder abuse, rape, or assault to the police. Frequently victims believe that they are the only ones who have ever had this happen to them or that it was their fault for some reason. Both of these feelings are understandable but completely incorrect. The support of others is usually welcomed, even if not sought. The police will be able to refer victims to support agencies even if the victim chooses not to press charges.

While it may seem oversimplified, a good rule to follow in preventing many assaults is to trust your instincts. *If something feels wrong about the situation, it probably is.* Get out of the situation and into a location where there are other people. Never be embarrassed or ashamed to make a scene or to call the police.

For more information on preventing assaults, contact your local police department, state council for crime prevention, or the National Council for Crime Prevention.

RECREATIONAL SAFETY

Recreation can be very hazardous. Outside of the work environment, more accidents occur in the pursuit of recreation than in any other activity. Many of the recreational activities that we choose gain their thrill from the risks associated with them. In this section we cannot discuss all recreational activities and their risks, but we can address some of the most common activities. The most important things to do in preventing accidents and injuries in most recreational activities are these: (1) Receive formal training in how to do the activity correctly and safely. (2) Prepare yourself physically and mentally for the activity. (3) Use good-quality equipment, check it frequently for damage, and keep it in good repair. (4) *Never* mix alcohol or drugs with recreational activities. (5) Be trained in first aid, CPR, and injury prevention. And lastly, (6) *know your limits and stay within them.*

HIKING AND BACKPACKING

Never hike alone. Tell others where you will be going and when you will return. Always take any needed medications in case something happens and you are unable to return as scheduled. Whenever hiking in unfamiliar areas, carry a map and compass and know how to use them. Be prepared for the worst expected weather, not the best. Always carry a survival/first aid kit with you.

HUNTING AND FISHING

When not in use, equipment should be stored properly. Always unload guns when not actively hunting or when crossing fences, streams, or ditches. Be aware of others around you when casting or shooting. Take hunter safety classes every 3 to 5 years. Store guns and ammunition separately and locked away to limit access to them. Take a class and receive

In all recreational activities, be aware of the hazards associated with the activity, plan how to prevent problems, and identify where to get help if it is needed.

proper training before attempting to reload your own ammunition. Follow the recommendations for hiking and backpacking also.

BICYCLING

Always wear an ANSI-recognized bicycle helmet. Follow all traffic laws; bicycles are considered vehicles. Dress appropriately for temperatures. If you are riding at a speed of 15 miles an hour and going into a 5-mile-an-hour breeze, the windchill would be equivalent to that of a 20-mile-per-hour wind. Have periodic tune-ups performed on your bike to insure that all parts are working properly. When riding in dim light or at night, be sure to have properly operating lights and reflectors. Wear clothing that will increase your visibility to others. Never wear earphones or other devices that will impair your hearing or vision.

JOGGING AND WALKING

Wear adequate clothing, remember that it is easier to remove clothing than to put on clothing that you do not have. Wear clothing that increases your visibility to others. When walking or jogging in dim light or at night, wear or carry lights and/or reflectors. Always tell someone your route and when you expect to return. When choosing a new route, always drive the route first to look for hazards, including dogs, rough terrain, and possible areas for mugging, and note locations where help is available. Never jog or walk alone. Do not wear clothing or earphones that obstruct your vision or hearing. When on vacation or traveling, always ask local running/walking clubs for suggested routes near your hotel. Ask

HEALTH UPDATE

Who Pays for Emergency Response?

Many response agencies, including law enforcement, search and rescue, and fire departments, are beginning to charge individuals for the services they provide if the individual can be shown to have been negligent or in some way responsible for their problem. A 2-day search for a lost hunter, hiker, or cross-country skier can cost thousands of dollars in worker hours and equipment. Many national parks have instituted policies, or are looking at, requiring individuals using backcountry areas to purchase short-term insurance policies or show proof of insurance to cover expenses of rescuing the individual if needed. In one instance in Idaho, a family whose car had mechanical problems and started a forest fire was billed for the cost of fighting the fire. Cost recovery is leading to our taking much more responsibility for our actions.

hotel personnel for information on suggested routes. Watch for other hotel guests that jog/walk and talk to them about routes, or you may ask to join them.

SWIMMING

Learn how to swim and stay within your limits. Always check out the water for depth, temperature, and underwater hazards such as plants, trees, or structures. Be aware of low head dams, spillways, diverters, or other structures that can unexpectedly change currents and trap you. Only dive in designated areas. Never swim alone, and whenever possible have someone out of the water watching those in the water. Be familiar with currents and tides and how they will affect you. Most drownings of persons of traditional college age involve alcohol or drug use; avoid this behavior. Follow all signs and posted warnings. Maintain constant observation of children even if they are in shallow water. Use personal flotation devices (life vests). Do not overload rafts, boats, or other flotation devices.

TRAVEL SAFETY

Travel safety is something that many people either take for granted or choose not to consider. The consequences of either attitude can range from discomfort to death. Most of our travels are by automobile or aircraft, so those are the two modes we will discuss. These same concerns can also apply to travel by train, bus, or boat.

TRAVEL BY AIRCRAFT

Always carry a bag with you. Whenever you check your bags there is a chance of being separated from them or of someone going through them. In your carry-on bag take all medications you need, any personal needs such as contact lens solution and storage case, identification, money, and traveler's checks. Other things to consider putting in your carry-on bag are things to increase your comfort, such as toothbrush and paste, deodorant, a small bar of soap, and a change of clothes.

As soon as you get settled into your seat, identify the two exits nearest you and determine which is the best in an emergency. Things to consider include proximity, ease of opening, who would be opening it (a trained flight attendant or an untrained passenger who might not have read the passenger safety card), the age and health of passengers between you and the exit, and any obstructions, such as the beverage cart. When choosing your seat assignment, choose a seat near an exit and know how to operate the exit.

If a high-jacking should occur, there are a few basic rules to observe. First, don't be a hero. Never confront the high-jackers or other passengers. Try to blend in. Always look down. Know where the exits are. Have a plan for what to do if they start shooting people or detonate a bomb or people start running; don't think you will suddenly know what to do when things start happening all around you.

TRAVEL BY AUTOMOBILE

Have your car checked out before you leave on an automobile trip and take the advice of a trained mechanic. Having something repaired before the trip is less time consuming and less expensive than breaking down on a highway far from home, being towed to the nearest town, and waiting for parts. Also remember that the local Ford dealer in a small town is not going to have those special German wheels or a Porsche carburetor. Plan your route and stops ahead of time. Give a copy of your route and schedule to a friend in case someone must get in contact with you. Stop frequently, even if it is just to walk around the car a couple of times. Check in with others at least every other day to get important messages and to let them know you are all right. Do not travel alone. Plan where to stay, do not leave it to luck. Plan how you will get help if you need it.

If your car does break down, try to get well off the road. Be aware of where you stopped. Are you just over the top of a hill or around a corner? Is it foggy, raining, or snowing? All of these things will reduce the warning other cars have that you are stopped. Warn oncoming traffic with your emergency flashers as well as flares or reflectors in the direction of oncoming traffic. If your car is stranded in a traffic lane, get out and stand well off the road. If your car is well off the road, stay in your car with doors locked. If someone stops to help you, it is usually best to have them send you qualified help (police, a tow truck, etc.) rather than go with them for help. You are usually better off to stay with your car and wait for help than to walk around looking for assistance.

MOTEL AND HOTEL SAFETY

There are several things to be concerned about while at a hotel. The first thing is, when making reservations or checking in, always request a room below the fifth floor. Most deaths in hotel fires involve guests above where standard rescue and fire-fighting equipment is effective. Also, if possible, stay above the first floor to reduce the access for thieves from outside. If they offer a nonsmoking wing, request a room there. Many fires start from guests smoking in bed. On the way to your room, familiarize yourself with the layout of the hotel. Having to evacuate your room into a dark or smokey corridor can be very disorienting. Notice where the emergency exits are and any alcoves or hallways you could get lost in between your room and the exit. Notice if there are fire extinguishers in the hallway and where they are in relation to your room. Look for the fire alarms or sirens to see that one is close enough to your room to be heard. Locate the nearest alarm pull station in case of a fire.

Once you are in your room, familiarize yourself with the room itself. Remember that frequently there are no lights in an emergency. Note where the extra towels and blankets are—they might be critical in an emergency. Always carry a small flashlight in your luggage that you can use if the power goes out. As soon as you have settled in, take valuables such as cameras and extra money to the front desk to be kept in the hotel safe. Never leave your door open even just to go to the ice machine. Whenever you are in the room, keep the security lock fastened also. Never open your door to anyone until you have seen them through the peephole, and always be cautious even of hotel employees unless you have requested their assistance.

When leaving the hotel in an unfamiliar city, always ask directions even if you think you know where you are going. Inquire of the hotel staff as to the safety of walking near the hotel and of using transit systems. Many hotels provide transportation for their guests to local malls and eating establishments; if your hotel does, use those services. If you are a jogger, you may want to watch for other guests who jog and join them so that you will not have to jog alone. Inquire with hotel staff and/or the local running club for good routes near the hotel. If you do jog or walk alone, leave your route and expected return time with the hotel staff and let them know when you return.

If the fire alarm is sounded while you are in your room, always evacuate no matter how inconvenient it is. When leaving, take your room key with you and lock your door. Prior to opening the door, feel it for heat. If the door is hot or the corridor is full of smoke and fire, stay in your room. If you are trapped in your room, hang a towel out of your window to indicate that you are in there. Try to call the front desk to inform them that you are trapped. Immediately fill the bathtub with water that you can use to wet towels and blankets if you need to. If smoke begins to come into the room under the door or through air vents, try to seal them with wet towels or bedding. If your room begins to fill with smoke, open a window a small amount. Smoke and flames can enter the room from the outside, also, so open the window only a small amount and only if necessary. Try to attract the attention of people outside the hotel to arrange your rescue. Once outside the hotel, do not reenter until you are told it is safe by hotel personnel and others have entered.

WORKSITE SAFETY

You have the right to a safe workplace. By law, an employer must, within reasonable limits, make your work environment safe. Most of us spend more time at work than at any other activity except possibly sleep. This means that a common place for accidents and injuries is at work. There are many state and federal agencies whose responsibility is to ensure a safe work environment for all of us, but the reality is that these agencies are too understaffed and underfunded to actually visit all worksites. It is the responsibility of each employee to report hazards to supervisors and to work as safely as possible. When injuries and work-related illnesses do occur, workers' compensation laws insure that we will receive adequate medical care at no cost to the employee.

The leading cause of occupation-related deaths is automobile accidents. Most companies have specific safety policies and educational programs related to automobile use at work. If you drive a vehicle of any kind and are unaware of the company's vehicle safety program, you should ask your supervisor about it. Basic automobile safety procedures as outlined in the "Automobile Safety" section of this text should be followed, including wearing seat belts and doing ongoing vehicle maintenance.

Among the fastest growing occupational health concerns are repetitive-motion injuries and workplace ergonomics. Making the work station fit the employee instead of the employee's fitting the work station reduces many disabling injuries. Also, process assessments are becoming very common. What you do and how you do it are reviewed to identify any repetitive motions, hazardous activities, chemical exposures, or unnatural movements that you must do. These problems are then engineered out of the process to make it safer.

If you work with any chemicals, you should be trained in how to use them safely, what protective equipment is required, how to recognize an exposure to the chemicals, and how to use the Material Safety Data Sheets. These and other requirements are part of the Hazard Communication Standard that most employers must comply with.

No employee should ever alter or remove any safety devices on equipment they use. Things such as guards and systems that require both hands to operate are designed to protect the user, and serious injury can occur when they are altered.

People who work in office settings frequently believe they are not at risk. This is an incorrect assumption. Office workers are frequently burned, shocked, and hit by falling objects. They have a high incidence of carpal tunnel syndrome and other repetitive-motion injuries from typing and word processing. They are frequently exposed to chemicals in photocopy machines and cleaning processes. The issue of secondhand smoke is more common in office environments, and many companies are banning smoking in all areas of their facilities.

It seems that no matter what the job, there are health concerns that must be addressed. There are responsibilities that both the employer and the employee must fulfill. Each of us needs to be more aware of potential hazards at work and must report unsafe conditions, accidents, near accidents, and injuries to the appropriate person where you work. For more information on occupational and worksite safety, contact your state or federal office of the Occupational Safety and Health Administration (**OSHA**).

PLANNING FOR EMERGENCIES

It is important to recognize that everything we do in life has some risk. We each decide how much risk we are willing to accept based on what the reward is for taking that risk. Most of us will risk crossing a street on foot to buy a hamburger if we are hungry. Many of us would not accept that risk just for a hamburger if it required us to cross a busy freeway. There are things that we can do to lessen our risk and to mitigate the circumstances if something does go wrong. These basic steps can be applied to all situations. How in-depth or elaborate we get will vary based on each situation. Your preplanning for going to the grocery store will be much less formal and much less involved than it would be for a boat trip down the Amazon River; a trip out-of-state to a relative's for Thanksgiving would fall somewhere in between.

The first thing to do when planning any activity is to recognize that all activities have risks. Identify the most common or most likely problems that could occur in the activity. Try to think of ways to prevent them from occurring. Act to prevent any problems that would have significant effects. One problem that can occur while you are driving to the grocery store is a flat tire. It might be worth checking to see that the spare tire is in good condition, but it might not be worth buying four new tires.

Homicide in the Workplace

According to an alert published by the National Institute for Occupational Safety and Health (NIOSH), for the period 1980–89 the leading cause of work-related deaths for females was homicide. The homicide rate for male workers was three times that of female workers. Homicide was the third leading cause of death overall. Nearly half of all occupational homicides occurred among workers aged 25 to 44. Retail trades and service industries experienced the most occupational homicides (see National Institutes of Health 1993). These statistics are particularly significant to college students and recent graduates. Many students are either working their way through school or preparing for occupations in the retail or service industries. We are frequently reminded of the violence in our society. We take precautions to protect ourselves at home and in our daily activities, but most of us seldom associate it with our jobs. This can be a fatal mistake.

The next thing to do is to identify how you would get help if a problem does occur. If your trip is across campus, you may want to think of where phones are or what buildings will be open that you could get help in. If it is a week-long backpacking trip into remote wilderness, you might want to arrange to have a radio with you. Do not just assume that there will be pay phones or that people will stop to help you or allow you in their house.

Identify what resources you have and what resources you will need. Do you have a jack and spare tire? Is there someone who can walk across campus with you? Should you pack your first aid kit or tire chains? There is nothing as important as the item you do not have in an emergency.

Lastly, identify what you can do to recover from this problem more quickly and easily. If you have to go to the hospital, who could fill in at work for you or take notes in your classes? Is there a local crisis line or rape crisis center? If your home or apartment is uninhabitable, who could you stay with?

DEALING WITH EMERGENCIES

If you find yourself in an emergency, there are some steps you can take to get you through the emergency. First, recognize that you are in an unsafe situation. Maybe it is the people, the

OSHA
Occupational Safety and Health Administration.

PERSONAL SKILLS AND EXPERIENCES

PNI and Safety Issues

It was a beautiful early fall afternoon. A father and his 12-year-old son were working together repairing fences in the pasture that they would soon be moving horses into. It was hard work, but it would only take 2 or 3 days. At around 6:30 P.M. the father experienced a heart attack and collapsed, quickly going unconscious. The son ran half a mile to the barn and called for an ambulance. By the time he returned, his father was quite gray and limp. The son held his father's head in his lap and cried until the ambulance arrived 20 minutes later. The father was transported to the nearest hospital, where he was pronounced dead.

Over the next 2 years the son dealt not only with the death of his father but also with the guilt of not having known CPR, not having been able to run as fast as he would have liked, and having had to stop and catch his breath while he was running. The son "put on weight," had difficulty sleeping, developed arthritis, had difficulty with relationships, and questioned God. During that time he often said that he could have dealt with the death of his father if he had known what to do—it was the helplessness that affected him.

Body

There are a lot of things that could have been done differently in the above situation. The father could have been in better shape. The son could have been in better shape. The father's diet contributed to the heart attack. The son responded to the guilt with physical ailments, including weight gain and joint pain. This is a good example of how by optimizing our physical health we can prevent, respond better to, and recover more quickly from accidents and illnesses.

Mind

Had they prepared for possible problems, the response might have been faster. The son could have learned CPR and been prepared to perform it. The father could have recognized how he was feeling and stopped working before the heart attack. The father could have learned the risk factors for heart attack and made some lifestyle changes.

Soul

Fear of caring for anyone, fear of being alone with people, questioning God and the meaning of life—all of these were normal responses to this challenge. They could have all been reduced had the son been more confident in his beliefs. The ultimate had to be the father's sudden confrontation with his beliefs about what happens after death and how he lived his life.

The goal here is not to dwell on the past but to learn from it. How can experiences like this make us stronger and better prepared for the future? We all have experiences to grow from. The key is to prevent and/or lessen the negative experiences associated with accidents, assaults, and other safety-related issues.

surroundings, the weather, or some other factor. One frequent problem is that we do not recognize, or, more importantly, act on our recognition, that we are in a bad situation until it is too late. Second, stay calm. We do not think at our best when we are too excited. Third, determine whether you are in immediate danger. In most cases we have time to think and react to the situation. Fourth, even if you are in immediate danger, take a few seconds to think about what you are going to do. Very few situations do *not* allow you time to think. Fifth, identify your resources, both internal and external. What characteristics do you have that will help you? Who else is around? Is there shelter or a phone? Sixth, identify what your options are and what the risks of each of them are. Most situations have a variety of possible solutions but there are positives and negatives to these solutions. Last, make a plan of action and act on that plan. This will be an informed, well thought out plan, even if it was developed in a few seconds. Having a plan is always better than random actions.

This model works well in almost all situations. It can be applied to everything from a situation of possible assault to spouse abuse, being trapped in a flood, being in an accident at work, or almost any other situation you may find yourself in.

TAKE ACTION

1. Think back to an unsafe situation that you have been in. In writing, describe that situation and go through the steps of the model, regarding that situation. Identify what your resources and risks, options and plans, were.

2. Pick three activities and do a written safety plan for each one. Choose one everyday activity, such as going to class at night or driving to the mall or simply arriving home. Then choose a recreational activity that you like, such as going to a concert, fishing, boating, or traveling. The last activity should be an activity that is high-risk—something that you do but do not like to because it scares you.

SUMMARY

1. We face many hazards on a daily basis. These hazards are found at home, at work, while traveling, and during recreational activities. The hazards include accidents, injuries, assault, property damage, and natural disasters.

2. It is impossible to be risk-free. However, there are many things we can do to reduce the risks that we face. This includes determining what is acceptable risk for each of us.

3. Awareness of risks and preplanning in order to reduce our risk and to be prepared for emergencies are important steps to take in order to increase our personal safety.

4. While risk reduction is the most important action we can take, we still need to know what to do after an incident occurs. Learn first aid and CPR. Know what resources are available to you, both on campus and in your community.

5. Cars provide us with tremendous freedom and opportunities, but they also present us with many hazards and risks.

6. Many hazards at home come on over time. These are frequently overlooked unless we take time to do occasional safety walk-throughs of our home. These should include indoor and outdoor assessments.

7. We often feel safe and comfortable on campus. We have set routines and know where we are supposed to be and what we are supposed to be doing. These are exactly the reasons why crime and assault are on the rise on many campuses.

8. By their very nature, many of the recreational activities that we participate in have risks associated with them. We can reduce these risks by preplanning and choosing lower-risk activities.

9. Even with all of the attention that safety receives at most worksites, occupational accidents are still a leading cause of injury and disabilities in the United States. All employees have a responsibility to report hazards to their supervisors and to follow all safety rules, regulations, and policies.

10. Alcohol and drugs (both prescription and recreational drugs) have a major affect on our personal safety. They influence how we behave and how others behave around us. By impairing the user's judgment, they increase the risk to the user and to others.

11. Take control of your life. Make safety a part of all decisions you make. By taking a moment to consider safety factors, you can save days, weeks, or months of recovery time. The knowledge you gain from this chapter is useless unless you take action.

COMMITMENT ACTIVITIES

1. Take first aid and CPR classes and stay certified. These classes may be offered on your campus or through local resources such as hospitals, the American Red Cross, or the American Heart Association.

2. Take the Health Assessment quiz in this chapter and select three to five questions for which you did not give the answer indicating safe behavior, and make the appropriate corrections to your life.

3. Organize a group of your friends and/or associates and invite the local law enforcement agency or rape crisis center to talk to you about preventing assault.

4. Use the Home Safety Walk-Through Checklist in this chapter to evaluate your home, apartment, or dorm. Identify the areas that are putting you at risk, prioritize them from highest risk to lowest risk, and pick five to correct.

5. Complete a hazard analysis of your next recreational activity. Identify all of the problems that might occur, and determine how to reduce or eliminate these problems and how you will handle them if they occur.

6. Organize or volunteer to be on a safety committee at your place of employment.

REFERENCES

American Academy of Orthopaedic Surgeons. 1992. *Emergency Care and Transportation of the Sick and Injured.* American Academy of Orthopaedic Surgeons.

Doniger, M. 1990. "Making Your Home Fall-Safe." *National Institutes of Health—Healthline,* April.

Emergency Cardiac Care Committees, American Heart Association. 1992. "Guidelines for Cardiopulmonary Resuscitation and Emergency Cardiac Care." *Journal of the American Medical Association* 268: 2172–83.

National Institutes of Health. 1993. "Homicide in the Workplace." *National Institutes of Health Alert.*

National Safety Council. 1991. *Introduction to Occupational Health and Safety.* Itasca, IL: National Safety Council.

National Safety Council. 1993. *Accident Facts—1993.* Chicago: National Safety Council.

ADDITIONAL READINGS

American Red Cross. 1993. *Community First Aid and Safety.* St. Louis: Mosby Lifeline. A good basic first aid textbook. This book is designed to accompany a Red Cross class but can stand well on its own. It also addresses injury prevention.

National Safety Council. 1993. *Accident Facts—1993.* Chicago: National Safety Council. This annual edition covers accidents, injury, and illness rates in a variety of settings.

National Safety Council. *Occupational Safety and Health Series.* 3 vols. Chicago: National Safety Council. This is a series of three books that address the basics of safety and health as related to the worksite setting. These are excellent for companies just starting a safety program with the help of a safety professional.

Most of the agencies suggested throughout the chapter have literature and lending libraries that you can use.

LIFESTYLE CONTRACT

By reading and working through the activities in the chapters on consumer health, you should have a good understanding of:

1. The influence of advertising on consumer health decisions as well as ways to evaluate advertising
2. Guidelines for the use of OTC and prescription drugs
3. Available consumer protection and ways for consumers to take action
4. Decisions that need to be made related to medical care
5. Alternative medical systems
6. Options for paying for medical care
7. The threat of quackery and how to deal with it

There has also been an opportunity to assess your feelings about many consumer health issues. Health-producing behaviors are enhanced by wise consumer health decisions. Examples of such decisions relate to every chapter of this book.

Since consumer health decisions are so basic to total health, it is appropriate to consider ways to strengthen your well-being related to consumer health. The prevention model presented in chapter 2 provides the framework within which to consider the relevance of the issues presented in this section.

Lifestyle Contracting Using Strength Intervention

I. Choosing the desired health behavior or skill.

A. Keeping in mind the purposes in life and goals you identified in the mental health chapter, consider one or two health behaviors related to consumer health that will help you reach your goals. In order to assess the likelihood of success, ask yourself questions similar to those used in previous sections such as:

1. Is my purpose, cause, or goal better realized by the adoption of this behavior?

_____ yes _____ no.

2. Am I hardy enough to accomplish this goal? (This means I feel I can do it if I work hard, I am in control of what needs to be done, I am committed to do it, and the goal is a challenge for me.)

_____ yes _____ no.

3. Is this a behavior I really want to change and that I feel I can change?

_____ yes _____ no.

4. Do I first need to nurture a personal strength area?

_____ yes _____ no.
(If yes, be sure to include this as a part of the plan.)

5. Do I need to free myself from a bad habit in order to accomplish this goal?
_____ yes _____ no.
(If yes, be sure to include this as a part of the plan.)

6. Have I considered the results of the assessments in the two consumer health chapters?

_____ yes _____ no. These results may be helpful in developing a plan.

("Yes" answers to the first three questions are a must in order to be successful. It might be wise to consider a different behavior if you cannot honestly answer "yes" to these questions. Your answers to questions 4–6 ought to provide information for consideration in your plan.)

B. Behaviors I will change (no more than two)

_____

_____

II. Lifestyle Plan

A. A description of the general plan of what I am going to do and how I will accomplish it. (Consider successes you may have had in the past, since they may help you develop the best ways to carry out this plan.)

_____

_____

_____

_____

_____

_____

B. Barriers to accomplishment of the plan (lack of time, feelings of others, hesitation to take action, motivation, etc.)

1. Identify barriers: _____

_____

_____

_____

2. Means to remove barriers (use problem-solving skills or creative approaches such as those described in the mental health chapter)

_____

_____

_____

_____

C. Implementation of the plan.

1. Substitution (putting positive behaviors in place of negative ones) _____

_____

(Continued on page 22.18)

LIFESTYLE CONTRACT

2. Linking behaviors _____

_____

3. Combining a strength and a weakness _____

_____

4. When _____

5. Where _____

6. Preparation _____

_____

7. With whom _____

III. Support Groups

    A. Who: _____

_____

    B. Role: _____

_____

    C. Organized support: _____

_____

IV. Trigger responses: _____

_____

_____

  V. Starting date: _____

VI. Date/Sequence the contract will be reevaluated: _____

_____

VII. Evidence of reaching goal: _____

_____

VIII. Rewards when contract is completed: _____

_____

IX. Signature of client: _____

  X. Signature of facilitator: _____

XI. Additional conditions/comments: _____

_____

_____

Nutrition and Weight Control

TABLE A.1 VITAMINS

Nutrient	Good Sources	Major Functions	Deficiency Symptoms
Fat-Soluble Vitamins			
Vitamin A	Milk, cheese, eggs, liver, and yellow/dark green fruits and vegetables	Required for healthy bones, teeth, skin, gums, and hair; maintenance of inner mucous membranes, thus increasing resistance to infection; adequate vision in dim light	Night blindness, decreased growth, decreased resistance to infection, rough-dry skin
Vitamin D	Fortified milk, cod liver oil, salmon, tuna, egg yolk	Necessary for bones and teeth; needed for calcium and phosphorus absorption	Rickets (bone softening), fractures, and muscle spasms
Vitamin E	Vegetable oils, yellow and green leafy vegetables, margarine, wheat germ, whole grain breads and cereals	Related to oxidation and normal muscle and red blood cell chemistry	Leg cramps, red blood cell breakdown
Vitamin K	Green leafy vegetables, cauliflower, cabbage, eggs, peas, and potatoes	Essential for normal blood clotting	Hemorrhaging
Water-Soluble Vitamins			
Vitamin B_1 (Thiamine)	Whole grain or enriched bread, lean meats and poultry, organ fish, liver, pork, poultry, organ meats, legumes, nuts, and dried yeast	Assists in proper use of carbohydrates; normal functioning of nervous system; maintenance of good appetite	Loss of appetite, nausea, confusion, cardiac abnormalities, muscle spasms
Vitamin B_2 (Riboflavin)	Eggs, milk, leafy green vegetables, whole grains, lean meats, dried beans and peas	Contributes to energy release from carbohydrates, fats, and proteins; needed for normal growth and development, good vision, and healthy skin	Cracking of the corners of the mouth, inflammation of the skin, impaired vision
Vitamin B_6 (Pyridoxine)	Vegetables, meats, whole grain cereals, soybeans, peanuts, and potatoes	Necessary for protein and fatty acids metabolism, and normal red blood cell formation	Depression, irritability, muscle spasms, nausea
Vitamin B_{12}	Meat, poultry, fish, liver, organ meats, eggs, shellfish, milk, and cheese	Required for normal growth, red blood cell formation, nervous system and digestive tract functioning	Impaired balance, weakness, drop in red blood cell count
Niacin	Liver and organ meats, meat, fish, poultry, whole grains, enriched breads, nuts, green leafy vegetables, and dried beans and peas	Contributes to energy release from carbohydrates, fats, and proteins; normal growth and development, and formation of hormones and nerve-regulating substances	Confusion, depression, weakness, weight loss
Biotin	Liver, kidney, eggs, yeast, legumes, milk, nuts, dark green vegetables	Essential for carbohydrate metabolism and fatty acid synthesis	Inflamed skin, muscle pain, depression, weight loss
Folic acid	Leafy green vegetables, organ meats, whole grains and cereals, and dried beans	Needed for cell growth and reproduction of red blood cell formation	Decreased resistance to infection
Pantothenic acid	All natural foods, especially liver, kidney, eggs, nuts, yeast, milk, dried peas and beans, and green leafy vegetables	Related to carbohydrate and fat metabolism	Depression, low blood sugar, leg cramps, nausea, headaches
Vitamin C (ascorbic acid)	Fruits and vegetables	Helps protect against infection; formation of collagenous tissue; normal blood vessels, teeth, bones	Slow healing wounds, loose teeth, hemorrhaging, rough-scaly skin, irritability

TABLE A.2   RECOMMENDED DIETARY ALLOWANCES,[a] REVISED 1989

Category	Age (Years) or Condition	Weight[b] (kg)	(lb)	Height[b] (cm)	(in)	Protein (g)	Fat-Soluble Vitamins Vitamin A (μ RE)[c]	Vitamin D (μg)[d]	Vitamin E (mg α-TE)[e]	Vitamin K (μg)
Infants	0.0–0.5	6	13	60	24	13	375	7.5	3	5
	0.5–1.0	9	20	71	28	14	375	10	4	10
Children	1–3	13	29	90	35	16	400	10	6	15
	4–6	20	44	112	44	24	500	10	7	20
	7–10	28	62	132	52	28	700	10	7	30
Males	11–14	45	99	157	62	45	1,000	10	10	45
	15–18	66	145	176	69	59	1,000	10	10	65
	19–24	72	160	177	70	58	1,000	10	10	70
	25–50	79	174	176	70	63	1,000	5	10	80
	51+	77	170	173	68	63	1,000	5	10	80
Females	11–14	46	101	157	62	46	800	10	8	45
	15–18	55	120	163	64	44	800	10	8	55
	19–24	58	128	164	65	46	800	10	8	60
	25–50	63	138	163	64	50	800	5	8	65
	51+	65	143	160	63	50	800	5	8	65
Pregnant						60	800	10	10	65
Lactating	1st 6 months					65	1,300	10	12	65
	2nd 6 months					62	1,200	10	11	65

[a]The allowances, expressed as average daily intakes over time, are intended to provide for individual variations among most normal persons as they live in the United States under usual environmental stresses. Diets should be based on a variety of common foods in order to provide other nutrients for which human requirements have been less well defined. See report for detailed discussion of allowances and of nutrients not tabulated.

[b]Weights and heights of reference adults are actual medians for the U.S. population of the designated age, as reported by NHANES II. The median weights and heights of those under 19 years of age were taken from the National Center for Health Statistics. The use of these figures does not imply that the height-to-weight ratios are ideal.

[c]Retinol equivalents. 1 retinol equivalent = 1 μg retinol or 6 μg β-carotene. See report for calculation of vitamin A activity of diets as retinol equivalents. μg = microgram, or one millionth of a gram.

[d]As cholecalciferol. 10 μg cholecalciferol = 400 IU of vitamin D.

[e]α-Tocopherol equivalents. 1 mg d-α tocopherol = 1 α-TE. See report for variation in allowances and calculation of vitamin E activity of the diet as α-tocopherol equivalents.

Reprinted with permission from *Recommended Dietary Allowances, 10th Edition,* © 1989 by the National Academy of Sciences. Published by National Academy Press.

TABLE A.2   RECOMMENDED DIETARY ALLOWANCES,[a] REVISED 1989—CONTINUED

Water-Soluble Vitamins							Minerals						
Vitamin C (mg)	Thiamin (mg)	Riboflavin (mg)	Niacin (mg NE)[f]	Vitamin B6 (mg)	Folate (μg)	Vitamin B12 (μg)	Calcium (mg)	Phosphorus (mg)	Magnesium (mg)	Iron (mg)	Zinc (mg)	Iodine (μg)	Selenium (μg)
30	0.3	0.4	5	0.3	25	0.3	400	300	40	6	5	40	10
35	0.4	0.5	6	0.6	35	0.5	600	500	60	10	5	50	15
40	0.7	0.8	9	1.0	50	0.7	800	800	80	10	10	70	20
45	0.9	1.1	12	1.1	75	1.0	800	800	120	10	10	90	20
45	1.0	1.2	13	1.4	100	1.4	800	800	170	10	10	120	30
50	1.3	1.5	17	1.7	150	2.0	1,200	1,200	270	12	15	150	40
60	1.5	1.8	20	2.0	200	2.0	1,200	1,200	400	12	15	150	50
60	1.5	1.7	19	2.0	200	2.0	1,200	1,200	350	10	15	150	70
60	1.5	1.7	19	2.0	200	2.0	800	800	350	10	15	150	70
60	1.2	1.4	15	2.0	200	2.0	800	800	350	10	15	150	70
50	1.1	1.3	15	1.4	150	2.0	1,200	1,200	280	15	12	150	45
60	1.1	1.3	15	1.5	180	2.0	1,200	1,200	300	15	12	150	50
60	1.1	1.3	15	1.6	180	2.0	1,200	1,200	280	15	12	150	55
60	1.1	1.3	15	1.6	180	2.0	800	800	280	15	12	150	55
60	1.0	1.2	13	1.6	180	2.0	800	800	280	10	12	150	55
70	1.5	1.6	17	2.2	400	2.2	1,200	1,200	320	30	15	175	65
95	1.6	1.8	20	2.1	280	2.6	1,200	1,200	355	15	19	200	75
90	1.6	1.7	20	2.1	260	2.6	1,200	1,200	340	15	16	200	75

[f] 1 NE (niacin equivalent) is equal to 1 mg of niacin or 60 mg of dietary tryptophan.

TABLE A.3   MINERALS

Nutrient	Good Sources	Major Functions	Deficiency Symptoms
Calcium[a]	Milk, yogurt, cheese, green leafy vegetables, dried beans, sardines, and salmon	Required for strong teeth and bone formation; maintenance of good muscle tone, heartbeat, and nerve function	Bone pain and fractures, periodontal disease, muscle cramps
Iron	Organ meats, lean meats, seafoods, eggs, dried peas and beans, nuts, whole and enriched grains, and green leafy vegetables	Major component of hemoglobin, aids in energy utilization	Nutritional anemia and overall weakness
Phosphorus[a]	Meats, fish, milk, eggs, dried beans and peas, whole grains, and processed foods	Required for bone and teeth formation, energy release regulation	Bone pain and fracture, weight loss, and skin problems
Zinc	Milk, meat, seafood, whole grains, nuts, eggs, and dried beans	Essential component of hormones, insulin, and enzymes; used in normal growth and development	Loss of appetite, slow-healing wounds, and skin problems
Magnesium[a]	Green leafy vegetables, whole grains, nuts, soybeans, seafood, and legumes	Needed for bone growth and maintenance, carbohydrate and protein utilization, nerve function, temperature regulation	Irregular heartbeat, weakness, muscle spasms, and sleeplessness
Sodium[a]	Table salt, processed foods, and meat	Body fluid regulation, transmission of nerve impulse, heart action	Rarely seen
Potassium[a]	Legumes, whole grains, bananas, orange juice, dried fruits, and potatoes	Heart action, bone formation and maintenance, regulation of energy release, acid-base regulation	Irregular heartbeat, nausea, weakness

[a]Macromineral

From Werner K. Holger, *Lifetime Physical Fitness and Wellness.* Copyright © 1990 Morton Publishing Company, Englewood, Co. Reprinted by permission.

TABLE A.4   INFORMATION SOURCES ON EATING DISORDERS

American Anorexia/Bulimia Association, Inc.
133 Cedar La.
Teaneck, NJ 07666
(201) 836–1800

Anorexia Nervosa and Associated Disorders, Inc.
P.O. Box 271
Highland Park, IL 60035\
(312) 831–3438

Anorexia Nervosa and Related Eating Disorders, Inc.
P.O. Box 5102
Eugene, OR 97405
(503) 344–1144

Bulimia, Anorexia Self-Help
6125 Colayton Ave., Suite 215
St. Louis, MO 63139
(800) 227–4785

National Anorexic Aid Society, Inc.
550 S. Cleveland Ave., Suite F
Westerville, OH 43081
(614) 436–1112

Health Objectives for the Nation

In 1979, the Department of Health and Human Services made public the "1990 Objectives for the Nation." Using the 1990 objectives as a foundation, in 1990 the year 2000 health objectives for the nation were presented in a publication entitled *Healthy People 2000: National Health Promotion and Disease Prevention Objectives*. These objectives outline the health goals for the country and also identify the health risk factors to eliminate in order to accomplish these objectives. Three broad goals were proposed to serve as overall measures of the nation's health. They were by the year 2000 to

1. Increase the span of healthy life for Americans
2. Reduce health disparities among Americans
3. Achieve access to preventive services for all Americans

The specific priority areas to accomplish these goals were grouped in the four categories of health promotion priorities, health protection priorities, preventive services priorities, and surveillance and data systems priorities as follows:

HEALTH PROMOTION PRIORITIES

1. Physical activity and fitness
2. Nutrition
3. Tobacco
4. Alcohol and other drugs
5. Family planning
6. Mental health and mental disorders
7. Violent and abusive behavior
8. Educational and community-based programs

HEALTH PROTECTION PRIORITIES

9. Unintentional injuries
10. Occupational safety and health
11. Environmental health
12. Food and drug safety
13. Oral health

PREVENTIVE SERVICES PRIORITIES

14. Maternal and infant health
15. Heart disease and stroke
16. Cancer

17. Diabetes and chronic disabling conditions
18. HIV infection
19. Sexually transmitted diseases
20. Immunization and infectious diseases
21. Clinical preventive services

SURVEILLANCE AND DATA SYSTEMS

22. Surveillance and data systems

Approximately four hundred objectives are listed for the nation. Sample objectives related to some of the chapters in this book include

1. Reduce overweight among people ages 20 through 74 to a prevalence of no more than 20 percent. (Baseline: 25.7% in 1976–80)
2. Increase to at least 50 percent the proportion of people age 6 and older who regularly perform physical activities that maintain muscular strength, muscular endurance, and flexibility. (Baseline data unavailable)
3. Reduce cigarette smoking to a prevalence of no more than 15 percent among people age 20 and older. (Baseline: 29.1% in 1987)
4. Reduce alcohol-related motor vehicle crash deaths to no more than 0.9 per 100 million vehicle miles traveled (VMT) and to 8.5 per 100,000 people. (Baseline: 1.2 per 100 million VMT and 9.7 per 100,000 people in 1987)
5. Reduce pregnancies among girls age 15–17 to no more than 55 per 1,000. (Baseline: 73.2 pregnancies per 1,000 in 1982)
6. Reduce rape and attempted rape of women age 12 and older to no more than 107 per 100,000 women. (Baseline: 119.7 per 100,000 in 1986)
7. Increase to at least 40 percent the proportion of people age 65 and older who participate in moderate physical activities 3 or more days per week for 20 minutes or more per occasion. (Baseline: 31% in 1985)
8. Increase to at least 90 percent the proportion of people who live in air quality reporting areas that have not exceeded the Environmental Protection Agency standard for ozone in the previous 12 months. (Baseline: 68 air quality reporting areas, with 113 million people exceeding the standard in 1985–87)

9. Reduce influenza-associated deaths among people age 65 and older to no more than 40 per 100,000 people. (Baseline: 70 per 100,000 in 1987)

10. Reverse the rising trend in the incidence of AIDS cases and reduce annual incidence to no more than the projected number of 80,000 new cases in 1992. (Baseline: 32,971 cases in 1988)

11. Reduce gonorrhea to an incidence of no more than 225 cases per 100,000 people. (Baseline: 297 per 100,000 in 1988)

12. Reduce the mean serum cholesterol level for people age 20 and older to no more than 200 mg/dL. (Baseline: 213 mg/dL in 1976–80)

13. Reduce breast cancer deaths to no more than 25.2 per 100,000 women. (Baseline: 27.2 per 100,000 in 1986)

14. Reduce to no more than 60 percent the proportion of adolescents age 15 who have experienced dental caries (cavities) in permanent teeth. (Baseline: 78 percent in 1986–87)

15. Reduce to at least 35 percent the proportion of people age 18 and older who experience adverse health effects from stress. (Baseline: 44 percent in 1985)

Some of the groups that have helped and are helping to accomplish these goals are federal, state, and local organizations as well as private and voluntary groups. Some organizations where students can receive complimentary information about particular health problems are listed below.

Voluntary Organizations

- Alcoholics Anonymous
  P.O. Box 459, Grand Central Annex
  New York, NY 10017
  (212) 686–1100

- Al-Anon Family Group Headquarters
  314 W. 53rd St., 2nd floor
  New York, NY 10012
  (800) 356–9996 (212) 245–3151
  (in New York and Canada)

- American Cancer Society
  19 W. 56th St.
  New York, NY 10019
  (212) 586–8700

- American Dental Association
  211 E. Chicago Ave.
  Chicago, IL 60611

- American Diabetes Association
  One W. 48th St.
  New York, NY 10020
  (800) 232–3472

- American Dietetic Association
  430 N. Michigan Ave.
  Chicago, IL 60611

- American Heart Association
  7320 Greenville Ave.
  Dallas, TX 75231
  (214) 750–5300

- American Lung Association
  1740 Broadway
  New York, NY 10019
  (212) 315–8700

- American National Red Cross
  17th and D Streets, NW
  Washington, DC 20006
  (202) 737–8300

- The Arthritis Foundation
  1314 Spring St. NW
  Atlanta, GA 30309
  (404) 837–3240

- Council on Family Health
  633 Third Ave.
  New York, NY 10017

- National Mental Health Association
  1021 Prince St.
  Arlington, VA 22314
  (703) 684–7722

- National Association for Sickle Cell Disease, Inc.
  245 S. Western Ave. Suite 206
  Los Angeles, CA 90006

- National Consumers League
  1028 Connecticut Ave., NW, Suite 522
  Washington, DC 20036

- National Council on Alcoholism
  733 Third Ave.
  New York, NY 10017
  (800) 622–2255

- National Foundation-March of Dimes
  1275 Mamaroneck Ave.
  White Plains, NY 10605
  (914) 428–7100

- World Health Organization
  1501 New Hampshire Ave., NW
  Washington, DC 20036

Government Agencies

- Consumer Information Center
  18th and E Streets NW
  Washington, DC 20405
  (202) 566–2794

- Environmental Protection Agency
  Public Information Center
  PM 211–B
  401 M St. NW
  Washington, DC 20460
  (800) 368–5888

- Food and Drug Administration
  Office of Consumer Affairs
  5600 Fishers Lane
  Rockville, MD 20857
  (301) 443–3170
- National Center for Alcohol Education
  1601 N. Kent St.
  Arlington, VA 22201
- National Cancer Institute
  9000 Rockville Pike
  Bethesda, MD 20014
  (301) 496–6641

- Centers for Disease Control
  Public Inquiries Office
  1600 Clifton Rd. NE
  Building 1, Room B63
  Atlanta, GA 30333
  (404) 639–3534

GLOSSARY

abortion
The premature expulsion of a fertilized egg, embryo, or fetus from the uterus.

abstinence
Refraining from drinking any alcoholic beverage.

acid rain
Rain that has a pH of less than 5.6.

acquired immunodeficiency syndrome (AIDS)
A breakdown in the body's natural defenses that is spread through the exchange of bodily fluids (in sexual intercourse, needle sharing, etc.) and is often fatal. There is no known cure.

acrophobia
Fear of high places.

active listening
Paraphrasing a speaker's words to be sure that the message was understood.

active immunity
Immunity to a disease, derived from having had either the disease or an injection of the infectious organism.

acupuncture
A medical technique that involves inserting and manipulating needles in the body to relieve pain and treat disease.

adaptive stress
Stress due to the attempt to maintain equilibrium or homeostasis in the face of change.

adipose tissue
Body tissue composed of fat cells.

adipose cells
Cells that store bodily fat. These can increase fifty times in size, and new adipose cells are created when existing cells are full. Fat cells.

adulterated
Made impure by the addition of another substance.

aerobics
Any form of total-body activity that raises the heart rate but does not produce oxygen debt (any longer-duration, moderately intense activity rather than shorter-duration, high-intensity activity).

ageism
Discrimination based on age.

aggressive behavior
Expressing views and opinions in ways that diminish the views and feelings of others.

aging
The process of growing older.

alarm stage
The first stage of the general adaptation syndrome, characterized by an immediate increase in muscle tension, heart rate, blood pressure, brain activity, and other physical peaking responses.

alcoholism
Loss of control in drinking; the inability to refrain from drinking; the inability to stop drinking before becoming intoxicated.

allopathic physician
A physician who has received a medical doctor degree (M.D.).

alpha-fetoprotein (AFP)
A test done during early stages of pregnancy to detect neural tube defects.

Alzheimer's disease
A dementia marked by a distinctive, detectable loss or change of nerve cells.

ambulatory-care center
A center that provides treatment for minor medical problems without an appointment.

amenorrhea
Absence of menstruation.

amino acids
Chemical compounds that are the constituents of proteins. The nine essential amino acids cannot be synthesized by the body and must be obtained in the diet; foods containing all nine of these are called "complete proteins."

amniocentesis (amniotic tap)
Analysis of amniotic fluid taken from the intrauterine environment in order to detect fetal defects.

amniotic fluid
The fluid surrounding the fetus in the uterus.

amphetamines
Stimulant drugs used to combat fatigue and suppress appetite; as drugs of abuse, commonly called "uppers."

anabolic steroids
Substances derived from the male hormone testosterone; used to increase muscle bulk, but with serious side effects.

analgesics
Medicines that relieve pain; painkillers.

aneurysm
A ballooning out of a vein, an artery, or the heart, due to a weakening of the wall by disease, traumatic injury, or an abnormality present at birth.

angel dust
The street name for phencyclidine, a hallucinogenic crystalline powder that produces bizarre and volatile effects.

angina
Chest pain associated with heart disease; can be brought on by smoking.

angiography
A diagnostic procedure through which the chambers and blood vessels of the heart are examined.

angioplasty
The process of clearing arteries using a balloon-type instrument on the end of a wire, much like cleaning a pipe with a plumber's snake.

animal parasite
Any animal (worms, lice, protozoa, etc.) that feeds on other organisms.

anorexia nervosa
A condition in which the individual severely limits caloric intake due to appetite suppression; sometimes described as self-induced starvation. Can be fatal.

Antabuse
A drug that in combination with alcohol causes nausea, dizziness, and heart palpitations; used to deter persons from drinking.

antibodies
Substances manufactured by the body to destroy invading organisms.

anxiety-prone personality
A tendency to see problems as being worse than they actually are.

aphasia
Loss of the ability to speak, usually caused by stroke.

arteriosclerosis
A group of diseases characterized by the shrinking of, and loss of elasticity in, artery walls.

arthritis
A chronic disease characterized by inflammation of the joints.

artificial insemination
The introduction of sperm into a woman's vagina by means of a syringe.

asexual
Without sexuality.

assertiveness
A mean between aggressiveness and passivity, in which people feel comfortable enough with themselves that they can freely express to others their own feelings and thoughts.

assessing
Determining one's personal strengths, motivations, existing support systems, barriers to lifestyle change, and factors that determine one's comfort and happiness.

asthma
A disease or allergic response characterized by bronchial spasms and difficulty in breathing.

astraphobia
Fear of thunder and lightning storms.

atherosclerosis
A disease state in which fat deposits (plaques) collect on artery walls, narrowing the arteries and sometimes leading to heart attack.

atrophy
A decrease in size (as of muscle cells).

attitudes
Feelings about facts and behaviors.

aversion therapy
A type of treatment in which a specific behaviorin this case, smokingis made undesirable through negative reinforcement.

bacteria
Microscopic organisms that cause disease.

bag
A single dosage unit of heroin.

balanced adjustment
Returning to the same level of functioning one was at prior to a life event.

barbiturates
Sedative-hypnotic depressant drugs; as drugs of abuse, commonly called "downers."

barriers to change
Aspects of your lifesuch as finances, working hours, or lack of social supportthat might require you to revise your plan for changing a health behavior.

basal body temperature (BBT) method
A method of birth control based on keeping track of the female's temperature changes during her menstrual cycle in an attempt to pinpoint ovulation.

basal-cell cancer
A type of skin cancer.

benign tumor
An uncontrolled growth of cells that is not malignant but can disturb the function of an organ.

benzodiazepines
A general classification of tranquilizers that includes the most widely prescribed, Valium and Librium.

bereavement
The loss we experience when someone close to us dies.

bestiality (zoophilia)
Sexual contact with animals.

beta cells
The cells in the islets of Langerhans of the pancreas that produce insulin.

bioecological stressors
Environmental or nutritional stressors, such as noise or a lack of nutrients.

biofeedback
Electronic feedback about bodily functions from machines that measure those functions. Used to observe physiological reactions to thought processes and for controlling the stress response.

biological dimension of human sexuality
Aspects of sexuality involving physiological responses, reproduction, puberty, pregnancy, and growth and development.

biopsy
A surgical procedure in which a small section of a tumor is removed and microscopically examined for possible cancer.

biorhythms
The natural physical, emotional, and mental highs and lows in our lives, which potentially can be charted and assessed.

birthing center
A medical facility with a homelike atmosphere that is used for delivering babies.

bisexuality
Having sexual desire for members of both sexes.

blood pressure
The force exerted by flowing blood against the artery walls.

blood alcohol concentration (BAC)
The percentage of alcohol in the blood; usually measured in suspected drunken drivers.

body composition
The percentage of fat versus lean tissue.

body mass index (BMI)
Weight in kilograms divided by the square of height in meters.

boredom
A lack of eustressors; weariness and restlessness in reaction to monotonous, unchallenging tasks.

brainstorming
Listing all solutions that come to mind, and evaluating them only after you're done listing.

breathalyzer
A machine used to determine a person's blood alcohol content; usually used with drivers suspected of being drunk.

breech birth
A birth in which the buttocks of the fetus are positioned to be delivered first.

bronchitis
Inflammation of the bronchial tubes in the lungs.

building on success
Using what you learned in previous successful attempts at changing your health behavior to change another health behavior.

bulbourethral glands (Cowper's glands)
Tiny pea-shaped organs located below the prostate that secrete a fluid during sexual arousal.

bulimia
A condition in which the individual periodically binges and purges, out of an obsessive fear of becoming fat.

bypass surgery
A surgical technique in which cardiologists take blood vessels from another part of the body and use them to replace obstructed coronary arteries. In single, double, triple, and quadruple bypasses, surgeons replace one, two, three, or four arteries, respectively.

caffeinism
Acute or chronic overuse of caffeine, and resultant caffeine poisoning; symptoms include anxiety, mood changes, sleep disturbances, and other psychophysical complaints.

calcium
The most prevalent mineral in the human body, mostly contained in the bones and teeth. Necessary for the growth and maintenance of strong bones and teeth; also assists in blood clotting, regulation of intercellular fluid flow, nerve impulse transmission, and maintaining a regular heartbeat. Might help prevent several cancers and hypertension. Deficiency can result in osteoporosis in older women.

calendar method
Keeping track of the number of days in the menstrual cycle in an attempt to pinpoint ovulation.

cancer
A group of diseases characterized by the uncontrolled growth and spread of abnormal cells.

cancer in situ
Localized cancer that has not spread.

candidiasis (monilia)
A common vaginal yeast infection caused by flourishing Candida albicans due to an upset in a woman's internal balance.

cannabinoids
Chemicals found in marijuana.

Cannabis sativa
The Indian hemp plant that produces marijuana and hashish.

carbohydrate loading
A dietary practice some athletes use to prepare for competitive events. A severe reduction in caloric intake for several days prior to the event is followed by a very large intake of carbohydrates on the day prior to the event the caloric reduction is meant to "empty" cells so that the large intake of carbohydrates can fill the cells with pure glycogen. No longer recommended.

carbohydrates
Nutrients that supply most of our energy for daily activities. Carbohydrates supply 4 calories per gram.

carbon monoxide
A deadly gas that is a by-product of burning tobacco.

carcinogens
Substances that stimulate the development of cancer.

cardiopulmonary resuscitation (CPR)
An emergency measure to artificially maintain breathing and heartbeat.

cardiovascular disease
Disease of the heart and blood vessels.

carotid endarterectomy
Surgery used to remove plaque buildup in the carotid arteries of the neck.

caveat emptor
"Let the buyer beware."

cerebral embolism
A clot that is carried to the brain, where it blocks a small artery.

cerebral hemorrhage
Bleeding from a diseased artery that damages surrounding brain tissue.

cerebral thrombosis
The formation of a blood clot that blocks one of the arteries that supply blood to the brain.

certified nurse-midwife (CNM)
A licensed nurse with a graduate degree and national certification who may operate an independent practice for maternity and gynecological care.

cervical mucus method (vaginal mucus method)
Checking cervical mucus in an attempt to pinpoint ovulation.

cervical cap
A rubber, plastic, or metal contraceptive device that fits snugly over the cervix.

cesarean section
The delivery of a baby through a surgical incision made in the mother's lower abdomen and uterine wall.

chancre
The first outward symptom of syphilis; a small, painless sore.

chemotherapy
The use of specific drugs to treat a disease.

chicken pox
A disease caused by a virus and resulting in a rash, skin eruptions, and fever; itching may be severe but can be treated with antihistamines and taking warm baths with baking soda.

child language
Terms parents often use with children to refer to body parts or body functions.

children of alcoholics (COAs)
People who grew up in dysfunctional families in which one or both parents were alcoholics.

chiropractic
A system of manipulative treatment, based on the teaching that all diseases are caused by impingement on spinal nerves and can be corrected by spinal adjustments.

chlamydia
A disease that is symptomatically similar to gonorrhea. It results in the infections of several pelvic areas and sometimes in scarring and damage to some of the reproductive organs.

chloasma
Commonly, a yellow to brown patch of pigmentation ("the mask of pregnancy") on the faces of pregnant Caucasian women; disappears when the pregnancy is over.

chloral hydrate
The oldest synthetic sleep-inducing drug.

chlorine residual
Chlorine that is left in a water system to destroy any remaining bacteria.

cholesterol
A waxy fatlike substance that circulates in the blood; cholesterol buildup (plaque) on artery walls has been implicated in atherosclerosis. Found only in animal food sources.

chorionic villi sampling (CVS)
The method of removing pieces of the villi (thin tissue) protruding from the chorion (outer layer of the amniotic sac) and analyzing it for fetal abnormalities.

chromosomes
The part of the cell that contains the hereditary factors (genes).

chronic bronchitis
Persistent inflammation of the mucous membrane of the bronchi, evidenced by continual coughing and discharges.

chronic disease
A drawn-out disease that cannot be cured.

cilia
Hairlike processes, as in the bronchi, that move mucus, pus, and dust particles upward and out.

circumcision
Surgical removal of the foreskin of the penis.

cirrhosis
A disease of the liver, manifested by scarring, that might be caused by excessive alcohol consumption.

class action suit
A suit in which one person takes legal action on behalf of all who have had the same problem.

claustrophobia
Fear of enclosed places.

Clean Air Act (CAA)
A law that establishes emission standards and air standards for seven pollutants.

clinical psychologist
A person with a Ph.D. degree who specializes in emotional and psychological adjustment.

clove cigarettes
Sometimes called "Kreteks," these contain about 60 percent tobacco, 40 percent ground cloves, and about twice the amount of tar and nicotine as most U.S. cigarettes.

codeine
A narcotic drug used to relieve moderate pain.

codependency
A condition in which people who are in a relationship with a problem drinker or alcoholic are so entrapped by love and concern for the person that they lose their own identities in the process of trying to help.

cohabiting
Living together without being legally married.

coitus interruptus
Withdrawal of the penis from the vagina before ejaculation.

coliform bacteria
A group of bacteria whose presence in drinking water is suggestive of fecal contamination.

collateral circulation
Circulation of the blood through smaller vessels when a major vessel has become blocked.

colostomy
Surgical removal of the rectum and part of the colon.

combination pill
A birth-control pill that contains both progesterone and estrogen and works by suspending ovulation.

communicable disease
A disease that can be passed from one person to another.

commuter marriage
A marriage in which spouses establish separate households and live apart for periods of time.

complementary factors
Characteristics by which people supplement each other.

complex carbohydrates
Carbohydrates, including starch, fiber, and glycogen, composed of three or more simple sugars bonded together.

conception
Fertilization of an egg by a sperm resulting in pregnancy.

condom (rubber)
A latex sheath that covers the penis and catches ejaculated sperm; a birth-control device for men.

condyloma
A sexually transmitted anal or genital wart caused by human papillomavirus, treated with Podophyllin.

congenital polyposis
A congenital disease in which a number of polyps grow in the colon and rectum.

congestive heart failure
A condition in which the heart cannot pump the required amount of blood, causing fluid to collect in the abdomen, legs, and/or lungs.

contagious disease
A communicable disease.

contraceptive
Any birth-control method or device.

contractual marriage
A marital relationship in which the partners agree to periodically review their marriage contract.

coronary
The general term for heart attack.

coronary circulation
The heart's independent circulatory system, which is strengthened through regular total-body exercise.

crabs
Insect parasites that can be passed from one person to another during close bodily contact; another name for pubic lice.

crack
A freebased version of cocaine that is extremely potent, quick acting, addicting, and dangerous.

crank
Another nickname for the stimulant methamphetamine, or "speed."

creative personal problem solving
A cognitive-affective-behavioral process through which an individual identifies effective means of coping with problems encountered in everyday living.

cremation
The process of burning a corpse in a furnace to reduce it to ashes.

criteria air pollutants
A group of substances identified under the Clean Air Act for which outside air standards are set. The substances include carbon monoxide, lead, nitrogen dioxide, hydrocarbons, ozone, particulates, and sulfur dioxide.

cross-tolerance
The condition in which tolerance to one drug carries over to another drug in the same group.

cryonic suspension
Deep-freezing human corpses in case, when a cure has been discovered for the condition from which the person died, the person can be revived and cured.

cryotherapy
The destruction of cells through extreme cold.

culture
The shared practices, rules, values, and beliefs of a large group of people.

cunnilingus
Oral sexual stimulation of the female genitals.

date rape
Raping a person one is on a date with or otherwise socially engaged with; acquaintance rape.

decibel (dB)
A numerical expression of the relative loudness of sound.

decision tree
A diagram of the possible choices and steps involved in making a decision.

dehydration
The removal of water from body tissues. Common when water intake is low or temperatures are high, resulting in perspiration. Severe dehydration can be fatal within hours. An adult should drink 10 cups of water or other noncaffeinated, noncola liquid each day.

delirium tremens (d.t.'s)
Hallucinations and convulsive seizures that occur during withdrawal from alcohol.

delta-9-tetrahydrocannabinol (THC)
The major psychoactive drug found in marijuana.

delusions
False beliefs that can occur in users of hallucinogens.

dementia
A loss of mental functions, including memory loss, loss of language functions, inability to think abstractly, personality change, or inability to care for oneself.

depressants
Drugs used to decrease nervous or muscular activity; as drugs of abuse, commonly called "downers."

designer drugs
Many of these drugs use as their chief ingredient fentanyl, or a derivative, which produces a drug that is a hundred times as strong as morphine and twenty to forty times as strong as heroin. Designer drugs can imitate narcotics, cocaine, or hallucinogens.

detoxification
The process of eliminating a drug from the user's body.

diabetic coma
A comatose state resulting from ketosis, the conversion of sugar buildup in a diabetic person's bloodstream into ketone bodies.

diaphragm
A round, latex, dome-shaped birth-control device for women that covers the entrance to the uterus (cervix); used with spermicidal jelly or foam.

diastolic pressure
The lowest point of blood pressure, measured when the heart relaxes.

diethylstilbestrol (DES)
A synthetic estrogen used as a "morning-after" pill.

digestion
The processes by which the body breaks down food to extract the nutrients it needs for energy, renewal, and growth.

dilation and curettage (D&C)
An abortion procedure that must be performed in the first 12 weeks of pregnancy; the procedure is also used to relieve excessive menstrual bleeding.

Dilaudid
A synthetic drug of abuse.

direct euthanasia
Administering a lethal injection, or performing some other action to cause death, in order to free a dying patient from suffering.

disaccharides
Simple carbohydrates, including sucrose, lactose, and maltose, formed from two monosaccharides.

disorganization
A temporary state that arises when one or more of the components of health become disrupted.

disruption
A life event that can cause an individual to become out of balance and unable to function effectively.

distress
Negative stress.

diuretic
A type of medication that causes the body to eliminate water through urination.

DNA
A nucleic acid found in all living cells that carries the organism's genetic information.

Down syndrome
Congenital mental retardation and physical deformities caused by the presence of an extra chromosome in chromosome pair 21.

duration
How long an exercise workout lasts.

eating disorders
Psychological disorders about food that appear to be culturally determined by our society's preoccupation with thinness.

eclampsia
Preeclampsia plus convulsions or coma; can be fatal.

ecstasy
Also called "MDMA," this hybrid cross between amphetamines and the hallucinogen mescaline acts much like cocaine.

ectopic pregnancy
A pregnancy in which the fertilized egg implants outside the uterus.

ego defense mechanism
A defensive, often unconscious, way of dealing with perceived inadequacies or stressors.

ejaculation
The expulsion of semen from the penis, usually accompanying orgasm.

electrocardiogram (EKG)
A test that measures electrical impulses in the heart, to determine whether the heart is malfunctioning.

electrocoagulation
Destruction of tissue by the use of intense heat.

electroencephalogram (EEG)
A machine that records and displays brain-wave patterns.

embalming
The process of removing blood from a dead person and replacing it with preserving fluid.

embolus
A wandering blood clot.

embryo
The unborn young from approximately 1 week after fertilization to about 8 weeks after fertilization.

embryonic stage
The first 2 months of pregnancy.

emotional health
The ability to express emotions comfortably and appropriately.

emphysema
A chronic disease of the lungs that affects the air sacs, causes breathlessness, and can lead to death.

empowerment
A process or mechanism by which people, organizations, and communities gain mastery over their affairs.

empty calories
Calories from foods, such as sugary snacks, that have no nutritive value (no vitamins, minerals, or protein).

enabling
A constellation of ideas, feelings, attitudes, and behaviors that unwittingly allow and/or encourage alcohol problems to continue or worsen by preventing the alcohol abuser from experiencing the consequences of his or her drinking behavior.

endometrium
The lining of the uterus.

Environmental Protection Agency (EPA)
A federal agency responsible for the protection of air and water, and other environmental concerns.

enzymes
Proteins that catalyze biochemical reactions, such as digestion, in the body.

epidemic
An outbreak of disease within a specified geographical area.

epididymis
A coiled tube between the seminiferous tubules and the vas deferens where the sperm mature.

episiotomy
An incision made in the woman's vaginal tissue before she gives birth, to prevent its tearing during childbirth.

erotic phone calling
Obtaining sexual pleasure from a distance; also done by letter writing, etc.

essential hypertension
High blood pressure, the cause of which is unknown.

estrogen
A female hormone, possessed in different degrees by both women and men, that aids in various bodily processes, such as promoting a healthy uterine lining for egg implantation.

ethyl alcohol
A colorless liquid (C2H5OH) that is the intoxicating ingredient in alcoholic beverages and is produced in the fermentation of grains and fruits.

euphemisms
Inoffensive expressions (such as making love and sleeping together) used to avoid use of more explicit terms.

euphoric
Characterized by a feeling of extreme well-being.

eustress
Positive stress.

evaluation
The second stage in making a health decision, in which we gather relevant information, analyze the possible choices, and decide on the best alternative.

excitement phase
The initial phase of human sexual response. Bodily changes include increased blood flow, vaginal lubrication, and penile erection.

exhaustion stage
The third stage of the general adaptation syndrome, characterized by the fatiguing of organs and a depressed immune system, with resultant disorders of the organs.

exhibitionism
Achievement of sexual gratification by displaying one's genitals to observers.

exposure
Along with dose, one of the two factors that determine toxicity. Exposure can occur through direct contact or inhalation.

extended family
Parents, children, and other relatives living together under one roof.

factitious disorder
A condition in which people literally make themselves sick to gain sympathy or enjoy some other emotional reward.

faith healing
Techniques based upon the belief that the mind controls the body and can cure disease through divine help.

fat
An essential nutrient for proper functioning of the body, fats protect the vital organs, provide insulation, enhance the taste of food, and transport the fat-soluble vitamins. Fats supply 9 calories per gram.

fat-cell hypertrophy
The filling of fat cells with fat.

fat-soluble vitamins
The vitamins (A, D, E, and K) that are stored in and transported by fat cells. Because these are stored in the body, it is not necessary to consume them every day, and high supplemental doses can be toxic.

faulty adjustment
Emerging from a life event with fewer protective skills than one had before the event.

FDA
Food and Drug Administration.

Federal Water Pollution Control Act
A law enacted in 1948 that announced the first national goals for water quality.

fellatio
Oral sexual stimulation of the male genitals.

FEMA
Federal Emergency Management Administration.

fentanyl
A psychoactive substance that is the basis for some designer drugs.

fetal alcohol syndrome (FAS)
Irreversible damage to the fetus caused by the mother's heavy use of alcohol during pregnancy.

fetal stage
The stage of pregnancy from the beginning of the third month until birth.

fetishism
Sexual fixation on an object other than a human being.

fetoscopy
The insertion of a viewing instrument into the womb to observe the fetus.

fetus
The unborn young from about 8 weeks after fertilization until birth.

fiber
A form of complex carbohydrate found in plant cell walls. Insoluble fiber, found in beans and whole grains, aids digestion and might be protective against cancer. Soluble fiber, such as guar, psyllium, and pectin, might help control diabetes and lower cholesterol.

fight-or-flight response
The alarm stage of the stress response; involuntary physiological response to sudden danger, characterized by quick action.

flashbacks
The recurrence of effects experienced on drugs, such as the intensification of colors, the apparent motion of a fixed object, or the mistaking of one object for another.

follicle
Small saclike structures in the ovary that contain developing egg cells.

follicle-stimulating hormone (FSH)
A hormone secreted by the pituitary gland that stimulates the egg follicles.

freeing
Achieving freedom from disabling habits.

frequency
Number of exercise workouts per week.

frottage
Obtaining sexual pleasure by rubbing against another person.

frustration
Being thwarted in one's pursuit of a desired goal.

FTC
Federal Trade Commission.

fungi
Parasitic organisms of simple structure that live in soil, rotting vegetation, and bird excreta.

gas chromatography/mass spectrometry (GC/MS) tests
An accurate drug-testing technique that breaks down each drug and spreads each substance on a printout for easy identification.

general adaptation syndrome (GAS)
The three stages through which our bodies respond to stress: alarm, resistance, and exhaustion.

generic drugs
Similar compounds that are not necessarily produced under the same brand name.

genetic counseling
Discussing one's hereditary characteristics with a trained counselor before deciding whether to have children.

gerontologist
One who studies aging.

gerontology
The study of aging.

glomeruli
A small cluster of capillaries located at the beginning of each uriniferous tubule in the kidney. Its function is to filter and remove wastes from the blood.

glucose
A simple, monosaccharide carbohydrate found in molasses, corn syrup, honey, and fruits.

glycogen
The form of complex carbohydrate into which the body converts excess glucose to store it. The body converts glycogen back into glucose when it needs a source of quick energy.

gonorrhea
One of the sexually transmitted diseases; the most frequently reported communicable disease.

gout
A form of arthritis that commonly affects the joints of the feet, especially the big toe.

greenhouse effect
The effects that the accumulation of carbon dioxide and other gases in the earth's atmosphere has on the balance between the energy the earth receives from solar radiation and the energy it loses by radiation from its surface back into space.

Grey Panthers
A political organization designed to combat ageism and old-age stereotyping.

grief
Intense emotional suffering that is a normal reaction to bereavement; its physical symptoms include a tight throat, shortness of breath, the need to sigh, and feelings of emptiness.

habit
An action that is performed routinely and without thought.

hallucinations
Visions or imaginary perceptions.

hashish
The resin of the cannabis plant; a drug of abuse.

hazardous air pollutants
Substances in the air that are generally considered carcinogenic. The EPA has identified six such substances: asbestos, benzene, beryllium, mercury, radionuclides, and vinyl chloride.

health
Well-being in all dimensions of life.

health maintenance organization (HMO)
A prepayment plan for medical care.

heart attack
The death of part or all of the heart muscle due to cardiovascular disease; also known as myocardial infarction.

hemodialysis
The use of an artificial kidney machine to purify blood when the person's kidneys have failed.

hemoglobin
An iron-containing compound in red blood cells that transports oxygen to the cells.

hemorrhoids
Swollen veins in the anal area that can cause swelling, pain, and bleeding.

hepatic failure
Failure of the liver to function properly.

hepatitis
A disease of the liver, of two types—infectious (hepatitis A) and serum (hepatitis B).

herbal medicine
The use of naturally occurring plants, roots, and seeds to fight disease.

heroin
A synthetic narcotic drug of abuse.

herpes genitalis
An incurable sexually transmitted disease characterized by cold-sore-like blisters caused by the herpes simplex virus

herpes simplex virus type 2
This virus causes herpes and is related to the virus that causes cold sores, fever blisters, and shingles. Blisters appear on the genitalia, and symptoms can last from one to three weeks. Recurrence is probable, and the disease is incurable.

hertz (Hz)
A measure of how irritating and damaging sound is. Hertz is the pitch of sound as indicated by the speed of the vibrations.

heterosexuality
Having sexual desire predominantly for members of the opposite sex.

high-density lipoprotein (HDL)
Considered "good" cholesterol, HDL removes other kinds of cholesterol from artery walls and transports it to the liver, where it is processed and excreted.

homeopathy
Medical treatment based on the premise that administration of minute doses of various substances will energize the immune system to fight disease.

homophobia
Fear of, hatred toward, or discrimination against homosexuals; a fear of homosexual feelings in oneself.

homosexuality
Having sexual desire predominantly for members of one's own sex.

hormone
A chemical glandular secretion that regulates or stimulates bodily processes.

hospice
Care for the terminally ill in the home, or in a homelike setting, when attempts at a cure have been abandoned and the focus of care is on keeping the dying person comfortable and free from pain.

host liability
The legal responsibility of individuals who provide drinks to their guests. Courts have found hosts liable for individuals who have left the drinking occasion and later were responsible for traffic accidents.

human chorionic gonadotropin (HCG)
A hormone produced by the placenta once implantation has occurred.

human growth hormone (HGH)
A growth-promoting hormone that occurs naturally in the body. It is sometimes abused and can result in giantism and other problems.

human immunodeficiency virus (HIV) infection
An infection that is present in persons who test positive for the AIDS virus, but symptoms are less severe than those of AIDS.

hydrocarbons
Organic compounds of hydrogen and carbon that have a high energy content and are often used as fuel.

hydroponics
The technology for growing plants (including marijuana) in nutrient solutions, with or without dirt as a medium or support.

hydrostatic weighing
Underwater weighing, indicating overall body density compared to water density, and body weight compared to body volume.

hypertension
Chronically high blood pressure, usually associated with arterial disease.

hypertrophy
An increase in size and strength (as of muscle fibers).

hypnosis
A physically induced altered state of consciousness in which the person can respond, within limits, to suggestions.

hypoglycemia
Low blood sugar.

hysterectomy
The surgical removal of the uterus.

hysterotomy
A method of abortion in which an incision is made in the woman's abdominal wall and the fetus is removed.

ice
A crystalline rock form of methamphetamine (speed) that is more powerful and more addicting than the original methamphetamine.

illness stage
The disease stage in which specific symptoms begin to appear.

imagery
What one sees, hears, smells, tastes, and feels through the mind's eye; meaningful fantasizing or daydreaming.

immunization
The administration of a vaccine that prevents a person from getting a particular disease.

immunoassay
A somewhat unreliable drug-testing technique that uses antibodies that bond to the drugs being tested for.

immunosuppressive drugs
Drugs that suppress the immune system to prevent the body from rejecting a transplant organ.

impact
The amount of stress the body, especially the joints and bones, receives during activities like aerobics.

implementation
The third stage in making a health decision, in which we put into practice a decision we have reached through analysis and learning.

incest
Sexual abuse of children by close relatives.

incubation stage
The disease stage between the time of infection and the appearance of symptoms.

indirect euthanasia
Removing life-support systems from an individual so that she or he can die naturally.

infectious
Contagious; communicable.

infertility
The inability to reproduce.

influenza
An infectious respiratory disease caused by a virus.

injectable
Long-acting injectable contraceptive.

insomnia
Difficulty sleeping.

insulin
A hormone produced by the pancreas.

insulin reaction
A condition that occurs when the blood sugar level becomes too low; calls for immediate ingestion of certain carbohydrates. Insulin shock.

intensity
The repetitions and force used during exercise. The appropriate intensity is enough exercise to condition the muscles and cardiovascular system without overextending the body.

interferon
A chemical in our bodies that gives us natural immunity to specific diseases.

internal medicine
A medical specialty in which the physician deals with the functions of the internal systems of the body.

intoxication
The depressant effects of alcohol upon the central nervous system; drunkenness.

intrauterine device (IUD)
A small plastic or stainless steel contraceptive device that is placed inside a woman's uterus by a physician.

introspection
The experience, often triggered by a need to cope, of assessing one's personal resources, traits, and past experiences in order to deal with adversity.

involuntary smoking (passive smoking)
Involuntarily inhaling smoke in the air from a person nearby who is smoking.

iron
A mineral whose main function is to make hemoglobin. Found in animal organs (which are high in saturated fat), leafy green vegetables, whole grains, dried fruits, and legumes. Deficiency is common.

isokinetic activities
Exercises that involve a constant speed of muscular contraction against a variable resistance.

isometric activities
Exercises that involve exerting muscular force against an immovable object to produce muscular contraction but no joint movement.

isopropyl alcohol
Rubbing alcohol; also used to cleanse and disinfect.

isotonic activities
Exercises that involve exerting muscular force throughout the range of motion of a joint.

Jarvik-7 artificial heart
An artificial heart that temporarily replaces a real heart until a donor can be found. The revised versions of the original Jarvik include the Jarvik-7, the Jarvik 7-70 and the Utah 100 Artificial Heart.

jaundice
A yellowing of the skin or eye tissue.

Kaplan's triphasic model
A model of human sexual response as consisting of three phases: desire, excitement, and resolution.

ketosis
In unmanaged diabetes, an excess of buildup of ketone bodies in the blood, which can cause coma or death.

kidney transplant
The implantation of a donor kidney when the patient's original kidneys have failed. Survival rates are vastly and steadily improving. Donor and recipient kidney tissues must match.

kilocalorie (kcal)
The amount of heat needed to raise 1,000 grams of water 1 degree Celsius.

labor
The process of childbirth.

lactation
Breast-feeding.

lactogenesis
The initiation of a woman's milk production after she delivers a baby.

Lamaze method
A type of natural childbirth based on exercises in relaxation, breathing, and concentration on muscular contractions.

large intestine
The lower end of the alimentary canal, below the small intestine. Solid waste moves from the small intestine to the large intestine, where it remains for 1 to 3 days.

law of reversibility
The principle that a significant decrease in physical capacity will occur within days after training is stopped ("Use it or lose it").

lesion
An abnormal change in an organ due to injury or disease.

leukemia
Cancer of the blood-forming tissues.

Librium
A widely prescribed minor tranquilizer used to treat anxiety.

licensed clinical social worker
A person with academic training in social work who specializes in emotional or psychological adjustment.

life events
Challenges and stressors, both positive and negative, that can cause disruption or changes in our lives.

lifestyle contracting
Making a personal plan for improving health behaviors.

limerence
The quality of sexual attraction based on chemistry and sexual desire.

linking behaviors
Performing two or more activities simultaneously to increase the likelihood that you will reach your goal.

lipoprotein
A substance, composed of protein, triglyceride, and cholesterol, that transports cholesterol in the bloodstream; a fatty protein. There are three kinds: high-density, low-density, and very-low-density lipoproteins.

living will
A document that states what medical interventions a person does or does not want to be taken if that person becomes incapacitated and cannot participate in decisions about his or her medical care.

locus of control
An individual's balance between internal and external control. With internal control, people perceive themselves as the masters of their own fate and outcomes as the results of their own actions. With external control, people perceive themselves as the products of their environment and their role models, their actions as directed by others, and the outcomes of their actions as due to chance or powerful others.

loneliness
A lack of the stimulations provided by close friendships.

low-density lipoprotein (LDL)
Considered an undesirable form of cholesterol, LDL has been implicated in the formation of arterial plaque (atherosclerosis).

luteinizing hormone (LH)
A hormone secreted by the pituitary gland that, in the female, causes ovulation.

Lyme disease
An infectious disease, caused by a spirochete transmitted by a tick, that develops in three stages(1) rash, (2) heart problems, and (3) arthritis.

lysergic acid diethylamide (LSD)
A hallucinogenic drug of abuse.

mainlining
Intravenous drug injection.

malignant tumor
A cancerous growth.

mammogram
An X ray of the breast; more effective than a self-administered breast exam because it can detect extremely small breast cancers before they grow large enough to be detected by touch.

marijuana
A drug of abuse derived from Cannabis sativa.

masochism
Sexual gratification from experiencing pain.

masturbation
Self-stimulation for sexual pleasure.

maximal aerobic power
The level of exertion at which, despite harder efforts, the heart and circulation cannot deliver more oxygen to the tissues without approaching exhaustion.

medical-scientific language
Concrete, technical terminology.

Medicare
A federally administered medical assistance plan for persons over the age of 65.

meditation
The skill of focusing (on a mantra, for instance) to reach a state of relaxation.

melanoma
A form of skin cancer, usually malignant and involving dark pigmentation.

menarche
The onset of menstruation.

menopause
The permanent cessation of menstruation; usually occurs between the ages of 45 and 55.

menstrual cycle
The cycle of menstruation, usually lasting about 28 days, beginning with the first day of menstrual blood flow.

menstruation
Periodic discharge of blood from the uterus through the vagina.

mental health
The capacity to cope with life situations, grow emotionally through them, and develop to your fullest potential.

mental illness
The inability to cope with life situations.

mescaline
A hallucinogenic drug of abuse, derived from the peyote cactus.

metastasis
The movement of detached cancer cells to other parts of the body through the bloodstream.

methadone
A synthetic narcotic drug of abuse; used as a treatment for heroin addiction.

methamphetamine
A stimulant drug of abuse; also called "speed."

methyl alcohol
Wood alcohol; an extremely poisonous liquid used in many industrial products.

mifepristone (RU 486)
A chemical that blocks the hormonal action needed to begin or sustain pregnancy.

minerals
Inorganic elements necessary for essential metabolic functions. Macrominerals (e.g., calcium, magnesium, sodium, potassium, phosphorus, sulfur, chlorine) are required in relatively large amounts. Trace minerals (e.g., iodine, iron, cobalt, copper, manganese, zinc) are required in much smaller amounts.

minipill
A birth-control pill that contains only progestin. The progestin inhibits implantation and causes the cervical mucus to become thicker, making it more difficult for sperm to get through.

miscarriage (spontaneous abortion)
A naturally occurring abortion.

mononucleosis
A viral infection of the lymphatic system. Medication is not helpful; recovery is attained through rest.

monophobia
Fear of being alone.

monosaccharides
Simple carbohydrates with a molecular structure containing only one sugar molecule.

monounsaturated fat
Monounsaturated fatty acids, which are liquid at room temperature and found in plant sources, such as olive and canola oils. A healthy source of dietary fat when not heated.

moral dimension of human sexuality
Basic questions of right and wrong regarding sexuality.

morning sickness
A condition of nausea and vomiting common early in pregnancy.

morphine
A narcotic drug used to relieve pain; it can also be abused.

motivation
The feeling of being impelled or of desiring to do something that leads you to engage in an activity.

mourning
Social customs for bereavement, such as wearing black and having funerals.

multiphasic pill
A birth-control pill that varies the amount of estrogen and progesterone throughout the menstrual cycle to more closely match the naturally occurring amounts of these hormones in the female.

myocardial infarction
Heart attack.

mysophobia
Fear of contamination or germs.

NAD
National Advertising Division of the Better Business Bureau.

narcotics
Drugs of abuse that contain opium and opium derivatives.

natural childbirth
Drug-free childbirth.

NF
National Formulary.

nicotine
An alkaloid poison; the addictive drug that is in tobacco.

nicotine gum
Sold under the name Nicorette, a gum that contains about 2 milligrams of nicotine and is designed to substitute for smoking cigarettes.

nicotine skin patches
Nicotine-containing patches placed on the arm that deliver about 1 milligram of nicotine per hour as a substitute for smoking.

nonbarbiturates
Depressant drugs such as methaqualone (Quaalude) and glutethimide. These drugs produce a calming effect and relieve anxiety and tension without inducing a hypnotic state.

nongonococcal urethritis (NGU)
Several diseases, including chlamydia, are included among the nongonococcus urethritis diseases because they cause the inflammation of the urethra but not by gonococcus bacteria.

norms
Cultural expectations.

nuclear family
Parents and children living together under one roof. Also called "conjugal family."

nurse practitioner
A registered nurse with advanced training in a particular medical specialty.

nurturing
Giving care and attention to the factors that produce strength in life.

nutrients
The nourishing elements in foods, including carbohydrates, proteins, fats, vitamins, minerals, and water. The body needs over forty nutrients for proper functioning and good health.

nutrition
Eating a diet that is rich in the nutrients needed for good health.

nymphomania
Extremely high sex drive in women.

obesity
Being 20 percent over desirable weight.

obstetrics and gynecology
Obstetrics is the medical specialty of caring for women during pregnancy, childbirth, and after birth. Gynecology is the medical specialty dealing with the health of the female reproductive organs.

occult blood
Blood in such minute quantities that it can be seen only by microscopic examination.

occupational health
Having feelings of comfort and accomplishment related to your daily tasks.

oligospermia
Low sperm count.

ophthalmologist
A medical doctor who treats and performs surgery for eye disorders.

opiates
Natural or synthetic derivatives of the drug opium, which is derived from the poppy plant.

optimism
The perception that experiences and events will turn out for the best.

optimizing
Striving to reach high-level health in one health component at a time.

optometrist
A nonmedical trained person who specializes in measuring visual acuity and in vision correction.

oral contraceptive
Birth-control pills; the pill.

oral-genital contact
Use of one partner's mouth to sexually stimulate the other partner's genitals.

organ donor card
A card indicating that, upon the bearer's death, specific organs are to be donated for organ transplants or research.

orgasm
The peak of pleasure in sexual excitement; the third phase of human sexual response.

OSHA
Occupational Safety and Health Administration.

osteoarthritis
A type of arthritis characterized by degeneration of the joint cartilage.

osteopathic physician
A physician who has been trained in a college of osteopathic medicine.

osteoporosis
A disease in which the bones lose bone material and become very porous and fracture easily. Especially prevalent in postmenopausal women. Preventive measures include regular lifelong calcium intake, weight-bearing exercise, and moderation of protein intake; after menopause, estrogen therapy is often used to increase the rate of calcium absorption.

OTC
"Over-the-counter" generally refers to drugs.

ovary
A gland in the female that contains eggs (ova) and certain hormones.

overload principle
The principle that improvement of a selected physical capacity requires that stress be placed on the relevant part of the body.

overstimulation
A level of demands placed on an individual that exceeds that individual's capacity to respond.

overweight
Being 10 percent over desirable weight.

oviduct (fallopian tube)
A pair of tubes in the female by which ova travel from the ovary to the uterus.

ovulation
The release of an egg from an ovary.

ovum
Egg.

oxygen debt
The amount of oxygen used during recovery from physical activity above the amount normally used during that same time at rest.

ozone layer
Part of the stratosphere that acts as a shield protecting against the sun's ultraviolet light.

pancreas
A long gland behind the stomach that secretes digestive enzymes as well as hormones, such as insulin.

Pap test
The microscopic examination of cells removed from an organ (usually the cervix of the uterus) for signs of cancer.

paraphilia
Various forms of sexual desire or love (philia) beyond the usual (para-).

paraquat
A defoliant (plant killer); very poisonous.

particulate matter
Minute, harmful substances in cigarette smoke.

patient-admission privileges
The rights of a physician to admit patients to certain hospitals.

pediatrics
The medical specialty dealing with the treatment of children.

pediculosis pubis
A sexually transmitted disease caused by crabs or public lice, pinhead-sized insect parasites that live in the hairy parts of the body, usually around the genitalia. Some people have no symptoms, while others experience intolerable itching from these parasites.

pedophilia
Adults using children as sexual objects.

pelvic inflammatory disease (PID)
Inflammation of the female genital tract; a complication in sexually transmitted diseases.

peptic ulcer
An ulcer in the stomach area.

perinatal death
The death of an infant within hours or days after its birth.

peyote
A form of cactus; mescaline is derived from its buttons.

phencyclidine (PCP)
A hallucinogenic drug of abuse; also called "angel dust."

photochemical smog
The primary air pollutant; the product of sunlight acting on automobile and industrial exhausts.

physical fitness
A state of physical well-being currently believed to consist of muscle strength, muscle endurance, flexibility, body composition (degree of fatness), and cardiorespiratory endurance.

physical health
Efficient bodily functioning, resistance to disease, and the physical capacity to respond appropriately to varied events.

physician assistant (PA)
A trained assistant who, under the supervision of a physician, does many basic tasks of a physician.

physiological dependence
A condition in which a person has a biochemical need to continue using a particular drug in order to prevent withdrawal symptoms.

placebo effect
Subjects' showing improvement (e.g., after taking sugar pills) just because they expect to improve.

placenta
The organ that connects the fetus to the uterus through the umbilical cord.

placenta previa
Partial or total obstruction of the cervical opening by the placenta.

planned disruption
Intentionally orchestrated life events and challenges that, after some adjustment, will help us to function comfortably at a higher level.

plateau phase
The second phase of human sexual response, involving intensification of the responses begun in the excitement phase.

point-of-service plan (POS)
A medical-care plan combining some features of HMOs and PPOs.

polyunsaturated fats
Polyunsaturated fatty acids, which are liquid at room temperature and found in plant sources, such as safflower, corn, and soybean oils. A healthy source of dietary fat when not heated.

pornography
Pictures or words intended to arouse sexual desire; often distinguished from erotica and artworks as being offensive, obscene, or harmful.

positive addictions
Activities that an individual participates in regularly that make that person stronger.

positive reinforcement
A technique in which the positive aspects of a person's endeavor to break a habit—in this case, smoking—are rewarded.

positive verbalization
The experience of saying, thinking, or writing down positive things about personality traits or skills that one likes about oneself and frequently reflecting on these traits and skills.

potassium
A mineral that works with salt to maintain normal heartbeat and nourish the muscles. Found in vegetables, oranges, whole grains, and sunflower seeds. Deficiencies can cause heartbeat irregularities, insomnia, and nervous disorders.

preeclampsia
Pregnancy-induced hypertension accompanied by swelling of the face, neck, and upper extremities.

preferred provider organization (PPO)
A group of physicians and facilities that contract with an employer to give subscribers specific services at a price (often discounted) agreed upon in advance.

pregnancy
The condition of having unborn young in the body.

premenstrual syndrome (PMS)
Physical and emotional symptoms that can occur before menstruation and that can sometimes be disabling.

prenatal care
Care prior to birth.

prenuptial agreement
Arrangements made prior to marriage, by those planning to marry, regarding assets, conditions of the marriage, situations that might arise, possible breakup, and other personal aspects of the relationship.

preparation
Securing the aids—such as equipment, information, or social arrangements with other people—you need in order to be successful in changing your health behaviors.

primary prevention
Prevention of a disease before symptoms occur.

principle of specificity
The principle that you must train specifically for the gains you wish to achieve (e.g., strength or endurance).

problem drinking
Repetitive use of alcohol that causes physical, psychological, or social harm to the drinker or to others.

problematic adjustment
Responding to a life event with behaviors—such as drug abuse, violence, or suicide attempts—that indicate a need for psychotherapy.

prodromal stage
The disease stage during which nonspecific symptoms appear.

progesterone
A hormone that, in the female, works with estrogen to prepare the uterine lining for pregnancy.

proof
The measure of a beverage's alcoholic content, equal to roughly twice the percentage of alcohol in the beverage.

prostaglandins
Fatty acid substances found naturally in the body. It might be possible to use these to induce labor during an abortion (still in research stage).

prostate gland
A male organ located below the bladder; it secretes fluid that is part of semen.

prostitution
Any situation in which one person pays another person for sexual gratification.

protective skills
Skills you can use to protect yourself from problems.

proteins
Essential nutrients that are a part of nearly every cell in the body. Proteins primarily function to build and repair body tissues, but they also help protect us from disease, regulate body functions, control biochemical bodily processes, and provide extra energy. Protein supplies 4 calories per gram.

protozoa
One-celled animal parasites.

pseudostressors
Dietary substances that can produce, in certain individuals, effects similar to those caused by stress.

psilocybin, psilocyn
Hallucinogenic drugs of abuse extracted from the psilocybin mushroom.

psychiatry
The medical specialty dealing with the diagnosis, treatment, and prevention of mental illness.

psychoactive substance dependence
A maladaptive pattern of psychoactive substance use indicated by the presence of at least two of the following: (1) The substance is taken in larger amounts, for a longer time, than the user intended; (2) a persistent desire for the substance, with unsuccessful efforts to cut down or control substance use; (3) a great deal of time spent in activities necessary to get, take, or recover from the substance; (4) frequent intoxication (drugged state) or withdrawal symptoms when the user is expected to fulfill a major role at work, school, or home; (5) important social, occupational, or recreational activities abandoned or reduced because of the substance use; (6) continued substance use despite knowing that one has a persistent or recurrent social, psychological, or physical problem that is caused or exacerbated by the use of the substance; (7) marked tolerance; (8) the substance is often taken to relieve or avoid withdrawal symptoms; (9) symptoms of disturbance have persisted for at least one month or have occurred repeatedly over a longer period of time.

psychoanalysis
A type of psychotherapy in which patients reflect on their lives in order to find solutions to problems.

psychogenic psychosomatic disorders
Structural or functional disorders, such as migraine headaches, ulcers, and asthma, that are worsened or caused by mental or emotional distress.

psychological dependence
A condition in which the user's craving for a particular drug is so intense that it alters the user's behavior.

psychological dimension of human sexuality
People's attitudes and feelings about themselves and others, regarding sexuality.

psychoneuroimmunology (PNI)
The study of the way we think (psycho-, "mind"), the effects of our thinking on our nervous system (neuro-,), and the effects of our nervous system on our immune system (immunology).

psychosomatic diseases
Physical symptoms that have an emotional or mental origin.

psychotherapy
Any mental method of treating a disease, especially nervous disorders.

quack
A person who uses discredited or unproven methods or devices to diagnose and/or treat diseases or disorders.

quackery
Methods and/or devices used to deceive the public about health/medical care.

radioactive pollution
Damage to an aquatic ecosystem through the addition of radioactive matter into a natural body of water.

radon
A naturally occurring gas that results from the radioactive decay of naturally occurring radium.

rape
Forcible sexual intercourse.

rapid eye movement (REM) sleep
A stage of sleep that almost always includes dreaming.

recognition
The first stage in making a health decision, in which we become aware that there are ways to promote our health or reach a goal, and that we must make a decision.

Recommended Dietary Allowance (RDA)
The recommended nutrient intake that meets the needs of almost all people of the given gender and age group.

recovery stage
The disease stage in which the body's defenses begin to overcome the microbes or the symptoms begin to disappear.

recycling
The reuse of specific materials, such as the aluminum in cans.

refractory period
The period following male ejaculation during which the male is unable to have another erection.

rehabilitation
The process of restoring a person's bodily or psychological functioning so that she or he can live a healthier life.

resiliency
The ability to prevent or bounce back from a disruption.

resilient adjustment
The process of coping with a disruptive, stressful, or challenging life event so that one has more protective and coping skills after the event than one had before it.

resistance stage
The second stage of the general adaptation syndrome, characterized by the body's attempting to return to homeostasis by building energy stores and hormones.

resolution phase
The fourth phase of human sexual response, when the body tends to return to its preexcitement state.

responsible drinking
Making provision to be taken home if planning to drink, understanding limits through calculating blood alcohol concentration, and recognizing when enough alcohol has been consumed.

responsible hosting
Demonstrating concern and care for people attending social events you are hosting, making sure that if they become intoxicated, they will get home safely.

review
The fourth stage in making a health decision, in which, after putting a decision into practice, we engage in periodic review of our progress.

reward
An enjoyable gift, consistent with your health behavior goal, that you give yourself when you have accomplished your goal.

Rh incompatibility
A condition in which the mother's blood is Rh negative and her fetus's blood is Rh positive. This can create complications in future pregnancies because the mother's body develops antibodies in response to the child's positive Rh factor.

rheumatic heart disease
An inflammatory disease centered in the valves of the heart.

rheumatoid arthritis
The most crippling form of arthritis, characterized by inflammation of the joints, stiffness, swelling, and pain.

rhythm method (fertility awareness method)
A method of birth control based on abstinence from intercourse during the woman's fertile period.

rickettsias
Just barely visible with a light microscope, these minute bacteria-like organisms must be in contact with living tissue and cannot be grown in a laboratory. They grow in the intestinal tracts of insects called "vectors," are considered borderline between bacteria and viruses, and might cause such diseases as typhus and Rocky Mountain spotted fever.

risk assessment
In the study of environmental health, the scientific estimation of the likelihood of health problems' occurring as a result of exposure to chemicals.

sadism
Sexual gratification from inflicting pain on another person.

saline induction
A type of abortion in which a saline solution is injected into the amniotic sac; used during the second trimester of pregnancy.

sanitary landfill
An area where solid waste is buried.

saturated fat
Saturated fatty acids, which come mainly from animal sources and are solid at room temperature. They have been implicated in heart disease and should be kept to a minimum in the diet.

satyriasis
Extremely high sex drive in men.

secondary prevention
Treatment of a disease at an early stage in an attempt to keep it from worsening.

self-actualization
Fulfilling one's human potential along with fulfilling one's basic needs (physiological needs and needs for safety, love, and self-esteem).

self-efficacy
The conviction that one can accomplish a desired outcome.

self-esteem
Feelings of self-worth, self-confidence, and satisfaction with oneself.

seminal vesicles
A pair of glands in the male that provide a portion of the ejaculate that contributes to the activation of the sperm.

seminiferous tubules
Coiled tubes in the testis in which the sperm are produced.

set point theory
The theory that the body has an internal control mechanism that helps it maintain a certain level of body fat.

sexual abuse
Forcing sexual behavior on another person against that person's will.

sexual dysfunction
Chronic inability to respond sexually in a way that one finds satisfying.

sexual harassment
Any harassment of other people related to sexuality; includes verbal abuse, sexist remarks, unwanted physical contact, leering, ogling, catcalls, demands for sexual favors in return for favorable treatment, a hostile environment, and physical assault.

sexuality
A four-dimensional (social, psychological, moral, biological) aspect of each person's personality that influences the person's total well-being.

sexually transmitted diseases (STDs)
Diseases spread by sexual contact, including gonorrhea, syphilis, and herpes genitalis; venereal diseases.

sidestream smoke
Smoke that comes directly from the sourcesuch as a cigarette, cigar, or pipe or a smoker's exhalationand still contains the negative elements of tobacco smoke.

similarity factors
Characteristics in which people are alike.

simple carbohydrates
Sugars that are found naturally in fruit, milk, and some vegetables; assimilated quickly, providing immediate energy.

single-parent family
Family with only one parent.

sinsemilla
Marijuana grown with high-tech hydroponics that produces much higher THC levels than in marijuana grown in natural mediums.

sinusitis
Inflammation of the sinuses.

skinfold technique
The use of calipers to measure the amount of subcutaneous fat to determine percent body fat.

skin popping
Injecting a drug directly under the skin.

small intestine
A narrow, 10-foot-long portion of the alimentary canal, extending from the stomach to the large intestine, where almost all digestion takes place. Enzymes from the intestinal walls and the pancreas break down food into nutrients, which are absorbed from the small intestine into the bloodstream.

smokeless tobacco
Tobacco that is used orally. It comes in snuff, looseleaf, and plug forms.

snuff
A type of tobacco that is inhaled through the nostrils, chewed, or placed against the gums.

social dimension of human sexuality
The sum of all the cultural factors that influence a person's thoughts and actions regarding sexuality.

social health
Good relations with others, the presence of a supportive culture, and successful adaptation to the environment.

social pressure
The belief that you must go along with or rebel against others' actions or expectations.

sodium
A component of table salt (sodium chloride). Necessary for many bodily functions. RDA is 200 milligrams per day. Overconsumption can result in hypertension as well as deplete the body's reserves of potassium.

sodomy
Anal intercourse. The term is often applied disparagingly to any sexual practices believed not to be "normal."

somatogenic psychosomatic disorders
Disorders that occur when the body's resistance (immune system) is weakened as a result of stress.

sperm
Reproductive cells in the male.

spermicide
Sperm-killing chemical.

sphygmomanometer
An instrument used to measure blood pressure.

spiritual health
The ability to discover and express your purpose in life; to learn how to experience love, joy, peace, and fulfillment; and to help yourself and others achieve full potential.

sponge
A relatively new contraceptive device that absorbs and kills sperm and serves as a barrier.

spontaneous remission
The reversal or cure of disease without medical intervention.

spot reduction
Losing fat from localized areas of the body, which is not possible—fat is lost over the body as a whole, not in isolated areas.

squamous-cell cancer
A type of skin cancer.

stages of alcoholism
Stages in the gradual decline from social drinking to alcoholism: The early stage involves increased drinking and tolerance; in the middle stage, one conceals one's drinking, drinks alone, doesn't function normally, and feels bad; in the final stage, one lives to drink and goes through extreme personality changes.

stages of dying
Five predictable, but not universally applicable, psychological stages a person passes through in the course of a terminal disease: denial, anger, bargaining, depression, and acceptance.

staleness
Feeling tired and slow and as if you are not making progress in your exercise program.

starch
A form of complex carbohydrate found in such foods as whole-grain bread, potatoes, rice, and vegetables. An important, highly nutritious part of the diet.

starting date
The date you select to start working at changing your chosen health behavior.

stepfamily
A family in which one or both parents have children from a previous marriage.

sterilization
A surgical procedure that renders the individual incapable of reproduction.

stillbirth
The birth of a dead infant.

stoma
An artificially created opening, such as an opening in the abdominal walls through which bodily wastes are excreted.

stomach
A principal digestive organ, part of the alimentary canal, located in the abdomen above the small intestine, where enzymes and stomach acids mix with food to start breaking down the food in order to extract nutrients from it.

street language
The slang language of peers and age groups slightly older; used in graffiti.

strength intervention
Influencing health behaviors by building on existing strengths.

stress
A nonspecific physiological response of the body to any demand made upon it.

stressor
A person, situation, or thought that triggers the stress response.

stress response
The physiological arousal that occurs as a result of stressors.

stretching
Slow, gradual extension of muscle groups to warm them up before exercise in order to improve performance and diminish the chance of injury during physical activity.

stroke
A cardiovascular disease in which the blood supply is cut off to a portion of the brain, causing paralysis, aphasia, and/or death.

subcultures
Smaller groups within a society that might have distinct practices that set them apart from other groups, even though they share the society's major cultural values.

subcutaneous fat
Fat beneath the skin.

substitution
Substituting positive behaviors for negative behaviors or for nonproductive time.

suction curettage
A type of abortion in which the uterine contents are sucked out through a narrow tube; the abortion method that is most widely used up through the twelfth week of pregnancy.

sudden infant death syndrome (SIDS)
A syndrome that occurs among apparently healthy babies, generally between one and three months of age, involving sudden death without warning, usually while the infant is sleeping.

sugar
Sweet, water-soluble, simple carbohydrates, including monosaccharides and disaccharides.

suicide
Intentionally killing oneself.

support group
A group of people from whom you derive comfort, support, happiness, and inner strength, and who can help you in your pursuit of improved health behaviors.

surgery
The medical specialty dealing with operative procedures for correction of disease or deformity.

surgicenter
A center capable of providing minor, low-risk, outpatient surgery.

susceptible host
An organism that is vulnerable to harboring and nourishing a parasite.

swinging
A mutual agreement in which a married couple opens up their relationship to include sexual encounters with others.

symptothermal method
The combination of BBT and cervical mucus methods.

synergistic effect
The result when the effects of two drugs used in combination are greater than the sum of their individual effects when used separately; a multiplying of effects.

syphilis
A sexually transmitted disease caused by a bacterium (Treponema pallidum), with an incubation period of 12 to 20 days.

systolic pressure
The highest point of blood pressure, measured when the heart contracts.

tar
A dangerous and carcinogenic chemical constituent of tobacco smoke.

target zone
A level of exertion at 60 to 80 percent of the individual's maximal aerobic power.

teetotalers
People who never drink alcoholic beverages.

temperament
The mental mechanisms, traits, experiences, and complex intricacies of individuals that determine how they behave, feel, and think.

teratogens
Substances that can cause birth defects or diseases in infants.

tertiary prevention
Rehabilitation; the lessening or eliminating of the serious effects of a disease.

testes
Two oval glands in the scrotum that produce sperm and testosterone.

testosterone
The male hormone that promotes the development of the male sex drive characteristics and sex drive.

thanatologist
A person who studies death and dying.

"the cold"
The most common communicable disease. It is caused by viruses for which no vaccine has been developed.

thermal pollution
Damage to an aquatic ecosystem through an increase in heat in the water.

threshold
The safe level of exposure for a particular chemical as opposed to nonthreshold chemicals, which are dangerous at even very low doses.

thrombolic therapy
The use of drugs to dissolve blood clots.

thrombus
A blood clot, usually one located at the point where it was formed, in a blood vessel or a chamber of the heart.

time management
The systematic matching of prioritized tasks with available blocks of time.

tolerance
The body's tendency to become less responsive to certain substances after repeated exposure. A person with low tolerance for alcohol has noticeable physiological responses from drinking a small amount of alcohol; a person with high tolerance for alcohol must drink much more alcohol to have those responses.

toxemias of pregnancy
The hypertensive conditions of preeclampsia and eclampsia.

toxicity
How poisonous a chemical is, depending on exposure, dose, and negative effects.

tranquilizers
Depressant drugs used medically to relieve tension and anxiety; as drugs of abuse, commonly known as "downers."

trans fat
Unsaturated fat that might raise cholesterol as much as saturated fats do.

transsexual
A person who feels "trapped" in a body of the wrong sex.

transvestism
Sexual gratification from dressing like a member of the opposite sex.

trigger responses
Positive responses to triggers (items that remind you of your health behavior goal) that help you succeed at reaching your goal.

triglycerides
The major form (95 percent) of our dietary fat.

trimesters
The three 3-month developmental periods of pregnancy.

troilism
Having sexual relations with another person while a third person watches.

tubal ligation
A sterilization procedure for females in which the fallopian tubes are severed.

tumor
An abnormal mass of tissue.

Type A behavior pattern
A pattern of behavior characterized by competitiveness, impatience, polyphasic thinking (thinking of two or more things at once), a sense of time urgency, and open or inward hostility.

Type B behavior pattern
A pattern of behavior characterized by taking one thing at a time, effective concentration, flexibility, and equanimity in the face of uncompleted daily tasks.

type I diabetes
Also called "insulin-dependent diabetes mellitus," formerly called "juvenile-onset diabetes"; the more severe form of diabetes, characterized by an absolute lack of insulin.

type II diabetes
Also called "non-insulin-dependent diabetes mellitus"; accounts for 85 to 90 percent of all diabetes cases. Not as severe as type I, and usually appears later in life (generally after 40). Insulin is produced by the beta cells but is not sufficient to deal with the glucose load.

ulcerative colitis
Inflammation of the mucous lining of the large intestine.

ultrasound
The use of sound waves for medical detection and treatment purposes.

umbilical cord
The cord that carries nourishment from the mother to the fetus.

uremia
The accumulation of waste products in the body tissues.

urethra
The tube through which urine passes from the bladder out of the body.

urgent-care center
A center that provides treatment without an appointment for minor medical problems such as sprained ankles, sore throats, and cuts needing stitches.

USP
United States Pharmacopeia.

uterus
The stretchable, pear-shaped organ in the female in which the fetus develops before birth; the womb.

vaccine
A preparation of dead or live attenuated (weakened) viruses or bacteria used to prevent infectious disease by inducing active immunity.

vagina
The female organ that receives the penis during coitus and provides passage for the infant during birth.

vaginal douche
Directing a stream of water or other liquid into the vagina for sanitary or medical reasons.

Valium
A widely prescribed tranquilizer that causes drowsiness and respiratory depression.

value/behavior congruence
Harmony between what someone believes to be right and how that individual acts. Value/behavior congruence results in inner peace; incongruence results in feelings of guilt.

values
Ideas we believe in and cherish.

vas deferens
A pair of tubes in the male, extending from the epididymis to the prostate, that serve as passageways for the sperm.

vasectomy
A sterilization procedure for males in which the vasa deferentia are severed.

vasoconstrictor
A drug that narrows the blood vessels and reduces the oxygen supply.

vasodilators
Drugs or nerves that cause a widening of the opening of blood vessels.

vectors
Organisms that transmit disease from one host (person or animal) to another.

vegetarian
A person who eats a diet low in, or excluding, animal sources of food. Vegans eat only plants. Lacto-vegetarians eat plant foods and dairy products. Lacto-ovo-vegetarians eat dairy products, eggs, and plants. All these diets can be nutritious with careful food selection.

very-low-density lipoprotein (VLDL)
Considered an undesirable form of cholesterol, VLDL has been implicated in the formation of arterial plaque (atherosclerosis).

virus
The smallest intracellular infectious parasite that is capable of reproducing only in living cells. Viruses cause numerous diseases, including measles, mumps, AIDS, hepatitis, herpes, and rabies. Viruses are very difficult to control.

vitamins
Organic substances essential, in very small amounts, for bodily chemical reactions. Vitamins combine with enzymes to enable the body to use other nutrients. Found in all foods except sugar, alcohol, and highly refined fats.

voyeurism (scopophilia)
Generally, obtaining pleasure from watching people undress or engage in sexual behavior.

water-soluble vitamins
The vitamins, including the eight B vitamins and vitamin C, that are not stored in the body and need to be replenished every day. Regular overconsumption can produce physical ailments.

withdrawal
Symptoms that occur, due to physical dependence on alcohol, when an alcoholic person stops drinking. The symptoms range from a hangover to delirium tremens.

Zilbergeld and Ellison's model
A five-component model of human sexual response.

zygote
The single cell resulting from the union of an egg and a sperm, and the multicell organism that develops from cell division during the first week after fertilization.

CREDITS

TEXT, ILLUSTRATIONS

Chapter 1
Figure 1.4: Reprinted with permission from the *Journal of Health Education*, 21(6), 1990, pp. 33–39. *Journal of Health Education* is a publication of the American Alliance for Health, Physical Education, Recreation and Dance, 1900 Association Drive, Reston, Virginia 22091.

Chapter 5
Figure, page 5.8: From the State of Wisconsin, Department of Health and Social Services, Division of Health.

Chapter 6
Figure 6.4: From "Typical Size of One Serving" Copyright 1993 by Consumers Union of U.S., Inc., Yonkers, NY 10703-1057. Reprinted by permission from *Consumer Reports on Health*, September 1993. **figure 6.5:** From Nanci Hellmich, "Consumer Guide to Reading the New Food Label" in *USA Today*, December 3, 1992. Copyright 1992, USA TODAY. Reprinted with permission.

Chapter 7
Figure 7.2: From L. Zohman, M.D., *Beyond Diet: Exercise Your Way to Fitness and Heart Health*, CPC International, Englewood Cliffs, New Jersey. Reprinted by permission. **figure, page 7.15:** From "Building Strong Abdominal Muscles Three Ways" Copyright 1993 by Consumers Union of U.S., Inc., Yonkers, NY 10703-1057. Reprinted by permission from *Consumer Reports on Health*, April 1993.

Chapter 8
Figure 8.5: From National Eating Disorders Organization at Harding Hospital. (1994). Possible Signs and Symptoms Accompanying Weight Loss in Eating Disorders. In *Eating Disorders Information Packet*, Worthington, Ohio: NEDO. (For more information write NEDO, 445 E. Granville Road, Worthington, Ohio 43085, (614) 436-1112.) Reprinted by permission.

Chapter 10
Figures 10.5, 10.6: From William H. Masters and Virginia E. Johnson, *Human Sexual Response*, page 5. Copyright © 1966 Little, Brown, Boston. Reprinted by permission.

Chapter 11
Figures 11.1, 11.2, 11.5: From John W. Hole, Jr., *Human Anatomy and Physiology*, 6th ed. Copyright © 1993 Wm. C. Brown Communications, Inc., Dubuque, Iowa. All Rights Reserved. Reprinted by permission. **figure 11.6:** From Stuart Ira Fox, *Human Physiology*, 4th ed. Copyright © 1993 Wm. C. Brown Communications, Inc., Dubuque, Iowa. All Rights Reserved. Reprinted by permission. **figure 11.8:** From Kent M. Van De Graaff and Stuart Ira Fox, *Concepts of Human Anatomy and Physiology*, 3d ed. Copyright © 1992 Wm. C. Brown Communications, Inc., Dubuque, Iowa. All Rights Reserved. Reprinted by permission.

Chapter 12
Figure 12.5: Reproduced with the permission of The Alan Guttmacher Institute from Susan Harlap, Kathryn Kost, and Jacqueline Darroch Forrest, *Preventing Pregnancy, Protecting Health: A New Look at Birth Control Choices in the United States*, 1991, New York.

Chapter 19
Text, page 19.18: From *Newsweek*, May 12, 1986. © 1986, Newsweek, Inc. All rights reserved. Reprinted by permission.

Chapter 20
Figure 20.1: From McKenzie JF: A Checklist for Evaluating Health Information. *Journal of School Health*. Vol. 57, No. 1, January 1987, p. 31. Copyright, 1987. American School Health Association, P.O. Box 708, Kent, OH 44240. Reprinted by permission.

PHOTOGRAPHS

Part Openers
A: © Greg Greer/Unicorn Stock Photos; **B:** © Westlight; **C:** © David Young Wolff/Photo Edit; **D:** Lori Adamski Peek/Tony Stone Images; **E:** © Bill Bachman/Photo Edit; **F:** (Inset) © Tony Freeman/Photo Edit, (Full Page) © Robert G. Bishop/Tony Stone Images; **G:** © Jean Higgins/Unicorn Stock Photos; **H:** © Robert Brenner/Photo Edit

Chapter 1
Opener: © F. Reischl/Unicorn Stock Photos; **p. 1.4:** © David Young-Wolff/Photo Edit; **p. 1.5:** © D. Palais/Superstock; **p. 1.10:** © Paul Gerda/Leo de Wys, Inc.; **p. 1.11:** © Richard Hutchings/PhotoEdit; **p. 1.16:** © Tony Freeman/PhotoEdit; **p. 1.26T and p. 1.26B:** © Tony Freeman/PhotoEdit

Chapter 2
Opener: © Westlight; **p. 2.5:** © Tony Freeman/PhotoEdit; **p. 2.16L:** © Superstock; **p. 2.16R:** © Superstock; **p. 2.17:** © Chris Grajczyk/Viewfinders; **p. 2.22:** © E. Herwig/The Picture Cube

Chapter 3
Opener: © Robert W. Ginn/Unicorn Stock Photos; **p. 3.2:** The Kobal Collection; **p. 3.5:** © Superstock; **p. 3.8:** © David Young-Wolff/Photo Edit; **p. 3.13:** © Gregory Heisler/The Image Bank; **p. 3.21:** © Jean Higgins/Unicorn Stock Photos, Inc.

Chapter 4
Opener: © Karen Holsinger Mullen/Unicorn Stock Photos; **p. 4.8:** © Dion Ogust/The Image Works; **p. 4.9:** © Merritt Vincent/PhotoEdit; **p. 4.13:** © Jane Williams/Unicorn Stock Photos

Chapter 5
Opener: © Aneal Vohra/Unicorn Stock Photos; **p. 5.5:** © Karen Stafford Photography; **p. 5.6:** © Paul Gerda/Leo de Wys Inc; **p. 5.13L:** © W. Marc Bernsau/The Image Works; **p. 5.13R:** © Jean-Claude Lejeune

Chapter 6
Opener: © Martin R. Jones/Unicorn Stock Photos; **p. 6.8:** © Tony Freeman/Photo Edit; **p. 6.10:** © Felicia Martinez/Photo Edit; **p. 6.16:** © Michael Newman/Photo Edit; **p. 6.20:** © George Munday/Leo de Wys, Inc.; **p. 6.21:** © Greg Vaughn/Tom Stack & Associates; **p. 6.24:** © Richard Hutchings/Photo Edit

Chapter 7
Opener: © Lawrence Ruggeri/Uniphoto; **p. 7.2:** © James Marshall 1993; **p. 7.9:** © Jon Feingersh/Tom Stack & Associates; **p. 7.12:** © Robert Brenner/Photo Edit; **p. 7.16:** © Tom McCarthy/Unicorn Stock Photos; **p. 7.22:** © Superstock

Chapter 8
Opener: Uniphoto; **p. 8.2:** © Michael Siluk; **p. 8.7:** © James Shaffer; **p. 8.8:** © William Hopkins; **p. 8.12:** © T. Rosenthal/Superstock; **p. 8.16:** © Tony Freeman/Photo Edit

INDEX

A

Abdominal muscles, building, 7.15
Abortion
    future of, 12.18–12.19
    methods of, 12.17–12.18
Abstinence, 13.17, 16.25
Acceptance, dying and, 5.5
Accumeter Cholesterol Self-Test, 20.9
Acetaminophen, 20.5–20.6
Acid rain, 19.9
Acquired immunodeficiency syndrome. *See* AIDS
Acrophobia, 3.18
Action, in planned disruption, 2.21
Action on Smoking and Health (ASH), 14.14
Active environment, 7.21–7.22
Active immunity, 16.6
Active listening, 9.12, 9.18
Activity levels, 8.8
Acupuncture, 14.20, 21.10–21.11
Acute leukemia, 18.13
Adaptive stress, 3.8, 3.11
Addiction cycle, 15.6
Adipose cells, 6.14
Adipose tissue, 8.9
Adult Children of Alcoholics (ACOA), 13.23
Adult day-care centers, 4.12
Adulterated cocaine, 15.13
Advertising, 6.4
    consumer vulnerability and, 20.3, 20.16
    Federal Trade Commission and, 20.4
    problems with advertisements, 20.15–20.16
    of tobacco products, 14.12–14.14
Aerobic exercise, 3.16, 7.12, 8.10
African Americans, smoking and, 14.7
Age, alcoholism and, 13.9
Ageism
    combating, 4.10
    retirement and, 4.9–4.10
    stereotyping and, 4.9
Aggression, rape as, 10.15–10.16
Aggressive behavior, 2.24
Aging, 4.3–4.17
    ageism and, 4.9–4.10
    assessment for, 4.15
    exercise and, 7.4
    growing elderly population, 4.4–4.5
    help for elderly, 4.10–4.12
    lifestyle contract for, 5.21–5.22
    multidimensional perspective, 4.4
    myths about, 4.12–4.13
    nature of, 4.5–4.8
    nutritional needs and, 6.33

    personal skills in, 4.16
    preparation for, 4.7, 4.14
    sexuality and, 9.15–9.16, 9.18
    theories on, 4.8–4.9
    visualization of, 4.15
AIDS (acquired immunodeficiency syndrome), 16.4, 16.14–16.20, 16.26
    condom use and, 12.6
    drug use and, 15.23
    dying and, 5.6
    HIV virus and, 16.16
    methods of transmission, 16.17–16.18
    prevention guidelines, 16.18
    research in, 16.18–16.20
    social stigma of, 16.17
    tuberculosis in, 16.13
Airline flights, smoking ban on, 14.14
Air pollution
    global warming and, 19.13–19.14
    greenhouse effect and, 19.12
    health consequences of, 19.11
    kinds of, 19.10–19.11, 19.22
    nature of, 19.11
    ozone layer and, 19.12–19.13
    reducing, 19.14
Air travel safety, 22.12
Alarm stage, 3.4
Alcohol, 6.23
    absorption and metabolism of, 13.5
    assessment of consumption of, 13.11
    on college campuses, 13.20
    dependence on, 13.9
    drinking behavior and, 13.9–13.10
    effects on body, 13.6–13.8
    fetal alcohol syndrome and, 11.3, 13.20–13.21
    legislation of consumption, 13.19–13.20
    nature of, 13.4–13.5
    personal decisions about, 13.10–13.13
    pregnancy and childbirth and, 11.13–11.14
    psychoneuroimmunology and, 13.23
    relationships with alcoholics, 13.21–13.23
    weight control and, 8.9
    in workplace, 13.14
    See also Alcoholism
Alcoholics, profile of, 13.9
Alcoholics Anonymous (AA), 13.12, 13.14, 13.18
Alcoholism, 13.14, 13.16, 13.24
    assessment of, 13.15–13.16
    causes of, 13.16–13.17
    driving and, 13.18–13.19
    helping drinker, 13.22–13.23
    legislation of consumption and, 13.19–13.20

    social impact of, 13.18
    stages of, 13.17
    steps to, 13.14
    treatment and rehabilitation of, 13.17–13.18
Algor mortis, 5.4
Allergies, 18.20
Allopathic physicians, 21.3
Alpha-fetoprotein (AFP) testing, 11.16
Alternative medical systems
    acupuncture, 21.10–21.11
    chiropractic, 21.9–21.10
    faith healing, 21.12–21.13
    herbal medicine, 21.11
    homeopathy, 21.11–21.12
    understanding new procedures and, 21.9
Altruistic dreams (causes), 2.24–2.26
Alzheimer's disease, 4.6–4.7
Alzheimer's Disease and Related Disorders Association (ADRDA), 4.7
Ambisexuality, 10.12
Ambulatory-care centers, 21.7
Amenorrhea, 8.16, 12.5
American Association for the Advancement of Science, 12.16
American Association of Retired Persons (AARP), 22.10
American Automobile Association (AAA), 22.5
American Cancer Society, 14.19, 18.12
American Chiropractic Association, 21.10
American Civil Liberties Union, 10.13
American College of Sports Medicine (ACSM), 7.11
American Heart Association, 6.17, 17.6, 17.9, 22.4
American Hospital Association, 21.15
American Medical Association, 14.12
American Psychiatric Association, 10.11–10.12
American Psychological Association, 6.17, 10.11–10.12
American Red Cross, 22.4
Amino acids, 6.13, 6.30
Amniocentesis, 11.14, 11.15, 18.22
Amniotic fluid, 12.18
Amniotic tap, 11.14, 11.15, 18.22
Amphetamines, 15.14
Anabolic steroids, 7.5, 15.19, 15.20
Analgesics, 15.9–15.10, 16.10
Aneurysms, 17.4
Angel Dust (PCP, phencyclidine), 15.18
Anger, 2.16–2.17, 5.4
Angina, 14.6, 17.11
Angiography, 17.12
Angioplasty, 17.12

Organ donor card, 5.15, 5.16

Orgasm, 10.4–10.5

Orlistat, 8.11

OSHA (Occupational Safety and Health Administration), 22.14

Osteoarthritis, 18.23, 18.24

Osteopathic physicians, 21.3

Osteoporosis, 4.5–4.6, 6.19–6.20

Outpatient facilities, 4.12

Ovarian cancer, 18.7

Ovary, 11.2

Overload principle, 7.4

Overstimulation, 3.8, 3.10

Over-the-counter (OTC) drugs, 20.5–20.7, 20.16

Overweight, 1.4, 8.4

Oviduct, 11.4

Ovulation, 11.2, 11.4

Ovum, 11.8

Oxygen debt, 7.6–7.7

Oxygen intake, 7.6

Oxygen requirements, 7.7

Ozone layer depletion, 19.12–19.14

P

Pain relief, 20.5–20.6, 21.11

Pancreas, 6.6

Pancreatic cancer, 18.8, 18.12

Pap test, 18.10–18.12

Paralysis, sexuality and, 9.17–9.18

Paraphilias, 10.13–10.15

Paraquat, 15.8

Parental control, 9.15

Parental support, 9.15

Parenting, 9.12–9.15

Parkinson's disease, symptoms produced by MPTP, 15.11

Partial sit-up, 7.15

Particulate matter, 14.11

Passive smoking, 14.11–14.12, 14.21

Patient-admission privileges, 21.7

Patients, personal skills of, 21.5

Patient's Bill of Rights, 21.15–21.17

Paton, Colin, 5.15

PCP (Angel Dust, phencyclidine), 15.18

Peak performances, stress and, 3.4

Pediatrics, 21.4

Pediculosis pubis (crabs), 16.23

Pedophilia, 10.19

Peer pressure, smoking and, 14.9, 14.11

Pelvic inflammatory disease (PID), 12.4, 16.20

Pelvic tilt, 7.15

Penicillin, to treat gonorrhea, 16.20

Penile gonorrhea, 16.20

Penile urethra, 10.5

Peptic ulcer, 14.7

Perceptual management, 3.17

Perceptual stressors, 3.11–3.14, 3.22

Perinatal death, 5.14

Persistence, 3.12

Personal enrichment, of mind and soul, 2.6–2.22

Personality(ies)
  anxiety-prone, 3.14, 3.15
  designing fitness program and, 7.17

eating habits and, 8.9
  types A and B, 3.12–3.14

Personality theory of alcoholism, 13.10

Personal safety. *See* Safety

Personal strengths, assessment of, 1.20–1.22

Pessimism, 2.15, 2.16

Peyote, 15.17

Phencyclidine (Angel Dust, PCP), 15.18

Philip Morris Company, 14.12–14.13

Phobias, 3.18

Photochemical smog, 19.11

Physical activity, 1.4, 7.1–7.24
  adjusting lifestyle for, 7.21–7.22
  benefits of physical fitness, 7.2–7.4, 7.23
  cultural influences on, 7.20
  developing program of, 7.7–7.15
  during pregnancy, 11.14
  factors influencing, 7.16–7.17
  factors in program choice, 7.16–7.17
  happiness and, 7.17
  kinds of, 7.11–7.15
  lifestyle contract for, 8.22–8.23
  maintaining, 7.18–7.21
  major body systems and, 7.4–7.7
  personality and, 7.17
  promoting success of fitness program, 7.15–7.16
  sleep and, 7.22–7.23

Physical fitness, 7.2–7.4, 20.3

Physical health, 1.5

Physically challenged people, sexuality and, 9.17–9.18

Physical stressors, 3.4

Physician assistant (PA), 21.4

Physician-assisted suicide (PAS), 5.9

Physician-committed voluntary active euthanasia (PCVAE), 5.9

Physician/patient relationship, 21.3–21.4

Physician(s)
  allopathic and osteopathic, 21.3
  counseling by, 3.22
  HMOs and, 21.14
  home health tests and, 20.10
  shopping for, 21.7

Physician's Desk Reference (PDR), 20.8

Physiological dependence, 13.9, 13.24, 15.3–15.4

Physiological losses, with aging, 4.7

Physiological reactions to stimulants, 15.11–15.12

Pipe smoking, 14.8, 14.21

Placebo effect, 21.18

Placenta, 11.18, 12.18

Placenta previa, 11.13

Planned disruptions, 2.20–2.21, 2.27

Plant proteins, 6.13

Plateau phase of sexual response, 10.4

PNI. *See* Psychoneuroimmunology

Point-of-service plan (POS), 21.14

Poison Control Center, 22.3

Pollutants, 3.9, 19.20

Pollution, 19.15
  See also specific kinds of pollution

Polydipsia, 18.18

Polyphagia, 18.18

Polyunsaturated fats, 6.14

Polyuria, 18.18

Population control, 12.3

Population growth, 19.4–19.6, 19.22

Pornography, 10.21–10.22

Positive addictions, 2.19

Positive reinforcement, 14.16

Positive self-esteem, 2.11

Positive thinking, 1.24

Positive verbalization, 2.12

Postal Inspection Service, 20.12

Postmarital sexual behavior, 10.10

Potassium, 6.20–6.21

Preeclampsia, 11.17

Preferred provider organization (PPO), 21.14

Pregnancy, 11.9–11.17
  assessment for, 11.13
  determination of, 11.11
  fetal development in, 11.16
  maternal health problems in, 11.16–11.17
  nutritional needs and, 6.32–6.33
  potential complications of, 11.14–11.16
  prenatal care and, 11.11–11.14
  smoking and, 14.6, 14.8, 14.11, 14.21
  syphilis and, 16.22
  teenage, 10.8
  vegetarianism and, 6.30

Pregnancy test kits, 11.11, 20.10

Premarital conception and birth, 11.11

Prematurity, 11.13–11.14, 14.8

Premenstrual syndrome (PMS), 11.5, 11.6

Prenatal care, 11.11–11.14

Prenuptial agreement, 9.7

Prescription drugs, 20.7–20.8, 20.16

President's Council on Physical Fitness, 7.8

Primary prevention, 17.3, 17.18

Principle of specificity, 7.4

Problematic adjustment, 1.18

Problem drinking. *See* Alcoholism

Problem solving, 1.14

Prodromal stage of communicable disease, 16.7

Product terminology, FDA regulation of, 6.29

Professional help, 3.18, 3.22, 3.23

Progestasert (IUD), 12.11

Progesterone, 11.4, 12.5

Proof (beverages), 13.5

Prospective payment system (PPS), 4.11

Prostaglandins, 12.18

Prostate cancer, 18.8, 18.12

Prostate gland, 11.7

Prostatic problems, 9.16

Prostitution, 10.7, 10.21

Protective skills, 1.13

Proteins, 6.12–6.13, 6.31, 6.33

Protozoa, 16.6

Pseudo-Cushing's syndrome, 13.7

Pseudostressors, 6.31–6.32

Psilocybin, 15.18

Psilocyn, 15.18

Psychiatric social workers, counseling by, 3.22

Psychiatrists, 3.22

Psychiatry, 21.4

Psychoactive drugs, 15.1–15.24
  AIDS and, 15.23
  dependence and abuse, 15.3–15.6
  drug interactions, 15.21

Q: Why is this woman so happy?

A: Because she owns the *Decisions for Health Student Workbook*.

And she did well in her Personal Health class by using her **Student Workbook** to accompany her Bruess/Richardson *Decisions for Health* text. She was turned onto ***learning objectives*** to help her zero in on important information. Her professor and her peers were impressed by her ***expanded vocabulary*** and clear understanding of key terms. Each chapter was ***outlined for easy review*** so when quiz time rolled around, she was ready. And to help her prepare for exams, the Workbook provided ***review questions*** and ***sample test questions***. But most importantly,

she was able to take charge of her attitudes and behaviors about health with the ***decision worksheets***.

This workbook can't take the class for you, but it will put you in better shape for class participation, homework, quizzes, exams, and a better grade, just like it did for her.

Contact your bookstore manager and ask for **ISBN 25964, Student Workbook by Susan J. Laing.** Or call Brown & Benchmark Customer Service at 1-800-338-5371 ext. 3059.

Brown & Benchmark
PUBLISHERS